TX
723.5
.P6
S77
1993

PC

Chicago Public Library

R0126588310
Polish heritage cookery.

D1608981

POLISH HERITAGE COOKERY

Hippocrene is NUMBER ONE in
International Cookbooks

Africa and Oceania
Good Food from Australia
Traditional South African
   Cookery

Asia and Near East
The Joy of Chinese Cooking
The Art of South Indian Cooking
The Art of Persian Cooking
The Art of Israeli Cooking
The Art of Turkish Cooking

Mediterranean
Best of Greek Cuisine
Taste of Malta
A Spanish Family Cookbook

Western Europe
Best of Austrian Cuisine
A Belgian Cookbook
Traditional Recipes from Old
   England
The Art of Irish Cooking
Traditional Food from Scotland
Traditional Food from Wales

Scandinavia
Best of Scandinavian Cooking
The Best of Finnish Cooking
The Best of Smorgasbord
   Cooking
Good Food from Sweden

Central Europe
All Along the Danube
Bavarian Cooking
The Best of Czech Cooking
The Art of Hungarian Cooking
Polish Heritage Cookery
The Best of Polish Cooking
Old Warsaw Cookbook
Old Polish Traditions
Taste of Romania

Eastern Europe
The Cuisine of Armenia
The Best of Russian Cooking
The Best of Ukrainian Cuisine

Americas
The Honey Cookbook
The Art of Brazilian Cookery
The Art of South American
   Cookery

POLISH HERITAGE COOKERY

Robert & Maria Strybel

HIPPOCRENE BOOKS
New York

Copyright© 1993 by Robert Strybel

Illustrated Edition, 1997

Photography: Zbigniew Pomaski & Andrzej Karczewski; arrangement: Stanislaw Kwiatkowski, Master Chef of Forum Hotel in Warsaw

Illustrations: Anna Ratyńska

All rights reserved. No part of this book may be reproduced in any form, by any means, electronic or mechanical, including photo-copying, recording or by any data-storage and retrieval system without written permission from the author: Robert Strybel, ulica Kaniowska 24, 01-529 Warsaw, Poland.

Published by Hippocrene Books, Inc., in 1993

For information, address:
Hippocrene Books, Inc.
171 Madison Avenue
New York, NY 10016

Library of Congress Cataloging-in-Publication Data
Strybel, Robert.
Polish Heritage Cookery / Robert & Maria Strybel.
        p.   cm.
Includes bibliographical references and index.
ISBN 0-7818-0558-9
1. Cookery, Polish. I. Strybel, Maria. II. Title.
TX723.5.P6S77   1993
641.59438—dc20   92-34455   CIP

Printed in the United States of America.

BUSINESS/SCIENCE/TECHNOLOGY DIVISION
CHICAGO PUBLIC LIBRARY
400 SOUTH STATE STREET
CHICAGO, IL 60605
R0126588310

CONTENTS

400 SOUTH STATE STREET

We dedicate this book to our dear mothers, Alicja Derkacz and Angela Strybel, as well as to the memory of our late grandmothers, who lovingly introduced us to the wonderful world of Polish cookery.

Majka & Rob

FOREWORD

My wife and I would like to invite you to join us on a trip through the still largely unexplored world of Polish cookery. Before we do, permit me to make a few introductory remarks, provide a bit of background, and sketch a broader cultural context which hopefully will make your journey a little more meaningful. You may understandably be tempted to go straight to the recipe sections, but remember: by first familiarizing yourself with the basics of Polish cuisine and the workings of this books, you will find the individual recipes easier to follow. Perhaps this will also make you stop and give some thought to what the preparation and enjoyment of good, healthful food are all about.

WHY THIS BOOK WAS WRITTEN

It was back in 1970 that I first began working as a Warsaw-based American journalist for a string of U.S. newspapers from New York to California. In 1975, my writings on political developments, economic issues, the cultural scene and subjects of human and ethnographic interest were expanded to include a Polish Chef column, in order to help popularize Poland's still relatively unknown culinary heritage. This move immediately generated a surprising amount of "fan mail" from Polish-American readers interested in recipes for dishes their late *Babcia* (grandma) used to make. Many of the letters also contained the query: "Where can I get a copy of your cookbook?"

I repeatedly informed them that I had not written any such book. I patiently explained that the regular Polish Chef columns contained recipes gleaned from a variety of sources, including our own heirloom favorites. There were dishes sampled at rustic Polish inns and first rate restaurants, at elegant Warsaw banquets and that endless round of nameday parties hosted in Polish homes. (Poles do not celebrate birthdays but *imieniny*, namedays, i.e. the feastday of their patron saints.) Also included were recipes from a large variety of cookbooks, some more than a century old, and therefore often modified by us to better suit modern dietary requirements. There were dishes enjoyed by Poles across the country, as well as local favorites limited to a single region.

Still, no amount of clarification seemed to help. As new readers came across the Polish Chef column, many of them would invariably write to inquire: "Where can your cookbook be purchased?" At first, that recurring question seemed a bit puzzling, considering that there already were a number of English-language Polish cookbooks on the American market, some of them quite good. The answer was indirectly supplied by other readers who had specific recipe requests for *gałuszki, śliziki, lemieszka, pieróg, kołacz, tłuczeńce* and other dishes rarely encountered any more even in Poland. By and large, the Polish cookbooks available in America made no reference to these and many other dishes and were essentially variations on the "highlights of Polish cooking" or "my favorite recipes" theme. So it was that, 13 years after the first Polish Chef column appeared, my wife and I became convinced that there was definitely a demand for a Polish cookbook more extensive than any published in English to date. That in a nutshell was how *Polish Heritage Cookery* was born.

INITIAL ENCOUNTERS
WITH POLISH CUISINE

I grew up in Detroit's once predominantly Polish suburb of Hamtramck, surrounded by the flavors and aromas of *kapusta, czernina, gołąbki*, home-made *kiełbasa*, dried mushrooms, and golden, salt-pork nuggets sizzling in a skillet. The house was filled with an exceptionally heavenly aroma when Easter *babka* (yeast-raised egg-bread) was being baked. To this day, I also recall the mouthwatering fragrance of sauerkraut and mushrooms simmering in the kitchen on *Wigilia* (Christmas Eve). Wafting in from the kitchen on those cold winter nights was the aroma of pickled herring, of fish frying in a skillet and of freshly baked poppyseed cakes—all mingled with the nostalgic evergreen scent of the *choinka* (Christmas tree).

Then were the Polish weddings, for which Hamtramck has long been known. These were day-long or even two-day affairs back in the 1940's and 50's when I was growing up, and hearty ethnic dishes were their culinary mainstay. Somehow, one little boy always managed to get more powdered sugar from the *chruściki* on his spanking new navy-blue outfit than down the hatch, no matter how hard he tried not to. There were the endless christenings, First Holy Communion parties, and funeral banquets, all of which would have been unthinkable without traditional Polish food. I also cannot forget the many Polish sausage shops and bakeries along Hamtramck's main shopping street, Joseph Campau Avenue, which were so unlike the packaged lunch meat counter and baked goods section of the big supermarkets. You could walk down the street blindfolded, but the heartwarming fragrance of freshly baked rye bread and *rogale* (a kind of large crescent roll) let it be known that you were passing a *piekarnia* (bakery). The same was true of the sausage shops, where the heady, smoky, garlicky aroma of kiełbasa, prominently displayed on hooks for all to behold, mingled with the pungent tang of barrel-cured dill pickles and the deep, dusky smell of dried Polish mushrooms.

Like most Americans raised in an ethnic community, my culinary recollections center on my immigrant grandmothers. It was the Polish *babcia* that prepared the Old World soups from scratch, made her own soup noodles, and kept alive the many other foods and eating habits of her ancestral homeland. My late maternal grandmother, Babcia Kupczyńska, enriched the culinary repertoire of her eastern home province of Lublin with dishes from other parts of Poland which she first encountered in America. And so, in addition to such typical Lublin favorites as *biały barszcz* (white sour soup served at Easter) and *pieróg gryczany* (buckwheat pie), she also learned to prepare *czernina* (duck soup), a specialty of the Western Poznań region. But she never cared for the Poznań practice of flavoring *kiełbasa* with marjoram and used only salt, pepper and garlic. Both my grandmothers prepared such Polish standards as *gołąbki* and *pierogi*, but my paternal grandmother, Babcia Kazia, also filled the latter at times with meat—a practice rarely encountered in Polish peasant cookery. As a result of her upscale culinary interests, I was also exposed to fish in aspic, beef tongue in gray sauce, beef tripe with marrow dumplings, hot stuffed eggs, steak roll-ups, *pasztet* (pâté), and other dishes far less common on the Polish-American scene than the old rustic favorites.

During my first trip to Poland (1966), I encountered many of the old familiar dishes of my childhood and many new ones as well. I especially liked the clear, hot, ruby-red beet-flavored bouillon served in twin-handled broth cups with hand held mushroom-filled pastries on the side. I also enjoyed the grilled *kiełbasa* served at no-frills sidewalk stands on a paper plate with a splotch of mustard and a slice of rye bread, especially if there was a draft-beer stand somewhere nearby. A real eye-opener was the Polish penchant for the extensive, varied, and usually quite appetizingly presented *zakąski* (cold appetizers). The Polish Americans among whom I had grown up definitely preferred hot dishes. On the other hand, I was not as uninitiated as one Polish American friend from Philadelphia, who told this story about his first trip to Poland. Eager to sample the Polish dishes his mother used to make, he did not ever bother to scan the menu at Warsaw's elegant Hotel Europejski, and told the waiter: "I'll have some *gołąbki*." When the dinner-jacketed waiter replied: "We haven't any," he shot back: "Well, then let me have the *pierogi*." After striking out for the second time, he tried again: "How about some *kiełbasa* and kapusta," whereupon the waiter chidingly asked in impeccable English: "Sir, would you order a hot dog at the Waldorf Astoria?!"

I think I was indeed fortunate when, four years later, I first met Majka (short for Maria), a lovely Warsaw University student who was soon to become the future Mrs. Strybel. Besides her many other virtues, I admired her cultural versatility in which culinary skills and family concerns in no way contradicted intellectual interests or scholarly pursuits. In fact, while working on a Ph.D. in historical linguistics, after a long day of research in the dusty archives, Majka would like nothing better than coming home and trying out some new gourmet treat. Culture, after all, not only means an appreciation of fine music, the arts and literature. It also involves the culture of daily living, of which family togetherness and the enjoyment of fine home-made food are an important part. This view may have run counter to the thinking of the so called "moderns" and "trendies" who actually pride themselves on their culinary ignorance, as if knowing how to cook were something demeaning. In reality, a creative culinary flair is among the things that turn a household into a warm and inviting home, to which family members eagerly return and guests look forward to visiting.

Majka hailed from the small town of Turobin in the eastern voivodship (province) of Lublin and was born to a family that enjoyed good food. The years of economic collectivism and resultant mismanagement by the communist regime caused periodic food shortages for big-city dwellers, but food was rarely a problem in rural villages and small towns. Many residents had a henhouse or rabbit hutches in back of the house. Some would fatten their own pigs for the holidays. And others kept a cow and always had plenty of their own milk, butter, buttermilk, and cheese. Fruits and vegetables were abundant and the then unpolluted river nearby produced beautiful big pike and plenty of crayfish for anyone with patience to stalk his prey. Majka's late dad was an avid mushroom-picker, who regularly supplied the family with a bumper crop of King Boletes as well as lesser, albeit still very noble, species. In the surrounding forests, wild blueberries and blackberries were also there for the taking. At an early age Majka was already cooking dinner for her working parents. The years that followed enabled her to refine and expand the culinary techniques mastered during childhood. Among other things, she often consulted a notebook of favorite recipes left behind by her aunt, and many of them have found their way onto the pages of this book.

Just as my initial visit to Poland expanded my knowledge of the native cuisine, Majka's first trip to America also made a deep impression that would influence many of her cooking habits. She was especially struck by the abundance of convenience items and the practical approach to food displayed by many American cooks. This included the endless variety of conveniently pre-trimmed and packaged fresh meat and produce, the availability of every imaginable appliance and cooking aid and shortcut techniques that need not adversely affect the flavor or nutritional value of food. Rather than overusing highly processed foods and imitations, American-style convenience could mean something as simple as cooking a dish in a single pot, where the traditional Polish cook would dirty up half a dozen. It did not have to involve overpaying for inferior-tasting frozen potato pancakes but rather using a blender instead of the old knuckle-scraping grater to create your own batter.

It was in the U.S. that Majka began baking her *pieróg* in an American-style piepan, which makes it easier to slice and serve than out of the more traditional loafpan. Refrigerator crescent-roll dough was found to produce something more than simply passable *paszteciki*, and convenient sheets of frozen phyllo dough could be used with good results in *strudel*. Canned beets made a very good *ćwikła* and frozen spinach could be used to whip up a quick and easy mock cream of sorrel soup when genuine *szczaw* (sorrel) was not available. Canned fruit-pie fillings sped up the preparation of Old Polish dishes the manufacturer never even imagined, and the electric slow-cooker seemed expressly created for *bigos*. These and many other shortcuts are included in this book in addition to the more traditional techniques. The choice is yours!

HOW POLISH COOKERY DEVELOPED

Some say that the world's only truly distinctive cuisines are those of China and France. It cannot be denied that French and Chinese cuisine have made a bigger impact on the culinary life styles of more nations than any other, but it would be an exaggeration to claim that the food of all other countries is simply a poor imitation of the original. It would be more correct to say that native eating habits, largely determined by geography and culture, evolved over the centuries into something distinctly Russian, Danish, Portuguese, German, Polish or whatever as a result of contacts with diverse cultural currents. Foreign monks, merchants and invaders alike all made their imprint on native cookery, as did dynastic unions and, in Poland's case, its partition by three aggressive neighbors—Russia, Germany, and Austria—between 1772 and 1918.

Actually the food of medieval Europe was monotonously similar. The upper classes would gorge on joints of crudely roasted wild game, dripping with fat, and wash it all down with far too much beer, wine and mead. The serfs had to content themselves with root vegetables, legumes, groats and whatever they occasionally managed to poach in their lord's forest. Even as late as the 16th century Anne Boleyn, the short-lived queen of England, one of the wives of Henry VIII, usually breakfasted on a slab of salted fat back and a pitcher of beer. She was not alone. Until then, Europe's only major culinary innovation had been the exotic spices introduced as a result of the Crusades. Even these were initially used for medicinal purposes.

Following the spices, the first major impact on native Polish cookery was made by the Italian Princess Bona Sforza, who became queen of Poland when she married King Zygmunt the Old in 1518. She brought not only architects and artists from her native Italy but also vegetable seeds and expert cooks. It was she who first introduced the Poles to various greens and vegetables, although initially many courtiers balked at such unseemly innovations: "Greens are something fed to goats and rabbits, and vegetables are fit only for peasants!" Queen Bona's contributions live on not only in the many vegetable dishes now considered so typically Polish, but even in what some of them are called. *Kalafiory, pomidory,* and *sałata,* the Polish words for cauliflowers, tomatoes, and lettuce respectively, came directly from Italian. To this day, the standard soup greens (carrot, celeriac, parsley root, leek, and Savoy cabbage) are referred to in Poland as *włoszczyzna (*Italian stuff).

It was not until the 17th century that the fabled grand cuisine of France came into its own, initially also largely influenced by the Italians. The Polish tradition of having food blessed on Holy Saturday, known as *święcone,* seemed to have combined with the culinary extravagance of the French aristocracy in the Easter table laid out by Duke Sapieha during the reign of Władysław IV (1632-1643). A chronicler noted: "There stood four immense wild boars, one for each season of the year, and each was stuffed with ham, sausage, and suckling pigs, roasted all together—no mean feat by the master cook. In tandem there stood 12 fully roasted elk with gilded antlers, stuffed with such game as hares, bustards, heathcocks*, symbolizing the 12 months. Arranged all round were ample cakes, 52 in number for the weeks of the year, marvelous raised cakes, flat Mazurian cakes, and Samogitian loaves, all copiously studded with southern fruits. Behind them stretched 365 babas, as many as days in the year, richly adorned with icing inscriptions and swirls..." According to the chronicler, the table was laden with similarly symbolic drink, from the 12 silver amphoras of venerable old wine to 8,760 quarts of mead for the servants. That's how many hours there are in the year.

Such extravagance, however, existed only among the very wealthy and even then was reserved for special occasions. The more typical fare of Old Poland included tart soups (*barszcz*, *żur*) made with beet-sour, rye-sour or even pickle juice, *rosół* (meat broth) with barley, boiled beef with horseradish and other piquant garnishes, Hussar beef roast stuffed with onions, a wide variety of game dishes, *pierogi*, *kiełbasa* stewed with sauerkraut, *kiszka*, (groat, blood and variety-meat sausage), brine-curd dill pickles made without a drop of vinegar, *zrazy*, buckwheat groats, *bigos*, and dark rye bread.

A characteristic of Old Polish cookery was the extensive use of honey, raisins, poppyseeds as well as such spices as cloves, nutmeg, ginger, cinnamon, and pepper, not to mention such native herbs as caraway and saffron. "*Pieprzno i szafranno, mości waćpanno!*" ("Peppery and saffrony, my gracious lady!")—was the master's standing order to the kitchen staff. Among the favorites were dishes that were sweet, sour, winey, and spicy, of which boiled beef tongue in tangy, raisin grey sauce and braised goose in rich and fragrant black sauce were good examples. Since the Middle Ages, the Polish city of Toruń had been known for its *pierniki* (honey-spice cakes) which were not only eaten for dessert but were often ground and added to savory dishes. Imports included the New World turkey and French *pâté*, both of which were quickly Polonized into *indyk z sosem* (see poultry chapter) and *pasztet*.

In addition to direct borrowings, Poland adopted from France an artistic flair for preparation, decoration and presentation of food. This added a touch of refinement to the Polish banquet table, whose offerings nonetheless retained their essentially Polish character. Of wholly native origin, however, was that overpowering *polska gościnność* (Polish hospitality), which foreign visitors sometimes found overwhelming. Polish hosts seemed to bend over backwards to live up to such sayings as "*Gość w dom, Bóg w dom*" ("When a guest enters the home, God enters the home) or "*Czem chata bogata, tem rada*" (The cottage is glad to share all it possesses.") One foreign visitor to 17th-century Poland noted that this was the only country where "you go to bed sober and wake up drunk." His Polish hosts apparently were concerned by his restraint at supper and decided to drag him out of bed to the banquet table in the middle of the night. To this day, American visitors to Poland sometimes complain that "they try to wine and dine you to death."

---

* Bustards, heathcocks—*dropie, cietrzewie* (Old World game birds)

Polish cuisine is also permeated with symbolism and ritual. The Poles' most sacred meal of the year is *Wigilia* (Christmas Eve supper), which begins with the sharing of *opłatek*, a thin, white wafer sometimes referred to as angel bread, and is followed by an odd number of meatless dishes, each of which has its own religious significance. Also of great importance is the *święcone*, the blessed food eaten on Easter. Newlyweds are still traditionally greeted with bread and salt when they return home from church. Cyprian Kamil Norwid, the 19th-century poet forced to live out his days as a lonely exile in Paris, remembered his homeland in one poem as the country where a fallen morsel of bread is respectfully raised from the ground to show reverence for the gifts of God. Indeed, if a piece of "our daily bread" ever happened to fall, it was picked up with reverence, kissed and used to make the sign of the Cross. The author also remembered his grandmother first tracing a cross on the bottom of a big round loaf of crusty rye bread with her knife before pressing it to her breast and carving it up.

Backtracking a bit, we might recall that the oldest surviving Polish cookbook was *Compendium ferculorum albo zebranie potraw (Collection of Dishes)*, published in Kraków in 1682 by Stanisław Czerniecki, the court chef to a local aristocrat. It contains 100 recipes each for meat, fish, and dairy dishes, interspersed with numerous culinary hints and secrets. Other authors reworked it in various forms throughout the 18th century, but the next milestone in Polish culinary literature did not occur until 1788, when one Wojciech Wielądek published his *Kucharz doskonały (The Perfect Cook)*. It was the 19th century that first produced the definitive work on Polish cooking techniques, Lucyna Ćwierczakiewiczowa's *365 obiadów za 5 złotych (365 Dinners at 5 złotys apiece)*. Her recipes and culinary insights have become legendary, and her books, though now somewhat obsolete, continue to be reprinted. A typical cake recipe might start with the words "take 60 eggs...". Elsewhere, Ćwierczakiewiczowa urges readers to "have five kitchen maids beat the batter for three hours in earthenware bowls." Many other cooks of the day swore by Wincenta Zawadzka's 1854 *Kucharka litewska (The Lithuanian Cook)* which, despite its title, was addressed to chefs employed by Lithuania's largely Polish gentry and middle class. Jan Sztyler's modest *Kuchnia myśliwska (The Hunter's Cuisine)*, published in 1845, was the first Polish cookbook devoted exclusively to wild game dishes. Another leading cookbook in 19th-century Poland was Marta Norkowska's *Najnowsza Kuchnia (The Latest Cuisine)*. Growing literacy and changing lifestyles brought about a flood of new cookbooks in the 20th century, to mention only a few of the works of Maria Ochorowicz-Monatowa and Maria Disselowa. In post-World War II Poland, a special place is held by Irena Gumowska, who seems to turn out a new cookbook each year. She is rightly acclaimed as today's most prolific Polish food writer. Many of her valuable insights on food and nutrition have found their way onto these pages.

Perhaps it is now time to attempt a definition of Polish cuisine. Today *kuchnia polska* is a blend of hearty peasant dishes and more elegant gourmet fare, served with a flair and generous helping of hospitality. As evidenced by such qualifiers as Lithuanian, Ukrainian, French, Italian, Jewish, Bohemian, Bavarian, Greek, etc., used to describe individual dishes, it has succeeded in assimilating a broad cross-section of cultural influence, but has not lost its distinctly Slavic flavor in the process. In the most general of terms, Polish cuisine might be described as a middle-of-the-road European cuisine, meaning that it has wide potential appeal. It is less fiery than the food of Hungary and Mexico, less vinegary than German cookery, less starchy than that of Czechoslovakia, and not as sweet as traditional Jewish cuisine. On the whole, Polish food is a bit more inclined towards the tart and tangy than mainstream American cooking. This, however, refers only to the traditional American food scene before it succumbed to wide-ranging Continental, Oriental, Hispanic, and other foreign influences in the second half of the 20th century.

Among Poland's culinary contributions is the *baba* (tall yeast-raised egg bread), believed to have been taken to France by the exiled Polish King Stanisław Leszczyński (1677-1766) who became Duke of Lorraine. He may have also inspired a sauerkraut *ragoût* indigenous to that region of France and quite similar to *bigos*. The simple but elegant Polonaise butter-browned breadcrumb topping, which enhances the natural flavor of so many dishes, has made its way into menus across the globe. As home to Europe's largest Jewish community up until World War II, Poland exerted considerable influence on what is regarded today as traditional Jewish cuisine. *Kiełbasa* has become a household word in the U.S., and the shelves of American supermarkets regularly display pickle jars plastered with white Polish eagles and such words as *polskie ogórki* (Polish pickles) or *polski wyrób* (Polish made). *Pierogi* are gaining in popularity and turning up at deli counters and frozen food sections around the country.

The bakeries and meat markets in Polish ethnic neighborhoods are often among the best in a given metropolis, attracting customers of many different backgrounds. In the author's hometown of Detroit, Polish bakeries are literally besieged by lovers of light and luscious *pączki* (frosted fruit-filling doughnuts) on Shrove Tuesday, which has come to be known throughout the metropolitan area as *Pączki Day*. Many people in Buffalo take Easter Monday off to celebrate *Dyngus Day*, Polish follow-up festivities featuring a wide range of traditional Polish food. Many non-Polish Americans first acquired a taste for this cuisine at the various Polish Festivals that nearly always include ethnic food concessions. Others have enjoyed good Polish restaurants in Chicago, Milwaukee, New York, Detroit, Buffalo, Toronto, and other cities. Still others have found canned ham and pork loin imported from Poland to be more tender, juicy, and flavorful than their competitors. Many connoisseurs rank *Wódka Wyborowa*, along with its younger cousin *Polonaise* brand, among the world's finest. Yet, when all is said and done, there is no denying that Poland's culinary presence in the American mainstream has been negligible to date. Poland's population of 40 million is roughly the same as Spain's and far exceeds that of all the Scandinavian countries (Sweden, Finland, Norway, Denmark and Iceland) put together. Medieval Poland was the biggest kingdom in Europe, spanning the continent from the Black Sea to the Baltic. While the Polish-American community is now between 10 and 12 million members strong, many smaller ethnic groups boast more restaurants and cookbooks and much greater media exposure. In part, this is due to Poland's turbulent and tragic history, including the fact that it was forced to sit out the culturally prolific 19th century.

A visit to any American liquor shop will reveal shelves of vodka bottles plastered with two-headed tsarist eagles and Russian sounding names ending in -off. And yet, vodka as we know it today was first distilled in Poland, not Russia, in the 16th century. Imperial Russia first introduced the world to its own version of vodka, to its great gourmet specialty caviar, and its classic ballet during the 19th century when cultural penetration was achieving new heights. It was during that culturally expansive period that France taught gourmets the world over to appreciate truffles, *pâté de foie gras* and fine vintage wines. The British Empire spread the fame of Scotch whiskey, Yorkshire pudding, bagpipes, and foxhunts far and wide. Germany's Christmas cookies and Christmas trees, philosophers, and fine beers spilled far beyond its borders, as Italian opera, *antipasto* and *pasta* dishes found receptive admirers in many different countries. Dutch windmills, tulips, and wooden shoes, Spanish bullfights, *Flamenco* dancing and *gazpacho*, the Swedish *smorgasbord* and St. Lucy's Day, Hungary's *czardas* and goulash... these and other now familiar concepts and notions first gained international prominence during the 19th century, a time of unprecedented cultural exchange. Strauss waltzes, the Austrian operetta and the fashionable Viennese café circuit also helped to define the "good life" of that era. Few people remembered that a Pole named Kulczyński had set up Vienna's first coffeehouse in 1683. Not only the Polish origin of vodka, but even the Polish ancestry of Chopin, Madame Curie, and Copernicus remain largely unknown to this day.

Poles were in no position to correct such misconceptions, let alone share with others the best their heritage had to offer. Poland did not exist, having been swallowed up by the combined forces of Imperial Russia, Prussia, and Austria. Throughout the 19th century its people languished under foreign oppression, including forcible Russification and Germanization. Successive generations of freedom-fighters launched ill-fated insurrections against the invaders and many of Poland's finest sons were sent to Siberia or driven into exile in reprisal. For those who avoided that fate, restoration of Poland's independence became the chief preoccupation. Such niceties as cultural sharing indeed seemed to be out of place, when the nation's very survival was at stake. According to one old anecdote, the Nobel Prize Committee once announced an essay contest on the subject of elephants. The French contestant wrote a composition entitled "The Love Life of the Elephant", the German submitted a treatise devoted to "The Elephant and Its Philosophical Implications for Post-Neo-Classical Metaphysics" and the American penned a piece: "The Elephant and How to Make It Bigger and Better". The title of the Pole's essay was "*Słoń a sprawa polska*" (The Elephant and the Polish Question").

Foreign occupation and the resultant periods of privation entrenched the sanctity of food and encouraged frugality. They also elevated the home to the rank of a familiar and comforting bastion against the alien forces beyond its walls. Perhaps that is why Poles have never been really big restaurant-goers, and have generally preferred home entertaining. As a result, the Polish immigrants who began flocking to America in the late 19th century set up many schools and churches, bakeries and meat markets, but far fewer restaurants than other ethnic groups. This cultural difference between Poles and Americans is illustrated by the following comparison. If one American tells another: "Mr. Smith eats out four times a week," the response is likely to be "Lucky guy!" If a Pole were to say the same thing about a *Pan Kowalski* or *Nowak*, the most typical reply would be "That's too bad!" In a Polish listener this evokes pity, because it suggests someone whose wife has walked out on him or who otherwise has been deprived of regular, home-cooked meals. The bottom line is that Polish cuisine has received far less public exposure than that of many other ethnic groups.

FOOD MEANS CULTURE AND NUTRITION

A Polish-American couple that visited Poland for the first time in the 1980's shared the following experience with me. One morning they turned up unannounced at the village home of long-lost relatives they had never met, having taken the address off a yellowed envelope sent to their late mother and mother-in-law many years earlier. There was no end to hugging and kissing, and before they knew it, breakfast was on the table. There were scrambled eggs, rye bread and butter, hot tea with lemon, and a crystal decanter of home-made raspberry cordial to help wash it all down.

The couple was surprised that throughout the meal their hosts kept profusely apologizing for such meager fare. "Meager," the American visitor thought to himself, "why this is what we have for that big Sunday breakfast and stick to toast and cereal the rest of the week." To Poles, however, something so lowly and pedestrian as *jajecznica* is hardly fit for guests, especially visitors from America. The hosts in question would have liked to turn out a lavish spread, featuring ham and other cold cuts plus a colorful array of pickled mushrooms and vegetables. Eggs could be included, but in the form of butter-fried eggs stuffed in their own shells or, at the very least, hard-cooked ones laced with a creamy sauce. They had been unprepared, however, and besides, the visitors turned up during the financially-strapped summer months before the money for the cash crops had come in.

One Polish book on home entertaining contains the entry "Breakfast for foreign visitors." The meal in question includes such gourmet delights as caviar, smoked salmon, hot-steak roll-ups, and champagne. Naturally, such opulence would be reserved only for special occasions, but even on a daily basis Poles prefer to start the day with a meal of cheese, cold cuts or eggs, with the accompanying bread or rolls and butter, tea, coffee or cocoa. Today's American style "starch and sugar" breakfast of cereal, toast, sweet rolls, doughnuts etc., definitely has fewer devotees.

This particular cultural trait of Polish eating habits, the high protein breakfast, is also nutritionally sound. Polish nutritionists insist that a hearty breakfast is essential to start the day right and should comprise roughly one third of a person's daily food intake. Weight watchers are therefore advised to skip some other meal, never breakfast. For no matter how big a breakfast one eats, all the calories will be burned up in the course of normal daily activities.

At this stage, a word about Polish meal patterns is in order. The average Pole starts his day with *śniadanie* (breakfast) some time between 5 and 8 a.m. depending on his or her work schedule. First shift factory workers, for instance, punch in at 6 a.m. and office employees usually start work at 8 or 9 a.m. Somewhere between 9 and 11 a.m., workers and schoolchildren alike have their *drugie śniadanie* (second breakfast), similar to the American bag lunch. The main meal of the day is *obiad* (dinner), which is normally eaten between 1 and 5 p.m. This is the biggest meal of the day, accounting for 40-45% of a person's daily calorie intake. It usually consists of a big bowl (about 2 cups) of homemade soup, a main course, and dessert. These calories also will be burned up, as long as a person does not retire for the night within the next five to six hours.

The lightest meal of the day is normally *kolacja* (supper), served between 6 and 8 p.m. In some families this can be simply a re-run of breakfast (cheese, cold cuts, eggs), but could also include cold fish, aspic dishes, cooked vegetable salads, or sweet dishes like pancakes or rice baked with apples or other fruit. Nutritionally this makes sense, because a lighter meal toward the end of the day is much more easily burned up than a heavier one.

The misadventure of a Polish basketball team that toured the U.S. not long ago illustrates culinary cultural clashes devoid of nutritional implications. The cagers had ordered their meals at a restaurant along the way and had received their salads. Every so often the cook, who was holding up the main course, would ask the waiter whether they had finished their salads, only to hear: "They haven't even touched them." The Polish cagers and their coach were simply unaware of the fact that Americans tend to view their salad as a kind of appetizer eaten before the main course. Poles, by contrasts, always eat their main course together with their salad. The French do things still differently by eating their salad after the main course before the cheeses are served. These cultural differences are nutritionally irrelevant; the main thing being to get enough fresh greens and veggies down the hatch. Here Poles could stand to learn a thing or two from the French, Italians, and Americans who on the whole are much bigger salad-eaters.

Back in 1979, a friend invited me to a new Polish-American restaurant, Tutag's on the Hill, that had opened in Warren, Michigan. I ordered a serving of *pierogi* and was surprised when the waitress reappeared shortly to ask: "Mashed, baked, French fries, or American-fried potatoes?" Thinking that she has mistaken my order for someone else's, I told her that I was having the *pierogi*, but she only replied: "That's O.K. We serve potatoes with all our dinners." Although that seemed as incongruous as having a side order of rice with a serving of meat and rice gołąbki, it goes to show the kind of unusual hybrids that may emerge when different culinary habits come into contact.

On the health scene, a widely held notion is that Americans have never been as nutrition-conscious as in the final decades of the 20th century. Indeed, someone may peel a banana, wink and say "potassium". Others go around sprinkling oat bran over most everything, popping magnesium pills, or avoiding eggs like the plague. Most, however, know only a smattering of what good nutrition is all about. Their superficial knowledge is not acquired at academic courses in dietetics nor from serious literature on the subject, but usually comes from magazine articles, "miraculous" diet books, and above all, aggressive food commercials. A good example is the "great cholesterol scare".

Clogged arteries are an obvious health hazard, but cholesterol as such is a natural substance needed in proper quantities to promote the smooth functioning of the body's natural processes. The claim "contains no cholesterol" can be misleading when it is found on the label of nuts, popcorn, and other vegetable products that never contained any in the first place. Moreover, the cholesterol count listed on food products obscures the fact that individuals react differently to dietary cholesterol. Some people who are on a steady diet of foods high in cholesterol, apparently for a variety of genetic and other factors—notably strenuous exercise—show no elevation of blood cholesterol. Others who put themselves on fat-free crash diets find that their cholesterol level has actually increased. The reason is that in a fat-starved body the liver may step up its own cholesterol production to compensate. The only way to find out where you stand is to have your doctor give you a simple blood test. Then, follow his advice to the letter.

Periodic "break-throughs" widely publicized by the sensationalist media often create confusion rather than shedding new light on the problem. A recent report out of Denmark made the rounds of the international press. Researchers there found that the cholesterol level of a group of males dropped, even though they were on a steady diet of eggs, butter and pork, as long as they additionally consumed one ounce of fish a day. That meant as little as a few sardines, a small herring or several forkfuls of tuna fish. Even to those not partial to fish, it was a small price to pay for enjoying the kind of food they liked but had been afraid to eat. Yet before too many people could rush down to the supermarket and stock up on canned salmon and tuna, researchers in Atlanta reported completely different findings. Their test group had been fed nothing but fish for two weeks, but their cholesterol level did not drop one iota.

The bottom line of all this is that much more research is needed before the cholesterol question is fully explained. It is often noted that Eskimos, whose diet consists mainly of fish and seal, experience no cholesterol problems, because beneficial fish oils keep it in check. But how can one explain that the Tibetans, who eat no fish or vegetables whatsoever and consume only meat and grain products, are also largely untroubled by cardio-vascular disease? One can only conjecture at this point that in addition to dietary cholesterol, genetics, environment, and other factors play a role that requires much additional research.

Half-truths and misconceptions, deliberately promulgated by the food industry have created a confused public prone to successive scares, fads and crazes. Besides cholesterol, another dirty word is "calories" which even some educated people regard as units of fat. They have apparently forgotten their high-school chemistry and physics classes, where calories were correctly defined as units of energy. Calories turn into fat only when more are ingested than consumed. And despite the huge upsurge in consumption of "lo-cal" and "diet" products over the past decade, overall obesity in America has not declined.

A good example of food fallacies was the great popularity of a fast-food innovation known as "Chicken McMorsel" or something of the sort. Believing that "chicken is good for you", people wolfed down huge quantities of these tasty, crunchy nuggets, without realizing that they were made from fatty chicken skins and scraps which were then boiled in beef suet, one of the highest-cholesterol fats known to man. Non-dairy creamers were another such hoax. Since milk products contain cholesterol, people were led to believe anything labeled "non-dairy" must be a healthier alternative. The manufacturers were not about to set things straight, and for decades supplied the public with creamers containing highly saturated coconut and palm oil.

Mention could be made of the outlandish diet crazes that have swept the country in recent decades. There were egg diets, steak diets, grapefruit diets, high-protein and low-protein diets, plans based on high carbohydrate intake, as well as sugar-free, low-fat, and vegetarian regimens, even a drinking-man's diet that urged dieters to start the day with a Bloody Mary. The medical value of these crazes was questionable, and some actually proved harmful, especially when people put themselves on such diets without consulting a physician. Any abrupt change in normal eating habits is a shock to the system, and a diet top-heavy in any one food group can cause hazardous nutritional deficiencies and even serious damage to the liver, kidney, and other vital organs.

Ellen Goodman, a leading columnist, ran this delightful assessment of the current food scene in the *Boston Globe*:

"Eating in America today is like taking medicine. Pleasing our palates has become a secret vice, while fiber-fueling our colons has become a most public virtue. If we had a menu for the way we think about food, it would look like a prescription pad.... The only certified culinary cure of my childhood was chicken soup for the common cold. Things that were good for you came with a maternal stamp of approval. An occasional piece of liver. Endless glasses of milk.

"But somewhere along the way, we became a far more sophisticated, food-fixated culture.... Even television ads today read like entries in a medical journal. The caring American family is shown as they begin the day with a bowl full of antidotes for rectal cancer. That is followed almost immediately by a potion to prevent osteoporosis.... Oat bran is the current four-star item on the Nouvelle menu, having barely edged out calcium among the most culinary cautions.

"The food-is-medicine school offers a balanced diet of worries. We don't just concentrate on the bad things in food—from fat to Alar—we get obsessed with the good....

"But there is something missing in any cuisine that asks us to think of a banana as a portion of potassium. There is something skewed about an eating regimen designed to do the most for every part of your body except the tip of your tongue."

I take exception only to Ms. Goodman's allegation that food sophistication has increased, when in reality we are dealing with a pseudo-sophistication based on incomplete or otherwise misleading information. A case in point is the osteoporosis she mentions. It is true that with age people's bones decalcify and become porous. However, it is also true that a person's bone-building process usually ends in his or her teens, and a milk-rich diet during childhood and adolescence is about all that is needed in most cases to ensure strong, healthy bones. In later life, especially in old age when osteoporosis can become a problem, dietary factors do little to reverse this process. But the manufacturers are not about to publicize this fact, when those of the Social Security set are among their biggest customers.

Despite the efforts of the Federal Government, to mention only the Truth in Packaging Act, food-producers and advertisers have always found clever ways of deluding the consumer without actually running afoul of the law. Even back in 1951, Ellen and Vrest Orton noted in their delightful book, *Cooking with Whole Grains,* that one commercial baker had marketed something called "all-wheat bread". What the label said was 100% true: the bread in question was indeed all-wheat, meaning that it contained no rye, barley, corn or whatever. That sound-alike term made the average bread-customer think he was buying a whole-grain loaf. What he was actually getting was a bread made of refined white flour with perhaps a bit of molasses added to darken its color. Using real whole wheat flour would have increased the price of the loaf, thereby decreasing demand. It should be remembered that the America of 1951 was still on its white-bread binge and there was only a limited market for breads other than cotton-fluff stuff at that time.

An effective way to immunize yourself against all the TV hucksters, who want you to fall for their "new and improved" this or that, is to bear one thing in mind. The giant food industry is not concerned with your health, sensible nutrition, or convenience. It is only out to make money and will try to talk you into whatever it can get away with! Misleading packaging, exaggerated health claims, and other ploys are all part of the game.

The food industry not only uses high-pressure salesmanship to promote whatever it can make big money on, but has also been known to conveniently suppress information that does not serve its ends. Years of clever propaganda by the powerful citrus-growers lobby has convinced several generations of Americans that there is no better source of vitamin C than orange juice and grapefruits. The truth is that black currants have five times the vitamin C of oranges, strawberries have nearly twice as much, and both red and white currants have significantly more. In fact, even cabbage contains more vitamin C than lemons, oranges, or grapefruits. To put it another way, a 100-gram (about 3½ ounce) serving of fresh cole slaw provides 64% of the average person's daily requirement of vitamin C, whereas an equivalent quantity of grapefruit supplies only 54% thereof. Why don't the cabbage producers counterattack, you may ask. Well, I for one don't know if a cabbage-growers' association even exists, and if it is does, it certainly has failed to project its message to the general public. The following chart may come as an eye-opener to many.

Vitamin C in milligrams per 100-gram serving

Rose hips (Rosa rugosa)	800-1,200
Parsley (greens)	177.7
Black currants	177.1
Green peppers	107.4
Dill (greens)	100
Brussel sprouts	71.4
Kale	65.3
Strawberries	63.4
Spinach	48.8
Cabbage (white)	48
White currants	44.7
Red currants	44.4
Broccoli	46.2
Kohlrabi	44.6
Red cabbage	42.1
Savoy cabbage	42.1
Cauliflower	36.6
Oranges	35.3
Sorrel	35
Raspberries	31.3
Lemons	31
Grapefruits	25.6
Cranberries	22.8
Tomatoes	21.2
Blackberries	21
Blueberries (European wild)	14.7
Lingonberries (mountain cranberries)	11.7
Sour cherries	7.1

Want more examples? Why is the general American public unaware of the fact that rabbit meat supplies more protein per serving but contains less fat and cholesterol than chicken, beef, pork, or veal? Not to mention the fact that it is more easily digestible than any of the above and therefore recommended to those on bland or otherwise restricted diets. Since we have invoked the name of that culinary super-villain of the late 20th century, cholesterol, no one need be reminded of the oat-bran craze. Yet why is so little said about the cholesterol-controling properties of lecithin-rich flaxseed? Why are high-fiber and protein-rich buckwheat groats so little known?

Good nutrition is constantly stressed throughout this book. There is a colossal difference between balanced, common-sense eating habits and all the trendy, pseudo-diet and quasi-health innovations the advertisers try to foist on an unsuspecting public. Unfortunately, all too often they succeed. One way to avoid being conned and manipulated is to read the label. Not the "new and improved", "40% less calories", or "no cholesterol" splashed across the front, but the very fine print where the ingredients are listed. Before you drink the next can of diet soda or gorge on that container of artificial dessert topping, or some of the fake-fat desserts on the market, see if the ingredients don't sound like the inventory of a chemistry lab. The potassium hydroxide, disodium phosphate, adipic acid, fumaric acid, synthetic fats, gums, emulsifiers, chemical spoilage retardants, artificial sweeteners, imitation flavoring, artificial coloring, etc., would make most anyone lose his appetite.

True, these chemical additives have been cleared by the Food and Drug Administration which considers them fit for human consumption. So far! However, before you become convinced that the current artificial sweetener is not a health hazard, remember that the same authorities once permitted saccharine and cyclamates to be marketed until they were found to be cancer-causing. The same holds true for the bleached paper coffee filters which a generation of Americans nonchalantly used on a daily basis without suspecting they were harmful. The general rule of thumb, therefore, is to stick to real, natural foods refined as little as possible such as those found in the produce department, at the fresh meat and fish counter and among the staples (flour, grains, pasta, salt) in your supermarket. Only in rare cases are natural foods harmful. Obviously people with allergies should avoid certain foods and those suffering certain kidney ailments, for example, are advised against high-alkaline spinach, sorrel, rhubarb. On the whole, however, natural ingredients eaten in moderation seldom cause problems. It is the additives you must avoid. The apple remains one of God's most healthful gifts to humanity; it is the alar, a waxy coating that acts as a preservative, that may be carcinogenic.

The food philosophy behind our Polish Heritage Cookery perfectly coincides with the sentiments of Julia Child, one of America's top specialists in good food and nutrition, who says: "In the 70s, there was a tremendous interest in home cooking. Now people don't have time to cook—they say: Well, if you know how to cook, you can cook very fast, and using fresh, not processed foods, you know what you're getting because you choose them, and you know what's in them. Frozen food just doesn't have that wonderful fresh taste... I'm worried about our concern with nutrition—about people being afraid of eating because of the scare tactics and warnings on the TV ads. I hope we will have more scientific information and not go off on tangents. Moderation, weight-watching and exercise allow you to eat many things and maintain good health."

The exercise referred to by Ms. Child deserves a comment, although in our fitness-obsessed era it might appear that everything on this subject has already been said. In reality, a great many people seem to have quite a lopsided attitude toward exercise. I am sure you know people who surround themselves with every manner of push-button gadgetry. They mow their lawns by riding mini-tractors and hop into their cars when the place they are going is only half a block away. The cars, of course, are loaded down with automatic this, power that, and push-button something else, and when they get back they push another button for the automatic garage door to open. If you asked them about it, they would say it's to save time and effort. Chances are, most of the time they save is spent in an easy chair in front of the boob-tube. They probably use a remote-control channel-changer so they don't have to budge to switch programs. Eventually these same people, who do everything in their power to burn up as few calories as possible, notice that they are getting fat, flabby and out of shape. Do they change their daily routine to include more ordinary physical activity? Not on your life! They either go on some crash diet, sign up at a weight-control clinic, join an aerobics class or start going to a spa, fitness club, or gym. In other words, they pay a fortune for something they could correct on their own right around the house.

Besides doing sit-ups and push-ups at home and taking brisk walks, you can also burn up calories simply doing ordinary things without the aid of too much gadgetry. You might avoid hopping into the car when what you have to attend to is within reasonable walking distance, or mow the lawn if not with a manual mower, then at least with a power model that you actually have to walk behind. The kitchen provides many opportunities to exercise while doing something constructive, like using a hand-cranked meat-grinder, pounding cutlets, kneading yeast dough. Although this may smack of heresy by the standards of the advertising and convenience-product industry, what about scrubbing the floor on your hands and knees? For the able-bodied, it is marvelous exercise. Not only will the floor be cleaner than you ever thought possible, but many of those muscles which have fallen into disuse will get a good honest work-out. Instead of storing calories, you will be putting them to good use and your body will be the winner. The more different muscles, ligaments, and joints that are regularly exerted, the less chance there is of a painful sprain during that occasional stretch to reach something on the top shelf or some unusual bend or twist. Moreover, regular physical activity is an excellent way to keep cholesterol in check and promote many of the body's natural functions. It strenghtens the heart, increases the lungs' air capacity, improves circulation, promotes regularity and provides an overall sense of well-being. Aren't those reasons enough to choose a nice brisk walk the next time you are tempted to plop yourself in front of the TV set?

In addition to food fallacies, fad-inspired nutritional obsessions, and a one-sided view of exercise, industry opinion-molders have also worked overtime to entrench a self-serving approach to food preparation itself. Their classic battle cry has been "slaving over a hot stove" and, indeed, generations of Americans have come to believe that cooking means back-breaking drudgery. It should be remembered, of course, that said opinion-molders don't really care about anyone's time or convenience. They are interested in getting people to fall for the punch line that follows: "...Therefore use our new instant, just add hot water, stir and enjoy" or "pop our quickie dinner into the microwave" or "send away for one of our hot, home-delivered pizzas."

Cooking is not a form of enslavement or drudgery. It is also much more than following this or that recipe and slapping together something to keep body and soul together. Food preparation is a way of life, a frame of mind, a pleasant and rewarding pastime. It was no coincidence that the authors of America's top-selling, many time reprinted cookbook called their creation *The Joy of Cooking*. You will see their point when you begin regarding cooking as a creative cultural pursuit rather than a dreaded chore. It enables you to give reign to your artistic fantasy and imprint your own seal of personal achievement on your culinary creation. It can be an intellectual challenge, like when the fridge is nearly bare and you still succeed in whipping up a tasty gourmet treat.

With the proper attitude, cooking can be a good way to relax after a hard day's work. You simply have to regard it as a hobby the way some people think of gardening, tinkering, card-playing, stamp-collecting, music making, or various handicrafts.

Above all, nothing provides a greater sense of accomplishment than those smiles of approval on the faces of family and friends, especially when they ask for seconds. There is a great satisfaction in knowing that you made it yourself and enjoyed doing it.

If you keep an open mind and try to forget the years of commercial indoctrination, perhaps, this book can help make all that a reality. In many cases you may be surprised at how little time, money and effort it takes.

POLISH COOKERY—A CUISINE WHOSE TIME HAS COME

When we first set about preparing this book in 1987, we approached Polish cookery as just so many recipes for different ethnic dishes. In the course of extensive research, interviews, and experimentation, however, the pieces began to fall into place, and out of them emerged an entire philosophy underlying the Polish culinary heritage. Initially, we also wondered whether there was room in today's America for yet another ethnic cuisine. After all, the United States is now a virtual kaleidoscope of culinary offerings from nearly every corner of the globe. That is a far cry from my boyhood days in the Detroit of the late 1940's and early 50's, when about the only "ethnic" restaurants around were chop-suey joints and spaghetti parlors. Even the pizza was still in its infancy as far as mainstream America was concerned.

As we delved deeper into the workings of Polish cookery, we came to the conclusion that it indeed had a great deal to offer. Perhaps 20 or 30 years ago that might not have been the case, but many of the traits that form the Polish food philosophy fit in beautifully with the dietary, cultural, and economic requirements of turn-of-the-century America. To simplify things, let us take these attributes one by one.

VARIETY: Like any new ethnic cuisine, Polish cookery gives meal-planners a wide array of change-of-pace alternatives. This may be especially helpful to those who have fallen into a hamburger, chicken, fish, and macaroni & cheese rut, and those who often say: "I just don't know what to fix for dinner." (Incidentally, this book contains a number of new ways to prepare the above-mentioned foods). Polish cuisine will add variety to your culinary repertoire without revolutionizing your gastric system or depleting your pocketbook.

As has already been noted, Polish cookery is a middle-of-the-road cuisine, meaning that it is neither too highly seasoned, nor does it generally require exotic, expensive, or hard-to-get ingredients. Most dishes can be prepared with foods from the average supermarket. It can diversify your eating habits by using familiar ingredients in combinations you may not be used to. Prunes, for instance, beautifully bring out the flavor of roast pork and fowl. The most typical poultry stuffing is seasoned with dill, not sage. Duck seasoned with marjoram and stuffed with apples is another specialty, and boiled beef tongue in a tangy raisin sauce has been a favorite for ages. A broad spectrum of soups includes everything from clear, plain and flavored bouillons to hearty meal-in-a-bowl type soups. Among the old favorites, which are still very popular today, are cream of sorrel, dill pickle, vegetable-barley, sauerkraut, beet, and mushroom soups, to mention but a few. There is a head-spinning variety of appetizers and salads. Mushrooms, which are favored today by low-calorie enthusiasts, are used to flavor a great many dishes and are frequently the main event in Polish cuisine. There are noodle, dumpling and grain dishes of every description and a wide variety of pancakes and numerous egg and dairy dishes to choose from. There are also a great many cakes and desserts, some quite involved and others surprisingly simple. What could be easier than honeyed cucumbers or sugared tomatoes? The former tastes something like watermelon, only better, and the latter remind many people of red currants. Add to this a wealth of homemade beverages, cordials, jams, pickles, sausage, ham, and bread, and you can rest assured that everyone will find new food ideas, cooking techniques, and serving suggestions between the pages of this book.

NATURAL INGREDIENTS: In general, Polish cuisine prefers fresh, natural ingredients that have been "improved" upon and adulterated as little as possible. This is not to suggest that you should do all your shopping at a health, organic or natural-food shop, because of the outrageous prices. In most supermarkets, however, you can count on reasonably fresh raw materials in the produce department and at the meat and fish counters. When shopping for staples, stick to the basics and avoid the commercial combinations, packaged mixes, and convenience items. Not only are they laced with additives you probably don't need, but they are quite expensive. The slightest amount of processing or "improvement" on the basic product adds money to your food bill. So cinnamon sugar is more expensive than mixing your own sugar and cinnamon at home, and ounce for ounce tea bags coast more than loose tea. The use of basic natural ingredients gives you more control over what you prepare and serve your family. If you prepare your own low-calorie sour cream as suggested in the dairy chapter, it will contain only the additives found in the dairy sour cream and milk you start with. If you buy one of the commercial "lite" sour creams, you would have to be a graduate chemist to understand the fine print where the ingredients are enumerated.

We agree with Julia Child that frozen food lacks the taste of fresh food, but we would not want to dismiss deep-frozen products entirely. Especially good are plain frozen berries and vegetables—the kind without additional flavorings or sauces. At home you can doctor these up to taste like something straight from the garden, however, there is a slight loss of vitamins compared to fresh fruits and vegetables. Home-freezing is a good way to store many typical Polish foods like *pierogi, zrazy, gołąbki* and various baked goods. There is some controversy as to whether *bigos* can be stored frozen without its flavor being distorted. If you are fortunate enough to have a vegetable garden, berry bushes, and fruit trees, you can ensure fresh produce by using only natural fertilizers and eliminating or at least restricting the use of chemical pesticides. These penetrate to the very core of fruits and vegetables and no amount of scrubbing or peeling can remove them.

Poles' preference for natural ingredients is carefully guarded by Polish government health officials. Following the collapse of Communism in 1989, Poland's markets were flooded with enticingly packaged processed foods from the West. Some of them, however, were banned as being unfit for human consumption. One packaged soup mix from the Orient was found to contain more synthetic flavoring compounds than dried vegetables and noodles. A West European hot chocolate mix could not be marketed in Poland because it contained an impermissible additive. German bubble gum containing the harmful artificial sweetener cyclamate was taken off the market.

Incidentally, as this book was being prepared, a conference of health experts in Washington, D.C., reported that glutamates were not the harmless flavor-enhancers they were once thought to be. Most processed savory foods (frozen dinners, soup mixes, bouillon cubes, canned gravies, lunch meats, etc.) are generously laced with monosodium glutamate (MSG) and similar compounds. Oriental cookery adds it to most everything, and hence, the concept "Chinese restaurant syndrome", which includes everything from a dry throat and difficulty swallowing to dizziness and nausea, depending on the amount ingested and a given eater's allergic reaction. The Washington conference found that its systematic use could lead to far more serious problems. Although we were unaware of those findings when preparing the recipe sections of this book, we suggested only a sparing use of MSG especially in certain ground meat dishes. Whether you want to use it at all is entirely up to you. In general, one of the main principles of Polish cookery is: fresh and natural is best!

HIGH-FIBER DIET: As this book was being written, the U.S. Surgeon General issued a recommendation for Americans to eat more legumes, cereal dishes, whole-grain breads and high-fiber vegetables. This was an exact description of traditional Polish peasant cookery. Coarse dark breads, ryé-flour noodles, dried peas, beans, and lentils, prunes and other dried fruits, high-fiber vegetables, such as beets, carrots, rutabagas, and cabbages as well as groats of every kind, have been the dietary mainstays of the Polish peasantry for ages. Naturally, the more well-to-do classes looked down on such humble fare as they feasted on white rolls made from highly refined flour and other more "sophisticated" foods.

Little did they know that it was the commoners who had a far healthier diet. One of their favorites was the "king of grains", buckwheat groats, a delicious, dusky, nut-flavored cereal that was high in fiber, protein, B vitamins, and minerals. In fact, *kasza gryczana* cut across class boundaries and was equally at home in a peasant cottage and on the banquet table of the nobility. To this day it plays an important role in the Polish diet and deserves wide popularization in America where irregularity remains a serious problem. Buckwheat groats also add variety to those in the potato, rice, and pasta rut.

Other high-fiber products widely used by Polish cooks include whole dried yellow peas, dried white beans, Brussels sprouts, cauliflower, pumpkin, wild blueberries, red currants, gooseberries, apples, strawberries, and hazelnuts. The net result of the Polish high-fiber diet is that irregularity and the serious health problems to which it can lead is far less common in Poland than in the U.S. Besides the fiber content of the average Polish diet, the habit of eating soup on a daily basis and the wide use of sour milk (see below) also help to keep people regular.

HIGH-PROTEIN BREAKFAST: It has already been stressed in the preceeding section that a healthy, energy-producing breakfast should account for roughly one-third of a person's daily food intake. But knowing something in theory is one thing, whereas putting it into practice is quite another. What about those people who say: "I am never hungry in the morning" and opt for a zero-calorie breakfast of black coffee or skip the meal entirely? All one can say is: "If you haven't tried it, don't knock it!" Over the years, in our Warsaw home, we have hosted quite a few Americans who also included breakfast-skippers as well as toast and doughnut addicts. Those who stayed at least a week were soon into the swing of things and actually began looking forward to breakfast. One day they got creamed farmer's cheese with chives, assorted rolls, and white coffee. The next day there may have been hot *serdelki* (knackwurst) with mustard, a few radishes, rye bread, and tea with lemon. Then perhaps a continental breakfast of rolls, butter, jam, honey, and cocoa. The following day cold cuts and cheese may have turned up on the breakfast table. Other days there would be hot stuffed eggs in shells, smoked salmon, scrambled eggs with mushrooms, cold pâté with horseradish sauce or eggs in a glass Polonaise. Except for the occasional continental breakfast, the main high-protein course of the typical Polish breakfast is often followed up with a dessert of *babka*, *placek* (coffee cake) or the like. In winter, hot milk soups containing noodles, rice or groats are enjoyed by many. Polish men often like a really hearty Old Polish breakfast of *bigos*, pork cutlets or steak roll-ups, usually accompanied by rye bread and tea.

Getting back to our American house guests, many of them reported they had started eating big breakfasts after returning to the United States. The mechanics are quite simple. If you eat a good, hearty breakfast three or four days in a row, even though you are not really hungry, by the fifth day your stomach will start growling: "I want food!" early in the day. It is that easy to get into the habit of a good Polish breakfast!

SOUR MILK: Poles have a penchant for sour milk. This is really nothing more than uncooked yogurt made with fresh milk. For the benefit of queasy American eaters, the advertisers have worked overtime to pass their yogurt off as a kind of custard, pudding, or fruit dessert, but the fact is that yogurt is nothing more than fermented milk. It differs from Polish-style *zsiadłe mleko* in that it ferments while being heated, whereas sour milk clabbers at room temperature. Sour milk is easier to digest than fresh milk and it contains a treasure chest of valuable nutrients, described in greater detail in the dairy chapter.

Cold, creamy sour milk is a refreshing drink just as it is, although it can be additionally flavored with fruit syrup, beet sour or dill-pickle brine. (The "morning after" crowd finds the latter two versions an especially good thirst-quencher!) Stir a spoonful or two of cherry preserves into a cold glass of *zsiadłe mleko* and you have a sort of instant milk shake. Or whirl it in a blender with fresh or frozen sugared strawberries for a real frothy and fruity milkshake. A bowl of cold sour milk makes a meal in itself when served with hot boiled or fried potatoes, garnished with chopped dill, or buckwheat groats. It is also the basis of that refreshing, beautifully pink, cold beet and garden-green soup known as *chłodnik* as well as a number of other cold soups. There are many good reasons to get into the sour-milk habit, including the fact that it contains fewer chemical additives than commercial yoghurt, if made with store-bought milk and a little dairy sour cream, none whatsoever if you are able to get pure, fresh milk straight from the cow.

ON THE TART SIDE: Many, but certainly not all, Polish dishes are on the tart side, without really being vinegary. Although vinegar is used in marinated products like gherkins, pickled mushrooms, and spiced fruits, as well as various dishes, it is not the sole souring substance used in Polish cuisine. There is also lemon juice, but that is not all. An important ingredient used to impart a tart taste is *kwasek cytrynowy*, sometimes known in English as lemon sour or sour salt. Its generic name is citric-acid crystals, and they are repeatedly referred to on these pages. Usually only a pinch of these pure-white crystals is needed to give the desired tang to soups, sauces, and desserts. Citric acid is less harsh and therefore more stomach-friendly than distilled vinegar. Unlike lemon juice, it never takes on a bitter taste when cooked.

For ages, Polish cooks have also made use of other souring agents such as *żur* (rye sour), *kwas buraczany* (beet sour), *kwaśnica* (sauerkraut juice), and *serwatka* (whey). All of them are healthier than vinegar and contain important nutrients to boot. Sauerkraut juice, obtained when you drain sauerkraut, can be stored indefinitely in a sealed jar in the fridge. It is good for souring all savory foods; for a change of pace we suggest you to try it in place of vinegar the next time you prepare vinaigrette or other salad dressing. Rye sour, which is used in a traditional Old Polish soup, imparts a milder tartness than sauerkraut juice to all savory dishes. The same is true of ruby-red beet sour. Unlike the other colorless souring agents, it should be used only in dishes where a reddish hue is desired, such as *bigos* or stews. Whey, which you will have access to if you make any of the cheeses in the dairy chapter, is the mildest of the four and gives a nice, winey tang to whatever it is added. All four of the above tart liquids can be used as meat marinades.

GOURMET CUISINE: A great many misconceptions have grown up around the term "gourmet". When people hear someone speak of "gourmet food", "gourmet restaurant", or a "gourmet food shop", many immediately think of wildly overpriced, fancy dishes incorporating exotic ingredients in unusual combinations. Quail stuffed with truffles and flavored with cognac would certainly qualify, but a soft-boiled egg would not. They call to mind expensive caviar, capers, vintage wines, gourmet blends of coffee, imported English marmalade, tinned *pâté de foie gras* and the like. Polish cuisine also has its share of gourmet delicacies of this type. The following menu would surely satisfy the most discriminating epicurean:

HORS D'OEUVRES: Assorted canapés, skewered *hors d'oeuvres*, caviar and relishes. Apperitifs of choice.
COLD APPETIZER: Walleye in mayonnaise, veal roulade with lingonberry sauce, smoked goose breast, egg and tomato "toadstools", duck in Malaga aspic, hare pâté, assorted sauces, relishes, bread, rolls and butter.
HOT APPETIZER: Butterfried fresh wild mushrooms (boletes, meadow or lactarius mushrooms), crusty rolls.
SOUP COURSE: Strong beef bouillon served in twin-handled bouillon cups and garnished with chopped sorrel.
FISH ENTRÉE: Poached walleye Polonaise, buttered new potatoes.
MEAT ENTRÉE: Roast beef Hussar style, potato puffs, Brussels sprouts with creamy hot dill sauce, leek and apple salad garnished with chopped walnuts.
DESSERT: Brandied raspberry compote, baba au rum, coffee, brandy, liqueurs.

In this book you will find numerous examples of the kinds of food many people think of when the term "gourmet" is mentioned.

In reality, however, gourmet cuisine means any food that starts with the freshest quality ingredients and is handled with the utmost care. This can mean a sauce that is gently simmered a long time, delicately seasoned with just the right herbs and spices, or otherwise pampered to perfection. But no dish is more worthy of the gourmet label than a classic omelet which contains nothing but beaten eggs fried in butter and seasoned with a little salt, provided that the eggs were collected in the henhouse the same day and beaten the right number of times, that the butter was neither too hot or too cold, and the omelet was folded at precisely the right time. In effect, it is not how expensive or complicated a given dish is, but rather the combination of fresh ingredients and culinary expertise that goes into it. It should be served with a touch of elegance. This can mean the simple elegance of serving a plain dish, like the above-mentioned omelet, on one's everyday china, as long it is unchipped. On the other hand, even the fanciest and priciest concoction would loose its gourmet status if slopped onto a paper plate.

The elegant touches associated with gourmet cuisine are also evident in Polish cookery. Naturally, one would expect candles, flowers, the best china and cutlery, as well as artistically garnished serving dishes at a diplomatic banquet or dinner party in a well-to-do Polish home, but the flair for elegance has also trickled down to the more modest segments of society. Even in a humble Polish farmhouse, chances are that the host's favorite home made cordial will be served to the guests in a crystal carafe, and his wife will add an appetizing sprinkling of fresh dill to the hard-boiled eggs in sour cream sauce she brings to the table. A nice little touch found even in Poland's lowest-echelon eating place, the *bar mleczny*, is a fresh flower or other natural greenery on each table. This may be no more than a few daisies in summer, or dried wildflowers in spring, but it somehow makes the most ordinary dish tastes better. Plastic flowers would not be the same.

IMPROVISATION: As noted in the section on Poland's culinary development, at various points in this country's turbulent history sheer survival required a flexible, make-do attitude towards food. This, combined with the Poles' fierce individualism, has created a cuisine which puts a premium on inventiveness and improvisation. It would be hard to find two Polish homes that make their *bigos, pasztet, zrazy,* or cheesecake exactly the same way. We have encountered families where most everything served is on the bland side and others where herbs and spices are generously used. Regarding onions and garlic, our family tends towards the upper end of the scale. While other cookbooks may specify a bud of garlic, don't be surprised to find "1-3 buds garlic" in many of our recipes. We simply don't want to impose our particular tastes on anyone else and prefer to provide adequate leeway. Other recipes might say "season to taste with caraway seeds or marjoram" or "other flavoring possibilities include chopped blanched almonds or walnuts, raisins or candied orange rinds". As you follow any of the recipes, feel free to increase, decrease or entirely omit any seasoning according to personal preference.

Court bouillon (vegetable stock) is frequently called for in this book and traditionally is made with the standard soup greens: carrots, celeriac, parsley root, leek, and in some cases, Savoy cabbage or onions. If one of the ingredients is missing, make it anyway. If you have only onions, you can still make a stock. If you lack one of the ingredients called for in a given recipe, look around and chances are that you will find an adequate substitute in your cupboard, fridge, or freezer.

Except for baked goods, the proportions in most recipes are variable and depend mainly on personal preference and availability. This is specially true of soups, meat and vegetable dishes, casseroles, and various fillings. If you love sauerkraut dishes but want to cut down on meat, you can prepare a bigos containing only a little meat for flavoring. If you don't have as much farmer cheese on hand as called for in the recipe for cheese and potato pierogi, use what you have and perhaps add a little sour cream or grated yellow cheese to the filling. The various stews and fricassees are a specially good example of dishes where you can add, substract, or modify at will. Approaching cuisine as a creative challenge, not a cut-and-dried science, and viewing recipes as orientational guidelines rather than hard-and-fast rules is really what Polish cookery is all about. If you come up with your own way to make any of our recipes easier, tastier, or otherwise better, be sure to tell us about it by dropping us a line here in Warsaw or c/o the publisher.

CREATIVE LEFTOVERS: An important aspect of the art of improvisation is the creative use of leftovers. This can be among the most challenging and rewarding experiences, and it is also economical. To some people, the term "leftovers" means something old and inferior, but any surplus of cooked food that is properly stored in the fridge or freezer remains a valuable, high quality ingredient. Cooked meat, for example, opens the way for a variety of interesting fricassees, meat-filled *pierogi* or potato dumplings, *naleśniki* or *paszteciki*, not to mention cold meat salads and canapé spreads. The best *bigos* ever can be made by using frozen, cooked, cubed meat from roast pork, beef, veal, poultry and game that has accumulated over a several month period. This not only saves time, money and effort, but it ensures a great variety of meats, the hallmark of a good *bigos*.

You may say there is nothing to eat when you see little in the fridge except the cooked pasta from yesterday's spaghetti or some noodles left over from the beef Stroganoff. All you need, really, is an egg or two to turn them into a change-of-pace noodle cake which can be served with a sweet (fruit syrup, preserves, jam, fresh or frozen berries, canned pie filling) or savory (sauce, gravy, pork cracklings, stewed mushrooms) topping.

Leftover mashed potatoes can be the basis for potato dumplings or cutlets. Naturally, cooked rice or groats can re-emerge in any number of casseroles, limited only by your imagination. The head, tail, backbone and fins of a large fish being used for other purposes make a tasty fish chowder or aspic. The cured beets left over when making beet sour can be cooked up into a kind of *bigos*, alone or with the addition of some fresh cabbage. If there is nothing in the fridge but a small piece of *kiełbasa*, a few slices of ham or other cold cuts and a little bacon, you are set to make a good smoked-meat soup like pea, sauerkraut, bean, beet, or sour white soup. Stale white bread (French, Italian, Vienna) can be ground into crumbs, used in poultry stuffing or for Bohemian dumplings. Stale rye or black bread can also be ground, but strips thereof are added to one type of steak roll-ups and it is also used to make bread sour for use in *biały barszcz* (one kind of tart white soup). Do not hastily discard the marinades from your homemade or store-bought pickles, peppers, spiced fruits, marinated mushrooms, etc. They can be used to season and give a bright, new flavor twist to soups, salads, stews, meats, and other dishes. The apple peelings usually discarded whenever you prepare *szarlotka*, pie, or whatever, make both a mild cider vinegar and a caffeine-free tea. These and other suggestions on how to put leftover foods to good use are scattered throughout this book.

OVERLAP COOKERY: We have coined the term "overlap cookery" to describe a cooking technique long used by Polish cooks, although no special word for it exists in Polish. It is similar to creative use of leftovers with one important difference. As defined above, leftovers are foods uneaten at the previous meal or incidental by-products obtained during their preparation. Overlap cooking, by contrast, involves purposely preparing more than needed for a given meal with a view to putting the excess to some other use. It can also mean consciously planning the use of by-products from one course in other courses of the same meal or a subsequent repast.

Since it is more easily demonstrated than explained, here is one classic example. An American-style breaded pork chop is consumed and forgotten as part of a single main course. By doing things the Polish way, much more mileage can be obtained from the very same piece of meat. The Polish *kotlet schabowy* (breaded pork cutlet) is pounded, breaded, and fried, but the bones first removed from the chops make an excellent stock for clear red *barszcz* (beet bouillon). The cooked meat from the pork bones, together with some sautéed mushrooms can be ground into a filling for pastry turnovers (*paszteciki*) to accompany the *barszcz*. That's not all! The cooked beets can be grated and mixed with horseradish for a quick and easy *ćwikła*. (If canned beets are used, just the liquid can be added to the pork stock and the beets can be grated for *ćwikła*.) Moreover, the cooked soup greens (carrots, celeriac, parsley) can be diced, combined with an extra cooked potato or two, diced dill pickles, an apple or other crunchies for a nice mayonnaise-laced supper salad. How is that for not letting anything go to waste?

The other aspect of overlap cooking is deliberate overpreparing. For example, when preparing *crêpes (naleśniki)*, fry up several more than needed, roll them up in foil or plastic wrap, and refrigerate overnight. Next day, slice the rolled-up *crêpe*s into *crêpe* noodles for soup or to accompany your main course. Whole cooked potatoes and any plain cooked vegetables are good for any number of creamy, cold supper salads. Cooked rice or groats can form the basis for savory casseroles and cutlets as well as sweet desserts. Many other examples are included between the covers of this book, and chances are, once you get the hang of it, you will find new ways to practice this old culinary technique.

THRIFT: The times of trial that befell Poland over the ages forced all classes of society to cut down and make do. When things improved, some reverted to their wasteful ways, while thrift to others became second nature. The philosophy underlying this book is that both wasting food and overpaying are senseless. Delicious and healthful food need not cost a fortune; it does, however, require certain culinary expertise as well thrifty shopping. The first rule of thumb is to get to know your merchandise. The well known saying that "you get what you pay for" is often, but not always, true. Usually a top-of-the-line brand of preserves is close to what you could make at home in quality, whereas an economy product might contain more syrup than fruit. Both sausages prepared the traditional way by ethnic butchers as well as baked goods from a real bakery, although more expensive, far surpass the quality of their supermarket equivalents. On the other hand, many fruit canneries pack cans with the very same product, except that you will pay less for the ones with a supermarket chain's own label. In this case, the latter is the more sensible alternative.

I personally feel that most American beers taste pretty much the same, although there are exceptions such as Carling's Red Cap Ale. In Warren, Michigan, back in 1988 I whipped up a little Polish gourmet dinner for a few relatives and friends, and since it was a very hot day, cold beer was a much appreciated thirst-quencher. Rather than one of the highly advertised "premium" brews, I got a local budget brand, Altes Lager for 89¢ a quart. Undoubtedly the monogrammed, crystal pilsner glasses it was served in had something to do with how good it tasted. The same is true of wine. Many wines from California are extremely good and can hold their own against their French counterparts, although admittedly they may lack the snob appeal of the latter. Furthermore, one of the best all-round coffees on the American market these days is Maxwell House Rich French Roast. With it you can brew a delicious Polish-style cup of coffee without overpaying for gourmet shop blends.

Because food attitudes are changing, many things that yesterday were looked down upon as poor people's food may today be a healthier alternative. One example are the vegetable and cereal fillers that were once thought of as merely inexpensive "stretchers" added to sausage and various ground meat dishes. The same holds true for the many meat and vegetable dishes as well as the various meat and grain combinations which were once regarded as something fit only for the peasantry. They have now come into their own at a time when many people are consciously trying to limit their intake of meat, fat, and cholesterol. As seen in the preceding sections, the element of thrift weaves its way through other aspects of Polish cookery, including improvisation, naturalness, nutrition, and even gourmet cuisine. This means that a Polish approach to food preparation enables one to serve tasty, wholesome, nutritious, and artistically appealing food without going bankrupt.

GENERAL APPEAL: Polish cuisine has a great potential appeal to the general American public because it does not really come on strong in any one area. While some dishes tend to be on the tart side, as noted above, this is not to say that every Polish dish is mouth-puckering sour. In fact, you could choose recipes from this book for every day in a year that no one would regard as tart. For reasons that have already been discussed, Polish food encompasses a wide range of tastes and is not dominated by any one spice or condiment like curry powder, soy sauce, vinegar, jalapeño peppers, oregano, or the like. While many Polish dishes definitely have a distinct character all their own, others are neutral enough to suit even the most pedestrian palate. I have not met many Americans who did not like steak roll-ups, roast pork with prunes, fish Polonaise (with dill-flavored hard-boiled egg topping), boiled beef with horseradish sauce, breaded pork cutlets, roast chicken Polonaise (with dill-flavored, meat and bread stuffing), roast duck stuffed with apples, meat and/or mushroom filled pastries, hot stuffed eggs in their shells or spring vegetable soup, not to mention a host of cakes and desserts.

On the other hand, anyone who dislikes the taste of sauerkraut in any way, shape, or form will probably not take to *bigos*. But those who say its high acidity does not agree with them because they think of sauerkraut as something heated and served just as it comes from the can are in for a surprise. Polish cooks usually drain and rinse their sauerkraut, doctor it up with various ingredients, and let it simmer a good, long time. As a result, it loses much of its offending harshness and tastes a lot different than sauerkraut straight from the can. Many other Polish dishes would be appreciated mainly by gourmet, adventurous eaters, or those raised on them since childhood. These include such old favorites as tripe, *czernina* (a soup containing duck or goose blood), *chłodnik* (a cold beet & soup), certain sausages, and variety-meat dishes and sauces which by American lunchroom standards might indeed seem exotic.

This is largely a question of mind over matter. During my college days at Madison, Wisconsin, I had a friend who disliked liver and other variety meat (*podroby*), until one day I treated him to beef tongue simmered in a thick dark sauce. Since he loved gravies and thought he was eating veal, he enjoyed the meal very much and was surprised to learn what he had just eaten. When all is said and done, the broad cross-section of dishes presented in this book includes something for every palate. There are people who say: "I don't care for Polish food!", and usually they have in mind *kapusta, kiełbasa, gołąbki, pierogi,* and a few other common stereotypes. This book is also for them. You can use it to cook family dinners 365 times a year, throw banquets, and whip up simple snacks without anyone thinking of them as "Polish" until they learn otherwise. As a result, this may well be one of the few ethnic-flavored, general-purpose cookbooks on the market today.

DRAWBACKS: So far I have highlighted the positive traits of Polish cookery which can add taste, variety, and good nutrition to the standard American menu. Yet Polish cuisine also has its drawbacks. A common complaint of the cholesterol-minded is its copious use of eggs, butter, sour cream, lard, fat back and other such ingredients. Rich foods indeed typify the cuisine of the historically well-to-do classes, peasant emigrants in America, and many people living in Poland today. That is why our book does not promote a steady diet of such foods, and stresses the benefits of the traditional peasant cookery of yesteryear and those of its beneficial traits that have trickled into general Polish eating habits. The old 19th-century cookbooks that started recipes with "take 60 eggs and five pounds of butter..." were meant for cooks in the employ of gentry and wealthy townspeople (*mieszczanie*). Simple farmers also yearned for rich foods but seldom actually ate them. Poverty as well as frequent religious fasts combined to make Polish peasant fare surprisingly lean. A spoonful of pork cracklings, meat drippings, lard or butter to flavor a plate of potatoes, groats, or beans was more than offset by the coarse black bread and back-breaking farm work. All too often they had to content themselves with linseed or hemp oil for flavoring, and such food was referred to as *postne jedzenie* (fastday fare). At one time, even those who could afford it would not eat eggs or dairy products during Advent or Lent. Poorer farmers would regularly take eggs, milk, butter and cheese to market leaving only the whey and buttermilk for the family. About the only time most peasants ate their fill was at Christmas, Easter, the harvest feast, and occasional weddings and christenings. It is a steady diet of rich foods, not occasional overindulgence, that causes health problems. The typical Polish peasant diet comprised healthy but once socially frowned upon cabbages and root vegetables, as well as abundant wild mushrooms and berries.

This rather lean diet changed after the same peasants emigrated to America, got jobs in industry, and eventually were able to indulge the cravings that poverty had suppressed in the Old Country. The image of the meat-loving Polish-American blue-collar worker functions as a stereotype to this day. In Poland, meanwhile, the 1970's economic boom, fueled mainly by massive Western credits, changed eating habits to where many could afford meat three times a day.

Since good nutrition is a cornerstone of this book, we do not urge anyone to emulate bad eating habits whatever their source. In fact, these pages are sprinkled with nutritional tips, including the warning that people on cholesterol-restricted diets should avoid variety meats in general, and calf's brains in particular. The fact that about one-half of the meat consumed in present-day Poland is in the form of sausage and cold cuts, which are high in fat, cholesterol, and sodium, is surely nothing to be promoted. That does not mean, however, that a normal, healthy individual should never enjoy *kiełbasa* or ham. Although there are many entries in our salad chapter, the fact remains that Poles eat fresh greens less frequently and in smaller quantities than Americans, who do not consider a dinner complete without a nice tossed salad on the side.

Throughout our book we have sought to offset nutritionally less desirable cooking practices by proposing healthier alternatives. We frequently state "simmer in butter or oil", leaving the choice to you. Remember that margarine can be substituted in all cooking and baking where butter is called for. You can also replace eggs with Egg Beater or other such cholesterol-free substitutes. We have even shown ways to make yolk-free mayonnaise and low-fat sour cream at home. One unsuccessful experiment was our attempt at low-fat *skwarki*. Since golden nuggets of fried salt pork are such a common topping, we tried simmering some of the imitation bacon bits that Americans sprinkle on their tossed salads in a little salad oil, in hope that the smokey flavor would permeate the oil. The finished product did not resemble *skwarki* in the least and was downright awful.

Even the successful substitutes are rarely quite the same as the real thing. *Faworki* (angel-wing pastries) boiled in oil are simply not as tasty as those fried the traditional way in lard. Very often substitutes involve some sacrifice in flavor, texture and aroma, so ultimately you must decide what is preferable in a given case.

HOW TO USE THIS BOOK

When we set about writing a cookbook that would be a fairly complete compendium of Polish cookery spanning the past two centuries, we were confronted by a serious problem: how would we cram all the information we planned between the covers of a single book? One solution would have been to go into two volumes, but that would have created new complications with production and distribution as well as a higher retail price beyond the reach of many readers. We therefore decided to try and compress the text as much as possible. One feature of this approach which you will immediately notice is the wide use of abbreviations. Considering the number of times long words like "tablespoon", "teaspoon", and "temperature" are used in books of this type, this meant a considerable saving of space. Even short words like "cup", "pint" and "quart" appear with sufficient frequency to make a difference in a book of this size. The most common abbreviations used in this book are the following:

T. = tablespoon	lb. = pound
t. = teaspoon	oz. = ounce
c. = cup	temp. = temperature
qt. = quart	min. = minute, minutes
pt. = pint	hr. = hour
	hrs. = hours

In addition, we made it a point to render all quantities in numerals rather than words, and we are sure that everyone will know that "⅔ c." means "two-thirds of a cup". The telegraphic style that often drops out an "of" or "the" as in "a pinch or 2 cinnamon" should also present no problem. Another space-saving measure involved dispensing with all but the first customary paragraph indentations in the recipe text. This often made it possible to save nearly an entire line of print, because the last line in a paragraph sometimes comprised no more than one or two words.

The most radical space-saving measure, on which we deliberated the longest, was the decision to dispense with the practice of listing the ingredients at the top of each recipe. It is true that the overwhelming majority of cookbooks—whether American, Polish, Chinese, or whatever—employ this technique, but considering the two-volume alternative, we ultimately decided against it. For one thing, I had been writing the Polish Chef column for 16 years now without receiving any complaints about its no-ingredient-list format. Our decision to carry this approach over into this book was reinforced by one the most authoritative cookbooks ever published in America. We have in mind the *Gold Cook Book* by master chef Louis P. De Gouy who also dispensed with the ingredient list throughout his more than 1,200-page work. If, however, you feel thumb-tied without the customary list, we suggest you lightly underline the ingredients in pencil. We are convinced, however, that after following two or three recipes, glancing at the text to pick out the ingredients will become second nature and the pencil route will no longer be necessary.

All recipes and other entries are listed bilingually—first in English and then in Polish. Very often the English heading will be longer, because it has to describe what in Polish can be rendered by a single word. For instance, *BEET & HORSERADISH RELISH* is known in Polish simply as *ĆWIKŁA*, and *PYZY* have been rendered in English as grated potato dumplings. A slash appears in the heading to separate different names for the same food. So you will find *KUTIA/KUCJA* to denote two regional variations of a traditional wheat, honey, and poppyseed pudding served in eastern Poland on Christmas Eve. *SĘKACZ/DZIAD* means that the same cake goes under two different names.

Both the English and Polish headings are listed alphabetically in the index at the back of the book. Remember that Polish accented letters (ł, ż, ś, ć) are always listed after their non-accented equivalents, so *CZERNINA* will be ahead of *ĆWIKŁA* and you will encounter *LIKIER* before you run into *ŁAZANKI*. If you remember that your grandmother used to make barszcz but don't know what it is called in English, look under *BARSZCZ*. It will lead you to that section of the soup chapter where various white and red soups by that name are found. If you have a nice piece of pork and are wondering how to prepare it, look in the index under *PORK*. On the page it will direct you to, and on adjoining pages you will find grouped together a number of recipes to choose from.

A few words should be said about variables, whose understanding is absolutely essential to your quest for culinary expertise. Many recipes in this and other cookbooks may call for "about 1 c. water" or direct you to bake something "20 min. or until golden brown". It is true that various package mixes and other commercially prefabricated foods have been calculated rather precisely, but with basic, natural ingredients this is not always possible. A cup of flour may seem straightforward enough, except that a loosely packed cup suddenly grows smaller when it is tapped down even slightly. One person's idea of "simmer at medium heat" differs from someone else's, as does "set aside until cool enough to handle". Besides these subjective differences, there are variables over which the cook has little control. These include the quality, texture and moisture content of various ingredients, the hardness of the water you use, local elevation above sea level and the settings on your oven. When you set your oven at 375° does it actually produce exactly that temperature? This can be checked easily enough with a thermometer, but some of the other variables are more difficult to determine.

If you have a favorite brand of flour and usually turn out baked goods with excellent results, you may be surprised if you suddenly switch brands. The new brand may also be labeled "enriched all-purpose flour", but it may be just a shade more finely or coarsely milled, contain a different amount of gluten or simply come from wheat grown in slightly different soil and weather conditions. This may also be the case with many other seemingly ordinary products.

The point is to be aware of such variables as you follow these or any other recipes and make the necessary adjustment as you go. Knowing your ingredients and equipment is a good start towards acquiring a "feel" for cooking. When something seems to be browning too quickly, although the specified cooking time has not elapsed, reduce the oven temperature somewhat or loosely cover the food with a piece of aluminum foil. We have included such hints a number of times, but to do so in every recipe would have swelled the size of this already substantial volume.

Some people nowadays scoff at the way the old-timers approached cooking: "Take a little of this and a bit of that", or "mix until it is just right", or "add as much water as the dough will absorb". In many cases they were not far off the mark. What they were saying was that cooking requires a certain "feel" and knack, and even the best recipe is no substitute for that. For instance, no recipe for *pierogi* dough can give the exact amount of water needed to get it right, precisely because of such variables as the dryness and texture of the flour and the hardness or softness of the water. If the dough is damp and sticky, a bit more flour must be worked in. If it is dry and crumbly, additional moisture is needed. If you try a recipe the first time and it doesn't come out just right, don't be discouraged; try it again. Remember, even the best cooks started by preparing a given dish the first time, and they too got to where they are through trial and error.

In general this book promotes the use of fresh, natural ingredients, although at times we have called for convenience items or short-cut methods. It also calls for traditional techniques whenever these are superior. If a recipe states that a wooden spoon should be used or that something should be placed in a glass or crockery bowl, that means that a given food might adversely react to metal utensils. Unless otherwise specified, electric appliances can be used to chop, dice, shred, purée, pulverize, or whatever, when any of these techniques are called for. Sometimes you may find, however, that it is more convenient to chop a single onion on a cutting-board with a knife, rather than dirty up your fancy food-processor for such a small job. In our experience, such things as pâté and poppyseeds are best ground in a meat-grinder or—in the latter case—in a special poppyseed grinder. The blender will shred the meat for the pâté, but its texture won't be right. And the poppyseeds will just bounce off the sides without getting crushed.

This book also warns against traditional techniques that are nutritionally or otherwise unsound. In the "olden days", both in Poland and in Polish neighborhoods in the U.S., it was common to see berries and sugar turning into syrup in large glass vessels placed in sun-drenched windows. The syrup was delicious, but the direct sunlight destroyed most of its vitamin C. As to whether to soak liver in milk, it is a question of taste vs. nutrition. Yes, the milk blunts the liver's frequently bitter edge. At the same time, it washes out much of the iron which is the liver's most valuable mineral nutrient.

One final remark. I have no doubts whatsoever that as you follow the recipes in this book, you will hit upon helpful hints, short cuts and improvements the authors never thought of. When you do, be sure to pass them to others, for that's exactly as it should be. That is called progress.

* * *

If you have managed to wade through this far too lengthy foreword, I can only add:
GOOD COOKING! GOOD LUCK! and "SMACZNEGO"!

ROBERT STRYBEL
Warsaw, Summer 1992

SPICES, HERBS, SEASONINGS AND OTHER INGREDIENTS

The people of many different countries fry, braise, bake, or boil meat, fish, and vegetables in much the same way. Often it is the flavoring ingredients used to bring out their taste that makes a given dish distinctly Hungarian, Chinese, Italian, Polish, or whatever. We believe a closer look at some of these seasonings will increase not only your knowledge of Polish cooking but your overall culinary sophistication as well. Polish cooks are especially fond of marjoram, dill, caraway, juniper, allspice, and bay leaves, whereas mint is largely restricted to a few regions of the country. The smell of sage remind many Poles of sore-throat or toothache medicine.

Besides traditional herbs and spices, we have included a number of other ingredients, which come in handy in any kitchen. Especially worth looking into is sour salt (citric acid crystals) and other souring agents that are less harmful than vinegar. Although it should not be overused. Maggi seasoning is worth recommending as a convenient way of deepening the color and flavor of soups, gravies, and fricassees. It was also with your convenience in mind that we developed a series of homemade seasonings which will enable you to quickly impart a genuine Polish flavor to a variety of dishes.

Also included is an easy recipe for homemade frozen bouillon cubes. Their preparation requires a minimum of supervision, but they can be a real godsend when you want to whip up a quick homemade soup or gravy without reaching for something out of a can. Do not overlook the sections on salts, sweeteners, thickeners, and leavening agents, a basic knowledge of which every self-respecting cook should have at his or her fingertips.

TABLE SALT
sól kuchenna

When the term "salt" is used, nearly everyone thinks of fine, free-flowing kitchen salt. This is nothing more than sodium chloride ($NaCl$). Salt is often iodized (enriched with iodine) in areas whose atmosphere, water supply, and soil conditions lack this important micro-element. In addition to being the world's most widely used seasoning, which improves the flavor of all savory dishes, it is also an important preservative. With the advent of refrigeration this role has diminished somewhat, but without salt it would be impossible to cure ham, bacon, salt pork and other meats, salt herring, smoke fish, pickle mushrooms and vegetables, or brine-cure a host of other tasty and nutritious foods. The body may require up to 5 grams (about 1 t.) salt per day if strenuous work is being performed in hot weather, less for inactive individuals. Salt is absolutely essential to promote the body's natural function. The food scares of recent times have sent millions of Americans scrambling for chemical substitutes (including products based on ammonium or potassium chloride) or inclined them to eliminate ordinary salt from their diets. This should be done only on a doctor's specific advice. Too much salt, however, can be a health hazard because it causes the body to retain too much water, raises blood pressure and overtaxes the heart. The only way to determine what amount is right for you is to consult your physician. *Note*: Most of the recipes in this book have been salt-reduced, as we feel everyone can sprinkle his soup, sauce, meat or egg with a little extra if he or she so desires. On the other hand, it is nearly impossible to remove salt that has been added to food during cooking.

COARSE KOSHER SALT
sól gruba

This coarse-grained salt is obtained from sea-water and contains natural iodine and other natural minerals but no artificial additives. It is something used to sprinkle rolls and other baked goods. If you plan to prepare any homemade seasoned salts (described further on in this chapter), we recommend that coarse salt be pounded in your mortar or pulverized in your processor together with the other spices. *Note*: Pickling salt is another natural salt that is recommended when preparing dill pickles and other such products; it is finer-grained than coarse salt and therefore dissolves more readily in water and other liquids.

MONOSODIUM GLUTAMATE
glutaminian sodu

Long used in the Orient as a flavor-enhancer, these white crystals have made their way into kitchens the world over, and Poland's are no exception. Extracted from the vegetable protein found in soybeans, grain, and beets, M.S.G. has no discernable taste of its own but heightens the natural flavor of savory dishes, especially meats and meat-based soups and gravies. We recommend its sparing use, particularly in ground meat dishes like gołąbki, meatballs, kiszka, and kiełbasa, i.e. no more than ¼–½ t. per lb. of ground meat. Don't get into the habit of sprinkling it on every meat dish, because everything you cook will then end up with the monotonous taste of canned soup, frozen dinners and institutional food. *Note*: Since Oriental dishes are often heavily seasoned with M.S.G., those who make a steady diet of such food sometimes develop an allergic reaction (parched throat, difficulty swallowing) popularly known as the "Chinese restaurant syndrome".

BLACK PEPPERCORN
czarny pieprz ziarnisty

These familiar black grains are actually the dried berries of the pepper plant (piper nigrum). Several of them are added whole to most savory soups and marinades, allowing them to slowly release their flavor. They release even more flavor when cracked or partially crushed, but not ground, in a mortar, and in this form they may be used to season stews, goulashes, and similar dishes. Peppercorns are also used to make pieprzówka (Polish pepper vodka) which some people swear by as an upset-stomach remedy. In general, pepper promotes digestion by stimulating the flow of gastric juices and helps to preserve food which it seasons.

GROUND BLACK PEPPER
czarny pieprz mielony

Next to salt, ground black peppercorns are undoubtedly the most widely used seasoning in Polish and many other cuisines. Indeed, it would take quite some doing to count the number of times the expression "salt and pepper to taste" appears in this book. It is used to season soups (even when whole peppercorns are used in the stock), sauces, meat, fish, vegetables, and many other foods, including Poland's world-famous kiełbasa. Although chiefly confined to savory dishes, ground pepper is also used in some recipes for Polish honey-spice cake (piernik or miodownik). Nearly every cook has a pepper shaker nearby and it is a permanent fixture on many tables, but the most flavorful and aromatic pepper is that which is freshly ground. A few twists of a handy pepper mill will perk up the flavor of a vast array of foods. Whenever "pepper" is referred to in this book, it means ground black pepper unless otherwise specified.

WHITE PEPPER
biały pieprz

Whereas black pepper is made from underripe berries that are picked and allowed to blacken as they dry in the sun, white pepper is the fully ripe berry of the same plant from which the black outer shell has been removed. While white pepper is a bit milder in taste, it is more aromatic than black pepper. In general, the difference is not significant. Ground white pepper is chiefly used by gourmet cooks who want a pepper flavor in white sauces and other light-colored foods without the black specks of ordinary ground pepper.

ALLSPICE
ziele angielskie/pieprz angielski

The Polish name of this dried tropical berry (Pimenta officinalis) indicates the nationality of the spice merchants who first brought it to Poland, hence the spice was dubbed "English herb" or "English pepper." Its English name is more descriptive, since its fragrant aroma is reminiscent of various spices such as nutmeg, cinnamon, cloves, and juniper. Polish cookery makes fairly wide use of the whole allspice grains in small quantities (usually 1–3 grains) in soup, sauces, marinades, and various savory dishes. It is less frequently ground and used to season roast meat. Allspice is widely used in pickling.

BAY LEAVES
listki laurowe/bobkowe

The dry leaves of the bay plant (Laurus nobilis) give a pleasingly aromatic undertone to a wide variety of soups, gravies, meats, and sauerkraut dishes. Together with peppercorns and allspice, bay leaves are the basic spice used in nearly all meat stocks and court bouillon. Anywhere from ½–2 bay leaves, depending on how fragrant you like your food, will greatly enhance the flavor of stew, goulash, and bigos. They are also used in pickled vegetables, marinated mushrooms, and meat marinades. Although bay leaves are usually used whole or halved, powdered bay leaf is convenient for sprinkling roasts and various other savory dishes.

MARJORAM
majeranek

Next to pepper, marjoram (Majorana hortensis) is probably Poland's most widely used seasoning. Sometimes referred to as wild oregano in English, it is somewhat reminiscent of the oregano widely used in Italian cookery, but has milder and sweeter undertones. Polish cuisine makes use of marjoram to flavor pork, water fowl, game dishes, sauerkraut, certain soups (notably pea and tripe), pâtés, and certain types of kiełbasa. A pinch or two of this fragrant herb will perk up the flavor of stew, goulash, and other stewed meat and vegetable dishes as well as cooked vegetables and mushrooms. Although used generously with pork, duck, and goose, a light sprinkling of marjoram can brighten the taste of chicken, turkey, beef, and lamb. It is also used to season variety meats (kidney, hearts, lungs, poultry gizzards). Available in the spice section of your supermarket, you can also raise marjoram in your back garden. When mature, cut it, tie in bunches, and hang up to dry. When dried, sieve the marjoram and store in an airtight container.

CARAWAY SEEDS
kminek

These aromatic seeds (Carum carvi) are widely used in Polish cuisine. They are used in rye bread, pork dishes, sauerkraut, farmer's cheese, baked potatoes, sausage, as well as in various soups and sauces. Polish cookery even includes a caraway soup. Caraway seeds are used whole or ground, but in most dishes they are best crushed. Simply place several pinches in your mortar and pound them a bit until the seeds are broken into 2–4 pieces. This is the most economical way because just a few crushed seeds release a lot of caraway flavor. *Note*: Cumin, a close relative of caraway, is almost identical in taste and may be used interchangeably whenever caraway is called for. Caraway seeds are also used to make kminkówka (caraway vodka).

MILD PAPRIKA
słodka papryka

These are fresh, mild peppers of the Capsicum family that are dried and ground into a bright red powder and used as a seasoning. It is available in nearly all American food stores. Whenever we refer simply to paprika in this book, it is this seasoning that is called for. While Polish cooks use it less extensively than their Hungarian counterparts, for whom this is the No. 1 seasoning, they do use it to add color and flavor to a variety of foods. These include farmer's cheese, various hors d'oeuvres, goulash, meat, fish, eggs, vegetables, sauces, and soups like tripe. Before being used to lard meat, sticks of frozen salt pork may first be sprinkled with paprika for added flavor. *Note*: Paprika does not take well to high heat, turning dark and bitter. It is best to sprinkle hot dishes with paprika shortly before serving so it retains all its color and bouquet.

CAYENNE PEPPER
ostra papryka/pieprz turecki

This is the hot variety of the same plant from which mild paprika is derived. Because it is extremely fiery, a pinch or two is all that is needed to add a little zing to any of the dishes described above.

DILL SEEDS
nasiona kopru

Fresh garden dill (see below) is Poland's most popular herb. It is used to add color, flavor, aroma, and nutrition to a wide variety of dishes, but the dried dill seeds also have numerous applications. After drying, dill seeds lose some of their volatile oils and have flavor more reminiscent of caraway than fresh dill. As a result use them whenever you would caraway seeds. The scientific name for dill is Anethum graveolens.

FENNEL
koper włoski

The Polish name for fennel (Foeniculum vulgare) is "Italian dill" indicating that it is viewed as an import. In Poland it is more widely used for medicinal purposes than as a seasoning. Mothers regularly give their infants fennel tea for stomach aches and gas. It may be used in very small quantities on white meats, chicken, veal, fish but not all Poles like its sweetish, anise-like aroma.

BLACK CUMIN
czarnuszka

These black aromatic seeds (Nigella sativa) have essentially only one use in Polish cookery. Like caraway and poppyseeds, they are sprinkled on bread and rolls.

POPPYSEEDS
mak

Crushed poppyseeds, flavored with honey, raisins, nuts, etc., are widely used by Polish cooks in cakes and dessert dishes, mainly associated with Christmas. Whole poppyseeds (Papaver somniferum) are used primarily to sprinkle bread, rolls, and cakes and are mixed in with the batter of tort makowy (poppyseed torte).

SAVORY
cząber

This delightful peppery herb (Satureja hortensis), which you can grow in your own garden, is used largely, though not exclusively, to season legumes (beans, peas, lentils). Use several pinches to perk up the taste of otherwise bland, cooked, dried beans as well as cooked green or wax beans and pea, bean and lentil soup. It is also good in meat dishes, poached fish, meat or potato salads, poultry stuffing, mushroom dishes, and various cooked vegetables. Savory looses its flavor in cooking, so it should be added to hot dishes toward the end. Although the use of this herb is largely limited to the western Wielkopolska (Poznań) region, it deserves to be more widely promoted, since it blends so nicely with so many different foods. *Note*: Savory is recommended in salt-restricted diets, since its peppery zest seems to have a hint of saltiness about it that helps make flat-tasting, unsalted foods more palatable.

JUNIPER
jałowiec

The brownish- or bluish-black, pea-sized berries of this evergreen shrub (Juniperus communis) have a pungent, sappy, coniferous-forest aroma that enhances the flavor of game dishes and helps neutralize the excessively gamey flavor of wild meat and fowl. It can therefore also be used to tone down undesirable off-flavors in such dishes as stewed kidneys and roast mutton. Add 1–3 juniper berries to a pot of stewed sauerkraut or bigos to brighten their taste. A sprinkling of ground juniper will add a bright new flavor twist to nearly any meat dish, including poultry, beef, and pork. For a change of pace, add a pinch or two to cooked cabbage (white, red or Savoy) or beets. *Note*: Whole juniper berries are used to flavor homemade Polish juniper vodka (jałowcówka), which is produced commercially as Hunter's vodka (Wódka Myśliwska) and has a taste similar to British gin and Dutch genever. Ground juniper is also used to season certain types of kiełbasa, especially myśliwska (hunter's sausage).

CORIANDER
kolendra/kolender

These small, round, yellow seeds with their pleasantly piquant aroma instantly remind many people of honey-spice cake or gingerbread, and so they should. This spice (Coriandrum sativum) is among the flavor ingredients of piernik, as well as holidays cookies, marzipan (almond confection) etc. But coriander also imparts an interesting flavor to many savory dishes. It is usually included in dry ham marinade as well as in the vinegary marinades in which cucumbers, mushrooms, fruit and herring are pickled. A pinch or two of ground or crushed coriander will perk up the flavor of pork dishes, pâtés, pea, bean and lentil soup, beets, puréed apples, carrots, and cabbages.

LOVAGE
lubczyk

The dried leaves of the lovage plants (Levisticum) are a natural flavor enhancer for meat and meat-based stocks and gravies, but they should be used sparingly. A few pinches underscore the meat's natural flavor, but too much produces a heavy, overpowering taste that detracts from its goodness. This is the same flavor found in the Maggi seasoning which we frequently call for in this book. *Note*: As a cultural aside, we should point out that in the Middle Ages lovage was regarded as an aphrodisiac, but only due to a bit of linguistic confusion. Its late-Latin name, Levisticum, was interpreted to mean "love herb". As a result, other languages, including Polish, English, German (Liebstöckel), and Russian (lyubistnik) perpetuated this misconception. Its proper Latin name should have been Ligusticum, which means nothing more than something from the Roman province of Liguria, for lovage was popularly called "Ligurian parsley".

MINT
mięta

Polish palates and those of the English-speaking world, France, Italy and the Arab countries are poles apart (no pun intended!) as regards this refreshing cool-tasting herb (Mentha piperita). In the latter it is used in mint sauce for lamb and mutton, in salads, cooked vegetables, alcoholic beverages, and confections, as well as in general purpose seasoning, whereas in Poland it lacks universal appeal. In fact, chopped fresh or dried, crushed mint leaves are limited to a few regional dishes. In the northeast they are used to season dishes containing farmer's cheese and buckwheat groats. In the southern mountain region they are sometimes sprinkled on scrambled eggs. We find both these applications very tasty with one reservation: use only a pinch or two; if you overdo it, these dishes will end up tasting like mint-flavored toothpaste or mouthwash.

SAGE
szałwia

The fact that sage (Salvia officinalis) is widely used as a seasoning in America and chiefly for medicinal purposes in Poland can lead to some amusing situations. When many visiting Poles first bite into those over-saged American-style pork sausages or sagey poultry seasoning, they immediately think of toothache medicine! Indeed sage extracts are used to this day to relieve the pain of toothaches, gum disorders, and sore throats in Poland, hence this seemingly strange association. For some reason, sage was once used more widely than at present to season roast pork. A light sprinkle helps reduce the fishy flavor of less-than-really fresh fish. It was once also used in the western Wielkapolska region in sausages. When the authors spent two years in Bay City, Michigan (1977–79), they first encountered a locally produced kiełbasa nicely seasoned with both marjoram and sage. The first immigrants from Wielkapolska began arriving in the area in the 1870's, and they passed their sausage-making skills on to their offsprings. To this day, this little town's three major Polish meat markets (Krzysiak's, Łobodziński's, and Kłosowski's) continue to prepare a lightly saged kiełbasa quite different from that found in such Polonian centers as Detroit and Chicago.

MUSTARD SEED
gorczyca

These seeds come from two different basic plants. White or yellow mustard (Sinapis alba) has pale to medium yellow seeds, is used to make mild-tasting mustards and is the type most readily available in the spice section of American supermarkets. Brown mustard (Brassica nigra) has dark-brown seeds and is used to prepare sharp brown mustard. Whole white-mustard seeds are used in the preparation of pickles, pickled vegetables, and marinated mushrooms. Dry mustard (mustard seeds ground to a powder) can be used in small quantities to perk up the flavor of beef, pork, and poultry as well as hot and cold sauces. Some experienced Polish cooks lightly sprinkle chicken with dry mustard before roasting which brings out the flavor of this rather bland meat. Too much mustard will give the chicken an undesirable mustardy flavor.

SAFFRON
szafran

Saffron (Crocus sativus) comes from the stigmas of the autumn crocus and once was far more widely used in Polish cuisine than at present. For various reasons it deserves to be rediscovered. The bright orange color, pungently bitter taste, and ridiculously high price of saffron are misleading. Since only a pinch is used at a time, this herb gives dishes a pale, golden hue and soft, mellow taste, and a little goes a long way. Add a pinch to the water in which rice is being cooked and this common grain will turn into a gourmet delight. A pinch added to a broth or bouillon that is unappetizingly pale will give them a nice golden glow and elegant flavor. Saffron was once used to color egg breads (babka, placek, chałka) by cooks who wanted to skimp on eggs but still produce a beautifully golden-colored bread. This function seems to have regained its currency in today's cholesterol-wary times when many are cutting down on eggs, not to economize but for health reasons. Simply dissolve a pinch of saffron in a T. hot water and add to egg-bread dough. An egg bread containing only 2 eggs will come out looking as if it contained 6 or 8.

ROSEMARY
rozmaryn

Although widely used in the cuisines of France and Italy, in Poland rosemary (Rosmarinus officinalis) is mainly associated with the World War I-vintage soldier song that goes: *"O mój rozmarynie rozwijaj się..."* ("Bloom, my rosemary bush"). Some Polish cooks do make occasional use of it, especially with fatty pork or mutton roasts. Rosemary is best when combined with caraway and coriander. Rub roast (adding other seasonings like salt and crushed garlic if desired) and let stand 1 hr. before roasting.

THYME
tymianek

Thyme (Thymus vulgaris) is a seasoning whose aroma Americans immediately associate with pizza and other Italian foods. Thyme plays only a very marginal role in Polish cuisine. Because of its strong aroma, it should be used very sparingly. A pinch may be added to broths, bean dishes, sauerkraut, and roasts, especially game. It can also help to neutralize the inevitable fishy odor that appears when freshness declines.

BASIL
bazylia

Despite its wide use in France and Italy, this herb (Ocimum basilicum) is of only marginal importance in Polish cookery. Only a pinch or two suffice to season meat, poultry, fish, and game dishes. Also try it in cooked vegetables, tomato soup and broth, but very sparingly.

TARRAGON
estragon

The overpowering aroma of this herb (Artemisia draculunculus) has never really caught on in Polish cookery, although it would be difficult to imagine French cuisine without it. Some sophisticated Polish cooks use it to flavor vinegar. Simply add a sprig or two of fresh tarragon or a t. dried tarragon to 1 pt. distilled, wine or cider vinegar. In a week it will be ready to use in salads. For an interesting flavor twist, sprinkle Polish-style tomato salad (sliced tomatoes, salted, peppered and topped with chopped onions or chives) with a little of your estragon-flavored vinegar and several pinches of sugar.

DILL
koper

Dill (Anethum graveolens) is undoubtedly the most widely used garden green in Poland and even outstrips parsley, which is more popular in America. It is the principal flavor accent in Polish-style poultry stuffing, sliced cucumbers, and other salads, hot stuffed eggs in shells, fish Polonaise, cooked cabbage, and cold sauce. Use it as a garnish to improve the eye-appeal, flavor, and nutrition (vitamin C) of stews, cooked vegetables, mushroom dishes, savory soups, and sauces hot and cold. Few Poles could imagine summer without that all-time seasonable favorite: buttered, walnut-sized, new potatoes topped with the finely chopped, fragrant, and feathery leaves of fresh dill. It would be pointless to continue enumerating the many ways dill is used in Polish cookery, because they are amply described throughout this book. Since dill is not always as readily available in America as it is in Poland, it is worth growing your own so you can always have it on hand during the warm months. Even if you don't have a vegetable patch or herb garden, dill will grow nicely along a fence, behind the garage, or most anywhere else including a balcony flower-box. In winter it can be grown indoors. It can also be preserved by salting or freezing, although some of its fragrance will invariably be lost. The dried dill weed available in supermarket spice sections has very little true dill flavor and is not recommended. The only exception is in dry seasonings, where dill in dried, powdered form is most convenient. Fresh dill you dry yourself is still better that the store-bought kind.

PARSLEY
pietruszka

Parsley (Petroselinum crispum) is second only to dill as Polish cuisine's most widely used fresh garnish. The word "fresh" is very important, since both dill and parsley discolor and lose their flavor in cooking. They should, therefore, be sprinkled over hot dishes just before serving to release their full bouquet. Parsley may be used as a garnish together with or instead of dill in most dishes. One exception is chłodnik (cold beet or cucumber soup), where only dill accentuates its full flavor. Americans consider parslied potatoes normal, but once you try dill on buttered potatoes, you may never want to go back. Parsley may be salted, frozen or dried. It is best to dry your own, as the stuff marketed commercially as "parsley flakes" can be pretty tasteless.

CHIVES
szczypiorek

Chives (Allium schoenoprasum), finely chopped, impart a subtle zest to a wide variety of dishes. They are an especially desirable garnish for creamed farmer's cheese and egg dishes, but may be sprinkled over stews, soups, salads, and cold and hot sauces. Often they are used in combination with dill and/or parsley. Like the latter, they should not be cooked, but rather added to hot dishes just before serving. Chives are faintly reminiscent of but far more delicate than green onions. For breakfast, many Poles sprinkle finely chopped, fresh chives over buttered bread, which enhances its taste, appearance, and nutritional value.

CHERVIL
trybula

Chervil (Antrhiscus cerefolium) is a garden green somewhat reminiscent of parsley but with anise-like undertones. In Polish cuisine, it is used far less frequently than dill, parsley, or chives, but does not deserve to be totally ignored. Use chervil to garnish savory omelets, potato soup, cooked vegetable salads, fish, and other dishes according to preference. Sprinkle it over hot dishes just before serving.

GARDEN CRESS
rzeżucha

Garden cress (Lepidium sativum) should not be confused with watercress (Nasturtium officinale or *rukiew wodna*), with which Americans are more familiar. Poles generally consider watercress, a swamp weed that grows in polluted ponds, unfit for human consumption. By contrast, many of them prize garden cress as a green that adds zest to a variety of salads, canapé spreads, potatoes, meats, soups, etc. Poland's leading food authority, Irena Gumowska, recommends it for those on low-salt diets. Its pungent flavor simply creates the illusion that the dish with which it is garnished has already been salted and peppered enough. *Note*: Garden cress will grow indoors when its seeds are sprinkled over a piece of moist cotton. It also has a ritual significance and is used as a greenery in a plaster, plastic, wooden, or sugar lamb to form the main centerpiece of the *święconka* (Easter table). Oats are also used for this purpose.

CAPERS
kapary

The pickled immature buds of the subtropical flower (Capparis spinosa) have long been prized by Polish gourmets, although their high price and virtual unavailability were responsible for their disappearance from post-World War II Polish cookery. Chop or mash ½–2 t. capers and add to mayonnaise-based sauces (used with pâté and other cold meats), fish and meat salads, tomato dishes, and hot white sauces for a distinctive gourmet twist. *Note*: Don't be turned off by the seemingly exorbitant price for a tiny jar of capers, since you won't be using them every day. Even on a special occasion only a very few are needed.

POLISH "CAPERS"
polskie "kapary"

The scarcity of the real thing has produced an acceptable substitute. Rinse and dry ½ c. immature nasturtium (Tro-paeolum maius) pods. Scald with boiling water, bring to boil, and drain. In pot combine ¾ c. 6% vinegar, ¼ c. water, several peppercorns, 2 grains allspice, 1 bay leaf, several pinches coriander, a pinch of tarragon, 1 clove, 2–3 small onions, 2 t. salt and 1 t. sugar. Bring to boil, add a piece of lemon rind, cool to room temperature and strain. Add the nasturtium pods and slowly heat to near boiling. When cooled to room temp., transfer mixture to small jars, seal and store in fridge until needed. Use as above.

GARLIC
czosnek

This healthful and aromatic plant (Allium sativum) of the lily family is not used as widely by Polish cooks as by French or Italian counterparts, but it is an absolute must in many dishes. These include kiełbasa, roast pork, mutton, lamb, veal, waterfowl, and game, kołduny (lamb-filled dumplings), bigos, beets, spinach and such soups as pea, beet, and żurek. Rather than crushing garlic in a garlic press, Polish cooks more commonly mince it very fine, sprinkle with salt, mince again, and then mash it with the flat of a knife this way and that on a cutting board to obtain a garlic paste. Garlic powder lacks the aroma and flavor of fresh garlic, but is convenient in dry seasonings (see below).

ONION
cebula

Onions (Allium cepa) are both a vegetable and one of the most common flavoring ingredients in Polish and many other cuisines. Chopped or thinly sliced raw onions are used in various salads. Cooked in various ways they are used in preparing a wide variety of meat, fish, egg, and vegetarian dishes, soups, and gravies. Fried, chopped onions are a frequent topping for potatoes, dumplings, noodles, and groats. They add flavor to savory stuffings, fillings, potato pancakes, and mushrooms and are usually included in meat marinades and pickled vegetables. Like garlic powder, commercially available onion powder is handy for sprinkling over various dishes when fresh onions are lacking or there isn't time to peel, chop, and sauté them from scratch.

HORSERADISH
chrzan

This sharp, pungent, eye-watering root (Cochlearia armoracia) is usually used freshly grated or prepared, i.e. grated and marinated in vinegar. Despite its sinus-clearing potency, good horseradish should never be bitter, and the prepared variety should not be kept refrigerated more than a month. Beware of some inferior brands of prepared horseradish or horseradish sauce which may contain such fillers as turnips or rutabaga. Use prepared horseradish or horseradish sauce with beef, tongue, hard-boiled eggs, fish, ham and kiełbasa, and freshly grated horseradish in grated-vegetable salads, horseradish butter and ćwikla. A piece of horseradish root is often added to dill pickles and other pickled vegetables. Dry, powdered horseradish is useful as a seasoning. If not commercially available, you can easily make your own. Peel and dice a horseradish root and leave it outside (a windowscreen is good for this purpose!) until dehydrated and brittle. Then grate fine or pulverize in processor. Sift through sieve and store in air-tight container.

MUSHROOM POWDER
proszek grzybowy/mączka grzybowa

This is commercially available, but you can also make your own quite easily. If you use a lot of fresh mushrooms, especially recipes that call for only the cap, you will have plenty of stems left over. Simply dry these (see food-preservation chapter), pound in mortar to a powder or pulverize in processor, strain through fine sieve, and store tightly sealed. Several sprinkles will enhance the flavor of meat, soups, gravies, sauerkraut dishes, or wherever a mushroom aroma is desired.

CINNAMON
cynamon

The bark of this tree (Cinnamonum zeylanicum) which grows in Ceylon is widely used as a sweet and fragrant spice that does wonders for a wide variety of desserts and sweet dishes. These include fruit soups, compotes, cakes, puddings, sweet dishes made with apples, as well as hot spiced beer and wine. Cinnamon is one of the spices included in honey-spice-cake seasoning. As with most other spices, it retains its flavor best when kept in a tightly sealed container in stick form and freshly grated as needed. Since you do not need much, running the cinnamon stick over the grater several times is usually all it takes. Store bought ground cinnamon quickly loses its aroma. A piece of cinnamon stick is often added to spiced fruits. *Note*: Most of the cinnamon available in American food stores is a Chinese variety (Cinnamonum cassia), which is cheaper than the one from Ceylon (Sri Lanka). Only the most sensitive gourmet palate can distinguish the two.

CLOVES
goździki

These are the dried buds of a tropical plant (Syzygium aromaticum) which look like little black nails, hence in some Polish dialects they are mistakenly referred to as gwoździki (little nails). Alone, or in combination with cinnamon or other spices, cloves are widely used in compotes and other fruit dishes as well as in spiced fruit and pickled vegetables and mushrooms. They are one of the main ingredients in honey-spice seasoning used to flavor various Christmas cakes, Polish grey sauce, and certain, mainly hot, alcoholic beverages (honey-spice cordial, spiced wine and beer). In small quantities, cloves may be added to roast pork, mutton and game, red cabbage and marinated herring. Some cooks add a pinch of ground cloves to their pâté (especially if it contains wild game), head cheese, and buckwheat sausage (kiszka, kaszanka). Cloves are best kept whole. Pound 1 or 2 in a mortar when you need a pinch of ground cloves.

NUTMEG
gałka muszkatołowa

Nutmeg is the dried nut-like kernel of a tropical plant (Myristica fragrans). A few pinches of this fragrant spice are frequently added to puddings and other desserts, apple dishes, cakes, compotes, whipped cream, ice cream and hot, spiced wine. It is excellent in Polish-style poultry stuffing and pâtés. Gourmet cooks often add a pinch to poultry and veal dishes (especially breaded veal cutlets) and even fish. Instead of store-bought ground nutmeg, which quickly loses its aroma, it is best to store whole nutmeg kernels tightly sealed and run one over a grater a couple of times when a pinch of this spice is needed.

MACE
kwiat muszkatołowy

This is the blossom of the same plant which gives us nutmeg. Polish cooks sometimes flavor yeast-raised egg bread (babka, placek, bułka, strucla) with a pinch or two. Also puréed potatoes.

GINGER
imbir

Many Poles immediately associate the pleasingly pungent aroma of this tropical plant (Zingiber officinale) with Christmas baked goods, such as piernik and miodowniczki. It is also used to make a ginger cordial known as imbirówka. In savory Polish cooking, ginger (together with marjoram and paprika) is an absolute must in tripe, and is frequently sprinkled over roast duck or goose or used to season pâté. A sprinkle of ground ginger over fried liver will help to mellow its frequently bitter edge.

CARDAMON
kardamon

This spice (Ellettaria cardamonum) has a pungent aroma and a zingy taste and should be used sparingly. It will add zest to honey-spice cakes, marzipan, and fruit desserts like compotes. A pinch of ground cardamon will enliven the flavor of pea soup, beef stew, fish dishes, and pâtés. Some epicures are known to add ½ a pinch to strong black coffee.

VANILLA
wanilia

The inviting fragrance of this spice (Vanilla planifolia) fills nearly everyone with a warm feeling of old-style hospitality and homey contentment. It is therefore undoubtedly the most widely used flavoring in desserts and sweet dishes including cakes, puddings, ice cream, whipped cream, milk-based soups (e.g. zupa "nic"), compotes, confections, and curd-cheese dishes. Add a ½–1 inch piece of vanilla pod to compote while it cooks. A bit of the pod is also among the flavorings of that Old Polish, hot honey-spice cordial known as krupnik. For cakes and puddings, a bit of the pulp can be removed from the pod and mashed with sugar before adding. If you use store bought vanilla extract, make sure it says "real vanilla" on the label. Although "imitation vanilla extract" costs less, you would do well to avoid this synthetic compound, known as "vanillin", which will give your food a cheap commercial flavor. *Note:* you can easily prepare your own vanilla extract and be sure it contains no preservatives or other additives. Simply cut two vanilla pods into ½ inch pieces, place in a small jar, cover with 100 proof vodka or strong light rum or brandy, seal tightly, and store at room temp. Use as you would store-bought vanilla extract.

VANILLA SUGAR
cukier waniliowy

Vanilla sugar is often the most convenient form in which to use this flavoring, especially when sprinkling over cakes, desserts, sliced fresh fruit, or whipped cream. Since the store bought variety is frequently made with "vanillin" (imitation vanilla), you can easily prepare your own at home. Simply cut up 2–3 vanilla pods and combine in a jar with enough powdered sugar to fill it. Mix to evenly distribute vanilla, seal tightly and store in cupboard at room temp. Use a little to dust faworki (angel wings) and other cakes and desserts, using an ordinary sieve for this purpose. Add more powdered sugar to jar as needed, since the vanilla will retain its aroma a long time. When aroma becomes faint, add another cut-up vanilla pod.

* * *

HOMEMADE POLISH SEASONINGS
różne przyprawy domowe

In your supermarket's spice section you have undoubtedly run across seasoning products labeled Italian, Mexican, Chinese, Oriental, Cajun etc. Although you can always season foods from scratch with a pinch of this, a dash of that, and a sprinkling of something else, it is often convenient to have blends of the most typical herbs and spices at your fingertips. One such familiar blend used in Indian cookery is curry powder, which is a combination of coriander, cardamon, cayenne pepper, ginger, cinnamon, tumeric, and other ingredients. Until Polish-style seasonings become readily available in North America, the only alternative is to make your own. If you freshly crush or grind your ingredients, they will be better and more aromatic than those bought in a store. It is best to start with whole spices (grains, seeds, dried leaves) and pound them together in a mortar or whirl them to a powder in a food processor or electric spice mill. Sift through a fine sieve onto a clean sheet of paper. The particles remaining in the sieve that are too big to get sifted can be additionally pounded (if using mortar) and re-sifted. Fold paper in half lengthwise over the powdered spices and transfer to air tight container. Be sure to label the seasonings. *Note:* The proportions given below are for small quantities of seasoning because all ground herbs and spices lose their aroma when stored any length of time. It is best to prepare only the quantity you are likely to use within several months and make up a fresh batch when you run out. Naturally, it would be senseless to prepare seasonings for, let us say, lamb and mutton or duck and goose if you never prepare such dishes. An exception to this rule is Polish hunter's seasonings. Even if you never serve venison or hare, this delightful seasoning can be used to give an interesting twist of flavor to chicken, pork, beef, and other meats as well as soups and gravies. For variety, use it instead of Italian seasoning in such dishes as spaghetti, lasagne, or chicken cacciatore. (Incidentally, the latter is simply the Italian version of "po myśliwsku" or "hunter's style".) Also excellent in meatloaf and meatballs.

* * *

POLISH MILD HERB PEPPER
pieprz ziołowy łagodny

Following the instructions above, crush or grind and sift together: 2 t. savory, 2 t. marjoram, 1 t. caraway, 1 t. coriander, and 1 t. dry (not freshly grated or prepared!) horseradish.

POLISH SHARP HERB PEPPER
pieprz ziołowy ostry

Combine as above: 1 t. savory, 1 t. dry (pale yellow) mustard, 1 t. dry black mustard, 1 t. coriander and 1 t. cayenne pepper. *Note*: Herb pepper may be used in any recipe calling for ground black pepper as in the frequent directive: salt and pepper to taste. *Note:* Either of the above mentioned seasonings will give a peppery taste with interesting new overtones to everything from meat, fish, soups, and gravies to farmer's cheese and scrambled eggs. *Variation*: Fill your pepper shaker with 1 part of either of the above-mentioned herb peppers mixed with an equal part of ground black pepper.

POLISH PORK SEASONING
przyprawa do mięs wieprzowych

Combine: 1 T. marjoram, 1 t. paprika, 1 t. caraway, 1 t. sage (optional), 2 t. black pepper, 2 t. onion powder, and 1 t. garlic powder. *Note*: The perfect blend for roast pork, roast bacon, pork goulash, and bigos. Sprinkle a little over meat when preparing both Polish-style breaded pork cutlets and American-style breaded pork chops. It is also good in meatloaf, meatballs, and other ground meat dishes.

POLISH GARLIC-CARAWAY
SALT
sól czosnkowo-kminkowa

This is a simpler composition also meant mainly for pork dishes. Combine 1 T. (preferably coarse kosher) salt with 1 T. garlic powder and 2 T. caraway. *Note:* The coarse kosher salt should, of course, be crushed or processed to a powder with the remaining ingredients.

POLISH BEEF SEASONING
przyprawa do mięs wołowych

Combine: 1 T. onion powder, 2 t. black pepper, 1 t. dry horseradish, 1 t. savory, 1 t. marjoram, ½ t. lovage, and ¼ t. ground bay leaves. *Variation:* Replace the horseradish and marjoram with 2 t.–1 T. mushroom powder.

POLISH VEAL SEASONING
przyprawa do cielęciny

Combine: 1 T. paprika, 2 t. white pepper, 2 t. garlic powder, 1 t. onion powder, ½ t. coriander, and ¼ t. nutmeg. *Note:* Use in all veal dishes including American-style "city chicken".

POLISH LAMB AND MUTTON SEASONING
przyprawa do baraniny

Combine: 1 t. onion powder, 2 t. garlic powder, 2 t. black pepper, 1 t. rosemary, 1 t. marjoram, 1 t. juniper, and (optional) ½ t. coriander or cardamon.

POLISH FISH SEASONING
przyprawa do ryb

Combine: 1 T. white pepper, 1 T. dry dill leaves (not dill seed!), 1 T. paprika, 2 t. sage, 1 t. borage, 1 t. sour salt (citric acid crystals), and (optional) ¼ t. nutmeg. *Variation:* For a fuller-flavored fish seasoning, add 1–2 t. mild or sharp herb pepper (above). *Note:* Fresh fish may be seasoned with mixture before or after cooking.

POLISH POULTRY SEASONING
przyprawa do drobiu

Combine: 1 T. paprika, 1 T. dry dill leaves, 1 T. dry parsley leaves, 1 T. white pepper, 1 t. dry mustard and ½ t. nutmeg. *Note*: This seasoning is meant primarily for roast chicken and turkey, but it is also good in other poultry dishes (stews, ground patties, etc.) It can likewise be used in classic Polish poultry stuffing, but ideally some fresh chopped dill and parsley should be added. *Hint*: If you are roasting a chicken or turkey that is on the lean and dry side, combine ½–1 c. pan dripping with ½ t. poultry seasoning and (optional) 1–2 T. dry white wine. Use hypodermic needle to inject mixture into breast, thighs, drumsticks, and wings. Be sure to baste the bird frequently.

POLISH WATERFOWL (GOOSE & DUCK) SEASONING
przyprawa do drobiu wodnego (gęsi i kaczki)

Combine: 2 T. marjoram, 2 t. black pepper, 1 t. garlic powder, 1 t. ginger, 1 t. savory, and ½ t. cloves. *Optional*: ½–1 t. juniper may be included for a wild waterfowl accent. *Variation*: For a change of pace, season chicken or turkey with this blend.

POLISH HUNTER'S SEASONING
przyprawa myśliwska

Combine: 2 T. marjoram, 1 T. pepper, 1 T. onion powder, 1 T. garlic powder, 1 T. juniper, 1 t. caraway, ½ t. allspice and ¼ t. ground bay leaf. *Note:* This blend helps blunt the "gamey" flavor of all wildfowl and game dishes. It can also be used to prepare the marinade in which game should marinate anywhere from several hrs. to several days. In pot combine 1 c. each water, vinegar, and dry red wine with 1 T. hunter's seasoning and bring to boil. Switch off heat and let stand covered until cool. Pour over uncooked game, cover and refrigerate, turning meat over every so often. Adding chopped onions and soup greens is also recommended. You can also do the trick with a hypodermic needle, injecting some of the marinade into the depth of the meat. *Hint*: Our family loves game dishes but only occasionally has access to hare, pheasant, venison, or boar. Thus, we do the next best thing by using this seasoning on domestic meats. It makes chicken taste a little like pheasant or partridge, gives a hint of wild boar to pork roast and makes your beef somewhat reminiscent of venison, especially if you marinate them an hr. or so before cooking in a game marinade (see above).

POLISH PÂTÉ SEASONING
przyprawa do pasztetów

Combine : 1 T. pepper, 2 t. marjoram, 1 t. onion powder, 1 t. garlic powder (optional), ½ t. ground nutmeg. *Optional:* If you like a zestier pâté, you may add ½ t. coriander, cardamon, or cloves, or ¼ t. of each.

SEASONED SALTS
sole przyprawowe

For seasoned salts, crush 2–4 T. coarse kosher salt along with the other ingredients of any of the above mentioned seasonings (except garlic-caraway salt). *Note:* We prefer the unsalted seasonings, since sprinkling foods with salt during preparation or at the table allows everyone to adjust the flavor to his or her taste.

POLISH SAUERKRAUT SEASONING
przyprawa do kiszonej kapusty

Combine: 1 T. black pepper, 2 t. onion powder, 2 t. mushroom powder, 1 t. caraway, 1 t. marjoram and ¼ t. ground bay leaf. *Note:* Sprinkle a little over stewed sauerkraut, bigos, kapuśniak, and other sauerkraut dishes.

POLISH STEW & GOULASH SEASONING
przyprawa gulaszowa

Combine: 1 T. pepper, 1 T. paprika, 1 T. dry parsley leaves, 1 T. onion powder, 1 t. garlic powder (optional), 1 t. savory and 1 t. marjoram. *Note:* Use as desired to season Polish pork goulash, American beef stew, beef Stroganoff, and all such fricasseed dishes. *Variation:* ½–1 t. caraway may be included. For a zestier seasoning (especially good in Hungarian goulash), add 1–2 t. cayenne pepper.

MILD POLISH HONEY-SPICE CAKE SEASONING
przyprawa do pierników

Combine: 1 T. cinnamon, 1 T. cloves, 1 T. ginger and 1 T. vanilla sugar. *Variation:* 1 T. dry grated orange and/or lemon rind may be included in mixture.

PEPPERY POLISH HONEY-SPICE-CAKE SEASONING
przyprawa do pierników ostrzejsza

Combine: 2 T. cinnamon, 2. t cloves, 2 t. black pepper, 1 t. coriander (or cardamon) and ½ t. nutmeg. *Note:* Besides being used to season various honey-spice cakes (pierniki) similar to English gingerbread or French pain d'épice, this seasoning also flavors the Old Polish grey sauce used mainly with boiled beef tongue and poached carp. It is also used in sweet fish aspic and honey-spice cordial (krupnik).

POLISH SOUP & STEW SEASONING
przyprawa "Jarzynka" do zup i potraw

Although soups based on meat and/or vegetable stock are superior in flavor and nutrition, you may on occasion be in the mood for hot soup, but lack the time or ingredients to make it from scratch. In such cases, this seasoned soup base may be the next best thing. Start by drying about 6 T. beef bouillon crystals. Spread them out on a plate or board and keep them in a well-ventilated dry place until no longer sticky. Process to a powder with 2 diced dried carrots, 1 diced dry parsley root, 2 T. dry parsley leaves, 2 T. onion powder, 1 T. celery powder, 1 T. pepper, 1 t. allspice, and ½ t. ground bay leaf. *Optional:* Add 1 t. marjoram, 1 t. savory, 1 T. lovage and/or 1 t. M.S.G. if desired. Sift through sieve as with other seasonings and store in a tightly-sealed container in dry place. Add about 1 T. of mixture (more or less according to taste) to 4 c. boiling water, and proceed to make soup of choice as if using homemade stock. *Note:* Mixtures such as this have been marketed in Poland under such trade names as "Jarzynka" and "Vegeta." *Variation:* A little of this mixture will also enhance the flavor of soups, gravies, and fricasseed dishes which may taste flat even though they were made from scratch.

BOUILLON CUBES
przyprawa do zup w kostkach

We are no great fans of using chicken, beef, or vegetable bouillon cubes in nearly every soup, gravy, or stew as some people do, but they can come in handy in an emergency. Something much tastier and more natural (no artificial flavorings or preservatives!) are frozen homemade bouillon cubes (see below).

HOMEMADE FROZEN BOUILLON CUBES
wywar domowy mrożony

This practice may seem complicated and time-consuming, but it really isn't, since it will virtually cook by itself with a minimum of supervision. Fill a large, heavy, non-aluminum pot (at least 4-qt capacity) with soup bones. These can be of a single variety (beef, veal, chicken, etc.), but combinations do give especially good results. Particularly good are beef bones that contain marrow, veal knuckles and shin bones, pork knuckles and neck bones, and the usually less desirable parts of an old hen like necks, rumps, even feet. You can throw in fatty scraps trimmed from steaks and roasts, a dried-up piece of slab bacon, a piece of dried-up and otherwise unusable kiełbasa or ham, even the bone from a leftover roast from which most of the meat has been removed. However, a really good stock is made with uncooked bones, and smoked or cooked meats should only be an addition.

Cover with cold water and let stand 1 hr. Switch on heat to low and allow to come to a gentle boil. Skim off scum from surface until no more forms. Reduce to lowest heat or place pot on insulated pad. (Asbestos pads are no longer recommended due to there alleged cancer-causing properties!) Cover pot loosely with lid, allowing a crack to remain, and let simmer 2–5 hrs. In the meantime you can read a book, watch TV, mow the lawn or attend to other chores. Add 2 portions soup greens (2–3 carrots, 2 parsley roots with greens left on, a small celeriac or 3 stalks celery), 3 onions, 3 bay leaves, 10 peppercorns, 5 grains allspice, 1 large whole tomato and 2 T. salt. Add more water if necessary and continue simmering another 3 hrs. or longer. You cannot overcook a stock and 10–12 hrs. is not too long. Strain stock. If you like, use cooked vegetables, cooked meat attached to bones, or marrow in some other dish. If you have more than 1 qt. stock, cook it down. Cool to room temp., then refrigerate overnight. Remove congealed fat from top and freeze for future use for roux, gravy, or frying, or (if you are restricting your intake of animal fats) discard. Heat the stock just to liquefy and pour into ice-cube trays. Keep in freezer 24 hrs., then transfer frozen bouillon cubes to containers. They will be ready to use whenever you are making soup or gravy, or need stock in any other recipe. *Note:* if you look in your fridge, you may find more stock fixings than you had imagined. The odd turnip, celery tops, a leek, or just its green top that is useless for any other purpose, a portion of head lettuce that has turned slightly brown, a few of your beet leaves (but not the beetroots!), several radishes, even some onion skins, can all go into your stock pot. The result may be a deeper, darker, and tastier stock.

MAGGI EXTRACT/SEASONING
przyprawa "Maggi"

Invented by Swiss food-industry pioneer Julius Maggi (1846–1912), this dark liquid seasoning has enjoyed an international reputation for years. The company he started built one of its factories in Gdańsk, and to this day Maggi remains Poland's most popular liquid seasoning. Its dark hue and deep, dusky aroma, reminiscent of lovage and dried mushrooms, help deepen the color and round out the flavor of many soups, gravies, fricassees, and sauerkraut dishes. A sprinkling perks up the flavor of cooked rice, boiled meat, and many cooked vegetables. We refer to it interchangeably as Maggi extract or Maggi seasoning and frequently call for it in this book. Due to its versatility, it should definitely be found on your kitchen's condiment shelf, as it requires no refrigeration. *Note:* Many American cooks use

Kitchen Bouquet where Polish cooks would reach for the Maggi. If you do, be sure to use less, because Kitchen Bouquet is more concentrated. Soy sauce can also be used in place of Maggi, but only the mild American chop-suey-style is recommended. Japanese soy sauce and other Far Eastern imports are often flavored with exotic, oriental fruits and spices which do not necessarily fit the Polish palate.

LIQUID MUSHROOM EXTRACT
przyprawa grzybowa

Commercially available liquid mushroom extract is good to have on hand whenever you want to impart the flavor of dried Polish mushrooms to food but haven't the time to soak and cook them from scratch. Add a little to soups, gravies, sauerkraut, or wherever the aroma of King Boletes (Boletus edulis) is required. *Note:* You can achieve much the same effect by making your own frozen mushroom extract right at home. Soak 3 oz. dried Polish mushrooms in 3 c. water 2 hrs., then cook in same water until tender. Remove mushrooms and use in another dish. Strain the hot mushroom liquid through a paper coffee filter to remove all sediment, then boil down if necessary until there is no more than 1 c. liquid. When cool, pour into an ice-cube tray and keep it in the freezer 24 hrs. Then remove cubes and store in a plastic bag or container in freezer. Whenever you need mushroom flavor, simply add 1 or more cubes to soup, gravy, stew, etc.

CARAMEL COLORING
karmel

Although commercially available, it is more economical and easy to make at home. In a dry saucepan, caramelize 1 c. sugar, i.e. heat over low heat until sugar melts and turns very dark. Remove from heat and allow to cool slightly. Add 1 c. boiling water a little at a time, return to low heat, stir and continue adding water until it is all used up. Heat, stirring constantly, until the caked, browned sugar dissolves completely and you get a smooth dark liquid. Transfer to bottle, seal tightly and store at room temp. Use to color gravies, fricasseed dishes, sauerkraut, or wherever a darker color is desired. *Note:* Sugar loses most of its sweetness when it is caramelized. *Warning:* Be sure to add very little hot water at the start and only when caramelized sugar has cooled somewhat; otherwise you may get painfully splattered.

GRANULATED SUGAR
cukier rafinowany

This is what most everyone thinks of when the word "sugar" is mentioned. Unless otherwise specified, this is also what we have in mind whenever sugar is called for in this book. Scientifically known as sucrose, it is made from sugarbeets or sugarcane and granulated medium fine. It is found in sugarbowls the world over and has countless uses in cooking, baking, canning, and candy-making. Sometimes it is pressed into cubes, which is both a more elegant and economical way of furnishing sugar for sweetening hot beverages, notably tea and coffee.

SUGAR CRYSTALS
cukier kryształ

In Poland, this form of sugar is more expensive than the ordinary granulated variety although it is no better in sweetening power or purity. Its major claim to fame is elegance. The large, square, semi-translucent crystals of this sugar will shimmer by candlelight in a beautiful crystal sugarbowl and add a touch of classic refinement to any festive meal when the faworki or szarlotka are brought in, the aromatic espresso is served and the brandy is being poured. Sugar in this form is harder to come by in America.

POWDERED/CONFECTIONER'S SUGAR
cukier puder

Although we realize that technically there is a difference between the grainier powdered sugar and the flour-fine confectioner's sugar, we chose to use the former throughout this book, both because it is customary in American usage as well as being closer in spirit to the Polish "cukier puder." Whenever we call for powdered sugar, we mean what is commercially marketed as confectioner's sugar. Its finest variety is labeled 10X. Although it can be used in baking and beverage-sweetening in place of granulated sugar, powdered sugar is more frequently placed in a sifter or sieve and used to dust pastries (like faworki), fresh fruit, and other desserts, pancakes (naleśniki, racuszki), fruit-filled pierogi, and other sweet dishes.

CINNAMON SUGAR
cukier cynamonowy

Why overpay for the store-bought version of this item? It's childishly simple to prepare at home. Simply combine 2–3 T. ground cinnamon with 1 c. powdered sugar and store it in a tightly-sealed jar. Use it to dust cakes, puddings, crêpes, rice & apple casserole or whatever. *Note:* Vanilla sugar, which is used much the same way, has already been described earlier in this chapter.

ORANGE/LEMON RIND SUGAR
tarta skórka pomarańczowa /cytrynowa w cukrze

Scrub 2 oranges well with brush in hot soapy water, rinse and dry. Grate only the orange-colored rind, but not the white inner lining, which is bitter. Mix grated rind with 1

c. granulated sugar and store in tightly-sealed jar. Use 1–2 t. to flavor cakes, puddings, fruit fillings, etc. Lemon-flavored sugar is prepared the same way. If you like, combine grated rind of 1 orange and 1 lemon with the sugar for an all-purpose citrus-flavored seasoning.

HONEY
miód

The ancients hailed honey as "the elixir of eternal youth," and a cure "for what ails you." Among them were the Greek physician Hippocrates, who lived to be 111, and the mathematician Pythagoras, who died at 90. The prescription is simple: drink 1–2 T. honey dissolved in ½ c. warm (pre-boiled) water upon rising (before breakfast) and again before retiring at night. Besides being a common Polish breakfast food (spread on bread and rolls), it is the main seasoning in honey-spice cakes and is used to sweeten hot milk and sometimes even tea and hot beer. It is used to flavor miodówka (honey cordial, served at room temp.), as well as hot krupnik (honey-spice cordial) and mead (honey wine). Old Polish cooks used honey not only in stewed fruits and sweet dishes, but often added a spoonful or two to bigos and roast meat. Try this old treat: honeyed cucumbers. Simply drizzle cucumber spears with a little honey and enjoy. It's hard to believe that something this simple could be so delicious! The color and flavor of honey varies and depends on the type of blossom from which the bees obtained their nectar. Common varieties include mild, linden honey and dark, full-flavored buckwheat honey, which is said to have the greatest youth-restoring properties. Rapeseed honey in particular helps strengthen the heart muscle, and firtree honey is known to relieve respiratory conditions by virtue of containing bactericidal (germ-killing) and decongestive ingredients. Honey is often recommended to patients with liver, gallbladder, and ulcer conditions and can even help to relieve nausea during pregnancy. According to Irena Gumowska, Poland's leading food expert, 2 oz. honey a day helps to restore blood cells in post-operative patients and anemics. Athletes often find that it relieves fatigue, and children raised on honey are better developed and more resistant to illness. Although this is not a health book, we found it difficult to resist touching on some of the properties of miód, a true wonder food. *Warning:* All of the above applies of course only to 100% pure honey. Unfortunately, some of the lower-priced brands of honey on the supermarket shelf are adulterated with corn syrup, glucose, and other inexpensive "stretchers." The only way to be sure is to deal with a reputable merchant specializing in natural foods. You may pay a little more but you'll know you're getting the real thing.

ARTIFICIAL SWEETENERS
sztuczne środki słodzące

Unless you are under a doctor's orders, you would do yourself a favor by avoiding these entirely. The problem is really quite simple. The advertising industry has simply cashed in on America's weight-watching obsession by flooding the market with diet this, sugar-free that and low-calorie something else, and a gullible public has eagerly fallen for the pitch. Despite all the claims, statistics prove that the average weight of Americans did not go down during the 1980's when the hoopla was at its height. Artificial sweeteners are not only inferior in taste, but have proved to be health hazards. After saccharine was found to be cancer-producing, cyclamate was hailed as a healthy substitute, but in time it too was exposed as hazardous. Who knows what the long-range effects of the currently popular synthetic sweeteners will be? In addition, the synthetics do not supply the body with energy as natural sweeteners do. Used in moderation, honey and sugar do not cause obesity and are necessary to promote the body's natural functions. *Remember:* 1 t. sugar supplies only 17 calories and 1 t. honey has about 20, but the latter is such a treasure chest of healthful nutrients that its calorie content is of secondary importance.

VINEGAR
ocet

There is now a great variety of wine, cider, and herb vinegars on the market, but whenever we call for vinegar in this book it means, unless otherwise specified, white distilled 6% vinegar. This product has a multitude of uses. Without it, there could be no korniszony (gherkins), marinated mushrooms, pickled vegetables, spiced fruits, prepared horseradish, prepared mustard, Poland's favorite relish, ćwikła, and many other zesty, appetite-whetting go-togethers. In addition, vinegar is used to sour soups and sauces, season salads and marinate meat before cooking. Some Polish restaurants and family dinner tables include a cruet of vinegar as a standard fixture. Everyone may impart added tartness to a dish according to taste. Zimne nogi (jellied pig's feet) is one dish which most everyone sprinkles with a little vinegar, but others also add a little to various soups and fricasseed dishes. The authoress, for instance, enjoys dipping cold smoked kiełbasa in vinegar rather than the more conventional horseradish, mustard, or ćwikła. *Note:* Excessive use of vinegar is rather harsh on the digestive tract, as it destroys the beneficial bacterial flora needed to ensure proper digestion. Lemon juice and citric acid are friendlier substitutes (see below).

HOMEMADE APPLE VINEGAR
domowy ocet jabłkowy

Whenever you bake apple cakes (or pies) or make applesauce, you invariably end up with a good amount of apple peels that get thrown away. You can use them to make a tasty light vinegar in another illustration of the theme that Polish cooks let nothing go to waste. The apples should be scrubbed well to remove all traces of pesticides and protective substances. Place 3 lbs. apple parings in a large jar, add 4 heaping t. sugar and 1 qt. lukewarm pre-boiled water. *Optional:* some pear peels may also be used. Cover jar with gauze, fasten with rubber band, and leave in warm (higher than room temp.) place to ferment. When fermentation (active bubbling) ceases, the liquid becomes clear and sufficiently tart, strain through linen cloth into bottles, seal, and refrigerate. Use this vinegar to season salads and sour cooked dishes, but not for marinades, pickled fruits or vegetables.

HOMEMADE WINE VINEGAR
domowy ocet winny

Proceed as above, but when straining, leave bottles with ¼ c. head space. To each, add ¼ c. dry white wine. Use as above.

TARRAGON VINEGAR
ocet estragonowy

Wash and dry a handful of fresh tarragon leaves and chop coarsely. Place in qt. jar, add 3 peeled shallots (bulbs only) or other small onions, ½ t. sugar and ¼ t. salt. Fill jars with 6% distilled cider or white-wine vinegar—the store-bought variety is best for this recipe! Seal jar tightly and keep on a sunny windowsill for about 8 days. Strain through gauze or cotton into dark bottle and refrigerate or store in cool, dark cellar. A t. or so added to salads or to hot dishes (fried mushrooms, cooked green beans or asparagus, for example) just before serving will give them a gourmet twist that plain vinegar never could.

HERB VINEGAR
ocet ziołowy

In qt. jar combine 1 heaping T. fresh chopped dill and a similar amount of fresh, torn up marjoram, tarragon leaves, basil leaves, thyme leaves and chopped chives. Fill jar with 6% white cider or white-wine vinegar, seal and store at room temp. 10 days. Strain through cotton or gauze into bottles, preferably the dark-glass variety, and refrigerate or store in cool cellar. Use as above.

MARINADES AS A SEASONING
zalewy jako przyprawa

If you have stocked your pantry with homemade pickled fruits or vegetables, after you have used up a given item DO NOT DISCARD the leftover marinade. It is essentially a spiced vinegar solution which has additionally absorbed the flavor of the fruit or vegetable marinated therein. Simply strain into clean jar, seal and store in fridge until needed. Several spoonfuls will add zest to salads, roast meats, and other dishes. They range in flavor from tart and tangy (gherkin marinade) to sweet, slightly tart, and spicy (spiced fruit) with numerous shades in between. You can also use these marinades to prepare your own condiments like Old Polish plum sauce (something like a sweeter version of American steak sauce), homemade ketchup or mustard (see chapter on sauces).

CITRIC ACID CRYSTALS/SOUR SALT
kwasek cytrynowy

These white crystals, derived from citrus fruits and pineapples, can be used as a handy way to sour foods that is healthier than vinegar. Just a pinch may be all you need to impart the desired tartness to soups, sauces, cooked vegetables and fricasseed dishes, stewed fruits and compotes. You can make a stomach-friendlier variety of prepared horseradish by substituting a citric-acid solution for the vinegar. When peeling a large batch of apples, place the peeled ones in cold water soured with a few pinches of citric acid to keep them from turning dark while you work on the rest. In some ways these lemony crystals are preferable to freshly-squeezed lemon juice. For one, you use only as much as you need without worrying about what to do with any excess juice. Secondly, citric acid does not take on a bitter edge in cooking as lemon juice often can.

LIQUID LEMON SOUR
roztwór z kwasku cytrynowego

Bring 1 c. water to boil. Remove from heat, add 1 T. citric acid crystals and stir until dissolved. When cool, pour into bottle, seal and store until needed. Use instead of vinegar on salads, in marinades, or wherever tartness is desired without the harshness of distilled vinegar.

LEMON JUICE
sok z cytryny

In keeping with our "fresh and natural is better" philosophy, we naturally prefer freshly-squeezed lemon juice to the bottled, reconstituted variety, which may contain preservatives, artificial coloring, and other additives. Fresh lemon juice adds a bright tang to salads and is a welcome addition to many sauces, hot and cold. It may be used as a substitute for vinegar in nearly all recipes. It is best to add lemon juice to hot dishes (sauces, soups, fricassees etc.) when they are nearly done. Everyone knows what a sprinkle of lemon juice does for fried fish, but also try a little on breaded pork or veal cutlets just before serving. A little lemon juice added to cooked beets or red cabbage just before serving will not only give them added tang but will also help restore their bright color. Some people prefer lemon juice or lemon vinegar (1 part lemon juice, 1 part white vinegar) for seasoning jellied pig's feet and other aspics as a more subtle alternative to plain harsh vinegar.

RYEMEAL SOUR
zakwas na żur

Although used principally to prepare the classic Old Polish soups, żurek and biały barszcz, this tart liquid can also be an all-purpose souring agent for savory dishes, sour soups, gravies, fricassees, and cooked vegetables with as much as needed to achieve the tartness you desire. Its acidity is lower than that of commercial vinegar, so you can use it freely without fear of over-souring. It is surprisingly easy to make. In 1½ qt. jar place 1–1¼ c. rye meal (coarse rye flour) or rye flour, oat flour, or uncooked oatmeal. Mix in 1½ c. lukewarm pre-boiled water, stir into paste, then add another 2½ c. lukewarm pre-boiled water. *Optional:* 1 halved bud garlic may also be added. Cover mouth of jar with cheesecloth and let stand in warm (75°–80°) place several days until nicely soured. Strain through cotton-filled funnel into bottles, seal and refrigerate.

SAUERKRAUT JUICE
kwaśnica/sok z kiszonej kapusty

In the various sauerkraut recipes found in this book we have usually recommended reserving the drained sauerkraut liquid. Considering the wealth of vitamins and minerals it contains, it would be a shame to let it go down the drain. Simply store sauerkraut juice in sealed jar in fridge and use a little to sour most savory dishes. Use a few spoonfuls to baste roast pork, beef, fowl (especially goose), and wild game. You can give an interesting flavor twist to your vinaigrette (vinegar & oil dressing) by replacing the vinegar with sauerkraut juice. *Remember:* The juice of naturally-cured sauerkraut is a far healthier souring agent than commercial vinegar.

DILL-PICKLE BRINE
sok z kiszonych ogórków

The pleasantly tart, garlicky liquid left over from the brine-cured dill pickles is also a good, natural souring agent as well as a storehouse of healthful minerals. After a crock or jar of brine-cured dill pickles has been used up, strain the left-over liquid into a clean jar, seal and refrigerate until needed. Use it to flavor salads, soups, gravies, or cold sauces, and sprinkle it over roasts. It also adds tang to stews, goulash, and fricasseed dishes. Dill-pickle brine, sauerkraut juice, and rye-meal sour can also be used in meat-tenderizing marinades.

Note: Some Poles drink cold dill-pickle brine straight or mixed 50-50 with cold club soda as a refreshing morning-after pick-me-up.

WHEY AS A FLAVORING
serwatka jako przyprawa

Whenever you make your own cheese, its by-product known as whey, should definitely not be thrown out. Simply store it in a tightly-sealed jar in the fridge until needed. This mildly tart, winey liquid with slightly sweet undertones may be used in all cooked savory dishes in place of wine. Use a little to sprinkle on salads or roasts. Whey is also good to use for marinating meat.

BAKING POWDER
proszek do pieczenia

As the name implies, baking powder is used chiefly in baking as a leavening agent. Although there are a great many different products of this type on the market, whenever we refer to baking powder in this book it means plain (unflavored) double-acting baking powder. Typically, such a baking powder will contain sodium aluminum sulfate, calcium acid phosphate, and sodium bicarbonate with a little cornstarch added to prevent lumping.

BAKING SODA
soda jadalna

Baking soda is the popular name for sodium bicarbonate. Before the advent of such products as Bromo-Seltzer and Alka-Seltzer, a "bicarb" (sodium bicarbonate with soda water) was what people used to take to relieve a sour stomach. In Polish cuisine, its use is largely restricted to that of a leavening agent, and even there it is used less frequently than yeast or baking powder. The honey-spice cake (piernik) is undoubtedly the best-known Polish baked good that usually calls for baking soda. *Note:* The old practice of adding baking soda to dry beans while they cook is definitely not recommended, since it destroys all their vitamins and minerals.

YEAST
drożdże

Most everyone thinks of yeast in terms of bread-baking and beer-brewing, but only in recent decades have researchers begun to discover its unique nutritive and therapeutic value. Like honey, whose health-giving properties have been hailed since the dawn of civilization, yeast also deserves to be called a wonder food and a wonder drug at the same time. Yeast is the biggest source of the B vitamins, hence it has been successfully used in the treatment of nervousness, sciatica, digestive-tract disorders, migraine headaches, obesity, insomnia, and acne. It is rich in phosphorus, calcium, and iron, and supplies such essential trace elements as selenium and chromium rarely found in other foods. Selenium helps the elderly absorb vitamin E (the vitality vitamin) and chromium facilitates the body's absorption of glucose. As research continues into the actual mechanics of this process, evidence is mounting that yeasts's nucleic acids retard the degenerative aspects of aging by rejuvenating the body's own DNA (deoxyribonucleic acid) and RNA (ribonucleic acid). An easy way to ingest more yeast than is available in bread and beer is to dissolve a spoonful (brewer's yeast is best) in a glass of boiling milk or water and "pour it down the hatch" each day. Since this is not the most palatable of beverages, Gumowska suggests an edible, scrambled-egg-like alternative, which she calls "mock calf's brains".

MOCK CALF'S BRAINS
fałszywy móżdżek

In 2 T. soybean oil, sauté 2 chopped onions until golden and tender but still unbrowned. Add 2 cakes fresh yeast and, when they melt, stir in 1–2 egg whites, scrambling until set but still moist. Salt & pepper to taste and enjoy.

FRESH YEAST
drożdże świeże

We will not take sides in the ongoing debate as to whether fresh or dry yeast is superior. Advocates on both sides of the barricade can rightfully point with pride to the culinary masterpieces they have achieved with their chosen variety. One thing is certain, however: fresh yeast has a shorter life span and must not be used beyond the expiration date stamped on the cake. Whenever "1 cake yeast" is referred to in this book it means a ⅔ oz. square of fresh compressed yeast. To activate fresh yeast, mash with a little sugar, and dissolve mixture in lukewarm (80°) milk.

DRY YEAST
drożdże suche

Granulated dry yeast is preferred by some because it is easier to store and will keep in the fridge up to 1 year, but not beyond the expiration date stamped on packet. Whenever we call for "1 packet dry yeast", we are referring to the standard ¼ oz. envelope. Because its moisture has been removed, ¼ dry yeast has roughly the same leavening power as the standard ⅔ oz. cake of compressed fresh yeast. Dry yeast requires a somewhat higher temp.

and more liquid to become activated. Typically, 1 packet dry yeast is dissolved in about ⅔ c. warm (105°–115°) water.

WHITE BREAD CRUMBS
tarta bułka

Whenever any recipe in this book calls simply for "bread crumbs," it means dry, white, plain bread crumbs. Do not confuse them with the various flavored varieties on the market. Bread crumbs are used as a thickener in various foods, including ground meat dishes, certain types of dumplings, and even in homemade kiełbasa meant for rapid consumption. They are also used for breading meat cutlets, fish, and various vegetarian patties, as well as in that simple but elegant garnish known as Polonaise topping (butter-browned bread crumbs). If you prefer, you may use crackers or matzo meal instead, but personally, we like the ordinary plain bread crumbs best. *Note:* Actually it seems foolish to waste money on store-bought bread crumbs when the average household can easily prepare its own virtually free of charge. Rather than discarding leftover bread, set it aside to dry. When enough has accumulated, grind it up and store in container in a dry place. You can use French, Vienna, or American-style white bread, kaiser rolls, Polish crescents (rogale), hamburger buns, hot dog rolls, and perhaps even throw in those last few saltines at the bottom of the box. For extra-fine bread crumbs (especially good in breading), sieve the ground stale bread. Add anything left over in the sieve to your coarser crumbs which are good in poultry stuffing, ground meat dishes, etc.

BLACK-BREAD CRUMBS
razowiec tarty

These are prepared exactly the same way as white bread crumbs, except that stale black bread is used instead. Although far less frequently used than white bread crumbs, they are occasionally called for in certain cakes and puddings and are used in one of the many different fillings used to stuff steak roll-ups (zrazy zawijane). *Note:* Crumbs made from the lighter rye bread may also be used in such recipes. *Variation:* Black bread or rye bread crumbs would produce too overpowering an effect if used alone in breading, but 1–2 T. added to ½ c. white breadcrumbs will make for zestier breading which may be enjoyed by the more adventurous savory food lovers.

STALE EGG BREAD
czerstwa bułka drożdżowa

Stale egg breads and coffee cakes (babka, placek drożdżowy, chałka) should also not be discarded but rather saved in a container stored in a dry place. Instead of grinding, we suggest you simply break up the slices and store until ready to use. Only plain coffee cakes without fillings (fruit, poppyseeds, cheese, etc.) should be used for this purpose. Egg-bread crumbs are a good thickener in various puddings and dessert dishes and may be added to fruit fillings and sweet cheese pierogi. Stale egg-bread soaked in milk and ground is used in a popular Polish turkey stuffing.

FLOUR AS A THICKENER
mąka do zagęszczania

Ordinary white enriched flour is undoubtedly the most common thickener used in Polish cuisine. It is used to thicken and (when sour cream or milk is added) to cream soups, gravies, and fricassees. A little flour is often browned in fat to form a roux (zasmażka), although we have tried to cut down on this practice in our book whenever possible. You can feel free to sprinkle a little flour (but not too much at first) over any poultry stuffing, ground meat dish, casserole, or filling which is too soggy, as it will take up excessive moisture.

POTATO FLOUR/STARCH
mąka kartoflana

This is the second most commonly used Polish thickener. We have used the terms potato starch and potato flour interchangeably to mean one and the same very white and fine powder extracted from potatoes. It is used to thicken fruit soups as well as fillings and gravies (although ordinary flour is better for the latter), plays a role in baking (e.g. sand babka, sponge cake), gives certain dumplings (kluski śląskie) their spongy consistency, and serves as the basis for that Old Polish fruit gel known as kisiel. A little potato flour dissolved in an equal amount of water is often brushed on bread towards the end of baking to give it a nice, shiny crust. *Note:* You may use cornstarch in any of our recipes calling for potato flour.

COLD HORS D'OEUVRES, APPETIZERS & STARTER COURSES

In Polish-style entertaining, cold dishes far outstrip hot entrées in popularity and importance, hence the length of this chapter. The traditional *święcone* (Easter feast) is often comprised mainly or even exclusively of cold, hard boiled eggs, *kiełbasa*, ham, cold roast pâtés, aspic dishes, salads, and relishes. At weddings and nameday parties alike, it is the cold appetizer course that is the most costly and varied and usually lasts the longest. Especially in the warmer months, there is even a tendency to skip the hot course entirely by following up many long hours of cold entertaining with tea, coffee, dessert, and homemade cordials and brandy.

One of the reasons for this is the Polish style of drinking. Unlike people of the English-speaking world, Poles never went in much for just drinking to work up an appetite. Food and drink always went together and crystal carafes of homemade spirits or bottles of the store-bought variety continue to be prominently displayed on the banquet table. Rather than a soft drink chaser, Polish guests prefer to "bite down" each round of drinks with a bit of food, and cold appetizers are just the thing.

Polish cuisine distinguishes between *przekąski*, the tiny hors d'oeuvres, canapés, and other such finger foods served at cocktail parties, which are not too common in the first place, and *zakąski* or *przystawki*, more substantial cold dishes usually eaten with a knife and fork while seated. We have included some of both in this chapter, but it is the latter that plays the biggest role on the Polish culinary scene.

If you are new to cold Polish-style entertaining, why not start at your next dinner party by prefacing the main course with at least three or four cold dishes. For starters, these could be hard-cooked eggs dressed with an easy cold sauce (see following chapter), smoked fish, a cold meat platter, and a cooked-vegetable salad. In time, you can graduate to more involved dishes, like stuffed eggs and vegetables, *pâtés* and aspics.

Whatever cold dishes you choose, they must be tastefully trimmed and garnished with a dash of culinary flair, not just plopped on a platter. We suggest you consult the "platter-trimmers" entry in this chapter to see what we mean. Your reputation as "lord and lady of the manor" is at stake, because the beauty and elegance of the cold table that greets your guests often sets the tone for the entire evening's entertainment.

* * *

SKEWERED HORS D'OEUVRES
korki/koreczki

These fancy, colorful, little, shish kebab-style hors d'oeuvres can be the festive centerpiece of a cocktail party or other gathering where a full-course meal is not planned. Or, served with drinks, they can provide an eye and palate pleasing prelude to a banquet or dinner party. Basically, only your imagination is the limit to how many combinations you come up with. First of all, assemble some or all of the following ingredients: Polish canned ham (unsliced); Canadian bacon; canned pork loin; smoked kiełbasa; cold roast beef, pork, or veal; roast chicken or turkey; boiled or roast slab bacon; boiled beef tongue; marinated herring; smoked salmon; firm sardines; anchovy fillets; firm smoked fish; yellow cheese (tilsit, munster, edam, gouda, Swiss, brick, etc.); dill pickles; gherkins; spiced cherries (pitted); spiced plums; radishes; pickled cocktail onions; green, yellow, or mild red pepper; olives; capers; pickled mushrooms; pitted prunes; dried fruits; raisins; large canned peas; whole raw cranberries; cucumber; lemon; hard cooked egg whites....

The meat, fish, cheese, and pickles should be cut into small cubes. Olives may be halved, pickled onions, cranberries, and raisins can be used whole, and the other ingredients should be cut into pieces roughly the size of the cubes. Impale 4–5 different cubes and morsels on toothpicks, taking care to achieve contrasting colors and complimentary taste combinations. Stick an orange, grapefruit, or loaf of unsliced bread with skewered hors d'oeuvres. Some examples:

— radish, ham, pickled mushroom, cheese
— prune, kiełbasa, pickle, egg white, black-bread cube
— cranberry, roast, raisin, cheese, bell pepper
— cooked bacon, spiced plum, cheese, gherkin
— cocktail onion, smoked salmon, cucumber, caper

CANAPÉS
kanapki

Tiny, Polish-style canapés or open-face sandwiches may be served with the apéritif to whet the appetite of your dinner guests, or as the main snack at card parties, club meetings, or various informal gatherings. A tray or platter decoratively arranged with these colorful kanapki will add a festive note to any get-together and invite your guests to savor and socialize. Kanapki rarely exceed 2 inches in diameter, are often silver-dollar-sized or even smaller (bite-size). At least two different kinds of bread should be used: light and dark. In addition to commercially available party rye and similar rounds of white canapé bread, you can also prepare your own. Rogale (Polish-style large crescent rolls available in ethnic bakeries) as well as rod-type French bread (baguettes) can be sliced into thin rounds.

(Bakeries usually have commercial slicers and can do the job for you on request.) You can also slice away the crust from a whole, unsliced loaf of Polish rye bread, slice it, and cut the slices into circles, squares, or triangles. The canapé bread is usually spread with plain or flavored butter and topped with lettuce or other greens, cold meats, cheese, fish, or hard-boiled egg slices, and garnished with fresh or pickled veggies, sauces, and the like. Others are covered with a layer of canapé spread and decorated with colorful trimmings. Here are but a few of the many possibilities:

DILL BUTTER
masło koperkowe

Fork-blend ½ c. soft butter with 2–3 T. finely chopped fresh dill and salt & pepper to taste.

GARDEN-GREEN BUTTER
masło z zieleniną

Fork-blend ½ c. soft butter with 1 T. each finely chopped fresh dill, parsley, and chives. Salt & pepper to taste.

GREEN BUTTER
masło zielone

Wash and very finely chop enough fresh spinach to make 1 slightly heaped T. Cook in 1 T. boiling water, stirring frequently, until fully cooked. Sieve and fork-blend with garden-green butter (above).

HORSERADISH BUTTER
masło chrzanowe

Cream ½ c. soft butter, then blend in 1 T. freshly grated horseradish and 2 t. lemon juice plus a dash of salt. May be mixed in blender.

MUSTARD BUTTER
masło musztardowe

Fork-blend ½ c. soft butter with 1–2 T. brown prepared mustard, 2 t. lemon juice, and a dash of salt.

ANCHOVY BUTTER
masło sardelowe

Combine ½ c. soft butter with 3 or 4 mashed or ground anchovy fillets (canned). For a more pronounced anchovy taste, blend in a little of the anchovy oil. *Optional:* Sprinkle in a bit of lemon juice. *Note:* Commercial anchovy paste also may be used.

HERRING BUTTER
masło śledziowe

Soak 1 small herring in cold water overnight, then skin, bone, and mash or grind. Combine with ½ c. soft butter. *Optional*: A little lemon may be added.

CRAYFISH BUTTER
masło rakowe

With mortar and pestle or in food-processor pulverize ½ c. diced cooked crayfish meat. Fork-blend with ½ c. soft butter. *Optional:* A dash of lemon juice and/or a little finely chopped fresh dill may be added.

SHRIMP BUTTER
masło krewetkowe

Combine 3 T. or so ground, cooked or canned (drained) shrimp with ½ c. soft butter. Lemon juice and/or chopped dill optional. *Note:* Experiment a little and come up with some interesting combinations of your own. For instance, two mashed, hard-cooked egg yolks may be added to any of the above butters for a richer taste. 2–3 T. ground ham will enhance the flavor of the horseradish or mustard butter. Dill and/or chives will perk up the taste of all the fish butters above. An equal amount of ground, smoked fish may replace the shrimp in the last recipe. A t. of beet juice (from canned beets) will impart an interesting, pinkish hue to all of the above. Thinly spread on bread, the above butters generally serve as a canapé base, which is then covered with a piece of lettuce or a slice of cucumber, topped with a thin slice of meat, fish, hard-cooked egg or cheese, and appropriately garnished. The butter containing ham or fish may be layered a bit more thickly as canapé spreads in their own right.

HAM CANAPÉS
kanapki z szynką

Thinly spread bread with butter (plain or flavored with mustard or horseradish as above), top with a thin slice of ham the size of the bread and cover with a small slice of tomato, cucumber or radish. (If using unflavored butter, you can top the ham with a splotch of prepared horseradish.)

KIEŁBASA CANAPÉS
kanapki z kiełbasą

Top bread thinly spread with horseradish- or mustard-flavored butter with a slice of skinned, smoked kiełbasa. Garnish with a sliced, marinated mushroom, a dill pickle slice, or half a spiced plum. The garnishes for ham canapés are also good.

PÂTÉ CANAPÉS
kanapki z pasztetem

Spread bread thinly with plain or horseradish butter. Cover with a slice of pâté and garnish with a small slice of tomato or gherkin. Top with a dollop of mayonnaise.

ROAST-MEAT CANAPÉS
kanapki z pieczystym

Thinly spread bread with plain, mustard- or horseradish-flavored butter. Top with a thin slice of cold roast beef, roast pork, roast turkey, or chicken. Garnish with a small tomato wedge and strip of green pepper plus a dollop of mayonnaise, or with a dab of whole-style cranberry sauce and a sprig of parsley.

BEEF-TONGUE CANAPÉS
kanapki z ozorem

Thinly spread bread with unflavored butter. Top with a thin slice of boiled beef tongue, garnish with a slice of cucumber and/or radish, and add a dollop of horseradish or horseradish-flavored mayonnaise.

SPRAT OR SARDINE CANAPÉS
kanapki ze szprotkami lub sardynką

Thinly spread bread with plain, dill or garden-green butter, top with a piece of Boston or leaf lettuce the size of the bread, a drained smoked Baltic sprat (imported from Poland) or high-grade sardine, and a dollop of mayonnaise. Insert a tiny wedge of peeled lemon into the mayonnaise.

HERRING CANAPÉS
kanapki ze śledziem

Top thinly buttered bread with lettuce, a piece of salt-herring fillet (soaked overnight, skinned and boned), a wedge of tomato, hard-boiled egg, and cucumber slice topped with a dollop of mayonnaise. Drained, store-bought, marinated herring (out of a jar) may also be used.

SMOKED-SALMON CANAPÉS
kanapki z łososiem

Cover bread thinly spread with dill butter with a piece of lettuce, a slice of smoked salmon (lox), a small wedge of peeled lemon, and a radish slice.

SMOKED-FISH CANAPÉS
kanapki z wędzoną rybą

Layer thinly buttered bread with lettuce, a piece of smoked fish (boneless), a dill-pickle slice and/or radish slice, and top with a dollop of carrot-flavored mayonnaise. (Fork-blend ½ c. mayonnaise with 1 heaping T. grated raw carrot, ½ t. lemon juice, ½ t. sugar, and a dash of salt.) Fresh cooked fish may be used instead of smoked fish.

WHITE-CHEESE CANAPÉS
kanapki z białym serem

Top buttered bread with a thin slice of farmer cheese, sprinkle with salt & pepper, garnish with radish slice, sprinkle with chopped chives, and dust with paprika.

YELLOW-CHEESE CANAPÉS
kanapki z żółtym serem

Cover bread thinly spread with plain or mustard-flavored butter with a slice of yellow cheese, garnish with a strip of green pepper and/or radish, and dust with paprika.

EGG CANAPÉS
kanapki z jajkiem

Thinly butter bread with plain, dill or garden-green butter, top with a hard boiled egg slice, decorate with a splotch of mayonnaise (or a blend of mayonnaise and brown mustard) and a small thin radish slice stuck into the mayonnaise. Sprinkle with chopped chives and dust with paprika. *Note:* Lettuce and a hard-boiled egg wedge may be used to enhance the flavor and color of all of the above canapés. All may be sprinkled with chopped chives according to your own preference.

CANAPÉ SPREADS
pasty kanapkowe

In addition to the above solid ingredients, a variety of tasty homemade spreads can be used in preparing your kanapki. It is best to place a piece of lettuce between the bread and the spread, as applying the spread directly to the bread tends to make it soggy. As with all canapés, use your imagination to colorfully garnish them with slices or wedges of cucumber, radish, pickle, green pepper, marinated mushrooms, hard-boiled eggs, etc.

ROAST-MEAT SPREAD
pasta z pieczystego

Grind 1 c. or so diced roast meat (pork, veal, beef, fowl, or any combination thereof) with 2 hard-boiled eggs. Add 1 T. chopped fresh dill, parsley, or chives and fork-blend into a smooth spread with ½ c. mayonnaise, sour cream or soft butter. Salt & pepper to taste. *Optional:* Add 1–2 buds crushed garlic.

HAM SPREAD
pasta z szynki

Combine 1 c. ground boiled ham with 1 T. prepared horseradish and/or brown mustard, 2 T. soft butter, and a heaping T. mayonnaise or enough to get the right spreadable consistency.

KIEŁBASA SPREAD
pasta z kiełbasy

Mix together ¾ c. ground smoked kiełbasa (with skin removed), 1 T. horseradish, 1 T. chopped chives and 4 T. soft butter. Mayonnaise (¼ c. or so) may be used in place of the butter.

FRANKFURTER SPREAD
pasta z parówek

Combine ¾ c. ground skinless franks, skinned serdelki (knackwurst) or bologna with 1 small minced onion, 2 ground dill pickles (drained of excess juice) and ⅓ c. mayonnaise and/or sour cream. For added zest, include 1 T. brown mustard.

HERRING SPREAD
pasta śledziowa

Grind 2 salt-herring fillets (soaked overnight) and combine with 1 t. minced onion, 1 t. finely chopped chives, ½ t. lemon juice, and several T. mayonnaise, or enough to get a smooth spread. Soft butter may be used instead of the mayonnaise.

HERRING & EGG SPREAD
pasta śledziowa z jajkiem

Combine 2 ground salt-herring fillets (soaked overnight) with 2 ground hard-boiled eggs, 1 T. finely chopped chives, and ⅓ c. soft butter or mayonnaise.

HERRING, APPLE & PICKLE SPREAD
pasta śledziowa z jabłkiem i ogórkiem

Grind together 2 salt-herring fillets (soaked overnight) with 2 dill pickles, 1 peeled and diced apple, and 1 small onion. Fork-blend ⅓ to ½ c. mayonnaise with 1 t. brown mustard and 1 t. sugar and combine with ground herring mixture.

HERRING & CHEESE SPREAD
pasta śledziowa z twarogiem

Grind together 1 salt-herring fillet (soaked overnight), ¼ lb. farmer cheese, 1 small onion, and 1 hard-boiled egg. Mix well with ½ c. soft butter and salt & pepper to taste. For a smoother spread, blend in one or more T. sour cream.

FISH & CHEESE SPREAD
pasta rybno-twarogowa

Combine ¼ lb. ground farmer's cheese with ½ c. ground smoked or cooked fish, 1 T. finely chopped chives, and ½ c. soft butter. Salt & pepper to taste. Sardines or tuna fish may also be used.

SMOKED-FISH SPREAD
pasta z wędzonej ryby

Combine ¾ c. ground smoked fish with ¼ c. grated raw carrot, 1 t. lemon juice and ⅓ to ½ c. mayonnaise.

ANCHOVY SPREAD
pasta sardelowa

Grind 1 small can drained anchovy fillets with 1 small onion and 1 hard-boiled egg. Stir in several T. soft butter or mayonnaise to get the right spreadable consistency. Several t. finely chopped chives may be added.

CHICKEN-LIVER SPREAD
pasta z wątróbek kurzych

In 4 T. butter fry ⅓ lb. chicken livers and 1 diced onion until liver is tender but not overdone (cutting them in half should show a trace of pinkness). Grind with 1 hard-boiled egg, salt & pepper to taste, and combine with ⅓ c. or more mayonnaise or sour cream.

MUSHROOM SPREAD
pasta z pieczarek

Cook ¼ lb. fresh, sliced white mushrooms in 4 T. butter, along with 1 diced onion until tender. Grind with 1 hard-boiled egg, add 2 t. chopped fresh dill (or 1 t. each chopped dill, parsley, and chives), salt & pepper to taste, and mix well to a spreadable consistency with ⅓ c. sour-cream or soft butter.

WHITE-CHEESE SPREAD
pasta twarogowa

Combine 1 c. ground farmer cheese with 3 t. finely chopped chives and ½ c. sour cream. Mix thoroughly and season to taste with salt, pepper, and paprika. *Optional*: Grind 2–3 radishes with the cheese.

CHEESE & BUTTER SPREAD
pasta twarogowo-maślana

Mix thoroughly to get a spreadable consistency: 1 c. ground farmer cheese, ½ c. butter, 2 buds crushed garlic, and salt & pepper to taste. *Optional*: Add 1 T. finely chopped chives.

EGG & ONION SPREAD
pasta jajeczna z cebulką

Simmer 1 chopped onion in 2 T. butter until tender and combine with 1 c. ground hard-boiled eggs. Add 1 T. finely chopped dill, salt & pepper to taste, and mix all ingredients with ½ c. sour cream.

EGG & CHIVES SPREAD
pasta jajeczna ze szczypiorkiem

Mix thoroughly 1 c. ground hard-boiled eggs, 2 T. finely chopped chives, 1 t. brown mustard and ⅓–½ c. sour cream. Salt & pepper to taste. Mayonnaise may be used in place of sour cream. *Note*: For extra smoothness all the above spreads may be prepared in a blender.

* * *

COLD APPETIZERS/STARTER COURSES
zimne zakąski/przystawki

These appetizers are usually more substantial than bite-sized hors d'oeuvres or tiny canapés, and are usually served at table and eaten with knife and fork. We begin our presentation of these dishes with a few suggestions on how to enhance their elegance and eye-appeal.

PLATTER TRIMMERS
dekorowanie półmisków

The recipes for many of the cold dishes that follow include hints on garnishes and go-togethers. Nonetheless, we feel the culinary art of presentation deserves a few special remarks and specific examples. The realm of platter decorations affords a great opportunity for individual creativity. Most any edible can serve as such a garnish if artistically arranged and color-coordinated with the dish it is supposed to decorate. Brightly colored trimmings are ideal for dishes of a paler hue, and whites or pastels will strike a pleasing contrast with dark-colored foods.

GARDEN-GREEN DECORATION
zieleninka do dekoracji

These are by far the simplest and most common of platter trimmers. A lettuce-lined platter can be the platform on which a great variety of cold dishes are served, although you can save on lettuce by simply lining the rim of the platter with leaves. Sprigs of parsley or kale, feathery tufts of dill, or strands of chives can provide the finishing touch to many a platter. As shown on the accompanying illustration, even green onions can be fashioned into an interesting bouquet. Cut 1½–2 pieces of green onion into strips ¾ of the way down. Place in ice water for 30 min., remove and use to decorate platters.

RADISH ROSES & OTHER GARNISHES
różyczki i inne dekoracje z rzodkiewek

If you have skill and patience you can turn ordinary radishes into beautiful, flower-like decorations with a paring knife. We suggest you pick up a handy little device, available wherever cooking utensils are sold, which will greatly facilitate the creation of radish roses. Another way is to cut the radishes into petals (like the tomato shown at top of illustration). Keep in ice-cold water for 30 min. and the petals should blossom out. A radish swirl is made like the illustrated cucumber swirl by cutting thin radish slice halfway, i.e. from side to center, then gently standing it up with ends pushed in opposite direction. A radish cross, meant mainly to top individual portions of cold dishes, is made by cutting slots from side to center in 2 thin radish slices, then fitting slices into slots perpendicularly. The simplest of decorations are radish slices or half-slices. Whole radish slices make an interesting border around rim of platter, but its best to stick them onto a ribbon of mayonnaise from decorator tube to keep them in place. For a more economical border (using fewer radishes), line slices end to end. A more elegant border is made with overlapping radish slices arranged shingle fashion. In either case, a sprinkling of chopped greens of choice will enhance their appearance.

DECORATIVE CUCUMBERS
dekoracje z ogórka

Cucumbers may be turned into a number of interesting platter trimmers. The simplest are cucumber and radish slices used to make a border like that described for radishes (above). In fact, a very eye-appealing border can be achieved using alternating cucumber and radish slices. Cucumbers can also serve as serving bowls for savory sauces. Slice off ends of an average cucumber (so it can stand upright) and cut into 3–4 pieces. Scoop out pulp from 1 side to create a serving bowl. With vegetable-peeler remove vertical strips of peel from top to bottom for an interesting zebra effect. Various cutters, scoops, and knifes will enable you to produce cucumber cubes, balls, spears, etc., which have countless applications as decorative embellishments.

DECORATIVE BELL PEPPERS
dekoracje z papryki

Bell peppers—green, yellow or red—add colorful accents to platters whether cut into rings, spears or cubes. Especially worth recommending is their use as an interesting container for sauces and relishes. Simply cut pepper in half widthwise, scoop out and discard seed portion, stand upright and you get two little bowls for dressings, pickled mushrooms, zesty gherkins, etc. Such a bowl may be set at center of platter, surrounded by slices of the meat, fish or whatever its sauce is meant to accompany. The pepper shell can also serve as a "flowerpot" for a more extravagant, potted-palm decoration. Stand as many whole leeks as needed in pepper half. With scissors snip leaves lengthwise to get a palm tree effect.

DECORATIVE TOMATOES
dekoracje z pomidorów

The simplest tomato decorations are wedges, slices, or half-slices, which can be used to brighten tops or rims of filled platters. A sprinkling of chopped garden greens is also recommended. Try this easy tomato blossom: cut a small firm tomato vertically one way and then the other to form 4 wedges, but do not cut all the way through. Gently spread wedges apart, add a small piece of lettuce and insert a radish rose at center. Without the radish rose, the tomato blossom may be used to hold a portion of salad. A scooped-out tomato half or basket (see illustration) can serve as an interesting bowl for sauces or relishes. A platter centerpiece can easily be created by cutting tomato into wedges, without cutting all the way through, and inserting cucumber slices or green-onion spears into the cracks (see illustration).

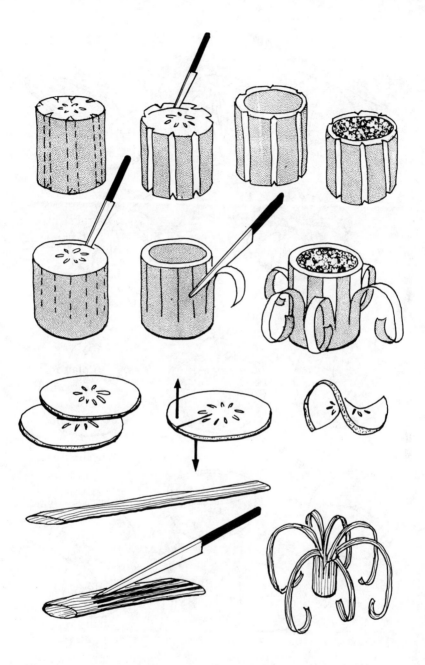

Top two rows show how a cucumber can be fashioned into an interesting sauce, relish and salad container by hollowing out the inside and decorating the exterior. A decorative cucumber swirl, used to embellish platters, is seen in third row, just above a green-onion bouquet or blossom which in Polish is called a "pióropusz" (head-dress).

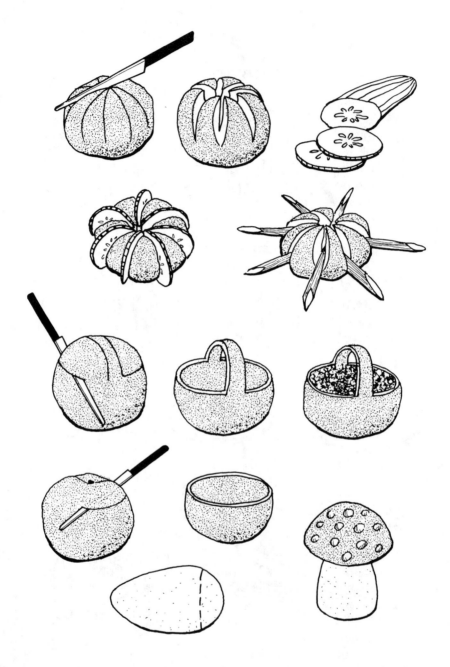

Cucumbers and green onions team up with the tomato to create platter decorations (top two rows). Preparation of a bright tomato basket for holding sauces and relishes is presented in third row. A tomato, hard-cooked egg, and a bit of mayonnaise is all that is needed to create a whimsical "toadstool" that is sure to be a conversation piece (bottom row).

CITRUS-FRUIT DECORATIONS
dekoracje z cytrusów

Before using any citrus fruits in their rinds, scrub well with plenty of soap and hot water, then scald with boiling water and dry. A lemon cut into 8 wedges may be arranged spoke-fashion in a circle (usually at center) or semi-circle (generally at 1 or both ends of platter). They may also be sliced into thin rounds or cut in half again into half-rounds. A lemon swirl is made the same way as a cucumber (see illustration) or radish swirl. Oranges may be used the same way, but are generally reserved for poultry. Lemons are used with fish, aspic dishes, meats, and salads. Rather than being discarded, squeezed-out lemon, orange, and grapefruit halves can serve as interesting bowls for tangy fruit sauces (currant, cranberry, lignonberry, plum, etc.) and spiced fruits. For added eye-appeal, cut a zigzag effect round the rim.

HARD-COOKED-EGG DECORATIONS
dekoracje z jaj

The illustrated egg & tomato "toadstool", described among the egg dishes in this chapter, is a guaranteed conversation piece, but hard-boiled eggs have many other uses as platter trimmers. The most common are wedges and slices, whose color is often brightened with a sprinkling of paprika or chopped garden greens. Cold stuffed eggs make an interesting border for a cold meat, fish, or salad platter. Chopped hard-boiled eggs are usually sprinkled over salad, but don't overlook the possibility of using them to trim a platter border. It's best to first line the border with a strip of mayonnaise from decorator tube so they keep in place.

OTHER PLATTER TRIMMERS
garnirowanie półmisków inaczej

Thin rounds of cooked carrots or drained cooked peas (fresh, frozen, or canned) make interesting decorations alone or in combination. For instance, arrange peas in rows or geometric designs resembling beads atop salads. An easy salad-topper is made with 4 carrot rounds with a pea at center. Use either or both as border trimmers, but remember to first apply a mayonnaise trail, so they don't go rolling into your guests's laps when the platter is passed round. Spiced cherries, plums, or pears, dill pickles, gherkins, brined apples, pickled mushrooms, spiced pumpkin cubes, sardines, sprats and anchovies, cubed boiled ham, pork loin, kiełbasa and cheese, as well as a great many other items too numerous to mention can help turn seemingly ordinary foods into gourmet delights. A decorator tube will enable you to turn plain or tinted gelled mayonnaise into flowers, swirls, and just about any other shape you happen to fancy. Beets are among the few foods not recommended as platter trimmers since they stain and cause unsightly red streaks in whatever food they touch. *Note:* The above are but a few suggestions which by no means exhaust the decorative cold-table repertoire of Polish cuisine. They may help enliven America's home-entertaining circuit where, under the guise of "casualness", food presentation can sometimes be dull and uninspiring. Obviously gourmet hors d'oeuvres and creative garnishes would be out of place at a family backyard picnic, but a touch of elegance and artistry wouldn't hurt at a dinner-party.

HARD-BOILED EGGS IN VARIOUS SAUCES
jaja w różnych sosach

With the proper presentation and a little flair, the lowly hard-boiled egg can become a gourmet delight worthy of its place among the smoked salmon, pâté, and other elegant dishes of your cold appetizer course. Simply place 8 hard-boiled halves cut side down on a lettuce-lined platter. Drench with sour cream and/or mayonnaise-based sauce of choice. Decorate platter with small tomato wedges, a row of overlapping radish slices, a few cucumber swirls, etc., and serve. For a larger platter, each row of hard-boiled egg halves can be dressed with a different, color-contrasting sauce, e.g. garden-green sauce, sour-cream sauce, mustard sauce, beet-relish sauce. *Note:* Depending on your dietary requirements, eggs may be drenched with sauce (allowing about ¾ c. sauce for 8 egg halves) or simply topped with a little dab thereof. Each dressed egg may be topped with a thin radish slice or radish cross. Light-colored sauces (sour-cream, mayonnaise, horseradish, mustard) may be garnished with a sprinkling of finely chopped garden greens or a dash of paprika.

EGG & TOMATO "TOADSTOOLS"
"muchomorki" z jaj i pomidorków

Although in terms of taste this novelty is little more than hard-boiled eggs and tomatoes dotted with a little mayonnaise, it can add a cute and colorful accent to any starter course or cold supper. Cut slice of white from both wider and narrower ends of 4 hard-boiled eggs to enable them to stand upright. On small serving dish, place 4 separate splotches (1 T. each) of mayonnaise which should "glue" them to platter. Cut 4 small, firm tomatoes (with a slightly larger diameter than the eggs) in half. From the stemless halves scoop our a little of the pulp to enable tomato to set firm on egg, forming a "toadstool." You may place a dab of mayonnaise at top of egg to "glue" the tomato half into place. Decorate tomato ("toadstool cap") with mayonnaise in decorator tube to produce the familiar red-cap toadstool of children's fairy tales. Finely chop the leftover slices of egg white and sprinkle over the "toadstool caps." Sprinkle the mayonnaise that has oozed out from the base of the "toadstool" with chopped chives to create a grasslike effect. *Note:* This may be served not only on their own serving dish, but can be placed at irregular intervals on a large platter containing cold meats, aspic dishes, assorted salads, etc. Small, squatty "toadstools" are made by using 1 egg for every 2 "muchomorki." After cutting egg in half widthwise, stand end with exposed yolk on mayonnaise dab on platter, and use only ⅓ of a tomato (stemless portion) for the cap.

GARNISHED EGGS & SMOKED SALMON
jaja z łososiem garnirowane

In bowl, combine 1 peeled, cored, diced, tart apple, 1 large diced dill pickle, ¼ c. grated celeriac (or finely diced celery stalk), ½ c. drained, canned baby peas, and 1 T. chopped parsley. Sprinkle with salt, paprika, and lemon juice, and gently toss ingredients with ½ c. mayonnaise. On platter, place 8 smallish leaves of Boston lettuce. Place on each hard-boiled egg half-wrapped in a thin slice of smoked salmon, and decorate each with ½ a thin lemon slice and a spring of parsley. Next to egg place a coop of salad topped with a small tomato wedge.

EGG & HAM ROLL-UPS
jaja w szynce/roladki

Cut 2 hard-boiled eggs into quarters lengthwise. Spread 8 thinly sliced 2 x 5 inch strips boiled ham (preferably Krakus brand) with a thin layer of prepared horseradish and a thicker layer of mayonnaise. Place egg quarter at end of each strip and roll up. Line the roll-ups down the center of a narrow platter. Decorate 1 side of platter with lettuce leaves and the other with tomato wedges. For added color, top each roll-up with a thin radish slice sprinkled with chopped chives.

EGGS & CAVIAR
jaja z kawiorem

Cut 4 slices French bread toast in half and then cut the halves in half again. Line a small platter with leaves of Boston lettuce so they protrude slightly beyond the rim. Cut 4 hard-boiled eggs in half lengthwise, remove a small slice of egg white from bottom so they don't wobble and line them up end to end in 2 rows on platter yolk side up. Top each yolk with as big a spoonful of caviar as you like (or can afford!) and insert a ¼ slice of lemon into each. Surround the platter with a border of toast. The sliced-off egg white may be finely chopped and sprinkled over the caviar. Served with ice-cold Wódka Wyborowa or champagne, this is a true gourmet delight.

CAVIAR-STUFFED EGGS
kawior w jajkach

Cut 4 slice French bread toast into 4 wedges each as above and line them up shingle fashion (with points overlapping) in 2 rows down center of platter. From 4 hard-cooked eggs remove a thin slice of white from wider end so they can stand upright. From narrower end remove a ½ inch slice to expose yolks. With small spoon gently scoop out yolks, taking care not to damage whites. Fill eggs with caviar and replace tops. Stand eggs up next to toast "shingles." Chop yolks with leftover white and heap in 4 little mounds on platter. Place a lemon wedge next to each egg. Decorate platter with greens, radish slices, etc.

CAVIAR-STUFFED EGGS ANOTHER WAY
kawior w jajkach inaczej

This is another delightful and elegant way to enjoy the superb taste of caviar, but it is a bit more economical because you simply use less of it. Cut 4 hard-boiled eggs into half lengthwise and remove a thin slice of white from bottoms so they don't wobble when placed yolk side up. Gently remove yolks and chop fine or mash. Add 4 scant t. caviar and toss with yolk very gently so as not to damage the roe. Fill eggs with mixture, insert a thin lemon wedge into each and serve with wedges of French bread toast.

ASSORTED EGG PLATTER
półmisek z jaj

Slice 8 hard-cooked eggs in half and remove a thin slice of white from bottoms so they don't wobble when placed yolk side up. Line a platter with leaves of Boston lettuce. Line the halves up in 4 rows and garnish each row as follows:
1st row: Top eggs with a thin slice of smoked salmon and decorate with a "star" made of 5 tiny strips of mild red pickled peppers. Insert a tiny lemon wedge into center of each star.
2nd row: Top eggs with a dollop of mayonnaise and cover with a horn-shaped roll of thinly sliced boiled ham; insert a sprig of curly parsley into each horn.
3rd row: Cover eggs with pieces of smoked Baltic sprats or sardines, top each with a tiny dollop of mayonnaise and insert tiny lemon wedge into it; on 1 side of fish slice place a few shavings of freshly grated horseradish, on the other ½ a thin radish slice.
4th row: Spread the eggs rather thickly with mayonnaise and garnish with grated yellow cheese; sprinkle with paprika; top each with a cucumber swirl made from a rather thin cucumber (see platter garnishes above).

EGGS IN TOMATOES
jajka w pomidorkach

Cut 4 small firm tomatoes (with a slightly larger circumference than peeled hard-boiled eggs) in half. Cut 4 peeled hard-boiled eggs in half widthwise. From each tomato half scoop out just enough pulp to make room for the egg half. Insert egg halves into tomatoes yolk side up. Place 4–6 thinly sliced slices boiled ham on top of each other, roll up starting at one of the narrow ends jelly-roll fashion, then slice into thin strips as you would egg noodles. Heap the ham strips on the egg-filled tomatoes. Place on lettuce-lined platter and drench with sauce made by fork-blending ¾ c. mayonnaise, 2 T. prepared brown mustard, ¼ t. salt, ¼ t. pepper, and 1 t. lemon juice. Garnish generously with chopped chives. *Note*: Freeze the scooped-out tomato pulp for tomato soup or other uses.

EGGS STUFFED WITH MUSHROOMS
jajka faszerowane pieczarkami

Wash well, dry, dice fine and sauté in 1 T. butter 6 large, fresh store-bought mushrooms. Sprinkle with salt and simmer until liquid evaporates, then set aside to cool. Peel 4 hard-cooked eggs, slice in half lengthwise, and scoop out yolks. Mash the yolks, add 2 T. sour cream, and the sautéed mushrooms, and mix until smooth. Salt & pepper to taste. Fill whites with mixture and decorate each egg half with a sprig of parsley.

EGGS STUFFED WITH SPRATS
jajka faszerowane szprotkami

Slice 4 peeled, hard-boiled eggs in half lengthwise and remove yolks. Mash yolks with 4–5 canned, smoked Baltic sprats (or sardines), and mix in 3 T. mayonnaise and 1 t. lemon juice. Fill decorator tube with mixture and fill the whites. Decorate each egg with a lemon wedge and strips of mild pickled red peppers.

EGGS STUFFED WITH HERRING
jajka faszerowane śledziem

Remove skin and bones from 1 small salt herring, soaked overnight in water, and dice fine. Cut 4 peeled, hard-boiled eggs in half lengthwise, remove yolks and mash them with the diced herring. Stir in 2 T. sour cream, ¼ t. paprika and 1 t. lemon juice and mix well until mixture is smooth. Fill whites with mixture. Sprinkle each egg with chopped fresh parsley and arrange on platter decorated with salted and peppered tomato wedges. *Variation*: Instead of herring, you may use 2–3 canned anchovy fillets.

EGGS STUFFED WITH SMOKED FISH
jajka faszerowane wędzoną rybą

Slice 4 peeled hard-cooked eggs in half lengthwise and remove yolks. Finely dice ¼ lb. smoked fish (with bones and skin removed) and mix well with 4 mashed egg yolks, 2–3 T. mayonnaise, 1 T. lemon juice and 1 T. finely grated raw carrot. Fill eggs with mixture, place on lettuce leaves, and decorate platter with small tomato wedges and parsley sprigs.

EGGS STUFFED WITH KIEŁBASA
jajka faszerowane kiełbasą

Peel 4 hard-boiled eggs, slice in half lengthwise, and remove yolks. Remove skin from ¼ lb. ready-to-eat smoked kiełbasa and grind together with the yolks and 1 small quartered raw onion. To ground mixture, add ¼ t. paprika, 2–3 T. mayonnaise or sour cream (or a little of both) and a pinch of salt if needed. Mix well and top eggs with mixture. With T. round mounds of kiełbasa mixture to resemble whole eggs. Place eggs on lettuce-lined platter and decorate each egg with a thin radish slice. Decorate platter rim with radish slices and top with grated yellow cheese. *Variation*: For milder-tasting stuffed eggs, use boiled ham in place of kiełbasa.

EGGS STUFFED WITH MEAT
jajka faszerowane mięsem

Here's a good way to use up that cooked leftover meat and achieve gourmet results at the same time. Grind ¼–⅓ lb. cooked pork, veal, beef or chicken or any combination thereof. Mash the 4 hard-cooked yolks, stir in 2–3 T. mayonnaise, add the ground meat, 1 T. chopped parsley, 1 t. prepared brown mustard or bottled horseradish, a pinch of pepper and, if needed, a little salt. Mix well and spoon mixture into hard-cooked egg-white halves. With spoon sculpt rounded mounds of filling equal in size and shape to the egg halves. Into each mound insert 2–3 thin radish slices and decorate platter with salted and peppered tomato wedges garnished with chopped chives or dill.

EGGS IN ASPIC
jajka w auszpiku

Soak ¾ T. gelatin in ½ c. cold vegetable stock until it expands. Separately, combine 1 c. vegetable stock with ½ t. tomato paste and 1 t. lemon juice. Add soaked gelatin and heat to just below boiling, seasoning to taste with salt & pepper. Add 2 T. hot liquid to 4 teacups and refrigerate until set. Into each cup place 1 hard-boiled egg half, yolk side up, top with 1 T. diced boiled ham, 1 T. drained canned baby peas, and 1 t. finely diced mild pickled red peppers. Cover with remaining gelatin mixture and refrigerate until set. When ready to serve, briefly dip teacups in boiling water and turn aspic molds out onto lettuce-lined platter down side up. Serve with sauce made by fork-blending ½ c. mayonnaise, 1 t. bottled horseradish and ½ t. lemon juice. *Optional*: For a gourmet twist cut 2 small firm tomatoes in half and scoop out pulp (reserving it for other uses). Place tomato halves next to each portion of aspic and fill them with the sauce.

EGGS IN FISH ASPIC
jajka w auszpiku rybnym

Soak ¾ T. gelatin in ½ c. cold fish stock, (see soups) until it expands. Separately, heat 1 c. strained fish stock, add gelatin, 1 t. lemon juice, and a pinch of salt if needed. Lightly beat 1 raw egg white and add to pot and continue heating until liquid becomes clear. Strain through sieve lined with several thicknesses cheesecloth and add 2 t. chopped fresh dill. Pour 2 T. liquid into each of 4 teacups and refrigerate until set. Into each teacup place a peeled, hard-boiled egg half and cover each with remaining gelatin liquid. Refrigerate until set. Meanwhile, dice cooked fish (from stock) to get about ½–¾ c., discarding bones and skin. Also dice 1 carrot from stock and 1 vinegar-cured dill pickle. In 2 c. lightly salted boiling water with a pinch of citric acid crystals added, cook 5–6 whole fresh cultivated mushrooms and combine with other diced ingredients. Add 4 T. drained canned baby peas and 4–6 T. mayonnaise. Mix gently so as not to crush peas, and salt & pepper to taste. Mound the salad at center of platter and surround with the aspic molds. Decorate each with lemon slices. *Variation*: Instead of serving clear aspic with salad, you may add the diced cooked fish and carrot directly to teacups, cover with gelatin liquid, and refrigerate to set. Serve with horseradish sauce.

EGGS IN MEAT ASPIC
jajka w auszpiku mięsnym

Soak ¾ T. gelatin in ½ c. cold strained meat stock (beef, pork, veal, or chicken) with congealed fat removed. (*Note:* If using a strong veal or chicken stock, which contains its own gelatin, gelatin may be reduced to 1½ t.) Combine another c. strained meat stock with ½ t. tomato paste, add gelatin mixture, heat to below boiling point, and season with ½ t. lemon juice, and salt & pepper to taste. Clarify liquid with beaten egg white as above and strain through cheesecloth. Add 2 T. liquid to each of 4 teacups and refrigerate until set. To each teacup add half a hard-cooked egg. Top each with several T. diced cooked meat and 1 T. drained canned baby peas. Fill with remaining gelatin liquid and refrigerate until set. Place on platter, decorate with tomato wedges, sliced radishes, and cucumbers, and serve with Tartar or horseradish sauce. *Note*: For smaller portions, prepare any of the above eggs in aspic in demitasses rather than full-sized teacups. This recipe will make 8 portions rather than 4.

QUAIL EGGS IN VARIOUS WAYS
jajka przepiórcze na różne sposoby

Tiny hard-boiled eggs may be used in any of the above egg recipes. They may be stuffed with any of the above fillings, although being so small, they require a steady hand. They can easily be drenched with various cold sauces, in which case do not cut them in half, but rather serve whole. In aspic dishes, use 3–4 halves per teacup or 2 halves per demitasse. You can also use hard-boiled quail eggs to decorate the rim of any cold chicken-egg platter, in which case dust them with paprika and/or sprinkle with chopped dill. If you use them to make tiny "toadstools", top each trimmed quail egg with half a small radish 'glued' into place with a dab of mayonnaise.

EGG "OYSTERS"
"ostrygi" z jaj

Before leaving our cold egg dishes, we present this unusual recipe which will probably be appreciated only by the vodka drinkers in your group. Fill crystal shot-glasses with ice-cold Wódka Wyborowa. Into identical glasses carefully deposit raw egg yolks from very fresh eggs, taking care that they do not break. To each raw egg yolk add ¼ t. olive oil, a sprinkle of lemon juice and a dash or two of Maggi seasoning. Sprinkle with salt & pepper. Have your guests pour their vodka "down the hatch" and follow up with the "oyster," which is also consumed in a single gulp. "Smacznego!"

SALT HERRING
śledzie solone

Barrel-cured salt herring, after being properly prepared, undoubtedly rank among Poland's favorite cold appetizers and may be served in a myriad of ways. Salt herring are generally available straight from the barrel at Polish, Jewish, and other ethnic markets. Sometimes you can get them in plastic bags of a lb. or so. Very good are Holland herring which come in small, plastic barrels with about 1 gallon capacity. Wherever you get them, the initial preparation is quite similar. Raw herring are heavily salted to prevent spoilage and tenderize the flesh. Therefore they first must be thoroughly de-salted. If the heads have been left on, cut them off before soaking. Soak herring in a sinkful or large pan of cold water about 24 hrs., changing water 2–3 times. *Optional*: After that, the herring may be soaked in milk to cover about 1 hr. You may soak the whole herring in water or clean it first. To clean, slit the belly, and remove the milt (from male herring) and roe (from female herring), setting it aside. Wash cavity well. Gently remove skin, taking care that the flesh does not stick to it. Herring may be cut into serving-size pieces with the bones left in, but your guests will have to fuss over them at table. It's better to remove the backbone and most of the thin bones will come with it. The roe is not very good, but many people like the milt. It can be sieved and used in the marinade or sauce, or it can be marinated separately and served to those who enjoy it. We prefer this method, because the milt makes for a cloudy marinade and may give the herring a strong, fishy taste.

MARINATED/PICKLED HERRING
śledź marynowany

Soak, clean, and fillet 4 salt herring as above and cut fillets into 2 inch pieces. Place in jar or crockery bowl with tight-fitting lid. In pot combine 1 c. water, 1 t.–1 T. sugar, 1 bay leaf, 5 grains allspice, 5 peppercorns, and 1 t. mustard seed, bring to boil, and simmer covered 3 min. Add 1 c. 6% distilled vinegar and bring to boil. Let stand covered until cooled to room temp. Pour marinade over herring, cover, and refrigerate 2–7 days. Before serving, garnish with onion sliced wafer thin or finely chopped.

HERRING MARINATED IN LEMON JUICE
śledź marynowany cytryną

Slice soaked, cleaned, filleted salt herring into 2 inch pieces. Place in jar or crockery bowl. In pot combine juice of 4 lemons, an equal amount of water, 2 sliced onions, 2 bay leaves, and 10 peppercorns. Bring to boil and cool. Pour over herring. Add several slices lemon, seal, and refrigerate at least 2 days before serving.

HERRING IN OIL
śledź w oleju

Soak, clean, and fillet 4 herring as usual and cut into 2 inch pieces. Place in jar or crockery bowl. Add 2 bay leaves and cover with olive oil or other high-grade oil, seal or cover tightly and refrigerate at least 24 hrs. before serving. To serve, place herring on serving dish, and garnish each piece with a little very finely chopped onion. This is the type of herring served in our household in Wigilia.

HERRING IN OIL WITH APPLES
śledź w oleju z jabłkami

Soak and prepare 4 salt herring as above. Scrub 1 lemon, scald with boiling water, and remove rind. Slice up lemon and cut each slice in half. Remove and discard seeds. In jar, alternate layers of herring with lemon slices and slices of 1 peeled tart apple. Add 5 peppercorns, 5 grains allspice, and 1–2 bay leaves. Cover with olive oil or other high-grade cooking oil, seal, and refrigerate at least 24 hrs. before serving. Serve without lemon or apple slices. If you like, decorate with fresh lemon slices.

PICKLED HERRING IN OIL
śledź marynowany w oleju

Cut 4 soaked, cleaned, and filleted salt herring into small pieces and toss gently with 2–3 onions sliced wafer thin. Transfer mixture to jar and cover with 6% distilled vinegar. Let stand 30 min, then drain off vinegar. Add 3 peppercorns, 2 grains allspice, and 1 bay leaf, and cover with high-grade oil. Seal and refrigerate at least 24 hrs. before serving. They will keep refrigerated up to a week. To serve, place herring on serving dish and garnish each piece with fresh finely chopped onion.

EASY PICKLED HERRING IN OIL
łatwy śledź marynowany w oleju

Even if you don't have ready access to barrel-cured salt herring or lack the time and energy to soak and dress them from scratch, you can still enjoy this tasty appetizer. Simply drain off the marinade from a jar of store-bought marinated herring and fill it with oil. Seal and refrigerate at least 24 hrs. On serving dish garnish each portion with finely chopped onion.

ROLLMOPS
rolmopsy

Soak and clean 4 salt herrings as above, but do not cut up. Place each of the 8 fillets on board, spread with Polish-style mustard, sprinkle with some finely chopped onions, and place a piece of dill pickle no larger than the herring fillet's wider end at 1 end. Roll up tightly, secure with toothpick, and place in jar. In pot combine 1 c. water, 1 bay leaf, 5 peppercorns, 3 grains allspice, 1 t. mustard seed, and 1 t.–1 T. sugar, depending on whether you prefer tart or slightly sweet rollmops. Add 1 c. 6% distilled vinegar and bring to boil. Cool to room temp. and pour over rollmops. Seal and refrigerate 2–7 days. To serve, garnish each rollmop with finely chopped onion.

ROLLMOPS IN OIL
rolmopsy w oleju

Spread 8 soaked and cleaned herring fillets (from 4 herring) with sharp brown mustard, roll up tightly, and secure with toothpick. Place in jar, add 2 bay leaves, and cover with oil. Seal and refrigerate 1–2 days before serving. To serve, place rollmops on serving dish, replace oily toothpicks with fresh ones, and garnish each rollmop with finely chopped onion.

ROLLMOPS WITH SAUERKRAUT
rolmopsy z kapustą

Prepare 8 fillets from 4 salt herrings as above. Chop fine ¾ c. drained sauerkraut and mix with 1 finely chopped onion and several T. oil. Place a little sauerkraut mixture at 1 end of herring fillets, roll up, and fasten with toothpick. Place in jar or crockery bowl. In pot combine ½ c. lemon juice (or 6% distilled vinegar), ½ c. water, 1 crumbled bay leaf, 10 peppercorns, and 1 sliced onion. Bring to boil, simmer briefly, switch off heat, and let stand covered until cool. Pour over rollmops, seal, and refrigerate at least 24 hrs. before serving.

ROLLMOPS WITH LEEK
rolmopsy z porami

Trim 2–3 leeks of green tops and root "whiskers" if still attached, wash well, and cook in boiling salted water to cover until tender. Remove and allow to cool. Soak and clean 4 salt herring the normal way, and remove bones to get 8 fillets. Place a piece of cooked leek at 1 end of each fillet and roll up. Secure each roll-up with a toothpick. In pot, combine ½ c. water, ½ c. 6% distilled vinegar, 5 peppercorns, 3 grains allspice, 1 bay leaf, and 2 t. sugar and bring to boil. Place rollmops in boiling marinade, cover, switch off heat, and let stand 5–10 min. Remove rollmops from marinade and let drain in colander until cool. Place rollmops on serving dish. Fork-blend 1 c. sour cream, 1 T. freshly grated horseradish (or 2 T. bottled horseradish), juice of ½–1 lemon, and 1 t. sugar. Drench rollmops with sauce.

HERRING & APPLES
śledź z jabłkiem

Slice 4 soaked, cleaned, filleted herring into ½ inch strips, and sprinkle with 1 T. oil. Peel a large tart apple and grate coarsely. Mix with 1 T. prepared horseradish, 1 T. lemon juice, and 2–3 T. sour cream or mayonnaise. On platter, place 4 small leaves of Boston lettuce, and mound ¼ of the herring strips on each. Top with apple mixture and decorate with strips of dill pickle and red mild pickled pepper.

CREAMED HERRING
śledź w śmietanie

Cut 4 soaked, filleted herring into 2 inch pieces and arrange on serving dish. Sprinkle each with a little (about ½ t.) lemon juice and top with wafer-thin onion slices. Fork-blend 1 c. sour cream with 1 t. powdered sugar and pour over herring. Refrigerate at least 1 hr. before serving. *Optional:* Just before serving, dust with paprika.

MAJKA'S CREAMED HERRING
śledź pani Majki w śmietanie

Soak, clean, and fillet 4 herring and cut into 2 inch pieces. Arrange on serving dish. Top herring with ½ c. peeled coarsely grated apple and ¾ c. finely chopped onion. Fork blend 1 c. sour cream with 1 T. Polish-style mustard and 1–2 t. powdered sugar. Pour over herring. Chill at least 1 hr. before serving. Decorate with thin onion slices and sprigs of parsley.

EASIEST CREAM HERRING
śledź w śmietanie najłatwiejszy

Whenever there isn't time to prepare these from scratch, take a shortcut using store bought marinated herring. (*Note:* We do not recommend store-bought creamed herring, as they contain a preservative to keep the cream from spoiling.) Drain 1 jar (about 1 c.) marinated herring and discard onions and spices. Plunge into cold water briefly and drain in colander. If herring are whole, cut into 2 inch pieces. Arrange on serving dish. Top herring with onion sliced wafer thin, and dress with ¾ c. fork-blended sour cream. *Optional:* 1 t.–1 T. sharp brown mustard may be added to sour cream.

CREAMED HERRING ANOTHER WAY
śledź w śmietanie inaczej

Soak, clean, and fillet 4 herring and cut into 2 inch pieces. Arrange on serving dish. Fork-blend ¾ c. sour cream, 2 T. freshly grated horseradish (or 4 T. prepared horseradish), 2 t. chopped parsley, 1 sieved hard-cooked egg yolk, 2 t. lemon juice, 2 t. powdered sugar, and several dashes pepper. Add ½ c. plumped raisins and drench with sauce.

HERRING IN SWEET CREAM
śledź w śmietance

Slice 4 soaked, cleaned, filleted herring in 2 inch pieces and alternate in jar with layers of onion sliced wafer thin. Sieve the milt and mix with 1 c. whipping cream (unwhipped). Add juice of 2 lemons. To jar, add 10 peppercorns and 1 bay leaf, and drench with cream mixture. Add several peeled lemon slices, seal, and refrigerate at least 24 hrs. before serving. *Optional:* 1–2 t. powdered sugar may be added to cream mixture.

HERRING IN MAYONNAISE
śledź w majonezie

In jar combine 4 soaked cleaned, filleted herring cut into 2 inch pieces with ½–¾ c. mayonnaise. Seal and refrigerate 24 hrs. Transfer to serving dish, garnish with chopped chives, and decorate with lemon slices. *Optional:* Adding 1–2 T. prepared horseradish to mayonnaise before mixing with herring will make them even tastier. *Note:* Store-bought marinated herring may also be dressed with mayonnaise (with or without horseradish) and served immediately.

HERRING & PICKLED MUSHROOMS
śledź z marynowanymi grzybkami

Prepare 4 salt herring and cut fillets into 2 inch pieces. Place in jar and cover with pickled mushrooms and their liquid. Seal and refrigerate at least 24 hrs. before serving. Place herring on serving dish, garnish with finely chopped onions, and decorate with mushrooms. *Note:* If you have no homemade pickled mushrooms left in your pantry, you can easily marinate a batch. Wash well about 12 oz. small, fresh mushrooms, and cook in boiling water 15 min. Transfer to jar with slotted spoon. Separately, combine in pot ½ c. water, ⅔ c. 6% distilled vinegar, 2 crumbled bay leaves, 10 peppercorns, 5 grains allspice, 3 cloves, and (optional) 1 t. dried cayenne pepper. Add 2 T. sugar, bring to boil, reduce heat, and simmer 10 min. covered. Set aside to cool. Pour over mushrooms, seal, and leave at room temp. at least 24 hrs. before pouring over herring.

HERRING MARINATED IN WINE
śledź marynowany w winie

Slice 4 soaked, cleaned, filleted salt herring into 2 inch pieces and place in jar. Add 5 peppercorns, 1 bay leaf, 2 cloves, and a pinch of thyme. In pot, combine 1 c. dry wine, ½ c. 6% distilled vinegar, and ½ c. water. *Optional*: Add 1–2 t. sugar if desired. Bring to boil, reduce heat, and simmer several min. Add 1 thinly sliced onion, switch off heat, and let stand covered until cool. Pour over herring, seal, and refrigerate at least 24 hrs. before serving.

HERRING & MUSHROOMS WILNO STYLE
śledź po wileńsku

Slice 1 lb. soaked, cleaned, filleted herring into ½ inch strips. Cook 3 oz. presoaked dried Polish mushrooms (boletes) in the water in which they have soaked until tender. Coarsely grate 2 carrots, cut 2 onions in half, and slice thin. Slice mushrooms into thin strips and sauté in 4 T. oil with onions and carrots until the latter are tender. Add about 3 T. mushroom liquid and simmer another 5 min. Set aside to cool. Place herring on serving dish and cover with mushroom mixture. *Optional:* 3 T. mayonnaise may be stirred into cold mushroom mixture before covering herring. Sprinkle with pepper. Cover tightly with plastic wrap and refrigerate at least 3 hrs. before serving. To serve, decorate with lemon slices.

HERRING IN LEMON ASPIC
śledź w auszpiku cytrynowym

Soak, clean, and fillet 4 salt herring as above and dice. In pot, combine 1 c. water, 5 peppercorns, 2 grains allspice, 1 clove, 1 bay leaf, ½ t. sugar, and 1 diced onion, bring to boil, and simmer 10 min. Add juice of 1 large lemon, bring to boil again. Soak 1½ t. gelatin (½ a packet) in a little cold water, add to hot marinade, and heat to just below boiling, stirring to dissolve gelatin. Pour 1 T. hot marinade into each of 8 demitasses and refrigerate until set. Add diced herring, several slices cooked carrot, and about 1 t. diced hard-cooked egg to each. *Optional:* 1 t. diced pickled mushrooms may also be added to each demitasse. Cover with strained gelatin mixture and refrigerate at least 24 hrs. before serving. Turn out onto lettuce-lined platter and decorate with mayonnaise in decorator tube, topping each aspic with radish slice.

FRESH MARINATED HERRING
świeży śledź marynowany

If you have no salt herring on hand, you can achieve a reasonable facsimile of marinated herring using fresh herring fillets. Line a cookery bowl with a thin layer of salt, add 1 lb. fresh herring fillet and cover with more salt, turning to make sure every surface is coated. (About ½ c. salt is needed for this recipe.) Cover and keep at room temp. for several hrs. or overnight. Next day rinse fillets and dry on absorbent paper. In pot, combine 1 c. water, 6–8 peppercorns, 3 grains allspice, 1 bay leaf, ½ t. mustard seeds, and 1 t. sugar. Bring to boil and simmer 3 min. Add 1 c. 6% vinegar and bring to boil. Switch off heat, cover, and let stand until cool. Through sieve, dust herring fillets with flour and fry in several T. oil until golden on both sides. Transfer to casserole or glass or crockery bowl or container with tight-fitting lid. In pan drippings, sauté 1 thinly sliced onion and 1 small thinly sliced carrot until tender, then pour over herring. Drench with cold marinade, cover and refrigerate, at least overnight before serving. They will be even tastier after longer marination. *Note:* Fish fillets other than herring may be prepared the same way.

CARP IN ASPIC
karp w galarecie

Soak 3 T. plain gelatin in 1 c. cold, pre-boiled water. Clean and rinse 2–2½ lb. carp, cutting off head and fins. Remove eyes from fish. In pot combine 6½ c. water, the fish head and fins, 3 carrots, 1 parsley root, 2 large onions quartered, 1 bay leaf, 5–6 peppercorns, 3 grains allspice, 2 t. salt, and 1 t. sugar. Bring to gentle boil, then cook on low heat covered 30 min. Slice the fish into 1–1½ inch steaks and add to pot. Cook 15–20 min., or until done. With slotted spoon gently remove fish and carrots. Strain stock through gauze into another pot. If there is less than 6 c., make up the difference with boiling water. To hot stock add gelatin mixture, stirring until fully dissolved. Add ¼ t. citric-acid crystals and salt and sugar to taste (if needed). Place pot into sink full of cold water. Cut the fish steaks in half and carefully remove bones. Arrange fish skin side up on deep oval platter, garnish with slices of cooked carrot (from the stock), and drench with slightly cooled stock to cover. Refrigerate until set. *Note:* Serve with cold horseradish or tartar sauce. *Variation:* Other garnish possibilities include hard-boiled egg slices, some drained canned peas, or strips of mild pickled red peppers. The finished aspic may be decorated with mayonnaise in a decorator tube. As a final touch, decorate the platter with lemon and tomato wedges and parsley sprigs. *Optional*: For a crystal clear aspic, clarify with egg white as described earlier.

OLD POLISH CARP IN ASPIC (WITH RAISINS)
karp w galarecie po staropolsku

Soak 3 T. gelatin in 1 c. cold pre-boiled water. Clean 2–2½ lb. carp and place its head (with eyes removed) and fins in pot. Add 6½ c. water, 3 carrots, 1 parsley root, 2 large quartered onions, 1 bay leaf, 6 peppercorns, 6 grain allspice, 2 t. salt, 3 T. sugar, and ½ t. homemade Polish honey-spice seasoning. Bring to gentle boil, cover, and cook on low heat about 40 min. Strain through gauze into another pot. To strained stock add fish sliced into 1–1½ inch steaks and ½ c. raisins and simmer 15–20 min. With slotted spoon, gently remove fish and set aside to cool. To 6 c. hot stock, add gelatin mixture, stirring until dissolved, ½ t. citric-acid crystals and, if necessary, a little salt and sugar to taste. Clarify with egg white and strain through gauze into another pot. Place pot in cold water to cool. Meanwhile, cut the cooked fish steaks into halves, carefully remove bones, and arrange on deep oval platter. Rinse raisins with boiling water, drain, and sprinkle them over and around fish. Drench with partially cooled stock, which should completely cover the fish. Refrigerate until set. Serve with horseradish-mayonnaise sauce. *Note:* We tried out this recipe for our cookbook and liked it so well that it has replaced the carp in aspic (above) as a permanent fixture at our Christmas Eve supper.

WALLEYE IN (DILL) ASPIC
sandacz w galarecie (koperkowej)

In 6–7 c. water, place head of 2–3 lb. walleye or northern pike, 1 bay leaf, 5 peppercorns, 3 grains allspice, and 2 t. salt. Bring to boil, then cover and simmer on low heat 30 min. Add 2 carrots, a slice of celeriac, 1 small parsley root (or a piece of parsnip), add 2 large quartered onions and simmer 10 min. more. Strain into another pot and in it cook fish cut into 1 inch pieces for about 20 min., or until fully cooked. Remove fish and carrots and set aside to cool. To stock add 3 T. gelatin soaked in 1 c. water and stir until completely dissolved, add ¼ t. citric-acid crystals and salt to taste if necessary. Clarify with egg white if desired. Stir in 1–2 T. chopped fresh dill, pour about 1 c. of mixture into deep platter or bowl and keep in fridge until gelled. Cool pot with remaining stock in cold water. Carefully remove bones from fish and place (whole or cut into smaller pieces) on platter. Decorate with sliced, cooked carrots and drench with remaining stock. Refrigerate until set. Serve with lemon wedges. *Note:* Other varieties of fish (whitefish, eel, perch, trout, cod, etc.) may also be used in the above aspic recipes.

INDIVIDUAL FISH-ASPIC MOLDS
tymbaliki z ryb

Fresh or frozen fillets are good in this recipe. In pot combine 5 c. water, 2 carrots, 1 small parsley root, 1–2 large quartered onions, 1 bay leaf, 5 peppercorns, 2 grains allspice, 1 clove, and 2 t. salt, and simmer 15–20 min. or until carrots are tender. Reserve carrots. Strain stock, discarding other vegetables and spices. In stock gently cook 1–1½ lbs. fresh or thawed frozen fish fillets 10–15 min. or until cooked but still firm. Remove fish with slotted spoon and set aside to cool. To stock, add a few pinches citric-acid crystals, ½ t. sugar, and a little salt if needed. Stir in 2½ T. gelatin pre-soaked in ¾ c. water. When completely dissolved, pour 1 T. of mixture into 8 or so demitasses, adding several carrot slices to each for color. Chill until set, then add flaked fish, some drained canned peas and/or chopped hard-boiled egg. Drench with stock to cover and refrigerate until set. To remove, dip demitasses in hot water briefly and turn down side up onto lettuce-lined platter or individual serving plates. Use decorator tube to decorate with horseradish-mayonnaise sauce, or simply spoon a little over each portion. Decorate with radish slices, cooked carrot slices (if some are left over), and lemon wedges. *Note:* Fish in Old Polish raisin aspic and dill aspic may also be prepared in individual serving-size molds.

STUFFED POACHED PIKE POLONAISE
szczupak faszerowany po polsku

Clean 3 lb. pike and scale carefully so as not to damage skin. Rinse well and pat dry. With sharp knife make a shallow incision round the head and gently peel off skin from head toward tail. A little flesh may cling to skin, but use the knife to prevent too much from being torn away. When you get to tail, cut away the backbone, leaving tail attached to skin. If there are any tears in skin, sew them up. Cut head from backbone, remove eyes and gills, and cook in 6 c. water with soup greens, 2 t. salt, several peppercorns and allspice grains, 1 bay leaf, and 1 clove on low heat for 1 hr. If you want the pike's mouth to be open for dramatic effect when you serve this dish, place a large radish or tiny raw potato therein before cooking. Meanwhile, gut pike, rinse well, and pat dry. Remove meat from backbone, taking care to discard any loose bones, and grind meat. Add 2 grated onions, 1 t. freshly grated or 2 t. prepared horseradish, ½ t. salt, and 2 pinches pepper. Cream 1 T. butter with 1 whole egg, add 2 T. rinsed, finely chopped raisins and add to the ground fish mixture. Stir in 6 T. bread crumbs and ½ t. powdered sugar. Mix well. Loosely fill casing-like pike skin with mixture, as it expands during cooking. Sew up head end. Remove pike head from stock with slotted spoon and refrigerate. Strain stock. Cook stuffed pike in strained stock in a long, narrow, fish-poaching pot if you have one on low heat for about 45 min. Switch off heat and let it cool to room temp. in covered pot. Remove fish from stock and refrigerate at least several hrs. To serve, remove threads and arrange slice rounds to resemble a whole pike belly side down. Squirt a dab of mayonnaise into eye sockets and insert a pea or cranberry into each. Decorate platter with curly lettuce leaves, radish slices, and lemon wedges. Serve with cold mayonnaise-horseradish sauce. *Hint:* For an added gourmet touch, use sauce in deco-rator tube to mask cuts between head and first slice as well as between remaining slices. This will give the pike an interesting zebra-like, vertical-stripe effect. Decorate with additional swirls and splotches according to your fancy. *Variation:* Carp and walleye are also good when prepared this way.

STUFFED POACHED PIKE ANOTHER WAY
szczupak faszerowany inaczej

Prepare exactly as above, but instead of raisins add 2 T. finely chopped dill or 1 T. chopped dill and 1 T. chopped parsley to stuffing.

STUFFED PIKE IN ASPIC
szczupak faszerowany w galarecie

Prepare as above, using either raisin or dill stuffing to fill fish skin. After cooked stuffed fish is chilled, slice into ¾ inch rounds and arrange down center of longish platter shingle fashion, i.e. with each slice leaning on the next. Soak 2½ T. gelatin in 1 c. cold, pre-boiled water. Heat fish stock and add boiling water if needed to make 5 c. Season to taste with salt, pepper, a few pinches sugar, ½ t. tomato paste, and a pinch citric acid. Add soaked gelatin, heat, and stir until completely dissolved. Clarify with beaten egg white. Cool to room temp., then chill until mixture just begins to gel. Pour over sliced fish rounds in platter and refrigerate until set. Serve with tartar sauce or mayonnaise-horseradish sauce.

STUFFED FISH IN ASPIC ANOTHER WAY
ryba faszerowana w galarecie inaczej

Prepare pike, walleye, carp, or cod as with stuffed pike in aspic (above), but stuff skin with filling made as follows. In 1 c. milk, soak 2 broken-up, stale kaiser rolls until soggy. Meanwhile, slice 2 onions and sauté in 2 T. butter until tender and transparent. Remove meat from backbone, watching for and discarding any loose bones, and grind together with soaked rolls and sautéed onions. Add 2 eggs, ½ t. salt, 1–2 pinches pepper, and (optional) 2 T. grated blanched almonds and several pinches sugar. Mix well, loosely fill skin with mixture, and proceed as above.

FISH ROULADE IN ASPIC
rolada rybna w galarecie

This is an easier way of getting the flavor of stuffed, poached fish. Rinse 1 lb. thawed frozen fish fillets and pat dry. Grind together with 1 medium onion and 2 T. chopped parsley and 1 T. chopped dill. To mixture, add 1 whole egg, ½ t. salt, 1–2 pinches pepper, several pinches paprika, 2 heaping T. bread crumbs. Mix well until uniform. On board form into a long roll 1½–2 inches thick. Wrap roll tightly in damp cheesecloth slightly longer than the roll. Tie both ends with string or strong thread. Tie roll in 2 or 3 more places so it retains its shape during cooking. Bring 4 c. water to boil in pot wide enough to accommodate roll without bending. Add 1 portion soup greens, several peppercorns and grains allspice, ½ a bay leaf, 1 pinch ground nutmeg, and ½ t. salt. Cook covered 20 min. As it cooks soak 1½ T. gelatin in ½ c. cold pre-boiled water. Strain stock, reserving carrots. Place tied fish roll in hot stock and cook on low heat 20-25 min. Gently remove from stock and let cool on rack. When cooled to nearly room temp., carefully remove cheesecloth and place fish roll in fridge for at least 1 hr., preferably longer. Meanwhile, to 3 c. hot stock, add gelatin and stir to dissolve. Season gelatin stock to taste with a little lemon juice and, if necessary, a bit of salt and sugar. Slice fish roll and arrange on deep platter. Decorate with carrot slices (from stock), several t. drained canned peas, and parsley sprigs. Cover with room temp. gelatin stock and refrigerate until set. Serve with tartar sauce or mayonnaise-horseradish sauce.

WALLEYE IN MAYONNAISE
sandacz w majonezie

Clean 3–4 lb. walleye or pike, leaving head attached. Remove eyes and gills. Place a large carrot in fish's cavity to help retain its shape and wrap fish in cheesecloth napkin. Place belly side down on poaching tray of fish-poaching pot. If you haven't got such a pot, a roaster long enough to fit over 2 burners of your range will do. The main thing is that the pot must be long enough so that the fish fits inside without bending. Make a vegetable stock with 1 carrot, 1 small parsley root, a slice of celeriac (or 1 stalk celery), 1 onion, 1 bay leaf and 20 peppercorns, cooking ingredients in 8 c. water containing 2 t. salt until carrots are tender. Cover fish with warm strained stock, bring to boil, reduce heat, cover, and simmer gently 20–30 min. (about 6–7 min. per lb.). Remove fish and let cool to room temp. Remove cloth and place fish belly side down on large serving platter. Meanwhile, soak 1½ T. gelatin in ½ c. cold pre-boiled water. Boil stock down to 3 c. and add gelatin, stirring until completely dissolved. Strain through fine sieve. When mixture cools to lukewarm, beat with hand-held electric mixer until it becomes white and foamy. Continue beating, adding ½ c. room temp. salad oil in a thin stream. Add juice of 1 lemon and 1 t. powdered sugar and beat a bit more. Chill mixture and spread it over the entire fish. Chill several hrs. before serving. Use cooked carrot slices, drained canned peas, capers, and plenty of imagination to decorate this culinary *Pièce de résistance* which is sure to draw raves from your banquet guests. Surround fish on platter with lettuce leaves and other greenery, various salads, and relishes. *Variation:* You can also use mayonnaise out of a jar, either plain or flavored with horseradish or chopped garden greens.

POACHED FISH FILLETS IN MAYONNAISE
filety rybne w majonezie

The above dish may be a spectacular table piece but it is rather messy to eat and guests will invariably have to pick fish bones from their portions. You can achieve much the same effect by using fillets. Wash and dry 1 lb. freshwater or ocean fillets, thawed if they are the frozen type, sprinkle with lemon juice, and refrigerate 1 hr. Place fillets in warm court bouillon, bring to boil, reduce heat and simmer on low heat 5–7 min. Remove with slotted spoon, cool to room temp., and chill. Place cold fillets on lettuce-lined platter and drench with sauce made by fork-blending ¾ c. mayonnaise with 2 T. chopped dill or 2 T. mixed chopped garden greens (dill, parsley, chervil, green onions, chives, garden cress). Top each portion with a lemon swirl, and place a salted and peppered tomato quarter to 1 side. *Variation:* Plain or horseradish-flavored mayonnaise is also good.

CARP AU BLEU
karp na niebiesko

Gut but do not wash a freshly killed 2–3 lb. mirror carp (the kind with almost no scales), leaving head attached. In pot, combine juice of 4 lemons (about 1 c.), 12 peppercorns, 1 crumbled bay leaf, and 1 T. salt. Add 1 large, thinly sliced onion, and bring to boil. Place carp on its side in fish-poaching pot, small roaster, or baking dish so that it fits snugly and scald with hot marinade. Cover baking container tightly with aluminum foil and bake in 375° oven about 30 min. After switching off heat, keep in oven another 20 min. Remove fish, place on dish, cover with plastic wrap, and refrigerate. Serve when thoroughly chilled with mayonnaise-based sauce of choice. *Note:* It is the acidity of the lemon juice (or vinegar which may be used instead) that turns the skin of the fish an interesting shade of blue and gives the meat its tang. Most any fish may be prepared this way if it is freshly killed and its slime has not been removed. Scaly fish (pike, walleye, perch, bass, etc.) should be cooked with scales left on.

TROUT AU BLEU
pstrągi na niebiesko

Gut 4 roughly ½ lb. rainbow trout, leaving heads attached and taking care not to rub off slime on skin. For best results, trout should be freshly killed. With large needle and strong thread, sew tail of each to gill so that trout forms a circle. Cook ½ portion soup greens with several peppercorns and 1 bay leaf in 4 c. salted water until vegetables are tender. Strain, discarding vegetables, add 1 c. wine vinegar. Place fish into this acidulated stock and simmer gently 8–10 min. Remove fish and let cool on rack, then chill in fridge. Turn out on lettuce-lined platter and dress with mayonnaise or serve it on the side.

MARINATED SALMON
łosoś marynowany

Cut 2 lbs. fresh salmon fillets into 2 x 4 inch rectangles. Carefully remove any bones still left inside. Sprinkle with salt and sauté in ½ c. olive oil on both sides until done but not overcooked. The salmon should remain firm and not fall apart. In 2 c. water cook 1 carrot and ½ a small celariac until tender. Strain stock, slice carrot and celeriac, and set aside. Combine ½ c. of the above stock with 2 c. dry white wine and juice of 3 lemons (about ¾ c.), 10 peppercorns, 2 bay leaves, 2 t. salt, a pinch of rosemary and tarragon, and 3 sliced onions; simmer until onions are tender. Set aside to cool. Carefully transfer salmon to a wide-mouthed jar, adding the oil in which it was sautéed. Add the cool marinade. Seal and refrigerate. Marinate at least 2 days before using. It will keep in fridge up to 10 days if you discard the onions.

SMALL MARINATED FISH
drobne rybki marynowane

Gut 1 lb. small fresh fish, discarding heads. You may use smelt, minnows, or undersize 3 inch panfish, but scaly species such as perch and bluegill should be scaled. Dry fish, sprinkle with salt and Polish fish seasoning or just salt & pepper, roll in flour (shaking off excess) and fry to a nice golden brown in oil. Set aside. To 1½ c. water add 1 t. salt, 1 t. sugar, 1 bay leaf, 5 peppercorns, and 1 grain allspice; simmer 10 min. Add 1–1½ c. 6% vinegar and bring to boil. Set aside to cool. Place fish in a wide-mouth jar and cover with cool marinade. Seal and refrigerate. After several days, the backbones will become soft enough to eat, and that is where all the mineral nutrients are. Fillets may be prepared the same way. A carrot and onion may be cooked until tender with spices and added to fish, but your marinated fish will not keep as long.

MARINATED EEL
węgorz marynowany

Skin, then gut 2–3 lbs. eel, cut into 2-inch pieces, wash and dry, sprinkle with lemon juice, and refrigerate ½ hr. In pot combine 6 c. water, 1 portion soup greens, 2 onions, 2 t.– 1 T. salt, several peppercorns and allspice grains, ½ a bay leaf and 2 cloves. Bring to boil, reduce heat and cook 20 min. Strain stock, add 1 c. dry white wine and juice of 1 lemon, place rinsed eel in stock, bring to gentle boil and cook on low heat 40 min. Switch off heat and let stand covered until cooled to room temp. Transfer eel to jar or crockery bowl, cover with stock, seal with plastic wrap and refrigerate overnight. Serve with cold mayonnaise-based sauce of choice. *Note:* Carp, pike, walleye, whitefish, catfish, trout, pike, cod, or other freshwater and ocean fish may be marinated this way. *Optional:* For added zing, add 1 t. Polish fish seasoning to hot marinade.

SMOKED FISH
ryby wędzone

Almost any fish can be smoked, but carp, whitefish and chubs are especially good, as are halibut and flounder. Smoked herring and mackerel can also be tasty, but tend to be on the dry side. Smoked eel is an exceptional treat and smoked salmon is in a class by itself (see below). You can try smoking your own (see chapter on sausage-making, curing and smoking) or rely on the smoked fish supplied by your fish market or delicatessen. As a cold appetizer, smoked fish offers wide possibilities. They may be served just as they are, with lemon wedges provided to bring out their taste, and they are excellent diced in salads, canapé spreads, stuffed vegetables, etc. Smoked fillets are available for those who don't care to mess with fish bones.

SMOKED SALMON
łosoś wędzony

Smoked salmon ranks among the most exquisite cold appetizers available. Slice thinly at an angle, arrange on lettuce-lined platter, and surround with lemon wedges. It is too good to smother with sauces or garnishes and should be served just as it comes, sprinkled with lemon juice to taste. Smoked salmon, widely known in the U.S. by its Yiddish name lox, is pricey, but as a gourmet treat for special occasions, many feel it is worth the expense.

FISH IN VEGETABLES À LA GREQUE
ryba w jarzynach po grecku

Wash 1 lb. fish fillets of choice, sprinkle with lemon juice, and refrigerate 30 min. Drain and pat dry, sprinkle with salt and Polish fish seasoning, dredge in flour, shaking off excess, and fry in several T. hot oil until golden on the outside and fully cooked on the inside. Place on serving platter. Separately, coarsely grate 2 carrots, 1 parsley root, and ½ a small celeriac. Dice 2 large onions. In skillet, heat 5–7 T. olive oil, add the grated vegetables and simmer, stirring frequently. When partially cooked, add 3 T. water and continue simmering until tender. Add 1 t. salt, 2 T. sugar, and ¼–½ t. pepper, 2 T. vinegar, 1 T. prepared brown mustard and ¼–½ c. tomato paste. Stir to mix ingredients and simmer 1 min. longer. Drench fish on platter with vegetable mixture. When cool, cover with plastic wrap and refrigerate overnight before serving. Serve cold, decorated with parsley sprigs. Even people who don't care for fish and aren't especially partial to vegetables often find this tangy combination quite delightful.

FISH PÂTÉ
pasztet rybny

In 5 c. water cook 2 carrots, 1 slice celeriac, 1 large sliced onion, 1 bay leaf, several peppercorns, a small bunch of parsley sprigs, a pinch of thyme, and 1 T. salt 20 min. Strain stock, discarding vegetables and spices. In stock poach 2 lbs. fish fillets until fully cooked and flaky. Soak 2 crumbled stale kaiser rolls in milk until soggy, squeeze out moisture and grind twice with cooked fish. Add 1 small grated onion and 2 buds mashed garlic. Mix well and season with 2 T. brown mustard, salt, pepper and paprika to taste and a dash or 2 of cayenne pepper for added zing. Mix in ¼–½ c. melted butter. Transfer mixture to buttered crockery bowl, smooth top with knife, and refrigerate until set. Serve cold with mayonnaise-based sauce of choice. *Variation:* for variety, grind ½ c. or so drained canned fish livers with fish.

CAVIAR
kawior

The best variety of this superb classic appetizer is the black caviar, made from the salted roe of the Russian beluga sturgeon, although Iranian caviar is also prized by many. Due to its high price, there are many less expensive substitutes including red salmon-roe caviar and Scandinavian caviar prepared from the roe of cod-family species. In this chapter's egg section, the use of caviar as an egg garnish is described. Hard-boiled eggs are a natural accompaniment to caviar, and very little is needed to enliven the rather bland taste of the eggs. If you truly appreciate this gourmet delight and can afford to splurge, serve it alone on a small glass or porcelain serving dish placed on ice. Surround with lemon wedges. Finely chopped hard-boiled eggs are often served on the side. Serve with plain or toasted French bread and well-chilled Wódka Wyborowa or champagne. Another way is to drain a small tin of caviar, mix gently with 1 t. olive oil and a little lemon juice and mound on a glass serving dish. Garnish with 1 small finely chopped onion, cover and chill well before serving. *Note*: For a homemade caviar substitute, try the next 2 recipes.

HOMEMADE CAVIAR SUBSTITUTE
niby-kawior

Wash and remove membrane from about 1 lb. fresh roe of Great Lakes sturgeon, carp, pike, cod or other large fish. In pot, combine 4 c. water, 10 partially crushed peppercorns, 4 T. salt, and ¼ t. saffron, bring to boil, simmer covered 5 min. and strain, discarding peppercorns. Place roe in crockery or glass bowl, bring spice stock to boil and pour it over roe. Cover and let stand 15 min. Drain through fine sieve so roe does not "escape". Mix roe with 1 finely minced onion, 2 T. oil, and 2 T. wine vinegar. Refrigerate several hrs. Serve on small glass serving dish garnished with chopped chives. As with real caviar, chopped egg may be served on the side.

HERRING-ROE "CAVIAR"
"kawior" z ikry śledziowej

Place roe from 4 salt herring in bowl with ½ c. milk and 1 large grated onion, cover and refrigerate 24 hrs. The roe of fresh herring may also be used, in which case heavily salt it and keep in covered bowl in fridge 24 hrs., then rinse well. After removing from refrigerator in both cases detach membrane from roe. Cream ⅓ c. room temp. olive oil and juice of 1–2 lemons (depending on tartness desired). Serve with French bread and dry white wine.

SARDINES
sardynki

These tasty little fish, which come in small tins ready to use, can help any hostess make an appetizer course in no time. At less formal gatherings, the opened tin may be placed directly on a small dish surrounded with leaves of curly lettuce and lemon wedges. If you prefer to remove them from the tin, do so very carefully so that the sardines remain intact. For an interesting effect, place sardines on small round dish in a circle with their tails meeting at center. Place a radish rose center and surround circle with lemon wedges. Another way is to form 2 semicircles or fans, garnishing one of them with chopped hard-cooked egg whites and the other with chopped hard-cooked egg yolks. Instead of eggs, each sardine may be topped with a thin strip of red mild pickled pepper. Sardines may also be lined end to end round the rim of a cold-fish platter, with small radish roses separating 1 fish from the next. The sardines may be decorated with a strip or squiggle of gelled mayonnaise from a decorator tube. Having been raised in a middle-class Detroit neighborhood in the 1950's, the author grew up thinking sardines were something poor people ate. The transient types who worked at a nearby car wash regularly made a lunch of a 12 ¢ can of sardines, a small loaf of cotton-fluff white bread and a bottle of beer or soft drink. A true eye-opener was that first trip to Europe (1966), where sardines have long graced the most elegant banquet tables from Italy to Scandinavia. Poland is no exception.

SPRATS
szproty

Sprats are little more than smoked sardines packed in a lightly aromatic oil, but that makes all the difference. Anyone who enjoys sardines is usually crazy about sprats. Among the best are the Smoked Baltic Sprats imported from Poland. Gently remove from the tin and arrange on serving dish, sprinkle with lemon juice and garnish with finely chopped onion or chives. Or, decorate each sprat with a splotch of mayonnaise and insert a tiny wedge (⅛ of a slice) of peeled lemon into it. You can also garnish them in any of the ways suggested for sardines (above).

GARLICKY SARDINES OR SPRATS
sardynki lub szproty czosnkowane

Open a tin of sardines or sprats and pour the oil into a cup. Add 1–2 buds crushed garlic to oil, stir and pour back over fish in tin. Cover with plastic wrap and refrigerate overnight. Next day, serve as you would ordinary sardines or sprats. We think you'll win rave reviews for this one!

ANCHOVIES
sardele

These highly salted small fish usually come tinned as flat fillets or tiny rollmops-type roll-ups with capers. Because of their price and their high salt content, they are usually used sparingly as a garnish and flavoring ingredient. They may also be presented on small serving dishes just as they come. A sprinkle of chopped chives will enhance the eye-appeal of the fillets. The roll-ups can be skewered on tooth picks and arranged on a large unpeeled cucumber slice.

FISH LIVER COCKTAIL
cocktail z wątróbek rybnych

Canned fish livers, especially cod, are not only a tasty and handy appetizer course ingredient, but are a true health food rich in vitamins A and D, phosphorous and other minerals, and additionally possess alleged cholesterol-lowering properties. Try versatile cod livers in the following cocktail. Line 4 wide-mouthed (not tulip-type) champagne glasses with thin slices of peeled cucumber. Sprinkle with lemon juice, a little salt and pepper and fresh chopped dill. Drain a tin of cod livers and cut each liver into 2–3 pieces. Arrange it at center of glasses and dress with mayonnaise-horseradish sauce. Place a wedge of hard-boiled egg to one side of liver and sprinkle egg with paprika. Chill before serving.

SHRIMP COCKTAIL POLONAISE
cocktail z krewetek po polsku

Proceed exactly as above, but use canned shrimp instead of fish livers. Into 1 c. mayonnaise-horseradish sauce stir 1 t. tomato paste which will give it a nice pinkish hue. *Variation*: Canned oysters or crabmeat may be used to prepare similar cocktails, dressed with either the plain or tomato-flavored mayonnaise-horseradish sauce. Garnish with chopped chives if desired.

COLD FISH PLATTER
zimny półmisek rybny

On large round or oval platter arrange different cold fish in rows or a geometric pattern. For example, make a cross of smoked-fish fillets and arrange servings of a different fish (sliced smoked salmon, poached fish in mayonnaise, marinated eel, individual fish aspics etc.) in each of its 4 corners. Decorate each fish with a different garnish, e.g. rows of overlapping radish slices (smoked fish), lemon slices (salmon), chopped chives (fish in mayonnaise), gelled-mayonnaise flower (aspic). Trim platter rim with alternating, overlapping cucumber and radish slices garnished with chopped chives, with a leaf of curly lettuce protruding at equal intervals. For additional decorating suggestions see platter garnishes in this chapter (between hors d' oeuvres and egg appetizers). For a large round platter, place a large scooped-out tomato half at center, fill it with cold mayonnaise-based sauce of choice and insert a serving spoon so guests can help themselves. Surround the tomato shell with a circle of individual fish aspics and arrange rows of other cold fish radiating from center to edge of platter spoke-fashion. Use different colored garnishes to put the final touch on your platter.

FISH SALADS
sałatki rybne

There is wide array of Polish-style fish salads which can enhance the most elegant appetizer course or, with bread and tea, make a complete supper. Look for recipes in the next chapter devoted to appetizers and cold-table salads.

COLD ROAST MEAT
zimne pieczenie

Besides egg and fish dishes, cold meats have long occupied an important place on the Polish starter-course spread. You can prepare these from scratch specifically for a given occasion, or you can simply put previously cooked frozen meat to good use with excellent effect. Frozen roast beef, veal, pork or turkey are exceptionally good, especially if neatly sliced before freezing. When preparing pâté, make a little more than you plan to use for a given occasion and freeze up the rest in one piece. Slice when thawed. These are not only a real godsend when unexpected visitors show up, but they will also enable you to throw a fabulous dinner-party in no time that will leave your guests full of admiration for your culinary expertise. Naturally, the sliced cold meats must be artistically arranged on platters and colorfully garnished. You may also cover them with aspic which will enhance their eye-appeal and keep them moist, fresh and tender. Cold meats, plain or in aspic, are traditionally served with prepared horseradish or horseradish sauce, other mayonnaise-based cold sauces (garden-green, tartar etc.) and marinated fruits, vegetables, and mushrooms. Ćwikła (beet and horseradish relish) is usually served with cold roast meats not encased in aspic.

ROAST PORK LOIN
schab pieczony

On a board mince 2–3 buds crushed garlic with 1 t. salt and mash with flat of knife into a paste. Rub mixture all over a 2–3 lb. boneless pork loin. Place on rack in roaster, cover and let stand 1 hr. Through sieve dust loin all over with flour and brown on all sides in several T. hot fat in skillet. Place fat side up on rack in roaster. Sprinkle with Polish pork seasoning. Place in pre-heated 450° oven, reduce to 350° and roast uncovered 1–1½ hrs. (about 30 min. per pound) basting occasionally with pan drippings. It is done if liquid that oozes out when meat is pricked is no longer pink. Remove from oven and cool to room temp. Refrigerate overnight. Slice cold. Arrange slices on platter and decorate with spiced plums and curly parsley. *Variations*: Pork loin may also be baked in heavy-duty aluminum foil which should be sealed at the top to prevent juices from escaping. Basting is unnecessary. *Note*: This is one of the most widely enjoyed cold meats on Poland's holiday, nameday, and dinner-party circuit.

ROAST PORK LOIN WITH PLUM GLAZE OR MUSTARD
schab pieczony z powidłami lub musztardą

Slice 2–3 buds garlic into 3-4 slivers each. Insert garlic slivers into incisions made on all sides of a 3–4 lb. pork loin with bone left in. Sprinkle all sides with salt, pepper and marjoram. Thinly spread entire surface of meat with about 4 T. homemade plum jam (powidła) or 2 T. brown prepared mustard mixed with 2 T. soft butter. Roast on rack in pan in 375° oven about 30 min. per lb. Test for doneness by pricking deeply with fork. When pinkish liquid does not ooze out, the meat is done. Cool to room temp. and chill well before removing bone. (Tasty morsels of meat will cling to the bone, so be sure to pick it clean before discarding.) Slice thin and serve as above.

POACHED PORK LOIN
schab gotowany

Rub washed and dried 2 lb. boneless pork loin with 2 cloves mashed garlic and let stand covered at room temp. 1 hr. Meanwhile, combine in a pot 6 c. water, 1 portion soup greens, 1 quartered onion, 1 bay leaf, 5 peppercorns, 5 grains allspice and 2 t. salt. Bring to boil. Add the pork loin to boiling pot and when boiling resumes cover, reduce heat to low and simmer 5–6 min. Switch off heat, do not remove cover and let stand at room temp. until completely cooled. Wrap loin in foil or plastic wrap and refrigerate overnight. Slice thin, arrange on platter and decorate with garnishes of choice. Serve with ćwikła, horseradish or horseradish sauce. *Note*: If you don't like a pork loin that may be a bit pink inside, after switching off heat, wrap pot in blanket and let stand 30 min. Then remove blanket and leave at room temp. until fully cooled.

ROAST PORK WILD BOAR STYLE
pieczeń wieprzowa na sposób dzika

Wash a 2 lb. pork roast (preferably ham portion) and place in pot. Separately, combine juice of 1–2 lemons, ½ c. dry white wine, 1 portion chopped soup greens, 2 sliced onions, 15 partially crushed (in mortar) juniper berries, 10 peppercorns, 10 grains allspice, 2 cloves, 1 bay leaf and a pinch of thyme. Bring to boil and scald pork with mixture. Cover and refrigerate 2 days, turning the meat several times a day to make sure all sides are evenly exposed to marinade. Remove meat from marinade and pat dry. Sprinkle with salt and dust with flour through sieve. Brown on all sides in skillet in 3 T. hot fat. Transfer to roasting pan, add ½ the strained marinade and place uncovered in pre-heated 400° oven. After 10 min. reduce to 350° and bake covered 45 min. Add the remaining strained marinade and bake another 20 min. or until done. Cool to room temp., then refrigerate overnight. Slice cold and serve with ćwikła, pickled mushrooms and horseradish sauce. Tangy cranberry-currant sauce is also good and can be placed at center of the platter in an orange shell.

ROAST FRESH BACON
boczek surowy pieczony

Wash and dry 2 lb. piece of fresh (unsmoked), lean slab bacon. Mash 2 buds garlic with 1 t. salt and rub bacon all over with mixture. Sprinkle with paprika and marjoram (or Polish pork seasoning) and refrigerate in covered container 2 hrs. Place on rack in pan and bake in pre-heated 375° oven about 1 hr., or until browned on the outside and soft like butter when pierced with a fork on the inside. Cool to room temp. and refrigerate overnight. Slice thin and arrange on platter. Serve with horseradish, ćwikła and pickled mushrooms. *Note*: Slab bacon may also be baked in heavy-duty aluminum foil.

BOILED SMOKED BACON
boczek wędzony gotowany

Combine 1 portion soup greens with 5–6 c. water and bring to boil. Use a pot wide enough to accommodate 2 lb. slab of bacon in 1 piece. Add 2 lb. slab smoked bacon, making sure it is covered with water, bring to boil again, reduce heat and simmer covered 1½ hrs.. Switch off heat and let bacon cool to room temp. in stock. Pat bacon dry and refrigerate overnight. Slice thin when cold and serve with mustard or horseradish. *Note:* Use diced soup greens for salad; the stock makes a good base for bean soup, kapuśniak, pea soup, barszcz, etc.

BOILED BEEF TONGUE
ozór wołowy gotowany

Scrub a beef tongue under cold running water, remove salivary glands if still attached and rinse well. Place in pot, add water to cover and cook covered on low heat about 3 hrs. replacing water that evaporates. Remove tongue and remove skin under cold running water. Return to stock. Add 1 portion soup greens, 6 peppercorns, 6 grains allspice, 1 bay leaf, 1 clove and 2 t. salt plus as much water as needed to cover and cook another hr. or until tongue is fork tender. Let tongue cool to room temp. in stock. Remove from stock, pat dry, wrap in plastic wrap and refrigerate overnight. Slice when cold into slices ⅛–¼ inch thick and arrange on platter decorated with cucumber swirls and strips of fresh green, yellow or red peppers. Serve with ćwikła, horseradish, horseradish sauce or pickled mushrooms and vegetables. *Note:* Smoked or corned beef tongue is cooked the same way but no salt should be added.

COLD BEEF TENDERLOIN
polędwica wołowa na zimno

Wash a 1½ lb. beef tenderloin and trim off fat and sinews. Pat dry. Finely mince 2–3 buds garlic and mash on board with flat of knife with 1 t. salt. Rub all sides of tenderloin with garlic paste. Dust generously with flour through sieve. Heat 4 T. oil or lard in skillet and brown tenderloin, turning to expose all sides to heat. When it is a nice golden brown, remove from skillet, cool to room temp, and refrigerate. It will still be quite rare on the inside and that's how gourmets prefer it. If you prefer it better done, simmer covered in skillet on low heat another 5 min. Slice thin when fully chilled and arrange on platter. Garnish as desired. Serve with Old Polish plum sauce or horseradish sauce.

BEEF ROULADE
rolada wołowa

With meat mallet pound a 2 lb. 1-inch thick piece of boneless beef (top round steaks are best) until about ¼ inch thick. Sprinkle with salt and spread with thin coating of prepared brown mustard. Place in fridge. Season ½ lb. ground pork with ½ t. salt and several dashes of your homemade pork, beef or hunter's seasoning. Add 5–6 washed, dried and finely chopped fresh cultivated mushrooms, 1 whole egg, 3 T. bread crumbs, 1 T. chopped parsley and ⅔ c. milk. Mix well to get uniform consistency. Spread pounded steak with mixture leaving a 1 inch space along the side towards which it will be rolled. Roll tightly, truss with string, sprinkle with salt and pepper, dust with flour and brown on all sides in 2–3 T. hot fat. Transfer to baking pan, add 1 c. water and 1 T. lard. Place in pre-heated 375° oven and reduce heat to 325° after 10 min. Cover and bake about 90 min. Cool to room temp, then refrigerate. When thoroughly chilled, remove string and slice ¼ inch thick. Arrange on platter with tomato wedges, radishes and lettuce in season, or with pickled mushrooms and vegetables in the winter months. Serve with horseradish sauce or plum sauce. Horseradish sauce may be served in a scooped-out green, yellow or red pepper and plum sauce in a grapefruit or orange shell.

BOILED BEEF ROULADE
rolada wołowa gotowana

Proceed as above. For variety and ease, spread pounded steak with homemade pâté, 4–5 inch squares of which are always good to have on hand in freezer. After rolling up tightly, wrap roulade in cheese cloth, tie both ends with string and truss it with several loops of string. Place roulade in hot meat stock to cover, bring to gentle boil and cook covered over med. heat 60–75 min. Remove from stock and let cool to room temp. on rack. Refrigerate overnight. Remove cheese cloth and slice when cold. Serve as above.

VEAL ROULADE
rolada cielęca

Pound 1½–2 lb. boneless veal round steak into rectangle about ¼ inch thick. Mince fine 2 buds garlic and mash with ½ t. salt. Spread upper surface of meat with garlic paste, cover with plastic wrap, and refrigerate while preparing stuffing. Mash 1 bud garlic with ½ t. salt and add to ½–¾ lb. ground uncooked veal along with ¼ t. paprika, 2 T. chopped fresh dill, 4 T. bread crumbs, ½ c. milk and 1 whole egg. Mix well to get a smooth, well-blended mixture. Spread pounded veal with mixture, leaving a 1-inch space along the end towards which meat will be rolled. Roll up tightly jelly-roll-fashion and truss with string. Sprinkle with salt and pepper, dust with flour and brown on all sides in skillet in several T. hot fat. Transfer to baking pan, add 1 c. water and place in pre-heated 400° oven. After 10 min. reduce heat to 325° and bake about 1 hr. under cover. Cool to room temp., refrigerate and slice when thoroughly chilled. Arrange on lettuce-lined platter garnished with radishes, cucumber slices and tomato wedges. Mayonnaise-based cold sauces and cranberry or currant sauce also make nice accompaniments.

CHICKEN OR DUCK ROULADE
rolada z kurczęcia lub kaczki

Cut off neck, butt, wing tips and drumsticks from a 3-4 lb. fryer-broiler (chicken) or duckling and freeze for stock or other use. Place bird on board breast side down and cut skin the full length of the back along spine. With small sharp knife cut meat away from bones until all has been removed. Place boned fowl skin side down on board. Since there will be more meat in some areas and less in others, cut pieces of meat from the abundant areas and transfer them to places where there is less meat attached to skin. The entire surface should be roughly uniform. Trim off uneven edges along sides to get a nice uniform rectangle. Cover with plastic wrap and refrigerate. In skillet saute 8 oz. washed, dried, chopped fresh mushrooms in 2-3 T. butter until moisture evaporates and mushrooms begin to sizzle. Grind mushrooms with fowl trimmings and ¼ lb. raw chicken livers. To mixture add 8 T. bread crumbs, ⅓ c. milk, ½ t. salt and ½–1 t. Polish poultry seasoning. Spread the fowl rectangle with stuffing, roll up tightly, truss well with string and brown on all sides in 2-3 T. fat. Transfer to baking pan, sprinkle with salt and dust with Polish poultry seasoning, add 1 c. water and 1 T. butter to pan and pop into pre-heated 400° oven. After 10 min. reduce heat to 325° and bake about 50-60 min. under cover. After cooling to room temp., refrigerate until fully chilled. Slice cold and arrange on lettuce-lined platter garnished with spiced plums, cherries, and pears. If desired, place an orange shell full of plain or zesty cranberry or currant sauce at center or off to one side of platter. *Note:* If using duck, trim and discard excess fat after boning bird and use Polish water fowl seasoning instead of poultry seasoning.

CHICKEN OR DUCK GALANTINE
galantyna z kurczęcia lub kaczki

A galantine is similar to a roulade except that it is boiled rather than baked. Bone chicken or duck as above, cover with plastic wrap and refrigerate. Place the leftover wing tips, drumsticks, neck and butt with soup greens and usual stock spices in 7 c. lightly salted water and cook 1 hr. In ½ c. stock soak 1 broken-up stale kaiser roll. When soggy, grind with boned fowl trimmings, ½ lb. boneless veal, ¼ lb. raw calf's liver and the chicken or duck liver. Grind mixture 2 more times. Add 2 whole eggs, a grating or 2 nutmeg and salt and pepper to taste. Mix well into uniform consistency, adding 3–4 T. stock. Place boned fowl on a rectangle of cheese cloth that protrudes several inches on all sides. Spread meat with stuffing and smooth out surface. Tightly roll up meat and wrap tightly in cheese cloth, tie both ends with string, and truss fairly tightly with loops of string at 1 inch intervals the length of the roll. Place in strained stock and cook covered 1½–2 hrs. *Hint*: It will cook nicely in loaf pan tightly covered with aluminum foil. Allow galantine to cool to room temp. in stock topped with small cutting board weighted down with something heavy. After removing from stock, allow to drip dry, then refrigerate. Slice when fully chilled. Serve as is or use stock to make an aspic and pour over sliced galantine. Decorate with spiced fruits before drenching with aspic and chill until set. *Variations*: For a zestier galantine, sprinkle ¼–½ c. diced zesty gherkins (korniszony) and/or marinated mushrooms, both well drained, over entire surface of stuffing before rolling up.

STUFFED GOOSE NECK
szyjki gęsie nadziewane

Carefully remove skin from goose neck so as not to damage it. Turn it inside out and scrape off fat. Rinse well, turn back to original position and sew up 1 end. Fill with either of the following stuffings:
Meat stuffing: Grind raw goose liver with 1 quartered onion and mix with ½ lb. ground pork or veal or ¼ lb. of each. Add 1–2 T. bread crumbs, 1 whole egg and salt and pepper to taste. Work well to thoroughly blend ingredients. *Optional:* 1 bud crushed garlic may be added.
Mushroom stuffing: Soak 2 broken-up stale kaiser rolls in 1 c. milk. Saute 1 finely minced onion in 2 T. butter until transparent. Add 4 oz. diced fresh mushrooms, sprinkle with salt and simmer with onion until mushrooms begin to brown. Grind soggy rolls and combine with mushrooms and onions. Add 2 whole eggs, 1 T. chopped parsley and salt and pepper to taste. Mix well to blend ingredients. Stuff gooseneck skin with either filling and sew up open end,

forming a kind of sausage. Place in greased baking pan and pop into pre-heated 375° oven. After 15 min. turn over and bake another 15 min. Skin should be crispy. When cool, chill in fridge. Slice into thin rounds and serve cold with cranberry sauce. *Variation:* Duck, chicken and turkey necks may be prepared the same way. Use the removed neck bones for stock.

COLD STUFFED VEAL BREAST
mostek cielęcy nadziewany na zimno

Have your butcher cut a pocket in a veal breast (about 5 lbs.). Wash well, pat dry, and rub meat inside and out with 1–2 cloves garlic mashed with 1 t. salt. For stuffing, combine 2 lbs. ground veal (or 1 lb. each ground veal and pork), 1¼ c. bread crumbs, 1¼ c. milk, 2 whole eggs, 2 buds crushed garlic, 1½ t. salt and 1 t. Polish veal seasoning. Work ingredients into a smooth and uniform stuffing. (*Optional:* Add ½ t. MSG.) Fill pocket with stuffing, press in and sew up with strong thread. Place in greased roaster, add 1 c. water, sprinkle with salt and paprika, cover with aluminum foil and bake in 325° oven about 2½ hrs., roughly 30 min. per lb. Cool to room temp. and refrigerate overnight. Slice rather thick (about ½ inch), taking care that stuffing does not fall out of rim of meat, arrange overlapping slices on round lettuce-lined platter and garnish with spiced cherries or plums. At center place a green pepper with top cut off and seed portion scooped out as your sauce bowl. Fill with mayonnaise-cranberry sauce, other mayonnaise-based sauce of choice or zesty cranberry or currant sauce. *Variation:* Fill veal breast with dill-flavored stuffing suggested for hot stuffed veal breast (see hot veal dishes).

HARE PÂTÉ
pasztet z zająca

This pâté is really good only when made with the dark-meat European wild hare. Wash the front portion of a dressed hare (save the more tender back portion for roast hare), place in pot with its heart, add 1 bay leaf, 5 peppercorns, 5 grains allspice and 2 t. salt, cover with boiling water and cook on low heat until tender (about 2 hrs.). In another pot cook in 6 c. water 2 lbs. pork with bone, adding 1 portion soup greens, 1 bay leaf, 5 grains allspice and 2 t. salt. Cook on low heat about 1 hr. Add 1 lb. smoked slab bacon and cook with pork about 50 min. Remove meat and bacon from stock and cut pork away from bones. In 2 c. pork stock soak 2 stale kaiser rolls. Remove hare from its stock and discard bones. In skillet lightly brown 2 sliced onions in 3-4 T. fat. Add hare liver and 1 lb. or slightly less chicken livers or calf's liver and sauté about 2 min. It should still be pink inside. Grind the cooked hare, pork, liver, onions and soggy rolls together 3 times. To mixture add 5 egg yolks, ½ t. freshly grated nutmeg, ¼ t. pepper, ½ t. MSG and salt to taste. Stir in about 3 c. stock and mix to blend ingredients. Gently fold in 5 beaten egg whites. Grease square or rectangular pan large enough so mixture is no more than 2 inches high, transfer mixture to pan and smooth top with moist hand. Bake in 350° oven about 1 hr. It is done when top is nicely browned and edges come away from the sides of the pan. After cooling to room temp. refrigerate overnight. Slice cold and serve with tartar sauce or horseradish sauce and spiced fruits.

RABBIT PÂTÉ
pasztet z królika

Under running water scrub 5 dried Polish (boletus) mushrooms well with brush and soak in 2 c. lukewarm water. Wash and cut up 2 lbs. dressed rabbit. In skillet melt 4 T. lard and brown 1½ lbs. cut up pork shoulder with bone left in. Transfer pork and drippings to pot. Add rabbit, 2 quartered onions, 1 bud garlic and t. salt, the soaked mushrooms and the water in which they were soaked. Add enough water to cover the meat and cook on low heat until fork-tender. Add ½ lb. pork liver and simmer 5 min. longer. Strain stock and add to it 2 stale kaiser rolls. Remove meat from bones and grind together with mushrooms, liver, onions and soggy rolls 3 times. Add leftover stock in which rolls were soaked, 4 egg yolks, 1 t. Polish pâté seasoning (or ½ t. grated nutmeg, ¼ t. pepper and ¼ t. paprika) and beat until smooth and creamy. Salt to taste. Fold in 4 beaten egg whites and mix gently. Transfer mixture to greased baking pan sprinkled with breadcrumbs, smooth top and bake in 325°–350° oven 50–60 min. until top is a nice golden brown. Reduce heat somewhat if top appears to be browning too fast. Cool and refrigerate. Slice when fully chilled, arrange on platter and garnish with tomato wedges and green-onion bouquets (see platter garnishes). Serve with mayonnaise-horseradish sauce or tartar sauce. *Variations:* Instead of greasing baking pan it may be lined with thin strips of bacon; top of pâté may also be covered with bacon strips. This technique can be used with all leaner pâtés not containing bacon or salt pork.

PORK PÂTÉ
pasztet z wieprzowiny

Wash 1½ lbs. boneless pork roast, cut up into large pieces, place in pot, add ½ t. salt, cover with water, and bring to boil. Reduce heat and skim off scum until no more forms and cook on low heat 1½ hrs. Add soup greens and ½ lb. piece of slab bacon or salt pork and cook another 30 min. Meanwhile, in several T. fat saute a large sliced onion until tender. Add ½ lb. pork liver or chicken livers, mix with onions and simmer about 3 min. Sprinkle with salt. Grind cooked meat, bacon, liver and onions twice. Season to taste with salt and add ¾–1 t. Polish pâté seasoning. Add 3 egg yolks, 6 T. fine bread crumbs, and 1 c. milk. Mix vigorously until smooth, fold in 3 beaten egg whites and mix gently. Transfer mixture to greased baking pan sprinkled with bread crumbs and bake in 325°–350° oven about 50 min. Cool, refrigerate, slice and serve as above. *Variation:* Pâté may also be cooked on stove top. Place mixture in loaf pan to a height of 1½–2 inches, cover tightly with heavy-duty aluminum foil, place pan in a larger pot of boiling water reaching ⅔ of the way up the side, cover with tight-fitting lid and cook on low heat 70–80 min.

MIXED-MEAT PÂTÉ
pasztet mieszany

Wash 3–4 dried Polish mushrooms (boletes) and soak in 1 c. lukewarm water overnight. Wash 1 lb. boneless beef, cut up into pieces, place in pot, cover with water, add 1 bay leaf and 5 peppercorns, 5 grains all-spice and 5 juniper berries and cook on low heat 1½ hrs. Add 1 lb. smoked slab bacon and ½ a portion of soup greens and cook another 30 min. In another pot cook in water to cover 1 lb. cut-up pork shoulder, ½ portion of soup greens, the mushrooms and their water, 1 t. salt, 5 peppercorns and 3 grains allspice until meat is fork-tender. Meanwhile, sauté 2 sliced onions in 2-3 T. fat until transparent, mix in ¾ lb. sliced calf's liver or whole chicken livers and simmer about 3 min. Sprinkle lightly with salt. Grind together 3 times cooked cooled beef and pork (with bones removed), mushrooms, bacon, and liver and onions. To mixture add 1 c. breadcrumbs soaked in 2 c. milk and 5 egg yolks. Mix vigorously until smooth and well blended, and season with 1 t. Polish pâté seasoning and salt to taste if needed. Fold in 5 beaten egg whites and mix lightly. Transfer mixture to greased baking pan sprinkled with breadcrumbs, smooth top and bake in 325°–350° oven about 1 hr. Top should be a dark golden brown, but lower heat during baking if it is browning too quickly–a rule of thumb that applies to all baked pâtés. Slice when fully chilled and serve as above. *Note*: There are no hard and fast rules on Polish-style pasztety and there are hardly two families that make it exactly the same. Feel free to modify ingredients according to preference and what you have on hand. Use slightly less bacon or salt pork for a leaner, drier pate, more liquid for a creamier texture and less for a firmer one. Besides Polish pâté seasoning, other flavoring possibilities include your homemade Polish pork seasoning, hunter's seasoning, poultry seasoning and waterfowl seasoning.

POULTRY PÂTÉ
pasztet z drobiu

Rinse well and dry 1 lb. chicken livers, removing any veins or membranes. In skillet saute 3 sliced onions in 4 T. hot fat until transparent, add livers, mix together and simmer 3–4 min. Sprinkle with salt. In another skillet or pot melt 2 T. butter, add about 1½ lbs. cooked poultry with bones removed (chicken, turkey, goose or duck) add ⅔ c. water and simmer covered about 10 min. Grind the liver, onions, and poultry 3 times. Add 2 whole eggs and vigorously mix with wooden spoon until smooth and creamy. Season with salt and pepper to taste and several pinches Polish poultry, waterfowl or pâté seasoning, if desired. Transfer mixture to well-buttered loaf pan and smooth top. Cover with heavy-duty aluminum foil and seal edges. Place loaf pan in pot of boiling water reaching ⅔ of the way up the loaf pan. Cover pot and cook on med. heat about 1 hr. It may also be baked in 350° oven, in which case pot with boiling water need not be covered. As with all pâtés, cool to room temp., refrigerate and slice when fully chilled. Arrange on platter, garnish with radish roses and cucumber swirls and serve with chive sauce, garden-green sauce or other such mayonnaise-based sauce of choice. *Note:* One or more types of poultry may be used according to preference and availability; chicken and turkey make a very mild pate; while duck or goose produce one with richer flavor.

PÂTÉ MADE FROM LEFTOVERS
pasztet z resztek

Although pâté is definitely a gourmet delicacy, that does not mean it is difficult to prepare or has to be expensive. A survey of the freezer in many families will turn up most of the ingredients you need, and eggs, bacon and onions are found in nearly every home, so you can make pasztet as often as you like. Cook 1 lb. slab of bacon with usual soup greens and spices in water to cover about 45 min. In 4 T. fat saute 2–3 sliced onions until transparent, add 1 lb. or so sliced liver (calf's, pork, baby beef, chicken) and simmer with onions several min. It should still be slightly pink on the inside. Sprinkle with salt. Grind the cooked bacon, liver, and onions and 1½–2 lbs. boneless cooked meat (pork, veal, beef, poultry, game in whatever proportion) 3 times. Season with salt and pâté seasoning, but taste ground mixture first because the cooked meats may already contain enough of their own seasoning. Soak ⅔ c. bread crumbs in 1½ c. milk and add to ground mixture together with 4 egg yolks and 1 c. bacon stock. Mix vigorously until smooth and creamy. Fold in beaten egg whites and mix lightly. (*Variation:* If time is at a premium beat in 4 whole eggs; although firmer in texture, your pâté will still be very good.) Transfer mixture to greased baking pan, smooth top and bake in 325°–350° oven 50–60 min. or until top is nicely browned. Cool, refrigerate, slice and serve as above. *Note:* For an everyday pâté not meant for company grind the soup vegetables together with the other ingredients.

GOOSE LIVER PÂTÉ POLONAISE
pasztet z gęsich wątróbek po polsku

This is a Polish version of France's legendary *pâté de foie gras* which incidentally is referred to in Polish as "pasztet strasburski" (pâté of Strasbourg). It uses unswollen goose livers, boletes instead of truffles and a touch of mead (honey wine) in place of cognac or red wine. Wash 3-4 dried Polish mushrooms (boletes) and soak in ½ c. lukewarm water several hrs. Add ½ c. milk and cook on low heat until tender. Remove mushrooms from liquid and set aside. Boil liquid down to 3 T. Sauté 1 sliced onion in 2 T. lard until transparent, adding a little water so it doesn't brown. Add 2–3 washed, dried and sliced goose livers and simmer with onions under cover about 8 min. on low heat. Add 1 t. mead or sherry and sauté 1 min. longer. Grind liver, onions and mushrooms 3 times. Stir in the mushroom liquid (3 T.), add ¼ lb. (1 stick) unsalted room-temp. butter and mix well to get a creamy mixture. Season with salt, pepper, ¼ t. freshly grated nutmeg and ½ t. ginger. Mound mixture on serving dish and decorate with lettuce leaves and radish roses. *Note:* This pâté is much richer and more "livery" than those presented above. If you prefer a milder-flavored pâté, grind together with the other ingredients 2-3 c. cooked, diced boneless chicken, turkey, veal or pork.

VEGETABLE ASPIC
galareta warzywna

In pot combine 2½ c. water, ½ portion soup greens, 1 bay leaf, 1 clove, 5 peppercorns, 1 grain allspice, and ½ t. salt and cook 40–50 min. Meanwhile, soak 1 T. gelatin in ½ c. cold pre-boiled water. Strain the stock of which there should be 1½ c. If there is less, make up difference with boiling water. Add gelatin mixture, heat aspic liquid without boiling and stir until gelatin is dissolved. Season with a pinch of citric acid crystals, a pinch of sugar and a pinch of pepper. For a more interesting color, add ½ t. caramel, ½ t. tomato paste or a pinch of saffron. Cool to room temp., chill slightly and use aspic to cover cold sliced meats, pâté, roulades, ham roll-ups etc. *Note:* For more flavor add 1 crushed beef or chicken bouillon cube during cooking. This is the simplest aspic recipe we know and the results are passable, but the meat-based aspics below are much tastier.

SOUP-BONE ASPIC
auszpik na kościach

Wash 1 lb. or so split soup bones. If you don't have a heavy meat axe, ask your butcher to split them. Place in pot with 6½ c. water and cook covered 3 hrs. At start of cooking skim off scum until no more forms. Add 1 portion soup greens, 1 bay leaf, 6 peppercorns, 3 grain allspice and ½ t. salt, cook 1 hr. longer. Strain stock. There should be just under 2 c. If there is more, cook it down. Soak 1½ t. gelatin in 5 T. cold water 10 min. Add to stock, stir to dissolve and add a pinch of citric acid crystals. Lightly beat 2 egg whites, add to stock, heat but do not boil, allow stock to become clear. Strain through linen napkin and season to taste with salt and pepper. To use, pour a little slightly chilled aspic onto serving platter no more than ⅛–¼ inch deep and refrigerate until set. Top with slices of cold meat, pâté, roulade, fried fish fillets, etc. and cover with remaining liquid. For a more colorful aspic, garnish meat or fish with hard-boiled egg slices, sliced cooked carrots, drained canned peas, zesty gherkins sliced into rounds, spiced fruits, etc. before covering with aspic liquid.

CALF'SFEET ASPIC
auszpik na nóżkach cielęcych

This is the tastiest of all clear aspics and requires no gelatin since it is made with gelatinous calf's feet. Rinse 1 lb. (more or less) split calf's feet and ½ lb. veal bones and cook covered on low heat 3 hrs. Add 1 portion soup greens, 6 peppercorns, 2 grains allspice, 1 bay leaf and ½ t. salt and cook another hr. Strain stock. Add 1–2 slightly beaten egg whites and heat to clarify. Strain through linen napkin and flavor with ½–1 t. lemon juice. This should give you about 2 c. aspic. Use as above. *Note*: For a completely fat-free soup-bone or calf'sfeet aspic, chill in fridge and discard fat that collects at top before using. *Variation:* 1 t.–1 T. dry white wine will add a bright accent to any of the above aspics.

TURKEY, GOOSE OR DUCK IN MALAGA ASPIC
indyk, gęś lub kaczka w maladze

Soak 1 t. gelatin in 2 T. cold water and dissolve in 1½ c. hot, clarified soup-bone or calf'sfeet aspic (see above). Mix in ½ c. Malaga wine and 1 t. powdered sugar. Pour mixture into 2 cups, placing 1 in fridge and leaving the other at room temp. On serving platter arrange slices of cold roast fowl. If using turkey, alternate slices of white meat and dark meat. Decorate with 3–4 varieties of drained canned fruit: pitted cherries, pitted purple plum halves, pear halves, peach halves or slices, pineapple slices, as well as peeled fresh orange sections or slices. With spoon top fowl and fruits with partially gelled aspic and refrigerate. When set, place the room-temp. aspic in fridge until slightly chilled but still unset and pour over platter. Refrigerate at least several hrs. until fully set. Before serving, decorate platter with lettuce leaves. Serve with plain or zesty cranberry sauce or cranberry-mayonnaise sauce. Currant sauce is also good.

JELLIED PIG'S FEET
galareta z nóżek/studzienina/"zimne nogi"

From the gourmet-type aspic dishes of high Polish cuisine, we move to the more salt-of-the-earth varieties typical of peasant cookery. Wash 1½ lbs. split pig's or calf's feet and place in pot with 10 c. water. Simmer on low heat, skimming off scum until no more forms. Add ½–1 lb. lean pork and cook on low heat another 1½ hrs. Add 1 portion soup greens, 1 bay leaf, 6 peppercorns, 2–3 grains allspice, and 1 t. salt and cook 1 hr. longer. By now meat should be falling off the bone. Strain. To stock add 1 t.–1 T. vinegar and 1–2 buds crushed garlic. Taste stock and season with salt and pepper if necessary. Remove meat from bone and dice. Cool stock to room temp. Arrange diced meat evenly in square or rectangular pan and drench with stock. Refrigerate overnight. Scrape off congealed fat from top and discard. Dip pan briefly in hot water to loosen jellied meat and turn out on platter of proper size. Cut into squares and serve with vinegar, lemon-vinegar or lemon juice provided in cruets. Some like this old-fashioned cold dish with horseradish.

GARNISHED JELLIED PIG'S FEET
galareta z nóżek z dodatkami

Although the plain jellied pig's feet above are tasty, personally we prefer this more colorful and varied aspic. Prepare as above, but first sprinkle pan with chopped parsley. Add some of the diced meat, interspersing it at intervals with hard-boiled egg slices and cooked carrot slices (from stock). Add some more meat, then a few more egg and carrot slices. Cover with cool stock and refrigerate until fully set. Overnight is best. *Optional:* Several zesty gherkins, sliced into thin rounds may also be added. Serve as above. *Note:* A combination of pig's and calf's feet may be used in both of the above recipes.

JELLIED PORK HOCK
galareta z golonki

Prepare as for plain or garnished jellied pig's feet, but use 1 large or 2 smaller pork hocks instead of pig's or calf's feet. *Variation:* A very tasty jellied dish can be made using 1 small pork hock, 1 pig's or calf's foot and an equal amount of lean pork. Otherwise, proceed as in preceding 2 recipes.

INDIVIDUAL CHICKEN ASPICS
tymbaliki/galaretka porcjowana z kurczaka

Cover 1 chicken leg (drumstick and thigh) with water and cook on med. heat ½ hr. Add ½ a portion of soup greens, ½ a bay leaf, 3 peppercorns, 1 grain allspice, 1 clove and ¼ t. salt and cook on low heat until meat comes away from bone and carrots are tender. Soak 1 T. gelatin in 3 T. cold pre-boiled water. Strain stock, of which there should be 2 c. If there is more, boil it down; if less than 2 c. make up difference with boiling water. Add gelatin to hot stock and stir to dissolve. Add 1 t. lemon juice, ¼ t. sugar and a dash or 2 salt if needed. Remove meat from bones and dice. Add ½ c. drained canned peas and sliced carrot (from stock). Toss gently and transfer mixture to tiny one-serving gelatin molds, tart pans or demitasses. Cover with aspic liquid and refrigerate until set. Before serving scrape off congealed fat and discard. Dip molds in hot water briefly and turn aspics out upside down on lettuce leaves. Place a lemon wedge on 1 side of each aspic and several spiced cherries on the other. Serve with mayonnaise- horseradish or other mayonnaise-based sauce of choice. *Variation:* Turkey, goose or duck may be prepared the same way; with goose or duck add several pitted prunes to stock with soup greens, then dice cooked prunes and add to aspic.

INDIVIDUAL FRUITED CHICKEN ASPICS
tymbaliki z kurczaka z owocami

Prepare as above, but instead of peas and carrots to diced cooked fowl, add about ½ c. drained canned peaches or pineapple.

PORK OR VEAL TONGUES IN ASPIC
ozorki cielęce lub wieprzowe w galarecie

Scrub 2 veal or pork tongues under running water and trim off salivary glands if still attached. Place in pot, add 5 c. water, bring to boil, reduce heat and simmer 60 min. Add soup greens, 1 bay leaf, 5 peppercorns and 3 grains allspice, ½ t. salt and (optional) for added zest 1 small dried chili pepper. Cook covered another 30–60 min. on low heat or until tongues are fork tender. Remove tongues from stock and peel off skins under cold running water. Return to stock, bring to boil, switch off heat and allow tongues to cool to room temp. in stock. Wrap tongues in plastic wrap and refrigerate at least several hrs. Slice at an angle ¼ inch thick and arrange on platter. Soak 2 T. gelatin in ½ c. cold stock. Strain stock and measure out 3½ c. If it has boiled out during cooking, make up the difference with boiled water. Add 1–2 t. lemon juice and several pinches sugar, salt and pepper to taste if needed and add ¼ t. MSG. Add gelatin to hot stock and stir to dissolve. Chill aspic stock slightly in fridge. Decorate sliced tongue with hard-boiled egg slices, sliced carrots and drained canned peas (several T.) and cover platter with cool aspic stock. Refrigerate until set. *Note:* All aspic dishes must be fully encased in gelatin, so choose a platter or other dish deep enough to accommodate the sliced meat and the aspic. Meat protruding through the aspic turns dark, dries out and looks unappetizing. Serve with horseradish or horseradish sauce.

BEEF TONGUE IN ASPIC
ozór wołowy w galarecie

Cook beef tongue as directed in recipe for boiled beef tongue earlier in this chapter. Otherwise, proceed as with veal or pork tongues in aspic. *Remember:* Beef tongue takes much longer to cook (3–4 hrs.) than veal or pork tongues, but cooking time can be cut in half in pressure cooker.

STEAK TARTARE
tatar/befsztyk tatarski

Trim fat and sinew from ¾–1 lb. beef tenderloin and grind. Add 1–2 t. prepared brown mustard, 1 T. olive oil, 1 t. Maggi seasoning, ½ t. salt and ¼ t. pepper. Mix well and divide into 4–5 portions. Roll into balls and place on serving platter (or individual plates), pressing down slightly to form a mound. Cover with plastic wrap and chill at least 30 min. To serve, make a well at top of each mound and deposit a fresh raw egg yolk in each. Next to each portion place a small mound (1 heaping t.) finely chopped onions and another of finely chopped dill pickles or zesty gherkins. Garnish egg yolks with a sprinkle of chopped chives and serve immediately. Polish rye or black bread and ice-cold Wódka Wyborowa are perfect accompaniments.

According to legend, this now world-famous cold steak dish originated in the eastern borderlands of medieval Poland which were repeatedly invaded by Tatar (also spelled Tartar) hordes. These ferocious horsemen, descended from the Mongolian hordes of Genghis Khan, were constantly on the move astride their fleet-footed ponies and seldom had time for a leisurely meal. Hence, they would place a piece of tough raw meat beneath their saddles. The constant pounding, heat and horse sweat served to marinate and tenderize the meat, which was then eaten uncooked.

STEAK TARTARE ANOTHER WAY
tatar/befsztyk tatarski

Trim fat and sinew from ¾–1 lb. beef tenderloin and chop very fine or grind. Salt and pepper to taste and form into 4–5 patties about 1¼ inch thick. Make a well in tops and deposit 1 raw egg yolk into each. Sprinkle yolks with paprika. Finely chop 1 onion and sprinkle with 2 t. wine vinegar. Surround yolks with concentric wreaths of chopped onion, chopped marinated mushrooms, chopped zesty gherkins, and sprinkle with capers. Add ¼ sardine, sprat or anchovy fillet to each portion and decorate with lettuce leaves, lemon wedges, and radish slices. On the side provide salt, pepper, paprika, vinegar, oil and Maggi seasoning, allowing your guests to additionally season their portions according to preference. *Note:* Guests mix the raw yolk with the ground steak and garnishes on their plates. *Variation:* Steak Tartare may be additionally seasoned with crushed garlic, chopped chives, parsley, garden cress, cayenne pepper and, in the absence of Maggi seasoning, soy sauce or Kitchen Bouquet.

POLISH IMPORTED CANNED HAM
polska szynka konserwowa

Unlike the cold courses that involve extensive preparation, Krakus brand imported Polish ham comes ready to use straight from the can. Time and again Krakus has beat out Danish, Dutch and other rivals at international food competitions as the leanest, meatiest, and tastiest canned ham available. Although the price per pound may seem higher than that of cheaper brands, there is no waste and very little gelatin, making it quite economical. It is also available at many delicatessens where you can buy as little as you need and have it sliced as thin as you like. On lettuce-lined platter arrange overlapping slices of ham down the center or roll them up into even rolls or trumpet-like horns. Garnish with radish roses, strips of mild red fresh or pickled peppers, cucumber slices, pickled mushrooms etc. The ham slices or rolls may be covered with aspic, in which case omit lettuce. Serve with horseradish, horseradish sauce or ćwikła.

POLISH IMPORTED CANNED PORK LOIN
polędwica konserwowa z Polski

Although not as well known in the U.S. as Polish canned ham, canned pork loin from Poland is also a superb cold meat that may be preferred by some. It is lighter in color and milder in flavor than ham, but also offers limitless opportunities for appetizer courses as well as simple cold suppers. It is available at delicatessens and butcher shops, especially in Polish ethnic neighborhoods where you can get it sliced to order. Serve cold and garnish as you would canned ham.

HAM OR PORK-LOIN HORNS WITH PEAS
rożki z szynki lub polędwicy z groszkiem

Spread 8 thin slices of canned Polish ham very thinly with prepared horseradish or prepared brown mustard. Roll each into a trumpet-like horn, closed at 1 end and open at the other. Combine 1 c. drained canned baby peas with 2 diced dill pickles, 1 diced hard-cooked egg (optional) and several T. chopped chives and /or diced radishes. Sprinkle with ½ t. powdered sugar and toss lightly so as not to damage peas. Add just enough mayonnaise to bind ingredients together and fill ham or pork-loin horns with mixture. Into each horn stick a radish slice or sprig of parsley and arrange on lettuce-lined platter. Each horn may be dressed with a little horseradish sauce, mustard sauce or other mayonnaise-based sauce of choice.

COLD-MEAT PLATTER
półmisek mięsny

It would be a rare Polish banquet, dinner-party, nameday gathering or holiday feast at Easter or Christmas (Christmas Eve being a meatless exception!) where only one cold meat was served. More often than not, various cold meats are arranged on a single large platter. There may be one platter for cooked, non-smoked meats (roasts, pâtés, tongue, roulades, etc.) and another for ham and other smoked meats and sausages. At smaller gatherings both smoked and non-smoked meats may be combined on a single platter. Besides ham and pork loin, other ready-to-eat cold Polish favorites include smoked pork tenderloin (polędwica wędzona—better known in North America as Canadian bacon), baleron (a smoked pork shoulder butt encased in bladder), ham sausage (kiełbasa szynkowa), hunter's sausage (kiełbasa myśliwska) and kabanosy (thin dried sausage). Whatever varieties you decide on, arrange them artistically on a platter in rows or concentric circles (on circular platter) with each slice overlapping the next and paler-colored meats flanking darker ones. Garnish imaginatively with greens, pickled mushrooms, marinated vegetables and spiced fruits. On a circular platter you may place a tomato, orange or pepper shell at center to contain the sauce.

COUNTRY-STYLE MEAT PLATTER
półmisek wyrobów wiejskich

For more informal gatherings, family suppers or community events with a definitely rural theme (like Dożynki—Polish harvest feast), a selection of more down-home-type meats would be called for. On a platter arrange slices of buckwheat sausage (kaszanka, kiszka), white and black head cheese (salceson), cold boiled or baked fresh kiełbasa, and ordinary, ready-to-eat smoked kiełbasa. To create a rustic climate, dispense with fancy platter garnishes and gourmet sauces, and serve with brown mustard, horseradish, dill pickles, sliced tomatoes and plenty of Polish rye and/or black bread and unsalted butter. A frothy stein of beer will help wash it all down nicely. *Note:* If interested in trying your hand at making some of these from scratch, see the chapter on sausage-making.

COLD SAVORY SAUCES, DRESSINGS & RELISHES

The great popularity of cold appetizers naturally led to a wide variety of sauces designed to make them more palatable and appetizing. Many of the same sauces can also be used as salad dressing. Although the prospect of making your own salad dressing may seem formidable at first, there really isn't much to it once you get the knack.

A great many of Poland's most popular cold sauces are based on sour cream or mayonnaise or a combination of the two. Even if you decide not to make your own mayonnaise or sour cream from scratch (although recipes for both are provided on these pages), you can easily whip up a gourmet sauce using the store-bought variety. A hard-boiled egg is just a hard-boiled egg—a bag lunch or picnic food—until you top it with a dollop of creamy sauce. What to do with that piece of cold leftover meat or fish from yesterday's dinner? The proper sauce and a little imagination can quickly turn it into an elegant cold appetizer or supper dish.

In addition to many super-quick and easy sauces, this chapter also includes recipes for more involved condiments, although they too are really not all that difficult. If you read on, you will find ways of preparing your own horseradish, ćwikła, mustard, and ketchup, not to mention pickled mushrooms and spiced fruits.

For the benefits of those who love creamy sauces, but prefer to stay away from foods high in calories and cholesterol, we have presented a number of low-fat substitutes, including yolk-less mayonnaise and no-fat yogurt as a replacement for sour cream. Whatever your dietary requirements and personal preferences, we are sure you will find entries in this chapter that facilitate meal-planning and add new flavor twists to your home-entertainment scene.

* * *

HOMEMADE MAYONNAISE
majonez domowy

It takes only a few minutes to make real mayonnaise right at home from scratch, and we are sure you'll agree that it is far superior in taste to the store-bought variety. The main thing to remember is that all ingredients should be at room temp. So take them out of fridge several hrs. before preparing. Oil must be added to yolks very gradually. Beat 1–2 large, raw egg yolks with wire whisk in one direction (or use electric mixer on low speed) until lemony, adding several pinches salt and about 1 t. lemon juice. Continue to beat and add in a very thin stream (or 1 t. at a time) 1 c. salad oil or olive oil. When nice and thick, season to taste with about 1 t. prepared brown mustard, a dash or 2 white pepper, 1 t. powdered sugar, and additional salt and lemon juice if needed. *Note*: If mayonnaise separates or curdles (as may occur if ingredients were not at same temp. or oil was added too fast), do not despair! Simply beat another egg yolk in a clean bowl and, when lemony, add a little of the curdled mayonnaise at a time, beating constantly. *Hint:* This thick mayonnaise is excellent for decorating platters, encasing a whole cold, poached fish or embellishing aspic dishes, but should be thinned down for use in salads. To do so, beat in ¼ c. or so of cold vegetable or meat stock or cold pre-boiled water.

BLENDER MAYONNAISE
majonez robiony mikserem

In blender, whirl 15 seconds or so 1 whole raw egg, 2 pinches salt, and 2 T. lemon juice. Continue blending and add in very thin stream 1 c. salad oil or olive oil until you get a thick mayonnaise. Do not overblend. When it gets very thick, it may be better to switch blender on and off to stir down mayonnaise. Season with 1 t. powdered sugar, 1 t. prepared brown mustard, and a pinch or 2 white pepper. *Note*: To thin, add slowly ¼–½ c. cold strained meat stock (with fat removed) or vegetable stock and blend a bit longer.

MAYONNAISE (ROUX & STOCK METHOD)
majonez na zasmażce

Beat 1 raw egg yolk until lemony, gradually adding, ½ t. salt, 2 t. lemon juice, and 1 T. prepared brown mustard. Continue beating (with whisk or electric mixer), while adding ½ c. oil in thin stream. When mayonnaise thickens, add 1 t. powdered sugar and several pinches white pepper. Chill in fridge. Meanwhile, melt 3 t. butter in saucepan, stir in 4 T. flour, and heat until bubbly but unbrowned, stirring constantly. Dilute with 1 c. strained beef stock (with fat removed) and bring to boil, stirring well until smooth. Cool to room temp., then refrigerate. Beat cold mayonnaise, gradually adding cold stock until mixture is smooth and creamy. Season to taste if necessary with salt, white pepper, lemon juice, and powdered sugar.

YOLKLESS MAYONNAISE
majonez bez żółtek

Beat 2 egg whites lightly in blender. Add ¼ t. salt and 1 t. lemon juice and whirl briefly to blend. Gradually add in thin stream while whirling ½ c. sunflower or soybean oil. When thick, add ½ t. lemon juice and a little cold pre-boiled water. Season to taste with 1 t. or so powdered sugar, several pinches white pepper, 1–2 t. brown prepared mustard and a bit more lemon juice if desired.

FLAVORED MAYONNAISE
majonez o różnych smakach

Homemade mayonnaise prepared in any of the ways given above as well as the bottled, store-bought variety may be flavored in a number of interesting ways. Some possibilities:

MUSTARD MAYONNAISE
majonez musztardowy

Into 1 c. homemade or store-bought mayonnaise, fork-blend 3–4 T. prepared brown mustard. Season to taste with additional salt and sugar if desired. Excellent on hard-boiled eggs and cold meats like ham and beef tongue.

HORSERADISH MAYONNAISE
majonez chrzanowy

Depending on the potency of the horseradish you have on hand and the sharpness you desire, fork-blend 1 c. mayonnaise with 3–5 T. prepared non-creamed-style horseradish. Good on hard-cooked eggs, cold meats, and fish. A bit of powdered sugar may be added if desired.

BEET MAYONNAISE
majonez ćwikłowy

Beat into 1 c. mayonnaise several T. beet juice from plain canned beets or pickled beets which will produce a delightfully pinkish mayonnaise with an interesting flavor twist. For added tang, flavor mayonnaise with several T. ćwikła (beet & horseradish relish) forced through sieve. Sweeten slightly if desired. The perfect accompaniment to cold pork.

HORSERADISH-TOMATO MAYONNAISE
majonez chrzanowo-pomidorowy

Fork-blend 1 c. mayonnaise with 1 T. tomato paste (or 3 T. ketchup) and 2–3 T. prepared horseradish. Season to taste with a little lemon juice and white pepper. Excellent on cold fish, fish livers, shrimp, and crabmeat.

GREEN MAYONNAISE
majonez zielony

In pot, combine 4 T. washed, finely chopped spinach and 3 T. water or milk. Simmer covered several min. until tender, then allow to cool. Sieve spinach, fork-blend with 1 c. mayonnaise and season with a bit of lemon juice, salt, and sugar if desired. Chill and serve with hard-cooked eggs or cold fish.

GARDEN-GREEN MAYONNAISE
majonez z zieleninką

Fork-blend 1 c. plain or green mayonnaise (above) with ½ c. finely chopped fresh greens: parsley, dill, chives, garden cress, chervil, and tarragon in whatever proportion you prefer. If fresh tarragon is not available, a pinch of dry tarragon will do. Season to taste with lemon juice, salt, white pepper, and powdered sugar. A great accompaniment to hard-boiled eggs and cold fish. *Variation*: Add 1 bud crushed garlic to sauce.

HERB MAYONNAISE
majonez ziołowy

Fork-blend 1 c. mayonnaise with 1 t. of your homemade Polish herb pepper, beef seasoning, poultry seasoning, wildfowl seasoning, fish seasoning or hunter's seasoning. For added sharpness, add a pinch or 2 cayenne pepper. Season to taste with lemon juice, salt, pepper, and powdered sugar. Serve with hard-cooked eggs or cold meat or fish.

LEMON MAYONNAISE
majonez cytrynowy

Fork-blend 1 c. mayonnaise with juice of ½ lemon. Add several pinches powdered sugar. Serve with cold veal or fish.

CRANBERRY MAYONNAISE
majonez żurawinowy

In blender, purée ¼ c. whole-style canned cranberry sauce. Fork-blend with 1 c. mayonnaise, 1 t. prepared horseradish, and a sprinkling of lemon juice. If too tart for your taste, add a pinch or 2 powdered sugar. Excellent with cold poultry.

BASIC MAYONNAISE SAUCE
sos majonezowy podstawowy

Mayonnaise makes an excellent base for a variety of delicious cold sauces which in America would probably be referred to as dressings. They will add a gourmet touch to your cold buffet or starter course, although most take only a few seconds to prepare. Simply fork blend ¾ c. mayonnaise with ¼ c. dairy sour cream, 1–2 t. prepared brown mustard, ½–1 t. lemon juice or vinegar and a little salt, white pepper, and powdered sugar to taste. Just as it is, this basic sauce is a great accompaniment to hard-boiled eggs, cold meats, and fish as well as starter-course or cold-supper salads (see following chapter). Or, it can be the basis for the sauces presented below. *Note*: Miracle Whip or similar salad dressings may be used in place of mayonnaise if you like, but omit the sugar whenever it is called for; also, use a trace more lemon juice or vinegar to blunt this dressing's sweet edge.

DIET BASIC MAYONNAISE SAUCE
sos majonezowy podstawowy dietetyczny

If you are calorie and/or cholesterol-conscious, prepare the above sauce using ¾ c. lite mayonnaise and ¼ c. low-fat or no-fat plain yogurt. It may not be quite as tasty as the original, but the various flavorings given below may disguise it sufficiently to make a more than passable substitute. *Note:* You can easily whip up a less drastic diet version of this sauce by combining ⅓ c. regular mayonnaise, ⅓ c. lite mayonnaise, ⅛ c. sour cream and ⅛ c. low-fat yogurt, plus the mustard, lemon juice, salt, white pepper, and powdered sugar indicated above.

MUSTARD SAUCE
sos musztardowy

Fork-blend 1 c. basic mayonnaise sauce with 2-4 T. prepared brown mustard (preferably Polish or Düsseldorf type). Great with hard-cooked eggs, cold ham and tongue.

CHIVE SAUCE
sos szczypiorkowy

Fork-blend 1 c. basic mayonnaise sauce with ¼–½ c. finely chopped fresh chives, green onions or scallions, or any combination thereof. Season with a little lemon juice if desired. Good on hard boiled eggs, cold meat and fish.

HORSERADISH SAUCE
sos chrzanowy

Fork-blend 1 c. basic mayonnaise sauce with 2 T. freshly grated horseradish root or 4–5 T. prepared non-creamed horseradish. This zesty sauce will perk up the flavor of hard-cooked eggs, pâtés and other cold meats as well as aspic dishes. Also good on cold fish.

GARDEN-GREEN SAUCE
sos z zieleniną

Fork-blend 1 c. basic mayonnaise sauce with ¼–½ c. finely chopped chives, parsley, dill, garden cress, chervil, and tarragon in any proportion you like. Feel free to omit any greens you don't particularly care for or don't have on hand. *Optional*: A little finely chopped fresh spinach, sorrel, or unwilted (preferably freshly picked) leaves of baby radishes may also be added. 2–3 finely grated radishes and/or 1 bud crushed garlic are additional possibilities. A tasty and vitamin-rich accompaniment to hard-boiled eggs, cold fish meats and aspic dishes.

EASTER SAUCE
sos do święconego

Fork-blend ¾ c. basic mayonnaise sauce with ¼ c. sour cream, 2 ground or finely diced hard-cooked eggs, 1 finely diced dill pickle, 1 T. prepared horseradish, 2–3 T. chopped chives and (optional) 1 T. chopped garden cress. This sauce is used to add zest to święcone, the hard-cooked eggs and cold meats of the traditional Polish Easter feast.

BEET & HORSERADISH SAUCE
sos ćwikłowy

Fork-blend 1 c. basic mayonnaise sauce with 3–5 T. ćwikła (beet & horseradish relish). This is also a proper accompaniment to traditional cold Easter treats and its pleasing pinkish hue contrasts nicely with the whitish, green-flecked Easter sauce above.

COLD TOMATO SAUCE
zimny sos pomidorowy

Fork-blend 1 c. basic mayonnaise sauce with 2 T. tomato paste or 4 T. ketchup and 1–2 t. prepared horseradish. Flavor to taste with a bit of powdered sugar, lemon juice, and cayenne pepper if desired. Excellent for dressing cold fish and seafood, including shrimp cocktail.

CAPER SAUCE
sos kaparowy

Chop fine 2–3 T. capers and fork-blend with 1 c. basic mayonnaise sauce. Good on hard-cooked eggs as well as cold meat and fish.

ANCHOVY SAUCE
sos sardelowy

Finely chop 3 canned anchovy fillets and sieve into 1 c. basic mayonnaise sauce. Fork-blend briefly and flavor with a sprinkling of lemon juice. Serve with hard-cooked eggs, mild-tasting cold meats, and aspic dishes.

ZESTY GHERKIN SAUCE
sos korniszonowy

Chop fine 3–4 zesty gherkins and fork-blend with 1 c. basic mayonnaise sauce. For added tang, blend in 1–2 t. of the gherkin marinade. Good with hard-boiled eggs as well as cold meat and fish.

PICKLED-MUSHROOM SAUCE
sos z grzybkami

Fork-blend 1 c. basic mayonnaise sauce with ¼–⅓ c. finely chopped pickled mushrooms, adding enough of the marinade (several t.) to get the tang you desire. Serve with cold roasts, especially pork, beef and game.

EASY TARTAR SAUCE
sos tatarski łatwy

Fork-blend 1 c. basic mayonnaise sauce with ¼ c. finely chopped zesty gherkins or vinegar-marinade dill pickles, ¼ c. finely chopped pickled mushrooms, 1 mashed hard-cooked egg yolk, 1 t. prepared horseradish, 1 T. chopped chives, 1 t. prepared brown mustard and salt, pepper, and powdered sugar to taste. *Note*: Whereas in America tartar sauce is a standard accompaniment to hot fried fish, in Polish tradition it is served almost exclusively with cold dishes, notably pâté, hard-cooked eggs, cold meat, and fish as well as aspic dishes.

CLASSIC TARTAR SAUCE
sos tatarski tradycyjny

Combine 2 sieved, hard-cooked egg yolks with 1–2 T. prepared brown mustard and 2 raw egg yolks and mix vigorously until smooth. Mixing constantly (with wire whisk or electric mixer) add 1 c. olive oil or other salad oil in a thin stream until mixture becomes thick and fluffy. Add 4 finely chopped zesty gherkins, ¼ c. finely chopped pickled mushrooms, 2 T. finely chopped capers, 2 finely chopped hard-cooked egg whites, 1 t. chopped parsley, 1 t. chopped chives and salt, pepper, lemon juice, and powdered sugar to taste. Fork-blend briefly, chill, and serve. *Remember*: For best results, all ingredients should be at room temp.

BLENDER TARTAR SAUCE
sos tatarski robiony mikserem

In blender, whirl together for 10–15 seconds 2 whole eggs, 2 T. lemon juice, ¼ t. salt, and 2 t. brown mustard. Continue blending while adding 1 c. olive oil or salad oil in thin stream. When oil has been absorbed, switch off blender and let mixture settle briefly. Whirl 1–2 more times in short spurts of several seconds. Transfer mixture to mixing cup and season to taste with salt, pepper, and powdered sugar. Stir in 2 finely diced dill pickles, 1 finely chopped hard-cooked egg, 1 small grated onion, 2 T. capers, 1 T. chopped chives, and 1 T. chopped garden cress.

SOUR CREAM SAUCE
sos śmietanowy

In addition to mayonnaise-based sauces, cold dressings made with sour cream have long been popular in Poland. They are not only extremely delicious but also very easy to prepare. This recipe is a good example. Simply fork-blend 1 c. dairy sour cream with 2 t. vinegar or lemon juice, 2 t. brown prepared mustard, ½ t. salt, a dash or 2 white pepper, and (optional) ½–1 t. sugar. Good on hard-cooked eggs, herring, cold cooked fish, and salads. *Note*: Use no-fat yogurt instead if dieting.

SOUR CREAM-MAYONNAISE SAUCE
sos śmietanowy z majonezem

Fork-blend ½ c. sour cream with ⅓–½ c. mayonnaise, 1 t. lemon juice, 1–2 t. brown prepared mustard, ¼ t. salt, a pinch or 2 white pepper and (optional) ½–1 t. sugar. An excellent dressing for vegetable and potato salads; also good with hard-cooked eggs, herring, and cold cooked fish.

MUSTARD-SOUR CREAM SAUCE
sos musztardowy na śmietanie

Fork-blend 1 c. dairy sour cream with 3–5 T. prepared brown mustard, ¼ t. salt and 1 t. or so powdered sugar and serve with hard-cooked eggs or cold meats. *Optional:* 2 mashed or ground hard-cooked egg yolks may be added.

SOUR CREAM & CHIVE SAUCE
sos szczypiorkowy na śmietanie

Mix 1 mashed hard-cooked egg yolk with 1 T. prepared brown mustard and 1–2 t. powdered sugar into smooth paste and fork-blend with 1 c. sour cream. Add 2–3 T. chopped chives and season to taste with salt, lemon juice, and a bit more powdered sugar if needed. Perfect on hard-cooked eggs and cold meats. Often served on Easter. *Note*: This and other sour cream sauces may be made with ¾ c. sour cream and ¼ c. mayonnaise which mellows the tartness of the sour cream.

SOUR CREAM & EGG SAUCE
sos śmietanowy z jajami

Fork-blend 1 c. sour cream with 2 ground or well-mashed hard-cooked eggs. Season to taste with salt, white pepper, lemon juice, and (optional) powdered sugar. This is another typical Easter sauce.

SOUR CREAM & HORSERADISH SAUCE
sos chrzanowy na śmietanie

Scald 2–3 T. freshly grated horseradish with 3–4 T. hot meat stock. Meanwhile, mash 2 hard-cooked egg yolks and mix with 2–3 T. sour cream into a smooth paste. Add ¾ c. sour cream and horseradish mixture and fork-blend. Season to taste with salt, lemon juice, and powdered sugar. Excellent on hard-cooked eggs and cold ham, hence its frequent use at Easter time. *Optional*: For added zing, blend in 2 t.–1 T. prepared brown mustard. *Note*: If you don't have freshly grated horseradish, use 4–5 T. prepared non-creamed horseradish and omit the meat stock.

SOUR CREAM, APPLE & HORSERADISH SAUCE
sos chrzanowo-jabłkowy na śmietanie

Fork-blend 1 c. sour cream with 2–3 T. freshly grated horseradish or 4–6 T. prepared non-creamed horseradish and 1 peeled, grated, tart cooking apple. Season to taste with salt, powdered sugar, and lemon juice. Excellent with ham and other cold meats.

SWEET CREAM & HORSERADISH SAUCE
sos chrzanowy ze śmietanką

Fork-blend ¾ c. ice-cold whipping cream with 2–3 T. freshly grated horseradish or 4–6 T. prepared non-creamed horseradish. Season to taste with salt, white pepper, powdered sugar, and lemon juice. *Variation*: Partially whip the cream, add horseradish and seasonings, and whip a while longer for a fluffier sauce. Excellent with ham and other cold smoked meats and sausages. *Note:* For a more potent sauce, use 1 part cream and 1 part prepared horseradish and season to taste.

PREPARED HORSERADISH
chrzan z octem

In pot, bring to boil ¼ c. 6% distilled vinegar, ¼ c. water, ¼ t. salt, and 1 t. or more sugar. Simmer covered several min. and set aside to cool. Wash and peel a small horseradish root (about ¼ lb.). Transfer marinade to bowl and into it grate the root on fine side of hand-held grater. This should be done at an open window, because the fumes can be overpowering. Mix grated horseradish with marinade, pack into a jar, seal, and refrigerate until ready to use. Serve as is with cold ham or cold or hot kiełbasa and use in any recipe calling for prepared horseradish. *Hint*: We usually cube the peeled horseradish root and grind it in a hand-cranked meat-grinder into a plastic bag that contains the marinade and is fastened to mouth of grinder with a rubber band. That way the fumes don't get to you. You may also whirl the cubed horseradish in blender. *Note*: Adding a peeled, grated apple will produce a milder horseradish.

OLD POLISH BEET & HORSERADISH RELISH
ćwikła po staropolsku

Wash and peel 4–5 beets and cook in 6 c. water until tender (35–60 min. depending on size of beets). Drain beets, reserving liquid for beet soup. Coarsely grate, dice, or thinly slice beets (on slicer blade of grater) and combine with ¼–½ c. prepared horseradish and 1 peeled, grated apple. Separately, combine in small pot ¼ c. 6% distilled vinegar, ¼ c. beer, ½ t. dill seed lightly crushed in mortar. Add 1 t. salt and 2–3 t. sugar, bring to boil, reduce heat, and simmer covered 5 min. Cool. Pour over beet mixture, cover, and refrigerate overnight before serving.

EASY BEET & HORSERADISH RELISH
ćwikła najłatwiejsza

Combine 2 c. coarsely grated drained canned beets (reserving liquid for soup) with ¼–½ c. prepared horseradish. In pot, combine ¼ c. 6% distilled vinegar, ¼ c. water, ½ t. salt, 2–3 t. sugar and ¼ t. slightly crushed caraway seeds or ground caraway. Bring to boil, cover, and simmer on low heat 5 min. and let cool to room temp. Pour over beet mixture, cover, and refrigerate overnight.

CREAMY PLUM SAUCE
sos śliwkowy ze śmietaną

Fork-blend vigorously or mix in electric mixer ¾ c. Polish plum jam (powidła) with ¼ c. prepared horseradish. Mix in ½ c. sour cream, juice of ½ lemon, and salt to taste. Serve with cold meats.

VINAIGRETTE (LEMON & OIL DRESSING)
vinaigrette/winegret

In small bowl, beat 3 T. lemon juice or wine vinegar with ¼ t. salt, ⅛ t. white or black pepper, and (optional) ½ t. sugar. Gradually add 6 T. olive oil or other salad oil, beating constantly with wire whisk. Use immediately to dress potato salad, lettuce and other salads. *Variation*: Add 2–3 T. finely chopped greens: parsley, dill, chives, chervil, and tarragon.

MUSTARD VINAIGRETTE
vinaigrette z musztardą

In small bowl beat with wire whisk 1½ T. lemon juice or wine vinegar with ¼ t. salt, ⅛ t. pepper, and (optional) ½ t. sugar. Mixing constantly, add 1½–2 T. brown prepared mustard and 6 T. olive oil or other salad oil of choice. Use as above.

VINAIGRETTE WITH EGG YOLK
vinaigrette z żółtkiem

In small bowl mash 1 hard-cooked egg yolk well and mix with 2–3 T. lemon juice or wine vinegar into a smooth paste. Add ¼ t. salt, ⅛ t. pepper, and 6 T. olive oil or other salad oil, mixing constantly. Used mainly to dress cooked-vegetable salads, especially potato salad. *Optional*: A sprinkling of finely chopped garden greens will enhance the appearance, taste, and aroma of this sauce. *Note*: Feel free to add 1–2 T. dry red or white wine to any of the above vinaigrettes. For added zip, season with ¼ t. Polish hunter's seasoning.

OLD POLISH PLUM SAUCE
staropolski sos śliwkowy

In pot, combine ½ c. Polish plum jam (powidła), ½ c. tomato paste, and ¾ c. spiced-plum marinade. Bring to boil, reduce heat and simmer several min., stirring frequently. Add ½ t. salt, ½ t. Polish hunter's seasoning, and a little more spiced-plum marinade, if needed, to get a thick, pourable sauce. Add 1–2 buds crushed garlic, simmer 10 min. longer, then cover and let stand until cooled to room temp. Transfer to jar, seal, and refrigerate. Use with cold meats or as a glaze for roast pork or poultry. Also, try it with steak, since it is quite similar in taste and texture to some American steak sauces. *Note*: Unsweetened powidła is best in this recipe. If you have only the type containing sugar, use a non-sweet marinade (from pickled mushrooms, zesty gherkins, etc.) instead of the sweeter, spiced-plum marinade. You can also add several t. vinegar to sauce as it cooks to get the taste you want. This sauce should have sweet undertones without actually tasting decidedly sweet.

TANGY TOMATO SAUCE (POLISH KETCHUP)
pikantny sos pomidorowy

In pot combine 1 c. tomato paste and 1 c. spiced-plum marinade. Stir well and bring to boil. Reduce heat and simmer covered 5 min. Add ½ t. salt and ½ t. Polish beef, pork, or hunter's seasoning and simmer a while longer. The sauce should have the thickness of ketchup. If it is too thick, dilute with a little more spiced-plum marinade or—if you find the sauce sweeter than you like—with a little boiling vinegar. Simmer a bit longer, cover, and let stand until cooled to room temp. Transfer to jar, seal, and store. Use as you would ketchup. *Optional*: Add 1–2 buds crushed garlic or ¼ t. garlic powder. *Variation*: For a less sweet-tasting tomato sauce, use pickled-mushroom marinade or gherkin marinade in place of spiced-plum marinade.

TANGY FRUIT SAUCE
pikantny sos owocowy

With electric mixer, mix until blended ½ c. black-currant, blackberry, or cherry preserves or jam with juice of ½ lemon, juice of ½ orange, ¼ t. each grated lemon and orange rind, 1 T. finely chopped onion (scalded with boiling water in strainer and drained), 1 jigger red wine (sweet or dry), 2 T. prepared brown mustard, and salt & pepper to taste. Serve with cold or hot game dishes, duck, and goose.

LINGONBERRY & PEAR SAUCE
borówki z gruszkami

This is one of Poland's favorite cold fruit sauces served with poultry and game dishes much the way cranberry sauce is served in America. The only problem is that fresh lingonberries (also known as cowberries and mountain cranberries or by their scientific name: Vaccinum vitis-idaea) are harder to find in the U.S. If you do get them, make a hot syrup from 1 c. water and ½–¾ c. sugar. When sugar dissolves and syrup is boiling, add 3 peeled diced pears. Simmer about 15 min., then add 3 c. washed and drained lingonberries. Cover and cook on low heat about 20 min. Let stand covered until cooled to room temp., then transfer to jar, seal, and refrigerate. *Note*: You may only manage to find lingonberry jam or preserves in a European import shop, but you can still come up with a passable substitute for the sauce cooked from scratch. Whirl in blender 1 c. lingonberry jam, 1 c. drained canned, pear halves, and juice of 1 lemon. This sauce should be sweet & sour. If too sweet, sour with a bit more lemon juice; if too tart, stir in some pear juice.

LINGONBERRY, APPLE & HORSERADISH SAUCE
borówki z jabłkami i chrzanem

Whirl together in blender 1 c. lingonberry jam or preserves, ½ c. applesauce, 3 T. prepared horseradish juice, and grated rind of 1 lemon and 1 jigger red fruit wine. Season to taste with salt, powdered sugar, and a little prepared brown mustard (about 1 t.). Excellent with game dishes and fowl. *Note*: If lingonberry jam or preserves are not available, cranberry jam or whole-style canned sauce may be used instead.

ZESTY CRANBERRY-CURRANT SAUCE
sos żurawinowo-porzeczkowy

In blender, combine 1 c. whole-style canned cranberry sauce, ½–1 c. red-currant jelly, juice of ½–1 lemon, and 2 t. prepared brown mustard and blend a few seconds until smooth. Season with a pinch or 2 salt if desired. Chill and serve with game and poultry. *Optional*: A jigger sweet red wine may be added to sauce. *Variation*: Zesty cranberry sauce is made the same way by omitting currant jelly and adding a bit of sugar.

TANGY CHERRY SAUCE
sos wiśniowy

Do not use a blender on this one, because cherries should remain intact. Simply mix together gently 1 c. canned cherry-pie filling with juice of ½ a lemon, 1 t. prepared horseradish (optional), ¼ t. Polish honey-spice cake seasoning, and a dash of salt. Serve with hot or cold pork, game dishes, and poultry. *Note*: This and the other tangy fruit sauces given above may be served in orange shells placed at center of serving platter.

HOMEMADE REGULAR MUSTARD
domowa musztarda stołowa

In pot combine ½ c. water, ½ c. 6% distilled vinegar, 2–3 T. sugar, and ½–1 t. salt. Bring to boil, reduce heat, and simmer at a gentle boil several min. Into boiling marinade, stir ½–¾ c. white dry mustard (sometimes known as English mustard), and simmer on very low heat (a double boiler is good) about 5 min., whisking constantly. Remove from heat and continue whisking (or beat at low speed of electric mixer) until cooled to room temp. Beat in 2 T. salad oil. If mustard appears too thick, beat in a little cold pre-boiled water. *Note:* If there is too much liquid, it may separate when mustard is refrigerated, but that's no problem at all. Simply fork-blend mustard before serving. Fill small jars with your prepared mustard, seal, and refrigerate.

HOMEMADE SHARP MUSTARD
domowa musztarda ostra

Proceed exactly as above, but use ½ c. dry white mustard and ¼ c. dry brown mustard. For even sharper mustard, use 1 part of each.

HOMEMADE HORSERADISH MUSTARD
domowa musztarda chrzanowa

Into homemade mustard, prepared in either of the ways presented above, stir from 1 heaping t.–1 heaping T. prepared horseradish.

HOMEMADE OLD POLISH MUSTARD
domowa musztarda staropolska

In pot lightly brown 3–4 T. honey. Add ¼ c. beer, ¼ c. water, ½ c. 6% distilled or cider vinegar, 1 t. salt, 2 peppercorns, 1 clove, and a small piece of bay leaf. Bring to boil and simmer 10 min. Strain, discarding spices. Bring strained marinade to boil and stir in ½ c. dry white mustard and ¼ c. dry brown mustard. Cook on very low heat about 5 min., whisking as it simmers. Switch off heat and continue whisking or beat with electric mixer until cooled to room temp. Beat in 2 T. horseradish juice (place prepared horseradish in sieve and press out juice with back of spoon) and 2 T. olive oil. If thicker than you like, beat in a little cold pre-boiled water. Seal in jar and refrigerate. *Note*: Use this or any of the other above mustards in any recipe calling for prepared mustard.

HOMEMADE CREAMY MUSTARD
domowa musztarda kremowa

Into homemade regular mustard (1st recipe) stir 1 heaping T. mayonnaise. For a sweeter taste, add 1–2 t. powdered sugar.

HOMEMADE MUSTARD IN OTHER WAYS
domowa musztarda jeszcze inaczej

As is the case with most condiments, mustard affords ample opportunities for creative improvisation. Feel free to alter the above proportions for a sharper or milder, tarter or sweeter, thicker or thinner mustard to suit your taste. Try using tarragon vinegar or wine vinegar, or flavoring your mustard with a pinch or 2 garlic powder or onion powder. Some prepared horseradish may be added to any of the above, not only the horseradish mustard. A t. potato starch dissolved in ¼ c. cold water and added to hot mustard as it simmers is not only an economical "stretcher" but also mellows its sharpness and makes it glossy. A T. dry wine beaten into mustard is another possibility.

CRAYFISH BUTTER
masło rakowe

Bring 1 gallon water containing 2 T. salt and a bunch of dill to boil. Under cold running water scrub well with brush 24 crayfish, removing black intestinal vein by twisting tail fin and easing it out. Place in boiling water and cook 20 min. Remove with slotted spoon, spill out water, and, when crayfish are cool enough to handle, remove all meat from claws and tails (use meat for some other dishes). Run crayfish shells through grinder. In skillet, melt 1 lb. unsalted butter, add ground crayfish shells and simmer about 10 min., stirring constantly. Add 2 c. water and continue simmering until butter floats up to top. Switch off heat and let cool, then scoop butter from top of mixture into bowl and refrigerate. Ground shells should remain at bottom of skillet and should be discarded. Use in any recipe calling for crayfish butter which adds a superb flavor to various sauces and dishes. *Note*: Divide crayfish butter into 2–3 T. portions, wrap in plastic wrap, and freeze. It'll be ready when you need it.

HURRY-UP PICKLED RELISHES
marynaty naprędce

In the chapter on pickling and bottling, we present traditional recipes for pickled vegetables and mushrooms as well as spiced fruits which are a standard fixture of the Polish cold starter course. When prepared and bottled from fresh produce in late summer and early autumn, they will provide loads of tangy, colorful garnishes for months of winter and spring entertaining as well as quick family-meal preparation. But if you have failed to stock your pantry for whatever reason or, you did put up jars of homemade pickled things, but have since run out—all is not lost! The following are a few quick and easy ways of producing a reasonable substitute hours before your guests arrive.

EASY PICKLED MUSHROOMS, TART TYPE
łatwe grzybki marynowane na kwaśno

In mortar, partially crush 6–8 peppercorns, 3–4 grains allspice, and 2 broken up bayleaves. In pot combine ½ c. 6% vinegar, ½–⅔ c. water, the above spices, 1 quartered onion and 1 T. salt. Bring to boil, reduce heat, cover, and simmer on low 15 min. Switch off heat and let stand covered until cooled to room temp. Meanwhile, drain an 8 oz. can of button mushrooms (reserving liquid for soup or gravy), and transfer mushrooms to a clean jar. Cover with strained marinade, seal, and refrigerate. Ready to serve in 2–3 hrs.

EASY PICKLED SWEET & SOUR MUSHROOMS
łatwe grzybki marynowane słodko-kwaśne

In mortar, partially crush 5 peppercorns, 2 grains allspice, 3–4 cloves, and 1–2 broken-up bay leaves. In pot, combine ⅓ c. 6% vinegar, ⅔ c. water, the above spices, 1 T. sugar, and 2 t. salt. Bring to boil, then reduce heat and simmer under cover 15 min. Let stand covered until cooled to room temp., then pour over 8 oz. drained, canned button mushrooms in jar. Seal and refrigerate. Prepare at least 3 hrs. before your dinner party is due to begin.

QUICK SPICED PEARS
gruszki w occie na chybcika

In mortar, partially crush 10–12 cloves, 5 peppercorns, 2 grains allspice, 2 broken-up bay leaves, and a small piece of cinnamon bark. In pot, combine ⅔ c. water, ⅓–½ c. 6% vinegar, the above spices, and 2–2½ T. sugar. Bring to boil, then simmer covered on low heat 15 min. and let stand at room temp. until cool to touch. Drain a large can of pear halves (reserving liquid for other uses), and gently transfer pears to serving bowl. Cover with strained marinade, seal with plastic wrap, and refrigerate 2–3 hrs. When ready to serve, drain off marinade. *Note*: Store marinade in sealed jar in fridge; it can be re-used for another batch of canned pears, but first simmer it with 1–2 T. vinegar.

HURRY-UP SPICED CHERRIES OR PLUMS
czereśnie lub śliwki w occie naprędce

Proceed exactly as with spiced pears (above), but use canned black cherries or canned purple plums. Reserve the liquid for desserts (fruit gelatin, jelly-pudding, fruit sauce) or a refreshing fruit drink made by mixing the liquid with an equal part of cold pre-boiled water or bottled sparkling water. *Note*: In all 3 above spiced-fruit recipes, if you don't have time to crush whole spices, simply add a slightly heaped t. Polish honey-spice cake seasoning to marinade and simmer as directed.

24-HOUR DILL PICKLES
ogórki kwaszone jednodobowe

Wash 1½ lbs. 3 inch long, preferably freshly picked pickling cucumbers. Cut off ends, cut cucumber in ½ widthwise and prick each piece with toothpick in 10 places. Make a ¼ inch layer of pickling salt in glass bowl, add the cucumbers, and cover with salt so they don't show through. Cover and let stand at room temp. 1 hr. Meanwhile, in pot combine 2½ c. water, ½ c. 6% distilled vinegar, 1 crumbled bay leaf, 3 T. pickling salt, and 1 t. sugar. Bring to boil and simmer covered on low heat 10 min. Rinse cucumbers of salt, scald a clean qt. jar with a little boiling water, place cucumbers in jar, add 1 t. dill seed, 3 peppercorns, 1–2 buds of garlic, sliced, 1 grain allspice, and 1 heaping T. prepared horseradish and cover with hot marinade. Pour marinade over cucumbers slowly so jar doesn't crack. Seal and leave at room temp. at least 24 hrs. Chill before serving. *Note*: If you have a cherry tree or some grapevines in your back garden, you can add 2–3 cherry leaves or 1 grape leaf to jar before adding marinade.

SPEEDY ZESTY GHERKINS
korniszony błyskawiczne

We have used the term "zesty gherkins" throughout this book to describe the sharp and tangy little pickles Poles call "korniszony" to distinguish them from the sweet gherkins found in every American supermarket. To prepare them the traditional way, see chapter on pickling and bottling. If you need them in a hurry, you can easily modify store-bought sweet gherkins as follows: Drain 1 jar store-bought sweet gherkins and discard marinade. In pot, bring to boil 1 c. distilled 6% vinegar, ½ c. water, 2 T. salt, 6 partially crushed peppercorns, 2 grains partially crushed allspice, 2 broken-up bay leaves, and 2 chopped dry cayenne peppers. Reduce heat and simmer covered 1 min. When cool, pour marinade over gherkins, seal and refrigerate. Ready in 1 hr. *Note:* Prepare only the amount you need for a given occasion. Storing them in this strong marinade may make the gherkins unpalatably overpowering.

COLD-APPETIZER & SUPPER SALADS

The salads presented in this chapter are by and large a part of Poland's cold-appetizer syndrome, because they are usually served along with the cold egg, meat, and fish dishes of the starter course. Some of the heartier egg, meat, fish, or cheese salads could be nice light suppers in themselves, when served with bread, butter, and hot tea.

Present-day Polish cookery distinguishes between the *sałatka*, a salad made chiefly from cooked vegetables and other cooked ingredients, and *surówka* (from "surowy" meaning "raw"), which encompasses fresh salads make with greens, grated vegetables, and the like. The latter are included in a different chapter which we have entitled "Dinner Salads", since they usually accompany the main meal of the day. By these standards, America's potato or bean salad would qualify as a *sałatka*, whereas the ubiquitous tossed salad would be termed a *surówka*. Just to confuse things a bit, back in the 19th century, the term *sałata* (which today refers only to lettuce) was used to mean any kind of salad, and old cookbooks contain such entries as *sałata z kartofli* (potato salad) and *sałata z raków* (crayfish salad).

By far the most popular salad of this type today is the mixed vegetable salad, similar to American potato salad, but diced finer and containing much more than just potatoes. Nearly all the recipes in this chapter are largely orientational, meaning you can feel free to mix, add, or modify ingredients according to preference. In fact, if you peruse the following pages, you may be surprised to learn that many *sałatki* can be whipped up without having to chase around for special ingredients. Chances are, you already have the fixings for some of them on hand, be it canned goods, lunch meat, some radishes or green onions in your fridge's crisper drawer, yesterday's leftover cooked vegetables, mayonnaise, mustard, or whatever.

You may not care for every item in this chapter, and that's only normal, for some people may not like a certain ingredient or it may not like them. But we are certain that you and your family will really go for some of them. So follow selected recipes as closely as you like, or be creative, experiment and improvise. Either way, you will be very Polish!

* * *

MIXED VEGETABLE SALAD
sałatka jarzynowa

The secret of a good Polish vegetable salad is to have all the ingredients diced very fine—no larger than a green pea. In salad bowl, combine 1 c. peeled diced apples, ½ c. diced onion, ½ c. peeled, diced, brine-cured or vinegar-type dill pickles, 5–6 diced pickled mushrooms, 1 c. diced cooked potatoes, 1 c. diced cooked carrots, 1 c. cooked or canned onion, ½ c. peeled, diced, brine-cured or vinegar-type dill pickles, 5–6 diced pickled mushrooms, 1 c. diced cooked potatoes, 1 c. diced cooked carrots, 1 c. cooked or canned drained navy beansor canned drained peas (or ½ c. of each). Toss ingredients gently to mix and dress with 1¼ c. basic mayonnaise sauce (see preceding chapter). Transfer to lettuce lined platter and pour another ¼ c. sauce over top. Decorate with hard-cooked egg wedges, tomato wedges, or radish roses or slices. *Note*: Salads like this are found at the cold-starter course of nearly every Polish nameday party, wedding, Easter feast, and other festive occasions. The proportions are strictly orientational, so feel free to omit, add, or limit according to personal preference.

QUICK MIXED VEGETABLE SALAD
sałatka jarzynowa naprędce

A very tasty vegetable salad can be whipped up in no time at all, using the ingredients you are likely to have on hand. If you follow the advice frequently offered in this book, you will often have cooked soup greens left over from broth or aspic dishes. Dice the carrots, parsley root, and celeriac from 1 or 2 portions of cooked soup greens, add 2–3 leftover cooked potatoes, which should also be diced. Throw in a drained can of peas or peas & carrots, a couple of diced dill pickles, a few diced pickled mushrooms and spiced plums if you have them, 1–2 diced hard-cooked eggs, and a diced onion or bunch of chopped green onions. A few odd radishes in your crisper drawer? Dice them up too for added crunch. Toss lightly and lace with basic mayonnaise sauce as above. Decorate with chopped parsley, if you have some on hand, or chopped chives or dill. A little diced fresh green pepper or pickled pepper, some diced yellow cheese—only your imagination and what you have on hand will limit your creativity!

TWO-COLOR VEGETABLE SALAD
sałatka jarzynowa dwukolorowa

Prepare vegetable salad according to either of the above recipes. Divide into 2 parts. Dress 1 part with basic mayonnaise sauce and sprinkle with chopped parsley. To the other part add ½–¾ c. diced, cooked or canned, drained beets and toss lightly. Dress with mayonnaise based horseradish sauce. The salad containing beets will take on a nice, pinkish hue. If you have a two-compartment serving dish, fill each compartment with a different version of your salad. Decorate the pink salad with beet roses and the light-colored one with hard-cooked egg slices or cooked carrot slices.

SPRING SALAD
sałatka wiosenna

Combine 1 c. chopped green onions (greens and bulbs), 1 c. diced radishes, 1 c. diced peeled cucumber, and 3–4 chopped hard-boiled eggs. Dress with about 1 c. basic mayonnaise sauce, garden-green sauce, sour-cream sauce, or sour cream-mayonnaise sauce. *Variation*: Replace the hard-cooked eggs with ¾–1 c. diced yellow cheese.

CREAMY POTATO SALAD
sałatka z kartofli

Chop 1 onion, sprinkle with ½ t. salt and 2 T. vinegar, and let stand 1 hr. Drain onion in sieve and combine with 2½ c. diced or sliced potatoes cooked in jackets. (*Note:* Potatoes used in all salads are best when cooked in jackets and peeled when cold). Dress with ½ c. or so basic mayonnaise sauce, chive sauce, garden-green sauce, or mustard sauce.

POTATO SALAD VINAIGRETTE
sałatka z kartofli z winegretem

Combine 2 c. dice potatoes cooked in jackets and peeled, ½ c. diced peeled apples, ½ c. diced onion, and (optional) 1–2 diced dill pickles. Mash 1 cooked egg yolk and mix with ½ c. mustard vinaigrette until well blended. Pour over potato mixture in serving dish. Garnish with chopped chives.

CREAMY POTATO SALAD VINAIGRETTE
sałatka z kartofli z winegretem śmietanowym

Combine about 2½ c. sliced potatoes cooked in jackets and peeled with ½ c. onions cut in ½ and sliced wafer thin. Mash 1 hard-cooked egg yolk with ¼ c. mustard vinaigrette and stir in ⅓ c. basic mayonnaise sauce or sour cream-mayonnaise sauce. Dress potatoes and onions with sauce.

POTATO SALAD WITH WINE
sałatka z kartofli z winem

Cook 1 lb. small potatoes in jackets until tender. Peel under cold running water, slice while hot, and sprinkle with 3 T. dry white wine. Let stand 30 min. Meanwhile, cook 1 small whole unpeeled celeriac in boiling water until tender, peel under cold running water, and sieve it. Mix sieved celeriac well with ½ c. vinaigrette and toss with potatoes. Sprinkle with chopped dill, parsley, and chives.

POTATO & HERRING SALAD
sałatka z kartofli ze śledziem

Rinse under running water but do not soak 1 salt herring. Remove skin and bones and dice. Combine herring with 2½ c. cold diced potatoes cooked in jackets and peeled along with 1 chopped onion. Dress with ½ c. unsalted basic mayonnaise sauce, transfer to lettuce-lined serving dish, and pour a little more sauce over top. Garnish with hard-boiled egg wedges and radish slices and sprinkle with chopped chives. Do not salt!

POTATO & MUSHROOM SALAD
sałatka z kartofli z grzybami

Wash well, dry, and dice 8 oz. fresh cultivated mushrooms and sauté in 2 T. oil on low heat about 10 min., or until liquid evaporates. Set aside to cool. Combine mushrooms with 1 lb. cold, sliced potatoes (cooked in jackets and peeled), ½ c. diced, cooked celeriac, and 1 chopped, raw onion. Toss lightly and dress with about ½ c. basic mayonnaise sauce or mustard sauce. Pour a little more sauce over top in serving dish, sprinkle with chopped garden cress, and decorate with hard-cooked egg wedges sprinkled with paprika.

POTATO & WAX BEAN SALAD
sałatka z kartofli i fasolki szparagowej

Combine 2 c. diced potatoes cooked in jackets and peeled with 2 c. cooked or canned and drained wax beans, cut in ½. Scrub but do not peel 1 small celeriac and place in boiling water 2 min. Peel celeriac under cold running water and grate. Mix with potatoes and beans, add 2 sliced hard-boiled eggs, and dress with ½ c. basic mayonnaise sauce or herb mayonnaise. Decorate with tomato slices and sprinkle with chopped chives.

GREEN-PEA SALAD
sałatka z zielonego groszku

Combine 2 c. drained canned baby peas with 1–2 peeled diced apples and dress with about ½ c. plain or flavored mayonnaise sauce, horseradish sauce, mustard sauce, or other mayonnaise-based sauces of choice.

CRUNCHY GREEN-PEA SALAD
sałatka z zielonego groszku chrupiąca

Combine 2 c. drained, canned baby peas with 1 peeled, diced apple and another c. or so of any or all of the following "crunchies" finely diced: dill pickle, fresh peeled cucumber, radishes, onion, green onions. Mild-tasting peas blend perfectly with a wide variety of ingredients, so feel free to add some diced ham or leftover cooked meat, a hard-boiled egg or two, some diced yellow cheese or diced firm tomatoes. Dress with mayonnaise-based sauce of choice.

NAVY-BEAN SALAD
sałatka z białej fasoli

Combine 2 c. cold cooked or canned and drained navy beans or pea beans with ½ c. chopped onion and (optional) 1 peeled, diced apple. Dress with ⅓–½ c. vinaigrette, basic mayonnaise sauce, mustard sauce, or horseradish sauce. Garden-green sauce is another possibility. *Variation*: Substitute beans for peas in crunchy green-pea salad (above). *Note*: As with all bean dishes, a pinch or 2 savory will enhance the flavor of this salad.

BEAN, POTATO & PEPPER SALAD
sałatka z fasoli i kartofli z papryką

In salad bowl, combine 1 c. cooked or canned and drained navy beans or pea beans, ¾ c. diced, cooked potatoes, 1 peeled, diced apple, 1 diced green bell pepper (with seeds removed), 1 diced pickled pepper, and (optional) 2–3 diced zesty gherkins. Toss ingredients lightly and place in serving dish. Mash 1–2 buds garlic and mix with ¾ c. chive sauce. Pour sauce over salad, cover with plastic wrap, and chill in fridge 2–3 hrs. before serving. Decorate with parsley sprigs, green-pepper rings, and radish slices.

WAX-BEAN SALAD
sałatka z fasoli szparagowej

Cook 1 lb. wax beans in lightly salted water with 1 t. sugar until tender and drain. Mash 1 bud garlic with ¼ t. salt and add to ½ c. plain vinaigrette. Season with a pinch of savory and pour over still warm beans in serving dish. Cover with plastic wrap and refrigerate 2–3 hrs. before serving. Decorate with parsley sprigs. *Variation*: A small diced onion may be added to beans before drenching with sauce. *Note*: Drained canned wax beans may also be used as well as cooked or canned green beans.

BEET SALAD
sałatka z buraków

Cook 2 large beets in skins in lightly salted boiling water until tender (35–60 min.). When cool, peel, rinse, and cut into 1 inch sticks. Add 1 peeled apple and 1 large brine-cured dill pickle—both cut into 1 inch sticks. Dress with ½ c. or more horseradish sauce.

BEET & EGG SALAD
sałatka z buraków z jajami

Combine 2 c. cooked, diced beets with 1 peeled, diced apple, ½ c. diced vinegar-type dill pickles, 1 small leek (white portion only) sliced into wafer-thin rounds, and 2 diced, hard-cooked eggs. Sprinkle with salt & pepper and dress with several heaping T. mayonnaise. Decorate with hard-boiled egg wedges. *Note*: Drained, canned beets may be used in both of the above recipes.

CAULIFLOWER & CELERIAC SALAD
sałatka z kalafiorów i selera

Cook 1 small, unpeeled celeriac in boiling water until tender. When cool, peel and grate coarsely and combine with 1 peeled, coarsely grated apple. Line serving bowl with lettuce leaves, on them arrange about 3 c. cooked cauliflower flowerlets, top with celeriac-apple mixture, and dress with ¾ c. basic mayonnaise sauce. Garnish with chopped parsley.

CAULIFLOWER SALAD
sałatka z kalafiorów

Arrange 3 c. or so cold, cooked cauliflower broken up into flowerlets on lettuce-lined serving dish. Season with salt, pepper, and a pinch of sugar, top with 1 diced, hard-boiled egg, and dress with basic mayonnaise sauce. Garnish with chopped chives. *Variation*: Dress with mustard vinaigrette.

LEEK, POTATO, & EGG SALAD
sałatka z porów, kartofli i jaj

Slice 2 washed and dried leeks (white portions only) into wafer-thin rounds and sprinkle with a little lemon juice. Combine with 3–4 small cooked, peeled potatoes thinly sliced, and 2 sliced hard-boiled eggs. Dress with basic mayonnaise sauce, chive sauce, garden-green sauce or herb sauce.

LEEK, POTATO & CHEESE SALAD
sałatka z porów z serem

Cut 2 washed leeks (with green portion discarded or reserved for soup) in ½ lengthwise and wash well to remove any embedded dirt. Dry and again cut each of the 4 pieces in ½ lengthwise to get 8 sticks. Place sticks side by side and cut into small nuggets. Toss with 1 c. diced yellow cheese and 1 peeled, diced tart cooking apple. Dress with plain mayonnaise and garnish with chopped chives.

CELERIAC SALAD
sałatka z selera

Peel 1 med. celeriac and cook in lightly salted boiling water until tender. Cool under cold running water and dice fine, sprinkling with lemon juice to prevent discoloration. Combine with 1 peeled, diced apple and 1 diced dill pickle (vinegar type). Sprinkle with salt & pepper and dress with mayonnaise. Divide into portions by placing a mound or scoop of salad on lettuce leaves. Grind 10 walnut meats and sprinkle a little over each portion.

ASPARAGUS SALAD
sałatka ze szparagów

Cook a tied bunch of asparagus spears (about 1 lb.) in boiling, salted water with 1 t. sugar added until tender, about 20–30 min. Drain, cool, and cut into smaller pieces. (***Note***: Drained canned asparagus may also be used). Arrange on serving dish, top with 2 diced hard-cooked eggs, garnish with 2 T. chopped chives, and lace with mayonnaise seasoned with a little salt and sugar.

ASPARAGUS SALAD VINAIGRETTE
sałatka ze szparagów z winegretem

Cook, drain, cool, cut, and arrange asparagus on serving dish as above but dress with ⅓–½ c. plain vinaigrette fork-blended with 2 T. canned tomato sauce. Garnish with chopped hard-boiled eggs and decorate with parsley sprigs.

ASPARAGUS & APPLE SALAD
sałatka ze szparagów z jabłkiem

Combine 1 lb. cooked, cut-up asparagus with 1 peeled, diced apple and 4 T. finely chopped walnut meats. Divide into portions and place each on a lettuce leaf. Dress with mayonnaise and decorate each portion with hard-boiled egg wedges and tomato wedges.

ASPARAGUS & HAM SALAD
sałatka ze szparagów z szynką

Divide cooked, cut-up asparagus into portions and place each on lettuce leaf. Evenly distribute 1 c. diced, boiled ham and 2 diced, hard-boiled eggs over portions and dress with mustard mayonnaise. Garnish with chopped parsley.

EGG SALAD
sałatka z jaj

Cut 5 hard-cooked eggs into 4 wedges each, then cut each wedge in ½ widthwise. Arrange on lettuce-lined serving dish, taking care that yolks do not separate from whites. Coarsely grate 2 peeled apples and sprinkle with lemon juice so they don't turn dark. Spread grated apples over eggs and dress with about ¾ c. sour cream & horseradish sauce.

EGG & POTATO SALAD
sałatka z jaj z kartoflami

Combine 2 finely chopped onions with 1 T. lemon juice, ½ t. powdered sugar, and ¼ t. salt, cover, and let stand 20 min. Meanwhile, cook 3 med. potatoes in jackets, peel when cool, and dice. Combine potatoes with 4–5 diced hard-cooked eggs, 2 peeled, diced tart apples, and drained onions. Toss lightly, salt & pepper to taste, sprinkle with 2 T. chopped chives, and dress with ½–¾ c. plain mayonnaise. Decorate with parsley sprigs.

CHEESE SALAD
sałatka z sera

Combine 1 c. diced yellow cheese, 1 peeled, diced apple, 1 diced mild red pepper (with seeds removed), and 1 c. drained canned baby peas. Sprinkle with salt & pepper, garnish with 1 T. chopped parsley, and lace with plain mayonnaise to taste. Transfer mixture to lettuce-lined serving dish, garnish with 1 chopped hard-cooked egg, and decorate with tomato wedges.

CHEESE & HAM SALAD
sałatka z sera i szynki

Combine 1 c. diced yellow cheese, ½ c. diced boiled ham, and ½ c. drained canned baby peas. Dress with ½ c. or so mustard mayonnaise. Decorate top of salad with radish slices and surround with radish roses. *Optional*: For added crunch, toss in 6–8 diced radishes.

HERRING SALAD
sałatka śledziowa

Soak 2 salt herring in water overnight. Dry, skin, remove bones, and dice or cut into thin strips. Combine herring with 3 potatoes, cooked in jackets and peeled when cold, 2 chopped onions, 2 diced brine-cured or vinegar-type dill pickles, 1 large peeled, diced apple, and 1 c. drained canned baby peas. Toss lightly so as not to damage peas and dress with 1 c. basic mayonnaise sauce or mustard. Serve on lettuce-lined dish decorated with brightly colored garnishes: radishes, strips of red pepper, or tomato wedges.

HERRING & BEAN SALAD
sałatka śledziowa z fasolą

Soak 2 salt herring overnight in cold water, then skin, fillet, and cut into thin strips. Finely chop 2 onions, sprinkle with 1 t. sugar, and stir in ⅓ c. basic mayonnaise sauce. Peel and dice 2 apples, sprinkle with several t. lemon juice, and mix with onion mixture. Add the herring, 1 c. cooked or canned and drained pea beans, and 3 chopped hard-boiled egg whites.

Sprinkle with 1 T. chopped parsley and chives and toss to blend ingredients. Transfer to serving dish, drench with ⅓ c. basic mayonnaise sauce, and top with 3 sieved, hard-boiled egg yolks. Garnish with another T. chopped parsley and chives.

HERRING & VEGETABLE SALAD
sałatka śledziowa z warzywami

Dice 2 beets (cooked in jackets and skinned when cool), 2 cooked carrots, and 1 peeled apple. Sprinkle diced vegetables with several t. lemon juice. Add 1 c. cooked or canned drained pea beans or navy beans, 2 chopped onions, and 3 T. chopped parsley. Sprinkle with 4 T. olive or other salad oil, add 2 herring (soaked overnight in water, filleted, and cut into strips), and toss ingredients. Place on serving dish and provide basic mayonnaise sauce on the side for your guests to help themselves. *Variation*: 1–2 peeled, diced potatoes cooked in jackets may also be added.

MOCK LOBSTER POLONAISE
"homar" po polsku

This gourmet salad is in a class of its own. Although not too pricey and easy to prepare, it can grace the most elegant dinner-party and may well leave your guests convinced they are feasting on lobster. Chances are they'll help themselves to seconds and ask for the recipe. Remove skin and fishbones from 1 lb. smoked halibut. Place in bowl and with 2 forks break meat into small pieces. Add 2 raw, finely grated carrots and toss with fish. Add juice of 1 lemon and 1 c. mayonnaise and mix. Cover and refrigerate 2 hrs. before serving. Serve on dish decorated with curls of Boston lettuce. That's all there is to it! *Note*: Other smoked fish like cod may be used, but only smoked halibut makes this dish what it is.

CRAYFISH SALAD
sałatka z raków

Remove meat from 10–15 crayfish (cooked in boiling water with dill the normal way) and arrange in serving dish. Add 2 diced potatoes (cooked in jackets and peeled when cool) and 2 diced, hard-boiled eggs. Dress with ⅓ c. mustard vinaigrette or mayonnaise vinaigrette. Rim serving dish with cucumber swirls and sprinkle salad with chopped dill and parsley.

SMOKED-EEL SALAD
sałatka z wędzonego węgorza

Skin and remove backbone from 1 smoked eel and dice meat. Dice 1 cooked celeriac, 2–3 potatoes cooked in jackets, and 2–3 peeled apples. Sprinkle vegetables and apple with juice of ½ lemon and diced eel with several pinches savory. Combine ingredients, season with salt & pepper, and dress with about ½ c. basic mayonnaise sauce. Cover and refrigerate 1–2 hrs.

SMOKED-FISH SALAD
sałatka z ryby wędzonej

Combine 1 c. diced, cooked potatoes, 1 med. chopped onion, and 1 c. or so diced, smoked fish (with skin and bones removed). Dress with ⅓–½ c. vinaigrette with egg yolk. Garnish with 1 chopped hard-boiled egg and a little chopped parsley. *Variation*: Dress with basic mayonnaise sauce or mayonnaise vinaigrette. *Note*: Although any smoked fish may be used in this salad, we feel smoked carp or whitefish are best of the fresh water fish and smoked halibut or cod of the ocean variety. Those preferring a leaner fish should like smoked mackerel or herring.

FISH SALAD
sałatka rybna

A tasty salad can be prepared using leftover cooked fish. When preparing fried fish for dinner, why not fry up 2–3 extra fillets, refrigerate them overnight, and use them in this recipe for the following day's supper? Simply combine 1 c. diced, cooked fish fillets with 2 diced, cooked potatoes, ½ c. diced dill pickles (vinegar type), and 1 peeled, diced apple. Sprinkle with a little lemon juice and dress with mayonnaise-based sauce of choice. *Variation*: Feel free to add other ingredients to this versatile salad like some drained canned peas or peas & carrots, a diced, cooked, or canned beet, a chopped onion or green onions, a few diced radishes, etc. For a gourmet touch, sprinkle diced fish with 2–3 T. dry white wine and let stand 15 min. Then drain and combine with other ingredients as above.

FISH & MUSHROOM SALAD
sałatka rybna z grzybami

Combine 1 c. diced, smoked fish or cooked fillets with 12 finely diced, pickled mushrooms, 2 chopped onions, 1 peeled, diced apple, and about 4 T. chopped chives. Dress with ⅓ c. plain vinaigrette and serve on lettuce-lined dish decorated with tomato wedges.

MAYONNAISE FISH SCOOPS
majoneziki z ryb

Although not a true salad, these interesting cold appetizers are a nice addition to your starter-course spread and let you put that leftover cooked fish to good use. With a fork, break up several cold, fried, or poached fish fillets into flakes. Sprinkle with some lemon juice and chopped dill, and add just enough mayonnaise to bind fish together. Use ice-cream scoop to scoop portions onto lettuce leaves. Pour a little fork-blended mayonnaise over each scoop, garnish with chopped chives, and decorate with radish slices. Surround scoops with hard-boiled egg wedges dusted with paprika and salted and peppered tomato wedges.

MUSHROOM SALAD
sałatka grzybowa

Sauté 1 c. chopped onion in 2 T. oil until tender but unbrowned. Add 3 med. cooked cold potatoes, diced, and toss with onions. Cover and set aside to cool. Cut 2 c. drained, pickled, or brined mushrooms into strips, and combine with cold onion and potatoes, 1 c. peeled, coarsely grated apple, and 2 buds crushed garlic. Toss to blend ingredients and dress with mayonnaise. Serve on lettuce leaves and decorate salad with several whole pickled or brined mushrooms.

MEAT SALAD
sałatka mięsna

Soak 6–8 prunes in water 1 hr. Drain, dry, remove pits, and dice. While they soak, combine 1–1½ c. diced, cooked pork or veal, 2–3 diced, cooked potatoes, 3 diced dill pickles, 2 peeled, diced apples, 1 small cooked celeriac, peeled and diced, 1 c. drained, canned peas & carrots. Add diced prunes, 1 finely chopped onion, and 2–3 buds crushed garlic. Toss lightly to blend ingredients, season to taste with salt, pepper, a pinch or so sugar, and a sprinkle of lemon juice. Dress with ¾ c. mustard sauce. Mound salad on lettuce-lined serving dish and pour over another ⅓ c. sauce. Sprinkle with chopped chives, place a radish rose at center of mound and decorate salad with thin rounds of cooked carrot and/or strips of fresh or pickled red peppers.

EASIER MEAT SALAD
sałatka mięsna łatwiejsza

If you don't have all the above ingredients on hand or don't care for such a big variety, this meat salad is also very tasty and so simple to whip up. Simply combine 1½ c. diced, cooked

cooked veal or pork with 1½ c. drained, cooked frozen, fresh or canned peas and ½ c. diced mild red pepper (with seeds discarded). Salt & pepper to taste and dress with ½ c. plain, mustard, or horseradish mayonnaise. On serving dish, decorate with Boston-lettuce leaves and radish roses. *Optional*: For added color, zest, and crunch, feel free to add any of the ingredients recommended for the meat salad above.

POULTRY SALAD
sałatka z drobiu

Combine 1½ c. diced boneless cooked chicken, turkey, goose, or duck (or any combination thereof) with 5–6 diced, pitted, spiced plums, 1 peeled, diced apple, 1 diced hard-boiled egg, and ½ c. drained, canned (or cooked frozen or fresh) peas. Toss ingredients lightly, salt & pepper to taste, and dress with ½ c. or so mayonnaise. Mound particles on lettuce leaves, surround with tomato wedges, and decorate with parsley sprigs.

HAM SALAD
sałatka z szynki

Combine 1½ c. diced boiled ham, 1 c. cooked, diced potatoes and 3–4 diced dill pickles. Dress with about ½ c. plain or mustard vinaigrette with 1–2 buds crushed garlic added, mayonnaise vinaigrette, basic mayonnaise sauce, mustard mayonnaise, or horseradish mayonnaise. Sprinkle with about 1 T. chopped parsley. Mound on serving dish rimmed with alternating cucumber and radish slices.

AUTUMN (BEEF) SALAD
sałatka jesienna (z wołowiną)

Peel and coarsely grate 1 uncooked celeriac and mix with 2 peeled, diced apples. Sprinkle with juice of ½ lemon. Finely chop 1 onion and 1 bud garlic and mix with apple-celeriac mixture. Add 2 c. cold diced roast beef and 2–3 T. chopped parsley. Toss, salt & pepper to taste, and dress with ½ c. plain vinaigrette. Refrigerate at least 1 hr. before serving. *Variation*: Use diced boiled beef tongue in place of roast beef.

SAUSAGE & CELERIAC SALAD
sałatka z kiełbasy i selera

Cook 1 med. unpeeled celeriac in boiling water until cooked but still firm when pierced with knife, peel under cold running water, dice and sprinkle with lemon juice. When cool, combine with 1 c. skinned, diced, garlicky smoked kiełbasa (krakowska is very good) and 2–4 diced, cooked potatoes. Sprinkle with 1–2 T. chopped garden cress and dress with about ½ c. plain or mustard vinaigrette. Salt & pepper to taste if necessary. Refrigerate at least 1 hr. for flavors to blend. *Note*: Stalk celery is not widely used in Polish cuisine, but feel free to use it in place of celeriac if you haven't got the latter on hand.

FRANKFURTER & TOMATO SALAD
sałatka z parówek i pomidorów

Combine 4–5 high quality, diced skinless frankfurters (or equivalent amount of skinned knackwurst, bologna, or canned luncheon meat like Treet or Spam) with 4–5 small firm tomatoes, diced, and 1 chopped onion. Toss ingredients and transfer to lettuce-lined serving dish. Season to taste with salt, pepper, sugar, and wine vinegar. *Variation*: If 1 or 2 unexpected guests arrive, add 2–3 diced, cooked potatoes to above ingredients and dress with mustard vinaigrette. It will also be very good.

CRUNCHY FRANKFURTER SALAD
sałatka z parówek chrupiąca

Combine 4 diced, skinless franks (or similar meat as above) with 4 chopped green onions (greens & bulbs), 1 bunch thinly sliced radishes, 3 small, diced, firm tomatoes, 1 med. peeled cucumber, diced, and (optional) 1–2 diced dill pickles. Toss ingredients and transfer to serving dish. Decorate with curly lettuce leaves. Fork-blend ½ c. mustard vinaigrette with 1 T. Polish plum sauce and pour over salad. Refrigerate 1–2 hrs. before serving so that flavors may blend.

MAYONNAISE MEAT SCOOPS
majoneziki z mięsa

Anywhere from 1 to several c. diced, cooked meat can be used in this recipe. This can be leftover pork, veal or beef, poultry, ham or any combination thereof you like. If diced meat is not highly seasoned, you may want to salt & pepper to taste. If you like your food on the zesty side, several dashes of Polish hunter's seasoning or one of your other homemade seasonings is recommended. To meat add just enough mayonnaise to bind meat together, mix well, and chill 1 hr. Use ice-cream scoop to scoop portions of salad onto lettuce leaves. Spoon a little more mayonnaise over each and garnish with chopped greens of choice.

COLD STUFFED TOMATOES
pomidory faszerowane na zimno

Wash and dry 8 small, firm tomatoes. Cut off tops about ¾ of the way up and scoop out most of the pulp, leaving a little around the walls so tomatoes retain their shape. Invert tomatoes cut side down to allow moisture to drain (about 30 min.). Fill tomatoes with salad of choice, so it protrudes about ½ inch. We are partial to green-pea salad, to which a little diced ham may be added, but any of the mayonnaise-based meat, fish, or even vegetable salads make a good filling for stuffed tomatoes. Replace top tomato slices, arrange tomatoes on lettuce-lined serving dish, and chill 1–2 hrs. Just before serving, decorate tops and sides of stuffed tomatoes with mayonnaise in decorator tube. *Note*: Freeze up the leftover tomato scoopings for use in sauces, soups, and gołąbki.

TOMATOES LACED WITH EGGS
pomidory przekładane jajkiem

Wash and dry 4 firm med. tomatoes. Stand each stem side down and cut into vertical slices about ¼ inch apart but only ¾ of the way down so tomatoes hold together. Into each opening insert a hard-boiled egg slice. Place tomatoes on lettuce leaves and decorate with mayonnaise in decorator tube. *Variation*: Fill alternating openings with hard-boiled egg slices and meat, poultry, or fish salad (mayonnaise type).

COLD STUFFED CUCUMBERS
ogórki faszerowane na zimno

Wash, dry, and peel 4 small cucumbers. Cut in ½ lengthwise and with spoon scoop out and discard pulpy seed portion. Fill cucumbers with mayonnaise-laced meat, poultry, or fish salad of choice so that it is slightly heaped. Arrange on platter decorated with tomato, hard-boiled egg wedges, and curly lettuce leaves, and chill at least 1 hr. before serving.

STUFFED CUCUMBER "CORKS"
korki z ogórków faszerowane

Wash, dry, and peel 1 large cucumber. Cut into 2 inch pieces. Stand each piece up and scoop out pulpy seed portion and some of the dry flesh, leaving about ½ inch at bottom. Fill cucumber "corks" with meat, poultry, or fish salad of choice (but only the mayonnaise variety) so it protrudes at the top. Round the tops with spoon and stick a tuft of dill or sprig of parsley in each. Chill at least 1 hr. before serving. *Variation*: For an interesting, zebra-like color contrast, do not peel cucumbers. After cutting into 2 inch pieces, use potato-peeler to remove vertical strips of skin at regular intervals. This produces a bar effect of alternating pale-green cucumber and dark-green skin. (See illustration in appetizer chapter.)

CUCUMBERS STUFFED WITH CHEESE
ogórki nadziewane twarogiem

Season 1½ c. ground or finely grated farmer's cheese with salt, pepper, and paprika to taste, add 3–4 T. chopped chives, and 2 heaping T. mayonnaise. Mix until blended, adding just enough sour cream to get a thick, smooth mixture. Use cheese mixture to stuff cucumbers prepared as for cold stuffed cucumbers or stuffed cucumber "corks" (above). Chill 1–2 hrs. before serving. Serve on lettuce leaves in a ring of overlapping radish slices.

PEPPERS STUFFED WITH CAULIFLOWER
papryka nadziewana kalafiorem

Cut 4 med. green, yellow, or red bell peppers in ½ widthwise to form 8 salad cases. Remove seed portion, rinse, and dry. Fill peppers with cauliflower salad (presented earlier in this chapter) and chill at least 1 hr. before serving. Serve with color-contrasting garnishes. *Variation*: Peppers are also good stuffed with mayonnaise-laced meat, poultry, or fish salad of choice.

COLD STUFFED CELERIAC
selery faszerowane na zimno

Cook 4 small to med. unpeeled celeriacs in boiling water until tender but still firm, and set aside to cool. Peel, cut in ½, and use spoon to scoop out some of the flesh to make an indentation. Dice the scoopings and combine with 1–1½ c. cooked, diced meat (any combination of roasts, ham, kiełbasa, etc. is good), 1 peeled, diced apple and several diced, zesty gherkins or marinated mushrooms. Mix with mayonnaise and mound portions of salad in celeriac halves. Chill at least 1 hr. before serving. Serve each portion on a lettuce leaf and garnish with chopped chives.

HOT APPETIZERS & HORS D'OEUVRES

Hot starter courses were in their prime in a slower-paced era, when the more well-to-do had time for leisurely socializing that lasted for hours on end. At one time, in fact, there were often several such hot entrées—egg dishes, fish, meat—brought in by servants one by one, as the *podczaszy* (cup-bearer) made sure no guests had an empty glass. And this, it should be remembered, was all before the main hot course of the evening!

Today, such entertaining is largely confined to the diplomatic circuit, but there may be times when you might like to surprise your guests with at least one hot starter course. Actually, we faced a dilemma whether or not to even include this chapter. After all, many of the fancier egg dishes and nearly all the hot meat, poultry, game, and fish selections could double as hot appetizers. The major difference from the main course is that the portions are somewhat smaller, and starter courses are normally not served with all the main course accompaniments such as potatoes, cooked vegetables, salad etc.

On the other hand, the entries in this chapter can also be served as a hot supper and need not be preceded by cold appetizers and soup, nor followed by a main course. Whatever your preference, we strongly recommend you try a truly delightful Polish favorite, hot stuffed eggs in shells, which we have used to kick off this chapter.

Also very nice are the savory puff pastries, tarts and pies, the pan-fried mushrooms, and a few gourmet fish dishes not found in the fish chapter. Steak fanciers will enjoy the flaming beefsteak, beef Stroganoff, and tenderloin tips, and those with a Polish palate will be partial to the bigos served up in a seashell or stoneware bowl. In fact, upon reconsidering, we think you will find enough worthwhile entries in this chapter to warrant its inclusion in this book. And we hope cocktail party devotees will enjoy some of the hot, one-bite hors d'oeuvres found at the very end.

* * *

HOT STUFFED EGGS IN SHELLS
jajka faszerowane w skorupkach

Hard boil 4 eggs and cool in cold running water. Wipe eggs. Take hold of egg set on firm dish-towel-covered table or counter-top, and give it a swift tap along its length with a sharp, thin, preferably heavy knife, then quickly cut it through lengthwise, shell and all. (Do not use knife with serrated blade!) With small spoon, gently scoop out cooked yolks and whites, taking care not to damage shell. Discard any loose, jagged splinters around edge of shells. Chop egg whites and yolks very fine or grind. Stir in 1 heaping T. soft butter, and 1

T. chopped chives, 1 T. chopped dill and salt & pepper to taste. (*Variation*: Instead of butter, use 1 heaping T. sour cream). Mix well. Stuff egg shells with mixture, pressing down gently. Dip in bread crumbs, pressing down gently and shaking off excess. These may be prepared several hrs. ahead of time and refrigerated until ready to use. Just before serving, sauté egg halves open-side-down in 1–2 T. butter. They are ready when a golden-brown crust forms at bottom and shells are hot to the touch, meaning their contents have been sufficiently heated through. Serve immediately with French bread. These eggs may also be served as an accompaniment to soups, especially clear beet soup, broths, and sorrel soup. *Note:* Another version of this tasty dish, made with sautéed onions, is found in the egg chapter of this book.

OMELETS, STEAMED PUDDINGS & SOUFFLÉS
omlety, budynie, suflety

Most savory omelets, steamed puddings (cooked in boiling water in pudding molds), and soufflés make an excellent light starter dish to precede your main course. Suggested recipes are found in the egg chapter and elsewhere in this book.

HOT HERRING ROLL-UPS
ruloniki śledziowe na gorąco

Rinse and dry 1 lb. fresh herring fillets, sprinkle with salt & pepper, and refrigerate 30 min. On each fillet, place a thin slice of bacon the length of the fillet. Place a pitted prune at one end and roll up tightly, fastening roll-up with toothpick. Generously butter a heat-proof baking dish, arrange roll-ups therein, and bake in 325° oven about 30 min. Serve in dish in which they were baked.

BAKED SOLE WITH MUSHROOMS
sola zapiekana z pieczarkami

Place 1 lb. sole fillets in buttered baking dish, sprinkle with salt, 1 T. dry white wine, 1 T. lemon juice, and top with about 12 oz. washed, dried, and sliced fresh mushrooms. Dot with butter, season with pepper and/or Polish fish seasoning, and pour 1 c. coffee cream over everything. Bake at 350° about 20 min. After carefully transferring to serving platter, sprinkle with paprika, and brown slightly under broiling flame of oven. *Note*: Flounder fillets may be prepared the same way.

This illustration shows the step-by-step preparation of hot stuffed eggs in shells—one of Polish cuisine's tastiest hot appetizers which also makes a nice supper dish.

CARP POACHED IN BLACK SAUCE
karp w czarnym sosie

For this Old Polish delicacy you will need a live 2–2½ lb. carp and its blood. If you are too squeamish to bleed it yourself, have your fish monger collect the blood in a jar containing 1 T. lemon juice (to prevent curdling). While you're at it, have the fish filleted. Rinse and dry fillets, sprinkle with salt, and refrigerate 1 hr. Meanwhile, in pot combine 2 c. water, 2 coarsely chopped onions, 4 peppercorns, 4 grains allspice, 1 bay leaf, ½ t. salt and ¼ t. each ginger and marjoram. Cook until onions are tender, then strain, discarding spices and sieving the onions into strained stock. Add 1 c. dark beer (porter, bock, stout), stir in the blood, bring to boil, add the fillets and simmer on very low heat 15–20 min. Make a white roux with 2 T. butter and 1 T. flour, dilute with 2–3 T. dry red wine, add a little sauce from fish, and simmer several min., whisking until smooth. Add to pot together with 3 T. ground walnuts and about 1 t. sugar. Simmer gently about 5 min. Transfer fish to platter and pour sauce over it.

OLD POLISH PIKE IN RAISIN SAUCE
szczupak po staropolsku

Place trimmings (backbone, head with eyes removed, tail) of a very fresh, filleted, 3 lb. pike in pot, cover with 3½ c. water, add ½ t. salt, and simmer 20 min. Add 3 carrots, 3 onions, a bunch of parsley, 2 bay leaves, 4 cloves, a tiny splinter of cinnamon bark, and a pinch of grated nutmeg, and cook on low heat until carrots are tender. While it cooks, salt and refrigerate pike fillets. Strain stock, sieving carrots and onions back into pot, but discarding spices. Place fillets in hot stock, add ½ c. dry white wine, 2 T. olive oil, 2 heaping T. raisins, 1 peeled, sliced onion, and 1 t. sugar. Cook covered on very low heat 20 min. Meanwhile, prepare roux with 2 T. butter and 1 T. flour, dilute with 1 c. hot stock, simmering several min. and whisking until smooth, then add to pot. Bring to boil once. Transfer fish with slotted spoon to serving platter and drench with sauce.

HALIBUT IN WALNUT SAUCE
halibut w sosie orzechowym

Wash and dry 1 lb. halibut fillets. Mince fine 1 bud garlic, mash with ½ t. salt, rub fillets with mixture, sprinkle with lemon juice, and refrigerate 30 min. In pot combine 1½ c. water, ½ c. dry red wine, 1 coarsely chopped onion, 1 t. chopped parsley, 3 cloves, and ¼ t. pepper, and simmer covered about 20 min. Add fillets and simmer another 15–20 min. covered. Carefully transfer fish to warmed serving dish and keep warm in oven. To stock add 1 bud minced garlic and ½ c. ground walnuts and bring to boil. Pour sauce over fish and serve at once.

WALLEYE IN GREEN SAUCE
sandacz w zielonym sosie

Poach 1 lb. walleye fillets in 3 c. strong court bouillon about 15 min., or until fully cooked (1 lb.), but still firm. As they cook, make a white roux with 3 T. butter and 2 T. flour, stirring in 1 c. hot fish stock and simmering several min. When smooth, stir in ½ c. fork-blended sour cream and ¼ c. dry white wine. Bring to boil, then switch off heat. Season to taste with salt, pepper and lemon juice and add 3 T. finely chopped parsley, dill, and chives. Remove cooked fish with slotted spoon to platter and drench with hot sauce.

BRAISED COD IN LEMON SAUCE
dorsz w sosie cytrynowym

Rinse and dry 1 lb. cod fillets, salt & pepper, and sauté in 3–4 T. butter or oil (skin side first if unskinned fillets are used!) until nice and golden on the outside but still uncooked on the inside. Transfer fish to pot. In same skillet, sauté 1 finely chopped onion and 1 T. butter until tender and golden and add to fish. Add ¾ c. court bouillon and ¼ c. dry white wine, ¼ t. ground nutmeg and ¼ t. ginger, and simmer covered on low heat about 10 min. Transfer fish to platter and keep warm in 150° oven. Make the white roux with 1 T. butter and 2 t. flour, dilute with a little stock, and simmer briefly, whisking until smooth. Stir into pot, add 2 t. grated lemon rind (zest), and bring to boil. Add juice of ½ lemon and 1 T. chopped parsley. Stir and adjust seasoning with salt and a little sugar. Drench fish with hot sauce on platter.

SALT COD IN CREAM SAUCE
sztokfisz w sosie śmietanowym

Soak 1 lb. dried salt cod in cold water 48 hrs., changing water 2–3 times. A quicker way is to pound the salt cod vigorously with flat side of kitchen mallet until it swells. This loosens the salt and usually makes an overnight soaking in cold water sufficient. Cut up into small pieces, place in pot, add 8 c. unsalted court bouillon, and simmer gently about 30 min. Meanwhile, make a roux with 1 T. butter and 2 t. flour, add 1 T. chopped parsley, and stir in 1 c. sour cream. Simmer gently, whisking until smooth. Fork-blend 2 eggs yolks with 2 T. of sauce and return to pot. Drain cod and break up into flakes, add to sauce, season with a grating of nutmeg (run whole nutmeg over grater once or twice), and heat well but do not boil. Arrange ring of cooked rice on platter and pour creamed cod into center.

BOILED CRAYFISH
raki z wody

Since the Baltic was never home to crabs, shrimps, or lobsters, these pricey imported delicacies were available only to Poland's privileged few. Still both noblemen and peasants alike were able to feast to their heart's content on a local substitute, the crayfish, found in abundance along the shores and shallows of Polish lakes, ponds, and streams. Since each crayfish contains only a few morsels of tasty meat in its tail and paws, quite a few must be gathered to make a meal. To prepare, keep 40–60 live crayfish in a large pan or tub of cold water several hrs. so they can clean themselves out. (*Note:* Some people add a handful of salt to speed up the process, but purists frown on this method because it kills the crayfish which, they insist, must be cooked live.) Whichever method you choose, in large pot bring to boil 2 gallons of water containing 3–4 heaping T. salt and 1–2 bunches of dill. Scrub crayfish with brush under cold running water, rinse well, and drop into boiling water one by one so boiling does not stop. Cook about 15 min. from the time the last crayfish was added. Remove crayfish with slotted spoon and drain in colander. Bring a steaming, mounded platter of these crimson crustaceans (they turn red during cooking like lobsters!) to table for your guests to enjoy. *Note:* In addition to this dramatic presentation and the great taste of boiled crayfish, they also make for a culinary adventure and are a great ice-breaker. Soon, even the stodgiest of dinner guests will be good-naturedly debating on the best way to dismember these crustaceans and get at their tasty meat. At Polish gatherings, the host and/or guests are likely to intersperse the proceedings with periodic calls of *"Raki lubią pływać!"* ("Crayfish like to swim!")—the signal for yet another round of wódka. We strongly advise against observing the principle of some crayfish-lovers: a shot of wódka for each crayfish. The results could be disastrous, considering that 12–15 crayfish make up a single serving.

CREAMED CRAYFISH POLONAISE
raki po polsku

Cook 30–40 crayfish as above. Drain. Remove black intestinal vein by twisting tail fin and easing it out. Remove meat and heat gently with 2–3 c. basic white sauce. Sprinkle with 2 T. chopped dill and serve on platter in a ring of cooked Kraków groats or saffron rice.

CRAYFISH À LA RADZIWIŁŁ
raki à la Radziwiłł

Rub 4 bowl-sized seashells or individual stoneware dishes generously with butter. Into each place meat of about 10 crayfish cooked as above. Sprinkle with salt & pepper, top each portion with heaping T. sour cream, sprinkle with grated yellow cheese (about ¼ c. per bowl) and 1 t. ground blanched almonds. Bake in 375° oven about 20 min. or until lightly browned and serve immediately. *Note:* For other hot starter courses served in seashells or stoneware bowls see below.

CRAYFISH WILNO STYLE
raki po wileńsku

Fill 4 generously buttered seashells or stoneware bowls with meat of about 10 crayfish each. Sprinkle each with 1 t. prepared horseradish or ½ t. freshly grated horseradish root and 1 t. ground walnuts. Salt & pepper lightly. Fork-blend 1 c. sour cream with 2 egg yolks and drench individual portions with mixture. Bake in 375° oven 20–25 min. Sprinkle with chopped parsley before serving.

STUFFED CRAYFISH
raki nadziewane

Cook 20 larger crayfish as above. Remove and discard black intestinal vein. Remove meat and set aside. Clean out crayfish shells, discarding pincers (or saving them for crayfish butter). In dry skillet combine ½ c. Kraków groats with 1 beaten egg; heat until groats are evenly coated with egg and dry, stirring constantly. Transfer mixture to small pot containing 1 c. boiling water, add ¼ t. salt and 1 T. butter, and pop into 375° oven covered for 30 min. or until groats are cooked. When cool, mix in 1 egg, 1 T. chopped dill and/or parsley, diced crayfish meat, and salt to taste if needed. Fill shells with mixture and place snugly in baking dish. Add 1 c. court bouillon and 2–3 T. crayfish butter (see cold sauces). Cover and simmer about 15 min. Serve immediately on platter garnished with sprigs of dill. *Note:* At elegant banquets, stuffed crayfish are sometimes used to rim platters on which fish dishes are served.

CRAYFISH & MUSHROOM FRICASSEE
potrawka z raków z pieczarkami

Sauté 8 oz. washed, dried, sliced, fresh mushrooms in 1 T. butter until tender, about 10–15 min., or until moisture evaporates. Add 2 T. court bouillon, 1 T. crayfish butter, meat of 20 cooked crayfish, and 2 c. basic white sauce with 1–2 raw egg yolks added. Season to taste with salt & pepper, and sprinkle with 1 T. each chopped dill and parsley. Simmer briefly and serve over rice or egg noodles.

FRICASSEES BAKED IN SEASHELLS OR STONEWARE BOWLS
potrawki zapiekane w muszelkach lub kamionkach

Portions of fricasseed dishes baked in real bowl-sized seashells make for an elegant starter course at any dinner party. If such shells are not available, stoneware, or other heatproof (glass, crockery etc.) bowls may be used. These are small more than little casseroles, served in the same containers in which they were baked, but somehow they always seem to add a special, festive touch. Almost any creamed or fricasseed dish may be served in this way, including creamed mushrooms, stews, tripe, and bigos. Simply fill shells or heatproof bowls with portions of cold, fully cooked, stewed dish, and bake in 375° oven 20–30 min. or until top begins to brown slightly. Bowls containing creamed mushrooms or tripe may be sprinkled with bread crumbs and grated yellow cheese before baking. A whole button mushroom, cap side up, may be placed at center of bowls containing bigos before baking. If using uncooked mushrooms, brush with oil or melted butter before baking.

MUSHROOMS À L'ESCARGOT (SNAIL FASHION)
pieczarki à la ślimaki

Wash 20 fresh cultivated mushrooms and cut off stems (which should be reserved for some other dish). Mince fine 3 buds garlic and mash on cutting board with ½ t. salt into a paste. Combine garlic paste in small bowl with 5 T. butter, 1 t. lemon juice, and a pinch of pepper. Spread a little mixture on the underside of each mushroom cap and place in baking dish cut side up. Just before serving, pop into 375° oven and bake about 20 min. Serve immediately.

BUTTER-FRIED MUSHROOMS
pieczarki lub rydze z patelni

Being light and non-filling but very tasty, mushrooms are a natural for hot starter courses which are meant to stimulate the appetite, not satiate it. Particularly good are domestic white mushrooms or wild milky caps (rydze), simply fried to a nice golden brown in butter (see mushroom chapter). If you have a nice company-quality skillet, use it to fry mushrooms and bring them to the table right in the skillet, inviting guests to help themselves. Provide good rye or French bread to sop up the buttery drippings which will have taken on a nice reddish hue if milky caps were used.

BEEF STROGANOFF
boeuf à la Stroganow

Although named after a 19th century Russian nobleman-diplomat, this exquisite dish entered Poland's culinary repertoire not directly from neighboring Russia but via Paris, as reflected by its French-sounding name. In Poland it is served almost exclusively as a hot starter dish, usually in individual stoneware bowls. Trim 1 lb. beef tenderloin of any sinews, wash, pat dry, and cut in ½ inch slices. Pound with meat mallet and cut into ½ inch strips. Sauté in several T. butter until lightly browned on both sides but still raw on the inside and transfer to pot. In same drippings, sauté 8 oz. washed, sliced, fresh, cultivated mushrooms until moisture steams away and mushrooms turn a nice golden brown. Add mushrooms to meat. Add a little more butter to skillet and sauté 2 onions sliced wafer thin until tender and slightly browned. Combine meat, mushrooms, and onions, stir in 1 c. sour cream fork-blended with 1 T. flour, and simmer on low heat about 5 min. Season to taste with salt & pepper. A sprinkling of chopped dill is recommended just before serving.

TENDERLOIN TIPS POLONAISE
tournedos po polsku

Pound to ½ their original thickness four 1 inch thick slices of beef tenderloin (tip end). With knife blade, even up ends into circular cutlets. In skillet, sauté 12 oz. washed, sliced, fresh, cultivated mushrooms until moisture evaporates and they begin to sizzle. Set aside and keep warm. Slice French bread 1 inch thick, remove crusts and scoop out an indentation at center. (Reserve crusts and bread scoopings for later use as bread crumbs in ground meat dishes etc.) Fry bread slices scooped-side-up in a little butter or oil until bottom is golden brown, with mushrooms in the indentation at top. *(Note:* The bread slices should be roughly the size of your tenderloin cutlets.) Sprinkle meat with Polish beef seasoning, dust with flour through sieve, and fry in 1 T. hot lard on both sides until as done as you like. Place steaks on top of toasted, mushroom-filled bread slices (which should have been kept warm in a 150° oven) and serve immediately. Next to each portion place a baked tart shell filled with tangy cranberry-currant sauce or lingonberry sauce (see cold savory sauces).

MINCED BEEFSTEAK FLAMBÉ
befsztyk siekany płonący

Trim 1 lb. beef tenderloin of any sinews, wash, dry, and grind coarsely together with 1 small to med. onion. Mix meat well with 2 raw egg yolks, 3 T. olive oil, 4 T. grated yellow cheese (preferably tilsit), 1 t. chopped parsley, and salt & pepper to taste. Form into 8 small oval patties, sprinkle tops with a few drops lemon juice, and place in heat-proof serving dish. Pour ¼ t. 190-proof grain alcohol over each patty, ignite, and bring flaming to table. When flames die out, they are ready to eat. Provide Old Polish plum sauce on the side. *Variation:* If you find these too rare, brown briefly in oiled skillet before adding alcohol and lighting.

HOT HAM ROLL-UPS
roladki z szynki na gorąco

Combine 5 T. butter, 8 T. grated yellow cheese, and 4 T. ground walnuts. Spread 8 thin slices boiled ham with mixture, roll up tightly, and place in greased baking dish. Shortly before serving pop into 375° oven for 10 min. Serve immediately in baking dish. *Optional:* For a flambé effect, mix 2 t. brandy with 2 t. grain alcohol, sprinkle roll-ups with mixture, light, and bring flaming to table.

HUNTER'S BIGOS (MEAT & SAUERKRAUT STEW)
bigos myśliwski

Dice ¼ lb. salt pork and ¼ lb. slab bacon (minus rind) and fry up together into golden nuggets. Remove nuggets and set aside. In drippings, brown lightly 3–4 diced onions. Drain (reserving juice) 1 qt. sauerkraut, rinse in cold running water, and allow to drip dry. Shred 1 small head cabbage, scald with boiling water, bring to boil, and simmer 5 min. Drain. Combine cabbage, sauerkraut, onions, and browned salt-pork and bacon nuggets. Dice 8 oz. pitted prunes and add to mixture. Cut 1½–2 lbs. pork into small cubes. Place a layer of sauerkraut mixture in enameled pot or Dutch oven, add a layer of meat, then a layer of sauerkraut, a layer of skinned, sliced, smoked kielbasa, then sauerkraut, and continue layering until ingredients are used up. You will need about 1 lb. kielbasa, and top layer should be sauerkraut. Add 1 c. meat stock or water and cook uncovered on med. heat about 30 min. Then reduce heat as low as possible and simmer 2 hrs. After 1st hr., cover. Stir occasionally to prevent scorching. Cool to room temp. and refrigerate overnight. Next day, simmer on very low heat on stovetop or in 325° oven 2–3 hrs. After 1 hr. add ½ c. dry red wine and season with Polish pork seasoning, hunter's seasoning or sauerkraut seasoning according to preference. Refrigerate overnight again. When ready to serve, fill stoneware or other individual heatproof bowls with cold bigos, top each portion with 3 thin slices skinned, smoked kielbasa and a pre-soaked, pitted prune and heat in 350° oven 20–30 min. Serve with rye and/or black bread and żubrówka (bison-grass vodka) or jałowcówka (juniper vodka). *Note:* Several other recipes for bigos are found in this book (consult index).

HOT STUFFED VEGETABLES
warzywa faszerowane na gorąco

Cucumbers, tomatoes, onions, kohlrabi, and other vegetables stuffed with meat, mushrooms or other fillings and baked in an oven, make a nice, light starter course to whet the appetite. For recipes, see meat & vegetable dishes.

HOT STUFFED PUFF-PASTRY SHELLS
ptysie faszerowane

This is another light and elegant hot starter course. Prepare puff-pastry shells as indicated for cream puffs (p. 685) using ½ c. water, ½ stick butter, ½ c. flour, 2 eggs, and ¼ t. salt. Form as directed and bake 8 shells. Cool, cut off tops ⅔ of the way from bottom, i.e. top should comprise ⅓ of the puff pastry. Fill bottom with non-drippy filling of choice (wet fillings will make the shell soggy!) replace tops, and bake in 400° oven 5–6 min., just long enough to thoroughly heat filling and lightly brown pastry. Serve immediately.

HOT PUFF PASTRIES STUFFED WITH HAM
ptysie faszerowane szynką

Make a white roux with 3 T. butter and 3 T. flour, dilute with 1 c. milk, and slowly bring to boil, whisking constantly. Remove from heat. Add ¼ lb. finely diced boiled ham (Polish canned ham is best in all recipes calling for boiled ham), 5 T. grated yellow cheese, a pinch of grated nutmeg, and salt & pepper to taste. Mix ingredients and allow to cool. Fill pastries and bake as above.

HOT PUFF PASTRIES WITH POULTRY FILLING
ptysie faszerowane drobiem

In bowl, combine 1½–2 c. cooked, diced chicken or turkey and 1 small grated onion. Forkblend ½ c. sour cream with 3 T. flour, stir in ½ c. hot milk and gently bring to boil, whisking until smooth. Add diced poultry and grated onion and bring to boil, stirring constantly. Switch off heat and add 3–4 T. drained, cooked (fresh or frozen) peas or canned peas, 5 T. grated yellow cheese, 1 T. chopped dill and/or parsley, ½ t. Maggi seasoning, a dash of paprika, and salt to taste. Mix lightly so as not to crush peas, heat a few seconds without boiling, and allow to cool. Stuff pastry shells just before baking.

HOT MUSHROOM-FILLED PUFF PASTRIES
ptysie faszerowane pieczarkami

Wash well, dry and dice 8 oz. fresh, cultivated mushrooms. Sauté in 3 T. butter with 1 finely chopped onion until moisture evaporates and mushrooms take on a light, golden hue. Cool slightly and stir in 1 raw egg yolk. Salt & pepper to taste. (*Optional:* Add a little chopped dill and/or parsley.) Stuff pastry shells with mixture and bake as above just before serving.

HOT PUFF PASTRIES FILLED WITH BIGOS
ptysie nadziewane bigosem

Reheat enough bigos (prepared as in recipe above or others in this book) to fill 8 puff-pastry shells. Place in sieve; with back of large spoon press out as much moisture as possible, i.e. until dripping stops. Fill pastry shells with bigos and bake immediately.

HOT PUFF PASTRIES FILLED WITH CALF'S BRAINS
ptysie z móżdżkiem cielęcym

Prepare calf's brains with eggs (see meat dishes) and fill pastry shells with mixture. Bake as above. *Note*: The above are only a sampling of the types of fillings that can be used in these tasty and elegant pastries. If you page through this book, you will undoubtedly come across many other fillings and fricasseed dishes that could be used to stuff puff-pastry shells, so don't be afraid to experiment!

* * *

HOT DUCK PIE
pasztet z kaczki w cieście

Cut up 1 cold roast duck into thin slices, strips, and small bits and pieces, cut away from hard-to-get places, place in skillet with ½ c. pre-soaked, pitted prunes and 1 c. hot water. Simmer covered until prunes are very tender. Meanwhile, sift 2½ c. flour onto board, cut in about 2 sticks butter, add 2 eggs, 5 T. sour cream, and a pinch of salt; quickly work by hand into a dough. Roll into ball, wrap in foil and refrigerate 1 hr. Roll out dough about ⅛ in. thick, cut into 2 circles, the larger of which should fit bottom and sides of spring form pan. Trim away excess dough extending beyond pan, prick bottom and sides with fork in several places, and pop into 400° oven for about 5 min. to set. In the meantime, dice prunes or cut into strips. Pour duck drippings into saucepan and thicken with about 1 T. flour, simmer several min., whisking until smooth and bubbly. If necessary, season sauce to taste with salt and wildfowl seasoning. Layer duck and prunes in partially baked pastry shell. Cover with remaining dough circle, trimming away any excess dough and sealing edges together. Puncture dough with fork in several places to allow steam to escape. Use dough trimmings to cut out decorative crescents, circles, stars, diamonds, etc., and stick them onto crust. Brush crust with an egg slightly beaten with 1 T. water and bake in 400° oven about 50–60 min. Reduce heat if top crust browns too quickly and, if necessary, loosely cover with a piece of aluminum foil. When done, remove sides of pan and place pie, on pan bottom, on round serving dish. Slice and serve piping hot with spiced fruits, pickled pumpkin, and the like on the side. *Note:* Ideally this type of pie should have a high, rounded top, meaning the duck filling should be mounded rather high. You may have to use more than 1 roast duck to achieve this effect or feel free to add some thinly sliced roast pork which blends nicely with duck. Goose pie is prepared exactly the same way.

HOT CHICKEN & MUSHROOM PIE
pasztet z kurczęcia w cieście

Slice up a cold roast chicken (fryer-broiler type) and prepare pastry shell as above. Wash, dry, slice 8–12 oz. fresh, cultivated mushrooms. In skillet melt 2 T. leftover fat from roasting pan and sauté mushrooms therein until tender (about 10 min.). In partially baked pastry shell, layer cold slices, strips, and pieces of chicken and sautéed mushrooms, sprinkling each layer with a little chopped dill. Pour about 1 c. basic white sauce (preferably made with leftover pan fat from chicken) over filling. Use just enough to coat chicken and mushrooms which should not be swimming in sauce. Cover with remaining dough circle and proceed as above. Serve with lettuce salad.

HOT PORK PIE
pasztet z wieprzowiny w cieście

Cut up enough roast pork into small thin slices, strips, and assorted pieces or, if you prefer, dice uniformly to make a high mound in partially-baked pastry shell as above. In saucepan, combine ½ c. pork pan drippings with ½ c. water and bring to boil. Add 1 c. peeled, sliced pears or apples (or some of each), and sauté in drippings briefly. Remove fruit and layer with pork in pastry shell. Stir 1 T. flour into drippings and simmer several min., whisking into a smooth sauce. Pour it over pie filling, cover with remaining dough circle, and proceed as above. *Note:* If desired, this and the other savory pies presented here may be served with extra sauce in gravy-boat with which guests may drench their individual portions to taste.

HOT CRAYFISH & PIKE PIE
pasztet z raków i szczupaka w cieście

For this version you will need the meat from about 30–40 crayfish, cooked the normal way in boiling salted water with dill, depending on their size. The important thing to remember is that there should be enough filling for a high, rounded pie. Layer about 1–1½ lbs. flaked or diced, poached pike fillets (or other freshwater fillets) with cooked crayfish meat, sprinkling with a little chopped dill. (*Optional:* 1–3 sliced hard-boiled eggs may be layered in between.) Drench with about 1 c. hot basic white sauce, flavored with a little extra lemon, cover with remaining dough circle, and proceed as above. *Note:* Canned crabmeat may be used instead of crayfish. *Variation:* 1 chopped onion sautéed in a little butter and/or about ¾ c. cooked, drained fresh or frozen, or canned baby peas may be added to filling.

Serve with hot truffle or mushroom sauce if desired. ***Optional:*** For dramatic effect, place a whole cooked crayfish (which should be nice and red) on a lettuce leaf or surround by parsley sprigs on top of the pie before bringing it to the table.

HOT VEAL & HAM PIE
pasztet z cielęciny i szynki w cieście

Dice coarsely or fine enough cold roast veal and boiled ham to fill partially baked pastry shell as indicated above. In several T. butter simmer 8 oz. fresh, washed, drained, sliced mushrooms with 1 chopped onion and 1 bud mashed garlic until done. Season with salt, pepper, and a pinch nutmeg. Combine veal, ham, mushrooms, and 2 beaten eggs. Use mixture to fill partially baked pastry shell and proceed as above. Serve with hot white sauce flavored with a cooked, diced truffle or 1 T. or so capers.

HOT SAVORY TARTS
kruche babeczki nadziewane

Sift 1 c. flour onto board, sprinkle with a pinch salt and cut in 3/4 stick butter. Sprinkle with 2½ T. water and work into dough with fingertips. Form into ball, cover with foil, and refrigerate 30 min. In the meantime, prepare filling (see note). On floured board roll dough out about ⅛ inch thick. Arrange small tart pans in cluster and cover them with dough sheet carried on rolling pin. Run rolling-pin over dough on tart pans, pressing down to cut out circles. Press dough circles into individual tart pans, pierce dough in several places in tart pans, and bake in 375° oven about 15 min. or until dough turns golden. Remove from pans when cool and fill with filling of choice. Just before serving, pop into 400° oven for 5 min. or heat in microwave if you like. ***Note:*** Fillings recommend for puff-pastry shell may be used in savory tarts.

HOT HORS D'OEUVRES
gorące przekąski

Only a few hot hors d'oeuvres are being listed for several reasons. Unlike hot starter courses eaten at the table with knife and fork, these are hot, bite-sized morsels served to guests at occasional stand-up cocktail parties, which are not really an important part of Poland's culinary lifestyle. Whereas platters of canapés and other cold hors d'oeuvres are placed round the room for guests to nibble on at their leisure, hot przekąski must be brought in from the kitchen sizzling hot and served immediately. They were therefore more in their element in the days of servants who could approach individual guests with various hot platters. Still, if you are determined to provide a hot hors d'oeuvre, here are a few suggestions.

HOT PRUNE & BACON ROLL-UPS
koreczki ze śliwek na gorąco

Cut thinly sliced bacon into twelve 4 inch strips. Gently remove pits from 12 prunes, pre-soaked 10 min. and thoroughly dried. Slip a whole blanched almond into the opening where the pit used to be, roll prune tightly in bacon strip, fasten with 2 toothpicks, and bake in 375° oven about 25 min. or until bacon is browned. Serve at once in heat-proof dish in which they were baked.

FRIED BREADED PRUNES
śliwki panierowane smażone

Scald 12 prunes and drain. Carefully remove pits and replace them with a whole blanched almond. Impale each prune on fork, dredge in flour, dip in beaten egg, and roll in bread crumbs, shaking off excess and gently pressing the breading in with fingers so it doesn't fall off during frying. Fry breaded prunes on all sides in butter to a nice golden brown. Stick in a toothpick, cocktail pick, or other small skewer and serve piping hot.

BREADED-MUSHROOM HORS D'OEUVRES
pieczarki panierowane na przekąskę

Wash well 12 med. fresh cultivated mushrooms, cut off stems even with cap, and wipe dry. (Reserve stems for some other dish.) Beat 1 egg with 2 T. milk, ¼ t. salt, and a pinch pepper. Dip mushrooms into egg mixture one at a time, making sure all sides are coated, then roll in bread crumbs. Fry in butter or butter and olive oil combination until nicely golden brown on all sides. Serve at once impaled on toothpicks.

HOT STUFFED MUSHROOMS
pieczarki faszerowane

Wash well 12 med. fresh cultivated mushrooms and cut off stem below cap line to form an indentation. Dry and set aside. Dice the mushroom stems fine and sauté in 2 T. butter with a finely minced onion until onion is transparent. Add 3 T. finely diced boiled ham and simmer briefly. Remove from heat and cool. Add 2 T. bread crumbs and 1 whole egg, mix well, and salt & pepper to taste. Fill cap bottoms with mixture, mounding and pressing it down slightly. Sprinkle with a little grated yellow cheese, arrange in baking dish, and bake in 375° oven about 20 min. Serve at once.

HOT STUFFED MUSHROOMS ANOTHER WAY
pieczarki faszerowane inaczej

Proceed as above, but prepare filling with 1 ground hard-boiled egg and 1 t. chopped dill in place of the boiled ham. *Note:* Instead of baking, both versions stuffed mushrooms may be dipped in beaten egg, rolled in bread crumbs, and fried in butter to a nice golden brown. Fry stuffed side first, then the top.

FRIED SAUSAGE APPETIZER
kiełbasa smażona na przekąskę

Skin about ½ lb. smoked, ready-to-eat kiełbasa and cut into small ½ inch cubes. Brown on all sides in a little lard or oil, stick with toothpicks, and serve at once, providing a dish of brown prepared mustard or cold mustard sauce for guests to dip their sausage cubes into. *Variation:* To browning sausage cubes add 1 small cooked or canned button mushroom per cube of kiełbasa. Impale 1 each on toothpick.

HOT SKEWERED HORS D'OEUVRES
szaszłyczki na przekąskę

On toothpicks impale a tiny cube of boiled ham, small button mushroom (fresh or canned), small cube of cold boiled bacon, and a piece of pitted prune (pre-soaked and dried). Brush lightly with olive oil and broil until lightly browned and sizzling. Serve immediately. *Note:* Be sure at least ¼ inch of toothpick protrudes so guests will have something to hold the hors d'oeuvre by.

SOUPS-HOT & COLD, SAVORY & SWEET

Unlike many Americans, Poles do not consider soup primarily as a cold-weather warmer-upper or something to wash down a mid-day sandwich with occasionally. Soup to this day is the normal first course at *obiad*, the main meal of the day. At Sunday dinner, it may be the second course, sandwiched in between a cold appetizer and the main hot course.

A big bowl of soup (the average portion is 1½–2 cups) is one of the things that helps prevent the "irregularity"—to use the well-known euphemism—that may result from too dry a diet. In poorer families, it serves as an effective filler, after which a token main course may suffice to keep body and soul together. Many of the thick and hearty peasant soups, to mention only *grochówka* (pea soup), *kapuśniak* (sauerkraut soup), and *krupnik* (barley soup) are a meal in themselves when served with bread or potatoes.

The length of this chapter, together with its follow-up devoted to soup garnishes and accompaniments, attests in itself to the role that *zupa, polewka, rosół,* and many others play in Polish cuisine. We have included often more than one version of all the old favorites, including *barszcz* (beetroot soup), *żur* (sour rye-meal soup), *czernina* (duck soup), *zupa szczawiowa* (sorrel soup), and many more. They range from the rustic *kartoflanka* (potato soup) to the dainty hot clear soups usually served at dinner-parties in large teacups or twin-handled *barszcz* cups.

"It's too hot a day for soup," you say? Not in Polish cookery, where summer favorites include a variety of cold savory soups (*chłodniki*) and sweet fruit soups (*zupy owocowe*). If you've got a youngster who doesn't care for soup, we'll bet he'll be crazy about that sweet and custardy *zupa "nic"*, served ice cold with frothy, snow-white dumplings floating inside.

If you like soup but associate its preparation with "slaving over a hot stove", do not despair, and do not reach for one of those "M-m-m good" cans or that artificial-tasting instant powder. Most Polish soups require little supervision and largely cook themselves, leaving you free for other pursuits. If you don't even have time to peel the soup greens or wait for the soup bones to cook, you should really look into making your own frozen bouillon as indicated in the first chapter on spices, herbs, seasoning, etc. That way you can whip up home-made soup in a matter of minutes.

* * *

VEGETABLE STOCK/COURT BOUILLON
wywar z włoszczyzny

Although not a dish in itself, this vegetable stock is the base for most Polish meatless soups, not to mention poached fish and aspic (jellied) dishes. Together with meat stock, court bouillon will be repeatedly called for in most of the recipes below, so it's a good idea to make its preparation almost second nature. Pour 8 c. cold water into pot. Add 2-3 peeled, medium sized (about 6 inches long) carrots, a slice of celeriac (root of celery), 1 leek, 1 small parsnip (parsley root), 6-8 peppercorns, 1-3 grains allspice, ½-1 bay leaf and 1 T. salt; cook until vegetables are tender. In a few soups (notably Ukrainian barszcz), the soup vegetables also include a slice of Savoy cabbage. Use the vegetables whole or diced. The diced vegetables are left in many of the hearty country-style soups, but removed from the more elegant ones. Rather than discarding the cooked vegetables, they may be diced and used in various mayonnaise and/or sour cream-laced, diced-vegetable salads (see cold-table salads). *Note:* If celeriac (seler) is not available, 2-3 stalks celery, including tops, may be used instead. An onion can take the place of leeks. If a strong court bouillon is called for (as in aspic dishes), simply increase the amount of vegetables to 3 carrots, a thicker slice of celeriac (or 3 stalks celery), 2 parsnips and 2 leeks (or 2 onions). Also increase the amount of spices by one-half. In general, let your own taste preferences guide you in increasing or decreasing the amount of vegetables and spices called for in this and other recipes. Taste is a highly individual matter, hence flavoring ingredients should be adjusted accordingly.

MEAT STOCK
wywar z mięsa

Most Polish meat-based soups start with this stock. Into 9 c. cold water place about 1 lb. pork, beef, veal, or chicken, including attached bones, or 1½ lbs. soup bones. The bones left after cutting the meat away from pork chops to make kotlety schabowe (breaded pork cutlets) make an excellent stock. Bring to boil, then reduce heat and simmer gently 60 min., skimming off foam with a slotted spoon until no more appears. Add soup vegetables and spices (as above) and simmer another 30 min., or until vegetables are tender. If using meat, remove it from stock, and use it for your main course with the sauce of your choice. It may also be ground and used in various pierogi, naleśniki, paszteciki, etc. If you have made your stock with soup bones, remove and dice all meat and return it to the pot. If you are weight or cholesterol conscious, strain the stock and, when cooled to room temp., refrigerate overnight. When ready to use, remove all but about 1 T. of the solidified fat at the top.

SMOKED-MEAT STOCK
wywar z wędzonki

Cover a 1-2 lb. hambone, or equal amount of smoked-porkchop bones, smoked-porkhock bones, or the rind and bones from slab bacon with 9 c. water and cook on low heat 3-4 hrs. If using bacon rind, it should be cooked until very tender and no longer rubbery. Any combination of the above may also be used. After about 2 hrs., add the standard portion of soup vegetables (carrot, celeriac, parsnip, leek) or simply 2 onions, plus a bay leaf and a half dozen peppercorns. The stock can also be made from 2 c. or so sliced, smoked kiełbasa, in which case only about 1½ hrs of cooking is required. This is an excellent way to put leftover lunch meat to good use: the end portion of a smoked ham, a few dried-up slices of non-Polish sausage, salami, bacon, or whatever. Smoked-meat stock is especially good for making żurek, red or white barszcz, cabbage, sauerkraut, pea, bean, and lentil soups. Taste the stock before adding any salt.

FISH STOCK
wywar z ryby

Wash well and remove the eyes and gills from the heads of 1-2 large freshwater fish (carp, pike, walleye, bass, whitefish) and cover with 6 c. water. Bring to boil, then reduce heat and skim away foam until no more forms. Add standard portion of soup vegetables, 1-2 quartered onions, 1 bay leaf, 6 peppercorns, and 2 t. salt; simmer on low heat 1 hr. or until head falls apart easily. If you've got no large fishheads, you can use 6-10 whole panfish (perch, bluegill, sunfish, crappie, chub) or 15-20 smelt or minnows. In addition to various fish chowders, this stock is also used to make the clear red barszcz served on Wigilia (Christmas Eve). *Note:* All the above stocks can be frozen and ready to use when you make your soup. This is a great time-saver, as most soups (pea, bean, and lentil are exceptions) can then be cooked in 20-30 min. To freeze stock, strain, removing vegetables, bones, and spices. To save space in your freezer, it is best to boil it down to about 3 c. The water can be replaced when cooking your soup.

RYEMEAL OR OATMEAL SOUR
zakwas na żur

Scald a crockery bowl (not metal!) or glass jar with boiling water and pour off. Pour in 2 c. rye flour, oat flour, or rolled oats and add 4–6 c. lukewarm, pre-boiled water. Cover with cheesecloth (if using a jar, the cloth can be fastened with a rubber band) and let stand at room temp. 3-4 days or until quite sour. If any mold begins to form at top, simply skim it away, as it is not harmful. Strain mixture through cheesecloth or gauze-lined funnel into bottles, seal and refrigerate until ready to use. It will keep for months.

RYEMEAL OR OATMEAL SOUR ANOTHER WAY
zakwas na żur inaczej

For a more savory żur pour 2 c. rye flour, rye bran, oat flour, or rolled oats into pre-scalded container as above. Add 2 c. hot water and stir to form a thick paste, then allow to cool. Add a slice of stale Polish rye or black (razowy) bread, or only the crust, 2 buds chopped garlic (or 1 small chopped onion), and 1 t. marjoram, cover with 4 c. lukewarm, pre-boiled water. Cover with cheesecloth and leave at room temp. 3-4 days or until nice and tart. Strain through cheesecloth into bottles, seal, and refrigerate. Adding bread speeds up the fermentation process.

BREAD SOUR FOR WHITE BARSZCZ
zakwas chlebowy na biały barszcz

Place 8-10 slices stale Polish rye and/or black bread in pre-scalded glass or crockery container. Cover with 6 c. lukewarm, pre-boiled water. Cover mouth of container with cheesecloth and let stand at room temp. 3-4 days or until nice and sour. Strain through cheesecloth into bottles, seal, and refrigerate until ready to make your barszcz.

BEET SOUR
kwas burakowy

Peel and thinly slice about two lbs. beets and place in large crockery bowl, earthenware crock, or glass jar. Add 1-2 slices stale Polish rye or black bread, 2 buds chopped garlic, 1 t. sugar, and 1 T. salt. Cover with 2½ qts. pre-boiled lukewarm water. Cover mouth of container with cheesecloth or dish towel and let stand at room temp. 4-5 days until pleasantly tart. Strain through cheesecloth-lined funnel into bottles, seal and refrigerate. Use for making barszcz czerwony (beet barszcz).

BEEF BROTH
rosół wołowy

Cook 1 lb. or so beef with bone attached in 8 c. water about 1½ hrs. or until meat is fairly tender. Cut an onion in 2, impale on fork, singe over flame (or by placing directly on the heating ring of electric range) until partially blackened, and add to broth. Add the standard soup vegetables, this time including a slice of Savoy (crinkly) cabbage, plus ½-1 bay leaf, 3 grains allspice, 2 t. salt and 6 peppercorns. Cook another 30 min. or until vegetables are tender and meat comes away from bone easily. Strain, removing vegetables and spices, but reserving carrot. One dried Polish mushroom, pre-scalded in ½ c. water several hrs. then added to soup pot along with the mushroom water at the start of cooking, will enhance the flavor of your broth. Before serving, sprinkle in 1 T. freshly chopped parsley. This makes for a hearty cold-weather warmer-upper when served over egg noodles, poured-batter noodles, or rice. A pinch of savory and 1 t. Maggi extract will perk up its flavor even more. Serve the boiled beef as your main course with horseradish sauce or grind it for use in pierogi, pastry turnovers, naleśniki, etc. *Note*: Since beef broth can be on the fat side, it's a good idea to prepare it a day ahead, refrigerating overnight and removing most of the solidified fat. This should not be discarded but frozen and saved for future use. A T. or 2 is great for gravies, to simmer onions in, or flavor various dishes.

CHICKEN SOUP
rosół z kury

Place cut-up 2 lb. stewing chicken including gizzard and heart in pot, cover with 8 c. cold water, add 1 T. salt, and cook under cover on low heat 1½ hrs. Add soup vegetables (minus cabbage), 6 or so peppercorns, and ½-1 bay leaf, plus 1 onion singed over flame, and cook 30 min. longer or until vegetables and meat are tender. Sprinkle with a T. fresh chopped parsley and/or dill and serve over egg noodles, poured-batter noodles, rice or liver dumplings. If you like, slice the cooked carrot and add to soup bowls. If the soup is too fat for your liking, prepare a day ahead, refrigerate overnight, and remove solidified fat. Like the beef fat (above), it should be frozen for use in gravies, etc. The boiled chicken can be used in main-course dishes such as kura w potrawce (chicken stew), as well as being ground for use in pastry turnovers, chicken & barley gołąbki, and similar ground-meat dishes.

FRYER-CHICKEN SOUP
rosół z kurczęcia

The most flavorful chicken soup is made with a mature stewing chicken, but fryers are more widely available, have less fat, and take less time to cook. Place a cut-up 1-1½ lb. fryer in pot, cover with 8 c. water, add 1 T. salt, and cook on low heat about 45 mins. Add soup vegetables, flame-singed onion, 6 peppercorns and ½-1 bay leaf, and cook another 15-20 min. or until chicken and vegetables are tender. Since soup made from fryers can be on the pale side, adding a whole tomato with the other vegetables will give it a nice, golden tinge and more savory flavor. Serve over noodles, rice, etc., and sprinkle with a little chopped parsley and/or dill before serving. *Note:* If you prefer to roast your fryer, make the soup only with the neck, rump, wings, gizzard, perhaps several other gizzards, or 2-3 extra chicken backs. Low-cost chicken parts like backs, necks, and gizzards alone make excellent soup since they have lots of flavor.

BEEF & CHICKEN BROTH
rosół z wołowiny i kury

Cover ¾ lb. beef with bones with 8 c. water, bring to boil, reduce heat, and skim off scum until no more forms. Cook about 1 hr. Add ¾ lb. fryer or stewing-chicken parts and 1 T. salt and cook another hr. Add soup greens and spices and cook until vegetables and meat are tender. Sprinkle with a little fresh chopped parsley and serve over egg noodles, poured-batter noodles, rice, or cream of wheat dumplings. A pinch of savory and rosemary will add zest to this nutritious and satisfying soup which combines the best of beef broth and chicken soup. Use boiled meat for other dishes.

ROYAL BROTH
rosół królewski

Prepare beef & chicken broth as above and strain. Bring to boil and add 8 oz. fresh mushrooms, washed well and cut into thin strips. Scald ¼ lb. chicken livers with boiling water, dice fine and add to broth. Cook 15 mins. Add 1 c. finely diced cooked chicken, 1 t. Maggi extract, 1-2 T. chopped parsley and salt & pepper to taste. A jigger of dry white wine may be added. Serve over noodles of choice for a change-of-pace soup with a gourmet twist.

BEEF BROTH À LA LESZCZYŃSKI
rosół à la Leszczyński

Prepare beef broth and season according to preference. Serve hot over liver dumplings (see soup accompaniments section). This soup was the favorite of the 18th-century Polish gourmet-monarch, King Stanisław Leszczyński, after whom it was named.

BEEF BROTH HUSSAR STYLE
rosół po husarsku

Scald 2 tomatoes with boiling water and remove skins. Dice and add to 6 c. beef broth with meat removed and diced soup vegetables left in. Add ½-¼ c. ready-to-eat ham, finely diced, and cook 10 mins. Before serving over egg noodles, add 2 buds mashed garlic, 1 t. Maggi extract, and salt & pepper to taste. This zesty and hearty broth was named after the valiant, bewinged horsemen (Hussars), whose exploits included the defeat of the Turks at the gates of Vienna in 1683 under Poland's King Jan Sobieski.

VEAL BROTH
rosół cielęcy

In 7–8 c. water cook 1½ lbs. veal 1 hr. Add standard soup vegetables and spices and cook ½ hr. longer or until meat and vegetables are tender. Strain. Wash ¼ c. rice or more under running water in sieve and add to broth. Cook about 20 min. or until very soft. Serve with sliced, cooked carrots and garnish with greens if you like. This nutritious but delicate broth is frequently served to convalescents and others requiring an easily digestible diet. Therefore use spices and salt accordingly.

PORK BROTH WITH POTATOES OR DUMPLINGS
rosół wieprzowy z kartoflami lub pierożkami

In pot combine 1 lb. pork neck bones or ribs, 1 small beef soup bone, 1 onion, a piece of bay leaf, 1 dried Polish mushroom, 5 peppercorns, 2 t. salt, and 8 c. water. Bring to boil, reduce heat, and skim off scum until no more forms. While stock simmers finely dice 1–2 chicken livers (or equivalent amount of pork or calf's liver) and sauté in T. butter with 1 grated onion and 1 grated carrot until nicely browned. Add to stock along with 1 whole unskinned tomato and 3–4 prunes. Cook 1½–2 hrs. or until meat falls away from bone. Strain, dice meat and mushroom, and return to stock. Adjust to taste with salt, pepper and about 1 t. vinegar (a pinch or 2 MSG won't hurt!) and serve over diced cooked potatoes. *Variation:* Combine finely diced or ground meat and mushroom with 1 diced onion sautéed in 1 T. butter, add enough bread crumbs to get a firm filling, and use mixture to fill tiny pierożki. Cook these in boiling salt water, drain, and serve in broth. *Note:* This and most other soup recipes given here are supposed to produce roughly 6 c. ready-to-eat soup or about 4 servings. Since some liquid evaporates during cooking, add enough boiling water to make 6 c. whenever you end up with less.

RABBIT BROTH
rosół z królika

Wash and dry 1½–2 lbs. dressed cut-up domestic rabbit, place in pot, add 8 c. cold water, 2 t. salt, 5 peppercorns, 3 grains allspice, and 1 bay leaf, bring to boil, reduce heat, and simmer covered 60–90 min. Add 1 portion diced soup greens and 1 unpeeled, halved, flame-singed onion and simmer covered another hr. Strain. Clarify with egg white if desired. Salt & pepper to taste and serve in bowl over noodles of choice or in teacups with soup pastries on the side. In either case, garnish with chopped parsley. *Note*: Use the cooked rabbit for your main course (see poultry & rabbit chapter). Rabbit broth ranks with veal broth as a very delicate and tasty soup ideal for convalescents. This stock may be used as the basis for any variety of savory soups (tomato, beet, sorrel, vegetable, barley, etc.).

OLD POLISH BROTH-ENRICHER
rosół rumiany

Although this is neither a soup nor a soup garnish, we have included it here because it is a handy way used by old Polish cooks to give unappetizingly pale broths a deeper color and richer taste. Melt 2 T. butter in saucepan. Add 1–2 finely diced chicken livers (or 1 diced goose liver, equivalent amount of pork or calf's liver or raw ground meat), 1 finely minced onion, and 1 med. coarsely grated carrot. Simmer until butter and other ingredients are fully browned, but not burnt, and add to broth midway through cooking. *Note:* Other ways of improving the color of broth is to add a whole unpeeled tomato, pinch of saffron, a little caramel coloring, Maggi seasoning, or Kitchen Bouquet, crushed bouillon cubes or bouillon granules (crystals). Try them all and judge for yourself which way is best. Incidentally, this broth enricher is incorporated in the above recipe for pork broth, but feel free to use it in any chicken, beef, veal, or other meat-based broths. Do not add broth enricher to wildgame broths which, if anything, already have too much flavor and often need to be toned down (see below).

WILDFOWL BROTH
rosół z dzikiego ptactwa

A tasty broth can be made from many gamebirds including pheasant, grouse, partridge, quail, wild dove, snipe, and woodcock. Place in pot about 1½ lbs. dressed and washed wildfowl of choice, add 1 dried bolete, standard soup spices plus (optional) 2–3 crushed juniper berries, 1 T. salt, and 8 c. cold water. Bring to boil, skimming off any scum, reduce heat, and simmer 1 hr. Add one portion soup greens, including Savoy cabbage and 1 onion, and cook another hr. Strain. Season to taste with salt, pepper, a pinch marjoram, and (optional) 1 jigger dry white wine. Serve over noodles, rice, or groats of choice and garnish with chopped parsley and or dill. *Note:* Either dice meat and return to broth or use it in a fricassee-type dish.

WILDGAME BROTH
rosół z dziczyzny

Dark-meat game such as hare, venison, elk, boar, even bison may be used to prepare a broth whose often strong gamey flavor is not to everybody's liking. Prepare as you would beef broth, but to help offset any off-flavors use Savoy cabbage and 1–2 onions with soup greens and add several crushed juniper berries to the standard spices. Adding 1–2 dried

Polish mushrooms at start of cooking is also not a bad idea. Wildgame may also require longer cooking than beef. Season with salt, pepper, ½–1 t. Polish hunter's seasoning, a little MSG, and a jigger dry red or white wine. A little Maggi seasoning also won't hurt. Serve over noodles, groats, or cooked potatoes, and garnish generously with chopped garden greens. *Optional*: Add 2–3 prunes at start of cooking.

BEEF BOUILLON
bulion wołowy

Bouillon is a strong clear broth often served in teacups ahead of the main course as an appetite stimulant. It is also the traditional food of convalescents, and a thermosful of steaming bouillon is a great warmer-upper for those engaged in cold-weather activities. A Polish cookbook published in the mid-19th century claimed that a truly good bouillon required 1 lb. of beef per serving. The following is a slightly scaled-down version that we feel is better suited to today's tastes and calorie requirements. Cut 2 peeled onions in ½ and singe over flame, on heating coil of electric range or in a dry frying pan until blackened rings appear. Wash 2–3 lbs. beef (with bone and some suet attached), in hot water place in pot, add 8 c. water, slowly bring to boil and cook at gentle boil about 15 min., skimming off scum. Remove meat and rinse under cold running water. Strain stock into another pot, add the meat, 2 t. salt, the onions, 2–3 carrots, 1 parsley root, ½ a celeriac (or 2 stalks celery including the leaves), ½–1 leek and a sprinkling of parsley greens. (*Optional:* For a pungent touch, add 1 small turnip or a slice of rutabaga.) Bring to a boil, reduce heat slightly, and cook at a gentle boil for 20 min., then reduce heat, cover and simmer on low until meat falls away from bone. Strain (use meat for some other dish) and allow to cool. Remove fat from top when cooled to room temp. If you want no fat at all, refrigerate overnight and remove congealed fat the next day. To clarify, add 2 slightly beaten egg whites to room temp. stock, gradually bring to a slow simmer, not to a boil, and simmer 10–15 min. without stirring. Strain through sieve lined with linen napkin, dish towel, or several thicknesses of cheesecloth. Season to taste with salt, pepper, a little MSG, and (optional) a sprinkle of lemon juice. Serve in teacups garnished with a trace of very finely chopped parsley and/or dill, or in bowls with egg-thread noodles, rice, or sago which should be cooked separately, not in the stock, because it may lose its clarity. *Note:* For a more aromatic bouillon, add several peppercorns and allspice grains and ½–1 bay leaf at the start of cooking.

BROWN BOUILLON
bulion rumiany

Wash 3 lb. piece of nice beef containing bone and suet. Trim off the suet and place in a pot with several carrots and 2 halved singed onions. Place meat on top, add 1 lb. veal with bone or a split calf's foot and a piece of smoked ham equivalent to 1 c. (The veal and ham are optional.) Add enough cold water just to cover and cook on med. heat until meat and vegetables are slightly browned, i.e. until water evaporates and ingredients just begin to sizzle. Cover with 8 c. water, bring to gentle boil, and skim off any scum. Add 1 portion soup greens (with or without Savoy cabbage), several grains allspice and peppercorns, ½ a bay leaf, several pinches marjoram, and 2 t. salt plus a whole unskinned tomato. Simmer until meat comes away from bone (2–3 hrs). Strain, de-fat, and clarify as above. Season with salt, pepper, and a little MSG as needed. For a darker bouillon, add several drops caramel coloring. To serve, place a raw unbroken egg yolk in each teacup, sprinkle with a pinch of finely chopped parsley and/or dill, and drench with steaming bouillon. May be served in bowls with egg-thread noodles, rice, or sago.

TART BROWN BOUILLON
bulion rumiany kwaskowaty

Soup vegetables such as carrots, parsnips, and onions usually gave a bouillon a sweetish tinge not everyone likes. You can offset it by adding a little sauerkraut juice to bouillon during last ½ hr. For a decidedly tart bouillon, use a little more sauerkraut juice.

BOUILLON WITH VEGETABLES
bulion z jarzynami

Prepare beef bouillon or brown bouillon as above, but remove carrots as soon as they are tender and dice or slice into thin rounds. Distribute them evenly in soup bowls and to each add some separately cooked, diced vegetables such as cauliflower, green or wax beans, asparagus or kohlrabi, even diced, cooked potatoes. Garnish with chopped parsley.

EASY GOURMET BOUILLON
bulion wyborny na poczekaniu

In pot combine 1 lb. ground meat (ground beef or beef-pork-veal meatloaf mixture), ½ t. Polish beef seasoning, 1 crushed beef bouillon cube, 2 crushed vegetable bouillon cubes, and 2 pinches grated nutmeg. Add 6 c. cold water, bring to boil, breaking up meat with fork, and cook on med. heat about 30 min. Strain broth (use meat for some other dish). Season to taste with salt & pepper, a pinch or 2 MSG, and ½–1 t. Maggy seasoning. In each teacup deposit a raw unbroken egg yolk, garnish with chopped dill, and drench with hot bouillon. May be served with butter-fried croutons. Who said gourmet dishes had to be complicated and time-consuming?! *Note:* Naturally you can add all or some of the standard soup greens, diced or coarsely grated, at start of cooking if you have them on hand. Also, skim off scum if it appears. If bouillon is sweeter than you like, season with a sprinkle of lemon juice.

CLEAR BEET BARSZCZ
barszcz czysty czerwony

Soak 1–3 dried Polish mushrooms in c. water several hrs. or overnight and cook in same water until tender. Reserve the cooked mushrooms for paszteciki (pastry turnovers). Bring 4 c. court bouillon, meat stock, or smoked-meat stock (see above) to boil, add the mushroom water, 2 peeled, coarsely grated raw beets, and simmer 15 min. Add 1–2 c. beet sour according to the tartness you like and strain. Add 1–2 buds minced garlic, 1 t. sugar and (optional) 1 jigger dry red wine. Instead of the wine, 1–2 peeled, diced cooking apples added with the beets will give your barszcz a special tang. Salt & pepper if needed. Serve hot in teacups with pastry turnovers.

CLEAR BEET BARSZCZ OLD POLISH STYLE
barszcz czysty staropolski

Bake 4 beets in oven until tender, cool, peel, and grate. Place in soup kettle along with 2 peeled, grated apples. Scald with 6 c. meat stock, add ¼ c. dry red wine, 1 crumbled bay leaf, 1 t. sugar, ¼ t. marjoram, and salt to taste. Simmer 5 min. and strain. To strained barszcz add 3 T. raisins and let them soak therein several min. Sour to taste with a little freshly squeezed lemon juice. Serve with kulebiak (cabbage pie).

CLEAR BEET BARSZCZ THE EASY WAY
barszcz czysty łatwy

Dissolve 3–4 bouillon cubes in 4 c. water, add 1–2 c. sliced canned beets including the beet liquid, and bring to boil. Sour to taste with several pinches citric-acid crystals, also known as sour salt (kwasek cytrynowy), add 1 t. sugar, 1 t. Maggi extract, a dash of garlic powder, salt & pepper. A jigger or dry red wine of a heaping T. applesauce may also be added. Instead of citric acid crystals, the barszcz may be soured with a little sauerkraut juice or dill-pickle juice. This short-cut method is definitely not as good as the barszcz made from scratch, so use it only in emergencies!

CLEAR BEET BARSZCZ FOR WIGILIA
barszcz czysty wigilijny

Soak 2–4 or more dried Polish mushrooms in 1 c. water several hrs. or overnight and cook in same water until tender. Reserve mushrooms for uszka (mushroom-filled soup dumplings). In 6 c. vegetable stock or fish stock (or 3 c. of each) cook 2–4 coarsely grated raw beets (the amount depending on the "beetiness" desired) about 10 min. Add mushroom water and sour to taste with beet sour. Simmer briefly but do not boil. Add 1–2 buds minced garlic, 1 t. sugar (more or less to taste), 1 jigger dry red wine, salt & pepper. A t. Maggi extract and 1 t. fresh or rinsed salted dill may be added. Season this extra special once-a-year soup carefully to enhance that earthy beet flavor with just the right sweet, sour, and winey dimension, highlighted with a trace of dusky Polish mushrooms. Strain and serve in bowls, each containing 3–6 uszka. This is the traditional soup at Christmas Eve supper.

CREAMED BEET BARSZCZ
barszcz zabielany

Scrub 4 beets and bake in oven until tender; when cool enough to handle, peel, slice very thin, or grate coarsely. Bring 6 c. meat stock or court bouillon to boil, add beets, and cook 10 mins. One or more pre-soaked and cooked dried Polish mushrooms plus the water may be added. Sour to taste with beet sour or sauerkraut juice (pickle brine, several pinches of citric acid crystals, or vinegar may also be used for souring instead), and add about 1 t. sugar and salt & pepper to taste. Fork-blend ½ c. or more sour cream with 2 T. flour until smooth and gradually add to soup. Simmer briefly and serve garnished with freshly chopped dill and/or parsley. *Note:* Since this method of creaming is used with Polish soups, it should become second nature. If the sour cream & flour mixture is added to hot soup too quickly, it will curdle. After fork-blending until lump-free, gradually add up to 1 c. of hot soup, one T. at a time to mixture, stirring constantly. The soup should not be boiling; in fact it's best to remove it from heat and let it stand several min. Gradually add the smooth sour cream & soup mixture to pot. Simmer briefly but do not bring to violent boil. If you're a beginner and can't seem to get rid of all the lumps in the sour cream & flour mixture, after mixing with 1 c. hot soup, pour it into your soup pot through a fine sieve. Then partially immerse the sieve in the soup and stir with teaspoon until lumps are broken up and forced through sieve.

UKRAINIAN BEET BARSZCZ
barszcz ukraiński

Soak ½–¾ c. navy beans in 1 qt. water overnight, then cook in same water until tender. Drain and set aside. Bake 2 med. beets (more or less depending on how beety a barszcz you like) in oven until tender, cool under cold running water, peel, and grate coarsely. In 6 c. hot, smoked-meat stock containing diced soup vegetables including Savoy cabbage, cook the beets, 1–2 c. shredded cabbage and 2 peeled, diced raw potatoes, simmering gently until vegetables are tender. Sour to taste with beet sour, sauerkraut juice, pickle brine, etc. Cream with ½–1 c. sour cream fork-blended with several T. flour. Add beans and simmer briefly.

Since the smoked-meat stock may already be salty and spicy enough, taste soup before adding salt & pepper. A pinch or 2 marjoram may be added for flavoring. Especially if served with the diced, smoked meat used to make the stock, this is a hearty meal in a bowl for a cold winter's day. *Optional:* For deeper color and flavor, 1–2 T. tomato paste may be stirred in.

BEET BARSZCZ PEASANT STYLE
barszcz gospodarski

Bake 4 unskinned beets in oven until tender, then cool, peel, and coarsely grate. Add to 7 c. hot meat stock along with 2 peeled, coarsely grated apples, sour to taste with beet sour and simmer on low heat 5 min. Cover, set aside, and allow to "age" 3–4 hrs. Scald 2 tomatoes to remove skins. Dice tomatoes, 1 peeled cucumber, and 1–2 onions and simmer in skillet in 2–3 T. butter (or the fat removed from cold meat stock) until tender. Heat soup, add the sautéed vegetables, 1 c. cooked (or drained canned) navy beans, 1 c. or more cooked, diced potatoes, about 1 t. sugar, and salt & pepper to taste. Cream with ½ c. sour cream fork-blended with 2 T. flour as usual and simmer briefly. *Note:* In all beet barszcz recipes, the beets may be either baked or boiled in their skins and then skinned, grated, and added to the stock, or they can be grated raw and cooked in the stock. Using raw beets, however, will give your barszcz an "earthy" taste that not everybody likes.

BEET BARSZCZ WITH PICKLES
barszcz z ogórkami

Bake 4 beets in oven until tender, then remove skin and grate. Peel 2–3 brine-cured dill pickles, grate coarsely, and simmer several mins. in 2 T. butter. Add to 6 c. court bouillon along with ½ lb. skinned, sliced, smoked kiełbasa and cook under cover on low heat 20–30 mins. Add the grated beets and stir. Cream with ½ c. sour cream fork-blended with 2 T. flour, add 2 t. chopped fresh dill and 1 bud garlic mashed into a paste with ½ t. salt. Adjust taste with a little pepper and about 1 t. sugar. If not as tart as you like, add a little pickle brine. Serve with boiled potatoes on the side.

WHITE BARSZCZ
biały barszcz

Sour 4–5 c. smoked-meat or meat stock with bread sour to taste and simmer briefly. Cream with ¾ c. sour cream fork-blended with 2–3 T. flour, add 2 buds minced garlic, and season to taste with salt & pepper and a pinch of marjoram. This soup should be definitely on the tart side so be sure to use enough of the bread-sour liquid. The white barszcz should contain the diced meat or kiełbasa on which the stock was made. Serve hot over hard-boiled egg slices in soup bowls. You may also add diced farmer's cheese, cubed stale rye or black bread, and a little freshly grated or prepared horseradish to taste. This tart and savory soup is traditionally served in parts of Eastern Poland for Easter. *Note:* This soup is frequently made with the water in which fresh or smoked kiełbasa was cooked. Even when not planning to make soup immediately, the water you cook your kiełbasa in should always be saved as a rich and flavorful stock for future use. Simply refrigerate, remove fat from top (which can also be saved for frying), and freeze.

WHITE BARSZCZ THE EASY WAY
biały barszcz łatwy

When in a hurry or out of bread sour and stock, you can still enjoy a short-cut version of this tangy hot soup. In pot combine 5 c. water, 1 chopped onion, 2 buds minced garlic, and 1–2 T. of the frozen kiełbasa fat (see above). Bring to boil, reduce heat, and simmer under cover 15 mins. Cream with ½ c. sour cream fork-blended with 2 T. flour and season to taste with salt, pepper, and a pinch of marjoram. Sour with a few pinches of citric acid crystals or—as a last resort—with a little vinegar. Serve piping hot over hard-boiled egg slices or any of the accompaniments in the preceding recipe.

RYEMEAL SOUP OLD POLISH STYLE
żur staropolski

Heat 4 c. smoked-meat stock, with diced meat left in, to boiling. Add 2 buds minced garlic and—for added aroma—½ a crumbled bay leaf. Add 1–2 c. ryemeal or oatmeal sour to get the tartness you desire. First shake the bottle containing the refrigerated ryemeal or oatmeal sour, because the floury sediment at bottom gives the soup more body and flavor. Salt & pepper to taste as needed. Serve hot with a dish of mashed potatoes, garnished with fried bacon bits and the drippings, on the side. A T. sour cream may be added to each bowl. This soup can also be made (and is very good!) with the water you cooked kielbasa in. If soup is too thin, stir 1 T. or so flour into a c. of soup until smooth and return to pot. Simmer briefly.

RYEMEAL SOUP KRAKÓW STYLE
żurek krakowski

Sour 4–5 c. smoked-meat stock to taste with rye sour, add 4 buds minced garlic, 2 crushed grains allspice, and ½ a crumbled bay leaf and simmer 5 mins. Serve over hard-boiled egg slices. Eat with rye bread or a side dish of potatoes. A hot bowl of this and other żurs are sometimes served at the end of balls and parties that last "...do białego rana" (till the break of day). This tart and tangy soup is regarded as a good eye-opener that also quenches the thirst acquired after a night of partying!

RYEMEAL SOUP COUNTRY STYLE
żur wiejski

In 6 c. smoked-meat stock cook 1 chopped onion and 4–5 peeled, diced potatoes until tender. Add 2 buds minced garlic, sour to taste with ryemeal sour and simmer several mins. Fry up ¼ lb. diced bacon into crunchy nuggets and add 1–2 spoonfuls to each bowl of soup.

LENTEN RYEMEAL SOUP
żur postny

Sour 4–5 c. strained court bouillon with ryemeal or oatmeal sour to taste, add 2–3 buds minced garlic and, for added zest, 2–3 peppercorns and ½ a bay leaf. (**Remember:** The court bouillon was already made with these spices!). Simmer 5 min. Fork-blend 2 T. flour with 1 c. of the soup until lumpfree and return to pot. Simmer a while longer. Season to taste with a pinch or two of marjoram and salt & pepper to taste. Serve with boiled or mashed potatoes, dotted with butter, on the side. Another way is to cook 3–5 peeled, diced potatoes in the court bouillon and serve them in the soup. This tart soup is fine for a change of pace, but it would be pretty hard to make a steady diet of it the way the Poles of yesteryear did during Lent. No wonder the end of Lent was marked by youngsters with a mock "funeral" of sorts, at which they buried herring bones and dumped out a pot of the meatless żur! Nowadays, stirring in ½ a c. of sour cream is recommended.

RYEMEAL SOUP WITH MUSHROOMS FOR WIGILIA
żurek wigilijny z grzybami

Soak 4–5 dried Polish mushrooms in 1 c. water overnight. Add to 4 c. strained court bouillon, including the water in which they soaked, and cook until mushrooms are tender. The mushrooms may then be diced and returned to soup or used in other Wigilia dishes like pierogi, sauerkraut, or kulebiak (cabbage pie). Sour to taste with ryemeal or oatmeal sour, add 1–2 buds minced garlic, and simmer a few mins. longer. Salt & pepper to taste. If you like, thicken with 1–2 T. flour, fork-blended with a c. of the soup. For a richer taste, fork-blend ½ c. sour cream with the flour, add 1 c. of soup, stir until lump-free and add to soup. *Optional:* 1–2 T. fine barley may be added at start of cooking.

DUCK OR GOOSE (BLOOD) SOUP
czernina/jusznik

Collect the blood of a freshly killed duck or goose and stir in ¼ c. 6% vinegar. Seal and refrigerate until ready to use. In pot combine duck or goose wings, neck, rump, heart, and gizzard with 8 c. cold water. Bring to boil, skimming off scum until no more forms, reduce heat and simmer 1 hr. Add several peppercorns, cloves, and allspice grains and ½–1 bay leaf plus the standard portion of soup greens (minus Savoy cabbage) and simmer another 1–1½ hrs. or until meat easily comes away from bone. Dice giblets, remove meat from bones, dice, and return to strained stock. The soup vegetables may be diced and returned to pot or used in another dish according to preference. Add about 2 c. dried fruit: prunes, apples, pears, raisins, and simmer another 15–20 min. Fork-blend 2–3 T. flour with blood & vinegar mixture, add about ½ c. stock 1 T. at a time, stirring constantly, then return to pot. Season with salt, pepper, a pinch or 2 ground juniper berries (optional), sugar, and a bit more vinegar if needed to get a sweet, sour, winey flavor with subtly spicy undertones. Simmer gently several min. and serve with egg noodles, noodle squares, grated-potato dumplings or cooked, diced potatoes. *Variation:* Fork-blend ½ c. sour cream with flour and blood & vinegar mixture before adding to stock.

DUCK OR GOOSE (BLOOD) SOUP WITH PORK RIBS
czernina na żeberkach

If you get an urge for this soup when you don't want or have a whole duck or goose, and if you live in or near a Polish neighborhood, you may be able to get a jar of blood & vinegar mixture at a local poultry market. Proceed as above, but instead of duck or goose trimmings and giblets, cook 1½ lbs. pork ribs in 8 c. water until they come away from bone. Dice meat, return to stock. Cook, season, and serve czernina as in first recipe. *Note:* besides having many devotees, czernina (the spelling is "czarnina" in peasant dialect) once also had a ritual significance in Poland. For it was the legendary "czarna polewka" (black pottage) served to an unsuccessful suitor to let him know his advances were not welcome.

TART AND TANGY PORK & PRUNE SOUP
kwas/kwaśne

Start with 6 c. meat stock made with pork bones. Remove meat from bones, dice, and return to pot. Add 1 c. prunes and ½ c. raisins (optional) and simmer 15 min. Sour to taste with ryesour or vinegar and add a little sugar to achieve the sweet & sour flavor you desire. Season with ½ t. or more marjoram and salt & pepper to taste. Thicken with 1–2 T. flour and simmer briefly. Serve over grated-potato noodles. We first encountered this unusual soup not in Poland, but in Bay City, Michigan, where it was still being prepared 100 years after being brought to America by immigrants from rural areas of the Poznań region. One local resident referred to it as "something like czernina, but without the blood."

TRIPE SOUP
zupa z flaczków

Soak 2 lbs. beef tripe in cold water 2 hrs. Scrub well, rinse and place in soup pot. Scald with boiling water, bring to boil, and cook 20 min. Drain, rinse in cold running water, then scald again and cook 3–4 hrs. or until tripe is tender, slice it into strips about 2 inches long and ½ an inch wide. Add to 7–8 c. beef stock with meat removed from bones, diced, and returned to pot. The soup vegetables should be cut into strips. Simmer 15 min. Season to taste rather generously with salt & pepper, marjoram, ginger, nutmeg, paprika, and 1–2 t. Maggi extract. Put these spices at table so your guests can season it additionally to taste. In 2 T. butter simmer 2–3 T. flour, stirring into a thick paste; dilute with 1 c. hot soup, stirring until smooth, then return to pot. Simmer several more min. Serve with or without marrow dumplings. In Warsaw, each bowl is topped with a little grated yellow cheese. This is a hearty he-man dish that begs for a glass of chilled vodka or a frosty stein of beer to wash it down! *Note:* The rather long cooking time can be cut in half if you use a pressure cooker. It will take next to nothing to prepare if you can get ready cooked tripe.

CABBAGE SOUP
kapuśniak z białej kapusty

Discard discolored outer leaves of a 1 lb. head of cabbage. Shred the cabbage, finely grate the core, scald with boiling water to cover, bring to boil, and simmer 5 min. Drain. Add to pot containing 8 c. meat stock or smoked-meat stock, including the diced meat but minus the soup vegetables. Cook on low heat uncovered 30 min. Scald 2 tomatoes with boiling water to remove skins and add to soup pot along with 4 peeled, diced raw potatoes and cook another 30 min. Fry up 4–5 slices diced bacon, stir in 2 T. flour and simmer until nicely browned, then dilute with 1 c. soup, stirring until lump-free and add to soup. Simmer several min. more. Season to taste with salt & pepper and a little lemon juice, vinegar, or citric acid crystals. Ryemeal sour or sauerkraut juice may also be used to sour taste. *Note*: If using smoked-meat stock, taste soup before seasoning.

CREAMED CABBAGE SOUP
kapuśniak zabielany

Shred, scald, and drain 1 lb. cabbage as above and cook in 8 c. meat stock or smoked-meat stock, containing diced meat and soup vegetables, 30 min. Add 3–4 peeled, diced raw potatoes and cook another 30 min. or until cabbage and potatoes are fully cooked. Fork-blend ½ c. sour cream with 2 T. flour, dilute with 1 c. soup, and add to soup. Season with salt & pepper and a pinch of citric acid crystals, lemon juice, vinegar, etc. Simmer a bit longer.

SAUERKRAUT SOUP
kapuśniak z kiszonej kapusty

Drain ½ qt. sauerkraut, reserving liquid. Rinse in cold water, drain in colander, squeeze out excess moisture, and slice quite fine. If the sauerkraut is very sour, scald with boiling water in pot, bring to boil, and simmer 5 min. then drain. Add sauerkraut to 7 c. meat stock or smoked-meat stock, including the diced meat, and cook uncovered 60 min. Fry up 4–5 sliced diced bacon and brown 2 T. or so flour in the drippings, stirring to a smooth roux. Stir in 1 c. soup and when smooth add to soup pot. Season with several dashes of pepper, ¼ t. caraway, and simmer a while longer. Add 1 t. sugar. If your kapuśniak is not as tart as you like, add a little reserved sauerkraut juice. Boiled potatoes can be served on the side or in the soup, whichever you prefer. Adding 1–2 presoaked dried Polish mushrooms at start of cooking will improve the flavor. ½–1 t. Maggi extract may be added at the end instead.

CREAMED SAUERKRAUT SOUP
kapuśniak "parzybroda"

Drain ½ qt. sauerkraut, rinse in cold water, drain in colander, squeeze out excess moisture, and slice fine. Add to 6 c. smoked-meat stock, including diced smoked meat and soup vegetables, and cook about 50 min. Scald 2 tomatoes with boiling water and remove skins. Dice tomatoes and add to soup, cooking another 15 mins. Fork-blend 1 c. milk, ½ c. sour cream, and 2 T. flour until smooth and add to soup along with 1 bud minced garlic. Simmer briefly. Add 1 t. sugar and salt & pepper if needed. Serve with boiled potatoes on the side or rye bread as a hearty cold-weather treat. *Note:* "Parzybroda", this soup's humorous nickname, literally means "chin-scorcher".

LENTEN SAUERKRAUT SOUP WITH MUSHROOMS
kapuśniak z grzybami postny

Soak 5–6 dried Polish mushrooms in 1 c. water several hrs. or overnight. Add mushrooms and their water to 5 c. water along with the soup vegetables and spices for court bouillon and cook until mushrooms are tender (30 min. or so—the exact time will depend on the age and dryness of the mushrooms). Remove mushrooms, dice, and return to pot. Drain, rinse well, drain, squeeze dry, and chop ½ qt. sauerkraut, add to stock and cook about

60 min. or so longer. Toward end of cooking, brown 1 diced onion in 2 T. butter and add to soup. Season to taste with salt & pepper and ½–1 t. Maggi extract. Cream soup with ½ c. sour cream fork-blended with 2. T. flour. Simmer several more min. Meatless, mushroom-flavored soups such as this were traditionally served during Lent and Advent. This one is especially good with boiled potatoes in jackets (kartofle w mundurkach) on the side.

VEGETABLE-BARLEY SOUP POLISH STYLE
krupnik polski

Cover ¼–½ c. barley with 3 c. cold water and set aside. Prepare 8 c. meat stock or court bouillon the normal way but add 4–5 presoaked, dried Polish mushrooms. The vegetables should be diced. Drain the soaked barley (discarding the water) and add to soup. Add 2–4 peeled, diced, raw potatoes and simmer until barley and potatoes are tender. If using soup bones, remove any meat found thereon, dice, and return to soup. If using court bouillon (meatless vegetable stock), add 2 T. butter. *Optional*: Cream with ¼ c. or so sour cream. Season to taste with salt & pepper and garnish with a little freshly chopped dill and parsley. The amount of barley depends on the thickness you prefer. Prepare only as much as you can eat in one day, because refrigerating turns this soup into a thick porridge. Naturally, you can dilute it with a little water, but it won't be as good.

TURKEY OR GOOSE-FLAVORED BARLEY SOUP
krupnik na kościach indyczych lub gęsich

After some festive occasion, you may not know what to do with that roast turkey or goose carcass that has been nearly picked clean and is just cluttering up your fridge. Never fear, Polish cookery has the answer! There is still enough meat and plenty of flavor in the bones to make this delicious soup. Simply cut up the carcass to fit in a soup pot, add 1 bay leaf, 4 peppercorns, and 2 grains allspice, cover with 8–10 c. cold water, bring to boil, reduce heat and simmer under cover for a long time, 2–3 hrs. is fine. The longer it simmers, the more flavor will be extracted. Remove all meat from bones, dice, and return to pot, discarding bones. Add diced, uncooked vegetables: 2 carrots, a slice of celeriac or 2 stalks celery, 1 small parsnip or parsley root, 1 leek or 1 onion, 3–4 potatoes, plus 3–5 presoaked, dried Polish mushrooms and the mushroom water, and ¼ c. or more barley, soaked in cold water 10 min. and drained. Cook until vegetables, mushrooms, and barley are tender (about 30 min.). Salt & pepper to taste and (optional) add a pinch of savory. Serve as is, or cream with ¼ c. or so sour cream. Garnish with chopped parsley and/or dill. Turkey bones make an excellent stock for other soups as well.

CREAM OF WHEAT OR OATMEAL SOUP
zupa z kaszki manny lub płatków owsianych

Although the English translation of this soup may sound none too enticing, this can be a nice change-of-pace dish during cold weather. Both cream of wheat as well as oatmeal have little characteristic flavor of their own, but they do add body to and highlight the flavor of your meat, vegetable, and mushroom stock. Simply proceed as with either of the barley soups above, but instead of barley, add ¼ c. or so uncooked cream of wheat or oatmeal. Both cereals require only a few min. of cooking. Season to taste as above. *Note:* 1–2 T. uncooked cream of wheat may freely be added to most any Polish-style vegetable or mushroom soup.

SPLIT PEA SOUP
zupa grochowa/grochówka

In 7–8 c. smoked-meat stock, containing the diced meat and vegetables, cook 1–1½ c. dry split yellow peas 30 min. Add 3 peeled, diced uncooked potatoes and simmer covered another 30 min. or until peas fully disintegrate. Season to taste with salt & pepper, ½–1 t. marjoram, and 1 bud minced garlic. For a thicker soup, make a roux from 2 T. bacon drippings and 2 T. flour, stirring in 1 c. hot soup until a smooth sauce forms. Add to soup and simmer a bit longer. For added flavor, add 1 pre-soaked Polish mushroom at start of cooking. When tender, dice it and return to soup. This savory, hearty soup is a real man-pleaser and is one of the author's all-time Polish favorites. It is truly a meal in a bowl, especially after a second helping. If you haven't the time to follow the above recipe, simply place the peas, 2 quartered onions, ½ lb. or more sliced, smoked kielbasa and the spices in a pot, cover with 2 qts. water, bring to boil, set heat as low as possible, and forget it for the next 2 hrs. or so. Using an electric slow-cooker is another possibility.

SPILT PEA SOUP PURÉED
zupa grochowa przecierana

Prepare soup as in the above recipe, but when ingredients are fully cooked, remove the smoked meat and spices and strain soup through a sieve. With wooden spoon, mash and force through the diced vegetables, scraping the bottom of sieve every so often. (Reserve the meat and mushroom, if you used one, for some other dish.) Unlike the hearty country-style pea soup (above), this is a daintier, smooth and creamy dish. Serve with butter-fried white bread croutons (grzanki).

MEATLESS SPLIT PEA SOUP WITH MUSHROOMS
grochówka postna z grzybami

Prepare 8 c. court bouillon including 4–6 pre-soaked, dried Polish mushrooms. Add 1–1½ c. dry split yellow peas and cook covered until they fully disintegrate (about 1 hr.). Brown 1 chopped onion in 2 T. butter, stir in 1–2 T. flour, adding 1 c. soup and add mixture to soup. Remove mushrooms, chop, and return to soup. Add 1 bud minced garlic, ½ t. marjoram, a pinch of savory (optional), and salt & pepper to taste. Simmer a while longer. 2–3 peeled, diced potatoes may be added and cooked in soup until tender (about 15 min.). In some families, this is one of the soups served on Christmas Eve.

BEAN SOUP
zupa fasolowa

Soak 1–1½ c. dry navy beans or lima beans overnight in 2 qts. lukewarm water. Next day, cook in same water until tender. This may take anywhere from 1–3 hrs., depending on the type and dryness of the beans you use. Drain beans and add to 6 c. smoked-meat stock. If you have no smoked-meat stock on hand, fry up 5–6 slices diced bacon with 1 chopped onion and add along with 1 c. raw chopped onions, 1 bay leaf, 6 peppercorns, 3 grains allspice, and the drained cooked beans to 6 c. water. Simmer 15–20 min. Season with salt & pepper, 1–2 buds minced garlic, 1 t. marjoram, and a pinch or 2 savory. ½–1 t. Maggi extract may also be added. Fork-blend 2 T. flour with 1 c. soup until lump free and add to pot. Simmer a few min. longer. Serve as is or over zacierka (grated-dough noodles).

LENTIL SOUP
zupa z soczewicy

Soak ¾ c. lentils in 1 qt. water 2 hrs., then cook in same water until tender. Cooking time will depend on the type of lentils you use. To 6 c. smoked-meat stock, including diced meat and soup vegetables, add the cooked, drained lentils, 3 peeled, diced raw potatoes, 1 t. marjoram and cook until potatoes are tender. Brown 2–3 T. flour in 2 T. bacon drippings, stir in 1 c. soup until lump free and add to soup pot. Season with salt & pepper, a pinch or 2 savory, 1 bud minced garlic, and 1 t. Maggi extract. *Optional*: Add 1 t. vinegar to perk up the flavor. Garnish with a little fresh chopped parsley, if you like.

CLASSIC POLISH MUSHROOM SOUP
zupa grzybowa

Soak 1 oz. dried Polish mushrooms in 2. c. water several hrs. or overnight, then cook in the same water with 1 quartered onion until tender. Chop mushrooms and add along with the mushroom water to 6–7 c. court bouillon or meat stock. Simmer briefly. Fork-blend ½–¾ c. sour cream with 3 T. flour, dilute with 1 c. soup and add to pot. Season with salt & pepper, garnish with 1 T. fresh chopped dill, and add 1–2 T. butter. Serve over egg noodles, egg noodle squares (łazanki), or poured-batter noodles. *Optional:* For a heartier soup, cook 1 c. peeled, diced uncooked potatoes in it before adding the sour cream. 1–2 T. barley (soaked in water 15 min. and drained) may be cooked in soup until tender instead of or in addition to the potatoes. If adding potatoes or barley, add an extra c. water to pot.

CLEAR MUSHROOM SOUP
zupa grzybowa czysta

Soak 1 oz. dried Polish mushrooms in 3 c. water several hrs. or overnight. Add 1 chopped onion, and cook covered in same water until mushrooms are tender. Slice mushrooms into thin, long strips, and add to 6 c. strained court bouillon. Simmer briefly, salt & pepper to taste, and serve over łazanki (egg-noodle squares) or other egg noodles. A little freshly chopped parsley and/or dill may be sprinkled in just before serving. This is a classic Wigilia soup.

TART MUSHROOM SOUP
kwasówka

As always with dried mushrooms, scrub and rinse under cold running water to remove hidden grit 1 oz. dried boletes. Soak in 1½ c. water several hrs., then cook in same water until tender. Slice mushrooms into thin strips and combine together with their water with 5–6 c. meat or vegetable stock, including diced soup vegetables. Add 1 c. sauerkraut juice and simmer briefly. Make a golden roux with 1½ T. butter and 2 T. flour, add 1 c. soup and simmer briefly, whisking until smooth. Add to pot, simmer briefly, and salt & pepper to taste. Serve with potatoes.

TART MUSHROOM & BEAN SOUP WITH DUMPLINGS
kwasówka z fasolą i kluskami

Soak 1 c. dried navy or pea beans in 5 c. water overnight, then cook in same water until tender. Soak 1 oz. dried boletes several hrs. in 2 c. water and cook until tender. In separate pot combine mushroom water with enough bean water to make 6 c. Use mushrooms to prepare mushroom soup dumplings (see soup garnishes), which should be cooked separately, drained, and added to soup when ready to serve. To stock add 1 c. sauerkraut juice and cooked beans. Bring to boil and simmer 10 min. In saucepan, brown 1 finely chopped onion in 2–3 T. lard, sprinkle in 2 T. flour, brown slightly, stirring into a smooth roux, and dilute with a little stock. Add to pot and simmer briefly. Season with salt, pepper, and a pinch or 2 ground caraway. Place mushroom-soup dumplings in bowls, drench with hot soup, and sprinkle with chopped dill and parsley. *Note:* Both these tart mushroom soups hail from western Poland's Wielkopolska (Great Poland) region, whose capital is Poznań. The latter soup in particular is a hearty and filling meal in a bowl!

FRESH MUSHROOM SOUP
zupa ze świeżych grzybów

Use 12–16 oz. wild mushrooms such as boletes (borowiki) or honey mushrooms (opieńki), also known locally as "stumpers", or the white store-bought mushrooms (pieczarki). Wash and rinse mushrooms very thoroughly, chop or slice thin, and sauté under cover in skillet along with 2 chopped onions, ½ c. water and 2 T. butter about 20 min. or until mushrooms are fully cooked. Transfer mushrooms to 6 c. court bouillon or meat stock (strained or with diced soup vegetables left in). Fork-blend ½–1 c. sour cream with 3 T. flour, add 1 c. soup stirring until lump-free, and add to pot. Simmer several min., salt & pepper, and serve over any type egg noodles or diced, cooked potatoes. Garnish with a little chopped fresh dill and/or parsley. *Optional:* 1 c. peeled, diced raw potatoes may be cooked in soup until tender. For a deeper flavor, add 1–2 pre-soaked, dry Polish mushrooms, cooked until tender in 1 c. water and diced.

MUSHROOM SOUP THE EASY WAY
zupa grzybowa uproszczona

Soak 1–3 dry Polish mushrooms in 1 c. water several hrs., then cook in same water with 1 chopped onion until tender. Dice mushrooms and add along with mushroom water to 4 c. cream of mushroom soup prepared according to directions on can or packet. Season to taste with salt & pepper, add ¼ t. vinegar, garnish with chopped dill and/or parsley, and serve over egg noodles of any type or cooked, diced potatoes. No one will know that you didn't make it entirely from scratch! You can also simmer 3–4 sliced fresh mushrooms and 1 chopped onion in 1 T. butter under cover about 10 min. and add to soup.

ONION SOUP POLISH STYLE
zupa cebulowa po polsku

Chop 5–6 onions (about 1 lb.) and simmer in 3 T. butter until transparent and golden but not browned. Transfer to 6 c. court bouillon containing the diced vegetables and cook 15 min. Force through sieve or mix until smooth in blender. Fork-blend ½ c. sour cream with 2 T. flour, stirring with 1 c. soup until smooth, then return to soup pot. Season to taste with salt & pepper, a pinch or 2 sugar, and ½ t. or so Maggi extract. Garnish with chopped parsley and serve with croutons. This will be quite different than the dark and thin French onion soup you may be used to, but we think you'll enjoy it for a change. It can also be made with meat stock.

OLD POLISH ONION & BREAD SOUP
zupa cebulowa po staropolsku

Remove skin from 4–5 slices Polish-style bakery rye bread, cut into croutons of whatever size (because they'll get lost in the sieving), and heat in 2 T. butter until lightly browned and crunchy. Set aside. Dice ½ lb. onions (about 5 med. onions), and sauté in 2–3 T. butter until tender and slightly browned. Combine onions and croutons in pot, add 6 c. water, and cook about 30 min. Sieve mixture or whirl in blender. Mix 1 c. coffee cream with 4 raw egg yolks until blended and add to sieved mixture. Heat gently without boiling, salt to taste, and serve with noodle squares.

PUMPKIN SOUP
zupa z dyni

Remove the skin from a fresh pumpkin and cut into ½ inch cubes. Place 2–3 c. pumpkin cubes in pot, add ½ t. salt and 1 c. water, bring to boil, reduce heat, and cook about 5 min. or until pumpkin is soft. Drain. Mash pumpkin with potato-masher and add to 4 c. boiling milk. Fork-blend 1 egg, 3 T.flour, and a pinch of salt into a smooth batter and pour in a thin stream into boiling soup. Cover and cook on low heat 3–5 min. Allow your diners to sugar it in their bowls to taste. It may also be flavored with a pinch of cinnamon or nutmeg or a drop or 2 of almond extract. Instead of the poured-batter noodles, it may also be served with rice or millet porridge (kasza jaglana). Canned pumpkin may also be used.

VEGETABLE SOUP
zupa jarzynowa

Bring 2 qts. water, with 1 T. salt added, to boil. Add 3–4 carrots, 2 stalks celery, 1 parsley root, and 1 leek (or 1 onion)—all vegetables diced, plus 1 c. fresh or frozen peas. Cook on low heat 20 min. then add 2 c. cauliflower, broken up into flowerlets, and 1 c. peeled, diced potatoes and cook about 15 min. longer, or until all vegetables are tender. Fork-blend ¾–1 c. sour cream with 3 T. flour, dilute with 1 c. soup, stirring until smooth, then add to soup pot. Simmer briefly, salt & pepper to taste, and just before serving, garnish with 1 T. chopped dill. This soup is among the authors' favorites, and we're sure your gang will also ask for seconds. *Note:* This soup can also be made with meat stock. Other vegetables may also be added, especially: kohlrabi, cabbage, turnip, or wax beans.

CAULIFLOWER SOUP
zupa kalafiorowa

Wash 1 cauliflower (about 1 lb.) and break up into flowerlets. Cook in 7 c. strained court bouillon with ½ t. sugar added about 20 min. or until tender. Cream with ¾ c. sour cream fork-blended with 2–3 T. flour. Simmer a few min. Garnish with 1 T. chopped dill or ½ t. dill and 1½ t. chopped parsley. Naturally, salt & pepper to taste.

KOHLRABI SOUP
zupa z kalarepy

Peel and dice 1 lb. preferably young kohlrabi, and cook in 6–7 c. meat stock uncovered about 20–30 min. or until tender. (Vegetables of the cabbage family like kohlrabi, cauliflower, Brussells sprouts, etc. are best cooked uncovered, at least at the beginning, to get rid of the strong "cabbagey" odor.) Cream as usual with ¾ c. sour cream fork-blended with 2–3 T. flour. Salt & pepper, simmer briefly, and top with a little chopped dill before serving. For puréed kohlrabi soup, mash and force the cooked kohlrabi through sieve, then proceed as above.

DILL SOUP
zupa koperkowa

Dissolve 3 T. flour in ½ c. cold water, add to 6 c. strained meat stock, and bring to boil. Beat 1–2 raw egg yolks with 1 T. soft butter and gradually add 1 c. hot soup, stirring constantly. Stir in ½ c. sour cream and when mixture is smooth, return to soup pot. Simmer 1 min. or so but do not boil. Switch off heat, add 3–4 T. finely chopped fresh dill, stir, cover, and let stand 2–3 min. Serve over poured-batter noodles.

POTATO SOUP
zupa kartoflana/kartoflanka

In 6 c. strained court bouillon or meat stock, cook 2-3 c. peeled, diced, uncooked potatoes 15 min. or until tender. Brown 1-2 finely chopped onions in 2 T. butter or other fat and add to pot. Cream with ¾ c. sour cream fork-blended with 2 T. flour and add to soup. Simmer briefly, salt & pepper to taste, and (optional) add ¼ t. ground caraway. Garnish with a little chopped dill and/or parsley. Serve over crêpe noodles (makaron z naleśników), grated-dough noodles, or other egg noodles of choice. *Optional*: 1 pre-soaked dry Polish mushroom, cooked in 1 c. water, may be added along with the water in which it cooked. The diced vegetables and/or meat from your stock may be added to soup.

OX-TAIL SOUP
zupa ogonowa

Place a 1 lb. ox tail in pot, cover with 2 qts. water, add 1 bay leaf, 3 grains allspice, and 6 peppercorns, and bring to boil. Skim off foam until no more forms, then reduce heat, cover, and cook on low heat 90 min. Add standard soup vegetables, diced, and 2 peeled, diced raw potatoes, 2 t. salt, and cook until tender. Simmer 1 finely chopped onion in 1 T. butter, add 2 T. flour and simmer until slightly browned. Dilute with 1 c. soup, stirring until lump-free, and add to pot. Simmer briefly. Salt & pepper, season with about ½ t. paprika. Remove any meat from tail, dice, and return to soup. Garnish with a little chopped parsley and serve over egg noodles.

CARAWAY SOUP
zupa kminkowa

To 6 c. meat or smoked-meat stock (with vegetables and spices removed but diced meat left in), add 2 T. caraway seeds and simmer under cover 20 min. Brown 2 T. flour in 2 T. butter, stir in 1 c. soup and, when lump-free add to pot. Simmer several min. longer. Garnish with chopped parsley. Salt & pepper to taste and serve over egg noodles of choice or cream of wheat dumplings. If you like, stir in ½ c. sour cream.

DILL PICKLE SOUP
zupa ogórkowa

To do this creamy, tart, and zesty soup up right, you will need some genuine Polish-style, brine-cured dill pickles (ogórki kiszone). The vinegar-cured variety you get at the supermarket will not do, even if they have "polish wyrób", "polskie ogórki", and white eagles all over the label! Peel 4–5 brine-cured dill pickles, grate coarsely, and add to 6 c. meat stock. Add 2 c. peeled, diced potatoes, cover, and cook on low heat about 30 min. Salt & pepper to taste and, if not as tart as you like, sour to taste with a little dill-pickle brine. Fork-blend ¾ c. sour cream with 2 T. flour, stir in 1 c. soup and, when lump-free, add to pot. Simmer several min. more. This soup is a Strybel family favorite and is usually made from the pork bones from which cutlets are cut away. The dill-pickle soup is a nice prelude to the second course: breaded pork cutlets (kotlety schabowe), mashed potatoes garnished with pan drippings, and sliced tomatoes (in summer) or grated carrot, apple & horseradish salad (in winter).

TOMATO SOUP
zupa pomidorowa

To 6 c. meat stock (preferably made with pork bones) add 1½ lbs. peeled, diced, fresh tomatoes, 3 c. canned, stewed tomatoes or 3 oz. tomato paste and simmer 15 min. Salt & pepper to taste. Fork-blend ¾ c. sour cream with 3 T. flour, stir in 1 c. soup, and add to soup pot. Simmer a few min. longer. If you like, adjust to taste with ¼–½ t. sugar. Garnish with a little fresh chopped parsley and serve over rice, egg noodles, or poured-batter noodles. ½ t. Maggi extract will enhance your soup's flavor.

CLEAR TOMATO SOUP
zupa pomidorowa klarowna

Wash and dice 1 lb. tomatoes, unpeeled, and simmer 1–2 min. in pot with 2 T. butter, stirring constantly. Cover with 5–6 c. strained court bouillon and cook 15 min. Strain through sieve that will retain the tomato skins and seeds. Salt & pepper to taste, add about ½ t. sugar, ½ t. Maggi extract and (optional) a jigger dry white wine. Serve this elegant soup with butter-fried white bread croutons or puff-pastry pellets (groszek ptysiowy).

TOMATO SOUP QUICK & EASY
zupa pomidorowa naprędce

Dissolve 3 beef or vegetable bouillon cubes in 2 c. hot water, add 2–3 c. tomato juice, and heat to boiling. Remove from heat. Fork-blend ½ c. sour cream with 2 T. flour, dilute with 1 c. hot soup, stir until smooth, and return to pot. Add 1 T. butter and simmer 1 min. Salt & pepper to taste, garnish with 1 T. chopped parsley, and serve over rice or egg noodles of choice. Although this takes no longer to prepare than canned soup, it has a much more homemade flavor. Whip up a batch when you have some rice or noodles left over from yesterday's meal.

LEEK SOUP
zupa z porów

Remove "whiskers" and hardened root portion from 3-4 leeks, cut away, and discard greens (upper part), cut lengthwise, wash well under cold, running water and chop. Cook in 6 c. boiling court bouillon or meat stock 15 min. or until leeks are fully cooked. Fork-blend ½ c. sour cream, 1 raw egg yolk, and 2 T. flour, dilute with 1 c. soup, stir until smooth, and gradually add to soup, stirring constantly. Simmer briefly. Salt & pepper to taste. ½ t. Maggi extract may be added to improve flavor. Garnish with a little chopped parsley and/or dill. *Optional:* 1 c. peeled, diced potatoes may be cooked in the stock along with the leeks.

SORREL SOUP
zupa szczawiowa

Wash well ½ lb. sorrel, trim away stems, chop, add to skillet along with 1 T. butter and 3 T. water and simmer on low heat under cover 10 min. Force mixture through sieve into 4 c. strained meat stock and simmer a few min. longer. Dissolve 3–4 T. flour in 2 c. milk and add to pot. Simmer briefly, then remove from heat. Fork-blend 2 raw egg yolks with 1 T. soft butter, adding several T. soup and stirring until smooth. Add to pot. Salt & pepper to taste and serve over hard-boiled egg slices. Instead of the eggs, it may be served over rice or with croutons.

SORREL SOUP ANOTHER WAY
zupa szczawiowa inaczej

Wash ½ lb. sorrel as above, chop very fine or run through meat grinder, and add to 5 c. boiling meat stock. Reduce heat and simmer under cover 15 min. Add 3 T. flour dissolved in 1 c. milk, season to taste with salt & pepper, and bring to boil. Remove from heat. Fork-blend ½ c. sour cream with ½ c. soup, adding 1 T. of the hot soup at a time and stirring constantly. Add to pot. Garnish with a little chopped fresh dill and parsley and serve over hard-boiled egg slices. *Optional:* Add 1 c. peeled, diced, raw potatoes to stock along with the sorrel. However it is prepared, creamy, tart, and tangy, sorrel soup is a Polish favorite well worth looking into. Since sorrel may not be easy to come by in your supermarket's produce department, it's a good idea to grow it in your vegetable garden. Sorrel concentrate may be found in Kosher delicatessens, but garden-fresh sorrel is best.

MOCK SORREL SOUP
zupa szczawiowa fałszywa

Cook 1 c. frozen chopped spinach in 4 c. water under cover 15 min., then blend in blender until smooth. Add to 1 can cream of potato soup, prepared according to directions. Simmer several min. Sour to taste with citric acid crystals, salt & pepper. For a richer taste, fork-blend 1 heaping T. sour cream with ½ c. hot soup and return to pot. Garnish with a little chopped dill and/or parsley and serve over hard-boiled egg slices.

PURÉED BABY PEA SOUP
zupa purée z młodego groszku

Shell, wash, and drain enough baby peas to make 2 c. and cook in 6 c. meat or vegetable stock until done (15–20 min.). Strain and sieve peas back into pot. Make a white roux with 2½ T. butter and 2 T. flour, stir in ½ c. coffee cream or half & half, simmer briefly, whisking until smooth, and stir into soup. Beat 2 egg yolks with a little soup and add to pot. Heat soup without boiling. Season with salt to taste and about 1 t. sugar. Serve with puff-pastry pellets or croutons.

GARDEN-GREEN SOUP
zupa z zieleniny

Wash well and chop fine 1 med. head Boston lettuce. Remove stems from 1 handful sorrel and 1 handful spinach, wash well, and chop fine. Combine greens in colander and rinse under cold running water. Drain, put in pot, and scald with 6 c. boiling meat stock. Simmer 30 min. Salt to taste. Fork-blend 1 c. sour cream, 2 egg yolks and 2 T. flour until smooth. Gradually stir in 1 c. hot soup and, when fully blended, add to pot. Simmer briefly, garnish with 1 T. or more chopped dill and parsley, and serve over farina (cream of wheat) squares.

CUCUMBER SOUP
zupa ze świeżych ogórków

This soup is similar to the one above, except that it contains cucumbers and chives, but no spinach. Peel 1 lb. cucumbers, cut in ½ lengthwise, then cut each piece in half again. Scoop out seeds. Slice thin, place in pot, add 3 T. butter, and sauté several min. Add 1 handful trimmed, washed, and finely chopped sorrel, 1 med. head washed and chopped Boston lettuce, a heaping T. each chopped chives, dill, and parsley. Mix ingredients and continue sautéing until cucumbers are very tender. Scald with 6 c. vegetable stock, bring to boil, and remove from heat. Fork-blend ½ c. sour cream, 2 egg yolks, and 2 T. flour and stir into soup. Simmer briefly and salt & pepper to taste. Serve with rye-bread croutons.

BEER SOUP
polewka piwna

Bring 4 c. beer just to the boiling point, then cover and set aside. In mixing bowl beat 1 c. sour cream, 4 raw egg yolks, and 1–2 T. sugar until smooth. Gradually add the hot beer in a thin stream, stirring constantly so mixture doesn't curdle. Heat but do not boil. Add a pinch or 2 cinnamon and serve over cubed farmer's cheese and rye-bread or white-bread croutons fried to a golden brown in butter.

BEER SOUP WITH CARAWAY
polewka piwna z kminkiem

In pot combine 5 c. beer, 1 c. water, 3 slices black bread (with crust removed), 2 T. butter and 1 t. caraway seeds. Bring to boil, reduce heat, simmer 10 min. Force through sieve, add 1 t. sugar and salt to taste. Serve with butter-fried rye-bread croutons sprinkled with grated yellow cheese. *Note*: This is but a small sample of the various beer soups widely served in the Poland of yesteryear, especially during Lent.

CREAMED FISH CHOWDER
zupa rybna

The heads of 1–2 pike are excellent for this dish but other large fish (carp, walleye, whitefish, sturgeon, lake trout, etc.) are also good. Wash the heads well, salt generously inside and out, and refrigerate in covered container overnight or several hrs. Rinse the head well, remove eyes and gills, place in pot, and cover with 8 c. court bouillon. Add 2 diced onions, bring to boil, skim away scum until no more forms, then simmer covered at least 1 hr. preferably longer, until head almost falls apart. Remove all meat from head, dice, and set aside. In soup, cook 1 c. peeled, diced potatoes about 15 mins. or until tender. Fork-blend ¾ c. sour cream with 2 T. flour, add 1 c. hot soup, and stir until smooth, then return to pot. Add the diced, cooked fish. Salt & pepper to taste, add a pinch of nutmeg, 1 t. lemon juice or vinegar, and sprinkle with 1 T. fresh chopped dill. This soup can also be made with half a dozen or so small panfish (perch, bluegills, chubs, etc.) Cook them whole (with eyes and gills removed) in court bouillon 1 hr. then force through sieve which will retain the bones and fins.

STURGEON SOUP
zupa z jesiotra

A cookbook published in Warsaw in 1906 called for an entire sturgeon to be cooked in court bouillon, but we suggest you content yourself with a sturgeon head or 1–2 heads of some other large fish. After an overnight or several-hr. salting, remove eyes and gills, rinse well, and cook in 8 c. court bouillon with a bay leaf added. After skimming away scum, cover and cook on low heat up to 90 min. or until head readily falls apart. Remove meat from head, dice, and set aside. Add 1 T. butter, 2 jiggers Madeira wine, and 1 peeled lemon, sliced thin. Salt & pepper to taste. Return diced fish to soup, garnish with a little chopped fresh dill and parsley, and serve over grated-dough noodles. These may be cooked separately in boiling salted water or in the boiling soup. *Variation:* Instead of the Madeira, add 2–3 t. freshly grated horseradish.

ROYAL FISH CHOWDER
zupa rybna po królewsku

Simmer 8–10 pitted prunes in ½ c. water under cover 15 min. or until they disintegrate and then force through sieve. Salt 1 lb. cleaned carp or other freshwater fish overnight or several hrs. Cut into chunks and cook in 6 c. court bouillon 30 min. Carefully remove all bones, and watch out for the tiny Y-bones if using carp. Dice and return to stock. (The heads of 2 carp or other large fish may be used instead but must be cooked 60 min. or longer.) Add the puréed prunes, ¼ c. pre-soaked and drained raisins, and 1 oz. ground, blanched almonds. Season to taste with salt & pepper, ¼ c. dry red wine, and a little sugar and lemon juice to achieve a balanced sweet, tart, and tangy taste. Serve over grated-dough noodles or with butter-fried white-bread croutons. This chowder reflects the somewhat exotic taste combinations favored by the Polish nobility of yesteryear, and we think you may enjoy it for a change of pace.

FISH BROTH WITH DUMPLINGS
rosół z ryby z pulpetami

After a salting of at least several hrs. rinse 1 lb. freshwater fish (carp, pike, or panfish), cut up and cook in 6 c. court bouillon along with 2 quartered onions 30 min. (Fillets may be used but cooking time should be reduced to 20 min.). Strain, reserving cooked fish for fish dumplings (pulpety z ryby). Add 1 T. butter and season to taste with salt & pepper, a pinch of sage and nutmeg, 1–2 t. lemon juice, ½ t. Maggi extract, and (optional) 1 bud minced garlic. Simmer briefly and garnish with 1 T. or more finely chopped dill. Serve with 4–6 fish dumplings per bowl.

CRAYFISH SOUP
zupa rakowa

Keep 20–25 live crayfish in a bucket or large pot of cold water 2–3 hrs. letting them "clean themselves out". Wash each under cold running water and place the live crayfish in 2 qts. salted boiling water containing a bunch of fresh dill. Reduce heat and cook covered 15 min. Remove and discard the black intestine from each crayfish, take out meat from the shells, and place in 5 c. cold, strained court bouillon. Grind the shells, place in separate pot with 3 T. butter and 1 c. court bouillon or beef stock, simmer until a reddish "crayfish butter" floats to top, and spoon it into court bouillon. Strain remaining mixture into court bouillon through sieve fine enough to retain the crushed shells. Heat soup to boiling, cream with ¾ c. sour cream fork-blended with 3 T. flour, salt & pepper to taste, garnish with 2–3 T. chopped dill, and serve over rice. The ordinary crayfish caught in lakes and ponds can be turned into this true gourmet delicacy.

WHEY SOUP WITH RAISINS
zupa z serwatki z rodzynkami

Heat 1½ qts. sour milk without boiling until curds come to top. Strain through fine sieve until dripping stops, retaining the liquid (whey). To whey add 1–2 heaping T. raisins and a little sugar to taste. Bring to boil and serve topped with the farmer's cheese you have made. *Optional:* Stir ½ c. sour cream into hot whey before adding cheese. *Note:* If you are nutrition-conscious, you should definitely not overlook this and other dishes based on whey, a true storehouse of important vitamins and minerals. What's more, whey has a pleasantly winey tang that is easy to like!

WHEY SOUP WITH RICE
zupa z serwatki z ryżem

Lightly beat 1 qt. sour milk and heat gently without boiling until curds separate from whey and float up. Strain through fine sieve, retaining whey. When dripping stops, transfer whey to pot, add 1 c. boiling water, bring to boil, reduce heat, and stir in ⅛ c. sour cream fork-blended with 2 T. flour. Simmer briefly, remove from heat, and beat in 2 raw egg yolks beaten with little boiled water. Pour over cooked rice in bowls and top with your crumbled, homemade farmer's cheese. Season with a little salt and sugar.

POTATO SOUP WITH WHEY
kartoflanka na serwatce

Peel, dice, and cook 7 med. potatoes in 3 c. vegetable stock until tender but still firm. Add 4 c. whey. Fork-blend ¾ c. sour cream with 2–3 T. flour and mix with 1 c. soup. Bring soup to boil, add sour cream mixture, and simmer several min. Salt to taste. Serve garnished with chopped dill. Season with a pinch or 2 ground caraway if desired.

HOT OR COLD BEET SOUP WITH WHEY
barszcz lub chłodnik na serwatce

Bring 3 c. whey to boil, remove from heat, and stir in 3 T. flour, mixing until smooth and free of lumps. Bring to boil again and set aside. Gradually stir in 2 c. buttermilk and ½–1 c. beet sour—enough to give the soup a nice pink color and tangy taste. Heat but do not boil, sprinkle with chopped dill, and serve with boiled potatoes on the side, garnish with fried salt-pork nuggets and as much of their drippings as you like. *Variation:* Chill soup and serve cold over hard-boiled egg slices.

HOT OR COLD WHEY & PICKLE SOUP
zupa lub chłodnik ogórkowy na serwatce

Proceed exactly as above but use about 1 c. strained juice of brine-cured dill pickles in place of beet sour. Taste before salting, because the pickle brine may be sufficiently salty to season your soup. Serve hot or cold as above.

LITHUANIAN COLD BEET & VEGETABLE SOUP
chłodnik litewski

Wash well and finely chop 1 c. baby beet greens and the roots that go with them. (The immature beet roots should be smaller than radishes). Place in pot, cover with 2 c. boiling water, and simmer covered 15 min. (*Optional:* For a more exquisite chłodnik, simmer with ½–¾ c. finely chopped boiled ham or cooked veal, or ½ c. chopped cooked crayfish meat or shrimp.) Cool. Beat or blend until smooth and creamy 4 c. sour milk and ½ c. sour cream. In cookery bowl combine the cooked baby beets, sour milk mixture, 1 peeled, finely chopped, or grated cucumber, 1 bunch radishes, 1 bunch green onion (all finely chopped). Add 2–3 T. finely chopped dill, 1–2 buds minced or crushed garlic, salt & pepper to taste, add 1 t. sugar and sour to taste with a little beet sour (kwas burakowy), sauerkraut juice, dill-pickle brine, or vinegar. Mix ingredients, cover, and refrigerate overnight. Serve cold over hard-boiled egg slices. To get the right deep-pink color, add the juice of 1 raw grated beet or a little beet juice from canned beets.

LITHUANIAN COLD BEET & VEGETABLE SOUP THE EASY WAY
chłodnik litewski łatwy

In mixing bowl combine 1 peeled, chopped cucumber, 1 bunch each chopped radishes and green onions, 2–3 chopped dill pickles, and 3 T. chopped dill. Pour in 4–5 c. buttermilk, 1–2 c. canned beet juice, mix ingredients, season to taste with salt & pepper, garlic powder, several pinches sugar, and a sprinkle of vinegar. Cover and refrigerate overnight. Serve cold over hard-boiled egg slices. As above, diced ham, veal, crayfish, or shrimp may be added for better flavor.

COLD CUCUMBER SOUP
chłodnik ogórkowy

In bowl, combine 2 peeled, thinly sliced, or coarsely grated cucumbers, 1 bunch green onions (green tops and white bottoms) chopped, 2 coarsely grated dill pickles, and 2–3 T. fresh chopped dill. Cover with 6 c. sour milk, beaten until smooth. Add 1 c. dill-pickle juice (or more to taste), and salt & pepper. Cover and refrigerate overnight. Serve cold over quartered hard-boiled eggs.

GREEN COLD & CREAMY SOUP
chłodnik zielony

In blender combine 2 c. sour milk, 1 bunch chopped green onions, 3 T. chopped dill, 2 T. each chopped chives and parsley, 2 diced dill pickles, ½ c. dill-pickle juice, 1 bud crushed garlic, and 1 t. salt. Blend until smooth and stir into 4–5 c. sour milk, beaten, or buttermilk. Refrigerate overnight. If you like, season to taste with a little sugar, a pinch of pepper, and as much sauerkraut juice as needed to get the tartness you desire. Serve cold over sliced or quartered hard-boiled eggs. *Optional:* A handful washed and finally chopped sorrel leaves and even several leaves of finely chopped Boston lettuce may be added. This is a gold mine of vitamins, mineral, and protein in a bowl that is also refreshingly cool on a hot summer's day.

COLD APPLE SOUP
chłodnik jabłkowy

Cover 1½ lbs. peeled, sliced apples and a small piece of orange rind (with white inner skin removed) with 5 c. water. Bring to boil; reduce heat, and cook covered 10 min. Force mixture through sieve and set aside to cool. Beat 3 raw egg yolks with 3–5 T. sugar until smooth and creamy and combine with soup. Add ½ t. vanilla extract or several pinches cinnamon, whichever you prefer, mix well and chill. Serve cold with puff-pastry pellets or butter-fried white bread croutons.

BLUEBERRY SOUP, HOT OR COLD
zupa z czarnych jagód

Cook 1 pt. washed and drained blueberries in 5 c. water about 10 min., sugar to taste. Dissolve 2 T. flour or potato flour in ½ c. cold water and stir into soup. Simmer a few seconds, then remove from heat. Fork-blend ¾ c. sour cream to liquify and dilute with 1 c. soup, stirring constantly until smooth. Add to soup when it has cooled somewhat. Season with a pinch of cinnamon if you like. Like most fruit soups, it may be served hot, warm, at room temp, or chilled. Serve with butter-fried white-bread croutons or puff-pastry pellets. If served hot, the egg noodles of your choice are a good accompaniment.

COLD STRAWBERRY-GOOSEBERRY SOUP
chłodnik z truskawek i agrestu

Wash and remove stems from 3 c. gooseberries and cook in 2 c. water and 3–4 T. sugar under cover about 20 min. Force through sieve. In blender, blend to a pulp 2 c. washed, hulled, uncooked strawberries and add to gooseberry mixture. Bring 2 c. milk and 1 c. coffee cream to boil and stir into fruit. Sweeten to taste with a little extra sugar if needed and chill. Serve cold with puff-pastry pellets, butter-fried white bread croutons, or egg noodles.

MIXED FRUIT SOUP
zupa z różnych owoców

In 4 c. water and 3–4 T. sugar, cook fruit of choice (apples, pears, plums, strawberries, blueberries, blackberries, raspberries, rhubarb, etc.) 15 min. Use anywhere from 3–5 c. fruit, depending on how strong you want your soup to be. For a purée-type soup, the apples and pears may be quartered and cooked unpeeled, since cooked fruits are forced through sieve which retains skins, cores, and seeds. If you prefer to have pieces of fruit in the soup, then peel and dice apples and pears. Dissolve 1–2 T. potato flour in ½ c. cold water, stir in ½ c. coffee cream or sour cream and 1 c. hot soup, and add mixture to pot. Season with a pinch of cinnamon or ground cloves if desired. Simmer briefly. Serve with butter-fried croutons, puff-pastry pellets, or egg noodles. The soup may be served hot, warm, at room temp. or cold. Since tastes vary, each diner may add additional sugar to his soup bowl. *Note:* Instead of whitening the soup, you can provide sour cream or half and half at table.

HOT APPLE SOUP WITH POTATOES
jabłczanka z kartoflami

Peel and slice 1½ lbs. apples and cook in 3 c. water 15 min. Force through sieve or leave apple slices intact, whichever you prefer. Add 2 c. water, 3 T. sugar or so, and bring to boil. Dissolve 2 T. flour in ½ c. cold water, stir in ½ c. sour cream (or ½ c.. plain yogurt if you are watching your weight) and, when mixture is smooth, add to soup. Bring to gentle boil. Season with a pinch of salt and a sprinkle of nutmeg or cinnamon. Serve with a dish of hot mashed potatoes dotted with butter on the side.

PEAR & APPLE SOUP
garus

Scrub well 4 apples and 4 pears. Cut in ½ without peeling and scoop out seed portion. Place in pot, cover with 6 c. water, add 2 crushed cloves and a small piece of cinnamon bark, and cook until fruit is soft (10-15 min.). Strain into another pot and sieve in cooked fruit. Add about 1 T. sugar (this soup should not be very sweet!) and bring to boil. Fork-blend 1 c. milk with 1 egg and 2 T. flour until smooth, gradually add 1 c. hot soup, stirring until smooth, then add to pot. Simmer briefly and serve with croutons or over-cooked, diced potatoes.

PLUM SOUP FROM MAŁOPOLSKA
pamuła śliwkowa

In pot combine about 1 lb. washed and drained whole fresh plums, preferably węgierki (Italian plums), 6 c. water, several cloves, a chip of cinnamon bark, and 2 T. or so sugar. Cook until plums fall apart. Strain and sieve mixture into another pot, stir ½ c. sour cream fork-blended with 1–2 T. flour, stir into soup, bring to boil, and serve with croutons or cooked diced potatoes. *Note:* Both this and the pear & apple soup (above) hail from the Małopolska region of southern Poland, also known as Galicja.

PEAR & BUTTERMILK SOUP
zupa gruszkowa na maślance

Peel and slice 1 lb. pears and cook with 2 cloves in 3 c. water 10 min. Force through sieve or leave pear slices intact. Mix 2 c. buttermilk and 2 T. flour dissolved in ½ c. cold water and bring to boil. Add cooked pears, 3 T. sugar or more to taste, and a pinch of cinnamon. Serve hot or cold over egg noodles or croutons.

PRUNE OR DRIED-FRUIT SOUP
zupa z suszonych śliwek lub suszu

Soak 8 oz. prunes in 6 c. water 2 hrs., add 2 cloves, a piece of lemon or orange rind (with white inner skin removed), and cook in same water until tender (about 15 min.). Add 1 T. potato flour dissolved in ½ c. cold water, sugar to taste, and heat briefly. Serve hot over rice or with butter-fried white bread croutons or puff pastry pellets. *Variation:* Use 4 oz. prunes and 4 oz. mixed dried fruit. Some families serve this soup instead of dried-fruit compote (kompot z suszu) on Christmas Eve. For a richer taste, fork-blend 1 raw egg yolk with ½ c. coffee cream, stir in 1 c. hot soup, and add mixture to pot. A pinch of cinnamon may also be added.

POLISH PLUM-JAM SOUP
zupa z powideł/powidlanka

In pot, combine 1 c. thick Polish plum jam (powidła), a pinch of cinnamon and/or ground cloves, and 4-5 c. water and bring to boil. Dissolve 1 T. potato flour in ½ c. cold water and add, stirring well. Simmer briefly. Sweeten to taste with a little sugar if necessary and serve hot with croutons or over egg noodles. *Optional:* ½ c. sour cream may be stirred into soup or a dollop may be added to each bowl.

COMPOTE OR FRUIT-SYRUP SOUP
zupa z kompotu

If your family uses a fair share of canned fruit, you may have more fruit syrup left over than you know what to do with. Rather than being thrown out, it can be the basis for a variety of fruit soups, limited only by your imagination. Simply combine 3–4 c. fruit juice from canned peaches, plums, pears, cherries, etc. (or any combination thereof) with 1–2 T. potato flour dissolved in ½ c. cold water, and bring to boil. ¼–½ coffee cream may be added for a creamed fruit soup. Add ½–1 c. of the fruit, diced, and serve hot or cold over egg noodles or with croutons.

RHUBARB SOUP
zupa rabarbarowa

Wash and dice 1 lb. young rhubarb and cook in 3 c. boiling water about 15 min. Force rhubarb through sieve or leave it intact. Dissolve 1–2 T. flour in c. cold milk, add to rhubarb and bring to boil. Remove from heat. Cream with ½ c. liquified sour cream or 2 egg yolks beaten with 1 T. sugar and ½ c. milk. Sweeten to taste with sugar as needed. Serve hot or cold with choice of traditional fruit-soup accompaniments. Since this soup often comes out an unattractive, whitish gray, a little juice from canned cherries will give it a more pleasing pinkish hue.

STRAWBERRY-RHUBARB SOUP
zupa truskawkowo-rabarbarowa

Cook only ½ lb. rhubarb in 2 c. water as above. Add 1–2 T. flour dissolved in ½ c. cold water, 2 more c. water, and bring to boil. Mash 1 pt. hulled, washed, fresh strawberries in blender and stir into hot soup but do not cook. Sugar to taste, stir in ½ c. fork-blended sour cream, and serve hot or cold over egg noodles, rice, or croutons.

"NOTHING" SOUP
zupa "nic"

Beat 2 egg whites to a stiff froth, adding 2 T. sugar, and beating until froth becomes glossy. Spoon mixture into 5 c. boiling milk. Simmer briefly, then turn froth dumplings over with fork, cover, and cook several mins. Remove with slotted spoon to serving bowls. Beat 4 egg yolks with 4 T. sugar until almost white. To hot milk add 1 t. vanilla extract and pour in thin stream into yolk mixture, stirring constantly so it doesn't curdle. (A wire whisk is good for this purpose.) Chill well. Serve cold with a few froth dumplings per bowl. Some say this soup is called "nic" because it requires "nothing" special except the ingredients found in every home. Others claim the reason is that it is "nothing but delicious." Whatever the case, this is something like a cold, liquid custard which your children will surely enjoy. A pinch of cinnamon or nutmeg may be added.

ALMOND SOUP
zupa migdałowa

Grind 1–1½ c. blanched almonds and scald with 6 c. boiling milk. Dissolve 1 T. potato flour in 1 c. milk and add to almond mixture. Bring to boil and remove from heat. Add ½ c. raisins, 1 c. cooked rice, cover, and let stand 5 mins. Sweeten to taste with several T. sugar and, for a more intensive almond taste, add ½ t. almond extract. For a richer taste and a nice golden hue, fork-blend 2 raw egg yolks with 3–4 T. cold milk and add. This time-honored dessert soup has been among the sweet dishes served at Wigilia.

POPPYSEED SOUP
zupa z maku

Rinse 1 c. poppyseeds in several c. waters, draining each time in sieve. Place poppyseeds in bowl, cover with 4 c. cold water, and soak overnight. Next day drain, grind 2–3 times with 1 oz. blanched almonds. To 5 c. milk add 3 cloves and a small piece of cinnamon bark, and bring to boil gently, stirring to prevent scorching. Stir in poppyseed mixture and simmer several min. Sweeten to taste with a little sugar and add a pinch of salt if desired. Serve over egg noodles. *Note:* This soup, like other poppyseed dishes, is sometimes served on Christmas Eve.

MILK SOUP
zupa mleczna

If you grew up in a real Polish home, a bowl of hot milk with rice or noodles, served on cold winter mornings, may well bring back fond childhood memories. Milk soups are a snap to prepare and easy to enjoy. Simply pour milk in pot (1–1½ c. per serving), add about ½ c. cooked rice or egg noodles (left over from yesterday's dinner), heat to boiling, and serve. A pat of butter may be added to each bowl. Sweeten with sugar or salt to taste.

MILK SOUP WITH POURED-BATTER NOODLES
lane kluski na mleku

Place 3 T. flour in cup, add 1 raw egg, ⅛ t. salt, and beat with fork until you get a smooth, pourable batter. If batter is on the thick side because, for instance, you have used a very small egg, stir in 1 T. cold milk. Pour batter in a thin stream all over the surface of

4 c. boiling milk. Stir gently, cover, and cook about 2 min. Let your gang salt or sugar the hot soup in their bowls according to preference. The author, for one, prefers salted milk soups, while others in the family like theirs sweet. A pat of butter may be added to bowls.

MILK SOUP WITH GRATED EGG-DOUGH NOODLES
zacierki jajeczne na mleku

Mix ¾ c. flour with 1 egg and form into a ball of stiff, dry dough. If it is sticky to the touch, add a bit more flour. If it is very dry and crumbly (for example, if you have used a very small egg), add ½–1 t. water to bind it together without making it sticky. Grate on to floured board, sprinkling with a little of flour to prevent noodles from sticking together. Add to 4–5 c. boiling milk, bring to boil again, reduce heat, and cook under cover 4–5 min. Salt or sugar according to preference. This type of noodle is sometimes known in English as egg-barley.

MILK SOUP WITH CREAM OF WHEAT
kasza manna na mleku

Mix ¾ c. uncooked cream of wheat with 1 c. water and ½ c. milk, bring to boil, reduce heat and cook under cover 15 mins. If it gets too thick, add a little boiling water. Stir in 3 c. hot milk and sugar to taste. To shorten cooking time, use instant cream of wheat.

MILK SOUP WITH OATMEAL
płatki owsiane na mleku

Mix ½–⅔ c. uncooked oatmeal with 2 c. cold water, add a dash of salt and cook on low heat 10 min under cover. Mix with 3 c. hot milk. Salt or sugar to taste. A pat of butter may be added to each serving.

MILK SOUP WITH MILLET GROATS
kasza jaglana na mleku

Mix ½ c. millet groats (available at many European-style delicatessens) with 3 c. cold water, bring to boil, reduce heat, and cook under cover 20 min. or until done. Drain and combine with 3 c. hot milk. Sugar to taste and (optional) add a pat of butter to each bowl.

SOUP GARNISHES & ACCOMPANIMENTS

Any nation that goes in for soup the way the Poles do would have had to develop a similarly impressive array of accompaniments. These include a wide variety of noodles and dumplings, croutons, groats, rice, potatoes, and pastry pellets—something like oyster crackers, only better! Hard-boiled eggs are a fairly common garnish and cheese is sometimes used as well.

While the above are garnishes added to the soup itself, there are also special pastries and pies eaten on the side, to mention a few *paszteciki* and *kulebiak*. *Żur*, Poland's traditional, tart, rye-meal soup, is often served with a side dish of hot potatoes drenched with fried salt-pork or bacon nuggets.

About the easiest soup garnish you can make from scratch are *lane kluski* (egg-batter noodles) which require little more than beating an egg or two and some flour with a fork and pouring the mixture into boiling soup where it cooks in a matter of seconds. Sometimes even less effort is required, like pouring hot soup over some of yesterday's leftover rice or noodles.

* * *

EGG-BATTER NOODLES/POURED-BATTER NOODLES/
EGG-DROP NOODLES
kluski lane

Fork-blend 2 eggs with 6 T. flour and ⅛ t. salt until air bubbles appear. Pour batter in a thin stream into boiling soup, broth, or water, and cook 2–3 min., stirring carefully. The taste will not be impaired, but cooking these noodles in a broth or other clear soup may make it cloudy, so it's better to cook them in boiling salted water and remove with slotted spoon when done. Serve with broth, tomato, potato, bean, and mushroom soups.

EGG-BATTER DUMPLINGS
kluski kładzione

Beat 1 egg with ¼ c. water, add ⅛ t. salt, and stir in 1 c. flour. Beat with fork until lump-free and glossy, striving to work as much air as possible into batter. With spoon scoop up smallish oblong dumplings and drop into boiling salted water, dipping spoon into boiling water between each new addition. Cook about 5 min., testing one for doneness. Serve in potato, bean, goulash, or other non-clear soups of choice.

FRIED EGG-BATTER NOODLES
kluski lane smażone

Beat 2 eggs with 2 T. flour and ¼ t. salt, adding 1 t. very finely chopped parsley. When batter is smooth, beat in 1½ t. rum. In skillet, melt 2 T. lard or heat 2 T. oil. Transfer batter to colander held over hot skillet and stir to allow it to drip onto hot surface. Fry until noodles are golden but still unbrowned. Serve with pea, tomato, or dill-pickle soup.

EGG-THREAD NOODLES
niteczki z jaj

Beat 1 egg with a pinch of salt to obtain uniform consistency. In thin stream pour into boiling broth. These will cook in a matter of seconds. Cook these noodles in only the amount of broth or other clear soup that you plan to serve immediately, as they do not keep well.

FRENCH EGG DUMPLINGS
kluski półfrancuskie

Cream 4 T. room temp. butter, adding 3 eggs one by one and mixing vigorously the whole time. Stir in ½ c. flour, ⅓ t. salt, and ½ c. water, mixing to achieve a uniform consistency. Drop spoonfuls of batter into boiling salted water, dipping the spoon in the water before adding another dumpling. Cook covered 2–3 min., testing one for doneness. Serve with creamed soups.

FLUFFY FRENCH DUMPLINGS
kluski francuskie

Cream 5 T. room-temp. butter, adding 3 egg yolks one by one and mixing until fluffy. Fold 3 stiffly-beaten egg whites and 8 T. flour into batter, mixing lightly. Drop spoonfuls of batter into boiling salted water, dipping spoon in hot water between each new addition. Cook under cover about 2 min. Serve with clear soups.

SCALDED EGG DUMPLINGS
kluseczki parzone

To 1 T. clarified butter add 2 T. boiling water, sprinkle with 3 T. flour and remove from heat. Beat in 1 whole egg, mixing until it fully blends with flour mixture. Add 1 egg yolk and a pinch of salt and mix until fully blended. Cover and refrigerate until ready to use. Shortly before serving, scoop up small oblong dumplings with spoon and cook in boiling salted water until they float up.

CREAM OF WHEAT DUMPLINGS
kluski kładzione z manny

Cream 2 T. room-temp. butter, gradually adding 2 egg yolks one by one and mix until uniform. Fold in 2 beaten egg whites, 3 T. flour and 3 T. uncooked cream of wheat. Add ⅓ t. salt and mix gently. Spoon mixture into boiling salted water, reduce heat to gentle, rolling boil, and cook covered until done (several min.). Test one for doneness. *Note:* Feel free to perk up the flavor or these and other plain soup dumplings with a little chopped parsley and/or dill, a pinch of pepper, nutmeg, or other seasoning according to preference. Serve with broth, caraway, or mushroom soup.

LIVER DUMPLINGS
kluski wątrobiane

Trim 3–4 chicken livers of any veins or membranes and grind. Cream 2 T. room-temp. butter with 2 egg yolks, add the liver, and continue mixing. Season with ¼ t. salt, a dash or 2 pepper, and (optional) a pinch of nutmeg. Fold in 2 beaten egg whites and sprinkle in 5 T. flour. Mix gently to blend ingredients. Drop spoonfuls of mixture into boiling salted water, dipping spoon in the water between additions. Cook 6–10 min. depending on size. Test one for doneness. Drain, place in soup bowls, and drench with hot broth.

LIVER & BREAD CRUMB DUMPLINGS
kluski wątrobiane z tartą bułką

Sauté 1 chopped onion in 2 T. butter until tender but unbrowned. Combine onion with 3 chicken livers and dice together, then force mixture through sieve. Separately, cream 1 egg yolk, add the liver, season with a little salt and marjoram, fold in 1 beaten egg white, and 4 T. bread crumbs. Mix to combine ingredients. Place spoonful into gently boiling water. If it does not fall apart, mixture is of proper consistency. If it does fall apart, stiffen batter with a bit more bread crumbs or a little flour. Cook 5–6 min.

MUSHROOM SOUP DUMPLINGS
kluski z grzybów

Cream 4 t. room-temp. butter with 1 egg yolk. Add 1 t. finely chopped parsley, ¼–⅓ c. ground, cooked mushrooms, and salt to taste. Mix well, fold in 1 beaten egg white and 2 T.

sifted flour, and mix again to blend ingredients. Add spoonfuls of mixture to boiling salted water and cook 10 min. or so. Serve in broth or other clear non-mushroom soups.

GRATED-POTATO SOUP DUMPLINGS
kluski z tartych kartofli do zup

Peel and grate 2–3 med. potatoes, transfer to sieve, and collect drippings. When leftover liquid settles, carefully pour off clear liquid at top, but add the starchy sediment to grated potatoes. Combine with ¾ c. flour (or ½ c. flour and ¼ c. bread crumbs), 1 egg and ½ t. salt, and work into uniform dough. On floured board form dough into thin ½ inch roll and slice at angle into ½ inch dumplings. Drop into salted boiling water and cook about 5 min. after boiling resumes. Drain in colander. These are especially popular in the Poznań region where they are served with czernina (duck soup) and sauerkraut soup. Also good in strong broths.

POTATO BROTH DUMPLINGS
kluski kartoflane do rosołu

Cream 4–5 t. room-temp. butter with 1 egg yolk, mix in 1 med. cold cooked potato mashed very fine, fold in 1 beaten egg white and 2 T. flour. Mix lightly and cook spoonfuls of mixture in boiling broth about 2 min.

CUSTARD CUBES
mleczko do zupy

Beat 1 egg and 1 additional yolk with 1 c. whole milk, adding a pinch or 2 salt and (optional) 1 pinch nutmeg. Fill tiny glass bowls or demitasses with mixture ¾ full and cook over steam until set. If you don't have a steamer pot, place in colander over boiling water in pot and cover with tight-fitting lid. When set, chill. Just before serving, remove custard and cut into cubes. Serve in tomato, sorrel, dill-pickle, or spring vegetable soup or in broth.

"NOTHINGS"/BAKED EGG-WHITE PUFFS
"nic"

Beat 2 egg whites to a stiff froth, gradually adding 6 T. sugar and beat continuously until mixture becomes quite firm. (*Hint:* A good way to do this is in a double boiler over boiling water.) Line baking sheet with parchment. Place egg-white mixture in decorator tube or simply roll up a sheet of plain writing paper into a horn for the same purpose. Squeeze cherry-sized or smaller globs of mixture onto parchment and bake in 325° oven until hard and fully dry. If puffs stick to the paper, moisten its bottom side and they should pull free. *Optional:* 1–2 t. vanilla sugar may be added while beating. Serve in "nothing" soup and fruit soups. These puffs can be stored in dry place in sealed container indefinitely, so make up a batch whenever you have leftover egg whites on hand.

GRATED EGG NOODLES/EGG BARLEY
zacierka do zup

Sift ⅔ c. flour onto bread board, add 1 egg, 2 T. water, and ¼ t. salt. Work ingredients into a stiff dough, sprinkling with flour. Roll into a ball and grate on coarse side of grater directly into boiling salted water or soup. Cook several min. until tender. If cooking in boiling water, drain and serve with bean, pea, or potato soup.

GRATED EGGLESS NOODLES
zacierka bez jaj

Eliminate egg from above recipe and increase the amount of water to get a stiff, non-sticky dough. Grate into boiling salted water and cook as above. It is best not to cook these in broth because they will make it cloudy. *Note:* Both of the above grated noodles are often cooked in hot milk as a breakfast soup.

SUET BALLS
pulpety z łoju

Sauté 1 chopped onion in ½ T. fat until tender and grind together with ½ lb. beef suet. Add 1 c. bread crumbs, 3 eggs, ½ t. salt, ¼ t. pepper, ¼ t. grated nutmeg, and 1 T. finely chopped parsley. Mix well, roll between floured hands into cherry-sized balls and drop into boiling salted water. Cook 6–9 min., testing one for doneness. Drain and serve with tripe (flaki).

SUET & MARROW BALLS
pulpety z łoju i szpiku

Grind ⅓ lb. beef suet with 2 oz. marrow, add 2 eggs, and mix to blend ingredients. Add 5–6 T. bread crumbs, 1 T. finely chopped parsley, ½ t. salt, ¼ t. pepper and a pinch or 2 grated nutmeg, mixing ingredients well. Between floured hands roll into cherry-sized balls and cook in boiling salted water 6–9 min. Drain and serve with tripe.

BUCKWHEAT SAUSAGE FOR TRIPE
kiszka do flaków

Pour ½ c. Kraków (fine) buckwheat groats into 1 c. boiling water and cook until it is thick. Transfer to plate and allow to cool. Sauté 1 chopped onion in 1 T. lard or salt-pork drippings until tender. To cold buckwheat mush add the onions, ¼ lb. raw ground pork, ¾ t. salt, 1 t. marjoram, and ½ t. ginger. Mix well and use mixture to stuff sausage casing. Tie both ends with strong thread, plunge into boiling water, and cook on low heat uncovered 30 min. Turn sausage over during cooking. Remove sausage from pot and plunge into cold water briefly. When cool enough to handle, slice into rounds, which are used to decorate the rim of your tripe platter.

FORCEMEAT BALLS
pulpety z mięsa

Slice an onion and sauté until golden in 1 T. fat. Soak 1 small slice stale French bread (½ a kaiser roll, etc.) in ½ c. milk. When soggy, grind together with the sautéed onion and about ⅓ lb. cooked meat. (Veal or poultry are best, but beef or pork will also do, as will any combination of these.) To mixture add 2 eggs, ½ t. salt, a dash or 2 pepper, 1 pinch nutmeg, 1 T. finely chopped parsley, and 2 T. bread crumbs. *Note:* Any of your homemade Polish meat seasonings are another flavor possibility. Mix well and roll between hands into cherry sized balls. Dip in flour, roll again snowball-fashion, and drop into boiling water. Cook 5–6 min. Drain and serve with bouillon or other clear soups.

RAW FORCEMEAT BALLS
pulpety z surowego mięsa

Combine ½ lb. raw ground veal, pork, and beef (the popular meatloaf mixture) with ½ c. bread crumbs, 2 eggs, 2 T. melted butter, 1 T. finely chopped parsley and/or dill, ½ t. salt and ¼ t. homemade herb pepper. Work into a uniform mixture and form into cherry-sized balls between floured hands. Cook in boiling salted water 10–15 min. Serve with clear soups as well as smooth creamed soups.

LIVER BALLS
pulpety z wątróbki

Sauté 1 sliced onion in 1 T. fat until tender. Trim away any veins or membranes from ¼ lb. chicken or calf's liver and grind together with the onions. Add 2 egg yolks, 6–8 T. bread crumbs, ½ t. salt, a pinch of pepper, and a pinch of ground coriander. Mix well to blend ingredients. Fold in 2 stiffly-beaten egg whites and mix gently. Between floured hands roll into cherry-sized balls and cook in boiling salted water 6–9 min. Serve with broth and tripe.

FORCEMEAT BALLS STUFFED WITH LIVER
pulpety nadziewane wątróbką

If you think that the preceding soup-ball garnishes are too much bother, then this recipe is not for you, because it is even more involved. But maybe for some special occasion when you feel extra-ambitious—who knows? Trim off crust from 1 slice French bread and soak in ¼ c. milk. Squeeze out excess milk and grind bread together with ¼ lb. cooked white chicken or turkey meat. Grind mixture again and refrigerate until completely chilled. Stir in ¼ c. whipping cream (unwhipped), sprinkle with salt, and mix well to obtain a smooth texture. Separately, trim 1 raw goose liver of any veins or membrane and place in saucepan containing 1 T. melted butter. Sauté with 1 T. finely chopped onion and 1 t. chopped parsley, but do not overcook. Transfer to mortar and pound vigorously, then force through sieve. Sprinkle mixture with a little salt. Roll ground chicken (or turkey) mixture into balls slightly larger than cherries, then flatten into patties. Place a little liver filling at center, fold in half, and between floured palms roll into balls. Cook in boiling salted water about 6–7 min. Drain and serve on gourmet occasions in clear broth. *Note:* These forcemeat balls can be made with cooked ground meat other than chicken or turkey and may be stuffed with chicken or calf's liver, if goose liver is not available.

FISH BALLS/DUMPLINGS
pulpety z ryby

Sauté 1 sliced onion in 1 T. oil until tender. Grind together with ¼ lb. boned, skinless fresh or frozen fish. Add 1 egg, 1 T. finely chopped fresh dill, ½ t. salt, a pinch of pepper, and/or ¼ t. homemade Polish fish seasoning, and about 4 T. bread crumbs. Work ingredients into uniform consistency and form cherry-sized balls between hands. Roll in flour, pressing it in by rolling balls again between hands snowball-fashion. Cook in boiling salted water 5–7 min., drain, and serve in fish soup.

THIN EGG NOODLES
makaron do rosołu

For generations, these homemade egg noodles have been a Polish Sunday dinner classic served with chicken soup or beef broth. They are both tastier, more natural (no artificial additives!), and more economical than the store-bought variety, and we're sure you'll enjoy them as much as we do. Here are four versions ranging from rich to lean:

— 2 c. flour, 3 eggs, ½ t. salt;
— 2 c. flour, 2 eggs, 1 yolk, ½ t. salt;
— 2 c. flour, 2 eggs, 4–6 T. water, ½ t. salt;
— 2 c. flour, 1 egg, about ¾ c. water, ½ t. salt.

Sift flour onto board and make a well at center. Break eggs into well, sprinkle with salt and, if recipe calls for water, add it lukewarm. Mix by hand and work into a uniform dough. Knead dough on floured board until it becomes smooth and elastic. Roll out as thin as possible and leave the rolled-out dough sheet on floured board to dry about 30 min. Do not overdry, because it will crack when you try to roll it. Roll dough sheet up tightly and slice very thin. The sliced noodles should be scattered over floured board while you slice the rest. Leave noodles scattered loosely over entire surface of board to dry about 30 min. Cook in boiling salted water 5–10 min., depending on thickness. Drain in colander and serve in broth, fruit soup, mushroom soup, tomato soup, and others. *Note:* If making a supply for future use, let it dry several hrs., then store in cupboard in paper sack.

SOUP NOODLES
kluski do rosołu

Prepare noodle dough according to any of the four sets of ingredients above. Roll out slightly thicker than paper thin and, after dough sheet has dried 30 min., roll it up and slice ⅛–¼ inch wide. Let dry on floured board and cook as above. *Remember:* These heavier noodles will take a little longer to cook, so test them for doneness.

SOUP NOODLE SQUARES
łazanki do zupy

Prepare dough as for thin egg noodles (above). After dough sheet has dried 30 min., cut it into strips ½ inch in width. Place 5–6 strips on top of each other and cut through to board to form ½ inch squares. Continue until all dough has been cut up. Scatter over floured board and let dry 30 min., then cook in salted boiling water 5–10 min. or until tender. Drain in colander, rinse with boiling water, and allow to drip dry. These noodle squares are often served with clear mushroom soup on Christmas Eve. They are also good in bean, potato, and other soups according to preference.

"LITTLE EAR" SOUP DUMPLINGS
uszka

The mushroom-filled version of these dainty little dumplings are the classic accompaniment to the clear beetroot barszcz served on Christmas Eve. Sift 1 c. flour onto

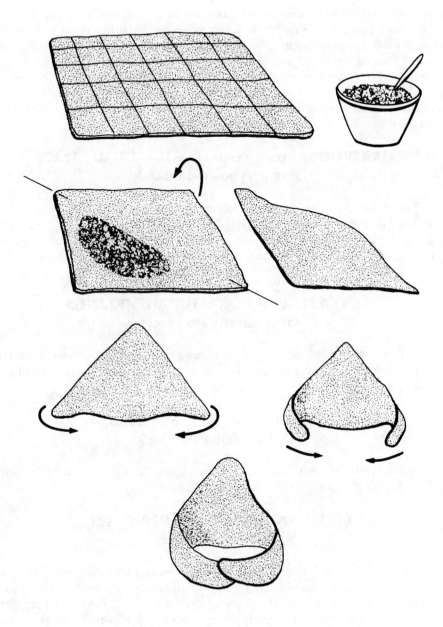

The formation of uszka ("little ear" soup dumplings) is easier to illustrate than to describe.

bread board and make a well at center. Break 1 egg into well, sprinkle with ¼ T. salt, and mix into a dough, adding only as much water as needed (several T.) to bind ingredients. Knead dough until it is elastic and glossy, then roll out thin on floured board. Cut dough sheet into 1½ inch squares. Place a little filling slightly off center, fold in half to form a triangle, and pinch edges together. *Hint:* Dip fingers in egg white to ensure a perfect seal. Gently pull the 2 bottom corners together and join by pinching. Cook in boiling salted water 2–4 min. from the time dumplings float up. Remove with slotted spoon and serve in clear beetroot soup or broth.

MUSHROOM FILLING FOR SOUP DUMPLINGS
farsz grzybowy do uszek

Scrub 2 oz. dried Polish mushrooms (boletes), soak overnight in 3 c. water and cook in same water until tender. (Reserve mushroom liquid for use in soups, gravies and sauerkraut dishes.) In 1 T. butter or oil sauté 1 sliced onion until tender. Grind mushrooms and onion, add 1 egg white, 2 T. breadcrumbs or more, salt & pepper to taste and mix well. Use to stuff "little ear" soup dumplings.

MEAT FILLING FOR SOUP DUMPLINGS
farsz mięsny do uszek

Fry up 1 heaping T. diced salt pork with 1 chopped onion until tender. Grind together with ½ lb. cooked beef or pork (or some of each). Add 1 egg, 1–2 T. bread crumbs, and salt & pepper to taste. Mix ingredients well and use to fill soup dumplings.

OTHER SOUP-DUMPLING FILLING
inne nadzienia do uszek

Uszka may also be stuffed with any of the savory fillings recommended for crêpes (naleśniki) or pierogi (see chapter on dumplings and noodles).

LITHUANIAN SOUP DUMPLINGS
kołduny litewskie

Sift 2 c. flour onto bread board, make a well at center, break an egg into it, sprinkle with ½ t. salt, and combine ingredients, gradually sprinkling with enough water to achieve a pierogi-dough consistency. Knead dough on floured board until smooth and elastic and roll out very thin. Use a wine glass 1 inch in diameter to cut dough into circles. Place a little filling on circles, leaving a ¼ inch space around the edge. Cover with another circle and seal together by pinching. Another way is to use a juice glass or biscuit-cutter about 1½ inches in diameter to cut out circles. Place filling just off center, fold in half, and seal by pinching. A third way is to cut dough sheet into 1 inch squares, fill, and fold in half to form triangle, sealing as above. Cook in boiling salted water in batches, so as not to crowd in pot, 3–5 min. from the time boiling resumes. Remove with slotted spoon and serve in broth or bouillon. *Note*: Besides being a soup garnish, kołduny are often served as a main course drenched with melted butter.

CLASSIC LITHUANIAN DUMPLING FILLING
farsz do kołdunów klasyczny

Grind ¼ lb. each boneless lamb (preferably leg portion), beef tenderloin, and beef suet. (Store-bought ground lamb and fatty hamburger may be used instead, in which case omit the suet.) Add 1 finely grated onion and 1 bud minced garlic mashed with ¾ t. salt. Sprinkle with pepper and about 1 t. marjoram. Mix well, adding about 2 T. water.

LITHUANIAN DUMPLING FILLING WITHOUT SUET
farsz do kołdunów bez łoju

Soak 6 dried Polish mushrooms in a little water overnight and cook until tender in same water. Grind mushrooms together with ¾ lb. beef tenderloin or cheaper cut of beef. Add 1 finely grated onion, 1 bud garlic mashed with ¾ t. salt, ¼ t. pepper, and ½ t. marjoram. Mix well.

CROQUETTES
krokiety

A good time to prepare these tasty, crispy croquettes is whenever you have some leftover naleśniki. Simply spread the crêpes with filling of choice, leaving 1 inch space around the edge. Fold 2 sides over filling to meet at center. Then roll up tightly lengthwise jelly-roll fashion. Dip the croquettes in beaten egg and roll in bread crumbs. Fry in hot fat on both sides to a nice golden brown. Drain on absorbent paper and serve hot with clear beetroot soup or other clear soups.

CROQUETTE FILLINGS
nadzienia do krokietów

Cooked ground meat, mushrooms, and stewed sauerkraut (usually with mushrooms) are the most common croquette fillings. But feel free to use any of the other fillings given for pierogi and naleśniki (see section on dumplings, noodles, & pancakes). Egg & rice filling is very good. The fish filling recommended for kulebiak (soup pie) is another possibility. Leftover bigos—why not? Croquettes seem to invite culinary creativity by their very nature.

CRÊPES NOODLES
makaron naleśnikowy

This is an easier way to use up leftover naleśniki. Simply place 3–4 crêpes on top of one another, roll up tightly and slice into thin noodles widthwise. Place batches of noodles in soup bowls and drench with piping hot bean, mushroom, tomato, or sorrel soup. Cold fruit soup is another possibility.

BATTER-FRIED MUSHROOMS
grzybki smażone w cieście

Soak 12 large dried Polish mushroom caps in water overnight. Next day, add a little salt and cook in same water until tender. Remove mushrooms and dry. (Use liquid for clear beet root soup.) Prepare crêpe batter by beating 2 eggs and gradually adding 6 T. sour cream, 10 t. flour, ½ t. salt, and ½ t. baking powder. In large skillet heat ½ c. oil. Place mushrooms in batter and remove them with fork one by one and fry in hot fat. Since the batter tends to flow down to bottom, pour a few t. over top of mushrooms as they fry. When bottom is golden brown, turn mushrooms over and fry other side. Drain on absorbent paper and serve with clear Christmas Eve barszcz. *Note:* Back in 1980 the authoress didn't have time to prepare the traditional uszka for Christmas Eve supper and she tried this recipe instead. Batter-fried mushrooms have been a Wigilia standard in our household ever since.

PUFF-PASTRY PELLETS
groszek ptysiowy

In pot, heat ½ c. water, ½ stick butter, and ¼ t. salt. When it comes to a boil, remove from heat and add ½ c. flour. Mix well so there are no lumps. Return to heat and, stirring constantly, cook about 2 min. or until mixture comes away from sides of pot and resembles whipped potatoes. Remove from heat, add 1 egg, and mix by hand until fully blended. Add another egg and mix until blended. Transfer mixture to decorator tube and squeeze out tiny pea-sized balls onto lightly greased baking sheet. Bake in hot 400° oven 10–15 min. or until pellets turn golden. Serve in cold fruit soups, cream of (domestic) mushroom, bean, puréed pea, and other puréed soups.

SOUP EGG-CAKE CUBES
grzybek do zup

Beat 2 egg yolks with ¼ t. salt. Add 3 T. flour and ½ c. milk and continue beating until smooth. Fold in 2 beaten egg whites and mix lightly. Heat 1 T. fat in skillet, add egg mixture, and cook until it is lightly browned. Flip over and lightly brown other side. Slide egg cake onto board, dice or slice into strips, and serve with sorrel, dill, or tomato soup.

BAKED SOUP SPONGE CAKE CUBES
grzybek biszkoptowy

Here is a sweeter grzybek excellent in fruit soups. Beat 2 egg whites to a stiff froth, add 2 T. sugar, and beat a while longer. While beating, gradually add 2 egg yolks, and 2 T. flour. When mixture is fluffy, transfer to buttered skillet or baking sheet, pop into 350° oven, and bake until golden. Just before serving dice or cut into strips.

RICE OR GROATS AS SOUP GARNISH
ryż lub kasza do zup

Rice, barley, and buckwheat groats are also used in various soups. Since the recipes are given in the chapter on groats and grain dishes, we will not repeat them here. Rather than preparing them from scratch, it is best to cook the appropriate soup when you have rice or groats left over from the previous day's meal. Cooked rice is a traditional garnish for tomato, lemon, and sorrel soup. Cooked groats may be added to tomato and other vegetable soups.

BROWNED RICE
ryż rumiany

Wash and drain ⅓ c. rice. In saucepan, melt ½ T. butter, add the rice, and sauté as for a roux, stirring constantly so that rice gets evenly browned. Add 1 c. broth and cook until rice is tender. Serve with broth or other clear soups.

FARINA OR KRAKÓW-GROAT CUBES
kostka z manny lub kaszy krakowskiej

In pot, combine ½ c. farina (cream of wheat) or fine buckwheat groats with ½ c. cold water to soak briefly. Separately, bring to boil 1 c. water containing ½ t. salt and 1–2 T.

butter. Add soaked rice or groats to boiling water. When boiling resumes, reduce heat to minimum and cook, stirring occasionally, until you get a smooth mush. *Optional:* Stir in 2 T. finely chopped parsley and/or dill. Pour hot mixture onto large, moist plate (rinsed in cold water) and spread it with knife into ½ inch thick layer. When cooled to room temp., chill in fridge. Cut into ½–1 inch cubes, distribute among soup bowls, and drench with hot broth, tomato soup, or mushroom soup—especially the clear varieties.

SAGO
sago

Largely unavailable and unknown to Polish cooks of the post-World War II period, these tapioca-like beads were once favored as a soup additive. Soak ⅓ c. sago beads (pearls) in ⅔ c. water 1 hr. or until it is all absorbed. Cook in soup or separately in boiling water, drain and add to soup, especially broths and bouillons. *Note:* Pearl tapioca may be used the same way.

FILLED SOUP PASTRIES/PIES
paszteciki

These little, hand-held pastries have long been a favorite accompaniment to clear soups served in teacups at elegant banquets and dinner-parties. In Warsaw, cooks who don't have the time to prepare them from scratch often buy these flaky little pies at the fashionable pastry shop of the Hotel Europejski, located on historic Krakowskie Przedmieście street. They are usually filled with mushrooms, or hard-boiled eggs, but many other fillings are possible. In fact, they offer an interesting opportunity to utilize various leftovers with gourmet effects. One problem we have encountered with paszteciki is linguistic rather than culinary in nature: what to call them in English? We have encountered attempts to render them as pastries, pasties, pies, turnovers, cakes, tarts, rolls, roll-ups, filled buns—you take your pick! Whatever you may call them, we are certain they will become one of your favorites. Of the many Polish dishes we have treated our American friends to over the years, paszteciki won the raving approval of 99 and 44/100 percent. Here are some ways to make them.

BUTTER-DOUGH SOUP PASTRIES
paszteciki maślane

Sift 1⅔ c. flour onto board, cut in 2 sticks butter, add ½ c. sour cream, 1 egg, 1 egg yolk and ¼ t. salt. Quickly work ingredients into a dough but do not knead. Cover and refrigerate

1 hr. Roll out on floured board into a rectangle 3–4 inches wide and ¼ inch thick. Run a strip of filling down the middle from end to end. Fold 1 side of dough over filling rather tightly so it overlaps the other side by about ½ inch and place roll seam side down. Cut roll into 2 inch cakes, place on greased baking sheet. Pop into pre-heated 450° oven and bake 20 min. or until nicely golden brown. Serve hot with clear red barszcz or broth.

YEAST-RAISED SOUP PASTRIES
paszteciki drożdżowe

In bowl, mash ½ cake yeast with ½ t. sugar, add ⅔ c. lukewarm milk and ¾ c. flour, mix ingredients, cover, and let rise in warm place 20–30 min. Add 1 egg, ½ t. salt, and 1 c. sifted flour. Blend ingredients with hand and knead until dough no longer sticks to hand and comes away from sides of bowl. Gradually add 5 T. melted butter and continue kneading until dough is smooth and glossy. Cover with napkin and let stand in warm place until doubled in bulk. Transfer dough to floured board and roll out ⅛–¼ inch thick into a rectangle 3–4 inches wide. Run a strip of filling down the center lengthwise from end to end, fold 1 long side of dough over filling so it overlaps the other side by ½ inch, and set the roll on board seam side down. Cut roll into 2 inch cakes, place on greased baking sheet in warm place to rise. Brush cakes with beaten egg and pop into pre-heated 400° oven. Bake 20–30 min. Use toothpick to see if done. Serve hot with clear soup.

FLAKY SOUP PASTRIES
paszteciki półkruche

Sift 2 c. flour onto bread board, place 1½ sticks of not-too-cold butter on top, sprinkle with ½ t. salt and 2 t. baking powder. With knife, chop to blend ingredients. Add 2 eggs and 2 T. sour cream and work into a dough. Roll out on floured board into a ¼ inch thick rectangle whose shorter sides measure about 8 inches. Cut rectangle lengthwise in two. Run the filling lengthwise down center of each rectangle. Fold one long side over filling so it overlaps the other side by ½ inch and set roll on board seam side down. Slice into 2 inch cakes, place on greased baking sheet, brush each pastry with beaten egg and bake in 375° oven 20–25 min. Serve as above.

EASIEST SOUP PASTRIES
paszteciki najłatwiejsze

When pressed for time, try this super-easy method using store-bought refrigerator crescent-roll dough. Remove dough sheet from package and place on lightly floured board.

Lightly sprinkle manufacturer's perforations with a little flour, then press down with thumb to obliterate them. Cut into 2 rectangles. Run filling lengthwise down center of each, fold over as above, place seam side down and cut into 1–1½ inch cakes. Bake according to directions on package and serve hot with clear soups. Chances are, nobody will even suspect that you didn't make them from scratch!

FRESH MUSHROOM FILLING FOR SOUP PASTRIES
farsz pieczarkowy do pasztecików

In 3 T. butter or other fat sauté 1 lb. washed, sliced, fresh mushrooms and 2 chopped onions, adding ½ t. salt, until moisture evaporates and mushrooms begin to sizzle. Grind, add 1 egg, 2 T. bread crumbs, ¼ t. pepper and a pinch of savory, mix well and use mixture to fill any of the 3 types of soup pastries presented above.

MEAT FILLING FOR SOUP PASTRIES
farsz mięsny do pasztecików

Sauté 2 sliced onions in 2–3 T. fat until tender and grind with about 1 lb. cooked pork or beef. Add 1 egg, salt & pepper to taste, and (optional) season with a little of your homemade pork, beef, or hunter's seasoning. Add 2 T. bread crumbs and mix well.

MEAT & MUSHROOM FILLING FOR SOUP PASTRIES
farsz mięsno-pieczarkowy do pasztecików

Prepare filling as above, but using about 8 oz. fresh mushrooms and ½ lb. cooked beef or pork. *Note*: Cooked veal, chicken, or turkey, or any combination of meats, can also be used. Other fillings given for kulebiak, pierogi, and naleśniki are also good.

BAKED PIEROŻKI AS SOUP ACCOMPANIMENT
pierożki pieczone do zup

Prepare dough in any of the 3 ways given for paszteciki (above). Either cut rolled-out dough into larger circles with water glass or biscuit-cutter, place a spoonful of filling at center, fold in half and seal edges by crimping, or cut out smaller circles with juice or wine glass, place a little filling on half of them, cover with remaining dough circles, and seal edges by pinching. Bake like paszteiki. *Note:* If using yeast-raised dough, remember to let pierożki rise in warm place before brushing with beaten egg and baking.

ROLLED PIEROŻKI WITH SALT PORK
pierożki zwijane ze słoniną

Prepare dough as for yeast-raised soup pastries and set aside in warm place to rise. Meanwhile, finely dice ½ lb. salt pork, place in pot, add 2 finely chopped onions, ½ t. salt (if using unsalted fat back) and ¼ t. pepper. Heat on low until salt pork becomes transparent without melting, stirring frequently. Stir in ½ c. bread crumbs and mix well. Set aside. Roll risen dough out ¼ inch thick, cut into rounds with glass or biscuit-cutter, spread surface with salt-pork filling, and roll up like tiny crêpes. Place on baking sheet to rise in warm place, then brush with beaten egg and bake in 400° oven about 20 min.

ONION OR CABBAGE CAKES
kołaczki z cebulą lub kapustą

Mash ½ cake yeast with 1 t. lukewarm milk, add ½ t. flour, and ½ t. sugar and set aside to rise. Sift scant 2 c. flour into bowl, make well at center, add risen yeast mixture, 2 egg yolks, 1 T. sugar and 1 t. salt. With spoon mix ingredients, gradually adding about ¼ c. lukewarm milk. After working ingredients into a dough, knead about 10–15 min. or until dough becomes glossy and air bubbles appear. Add 2 T. melted butter and knead until fully blended. Smooth surface of dough with buttered hand, cover, and let rise in warm place about 1 hr. Roll dough out about ⅓ inch thick, cut into circles, and place on greased baking sheet in warm place to rise. Make indentation at center of each cake, brush with egg white, and fill indentation with onion or cabbage filling. For onion filling, slice 2–3 onions (depending on size) wafer thin and scald with boiling water. Drain in colander and sauté in 3 T. butter until tender but still unbrowned. Season with salt & pepper and a pinch of sugar. Bake in 400° oven 20 min. or until nicely browned. *Note:* For cabbage kołaczki, use cabbage filling given for kulebiak (below).

YEAST-RAISED FILLED LOAF/PIE
kulebiak drożdżowy

Mash ½ cake yeast with 1 t. sugar, add ½ c. lukewarm milk and ½ c. flour, mix, cover, and let stand in warm place 15–20 min. Into bowl sift 1½ c. flour, add yeast mixture, ½ t. salt, 1 beaten egg, and 1 beaten yolk, and work ingredients into a dough. Knead until dough no longer sticks to hand and sides of bowl. Add 3 T. melted butter and knead until dough becomes smooth and glossy. Form dough into ball and leave in bowl in warm place to rise. When it doubles in bulk, transfer to floured bread-board and roll out into rectangle ⅓ inch thick. Spread filling of choice (see below) on dough up to 1 inch from edges. Roll long side up jelly-roll fashion, and place on board seam side down. Press down ends and tuck underneath. Transfer to greased loaf pan, cover with clean dish towel, and let rise in warm place. Brush with beaten egg and bake in 400° oven about 1 hr. If it is browning too quickly, reduce heat. Remove from oven and while still hot, brush surface with a piece of cold butter impaled on fork. Slice and serve with clear soups.

FLAKY YEAST-RAISED FILLED LOAF/PIE
kulebiak krucho-drożdżowy

This no-knead yeast loaf is less reminiscent of the traditionally light yeast-raised dough and tends to resemble a crumbly pastry. Mash ½ cake yeast with ½ t. sugar and let stand 2 min. Sift 2 c. flour onto bread board, top with 7 T. butter, and cut in with knife or pastry blender. Add 1 egg, 1 yolk, yeast mixture, 4–5 T. sour cream, and ½ t. salt; mix with pastry blender until ingredients stick together. Quickly work into a dough on floured bread board, sprinkling with a little flour, and roll out ⅓ inch thick into a rectangle. Spread with filling up to 1 inch from edges, roll up, transfer to greased loaf pan, cover with towel, and let rise in warm place until nearly doubled in bulk. Brush with lightly beaten egg white and bake in 400° oven about 1 hr.

FRENCH-PASTRY FILLED LOAF/PIE
kulebiak z ciasta francuskiego

Sprinkle 2¼ sticks butter with 5 T. flour, blend with pastry cutter into uniform mixture, form into a square and chill in fridge. Meanwhile, sift 1¼ c. flour onto breadboard, add 1 egg, and work into dough with knife or pastry blender, adding in a thin stream 1 c. water containing 2 t. vinegar and ¼ t. salt. Work ingredients well into a dough, cover with dish towel, and let stand 15 min. Roll dough into a square twice the size of the chilled butter square. Place butter square on top of dough square, fold dough over butter envelope fashion, and roll out in one direction (away from yourself) into a rectangle. Fold in three, wrap in dish towel, and chill in fridge 15 min. Roll out again, fold in three, wrap in towel, and refrigerate another 15 min. Repeat 2 more times. Divide dough into two uneven parts: ⅓ and ⅔. Roll out ⅓ inch thick into rectangles. Place filling of choice on smaller rectangle up to 1 inch from edges. Cover with larger rectangle and join top and bottom dough rectangles by pinching edges together. Brush with beaten egg, transfer to greased loaf pan, and pop into 480° oven. Bake 15 min., then reduce heat to 390° and bake another 10–15 min.

MUSHROOM FILLING FOR FILLED LOAF/PIE
farsz pieczarkowy do kulebiaka

Wash, dry, and dice 1 lb. fresh cultivated mushrooms. In skillet, melt 2–3 T. butter, add mushrooms, sprinkle with ½ t. salt and ¼ t. pepper, and sauté, stirring occasionally until all moisture evaporates and mushrooms just begin to sizzle. Remove from heat. Separately, sauté

1 chopped onion in 1 T. butter until tender and stir into mushrooms. 1–2 T. bread crumbs may be added. If desired, sprinkle with 1 T. chopped dill and/or parsley.

MUSHROOM & CABBAGE FILLING FOR LOAF/PIE
farsz z kapusty i pieczarek do kulebiaka

Shred 1 lb. cabbage, scald with boiling water to cover, bring to boil, cook several min., and drain. Cook cabbage in fresh boiling salted water until tender. Drain in colander. Meanwhile, sauté 8 oz. fresh sliced mushrooms in 2 T. butter until moisture evaporates, stirring frequently. Combine cooked cabbage and mushrooms and run through coarse blade of grinder. Add 1 T. chopped parsley and 4 T. bread crumbs, mix well, and salt & pepper to taste.

MUSHROOM & SAUERKRAUT FILLING
farsz z kiszonej kapusty i grzybów do kulebiaka

Soak 5–6 dried mushrooms overnight and cook in same water until tender. Drain 1 pt. sauerkraut, rinse, drain, press out moisture, chop, place in pot, add mushroom liquid, and cook until tender. Add a little extra water if mushroom liquid evaporates before sauerkraut is tender. Steam off excess moisture. Sauté 1 chopped onion in 1 T. fat until tender and add sauerkraut together with chopped mushrooms. Salt & pepper to taste. *Note:* 8 oz. fresh sautéed mushrooms may be used instead of cooked dried mushrooms. For non-fast days, add ½–1 c. diced ham or other smoked meat.

RICE & MUSHROOM FILLING FOR LOAF/PIE
farsz z ryżu i grzybów do kulebiaka

Soak 5–6 dried mushrooms overnight and cook in same water until tender. Steam off all but a little of the liquid. Sauté 1 chopped onion in 1 T. fat until tender. Dice the cooked mushrooms and add together with the leftover mushroom liquid to 2 c. cooked rice. Add the sautéed onions, 2 finely diced hard-boiled eggs, 1 T. dill and/or parsley finely chopped and salt & pepper to taste. Mix to combine ingredients. *Variation:* 8–12 oz. fresh mushrooms, sautéed in a little butter and diced, may be used in place of cooked dried mushrooms.

GROAT & MUSHROOM FILLING FOR LOAF/PIE
farsz z kaszy i grzybów do kulebiaka

Soak 5–6 dried boletes overnight in 1½ c. water, add ½ t. salt, and cook in same water until tender. Add enough water to mushroom liquid to make 1¾ c., add 1 T. butter, bring to boil, and gradually add 1 c. buckwheat groats. Reduce heat, cover, and cook until liquid is absorbed. Transfer pot to 350° oven for 30 min. Add the mushrooms, finely chopped, season with salt, pepper, and (optional) a pinch finely chopped fresh or dried mint leaves and mix well. *Variation:* For non-fast days, add 1 c. finely diced cooked pork.

FILLING À LA POTOCKI FOR LOAF/PIE
farsz à la Potocki do kulebiaka

Combine ¾ lb. cooked chicken, ½ lb. cooked ham or other smoked meat, and 2 hard-boiled eggs—all finely diced or coarsely ground. Add 1 T. chopped parsley, mix well, and salt & pepper to taste.

FRANKFURTER FILLING FOR LOAF/PIE
farsz z parówek do kulebiaka

Grind ½ lb. high-quality frankfurters, 2 hard-boiled eggs, and 1 chopped sautéed onion. Add 5 T. bread crumbs soaked in ⅓ c. milk, 4 T. raisins, and 1 T. chopped parsley. Mix well and salt & pepper to taste.

FISH FILLING FOR LOAF/PIE
farsz rybny do kulebiaka

This is a good way to use up that leftover fried fish. Dice fine or grind coarsely 1 lb. fried fish fillets and combine with 2 c. cooked rice and 2 chopped onions sautéed in 2–3 T. butter. Add 1 T. chopped dill and salt & pepper to taste. *Variation:* Cook 1 c. shredded cabbage in boiling salted water until tender, drain well, and add to filling. 1–2 chopped hard-boiled eggs may also be added.

SAVORY STRUDEL AS SOUP ACCOMPANIMENT
strudel do zup

This classic Central European pastry is usually filled with apples, raisins, nuts, etc., but the soup-loving Poles have also come up with savory versions of strudel, ideally suited to bite their clear soups down with. Since making strudel dough from scratch is a monumental culinary challenge, requiring at least 2 people to do the stretching (although we have included the recipe in the cake & pastry chapter), we suggest getting some ready-to-use strudel dough.

CALF'S BRAIN STRUDEL
strudel z móżdżkiem

Trim 1 calf's brain of any membranes and dice. Sauté 1 chopped onion in 3 T. butter until tender, add the brains, and sauté 5–6 min. Add ¼ c. fork-blended sour cream, season with salt & pepper, and simmer briefly until brains turn white and firm up. Set aside to cool. Sprinkle a roughly 6 x 6 inch square of strudel dough with 1 T. chopped fresh parsley and ¼ c. bread crumbs. Cream 2 egg yolks until white and beat 2 egg whites to a stiff froth and spread over dough. Evenly spread the brains over surface and roll dough up jelly-roll fashion. Place on greased baking sheet, brush top with butter. Bake in 400° oven 15–20 min. Reduce heat to 350°, brush with a bit more butter, and bake another 10 min. or until nicely browned. *Note*: Be careful not to let it burn; treat temp. and baking time only as orientational guidelines, not dogma!

SPINACH STRUDEL
strudel ze szpinakiem

Wash and remove stems from 2 lbs. fresh spinach. Place in pot, scald with 4 c. boiling water, and cook on med. heat about 10 min. Drain, force through sieve, or chop in blender. In skillet briefly simmer 2 T. flour in 4 T. butter without browning, stir in ¼ c. sour cream, add the spinach, salt & pepper to taste and simmer briefly, mixing well. Set aside to cool. Stir in 3 egg yolks and 3 whites beaten to a froth, mix lightly and spread mixture over strudel dough. Roll up, place on greased baking sheet, brush with butter and bake as above. During baking, baste with a little liquified sour cream. *Note:* Strudel is also good with cabbage, sauerkraut, mushroom, meat, and other fillings recommended for kulebiak (above).

SALTY STICKS/PASTRY FINGERS
słone paluszki

Mix 2 c. flour with 2 t. baking powder and sift together onto bread board. Cut in 1 stick (½ c.) butter with knife or pastry-blender, add 1 egg, 2–3 T. sour cream and quickly work ingredients into a dough. Refrigerate 30 min. Roll out ⅛ inch thick and cut into sticks ¼ wide and about 2½ inches long. Brush sticks with beaten egg and sprinkle with one of the following: coarse kosher salt; table salt & caraway seeds; table salt & poppyseeds; or table salt & grated yellow cheese. Bake in 375°–400° oven 10–15 min. until golden. *Note:* Overbaking will make them bitter. They make a simple but elegant accompaniment to clear barszcz and puréed soups.

YEAST-RAISED STICKS/FINGERS
paluszki drożdżowe

Sift 1½ c. flour into bowl. Separately, dissolve ⅓ cake yeast in ½ c. lukewarm milk, add to flour, mix, and let rise. When mixture rises, add ½ c. sour cream, 1 egg yolk, ½ stick (¼ c.) melted butter, and ½ t. salt. Work ingredients into a dough and knead briefly. Pinch off pieces of dough and between palms of hands roll them into pencil-thin sticks about 3–4 inches in length. Brush with lightly beaten egg white. Sprinkle with caraway seeds, poppyseeds, or black cumin, according to preference, and place on greased baking sheet. Bake in 390° oven just until the sticks turn golden. Serve with clear beet or clear tomato soup, as well as with other soups served in teacups or twin-handled barszcz cups.

FRENCH OR RYE-BREAD CROUTONS
grzanki z bułki lub chleba

Trim crusts from 6–8 ½-inch thick slices of French or Polish rye bread. (Croutons made from that soft American-style white bread lack body and turn mushy in the soup!) In large skillet melt 3 T. butter. Cut bread into ½ inch cubes and add to skillet, tossing gently to coat with butter as evenly as possible. Simmer on med. heat, turning croutons so all sides get nicely browned. Transfer to platter and serve with puréed vegetable soups, mushroom soup, or fruit soups. Both French-bread and rye-bread croutons are suitable for savory soups, but only the former are used with fruit soups. *Variation:* Another way is to lightly butter the crustless bread slices on both sides, cut into cubes, and bake in 375° oven until browned. *Note*: Interesting round croutons can be made using Polish bakery crescents (rogale).

SWEET SOUP CROUTONS
grzanki do zup słodkich

Cubes of egg bread (chałka, placek, babka) or plain sweet rolls (minus any fruit, cheese, or poppyseed fillings!) can be browned in skillet or oven as above and served with fruit soups or other sweet soups. *Variation:* Cut egg bread or rolls into cubes and let stand overnight to turn stale. Line cubes in 1 layer in baking pan, sprinkle with 3–4 T. milk, and dust with a little powdered sugar. Bake in 375° oven about 10 min. or until slightly browned.

DEVILISH CHEESE CROUTONS
grzanki z serem/diablotki

Trim crusts from 6–8 ½-inch thick slices French bread and cut into 1 inch cubes. You can also use Polish bakery crescent rolls (rogale) and slice them into rounds ¼–½ inch thick.

In cup, fork-blend 1 T. soft butter with 1 raw egg yolk and 6 T. grated sharp yellow cheese. Spread one side of bread squares or rounds with mixture, place on greased baking sheet and bake in 375° oven 5–10 min. Serve immediately with broth and other clear soups, onion soup, mushroom soup, and savory puréed soups.

DEVILISH CHEESE CROUTONS ANOTHER WAY
diablotki inaczej

Prepare 1 inch French-bread squares as above and sauté briefly in 3 T. butter in skillet only long enough for squares to evenly absorb the butter, but do not brown. Transfer to baking dish in a single layer, sprinkle with sharp grated cheese, and bake in 375° oven 5–10 min. or until nicely browned. *Optional:* For added zest, sprinkle bread squares with tiny pinches of cayenne pepper.

HARD-BOILED EGGS AS SOUP GARNISH
jaja na twardo jako dodatek do zup

Hard-boiled eggs—whole, halved, quartered, or sliced—are a common garnish for a number of popular Polish soups. These include sorrel soup, creamed beet soup, beet-green soup (boćwinka), tart and tangy żurek and biały barszcz (both of which are sometimes referred to as Easter soups), and cold beet and cucumber soups (chłodnik). Allow ½–1 egg per serving.

FRIED HARD-BOILED EGGS AS SOUP GARNISH
jaja na twardo podsmażane

Remove shell from 2 hard-boiled eggs (allowing ½ an egg per serving). Slice eggs in half lengthwise, scoop out yolks, and set whites aside. In saucepan melt 2 t. butter, add yolks forced through sieve, 1 pinch chopped dill, 1 t. sour cream, and a pinch of salt. Simmer briefly, stirring to blend ingredients. Fill egg cavities with mixture, pressing down with flat of knife so it is level with egg. Brush filled sides of egg halves with 1 lightly beaten egg white, dip in bread crumbs, and sauté breaded side down in a little butter until a golden-brown crust forms. Serve with broth, clear beet soup, and other clear soups served in teacups.

SHIRTED (POACHED) EGGS AS SOUP GARNISH
jaja w koszulkach do zup

Bring 3 c. water and 2 t. salt to boil. *Optional:* For zestier-tasting eggs, also add 1½ T. 6% vinegar. Break 4 eggs into separate saucers or demitasses and slip into boiling water from just above surface. Reduce heat, cover, and cook ½–1 min. Carefully remove with slotted spoon and transfer to soup bowls, then drench with hot broth or clear beet root soup. These eggs are also good with sorrel soup. *Note*: Since these eggs are just barely set, they are extremely fragile and must be handled with great care. The trick is to keep the egg intact so that your guests can break into them and let the liquidy yolk flow into their soup.

POTATOES AS SOUP GARNISH
kartofle do zup

In Polish peasant cookery, diced cooked potatoes are sometimes added to soups. Simply dice 1 med. cooked potato per person, place in soup bowls, and drench with hot soup. Broth and duck soup (czernina) are probably the most common soups garnished with potatoes. *Variation:* Boiled or mashed potatoes are often served alongside rather than in żurek (rye-meal soup) as well as sour milk and buttermilk eaten soup-fashion from a bowl. Such potatoes are usually garnished with golden salt-pork or bacon nuggets and their drippings or, on fast days, with melted butter.

HOT MEATS & MEAT DISHES

A hot meat as the main course has long been the crowning touch on the traditional Polish banquet table, following the long round of cold dishes, toasts, soups, and hot fish appetizers. To this day, to a great many Poles, dinner is not dinner unless there is meat to follow the customary soup course. Back in the 15th and 16th centuries, French visitors to Poland complained that their hosts served too much meat and not enough fish. Italian travelers missed their vegetables, breads, and pasta dishes. But since good drink flowed freely, foreign guests dug in with relish and marveled at the Poles' hospitality.

Although things were quite different among the peasantry, the less fortunate classes also dreamed of meat as a coveted and hard-to-get delicacy. On a daily basis they often had to content themselves with a spoonful of fried salt-pork nuggets or meat drippings with which to flavor their soups, groats, or dumplings. They therefore looked forward to the harvest feast, Christmas and Easter, as well as weddings and other celebrations, when they could feast on meat to their heart's content. Poles in America are widely known as a meat-loving lot, as attested to by the excellent sausage shops and meat markets traditionally found in Polish ethnic neighborhoods. It was in America that the immigrants of chiefly peasant stock, who began arriving in the late 19th century, were able to satiate their appetite for meat.

Unlike people of the English-speaking world, when a Pole speaks of meat, he thinks mainly of pork, not beef. The breaded pork cutlet (*kotlet schabowy*) in terms of general appeal among Poles could be compared to the popularity of roast beef in America. A very old Polish favorite is roast pork loin with prunes, and boiled pork hocks and pork ribs baked in sauerkraut also have many devotees.

Although beef may not rate No.1, Polish cuisine has developed a number of interesting beef dishes, including roll-ups, stuffed roasts, braised collops (pounded beef cutlets stewed in gravy), boiled beef, and beef tongue. The latter is often served with a tangy raisin gravy known as Old Polish grey sauce.

Also popular are tasty veal dishes such as roasts, breaded cutlets, and various fricassees. Lamb and mutton have never achieved the popularity they enjoy elsewhere in Europe, but a number of interesting ways of preparing them have been included in this chapter nonetheless.

Meat is an indispensable energy food that supplies the body with protein, vitamin B, and iron. Generous helpings are recommended to growing youngsters and adolescents, young adults, people of robust health, and those engaged in strenuous physical activity. Those who lead a more sedentary existence or have various health problems are often advised to cut down on red meat. Such people might do well to consider the various fricassee-type dishes where the amount of vegetables, mushrooms, or other non-meat additives can be freely increased to taste. Those who must restrict their intake of dietary cholesterol should also consider lean, ground meat dishes containing cereal, bread, or vegetable fillers.

But, whatever your taste or dietary requirements, we are sure you will find recipes that meet with your approval among the repertoire of traditional and modified Polish meat dishes on the pages that follow.

* * *

ROAST BEEF AU JUS
pieczeń wołowa we własnym sosie

Pound a 1½ lb. beef rump or chuck roast with rolling pin or flat side of meat mallet. Lard with larding needle (see illustration) or use scalded stick, long narrow knife, or skewer to make 6–8 incisions the length of the roast. Cut 6–8 sticks of salt pork the length of the roast, and force them into the incisions. (Salt-pork sticks will be easier to handle if frozen overnight.) Place meat in crockery baking dish, scald with ¼ c. boiling vinegar, sprinkle with salt & pepper, cover, and refrigerate several hrs. or overnight. Roll meat in flour and brown on all sides in 4–5 T. lard or oil. Transfer to baking dish or Dutch oven. In pan drippings brown 2 sliced or coarsely chopped onions and pour over meat. Add 1 c. water, ½ a crumbled bay leaf, and 4 grains each allspice and peppercorns. Simmer covered in Dutch oven on stove top or bake in 325° oven 1½–2 hrs, or until tender. Replace any liquid that evaporates during cooking. When done, slice thin. Force pan drippings through sieve, add 1 T. flour, and simmer briefly, then pour over beef slices. All beef roasts are tastier and more tender if refrigerated overnight, sliced when cold, and then reheated in pan drippings or gravy. Serve with potatoes, groats or noodles. Braised beets or cooked vegetables of the cabbage family are always a good accompaniment to beef. *Note*: Feel free to use your Polish beef seasoning in all beef recipes.

ROAST BEEF WITH MUSHROOMS
pieczeń wołowa z grzybami

Soak ½–1 oz. dried Polish mushrooms in 2 c. water 2 hrs, then cook in same water 15 min. Prepare roast as above. After transferring browned roast to baking dish and smothering in onions, add the mushrooms, chopped or sliced into thin strips, and the water in which they cooked. Cook as above. When done, serve as is or combine drippings with ¾ c. sour cream fork-blended with 2 T. flour. Simmer briefly, salt & pepper to taste, and pour sauce over sliced beef.

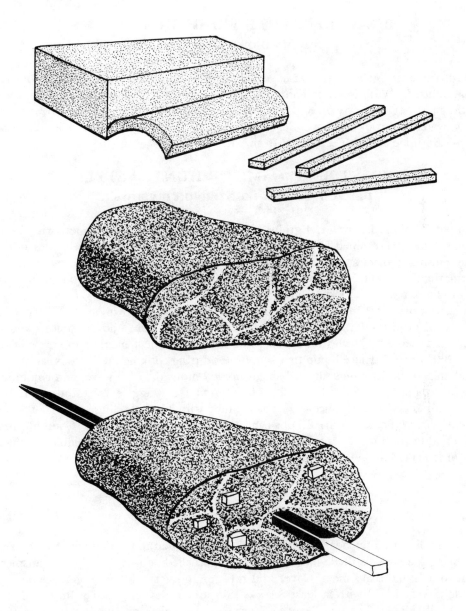

Roasts, especially beef and wild game, are frequently larded to ensure juiciness. This is best accomplished with a larding needle (bottom). If one is not available, fat back should be placed in freezer overnight after being cut into sticks (top). When frozen stiff, they will easily slip into incisions made through the meat with a skewer, clean stick or other such instruments.

ROAST BEEF WITH FRESH MUSHROOMS
pieczeń wołowa z pieczarkami

Prepare meat as above. (If you have a very juicy and tender roast, the salt-pork larding may be omitted.) Wash well and chop 8 oz. fresh mushrooms, simmer in 3 T. butter or oil until they just begin to brown. Add to roast in baking pan along with the browned onions and 1 c. water and cook as above. Serve as is or with sour-cream sauce as in above recipe. *Optional:* Sprinkle with 1 T. chopped fresh parsley.

ROAST BEEF, GAME OR HUNTER STYLE
pieczeń wołowa na dziko/po myśliwsku

In pot, combine 1 c. water, 4 grains crushed allspice, 6 crushed peppercorns, 3 crushed juniper berries, 1 crumbled bay leaf, and 1 sliced onion. (*Note:* Crushed does not mean ground; crush in mortar so that each grain breaks up into 4–6 pieces, releasing all its flavor.) Bring marinade to boil. When cool, add ¼ c. 6% distilled vinegar and pour over 1½–2 lb. rump or chuck roast in crockery bowl. Cover and refrigerate 2–3 days, turning meat over each day. Remove meat from marinade, dry, roll in flour, and brown on all sides in 4 T. lard or oil to seal in juices. Transfer to Dutch oven or baking dish. Add the onions and spices from marinade and 1 c. water and cook 1½–2 hrs. on low heat in stove-top Dutch oven or bake in 350° oven. Replace liquid that evaporates during cooking and turn meat over once. When done, strain drippings, discard spices, force onions through sieve, and combine with ¾ c. sour cream, fork-blended with 2 T. flour. Add 1 t. Maggi extract and a little of the marinade for added zest. If sauce is too thick, dilute with a little boiling water. Salt & pepper to taste. *Optional:* Soak 1–2 dried Polish mushrooms in 1 c. water 2 hrs. Chop mushrooms fine and add to roast at start of cooking. Instead of plain water, add the liquid in which the mushrooms soaked and enough water to total 1 c.

BEEF POT ROAST IN TANGY SAUCE
sztufada

Pound 2 lb. or larger beef rump or chuck roast. (Rolled roasts tied with string are very good.) Bring ¼ c. 6% distilled vinegar and several crushed peppercorns, grains allspice and bay leaf to boil and scald meat. Cover and refrigerate overnight or longer. Remove from marinade, dry and lard with at least 8 sticks salt pork rolled in paprika. Roll in flour and brown on all sides in hot fat. Transfer meat to baking dish or Dutch oven and add the drippings. Add 1 standard portion of diced soup greens (carrot, celery, parsnip, leek), 1–2 onions and (optional) 1 small kohlrabi and 1 small beet. Pour in 1 c. water and simmer covered on low heat or bake in 325° oven about 2 hrs, or until tender. When roast is done, force pan drippings through sieve. If you have not used a beet among the vegetables, add 1–2

T. tomato concentrate and simmer sauce briefly. Thicken with a little flour as needed or add a bit of boiling water if too thick. Salt & pepper to taste and pour over sliced roast. For a richer sauce, stir in a heaping T. sour cream. *Note:* In all roast beef recipes, for best results cook meat a day ahead and refrigerate overnight, as it slices best when cold. When ready to serve, place the slices in sauce or drippings and simmer 10–15 min.

ROAST BEEF HUSSAR STYLE
pieczeń wołowa po husarsku

Beat a 3–4 lb. beef rump or chuck roast with rolling pin. Sprinkle with salt and flour and brown on all sides in hot fat to seal in juices. Transfer to Dutch oven or roaster, add the drippings and ¼ c. water and cook on low heat about 2 hrs. or until tender, replacing liquid that evaporates. Meanwhile, combine ½ c. bread crumbs (white, rye or 1 part each) with 3 T. soft butter and 2 finely grated onions. Mix ingredients and salt & pepper to taste. When meat is tender slice fairly thin, leaving every 2nd slice not cut all the way through. Stuff bread-crumb mixture into these pockets and fasten with toothpicks. Return meat to pot in its original shape, cover and simmer about 30 min. A little flour may be added to drippings and simmered briefly for the sauce. Serve with stewed sauerkraut, red or white cabbage or Brussels sprouts and boiled potatoes.

ROAST BEEF STUFFED WITH HORSERADISH
pieczeń wołowa nadziewana chrzanem

Proceed as with Hussar-style roast (above). When meat is tender, slice thin, leaving every 2nd slice not cut all the way through. Fill pockets with following mixture: ⅓ c. freshly grated horseradish root, ⅓ c. white bread crumbs, 1 egg, ¼ t. salt, 1 t. sugar and 2–3 T. sour cream—enough to get a thick filling. Braised beets are a good go-together.

BEEF COLLOPS STEWED IN SOUR CREAM
bitki w śmietanie

Cut 2 lbs. round or flank steak into 1½–2 inch squares. With kitchen mallet moistened with water pound the pieces until about ¼ inch thin but unbroken. Salt, roll in flour, and brown briefly in 5 T. lard or oil on both sides. Transfer to baking dish. In drippings brown 1–2 sliced onions, then add to meat along with 1 c. water and 3 crushed peppercorns and grains allspice plus 1 crumbled bay leaf. Simmer on low heat under cover on stove top or bake in 350° oven 1–1½ hrs, or until tender. Fork-blend 1 c. sour cream with 3 T. flour and drench meat. Simmer another 15 min. Salt & pepper to taste. Serve with buckwheat groats, barley, or noodles and sliced tomatoes.

BEEF COLLOPS AU JUS
bitki w sosie własnym

For a change of pace (or, if you are watching your weight or restricting cholesterol), proceed as above, but do not add sour cream and flour mixture. *Bitki* is short for *bite zrazy* (pounded fillets).

BEEF COLLOPS WITH MUSHROOMS
zrazy wołowe z grzybami

Soak ½–1 oz. dried Polish mushrooms in 2 c. water several hrs. or overnight, then cook in same water until tender. Brown 2 coarsely chopped onions, in 2 T. fat. Prepare steak fillets as bitki (above). To meat in baking dish add sliced, cooked mushrooms and the liquid in which they cooked plus the onions. Cook covered on low heat 1–1½ hrs. or until tender. Serve as is or add 1 c. sour cream fork-blended with 2–3 T. flour, and simmer briefly until gravy is thick and bubbly. Salt & pepper to taste. If gravy is too thick, dilute with a little boiling water.

BEEF COLLOPS WITH FRESH MUSHROOMS
zrazy wołowe z pieczarkami

Prepare zrazy as above and place in baking dish. Wash well and slice or dice 8 oz. fresh mushrooms, place in skillet with 2 coarsely chopped onions, and 2 T. butter and simmer under cover 5 min. Add to baking dish together with 1 c. water, cover, and bake in 350° oven 1–1½ hrs. or until tender. Salt & pepper. Serve as is or drench with 1 c. sour cream fork-blended with 2–3 T. flour and simmer several min. longer. A t. Maggi extract may be added. Dilute sauce with boiling water if too thick. Buckwheat groats and braised beets are classic accompaniments to this and other Polish-style beef dishes.

BEEF COLLOPS À LA NELSON
zrazy po nelsońsku

Slice 1½ lbs. beef tenderloin (polędwica) ½ inch thick, cut slices in half, and pound with meat mallet until thin but unbroken. Cook ½ oz. dried Polish mushrooms (pre-soaked 2 hrs. in 2 c. water) about 30 min. covered, or until tender. Peel and slice about ¼ inch thick 3 lbs. potatoes and cook in boiling salted water 5 min., then drain. Sprinkle meat with freshly ground pepper and flour and brown in 6 T. hot oil or lard on both sides. Remove meat and brown thinly sliced onions in same drippings, adding 1–2 T. butter if more fat is needed. Butter a baking dish generously. Line the bottom with a layer of potatoes, top with meat, onions, and chopped mushrooms, and continue layering until all ingredients are used up. Sprinkle each layer with salt & pepper. The top layer should be potatoes. Fork-blend 1¼ c. sour cream with 2 T. flour, stir in the liquid in which the mushrooms were cooked, and pour over the potatoes in baking dish. Bake covered in 400° oven about 30 min. Red cabbage & apple salad will nicely enhance this truly tasty dish.

BEEF COLLOPS À LA NELSON–ECONOMICAL VERSION
zrazy po nelsońsku oszczędniej

Instead of expensive beef tenderloin, you can use round or flank steak beaten very well. If you do not have Polish dried mushrooms, use 8–12 oz. fresh mushrooms. Cook them in boiling salted water several min., drain, and slice before adding to baking dish. To the sour cream you can add ½ t. liquid mushroom extract or 1 t. Maggi extract. *Note:* Dieters may use plain yogurt in place of sour cream in this and other dishes (see "Milk, Dairy Products, & Cheese Dishes").

STEAK ROLL-UPS
zrazy wołowe zawijane

Cut 2–3 lbs. round steak into 2 by 3 inch pieces. Salt & pepper and pound with meat mallet, occasionally dipped in water, until steak slices are quite thin. Spread with filling of choice (see below), roll up tightly, and fasten each roll-up with 2 toothpicks or tie with strong white thread. Roll in flour and brown on all sides in 5–6 T. lard or oil. Transfer to baking dish, add 2 c. water or beef bouillon, cover, and bake in 350° oven 1½ hrs. To serve, pour pan drippings over meat on platter. *Optional:* Fork-blend ¾ c. sour cream with 2 T. flour until lump-free, stir into pan drippings, and simmer a min. or so. Season to taste with salt and your homemade Polish beef seasoning. Dilute with a little boiling water if too thick. The classic side dishes for this Old Polish favorite are buckwheat groats and braised beets. A sliced-tomato salad, dressed to taste with salt, pepper, lemon juice, and a sprinkle of sugar, is also nice. *Note:* Toothpicks or thread should be removed from roll-ups before serving.

WARSAW-STYLE ROLL-UPS WITH BREAD & ONION FILLING
zrazy zawijane po warszawsku

Simmer 1–2 finely chopped onions in 3 T. butter, lard, or oil until transparent. Remove from heat, stir in ¼ c. bread crumbs, salt & pepper. Spread mixture thinly over steak slices, roll up, and proceed as above.

BLACK BREAD ROLL-UPS
zrazy zawijane z razowcem

At one end of each pounded steak slice place a piece of uncooked bacon across the width of the meat, a stick of stale black bread, and a little minced onion.

STEAK ROLL-UPS WITH PICKLE & SALT PORK
zrazy zawijane z ogórkiem i słoniną

Thinly spread each steak slice with sharp brown mustard. At one end place a piece of dill pickle and a stick of salt pork across the width of the meat (a piece of uncooked bacon may be used instead) and roll up tightly.

STEAK ROLL-UPS WITH ONION & SALT PORK
zrazy zawijane z cebulą i słoniną

Spread each steak slice with a thin layer of sharp brown mustard. At the end of each piece place a stick of salt pork and a strip of onion. In this and the above 2 recipes a stick of skinned, smoked kiełbasa may be used in addition to or in place of the salt pork or bacon for a zestier flavor.

STEAK ROLL-UPS WITH SAUSAGE À LA ZAGŁOBA
zrazy zawijane à la Zagłoba

Remove casting from ¼ lb. or slightly more uncooked fresh kiełbasa and mix with 2–3 T. finely grated horseradish root (or prepared horseradish), 1 grated onion, 3 T. black bread crumbs, and 1 T. sour cream. Spread steak slices with a thin layer of mixture and season each with a dash of nutmeg. Roll up and proceed as above. When cooked, add 1–2 T. tomato concentrate to pan drippings and simmer briefly. Pour over roll-ups on serving platter. *Note:* This tasty concoction was named after Onufry Zagłoba, the humorous, boastful "old warrior" in the historical *Trilogy* of Nobel Prize-winning novelist, Henryk Sienkiewicz (1846–1916).

STEAK ROLL-UPS WITH MUSHROOMS
zrazy zawijane z grzybami

Soak ½–1 oz. dried boletes (mushrooms) in 2 c. water 3 hrs. then cook in same water until tender. Run mushrooms through meat grinder. Brown 2 finely chopped onions in 3 T. butter and combine with mushrooms. Add 2 T. white bread crumbs and salt & pepper to taste. Roll up and proceed as above, but instead of adding 2 c. water to baking dish, add the liquid in which the mushrooms were cooked and enough water to make 2 c.

STEAK ROLL-UPS WITH FRESH MUSHROOMS
zrazy zawijane z pieczarkami

Wash well and chop fine 8 oz. fresh mushrooms and brown in 4 T. butter or oil with 2 finely chopped onions. Remove from heat and stir in 1 raw egg yolk, 1 T. chopped fresh parsley, and 2 T. bread crumbs or more—enough to get a moist filling. Salt & pepper to taste and proceed as above. When tender, add 1 jigger dry white wine and ¾ c. sour cream, fork-blended with 2 T. flour. Simmer briefly.

STEAK ROLL-UPS WITH LIVER FILLING
zrazy zawijane z wątróbką

Grind or chop very fine ¼ lb. or more raw calf's or chicken liver. Combine with 1–2 T. grated onion, 1 T. chopped fresh parsley, and 4 T. butter. Salt & pepper to taste.

CHOPPED STEAK ROLLS
zrazy siekane duszone

Crumble 1 stale kaiser roll (stale hamburger bun or French bread is also good) into ½ c. milk and let stand 10 min., then run through meat grinder. By hand combine ground soggy roll with 1½ lb. ground round or sirloin steak or hamburger. Add 1 whole egg, 2 T. chopped fresh parsley, and mix ingredients into uniform mass; salt & pepper to taste. On board, form mixture into 2 or more 1½-inch rolls and cut into 3 inch pieces. Roll between hands, dip in flour, and brown on all sides in several T. hot lard or oil. Transfer to baking dish, add pan drippings and 1 c. water, and bake covered in 350° oven 35–40 min. Replace any liquid that evaporates during baking. For a gourmet twist, add 1 T. dry red wine towards end of baking. A mashed clove of garlic also wouldn't hurt. Serve as is with potatoes, rice, or buckwheat groats, or stir 1 heaping T. sour cream into drippings and simmer briefly until bubbly.

CHOPPED STEAK ROLL WITH ONIONS
zrazy siekane duszone z cebulą

This dish may be prepared in 1 of 3 different ways:
1) Proceed as above but to meat mixture add 2 T. grated onion.
2) After browning steak rolls in fat, brown 1–2 slices onions in same drippings and add to baking dish.
3) In several T. butter brown 2 finely chopped onions and stir in 2 T. bread crumbs. Salt & pepper and use mixture to fill uncooked chopped steak rolls. Seal well so filling is on the inside, roll in flour, brown, and proceed as above.

MUSHROOM-FILLED CHOPPED STEAK ROLLS
zrazy siekane nadziewane grzybami

Prepare meat as above but fill meat rolls with dried or fresh mushroom filling as for steak roll-ups (zrazy zawijane z grzybami or z pieczarkami) above.

CHOPPED STEAK WITH MUSHROOMS
zrazy siekane z grzybami

Prepare 1½ lbs. ground round, sirloin, or hamburger as for chopped steak rolls (above), or use the meat as is with no additional ingredients. Form meat into ¾–1 inch thick, 3–4 inch long oval patties. (If meat is unflavored, salt & pepper each piece.) Roll in flour and brown on both sides in 4–5 T. hot lard or oil. In same drippings brown 8 oz. chopped or sliced fresh mushrooms and 1–2 chopped onions. Transfer meat to baking dish, top it with browned mushrooms and onions, add 1 c. water, and bake in 350° oven covered about 30 min. This dish will be even tastier if you use dried mushrooms (about ½ oz.). As always, they should be soaked in 2 c. water 2 hrs., cooked in the same water, chopped, and added to browning onions. Pour the mushroom water over the meat in baking dish, adding only enough water to make 1 c. liquid. Serve as is or drench with ¾ c. sour cream fork-blended with 2 T. flour. Simmer briefly until thick and bubbly. Serve with potatoes or buckwheat groats, cooked beets of choice, or a cooked vegetable of the cabbage family. *Note:* If you are out of both dried and fresh mushrooms, you can use about 3 oz. canned mushrooms (including the liquid) instead.

CHOPPED STEAK IN SOUR CREAM
zrazy siekane w śmietanie

Prepare oval ground steak patties as above and transfer to baking dish. Brown 2 sliced onions in 2 T. lard or oil and add to meat together with ¾ c. water. Cover and bake in 350° oven 30–35 min. Fork-blend ¾ c. sour cream with 2 T. flour and add to dish, mixing with drippings to form a sauce. Salt & pepper and simmer until thick and bubbly. Sprinkle with 1–2 t. chopped fresh parsley and serve with any of the above accompaniments.

BEEF TENDERLOIN À LA VARSOVIENNE
polędwica po warszawsku

Rub a 1½ lb. whole beef tenderloin with 1–2 buds mashed garlic. Roll in flour and brown in very hot lard or oil (about 5 min.) on all sides until a crust forms to seal in the juices. The tenderloin must still be completely raw inside. Refrigerate covered overnight. When ready to use, cut tenderloin into 1–1¼ inch steaks and fry briefly on both sides in 2–3 T. very hot oil. Actual cooking time depends on whether you want your steaks rare, medium rare, or medium well. Even in the latter case, the steak should still retain a trace of pinkness on the inside. Cooking them until well done is truly a waste of such fine meat. Each portion may be topped with a pat or ball of horseradish butter, chive butter, or green butter, according to preference. Serve with a fresh green salad and rice or French fries. This fairly simple dish, which was conceived by the authors of this book and named after the city where it originated, is sure to please the most fastidious steak-lovers. Pre-browning the entire tenderloin seals in the juices is much better that throwing raw steaks into a hot skillet, and the overnight refrigeration helps tenderize the meat.

TENDERLOIN STEAK—THE TRADITIONAL WAY
befsztyk z polędwicy

Slice 1½ lb. beef tenderloin into 1 inch steaks. With flat of knife even out the sides of each steak to form more or less regular rounds. Heat 3 T. lard in skillet and, when very hot, fry the meat several min. on both sides to get the degree of doneness you prefer. Before turning over steaks, sprinkle top side with freshly ground pepper. Salting steaks during cooking may make them tough, so allow dinner guests to season the portions on their plate. Serve with potatoes or rice, and a salad: sliced tomatoes in summer and grated carrot, apple, and horseradish salad in winter. As for cooked vegetables, Brussels sprouts or cauliflower nicely complement this dish.

BEEF TENDERLOIN, PRE-MARINATED
befsztyk z polędwicy z marynaty

Place 1½ lb. whole beef tenderloin in crockery or glass (not metal!) bowl. Sprinkle with juice of ½ a lemon or scald with 2 T. vinegar, brought to boil with 2 T. water. Sprinkle meat with crushed or powdered bay leaf, freshly ground pepper, and a little marjoram, or use your homemade beef seasoning. Rub spices into meat by hand, making sure all sides have been covered. A bud of mashed garlic may also be rubbed into meat. Pour 4–5 T. salad oil over meat (genuine olive oil is best!), surround with sliced onions, cover and refrigerate overnight. Next day, remove spices and onions, dry meat, slice into 1 inch thick steaks and fry in 3 T. very hot lard on both sides, cooked to your taste. Sprinkling meat with flour before frying will help seal in juices. Steak pre-marinated this way can also be cooked on a charcoal grill. Each portion of this and other steaks may be topped with a pat or ball of butter flavored with horseradish, anchovies, or garden greens.

TENDERLOIN STEAK, CUBED
brizol z polędwicy

Slice 1½ lb. whole beef tenderloin into 4–5 portions. On moistened cutting board pound steaks with meat mallet, dipped in water, into rounds less than ¼ inch thick. Meat may be peppered before or after pounding. With flat of knife even out edges so that portions are circular in shape. Sprinkle with flour on both sides and fry in 4 T. hot lard until nicely browned on the outside but still pink on the inside.

TENDERLOIN STRIPS SMOTHERED IN ONIONS
potrawka z polędwicy

Slice thin 1½ lb. beef tenderloin, cut slices into strips, place in crockery bowl, and pour 3 T. salad oil and 2 T. Maggi extract or soy sauce over it. Refrigerate covered over night. Next day, brown 1½ lbs. sliced onions in 4–5 T. oil. Add meat and marinade, toss with fried onions, add 1 T. water, and cook on fairly high heat, stirring constantly 2–3 min. The meat should be still quite pink on the inside. Pepper, add 2 T. tomato concentrate or ketchup, and serve over rice with a crispy salad on the side. *Note:* This simple but elegant dish—a specialty of Warsaw's Hotel Europejski—is also a frequent dinner party offering at the Strybel home, and we think you'll like it too.

RUMPSTEAK
rumsztyki wołowe

Trim a 1½ lb. piece of beef rump of excess fat and veins and cut against grain into thin slices. Pound thin with moistened mallet. With flat of knife, form portions into oval steaks. Sprinkle with freshly ground pepper, dust with flour, and brown on both sides in several T. hot fat. Sprinkle with a little court bouillon or beef broth, cover, and simmer on low heat several min. Garnish with chopped parsley and serve with puréed potatoes and a seasonal vegetable and salad.

RIB STEAK SMOTHERED IN ONIONS
rozbratel z cebulką

Remove bones and trim away excess fat from 1½ lbs. rib steaks. Pepper steaks and pound with moistened meat mallet until ½ inch thick. Sprinkle with flour and fry in several T. hot lard on both sides until still pink inside. Separately, fry 2–3 sliced onions until nicely browned. To serve, top each steak with a portion of fried onions.

BEEF STEAK WITH HORSERADISH
antrykot

Proceed as above, but omit onions. Top each portion with a little freshly grated horseradish root and a pat of chive butter or garden-green butter.

BEEF STEW
gulasz wołowy

Roll 1½ lbs. cubed stewing beef in flour and brown on all sides in 4 T. lard. Transfer to Dutch oven or baking dish. In same drippings partially brown 3–4 diced onions, then add to meat with 1 c. water. Simmer in covered Dutch oven on stove top at low heat or bake covered in 375° oven 2 hrs. or until meat is fork tender. Replace any liquid that evaporates during cooking. Fork-blend 1 heaping T. sour cream, 1 level T. tomato concentrate, ½ t. paprika, and pour over meat. Simmer until thick and bubbly and salt & pepper to taste. Thin sauce with a little hot water if too thick. Garnish with a little chopped parsley and/or dill and serve over noodles of choice. *Variations:* Gulasz and other potrawki (fricassees) afford the cook an almost endless array of flavor twists that ensure he or she won't end up serving up the same old dish over and over again. Here are but a few suggestions.

1) After browning meat, add 1 or 2 thinly sliced carrots to pot.
2) Brown 8 oz. chopped fresh mushrooms with the onions and add to browned meat.
3) Add ½ oz. chopped, cooked, Polish dried mushrooms to the meat, including the liquid in which the mushrooms were cooked. Omit the paprika and tomato concentrate.
4) Omit the tomato concentrate and drench the meat at the end of cooking with ¾ c. sour cream fork-blended with 1–2 T. flour. Thin sauce with hot water if necessary.
5) Instead of 1 c. water, use ½ c. beer and ½ c. water at start of cooking.
6) Add ¼ c. grated dill pickles to meat at start of cooking.
7) Instead of or in addition to the paprika, add one of the following spices: ½ t. marjoram, ½ t. caraway, ¼ t. savory, ¼ t. thyme, or 1 crumbled bay leaf. About ½ t. herb pepper. Beef seasoning, goulash seasoning or hunter's seasoning are also possibilities.
8) Other vegetables that can be added to your stew include kohlrabi, celery, and green peppers. But remember: genuine Polish style stew never contains potatoes!
9) Add 1–2 T. dry red wine to sauce when meat is tender.
10) Before flouring and browning the meat, refrigerate it overnight in a marinade like that recommended for beef tenderloin, pre-marinated (p. 253).

BEEF SHISH KEBABS
szaszłyki wołowe

Cut 1½–2 lbs. beef tenderloin (or use a less expensive cut like sirloin) into 1 inch squares and pound with meat mallet. In crockery bowl, place the meat slices one on top of the other, sprinkling each with pepper, a little thyme and/or marjoram, lemon juice, and oil. Cover and let stand at room temp. 3 hrs. or up to 2 days in refrigerator. Cut sliced, uncooked bacon into pieces the length of the steak and choose firm tomatoes, onions, and fresh mushroom caps of approximately the same size. Thread the meat, bacon, sliced tomatoes, sliced onions (the tomatoes should be sliced about ½ inch thick, the onions much thinner), and mushroom caps onto skewers rather tightly. Fry in 4 T. lard on all sides until tender. Another way is to brush with oil and cook in home rotisserie or over charcoal grill. Serve immediately with cooked rice and a lettuce salad. This is but one version of the Middle Eastern favorite that has enriched the cuisine of Poland and many other countries as well.

KIEŁBASA SHISH KEBABS
szaszłyki z kiełbasą

On skewers intersperse the ingredients above with ½ inch slices of skinned, smoked Polish sausage. It may be used in addition to or instead of the beef.

BOILED BEEF
sztuka mięsa

In soup kettle, place 2–3 lbs. beef chuck, rump, shank, or short ribs. Scald with boiling water to cover and cook about 90 min., skimming away scum until no more forms. Add standard portion of soup greens (carrot, parsley root, celeriac or celery, leek, and a good-sized wedge of Savoy cabbage) and spices (6 peppercorns, 3 grains allspice, and 1 bay leaf). An onion, cut in half and singed over flame, may also be added. Cook another hr. on low heat, or until meat is fork tender. (The stock makes an excellent beef broth). Slice the meat and drench with horseradish sauce on platter. Serve with mashed potatoes and the boiled vegetables from broth. *Note:* You can cut cooking time in half by using a pressure cooker.

BEEF TONGUE IN POLISH GREY SAUCE
ozór wołowy w szarym sosie

Place 1 beef tongue in soup kettle, scald with plenty of boiling water, and cook 2 hrs. Add 6 peppercorns, 3 grains allspice, 1 clove, and 1 bay leaf. For added zest, a cayenne pepper in whole or part may be added. Add 1 portion diced soup greens and 1 T. salt and continue to cook (roughly ½–1 hr. depending on size and toughness of tongue) until it is fork tender. Remove skin under cold running water. If it comes off easily, the tongue has been fully cooked. Cut tongue into ½ inch thick slices and return to stock. Meanwhile, prepare the sauce. Caramelize 1 T. sugar in dry saucepan, add 4 T. boiling water, stirring until carmelized sugar dissolves. Set aside. Brown 3 T. flour in another dry skillet, add 2 T. butter and, when it melts, add the caramel liquid and about 2 c. tongue stock. Add ½ c. raisins, 2 t. lemon juice, and ½ t. honey-spice cake seasoning. *Note*: If you have not home-blended a supply of this seasoning as recommended, add ⅛ t. ground cloves, ⅛ t. ginger, and a dash of cinnamon and nutmeg. *Optional:* Add 1 jigger dry red wine and/or 1 T. powidła (plum jam). Simmer sauce a few min. until smooth and bubbly and salt & pepper to taste. If necessary, thin with a little tongue stock. Place sliced hot tongue on platter and drench with sauce. Serve with mashed potatoes and a salad.

BEEF TONGUE IN HORSERADISH SAUCE
ozór wołowy w sosie chrzanowym

Cook beef tongue as above. To make the sauce, melt 2 T. butter in saucepan. Fork-blend ¾–1 c. sour cream with 3 T. flour until lump-free and add to sauce pan. Stir in enough hot tongue stock to get the thickness you desire. Add 3–6 T. freshly grated horseradish root or prepared horseradish (the amount depends on the potency of your horseradish and how hot you want your sauce to be!), salt & pepper, sugar to taste, and simmer about 1 min. Pour over sliced tongue on platter. *Optional:* The sauce will be even tastier if you fork-blend 1 raw egg yolk with the sour cream. Mustard sauce and gherkin sauce are other possibilities. *Note*: Slice boiled beef (p. 256) may also be served with any of the sauces recommended for tongue. Use the tongue stock as a soup base.

STEWED BEEF KIDNEY
cynadry wołowe duszone

Cut away any fat still attached to 1½ lbs. beef kidneys. Slice each kidney in half and soak in plenty of cold water 1 hr. Transfer kidneys to pot containing 8 c. fresh cold water, bring to boil, simmer several min. and drain. Repeat 1 or 2 more times, using fresh cold water each time. Drain kidneys. When cool, cut into thin slices, sprinkle with flour, and brown in 3 T. lard on all sides. Midway through browning, add 2–3 diced onions, mixing and browning with meat. Add 1 c. or more beef bouillon (tongue stock is good!), cover, and simmer on low heat 1–1½ hrs., or until tender. Replace liquid that evaporates during cooking. Stir in 1–2 T. tomato concentrate or ketchup, 1 jigger red or white dry wine, 1 heaping T. sour cream, and salt & pepper to taste. Simmer 1 min., stirring to a smooth, pourable sauce. If too thin, sprinkle in a little flour and simmer briefly. Before serving, sprinkle with fresh chopped parsley. Serve with buckwheat groats, or barley and a dill pickle or dill pickle salad.

BEEF KIDNEY WITH MUSHROOMS
cynadry wołowe z pieczarkami

Trim, soak, par-boil, slice, and brown beef kidneys as above, but add 2 chopped onions and 8 oz. washed, fresh, sliced mushrooms. Add 2 c. bouillon and ½ t. Maggi extract and simmer under cover until meat is tender. Serve as is, or drench with ¾ c. sour cream fork-blended with 1 T. flour or more. Simmer 1 min. and salt & pepper.

BRAISED BEEF HEART
serce wołowe w sosie

Remove all tubes from 1 beef heart and wash thoroughly. Place heart in pot, cover with cold water, bring to boil, then reduce heat, cover, and simmer about 2½ hrs. Replace water that evaporates. Add 1 portion soup greens, several peppercorns, 1 bay leaf, 2 grains allspice, and 1 clove; continue simmering until heart is tender. Remove heart and, when cool enough to handle, remove and discard all fat and hard matter. Slice heart and simmer briefly in brown gravy, hot cream sauce, or other hot sauce of choice. Use heart stock where sauce recipe calls for meat stock. *Note:* In general, beef heart requires slow long cooking, because it is on the tough side, but can be very tasty if properly prepared. It should be avoided by people with above-normal cholesterol levels.

ROAST VEAL
pieczeń cielęca

Slice 2–3 buds garlic into quarters. Make 1 inch deep incision on all sides of a 3 lb. veal rump or arm roast (the rolled, string-tied roasts are good!) and force pieces of garlic into each incision. Into roaster or baking dish pour 2 c. boiling water, add 1 T. salt, place roast into water, and let stand 25 min. Then add 1 T. lard, place 2–3 strips uncooked bacon on top of meat. Roast uncovered in pre-heated 400° oven 30 min., basting with pan liquid twice. Top meat with 2 T. butter, cover, reduce heat to 325° and bake about 1 hr. longer, or until tender, basting occasionally. Salt & pepper. Let roast set at room temp. about 15 min. before slicing. Serve with mashed potatoes, using pan drippings to flavor them instead of gravy, creamed or floured peas & carrots, and a lettuce salad. You can also refrigerate the unsliced roast overnight, slice when cold, and reheat in pan drippings when ready to serve.

STUFFED VEAL ROAST
pieczeń cielęca nadziewana

Roast veal as above or proceed as follows. Beat an unrolled 3 lb. veal roast on all sides with rolling pin. Rub all over with 1–2 buds mashed garlic and sprinkle with salt & pepper or Polish veal seasoning. Sprinkle all sides with flour and brown in about 4 T. hot lard or oil. Transfer to roaster, drench with drippings (from browning), sprinkle with several T. water, and bake covered in 325° oven 2–2½ hrs. or until tender. Baste with pan drippings occasionally and replace any liquid that evaporates. When roast (prepared in either of the two ways) is done, remove to cutting board, and allow to stand about 15 min. Meanwhile, prepare stuffing. Brown 2 finely diced onions in 2 T. butter. Add 3–4 T. bread crumbs, 1 raw egg yolk, and enough sour cream to get a thick, moist filling. Add 1 T. or more fresh chopped dill, 1 t. fresh parsley, a pinch or 2 nutmeg, and salt & pepper to taste. Combine ingredients well. Slice roast fairly thin at an angle, leaving every second slice not cut all the way through. Fill the pockets (the slices not cut all the way to board) with filling. Fasten with toothpicks in the form of the original roast, return to roaster, and bake covered for another 30 min.

STUFFED VEAL BREAST
mostek cielęcy nadziewany

Have your butcher cut a pocket in a 4 lb. veal breast. Into bowl containing 1 c. milk crumble 3 stale kaiser rolls (French bread etc.). When soft, run through meat grinder with ¼ lb. calf's liver or chicken livers. Partially brown 2 finely chopped onions in 2 T. butter. Combine bread & liver mixture with onions and drippings, add 2 raw egg yolks, 1 T. fresh chopped dill, 1 t. fresh chopped parsley, and 3 T. bread crumbs. Fold in 2 egg whites beaten to a froth, mix ingredients well, add a dash of nutmeg and salt & pepper to taste. (*Note*: Instead of liver, you can use ¼ lb. ground veal or ground pork.) Fill pocket with stuffing and sew up. Melt 4 T. lard in roaster, add meat, sprinkle with water, and roast uncovered 1½ hrs., basting frequently with pan drippings. Cover and roast another 1½ hrs. or until meat is tender. An oven temp. of 325° is best. Let veal breast stand 15 min. at room temp. before slicing. Slice carefully so the stuffing does not fall out of the rim of meat. For best results, slice when cold, then reheat in pan drippings. Serve as is or add a little boiling water to pan drippings, stir ¾ c. sour cream fork-blended with 1 T. or so flour, and simmer several min. Salt & pepper to taste and pour over sliced meat on platter. Serve with potatoes, peas, and leek salad.

VEAL CHOPS WITH MUSHROOMS
kotlet cielęcy z pieczarkami

Pound 1½ lbs. veal chops until ½ inch thick. Roll in flour and fry in several T. lard or oil until tender. Separately, brown in 3 T. butter 8 oz. washed, chopped mushrooms and 1 chopped onion. Top meat with mushrooms, add 1 t. tomato concentrate or ketchup, and ½ t. Maggi extract; cover and simmer 2–3 min. Garnish with chopped fresh parsley and salt & pepper to taste. Serve with rice or potatoes. Cauliflower Polonaise is a nice side dish (p.520).

BREADED VEAL CUTLETS À LA VIENNOISE/WIENERSCHNITZEL
sznycel cielęcy po wiedeńsku

Cut away bones from 1½ lbs. veal chops. (Use bones for making soups.) With moist meat mallet beat cutlets to a thickness of about ¼ inch. Sprinkle with salt, dip in flour, beaten eggs and bread crumbs, pressing breading in with hand so it doesn't fall off during frying. Fry in 4–5 T. hot lard until nicely golden on both sides, then reduce heat and continue cooking until done. In separate skillet, fry in butter as many eggs sunny-side-up as there are cutlets. To serve, place a fried egg on top of each cutlet, also a lemon slice and a ball of chive butter. Serve with mashed potatoes (flavored with pan drippings), peas, or spinach, and a grated vegetable salad. This popular gourmet dish, which originated in Austria, has long been a favorite on Poland's culinary scene. It will undoubtedly become one of your family's favorites, as well!

CALF'S FEET FRIED IN BATTER
nóżki cielęce smażone w cieście

Place 4 calf's feet in pot, scald with about 6 c. boiling water, bring to boil, and drain. Cut feet lengthwise, place in boiling salted water, and cook 1½ hrs. Add 1 portion soup greens, crumbled bay leaf, 3 grains allspice, and 6 peppercorns; cook until meat comes away from bone. Drain. (Use stock as soup base.) Remove bones and cut each foot into 2 rectangles of meat. Allow meat to drip dry in colander, then place flat on cutting board. Cover with another cutting board, weighted down with something heavy, and allow to cool. Meanwhile, prepare batter: mix 1¼ c. flour with 2 egg yolks, 2 T. salad oil, and about ½ c. water. Salt lightly and fold in the 2 beaten egg whites. Salt & pepper meat, dip in batter, and fry in 4 T. hot lard on both sides to a nice golden brown. Serve with rice and a tangy salad.

STEWED VEAL
potrawka cielęca

Scald 1½ lbs. veal arm, blade, or rump roast (with bone attached) with 6–8 c. boiling water, bring to boil, reduce heat, and simmer under cover 1 hr. Add soup greens and spices (peppercorns, allspice, bay leaf) and continue cooking until meat is tender. Drain meat, cut away from bone into small cubes, place in skillet, and stew with any of the below.

VEAL STEWED WITH MUSHROOMS
potrawka cielęca z grzybami lub pieczarkami

Brown 8 oz. washed, chopped, or sliced fresh mushrooms in 4 T. butter with 1–2 chopped onions, combine with diced veal in skillet, add 2 c. stock (in which veal was cooked), cover, and simmer 20 min. Add ½ t. Maggi extract, salt & pepper to taste, stir in 1 heaping T. sour cream, and sprinkle in enough flour to form a thick sauce. This dish will be even better if you use home-canned wild mushrooms. To diced veal in skillet add 2 finely chopped onions browned in 2 T. butter and 2 c. home-canned wild mushrooms, including the liquid. Simmer under cover about 20 min. The home-canned mushrooms may be sufficiently salty, so taste the dish before adding additional salt. Pepper and thicken sauce with a little flour if necessary. *Optional:* Stir in 1 heaping T. sour cream. Simmer briefly and serve over rice or egg-batter dumplings. Cooked cauliflower goes well with your stewed veal.

VEAL STEWED WITH VEGETABLES
potrawka cielęca z jarzynami

Brown 1–2 finely chopped onions in 3 T. butter. Remove from heat and stir in 3 T. flour, gradually adding 2 c. veal stock. Simmer while beating with wire whisk about 5 min. In cup fork-blend ½ c. sauce, slightly cooled, with 1 raw egg yolk and return to saucepan. Salt & pepper sauce to taste and pour over diced veal, diced vegetables from stock, and ½ c. canned peas, drained. Heat but do not boil and garnish with a little chopped parsley and/or dill.

VEAL STEWED WITH PRUNES & RAISINS OLD POLISH STYLE
potrawka cielęca po staropolsku

Soak 8 prunes in c. water 30 min., remove pits, chop fine, and cook in several T. water until tender. Set aside. Soak ¼ c. raisins in ¾ c. water. In saucepan combine 3 T. melted butter with 3 T. flour and simmer but do not brown. Add 1½ c. veal stock and simmer 10 min., beating frequently with wire whisk. Add the stewed prunes, drained raisins, 1 jigger dry white wine, 1 T. honey and juice of ½–1 lemon (depending on tartness desired). Simmer briefly, salt & pepper to taste, and pour over diced veal. Heat thoroughly but do not boil. This now rather exotic dish is typical of the kind of delicacies favored by the Old Polish nobility of yesteryear.

VEAL STEWED WITH GOOSEBERRIES
potrawka cielęca z agrestem

In small pot melt 2 T. butter, add 1 c. washed, drained, ripe gooseberries and simmer with butter, adding ¼ c. veal stock and stirring frequently. Sprinkle in 1 T. flour, stirring to form lump-free sauce. Dilute gooseberry mixture with several T. stock if necessary. Place hot diced or sliced veal on platter, salt & pepper, and drench with hot gooseberry mixture. For a sweet & sour taste, adjust flavor of gooseberry sauce with a little sugar and lemon juice.

VEAL STEWED WITH APPLES
potrawka cielęca z jabłkami

Peel and coarsely grate 2 apples and cook in ½ c. veal stock until soft. Add diced veal and soup vegetables (the latter forced through sieve). In saucepan melt 3 T. butter, stir in 3 T. flour, and simmer but do not brown. Add ½ c. sour cream and enough veal stock to get a thick sauce and simmer 5 min., mixing occasionally with wire whisk. Add veal and apple mixture and heat thoroughly. Salt & pepper to taste. Serve with rice, barley, or egg batter dumplings, and a grated vegetable salad.

VEAL IN LEMON-DILL SAUCE
potrawka cielęca w sosie cytrynowo-koperkowym

Melt 3 T. butter, add 3 T. flour, and simmer, stirring until smooth, but do not brown. Stir in 1 c. veal stock and bring to boil. Remove from heat. Stir in ½ c. sour cream, juice of ½ lemon, 1 t. sugar, and 2–3 T. fresh chopped dill. Simmer briefly but do not boil. Fork-blend ½ c. of the sauce, slightly cooled, with 1 raw egg yolk and return to saucepan. Dilute with a little veal stock if too thick. Add the diced veal and heat through but do not boil. Serve with rice, barley, or noodles and a crispy salad.

VEAL GOULASH
paprykarz cielęcy

Partially brown 2 chopped onions in 3 T. butter. Add the diced veal, ¾ c. veal stock, 2 buds mashed garlic, 1 t. mild paprika, ¼ t. cayenne pepper (more or less, depending on how hot you like your food), salt & pepper. Simmer covered about 15 min. Fork-blend ½ c. sour cream with 2–3 T. flour, add to skillet and simmer briefly. If necessary, dilute with a little veal stock to get a nice, pourable consistency. Serve with egg-batter dumplings and sauerkraut salad. *Variation:* Brown 6–8 oz. fresh chopped mushrooms with the onions, then proceed as above.

VEAL COLLOPS WITH MUSHROOMS
bitki/zrazy cielęce z pieczarkami

Cut away meat from 1½ lbs. veal chops. You can also use veal round steak in this recipe, in which case cut meat into roughly 2 inch squares or 1½ x 2½ inch rectangles. Pound meat with moistened meat mallet. Sprinkle with salt and flour and brown meat on both sides in 4 T. lard or oil. (You may also use 2 T. butter and 2 T. oil, as butter alone tends to burn.) Transfer meat to baking dish, add pan drippings and several T. water, and bake covered in 325° oven about 30 min. It can also be simmered on low heat in a heavy (preferably cast-iron) skillet or Dutch oven on stove top. Meanwhile, chop or slice 4–8 oz. fresh mushrooms, place in separate pot containing 1 c. meat stock (or 1 c. water and 1 bouillon cube), salt and cook covered about 20 min. Add mushrooms to meat and bake covered another 30 min., or until meat is tender. Add 1 jigger dry white wine and 1 T. potato starch dissolved in ¼ c. cold water and bring to boil. Salt & pepper to taste and serve with rice or noodles with a radish salad on the side.

VEAL COLLOPS AU JUS
bitki/zrazy cielęce we własnym sosie

Prepare 1½ lbs. veal chops or veal round as above. After browning meat and transferring to baking dish, in same fat brown 1–2 thinly sliced onions. Add onions to meat along with 1 c. meat stock and simmer under cover 45–60 min., or until tender. Sprinkle with a little flour, combining it with pan drippings and simmer briefly. Salt & pepper to taste and serve with Kraków groats or noodles. Creamed peas & carrots make a nice accompaniment.

VEAL COLLOPS IN SOUR CREAM
bitki/zrazy cielęce w śmietanie

Proceed as above, but instead of sprinkling meat with flour, drench it with ½–¾ c. sour cream fork-blended with 2 T. flour. Simmer briefly and salt & pepper. Garnish with a little chopped dill and/or parsley.

VEAL ROLL-UPS À LA POLONAISE
zrazy cielęce zawijane po polsku

Pound 1½ veal chops (with bones removed) or veal round steak cut into 1½ x 2½ inch pieces until very thin but still unbroken. Brown 1 finely chopped onion in 2 T. butter. Soak 1 kaiser roll in milk until soggy and run through meat grinder with browned onions. To mixture add 1 T. bread crumbs, 2–3 T. raisins (pre-soaked and drained), 1 T. chopped parsley, 1 raw egg yolk, and a dash of nutmeg. Mix ingredients well and salt & pepper to taste. Spread meat with filling, roll up tightly, and fasten with toothpicks or tie with strong thread. Salt & pepper roll-ups, roll in flour, and brown on all sides in hot oil and butter (about one part of each). Transfer to baking dish, drench with pan drippings, add 2 c. meat stock, and simmer covered 45–60 min., or until tender. Drench with ¾ c. sour cream fork-blended with 2 T. flour. Simmer until thick and bubbly, adding a little stock or hot water if sauce is too thick. Season with ½ t. Maggi extract and salt & pepper. Serve with rice, barley, or Kraków groats, boiled vegetables and non-creamed salad.

VEAL ROLL-UPS WITH HAM
zrazy cielęce zawijane z szynką

Pound 1½ lbs. de-boned veal chops or veal round steak as above. On each piece of meat place a slice of boiled ham (Krakus canned ham from Poland is best!), roll up and fasten with toothpicks or tie with strong thread. Sprinkle with flour and brown on all sides in 4 T. lard, oil, or part each oil and butter. Transfer to baking dish. In drippings brown 1 thinly sliced onion and add to meat. Fork-blend 1 c. stock or water with 2 T. tomato concentrate and pour over meat. Simmer covered 45–60 min. or until tender. Fork-blend ½ c. of the pan sauce with 2 T. flour, ½ t. paprika, and ½ t. sugar and salt & pepper to taste. Pour over meat and simmer 2–3 min. Garnish with chopped dill and serve with rice, barley, or egg-batter dumplings, together with boiled vegetables and non-creamed salad. *Note:* Veal roll-ups can also be prepared with any of the fillings recommended for beef steak roll-ups.

MINCED VEAL CUTLETS
kotlety cielęce siekane

Soak broken-up, stale kaiser roll (hamburger bun, French bread, etc.) in ½ c. milk until soggy, then run through meat grinder. Combine well with 1–1½ lbs. ground veal and 1 whole egg and work well into a uniform mass. Salt & pepper. *Optional:* 1–2 T. grated onion may be added. Also, the egg white may be beaten separately and folded into mixture. Form and roll between palms snowball-fashion. Roll in flour and bread crumbs, pressing in breading with hands, and fry in 4 T. hot fat of choice on both sides, flattening slightly with spatula. Polish kotlety siekane are not perfectly round meatballs, but rather thick, oval-shaped patties. After both sides have browned nicely, reduce heat, cover, and simmer about 15 min. Serve with mashed potatoes, sprinkled with pan drippings, and a cucumber or lettuce salad laced with sour cream.

VEAL MEATBALLS, STEWED
klopsiki cielęce duszone

Prepare meat as for minced veal cutlets (above). Form meat into walnut or golfball-sized balls, roll in flour, and brown on all sides in 4 T. hot lard, or oil and butter. Transfer to baking dish. In drippings brown 1 finely chopped onion. Add to meat together with ½–1 c. stock or water, ½ t. Maggi extract, and salt & pepper. Cover and simmer on low heat 20–30 min., replacing liquid that evaporates. Fork-blend 1 heaping T. sour cream with 2 T. flour and several T. pan drippings and add to meat. Simmer briefly and dilute with a little stock or hot water if too thick. Salt & pepper and garnish with a little chopped dill. Serve with rice, potatoes, or noodles, and a crispy, non-creamed salad.

BREADED GROUND VEAL CUTLETS À LA POJARSKI
kotlety pożarskie

Soak broken-up, stale kaiser roll in ½ c. milk and run through meat grinder. Mix with 1 lb. or so ground veal and run entire mixture through grinder again. Salt mixture, add 1–2 t. chopped dill, 1 T. or slightly more melted butter, and fold in 2 stiffly beaten egg whites. Mix with hands until ingredients are fully blended and somewhat fluffy, adding 1 or more T. milk as needed. Between moistened palms form meat into 3 inch rolls about ¾ inch thick. Dip in beaten eggs, roll in bread crumbs, press in breading, and fry in 2 T. butter on medium heat until golden on both sides. Place a pat of butter on each cutlet, cover, and bake in pre-heated 350° oven 15 min. Serve with mashed potatoes (sprinkled with pan drippings), cooked cauliflower or asparagus, and a lettuce or grated-vegetable salad.

BREADED GROUND VEAL CUTLETS À LA MINISTRE
sznycel cielęcy ministerski

Cut a fresh kaiser roll or other bun into 1 inch long strips to resemble the shoestring potatoes sold at snack counters. Leave out overnight to turn stale or heat in warm oven to dry thoroughly. Prepare meat as for Pożarski cutlets (above), but use 1 whole egg (instead of 2 beaten egg whites) and omit dill. Form meat into round 3 inch patties about ¾ inch thick. Dip cutlets in flour, beaten eggs, and the stale bread strips mixed with several T. bread crumbs. Fry on medium heat in 3 T. oil until they are a nice golden brown on both sides. Top each cutlet with a pat of butter, cover, reduce heat as low as possible, and simmer 2 min. longer. Serve with mashed potatoes (flavored with pan drippings instead of gravy), cooked string beans, peas or carrots, and cucumber & sour cream salad.

VEAL SAUSAGE ROLLS
frykadelki cielęce

Prepare meat mixture as above. Between palms roll meat into the shape of small frankfurters about 4 inches long and ¾ inch thick. Roll in bread crumbs, pressing them taking care that the meat rolls retain their sausage-like shape. Fry in 4 T. hot lard or oil until nicely browned on all sides, then reduce heat and continue cooking until done. A total cooking time of 15 min. should be more than sufficient.

POACHED VEAL MEATBALLS
pulpety cielęce

Prepare meat mixture as for any of the meatballs and ground cutlets above, but omit spices except for a little salt. Roll into golfball-sized meatballs between floured palms and set aside. In 5 c. water cook 1 portion standard soup greens. When vegetables are tender, add 2 t. salt and poach the meatballs in the water (with or without the vegetables) about 10–15 min. Test one for doneness. Remove meatballs to platter with slotted spoon and surround with the vegetables. *Optional:* Dot with butter on platter. This light and highly digestible dish is often served in Poland to small children or convalescents on a restricted diet.

POACHED VEAL MEATBALLS IN SAUCE
pulpety cielęce w sosie

Prepare and cook meatballs in vegetable stock as above. Drain. Drench with any of the sauces recommended for meatballs browned in fat: sour cream, mushroom, dill, tomato, etc. Use vegetable stock in which meatballs were poached in the sauce. Poached meatballs in sauce naturally have more calories and cholesterol than the plain ones, but they are less fattening and more digestible than those browned in fat.

CALF'S LIVER SAUTÉ
wątróbka cielęca sauté

Sprinkle 1 lb. sliced calf's liver with pepper and a pinch or 2 ginger. Roll in flour and brown in 4 T. medium hot lard (or 2 T. oil, 2 T. butter) on both sides. Add 2–3 thinly sliced onions, brown briefly in pan drippings with the liver, then cover, reduce heat, and simmer until liver is cooked. Liver should not be overcooked and should still show a trace of pinkness inside, so cut one of the slices in half to check. Salt only after cooking. Serve immediately with egg-batter noodles or rice and braised beets.

CALF'S LIVER STEWED IN CREAM
wątróbka cielęca w śmietanie

Pepper 1 lb. sliced calf's liver and roll in flour. In skillet melt, but do not brown, 1 T. butter, tilting skillet to butter entire surface. Place the liver in skillet, drench with ¾ c. sour cream (liquified by fork-blending) and simmer under cover about 10 min. Salt and serve with mashed potatoes or groats and beet & apple salad.

CALF'S LIVER STEWED IN VEGETABLES
wątróbka cielęca duszona w jarzynach

Slice thin 2 onions, 1 carrot, 1 small parsley root, and dice a small piece of celeriac (or small stalk celery). Dice ¼ lb. salt pork and brown in skillet. Add vegetables and simmer under cover 5 min., stirring occasionally. Smother 1 lb. sliced calf's liver with vegetables, pepper, and sprinkle with 3 crushed juniper berries. Cover and simmer 5 min. or until liver is cooked but still faintly pink inside. Sprinkle with 1 T. flour, stir in 3 T. sour cream, and simmer briefly. Salt & pepper. Serve with noodles and sauerkraut salad.

BOILED VEAL TONGUE
ozorki cielęce gotowane

Scald 1½ lbs. veal tongues with 6 c. boiling water, boil and cook on medium heat 15 min. Skim away scum. Add 1 portion soup greens, 1 bay leaf, 4 grains allspice and 1 T. salt, cover and simmer 1–1½ hrs. or until tender. Remove skin from tongues under cold running water, slice, and return to stock while you prepare sauce. Place slices of hot, drained tongue on serving platter, surround with soup greens, and drench with horseradish, mustard, tomato, or grey sauce. Gherkin sauce is another possibility. Serve with mashed potatoes and a crunchy non-creamed salad. Veal tongues may also be corned for added zest and a pink, ham-like hue. See smoked beef tongue.

VEAL HEARTS WITH MUSHROOMS
serca cielęce duszone z pieczarkami

Cut 1–1½ lbs. veal hearts into cubes, removing veins and any fat. Place in pot containing 8 c. cold water, bring to boil, and cook 30 min. Add 1 bay leaf, 4 grains allspice, and 1 T. salt, and simmer another 30 min., or until tender. In skillet partially brown 2 chopped onions and 4–8 oz. fresh chopped mushrooms in 3 T. butter. Add the cooked veal hearts and about 1 c. of the stock in which they cooked, cover, and simmer 10 min. Uncover and allow most of the moisture to evaporate. Salt & pepper, sprinkle with 1 T. flour, stir in 2–3 T. sour cream, and simmer briefly. Garnish with a little chopped parsley and/or dill. Serve with mashed potatoes and spinach Polonaise.

STEWED VEAL KIDNEYS
cynaderki cielęce duszone

Remove membrane and fat from 1½ lbs. veal kidneys if still attached. Make a deep slit in the kidneys lengthwise and soak in plenty of cold water 3 hrs. changing water 2 or 3 times. Scald the kidneys with 6–8 c. boiling salted water, bring to boil, and cook 10 min. Remove kidneys, pour away water, and slice kidneys thin when they have cooled. Place kidneys in pot, cover with cold water, and bring to boil. Meanwhile, brown 2–3 sliced onions in 3 T. lard and add to kidneys. Salt, cover, and simmer on low heat until kidneys are tender. Add 1 bud mashed garlic, ½ t. Maggi extract, 1 T. dry wine (optional), and pepper to taste. Sprinkle with 1 T. flour and simmer briefly. During cooking, any evaporated liquid should be replaced. Garnish with fresh chopped parsley and serve with puréed potatoes and cwikła. *Variation:* Kidneys are also delicious simmered in mushrooms and onions like veal hearts (above) or in tomato sauce.

CALF'S BRAIN WITH EGGS
móżdżek cielęcy z jajkami

To 4 c. boiling water add 2 T. salt, 2 T. vinegar, and bring to boil. Add 1 lb. calves brains and blanch until they turn whitish. Remove brains and set aside to cool. Dice brains, discarding any membranes, veins, or gristle. Brown 2 finely diced onions in 3 T. butter, add diced brains, and simmer briefly. Stir in 3–6 beaten eggs and cook as you would scrambled eggs until set but still moist. Salt & pepper to taste and sprinkle with chopped chives or parsley. This dish makes a nice Sunday brunch, served with plenty of crusty French bread, sliced tomatoes on the side, and a big pot of steaming white coffee (biała kawa) to wash it all down.

CALF'S BRAIN CUTLETS
kotlety z móżdżku cielęcego

Blanch 1 lb. calves brains in 4 c. boiling water, containing 2 T. salt and 2 T. vinegar, as above. Remove from pot and set aside to cool. This time, however, slice brains into small cutlets (patties), discarding membrane, veins, and gristle. Salt & pepper, dip in beaten eggs, roll in bread crumbs, pressing in breading and brown on both sides in 2 T. oil and 2 T. butter, then reduce heat and simmer a while longer. Serve with tartar sauce.

CALF'S BRAIN WITH MUSHROOMS
możdżek cielęcy z pieczarkami

Blanch ¾ lbs. calves brains as above, then set aside to cool. Lightly brown 2 finely chopped onions in 2 T. oil and 2 T. butter. Add 4–8 oz. finely chopped fresh mushrooms, mix with onions, add 3–4 T. broth (homemade or made with bouillon cube) and simmer covered about 15 min. or until mushrooms are tender. Meanwhile, dice brains, discarding membrane, veins, and any gristle, and add to mushrooms. Pepper and simmer briefly. Sprinkle with 1 T. flour and toss ingredients to fully absorb it. Drench with ½ c. fork-blended sour cream and simmer a while longer. Salt & pepper to taste. Serve with rice and lettuce with vinaigrette.

VEAL LUNGS IN TANGY SAUCE
płucka cielęce na kwaśno

Rinse 1½ lbs. veal lungs and cut off windpipe if still attached. Chop 1 portion soup greens, place in soup kettle, scald with 6–8 c. boiling water, and bring to boil. Add the lungs, 1 bay leaf, and 4 peppercorns and simmer covered 1 hr. or until lungs are fully cooked. Simmer 2 chopped onions in 3 T. lard or oil and butter, sprinkle in 3 T. flour, and add enough stock (in which lungs and vegetables were cooked) to get a nicely pourable sauce. Simmer several min. Salt and season to taste with a little vinegar (start with 2 t.) and sugar to get a nice sweet & sour taste. In cup, fork blend 1 raw egg yolk with ½ c. of slightly cooled sauce, and return to pan. Slice the lungs into thin strips and add to sauce. Simmer briefly. Serve with potatoes or rice and a grated-vegetable salad. *Variation:* Instead of egg yolk, you can use ½ c. sour cream for the sauce. The cooked soup vegetables may be added to this dish.

ROAST PORK
pieczeń wieprzowa

Salt & pepper 3–4 lbs. pork roast (shoulder or picnic roasts with bone are good, as are rolled boneless roasts), sprinkle with flour and brown on all sides in 3 T. hot lard. Place in roaster fat side up. In pan drippings brown 2 sliced onions. Top roast with onions, add pan drippings and 3 T. water, sprinkle with caraway seeds (about ½ t.), and bake covered in pre-heated 325° oven 2–2½ hrs., basting occasionally and replacing evaporated pan liquid with water. Roast is fully cooked when a fork goes in easily and the liquid trickling out of the puncture is no longer pinkish. About 40 min. before end of cooking, you may add some small peeled potatoes to roaster, if you like. Remove roast and allow to set 15 min. at room temp. and it'll be easier to slice. Serve with stewed sauerkraut or braised red cabbage and/or a grated, horseradish-flavored vegetable salad. Several variations on this basic recipe follow.

ROAST PORK IN VEGETABLE SAUCE
pieczeń wieprzowa duszona w jarzynach

Make 6–8 1 inch-deep incisions in roast and force a halved or quartered garlic bud into each. Sprinkle with flour and brown as above. In pan drippings, partially brown 2 sliced onions and 1 portion soup greens, diced. Sprinkle meat with marjoram (about 1 t.), smother with vegetables, add 2 c. water, cover, and bake in pre-heated 325°–350° oven until fully cooked. Force vegetables and drippings through sieve or blend in blender. Sprinkle with 1 T. or so flour and add enough boiling water to get a smooth, pourable sauce. (*Optional:* Add 1 T. tomato concentrate or ketchup. Simmer several min. and salt & pepper to taste.) Pour over sliced roast on platter.

ROAST PORK & SAUERKRAUT
pieczeń wieprzowa w kiszonej kapuście

Salt & pepper, then sprinkle with flour 3–4 lb. pork roast of choice, brown all over in 3 T. hot lard, and transfer to roaster. In pan drippings brown 2 sliced onions. Sprinkle roast with caraway seeds, top with browned onions, and let stand. Meanwhile, drain 1 qt. sauerkraut, rinse in plenty of cold water, drain, and chop coarsely. Add to pot with 5 c. cold water, bring to boil, and cook 10 min. Drain. Smother roast with sauerkraut, add 3 T. water, cover, and bake as above.

ROAST PORK À LA WILNO IN WINE MARINADE
pieczeń wieprzowa po wileńsku

Sprinkle 3–4 lb. pork roast generously with pepper, marjoram, paprika, and caraway seeds and rub in well. Cover roast with lemon slices and drench with 1 c. dry white wine. Cover and refrigerate 24 hrs. Turn meat over once or twice, placing lemon slices on top. Remove from marinade, pat meat dry, sprinkle with flour, and brown on all sides in 3 T. hot lard. Transfer to roaster, sprinkle with pan drippings and several T. wine marinade. Bake covered until fully cooked in 325° oven, basting occasionally with pan drippings. After 1½ hrs. add 1 c. prunes, pre-soaked 15 min. in water and drained. (Using pitted prunes will make things easier.) Force pan drippings through sieve or blend in blender. Add 1–2 T. flour and enough water to make a pourable sauce and simmer 5 min. Add ½ t. Maggi extract and salt & pepper to taste. Serve with rice and lettuce & sour cream salad.

ROAST PORK IN PLUM SAUCE
pieczeń wieprzowa w sosie powidłowym

Make 5–6 1 inch deep incisions in 3–4 lbs. pork roast and force a garlic half or quarter into each. Rub meat all over with salt, pepper, and marjoram, top with raw sliced onions, cover, and let stand at room temp. 1 hr. In saucepan bring to boil ½ c. water, ¼ c. powidła (thick Polish plum jam) or domestic plum jam, 1 t. Maggi extract, and 1 T. vinegar plus a pinch of ground cloves. Sprinkle roast with flour, brown on all sides in 3 T. hot lard, transfer to roast, and drench with plum sauce. Brown onions in pan drippings and pour over meat. Bake covered in 325° oven, replacing evaporated liquid and basting occasionally. Serve with rice sprinkled with pan drippings, Brussels sprouts, and radish salad.

ROAST LOIN OF PORK WITH PRUNES
schab pieczony ze śliwkami

Rub a 3–5 lb. pork loin with 1–2 buds crushed garlic, salt, pepper, paprika, and marjoram. (*Note:* Instead of garlic and spices, in this and other pork dishes you can use your homemade Polish pork seasoning.) Place meat in roaster, top with 2–3 sliced onions, cover, and let stand at room temp. 1 hr. or refrigerate overnight. Set aside onions, sprinkle loin with flour and brown on all sides in 3–4 T. hot lard. Return to roaster. In pan drippings brown the sliced onions and add to meat. Add 1½ c. water and roast covered in pre-heated 375° oven 1 hr., basting occasionally with pan drippings. Soak 2 c. prunes (with pits left in) in cold water 15 min., drain, and add to roaster adding more water if needed. Cover and reduce heat to 325° and bake another 1–1½ hrs. or until fully cooked. You may cut the loin in two to check how it is being cooked. Remove loin and allow to set at room temp. 15 min. before slicing. It will be even better if refrigerated overnight, sliced when cold, and reheated in pan drippings. This Old Polish gourmet dish ranks among the author's family and dinner-party favorites. Serve with saffron rice and a tomato, cucumber, and onion salad laced with sour cream. We usually place the rice on a very large, old-fashioned platter, run the sliced pork loin down the center, and garnish it with the pan drippings and prunes.

ROAST LOIN OF PORK WITH RAISINS
schab pieczony z rodzynkami

Prepare like roast loin of pork with prunes, but sprinkle browned meat with 1 jigger dry white wine and 1 c. water. Instead of the prunes, add 1 c. raisins. Otherwise proceed as above.

ROAST LOIN OF PORK WITH SOUR-CURED APPLES
schab pieczony a kwaszonymi jabłkami

Rub a 3–5 lb. pork loin with salt, pepper, and 1 bud mashed garlic. Cover and let stand at room temp. 1 hr. or in refrigerator overnight. Sprinkle with flour and brown on all sides in 3–4 T. hot lard. Transfer to roaster. Brown 2 sliced onions in the pan drippings and add to roaster along with ½ c. water, bouillon or beer, and bake covered in 325° pre-heated oven 1½ hrs. If you failed to put up a supply of sour-cured apples last autumn, no matter. Dissolve 3 T. sugar, 1 T. salt, and 1 t. citric acid crystals in 1 c. hot water and add to 1 qt. cold water in pot. Peel, quarter and remove core from 2 lbs. apples, placing the peeled quarters into the brine. Let apples stay in brine at least 30 min., then drain and add to roaster. Sprinkle meat with 1 t. caraway seeds, cover, and bake another hr. or so, or until meat is tender. After slicing meat, top each slice with a spoonful of the stewed apples. Serve with boiled potatoes sprinkled with pan drippings and garnished with chopped dill. *Note:* This dish can also be made using fresh apple quarters.

ROAST LOIN OF PORK WITH MUSHROOMS
schab pieczony z pieczarkami

Combine 1 t. Maggi extract, 1 t. salt, 1 bud mashed garlic, ½ t. paprika, and ¼ t. pepper. Rub a 3–5 lb. pork loin all over with mixture and let stand covered at room temp. 1 hr. Sprinkle loin with flour and brown in 4 T. hot lard. Place in roaster. In drippings brown 2 sliced onions and add to roaster together with 1 c. water. Roast covered in pre-heated 375° oven 30 min., sprinkling meat with water occasionally, then cover, reduce heat to 325°, and cook another hr. basting with pan drippings occasionally. Add 8 oz. fresh, washed, chopped mushrooms and cook 30 min. more. It is best to remove meat when it is still slightly underdone, refrigerate overnight, slice when cold, and simmer it in pan drippings and mushrooms until fully cooked just prior to serving. Serve with mashed potatoes and sliced tomatoes.

ROAST LOIN OF PORK WITH POTATOES
schab pieczony z kartofelkami

Rub pork loin with salt, and Polish pork seasoning, sprinkle with flour and brown in hot fat as above. Transfer to roaster, top with 2 raw onions, sliced, add 3 T. water, and roast uncovered in 375° oven 30 min., then reduce temp. to 325° and continue cooking about 1 hr., basting occasionally. Replace liquid that evaporates. Add about 2 lbs. small peeled potatoes, sprinkle meat with 1 t. caraway seeds, and bake covered another 45 min.–1 hr. or until meat is fully cooked. Place the sliced loin on platter, surround with potatoes which should be garnished with chopped dill and/or parsley. Serve with stewed sauerkraut or sauerkraut salad, braised red cabbage or red-cabbage salad. This simple, country-style dish is sure to satisfy the hearty eaters in your gang.

ROAST LOIN OF PORK BAKED IN FOIL
schab pieczony w folii

Place your pork loin on a double thickness of heavy-duty aluminum foil. Rub in 1–2 buds mashed garlic, salt, pepper, and marjoram. Line top and sides with raw onion slices. Wrap in the foil and seal tightly at top, leaving just a little head space. Place meat in roaster, add 1 c. water to roaster, and roast uncovered in pre-heated 325°–350° oven 2–2½ hrs. or until tender. Since this method does not require overnight aging, browning, or basting, you may find it more convenient than the traditional way. The foil seals in the juices.

ROLLED PORK LOIN STUFFED WITH SAUSAGE
rolada wieprzowa nadziewana kiełbasą

Pound a 2–3 lb. boneless pork loin with meat mallet until about ½ inch thick. Spread meat with ½ lb. fresh kielbasa removed from casing. Roll meat up and tie with string. Roll in flour and brown in 4 T. hot lard on all sides, including ends. Transfer to baking dish. Sprinkle with salt, pepper, and paprika, top with sliced onions, add ¾ c. water, and bake covered in 325° oven about 2 hrs. or until tender. Replace liquid that evaporates during baking. Cool to room temp. and refrigerate overnight. Remove string. To serve hot, slice thin and reheat in pan drippings. Excellent with boiled potatoes, stewed sauerkraut, and/or ćwikła. This meat also bakes well in aluminum foil.

BREADED PORK CUTLETS
kotlety schabowe

Cut meat away from 1½ lbs. center-cut pork chops. (The bones make an excellent soup stock!) Sprinkle the cutlets with salt and (optional) 1 bud mashed garlic or a trace of garlic powder. A pinch of marjoram, paprika, or homemade Polish pork seasoning are other possibilities, but season the cutlets sparingly. Pound with moistened meat mallet until just under ¼ inch thick. After pounding, a large cutlet often covers an entire dinner plate. Dip in flour, beaten eggs, and bread crumbs. Press breading in with hand. Fry in 3 T. or so medium hot lard until nicely golden brown on both sides. Depending on the tenderness of the meat, the thickness of the cutlets, and the temp. of the fat, about 5–7 min. frying time per side should suffice. The cutlets may be served straight from the skillet, but most Polish cooks prefer to "dodusić", or simmer them additionally so they steam a bit and become extra flavorful and tender. To do so, simply transfer fried cutlets to a pot or baking dish, spoon some of the pan drippings over them, cover and simmer in pre-heated 325° oven 15–20 min. Serve with boiled or mashed potatoes, and in summer with boiled, walnut-sized new potatoes. Spoon pan drippings over potatoes and garnish with chopped dill. Stewed sauerkraut or braised cabbage are among the traditional vegetable accompaniments. Cucumber or lettuce salad dressed with sour cream in summer and grated carrot, apple & horseradish or radish salad in winter nicely enhance this traditional Polish favorite. Although this recipe has been inconspicuously tucked away among roast pork loins, meatballs, and stews in this particular cookbook, it's worth mentioning that this is modern-day Poland's most popular meat dish. It's somewhat like the way most Americans are crazy about steak!

BREADED PORK CHOPS
kotlety wieprzowe z kostką

In this recipe you can use a less expensive variety than center-cut pork chops, like pork sirloin or rib chops or even pork steak. Leave the bones attached to meat and pound meat a little with moistened meat mallet, but do not flatten as much as for breaded pork cutlets above. Salt & pepper. Melt 1 T. butter in saucepan and simmer 1 T. grated onion in it until golden but not browned. When cool, add simmered onions and drippings to 2 whole eggs; beat well. Dip chops in flour, beaten eggs, and bread crumbs, pressing in breading. Fry in 3 T. medium hot lard on both sides to a nice golden brown. Simmer additionally in oven as above, if you like.

PORK STEAK & ONIONS
stek wieprzowy duszony z cebulką

Pound slightly the meaty part (not the bones!) of 1½ lbs. pork steaks. Salt & pepper, sprinkle with flour, and brown in 2 T. hot lard. Separately brown 3–4 thinly sliced onions in 2 T. hot lard. Top with pork steaks with the onions, add 2–3 T. water or beer, and simmer covered on low heat about 1 hr. or until meat is fork tender. Serve with mashed potatoes and dill pickles or dill-pickle salad.

BRAISED PORK COLLOPS
bitki wieprzowe duszone

Remove bones from 1½ lbs. pork chops or slice other boneless cut into ½ inch thick 1 x 2 inch pieces. With moistened meat mallet pound until very thin. Mash 2 buds garlic and mix with ¼ t. marjoram, ¼ t. Maggi extract, and a pinch of sage and rosemary. Spread each fillet with a little of the herb mixture and stack them one on top of the other. Refrigerate in covered container or wrapped in foil 1 hr. Brown in 3 T. lard or oil on both sides and transfer to pot with tight-fitting lid. Top with 1 minced onion, add 1 c. meat stock or court bouillon and simmer covered on low heat until meat is tender (about 1 hr.). Replace evaporating liquid with water. Uncover and allow most of the liquid steam away. If you want a sauce, omit last step and sprinkle in a little flour to thicken pan drippings. Simmer briefly. Salt & pepper to taste. Garnish with a little chopped parsley and chives just prior to serving. Serve with rice and green-onion or leek salad.

PORK ROLL-UPS WITH MUSHROOMS
zrazy wieprzowe zawijane z pieczarkami

Pound 1½ lbs. de-boned pork chops or other cut of pork into thin cutlets as above. Run a piece of uncooked bacon down the center of each cutlet lengthwise and roll up. Finely dice a small piece (about ⅛ lb.) salt pork and fry until nuggets are golden brown. Remove salt-pork nuggets and set aside. Dredge roll-ups in 1 heaping T. bread crumbs mixed with an equal amount of flour, gently shake off excess breading, and brown on all sides in the hot salt-pork drippings. For easier handling, the roll-ups may be fastened with toothpicks or tied with thread, but be sure to remove these before serving. Transfer browned roll-ups to pot, add the drippings, salt-pork nuggets, 4 oz. finely chopped fresh mushrooms, and 3 T. water and simmer covered on low heat about 20 min. Add 1 grated onion and 1 stalk grated celery, mixing ingredients gently, add a little more water, and continue simmering until meat is tender. Salt & pepper to taste and serve with puréed potatoes and a crispy salad dressed with vinaigrette.

BREADED PORK ROLL-UPS À LA UHLAN
zrazy wieprzowe po ułańsku

Remove bones from 1½ lbs. pork chops and pound each cutlet well until thin but unbroken. For smaller and daintier roll-ups, cut each pounded cutlet in half. Sprinkle each with salt, pepper, and marjoram, spread with a thin layer of powidła (plum jam), place a strip of uncooked bacon, a slice of smoked Polish sausage, and a piece of onion at one edge and roll up tightly. You may fasten each with 2 toothpicks, but you can also do without these. Dredge roll-ups in flour, beaten egg, and bread crumbs, pressing in breading and carefully place in medium hot fat seam-side down. The hot fat should set the breading and prevent the roll-up from coming undone. Fry in about 4–5 T. lard until nicely golden brown on all sides, then reduce heat, and cook until meat is tender. About 12–15 min. cooking time should be sufficient. Transfer to pot or baking dish, sprinkle with several T. drippings, cover, and allow to simmer another 15–20 min. in 325° oven. Serve with rice sprinkled with pan drippings, and leek or green-onion salad.

BREADED PORK ROLL-UPS MINER'S STYLE
zrazy wieprzowe zawijane górnicze

Soak ½ oz. Polish dried mushrooms in 2 c. water for 2 hrs., then cook in same water until tender. Chop mushrooms fine and return to liquid. Drain about 1 c. sauerkraut, rinse in cold water, drain, squeeze out moisture, and chop. Place in pot, scald with boiling water to cover and cook uncovered. When most liquid evaporates, add the mushrooms and mushroom water. In saucepan brown 1 small chopped onion in 1 T. butter. When most of the liquid has evaporated from sauerkraut, add to onions and simmer until almost dry. Season with salt, pepper, a little sugar and sprinkle in 1 T. flour or bread crumbs. Place in sieve and press out moisture. Pound and season 1½ lbs. de-boned pork chops as above. Spread each with sauerkraut mixture, keeping it away from the edges. Roll up tightly, dip in flour, beaten egg, and bread crumbs, and proceed as above. Serve with potatoes and ćwikła. *Variation:* The roll-ups can also be made with a fresh-cabbage filling. Scald 2 c. shredded fresh cabbage with 2 c. boiling water, bring to boil, and simmer several min. Drain well. In skillet, lightly brown 1 minced onion and (optional) several finely chopped fresh mushrooms in 1–2 T. butter. Add cabbage and simmer under cover 15 min., then uncover and allow most moisture to evaporate. Drain, pressing out moisture with spoon. Add 1 T. flour or bread crumbs, salt & pepper. 1 t. chopped dill may be added to cabbage filling.

BREADED PORK ROLL-UPS "CORDON BLEU"
zrazy wieprzowe zawijane "cordon bleu"

Cut meat away from 1½ pork chops or cut slices of meat of similar size from a less expensive cut of pork. With moistened meat mallet pound the meat until thin but unbroken. Sprinkle with salt, pepper, and a pinch of marjoram. Instead of marjoram, a pinch of thyme or ground coriander is also good. Cover each cutlet with a thin slice of yellow cheese: edam, gouda, tilsit, or munster. Roll the meat slices up tightly. You may but need not fasten the roll-ups with toothpicks or tie with strong thread. Dip in beaten eggs and roll in mixture consisting of 1 part bread crumbs and 1 part flour. Make sure the roll-ups are evenly coated with breading, including the ends, and press it down by hand. Fry in 6 T. or so hot lard until nicely browned on all sides, then reduce heat and cook until meat is tender. Serve with rice, cauliflower and sour cream-laced salad. This is the author's own adaptation of a well-known French dish usually made with veal.

BREADED PORK ROLL-UPS "IMPERIAL"
kotlety "imperial"

Pound 1½ lbs. de-boned pork chops or other cut of pork quite thin. Larger pieces of meat are better for this dish, so your pounded cutlets end up the size of a dinner plate. Salt

& pepper and rub pounded cutlets with 1 bud mashed garlic. Run ½ c. cold unsalted butter and an equal amount of boiled ham and yellow cheese through grinder. Lightly toss mixture to combine ingredients evenly and spread over ½ of each cutlet. Roll up tightly, dredge in flour, dip in beaten eggs, and roll in bread crumbs, pressing in breading. Place seam-side down in hot fat reaching ¾ of the way up the roll-ups and fry until a deep golden brown on all sides. Remove to absorbent paper to take up excess grease and serve immediately. Rice or mashed potatoes, wax beans, and a radish salad make nice companions. This gourmet dish is a specialty of the Hotel Novotel in Olsztyn in the heart of Poland's forested Mazurian Lake District.

PORK STEW
gulasz wieprzowy

Dice about ⅛ lb. white salt pork and fry in large, heavy skillet or Dutch oven until light brown. Remove fried salt-pork bits. Sprinkle 1½ lbs. boneless pork, cut into roughly ¾ inch cubes, with salt, dredge in flour (or shake meat with flour in plastic bag) and brown on all sides in the hot salt-pork drippings. (If you have no salt pork on hand, brown meat in 4 T. lard or oil.) Add 3 sliced or coarsely chopped onions, and fry with meat until onion is golden or just slightly begins to brown. Reduce heat, add fried salt-pork nuggets, ½ t. caraway seeds, and ¾ c. liquid: court bouillon, beer, or water (or 1 part beer and 1 part water). Cover and simmer on low heat about 1 hr. or until meat is tender. Stir ingredients occasionally and replace evaporating liquid with water so your stew doesn't burn. Thicken pan liquid with a little flour, salt & pepper to taste, and simmer briefly. Serve with potatoes, noodles, or barley, and a carrot, apple & horseradish salad, or lettuce dressed with sour cream. *Optional:* When meat is tender, stir in 1 heaping T. sour cream and/or 1 level T. tomato paste. Ketchup is also good.

PORK STEW WITH CARROTS
gulasz wieprzowy z marchewką

Proceed as above, but instead of 3 onions, lightly brown 1 coarsely chopped onion and 2 thinly sliced carrots with meat. Omit caraway seeds. When meat is tender, add 1 t. lemon juice and prepare sauce as above. Before serving, sprinkle with chopped fresh parsley.

PORK STEW WITH SAUERKRAUT
gulasz wieprzowy z kapustą kiszoną

Rinse 1 c. sauerkraut in cold water, drain, squeeze dry, chop fine. Proceed as in first pork stew recipe but brown the sauerkraut and onions with the meat. Add ¼ t. caraway seeds and ¾ c. liquid and simmer under cover on low heat 1 hr. When meat is tender sprinkle with ¼ t. paprika, stir in heaping T. sour cream, and simmer until sauce is smooth and bubbly, thickening it with a little flour as needed. Salt & pepper to taste.

PORK STEWED WITH KOHLRABI
gulasz wieprzowy z kalarepą

Salt 1½ lbs. cubed, boneless pork, dredge in flour, and brown on all sides in hot lard or salt-pork drippings. Add 2 coarsely chopped onions and simmer with meat until golden. Reduce heat, add 2–3 small, peeled, spring kohlrabi, diced, add ½ c. court bouillon or water, cover, and simmer on low heat about 1 hr. Replace evaporating moisture with water. When meat is tender, thicken pan liquid with a little flour, salt & pepper, and garnish with a little chopped fresh dill just before serving. *Note:* Unlike American-style stews, which often contain everything but the kitchen sink, Polish gulasz is seldom made with more than 1–2 different vegetables. In addition to the above, you can come up with many variations of your own. After browning the pork and onions and simmering in a little liquid about 30 min., you can add string or wax beans cut into 1 inch lengths, brussels sprouts, small flowerets of cauliflower, diced turnips, parsnips, celery, even a few whole or halved small radishes. A sprinkling of homemade pork seasoning or (for variety) hunter's seasoning will enhance the flavor of any of the above stews.

PORK STEWED WITH MUSHROOMS
wieprzowina duszona z grzybami

Salt, dredge in flour, and brown in hot fat 1½ lbs. cube, boneless pork; add 2 diced onions and simmer until golden. Add 1–2 c. home-canned wild mushrooms including the liquid. If the mushrooms are on the large side, slice or dice them first. Simmer under cover on low heat about 1 hr. Serve as is, after salting & peppering to taste, or stir in 1 heaping T. sour cream. Simmer briefly and thicken sauce with a little flour. This dish can also be made with fresh mushrooms. Simply brown 4–8 oz. fresh sliced or diced mushrooms with 1–2 coarsely chopped onions in the drippings the meat was browned in. Add ½ c. water and 1 t. Maggi extract and simmer covered with pork on low heat 1 hr. Thicken sauce with a sprinkling of flour. A T. sour cream is optional.

PORK STEWED WITH APPLES
wieprzowina duszona z jabłkami

Sprinkle 1½ lbs. cubed, boneless pork with salt, roll in flour, and brown in 3 T. or so hot lard or salt-pork drippings. Bacon drippings are also good. Add 1 chopped onion and simmer until golden with the meat. Add ½ c. court bouillon or water and simmer covered on low heat 45 min. Add 2–3 peeled, diced, fresh or sour-cured apples. Toss apples with meat, sprinkle with a little marjoram, and simmer covered another 15 min. or until meat is very tender.

PORK & PEAS OR BEANS
wieprzowina z grochem lub fasolą

Soak 1–1½ c. dried whole yellow peas, dried navy beans, pea beans or lima beans in 6 c. cold water overnight. Next day, cook in same water until tender, adding ½ a bay leaf, if you like. Beans should be cooked uncovered on very low heat to prevent them from bursting. Cooking time may range from 30–60 min., or even longer, depending on the size and dryness of the peas or beans. When fully cooked, drain in colander. Brown 1½ lbs. cubed, boneless pork in 3–4 T. lard or salt-pork or bacon drippings on all sides. (Meat may be dredged in flour first, but it isn't necessary in this particular dish.) Add 2–3 chopped onions. When onions are golden or just begin to brown, add ¾ c. court bouillon or beer and simmer covered 50 min. Add drained peas or beans, toss with meat, and continue simmering under cover 15 min. Meanwhile, combine 1–2 T. sharp brown mustard, 2–3 T. plum jam (Polish or domestic), 2 t. marjoram, 1 t. Maggi extract, ¼ t. salt, ¼ t. pepper, and 1–3 buds mashed garlic. Mix with several T. of pan liquid and add to meat and beans. Simmer until meat is very tender. This dish is very good when baked in an oven. Adjust flavor with about 1 t. lemon juice or vinegar, or 1–2 T. pickle juice from brine-cured dill pickles. This dish should be just faintly sweet & sour. Thicken sauce with a little flour if necessary. *Note:* If you don't have the time to cook beans from scratch, use drained canned beans instead.

PORK & PEARS
wieprzowina z gruszkami

Place 1½–2 lbs. pork steaks into soup kettle, add 1 portion soup greens, diced, 2 t. salt, and cover with 4 c. cold water. Bring to boil, skimming off scum until no more forms, then reduce heat and simmer covered about 1 hr. Add 1½ lbs. peeled, cored pear halves. Pears should be on the firm, even hard side, not the soft and juicy variety. Cover and cook 15–20 min. or until meat and pears are tender. Meanwhile, in saucepan brown 2 T. flour slightly in 2 T. butter. Add 1½ c. of the stock and simmer, stirring constantly until smooth and bubbly. Add 1 crushed bouillon cube and simmer until it is fully dissolved. Season sauce to taste with salt, pepper, sugar, and lemon juice for a sweet & sour taste. Carefully remove meat with slotted spoon to platter, top with pear halves, and drench with sauce. This is an old dish from Silesia (Śląsk) that is great with Silesian bread dumplings (p. 479).

TRIPE-STYLE PORK
wieprzowina à la flaczki

Cut 1 lb. boneless shoulder pork into thin strips about 1 inch long resembling cut-up tripe. Sprinkle with paprika and flour and brown briefly in 3 T. hot lard. Transfer to pot together with the drippings, add 1 c. meat stock, 1 T. marjoram, ½ t. pepper, and ½ t. ginger, and simmer on low heat covered about 20 min. Add 1 portion soup greens and 3 onions—all vegetables cut into thin sticks no more than 1 inch long or coarsely grated. Add to pot 2 c. hot stock and 1–2 T. butter and simmer under cover another 30 min., or until meat and vegetables are very tender. Thicken sauce with a little flour and season to taste with salt, pepper, paprika, a little cayenne pepper, and Maggi extract. This dish should definitely be on the hot & spicy side. Serve with noodles as a main course or dilute with several c. boiling water and serve as a hearty soup. Either way, individual portions may be garnished with a little grated yellow cheese of choice. This dish is sure to go over with those who enjoy the spicy tang of Polish-style flaczki but may be squeamish about eating a real cow stomach!

BOILED BACON
boczek gotowany

Place a 1½ lb. piece of smoked slab bacon in pot and scald with 6 c. boiling water. Add 2 whole onions, 6 peppercorns, 1 bay leaf, and 2 grain allspice. 1–2 juniper berries may also be added. Bring to boil, skim off scum, if any, until no more forms, reduce heat, and cook on low heat 1–1½ hrs. or until bacon is fork tender. Replace water that evaporates. When cooked, leave in pot about 10 min. Cut off bottom rind and slice bacon about ¼ inch thick. Serve with stewed sauerkraut or pea purée. Save the stock for one of your favorite smoked meat-based soups. First, however, chill stock to remove congealed fat.

ROAST BACON
boczek pieczony

Scald a 1½ lb. piece of slab bacon with boiling water and cook 20 min. Transfer to baking dish. Bacon may be placed on a rack to keep it out of the drippings. Sprinkle all over with marjoram, paprika, pepper, and caraway seeds, rub with 2–3 buds crushed garlic, top with onion slices, and bake in 325° oven 1–1½ hrs. or until fork tender. At start of baking, sprinkle with water and baste occasionally with pan drippings that form. Turn bacon over at least once. Slice and serve as above.

BOILED PORK HOCKS
golonka wieprzowa

Wash 2–3 lbs. pork hocks. If any bristle is still attached, singe it off over flame before washing hocks. Place in soup kettle, scald with 2 qts. boiling water, and add 1 T. salt, and bring to boil. Skim off scum, reduce heat, cover, and cook 1½ hrs. Add 1 bay leaf, 4–6 peppercorns, and (optional) ¼ t. tarragon. Also add 1 portion soup greens, diced, and 1 quartered onion. Cover and continue simmering until meat is tender. It is fully cooked when it easily comes away from bone. At the end of cooking add 2 crushed buds garlic and simmer several min. more. Switch off heat and allow hocks to rest in stock about 5 min. Serve with boiled or mashed potatoes and/or pea purée. Prepared horseradish and brown mustard are also frequent accompaniments. This hearty he-man dish almost begs for a glass of vodka or a frosty stein of beer to wash it down! Use the stock, after de-greasing, for making barszcz, żurek, kapuśniak or grochówka.

PORK HOCKS & SAUERKRAUT
golonka duszona w kapuście

Cook pork hocks as above 1½ hrs. Drain 1 qt. sauerkraut, reserving liquid. (A little reserved sauerkraut juice may be added at end of cooking if the dish turns out not as tart as you like.) Rinse sauerkraut in plenty of cold, running water, drain in colander, and squeeze out excess moisture. Place in a pot, scald with boiling water, and after boiling resumes, cook uncovered 15–20 min. Drain and add to pot in which pork hocks have cooked 1½ hrs. Add spices as above. The drained sauerkraut juice may also be added uncooked for a sharper sauerkraut taste. Cook with hocks another 1–1½ hrs. or until meat is very tender. Transfer hocks and sauerkraut to colander, retaining liquid that drips out. To about 1 c. of the liquid add 1 t. Maggi extract, ¼ t. pepper, 1 t. sugar, 2 buds mashed garlic, and (optional) ¼ t. caraway seeds. Stir in 2 T. flour, stirring until lump-free. Place drained hocks and sauerkraut in clean pot, drench with sauce and simmer several min. Serve with boiled potatoes.

PORK RIBS & SAUERKRAUT
żeberka wieprzowe w kapuście

Cut 2–3 lbs. pork ribs into 2-rib pieces, salt & pepper, dredge in flour, and brown on both sides in 3 T. hot lard. Transfer to Dutch oven or baking dish. In drippings brown 1–2 sliced onions. Add onions and 2 c. water to meat and simmer under cover on low heat about 60 min. You can also bake ribs covered in 325° oven. Whether cooking on stove top or in oven, be sure to replace evaporating liquid so ribs do not burn. Meanwhile, drain 1 qt.

sauerkraut, rinse in cold water, drain well, place in separate pot, scald with boiling water to cover, and cook uncovered 30 min. Drain. In baking dish, alternate layers of sauerkraut and ribs, with the kraut forming the top and bottom layers. Sprinkle with a little pepper, about 1 t. sugar and (optional) ¼ t. caraway seeds. Add 1–2 buds crushed garlic and drench with 1 c. of the rib pan drippings and as much of the cooked-sauerkraut liquid as needed to ensure proper moisture. Bake covered in 325° oven 60 min. or until ribs easily come away from bone. Serve with boiled potatoes. Small, peeled potatoes may be placed in baking dish with ribs & kraut about 30–40 min. before end of cooking. When meat is tender, sprinkle in a little flour, mix, and simmer briefly with sauerkraut.

MEATLOAF
klops/pieczeń rzymska

Crumble 1 stale kaiser roll (or a piece of stale French bread, hamburger bun, etc., of similar size) into bowl and add ½ c. cold milk. Let soak 10 min., then squeeze out excess moisture and run through meat grinder. Combine with 1–1¼ lbs. raw ground pork, 1 finely minced onion simmered until golden in 1 T. butter, 1 raw egg, and salt & pepper to taste. Mix well by hand and form into an oval loaf. Grease bottom of baking pan and place meatloaf therein. Sprinkle with several T. water and bake in 350° oven about 1 hr., basting occasionally with pan drippings and replacing evaporating liquid with water. For easier slicing, allow to rest 10 min. after removing from oven. Serve as is with mashed potatoes or buckwheat groats. Floured peas & carrots or braised beets make a nice side dish, as does leek or radish salad.

Variations:
1) For a finer-textured meatloaf, run ground meat and soggy roll through meat grinder a second time.
2) Instead of ground pork alone, use a combination of ground beef & pork or pork, beef & veal.
3) Season meat mixture with 1–2 buds crushed garlic and your homemade Polish pork seasoning or hunter's seasoning. A little paprika is another possibility.
4) For a sharper taste, add 1 raw grated onion to meat mixture instead of the minced onion simmered in butter.
5) For a crustier meatloaf, first sprinkle your formed loaf with flour and brown on all sides in hot lard.
6) If an extra guest is coming to dinner, add another egg and 2 T. bread crumbs to raw meat mixture.
7) Meatloaf will not require basting if baked in aluminum foil.
8) Use the pan drippings as a base for making sour cream, tomato, or mushroom sauce.

MEATLOAF STUFFED WITH MUSHROOMS
klops nadziewany grzybami

Soak ½ oz. Polish dried mushrooms in 1½ c. water 2 hrs. then cook in same water until tender, replacing liquid that evaporates. Chop mushrooms fine. In skillet combine 4 oz. washed, chopped, fresh mushrooms and 1–2 chopped onions and simmer in 2 T. butter under cover about 15 min. Add the cooked, dried mushrooms, simmer a bit longer, allowing excess moisture (if any) to evaporate. Add 2 T. bread crumbs and salt & pepper to taste. Prepare meat as above, form it into a 1 inch thick rectangle on cutting board, run the mushroom mixture down the center lengthwise, and fold meat over to form a loaf. Pat it and press it down well on all sides. Bake as above. When meatloaf is done, combine pan drippings with reserved, dried-mushroom water and 1–2 heaping T. sour cream. Add a little flour and as much boiling water as needed to get a thick, pourable gravy. Salt & pepper to taste and add ½ t. Maggi extract. The mushroom surprise inside and the rich gravy can turn this old standby into a surprise treat. A small raw egg may be added as a binder to the mushroom mixture before filling the meatloaf.

GROUND PORK CUTLETS
kotlety wieprzowe mielone

Prepare meat mixture as for meatloaf (above), using ground pork, pork & beef, or pork, beef, & veal. Form meat into oval patties about 2–2½ inches long and ¾–1 inch thick. On cutting board use flat of knife to give cutlets a uniform shape. Brown on both sides in fairly hot lard (about 3 T.), then reduce heat, cover, and simmer 10–15 min. A little water (1–2 T.) may be added before simmering under cover. Some Polish cooks like to oven-simmer the cutlets for added lightness and flavor. To do so, simply transfer browned cutlets to baking dish, add several T. pan drippings and 1–2 T. water, and bake in 325° oven covered 15–20 min. Serve cutlets with mashed potatoes sprinkled with pan drippings, a cooked vegetable, and a tangy salad. *Note:* For crustier cutlets, dredge in flour & bread crumb mixture before browning in hot fat.

MEATBALLS IN SOUR CREAM
klopsiki w śmietanie

Soak 1 stale kaiser roll in ½ c. water, milk, or (for richer flavor) evaporated milk or coffee cream. When soggy run through meat grinder. Combine with 1–1¼ lbs. ground pork, pork & beef, or pork, beef, & veal. Add 1 raw egg and 1 grated onion, either raw or simmered in a little butter. For lighter meatballs, add only the yolk and fold in the egg white beaten to a stiff froth. Mix all ingredients well and salt & pepper to taste. If mixture feels too mushy, add 1–2 T. bread crumbs. If it is too stiff, add the milk in which the stale roll was soaked. Moisten hands and roll meat between palms into golfball-size meatballs. Brown on all sides in 2–3 T. hot lard. The meatballs may be dredged in flour & bread crumb mixture before browning. Transfer to baking pan, add 2 T. water, and bake in 325° oven 30 min. Combine pan drippings with ¾ c. sour cream, fork-blended with 2 T. flour, and some boiling water if needed to get a thick, pourable sauce. Drench meatballs with mixture and simmer several min. longer. Salt & pepper to taste and garnish with chopped greens: parsley, dill, chives, or any combination thereof. Serve with mashed potatoes or buckwheat groats, braised beets, and a non-creamed salad. Meatballs are also excellent in mushroom sauce. Make it from scratch, using Polish dried and/or fresh mushrooms or use the short-cut method below.

MEATBALLS IN MUSHROOM GRAVY THE EASY WAY
klopsiki w sosie grzybowym naprędce

Prepare, brown, and simmer meatballs as above. Combine drippings with 1 can cream of mushroom soup, 1 t. liquid mushroom extract (if unavailable use 1 t. Maggi extract), a generous sprinkling of pepper (preferably freshly ground), 1 t. lemon juice, and enough boiling water to get a thick, pourable gravy. Drench meatballs in skillet with gravy, cover, and simmer 5 min. Garnish with chopped parsley and serve as above. No one will know your sauce came out of a can. Another way is to soak 1–3 dried Polish mushrooms in 1 c. water before going to work. When you return, cook them in same water until tender, dice fine, and add to above sauce instead of the liquid mushroom extract.

GROUND CUTLETS, MEAT ROLLS, PATTIES, MEATBALLS, ETC.
kotlety-kotleciki, zrazy-zraziki, bitki, sznycelki, klopsiki, pulpety, frykadelki

This entry will not be another recipe, but an attempt to clear up the confusing terminology surrounding the various Polish ground meat dishes.

KOTLETY: Strictly speaking, the Polish kotlet is a solid piece of meat usually pounded thin as in the classic kotlet schabowy (breaded pork cutlet). But often it designates a ground cutlet with the words skiekany or mielony (minced or ground) added or simply implied. It is usually oval, anywhere from ¾–1 inch thick and between 2–4 inches in length.

KOTLECIKI: The diminutive of kotlet indicates a smaller oval patty, measuring perhaps 1½–2½ inches in length.

ZRAZY: These are slices of solid, unground meat pounded very thin and sometimes referred to in English as collops. If we preface the zrazy with the adjective siekany or mielony it comes to mean a ground oval patty, possibly a hair thinner than the kotlet siekany (above), or a ground meat roll measuring roughly 1 x 3 inches. Like the solid meat zrazy zawijane (roll-ups), the ground meat rolls may also be filled.

ZRAZIKI: This is simply a smaller version of the zrazy.

BITKI: This term is short for bite zrazy (pounded fillets) but is also used to designate a thick oval patty (like zrazy siekane) or a slightly flattened meatball.

SZNYCELKI: In southern Poland, this term is used to designate any of the above ground meat dishes.

KLOPSIKI: This is the traditional meatball, ranging in size from that of a small walnut to that of a small apple. It is rarely perfectly round, as it gets slightly flattened with the spatula during browning.

PULPETY: This is also a meatball, but rather than being fried or simmered, it is usually poached (boiled) in water or court bouillon.

FRYKADELKI: These are made with the same ground meat mixture as the above, but are shaped like sausages (without the casing), measuring 4–5 inches in length.

Whether the above explanation seems straightforward or confusing, all this unfortunately is simply theory. In reality, most of these terms vary from region to region and from one home to the next. Don't be surprised, therefore, if a Polish restaurant or household you visit serves something this book refers to as klopsiki (meatballs), but calls them kotleciki, zrazy, or bitki. Different Polish cookbooks also tend to use these terms interchangeably.

VARIOUS MINCED CUTLETS, MEATBALLS, ETC.
kotleciki, zraziki, klopsiki na różne sposoby

Prepare meat mixture by combining 1–1¼ lbs. ground pork, pork & veal, pork & beef, or a combination of all three with ground, soaked roll, 1 grated onion (simmered in butter or raw), 1 whole egg, and flavorings of choice. Form into any of the above shapes and proceed according to one of the following:

1) Roll in flour and/or bread crumbs, brown in 2–3 T. hot fat, then add 1–2 T. water, reduce heat, and simmer covered about 15 min.

2) After browning the meat, add 1–2 chopped onions and/or 4 oz. fresh chopped mushrooms, brown briefly in drippings, then add 1–2 T. water, cover, and simmer on low heat about 20 min.

3) Proceed as in first variation. When meat has simmered under cover about 10 min., drench with mushroom sauce, tomato sauce, horseradish sauce, or mustard sauce, and simmer another 5 min. or so.

4) Prepare according to any of the chopped steak or veal recipes such as mushroom-filled chopped steak rolls, breaded ground veal cutlets à la ministre.

5)   Use a little imagination to come up with your own creative ways of preparing these various meat rolls, cutlets, patties, and meatballs. Fry them breaded or fill them with strips of cheese and/or ham. Although dill sauce and lemon sauce are normally reserved for veal dishes, try them with pork patties or meatballs, as well. Almost any tangy sauce will give bland-tasting meatballs or meat rolls added zing. When cooking with versatile ground meat, only your imagination is the limit!

When all is said and done, however, undoubtedly the best known Polish culinary contribution made of chopped and/or ground meat is kiełbasa, that juicy, savory, pleasantly garlicky sausage that is enjoyed by most everyone. If you want to try your hand at making your own, see the chapter on sausage-making and meat-curing. However, many Polish meat markets in the larger North American cities and some smaller towns as well offer various kinds of Polish sausage ranging from satisfactory to excellent. The brands sold in big supermarkets do not always live up to their name, even when the packages are plastered with Polish white eagles and such words as "polska kiełbasa" or "polski wyrób." Most varieties of kiełbasa are meant to be eaten cold; these are discussed in the chapter devoted to appetizers. Presented below are several ways of serving hot Polish sausage as a main dinner course or a hot supper.

BOILED FRESH SAUSAGE
biała kiełbasa

Place about 2 lbs. fresh Polish sausage in pot, add enough boiling water to cover, plus 1 quartered onion, several peppercorns, 1 t. marjoram, ½ a bay leaf according to preference. Especially if your sausage is on the bland side, the addition of spices will help replace the seasoning that boils out during cooking. Cover and simmer on very low heat about 30–50 min., or until the kiełbasa is tender. Too rapid boiling may cause the sausage to burst. You can prevent this by pricking the sausage at intervals with a pin or toothpick before cooking. Serve with boiled potatoes and ćwikła or simply with crusty rye bread and prepared horseradish. This dish is an Easter "must" in many Polish homes. Save the water for white or red barszcz, żurek, pea soup or kapuśniak.

BAKED FRESH SAUSAGE
biała kiełbasa pieczona

Place 2 lbs. fresh Polish sausage in shallow baking dish. Prick at intervals with pin or toothpick to prevent bursting. Add enough cold water to obtain a depth of about ½ inch, cover, and bake in preheated 350° oven about 30 min. Turn sausage over, sprinkle with marjoram, replace evaporated water, and bake uncovered until it becomes a nice ruddy brown. Serve as above or with stewed sauerkraut. *Note:* The kiełbasa will be even tastier if you simmer it in one part beer and one part water, instead of plain water.

FRESH SAUSAGE STEWED IN BEER
biała kiełbasa duszona w piwie

Place 2 lbs. fresh sausage in pot, cover with beer, add 1 mashed bouillon cube and 1–2 finely chopped onions, bring to boil, and simmer on low heat covered 30 min. Add 1 t. sugar, 2 t. freshly squeezed lemon juice, and simmer another 15–20 min. Combine sieved pan drippings with 2 T. flour or enough to get a smooth, pourable sauce. Simmer briefly and pour over sausage on platter. Serve with mashed potatoes or barley. This is a slightly modified version of a recipe found in *Praktyczny kucharz warszawski* ("The Practical Warsaw Cook"), a cookbook published in Warsaw in 1905. The modification involved omitting the butter called for in the original recipe. We felt that the sausage's own fat would make this dish sufficiently rich for today's tastes and calorie-conscious eaters.

FRESH SAUSAGE IN OLD POLISH SAUCE
biała kiełbasa w sosie po staropolsku

Place 2 lbs. fresh Polish sausage in pot, scald with 1½ c. boiling water, and bring to boil. Sprinkle sausage with marjoram (generously) and paprika (sparingly), and smother with 2–3 finely chopped onions. Add 1½ c. beer and simmer covered on low heat 45–60 min. Force onions and pan drippings through sieve or blend in blender until smooth. Stir in 2 T. flour or as much as needed to get smooth sauce and dilute with a little boiling water if needed. Simmer in saucepan several min. until thick and bubbly. Season to taste with a little vinegar and sugar to achieve the sweet and sour flavor you want. Salt & pepper if necessary, but taste the sauce first, since it may be salty and peppery enough. A pinch of saffron may be added, as well as ¼ c. raisins (both optional). Pour sauce over portion-size pieces of kiełbasa on a platter and serve with potatoes or barley. The saffron, raisins, and barley are dead giveaways that this somewhat exotic, centuries-old recipe goes back to an era when such combinations were popular. Halbański's *Leksykon sztuki kulinarnej* ("Lexicon of Culinary Art") refers to it as kiełbasa po polsku, otherwise known as wereszczaka. It was reportedly named after Wereszczaka, court chef to the Saxon Kings who ruled Poland from the late 17th century on through the better part of the 18th century.

FRESH SAUSAGE & SAUERKRAUT
biała kiełbasa z kapustą

Drain 1 qt. sauerkraut, reserving liquid. Rinse in cold water, drain, squeeze dry, and chop coarsely. Transfer to pot, scald with boiling water to cover and, after boiling resumes, reduce heat and cook uncovered 30 min. Meanwhile, place 2–3 lbs. fresh sausage in shallow pan, add 1 c. water, and bake uncovered in pre-heated 350° oven. After 20 min. turn sausage over and continue baking until nicely browned. Add a little more water if needed so kiełbasa doesn't burn or stick to pan. Place ½ the sauerkraut in baking dish, cut the sausage into 3–4 inch pieces and place on sauerkraut, top with remaining kraut, and bake covered in 325° oven 45 min. or until sausage & sauerkraut are as tender as you like. In dry saucepan lightly brown 2 T. flour, add ½ c. liquid from baking dish, 1 t. sugar, 1 t. Maggi extract, and a little Polish sauerkraut seasoning to taste. If you like, you might also add ¼ t. caraway seeds. Stir liquid until smooth and pour over sauerkraut. Toss ingredients lightly to blend with sauce and bake uncovered another 10 min. Switch off heat and let dish remain in oven a while longer. As with all sauerkraut dishes, this will taste even better if refrigerated overnight and warmed up the next day. *Optional:* To give the sauerkraut a nice color and added tang, add 1 T. tomato paste or ketchup to the sauce. Serve with boiled potatoes. This dish was a standard at weddings and other celebrations among the peasantry of Old Poland, hence its continued popularity among our American Polonia.

FRESH SAUSAGE IN TOMATO SAUCE
biała kiełbasa w sosie pomidorowym

In pot scald 2 lbs. or so fresh kiełbasa with boiling water to cover, bring to boil, reduce heat, and cook covered 30 min. Meanwhile, brown 2–3 finely chopped onions in 2 T. butter. In dry saucepan brown 2 T. flour and add to onions together with 2–3 oz. tomato paste and enough of the kiełbasa water to obtain a smooth, pourable sauce. For a richer taste, stir in 1 heaping T. sour cream. Mix well, season to taste with salt, pepper, a little sugar and lemon juice, and 1–2 buds crushed garlic. Several pinches marjoram may be added. Simmer sauce several min. and pour it over the drained cooked sausage, cut into 3–4 inch pieces. Simmer 5 min. and serve with mashed potatoes or rice.

FRESH SAUSAGE IN GREY SAUCE
biała kiełbasa w szarym sosie

Cook the fresh sausage in boiling water to cover as above. Meanwhile, in saucepan combine 1 heaping t. sugar with ¼ t. water and simmer until sugar is caramelized or browned. Add ⅓ c. boiling water and cook until caramelized sugar fully dissolves. In another dry saucepan, brown 3 T. flour, add 2 T. butter, mixing well as it melts, then add the caramelized-sugar liquid and enough of the kiełbasa water to get a nice, pourable sauce. Season sauce to taste with salt, pepper, and lemon juice to get the sweet & sour taste you want. A jigger of mead (miód pitny, imported Polish honey wine) may be added. Simmer several min. and pour over kiełbasa, cut into 3–4 inch pieces. Simmer another 5 min. or so.

Serve with mashed potatoes. *Note*: You will find several recipes for grey sauce, an Old Polish specialty, in this book. It is frequently served with beef tongue and carp. *Note:* Boiled fresh kiełbasa may also be served with horseradish, mustard, or gherkin sauce.

BOILED SMOKED SAUSAGE
kiełbasa wędzona gotowana

Cut 2 lbs. smoked Polish sausage into 3–4 inch pieces, place in pot, cover with cold water, bring to boil, reduce heat, and cook covered about 1 hr. *Optional*: A quartered onion, ½ a bay leaf, and several peppercorns and grains of allspice may be added. Serve with stewed sauerkraut, boiled or mashed potatoes, ćwikła, or prepared horseradish. Save the water for your favorite smoked-meat based soup. Sauerkraut is also very good cooked in the kiełbasa stock.

BAKED SMOKED SAUSAGE
kiełbasa wędzona pieczona

Place a 2 lb. ring of smoked Polish sausage in a shallow baking pan, add 1 c. water, pop into pre-heated 325° oven, and bake uncovered about 1 hr. There should be sufficient drippings in the pan, but if all liquid steams away before end of baking, add a little more water. The kiełbasa is done when the skin becomes crackly but soft to the bite. Proper baking will make even tough casing palatably tender. Cut into portions and serve with potatoes, stewed sauerkraut, and ćwikła. It is great for a simple supper with only rye bread and horseradish or brown mustard.

SMOKED SAUSAGE & SAUERKRAUT
kiełbasa wędzona z kapustą

Boil or bake 2–2½ lbs. smoked Polish sausage as above, but only 30 min. Meanwhile, prepare 1 qt. sauerkraut as in fresh sausage & sauerkraut. Cut the partially cooked sausage into 2–4 inch pieces, mix with sauerkraut in roaster or baking dish, cover and bake in 325° oven 1 hr. or longer. Season as in fresh sausage & sauerkraut. For best results, prepare a day ahead. When baking is completed, switch off heat and leave the dish in oven 1–2 hrs. Remove and allow to cool to room temp., then refrigerate overnight. Reheat in same pan just prior to serving and serve with boiled potatoes or rye bread. The flavor of all sauerkraut dishes improves with each reheating.

SMOKED SAUSAGE & YOUNG CABBAGE
kiełbasa duszona z młodą kapustą

Skin and slice thin 1 lb. smoked Polish sausage, place in large pot, cover with water, bring to boil, then reduce heat and simmer covered about 30 min. Shred about 1½–2 lbs. young cabbage, whose leaves are looser, more tender, and a darker green than mature cabbage. Mix shredded cabbage with sausage, add a little water if needed, and cook several min. on high heat uncovered, then reduce heat, cover and simmer until cabbage is tender. This should take only a few min., because the young cabbage cooks quickly. In saucepan saute 1 small minced onion in 1 T. butter until tender and golden but not browned, stir in 2 T. flour and enough of the sausage & cabbage liquid from pot to form a thick sauce. Pour sauce over sausage & cabbage and simmer briefly. Season to taste with salt, pepper, lemon juice, (or vinegar) and a little sugar. *Optional:* garnish with 1 T. chopped dill. Served with boiled, dilled new potatoes, this is a summertime favorite in the Strybel household on either side of the Atlantic.

VARIOUS SAUSAGE CASSEROLES
różne zapiekanki z kiełbasą

Smoked kiełbasa is a versatile ingredient in any number of casseroles. First remove the skin from ½–1 lb. of smoked Polish sausage. (You need not remove the skin if using pre-baked smoked or fresh kiełbasa.) Slice thin and brown on one side in 2 T. lard, butter or oil. Turn sausage slices over, add 1–2 finely chopped onions and continue to simmer until onions are golden and just begin to brown. Then, proceed as follows:

SAUSAGE & POTATO CASSEROLE
zapiekanka z kiełbasą i kartoflami

Slice or dice 4–8 cold, cooked potatoes and mix with the browned sausage, onion, and drippings. Sprinkle with salt, pepper, and marjoram, and transfer mixture to buttered casserole. Fork-blend ½–1 c. sour cream with 1 T. flour and pour over potato & sausage mixture. Cover and bake in 325°–350° oven 30–40 min. *Variation:* Instead of marjoram, sprinkle with a ½ t. caraway seeds. Omit the sour cream and sprinkle casserole with 1–2 T. vinegar, 4 T. water, and 1–2 t. sugar. Bake as above, adding a little water if mixture begins to sizzle. This dish is somewhat reminiscent of hot German potato salad. Sprinkle with a little flour if desired, toss gently, and simmer a bit longer.

BEANS & SAUSAGE
kiełbasa zapiekana z fasolą

Combine browned sausage, onions, and drippings with 2–4 c. cooked navy beans. (These may be cooked from scratch or out of a can, but either way they must be well drained before adding to sausage). Add 1 small can baked beans or pork & beans, sprinkle with salt, pepper and marjoram and/or savory, and transfer mixture to buttered casserole. Separately, fork-blend ¼ c. water, 2 T. vinegar, and 2 t. sugar and add to beans. Cover, bake in 325° oven 30–40 min. For added zest, 1 T. brown prepared mustard may be added.

STRING BEANS & SAUSAGE
kiełbasa z fasolką szparagową

Mix sausage & onions with 3–5 c. yellow or green cooked string beans (canned are good, but drain well). Sprinkle with salt, pepper, and savory, a little vinegar (about 1 T.) and sugar (1 t. or more). Place mixture into buttered casserole, dot with butter, add several T. meat stock, court bouillon or water, sprinkle with bread crumbs, and bake covered in pre-heated 325° oven 30 min. *Note:* In place of the string beans, other cooked vegetables like Brussels sprouts or cauliflower may be used. Leftover cooked noodles or macaroni are another possibility. When cooking with versatile Polish sausage, only your imagination and the ingredients you have on hand set the limit!

BATTER FRIED SAUSAGE
kiełbasa smażona w cieście

In bowl combine 1¼ c. flour, 2 raw egg yolks, 8 T. water, and 2 T. salad oil. Mix until you get a smooth batter. Beat 2 egg whites to a froth, fold in and stir to distribute evenly, and salt lightly. Cut 1½ lbs. baked, smoked kiełbasa into ¼ inch slices or 1 inch pieces. Roll in flour, impale on fork, and dip in batter. Brown in fairly hot oil until golden on all sides, then reduce heat, cover, and simmer 5 min. or so. This can be a main dinner course when served with potatoes and cole slaw, a nice breakfast or supper dish, served with horseradish or mustard and bread, or a hot hors d'oeuvre. In the latter case, use sliced sausage and stick the fried rounds with toothpicks for a bite-sized snack.

GRILLED POLISH SAUSAGE
kiełbasa z rusztu

Cut as much smoked Polish sausage as needed (allowing ¼–½ lb. per person) into 3–4 inch pieces. Place on charcoal grill positioned a fair distance away from the glowing embers.

If the grill is too close to the flame, the sausage will burn on the outside without cooking evenly. Grill until sausage is a deep, ruddy brown on all sides. You can shorten cooking time and ensure more even cooking if you score the sausage half way through on one side at ¼ inch intervals. Serve with horseradish or brown mustard, rye bread, and sliced tomatoes and/or vegetable salad.

KIEŁBASA SHISH KEBAB
szaszłyk z kiełbasy

Slice 2 lbs. smoked Polish sausage about ¼–½ inch thick and stick on skewers, interspersing with onion slices the size of the sausage and squares of sliced bacon. Place on charcoal grill not too close to embers and turn frequently until nicely browned. Better yet, cook on rotisserie. *Variation:* Intersperse ingredients above with cubes of beef tenderloin and/or squares of green pepper. Sprinkle with maggi extract and cook on charcoal grill or rotisserie until tender. Cheaper cuts of steak may also be used, but these should be marinated overnight in any of the oil-based marinades recommended for roast beef or in a commercial, meat-tenderizing marinade. For an added gourmet touch, include a few fresh mushroom caps on the skewers.

LARDED PORK LIVER IN SOUR CREAM
wątróbka wieprzowa szpikowana w śmietanie

Wash a 1–1¼ lb. piece of pork liver, removing veins and membrane. Pat dry. Lard with about ⅛ lb. salt pork, cut into thin strips about 2½ inches long. (See roast beef au jus for detailed larding instructions). Sprinkle liver with pepper and ginger, roll in flour, shaking off excess, and brown in 2 T. hot lard or oil on all sides. Reduce heat, add ½ c. water, cover, and simmer on low flame about 15 min. Turn liver over once during cooking. In cup, fork-blend pan drippings, ½ c. sour cream and 1 T. flour until smooth, salt & pepper and pour over liver. Simmer briefly. Slice liver, place on platter, and drench with sauce. Garnish with chopped fresh parsley. Serve with rice or potatoes and non-creamed in-season salad of choice.

BREADED PORK LIVER
wątróbka wieprzowa panierowana

Remove veins and membrane from 1–1¼ lb. pork liver and slice into ½ inch thick cutlets. Sprinkle with pepper and ginger and pound lightly with meat mallet on both sides, but not as thin as for breaded pork cutlets. Dredge in flour, beaten eggs, and bread crumbs, pressing in breading so it doesn't fall off when frying. Brown in 3 T. fairly hot lard or oil on both sides, then reduce heat and simmer several min. longer. Liver should still be faintly pink inside, so cut one of the slices in half to check for doneness. Sprinkle with salt just before serving. For an Old Polish touch, serve with saffron rice. Tomato & onion salad is also a nice side dish for pork liver.

PORK HEART STEW
gulasz z serc wieprzowych

Cut 1–1¼ lbs. pork hearts into cubes, removing all arteries. Place in pot with 6 c. cold water, add 1 T. salt and, after bringing to boil, reduce heat and simmer covered about 2 hrs. Add 1 standard portion soup greens, 1 bay leaf, and 2 grains allspice. Continue cooking until meat and vegetables are tender. Meanwhile, sauté 2 chopped onions and 4–8 oz. chopped or thinly sliced fresh mushrooms in 2 T. butter until tender. Strain stock and add the cooked hearts and vegetables (diced) to mushrooms & onions in skillet. Add 1 c. heart stock, cover and simmer 15 min. Fork-blend ½ c. sour cream with 1 t. Maggi extract and 2 T. flour and add to skillet. Simmer a bit longer, salt & pepper to taste and garnish with freshly chopped garden greens (parsley, dill or chives or any combination thereof). Serve over egg noodles or dumplings of choice together with a crispy, non-creamed salad. Reserve the stock for soup.

TART & TANGY PORK LUNGS
płucka wieprzowe na kwaśno

Remove windpipe, if still attached, from 1½ lbs. pork lungs. Scald with 5 c. boiling water, bring to boil, drain, then cover with 5 c. cold water and cook covered on low flame 45 min. Add 1 portion soup greens and continue cooking under cover until lungs are fully cooked (about 30 min.). Meanwhile, lightly brown 1–2 chopped onions in 3 T. butter, add 2 T. flour, brown slightly, then stir in 1 c. lung stock. Remove lungs from stock, dice, or cut into small cubes and add to skillet. Season with salt, pepper, marjoram, a dash of nutmeg, and enough lemon juice to get the tart flavor you want. For a sweet & sour taste, add 1 t. or so sugar. Simmer briefly and serve with potatoes and grated-vegetable salad of choice.

PORK TONGUES IN TOMATO SAUCE
ozorki wieprzowe w sosie pomidorowym

Wash 1½ lbs. pork tongues and cut away salivary glands if still attached to he base. Place in pot, scald with 8 c. boiling water, bring to boil, add 1 portion diced soup greens, 1 bay leaf, 3 grains allspice, and 1 T. salt and cook covered 1–1½ hrs. or until tongues are fork tender. Remove skin from tongues under cold running water, then return them to stock. Meanwhile, prepare sauce as follows. Sauté 1 finely minced onion in 2 T. butter until golden, but not browned. Sprinkle in 3 T. flour and brown slightly, stirring constantly. Dilute with 1–1½ c. tongue stock. Stir in 3–5 T. tomato concentrate (depending on whether a mild or more intensive tomato flavor is desired), season with salt, pepper, and a little sugar. Bring to boil and simmer briefly. Fork-blend ½ c. sour cream with several T. of the hot sauce, then add to skillet. Slice the tongues, add to sauce, and simmer several min. Serve with rice or potatoes and a crunchy salad. Pork tongues may also be served with horseradish, mustard, or gherkin sauce. The gray sauce, usually served with beef tongue, is another possibility.

BATTER-FRIED PORK TONGUES
ozorki wieprzowe smażone w cieście

Cook 1½ lbs. pork tongues until tender in water with soup greens and spices as above. Remove skin under cold running water, and set tongue aside to cool. Cut into ½ inch thick slices. Prepare batter as for batter-fried sausage (p. 291). Dredge tongue slices in flour, impale on fork, and dip in batter, then fry in fairly hot lard or oil to a nice golden brown. Drain on absorbent paper to remove excess grease. Serve with hot or cold horseradish sauce or tartar sauce, mashed potatoes and sliced tomatoes.

PORK BRAINS
móżdżki wieprzowe

Prepare according to any of the recipes given for calves brains.

ROAST SUCKLING PIG
prosię pieczone

We conclude our review of pork dishes with a rare treat that once graced the banquets of the Old Polish nobility and was the centerpiece of the tantalizingly colorful święconka (Easter) table. If you can get a 5–7 lb. suckling pig, treat your dinner guests to this time-honored delicacy. Rub the cleaned piglet inside and out with salt, pepper, marjoram, and (optional) 1–2 buds mashed garlic. Place in covered container and let stand at room temp. 1 hr. Stuff with dressing of choice (see below), sew up, and place a small raw potato in piglet's mouth. Cover ears and tail with oiled paper, tied in place with string so they don't get scorched during roasting, and brush all over with olive oil. (Old Polish cooks preferred butter, but it tends to burn.) Place piglet in roaster on rack with forelegs bent back at the knee as if kneeling. Roast in pre-heated 375° oven uncovered, basting every 15-20 min., about 2½ hrs. or until tender. Replace evaporating pan drippings with water. When piglet turns a nice golden orange, prick it with fork. If the fork goes in easily and a clear, golden juice drips out, your piglet is cooked. Remove potato from mouth and replace with a small apple. Also remove the oiled paper from ears and tail. Place the roast suckling pig on a lettuce-lined platter surrounded by small apples. Carve at table. At Eastertime, place a pisanka (painted Easter egg) in the pig's mouth instead of the apple.

—bread & liver dressing: Soak the liver from your suckling pig and ¾ lb. calf's liver in 3 c. milk 1 hr. Soak 4–6 stale, crumbled kaiser rolls in 2 c. milk until soggy. Run the liver and soggy rolls through meat-grinder. Cream 4–6 T. butter, gradually adding 4 raw egg yolks. Combine with liver & bread mixture, fold in 4 beaten egg whites, season with salt, pepper, and several dashes of nutmeg, and add just enough bread crumbs to get a soft and moist mixture.

—bread, liver & veal dressing: Proceed as above, but instead of calf's liver add ¾ lb. ground veal. Also add 2 T. chopped fresh dill and 1 T. chopped fresh parsley.

—buckwheat dressing: In pot, combine 3 c. water, 1 T. butter, and ½ t. salt. Bring to boil and add 1½ c. buckwheat groats. Cook on low heat until water is absorbed, then cover, place in oven, and bake at 325° oven 30 min. Cook the piglet's lungs (with windpipe removed) in boiling water to cover about 45 min., then run through meat grinder when cool. Scald the liver and grind. Dice ⅛ lb. salt pork and fry up into golden nuggets. Combine the buckwheat, salt-pork nuggets, and drippings, ground lungs and liver. Stir in 1 egg, or add just the yolk and beat the white to a froth before folding in. Season to taste with salt, pepper, and marjoram.

—apple dressing: fill the piglet's cavity with peeled, cored apple quarters.

—bread & apple dressing: Soak 2 stale kaiser rolls in ½ c. milk and, when soggy, run through meat grinder. Add enough peeled, diced apples to loosely fill cavity. Sprinkle sparingly with salt, pepper, and marjoram. ***Optional:*** ½ c. pre-soaked, drained raisins may be added. Instead of marjoram, season with several dashes of nutmeg. For a sweet undertone, add 1–2 t. sugar.

—noodle & ham dressing: Cook 1 pkg. egg noodles according to directions on package. Transfer to colander, drain, and chop coarsely. In skillet, melt 1–2 T. butter, add the noodles, and ½ lb. boiled ham, finely diced. Toss to coat with butter evenly, but do not cook. Stir in 2 raw eggs, mix well, salt & pepper, and stuff suckling pig with mixture. Several T. bread crumbs as well as a little chopped parsley or dill may be added to dressing.

* * *

ROAST LAMB
pieczeń barania

Beat a 3–4 lb. boned, rolled (string-tied) lamb shoulder roast on all sides with heavy rolling pin. (The light, flimsy, plastic rolling pins are next to useless.) Scald with ¾ c. boiling vinegar. Slice 4–5 buds garlic and 1 small onion into slivers, make scattered slits all over the roast with the tip of a sharp knife, and insert the garlic and onion slivers into them. Rub roast all over with salt, pepper, and marjoram, and let stand covered at room temp. 1 hr. Roast meat uncovered on rack in roaster in 350° oven 2–2½ hrs. At start of roasting, add several T. boiling water to roaster and baste occasionally with pan drippings. Roast is done when a fork goes in easily and a cloudy, pale-pink juice drips out of stab mark. Meat should still be faintly pink on the inside. For well-done roast, keep in oven a while longer. For a crispier skin, roast in 400° oven the first 15 min., then turn meat over and continue roasting at 350°. Remove roast from oven and allow to set 15 min. before slicing. Serve with mashed potatoes, sprinkled with some of the pan drippings, braised beets, or Brussels sprouts Polonaise and a zesty grated-vegetable salad containing horseradish.

ROAST LEG OF LAMB OR MUTTON, HUNTER'S STYLE
udziec barani na dziko

Pound a 5–7 lb. leg of lamb with rolling pin on all sides. It should not be flattened, but retain its original shape. In pot combine 6 peppercorns, 3 grains allspice, 2 crumbled bay leaves, and 8 juniper berries (all coarsely crushed in mortar, but not ground!). Add 1 t. ginger, ½ c. water, ½ c. dry white wine, and ¼ c. vinegar. Bring to boil and scald roast. Cover and refrigerate 2–3 days, turning meat over each day. Remove from marinade, pat dry, insert garlic slivers (using 3–5 buds) into scattered slits all over roast, rub with salt, and let stand 1 hr. covered at room temp. Roast on rack fat side up in roaster at 350° 3–4 hrs. With the fat on top, the roast will baste itself. When done, remove from oven and allow to rest 15 min. before slicing. Brown 3 T. flour in ¼ c. of the pan drippings, stirring until smooth and lump-free. Add 1 c. boiling water and as much of the strained marinade as needed to get the tangy taste you want. Season to taste with salt, pepper, and a little sugar. Simmer briefly and pour over sliced meat on platter. Serve with potatoes, buckwheat groats or barley, and braised beets or braised red cabbage.

LAMB FILLETS & CABBAGE
zrazy baranie duszone z kapustą

Trim excess fat from 1½ lbs. lamb leg steaks and remove the small round bone if still attached. Cut into 1 x 2 inch rectangles and pound with a moistened meat mallet until thin but unbroken. Sprinkle with salt & pepper and (optional) a little of your homemade hunter's seasoning or lamb & mutton seasoning (see section on spices & seasonings), dredge in flour, and brown on both sides in 3 T. hot oil. Transfer meat to baking dish. In pan drippings, lightly brown 3 small, sliced onions, and add to meat together with ½ c. water. Cover and bake in 325° oven about 1 hr., replacing any liquid that evaporates. Meanwhile, shred 1 small head cabbage (the wrinkly Savoy cabbage is good), scald with boiling water to cover, and cook 5 min. Drain and add to meat. Add ½ t. caraway seeds and 1 mashed bud garlic and bake until meat is very tender. Fork-blend 2–3 t. flour with ½ c. warm water and add to meat and cabbage. Season to taste with salt, pepper, and a little vinegar and sugar. Simmer briefly and serve with boiled potatoes.

BREADED LAMB CUTLETS
kotlety baranie panierowane

Remove meat from 1½ lbs. lamb chops and trim away any excess fat. Proceed as with breaded pork cutlets or breaded veal cutlets, but sprinkle with Polish lamb & mutton seasoning. Since most lamb chops have a piece of meat on each side of the bone, you can make two cutlets from each chop.

LAMB OR MUTTON STEW
gulasz barani

Cut 1½ lbs. boned lamb or mutton (leg or shoulder portion) into cubes the size of playing dice. Dredge in flour and brown on all sides in 2–3 T. hot oil. Add 3 sliced onions, toss with meat, and brown slightly. Salt & pepper, add 1 c. hot water, cover, and simmer on low heat 45–60 min., or until tender, replacing liquid that evaporates. Meanwhile, quarter 2–3 tomatoes, scald with boiling water to cover, and cook 15 min. Force through sieve and add to stew. Season with 1 t. paprika, ⅛–¼ t. cayenne pepper, a sprinkle of rosemary, lemon juice, and sugar. Sprinkle with a little flour—enough to form a nice, pourable sauce with the pan drippings and stir in 1 heaping T. sour cream. Simmer 1 min. and serve over rice, mashed potatoes, or egg-batter dumplings. Serve with green pepper, onion, & tomato salad.

DEVIL'S LAMB ROLL-UPS
"czarcie" zrazy baranie

Remove meat and trim away excess fat from 1½ lbs. lamb chops, or cut boneless lamb shoulder or leg into 1 x 2 or 1½ x 2½ inch rectangles ½ inch thick. With moistened meat mallet pound thin. In mortar, crush 4 juniper berries, 6 peppercorns, and 2 crumbled bay leaves and sprinkle each slice with mixture through sieve. Place slices one on top of the other, cover, and refrigerate 1–2 hrs. Scrape off spices, salt each cutlet, and spread with a trace of mashed garlic; place a piece of uncooked bacon and a slice of onion at the end of each piece and roll up tightly. These may be impaled on a long hot dog fork, brushed with oil, and cooked over an open fire, taking care that the meat doesn't burn. They can also be cooked on a charcoal grill. If you do so, use small metal skewers rather than toothpicks to fasten the roll-ups. More conventionally, you can fasten with toothpicks or tie with strong thread, dredge in flour, brown in several T. hot oil, then transfer to baking dish, add ½–¾ c. water, cover, and simmer on low heat 45–60 min. or until tender. In an outdoor picnic atmosphere, serve with potatoes cooked in the embers of a campfire, whole tomatoes and radishes. At home, a nice accompaniment is hot rice and sour-cream laced tomato, onion & cucumber salad.

LAMB STEWED WITH BEANS
baranina duszona z fasolą

Soak 1–1½ c. dried navy beans or pea beans overnight in plenty of water and cook in same water until tender (60 min. or longer depending on the dryness of the beans). Dice 1½ lbs. boneless lamb (leg or shoulder portion), sprinkle with salt & pepper, dredge in flour (optional), and brown on all sides in 2 T. hot oil. Add 3 coarsely diced onions, toss with meat and brown lightly, then add 1 c. water. Reduce heat and simmer covered 45–60 mins., or until meat is tender. Add the drained cooked beans. Season with salt, pepper, 1–2 buds mashed garlic, marjoram, savory, a little vinegar or lemon juice, and sugar. Continue simmering covered another 15–20 min. or transfer to baking dish and bake covered at 325° oven 20–30 min. *Optional*: Stir in 1–2 T. tomato concentrate or ketchup. Serve with a crunchy salad.

MEATBALLS, SHISHKEBABS, & OTHER LAMB DISHES
klopsiki, szaszłyki i inne potrawy baranie

Prepare lamb meatballs, patties, and chopped cutlets according to any of the recipes given for ground pork, beef and veal. The flavor of ground lamb is always enhanced by a little mashed garlic, marjoram, and/or rosemary in addition to the usual salt & pepper. Prepare lamb shish kebabs the same way as beef shish kebabs (p.256). It's worth bearing in mind that in the Middle East, where this delicacy originated, it was and continues to be made primarily with lamb. Lamb leg steak is excellent when prepared according to the recipe for pork steak & onions. Lamb can also be used in nearly all the recipes for cutlets, roll-ups, roasts, and stews in this book that call for pork, veal, and beef. This is also true of variety meats such as liver, tongue, kidneys, etc. Besides Polish lamb & mutton seasoning, your homemade pork seasoning and hunter's seasoning can also help spice up lamb dishes. Although Polish cookery makes use of lamb far less frequently than other meats, an old favorite is worth mentioning: (kołduny litewskie) lamb-filled dumplings, which are presented in the dumpling & noodle section of this book. *Note*: In general, the Polish language does not distinguish lamb and mutton, referring to the meat of both young and mature individuals of the species as *baranina*. If the necessity were to arise, however, the terms *pieczeń z jagnięcia* (roast lamb) or *kotlety jagnięce* (lamb cutlets) would be used.

HORSEMEAT
konina

Unlike such horsemeat-loving countries as Italy, Switzerland, France, Germany, Belgium, and Holland, the Polish people have never been especially fond of equine steaks and roasts. This is due more to sentiment than aversion. Poles have simply had a centuries-long "love affair" with the horse and consider it too noble an animal to butcher. Crack Polish cavalry units have thundered across the pages of this country's often turbulent history, and to this day Polish riders continue to win top honors at such equestrian events as Sopot's annual show jumping competition or the medieval knights' tournaments staged at Gołub-Dobrzyń. Poland also breeds some of the world's finest race horses, and the annual auction at Janów Podlaski regularly attracts buyers from Europe, the U.S., the Arab world, and many other places. Nonetheless, from a dietary standpoint, horsemeat would seem to have everything going for it. It contains next to no fat, hence a 100-gram serving (about 3 ½ oz.) has only 118 calories, compared with 213 for lean beef. Yet it supplies more protein, iron, and calcium than beef. *Note*: Horsemeat is extremely red and lean and has a sweetish taste not everyone likes. To prepare, it should be marinated, larded, seasoned with Polish beef seasoning or hunter's seasoning, and cooked like game-style beef or venison.

POULTRY & RABBIT

Poultry or domestic fowl continues to enjoy the status of "something special" in Polish cuisine. To many Poles, a roast fowl is associated with festive occasions such as holiday celebrations, banquets, or at least Sunday dinner at *Babcia's* (grandma's). Although now industrially mass produced, even the broiler-fryer (chicken) is more likely to be served on Sunday than on other days of the week.

Chicken and turkey are ideal for those who prefer a light and delicate meat that is easy to digest, while duck and goose would be more to the liking of people who enjoy robust, full-flavored dishes. Typical entrées include roast chicken Polonaise, stuffed with fragrantly dill-flavored bread & liver dressing. Roast turkey, often stuffed with a slightly sweet raisin & almond dressing, is a favorite for New Year's dinner.

Roast goose, stuffed with apples ,groats, or other dressings, is associated with winter holiday entertaining and in the olden days was traditionally served on St. Martin's Day (November 11). Roast duck stuffed with apples, accompanied with a glass of good red wine, is a specialty of some Polish restaurants and cafés and makes a nice after-theatre supper. Guinea fowl appears far less frequently, but also has its devotees.

Although poultry is usually roasted whole, it can also be prepared in a variety of other ways, notably braised with fruit, vegetables, or mushrooms into fricassee-type dishes. Cooked boneless fowl is sometimes ground and used in various minced cutlets, meatballs, croquettes, and the like. This enables the imaginative cook to come up with any number of thrifty and tasty meals.

The domestic rabbit is certainly not a fowl, neither is it a game dish, so it was only after some debate that we decided to include it is this chapter. Often overlooked by American meal-planners, rabbit has everything going for it in today's health-conscious times. Its delicate white meat is high in protein, but extremely low in fat and cholesterol. It is easy to digest and can thus be freely served to convalescents. Above all, it is extremely tasty and lends itself to a wide variety of dishes.

Rabbit hutches out behind the house or shed remain a common sight in rural and small-town Poland. While Poles eat nowhere the amount of rabbit that their French counterparts do. On the other hand, consumption of this delicious and healthful meat is higher in Poland than in America. Once you try it, we think you will get out of the pork, beef, and chicken rut and make rabbit a normal part of your family-dinner scene, particularly on those slightly special occasions, because like poultry, rabbit—baked, braised, fried, or whatever—also has a certain festive air about it.

* * *

ROAST STUFFED CHICKEN POLONAISE
kurczę z nadzieniem po polsku

Wash, dry, and salt 2½–4 lb. fryer-broiler chicken inside and out and set aside. Break up 1–2 stale kaiser rolls (or other stale white bread or rolls) into a bowl and cover with ½ c. milk. When they become soggy, run them through a meat grinder together with 1 raw chicken liver. Separately, cream 2–3 T. soft butter, adding 2–3 raw egg yolks one at a time and mixing constantly until smooth and creamy. Combine bread & liver mixture with yolk & butter mixture and fold in 2–3 egg whites beaten to a froth. Add 3 t. finely chopped fresh dill (or 2 T. dill and 1 T. parsley), season to taste with salt, pepper, and a dash or 2 nutmeg. You may increase or decrease the amount of stuffing, depending on the size of your chicken. Fill cavity no more than ½ to ¾ full, since the stuffing will expand during roasting. Don't worry if the dressing is much wetter and mushier than the typical American-style bread stuffing, because that's how it's supposed to be. During roasting it will become light and fluffy. If you like this traditional Polish dressing as much as we do, make a little extra and also force a thin layer of it with a teaspoon under the skin of the chicken's breast and legs. Sew up chicken. *(Optional*: Dust with a little paprika or your homemade Polish-style poultry seasoning.) Place chicken on rack in roasting pan, brush with butter, and roast in pre-heated 375° oven covered about 1½ hrs., or until tender. Baste frequently with butter and then the pan drippings that form. This classic Polish dish is one of our favorites, especially in the summer months when fresh dill is plentiful. We usually serve it with tiny, boiled new potatoes and cucumber & sour cream salad. *Note*: Instead of the stale rolls, about 1 c. dry bread crumbs, moistened with a little milk, can be used instead. For a richer-tasting stuffing, add about ¼ lb. raw ground veal.

ROAST CHICKEN WITH LIVER STUFFING
kurczę z nadzieniem wątrobianym

Soak 2 crumbled, stale rolls in ½ c. milk and, when soggy, run through meat grinder together with 4–5 raw chicken livers and 1 small onion. To mixture add 2 raw egg yolks, 3 T. melted butter, and 3 T. finely chopped dill and or parsley. Mix well, adding 2 T. milk (in which the rolls were soaked) and folding in 2 stiffly beaten egg whites. Salt & pepper to taste. Stuff chicken, sew up, and roast as above.

ROAST CHICKEN WITH RICE STUFFING
kurczę nadziewane ryzem

Cook chicken heart and gizzard under cover in a small amount of water 1 hr. or until tender, then run through meat grinder together with 1 raw chicken liver and 2 hard-boiled eggs. Combine with 2 c. cooked rice. Sauté 1 minced onion in 1 T. butter and add to mixture. Cream 2 T. butter, adding 2 raw egg yolks, one at a time. Add to mixture, fold in 2 beaten egg whites and 3 T. finely chopped dill and/or parsley. Salt & pepper to taste and stuff chicken with mixture. Roast as above. *Note*: Fine cooked barley or cooked fine buckwheat groats (*kasza krakowska*) may be used in place of rice.

ROAST CHICKEN WITH RAISIN STUFFING
kurczę z nadzieniem rodzynkowym

Cream 2 T. butter with 2 raw egg yolks and add to 2 c. cooked rice, 3 t. finely chopped parsley, and ¼ c. finely chopped or ground blanched almonds. Beat 2 egg whites to a stiff froth, adding 1–2 t. sugar towards the end, and fold into rice mixture. Soak ½ c. raisins in 1 c. water 15 min., drain well, and add to mixture. Season to taste with a little salt and a dash of nutmeg. Mix ingredients well and stuff chicken. Roast as above.

ROAST CHICKEN, PARTRIDGE STYLE
kurczę na sposób kuropatwy

Cream 2 T. butter with 2 raw egg yolks and mix with 1 c. bread crumbs, 1 grated onion and 3 T. chopped parsley. Beat 2 egg whites to a froth and fold in. Add enough milk to get a moist filling. Salt & pepper to taste and stuff salted chicken. Sew up. In mortar, finely crush 8 juniper berries and sprinkle over chicken. Top chicken's breast and legs with thin slices of salt pork and roast as above. Instead of the juniper alone, you may sprinkle bird with your homemade hunter's seasoning which contains juniper and other spices. Either way, your chicken will end up with a hint of the great outdoors, and your guests may believe they are feasting on partridge or pheasant. *Optional*: Before roasting, your chicken may be rubbed inside and out with 1–2 buds mashed garlic. Midway through roasting, you may also sprinkle it with a jigger of dry white wine or mead (Polish honey wine).

ROAST CHICKEN WITH MUSHROOM STUFFING
kurczę z nadzieniem pieczarkowym

Sauté 8 oz. sliced fresh mushrooms and finely chopped onion in 3 T. butter until tender. Combine with 2 c. cooked rice, 1 raw egg yolk, 1 beaten egg white, 2–3 t. finely chopped fresh dill and/or parsley and salt & pepper to taste. Stuff chicken and sew up. If any pan drippings remain from the mushrooms, pour them over the chicken. If not, melt 1 T. butter in the skillet in which they were fried to absorb all the mushroom flavor and pour it over the chicken. Proceed as above.

CHICKEN BAKED WITH MUSHROOMS
kurczę pieczone z pieczarkami

Wash, dry, and generously salt & pepper chicken inside and out. In 3 T. butter simmer 8–12 oz. washed, sliced, fresh mushrooms until tender. With slotted spoon transfer mushrooms to chicken's cavity but do not sew up. Place chicken in roasting pan, pour the mushroom pan drippings over it, add 1 c. water to pan, and roast in pre-heated 400° oven uncovered for 15–20 min. Cover, reduce heat to 375°, and bake another 30–45 min., or until tender. Serve with mashed potatoes or rice and a fresh salad of choice.

FRIED CHICKEN
kurczęta smażone

Salt 2 cut-up fryers or equal amount of your favorite chicken parts (drumsticks, breasts, wings, etc.) 1 hr. before cooking. Sprinkle with homemade Polish poultry seasoning, dredge in flour, dip in beaten eggs, and roll in bread crumbs until thoroughly covered. Press breading in gently by hand. Fry in about 4–5 T. hot oil or lard until nicely browned on all sides. Transfer to roasting pan, adding 1–2 T. water, and bake covered in pre-heated 375° oven about 30 min. Serve with potatoes and lettuce & sour cream salad.

BREADED CHICKEN ROLL-UPS À LA KIEV
kotlet de volaille

Remove the skin from 4 chicken breasts. Turn over and with sharp knife carefully remove the rib bones, leaving small wing bone intact. Gently beat only the bottom side of breasts (from which rib bones were removed) with mallet until about ¼ inch thick. Sprinkle with salt. Place a 2–3 T. strip of very cold, unsalted butter on each cutlet parallel to the wing bone and roll up tightly starting at the wing-bone end. Dredge in flour, dip in beaten eggs, and roll in very fine bread crumbs; repeat process to get an extra thick coat of breading. Sieve bread crumbs first if they are not very fine. Heat 5 T. high-grade salad oil (pure olive oil is best!), add 1–2 T. butter and fry roll-ups until nicely golden on all sides. Transfer to serving platter, dot with butter, and decorate with sprigs of parsley and lemon slices. This is a gourmet dish that will delight the most discriminating palate. The cutlet literally melts in your mouth and the fresh butter oozes out when you cut into it. Despite its French name (which simply means poultry cutlet), this dish originated in the formerly Polish city of Kijów and is known in the English-speaking world as chicken Kiev. Regardless of its citizenship, we're sure you'll find it well worth the effort. Serve with mashed potatoes or boiled new potatoes, sprinkled with the pan drippings and a little dill, plus such vegetable companions as peas, peas & carrots, floured carrots, Brussels sprouts, or asparagus with Polonaise topping. Lettuce or cucumbers dressed with sour cream are the perfect salad accompaniment

CHICKEN IN SOUR CREAM
kurczę w śmietanie

Cut up 1–2 fryers and salt well. Let stand 1 hr. at room temp. Place chicken in Dutch oven or other pot with tight-fitting lid, add 1 portion diced soup greens, ½ a bay leaf, 4–6 peppercorns, and 1–2 grains allspice. Scald with boiling water to cover and simmer under cover 1 hr. on low flame. When chicken is fork-tender, fork-blend 1 c. sour cream with 3 T. flour and add to pot, cover, and simmer another 10 min. Season to taste with salt, pepper, and a little lemon juice. *Optional*: For added zest, add 1 t. paprika, 1 t. Maggi extract, and several dashes cayenne pepper. Sprinkle with chopped fresh dill and serve with mashed potatoes or rice and a crispy, non-creamed salad.

CHICKEN & PRUNES
kurczę ze śliwkami

Cut up 1–2 chickens, sprinkle with ginger, rub with salt, cover, and refrigerate 1–2 hrs. Dredge in flour and brown on all sides in 2–3 T. hot fat. Transfer to pot, add 1 c. water, and simmer under cover on low heat 30 min. Add 4 oz. prunes and replace evaporated liquid. simmer another 30 min. or until chicken is tender. A T. dry red or white wine may be added towards the end. Arrange chicken on serving platter and top with prunes. Serve with rice and a grated-vegetable salad (in winter) or lettuce or cucumbers (in summer).

MINCED CHICKEN CUTLETS
kotleciki z kury

Cook a cut-up stewing chicken in 8 c. vegetable stock (court bouillon) 2 hrs. or until tender. Remove chicken, leaving wings, neck, rump, gizzard, and heart to cook another 30 min. Remove meat from bone and run through meat grinder with 1 stale roll, soaked 10 min. in ½ c. milk. Sauté 1 sliced minced onion in 1 T. butter until golden and add to ground chicken mixture together with 1–2 eggs, 2 T. chopped dill, 1 T. chopped parsley, salt, pepper, and a dash of nutmeg to taste. Add 1–2 T. bread crumbs, mix all ingredients well, and form into small, oval cutlets. Roll in flour (or, for a breaded coating, in flour, beaten eggs, and bread crumbs), and fry in several T. hot fat on both sides until a nice golden brown crust forms. Serve with potatoes and radish or leek salad. *Variation*: Vary the taste of your chicken cutlets by adding 4–8 oz. ground, butter-fried fresh mushrooms to the mixture. Another possibility is adding ¼–½ lb. raw ground veal to the ground chicken mixture. Different flavor twists can be achieved by sprinkling the meat mixture or the cutlets as they fry with poultry seasoning, waterfowl seasoning or hunter's seasoning. These cutlets are a tasty, practical, and economical way of using a mature stewing chicken, which may often be tough and stringy when unground, and getting a bowl of hearty chicken soup (the stock in which it was cooked) thrown into the bargain!

TRIPE-STYLE CHICKEN
kurczak à la flaczki

Divide fryer-broiler into quarters, place in pot, add 1 t. salt and 4 c. water, bring to boil, and cook about 30 min. Remove chicken and allow to cool. Remove the meat from bones. Slice meat and skin into thin 1 inch strips to resemble tripe. Return to pot, add 1 portion diced soup greens and 1 T. marjoram and cook uncovered another 30 min. or until meat is tender. In a saucepan, lightly brown 4 T. flour in 3 T. butter, gradually stirring in 1 c. hot stock, then add to pot. Add 2–3 t. Maggi extract, 1 t. paprika, ½ t. ginger, a pinch of nutmeg, a dash or two cayenne pepper (this dish should be on the hot and spicy side), and salt & pepper to taste. Portions may be topped with a little grated yellow cheese. Serve as a fricassee with mashed potatoes or, by diluting with 2–3 c. boiling water, as a hearty soup. This dish is sufficiently different to please the "not-chicken-again!" eaters in your gang as well as those who like the spicy flavor of Polish-style tripe but may feel uncomfortable about consuming cow stomachs.

STEWED CHICKEN GIZZARDS
żołądki kurze duszone

Cover 1–1½ lbs. chicken gizzards with cold water, bring to boil, then reduce heat, cover, and simmer 2 hrs. Add 1 portion diced soup greens, ½ a bay leaf, 4 peppercorns, and 1 grain allspice. Replace any water that has evaporated, and continue cooking until gizzards are fork tender. Remove gizzards and, when cool enough to handle, dice or slice and return to pot. At this stage, this versatile variety meat lets you prepare a stew suited to almost any mood or palate. Some examples:
–Fork-blend 2–3 T. flour with 1 c. of the pan liquid until smooth, return to pot, season with 1 t. Maggi extract, and salt & pepper to taste. A T. sour cream may be stirred in. Simmer briefly and serve over rice or noodles of choice.
–Fork-blend ½ c. sour cream with 2–3 T. tomato paste or ketchup and 2 T. flour, gradually adding 1 c. pan liquid. Return to pot. Season with salt, pepper, marjoram, paprika, and about 1 t. sugar. Simmer briefly.

–Stir in 1 T. tomato paste, 1 T. dry red or white wine, 2 t. vinegar, 1 t. sugar or slightly more, and salt & pepper to taste. Thicken sauce with 2 T. flour as above and simmer briefly. *Optional*: Add 1–2 t. paprika.

–Sauté 8 oz. sliced fresh mushrooms and 1 finely chopped onion in 2 T. butter until tender. Add to gizzards along with 1 t. Maggi extract. Fork-blend ½ c. sour cream with 2 T. flour, gradually stirring in 1 c. pan liquid. Add to pot, salt & pepper, and simmer briefly. Just before serving, garnish with a little chopped fresh parsley.

–To the basic recipe add 1 c. drained, canned peas and/or any cooked, leftover vegetables you happen to have on hand. Your imagination is the only limit on what you add and how you season this highly economical but very tasty variety meat.

FRIED CHICKEN LIVERS
smażone wątróbki kurze

Soak 1–1½ lbs. chicken livers in 2 c. milk in refrigerator up to 6 hrs. (This is not absolutely necessary, but it helps to blunt the bitter edge often encountered in chicken liver.) Drain and dry livers and dredge in flour. In 4–5 T. butter simmer 3 chopped onions until just transparent but still unbrowned. Add the livers and brown lightly on all sides, then cover, reduce heat, and simmer 8–10 min. (The chicken livers should still show a trace of pinkness inside.) Salt & pepper, sprinkle with 1 t. Maggi extract, and (optional) several pinches of ginger. Serve with rice and sliced tomatoes as a dinner course. This also makes a very nice Sunday after-church brunch when served with crusty French bread to sop up the drippings.

CHICKEN-LIVER SHISH KEBABS
szaszłyk z kurzych wątróbek

Drench 20 chicken livers with 2 c. milk and soak 30 min. Drain and pat dry. Cut sliced bacon into 20 1 inch squares and slice small onions into 20 thin rounds. (*Optional*: Cut green peppers into 20 small pieces the size of the bacon squares.) Mix 1 t. salt with ¼ t. paprika, ¼ t. nutmeg, and (optional) ¼ t. garlic powder or garlic salt. Slide the ingredients onto 4 skewers, sprinkle with spice mixture, and fry in several T. hot fat on all sides. They are done when the liver is still faintly pink on the inside. You can also brush the shishkebabs with melted butter or a butter & oil mixture and broil on charcoal grill or rotisserie. Serve with rice and tomato, onion & cucumber salad.

* * *

ROAST DUCK WITH APPLES
kaczka pieczona z jabłkami

Wash a 4–5 lb. duck and pat dry. Rub inside and out with salt, marjoram, and (optional) 1 bud mashed garlic. Place in covered container and let stand at room temp. 1 hr. Peel, core, and cut into quarters 2–2½ lbs. apples or enough to fill the duck's cavity. Sew up. Place duck on rack in roasting pan and roast in pre-heated 450° oven 10 min. Reduce to 350° and roast 80 min.–2 hrs. or until fork tender. Sprinkle with about 1 T. water at start of roasting and puncture with fork at intervals to release fat. Baste occasionally with pan drippings. Serve with mashed or boiled potatoes. Another way is to place small, peeled potatoes into the pan drippings during last ½ hr. of roasting. These may be sprinkled with caraway for added zest. Stewed red or white cabbage or braised beets are typical accompaniments. This is the classic Polish way of preparing duck and ranks among the authors' favorite dishes. It is a specialty of many better Polish restaurants and hotels, not to mention the quaint little Kamienne Schodki Café in Warsaw's Old Town Square, where the duck is served with a glass of dry red wine. A perfect combination! For variety, try seasoning your duck with your homemade Polish-style waterfowl seasoning instead of just marjoram.

ROAST DUCK WITH VEAL STUFFING
kaczka nadziewana cielęciną

Rub duck with salt inside and out and let stand 1 hr. Soak 1 c. bread crumbs in ½ c. milk until soggy. Mix with 1–1½ lbs. ground raw veal, 1 ground raw duck liver (pre-soaked in ½ c. milk 2 hrs.), 1 finely chopped onion simmered in 1 T. butter, and 2 raw eggs. For a fluffier stuffing, add only the yolks and then fold in the 2 beaten whites. Season to taste with salt, pepper, marjoram, several dashes nutmeg, and (optional) 1 t. sugar. Knead stuffing well, fill cavity no more than ¾ full, sew up, and roast on rack in uncovered roasting pan as above (about 20 min per lb.). Sprinkle with a little water and baste during roasting with the pan drippings that form. Prick duck with fork at intervals to allow excess fat to drip away.

ROAST DUCK WITH MUSHROOM STUFFING
kaczka z nadzieniem grzybowym

Soak 1 oz. dried Polish mushrooms in 4 c. water 2 hrs. Add duck heart and gizzard (which should be cut open to remove any seeds lodged inside) and cook covered 45 min. Add 1 portion diced soup greens and 2 t. salt and cook until all ingredients are tender. Drain, reserving liquid. If there is less than 2 c., add enough water to mushroom-giblet stock to make 2 c. and in it cook 1 c. buckwheat groats, Kraków groats, fine barley, or rice.

Meanwhile, finely chop mushrooms and giblets. Finely chop 1 onion and simmer in 1 T. butter until golden. When groats or rice are cool, combine with the mushrooms, giblets, cooked vegetables, sautéd onion, and 2 beaten egg yolks. Fold in 2 egg whites beaten to a froth. Add 2 T. finely chopped fresh dill or 1 T. dill and 1 T. parsley. Mix ingredients well, salt & pepper to taste, and fill duck no more than ¾ full. Sew up and roast as above. Serve with stewed sauerkraut or braised white or red cabbage.

ROAST DUCK HUNTER'S STYLE
kaczka na dziko

Place washed, dried duck in glass or crockery container with lid. In mortar coarsely crush 6 peppercorns, 5 juniper berries, 2 grains allspice, 3 crumbled bay leaves, 2 cloves, and 1 t. ginger. In pot combine 3 c. water, ⅓ c. vinegar, and 1 t. salt, add the crushed spices and 1 portion diced soup greens, bring to boil, reduce heat, cover, and simmer 10 min. When cool, pour mixture over duck, cover, and refrigerate overnight. Turn duck several times so that top, bottom, and both sides get the full benefit of marinade. Remove duck from marinade, dry, and rub with salt inside and out. Let stand 1 hr. Place on rack in roasting pan, surround with drained soup greens from marinade, and roast at 350° about 25 min. per lb. Sprinkle with a little marinade at the start, then baste occasionally with pan drippings that form. Meanwhile, cook the duck heart and gizzard in 3 c. water until tender, adding liver the last few min., since it cooks in a short time. Chop giblets and return to stock. When duck is done, fork-blend ¼ c. pan drippings with 3 T. flour, combine with giblet stock and simmer 10 min. Add 1 t. Maggi extract, ½ t. sugar, a little of the marinade, and salt & pepper to taste. Cut up duck, place on serving platter, and drench with the sauce. Sauce may also be served in gravy boat. Serve with potatoes, Brussels sprouts or red cabbage salad.

DUCK STEWED WITH APPLES, PEARS, ETC.
kaczka duszona z jabłkami, gruszkami itp.

Cut up duck, salt well, and let stand 1 hr. Place in pot, cover with boiling water, bring to boil, reduce heat, cover, and simmer 1 hr. Pour off all the pan liquid and cover with fresh boiling water and cook another hr., or until tender. (This updated version of the original recipe is suited to those who love the taste of duck but don't need the extra fat; the traditional way is to continue stewing the duck in its own, usually quite fat, drippings!) If you like, you may cool the duck until easy to handle and remove the bones and return to pot with about 1 c. drippings. Season with pepper and marjoram or waterfowl seasoning. Intersperse meat with 1–1½ lbs. peeled, cored, quartered apples or pears. Fresh, skinned peach quarters are also good. Cover and simmer another 15 min. or until fruit is fully cooked. Serve with potatoes or rice.

ROAST DUCK WITH CHERRIES
kaczka z wiśniami

Rub duck inside and out with salt & pepper and let stand 1 hr. Place on rack in roasting pan and roast in 350° oven about 25 min. per lb. or until tender. During roasting, baste with ½ c. dry red wine and later with the pan drippings that form. When duck is cool enough to handle, cut into portions and place in clean pot. Top with 1 lb. sour cherries with pits left in or removed, as you prefer. Add 1–2 T. sugar to ½ c. pan drippings and pour over cherries and duck. Cover and simmer 15–20 min., or until cherries are fully cooked. The rich, full-bodied flavor of duck is beautifully complemented by the delicately tart tang of fruit, hence it is called for in many Polish recipes for this juicy, tasty fowl. Instead of fresh cherries, you can use ¾ c. canned cherry-pie filling, but omit sugar.

DUCK STEWED IN CABBAGE
kaczka duszona w kapuście

Roast duck as above and, when cool enough to handle, cut into portions. Shred 1 small head red or white cabbage, combine in pot with 1 thinly sliced onion and ½ t. caraway, scald with boiling water to cover, and cook uncovered 10 min., stirring occasionally. Transfer cabbage to clean baking dish and intersperse with duck, cover and bake in 350° oven for 30 min. Season ½ c. drippings from pan in which duck was roasted with about 1 T. dry red wine, 1–2 t. vinegar, 2 t. or so sugar, and salt & pepper to taste; pour over duck and cabbage. Sprinkle with a little flour, mix in and allow to simmer a few more min. Serve with boiled potatoes.

DUCK STEWED WITH MUSHROOMS
kaczka duszona z grzybami

Soak ½–1 oz. dried Polish mushrooms in 2 c. water 2 hrs., then cook in same water until tender. Chop mushrooms and return to water. Generously salt & pepper cut-up duck and let stand 1 hr. Place in pot, scald with boiling water to cover, add 2 sliced onions, and simmer covered about 2 hrs. In saucepan, simmer 1 finely chopped onion in 4 T. duck drippings until tender, add the drained mushrooms, and simmer briefly. Transfer duck to baking pan, add onions, mushrooms, and the mushroom liquid; bake covered 20 min. in 350° oven. Fork-blend ½ c. sour cream with 2–3 T. flour, stir in 1 c. liquid from baking pan, and pour over duck. Salt & pepper to taste and simmer a few min. longer. Serve with mashed potatoes or buckwheat groats. *Note*: In place of or in addition to the spices indicated, for variety all of the duck recipes presented above may be seasoned with waterfowl seasoning or hunter's seasoning.

ROAST GOOSE WITH APPLES
gęś pieczona z jabłkami

Rub a 6–10 lb. goose inside and out with salt, pepper, marjoram, and (optional) 1–2 buds mashed garlic. Let stand at least 1 hr. before roasting. Better yet, refrigerate in covered container overnight. Fill cavity with peeled, cored apple halves and sew up. *Remember:* Your bird should be filled only ⅔–¾ full when using bread or cereal stuffing which tends to expand during roasting; the apples will shrink, so you can safely include as many as will fit. Place goose on rack in roaster and roast at 350° about 25 min. per lb. or until fork tender. When it begins to brown, sprinkle with a little water. Prick the goose with fork at intervals and it will baste itself during roasting. (*Variation*: In blender, blend 1 c. canned, whole-style cranberry sauce and mix with apples before stuffing.) Serve with boiled potatoes or raw-potato dumplings (pyzy) and stewed red cabbage or red cabbage salad. In Polish tradition, roast goose has long been a holiday delight served on festive occasions during the long autumn and winter months. The first such occasion was St. Martin's Day (November 11) which, in the older liturgical calendar, marked the final fling of feasting and merry-making before the penitential fasting of the then six-week-long Advent.

ROAST GOOSE WITH BREAD & APPLE STUFFING
gęś z nadzieniem jabłkowo-bułczanym

Remove excess fat from goose, dice very fine, and render (melt) in saucepan. Rub goose inside and out with salt, pepper, and marjoram; and let stand 1 hr. at room temp. or refrigerate overnight. Break up 2–3 stale kaiser rolls (French bread, etc.) and soak in 1 c. milk until soggy. In 2 T. rendered goose fat sauté 2 finely chopped onions and, when nearly tender, add the chopped goose liver which should not be overcooked. Run the liver, onions, and soggy rolls through meat grinder. Peel and coarsely grate 1½–3 lbs. apples and add to mixture together with ⅓–½ c. pre-soaked, well-drained raisins, 1 raw egg yolk, and 2–3 T. finely chopped fresh parsley. Fold in 1 beaten egg white, combine ingredients well, and season with salt, pepper, and nutmeg. Fill goose with mixture no more than ¾ full, sew up, and roast as above. Instead of water, the goose may be basted with a little red wine (¼–½ c.) during roasting. *Note*: Allow about 1 c. stuffing per lb. goose.

ROAST GOOSE WITH BEAN STUFFING
gęś nadziewana fasolą

Soak 2 c. navy or pea beans in 3 qts. water overnight, then cook in same water until tender. Drain. Rub goose generously inside and out with salt, pepper, basil, and 2–3 buds mashed garlic; let stand at room temp. 1 hr. or refrigerate overnight. Finely chop 2–3 onions and sauté in a little rendered goose fat until golden. Finely chop ¾–1 c. pitted prunes and cook in just a little boiling water until they disintegrate. Combine beans, onions, prunes, and ½ c. pre-soaked, drained raisins, salt & pepper lightly, stuff goose with mixture and sew up. Roast on rack in 325°–350° oven 2½–3½ hrs., or until tender, basting occasionally with water, wine, or beer and pricking with fork to release excess fat. *Note*: Before roasting goose, it is customary to cut off wings, neck, and rump and freeze for future reference. The wings are not very meaty, but together with the neck and tail they make an excellent stock for czernina and other soups. Moreover, the necks make an exquisite appetizer: stuffed goose necks(p.315). If the liver is not being used in stuffing, freeze it as well for future use in pâté and other dishes. It ranks among the best of all livers. The gizzard and heart should also be saved for stocks and stews.

ROAST GOOSE WITH MUSHROOM STUFFING
gęś z nadzieniem grzybowym

Prepare like roast duck with mushroom stuffing (p.307), but increase amount of stuffing and roasting time according to the size of your goose. It is done when fork tender and the juice that oozes out when meat is pricked with fork is no longer pink. In general, goose may be prepared according to any of the duck recipes presented above and vice-versa.

GOOSE STEWED WITH SAUERKRAUT
gęś duszona z kiszoną kapustą

Salt & pepper goose 1 hr. before roasting, then roast on rack in pan as above. Soak 1 oz. dried Polish mushrooms in 3 c. water 2 hrs. then cook in same water until tender. Chop and return to mushroom water. Drain 1 qt. sauerkraut, reserving liquid. Rinse in cold water; drain well, pressing out moisture by hand. Chop coarsely, place in pot, scald with boiling water to cover, and cook uncovered 30 min., adding more water if too much evaporates. Add mushrooms and mushroom water, season with a little pepper, and cook on low heat under cover another 30 min. In 3 T. goose drippings from roaster sauté 1 large finely chopped onion until tender and add to sauerkraut. When goose is nearly tender, remove from roaster and cut into portions. Remove some of the larger bones if you like. Place ½ the sauerkraut in a clean baking dish, sprinkle with ¼ t. caraway, add the goose, top with remaining sauerkraut, sprinkle with another ¼ t. caraway, cover, and bake in moderate oven 30–45 min. Serve with boiled potatoes. ***Optional***: A t. or so sugar may be added to sauerkraut before combining with goose in baking dish.

GOOSE UHLAN STYLE, WITH TANGY PLUM SAUCE
gęś po ułańsku

Rub goose inside and out with salt, pepper, and crushed cloves and let stand at least 1 hr. Fill goose cavity with 1 small, peeled, and diced celeriac (or 2 stalks diced celery including the leafy tops), 1 diced carrot, 1 chopped onion, and ½ c. fresh chopped parsley. Do not sew up. Place on rack in roaster and roast as in above recipes until meat is nearly tender. Cut cooked goose into portions and transfer to clean baking dish. Fork-blend ½ c. dry red wine, ½ c. powidła (or domestic plum jam), ¼ c. finely grated black bread and ½ c. goose drippings from roaster. Flavor with a little lemon juice and pour over goose. Cover and bake in moderate oven 30–45 min. Serve with mashed potatoes and tomato salad.

GOOSE STEWED WITH PRUNES
gęś duszona ze śliwkami

Cut up goose, sprinkle with salt, pepper, marjoram, and paprika and refrigerate in covered container several hrs. or overnight. Place in Dutch oven or other pot with tight-fitting lid, scald with boiling water to cover, bring to boil and simmer under cover on low to medium heat about 1½ hrs. Pour off the water. Replace with fresh cold water to cover, add 2 coarsely chopped onions, 12–16 oz. prunes (with pits left in), and 2–3 buds mashed garlic. Season with waterfowl seasoning and simmer under cover another hr., or until goose is tender. Serve over rice or potatoes.

GOOSE BRAISED IN BLACK SAUCE
gęś duszona w czarnym sosie

Collect blood of a freshly killed goose in jar and stir in several T. vinegar. Seal jar and refrigerate until needed. Meanwhile, trim away and discard visible fat from a cleaned, cut-up goose and soak in cold water about 1 hr. Remove from water, pat dry, rub with salt and let stand in covered Dutch oven at room temp. 1 hr. Scald with boiling water to cover, bring to boil, reduce heat and simmer covered 90 min. Drain, reserving liquid. Remove fat from top of liquid. (***Hint***: If you prepare it a day ahead and refrigerate overnight, the congealed fat will be easy to remove.) Cover goose in Dutch oven with degreased stock, add 2 t. salt, bay leaf, several peppercorns, 3 grains allspice and 3 cloves plus 1 portion diced soup greens. Add a little water as needed and simmer covered until meat is tender. Strain stock, discarding spices and vegetables. In 4 c. stock dissolve 3–4 T. flour, whisking until smooth. Add a heaping T. powidła (thick plum jam), 1–2 T. honey and the goose blood, rubbed through sieve. Gradually bring to boil, whisking constantly to get a smooth sauce. Salt & pepper to taste and season with about 1 t. ground ginger. If sauce is thinner than you like, thicken with a bit more flour. Sauce should have a sweet, sour, winey and mildly spicy flavor, so feel free to add several pinches ground cloves and/or honey-spice-cake seasoning and a bit of vinegar to get the right balance. Pour sauce over goose in Dutch oven, cover and simmer on very low heat about 10 min. and let stand covered another 5 min. for flavors to blend before serving. *Note:* This was a favorite banquet dish of Poland's 18th century royalty. If you like czernina (goose soup), chances are you will also enjoy this. To do things up right in the Old Polish manner, serve it with cooked barley or saffron rice instead of potatoes and provide a little ćwikła on the side.

ROAST GOOSE COUNTRY STYLE
gęś po wiejsku

Season goose with salt, pepper, and marjoram and let stand 1 hr. The previous day, cut several slices of French bread into small cubes and leave out overnight to dry. Chop 2–3 onions and sauté in a little rendered goose fat until golden. Run 3 hard-boiled eggs and the raw goose liver through meat grinder, combine with the dry bread cubes, onions, ground egg & liver mixture, 3–4 T. chopped parsley, and ⅔ c. sour cream. Salt & pepper to taste, toss ingredients lightly to distribute evenly and fill goose cavity. Sew up. Roast goose as in the other stuffed goose recipes above. Allow about 1 c. stuffing per lb. goose.

GOOSE KASHUBIAN STYLE, WITH POTATOES & RUTABAGA
gęś po kaszubsku

Salt cut-up goose and let stand at least 1 hr. Cut off fat, dice fine, and render. Dredge goose in flour and brown on all sides in hot goose fat. Transfer to pot, scald with boiling water to cover, and simmer covered 1½–2 hrs. or until nearly tender. Add 2 crushed bay leaves, 3 grains allspice, 1 level T. dill seed, and 1½ c. pickle juice (from brine-cured dill pickles). Top with 1½ lbs. or more peeled, diced, raw potatoes and 1½ lbs. peeled, diced, uncooked rutabaga. (If rutabaga is not available, turnips or kohlrabi may be used instead.) Salt & pepper and continue simmering under cover until goose is very tender. You can also bake this dish in a moderate oven. If you cannot prepare this dish a day ahead, pour drippings into container and place in freezer about 1 hr., or until fat congeals at top. Discard fat and combine remaining drippings in saucepan with 1–2 t. flour, stirring into a smooth sauce. Add a little boiling water if necessary to get a nice pourable consistency. Adjust taste with salt, pepper, and a little sugar. Arrange goose and vegetables on platter and pour hot sauce over the top. Serve with red cabbage & leek salad.

ROLLED ROAST GOOSE I, WITH GROATS & MUSHROOMS
rolada z gęsi I

Cut neck and wings from goose and set aside. Place goose breast side down on board and split down center of back with poultry shears. Spread skin side down. With sharp knife, carefully remove the bones and most of the meat, leaving a thin layer attached to skin. Sew up any breaks in skin with cotton thread. Rub skin with salt, marjoram, and 1–2 buds mashed garlic. Wrap in aluminum foil and refrigerate. Sprinkle the boned meat with salt, pepper, and marjoram and set aside. Place goose bones in pot, add ½–¾ oz. dried Polish mushrooms, pre-soaked 2 hrs. in 1 c. water, 1 portion soup greens, the heart, gizzard, neck, and wings and 1 bay leaf. Cover with cold water and cook on medium heat 2 hrs. Strain. Remove meat from bones and run through meat grinder with the giblets, mushrooms, raw goose liver, and uncooked goosemeat. Sauté 1 finely chopped onion in 1–2 T. rendered goose fat. Cook 1½ c. buckwheat groats in 3 c. goose-bone stock until light and fluffy and cool. Combine ground mixture with sautéd onion and groats, mix in 2 raw egg yolks, and 3 T. chopped fresh parsley, fold in 2 beaten egg whites, mix ingredients well, and salt & pepper to taste. Place stuffing on goose skin, roll up and sew up ends and seam. You may also tie it with string like rolled roasts. Place on rack in roasting pan and bake in 325° oven about 2 hrs. Sprinkle with water at start of roasting and baste with pan drippings. Serve with potatoes and red-cabbage salad.

ROLLED ROAST GOOSE II, WITH BREAD & VEAL
rolada z gęsi II

Split goose and remove bones and most meat as above. (Freeze bones, neck, wings and giblets for future use, but not the liver.) Remove goose fat, dice fine, and render. In it cook 8 oz. fresh, chopped mushrooms and 1 finely chopped onion. Soak ½ lb. stale French bread in 2 c. milk. When soggy, run through meat grinder with 1 raw goose liver, the raw goose meat and ¾ lbs. raw ground veal or pork. For finer texture, the mixture may be ground a second time. Add 2–3 T. chopped fresh dill, the mushrooms and onions, and 2 raw eggs. (Or, add just the yolks, beat whites, and fold in.) Season to taste with salt, pepper, and marjoram. Place stuffing on goose skin, roll up tightly, and truss with string. Rub skin with a little rendered goose fat, sprinkle with marjoram, wrap in aluminum foil, and bake in 350° oven about 90 min. Switch off heat and leave in oven another 30 min. Serve with potatoes, stewed sauerkraut, and sliced tomatoes. This rolled goose roast is also excellent sliced and served cold with cranberry sauce, spiced plums, etc.

STUFFED GOOSE NECK
gęsia szyjka faszerowana

Carefully remove skin from goose neck so as not to damage it. (Freeze neck for future use.) Turn neck skin inside out and scrape away the fat. Return to original shape. Soak ½ c. bread crumbs in ½ c. milk. Run small piece of unsalted pork fat (słonina) (about ⅛ lb.) through meat grinder with 4 oz. fresh, uncooked mushrooms and 1 raw goose liver. Combine ground mixture with ¼ lb. raw ground veal and the soggy bread crumbs with excess moisture squeezed out. Mix well and run entire mixture through meat grinder again. Mix in 1 whole egg and season to taste with salt, pepper, and nutmeg. Fill goose-neck skin with mixture. Tie both ends with string like sausage, puncture in several places to prevent bursting during cooking, and place in pot with boiling salted water. Cook covered on low heat 1 hr. Slice and serve with any of the accompaniments recommended with other goose dishes. To serve cold, place cooled neck between 2 boards and weight down lightly. Refrigerate overnight. Slice thin and serve as a cold cut.

GOOSE LIVER & ONIONS
wątróbka gęsia z cebulką

Dice 3–4 slices bacon and fry in skillet until fairly crisp. Remove bacon bits and set aside. Cut 2 onions in half, slice thin, and sauté in bacon drippings until golden. Remove onions and set aside. Slice 1 lb. goose liver into roughly uniform pieces about ¼ inch thick. Salt & pepper, sprinkle with flour, add 1 T. butter to skillet and brown liver in it on both sides over fairly high heat, then top with onions, reduce heat, add 1 T. water, and simmer covered several min. longer. *Variation*: Proceed as above but use only 1 onion. When liver is browned on both sides, add 1 peeled, coarsely grated apple, sprinkle lightly with marjoram, add onions, cover, and simmer briefly. Serve with rice or potatoes and a grated-vegetable salad.

GOOSE GIBLET STEW
gulasz z gęsich podróbek

Place 1½ lbs. goose giblets (gizzards and hearts or just gizzards) in pot, scald with 4 c. salted, boiling water and cook 90 min. Add several peppercorns, 1 grain allspice, 1 clove, and ½ bay leaf, plus 1 portion soup greens, diced, and cook until giblets are tender. Remove from heat. In skillet sauté 2 chopped onions with 8 oz. diced, fresh mushrooms in 3 T. butter. To mushrooms add diced giblets, soup vegetables (discard spices), 2 c. giblet stock, 1 t. paprika, and 1 t. Maggi extract, cover and simmer 15 min. Fork-blend ½–¾ c. sour cream with 2–3 T. flour, adding 1 c. stew liquid a little at a time until mixture is lump-free. Add to skillet, stir, season to taste with salt, pepper, and a little marjoram. Simmer for a few more min. A T. of sherry, Madeira, mead, or most any wine you happen to have on hand will add a gourmet touch to this tasty dish. Serve with noodles of choice and a crispy, non-creamed salad.

* * *

HEN TURKEY POLONAISE WITH RAISIN STUFFING
indyczka po polsku

Salt 8–10 lb. hen turkey, cover, and refrigerate at least 3 hrs. Crumble ½–¼ lb. stale French bread into bowl and drench with 2 c. milk. When soggy, run through meat grinder with raw turkey liver. Beat 3–4 raw egg yolks with 3–4 T. soft butter until thick and creamy; combine with ground mixture. Add 1 c. or more raisins, pre-soaked in water 10 min. and drained well, 1 c. blanched almonds, chopped, thinly sliced or ground, the remaining milk (in which the bread was soaked), about ½ c. bread crumbs, 3 T. chopped parsley, and fold in the stiffly beaten egg whites. Toss ingredients to mix, season with salt & pepper, about ¼ t grated nutmeg and ½ t. ground cloves. (*Optional*: For sweeter taste, add 3–4 T. sugar.) Press down on turkey breast bone to flatten carcass slightly. Fill cavity with stuffing or first run a thin layer of it between skin and meat. Sew up, tuck ends of drumsticks under skin flaps near tail. Place in roaster lined with strips of salt pork, place strips of salt pork on breast and drumsticks, brush all over with melted butter, add 2 c. water to roaster and roast in pre-heated 350° oven 3–4 hrs. (Exact roasting time is impossible to specify, but a rule of thumb is 20–25 min. per lb.; test a drumstick for doneness with fork.) During roasting, baste frequently with melted butter. Instead of adding water to pan, you can sprinkle the bird with a little water several times during first hr. of roasting, alternating with the melted butter. Later, baste with pan drippings that form. According to one school of thought, no water at all should be added. If turkey browns two quickly, you can cover roaster with aluminum foil or with the roaster lid. When turkey is done, remove from oven and let stand 20–25 min. before slicing. Serve with mashed potatoes, flavored with pan drippings (instead of gravy) or whole, peeled potatoes, cooked in pan drippings during last 30–40 min. of roasting. A natural accompaniment is Polish-style cranberry sauce or cranberry-currant sauce which is more intense, sweeter, and not gelatinous like its American counterpart. *Note*: Polish recipes have traditionally favored hen turkeys as being more delicate and tender. However, American turkeys are specially bred for tenderness and some are injected with fat to keep them juicy, so you really needn't go out of your way to find an indyczka. A commercially produced American Tom turkey will do just as well! Instead of stale bread, stuffing may be made with stale babka, chałka, placek or other such yeast-raised egg breads (coffee cakes).

ROAST TURKEY WITH LIVER STUFFING
indyk nadziewany wątróbką

Soak ½ lb. or so stale French bread (kaiser rolls, hamburger buns, etc.) in 2 c. milk. When soggy, run through meat grinder with ¼ lb. raw turkey, chicken, or veal liver. Beat 2–3 raw egg yolks with 2–3 T. soft butter until smooth, combine with ground mixture, add 4–5 T. chopped fresh parsley and fold in beaten egg whites (2–3). The milk in which the bread was soaked may be added together with ½ c. bread crumbs, or enough to make a very soft and moist but not runny stuffing. Season to taste with salt, pepper, and nutmeg. (*Optional*: ½ c. pre-soaked drained raisins may also be added to stuffing.) Stuff turkey with mixture, sew up, and roast as above. To make gravy, strain pan drippings and combine in bowl with 1 T. flour for each c. drippings. Beat with wire whisk, egg-beater, or electric mixer until smooth. Add 1 t. Maggi extract and salt & pepper to taste. *Optional*: A heaping T. sour cream and 1 T. chopped fresh parsley and/or dill may be added. Simmer until smooth and bubbly. Pour over sliced turkey and stuffing on platter or serve in gravy boat.

ROAST TURKEY WITH MUSHROOM STUFFING
indyk z nadzieniem pieczarkowym

Cook turkey gizzard, heart, and neck in 4 c. water along with 1 portion diced soup greens and several peppercorns and allspice grains 1–1½ hrs., or until giblets are tender. Soak ½ lb. stale French bread in 1½ c. milk. When soggy, run through meat grinder with giblets, soup greens, and raw turkey liver. Naturally, grind only the skin and meat of neck, discarding bones. In 3 T. butter simmer 12 oz. fresh, chopped mushrooms and 2 chopped onions until tender. Combine with ground mixture, add 2 beaten egg yolks, the leftover milk if any, several T. bread crumbs, 2 beaten egg whites, 2 T. each chopped fresh dill and parsley and salt & pepper to taste. A heaping T. sour cream may also be added. Fill turkey, sew up, and roast as above, basting alternately with melted butter and a little water (about 1 c.) and later with the pan drippings. During last ½ hr. of roasting, add another 12 oz. or more chopped or thinly sliced fresh mushrooms to pan drippings and let them simmer. Pour the pan drippings and mushrooms over the sliced turkey and stuffing on platter. Or, thicken with a little flour and sour cream, simmer briefly, season to taste, and serve in gravy boat. This dish is sometimes referred to as indyk po warszawsku (roast turkey à la Varsovienne).

OLD POLISH TURKEY IN GRAVY
indyk z sosem

Salt turkey and season inside and out with your homemade Polish-style poultry seasoning and refrigerate covered at least 3 hrs. Fill cavity with 1 portion diced soup greens, an additional onion, a small bunch of dill and parsley, and fresh herbs such as lovage or tarragon. Place in roaster, add 2 c. water to pan, brush turkey generously all over with melted butter, and roast in 350° oven, allowing about 25 min. cooking time per lb. Brush frequently with butter, then baste with pan drippings that form. Remove turkey from oven and allow to cool to room temp. Discard vegetables and herbs. Slice and reheat in pan drippings. Serve with cooked barley, rice or mashed potatoes and spiced fruit (plums, cherries, pears) on the side. Or, use spiced fruit to decorate serving platter. *Note:* In modern-day Polish, this dish would probably be called indyk w sosie własnym, but we have chosen, purely for cultural flavor, the version from the familiar old drinking song *"Pije Kuba do Jakuba,"* which contains the line: *"Indyk z sosem, zraz z bigosem jadły dawne pany, dzisiaj żaby i ślimaki jedzą jak bociany."* ("On turkey, collops, hunter's stew the lords of yore did lunch—Now like storks it's snails and frogs that they prefer to munch.") The song extols the simple, hearty food of the Old Polish nobility, while ridiculing the new-fangled French eating habits which were replacing it. The interesting thing is that already several centuries ago, when this song emerged, turkey was considered a time-honored Polish dish. It must have therefore made its appearance in Poland shortly after arriving in Europe from its native America.

CRISPY-SKIN ROAST TURKEY
indyk o chrupkiej skórce

Roast turkey with or without stuffing according to any of the above recipes. During last ½ hr. of roasting, remove salt pork if you have used it, brush turkey with melted butter, and sprinkle the bird all over with fine bread crumbs. After 30 min. in oven, this should give your turkey a crispy, golden-brown crust.

ROAST TURKEY WITH RICE & PRUNE STUFFING
indyk nadziewany ryżem i śliwkami

Chop 1–1½ c. pitted prunes, place in pot, cover with a little water, and simmer until tender. Cream 2 T. soft butter with 2 raw egg yolks. Simmer 2 finely chopped onions in 2 T. butter until golden. Combine 4–5 c. cooked rice with the cooked prunes and their juice, creamed butter and yolks and sautéd onions, then fold in 2 stiffly beaten egg whites. If mixture appears too moist, add several T. bread crumbs. Season to taste with salt, pepper, several pinches of marjoram, ½ t. grated lemon rind, and 1–2 t. sugar. Mix well, stuff turkey, and roast as above.

TURKEY FRICASSEE
potrawka z indyka

Cut up ¼ of an uncooked 8–10 lb. turkey into portions or use about 2½ lbs. of your favorite turkey parts. Salt well and sprinkle with your homemade poultry seasoning. Cover and refrigerate several hrs. Place turkey in Dutch oven or other pot with tight-fitting lid, scald with boiling water to cover, bring to boil, reduce heat, and simmer covered 1 hr. Add 1 portion diced soup greens plus an onion, cover, and cook until turkey is tender. Replace any water that has evaporated. Melt 3 T. butter in saucepan, stirring in 4 T. flour, and simmer briefly without browning. Gradually stir in 2–2½ c. stock in which the turkey was cooked, beating with wire whisk until smooth. Fork-blend ½–¾ c. sour cream with 1 raw egg yolk and gradually add 1 c. of the above sauce, one spoon at a time so cream and yolk do not curdle. Transfer turkey to baking dish, drench with sauce, and bake covered in 350° oven 15 min. Before serving, garnish with a little chopped dill and/or parsley. Serve with mashed potatoes or noodles and lettuce with vinaigrette. *Variation*: Add 8–12 oz. fresh sliced mushrooms to turkey as it stews in the water in Dutch oven.

VARIOUS LEFTOVER-TURKEY DISHES
różne potrawy z resztek indyka

Despite its status as a gourmet delicacy in Polish cuisine, in the U.S. turkey is a highly economical food with great versatility. Since all the meat is rarely consumed at a single family meal or even a dinner party, the leftovers offer a wide range of possibilities for future meal planning. After removing meat from bone, cut into small cubes and freeze for future use. Even when the carcass is picked clean, it still contains plenty of flavor for a delicious, savory broth. Simply place carcass in large soup kettle, add 1 portion soup greens, several grains allspice and peppercorns, 1 bay leaf, and 2 T. salt. Pour in 2–3 qts. water and heat to boiling. Reduce heat as low as possible, cover, and simmer several hrs. You can put it on before you leave for work in the morning. When you get home, you will have the perfect stock for whatever soup you care to make. You can, of course, freeze the stock for future use. Here are a few suggestions for using cooked leftover turkey:

TURKEY, POTATO, & MUSHROOM CASSEROLE
indyk zapiekany z kartoflami i grzybami

Soak ½ oz. dried Polish mushrooms in 1 c. water 2 hrs., then cook in same water until tender. Slice thin and return to mushroom stock. Sauté 1 chopped onion in 2 T. butter until golden. Generously butter a casserole and cover bottom with 3–4 thinly sliced cooked potatoes. Add ⅓ of the sautéd onions, 1 c. diced, cooked turkey, and ⅓ of the mushrooms. Salt & pepper and repeat 2 more times. Sliced potatoes should form the top layer. Fork-blend mushroom stock with 1 c. sour cream and pour over ingredients in casserole. Cover and bake in 350 ° oven 30–45 min. Sprinkle with chopped parsley before serving.

TURKEY & NOODLE CASSEROLE
indyk zapiekany z kluskami

Cook 1 pkg. flat egg noodles according to directions on pkg. Drain. Simmer 1 chopped onion in 1 T. butter until tender. Combine the drained, cooked noodles with onions, 2–4 c. diced, cooked turkey and 1 T. chopped parsley. *Optional*: 1 bud mashed garlic may be added. Season with salt, pepper, and homemade poultry seasoning and place in well-buttered casserole. Fork-blend ½ c. sour cream with ½ c. water and 1 t. Maggi extract. Pour over turkey & noodles. Top with ½ c. grated yellow cheese of choice, dot with butter, cover, and bake in 350° oven 30 min.

TURKEY GOULASH
gulasz z indyka

Melt 3 T. butter in skillet, add 3 chopped onions, and sauté until golden. Add 8 oz. fresh sliced mushrooms, mix with onions, and brown briefly on fairly high heat. Add 3 T. water, cover, reduce heat, and simmer 15 min. Add 3 c. or more diced, cooked turkey, 1 c. canned peas & carrots, drained, ¼ c. beer, 2 buds mashed garlic, 2 t. paprika, and salt & pepper to taste. Cover and simmer on low heat 15–20 min. Stir in 1 heaping T. or more sour cream and heat thoroughly. Serve over egg noodles with sliced tomatoes on the side.

HUNTER'S STEW WITH TURKEY
bigos z indykiem

Soak ½ oz. dried Polish mushrooms in 1 c. water 2 hrs., then cook in same water until tender. Chop mushrooms and return to mushroom stock. Drain 1 qt. sauerkraut, rinse in cold water, and drain again. Place in pot, scald with boiling water to cover, and cook uncovered 30 min. Shred 1 small head cabbage, scald with boiling water to cover, and cook uncovered 15 min. Simmer 1 chopped onion in 2 T. butter until golden. In casserole, combine the sauerkraut, cabbage, onions, mushrooms, and mushroom stock. Add 3–4 c. diced, cooked turkey and ½–¾ lb. skinned Polish smoked sausage, thinly sliced. Add 1 peeled, coarsely grated apple, 1 t. Maggi extract, 1 bud mashed garlic and salt, pepper, and a pinch of marjoram to taste. Mix ingredients well, cover, and bake in 325° oven 1 hr. When cool, refrigerate overnight. Bake another 50 min. before serving with boiled potatoes or crusty rye bread. *Optional:* a jigger dry white wine or ¼ c. beer may be added to the bigos before baking 2nd time.

TURKEY GIBLETS
podróbki indycze

Turkey livers, gizzards, and hearts can be used to prepare a variety of very tasty dishes. Cook them according to any of the recipes given for chicken or goose giblets.

ROAST PIGEONS
gołębie pieczone

Mince 2 buds garlic, add 1 t. salt, and mash with flat of knife into a paste. Rub 2 washed and dried pigeons with garlic paste inside and out and sprinkle with pepper. Let stand covered in refrigerator several hrs. Lard the meaty portions of bird with sticks of very cold or frozen salt pork. Place pigeons in roasting pan lined with thin slices of salt pork, cover birds with additional salt-pork slices, and roast in 350° oven 45–60 min. or until tender. Baste frequently with butter and pan drippings. Pigeons have delicious, dark meat somewhat reminiscent of beef, but they tend to be on the dry side so the larding and basting are necessary. Split the pigeons lengthwise with poultry shears and serve with mashed potatoes, sprinkled with pan drippings, and a crunchy, grated salad containing horseradish. *Optional*: These tasty birds are also excellent stuffed like roast stuffed chicken Polonaise (p.301) or roast duck with apples (p.307).

ROAST PIGEONS PARTRIDGE STYLE
gołębie à la kuropatwa

Rub 2 pigeons inside and out with crushed juniper or sprinkle with hunter's seasoning. Sprinkle each with 1 t. vinegar, place in covered container, and refrigerate 3 hrs. Lard with salt pork, sprinkle with salt, and roast in pan lined with sliced salt pork, in 350° oven 45–60 min., or until tender. Cooking time will depend on size and age of birds. Baste frequently with butter. When the birds are tender, brush with a final coat of butter, sprinkle with fine bread crumbs, increase heat to 375°, and brown several min. *Note*: 2 heaping T. finely chopped soup greens may be added to each pigeon cavity before roasting and pigeons may be surrounded with small, peeled potatoes of uniform size which will cook in the drippings. Pigeons prepared in this way will fool anyone into thinking he's feasting on roast partridge.

* * *

ROAST GUINEA HEN
perliczka pieczona

Rub washed, dried guinea hen inside and out with salt, pepper, and ginger (about 2 t.). Place in covered container and refrigerate 1 hr. Densely lard the bird's breast and thighs with thin sticks of salt pork. Fill cavity with some chopped parsley, chopped celery leaves, and 1 chopped onion. Line pan with slices of salt pork, place bird thereon, cover with a few more salt-pork slices, brush generously with butter, and roast in 350°–375° oven 1–1½ hrs. or until tender. Be sure to also generously brush the inside of bird with butter before roasting. Peeled potatoes may be baked in roasting pan in drippings. Serve with braised beets and cucumber salad. Use only a young guinea hen, as the male of the species and older hens can be tough and dry.

ROAST STUFFED GUINEA HEN
perliczka nadziewana

Your young guinea hen, pre-seasoned and well larded as above, may be stuffed with any of the stuffings recommended for chicken, duck, goose, or turkey, but quantity must be scaled down to fill cavity no more than ⅔ full. If using apples, entire cavity may be filled since they shrink during roasting. For variety, season bird with crushed juniper berries or hunter's seasoning. For an interesting twist, add 1 T. prepared horseradish to stuffing of choice. *Remember:* Stuffed birds take a little longer to cook!

* * *

ROAST RABBIT POLISH STYLE
królik pieczony po polsku

Cut ¼ lb. white salt pork into thin sticks and freeze overnight. With thin knife, metal skewer, or sharpened stick, make incisions in 3 lb. dressed rabbit (saddle and haunch portions) and lard with salt-pork sticks. In pot bring 3 c. water to boil with 6 peppercorns, 4 grains allspice, 2 crushed bay leaves, 3 juniper berries, 1 T. salt, and 1 t. sugar. Cover and cook on med. heat 5 min. Set aside to cool. When lukewarm, add 1¼–1½ c. 6% distilled white vinegar and refrigerate. Meanwhile, finely chop and mash with ½ t. salt, 2–3 cloves garlic, and rub mixture all over rabbit. Place rabbit in crockery (not metal!) bowl, cover all sides with 1 sliced onion, drench with cold marinade including spices, cover, and refrigerate 24–36 hrs. Remove rabbit from marinade, pat dry, rub all over with butter, place in greased baking pan, and pop into pre-heated 400° oven for 15 min. so it can brown. Reduce heat to 350°, sprinkle with a little marinade, and bake covered another 50–70 min. or until tender. Baste occasionally with pan drippings. When rabbit is tender, remove from pan, and keep warm. Fork-blend 1 c. sour cream with 2–4 T. flour until smooth and mix with pan drippings. Simmer several min. and salt & pepper to taste. Place roast rabbit on serving platter, and either drench with sauce or serve it separately in a gravy boat. Boiled potatoes and braised beets are good side dishes.

ROAST RABBIT SILESIAN STYLE
królik pieczony po śląsku

Salt & pepper 3 lb. dressed rabbit. Rinse 5–10 fairly young horseradish leaves under running water. Shake off excess moisture and use them to wrap the rabbit. Soak a clean linen dish towel in mixture of ½ c. water and ½ c. vinegar. Squeeze out excess moisture until towel is damp but not dripping and wrap the rabbit in it. Place in crockery bowl, cover with plate, and refrigerate 24–48 hrs. Remove rabbit from horseradish-leaf and towel wrapping, sprinkle all over with thyme and nutmeg, cover, and set aside. In skillet, fry 4 thick strips of bacon until partially browned but still not crumbly. Place rabbit in roasting pan, pour bacon drippings over it, and cover with bacon strips. Brown in pre-heated 400° oven 15 min., then reduce heat to 350°, sprinkle with a little water, cover and bake about an hr. or until tender, basting occasionally. When rabbit is done, remove from baking pan and allow to set 15 min. at room temp. Meanwhile, bring pan drippings to boil, thicken with a little flour, and add some water as needed to get a medium thick gravy. Salt & pepper to taste and simmer briefly. Slice the rabbit and place on heat-proof platter, drench with gravy, and bake in oven 15 min. Serve with Silesian potato dumplings and stewed sauerkraut.

ROAST RABBIT COUNTRY STYLE
królik pieczony po wiejsku

Rub dressed 3 lb. rabbit all over with salt & pepper. Place in crockery bowl. With wire whisk beat whey or sour milk until smooth and pour over rabbit to cover. A t. sugar or several drops fresh lemon juice may be added to whey or sour milk. Buttermilk may also be used as a marinade. Cover and refrigerate 24–48 hrs. Remove from marinade, pat dry, sprinkle with flour, and brown on all sides in hot lard or oil. Transfer to baking dish, drench with the pan drippings in which the rabbit was browned, add several T. water, and bake in 350° oven 90 min. or until tender, basting frequently. Replace pan liquid that evaporates with water. Divide cooked rabbit into portions and drench with pan drippings on platter.

FRICASSEED RABBIT POLONAISE
potrawka z królika po polsku

Place a 3 lb. cut-up rabbit into a pot of boiling salted water and cook, skimming off scum until no more forms. Dice 1 carrot, 1 small parsnip, 1 slice celeriac, 1 leek, ¼ head Savoy cabbage, 1 onion, and 1 kohlrabi (naturally, all peeled and washed), and add to pot. When boiling resumes, reduce heat and cook covered until meat is tender. Remove rabbit and transfer to heat-proof dish. In saucepan, melt 5 T. butter, stir in 5 T. flour, and brown slightly. Add enough of the rabbit-vegetable stock to get a nice, pourable sauce, stir until lump-free, simmer several min., and season to taste with salt, pepper, and sugar. Add the soup vegetables and simmer under cover 10 min. Then switch off heat and let stand. Beat 1 raw egg yolk and stir into sauce until fully blended. Sprinkle rabbit with chopped parsley, drench with vegetable sauce, and bake 15 min. in 375° oven. Serve with cooked pearl barley and sauerkraut salad.

STEWED RABBIT GREAT POLAND STYLE (WITH PRUNES)
królik duszony po wielkopolsku

Finely chop and mash with 1 T. salt 3 cloves garlic until a paste forms and rub a 3 lb. dressed rabbit on all sides with mixture. Sprinkle generously with (preferably freshly ground) pepper and paprika and rub spices into meat, making sure you don't miss any surface or crevice. Brush rabbit all over with oil, taking care that its entire area is covered. Slice 4 onions, 2 parsnips, and 1 med. celeriac; place rabbit in crockery bowl and smother it on all sides with the vegetables. Cover tightly with plate and refrigerate 24–36 hrs. When ready to use, wipe the rabbit with damp cloth. Dice ¼ lb. slab bacon and fry to a nice golden brown. Remove bacon nuggets and set aside. In drippings brown 2 thinly sliced onions and remove from skillet. Cut up the rabbit, salt & pepper, dredge in flour and brown on all sides in hot bacon drippings. Transfer to baking pan, add the onions, pan drippings, ½ c. pitted prunes, and 1 c. water. Sprinkle with ½ t. homemade hunter's seasoning and simmer covered on low heat until meat is tender. Serve as is with boiled or mashed potatoes and braised beets, or force drippings through sieve and combine with a little boiling water and enough flour to get a nice pourable gravy. Season to taste if necessary.

RABBIT STEWED WITH MUSHROOMS
królik duszony z grzybami

Proceed as above, but instead of prunes add 12 oz. or more washed, sliced, fresh, wild or store-bought mushrooms. Omit the hunter's seasoning and simply salt & pepper to taste.

RABBIT STEWED WITH APPLES
królik duszony z jabłkami

Marinate the rabbit 24–48 hrs. according to the horseradish-leaf method in roast rabbit Silesian style (p. 323). After removing rabbit from horseradish leaf, cut up meat into 6–8 pieces, salt & pepper all over, and dredge in flour. In skillet, melt 1 stick (¼ lb.) butter or margarine and brown the rabbit in it on all sides until a golden crust forms. If you have browned the rabbit in a heavy skillet with a tight-fitting lid, then leave it there, otherwise transfer rabbit to Dutch oven. Add 4 sliced onions, 1 t. marjoram, and 2 c. water, and simmer covered on low heat 40–45 min. or until nearly done. Replace any liquid that evaporates during cooking. Surround rabbit pieces with 1 lb. peeled, sliced apples, preferably the tart cooking variety. Cover and simmer about 15 min. longer or until meat is tender and apples are fully cooked. Cover rabbit with apple slices on serving platter and top with pan drippings. If you prefer a gravy, sieve the pan drippings, thicken with a little flour, add enough water to get a smooth, pourable sauce, simmer briefly until thick and bubbly, season with salt & pepper and (optional) 1 t. vinegar. Serve with cooked rice or boiled potatoes and a red-cabbage salad or cole slaw.

FRIED RABBIT COLLOPS (FILLETS) WARSAW STYLE
filety z królika po warszawsku

This recipe requires no pre-marination in vinegar marinade, whey, or horseradish leaves. Simply cut nice slices of meat from the saddle (middle) portion of your dressed rabbit. Salt & pepper and pound with meat mallet on both sides. Refrigerate 30 min. Sprinkle fillets with lemon juice, dredge in flour, and fry in ¼ lb. butter or margarine on both sides to a nice golden brown. Drain on absorbent paper and keep warm. Cut ¾ inch thick as many slices french bread as there are fillets and fry in the drippings until golden brown on both sides. Top each slice of fried toast with a fillet and serve with french fries, cranberry sauce, and cooked cauliflower.

RABBIT ROLL-UPS
zrazy zawijane z królika

From the saddle of a rabbit that has been marinated 24–48 hrs. according to any of the methods (vinegar, whey, garlic-onion-oil, or horseradish-leaf) presented above, cut 5–6 nice slices of meat. Pound well on both sides with meat mallet, sprinkle with salt & pepper, and (optional) a little hunter's seasoning. Refrigerate 15 min. Run 2 quartered onions, 6–8 fresh washed mushrooms, and any scraps of rabbit meat left over from slicing through meat grinder. Add 1 whole egg to ground mixture, salt & pepper to taste, and add enough bread crumbs to get a filling that is spreadably soft but not mushy. Spread meat with filling and roll up tightly, tying with strong thread. Brown on all sides in hot fat, then reduce heat, add 1½ c. meat stock or court bouillon, cover and simmer 45–60 min., or until tender. Sprinkle with 1 T. or so flour, stirring gently, and add enough hot water to get a nice, pourable sauce. Simmer briefly and serve with rice and lettuce & sour cream.

RABBIT MEATBALLS/MINCED CUTLETS
mielone kotleciki/sznycelki z królika

Ground dishes are a good way to make use of the less meaty and tougher front portion of the rabbit or of older animals too tough for roasting or stewing. Break up a stale kaiser roll into a bowl and cover with ½ c. milk. Chop 1 onion and simmer until transparent in several T. butter. Cut rabbit meat away from bone and discard all membranes. Run the meat (about 1 lb.), onions, and soggy roll through meat grinder twice. Stir in 1 egg, 1–2 T. water, and work by hand to fully blend ingredients. Season to taste with salt, pepper, and hunter's seasoning, and form between palms of hand into small, flattened meatballs. Roll in bread crumbs, pressing them in, and fry on both sides to a nice golden brown in ½ stick (⅛ lb.) butter or margarine or equivalent of bacon drippings, lard, or oil. Transfer to casserole, drench with pan drippings, add 1–2 t. boiling water, and bake covered in 350° oven 20–30 min. Serve with cooked barley or Kraków groats and braised beets or red-cabbage salad.

RABBIT MEATBALLS WITH MUSHROOMS
kotleciki królicze z grzybami

Soak 2–3 dried Polish mushrooms in 2 c. water several hrs. and cook in same water until tender. Chop mushrooms and return to water in which they were cooked. Prepare rabbit meatballs as above. After rolling in bread crumbs, brown lightly in fat, and stir in 8–12 oz. washed, drained, chopped, fresh mushrooms (store-bought or wild) and 1–2 chopped onions. Gently mix mushrooms and onions into meatballs and simmer under cover 10 min. Add the cooked, dried mushrooms and their water and simmer covered about 20 min. Fork-blend ½–1 c. sour cream with 2–3 T. flour, stir in several T. of the pan liquid, then add to rabbit. Salt & pepper and simmer several min. more. Just before serving, garnish with chopped parsley and/or dill (optional).

POACHED RABBIT FORCEMEAT BALLS
pulpety z królika

Prepare rabbit meatballs, but instead of browning in fat, cook in 5 c. boiling meat stock or salted boiling water. When boiling resumes, reduce heat, cover and cook 30–40 min. Remove with slotted spoon and serve with mashed potatoes and beets with apples diet style.

This is an easy-to-digest entrée ideal for those who should avoid fried foods. *Optional*: Serve with sour cream sauce, onion sauce, mushroom sauce, or brown gravy.

POACHED RABBIT & VEGETABLES
królik z wody z jarzynami

Place 1–1½ lb. boned rabbit with membranes and veins removed into a pot containing 6 c. cold water, bring to boil, and cook 30–45 min. Add 1 coarsely chopped onion and ¼ Savoy cabbage and cook 15 min. Add 1 sliced onion, 1 thick slice diced celeriac, 1 small diced kohlrabi, and 1 t. salt, and cook another 10 min. or until all vegetables are fork-tender. With slotted spoon remove meat and vegetables to serving platter, dot with unsalted butter, and garnish with chopped dill. Serve with boiled potatoes or rice. This highly dietetic dish is recommended by Polish doctors for gallstone sufferers, patients with arteriosclerosis, and intestinal complaints as well as diabetics. *Note*: A little milk or sweet cream may be added to the leftover stock which, after simmering and seasoning to taste, produces a light, digestible soup. It can be served with cooked rice and garnished with fresh chopped dill.

OTHER GROUND RABBIT DISHES
inne potrawy z mielonego królika

Use ground rabbit meat in any of the recipes for ground pork, veal, or beef, including anything from meatballs to gołąbki. Mild-tasting rabbit blends nicely with other meats, so try it in meatloaf, using 1 part rabbit to 1 part ground pork, veal, and/or beef. Another possibility is stuffed vegetables (peppers, onions, cucumbers, etc.). Rabbit meat is truly a health food that will reduce your fat and cholesterol intake when used in place of nearly any other meat. Non-dieters concerned mainly with taste should note that rabbit variety meats (liver, hearts, and lungs) are extremely delicious in various dishes.

WILDFOWL & GAME

A major role in satiating the appetites of the meat-loving Poles was once played by wild game. Wildlife of every type, including the now extinct aurochs (*tur*) and its cousin the bison (*żubr*), abounded in the vast, forested expanses of medieval Poland, once the largest country in Europe. A surviving "shopping list" from the sumptuous 1681 wedding feast hosted by the Potockis and Lubomirskis, two of Poland's most powerful aristocratic clans, included the following: 24 elk, 30 fallow deer, 45 roe-deer, 10 chamois, 4 wild boars, 300 hares, 2,000 partridges and as many grouse, 3,000 assorted smaller game birds, 100 wild geese, 800 wild ducks, and 12 bustards.

Game in Old Poland was the sole property of the nobleman, whose land it inhabited, and poachers faced punishment if caught. Still, hungry peasants would occasionally take their chances and set snares for hare and wildfowl. But after a successful hunt, commoners could expect to legally enjoy the fruits of their toil if they had served their masters as beaters, carters, bearers, cooks, or whatever.

Wildlife continues to enjoy popularity in today's Poland, although only those with a hunter in the family can feast on it with any regularity. One of Warsaw's better restaurants, Bazyliszek, specializes in such game dishes as roast boar, elk steak, and roast pheasant. To this day, some Polish cooks make an extra effort to obtain at least half a hare at Christmas time, insisting that it adds a special touch of the great outdoors to their holiday *pasztet*. Throughout December, the keen observer can spot unskinned hares hanging head down from high-rise windows and balconies as they "age" in the cold.

Epicures the world over delight in the robust, dusky flavor of game which contains much less fat than the meat of domestic livestock. The uninitiated, however, complain of its strong, musky odor. Such off-flavors or gaminess, as some call it, are more pronounced in older animals, but hunters and game cooks have found ways to deal with the problem. Older specimens also tend to be on the tough side and require special handling.

In general, bigger game should be gutted as soon as possible after being shot, and the gonads of male specimens should be removed at the very outset, lest they impart a strong, unpleasant odor to the entire carcass. For the same reason, the urine of freshly shot hares and wild rabbits should be removed immediately by holding the animal up by its forepaws and pressing on its bladder. They may then be hung up in the cold, unskinned and uneviscerated for several weeks, during which time the meat ages and becomes more tender. An easier way is to let it age in your freezer.

Young partridge, uneviscerated and unplucked, may require only an overnight hanging before being cooked, while older birds should be aged 4–5 days. A pheasant has hung sufficiently long when droplets of clear fluid appear on its beak. Detailed instructions on how to distinguish an old animal from a younger one and how to dress, age, or otherwise handle individual species transcend the scope of this book. If you're a hunter, these things are second nature. If not, you will probably be getting your game from a butcher—dressed, trimmed, frozen, and ready for marination and cooking.

We began this chapter with a few words on marination. In general, the older the animal, the stronger a marinade and the longer a marination period is required. Young game birds (partridge, grouse, quail, pheasant, etc.) usually require no marination whatsoever. Since game can be on the tough and dry side, larding is often recommended, as you will see on the pages that follow. You will be a step ahead in preparing a tasty game dish, if you have made a batch of homemade Polish hunter's seasoning (p. 58). As we have already noted, it can also be used to produce a hunter's-style version of domestic meat and fowl.

* * *

MARINATED WILD GAME
marynowanie/zaprawianie dziczyzny

Marination is often required to neutralize the musky, gamey flavor of wild game and to help tenderize it as well. There are a number of wet and dry marinades known to Polish cuisine, of which we present only the most common.

VINEGAR & HERB MARINADE
zaprawa z octu i przypraw

Bring to boil ⅔ c. water and ⅓ c. 6% vinegar. Add 6 peppercorns, 5 grains allspice, and 3 broken-up bay leaves; simmer under cover briefly. Add about ½ c. cleaned, diced soup greens (excluding Savoy cabbage) and 1 sliced onion. Cover and let stand until cooled to room temp. Pour over cleaned, washed game in crockery bowl, cover, and keep in cool place or in fridge as specified in a given recipe. Turn meat over occasionally. Allow about 1 c. marinade per lb. meat.

WINE & VINEGAR MARINADE
zaprawa z wina i octu

In pot combine ⅓ c. each dry red wine, vinegar, and water, and bring to boil. Remove from heat, cover, and let stand until cooled to room temp. When cool, pour over game in crockery bowl and keep in cool place or fridge. Turn meat over several times a day. The above quantities are for roughly 1 lb. meat.

WINE MARINADE
zaprawa z samego wina

Dry red wine with nothing else added is often used as a game marinade. *Hint*: The marination period can be substantially reduced if wine is injected directly into meat with hypodermic syringe.

VEGETABLE MARINADE
zaprawa z warzyw

Allow about 1 c. grated vegetables for each lb. meat. Coarsely grate roughly equal amount of onions, celeriac, parsley root, and carrot. Toss with juice of ½ lemon and about ¼ c. oil, seasoning with a little salt, pepper, sugar, ground allspice, and ground bay leaf. In crockery bowl, smother meat with mixture, cover, and refrigerate about 24 hrs.

BEER MARINADE
zaprawa piwna

Dice 2–3 onions, place in pot, add 1 c. 6% vinegar, and bring to boil. Remove from heat. When cooled to room temp. add 1 c. beer and 2–3 t. partially crushed spices (pepper, juniper, cloves, and ginger), 1–2 buds mashed garlic, and a little salt. Drench meat with mixture and refrigerate in covered glass or crockery bowl about 24 hrs., turning meat several times. This amount of marinade is for 2–4 lbs. of game.

RYE-SOUR MARINADE
zaprawa z zakwasu żytniego

A typical peasant marinade was rye-sour, the tart liquid formed when rye flour was allowed to ferment several days in a large amount of water (see soup chapter). Simply cover the meat with rye-sour in crockery bowl, cover, and refrigerate 12–24 hrs.

DAIRY MARINADE
zaprawa mleczna

Fresh or sour milk, buttermilk or whey, can also serve as a gentle marinade for both game and domestic meat. Simply cover meat with liquid in crockery bowl and refrigerate overnight. This is recommended mainly for young game, as the meat of older animals requires a stronger vinegar and/or wine marinade.

DRY HERB MARINADE
zaprawa sucha z przypraw

For each lb. game partially crush in mortar 5 peppercorns, 5 grains allspice, 1 t. juniper berries, 1 bay leaf, and a pinch of thyme. Rub spices into meat, intersperse with onion slices, and keep in covered crockery bowl in cool place 2–4 days. *Note*: Partially crushed juniper can be used alone, in which case use anywhere from 2 t. to 1½ T. per lb. of meat. Always use more for older, strong-smelling animals.

* * *

BRAISED HARE POLONAISE
zając duszony po polsku

Wash well, cut up, and rub with dry herb marinade (minus the onions) the saddle and hind legs of a nice hare. Place in crockery bowl, drench with ½ c. 6% vinegar, cover and refrigerate overnight. Remove from marinade, rinse well and soak in cold water 1 hr. Place in Dutch oven, cover with cold water, bring to boil, and drain. Cover with fresh cold water, add 1 bay leaf, 5 grains allspice, 5 peppercorns, 5 juniper berries, and about 2 t. salt. Bring to boil, reduce heat, cover, and simmer about 90 min. Add 2–3 chopped onions and continue simmering until hare is tender. Replace any liquid that evaporates. Fork-blend 1 c. sour cream with 2–3 T. flour, gradually stir in about 1 c. pan liquid, and add mixture to Dutch oven. Bring to boil, reduce heat, and simmer covered about 10 min. Stir in 2 t. Maggi seasoning and salt & pepper to taste. Serve with mashed potatoes and braised beets & apples. This is the authors' favorite way of preparing hare, since it comes out more tender and juicy than many other recipes. We often serve a leek salad on the side.

ROAST HARE IN SOUR CREAM POLONAISE
zając po polsku

In crockery or glass bowl drench the saddle and thighs (back portion) of a nice 6–7 lb. hare with wine & vinegar marinade. Cover, refrigerate, and marinade 2–4 days, turning meat over each day. Rinse hare, lard generously with salt-pork sticks, and sprinkle all over with salt. In roasting pan, melt 4 T. lard, place hare in pan, baste with lard (*Optional*: Cover with slices of salt pork), and bake in 350° oven about 2 hrs., or until tender. Baste frequently with pan drippings. When hare is fully cooked, remove from pan. When cool enough to handle, cut into portions. Fork-blend 1 c. sour cream with 2 T. flour and stir in the pan drippings. Salt & pepper to taste. If necessary, add a little boiling water to make a thick, pourable sauce. Return hare to pan, drench with sour-cream sauce, cover, and bake another 15 min. Serve with mashed potatoes and braised beets. This is the classic Polish way of serving hare, now Poland's most common wild-game dish. Be sure not to confuse the dark-meat, dusky-flavored European hare (*zając* in Polish, *Hase* in German, and *lièvre* in French) from the white-meat domestic rabbit (*królik*, *Kaninchen*, and *lapin* respectively). If you do not have access to imported European hares, the next best thing is America's major representative of the hare family: the western jackrabbit (Lepus californicus).

HARE IN CURRANT SAUCE
zając z sosem porzeczkowym

Marinate saddle of hare in wine & vinegar marinade overnight. Lard generously with salt pork, brush generously with butter, and roast in 350° oven about 2 hrs., or until tender, basting frequently with pan drippings. In pot, combine ½ c. dry red wine, ½ c. currant jelly, ⅛ t. each pepper, nutmeg, and cloves, and bring to boil. Add 1 t. prepared horseradish and the pan drippings. Pour over hare and bake covered another 15 min. Serve with hash-browned potatoes and red-cabbage salad.

HARE ROLL-UPS
zrazy z zająca zawijane

Cut small ¾ inch thick slices of pure meat (free of membranes, gristle, etc.) from the saddle of a young hare (jackrabbit), and soak in cold, fresh milk 1 hr. Dry. With moistened meat mallet beat each slice on both sides until very thin but still unbroken. Sprinkle with salt & pepper and (optional) hunter's seasoning, place a slice of bacon and a slice of boiled ham on each hare cutlet (the bacon and ham should be the same length as the meat), top with a slice of lemon (with rind and seeds removed) and 3–4 capers. Roll up tightly, tie with thread, sprinkle with salt, and brown on all sides in ¼ lb. melted butter. Reduce heat, cover, and simmer until tender, basting with the butter frequently and turning roll-ups over so they cook evenly. Serve with buckwheat groats and braised beets. After browning, the roll-ups may be transferred to baking dish, drenched with the butter, and baked covered in medium oven. They will be even better if 8–12 oz. sliced fresh mushrooms are added during last ½ hr. to simmer in the buttery pan drippings. A T. dry red wine may also be added towards the end.

ELK (jeleń)

WILD BOAR (dzik)

HARE (zając)

HARE MEAT LOAF
klops z zająca

Nearly all roast hare recipes call for the animal's meaty back portion (saddle and thighs). The less meaty front portion (ribs, shoulder, and forelegs) is usually reserved for ground dishes like pâté (see appetizers), meat loaf, and various minced cutlets and meatballs. The hare's giblets are very good in such dishes but they must be removed from a freshly killed hare to prevent spoilage and used immediately or frozen. Since the hare ages best when hung up intact, many cooks sacrifice the giblets, which must be discarded when the animal is finally gutted. But back to our recipe. . . . Remove all bones, tendons, gristle, etc., from the lungs, liver, and heart. Liver may be soaked in 1 c. cold milk 1 hr. Soak 3 stale kaiser rolls, broken up, in 1½ c. milk until soggy. Run the meat and giblets through a meat grinder with the soggy rolls, 1 lb. uncooked bacon, and 1 large skinned, brine-cured dill pickle. Simmer 2 finely chopped onions in 3 T. butter until golden and add to mixture. Add 1 t. lemon juice, grated rind of 1 lemon, 2 eggs, and salt & pepper. Mix well to combine ingredients evenly and add just enough bread crumbs to get a workable consistency. Line baking pan with strips of salt pork. Form meat mixture into a loaf and place on salt pork in pan. Top with additional slices of salt pork, sprinkle with 1 T. melted lard, and bake in 325° oven 1½ hrs. During baking, baste frequently with water and then with the pan drippings that form. The meat loaf slices best when cold. Place the cold slices in the pan drippings, drench with 1 c. sour cream, liquified by fork-blending, and allow to simmer several min. Salt & pepper to taste. Garnish with a little chopped fresh dill and/or parsley. Serve with buckwheat groats or mashed potatoes and grated carrot, apple, & horseradish salad.

ROAST WILD RABBIT
dziki królik pieczony

Rub cleaned wild rabbit (cottontail) with pepper, crushed or powdered bay leaf, 1 T. grated lemon rind, and 1 bud mashed garlic. Smother with 2 sliced onions, cover, and refrigerate overnight. Next day, salt rabbit. In baking dish lightly brown several slices salt pork, place rabbit on top of salt pork, cover with a stick (¼ lb.) butter, cover, and bake in 350° oven 1½ hrs., or until tender. Serve with potatoes, rice, or barley and a grated salad containing horseradish.

WILD RABBIT BAKED WITH MUSHROOMS
dziki królik z pieczarkami

Lard cleaned wild rabbit with salt pork. Melt 1 stick (¼ lb.) butter in baking dish, add rabbit, turning to ensure that all sides get nicely buttered. Add 1 chopped onion, 2 thinly sliced carrots, 12 oz. sliced fresh mushrooms, 5 peppercorns, 2 cloves, and 1 bay leaf. Pour in 1 c. water, cover, and bake about 90 min. in 350° oven or until meat is tender. Baste occasionally with sour cream (1 c.). When rabbit is done, salt and serve with boiled potatoes or noodles and lettuce with vinaigrette.

FRIED WILD RABBIT
dziki królik smażony

Cut up wild rabbit and drench with vinegar & herb or wine & vinegar marinade. Cover and refrigerate several hrs., turning the meat a few times. Dry well. Dredge pieces in flour, dip in 2 eggs, salted and beaten with 2 T. beer, then roll in mixture of 1 c. bread crumbs and ½ c. finely grated carrot. Press in breading so it doesn't fall off during frying. Brown on all sides in 5–6 T. hot oil until a nice golden crust forms, then reduce heat, cover, and simmer until meat is tender. Rubbing meat with 1–2 buds mashed garlic before breading will perk up the flavor of this tasty dish. Serve with fried potatoes and cucumber & sour cream salad.

MINCED WILD RABBIT CUTLETS
kotleciki z dzikiego królika

Soak cleaned, cut-up wild rabbit in milk overnight. Remove bones, ligaments, gristle, etc., so you have only pure meat. Run meat through meat grinder with ½ lb. salt pork and 1–2 onions. Add 2 beaten eggs and enough bread crumbs to get a workable consistency. Season to taste with salt, pepper, nutmeg, and a pinch of rosemary. Work well to blend ingredients and form into small, 2 inch oval patties about ¾ inch thick. Dip in 3 salted eggs, beaten with 2 T. beer, roll in bread crumbs, and fry until cooked through in several T. oil. Serve with mashed potatoes and leek & apple salad.

ROAST WILD BOAR
pieczeń z dzika

Remove veins from a 3–4 lb. leg or shoulder roast of a fairly young boar and place in non-metal bowl. Prepare vinegar & herb marinade, omitting vegetables, and scald meat with 3 c. boiling marinade. Cover and refrigerate 24 hrs. or longer. Dry meat, lard with salt pork, beat on all sides with rolling pin, sprinkle with flour, and brown on all sides in 5 T. hot lard until a golden crust forms. Add 3–4 chopped onions and brown briefly in pan drippings, then sprinkle meat with 1 c. water and 1 T. marinade, reduce heat and simmer covered 2 hrs. or until it is fully cooked. This can be done on stove top in Dutch oven or in covered baking dish in medium oven. Baste frequently with pan drippings. Cool roast to room temp. in covered baking dish, then chill in refrigerator. Slice thin when cold. Simmer boar slices in pan drippings several min. Fork-blend 1 c. sour cream, 2–3 T. tomato paste, and 1–2 T. flour. Combine with pan drippings and simmer several min. Add a little boiling water if needed to get a smooth, pourable gravy. Season to taste with salt & pepper. Serve with potatoes or buckwheat groats, braised beets, and non-creamed salad of choice.

ROAST BOAR IN CHERRY SAUCE
pieczeń z dzika z wiśniami

Proceed as above, except after slicing the cold meat, do the following. In pot combine 1 lb. pitted sour cherries, 1 c. dry red wine, grated rind of ½ a lemon, ⅓ c. ground, blanched almonds, 3 T. sugar, and a pinch or 2 ground cloves. Cook on medium heat until cherries are tender, then cover and set aside. Brown 2 T. flour in 3 T. butter and stir in ¾ c. strained pan drippings. Simmer until smooth and bubbly and combine with cherry mixture. Pour cherry sauce over sliced boar and simmer several more min. Serve with boiled potatoes and leek salad. *Note*: If you don't have fresh cherries, you can use 2 c. canned cherry-pie filling, but omit sugar and flour.

ROYAL BOAR STEW
królewskie ragoût z dzika

Cut 3 lbs. boar meat from neck or shoulder into ½ x 1 inch pieces, discarding any veins, gristle, etc. Rub meat with 1 bud mashed garlic and 1 crushed bay leaf. Place in crockery or glass bowl (a casserole dish is good), smother meat with 1 portion diced soup greens, and drench with 1½ c. dry red wine. Cover and refrigerate 2–3 days. Remove meat from marinade, dry, and brown on all sides in ½ c. hot lard. Transfer meat to baking dish, sprinkle with thyme, cover with marinade, including vegetables, and bake covered in slow oven until meat is tender. In 3 T. of the lard cook 8 oz. fresh sliced or chopped mushrooms. Make a roux from 1 T. flour and 1 T. butter and add to sieved vegetables (in which meat was cooked) along with the mushrooms. Simmer briefly, adding a little boiling water if needed to get a pourable sauce. Stew meat in sauce briefly and garnish with a little chopped fresh parsley. Serve with potatoes, groats, or rice and beet & horseradish relish (ćwikła).

ROAST BABY BOAR WITH POLISH STUFFING
warchlak z polskim nadzieniem

Salt a cleaned baby boar well and let stand 1 hr. Chop fine 2–3 onions and sauté until golden in 3 T. lard. Soak 2 c. bread crumbs in 1 c. milk. Grind the heart and liver. Cream ¼ lb. butter (½ c.) with 3 raw egg yolks. Combine ingredients, fold in 3 stiffly beaten egg whites, and season with salt & pepper, marjoram, several pinches of nutmeg, and several T.

chopped fresh parsley. Fill baby boar with mixture and sew up. Increase or decrease the amount of stuffing depending on the size of your animal. Roast on rack in pan uncovered in 350° oven, brushing often with melted lard and beer, then with the pan drippings. You will need about 1½–2 c. lard and the same amount of beer. Roasting time will depend on the size of your baby boar. It is done when fork tender and when juice that oozes out is no longer pink. *Note*: Baby boar can also be stuffed with any of the stuffings recommended for roast suckling pig.

MINCED BOAR ROLLS
zrazy mielone z dzika

Soak 2 kaiser rolls in 1 c. milk and, when soggy, run through meat grinder with 2 lbs. boneless boar meat and ¼ lb. salt pork. Finely dice a little more salt pork (a heaping T.), brown in skillet, add 1–2 finely chopped onions, and simmer until they just begin to brown. Add onions and salt pork to ground mixture along with 2 beaten eggs, 1–2 buds mashed garlic, and salt, pepper, and marjoram to taste (rather generously). Work mixture well and add about 1 c. bread crumbs, or enough to get a fairly firm consistency. Roll small pieces of mixture between palms into ¾ x 2 inch rolls, dredge in flour, and fry in 1 c. hot oil. After the outside browns, reduce heat and cook until done, testing one for doneness. Serve with buckwheat groats and braised beets. If you like, transfer meat to baking dish, drench with 1 c. liquified sour cream, and simmer covered about 15 min. in medium oven.

OTHER WILD BOAR DISHES
inne potrawy z dzika

In general, boar meat can be prepared like beef (roasts, steak roll-ups, pounded fillets) or pork (roasts, cutlets, loin, etc.), but remember it is tougher than beef and much leaner than pork. It is therefore a good idea to marinate and lard the meat before cooking or (in the case of cutlets, fillets, and roll-ups) give it an extra good pounding. Garlic, juniper, thyme, and rosemary are the ideal seasonings, or simply use your homemade hunter's seasoning. The variety meats (giblets) can be prepared like pork liver, heart, tongue, lungs, and brains, but liver should first be soaked in cold milk at least 1 hr. Ground boar can be prepared like any of the ground pork and beef dishes, but grind at least ¼ lb. salt pork with each 2 lbs. of boar meat so it doesn't turn out too dry. *Note*: If you're a hunter, you can take aim at wild boar in parts of the American South and Southwest, where this is not sport for the timid. A 300 lb. charging, wounded boar, grunting menacingly with tusks poised for action, has sent many a hunter scampering up a tree for safety. If this is not your cup of tea, you can get boar meat, usually frozen, at food shops specializing in wild game in larger American cities. Especially good are smoked boar ham and sausage.

VENISON IN SOUR CREAM
sarnina w śmietanie

Marinate 3 lb. piece of deer meat (leg portion) in vinegar & herb or vinegar & wine marinade 1–3 days, depending on age of specimen. Remove any veins and membranes, lard with salt pork, sprinkle with salt, and brown on all sides in 4 T. hot lard. Transfer to Dutch oven, add 1 c. water and several T. marinade, add 1 portion diced soup greens plus an onion or 2, and simmer under cover, basting occasionally with marinade. Cook on stove top or in 350° oven 1½–2 hrs., or until tender. Remove meat and let set at room temp. 20 min. Meanwhile, fork-blend 1 c. sour cream with 1–2 T. flour and mix with pan drippings. Simmer briefly, stirring constantly. Season to taste with salt, pepper, and 1 t. Maggi extract. Heat the sliced venison in the sour cream sauce and serve with potatoes or buckwheat groats, braised beets, or cooked vegetables of the cabbage family.

ROAST VENISON ROYALE
pieczeń sarnia po królewsku

Marinate, lard, and cook the venison as above. Brown 2 T. flour in 3 T. butter, stirring in 1 c. meat stock to form a smooth sauce. Add ¼ c. dry red wine and bring to boil. Add 1 thinly sliced lemon (with rind and seeds removed), ⅓–½ c. pre-soaked, drained raisins, and a heaping T. whole-style cranberry sauce. Simmer briefly and pour over sliced venison. Simmer about 5 min. Serve with fried potatoes and lettuce & sour cream salad.

VENISON STEW
gulasz z sarniny

Remove any veins and membranes from 2 lb. piece of venison (leg or shoulder portion), cut into small cubes, scald with 1½ c. boiling vinegar & herb marinade, cover, and refrigerate 2 hrs. Dry meat, sprinkle with rosemary, powdered juniper, and pepper, dredge in flour, and brown on all sides in 4–5 T. hot lard, adding 2 chopped onions when meat is browned on one side. Add several T. water, cover, reduce heat, and simmer until meat is tender. Add ½ lb. peeled, sliced apples, a heaping T. powidła (or domestic plum jam), ¼ c. ground, blanched almonds, and 2 T. grated black bread. Toss ingredients and simmer covered until apples are fully cooked. Serve with buckwheat groats or barley and grated vegetable salad of choice.

VENISON ROLL-UPS WITH MUSHROOMS
zrazy zawijane z sarniny z grzybami

Slice 2 lb. leg of venison into 2 x 3 inch rectangles about ½ inch thick. Remove any veins and membranes. Sprinkle with dry marinade and stack slices one on top of the other. Wrap in aluminum foil and refrigerate several hrs. Wash well ½ lb. wild mushrooms to remove all grass and sand. Chop and simmer with 2 chopped onions in ¼ lb. diced salt pork until mushrooms are tender. Remove from heat. Sprinkle with salt and caraway. Scrape spices from meat and wipe it with damp cloth. With meat mallet, pound the slices on both sides until very thin. To mushroom mixture add 1 beaten egg, mix well, and add 1 or more T. bread crumbs to get a soft stuffing. Spread meat with stuffing, roll up tightly, and tie with string or fasten with toothpicks. In Dutch oven, heat 4–5 T. lard and brown the rolls up on all sides. Add 2 chopped onions, ½ c. dry red wine, and bake in medium oven covered 1½–2 hrs. It may also be simmered on low in heavy covered skillet. When done, sprinkle with a little flour, and mix with drippings until absorbed. Season to taste with salt & pepper, about 1 t. sugar, and 2 t. lemon juice. Simmer briefly and serve with buckwheat groats or potatoes of choice and lettuce with mayonnaise. Good wild mushrooms to use in this dish are honey mushrooms (opieńki) or chantrelles (kurki), but the best of all is the bolete (borowik, prawdziwek). If none of these are available, you can always fall back on the white mushrooms from your produce department, but these are a bit too bland to stand up to full-flavored meat like venison.

MINCED VENISON ROLLS
zraziki z sarniny

Remove veins and membrane from 1 lb. boneless venison. Marinate for 1 hr. if it is from an older deer. Rinse. Run through meat grinder with ¾–1 lb. fatty boneless pork and 2–3 kaiser rolls, pre-soaked in 2 c. milk until soggy. Add 2 eggs and a raw grated onion. Mix ingredients well and add some bread crumbs if mixture appears too wet and mushy. Add grated rind of ½ a lemon and salt & pepper to taste. (*Optional*: Mince and then mash 2 canned anchovy fillets, mix with 2 heaping T. butter, and work into mixture. If you haven't any anchovies or don't care for them, add only the butter.) Knead mixture well and roll into 3 inch rolls about 1–1½ inches thick, small oval patties or meatballs, and fry in a little hot lard until golden brown on both sides and cooked through. Serve with mashed potatoes and stewed sauerkraut or cabbage. Also good is zesty cranberry sauce. (In blender, simply blend 1 c. canned whole-style cranberry sauce, 1 heaping t. prepared horseradish, 1 level t. sugar, and 1 t. lemon juice until smooth.)

OTHER VENISON DISHES
sarnina inaczej

Venison can be prepared according to the recipes given for beef, especially roll-ups, pounded fillets, roasts, stews, and ground meat dishes, but be sure to marinate the meat one way or another before cooking. The tastiest venison is provided by fawns and young does, but their availability in your area will largely depend on local hunting regulations. Deer variety meats are also good, especially the liver of young deer.

ELK STEAK
stek z jelenia

Cut 2–3 lbs. boneless leg of elk into portions. If the meat is from a young elk, you may omit the marination. Sprinkle the slices with pepper and thyme and pound with meat mallet to a thickness of about ¼ inch. Dredge in flour, shaking away excess, and brown in several T. hot oil. Scald 2–3 tomatoes with boiling water, peel and cut into quarters. Peel, core, and quarter 2–3 apples. Add to steak together with 1–2 jiggers dry red wine, cover and simmer on low heat until meat is tender. Season to taste with salt, lemon juice, and a little sugar. Serve with french fries (p. 450), cauliflower Polonaise (p. 520) and radish salad (p. 544). *Note*: Elk may be prepared the same way as deer meat (venison), but it may be a bit tougher. Your best bet is a young doe or a buck with only the first trace of sprouting antlers. In terms of eating enjoyment, buying frozen game is often a better alternative, since freezing tenderizes the meat.

ROLLED MOUFLON ROAST
rolada z muflona

Cut a 2–2½ lb. rectangular piece of boneless meat from the leg of a mouflon (wild sheep). Pound well with meat mallet to flatten. Rub with 2 buds mashed garlic, sprinkle with salt, and smear with 1 T. brown mustard. Clean well ½ lb. wild mushrooms, wash, rinse, and cook with 1 chopped onion in several T. butter until tender. When mushrooms have cooled, add 2 beaten eggs. Skin and chop 2 brine-cured dill pickles, skin and dice 1 knackwurst (serdelek), add to mushrooms, mix and spread over meat. Roll meat up tightly and tie with string. Brush generously with butter and bake in covered roasting pan in 350° oven 1½–2½ hrs., or until tender. Alternate brushing with butter and sprinkling with water during baking. When meat is tender, remove, and allow to set 20 min. at room temp. It will be even easier to slice when cold. Add 3 T. dry red wine and 1 T. flour to pan drippings and simmer until a nice, pourable sauce forms. Reheat sliced roast in sauce. *Note*: Mountain goat can be used in this recipe, but its meat is tough and could do with a little marination before cooking.

ROAST MOOSE
pieczeń z łosia

Scald a 4 lb. moose leg roast with 3 c. boiling wine & vinegar marinade and refrigerate in crockery bowl, tightly covered, 5–7 days, turning meat each day. When ready to use, cut at least ½ lb. salt pork into thin sticks. Roll salt-pork sticks in a mixture of salt, pepper, and marjoram, and lard the meat. If you don't have a larding needle (and these are hard to find even in Poland these days!), thread the salt-pork sticks on a thin wire skewer. Make deep incisions in meat the length of the sticks with a sharp, pointed narrow knife and force the salt pork all the way in. Hold the salt pork in with one hand and pull the skewer out with the other. Place meat in roasting pan. Brush all over with melted butter and bake covered in 325° oven 2½–3 hrs., or until tender. Use at least ¼ lb. butter for basting and alternate with sprinkles of marinade and then with the pan drippings. Allow meat to set at room temp. 20 min., then slice. Stir 2 T. flour into pan drippings and, when dissolved, add 1 c. sour cream. Whisk while simmering to get a smooth sauce, then simmer sliced meat in it several min. Serve with potatoes, groats, braised beets, or red cabbage salad. *Note*: Use only young moose meat as that from an old bull moose is tough and stringy and suitable for only ground meat dishes. Although moose are now a rarity in Poland, we have decided to include this recipe for both cultural and practical reasons. At one time moose was an important item in the diet of the Old Polish nobility, as attested to by the old adage: *"Musi pan wołu zarżnąć, gdy łosia nie dostanie."* ("The lord of the manor must butcher an ox, when moose cannot be had.") Secondly, who knows if copies of this book won't reach readers in such places as Alaska or northern Wisconsin or Ontario where moose are still abundant?

ROAST PHEASANT
bażant pieczony

Salt a cleaned pheasant inside and out and let stand 1 hr. Place a whole, peeled, raw potato and a small piece of salt pork into the cavity and sew up. Lard the breast and thighs with salt pork. Dice a small piece of salt pork (about 1 heaping T.), melt in saucepan but do not brown, add 4 T. butter, 4 crushed peppercorns, and small, sliced onion and simmer until onion is golden and just begins to brown. Transfer to baking dish, add pheasant and 1 c. meat stock and roast in 350° oven 1½–2 hrs., or until tender, basting frequently with pan drippings. Place the pheasant on one side, then the other during roasting so it gets nicely browned on all sides. Serve drenched with pan drippings along with potatoes (french fries are good), lettuce, and cranberry sauce.

PHEASANT (bażant)

WOODCOCK (słonka)

PARTRIDGE (kuropatwa)

GROUSE (jarząbek)

PHEASANT STEWED IN MEAD
bażant duszony w miodzie

Salt & pepper cleaned pheasant inside and out, sew up, place in baking dish, drench with ¼ lb. hot butter. Add a thinly sliced carrot and onion, ½ a sliced lemon (with rind and seeds removed), 1 bay leaf, 5 peppercorns and 2 cloves, plus ¼–½ c. mead (Polish honey wine). If miód pitny is not available, another sweet white wine may be used. Cover and bake in 325° oven 90 min., or until fork tender. Cut pheasant into portions. Add ½ c. sour cream to pan drippings and simmer until smooth, then add pheasant and simmer several min. longer. Serve with mashed potatoes or rice and sliced tomatoes.

ROAST STUFFED PHEASANT
bażant z nadzieniem

Stuff pheasant with any of the stuffings recommended for domestic poultry. Polonaise (bread & giblet) stuffing and apples (with or without a spoonful of cranberry sauce added) are especially good. Sew up. Lard with salt pork, and roast in 350° oven, alternately basting with pan drippings and sprinkling with red dry wine (about ¼ c.). Towards end of roasting, add 5 crushed juniper berries to pan drippings. Cut up pheasant and simmer in drippings several min.

STEAMED PHEASANT
bażant gotowany w parze

Line a baking dish just large enough to tightly enclose pheasant with thin slices of salt pork. Sprinkle with thyme, pepper, and 1 crushed bay leaf. Salt pheasant inside and out and place several sprigs parsley and a small quartered onion in cavity. Place pheasant in baking dish. Combine ½ c. flour with enough water to make a thick paste. Cover baking dish and seal the lid with the flour paste so no steam escapes during cooking. Place baking dish in a pan of water in oven and bake at 325° about 2 hrs. Discard the flour-paste crust around the lid. Remove pheasant and cut up. Add 2 T. sherry to pan drippings and simmer the pheasant therein several min. Serve with rice (saffron rice is an elegant possibility) and string beans & mushrooms.

ROAST GROUSE
jarząbek pieczony

Salt 2 cleaned, ruffed, or sharp-tail grouse inside and out and let stand 1 hr. Lard breasts with salt pork, cover birds with thin slices of salt pork, and (optional) tie with thread to keep them in place. Transfer to pan and drench with ¼ lb. hot butter. Roast in 350° oven, basting frequently with pan drippings and turning birds on all sides to brown evenly. Towards end of roasting add 5 crushed juniper berries, 5 crushed peppercorns, ¼ t. grated lemon rind, and 1 T. grated onion to pan drippings, and simmer grouse in their sauce a while until very tender. Serve with rice or potatoes and zesty cranberry sauce.

STEWED GROUSE
jarząbek duszony

Cut up 2 grouse into quarters, salt, and let stand 1 hr. In skillet, simmer 1 heaping T. diced salt pork (about ⅛ lb.) until pale golden and add ¼ c. butter. Simmer grouse in the fat, turning frequently. After 30 min., add ½ c. sweet cream, a pinch or 2 nutmeg, and ½ c. bread crumbs. Stir ingredients, cover, and simmer on very low heat until grouse is tender. Salt & pepper to taste.

GROUSE WITH HAM & MUSHROOMS
jarząbek duszony z szynką i pieczarkami

Cut up 2 cleaned grouse, sprinkle with salt, and brown on all sides in ¼ lb. or more butter. To prevent butter from burning, first heat 2–3 T. oil and then add butter. Remove grouse and set aside. In pan drippings simmer 4 oz. sliced, fresh mushrooms and ¼–½ c. diced, boiled ham. Add ¼ c. dry red wine and 1 crumbled bay leaf, place the grouse in sauce, cover tightly, and simmer on very low heat 1 hr. or until grouse is very tender. Serve with rice and mayonnaise-laced salad of choice. *Note*: Partridge may be prepared according to any of the above recipes for grouse which, in turn, can be cooked like any of the partridge dishes presented below.

PARTRIDGE IN SOUR CREAM
kuropatwy w śmietanie

With poultry shears split 2 partridges in half lengthwise. Salt & pepper and set aside. Meanwhile, melt 1 stick butter (¼ lb.) in heavy skillet and in it simmer 1 chopped onion until golden. Add the birds, basting with butter. Add 7 crushed peppercorns and 5 grains crushed allspice. Cover and simmer on low heat, basting with pan drippings and about ½ c. fork-blended sour cream until partridges are tender. In dry saucepan brown 2 t. flour, stirring in another ¼ c. sour cream. Add mixture to skillet, salt & pepper to taste, and simmer a bit longer. Garnish with a little chopped parsley. Serve with mashed potatoes and spiced plums, cherries or pears.

PARTRIDGE HUNTER'S STYLE
kuropatwy po myśliwsku

Salt and lard 2 partridges and brown on all sides in ¼ lb. hot butter. To each bird's cavity add 1 small sliced onion, a rye-bread crust, and 5 crushed juniper berries. Add ½ c. water to skillet, cover, and simmer until tender. Cut partridges into portions, sieve sauce, and pour it over the meat on platter. Serve with boiled potatoes and a vinegary salad.

PARTRIDGE STEWED IN SAUERKRAUT
kuropatwy duszone w kapuście

Lard 2 mature (larger) partridges, sprinkle with salt, and brown lightly in 4 T. fairly hot lard on all sides, adding 2 thinly sliced onions. Reduce heat, baste with drippings, cover, and simmer on low heat. Meanwhile, drain 1 qt. sauerkraut, rinse in plenty of cold water, squeeze out moisture in collander, and chop. Place in pot, add 1 c. meat stock, and cook 30 min. Add sauerkraut and 2 T. dry white wine to partridges and simmer until meat and kraut are done. Brown 1 T. flour in dry saucepan, stir in several T. pan liquid and add to sauerkraut. Simmer briefly. Season to taste with salt, pepper, 1 t. Maggi extract, and (optional) 1 level t. sugar. Several dashes mushroom powder or Polish sauerkraut seasoning also won't hurt. Serve with boiled potatoes. Instead of sauerkraut, this dish may be prepared with a small head of cabbage, nicely shredded, but cook in meat stock only 15 min. before adding to birds.

QUAIL WITH MUSHROOMS
przepiórki z pieczarkami

Sprinkle 8 quail with salt & pepper inside and out. In skillet melt 1 stick butter, add 2 small, thinly sliced onions and 4–8 oz. sliced fresh mushrooms. Sprinkle with 1 T. chopped parsley, place the quail on top and simmer 10 min., turning birds to brown lightly on all sides. Sprinkle with 2 T. flour, add 1 c. water and ½ c. dark beer (bock, stout, porter), and simmer under cover until birds are tender. They will be done in no time. Allow at least 2 quail per person, although a hearty eater can easily polish off half a dozen of these tasty little birds himself. Serve with potatoes or rice and tomatoes stuffed with pea salad.

QUAIL BAKED IN FOIL
przepiórki pieczone w folii

Sprinkle 8 cleaned quail inside and out with a little hunter's seasoning and salt. Into each cavity place a T. butter and 1 thin onion slice. Wrap each bird with a thin slice of salt pork and place on a square of alumium foil. Brush generously with melted butter and wrap in foil. Bake in 350° oven 25–30 min. Check one for doneness. Serve with potatoes cooked in jackets and Brussels sprouts Polonaise (p. 520).

QUAIL IN SAUERKRAUT
przepiórki w kapuście

Prepare like partridge stewed in sauerkraut, but use 6 quail. Cook sauerkraut in meat stock 45–60 min., or until fully cooked, before adding to birds.

ROAST WILD DOVE
dziki gołąb pieczony

Salt 2 cleaned wild doves, place ½ a stick butter in each cavity, and sew up. Wrap with slices of salt pork and tie with thread to keep them in place. Roast in 350° oven, sprinkling with a little water and then pan drippings that form, until birds are tender. Turn birds frequently during roasting so that all sides get nicely browned. Split doves in half with poultry shears, place on platter, and drench with pan drippings. Serve with boiled potatoes and floured carrots. Lettuce & radish salad dressed with sour cream or mayonnaise sauce is a nice accompaniment.

WILD DOVE IN CURRANT SAUCE
dziki gołąb w sosie porzeczkowym

Salt 2 wild doves and sprinkle with hunter's seasoning. It is best to lard the breasts of older birds with salt pork. Melt 1 stick butter in Dutch oven, add 2 thinly sliced onions, and brown the doves on all sides. Add ½ c. meat stock, cover, reduce heat, and cook about 45 min., turning birds frequently. In saucepan, combine ½ c. red-currant jelly, ¼ c. dry red wine and ¼ c. water, add grated rind of ½ a lemon, and bring to boil. Pour over the doves and continue simmering until they are nice and tender. Thicken sauce with 2–3 T. grated stale honey-spice cake (piernik). Serve with rice and grated carrot, celeriac, & apple salad.

STUFFED WILD DOVE
dziki gołąb nadziewany

Grind the livers, gizzards, and hearts of 2 wild doves along with 6 or so fresh boletes (or store-bought fresh mushrooms) and simmer in ½ stick butter about 5 min. Remove from heat. Add 2 beaten eggs, ½ c. bread crumbs, 3 T. milk, 1 grated onion, and mix ingredients well. Season with salt, pepper, and a pinch or 2 nutmeg. Stuff birds, sew up, and bake covered in 350° oven, drenched with at least ½ stick butter. Baste frequently with pan drippings and turn birds over to brown evenly. Serve with boiled potatoes and zesty cranberry sauce. Birds should be done in 1–1½ hrs.

ROAST WOODCOCK OR SNIPE
słonka lub bekas pieczony

Salt & pepper 8 cleaned birds with heads left on. Into each cavity place 2 crushed juniper berries, a pinch of chopped parsley, and 1 T. butter. Tuck the neck under each bird's right wing, wrap whole bird with a thin slice of salt pork, tie in place with strong thread, and bake in 1½ sticks butter in 350° oven about 30 min., turning occasionally. Remove thread, place cooked birds on a platter of saffron rice, and drench with pan drippings. The heads with their long pointed beaks will remain tucked under the wing for an interesting culinary effect. Woodcock and snipe may also be prepared according to any of the recipes for grouse, partridge, or quail. The breasts of larger birds can be larded with salt pork. Quail, woodcock, and snipe, wrapped with salt-pork slices can be roasted over a campfire on an improvised spit or in an electric rotisserie. In either case, they should be generously basted with butter during roasting.

ROAST WILD DUCK
dzika kaczka pieczona

Rub cleaned duck with salt and waterfowl seasoning or hunter's seasoning. Place in baking pan, brush with ½ stick butter, add 1 portion chopped soup greens, 1 t. grated lemon rind, and bake covered in 350° oven about 2 hrs. or until tender. During baking baste with another ½ stick butter and then with the pan drippings. Turn duck over once or twice. Occasionally sprinkle with dry red wine (about ¼ c.). This method is good for a younger, more tender wild duck. Serve with potatoes or rice and braised red cabbage.

ROAST WILD DUCK A DIFFERENT WAY
dzika kaczka pieczona inaczej

Boil the duck in water 20 min. Drain. When cool, lard with salt pork, sprinkle inside and out with salt, pepper, marjoram, and caraway. In Dutch oven, melt ½ stick butter, add 2 small, sliced onions, and 1–2 buds minced garlic. Brown onions partially, add duck, and brown in butter and onions 15 min. Add 1 c. meat stock, cover, reduce heat, and cook until duck is tender (1½–2 hrs.). You can shorten cooking time by cutting duck into portions first. Add 1 T. dry red wine and 1 t. Maggi extract to pan drippings, thicken with a little flour, and dilute with boiling water if necessary to get a smooth, pourable sauce. Simmer duck in sauce several min. Salt & pepper to taste. Serve with boiled potatoes and stewed sauerkraut & mushrooms.

WILD DUCK IN RED CABBAGE
dzika kaczka w czerwonej kapuście

Cut wild duck into portions. If it is on the lean side, lard breast and thighs with salt pork. Sprinkle with salt and 3–5 crushed juniper berries (or dust with hunter's seasoning). Melt ½ stick butter in Dutch oven and brown the duck in it on all sides. Add 1 c. meat stock or water, reduce heat, cover, and simmer on low heat 1½ hrs., replacing liquid that evaporates. Separately, shred 1 small red cabbage, mix with 1 chopped onion, scald with boiling water to cover, and bring to boil. Drain and add to duck. Toss ingredients so duck is smothered in cabbage, cover, and cook covered on low heat until duck is fork tender. Season to taste with salt, pepper, vinegar (1–3 T.), dry red wine (1–2 T.), and sugar (1–2 t.). Sprinkle with 2 T. flour, toss to absorb excess liquid, and simmer duck several more min. Serve with boiled potatoes sprinkled with caraway seeds. Wild goose is excellent prepared the same way, but double the amount of red cabbage and other ingredients proportionately.

BAKED WILD GOOSE
dzika gęś pieczona

Cut up wild goose, place in crockery bowl, drench with 1 c. wine & vinegar marinade. Cover and refrigerate overnight, turning goose several times. Remove from marinade, rinse in cold water, pat dry, and rub all over with salt, pepper, a little nutmeg and crushed cloves. Place in roaster, brush with 1 stick butter, cover, and bake in 350° oven 2–2½ hrs. or longer, depending on age and size of goose. Turn pieces over occasionally. Sprinkle with 1–2 t. water and reduce heat if necessary to prevent burning. When goose is tender, stir ½ c. liquified sour cream into drippings and simmer in sauce several min. longer. Serve with boiled potatoes or buckwheat groats and cooked vegetable. This way is best for an older wild goose.

WHOLE ROAST WILD GOOSE
dzika gęś pieczona w całości

Salt a young wild goose and sprinkle with caraway seeds or crushed caraway and pepper inside and out. Place in roaster, drench with 1 stick melted butter and roast at 350° about 25 min. per lb. or until fork tender. Sprinkle with water several times and baste often with pan drippings. Whole peeled potatoes may be added to roaster during last 30 min. or so to cook in the drippings. *Optional*: Stuff goose with peeled, cored apple halves before roasting and sew up. If you like, mix a heaping T. whole-style cranberry sauce or 1 pre-soaked, ground kaiser roll with apples before stuffing.

WILD GOOSE OR DUCK IN OTHER WAYS
dzika gęś lub kaczka inaczej

Wild goose and duck may also be prepared according to any of the recipes given for domestic goose and duck, but one thing should be borne in mind. Whereas domestic waterfowl often have too much fat, the meat of their wild cousins is on the dry side and requires larding with salt pork and basting with plenty of butter. The older wild birds in particular can usually do with some marination before cooking both to tenderize the meat and offset that excessively "gamey" flavor.

ROAST BEAR (WITH MUSHROOMS) POLISH STYLE
pieczeń z niedźwiedzia po polsku

Trim away and discard all visible fat from a 2–3 lb. boneless bear roast, preferably leg portion. Wash well, pat dry and cover with vinegar & herb or wine & vinegar marinade. Refrigerate 24 hrs. if using young bear meat and longer if your roast comes from an older animal. Remove from marinade, pat dry, sprinkle with hunter's seasoning, dust with flour and in Dutch oven brown all over in hot fat. Remove meat. In drippings lightly brown 2–3 sliced onions, then return meat, sprinkle with a little dry white wine, add 1 c. vegetable stock and simmer on very low heat under cover until tender, replacing liquid that evaporates. This may take 2–2½ hrs. for bear cub and an hr. or more longer for an older specimen. When roast is almost tender, add 8 oz. washed, trimmed and sliced fresh boletes or other wild mushrooms about 20–30 min. before cooking ends. Into pan drippings stir about ½ c. sour cream fork-blended with 1–2 T. flour. Simmer briefly, season to taste, thin with a little stock if needed and whisk into a smooth, creamy sauce. Slice roast and drench with sauce on platter. Serve with groats or potatoes and braised beets. Braised red or Savoy cabbage is also a good side dish.

HONEY-BRAISED BEAR PAWS
łapy niedźwiedzie w miodzie

This is one of those fabled dishes once enjoyed by the Old Polish nobility and kept alive today mainly by literature and legend. Skin, wash and scald 2 bear paws and remove tendons and sinews. Place in pot, cover with hot court bouillon and simmer covered on low heat until tender. Divide each paw into 4 and set aside. In skillet sauté in a little fat 2–3 sliced onions until tender and slightly browned. Dust with flour and toss to coat evenly, then add 1 c. coffee cream or half & half, 1/4 c. dry white wine, juice of 1 lemon and 1–2 t. capers. Simmer briefly and season to taste with salt, pepper and a little honey. Add the bear paws and simmer covered on very low heat about 10 min. Serve with potatoes and braised Savoy cabbage or a horseradish-flavored grated vegetable salad. *Note:* Since bears are now a protected species in Poland, we had originally not intended to include any recipes. Then we ran across an item in a major American newspaper about a resurging interest in bear meat and other exotic game. Throughout the northwoods of the U.S. and Canada bears are a far from extinct species, so hopefully the above two recipes may come in handy to some of our readers.

BISON POT ROAST PEASANT STYLE
pieczeń z żubra po chłopsku

Known in Polish as król puszczy (king of the wilds), the mighty forest-dwelling bison is a close cousin to America's plains-dwelling buffalo which has in recent years won new devotees for its lean and tasty meat. To prepare this old Polish peasant dish, trim 2½–3 lbs. boneless bison (buffalo) round steak of any membranes, place in glass or crockery bowl, cover with rye sour and refrigerate for 12–24 hrs. Remove meat from marinade, dry, dust with flour and brown on all sides in several T. hot fat in Dutch oven. As meat browns, add 2–4 chopped onions and allow to brown slightly. Reduce heat, sprinkle with several T. rye sour and simmer covered until tender. During cooking, sprinkle with a little sweet cream and baste with pan drippings that form. Pot roast may be cooked on stove top or in 350° oven according to preference. When meat is tender, slice thin against the grain and place in baking dish. Season with salt, pepper and (optional) a little Polish hunter's seasoning. Sieve pan drippings, add a little stock and flour as needed, bring to boil, reduce heat and simmer briefly, whisking to get a smooth pourable sauce. Season sauce, pour over sliced meat and bake in 375° oven about 10 min. Serve in baking dish with boiled potatoes and stewed sauerkraut on the side.

BISON STEAK À LA JAGIEŁŁO
befsztyk z żubra à la Jagiełło

The above peasant roast notwithstanding, in Old Poland bison was often the meat of royalty. This dish was named after the great 15th-century monarch Władysław Jagiełło, who joined the Polish Kingdom with the Grand Duchy of Lithuania to create the largest country in Europe. He was also an avid huntsman and lover of game dishes. Wash and remove membrane from a 1–1½ lb. bison (buffalo) tenderloin, slice into 1 inch steaks and pound with moistened meat mallet. Soak ½ c. pitted prunes in ½ c. warm water 5 min., then cook in same water until they disintegrate. Add 1 t. grated lemon rind, 1 T. freshly grated horseradish root, salt, pepper and lemon juice to taste and simmer briefly. Add ½ c. dry red wine, mix well and set aside. Salt & pepper steaks, dust with flour and brown in hot fat on both sides. Top with prune mixture, reduce heat and simmer several min. Serve with potato puffs and a grated vegetable salad.

OTHER BISON DISHES
inne potrawy z żubra

Bison meat may be prepared according to any of the recipes given for beef or venison. Larded roasts, collops stewed in sour cream, roll-ups with filling of choice and goulashes or fricassees are especially good.

MEAT & VEGETABLE
AND VEGETARIAN DISHES

Although meat has been regarded as the most coveted food since the dawn of Polish history, from the earliest times it was also known to be paired with different vegetables. Nobody way back then realized that vegetables helped to neutralize meat's natural acidity, but perhaps someone discovered that they eased the heartburn often caused by eating too much meat. Those less well off largely used vegetables as an economical "stretcher" when there wasn't enough meat to go round. In time people developed a taste for certain combinations, and perhaps that's how *gołąbki* were born.

Gołąbki (literally: little pigeons) have long been viewed as a dish typical of Polish and other Slavic cuisines, although similar foods are also found in other cultures, to mention only the Greek stuffed grape leaves. Even though Polish stuffed cabbage rolls filled with meat and rice are undoubtedly the most common in America, this particular dish offers endless possibilities limited only by personal preference, available ingredients and a given cook's culinary flair.

We therefore urge you to treat our *gołąbki* recipes only as general guidelines, not as hard and fast rules, and feel free to modify, "doctor up" or improve on this or that according to whim. Polish cooks, after all, have always regarded cooking as an art, not a science.

Stuffed cabbage rolls are only one of an extensive family of meat & vegetable dishes which include other stuffed vegetables as well as an endless array of fricassees and casseroles. Only some of them have been presented here because, as we have repeatedly stressed, creativity and individualism are the essence of Polish cookery. Any leftover cooked vegetables can be the basis for a new creation, if you throw in some diced cooked meat and/or cold cuts, stir in a spoonful of sour cream, simmer to heat thoroughly and blend flavors and season it all to taste. A sprinkling of garden greens is highly recommended.

The same holds true for purely vegetarian dishes made without meat, although Polish cooks often use meat drippings or fried salt-pork nuggets in their preparation. In addition to the vegetable cutlets, savory puddings and batter-fried vegetables included in this chapter, many of the items presented in the cooked-vegetables chapter as side dishes can also double as main hot-supper courses.

To end on a nutritional note, growing health awareness has turned yesterday's poor people's food into today's rational choice. For both meat & vegetable, as well as fully vegetarian dishes, are high in fiber, vitamins and other nutrients and help cut down on fat and cholesterol. Some researchers even claim that certain vegetables, notably beans, actually neutralize the effects of excessive cholesterol. We wouldn't go that far, but we do believe that this family of foods has a lot going for it by being tasty, nutritious and economical.

* * *

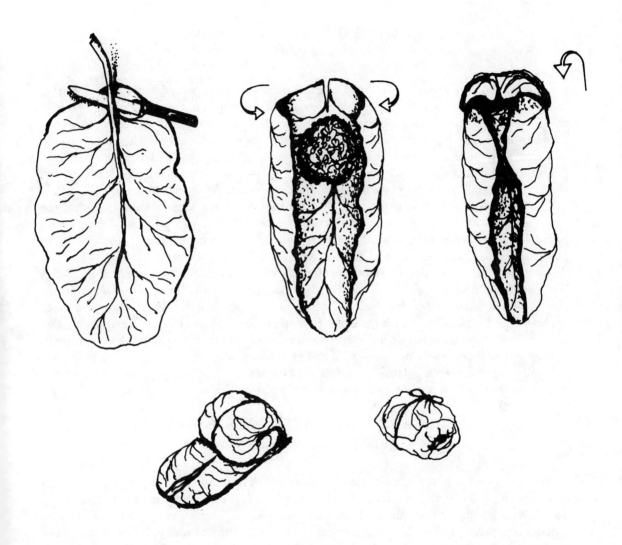

Shown above is the step-by-step preparation of gołąbki (stuffed cabbage rolls) which starts by wilting a cored head of cabbage in boiling water. Next the tough stem or vein is trimmed from the individual leaves which are topped at stem end with filling and rolled up as illustrated, tucking in the sides.

STUFFED CABBAGE ROLLS
gołąbki

Cut out the core from a 3 lb. head of cabbage and remove wilted outer leaves, setting them aside for later use. Place the cabbage core-side-down into a pot of boiling water to cover and cook several min. Remove the softened outer leaves and set aside. Continue cooking and removing leaves until you get to the undersized ones which should also be reserved. Trim the thick center vein from the bottom of each large leaf. Another way is to pound it a bit with a meat mallet to soften it, taking care not to damage the leaf. Place a roll (about 3 heaped T.) of filling (see recipes below) at center perpendicular to the stem. Fold sides of leaf over filling and then roll up, starting at the stem end. Some cooks tie the cabbage rolls with a thread, but this isn't really necessary if you carefully place them seam-side-down in roasting pan. Line the roaster with ½ the wilted, damaged, undersized or otherwise unused cabbage leaves, as this prevents your gołąbki from burning. Place the cabbage rolls in roaster side by side in preferably 2 but no more than 3 layers. Pour 2–3 c. liquid over the cabbage rolls. This can be court bouillon or meat stock, the water in which the cabbage was par-boiled (in which 1–2 bouillon cubes may be dissolved) or tomato sauce of choice (see below). Cover with remaining unused cabbage leaves to prevent scorching and bake in 350° oven (covered or uncovered) about 2 hrs. Switch off oven and let them stand at least 30 min. before serving. Serve with boiled, mashed or purée potatoes. Fresh salads are generally not served with gołąbki. This dish will be even tastier if refrigerated overnight and reheated the next day, allowing flavors to blend and mature.

CABBAGE ROLLS WITH RICE & MEAT
gołąbki z ryżem i mięsem

Simmer 1–2 finely chopped onions in several T. butter until golden and tender and combine with 2–3 c. slightly undercooked rice and ½–1 lb ground pork, pork & beef or pork, beef & veal combination. Mix in 1 raw egg and season to taste with salt, pepper and (optional) paprika. (Other flavoring possibilities include pork seasoning, hunter's seasoning and/or 1–2 buds mashed garlic.) Combine ingredients well and fill cabbage leaves as above. For cabbage rolls in tomato sauce, use any of the following: 1) fresh tomatoes, peeled, diced and simmered in a little cabbage water briefly; 2) canned stewed tomatoes; 3) canned tomato sauce; 4) tomato paste diluted to taste with cabbage water; 5) ketchup mixed with a little cabbage water; or 6) canned tomato soup, straight from the can or diluted with a little cabbage water. Whichever you prefer, pour a little tomato sauce of choice over each layer of gołąbki in roaster, but the most over the top layer. Salt & pepper each layer and bake as above. Another way is to bake gołąbki with 2 c. or so cabbage water. When cooked, fork-blend 6 T. tomato paste with 1 c. or so cabbage water and 1 T. flour until smooth, bring to boil, salt & pepper (a little sugar may also be added) and pour over cabbage rolls on serving platter. For a smoother, richer-tasting sauce, stir in a heaping T. sour cream. *Note*: Instead of tomato sauce, any of the following are also very good. Soak ½–1 oz. dried Polish mushrooms in 2 c. water 2 hrs., then cook in same water until tender. Chop mushrooms and distribute them evenly between layers of gołąbki in roaster. Combine ½ the mushroom liquid with 2 c. court bouillon, pour over cabbage rolls and bake. When nearly done, fork-blend remaining mushroom liquid with 1 c. sour cream and 1–2 T. flour, salt & pepper and pour over gołąbki. Allow to simmer 10–15 min. For sour cream sauce, fork-blend 1½ c. or more sour cream with 2–3 T. flour and enough cabbage water to get a thick, pourable sauce. Season with salt, pepper and Maggi extract or a bouillon cube dissolved in several T. hot water. Heat to boiling and pour over gołąbki. Simmer 5–10 min. Garnish with chopped parsley and/or dill just before serving. Instead of a thick sauce, for a change of pace bake the cabbage rolls with 2 c. or so meat stock court bouillon added. When cooked, dice and fry ¼ lb. white salt pork until you get golden, crunchy nuggets. Pour nuggets and as much of the drippings as you like over gołąbki on serving platter.

CABBAGE ROLLS WITH RICE & SAUSAGE
gołąbki z ryżem i kiełbasą

Substitute ½–1 lb. skinned, ground smoked or fresh kiełbasa or even knackwurst, frankfurters or bologna for the raw meat. Otherwise, proceed as above. Other possibilities include finely diced or ground cooked meat or smoked fish.

CABBAGE ROLLS WITH MEAT
gołąbki z mięsem

Soak 2 stale, crumbled-up kaiser rolls in ¾ c. milk until soggy. Simmer 1–2 finely chopped onions in several T. butter until they just begin to brown. Run soggy rolls through meat grinder, combine with the onions, ¾–1 lb. ground pork or pork & beef, 1 raw egg. Mix well and season with salt, pepper and (optional) pork seasoning or hunter's seasoning. Fill cabbage leaves with mixture and proceed as with cabbage rolls with rice & meat.

CABBAGE ROLLS WITH GROATS & MUSHROOMS
gołąbki z kaszą i grzybami

Soak 1 oz. dried Polish mushrooms in 2 c. water for 2 hrs. and cook in same water until tender. Reserve liquid, chop mushrooms fine and mix with 3 c. cooked buckwheat groats or fine barley. Add 2 chopped onions simmered in 3 T. butter, 1 T. chopped parsley and 2 eggs. You may first add just the yolks and then fold in the stiffly beaten whites. Add some bread crumbs if mixture is too wet and mushy. Season generously with salt & pepper and (optional)

1 t. Maggi extract. Fill cabbage leaves with mixture and bake with 2 c. cabbage water or court bouillon about 2 hrs. Fork-blend 1 c. sour cream with 1 T. flour, the mushroom liquid, 1 t. Maggi extract and bring to boil. Add 1 T. butter and salt & pepper to taste. Pour sauce over gołąbki in roaster and simmer briefly or over gołąbki on serving platter. *Note*: Instead of dried mushrooms, 12–16 oz. fresh mushrooms may be used. Chop the cleaned mushrooms and simmer in butter with the onions until tender, then add to groats. Add 1 t. mushroom extract to the sour cream sauce. In a pinch, you can use canned cream of mushroom sauce as your sauce base. Dilute it with enough of the cabbage water to get a thick, smooth sauce and season to taste with salt, pepper, 1 t. liquid mushroom extract and/or 1 t. Maggi extract. Bring to boil and pour over gołąbki. Such meatless cabbage rolls are sometimes served on Wigilia (Christmas Eve).

CABBAGE ROLLS KURPIE STYLE WITH CHICKEN & GROATS
gołąbki po kurpiowsku

Combine 2–3 c. finely diced or ground cooked, boneless chicken. (Cooked turkey, goose or duck may also be used.) Simmer 6 oz. chopped fresh mushrooms and 1 chopped onion in several T. butter until tender. Combine the above with 2 c. or more cooked buckwheat groats, 2–3 ground hard-boiled eggs, 1 raw egg, 1 T. chopped dill or parsley and season with salt, pepper, and several pinches marjoram. Mix well and fill cabbage leaves. Place in roaster, add 2 c. chicken stock and bake 1½ hrs. in 350° oven. As always, line the bottom of roaster and top the gołąbki with unused cabbage leaves to prevent scorching. Serve drenched with sour cream or mushroom sauce. This variety of cabbage roll is a specialty of the Kurpie district of northeast Poland.

CABBAGE ROLLS WITH MUSHROOMS
gołąbki z grzybami

Wash well and dice 1½ lbs. fresh wild mushrooms. Boletes (prawdziwki, borowiki) are best, but honey mushrooms (opieńki, podpieńki), morels (smardze), chantrelles (kurki), and others are also good. In a pinch, you can use the white, store-bought mushrooms. Simmer the mushrooms in 3–4 T. butter with 3 finely chopped onions 15–20 min. or until fully cooked. When cool, stir in ¾ c. bread crumbs and 1 large raw egg. Mix well. Salt & pepper rather generously and fill cabbage leaves with mixture. Place gołąbki in pan, dot each layer generously with butter, add 2 c. court bouillon or cabbage water and bake in 350° oven 1½ hrs. All gołąbki are tastier if allowed to remain in switched-off oven 20–30 min. before serving. Meanwhile, lightly brown 1 small, diced onion in 1 T. butter. Dilute with 1 c. court bouillon or 1 c. cabbage water in which 1 bouillon cube has been dissolved. Stir in ½ c. sour cream, bring to boil, salt & pepper to taste, and pour over cabbage rolls on serving platter.

CABBAGE ROLLS WITH MUSHROOMS & EGGS
gołąbki z grzybów i jaj

Soak 1 stale, broken-up kaiser roll in ½ c. milk until soggy and grind. Wash well and dice 12 oz. wild or domestic fresh mushrooms and simmer in 3–4 T. butter with 2 chopped onions 15–20 min., or until fully cooked. When cool, combine with ground roll, 3 T. uncooked instant cream of wheat and 3 finely chopped or ground hard-boiled eggs. Add 1 T. or more chopped parsley and/or dill, mix well, and salt & pepper to taste. Fill cabbage leaves with mixture. Place in roaster, add 2 c. court bouillon, and bake at 350° 1½ hrs. Drench with onion sauce on platter.

CABBAGE ROLLS WITH GROATS & CHEESE
gołąbki z kaszy i sera

Dice and lightly brown 1 fairly large onion in 3 T. butter. Combine with 3 c. cooked buckwheat groats and ½ lb. grated or ground farmer cheese (homemade or store-bought). Stir in 2 raw eggs and mix well. Season with salt, pepper, marjoram, and a little sugar. Fill cabbage leaves, place gołąbki in pan, add 2 c. court bouillon and bake in 350° oven about 1½ hrs. Drench with sour cream sauce and garnish with chopped dill on serving platter.

CABBAGE ROLLS WITH RICE & EGGS
gołąbki z ryżu i jaj

Cook 1–1½ c. rice in double the amount of court bouillon. When cool, combine with 4 finely chopped or ground hard-boiled eggs, 2 diced onions sautéd in 3 T. butter, 1 raw egg, and 2–3 T. chopped dill. Mix well and season with salt, pepper, and 1 t. Maggi extract. Fill cabbage leaves and bake in roaster (with 2 c. cabbage water added) at 350° 1½ hrs. Serve with sour cream sauce or tomato sauce. *Note*: For a change of pace, use fine cooked barley in this and other gołąbki recipes that call for rice.

CABBAGE ROLLS WITH HAM & MUSHROOMS
gołąbki z szynką i pieczarkami

Soak 1–2 stale, broken-up kaiser rolls in ½–1 c. milk until soggy and grind. Simmer 16 oz. chopped fresh mushrooms in 3 T. butter until fully cooked and combine with ground roll. Add ½–¾ lb. finely diced boiled ham, 2 raw egg yolks. Fold in 2 stiffly beaten egg whites, mix well and season with salt, pepper & nutmeg. Fill leaves with mixture and place in pan. Fork-blend 1 c. sour cream and 1 c. cabbage water with 3 T. flour and pour over gołąbki. Bake in 350° oven 1½ hrs.

CABBAGE ROLLS INTERLACED WITH SAUERKRAUT
gołąbki przekładane kwaszoną kapustą

Instead of any of the various tomato mixtures, add a tart twist to your rice & meat, rice & sausage, or meat gołąbki. Drain 1 pt. sauerkraut, reserving liquid. Rinse, drain, chop, and intersperse layers of gołąbki in roaster with sauerkraut. Mix 1½ c. cabbage water (in which the cabbage was par-boiled) with ½ c. sauerkraut liquid and 1 t. sugar. Pour over gołąbki and bake at 350° 2 hrs. The layers of sauerkraut may be sprinkled with salt, pepper, and caraway seeds, if you like. Serve as is or garnish with fried salt-pork nuggets and their drippings.

OLD POLISH (PORK & BARLEY) CABBAGE ROLLS
gołąbki po staropolsku

Finely chop 1–1½ lbs. pork including the fat. (Coarsely ground pork may also be used but the original Old Polish recipe calls for chopped pork!). Combine with 2 c. cooked pearl barley. Wash well, drain, and chop 8 oz. fresh store-bought or wild mushrooms and simmer under cover in several T. butter or lard with 1–2 finely chopped onions until tender. Combine meat & barley with mushrooms & onions, fold in 1–2 slightly beaten eggs, work by hand into uniform mixture, and salt & pepper to taste. Fill wilted cabbage leaves with mixture and roll up. Line bottom of roaster with damaged or undersized cabbage leaves (reserving some of them for the top), arrange cabbage rolls along bottom side by side, top with another layer of cabbage rolls, and scald with 1½ c. hot meat stock. Cover with remaining leftover cabbage leaves to prevent scorching, cover, and bake in 350° oven 1 hr. Add 2 c. rye sour and bake another hr. Switch off heat and allow to set in oven another 30 min. Remove to serving platter and drench with golden-brown salt-pork nuggets and their drippings.

RED CABBAGE ROLLS SILESIAN STYLE
gołąbki z modrej kapusty po śląsku

Remove the core from a 2 lb. head of red cabbage and immerse it cored-side-down in a pot of boiling, salted water to which 1 T. vinegar has been added. Bring to boil and cook several min. Remove wilted outer leaves and continue cooking until all nice-sized leaves are removed. Set leaves aside to drain. Meanwhile, crumble 3–4 stale kaiser or french bread type rolls into a bowl, cover with cold meat stock and allow to soak until soggy. Squeeze out excess moisture and grind. Combine with 1 lb. skinned, smoked kiełbasa chopped as finely as possible, 2 whole eggs, and 3–4 T. chopped fresh parsley. Work mixture by hand until ingredients are well blended and salt & pepper to taste. Fill and roll up cabbage leaves. In a Dutch oven lightly brown 1 heaping T. diced salt pork and line the cabbage rolls up along the bottom. Make no more than two layers. Scald with 3 c. hot meat stock, cover, and cook on med. heat on stove top or in moderate oven (350°) about 1½ hrs. In skillet fry up ¼ lb. diced slab bacon until nicely browned and somewhat crunchy. Remove gołąbki to serving platter carefully with slotted spoon and drench with browned bacon nuggets and their drippings.

SAVOY CABBAGE ROLLS
gołąbki z włoskiej kapusty

Wrinkly Savoy cabbage gives a daintier touch to this hearty peasant dish. Use it to prepare any of the above gołąbki recipes instead of ordinary white cabbage.But remember: the leaves are more tender, so less par-boiling is needed to wilt them. Or try the interesting recipe below which was specifically designed for Savoy cabbage.

BREADED CABBAGE ROLLS
gołąbki panierowane

Remove core from head of Savoy cabbage and par-boil to remove leaves as with ordinary cabbage. Then return removed leaves to pot and simmer on very low heat until they are fully cooked. Remove very carefully so they don't tear and drain on absorbent paper. Fill leaves with gołąbki filling of choice, although we personally feel these are best with the meatless mushroom or egg fillings. Handle with care because the fully-cooked leaves of Savoy cabbage are more fragile than those that are only wilted. Dredge in flour, dip in beaten eggs, roll in bread crumbs, gently pressing in breading, and fry in hot oil to a nice golden brown on all sides. We think you will enjoy these change-of-pace gołąbki.

STUFFED CABBAGE
kapusta faszerowana

Remove wilted outer leaves from a 2½–3 lb. cabbage. Cut cabbage into quarters, place in boiling salted water to cover, and cook 5–10 min. Drain in colander and, when cool enough to handle, press out excess water by hand, taking care not to damage leaves. Combine ¾–1 lb. ground, raw pork & beef, 1 ground kaiser roll (pre-soaked in milk), 1 raw egg, ¼ c. bread crumbs, and salt, pepper to taste. Add several T. milk if mixture is too stiff. With knife carefully spread thin layer of meat mixture between cabbage leaves. Some cooks then tie the cabbage quarters with thread, but if you place them close together in a tight-fitting baking pan, they shouldn't fall apart. Add 1 c. boiling water to pan and bake in 350° pre-heated oven 60–95 min., or until done, replacing liquid that evaporates. In saucepan lightly brown 3 T. flour in 2 T. butter, dilute with 2 c. meat stock or court bouillon, add 2 t. caramelized sugar dissolved in 2 T. hot water, and season to taste with salt, pepper, and a little vinegar. Pour off cabbage pan liquid, bring sauce to boil, pour over cabbage quarters, and bake in 375–400° oven 10–15 min. Serve with boiled, or purée potatoes.

STUFFED CABBAGE ANOTHER WAY
kapusta faszerowana inaczej

Proceed as above, but spread cabbage leaves with filling made as follows. Combine ¾ lb. ground pork, 1 c. cooked rice, 1 finely chopped onion lightly browned in 1 T. lard, 1 raw egg, 2 T. chopped parsley, and salt & pepper to taste. Bake in 350° oven, adding 1 c. meat stock, 60–90 min., or until tender, transfer to platter, and drench with tomato sauce. This tastes quite a bit like meat & rice gołąbki.

STUFFED CABBAGE LITHUANIAN STYLE
kapusta faszerowana po litewsku

Prepare cabbage as in the first stuffed-cabbage recipe (above), but fill with the following mixture. Mix ¾ lb. ground lamb with heaping T. diced beef suet that has been ground with 2 raw onions. Add ¼ c. bread crumbs, 2–3 buds crushed garlic, and 1 raw egg and work by hand to blend ingredients. Season with salt, pepper, and generously with marjoram. After spreading mixture between leaves, tie each quarter with a strong thread and brown on all sides in 3 T. hot butter. Transfer to baking dish. In butter drippings brown 1 T. flour and pour over cabbage. Add 1 c. boiling water to pan, cover, and simmer in 325° oven 65–90 min. or until tender. Transfer to serving platter, sprinkle with bread crumbs, and drench with pan drippings. *Note*: Both ordinary white cabbage as well as wrinkly Savoy cabbage may be used in the above stuffed-cabbage recipes, but it is best to choose a head that is not too tightly packed and has loose-fitting leaves.

STUFFED CABBAGE WITH MUSHROOM FILLING
kapusta faszerowana z nadzieniem grzybowym

Wash well, drain, and dice fine 6–8 oz. fresh, wild, or cultivated mushrooms, and simmer under cover in 3 T. butter and 2 T. water with 2 finely chopped onions 15 min., or until fully cooked. Uncover and steam off moisture. Combine with 1½ c. cooked rice, 2 raw eggs, and 2 T. chopped dill. Add some bread crumbs if mixture is too moist. Salt & pepper and spread mixture between cabbage leaves as above. Place tightly in baking pan. Brown 1 T. flour in

1 T. butter, dilute with 1 c. court bouillon, stirring until lump-free, and pour over cabbage quarters. Cover and bake at 350° 30–40 min., or until tender. On serving platter garnish with Polonaise butter-browned bread-crumb topping. *Note*: This dish can also be made with dried Polish mushrooms, pre-soaked, cooked, and finely chopped. Pour the mushroom liquid over the cabbage in baking dish and bake as above. Instead of the bread-crumb topping, this dish is delicious drenched with sour cream sauce (with the mushroom water added when using dried mushrooms).

ROGUE'S BEEF & SAUERKRAUT STEW
bigos hultajski

Rinse well 1 qt. sauerkraut, drain, place in pot, add 2 c. beef stock, 1 T. lard or salt-pork drippings, and salt & pepper, cook 30 min. Dice ¾ lb. boiled beef (cooked in the beef stock) and add to kraut. In 2 T. lard or salt-pork drippings brown ½ lb. skinned, sliced, smoked kiełbasa and add to pot. In the pan drippings, brown 1 chopped onion and 1 T. flour, add to pot and cook another hr. or so. Serve with rye bread or potatoes in jackets. This simplified version of Poland's famous bigos, combined with its intriguing name, conjures up images of a group of horse thieves, poachers or the like, huddled round a campfire and ready to break camp the minute the gendarmes or game wardens get too close for comfort.

STUFFED PEPPERS
papryka nadziewana

Cut the tops from 8–12 green peppers, scoop out seeds and membranes, wash well inside and out, and set aside to dry. Combine 2–3 c. cooked rice with ¾–1 lb. raw ground pork or pork & beef, 2–3 chopped onions slightly browned in 2 T. lard, 1 raw egg and salt, pepper, and paprika to taste. Mix well. Sprinkle inside of peppers with salt & paprika and fill with mixture. Place upright close together in baking pan, separating peppers from each other with ½ inch-thick tomato slices. Also place a tomato slice on top of each pepper. Pour 2 c. tomato juice over peppers, cover, and cook in 350° oven 45–60 min. or until fully cooked. Add a little water during baking if too much of the tomato juice evaporates. Beat ½ c. milk with 1 raw egg and 1 T. flour, season with salt & pepper, and pour over peppers. Brown uncovered about 10 min. Serve with potatoes or noodles. Although not as popular as gołąbki, this culinary import from Hungary and the Balkans has numerous enthusiasts in Poland and has been around as long as anyone can remember. *Variations*: Ground cooked meat (leftover roasts etc.) can be used instead of raw meat, and cooked fine barley can replace the rice. The peppers may also be stuffed with any of the rice fillings recommended for gołąbki.

STUFFED PEPPERS ANOTHER WAY
papryka nadziewana inaczej

Use 10 of the narrower, mild, yellow peppers that come to a point, remove tops, scoop out seeds, wash, and drain. Finely chop 2–3 onions and brown lightly in 5 T. oil. Add ½ t. paprika, ⅓ c. uncooked rice, and simmer in oil several min. Add 1 c. water, mix and cook on low heat 10–15 min., or until mixture thickens. Remove from heat, cover and let stand until cool. Add mixture to ½–¾ lb. ground pork or pork & beef, season with salt & pepper, and mix well. Fill peppers with mixture and lay them on their side in baking pan. Add 1 c. water and bake covered in 350° oven 45–60 min., replacing water that evaporates during baking. Fork-blend 1 c. plain yogurt with 1 raw egg yolk, 1 T. flour, and enough pan liquid to get a smooth, thick sauce. Salt & pepper to taste, simmer briefly, and pour over stuffed peppers on serving platter. *Optional*: Add 1 t. Maggi extract to yogurt sauce.

STUFFED KOHLRABI
kalarepa nadziewana

Wash and peel about 8 young, smallish kohlrabis and scoop out center. Cook the scooped-out portion in a little salted water until tender and drain. Soak 1 stale, broken-up kaiser roll in ½ c. milk until soggy and grind together with the cooked kohlrabi. Combine mixture with ¼ lb. ground pork, add an egg, mix well, and season with salt, pepper, and marjoram. Fill kohlrabi with mixture. Place kohlrabi upright in buttered baking dish close together, add enough water to reach halfway up the kohlrabi, along with 1 T. fat, and bake covered at 350° until fork tender. Fork-blend 1 c. sour cream with 1 T. flour and enough pan drippings to get a smooth, pourable sauce. Bring to boil and season with salt & pepper. Spill out pan drippings left in baking pan and drench kohlrabi with sour cream sauce. Bake uncovered in 375°–400° oven about 10 min., or until slightly browned. Sprinkle with chopped parsley and serve with potatoes and a non-creamed salad.

STUFFED ONIONS
cebula nadziewana

Remove skin and tough or yellowed layers from 12 fairly large onions of equal size. Place in boiling salted water to cover and cook on medium heat about 10 min. Remove from water and cool. Cut off tops and carefully scoop out insides, making sure to leave a sufficiently thick wall on all sides. Save scoopings. Sauté 4 oz. finely chopped fresh mushrooms in 2 T. butter and mix with 1–2 c. ground cooked meat and 1 c. cooked rice. Add 1 T. chopped parsley, 1–2 buds crushed garlic, and salt & pepper to taste. Mix well. Fill onions with mixture and top with a little grated yellow cheese of choice, place in baking dish, add 2 c. meat stock, court bouillon or water in which onions were par-boiled and bake covered at 350° 45–60 min. Meanwhile, chop onion scoopings and brown lightly in 2 T. butter, add 2 T. tomato paste and 1 T. flour, stirring in enough pan drippings to get a pourable sauce. Season to taste with salt, pepper, and a little sugar, and pour over stuffed onions. Bake another 10 min. Serve with potatoes or noodles.

STUFFED TOMATOES
pomidory faszerowane

Combine 2 c. ground cooked meat or ground cooked poulty giblets with 1½ c. cooked rice or 2 ground, pre-soaked kaiser rolls, 1 chopped onion sautéd in 2 T. fat, and 1 raw egg. Mix well and salt & pepper to taste. Wash 12 medium-sized tomatoes (about 2–2½ lbs.), remove green stems if still attached, and place stem-side-down on cutting board. With knife slice off tops about ¾ of the way up the tomato and scoop out most of the pulp, leaving a ½ inch wall. (Freeze scooping for future soup or tomato sauce.) Fill tomatoes with meat mixture, replace tops, pressing down on filling and bake in pre-heated 375°–400° oven 10–15 min. Add 1 c. water or meat stock to pan before baking. *Optional*: Before baking, drench tomatoes with ½ c. salted, fork-blended sour cream and sprinkle with 1 T. chopped dill.

STUFFED CUCUMBERS
ogórki faszerowane

Peel 2½ lbs. medium-sized cucumbers, slice in half lengthwise, and scoop out seed portion. Soak 2 stale, broken-up rolls in 1 c. milk until soggy and grind. Combine with ¾ lb. cooked ground pork or lamb, 1 chopped onion sautéd in 2 T. butter, and 1 raw egg. Season with salt & pepper. (If using lamb, add several pinches marjoram and rosemary plus 1–2 buds mashed garlic.) Mix ingredients well and fill cucumber halves. Place in pan, add 1 c. water or stock, and bake in pre-heated 375° oven 20–30 min. Fork-blend ¾ c. sour cream with 1 T. flour, salt & pepper, and 1 t. Maggi extract. Pour over cucumbers, then bake another 5 min. Just before serving, garnish with chopped dill and serve with boiled potatoes dotted with butter. *Note*: Zucchini, eggplant, summer squash, even a small pumpkin are also delicious prepared in this way. They should be split in half and seed portions should be removed before filling. Adjust cooking time to size of vegetable being used. Skinned, ground, smoked kiełbasa or ground frankfurters (knackwurst, bologna) may be used in place of meat in any of the above recipes. The meat & rice gołąbki filling is also very good in any of the above.

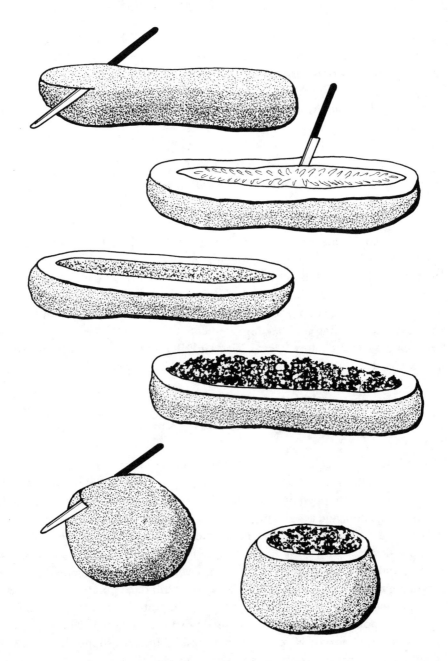

Cucumbers, tomatoes and other vegetables, stuffed with filling and baked, make a tasty and economical dish. Their preparation is illustrated above.

STUFFED POTATOES
kartofle nadziewane

Finely chop 6–8 oz. well-washed wild or store-bought fresh mushrooms and sauté in 3 T. butter or oil with 1 finely chopped onion until fully cooked and just lightly browned. Grind 2 kaiser rolls pre-soaked in milk and combine with mushroom mixture and ½ lb. ground raw pork. Add 1 raw egg, 1 T. chopped parsley, mix well, and salt & pepper to taste. Peel and wash 8 oblong potatoes (2–2½ lbs.) of roughly equal size. Cut in half lengthwise and scoop out most of the insides, leaving only a ¼ inch wall. (Use potato scoopings in soups, fricassee-type dishes etc.) Sprinkle potatoes with salt and fill with meat & mushroom mixture. Place in buttered baking dish, sprinkle with 2 T. or so melted butter and bake in 350°–375° oven until done. Serve in baking pan, sprinkled with chopped dill, with a crispy lettuce or cucumber salad on the side. *Variation*: For a meatless version of this dish, simply omit meat and increase amount of mushrooms to 12–16 oz.

POTATO CUTLETS
kotlety kartoflane

Cook 2 lbs. potatoes in jackets until tender, remove from water, and allow to cool. Peel and mash very thoroughly or grind. (Rather than cooking potatoes from scratch, personally we feel this dish is the perfect way to use up yesterday's leftover potatoes.) Sauté 2 finely chopped onions in a little butter until they just begin to brown and add to potatoes along with 2 eggs and 5 T. flour. Mix well, adding some bread crumbs if mixture appears too soft. Salt & pepper generously. Place mixture on lightly floured board, roll it into a 1½ inch thick roll and cut into 1½ inch pieces. Roll in bread crumbs and shape each piece into a small oval cutlet. (If you like, cutlets may be rolled in flour and dipped in egg wash and bread crumbs.) Fry cutlets in hot lard, butter, or oil & butter on both sides to a nice crusty golden brown. Serve straight from the pan or drench with mushroom sauce or sour cream sauce on platter. Sauerkraut salad or a grated-vegetable salad of choice makes a nice accompaniment. *Variations*: To potato mixture add any of the following: 1) ½–1 c. ground farmer's cheese; 2) ½–1 c. ground cooked meat of choice; 3) ¼ lb. or so raw ground meat; 4) in addition to salt & pepper, other good flavorings include chopped dill and/or parsley, marjoram, caraway seeds, homemade pork seasoning or hunter's seasoning.

CABBAGE CUTLETS
kotlety z kapusty

Coarsely dice 1 cabbage (about 2 lbs.), place in pot, scald with boiling water to cover, add 1 t. salt and cook until tender. Drain in sieve, pressing out as much moisture as possible. Finely chop 3 onions and brown lightly in 1 T. fat of choice. Grind cabbage and combine with the onions, ¾ c. bread crumbs, 2 eggs, and 1–2 T. chopped dill. Mix well and salt & pepper. Form into small oval cutlets, roll in bread crumbs, pressing in breading, and fry to a nice golden brown in 4–5 T. fat. Serve drenched with tomato sauce, mushroom sauce, or sour cream sauce and boiled or mashed potatoes. *Variations*: some ground cooked mushrooms (dried, fresh, or canned), a couple of ground, hard-boiled eggs, or a little ground cooked or raw meat may be added to mixture.

VEGETABLE CUTLETS
kotlety z jarzyn

Proceed as with potato or cabbage cutlets (above), using whatever cooked vegetables you happen to have on hand. Potatoes, cauliflower, cabbage, broccoli, brussels sprouts, kohlrabi, turnips, rutabaga, string beans, carrots, soup greens, etc., or any combination there of are good, but beets are not recommended. The best are plain, boiled vegetables. If you have leftover creamed vegetables, add 1 c. boiling water, heat to boiling, and drain well before using. Use the liquid to make a sauce. These cutlets are an excellent way to use up the leftover vegetables found in most kitchens.

VEGETABLE CROQUETTES
krokiety z jarzyn

Proceed according to any of the 3 preceding recipes, but form mixture into a long, 1 inch thick roll, and cut into 2–3 inch pieces instead of oval cutlets. Bread, fry, and serve as above.

LITHUANIAN SAUERKRAUT CUTLETS
kotlety z kapusty po litewsku

Soak ½–1 oz. dried Polish mushrooms several hrs., cook in same water until tender, chop, and return to liquid. Rinse 1 qt. sauerkraut in plenty of cold water, drain, press out moisture, place in pot, scald with boiling water to cover, and cook until tender. Sauté 1 minced onion in a little butter until golden. In dry saucepan, brown 2½ T. flour. Drain cooked sauerkraut, pressing out all moisture. Chop mushrooms fine and add to sauerkraut along with browned flour, 2 small eggs, ¼ c. bread crumbs, and pepper to taste. Form into 3–4 inch oval cutlets, roll in bread crumbs, pressing them in well, and fry in 4 T. lard until nicely browned on both sides. Serve with boiled potatoes garnished with golden salt-pork nuggets.

BEAN CUTLETS
kotlety z fasoli

Soak 2 c. dried navy beans in water overnight. Next day cook in same water until tender. Drain, cool, and run through meat grinder. Sauté 2 finely chopped onions in a little butter until tender and slightly browned and add to bean mixture together with 2 raw eggs, 1 T. chopped dill, 1 t. marjoram, and salt & pepper to taste. Mix well, adding some bread crumbs if mixture appears too moist. Shape into small oval cutlets, rolling in bread crumbs and pressing them in. Fry in 5–6 T. hot fat on both sides to a nice, crusty golden brown. Serve drenched with tomato sauce, with a grated-vegetable salad on the side.

UKRAINIAN BEAN CUTLETS
kotlety z fasoli ukraińskie

Soak and cook 2 c. dried navy beans as above. (In both this and the above recipe, canned drained beans may be used.) Soak 1–1½ oz. dried Polish mushrooms in 2 c. water 2 hrs., then cook in same water until tender. Grind drained beans and mushrooms, add 2 finely chopped onions sautéed in butter, 4 T. bread crumbs, 1½ T. potato starch, 3 raw eggs, and salt, pepper, and marjoram to taste. Mix well by hand and form into small oval cutlets. Roll in bread crumbs and fry in 4 T. hot fat until golden brown. Separately, melt 2 T. butter in saucepan, add 2 T. flour, and brown slightly. Fork-blend ¾ c. sour cream with the mushroom liquid and add to saucepan. Bring to boil, stirring constantly. Dilute with a little water if too thick, salt & pepper to taste, and pour over cutlets on platter. Serve with fresh non-creamed salad of choice.

BEANS & PORK CRACKLINGS
fasola ze słoniną

Soak, cook, and drain 2 c. dried navy beans as above. Dice ¼ lb. salt pork or bacon and fry until nuggets are crunchy and golden. Spoon the cracklings and as much of the drippings as you like over the beans. Season with salt, pepper, and marjoram and/or savory. *Optional*: Brown 1 minced onion along with the salt pork. With some rye bread and dill pickles this simple, stick-to-the-ribs peasant dish is a meal in itself, and its simplicity makes it ideal for camping trips. Naturally, canned drained beans, which only need to be heated through, may also be used.

BEANS IN TOMATO SAUCE
fasola w sosie pomidorowym

Soak, cook, and drain beans as above. Drench with about 2 c. hot tomato sauce (see sauce section). *Variation*: This dish will even be better if beans are first mixed with fried bacon bits (about ¼ lb.) before drenching with sauce.

BEAN CAKE
babka z fasoli

Soak, cook, drain, and grind beans as above. Finely chop 3 onions and simmer in 4 T. butter until tender and golden. Add 4 raw egg yolks, 4 T. grated yellow cheese (gouda, munster etc.) and the onions, mix extremely well. Fold in 4 stiffly beaten egg whites, lightly salted. Season generously with salt, pepper, and paprika, and turn mixture into well-buttered casserole. Bake uncovered at 350° 30–40 min., or until nicely browned. Remove from oven and let stand several min. to set. Loosen sides with knife and turn out on round platter upside down. Slice and drench each portion with hot tomato sauce or gherkin sauce.

CABBAGE PUDDING
budyń z kapusty

Shred 1 small cabbage (about 2–2½ lbs.) and add to 2 c. boiling milk. Cook cabbage in milk 15 min., then cover, reduce heat, and cook until tender. Drain and chop fine. Sauté 3 minced onions in 3 T. butter and, when they start turning golden, add the cabbage. Mix well and simmer covered on low heat several min. Cream 1 stick (¼ lb.) soft butter, gradually adding 5 raw egg yolks and mixing constantly. Combine cabbage and butter-egg mixtures and season to taste with salt, pepper, and a little sugar. Beat 5 egg whites to a froth, salt lightly, and beat a bit longer, then fold into mixture along with 1 c. bread crumbs and 2–3 T. chopped parsley and/or dill. Mix well and turn into metal pudding mold with snap-on lid. It should be no more than ¾ full. Place filled, sealed pudding mold in pot containing boiling water (which should reach ¾ up the side of the mold), cover pot and cook 60 min. (If you haven't got a classic pudding mold, simply transfer mixture to a pot in which it reaches ¾ of the way up the side.) Cover with tight-fitting lid, place in larger pot of boiling water, cover and cook. Turn the cooked pudding out onto a round platter, slice and serve with hot mushroom sauce or tomato sauce and potatoes. This dish can also be cooked in double boiler. *Optional*: ½–1 c. diced boiled ham may be added to mixture.

CAULIFLOWER PUDDING
budyń z kalafiora

Break up a washed 2 lb. cauliflower into flowerlets and cook in boiling salted water, uncovered until tender. Drain. (The leftover water can be used for a soup or sauce.) Cream 4 T. butter, adding 4 raw egg yolks one by one and folding in 4 beaten egg whites. Mix 4 T. flour with ¾ c. milk and bring to boil. Combine cooked cauliflower with milk sauce and egg mixture, adding 6 T. chopped dill and salt and a little sugar to taste. Butter pudding mold (or pot), sprinkle with bread crumbs, and fill ¾ full with mixture. Seal and cook 60 min. as above. Serve drenched with sour cream sauce. *Note*: Other vegetables like Brussels sprouts, broccoli, or spinach (pre-cooked in salted water until tender then drained well) can be used instead of the cabbage or cauliflower in the above two recipes.

CAULIFLOWER PIE
kalafiory w cieście

Cut 2 T. butter into 1½ c. flour, add 2 T. sour cream, 1 egg, and a pinch of sugar and quickly work into a dough. Cover and refrigerate 10 min. Roll out thin and line a loaf pan with most of the dough, leaving enough for the top. Bake in hot oven about 10 min. or until dough is golden. Separately, cook 1½ lbs. cauliflower broken up into flowerlets in boiling salted water until tender and drain. In saucepan, melt 1½ T. butter, sprinkle in 1½ T. flour and add ⅓ c. milk. Bring to boil, stirring constantly to ensure smoothness. Add cooked, drained cauliflower to sauce and allow to cool. Add 2 beaten eggs, 2 T. bread crumbs, 3 T. grated yellow cheese, 2–3 T. chopped dill, and salt, pepper, and a little sugar to taste. Transfer mixture to partially baked pastry shell, cover with remaining sheet of dough. Bake in 400° oven until top crust is golden brown. *Note*: If you have some leftover potatoes, peas & carrots, or other cooked vegetable, feel free to add them. You may well come up with an interesting new twist to this tasty dish. You may also make small individual pies instead of one loaf.

LIVER PUDDING
budyń z wątróbki

Remove any membranes from ¾ lb. calf's liver, cut into cubes and brown lightly in 1 T. butter together with 2–3 onions sliced wafer thin. Soak 1 stale, broken-up kaiser roll in ½ c. milk until soggy. Run the liver & onions and soggy roll through meat grinder. Cream 2 T. butter, gradually adding 4 raw egg yolks. Beat until fluffy and add to ground mixture. Add 3 T. chopped parsley, fold in 4 stiffly beaten egg whites (lightly salted towards end of beating), and season with salt, pepper, and a pinch of nutmeg. Mix well. Butter pudding mold and sprinkle with bread crumbs. Fill pudding mold with mixture no more than ¾ full, seal lid and cook in covered pot of boiling water 70–80 min. Slice and serve drenched with onion sauce or mushroom sauce and a fresh green salad. *Note:* The flavor will not be affected if you cook your pudding in an ordinary pot, but only a fluted pudding mold will give your final product the elegance of a tall, tapered babka.

POTATO & MEAT CAKE
baba kartoflana z mięsem

Place 1½ lb. pork ribs in 2 qts. water with 1 portion soup greens (or simply 1–2 onions), 5 peppercorns, 1 grain allspice, and half a bay leaf and cook covered 90 min. or until meat easily comes away from bone. Remove meat from bone, dice, and set aside. (Use the rib stock for soup.) Grate 2 lbs. peeled potatoes, transfer to sieve, and allow to drip dry. To grated potatoes add 3 eggs, the diced meat, 1–2 T. grated raw onion, 3 buds mashed garlic, 1 t. salt, and ½ t. pepper. Mix well and place mixture in well-greased pan. Choose the size pan that will allow potato mixture to have a depth of 1½–2 inches. Bake in 350° oven about 90 min. Slice and serve hot with sour cream. *Variation*: Instead of cooking ribs from scratch, you can use whatever cooked leftover meat you happen to have on hand, including poultry. You can also fry up ½–¾ lb. diced slab bacon and add the browned nuggets and 2–3 T. bacon drippings to grated potatoes. *Note*: One contemporary Polish cookbook advised that this dish should be washed down with hot, unsweetened mint tea, which aids digestion. Like other grated-potato dishes, this is a hearty, stick-to-the-ribs concoction not recommended for delicate eaters.

POTATO & SAUERKRAUT CAKE
baba kartoflana z kapustą

Rinse 1 pt. sauerkraut in plenty of cold water, drain in colander, and press out excess moisture. Place in pot, scald with 1½ c. hot meat stock (or 1½ beef or chicken bouillon cubes dissolved in 1½ c. boiling water), add 1 chopped onion, and 1 T. bacon drippings and cook 50 min. Add 1 peeled, diced apple and cook another 10–15 min. or until sauerkraut is tender. Drain cooked sauerkraut and press out excess moisture. Meanwhile, cook 5 peeled potatoes in boiling salted water to cover until tender, drain and mash thoroughly. Grate 5 peeled potatoes and drain in sieve. Combine the cooked and raw grated potatoes. Add 1 egg, 2 T. flour, 1 t. salt, and ¼ t. pepper. Mix well and transfer ⅔ potato mixture to well-greased baking pan. Top with sauerkraut and cover with remaining potato mixture. With wooden skewer (city-chicken stick), puncture holes in mixture all the way to bottom and drench with ¼ c. hot bacon drippings. Bake in 375° oven 1 hr. Slice and serve hot topped with browned bacon nuggets.

POTATO & MUSHROOM CAKE
babka kartoflana z pieczarkami

Cook 5–6 peeled potatoes in boiling, salted water, drain well and mash, adding 1½ T. butter and 5 T. chopped parsley. Wash well 16 oz. fresh store-bought mushrooms, dice, and sauté in 2 T. butter until tender. Add mushrooms to potatoes together with 4 raw egg yolks and 2 T. bread crumbs. Mix well and salt & pepper to taste. Beat 4 egg whites to a stiff froth, salt lightly, and beat some more, then fold into mixture. Transfer mixture to well buttered casserole and bake at 350° 35–40 min. Serve portions drenched with mushroom sauce or sour cream sauce, generously garnished with dill, and a crispy salad on the side.

POTATO & MUSHROOM CASSEROLE
kartofle zapiekane z grzybami

Wash well 16 oz. fresh, wild, or store-bought mushrooms, drain and dice. Chop 3 onions and brown lightly in 3–4 T. fat (butter, oleo, lard, or oil) along with the mushrooms, stirring constantly. Fork-blend ¾ c. sour cream until creamy and stir into mushrooms, simmer briefly, cover, and set aside. Peel and wash 2–2½ lbs. potatoes, slice, place in pot, scald with boiling salted water to cover, and cook about 10 min. Drain. Butter a casserole and line bottom with a layer of potatoes, salt & pepper, and top with a layer of creamed mushrooms, followed by potatoes and creamed mushrooms until all are used up. Top layer should be creamed mushrooms. Cover and bake in 350° oven 60–80 min. or until potatoes are tender. Before serving, sprinkle with chopped fresh parsley and/or dill.

ASSORTED CASSEROLES
zapiekanki różne

The potato casserole above is but one of countless possibilities. Feel free to improvise as Polish cooks long have done. Sliced potatoes (raw, par-boiled, or cooked) as well as any type of cooked noodles or macaroni can be the start of an interesting new dish. Place these in a well-buttered casserole, intersperse with chopped leftover cooked meat or fish. Chopped smoked kiełbasa, ham or other cold cuts can also be added. A finely chopped onion simmered in butter or some chopped, cooked, or canned mushrooms will improve the flavor of any savory casserole. If you're short on leftover meat, adding several sliced hard-boiled eggs will increase the nutritive value of your dish. The liquid you must add to your casserole so it doesn't burn may be 1–1½ c. fork-blended sour cream, milk (with 2–3 T. flour), leftover gravy or even some leftover soup. Your imagination and what you have on hand are the only limits on the combinations you can come up with. Naturally, you can alter the character of your casserole by the seasonings you choose. Besides salt & pepper, consider any of your home-made, Polish-style seasonings (except honey-spice cake seasonings), a dash or two of garlic or mushroom powder, a pinch of cayenne pepper for added zest, etc. A garnish of chopped fresh parsley, dill, and/or chives will enhance the flavor, aroma, and eye-appeal of any casserole.

FISH ENTRÉES

As a fisherman from way back, the author was particularly struck by one exhibit at Biskupin in western Poland, a reconstructed prehistoric lakeshore settlement first built by the ancestors of today's Poles around 600 B.C. Among the tools of those ancient lake dwellers was a huge fish hook of crudely smelted iron. Its size gives us some indication of how large were the sturgeon, sheatfish (European catfish) or perhaps pike that lurked in the deep at that time.

Fish continued to play an important role in the national diet over the centuries that followed Poland's emergence as an independent state in 966. Since Germany's aggressive eastward expansion restricted Poland's access to the Baltic—with the exception of herring, flounder, cod, and a few other species—it was freshwater fish that were held in the highest esteem. "In the preparation of fish Poles enjoyed renown from the earliest times and surpassed other countries in this regard", wrote the early-20th-century food expert Maria Ochrowicz-Monatowa in 1910.

Suffice it to say that fish has for centuries reigned supreme at the Poles' most solemn family gathering of the year: *Wigilia* or Christmas Eve supper. The *Wigilia* tables of the Old Polish nobility would boast 12 different fish dishes alone, but three or four kinds of fish could also be found in the lowly cottages of the peasantry. To this day, in addition to cold appetizers such as marinated herring and fish in aspic, one can find a number of fish entrées at this festive holiday repast. These may include breaded or batter-fried carp, carp in grey sauce, poached perch, or walleye topped with a buttery, dilled garnish of chopped, hard-boiled eggs, pike in horseradish sauce, or panfish stewed in sour cream.

Fish was important in this staunchly Catholic country as a dietary mainstay throughout Lent and Advent and on the many fast days and ember days that peppered the liturgical calendar. Tench stewed with cabbage was the traditional dish that helped poor peasants keep body and soul together in the lean period preceding the annual harvest. Fish also fits in nicely with Polish lifestyles as a traditional bite-down for vodka. To invite someone *na rybkę* amounts to saying "drop in for a drink", because *ryba lubi pływać* (fish like to swim).

Increasing your fish consumption is well worth considering for a variety of reasons. Fish is rich in protein, phosphorous, calcium, vitamins A and D, and other nutrients, but low in calories. Most fish require little actual cooking time, because they are never really tough the way meat can be. It should not be overcooked and is ready when it loses its glossy translucence and flakes readily. Above all, fish—if truly fresh and properly prepared—is downright delicious and easily surpasses other foods for overall eating enjoyment.

* * *

CHECKING FISH FOR FRESHNESS
sprawdzanie świeżości ryb

The best fish is freshly caught and cooked over a campfire at the lakeshore. Another way is to purchase your fish live, have it killed and dressed on the spot, and cook it shortly thereafter. If, however, you are getting fresh fish that has been killed ahead of time, be sure to check it for freshness before you buy it. The first check is the "nose test". If the fish has a strong fishy or otherwise unpleasant odor, don't buy it. The eyes should be bright and clear; if they are cloudy, beware! The gills of a truly fresh fish are a deep healthy pink or bright blood-crimson. If they have a sickly grayish or bluish tinge and show signs of deterioration, the fish is decomposing. *Remember*: Spoilage of fish starts from the head! For that reason, watch out for fish that has been beheaded or gutted, even if it is appetizingly displayed on crushed ice and garnished with parsley and lemon slices. A reputable fish merchant may have done this only for the customer's convenience, but this practice can also be an attempt to conceal a lack of freshness. To determine which is the case, assuming that the fish has passed the "nose test," press its flesh firmly with an index finger. The flesh of a fresh fish will quickly rebound. If the imprint remains, forget it!

FISH MARINADES
zaprawy do ryb

Unlike meat, especially wild game, fish does not need to be marinated to make it more tender. Older specimens like large pike may be tough, but are braised in fat to make them more palatable, rather than being pre-soaked in a marinade. However, dry marinades are often used to neutralize fishy odors or enhance the flavor of bland tasting species. Here are a few common methods of preparing fresh fish prior to cooking.

SALTING FISH
solenie ryb

Every fresh fish can do with a salting before cooking. Simply sprinkle all over with salt, cover and refrigerate about 1 hr. Then rinse away salt, pat dry, and cook as desired. *Optional:* in addition to salting, feel free to sprinkle fish with your homemade fish seasoning. For variety, use your hunter's seasoning.

ONION MARINADE FOR FISH
zaprawa z cebuli do ryb

In addition to salt, fish may be interspersed with thinly sliced onions before refrigerating. Use anywhere from 1–2 onions per lb. of fish.

VEGETABLE MARINADE FOR FISH
zaprawa z warzyw do ryb

A portion of coarsely grated soup greens, 1 chopped onion and several T. finely chopped dill and parsley will help neutralize the off-flavors of 2–3 lbs. of fish. Sprinkle fish with salt, pepper, or fish seasoning before smothering it with chopped greens and refrigerate 1 hr. or longer. An overnight marination is recommended for fish that is less than super-fresh. *Note*: The juice of 1/2 a lemon may be added to this or either of the above marinades.

SALT, VINEGAR & MILK BATH
kąpiel solno-octowo-mleczna

Freshwater fish, although freshly caught, may sometimes have a muddy or weedy smell. One way to deal with this is to keep them alive 2–3 days in fresh, cold, running water. Another way is to soak them, after cleaning, in any or all of the following "baths". Dissolve ¼–½ c. salt in a little hot water and add to 2 qts. ice-cold water. For vinegar bath, simply add ½ c. 6% vinegar to 2 qts. ice-cold water. This amount is for about 2 lbs. of fish. Place the fish in the solution for about 10 min. Longer soaking is not recommended. You can follow up either or both of these baths with a 15 min. soaking in cold milk to cover. Then pat dry and cook as desired. Seafood that is less than very fresh often has a cod-liver-oil scent about it, meaning that its oil has begun to turn rancid. In many cases it too may respond to this technique. *Note*: If using salt solution, do not salt fish during cooking.

FRIED CARP
karp smażony

Slice a 2–3 lb. carp into 1½ inch steaks, sprinkle with salt, and refrigerate 1 hr. or overnight in covered container. When ready to use, rinse off salt, and pat dry. Pepper lightly and dredge in flour or in a mixture of 2 parts flour and 1 part fine bread crumbs. (Rub bread crumbs through a sieve with a spoon to achieve the proper fineness.) Brown in 4–5 T. hot oil on all sides, then reduce heat and continue frying until fish is fully cooked. About 12–15 min. should suffice, but test a piece to make sure. You can serve the fish straight from the frying pan or do what many experienced Polish cooks do: transfer fish to baking pan, dot generously with butter, cover, and bake in a 300° oven another 15–30 min. Serve with boiled potatoes and prepared horseradish or easy horseradish sauce: fork-blend 2 heaping T. prepared horseradish (non-creamed variety) with 2 heaping T. sour cream, and season to taste with a little sugar, lemon juice, and a dash of salt. Many believe (and this includes the authors) that this simple recipe is the best way to prepare carp, Poland's most prized and expensive fresh water fish. Crispy, golden-brown "horse shoes" of fried carp are an absolute "must" on the Wigilia (Christmas Eve) table, even of families that can rarely afford it at other times of the year. According to one old folk belief, keeping a golden carp scale in one's purse ensures that it's full of money all year long. *Note*: The last slice of carp about 2 inches from the tail is full of tiny pinlike and Y-shaped bones, so it is best to freeze (rather than fry) the tail portion together with the head for fish chowder.

CARP WITH APPLES
karp z jabłkami

Slice carp into 1 inch steaks, salt, and refrigerate at least 1 hr. Sprinkle with pepper and a little marjoram, dredge in flour, and fry in 3 T. oil and 2 T. butter until nicely browned on one side. Turn fish over, smother with 1–1½ lbs. peeled, sliced apples, cover, reduce heat, and simmer about 20 min. Serve with boiled potatoes.

CARP WITH GRAY SAUCE
karp w szarym sosie

Use a whole 2–3 lb. carp or slice it into 1½ inch steaks. Salt and refrigerate 1 hr. Place fish in an oblong pan, preferably on a rack so it can be easily lifted out, add 5–6 c. hot court bouillon (vegetable stock), or enough to more than cover fish, and cook on low heat covered about 40 min. Gently transfer fish to platter, cover with aluminum foil, and keep in warm oven until sauce is ready. In skillet caramelize (brown and melt) 1 T. sugar, add several T. fish stock, and stir until caramelized sugar dissolves. Add 2 c. fish stock, ½ c. raisins, ¼ c. ground almonds, ¾ c. dark beer (or a jigger dry red wine), and simmer briefly. A T. powidła (or domestic plum jam) may also be added. In separate saucepan brown 3 T. flour in 3 T. butter, stirring in ½ c. sauce to get a smooth mixture, then combine with rest of sauce. Add ½–1 t. honey-spice cake seasoning (przyprawa do pierników) and season to taste with salt, pepper, and a little lemon juice. The sauce should have a balanced sweet & sour taste (or slightly more sweet than sour) with spicy overtones. Remove fish from oven and drench with sauce. Serve with mashed potatoes. *Note:* If you have a live carp, you can prepare this Old Polish specialty according to the original recipe. Grip fish in the middle of the back with its belly resting on a firm surface. Stun fish with 2–3 blows to the back of the head. Slit throat, hold fish head down, and collect blood in glass containing ½ T. vinegar. Stir blood & vinegar mixture into sauce towards the end, bringing to boil and simmering briefly.

CARP À LA JUIVE/JEWISH STYLE
karp po żydowsku

Cut cleaned carp into 1 inch steaks. Salt, pepper, sprinkle with 4–5 crushed cloves, and 1 T. vinegar, and refrigerate covered 1 hr. In 3 T. butter simmer 2 chopped onions until tender but not browned. Add ½ c. beer, bring to boil, and add fish. Cover and simmer on low heat about 30 min. Add ⅓ c. or more raisins and ½ t. grated lemon rind. Simmer briefly and serve with mashed potatoes.

CARP BAKED WITH ONIONS
karp pieczony z cebulą

Remove eyes and gills from 1 whole cleaned carp. Mince 2 buds garlic and mash with ½ t. salt. Rub fish inside and out with garlic mixture. Thinly slice 5–6 small onions, sprinkle with salt, pepper, and 1 t. sugar, and toss with 1 T. olive oil. Fill fish with onions and place in baking dish containing 2 T. olive oil. Brush fish with butter and bake in 400° oven. When skin begins to brown, sprinkle with a little water, reduce heat, and continue baking until fish is done. Serve with fried potatoes and carrot, apple, & horseradish salad.

BAKED STUFFED CARP
karp faszerowany pieczony

Cook 4–6 oz. cleaned, chopped mushrooms (boletes are best but the white store-bought kind are also good) in 2 T. butter and 1 T. water about 10 min. Salt & pepper. Cream 2 T. butter with 2 raw egg yolks, combine with mushrooms, ½ c. bread crumbs, and 2 beaten egg whites. Salt & pepper to taste. A T. or more chopped parsley and/or dill may be added. Mix ingredients well and fill a 2–3 lb. carp which has been salted and refrigerated 1 hr. Remove eyes and gills of fish. Sew up cavity. Place in well-buttered baking dish and brush generously with melted butter. Bake in 350° oven 45–50 min. or until fish is done. Baste with pan drippings. If they evaporate, sprinkle fish with water or court bouillon. *Optional*: Fork-blend ½ c. sour cream with 1 t. flour and ¼ t. salt and pour over fish. Bake another 5 min. Serve with boiled potatoes and lettuce with vinaigrette.

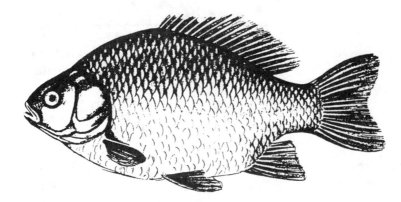

CRUCEAN (karaś)

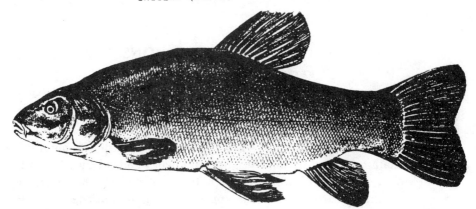

TENCH (lin)

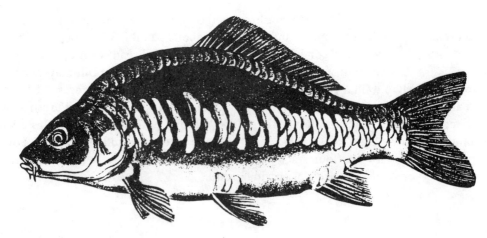

CARP (karp)

PIKE (szczupak)

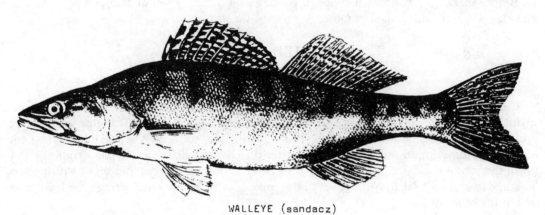

WALLEYE (sandacz)

PERCH (okoń)

CARP BAKED WITH HORSERADISH
karp pieczony z chrzanem

Remove eyes and gills from whole cleaned carp. Salt inside and out, sprinkle with 1 T. vinegar, and spread 1 T. freshly grated horseradish root or prepared horseradish inside cavity. Place fish in well-buttered baking dish, brush with butter, and bake in 350° oven about 45–50 min. basting frequently with butter and a total of 2–3 T. water. When fish is fully cooked, fork-blend ½ c. sour cream with 3–4 T. freshly grated horseradish or prepared horseradish. Season to taste with salt and sugar and pour over fish. Bake another 10 min. or so. Before serving, garnish with chopped parsley or a combination of chopped parsley, dill, and chives. Serve with boiled potatoes.

FRIED PIKE
szczupak smażony

Cut 2 small cleaned pikes weighing not more than 1½ lbs. each into 1 inch pieces, sprinkle with salt & pepper, dredge in flour, and fry in 1 T. oil and 2 T. butter until nicely browned on all sides. Reduce heat and simmer until fully cooked. When fish has browned, instead of simmering in skillet, you can transfer it to baking dish with the pan drippings and finish the job in the oven. Decorate fish on platter with lemon slices and serve with potato balls and sauerkraut salad. *Note:* A very large pike may be too dry and stringy for frying, so save it for other dishes.

BATTER FRIED PIKE FILLETS
filety ze szczupaka w cieście

Beat 2 eggs well, gradually adding ⅔ c. flour and ½ c. sour cream. Beat until you get a smooth, creamy batter, and add a pinch of baking powder at the end. Sprinkle 1½ lbs. pike fillets with salt & pepper or your homemade fish seasoning, impale each fillet on fork, dip in batter, and fry in hot oil about ¼ inch deep in the skillet. Fry on both sides until golden, then transfer to covered baking dish and bake in 350° oven another 20 min. or so. Test 1 piece for doneness. Serve as is or with hot horseradish or gherkin sauce and boiled potatoes or potato balls. *Note*: Any fresh water or ocean fillets may be prepared in this way.

PIKE IN HORSERADISH SAUCE
szczupak w sosie chrzanowym

Slice 1½–2 lbs. pike into 1 inch pieces, salt, and refrigerate 1 hr. in covered container or overnight. Bring 6 c. strained court bouillon (i.e. with soup greens and spices removed) to boil and cook the pike in it on low heat about 30 min. In skillet melt 3 T. butter, sprinkle in 2 T. flour, and stir until absorbed, then add several T. freshly grated horseradish root or prepared horseradish and ¾ c. sour cream. Stir constantly over low heat and gradually add enough fish stock (in which pike was cooked) to get a sauce of smooth, pourable consistency. Season to taste with salt, white pepper, lemon juice, and a little sugar. Gently transfer fish to baking dish, drench with sauce, and bake in medium oven 10–15 min. On serving platter sprinkle with parsley or dust with paprika. Serve with mashed potatoes and a non-creamed cole slaw. This is one of the traditional dishes of Wigilia (Christmas Eve), where pike ranks second only to carp in culinary importance. According to one old folk belief, this particular fish foretells what the future holds in store for the newly born Christ-child. If taken apart properly, the head of the pike can be shown to contain bones resembling the tools of the crucifixion: a cross, a ladder, a hammer, and nails.

STUFFED PIKE
szczupak faszerowany

Remove fins and tail from a 2 lb. pike. Carefully scrape away scales so as not to damage the skin but do not gut. Cut the skin all the way around the head and gently remove skin, cut it away from meat with a small, razor-sharp knife. This is easier to accomplish with one person holding the head as the other cuts away the skin. When the skin has been removed, set it aside. If there are any tears, sew them up. Gut the fish, wash well, and remove all the meat from bones. Cook pike head (with eyes and gills removed), backbone, and 1 portion soup greens, plus several peppercorns and allspice grains and a bay leaf in 6 c. water 1 hr., counting from when it first comes to a boil. Strain stock, removing all light meat from head and backbone. Soak 1–1½ stale kaiser rolls, broken up, in ½ c. milk. Slice 2 onions and simmer in 2 T. butter until golden and tender. When roll is soggy, run it through meat grinder with the fish and onions, then grind mixture a second time. Add 1 egg, 1 T. uncooked cream of wheat, and 3–4 T. milk. Season with salt, pepper, and a dash of nutmeg. Mix well and loosely fill pike skin. Sew up at both ends. Place in a pot containing the warm stock, heat gently to boiling, and cook on very low heat 1 hr. (Rapid cooking may cause the skin to burst. You can prevent this by doing the following: Wet a cloth napkin in the stock, place the stuffed pike on it, and roll up. Tie lightly with string in 4 places and cook in stock as above.) When cooked, slice at an angle into ¾ inch thick slices and serve with hot or cold horseradish sauce and boiled potatoes. *Note*: Walleye and cod may be stuffed the same way, but only if you have a live or freshly killed fish that has not been gutted.

WALLEYE POLONAISE, WITH EGG TOPPING
sandacz po polsku

This may well be one of the tastiest fish dishes you ever ate, so be sure to try it before going on to the recipes below! Slice a cleaned 2–3 lb. walleyed pike (known in parts of the U.S. Midwest and Ontario as pickerel) into 1 inch pieces, salt, and refrigerate 1 hr. Place fish in pan, drench with enough strong court bouillon to cover, and cook on very low heat 20–30 min. or until fish is done. Meanwhile, in 3 T. butter simmer 1 finely chopped onion until golden and tender but unbrowned. Remove from heat and add 4–5 finely chopped or ground hard-boiled eggs and 1 T. fresh chopped dill. Toss eggs with onions and butter drippings to coat evenly and warm through, but do not cook. Salt & pepper. Remove fish to serving platter with slotted spoon, sprinkle with a little lemon juice, and top with egg mixture. This simple but elegant and extremely tasty dish is likely to make fish lovers of those in your gang that say: "I don't care much for fish". Serve with fried potatoes and green onion salad or leek salad. Although the original recipe calls for poached fish (as above), this dish can also be made with fried fillets, which will be less messy to eat for those unaccustomed to picking out fish bones. See below.

WALLEYE POLONAISE ANOTHER WAY
sandacz po polsku inaczej

Salt 1½ lbs. walleye fillets and (optional) sprinkle lightly with your homemade Polish-style fish seasoning. Refrigerate 1 hr. Dredge fillets in flour, shake off excess, and fry in several T. hot oil until golden on both sides. When fully cooked, drain on absorbent paper, place on serving platter, sprinkle with lemon juice, and top with egg mixture as above. *Note*: Walleye, pike, or perch fillets may also be poached in court bouillon as in the first recipe, but cooking time should be reduced to about 15 min. You may also use high-grade ocean fillets, but they must be very fresh. This is yet another dish frequently featured at Poland's greatest fish feast: Christmas Eve supper.

FRIED BREADED WALLEYE
sandacz smażony panierowany

Salt a 2½ lb. walleye cut into 1–1½ inch pieces or 1½ lbs. walleye fillets and refrigerate 1 hr. Dredge in flour, dip in beaten eggs, and roll in a mixture of 1 part fine bread crumbs and 1 part flour. Press in breading and fry in ¼ inch hot oil on all sides until golden then transfer to baking dish, dot with butter, cover, and keep in 300° oven 20 min. Serve with prepared horseradish or cold horseradish sauce, boiled potatoes and stewed sauerkraut.

WALLEYE WITH FRESH MUSHROOMS
sandacz z pieczarkami

Salt 1½ lbs. walleye fillets and let stand in refrigerator 1 hr. Dredge in flour and brown on both sides in 3 T. hot oil until pale gold crust forms. Separately, cook 12 oz. cleaned, sliced, fresh mushrooms in 3 T. butter and 1 T. water until tender. Transfer fish to baking dish, top with mushrooms and pan drippings, salt & pepper, and bake covered 20 min. in 325° oven. Before serving, sprinkle with a little chopped parsley. Serve with mashed potatoes and green-onion salad.

POACHED TROUT
pstrągi z wody

Clean 2–2½ lbs. rainbow trout, but leave the heads attached. Cook the fish in hot, strong court bouillon on low heat about 30 min. The bouillon should barely simmer. Gently transfer fish to serving platter. Place a sprig of parsley in each mouth, drench fish with melted butter, garnish with a little chopped parsley, and surround with lemon wedges plus about 3 finely chopped hard-cooked eggs, salted and peppered, on the side. Some connoisseurs claim that this is the finest way to enjoy truly fresh fish, as there are no sauces, breadings, or heavy spices to disguise their subtle flavor. Whether or not you agree, this is certainly a light and highly digestible dish, frequently prescribed for those on fat-restricted or bland diets. Fish prepared in this way is very low in cholesterol if it is flavored with a little melted, unsaturated-type margarine instead of butter. Of course, you will have to sacrifice the flavor of unsalted, creamery-fresh butter which nothing else can match. The choice is yours! Personally, we prefer the trout recipe below.

TROUT SAUTÉ
pstrągi sauté

Salt 2–2½ lbs. cleaned and well-rinsed rainbow trout with heads left on, cover and refrigerate 1 hr. Sprinkle with a little white pepper if you like, dredge in flour, shaking off excess, simmer in 6 T. fairly hot oil on both sides to obtain a nice golden crust. Transfer to baking dish, dot with butter, cover, and bake in 350° oven 10–15 min. Serve on platter surrounded by dilled, buttered new potatoes and lemon wedges. Tomato salad makes a nice, fresh accompaniment. *Note*: Trout may be cooked entirely in skillet without baking.

FRIED PERCH
okoń smażony

Perch is an extremely popular and tasty fish, similar in taste to the walleye, to which it is related. (In Britain, the walleye is known as pike-perch.) Perch taste best when fried. If you don't like picking out bones, choose perch fillets. Salt an hr. before frying, sprinkle lightly with fish seasoning, and apply one of the following coatings before frying: 1) Simply dredge in flour and shake off excess, then fry until golden in ¼ inch hot oil. Since the flour gives only a thin coating, cooking time will be shorter than in the following 2 methods: 2) Dredge in flour, dip in beaten eggs (to which a T. beer may be added), roll in fine bread crumbs or a combination of flour and bread crumbs, and fry as above to a crusty golden brown: 3) Dip in batter prepared as for batter-fried pike above. Creamy horseradish & mayonnaise sauce will perk up the flavor of your fried perch. Simply fork-blend ¾ c. mayonnaise with a heaping T. prepared horseradish (non-creamed variety), season with salt, sugar, and lemon juice to taste and add 1–2 T. finely chopped chives. *Note*: Fried perch may be served straight from the skillet or kept in medium oven 10–15 min., dotted with butter, to become more succulent and delicious.

PERCH KASHUBIAN STYLE
okoń po kaszubsku

Salt and pepper 2 lbs. or so perch fillets, sprinkle with lemon juice, and wrap in uncooked sliced bacon. Place on rack in baking pan and bake in pre-heated 375° oven 20–25 min. or until done. Serve with dilled new potatoes and a tart lettuce & sour cream salad.

PERCH POLONAISE
okoń po polsku

Prepare like walleye polonaise (p. 381), preferably using perch fillets. Fillets may be poached or fried before garnishing with egg topping.

CRUCIANS IN SOUR CREAM
karasie w śmietanie

In presenting Poland's best-tasting pan fish, the karaś, we run into a major icthyological problem: the species is not found in the waters of North America and, as far as we know, it is not imported in frozen form. The crucian (scientific name: *Carassius*; sometimes nicknamed "black perch" or "German carp") is a round, flat, golden-tinged pan fish which at least three Polish cookbooks published in the U.S. have translated as "crappie". It is true that the *karaś* resembles America's crappie (also known as "calico bass") as well as the bluegill and sunfish in size and shape, but it is neither related to them (the crucian belongs to the minnow family, whereas the American pan fish is from the bass family), nor does it taste the same. All the scholarly mumbo-jumbo aside, you can approximate the Old Polish dish by substituting any of the above pan fish for the karaś. But, since picking small bones from fish smothered in sauce is a fairly messy proposition, we propose a better alternative. Salt 1½–2 lbs. perch fillets, place in strong court bouillon to cover, bring to boil, reduce heat, and simmer 10 min. on very low heat. Transfer fish to a well-buttered baking dish, pour 2 T. melted butter over fish. Fork-blend 1 c. sour cream with 1 T. flour and 2–3 T. fish stock until lump-free and pour over fish. Cover and bake in 375° oven about 20 min. Before serving, sprinkle with a little chopped dill, if you like. Serve with rice, noodles or potatoes, and a fresh non-creamed salad. As for sampling genuine crucians in sour cream, you will probably have to wait until you visit Poland, or at least Central Europe.

TENCH OR BULLHEAD IN BEER
lin lub sumik w piwie

The tench (scientific name: Tinca), another pan fish of the minnow family, has reportedly been transplanted to Oregon or thereabouts, but we haven't heard whether its adaptation has been successful. Until such time as the tench becomes plentiful in the New World, we propose making this dish with the good ol' American bullhead which, incidentally, has been transplanted to Poland and is thriving. Both the tench and bullhead are bottom-feeders, hence they often have a muddy taste. This can be largely eliminated using the triple-bath (vinegar marinade-brine-milk) method described in this chapter's introductory remarks. Having thus prepared 1½–2 lbs. of bullheads, remove the skin, sprinkle with salt, pepper, crushed cloves, and a little vinegar, and refrigerate 1 hr. Meanwhile, in skillet melt 3 T. butter and in it sauté 2 thinly sliced onions until tender and golden but still unbrowned. Add 2 c. strong court bouillon and 1 c. beer, bring to boil, add the fish, and simmer on the lowest flame possible about 20 min. Serve the fish as is with potatoes and cole slaw. If you'd like a sauce, brown 2 T. flour in 2 T. butter and stir in 2 c. of the bouillon-beer liquid in which your bullheads were cooked. Season to taste with salt & pepper, 1 t. Maggi extract, and a little lemon juice and sugar. Simmer several min. and pour over fish on serving platter.

TENCH OR BULLHEAD & SAUERKRAUT
lin lub sumik duszony w kapuście

Give 2–2½ lbs. bullheads the triple bath (see p. 375), then skin and cut fillets away from backbone. Pepper fillets generously, top with sliced onions, cover, and refrigerate 1 hr. Cook 1 oz. dried Polish mushrooms (that have soaked in 2 c. water at least 2 hrs.) until tender. Slice or chop and return to same water. Drain 1 qt. sauerkraut, rinse in plenty of cold water, drain again, squeeze out excess moisture, chop coarsely, place in pot, cover with mushroom stock, bring to boil, reduce heat, and cook 40 min. Salt the fillets, dredge in flour and brown in several T. hot oil on both sides until nice and golden. Separately, simmer 1 chopped onion in 2 T. butter until it just begins to brown, add the mushrooms, and simmer briefly, stirring constantly. In baking dish place a layer of sauerkraut, then fish, topped with mushrooms and repeat until you run out of ingredients. Sauerkraut should be the top layer. Sprinkle with 1¼ t. caraway seeds and 1 t. Maggi extract, cover, and bake in 375° oven about 20–30 min. Switch off heat and leave in oven another 15–30 min. for the flavors to blend nicely. Serve with boiled potatoes. As with all sauerkraut dishes, a t. sugar may be added before baking. *Note*: If the sauerkraut is too moist, sprinkle with a little flour. You can also fork-blend ½ c. sour cream with 1 T. flour and add to dish before baking. Bullheads are also good stewed in fresh red or white cabbage.

TENCH OR BULLHEAD TRIPE STYLE
lin lub sumik à la flaczki

Soak 2 lbs. bullheads in triple bath (see p. 375), remove skin, cut fillets away from backbone, and slice into ¼ inch tripe-style strips. Pepper and refrigerate 1 hr. Meanwhile in 5 c. water cook 1 portion soup greens, cut into triple-style strips, with 1 bay leaf, 6 peppercorns, and 2 grains allspice 1 hr. Melt 4 T. butter in skillet and sauté 1 sliced onion in it until golden. Remove onions from skillet and set aside. Sprinkle strips of fish with salt and paprika, dust with flour, and brown in the onion drippings until a golden crust forms on all sides. Add the fish and onions to the vegetables and stock, which should have boiled down to about 3–3½ c. Season with salt, pepper, marjoram, paprika, ginger, nutmeg, and 1 t. Maggi extract. This dish should definitely be on the sharp & spicy side, and marjoram is the dominant seasoning, so feel free to use 1–2 t. Simmer about 10 min. Fork-blend ¾–1 c. sour cream with 3 T. flour and add to pot. Simmer briefly. Transfer to serving platter, garnish with chopped parsley, and top generously with grated yellow cheese. Serve with mashed potatoes. *Optional*: Add 1–2 buds mashed garlic towards the end. For added zing, season with several dashes cayenne pepper.

BAKED CATFISH
sum pieczony

If you have a whole catfish, after cleaning it give it the vinegar-brine-milk bath (see p. 375). Then remove skin and backbone and slice into steaks. You can skip this procedure if using pan-ready fillets. Season the slices with salt and lemon juice and refrigerate in covered container 1 hr. Place in shallow pan, brush generously in butter, and bake in 350° oven 30–40 min., or until fully cooked. Drench with ½ c. fork-blended sour cream and bake another 5 min. Serve with potatoes and sauerkraut salad. *Note*: Catfish is also very good sprinkled with fish seasoning, dredged in flour, or breaded and fried. It can likewise be prepared according to any of the recipes given for bullhead.

CATFISH CUTLETS IN MUSHROOM SAUCE
zraziki z suma w sosie grzybowym

Cut 1½–2 lbs. cleaned, skinned, and boned catfish into large cubes, salt & pepper, sprinkle with juice of ½ a lemon, and refrigerate 2 hrs. Soak 1 oz. dried Polish mushrooms in 3 c. water 2 hrs., then cook in same water until tender. Chop mushrooms and return to stock. Soak 2 crumbled-up, stale kaiser rolls in ¾ c. milk until soggy. Run catfish and rolls through meat grinder, add 1 large or 2 small chopped onions browned in 2 T. butter, 2 eggs, 1 T. chopped parsley, and salt, pepper, and nutmeg to taste. Knead ingredients into a uniform mass and add some bread crumbs if mixture feels too mushy. Form into small oval cutlets, dredge in flour, and brown on both sides in several T. hot oil, then reduce heat, cover, and simmer about 15–20 min. Transfer to baking dish and dot with butter. Fork-blend 1 c. sour cream with 2–3 T. flour until smooth, then stir in the mushroom water. When mixture is lump-free, add the chopped mushrooms, and drench the fish with the sauce. Bake in pre-heated 375° oven about 20 min. Serve with potatoes or groats and a non-creamed, seasonal salad.

BURBOT—MANY DIFFERENT WAYS
miętus na różne sposoby

The freshwater burbot, like its cousin, the saltwater cod, is an extremely tasty and versatile fish which may be prepared in a great variety of ways. It is excellent fried (either floured, breaded, or battered), it is good for poaching (especially with Polonaise egg topping), baking, or broiling, and tastes great in cutlets prepared as above. Or try it according to the recipe below, taken from the rich repertoire of Polish-Jewish cookery.

BURBOT À LA JUIVE
miętus po żydowsku

Sprinkle 2–2½ lbs. filleted burbot with salt and lemon juice and let stand in refrigerator 2 hrs. Dredge in flour and fry in several T. hot oil until nicely golden on both sides. Transfer to baking dish. Chop 2–3 onions very fine and mix with 2 beaten egg yolks and ⅓ c. raisins (pre-soaked and well-drained). Season to taste with salt, pepper, and a little sugar and lemon juice. Pour mixture over fish and bake in 350° oven about 20 min. Serve with potatoes and sour cream-laced salad.

COD—MANY DIFFERENT WAYS
dorsz na różne sposoby

Like burbot, cod is an extremely versatile fish. It is excellent when very fresh, but its oil easily turns rancid, giving it an unpleasant cod-liver-oil taste. Besides frying, baking, poaching, and broiling, try it according to the recipe for pike in horseradish sauce and walleye with fresh mushrooms. *Note*: A slight cod-liver-oil smell does not mean the cod is unfit to eat. It can be largely eliminated by giving it the marinade, brine, and milk bath.

BAKED STURGEON
jesiotr pieczony

Sprinkle 2–2½ lbs. cleaned, sliced sturgeon with salt and several T. vinegar and refrigerate 1 hr. Place in baking dish, after rinsing of excess salt and bake in 375° oven 20 min. Fork-blend 1 c. sour cream with 1 T. or more chopped dill and salt & pepper to taste. Pour over fish, sprinkle with several T. bread crumbs, and bake until it begins to brown. Serve with potatoes or rice and a fresh vinaigrette-dressed salad. *Variation*: Cook 6–8 oz. sliced, fresh mushrooms and 1 small minced onion in 2 T. butter 10 min. Smother sturgeon with cooked mushrooms before adding sour cream.

STURGEON WITH RUDDY RAISIN SAUCE
jesiotr z rumianym sosem rodzynkowym

Cook 2–2½ lbs. sturgeon in strained court bouillon (made with an extra onion) to cover on very low heat 30–40 min. Meanwhile, in dry saucepan caramelize (melt and brown) 2 t. sugar. Add 2 T. water and simmer, stirring constantly, until caramelized sugar dissolves and a brown, clear liquid appears. Add 1 T. butter and 1 T. flour, stir constantly, and simmer until you get a smooth, thick paste. Stir in 2 c. sturgeon stock, bring to boil, and add 3 T. vinegar, ¼ c. dry red or white wine, ½ c. raisins, 1 thinly sliced lemon (with rind and seeds removed), and simmer 5 min. Season to taste with salt & pepper, and enough sugar to get a sweet, sour, and winey taste. Transfer cooked sturgeon to serving platter and drench with sauce. Serve with mashed potatoes. *Note*: As you have probably gathered, ruddy raisin sauce is another name for gray sauce which occupies an important place in Old Polish cuisine and has been mentioned on these pages more than once. The above recipe, incidentally, has been adapted from a cookbook published in the 19th century.

STURGEON PIE
jesiotr w pierogu

Dissolve 1 cake crushed yeast in 1 c. lukewarm milk and combine with about 4 c. flour, 2 eggs, 1 T. butter, and ½ t. salt. Beat with wooden spoon until dough no longer sticks to spoon. Set aside to rise. Meanwhile, simmer 2 lbs. sturgeon slices (that have been salted, sprinkled with lemon juice, and refrigerated 1 hr.) in 3–4 T. butter about 10 min. until partially cooked. Midway through add 2 finely minced onions and simmer with fish in butter drippings. Place dough on floured board. When it has risen slightly, stretch it out into a rectangle, sprinkling lightly with flour. On one half of the dough rectangle place half the fish, top with a generous layer of sliced, hard-boiled eggs, salt, pepper, garnish with fresh chopped dill, and sprinkle with several T. melted butter. Top with the remaining fish and cover with another layer of hard-boiled egg slices, salted, peppered, sprinkled with dill, and drenched with butter. Cover with the remaining flap of dough and seal the 2 halves together. Allow to rise in warm, draftless place about 1½ hrs. then bake in 350° oven about 1 hr. The crust may be brushed with beaten egg and sprinkled with bread crumbs. Serve hot as a meal in itself. *Note*: This pie can be made with any really fresh or fresh-frozen freshwater or saltwater fillets. It was once commonly served on *Wigilia* (Christmas Eve), especially along Poland's eastern borderlands, where it is usually referred to as kulebiak.

FRIED EEL
węgorz smażony

Cut 2–2½ lbs. cleaned, skinned eel into 2–3 inch pieces. If it has a muddy smell, give it the vinegar-brine-milk bath. Pat dry, sprinkle with salt, dredge in flour, dip in beaten eggs, and roll in bread crumbs and brown in 4 T. hot oil. Reduce heat and cook until done. On serving platter decorate with lemon wedges and sprigs of parsley. Serve with potatoes and tartar sauce. Since eel is one of the fatter fishes, many feel that poaching is a better way to prepare it.

POACHED EEL
węgorz z wody

Place 2–2½ lbs. cleaned, skinned eel, cut into 3 inch portions in pot, cover with 6 c. hot, strained court bouillon and cook on low heat about 20 min. On serving platter, sprinkle with lemon juice and garnish with chopped dill. Serve with potato balls Polonaise (topped with butter-browned bread crumbs) and a grated, mayonnaise-laced salad.

BATTER-FRIED FRESH HERRING
śledzie świeże smażone w cieście

Herring has traditionally been salted, marinated, rolled into rollmops, and served with oil or sour cream as a cold appetizer for so long that many people overlook the possibility of using it in its fresh state. If you can get some fresh or fresh-frozen herring fillets, try the following for next Friday's meal. Sprinkle fillets with salt and lemon juice and refrigerate 1 hr. Meanwhile, combine 2 raw eggs yolks, 2 T. oil, ⅓ c. flour and ¼ t. salt and beat into creamy batter. Beat 2 egg whites to a froth and fold in together with another ⅓ c. flour. Mix well. The dough should be thicker than that used for crêpes (naleśinki). If it is too thin, sprinkle in a bit more flour. Wipe the fillets dry, impale on fork, and dip into batter, making sure they are uniformly covered, and fry in 4–5 T. hot oil until nicely golden on both sides, then reduce heat and cook a while longer until done. Test one for doneness. Serve with gherkin sauce and buttered, dilled potatoes (new or old).

FRIED FLOUNDER
flądra smażona

Rinse 1½–2 lbs. cleaned flounder, pat dry, salt, sprinkle with lemon juice, and let stand in refrigerator 1 hr. Sprinkle with fish seasoning, dredge in flour, and fry in 5 or more T. hot oil until nice and golden on both sides, then reduce heat and cook until tender. After browning they may also be transferred to baking pan, dotted with butter, and baked in 350° oven 10–15 min. Serve with any of the accompaniments suggested for other fried-fish dishes. *Note*: Flounder may also be breaded or dipped in batter before frying. The authors of this cookbook were first introduced to this delicious fish in 1970, when honeymooning in Sopot, Poland's best-known seaside resort town. To this day, fried flounder fresh from the Baltic is sold there at sidewalk stands on paper plates, served only with a splotch of horseradish and rye bread. Delicious!

FRIED SMELT
stynki smażone

Salt 1½–2 lbs. cleaned smelt and let stand 1 hr. Drain off liquid that forms, pat dry, dredge in flour, dip in beaten eggs and beer (1 T. beer per egg), and roll in mixture of fine bread crumbs and flour. Fry in hot, fairly deep oil reaching ½ inch up the side of skillet, on both sides to a nice golden brown. Serve with cold horseradish sauce, potatoes, and lettuce & radish salad.

CRUNCHY-FRIED SMALL FISH
rybki smażone na chrupko

Every still-fisherman has a day when the only thing that seems to bite are undersized 2–3 inch panfish. If you throw them back, you may only be helping to keep the lake or pond overpopulated with stunted fish competing for an inadequate food supply. Especially since they make mighty good eating right at the lakeshore in camp-type conditions. Simply clean the baby perch, bluegill, rockbass, sunfish, or whatever, wash well, dry, sprinkle with salt & pepper, dredge in flour (or shake in a flour-filled plastic bag), and fry in very hot oil about ½ inch deep to a deep golden brown on both sides. Drain on absorbent paper, if you have it, and simply eat the entire crunchy fish like a snack food with a cold glass of beer. If you have enough, you can make a meal of them with rye bread and a tomato or dill pickle. *Note*:

If the fish are no more than 2–3 inches long and you fry them long enough, the bones will dissolve and can be eaten along with the fish, giving you the full benefit of the calcium, phosphorus, and other nutrients that normally are discarded. If you have some minnows and chubs left over in the bait bucket, clean and fry them too, along with the baby panfish.

MARINATED PANFISH
rybki marynowane

By rights, this recipe belongs in the cold-appetizer chapter, but since we're on the subject of fishing and panfish, we might as well pass along right here and now a little trick long known to Polish anglers and campers. It is especially good when you've caught more panfish than you can fry for supper and you have no way to refrigerate them. In pot combine 2 c. 6% distilled (white) vinegar and 2–3 c. water (depending on tartness desired). Add 10 peppercorns, 3–6 grains allspice, 2–3 crumbled bay leaves, 2 sliced onions, and (optional) 1 small sliced carrot, 1 T. salt, and 2–3 t. sugar or more. Bring to boil, simmer 5 min., remove from heat, cover, and set aside to cool. Salt 2–3 lbs. cleaned, well-rinsed, dried panfish of various species and size, in general not exceeding a length of 6 inches before the heads are removed. Fry in hot oil until golden brown on both sides and drain on absorbent paper. They should not be overfried. Some fishermen sprinkle the fish with flour before frying, but that causes the marinade to turn cloudy and unappetizing, so we don't recommend it. Place the fried fish head down in quart twist-off jars and cover with cool marinade, evenly distributing vegetables and spices. Seal and store. They will keep a week or longer without refrigeration, since the vinegar acts as a preservative. After several days the bones of the smaller fish will become soft (the bigger ones will take a little longer) and the entire fish can be eaten. Marinated panfish are reminiscent of pickled herring and some say they are even tastier.

CAMPFIRE-BAKED FISH
ryba pieczona w ognisku

Before moving on to other things, here is one final recipe from the Polish lakeshore circuit. Clean, remove head, and wash well a 1½–2 lb. fish. Pike, carp, walleye, bass, whitefish, trout, catfish, or any such freshly caught species is good. Salt & pepper inside and out, place on a horseradish leaf, insert ½ a stick of butter into cavity along with a few onion slices and a sprig of dill, if you have them. Rub the outside of the fish with butter and wrap in the horseradish leaf. Use more than 1 leaf if needed to cover the entire fish. Cover fish with a ½–¾ inch shell of damp, freshly-dug clay. After your campfire has died down, dig a hole at center and line with a layer of hot embers. Place the clay-encased fish inside and cover it with the remaining embers, then cover with dirt and pat down with shovel. Then, go for a hike or swim or take a trip to town. When you get back several hrs. later, break open the clay shell and enjoy this piping hot, mouth-watering delicacy. Instead of clay, you can wrap the fish in several thicknesses of aluminum foil, but first wrap it in horseradish leaves if available. They not only kill bacteria, but also impart a delightful flavor to the baked fish.

FISH ROLL-UPS
zrazy rybne zawijane

For this dish, use 1½–2 lbs. freshwater or saltwater fillets that include the skin. Pike, walleye, perch, and cod are especially good. Cut the fillets into roughly 2 x 4 inch rectangles if possible, place on board skin-side down and sprinkle with salt. Grate 2–3 onions and simmer until golden in 3 T. butter. (*Variation*: Simmer grated onions with about 6 finely chopped fresh mushrooms.) Remove from heat. Add 1–2 T. bread crumbs and 1 raw egg, sprinkle with pepper, and (optional) a little chopped dill and/or parsley. Mix well and spread fish slices with mixture. Roll up tightly and tie each roll-up with a strong cotton thread. Dip in beaten eggs, roll in fine bread crumbs, and fry to a nice golden brown in 2 T. oil and 3 T. butter. Transfer to baking dish. Add the pan drippings, a T. bread crumbs, juice of ½ a lemon, and ¼ c. court bouillon and bake covered in 350° oven 20–30 min. Serve with potatoes or rice and green-onion salad. *Note*: Warn your guests of the thread or, better yet, fasten roll-ups with toothpicks which are easily removed before serving.

MINCED FISH ROLLS
zrazy rybne siekane

Bake 2–3 whole onions in hot oven until tender, discard scorched outer skin, and run through meat grinder with 1½ lbs. skinned freshwater fillets. Mix in 1 raw egg and add enough bread crumbs to get a workable consistency. Knead well to combine ingredients, salt & pepper generously, and roll into thick rolls. Cut into 1 inch pieces and place in baking dish. Add 3 T. butter, ½ c. beer, and ½ c. court bouillon and bake in 350° oven 45–60 min. Before serving with potatoes and a salad, garnish with chopped dill. *Variation*: Brown 1 T. flour in 1 T. butter in saucepan, mix with pan liquid, season with salt, pepper, and a little lemon juice, bring to boil, and pour over fish rolls.

POACHED SALMON
łosoś z wody

Place 1½–2 lbs. fresh salmon fillets in 6 c. hot court bouillon and simmer on low heat about 30 min. Remove to serving platter, sprinkle with lemon juice, and drench with melted butter. For an elegant effect, surround the salmon, with potato balls Polonaise, finely chopped hard-boiled eggs, salted, peppered, and garnished with chopped dill, and radish roses. Serve fresh mushroom sauce in gravy boat.

GRILLED SALMON
łosoś z rusztu

Slice 2 lbs. whole, cleaned salmon into ¾ inch steaks, sprinkle with salt, and refrigerate 1 hr. Brush salmon steaks with butter and place on oil-brushed charcoal grill, far enough away from the hot embers so they do not get scorched. Grill about 10 min., then turn over and grill until done. The fish flakes easily when done. Do not overcook. Baste with butter a few times during cooking. On platter sprinkle salmon steaks with melted butter and decorate with lemon wedges. Serve with french fries, lettuce & vinaigrette salad, and preferably homemade tartar sauce. *Note:* Naturally, you can also place salmon steaks on a rack and broil them in your oven or electric broiler.

BUTTER-COOKED WHITEFISH
sielawa w maśle

Salt 2 lbs. cleaned whitefish and refrigerate 1 hr. Dredge in flour or a mixture of fine bread crumbs and flour. In skillet melt 3–4 T. butter and add the fish. Simmer on very low heat so that the butter barely bubbles and fish does not sizzle. About 10 min. per side should be more than enough. Fish is done when it flakes easily. Serve straight from the skillet garnished with lemon wedges. Pureed potatoes and lettuce & vinaigrette are excellent side dishes. *Variation*: After fish has simmered on one side 5 min., turn it over. Add 4–6 thinly sliced fresh mushrooms to skillet and allow to simmer butter with the fish another 5 min. Add 1 T. dry white wine, cover, and simmer another 10 min. or so. Switch off heat and allow flavors to intermingle a while longer. Serve with boiled new potatoes drenched with the pan drippings.

FISH MAZURIAN STYLE
ryba po mazursku

Soak 1 oz. dried Polish mushrooms in 2 c. water 2 hrs., then cook in same water until tender. Slice or chop mushrooms and return to water. Simmer 3 thinly sliced onions in 3 T. butter until golden and tender but still unbrowned. Salt 2 lbs. pike, walleye, or other freshwater or ocean fillets and refrigerate 1 hr. (If using ocean fillets, also sprinkle with lemon juice.) Dredge fillets in flour and fry in a little hot oil on both sides until golden. Transfer fish to baking dish. Skin 2 brine-cured dill pickles and slice into thin rounds. Combine pickles, sautéd onion, and drained mushrooms, and add to baking pan. Fork-blend ¾ c. sour cream with 1–2 T. flour, stir in the mushroom water, and season to taste with salt, pepper, and about 1 t. Maggi extract. When smooth, pour over fish. Top with a little grated yellow cheese and bake in 375° oven about 20 min. Serve with mashed potatoes and sauerkraut salad.

FISH TARTAR STYLE
ryba po tatarsku

Salt 2–2½ lbs. freshwater fillets (pike, walleye, sturgeon, or whitefish are best) and let stand 1 hr. in refrigerator. Meanwhile, grate 4 Spanish onions, place in sieve, and press down with wooden thumper or spoon to extract all the juice. Melt ½ a stick butter in large skillet with tight-fitting lid, place the fillets in the butter, drench with onion juice, (discard onion pulp left in sieve) and simmer on very low heat covered about 15 min. Add 2 c. fork-blended sour cream and simmer 10 min. longer, or until fish is tender. Transfer fish to warm platter. To sauce, add 1 thinly sliced lemon (with rind and seeds removed), 1 t. capers, and 6–10 thinly sliced olives. Bring sauce to boil, salt & pepper to taste, and pour over fish on platter. Serve with mashed or boiled potatoes and a non-creamed salad.

FISH À LA NELSON
ryba po nelsońsku

Soak ½–1 oz. dried Polish mushrooms in 2 c. water 2 hrs., then cook in same water until tender. Slice and return to liquid. Salt and sprinkle with lemon juice 2 lbs. very fresh fillets and let stand 1 hr. in fridge. Dredge in flour and fry in several T. oil until pale golden on both sides. They should be slightly undercooked, since the baking that follows will complete the cooking process. Set fillets aside. In same drippings sauté 1–2 thinly sliced onions until golden and tender. Cook 4–6 potatoes in skins and remove when still slightly underdone. Remove skins under cold running water and slice. Generously butter a baking pan, line bottom with a layer of potatoes, salt & pepper, cover with layer of fish, and top with mushrooms and onions. Dot with butter and repeat process, leaving some potatoes to make up the top layer. Fork-blend 1 cup sour cream with 1 T. flour and mushroom liquid and pour over the remaining ingredients. Bake in 350° oven 30–45 min. Sprinkle with chopped dill and/or parsley before serving. This delicious one-pan meal needs only a crunchy salad to round things out. *Optional*: 2–3 sliced hard-boiled eggs may be included among the layers before baking.

FISH GRECIAN STYLE
ryba po grecku

Cut 1 portion cleaned soup greens and 2–3 onions into thin strips about 1 inch long. Cook in skillet on low heat in 3 T. oil, adding 3 T. water when vegetables begin to brown. Salt and simmer until tender. Stir in 2–3 T. tomato paste and season to taste with salt, pepper, paprika, lemon juice, and a little sugar to get the zesty sweet & sour taste you want. For added zing 1–2 t. brown mustard may be added. Salt 2 lbs. fresh or fresh-frozen fish fillets of choice and refrigerate 1 hr. Dredge in flour and fry to a nice golden hue on both sides. In buttered baking dish layer the vegetables and fish, making sure that the top layer is vegetables. Bake in 350° oven 15–20 min. In some families, this delicacy is included among the fish dishes served on *Wigilia* (Christmas Eve). More often than not, it is served cold as an appetizer or starter course.

FISH À LA RADECKI
ryba à la Radecki

Simmer 2 lbs. of fish fillets of choice in court bouillon about 20 min. or until tender. Carefully remove fillets with slotted spoon and keep warm. Cool 2–3 c. strained stock (in which the fillets were cooked) to room temp. in freezer, then mix with ½ c. red currant jelly and ¼ c. dry red wine. In saucepan, melt 3 T. butter and simmer 3 T. flour in it but do not brown. Gradually add the stock, jelly, and wine mixture, stirring constantly. Beat with wire whisk to get a smooth sauce, season to taste with salt, pepper, lemon juice, sugar, and (optional) a pinch of ground cloves. Bring to boil. Either pour the hot sauce over the fish or warm up the fish in the sauce.

* * *

MUSHROOM DISHES

"Mushrooms abounded—round the fair damsels* the young men did throng;
Or vixens, as they're hailed in Lithuanian song.
They symbolize maidenhood, their flesh no maggot bites
And no insect thereon ever even alights.
The slender bolete maidens pursued instead,
That colonel of mushrooms as it's commonly said.
But all hunt for milky caps which, though not very tall
And largely unsung, are the tastiest of all..."

The above passage comes from the epic *Pan Tadeusz* by the great 19th century romantic poet, Adam Mickiewicz, and is one of many literary portrayals of Polish mushroom lore and legend. It is no wonder, for a certain magic has always surrounded *grzyby* in this heavily forested country.

Historically speaking, culinary lifestyles had run largely along economic and class lines. Whereas the nobility feasted on choice meats, rich cakes, and imported wines, the peasantry had to make do with groats, dumplings, cabbage, and coarse breads. Mushrooms were the great equalizer. They held a place of honor on the banquet tables of royalty, but were equally at home in the humble peasant cottage. They were there for the picking and, after a good warm rain, carpeted the forest floor and sprouted abundantly in meadows and at waysides.

To this day mushroom-picking remains a national pastime. In a good season, when the weather is right, a family can gather enough for the entire year. What isn't used at once is canned, brine-cured, pickled, or dried for the months ahead.

Fresh mushrooms are delicious in soups and stews as well as with scrambled eggs, and dried mushrooms are in a class by themselves. They greatly enhance the flavor in soups, gravies, and sauerkraut dishes, including *bigos*, which is known as Poland's national dish. Interestingly enough, the characteristic feature of Polish cuisine is that it regards mushrooms as not only a garnish or flavoring. Both fresh, wild and domestic, cultivated mushrooms as well as the reconstituted dry variety are often a meal in themselves, usually sautéed in butter or simmered in sour cream.

To Poles, the king of mushrooms is the *borowik* (*Boletus edulis*), commonly known in English as King Bolete. Its Polish name is derived from *bór* (coniferous forest) and aptly defines its preferred natural habitat. It is also referred to at times as *grzyb prawdziwy* (true

---

* Fair damsels—*krasnolice* (literally: beautiful women) and *lisice* (vixen) are regional slang for chanterelles.

mushroom) or *prawdziwek*, implying that all other species are definitely inferior. But many feel the fresh butter-fried *rydz* (Lactarius deliciosus) equals the fresh bolete in taste or comes in a close second. This was pointed out in the above-cited fragment of Mickiewicz's poem. It must have been a dissenter among those incorrigibly individualistic Poles that coined the saying: "*Lepszy rydz niż nic!*" (a milky cap is better than nothing).

Other desirable species include *pieczarka* (meadow mushroom), *kurka* (chanterelle), *maślak* (sticky bun), *gąska* (Tricholoma), *gołąbek (Russula)*, and *kania* (parasol mushroom). Although the *smardz* (morel) is also picked in Poland, it is ranked as a mediocre find, since there are many species that equal or surpass it in taste. In the U.S., by contrast, morels are among the most highly prized wild species. The boletus family also includes the *koźlarz czerwony* (orange bolete) and *koźlarz babka* (birch bolete). They are ranked fair to good but cannot compete with the King Bolete. Widely marketed in Poland as an economy version of the latter is the *podgrzybek (Boletus chrysenteron)* which grows in great abundance but is definitely inferior to the real thing.

The statement that mushrooms are "all flavor and no nutrition" or that they are non-fattening and therefore a perfect diet food is only partially true. Nutritionally they are low in protein, but they contain plenty of vitamin PP, provitamin D, minerals (notably zinc and copper), some B vitamins, and glycogen, a substance that promotes the body's natural functions. They indeed have very few calories and someone who ate nothing but boiled mushrooms would certainly lose weight. But the butter, cream, and other such embellishments with which they are often prepared definitely undermine their low-calorie status.

But no matter how you slice them (no pun intended!), mushrooms are simply great eating. We hope some of the following recipes will help make them a regular part of your homecooking and entertainment scene.

* * *

Before presenting some actual recipes, we feel any reader interested in picking, preparing, and/or eating mushrooms would do well to familiarize himself with the names of some of the better-known varieties. We have limited the chart below to those species found in both Poland and North America. For instance, we have omitted the *podgrzybek złotawy* (Boletus chrysenteron), which is very popular in Poland, where it passes as "a poor man's bolete." As far as we can determine, it grows in parts of North America, but for some reason is rarely picked. A full description of the various species, their natural habitats, and growing seasons as well as of mushroom-picking techniques far transcends the scope of this book. The following little chart is only a modest attempt to clear up some of the confusion over terminology and provide a few added pointers, but it is no substitute for a good mushroom atlas or guide. Any novice planning to take to the fields and forests in pursuit of these edible fungi should by all means take along an experienced mushroom-picker. Since edible mushrooms often have poisonous look-alikes, a cautious approach is very advisable.

COMMON POLISH NAMES	SCIENTIFIC NAMES	COMMON ENGLISH NAMES
BOROWIK, GRZYB PRAWDZIWY, PRAWDZIWEK	*BOLETUS EDULIS*	*KING BOLETE*

Note: This is undoubtedly the finest-tasting above ground mushroom known to man. Hence popular Polish terminology refers to the bolete as the only true mushroom, and the common English name gives it royal status. There is no more delectable and elegant gourmet delight than a dish of freshly picked boletes sautéed in butter and seasoned only with a little salt. It is the bolete that we primarily think of whenever imported dried Polish mushrooms are mentioned. Their dusky, nutlike taste and heavenly aroma turn an ordinary meal into a festive repast. If you get them in gourmet or import shops, you may run into such foreign names of the bolete as cèpe (French), porcino (Italian), or Steinpilz (German). The sight of this noble, brown-capped mushroom with its stocky tan stem growing under conifers gladdens the heart of mushroom-pickers the world over!

KOŹLARZ CZERWONY, GRZYB CZERWONY	*LECINUM AURANTIACUM*	*ORANGE BOLETE ORANGE-CAP MUSHROOM*

Note: Very tasty, although it cannot compare with the King Bolete, for no mushroom can! Grows mainly under pines and aspens. It has an orange cap and a brown and white speckled stem.

KOŹLARZ BABKA, KOŹLAK, KOZAK, PODBRZEŹNIAK	*LECCINUM SCABRUM*	*BIRCH BOLETE*

Note: Although inferior to the King Bolete, this is still a very good wild mushroom. Whereas most boletes grow in coniferous forests, this variety prefers birch groves. Except for its brown cap, the birch bolete is very similar to the orange bolete.

---------------------------	*BOLETUS MIRABILIS*	*ADMIRABLE BOLETE*

Note: This appears to be one of the few indigenously American boletes and is second in taste only to the King Bolete. It grows on or around stumps and logs (mainly hemlock, fir, and cedar) in the Pacific Northwest and Rocky Mountain states but is unknown in Poland, hence the lack of a common Polish name.

Some of Poland's better-known wild mushrooms: 1. *Lactarius* (rydz) are most delicious fried in butter; 2. *Butterball* (maślak), a member of the large boletus family; 3. King Bolete (borowik, prawdziwek), the country's most coveted mushroom; 4. Parasol mushroom (kanie) whose large cap is usually breaded and fried like a pork chop; 5. Tricholoma (gąska), a member of the agaric family; 6. Birch Boletes (koźlarz babka) prefer birch groves to coniferous forests; 7. Chanterelles (kurka) look like little golden trumpets; 8. Boletus Chrisenteron (podgrzybek) is a "poor man's bolete"; 9. Meadow mushroom (pieczarka), the wild version of the well-known white store-bought mushroom.

MAŚLAK ZWYCZAJNY	SUILLUS LUTEUS	BUTTERBALL, STICKY
MAŚLAK ZIARNISTY	SUILLUS GRANULATUS	BUN, GRANULATED
		BOLETE, PINE BOLETE

Note: Both these similar species are very tasty representatives of the large Boletus family, of which only a few examples are presented here. They mainly grow under pines, and pine needles are usually seen stuck to their sticky caps. In the author's home state of Michigan, butterballs and granulated boletes account for the largest volume of boletes gathered each autumn by local mushroom-pickers, most of whom are of Polish, other-Slavic, Lithuanian, or Italian ancestry.

PIECZARKA POLNA,	AGARICUS CAMPESTRIS	MEADOW MUSHROOM,
ŁĄKOWA		FIELD MUSHROOM,
		PASTURE MUSHROOM,
		COMMON MUSHROOM,
		WHITE MUSHROOM,
		PINK BOTTOM,
		BUTTON MUSHROOM

Note: This is the wild version of the white commercially produced mushroom found in the produce departments of supermarkets. As its name implies, it grows in fields and pastures, especially those in which horses graze. It is similar in taste and texture to the domestic variety but has more flavor.

PIECZARKA HODOWLANA	AGARICUS BISPORUS	WHITE MUSHROOM,
		CULTIVATED MUSH-
		ROOM, CHAMPIGNON
		DE PARIS

Note: This is what most Americans immediately call to mind when they think of mushrooms, quite unlike Poles whose thoughts first turn to the noble, wild-growing borowik (King Bolete). Although a bit short on flavor, fresh store-bought mushrooms are now used extensively in Polish cuisine and are above all prized for their convenience. They come cleaned and packaged in various-sized containers and are ready to fry, sauté, bake, braise, or broil. They are excellent in soups and sauces and are among the few species of mushrooms that can be eaten raw in salads, although this practice has not caught on in Poland.

**KURKA, KURZA NOGA,
PIEPRZNIK**

CANTHARELLUS CIBARIUS

**GOLDEN OR YELLOW
CHANTERELLE, EGG
MUSHROOM**

Note: This small, trumpet-shaped, egg-yolk-yellow mushroom has a slightly peppery taste, hence one of its Polish names, pieprznik, and its principal German name: Pfifferling. It is found in both leafy and coniferous forests. It is quite tasty.

**LEJKOWIEC DĘTY,
CHOLEWKA, SKÓRZAK**

**CRATERELLUS
CORNUCOPIOIDES**

**HORN OF PLENTY,
FAIRY TRUMPET,
TRUMPET OF DEATH**

Note: One of the common English names of this mushroom, trumpet of death, could easily scare off the uninitiated, but it is truly a misnomer. This horn of plenty is not only edible but can be downright delicious. Like the golden chantrelle, to which it is related, it is excellent fried, alone or with scrambled eggs, in stews, etc. It is chiefly found in hardwood or mixed forests and looks something like a brown, ragged-edged chantrelle.

RYDZ, MLECZAJ RYDZ

LACTARIUS DELICIOSUS

**MILKY CAP,
SAFFRON MILK CUP**

Note: This pale ruddy-orange mushroom with a concave cap is prized by some on par with the King Bolete. It grows mainly in spruce forests.

GOŁĄBEK

RUSSULA VESCA

RUSSULA MUSHROOM

Note: Related to the milky cap, the russula has a reddish-brown cap and a white stem and prefers the company of evergreens, oak, and beech.

GĄSKA ZIELONKA

TRICHOLOMA FLAVOVIRENS

**TRICHOLOMA
MUSHROOM**

Note: This greenish-yellow mushroom grows under conifers and deciduous trees.

**OPIENIEK, OPIEŃKA,
PODPIENIEK, PODPIEŃKA,
BEDŁKA PNIAKOWA**

ARMILLARIELLA MELLEA

**HONEY MUSHROOM
STUMPER**

Note: This tasty brown mushroom is often found growing in large quantities on or around stumps, hence its Polish names which mean "round the stump" or "under the stump." Considerable quantities of canned honey mushrooms are imported from Italy, where they are referred to as chiodini or funghi al naturale. In his "Mushrooms Wild and Edible" Vicent Maretka advises novices against picking these mushrooms in the wilds because they can easily be confused with the poisonous galerina.

SMARDZ	*MORCHELLA ESCULENTA*	*MOREL, HONEYCOMB MUSHROOM, PINE CONE FUNGUS*

Note: These mushrooms with a brown, conical, sponge-like cap are far more prized in America than in Poland, perhaps because there are simply more familiar and widely-picked species in the latter. Abundant during damp spring weather in woodlands and abandoned orchards.

PIESTRZENICA KASZTANOWATA, BABIE UCHO	*GYROMITRA ESCULENTA*	*FALSE MOREL, BRAIN MUSHROOM*

Note: Somewhat reminiscent of the morel, this mushroom has a cap resembling the wrinkled lobes of a brain. Its favorite habitat is the evergreen forest. Unless properly prepared, the false morel is poisonous. The mushrooms should be boiled in water about 20 min. and then drained before using like fresh mushrooms. An even surer way of removing the toxins is to dry these mushrooms.

BARANIOSZEK	*POLYSPORUS FRONDOSUS*	*HEN OF THE WOODS, CAULIFLOWER MUSH-ROOM*

Note: This edible fungus appears in the form of a cluster of overlapping greyish-brown caps that at first glance may look like a hen sitting in its nest. Poles perceive it as ram's fleece, hence its name, "little ram". Unfortunately, adverse ecological changes have made this mushroom rare in Poland. In the U.S. it is especially sought after by Italian-Americans, who look for it after autumn rains round the base of trees and stumps.

KANIA, SOWA, PARASOL	*MACROLEPIOTA PROCERA*	*PARASOL MUSHROOM*

Note: This tall brown mushroom with a large, flat, shaggy cap is a favorite in Poland. Just the cap is used which is breaded and fried in fat like a meat cutlet. It also grows in North America but tends to be avoided because of the fear of confusing it with the poisonous, green-gilled lepiota (Chlorophyllum molybdites). The latter is unknown in Poland.

HUBA SIARKOWA   *POLYSPORUS SULPHUREUS*   **SULPHUR-SHELF MUSHROOM, CHICKEN MUSHROOM**

Note: This edible fungus grows on the sides of trees and stumps in the form of numerous overlapping caps that are a bright orange on top and pale sulphur yellow underneath. In Poland, the large caps are breaded and fried in fat and come out tasting like white chicken meat. Cut up into chunks, the sulphur shelf also tastes like chicken in stews and casseroles.

SZMACIAK GAŁĘZISTY   *SPARASSIS CRISPA*   **CURLY SPARASSIS, CAULIFLOWER FUNGUS**

Note: A single cluster of this yellow or brown-yellow curly fungus, growing at the base of an evergreen, can weigh 10 or 20 lbs. or more and provide food for several meals. It keeps well under refrigeration, unlike most fresh mushrooms which should not be stored too long, and can be sautéed, used in stews, or dried.

SOPLÓWKA GAŁĘZISTA   *HERICIUM RAMOSUM*   **BEAR'S HEAD FUNGUS, ICICLE FUNGUS**

Note: These beautiful clusters of snowy-white icicles grow on the sides of trees. Both this and the related coral fungus (Hericium coralloides) are tasty when prepared in a variety of ways.

BOCZNIAK OSTRYGOWATY   *PLEUROTUS OSTREATUS*   **OYSTER MUSHROOM**

Note: These white, grey, or tan mushrooms grow in clusters on the sides of deciduous trees and are one of the few species that are unaffected by cold winter weather. Like the common white mushroom (Agaricus bisporus), the oyster mushroom is widely cultivated throughout the world. You can actually grow it in your garden on an old log or even on a bed of damp cut straw or ground corn cobs in your cellar. They are quite tasty and versatile in the kitchen, and the slightly fishy aroma can easily be disguised through the use of spices and other flavorings.

CZERNIDLAK KOŁPAKOWATY   *COPRINUS COMATUS*   **SHAGGY-MANE MUSHROOM INKY EGG**

Note: Since they readily grow on big-city lawns, in vacant lots, and at roadsides, these are often viewed by the uninitiated as an inedible nuisance. In reality, these mushrooms, with their shaggy, egg-shaped caps, are very delicious, but in attempting to prepare them one thing must be borne in mind. They must be cooked soon after picking before their caps turn into an ink-like substance. You can prevent this by refrigerating them submerged in cold water. Related species are the inky-cap mushrooms (czernidlak pospolity or Coprinus atramentarius) and glistening inky caps (czernidlak błyszczący or Corprinus micaceus). Both are tasty when cooked soon after picking but should not be consumed with alcoholic beverages.

PURCHAWKA	*LYCOPERDON, CALVATIA*	*PUFFBALL*

Note: Youngsters often like to give these large round fungi a good swift kick in order to see a cloud of smoke go up. At that stage, puffballs are no longer fit to eat. Only the young fungi are edible, when their insides are a nice cream-cheese white. This large family ranges from the golf-ball-sized gemmed puffball (purchawada chropowata or Lycoperdron perlatum) to the giant puffball (purchawada olbrzymia or Calvatia gigantea), which can weigh in at several pounds. Perhaps due to the available variety of superior-tasting mushrooms, these are not too widely collected in Poland. In the U.S., mushroom-hunters of Italian descent are especially fond of puffballs.

TWARDZIAK JADALNY	*LENTINUS EDODES*	*SHIITAKE MUSHROOM*

Note: These mushrooms are native neither to Poland nor North America and hail from the Far East. We have included them here, because fresh and dried shiitake are a reasonable substitute for boletes in any Polish recipe. You can also raise them at home (see below). They are second only to the white mushroom (Agaricus bisporus) as the world's most widely cultivated species, and their popularity continues to grow.

* * *

If you love mushrooms, but lack the desire or know-how to pick them in the wilds, and cannot afford the commercially available ones as often as you might like, you still need not do without. Try raising your own right at home. It is both simple and economical. Chances are there's a garden, nursery, or seed center nearby that supplies complete mushroom-growing kits at reasonable prices. They can also be mail-ordered through nursery and seed catalogues.

* * *

MUSHROOM PREPARATION
przygotowanie grzybów

If you pick wild mushrooms, they should be brushed free of soil, pine needles, and scraps of dry leaves or undergrowth before they land in your basket. It's also a good idea to use your mushrooming knife to trim away hardened stem bottoms, as well as wormy or discolored portions. That will save time when you're ready to clean your mushrooms for cooking. Store-bought fresh mushrooms are usually fairly clean already, but trim the bottoms if they are hardened. It is not recommended to soak mushrooms excessively, as they will become water-logged and lose some of their flavor and natural nutrients in the water. The best way to clean them is to wipe them with a damp cloth, but if they show signs of embedded dirt, you may wash them well and rinse in a colander under cold running water. You can also scald them in a colander with boiling water. Either way, allow the mushrooms to drip dry, then dry them with a towel. When they are completely dry, they are ready to use in any of the following recipes.

SAUTÉED BOLETES AU NATUREL
borowiki smażone

Use 1½ lbs. bolete caps of similar size if possible. If they are different sizes, use the smaller ones whole and cut the larger ones in half. Heat 5 T. lard (or olive oil), in large skillet and sauté the mushrooms until nicely golden brown on both sides. Do not crowd. A single layer of mushrooms should line the skillet's surface. If skillet is not large enough, sauté mushrooms in batches. When all are browned, combine them in skillet, add 1–2 T. butter, cover, and simmer on lowest possible heat 5 min. Toss them occasionally with wooden spoon. Transfer to serving dish, drench with pan drippings, and sprinkle with salt and pepper. Serve crusty French bread to sop up the drippings at casual family meals. On more formal occasions, place a slice of French bread, plain or toasted, on each plate, and top with a serving of mushrooms. That way your guests will be able to consume this delicacy more elegantly with knife & fork.

BOLETES SAUTÉED IN BUTTER
borowiki duszone w maśle

Plunge 1½ lbs. boletes into pot of boiling water and, when boiling resumes, drain. Meanwhile, melt 1 stick butter in large skillet. Add the still slightly damp mushrooms and toss gently with wooden spoon to coat with butter. Cover and simmer on very low heat 20 min., or until mushrooms are tender. Toss occasionally while they simmer. Salt & pepper and garnish with a little chopped dill and/or parsley if desired. Serve with potatoes or bread.

CREAMED BOLETES
borowiki w śmietanie

Slice 1½ lbs. boletes and simmer on low heat in skillet in 1–2 T. lard (or 1 T. lard and 1 T. butter). Add 1 T. grated onion and 1 T. water or stock, cover, and simmer on low heat 15 min. or until tender, sprinkling with salt towards the end. Sprinkle with a little flour, stirring until it is absorbed, and drench with ½–¾ c. fork-blended sour cream. Bring to gentle boil, stirring constantly, then switch off heat, cover and allow to rest several min. for flavors to mingle. Salt & pepper to taste and transfer to serving platter. *Optional*: Sprinkle with parsley and/or a little grated yellow cheese. Serve with mashed potatoes and a salad for a complete meal.

BOLETES IN CREAM SAUCE
borowiki w sosie śmietanowym

Proceed as above, but use only ½–¾ lb. fresh sliced boletes and ¾–1 c. sour cream. This is a good choice when you have only a small quantity of mushrooms. *Optional*: Flavor sauce with ½ t. liquid mushroom extract or Maggi seasoning. Serve over noodles, mashed potatoes, or buckwheat groats.

BOLETES & BACON
borowiki z boczkiem

In skillet brown ¼ lb. finely diced slab bacon. Remove browned bacon nuggets and set aside. In bacon drippings, sauté 2 finely chopped onions until golden, add 1½ lbs. sliced boletes, toss gently with wooden spoon to coat mushrooms, cover, and simmer on low heat, stirring occasionally. Cook about 20 min. or until tender. Add the browned bacon nuggets, sprinkle with ½ T. flour, stirring until it is fully absorbed, add 1 T. chopped parsley and (optional) 1 bud crushed garlic and simmer under cover another min. or so. This is a meal in itself with potatoes and a salad. It is also an interesting accompaniment to fried eggs.

BOLETES & ONIONS
borowiki z cebulką

Slice 3 onions wafer thin and sauté in 2½ T. lard (or olive oil) until golden. Add 1 lb. small boletes, sprinkle with 1 T. flour, stirring until absorbed, and simmer under cover on low heat, adding ½ c. chicken broth or meat stock. When mushrooms are tender, salt & pepper to taste. *Note:* This is meant primarily as a topping for meat or fish. If you want to serve it as a meal in itself, increase the mushrooms to 1½ lbs.

BOLETES STEWED IN WINE
borowiki duszone w winie

Dice 3 onions and brown in 2 T. lard. Stir in 1 lb. mushrooms, cover, and simmer 25 min. Add ½ c. dry white wine and 2 t. freshly squeezed lemon juice and simmer another 10 min.

Salt & pepper to taste and sprinkle with 2 T. chopped parsley. Serve as main course or as an addition to meat or fish.

BOLETE & HAM SUPPER-PARTY
borowiki z szynką na przyjęcie gości

Simmer 3 finely diced onions in 3 T. lard until golden. Dice 2 lbs. boletes, add to onions and toss lightly. Add 2 T. butter, sprinkle with a little salt (about ½ t.), and simmer on low heat under cover until mushrooms are tender (20–30 min.). At the start of simmering add 1–2 T. court bouillon (vegetable stock) or meat stock and another 2 T. or so as it cooks. Sprinkle mushrooms with 1 T. flour, add 2–3 c. diced boiled ham (preferably Krakus canned ham), salt & pepper to taste, toss ingredients, and simmer a bit longer. Remove from heat and stir in 2 beaten egg yolks. Heat well but do not bring to boil. Transfer to serving platter and sprinkle with chopped parsley. Serve with egg noodles and sliced tomatoes topped with chopped chives or onions.

BATTER-FRIED BOLETES
borowiki smażone w cieście

Plunge 2 lbs. bolete caps of similar size into boiling salted water and cook 5 min. from the time boiling resumes at a gentle, rolling boil. As they cook, beat 1 egg yolk with ½ t. salt until creamy. Continue beating and gradually add 5 T. flour and 1 c. milk (or ½ milk and ½ c. sour cream). Fold in 1 beaten egg white and mix lightly. Drain mushrooms and dry on absorbent paper or dish towel. Sprinkle mushrooms on both sides lightly with flour (through sieve), impale each on fork, dip in batter, and fry in hot lard oil (that is about ¼ inch deep) to a nice golden brown. Excellent as a supper course, light snack, or accompaniment to clear soups.

BOLETE CASSEROLE
borowiki zapiekane

Plunge 2 lbs. bolete caps into boiling salted water and cook 5 min. at gentle boil from the time boiling resumes. Drain and dry mushrooms. Using sieve, dust lightly with flour. Brown mushrooms lightly on both sides in 2 T. hot lard and transfer to baking dish. Sprinkle with salt & pepper. Make a paste from 2 T. flour and ¼ c. milk and heat in saucepan, stirring until smooth and lump-free. Stir in another ¾ c. milk and bring to boil. Remove from heat and beat in 2 egg yolks,, adding 5 T. grated yellow cheese (preferably tilsit). Salt & pepper to taste and pour mixture over mushrooms. Bake in 375° oven 20 min. or until surface begins to brown.

BOLETE & CHEESE CASSEROLE
borowiki zapiekane z serem

Take 2 lbs. fresh boletes of similar size if possible. Large mushrooms should be quartered, med.-sized ones cut in half, and small ones left whole. In 4 T. oil lightly brown 2 onions sliced wafer thin, add the mushrooms, salt & pepper, and simmer covered on low heat 20 min. or until tender. If moisture evaporates and they start to sizzle, sprinkle with a little water. Remove from heat, sprinkle with about 2 T. flour, and stir until it is absorbed. Add ¾–1 c. sour cream and 2 T. butter, stir to combine, and salt & pepper to taste. Transfer to baking dish. Mix 1¼ c. grated yellow cheese, and salt & pepper to taste. Transfer to baking dish. Bake in 375° oven 20 min. or until tops turn a nice golden-brown. Serve with hot noodles and sliced tomatoes.

BOLETES LITHUANIAN STYLE
borowiki po litewsku

Grease baking dish generously with butter. Line bottom with small fresh bolete caps—roughly 1 lb. Top with 1 diced onion and cover it with a thin layer of rye-bread crumbs (grated stale rye bread), then dot with butter. Add another layer of mushrooms, onions, rye-bread crumbs, and butter, and repeat until ingredients are used up. In addition to butter used from greasing dish, you will need about ½ a stick more, plus a total of 3 large onions and about 1 c. grated stale rye bread. Each layer of mushrooms should be lightly sprinkled with salt, and top layer should be rye bread crumbs dotted with butter. Bake covered in 325° oven about 40 min. or until mushrooms are fully cooked. *Note:* The use of raw onions and grated rye bread gives this peasant dish an earthy harshness that not everyone will appreciate. To tone it down a bit, simmer the mushrooms and onions briefly in butter before adding to baking dish and use ½ c. grated rye bread and ½ c. white bread crumbs.

ROTISSERIE-BAKED MUSHROOMS
borowiki z rożna

Impale about 16 fresh bolete caps on thin rotisserie skewers (too thick a skewer may cause the mushrooms to split and fall off!), brush lightly with olive oil, and cook on electric or charcoal-stove rotisserie until they are a nice golden-brown on the outside and fully cooked inside. Test one for doneness. When done, sprinkle with salt & pepper. Serve as an accompaniment to cooked meat, fish, or egg dishes. Or, simply serve with bread as a meal in itself.

BOLETE-KEBAB
szaszłyk z borowików

Proceed as above, but intersperse bolete caps with a similar-sized slice of green pepper, a thin slice of onion, and a square of sliced bacon. (This is one of the few recipes in this book that calls for store-bought sliced bacon, because it is very thinly sliced!). Each mushroom should be separated from the next by only one of the above ingredients: mushroom–pepper–mushroom–bacon–mushroom–onion–mushroom–pepper, etc. until all 16 bolete caps are used. Brush lightly with oil and cook on rotisserie until nicely browned and cooked through. Served with bread, Polish dill pickles, or sliced tomatoes, this is sure to be a hit at your next backyard cook-out! *Note*: You may substitute fresh white mushrooms, either store-bought (*Agaricus bisporus*) or wild (*Agaricus campestris*), for boletes in this and any of the above bolete recipes. In fact, nearly all fresh mushrooms are interchangeable, although in most cases you will detect differences in aroma, taste, and texture. The fact is that none of them can match the delicate gourmet taste of the borowik (King Bolete or Boletus edulis).

UTILIZING MUSHROOM STEMS
wykorzystanie trzonków grzybowych

Many of the more elegant recipes for boletes and other mushrooms call for only the caps. If you regularly enjoy these dishes, you will end up with a lot of extra stems. Although they are less eye-appealing than the gracefully rounded caps, they contain plenty of mushroom flavor and should certainly not be discarded. You can use them in soups, gravies, and stews, and many other dishes. One convenient way is to sauté them in butter, lard, or olive oil (or any combination of these fats) and freeze them for future reference. Simply thinly slice mushroom stems from top to bottom. If the stem gets harder to cut as you approach the base, cut the stem off at the point where it still slices easily. (The tougher pieces can be dried and pulverized into a mushroom powder excellent for seasoning). Sauté 1 c. soft stem slices in about 2 T. fat of choice until tender and fully cooked, sprinkle with salt & pepper, and set aside. When cooled to room temp., freeze sautéed mushrooms for use in soups, sauces, stews, casseroles, sauerkraut dishes, etc., whenever you like. Reheated, they can serve as a topping for meat, fish, or scrambled eggs.

BREADED BIRCH BOLETES
kozaki panierowane

Plunge about 12 caps of fair-sized birch boletes into boiling salted water and cook about 5 min. at a rolling boil from the time boiling resumes. Drain and dry on absorbent paper or dish towel. Dredge in flour, dip in beaten egg, and roll in bread crumbs, gently pressing in breading so it stays put. Heat ¼ c. olive oil or same amount lard in skillet and fry the breaded mushrooms on med. heat to a crispy golden-brown on both sides. Salt & pepper before serving.

ORANGE BOLETES & POTATOES
czerwone koźlarze z kartoflami

Chop 2–3 onions and simmer in 4 T. lard until transparent but still unbrowned. Add 2 c. diced raw potatoes, mix with onions, and cook on low heat, stirring frequently, until partially cooked. Par-boil 1 lb. sliced orange boletes in boiling salted water about 3 min. from the time boiling resumes, drain, dry on absorbent paper, and add to potatoes & onions. Turn up heat briefly, stir ingredients, salt & pepper, then reduce heat, cover, and simmer about 20 min. or until mushrooms and potatoes are fully cooked. Stir in ¾ c. sour cream and simmer briefly until it just begins to bubble. Serve with Polish rye or French bread. With a crisp salad or sliced tomatoes on the side, this is a complete meal. Garnish with chopped dill if desired.

MUSHROOM PIE
placek grzybowy

Cook 1 qt. small whole orange or birch boletes in boiling water 5 min. from the time boiling resumes. Drain well and chop fine. Sauté the chopped mushrooms together with 2–3 finely chopped onions in 3 T. butter until lightly browned. Remove from heat and add 2 beaten eggs, 2 T. sour cream, ½ c. bread crumbs, and 1 T. flour. Mix ingredients well, salt & pepper, and transfer mixture to buttered baking dish, sprinkled with bread crumbs, and bake in 350° oven 15–20 min. Turn the "pie" down-side-up onto serving platter and drench with sour-cream sauce.

HONEY MUSHROOMS SAUTÉED IN BUTTER
opieńki duszone w maśle

Finely dice 2 lbs. young honey mushrooms, combine with 2–3 chopped onions, and simmer in 2 T. lard, stirring to coat evenly. Briefly turn up heat, add 3–4 T. water, and when it boils, reduce heat, cover, and simmer 25 min. or until tender. Salt & pepper, sprinkle with

2 T. flour, and bring to boil. Add 2 T. butter and 1 T. each chopped dill and parsley and mix ingredients gently. Allow to rest covered 1 min. or so for flavors to blend. Serve with bread or mashed or whipped potatoes. *Note*: We specified young honey mushrooms, because the older ones may be tough. If you happen to run into these during your mushroom-picking excursion, feel free to pick them anyway, as long as they are not wormy or withered. You can dry and pulverize them into an excellent mushroom powder for seasoning meats, soups, gravies, and sauerkraut dishes.

PAN-FRIED MEADOW MUSHROOMS
pieczarki z patelni

Heat 3 T. lard in large skillet and add 1½ lbs. wild or cultivated white mushroom caps of roughly equal size. (If you use larger wild meadow mushrooms, you may have to skin them.) Fry on fairly high heat on both sides to a nice golden brown, then add 3 T. butter, remove skillet from heat, toss gently to coat mushrooms, and sprinkle with salt & pepper. Serve with french bread on the side or over toasted slices of french bread. The bread will soak up the mushroom drippings and be every bit as tasty as the pieczarki themselves. *Note*: Some Polish restaurants serve this as a hot appetizer. Dry white wine is the perfect accompaniment.

CREAM-STEWED MEADOW MUSHROOMS
pieczarki duszone

Thinly slice 1 lb. or slightly more whole white mushrooms (wild or domestic). Finely chop 1–2 onions and simmer in 3 T. fat (lard, oil, or butter; if using butter it's better to first heat lard or oil and then add the butter, since butter alone tends to burn). When onions just begin to brown, add the mushrooms, stir to coat with fat, add 2–3 T. water, cover, and simmer covered on low heat 15–20 min. or until tender. Sprinkle with salt & pepper. If there is still some liquid in skillet, let it steam away. Stir in ½ c. sour cream and simmer briefly, stirring constantly, but do not boil. Remove from heat. Stir in 1 raw egg yolk and mix until it is fully absorbed. Heat briefly without boiling and serve over noodles or whipped potatoes or with rye or french bread.

CREAM-STEWED MEADOW MUSHROOMS À LA VARSOVIENNE
pieczarki duszone po warszawsku

Slice 1½ lbs. meadow or domestic white mushrooms and simmer until golden but still unbrowned in 5 T. olive oil. Transfer to pot. Add 3 T. water, sprinkle with salt, cover, and simmer on very low heat 15–20 min., stirring occasionally. Stir in 1 c. fork-blended sour cream and simmer several min. longer. Salt to taste and serve with potatoes or noodles and a fresh non-creamed salad.

CREAMED MEADOW MUSHROOMS WITH WINE
pieczarki duszone z winem

Slice 1½ lbs. meadow mushrooms or their store-bought counterpart and simmer in ½ a stick butter, stirring constantly, until slightly browned. Remove from heat, sprinkle with 1 T. flour, stirring until absorbed, add 1–2 jiggers dry white wine, return to heat, bring to boil, reduce heat, and simmer 1 min. or so. Stir in 1 c. fork-blended sour cream and gradually bring to boil. Switch off heat, salt & pepper to taste, and garnish with 2 T. chopped parsley.

COOKED MUSHROOM SALAD
sałatka z pieczarek

Slice thin 1¼ lbs. white cultivated mushrooms, sprinkle with juice of ½ a lemon, and let stand several min. Cook in boiling salted water 15 min., then transfer to colander to drip dry and cool. Toss mushrooms with 3 chopped hard-boiled eggs and 3 T. olive oil, add 2 T. chopped parsley, and stir in ¼ c. mayonnaise or tartar sauce. Season to taste with salt, pepper, and a little lemon juice. Mound mixture on lettuce-lined serving dish, drench with fork-blended mayonnaise, decorate with radish slices, and garnish with chopped chives. *Note:* White mushrooms are served raw in salads in the U.S. and several other countries, but uncooked mushrooms are not part of the Polish culinary heritage.

MILKY CAPS FRIED IN BUTTER
rydze smażone w maśle

Melt ½–1 stick butter in large skillet and add 1–1½ lbs. milky caps (with stems removed). Fry cap-side-down on med.-heat until nicely browned, then flip over and brown the underside. Mushrooms should be done when all the mushroom liquid evaporates and only clarified, reddish-tinged butter remains in the skillet. Salt & pepper and serve immediately together with the drippings and bread. Although there are other ways of preparing this mushroom (see below), only frying them in butter really does justice to this tasty, reddish fungus.

MILKY CAPS STEWED WITH ONIONS
rydze duszone z cebulką

Heat 3 T. lard or olive oil in skillet and in it sauté 2–3 onions sliced wafer thin until golden but still unbrowned. Add 1–1½ lbs. sliced milky caps and 3 T. butter, reduce heat, cover, and simmer until fully cooked (15–20 min.). Uncover and allow any excess liquid to steam away. Salt & pepper and serve immediately. *Variation*: When mushrooms are tender, sprinkle with 1 T. flour, stir in ½ c. fork-blended sour cream, and simmer briefly until a thick, bubbly sauce forms. Garnish with chopped dill, if desired.

MILKY CAPS WITH SCRAMBLED EGGS
rydze z jajami

You may not always have on hand the 1–1½ lbs. fresh mushrooms called for in the above recipes. When you have a smaller quantity, this is a good dish to try. Heat 1 T. salt-pork drippings (or olive oil), add 2 T. butter, and 2 c. or so sliced milky caps. Simmer until nicely browned. Beat 6–8 eggs with 3 T. milk and pour over mushrooms. Sprinkle with salt & pepper and cook, stirring constantly like ordinary scrambled eggs. Serve with rye bread or potatoes.

MILKY CAPS À LA RADZIWILL
rydze à la Radziwiłł

Separate the stems from 1½ lbs. milky caps. Slice the stems into thin rounds and simmer in 3 T. butter with 2 finely chopped onions until nearly tender. Add the caps, sprinkle with 1 T. grated, stale black bread and the skinned and finely chopped meats of 5–6 walnuts. Stir in 1 T. tomato concentrate or several T. tomato sauce or purée, cover, and simmer on low heat 10–15 min., or until mushrooms are cooked. Salt & pepper to taste and serve with rice and a lettuce salad. *Note:* This seemingly unusual combination is quite typical of the kinds of dishes favored in the Polish manor houses of yesteryear. It also shows that milky caps were prized even by those who could afford the very best, for it was named after the Radziwiłłs, one of Old Poland's most illustrious aristocratic clans.

CHANTERELLES & BACON
kurki duszone z boczkiem

On low heat cook ¼ lb. diced slab of bacon until it just begins to brown. Add 2–3 diced onions and simmer until transparent. Add 1½ lbs. sliced chanterelles, mix gently with bacon & onions, and simmer covered on lowest possible heat, watching so they do not burn. When mushrooms are tender, stir in 1 bud crushed garlic, 2–3 T. chopped parsley and salt & pepper to taste. Simmer a bit longer for flavors to blend. Serve with fried eggs and rye bread or with potatoes and salad. *Variation*: Diced salt pork may be used instead of bacon in this recipe.

CHANTERELLES & VEGETABLE STEW
kurki duszone w jarzynach

Fry up ¼ lb. diced salt pork with 2 chopped onions until golden. Transfer to pot, add 4 c. sliced chanterelles, 2 med. thinly sliced carrots, 1 small sliced parsley root, and 4 peeled diced potatoes. (*Optional*: 1 T. grated celeriac may be added if desired.) Add 1 bud curshed garlic and ½ c. chicken broth or meat stock and simmer covered on low heat until mushrooms and vegetables are fully cooked. Salt & pepper to taste and garnish with fresh chopped dill. Serve with cucumber salad or brine-cured dill pickles. *Optional*: If you like a thicker sauce, sprinkle with 1 T. or so flour and simmer briefly until it is fully absorbed.

CHANTERELLES & SCRAMBLED EGGS
kurki z jajami

Prepare according to recipe for milky caps & scrambled eggs (p. 413).

CREAM-BAKED BUTTERBALLS
maślaki zapiekane w śmietanie

Peel the sticky skin from 1½ lbs. butterballs before washing. Drain and dry. Place mushrooms in pot and add 1 onion sliced wafer thin. Sprinkle with salt & pepper and simmer on low heat until mushrooms release their liquid. Transfer the caps (use stems in some other recipes) to a buttered baking dish and drench with 1 c. fork-blended sour cream. Mix 4 T. bread crumbs with 4 T. grated yellow cheese and sprinkle cream-drenched mushrooms with mixture. Bake in 350° oven until surface is nicely browned. Serve with boiled potatoes and fresh salads.

CREAM-STEWED MORELS
smardze duszone w śmietanie

Dirt tends to collect in the many crevices of these peak-capped spring mushrooms, so be sure to wash and rinse them well in a sieve under rapidly running cold water. After they dry, slice into thin rounds (horizontally). Sauté 1–2 chopped or thinly sliced onions in 3 T. lard or olive oil, add the mushrooms (1–1½ lbs.), sprinkle with 2–3 T. water or meat stock, and simmer covered on low heat 10–15 min. Sprinkle with 2 T. flour, stirring gently until absorbed, salt & pepper, and bring to boil. Remove from heat, stir in ½ c. sour cream, and simmer briefly until the sauce is thick and bubbly. Garnish with a little chopped parsley and dill and serve over mashed potatoes, rice, or noodles.

BREADED PARASOL MUSHROOM CUTLETS
kotlety z kani

Wash and remove the skin from 4 large or 8 smaller parasol-mushroom caps, or enough to serve 4 people. Plunge mushrooms into boiling salted water. When boiling resumes cook about 1 min. Drain and drip dry in colander. Dredge the dry caps in flour, dip in beaten egg, and roll in bread crumbs, gently shaking off excess. Fry to a nice golden brown on both sides in hot lard and/or olive oil about ¼ inch deep in skillet. Drain on absorbent paper, sprinkle with salt & pepper, and serve as you would breaded pork or veal cutlets. *Variation*: After mushroom cutlets are fried and drained on absorbent paper, transfer to serving platter, salt & pepper, dot with butter, and cover with aluminum foil. Keep in 325° oven 10–15 min. Remove foil, sprinkle generously with grated yellow cheese (preferably tilsit or Swiss a.k.a. Emmenthaler), and serve.

BREADED CHICKEN MUSHROOM CUTLETS
kotlety z huby siarkowej

We have called these colorful fungi that grow on trees chicken mushrooms, because their other name, sulphur-shelf mushrooms, just doesn't have the right ring to it and may turn people off. In reality, these mushrooms have a chicken-like texture and can be used in any recipe calling for chicken. According to Polish mycologist Prof. Grzywacz, they have a certain snob appeal about them and are thus prized by some of the country's trendy set. Prepare them according to the above recipe for breaded parasol mushroom cutlets. Sprinkle with savory for added flavor.

MINCED MUSHROOM PATTIES
mielone kotlety z grzybów

Cook 1½ lbs. fresh mushrooms in boiling salted water 15 min., then drain in colander and allow to drip dry and cool. (Almost any mushrooms can be used in this recipe, but the best are King Boletes, butterballs, birch boletes, orange boletes, milky caps, or meadow mushrooms; remember to peel off skin from butterballs and older meadow mushrooms before cooking.) Sauté 2 chopped onions in 2 T. lard or olive oil until tender, then grind the mushrooms together with sautéed onion. To mixture add 1 egg, ½–¾ c. bread crumbs, 1 T. chopped parsley, and salt & pepper to taste. (*Optional*: A pinch or 2 ground nutmeg may be added.) Work mixture well into uniform consistency and form into golfball-sized balls, flattening them slightly into oval cutlets. Dip in unbeaten egg whites (about 2 should suffice) and roll in bread crumbs. Fry in hot fat (lard, salt-pork drippings, bacon drippings, or olive oil) to a nice golden brown on both sides. Serve immediately as is or drenched with sour-cream sauce, with potatoes and a salad.

MINCED MUSHROOM PATTIES ANOTHER WAY
mielone kotlety z grzybów inaczej

Dice 1–1½ lbs. cleaned fresh, wild or domestic mushrooms and sauté in 3 T. butter until moisture steams away and mushrooms begin to sizzle. Remove from heat. In bowl, break up 2 stale kaiser rolls or equivalent amount of stale french bread, drench with 1 c. milk, and let stand until soggy. Squeeze excess milk from soggy rolls and grind together with the mushrooms and 1 large, quartered raw onion. To mixture, add 2 T. uncooked instant cream of wheat, 1½ T. potato starch (or cornstarch), 2 T. chopped fresh dill, 2 eggs, and salt & pepper to taste. Work mixture well by hand to fully blend ingredients and achieve a uniform consistency. Form into small oval cutlets as above, roll in bread crumbs, and fry in hot fat of choice until both sides are a nice, crusty golden brown. They may be served just as they come with potatoes and salad, or drench with hot sour-cream sauce, horseradish sauce, tomato sauce, or even mushroom sauce (made with dried boletes).

MUSHROOM GOULASH OR STEW
gulasz grzybowy

Plunge 1–1½ lbs. fresh, sliced or diced, wild or domestic mushrooms of choice into boiling salted water and cook about 2–3 min. from the time boiling resumes. Drain and drip dry. In 3 T. fat of choice sauté about 2 chopped onions until tender and transparent but still unbrowned. Add the mushrooms and simmer under cover on low heat about 15 min. Now only your culinary creativity and the ingredients you happen to have on hand limit the way you can go. You can add 1 c. diced cooked leftover meat, 1 c. cooked sauerkraut, several diced cooked potatoes and/or a small can of drained peas & carrots for color. Any diced leftover cooked vegetables are another possibility. Fork-blend ½–¾ c. sour cream with 1–2 T. flour and add to mixture. Simmer several min., season with salt, pepper, chopped dill, parsley, and/or chives. *Optional*: Other seasonings may include ½–1 t. paprika, ½–1 t. Maggi extract seasoning, a pinch or 2 marjoram and/or savory. Serve with noodles, potatoes, rice, or groats.

BEANS AND MUSHROOMS
fasola z grzybami

Cook about 1 lb. sliced fresh cultivated or wild mushrooms with 2 chopped onions sautéed in 3 T. lard, adding 2–3 T. water. Simmer on low heat under cover about 20 min., stirring occasionally. Uncover and allow excess moisture to steam away. Salt & pepper and serve over 4–5 c. cooked or canned drained navy beans. Season with several pinches savory or marjoram if desired. *Note:* This is a typical old peasant dish: simple, filling, and economical, especially since Polish country folk pick their own mushrooms in nearby fields and forests.

MUSHROOM PANCAKES
naleśniki ze świeżych grzybów

Plunge 1 lb. or less sliced fresh wild mushrooms of any species (except chanterelles!) into boiling salted water and cook 2–3 min. from the time boiling resumes. Drain, grind, transfer to pot or skillet, add 2 T. water, 1 T. butter, and simmer covered on very low heat about 20 min., stirring occasionally. Set aside to cool. Separately, beat 1 egg yolk with ½ t. sugar and ½ t. salt, stir in 1 c. sour milk and, beating constantly, gradually add 2 c. flour, sifted through sieve. When batter is smooth and creamy, add the mushrooms, a pinch or 2 salt and fold in 1 beaten egg white. Mix lightly. Spoon batter into hot lard or oil and fry to a nice golden brown on both sides. Drain on absorbent paper and serve immediately with sour cream.

MUSHROOM SAUSAGE
kiełbasa z grzybów

Plunge 2 lbs. fresh sliced wild mushrooms of 1 or several species (except chanterelles) into boiling salted water and cook at a slow rolling boil 5 min. from the time boiling resumes. Drain and grind coarsely. Into mixture stir 2 whole eggs and 3 finely chopped not-too-hard-boiled eggs. (Another way is to grind the hard-boiled eggs together with the mushrooms). Simmer 1–2 finely chopped onions in 2 T. bacon drippings until they just begin to brown around the edges. Add to mushroom mixture together with ¼ lb. ground uncooked slab bacon. Season with salt & pepper and work by hand into a uniform consistency. *(Optional:* 1 bud crushed garlic and a sprinkling of marjoram may also be added.) Stuff mixture into pork casing and tie at both ends. Place sausage into pot of cold water, add 1 T. salt, and cook at gentle rolling boil about 10 min. from the time boiling starts. Serve hot with boiled potatoes and creamed horseradish or ćwikła. It is also good cold, dressed with a little sour cream.

MUSHROOM PÂTÉ
pasztet z grzybów

Plunge 2 lbs. whole mushrooms into boiling salted water. When boiling resumes, cook at gentle rolling boiling 5 min. (King Boletes, white cultivated mushrooms, or a combination thereof are especially good.) Drain through colander and allow to drip dry. Cube ¼ lb. salt pork and run through meat grinder together with the mushrooms, then grind mixture again. *(Optional:* For a meat & mushroom pâté, grind 1–2 lbs. cooked diced meats [pork, veal, turkey, chicken, or any combination thereof] together with the mushrooms and salt pork.)

Add 2 egg yolks, ½ c. bread crumbs, and work well by hand until mixture is smooth and blended. Season to taste with salt & pepper and several pinches, preferably freshly grated, nutmeg. Fold in 2 beaten egg whites and mix lightly. Line baking pan with sliced bacon, place pâté mixture on top, and level off top with knife or spatula. Choose a pan that will make the mixture 1½–2 inches high. Cover with another layer of sliced, uncooked bacon and bake in 325° oven about 60 min. Slice when cold and serve with tartar sauce, horseradish sauce, or mayonnaise-sour cream sauce as a cold appetizer. *Variation*: 1–2 cooked and ground dried King Boletes (plus the water in which they cooked) or a t. of minced, canned truffles may be added (see below).

DRIED MUSHROOMS
grzyby suszone

Mushrooms suitable for drying include orange and birch boletes, meadow mushrooms, and butterballs (but they should first be peeled). White store-bought mushrooms can also be dried. When most people think of dried Polish mushrooms, which are frequently called for throughout this book, it is the noble borowik or prawdziwek (King Bolete a.k.a. Boletus edulis) that first comes to mind. No other mushroom can match it for its heady aroma and deep, dusky, Old World flavor. The price of commercially available dried King Boletes may appear staggering, but it should be remembered that they are the equivalent of 5–6 times that amount of fresh mushrooms. Also, just 1 or 2 dried boletes is all that is needed to flavor many soups, gravies, stews, casseroles, sauerkraut, and other dishes. Dried shiitake mushrooms, imported from Japan, are also good in Polish dishes.

RECONSTITUTING DRIED MUSHROOMS
przyrządzanie grzybów suszonych

To reconstitute 1 oz. dried mushrooms, rinse in pot of cold water, scrub each with brush under cold running water to remove hidden dirt, rinse again, drain, cover with warm water, and let stand 1–2 hrs. (*Variation*: 1 part milk and 1 part water may be used instead). Cook in liquid in which they have soaked on low heat anywhere from 30 min.–1 hr., or until they are tender. Use as you would fresh mushrooms, but be sure to reserve the liquid in which they were cooked, as it contains a great deal of flavor and nutrients. *Note*: Lucyna Ćwierczakiewiczowa, the "first lady" of 19th-century Polish cuisines provided the following way for reconstituting dried mushrooms. Scald 1–3 oz. sliced dried mushrooms with boiling water to cover and let stand 2–3 hrs. Drain, reserving liquid. Scald with boiling water again and let stand another hr. or so. Drain and combine leftover liquid with 1st liquid. Cover mushrooms with hot milk and let stand in warm place about 6 hrs., or until all or most of the milk is absorbed. Then use as you would fresh mushrooms. Her famous book, *365 obiadów* (365 Dinners), makes no mention of what to do with the leftover mushroom water, but we definitely advise against discarding it. Use it in soups, gravies, sauerkraut, and meat dishes, or freeze it for future use. *Hint:* The liquid in which dried mushrooms were soaked and cooked is often a little gritty due to sand hidden in the various crevices. One way to deal with this problem is to filter liquid through several thicknesses of cheesecloth or a clean dish towel, wringing out cloth to lose as little flavor as possible, or use paper coffee filter in sieve.

CREAMED DRIED MUSHROOMS
grzyby suszone w śmietanie

Reconstitute 1–2 oz. dried King Boletes (or other mushrooms) by soaking and cooking until tender as above. In 2 T. lard or 1 T. lard and 1 T. butter sauté 1–2 chopped onions until tender and just beginning to brown. Slice or dice the mushrooms and add to onions with 2–3 T. reserved mushroom liquid and simmer on low heat covered about 10 min. Fork-blend ½ c. reserved mushroom liquid (if there is more leftover, boil it down to ½ c.) with ½ c. or more sour cream and 2–4 T. flour until smooth and lump-free. Add to mushrooms and simmer several min. until sauce is smooth and bubbly. Salt & pepper to taste and garnish with chopped dill and/or parsley if desired. Serve as a main course over potatoes, groats, rice, or noodles, or as a topping for cooked meat or fish.

BREADED DRIED MUSHROOM CUTLETS
sznycle z suszonych grzybów

Soak 8 large dried King Bolete caps in warm water overnight. Next day, cook in same water until tender. Drain, reserving liquid for use in other dishes. Place hot cooked caps on cutting board, cover with another board, weight down with something heavy (e.g. a 2 qt. jar filled with water), and let stand until cool. Dredge in flour, dip in beaten egg, and roll in bread crumbs. Salt & pepper and fry in hot lard or oil to a nice golden brown on each side. On serving platter top each cutlet with a pat of butter and a slice of lemon. Serve with potatoes and salad.

MINCED MUSHROOM CUTLETS
kotleciki grzybowe

Soak and cook 1½–2 oz. dried mushrooms the usual way. When mushrooms are tender, remove from liquid and set aside. Crumble 1 stale kaiser roll or equivalent amount of stale french bread into mushroom liquid and let soak until soggy. Squeeze excess moisture from soggy roll and pass roll, the mushrooms, and 2 hard-boiled eggs through grinder. Sauté 1 large finely chopped onion in 1 T. fat until it just begins to brown and add to ground mixture. Mix in 1 raw egg and salt & pepper to taste. Work well into uniform mixture, roll into golfball-sized balls and flatten somewhat, roll in bread crumbs, and fry to a nice golden brown on both sides in lard or oil. Serve as is with potatoes and a salad or transfer to baking dish, cover, and keep in 325° oven 15–20 min. for flavors to blend.

MINCED MUSHROOM CUTLETS IN GRAVY
kotleciki grzybowe w sosie

Proceed as above, but instead of rolling cutlets in bread crumbs, roll in flour and fry in a little fat to a light golden brown on sides. Remove from heat. Combine mushroom liquid (left over from squeezing out the soggy roll) with a heaping T. sour cream and several T. flour, and fork-blend into a thick creamy sauce. Drench the mushroom cutlets with sauce and simmer on low heat covered 2–3 min. Season sauce to taste with salt & pepper, 1 t. Maggi seasoning, and (optional) 1 T. fresh chopped dill. Simmer briefly, stirring constantly. If sauce is too thick, dilute with a little boiling water. Cover and let stand several min. for flavors to mingle. A few pinches of savory will enhance this and other mushroom dishes.

DRIED MUSHROOMS, STEAK & ONION STYLE
befsztyki z grzybów

Soak 3 oz. large dried King Bolete caps in cold water about 2 hrs. Drain (reserving liquid for use in other dishes) and cover mushrooms with 1 c. milk. Let stand about 1 hr., then cook in the milk on low heat until tender. Drain (reserving liquid for other uses). Dry the caps on absorbent paper, then salt & pepper and sprinkle with sifted flour on both sides. Slice 1 large onion into thin rounds and sauté in several T. hot oil until tender. Remove onions and set aside. Heat the drippings, adding a little more oil as needed, and fry the mushrooms until nicely browned on both sides and serve smothered with onions. Potatoes and sliced tomatoes or a sauerkraut salad (in winter) are good side dishes.

DRIED MUSHROOM COLLOPS À LA NELSON
zrazy grzybowe po nelsońsku

Use 2 oz. dried Bolete caps. Soak and cook as above. Line bottom of buttered casserole with a layer of cold, cooked sliced potatoes, top with a layer of mushrooms, then a layer of sautéed, sliced onions. Continue layering until ingredients are used up, lightly salting and peppering each layer. Potatoes should make up the top layer. In pot, combine water in which mushrooms soaked and milk in which they cooked, bring to boil, and simmer covered 5 min. When cool, mix well with 1 c. sour cream and ½ c. strong beef stock. (1 beef bouillon cube dissolved in ½ c. boiling water may be used). Salt & pepper sauce to taste and pour it over casserole. Bake in 350° oven about 1 hr. You will need about 7–8 cooked med.-sized potatoes and 2 onions for this recipe. *Note:* If you're wondering who or what Nelson is, this and similar "po nelsońsku" dishes were named after Britain's heroic naval commander, Admiral Horatio Nelson (1758–1805). They enjoyed great popularity in well-to-do Polish homes throughout the 19th century. The Polonized version of this dish makes use of sour cream instead of the wine called for in the original recipe.

DRIED MUSHROOMS AND GRATED EGG NOODLES
zacierki z grzybami

Soak and cook 1 oz. dried mushrooms the usual way and leave them in liquid until ready to use. Meanwhile, make noodle dough by combining 2¼ c. flour with 2 eggs, 6 T. water, and ¼ t. salt. When fully blended, grate dough on coarse side of grater and scatter noodles over a floured bread-board to dry several min. Transfer noodles to large pot of boiling salted water and, when boiling resumes, reduce heat, cover and cook about 5 min. In skillet, melt a diced 2-inch square of salt pork, push golden salt-pork nuggets over to one side, and in drippings sauté 1 finely chopped onion. Remove mushrooms from liquid (reserving liquid for other uses), dice mushrooms, and stir into onions and salt-pork nuggets. Drain noodles and serve topped with mushroom mixture. Salt & pepper to taste. This is a simple but satisfying peasant dish. *Variation*: Instead of dried mushrooms, you can sauté 16 oz. fresh sliced mushrooms with salt pork and onions and use to top noodles.

SAUTÉED DRIED & FRESH MUSHROOMS
grzyby suszone duszone ze świeżymi

Unless you pick and dry your own mushrooms, you will probably find commercially available dried mushrooms rather pricey and, therefore, use them sparingly. If that is the case, this is a good way to "stretch" dried mushrooms without sacrificing too much flavor. Soak and cook ½–1 oz. dried King Bolete mushrooms and leave them in their water until ready to use. In skillet, melt 3 T. lard and fry 16 oz. chopped fresh store-bought mushrooms in it over fairly high heat, stirring frequently. When the mushrooms' natural moisture evaporates and they begin to sizzle, add 1 finely chopped onion, stir and brown over reduced heat. Remove from heat, dice the cooked dried mushrooms, and add to skillet. Simmer briefly with fresh mushrooms then add the mushroom liquid. Simmer until most of the liquid evaporates, then switch off heat, cover, and let stand several min. for fresh mushrooms to fully absorb the dried mushroom flavor. Salt & pepper to taste. Serve as is over cooked noodles, plain dumplings, potatoes, or rice, or as a topping for cooked meat, fish, or scrambled eggs. It can also serve as a filling for a plain omelet or crêpes (naleśniki). *Variation*: For creamed mushrooms, sprinkle cooked mushrooms with 1 T. or so flour, stir until it is absorbed, then stir in heaping T. sour cream and simmer on low heat until you have a creamy, bubbling sauce. A sprinkling of chopped dill and/or parsley is recommended. *Note:* Your guests may come away convinced that they have just feasted on expensive dried borowiki. This will be the case if you fry the store-bought mushrooms until they become quite dark. If you stew them over low heat in too much liquid, their familiar tan color will give them away.

SALT-CURED MUSHROOMS IN DIFFERENT WAYS
grzyby kiszone na różne sposoby

Salt-cured mushrooms may be used in most recipes for sautéed or stewed mushrooms, but they should first be rinsed well in cold water and then dried. For hints on how to salt-cure, dry, pickle, and preserve mushrooms in other ways, see chapter on food preservation.

TRUFFLES
trufle

These are the world's most expensive mushrooms, and their price is likely to keep growing as supplies dwindle due to land development and environmental pollution. The most sought-after varieties are found only in certain regions of France and Italy and, since they grow underground, specially trained pigs and dogs are used to dig them out. They have all but disappeared from contemporary Polish cookery, but references to them may be found in 19th- and early 20th-century Polish culinary classics. The legendary Ćwierczakiewiczowa, whose writings were chiefly addressed to chefs in the employ of wealthy merchants and landed gentry, supplied the following recipe in the 1911 edition of her famous cookbook: "Clean truffles with brush, rinse thoroughly, salt, cover with light Madeira, sprinkle with white pepper and cook about half an hour. When they are tender, drain and transfer to platter lined with a napkin. Serve young, fresh butter on the side." Feel free to try this dish if you are a millionaire and can afford to have fresh truffles flown in from France or Italy. If not, you may have to content yourself with a tiny 1½ oz. tin. At first glance, even that minute quantity may appear ridiculously overpriced. After all, for that price two people can enjoy a full-course dinner with drinks in a good restaurant. It should be remembered, however, that truffles go a long way. As little as ½–1 t. will impart their elegant fragrance to your pâté, poultry stuffing, canapé spread, and the like, and turn an ordinary omelet or even scrambled eggs into a gourmet delicacy.

GROATS & GRAIN DISHES

Despite the major inroads made by potatoes over the centuries, Poland continues to rank among Europe's top grain-eating countries. Only quite recently have other European countries and America begun to rediscover the interesting "new" taste and important nutritional benefits of groats, especially the whole-grain variety, which include fiber, minerals, protein, and even alleged anti-cholesterol properties.

But, as this book was being written (1988–1990), America had yet to discover that king of cereals, buckwheat groats, which can rightly be called "Poland's wonder grain"! Buckwheat groats have more protein than rolled oats, farina, barley, or rice, but are less starchy than rice or potatoes, and contain none of the cholesterol of egg noodles. They are also high in calcium, phosphorous, and iron, as well as B vitamins and vitamin PP. In addition, their high fiber content helps promote regularity—a serious problem to those who make a steady diet of "cotton fluff" (American-style white bread) and other mushy, starchy, over-processed foods.

Buckwheat groats are also proof that healthful foods need not taste like medicine. The fluffy kernels of cooked buckwheat have a pleasingly dusky or nut-like flavor that many may prefer to that of today's much vaunted wild rice. Buckwheat groats span class barriers and are equally at home in hearty peasant dishes as well as being the traditional accompaniment to more epicurean fare such as steak roll-ups, braised collops, and wild game.

Also included in this chapter are recipes incorporating barley, oats, rice, and even millet, although its popularity is now a mere shadow of its former self. The unusual cooked-wheat pudding, flavored with poppyseeds, honey and nuts, is traditionally served on Christmas Eve, to Poles the most festive day of the year. It is known as *kutia* or *kucja*.

If this book had been written a decade earlier, before the cholesterol scare and soluble-fiber craze had shaken American eating habits, we probably would not have included any dishes of the *prażucha*, *kulasza*, *lemieszka*, or *mamałyga* variety. These old-fashioned mushes, once eaten by the poorest peasant families, would simply have seemed too rustic and obsolete. Now, however, they may prove beneficial to those who are modifying their eating habits to include more cereals and vegetables in place of red meat.

Growing health awareness has also turned yesterday's "cheap cereal fillers" into today's healthful high-fiber additives. We have therefore included a number of ways to prepare traditional ground-meat dishes (meatloaf, meatballs, minced cutlets etc.) that are lower in cholesterol but every bit as tasty as the original.

* * *

BUCKWHEAT GROATS
kasza gryczana na sypko

In pot combine 3 c. water, 1 T. fat (salt-pork drippings or butter are best, but oil is also good), and ½–1 level t. salt and bring to boil. In sieve rinse 2 c. buckwheat groats under running water, drain well, and add to pot. When boiling resumes, reduce heat and cook under cover until all water is absorbed by groats. Transfer to 350° oven and bake covered about 45 min. This is a typically Polish accompaniment to steak roll-ups, beef and game dishes, meatballs and other meats, especially those served with gravy. Groats are also excellent with creamed mushrooms—a traditional Wigilia dish in some families. *Note*: Buckwheat groats come unroasted, medium roasted, and dark-roasted. We prefer the medium roasted variety, but the more robust, dark-roasted kind is also good. The unroasted variety tends to be bland, but it's all a matter of preference. These groats are also known in Polish as kasza hreczana or tatarczana.

FLUFFY BUCKWHEAT GROATS
kasza gryczana puszysta

Prepare as above, but after removing from oven, wrap pot tightly with an old newspaper, then with a dish towel, bath towel, and blanket. Place this bundle under a heavy pierzyna (feather bed), or smother it with large pillows and forget about it. If you prepare your kasza in this way before you go to work in the morning, it will still be hot and ready to serve for dinner.

BUCKWHEAT GROATS WITH MILK
kasza gryczana z mlekiem

Prepare buckwheat groats in either of the above ways and top with fried, golden salt-pork nuggets and as much of the drippings as you like. Serve with a bowl of cold sour milk or buttermilk in summer, and hot fresh milk in winter. On fast days, flavor the kasza with butter instead of salt pork. Since buckwheat groats are so rich in nutrients, this simple repast constitutes almost a complete meal.

BUCKWHEAT GROATS & CHEESE
kasza gryczana z serem

Top hot buckwheat groats with fried salt-pork nuggets and drippings and add 1–2 c. finely diced, crumbled, or grated farmer's cheese. As a change of pace, perhaps your family will enjoy this simple, old-fashioned peasant dish as much as ours does. Particularly in eastern Poland, this dish is often flavored with a light sprinkling of dried mint leaves.

BUCKWHEAT GROATS & FRIED EGGS
kasza gryczana z sadzonym jajkiem

Fry up ⅛ lb. (about 1 heaping T.) diced salt pork until golden. Remove salt-pork nuggets and set aside. In the drippings, fry 2–3 c. cooked buckwheat groats until fully heated through. Set aside and keep warm. Place the salt-pork nuggets in a clean skillet and heat until skillet surface is greased, then fry 4 eggs therein sunny-side up until the white is set. Divide the groats into 2 portions and top each with 2 fried eggs. Salt and pepper to taste and enjoy! In Poland this is a typical poor man's meal, of the kind served at a bar mleczny (milk bar), a low-cost, meatless eatery specializing in soups, dumplings, and dairy dishes. In our household, this is a favorite breakfast or supper dish. The above recipe serves 2, but if you are cholesterol conscious, you can use only 1 egg per serving.

GROAT & CHEESE CUTLETS
kotlety z kaszy i sera

Grind 3–3½ c. cooked, cold buckwheat groats (cooked barley may also be used) together with ¾ lb. cubed farmer's cheese. Mix in 2 whole eggs, work to blend ingredients, and salt & pepper to taste. (A sprinkle of dried mint leaves or several dashes of hunter's seasoning are other flavoring possibilities.) Form mixture into golf-ball-sized rounds and flatten into thick oval patties. Roll in bread crumbs and brown in fat or oil on both sides, transfer to baking dish, and bake covered in 350° oven 30–45 min. Serve drenched with hot mushroom sauce, sour cream sauce, or dill sauce. A grated vegetable salad in winter or sliced tomatoes in summer make perfect accompaniments.

GROAT & MUSHROOM CUTLETS
kotlety z kaszy i grzybów

Soak 1 oz. dried Polish mushrooms in 3 c. water several hrs., then cook in same water until tender. Simmer 1 finely chopped onion in a little butter or oil until golden. Grind 4 c. cooked buckwheat groats, the cooked mushrooms, and the onions. Add 2 beaten eggs and mix well to blend ingredients. Salt & pepper to taste and (optional) add 2–3 T. chopped parsley and/or dill. Form into thick oval patties, roll in bread crumbs, and fry to a nice golden brown on both sides in fat or oil. Serve drenched with mushroom sauce, incorporating the water in which the dried mushrooms were cooked.

GROAT & MEAT CUTLETS
kotlety z kaszy i mięsa

Simmer 2 finely chopped onions in 2 or more T. fat or oil until tender and golden. Grind 2 c. cooked buckwheat groats and combine with an equal amount of ground pork, veal, and beef blend used in meatloaf. Add the onions, 2 beaten eggs, 1 clove mashed garlic (optional), and salt & pepper to taste. (For variety, flavor with a little pork seasoning or hunter's seasoning.) Mix ingredients well, form into thick oval patties, roll in flour, and brown on both sides in hot fat or oil. Then, either cover skillet, reduce heat, and simmer about 20 min., or until meat is fully cooked, or transfer to baking dish and bake covered in 350° oven 30–40 min. Serve as is or whisk and heat pan drippings in saucepan with a little flour; add enough milk to get a nice sauce. Season it to taste with salt, pepper, Maggi seasoning (or a pinch of lovage), garlic powder, paprika or Polish hunter's seasoning. *Note*: This is not only an economical way to stretch ground meat dishes; these cutlets are healthier than all-meat patties by being lower in fat and richer in the fiber and nutrients for which buckwheat groats are well known! Excellent with mushroom gravy!

BUCKWHEAT-GROAT MEATLOAF
klops z kaszy i mięsa

Prepare ingredients as for groat & meat cutlets (above), but instead of forming patties, place mixture in greased loaf pan and bake in 350° oven about 1 hr. Weight-watchers, place mixture in ungreased loaf pan, add ½ c. boiling water, cover tightly with foil, and bake in 350° oven 1 hr.

BUCKWHEAT-STUFFED MEATLOAF
klops nadziewany kaszą

Crumble a stale kaiser roll into ½ c. milk. Simmer 1 chopped onion in a little butter or oil until tender and golden. Run soggy roll through grinder and combine with 1 lb. or so raw ground pork, veal, and beef combination (commonly known as meatloaf mixture). Add 1 raw egg, mix ingredients well, and salt & pepper to taste. Several dashes of Polish pork or hunter's seasoning and/or a bud of crushed garlic are recommended. Place half the mixture in a greased loaf pan and make an indentation down the center of the meat the length of the pan. Fill indentation with about 2 c. cooked buckwheat groats, cover with remaining meat mixture, and bake in 350° oven about 1 hr. Serve with creamy mushroom sauce incorporating the meatloaf pan drippings.

BUCKWHEAT SAUSAGE ("KISZKA") LOAF
kaszanka zapiekana w blasze

To make genuine kiszka or kaszanka (these terms are interchangeable in Polish) you need the blood, heart, lungs, liver, fat back, etc. of a freshly butchered hog. We have provided several such recipes in the sausage-making chapter of this book, but you can also try a simplified version of this old favorite using ingredients available at your local supermarket. Start by cooking 3 lbs. pork ribs in 8 c. water 1 hr., skimming off scum until no more forms. Add 2 t. salt, 2 onions, several peppercorns, and 1 bay leaf. Cook another hr., or until meat comes away from bones easily. Remove meat from bones, dice, and set aside. Bring 3 c. strained rib stock to boil, and add 2 c. buckwheat groats. Stir and cook on low to med. heat until liquid is absorbed; leave covered until cool. Grind 1–1½ c. raw liver (calf's, pork, baby beef, or chicken) and mix with groats. Add diced meat, 1 beaten egg, 1–2 t. marjoram, several pinches ground allspice, ½ t. MSG (Accent), and salt & pepper to taste. Mix ingredients well and transfer to greased loaf pan. Pack mixture into pan, level off top, and bake in 350° oven 60–70 min. Serve hot with horseradish or brown mustard, rye bread, dill pickles, and hot tea with lemon or cold beer. The buckwheat-sausage loaf may also be chilled, sliced when cold, and fried in butter or eaten cold.

NEAR-KISZKA
niby-kiszka

Here is another easy take-off on the kiszka theme. Sauté 1 finely chopped onion in 2 T. oil until transparent. Add 1 lb. rather fatty ground pork and brown lightly, breaking it up with fork. Add 3–4 ground chicken livers, toss with remaining ingredients, and simmer briefly. (Liver should still show a trace of pink.) Remove from heat. Season with about 2 t. salt, ½ t. marjoram, and ½ t. MSG. Combine with 3–4 c. cooked buckwheat groats or barley. Grease loaf pan, sprinkle bottom and sides with bread crumbs, and pack meat and groat mixture into it. Bake in 350° oven about 1 hr. Serve hot or cold as above. *Optional*: Adding about ½ c. browned salt-pork nuggets and several T. of their drippings to mixture will improve the flavor. *Variation*: If you have hog casings, you may loosely stuff them with mixture from this or the above recipe and tie ends with strong thread. Place in baking pan and bake in 350 oven 1 hr. After 30 min. turn over in pan. A little water may be added to pan to prevent scorching. This may not taste exactly like real kiszka, but it's the next best thing!

BOILED BUCKWHEAT CAKE KASHUBIAN STYLE
kiszka po kaszubsku

Bring 2¼ c. water and ½ t. salt to boil, gradually adding 1½ c. buckwheat groats. Reduce heat and cook covered until all water is absorbed. The groats should not be fully cooked.

Grate 2½ lbs. peeled raw potatoes (if you dice the potatoes, this can be done in a blender!) together with 2–3 onions. Mix the groats with the grated potatoes and onions and salt & pepper to taste. Transfer mixture to cloth bags about 4 inches in diameter. Do not pack bags tightly, as mixture will expand during cooking. Tie the bags shut and cook in boiling salted water 30 min. Immerse the bags in cold water for about 5 min. to cool. Remove and let them drip dry. Remove from bag, slice and serve with sour cream and a cup or bowl of hot fresh milk on the side.

BUCKWHEAT PIE LUBLIN STYLE
pieróg lubelski

This is a truly tasty and nutritious loaf filled with groats, cheese, and potatoes, which has been a favorite in the authors' families for generations. Both sides have links to Poland's eastern Lublin region where this pie originated. For the dough, cut ¼ c. lard and ¼ c. butter or oleo into 5 c. sifted flour on bread-board. Make well at center and place therein 2 egg yolks, 1 whole egg, ½ c. sour cream, 1 t. salt, 1–2 t. sugar, and 2 t. baking powder. Work ingredients into a uniform dough by hand, and towards the end gradually add about ¾ c. water. Set aside and prepare filling by combining 6 c. cooked buckwheat, about 2–3 c. ground farmer's cheese, and 1 c. mashed potatoes—the Polish kind with no milk or butter added. (*Note*: Feel free to vary the amount of cheese and potatoes according to preference or availability.) Add 2 eggs, ½ c. browned salt-pork nuggets, and 2–3 T. of their drippings. Mix well and season with salt & pepper, several pinches dried mint leaves, and ½ –1 t. MSG. Divide dough into 2 parts. Roll out each on lightly floured board into a rectangle about ¼ inch thick, i.e. considerably thicker than for American-style pie. Line 2 loaf pans with dough sheets, leaving a flap left over for the top. Place half the groat mixture in each dough-lined pan, cover with dough flaps, and pinch together with dough protruding from sides and ends. Brush with beaten egg, puncture crust with fork in about a doz. places for steam to escape, and bake in 400° oven about 1 hr., or until crust is nicely browned. Allow to cool somewhat before removing from pan. Slice carefully about 1 inch thick so filling does not fall out. Serve warm, cold, or reheated in frying pan in a little butter (or without butter in microwave). Hot milk or tea with lemon are perfect accompaniments for this pie, which makes a tasty and nutritious breakfast or supper. *Variations:* If you haven't the time to prepare dough from scratch, store-bought pie dough may be used. You may even dispense with dough entirely and bake mixture in a greased pan sprinkled with bread crumbs as a kind of casserole.

MODIFIED BUCKWHEAT PIE
pieróg inaczej

During one of her visits to the U.S, the authoress developed a modified, fat-reduced version of the above dish, which she bakes in an American-style pie pan. Prepare dough as above, but increase sugar to 1 T. and roll into 4 circles (two slightly smaller for the top as with American-style pies). Chop 4 med. onions and brown lightly in 3 T. oil. Mix with 8 c. cooked groats, 1–2 eggs, and salt & pepper to taste. Fill each pie shell with ¼ of the groat mixture, top with a ½ inch layer of mashed or crumbled farmer's cheese, cover each with remaining groats. Cover each pie with remaining (smaller) dough circle, trim away excess dough, and press edges together to seal. Brush crust with water, pierce with fork at roughly 1 inch intervals for steam to escape, and bake in 400° oven about 1 hr. or until crust is nicely browned. Serve as above.

KRAKÓW STYLE FINE BUCKWHEAT
kasza krakowska

Besides being unroasted, medium-roasted, or dark-roasted, buckwheat groats may be purchased whole or split. The finest milled variety is known as kasza krakowska and is prepared as follows. Mix 2 c. buckwheat with 1 egg white or 1 whole small egg to coat each grain, spread mixture thinly over the surface of a large skillet, and heat over low flame, stirring frequently until dry. In pot combine 3 c. water, ½–1 t. salt, and 1–2 T. butter, pork fat or oil. Bring to boil and gradually add the buckwheat. When boiling resumes, reduce heat to low and cook until water is absorbed. Cover, transfer to 350° oven, and bake about 45 min. After switching off heat, you can leave the pot in the oven another 15 min., but this is not necessary. Serve in any of the ways recommended for buckwheat groats. This kasza is especially good with mushroom sauce or any meat-based gravy.

FINE BUCKWHEAT & MUSHROOMS
kasza krakowska z grzybami

Soak 1 oz. dried Polish mushrooms in 2 c. water 2 hrs. or longer, then cook in same water until tender. Meanwhile, mix 2 c. Kraków-style buckwheat with 1 egg white or 1 small whole egg to coat, and dry in hot skillet as above. Pour the mushroom water into a pot and add enough boiling water to make 3 c. Bring to boil, add the buckwheat, the finely chopped mushrooms, 1 t. salt, and 1 T. butter, mix ingredients, bring to boil, reduce heat, and cook on low heat until water is absorbed. Cover and transfer to 350° oven and bake about 45 min. *Variation:* Another way is to place the pot containing the buckwheat into a larger pot filled with boiling water and cook 45–60 min. on stove top. Both pots should be tightly covered and boiling water should be replaced as it evaporates. Serve drenched with mushroom sauce or creamy dill sauce or with a bowl of cold sour milk on the side.

KRAKÓW BUCKWHEAT & MUSHROOM PUDDING
budyń z kaszy krakowskiej i grzybów

Prepare mushrooms and cook 2 c. fine-milled buckwheat as above. Simmer 1 finely chopped onion in 3 T. butter or other fat until golden and tender. In a bowl, beat 4 egg yolks until creamy, add the buckwheat-mushroom mixture plus the onions and pan drippings, mix well, and salt to taste. Beat 4 egg whites to a stiff froth and fold in. Grease a pudding mold and sprinkle with bread crumbs. Fill the mold with mixture no more than ¾ full, since it will expand during cooking. Seal and cook in covered pot of boiling water (reaching ¾ the height of the mold) about 1 hr. Replace boiling water that evaporates. *Variation*: Instead of dried mushrooms, 8–12 oz. fresh mushrooms can be used, which should be diced and simmered until tender with the onions. Serve hot with a creamy hot sauce or gravy and a fresh salad for a complete meal.

KRAKÓW BUCKWHEAT À LA ROYALE
kasza krakowska po królewsku

Mix 1 c. Kraków (fine buckwheat) groats with 2 beaten egg yolks to coat, place in dry skillet, and heat, stirring constantly until dry. Set aside to cool. Bring to boil 1½ c. milk containing 3 T. butter and add the groats. Stir to break up lumps and place pot into another larger pot of boiling water. Cover both pots and cook 30–40 min., stirring occasionally. (A double boiler may be used for this purpose.) Into cooked groats stir ¾ c. cherry preserves, ½ c. pre-soaked, drained raisins, a sprinkle of vanilla extract or vanilla sugar, a pinch of salt, and a little sugar to taste if desired. Transfer mixture to baking dish and bake in 375° oven 20 min.

MILLET GROATS
kasza jaglana

Bring 4 c. water containing 2–3 T. fat and 1 t. salt to rapid boil. In thin gradual stream, add 2 c. millet groats so boiling does not stop entirely. When all groats have been added, cook on low heat until water is absorbed. Then cover and bake in 350° oven about 45 min. Leave in oven another 15 min. after switching off heat. Serve as meal in itself, drenched with mushroom sauce or meat gravy, or serve as a side dish (instead of potatoes), especially with gravy-laced meat dishes. Although millet groats no longer enjoy the popularity they did in Old Polish cookery, they are chock full of vitamins and minerals and add a change-of-pace flavor to your meal-planning schedule. They will be even tastier if cooked in 1–2 c. milk and 2–3 c. water instead of plain water. The important thing is to use twice the amount of liquid as uncooked groats.

MILLET & PRUNE CASSEROLE
kasza jaglana zapiekana ze śliwkami

Scald 1 c. millet groats with boiling water and drain. In a pot combine 1 c. milk, 1.c water, 2 T. butter, ¼ t. salt, and 2 pinches of cinnamon, and bring to boil. Add groats, stir well, and cook on low heat, stirring frequently, until tender. Meanwhile, soak 1 c. prunes in very warm water 15 min. Drain, remove pits, and dice prunes. When millet is done, set aside to cool. Separately, cream 2 egg yolks with 2 T. butter and ½ c. sugar. Combine millet with egg mixture and prunes, and fold in 2 beaten egg whites. Transfer mixture to baking dish and bake covered in 350° oven about 1 hr. Serve sprinkled with a little powdered sugar and a little more cinnamon if you like.

BARLEY
kasza jęczmienna

Barley is available in whole grains with only the hull removed (pęcak or pęczak), split, or cracked in various degrees of coarseness (kasza łamana) or milled and polished into beads of various size which is then called pearl barley (kasza perłowa). For the coarser grinds, bring to boil 4 c. water with 2 T. fat and 1 t. salt, and add barley in a thin stream so boiling continues uninterrupted. If you add the cereal too quickly and boiling stops, the barley will stick together. Reduce heat and cook gently until all the liquid is absorbed. Cover and bake in 350° oven about 45 min. and leave in switched-off oven another 15 min. Serve as a simple meal in itself topped with fried salt-pork or bacon nuggets and the drippings. A finely chopped onion may be browned with the pork cracklings (optional). Use the cooked barley as a side dish with gravy-laced meat or mushroom dishes, or in any casserole in place of rice. The next time you make gołąbki (stuffed cabbage rolls), substitute barley for the rice. *Note:* To prevent finely-milled barley from sticking together, first coat with egg white or egg, and dry in hot skillet as with Kraków buckwheat (p. 429).

OLD POLISH BARLEY, BEAN & SAUSAGE CASSEROLE
kasza jęczmienna po staropolsku

Cook 2 c. cracked or pearl barley as above. In 3 T. fat, simmer 1 finely chopped onion until tender, adding 1 c. skinned, diced, smoked kiełbasa midway through. Remove from heat and stir in 1 T. tomato paste (or 3 T. ketchup) and 1 T. Polish plum jam (powidła). Toss mixture with 1–2 c. cooked or canned, drained navy beans and season to taste with salt, pepper, and marjoram. Generously butter a baking dish and sprinkle with bread crumbs. Add a layer of cooked barley, top with a layer of bean mixture, and continue alternating until ingredients are used up. The bottom and top layers should be barley. Smooth top of ingredients, drench with ¾ c. fork-blended sour cream, and bake in 375° oven about 45 min. Serve with a fresh salad.

WHOLE-GRAIN BARLEY
pęcak

In pot, combine 4½ c. water, 3 T. fat, and 1–2 t. salt. Bring to rapid boil and slowly add 1½ c. whole hulled barley. Stir. Reduce heat and cook over very low flame until all liquid is absorbed. *Remember*: With whole-grain barley, you use 3 times the amount of liquid as barley hence slightly longer cooking is needed for all the water to be absorbed. Transfer to 350° oven and bake tightly covered 40–50 min. Leave in oven another 15 min. after switching off heat. Serve like groats or rice.

WHOLE-GRAIN BARLEY & PEAS
pęcak z grochem

Soak 1 c. whole yellow dried peas in 4–5 c. warm water containing 1–2 t. salt overnight at room temp. Next day, stir peas and skim off any hulls or impurities that float up. Bring peas to boil in same water, add the rind from a 1 lb. slab of salt pork or bacon, reduce heat, and simmer until tender, anywhere from 2–3 hrs. Meanwhile, cook 1 c. whole-grain barley in 3 c. boiling water containing 1 t. salt and 2 T. fat as in above recipe. When peas are tender, drain in colander until dripping stops and combine with barley. Serve topped with golden salt-pork or bacon nuggets and the drippings, with or without browned chopped onion. Salt & pepper to taste. This was once a favorite dish of the poor Tatra Mountain folk, because it was simple, inexpensive, and filling.

CABBAGE ROLLS WITH PEAS & BARLEY
gołąbki z pęcaku i grochu

Although other gołąbki are listed in the meat & vegetable chapter, we decided to include the following version, which hails from the Małopolska region (southeastern Poland) among the barley recipes. A day earlier wash, rinse under cold running water, and drain 1 c. whole, dry, yellow peas. Soak in 5 c. water overnight, then cook in same water until tender. Drain. Separately, bring 1½ c. salted water to boil, gradually add ½ c. rinsed and drained whole-grain barley, reduce heat, and cook until liquid is absorbed. Meanwhile, dice about ⅓ lb. slab bacon and brown. Remove bacon nuggets and set aside. In bacon drippings brown 3 chopped onions. Mix peas, barley, and 1 beaten egg, add bacon, onions, and drippings, and season with salt, pepper & marjoram. Par-boil cabbage, fill leaves with mixture, and roll up as usual. Line baking dish with leftover cabbage leaves, place the cabbage rolls on top side by side.

Cover with 3 c. or so meat stock or court bouillon, top with another layer of cabbage leaves, cover, and bake in 350° oven 1½–2 hrs. On platter drench with tomato sauce and serve with boiled or mashed potatoes. This old peasant dish is both economical and filling.

MEAT & OAT CUTLETS
kotlety mięsno-owsiane

Scald ¾ c. rolled oats with 1½ c. hot milk, water, or milk & water combination, bring to boil, then reduce heat and cook gently, stirring frequently for about 10 min. Cover and set aside to cool. Combine cold oatmeal with equal amount fresh ground pork, veal, beef, or any combination thereof. Simmer 2 finely chopped onions in 3 T. fat until slightly browned and add to meat & oat mixture. Add 1 large or 2 small eggs, 1 bud crushed garlic (optional), and salt & pepper to taste. For variety, season additionally with your homemade Polish seasoning of choice: pork, beef, poultry or hunter's. Mix well to blend ingredients and roll into small meatballs or oval patties. Roll in bread crumbs, pressing them in, and brown in hot lard or oil on both sides, then reduce heat to low, cover, and simmer another 15 min. or so. Serve straight from the skillet with potatoes and a salad, or use the pan drippings to make a gravy. Simply fork-blend ½ c. sour cream with 2 T. flour and stir into pan drippings. Simmer briefly and dilute with a little boiling water to get a nice, pourable consistency. Season with salt, pepper, a t. Maggi seasoning, and a dash or 2 of any of your Polish seasonings. *Note*: At one time adding oatmeal or other cereal fillers to meatballs was viewed mainly as an economical "stretcher." Now we know this is actually a healthier alternative, because it replaces at least part of the meat's fat and cholesterol with high-fiber cereal.

BAKED WHEAT & BUCKWHEAT MUSH
prażucha

Prażucha (also known regionally as lemieszka and kulasza) and other dishes of this type were once known as filling and affordable foods used to keep body and soul together. While the English translation admittedly sounds far less appetizing than some of our other recipes, in today's natural-food and fiber-conscious era it could definitely prove more popular. To prepare this simple dish, mix 1½ c. ordinary enriched flour with 1½ c. buckwheat flour and place in large, deep skillet or Dutch oven. Heat, stirring constantly with wooden spoon, until flour turns a nice golden brown. Bring 4 c. water with 1 t. salt added to boil and gradually add the browned flour, stirring constantly with wooden spoon and obliterating any lumps that form. When mixture is smooth, cover and bake in 350° oven 20–30 min. Meanwhile, dice a 3 inch square salt pork or slab bacon and simmer until golden. Dip wooden spoon in drippings and scoop small, dumpling-sized portions of mush onto serving platter. Dip spoon in salt-pork drippings between each scoop. Drench the mush dumplings with salt-pork or bacon nuggets and drippings. Garnish with a little chopped parsley, dill, or chives. *Note:* Traditionally, mushes of this type were eaten for breakfast or supper with a bowl of hot fresh milk, cold sour milk, or buttermilk on the side. You can also serve it (minus the salt pork or bacon) as an accompaniment to gravy-laced meat dishes instead of potatoes, noodles, rice, etc.

MOUNTAINEER WHOLEWHEAT MUSH WITH EGG
kulasza góralska z jajecznicą

Bring 4 c. lightly salted water to boil and gradually add 3 c. whole-wheat flour, stirring vigorously with wooden spoon to break up any lumps until mixture is smooth. Reduce heat simmer a while longer until flour loses its raw taste. Cover and let stand briefly. Meanwhile, fry up 3 inch square diced salt pork or slab bacon to a nice golden brown, and in these nuggets and drippings fry 4–8 scrambled eggs. Dish mush into individual bowls, make an indentation at center with spoon, and evenly fill with scrambled eggs. May be served just with salt-pork or bacon nuggets and their drippings and topped with some mashed farmer's cheese or bryndza.

POTATO & RYE MUSH
prażucha żytnia z kartoflami

Peel 4 med. potatoes and cook in boiling salted water to cover. Drain and gradually add 4 c. warm milk, mashing to blend ingredients and heating to a gentle boil. Gradually add 2½ c. preferably coarsely ground rye flour, stirring constantly with wooden spoon until smooth. Allow to simmer a while, stirring to prevent scorching, until flour loses its raw taste. Salt to taste. Transfer to serving bowl and drench with golden salt-pork or bacon nuggets and their drippings. *Optional:* Some chopped onion may be browned in the drippings if you like. Each portion may also be topped with a dollop of sour cream. Serve with a cup or bowl of sour milk or buttermilk.

BUCKWHEAT & GRATED POTATO MUSH
prażucha gryczana z tartymi kartoflami

Scald 2 c. buckwheat groats with 2 c. boiling water and drain. Place groats in pot with 6 c. cold water, bring to boil, reduce heat, and cook on med. until done, stirring occasionally (10–15 min.). Stir in 2 c. grated raw potatoes including their liquid. Cook about 10 min., stirring frequently, or bake in med. oven. Serve with fried salt-pork or bacon nuggets and drippings (with or without browned chopped onions) or sour cream. Salt & pepper to taste.

BAKED CORNMEAL MUSH
mamałyga

Bring 6 c. water to boil, add 3–4 T. lard, and 1 T. salt, and gradually add 3 c. fine to med. cornmeal, stirring constantly. Cook covered on very low heat 10 min. without disturbing, then turn mixture over in pot and cook another 10 min. Mix and break up any lumps, then bake in med. oven about 30 min. Scoop small, dumpling-sized pieces onto serving platter and drench with fried salt-pork nuggets and drippings or melted butter. Also may be topped with crumbled bryndza or farmer's cheese. *Note:* This dish was a mainstay of the peasantry in the southeastern corner of Poland which bordered (before World War II) on Romania, where it originated.

BUCKWHEAT CAKE
pyza z mąki gryczanej

Place 4 c. buckwheat flour in bowl and scald with 1 c. hot melted lard, mixing to combine ingredients. Stir in ¾ c. flour, add 1 oz. crushed fresh yeast and 1 T. salt, stirring constantly and gradually adding about 2 c. warm water. Set aside in warm place to rise, transfer to greased baking pan and let rise again. Bake in moderate oven about 1 hr. Serve hot with sour cream and (optional) farmer's cheese or bryndza.

COOKED RICE
ryż na sypko

Wash 1 c. uncooked rice in sieve under cold running water and drain. In small pot with tight-fitting lid bring to boil 1¾–2 c. water containing 2–3 T. butter and ½ t. salt. Add the rice. When boiling resumes, stir briefly, reduce heat, cover, and cook on low heat 20–30 min. or until tender.

BAKED RICE
ryż wypiekany

Proceed as above, but when most water is absorbed, stir rice once, cover, and place in 375° oven. Bake about 20 min.

FLUFFY SELF-STEAMING RICE
ryż w dogotowywaczu

Wash 1 c. uncooked rice and drain. Bring to boil 2 c. water containing 2–3 T. butter, oleo, or lard and ½ t. salt. Add rice. When boiling resumes, stir, and cook covered on lowest possible heat 10 min. Do not uncover pot, but wrap it tightly in old newspaper or, better yet several thicknesses heavy-duty aluminum foil. Then wrap it in a towel, followed by a blanket, and smother it with a pillow or a featherbed. In 2–3 hrs. you will have the fluffiest rice you can imagine. It will still be hot in 8 hrs. This is sometimes called "working people's rice." You prepare it before leaving for work in the morning and it's ready to serve the minute you return.

COOKED RICE "BIG-WATER" METHOD
ryż w "dużej wodzie"

Wash and drain 1 c. rice as above. Bring to boil 8 c. water to which 2–3 T. butter and 1 t. salt have been added. Add the rice. When boiling resumes, cook uncovered about 17 min. Drain in sieve and rinse with a little cold water. Drain again, shaking sieve until dripping stops. *Note*: This method, favored by some older Polish cooks, guarantees that your rice will be moist, very tender, and not sticky. It also is less fattening because much of the starch is washed away compared with the "1 c. rice + 2 c. water" method. One nutritional drawback, however, is the fact that some of the mineral salts are also lost in the water.

RICE COOKED IN MILK OR STOCK
ryż na mleku lub rosole

You may cook rice according to the 1st method, using 2 c. milk instead of water or 1 c. milk and 1 c. water. Rice prepared in this way is generally used in sweet dishes and desserts. A flavorful savory rice can be prepared by substituting 2 c. strained broth or meat stock for the water.

SAFFRON RICE
ryż szafranny

Prepare rice as in the first method given but add a pinch saffron when uncooked rice is added to boiling water. This will give your rice a beautiful golden tinge plus a faintly exotic aroma. Saffron rice was a favorite of the Old Polish nobility and we sometimes serve it at dinner parties, especially with roast pork loin and prunes.

RICE & MEAT CASSEROLE
ryżowiec mięsny

Bring 10 c. water with 1 t. salt and 3 T. fat to boil. Add 1½ c. rinsed rice and, when boiling resumes, cook uncovered 10 min. Drain. In skillet, sauté 1 chopped onion in 2–3 T.

fat, add ½ lb. uncooked ground meat of choice (a pork, veal, & beef mixture is good) and brown lightly. Combine with rice, 2 eggs, 2 T. chopped dill or parsley, mix well, and season to taste with salt & pepper or one of your Polish meat seasonings. Grease baking dish and sprinkle with bread crumbs. Add mixture, even out the top, and bake in 420° oven 30 min. If top browns too quickly, cover. Serve with tomato sauce and a crispy salad.

RICE & COOKED MEAT CASSEROLE
ryż zapiekany z mięsem

This is a good way to use up meat leftover from the holidays. You can use roasts, boiled meat, ham, kiełbasa, or any combination thereof. Combine 1–3 c. of such cooked meat, finely diced, with 3–4 c. cooked rice, and season to taste with salt & pepper or a Polish seasoning of choice. The proportion of cooked meat to rice depends entirely on personal preference and the amount of leftovers you happen to have. Stir in about ½ c. strained meat or vegetable stock (court bouillon), or just enough to moisten mixture without making it appear wet. Transfer mixture to generously buttered baking dish. Fork-blend ½–1 c. sour cream with 1 raw egg yolk and ¼ c. grated yellow cheese. Pour over casserole, sprinkling with a little more grated cheese, and bake in 420° oven about 20 min., or until top is a nice golden brown. Turn out on serving platter or serve directly from baking pan and sprinkle with chopped greens of choice. Serve with a seasonal salad for a complete meal.

RICE & CALVES BRAIN CASSEROLE
ryż zapiekany z móżdżkiem

Rinse well and soak in cold water 30 min. ¾ lb. calves brains. Remove membranes and dice coarsely. Sauté 1 minced onion in 3 T. fat until golden, add brains, and simmer several min., stirring constantly. Season to taste with salt & pepper. In greased baking dish place 1½ c. cooked rice, top with brain mixture, and cover with another 1½ c. rice. Fork-blend ½ c. sour cream with 1 raw egg yolk and pour over mixture. Sprinkle with about ½ c. grated yellow cheese, preferably a sharper variety like tilsit. Bake in 400–420° oven 20–30 min. or until top turns golden brown. Sprinkle with chopped parsley before serving. *Note*: Chances are even your more squeamish guests will enjoy this dish, provided they don't know it contains calves brains!

RICE & MUSHROOM CASSEROLE
ryż zapiekany z pieczarkami

Wash well, drain, and slice thin or dice 12 oz. fresh cultivated mushrooms. In 3 T. butter simmer 1–2 chopped onions until transparent, add mushrooms, and sauté until liquid evaporates and mushrooms begin to sizzle. Stir frequently. Salt & pepper to taste and, for a more pronounced mushroom flavor, season with a little mushroom powder or liquid mushroom extract. Combine with 4 c. cooked rice, add 1–2 T. chopped dill and/or parsley, correct seasoning if necessary, and transfer mixture to greased baking dish sprinkled with bread crumbs. Fork-blend ½ c. sour cream with 1 raw egg yolk and ¼ c. bread crumbs with ½ c. grated yellow cheese and sprinkle over mixture. Dot with butter and bake in 400–420° oven 20–30 min. Serve with sliced tomatoes in summer and a grated-vegetable salad in winter for a complete meal.

RICE & TOMATOES
ryż z pomidorami

Wash and dice 2–3 med. tomatoes, place in pot, add 2 T. butter, 2 T. water, and ½ t. salt and simmer on low heat about 10 min. Sieve mixture into 4 c. cooked rice, stir in ¼ c. grated yellow cheese, add 1–2 T. chopped chives, and mix well. Transfer mixture to greased baking dish, top with ¼ c. grated yellow cheese, and bake in 400° oven 20 min. Transfer to platter and surround with cutlets or sliced roast.

RICE BAKED WITH PEAS
ryż z zielonym groszkiem

Place 1½ c. cooked rice in greased baking dish, add 2 c. cooked, drained peas (fresh or frozen are better than canned peas in this dish!), dot generously with butter. Salt & pepper to taste, sprinkle with 1 T. or so chopped dill, and cover with another 1½ c. cooked rice. Dot rice with a little more butter and bake in 400° oven about 30 min. *Note:* If rice is on the dry side, sprinkle with about ¼ c. meat or vegetable stock before baking. Place on serving platter and sprinkle with grated yellow cheese.

VARIOUS RICE CASSEROLES
różne zapiekanki z ryżem

Feel absolutely free to experiment and enhance any of the above rice casseroles with additional ingredients. Bland-tasting rice blends nicely with any variety of more distinctly flavored additions. You might want to add some diced, cooked meat to any of the rice & vegetable mixtures or use up some leftover cooked vegetables by baking them in your casserole. Use a little leftover soup instead of or in combination with the sour cream poured over casseroles before baking. A sprinkling of chopped dill, parsley, or chives will enhance both the flavor and looks of nearly every savory casserole. *Note*: Cooked barley may be used in any of the above dishes that call for cooked rice.

SWEET RICE DISHES
ryż na słodko

Besides savory casseroles, rice lends itself beautifully to a variety of sweet dishes, incorporating apples, cherries, raisins, and other fruits, honey, or preserves. They can be a light supper dish or a dessert and may be seasoned with cinnamon, nutmeg, or vanilla if desired. As a result, they have long been a favorite with youngsters, and some of them are traditionally served at the festive Wigilia (Christmas Eve) supper. *Note*: Cooked barley may be substituted for rice in any of these recipes.

RICE & FRUIT PRESERVES
ryż z konfiturami

Cook 1 c. rice according to "big-water" method and drain. Portion it out. Provide your favorite preserves (we think cherry or strawberry are best) allowing guests to spoon on as much as they like. Also provide whipped cream or sour cream as a topping. Rarely is anything so simple this good. *Variation*: Sliced, sugared strawberries or canned cherry-pie filling may be used instead of preserves.

RICE & APPLE CASSEROLE
ryż zapiekany z jabłkami

Cook 2 c. rice according to "big-water" method or in milk. Drain if cooked the first way. Coarsely grate 1½ lbs. peeled, cored apples, sugar to taste and add several drops vanilla extract. Generously butter baking dish, add a layer of rice, then some apples and continue layering until ingredients are used up. Top layer should be rice. Dot with butter and bake in 375° oven 30–40 min. Dust portions with powdered sugar and top with whipped cream. Coffee cream or half & half may be poured over servings instead. *Optional*: Sprinkle with several pinches cinnamon before or after baking. *Note:* Some families serve this dish on Christmas Eve.

BAKED RICE RING WITH FRUIT
wieniec ryżowy z owocami

Cook 1-1½ c. rice according to "big-water" method, drain, and cool slightly. Cream 3 egg yolks with 4 T. powdered sugar and mix with rice. Fold in 3 beaten egg whites and mix lightly. Generously butter ring mold and sprinkle with bread crumbs. Add rice mixture and level off top. Cover with aluminum foil and bake in pre-heated 375° oven about 30 min.

While it bakes, wash and drain 1–1½ lbs. fresh fruit: strawberries, raspberries, blueberries, etc. (Hull strawberries if necessary and cut each into quarters.) Transfer rice ring to round platter and fill opening with fruit. For decorative effect, run some of the berries round the rim of platter. Fork-blend 1–1½ c. sour cream with ½ c. powdered sugar and a bit of vanilla extract and pour over rice ring.

RICE & BERRY CASSEROLE
babka ryżowa z owocami

Cook 1–1½ c. rice according to "big-water" method or in milk. Allow to cool slightly, draining it first if made the first way. Cream 3 egg yolks with 4 T. powdered sugar, mix with rice, flavor with a little vanilla extract, and fold in 3 beaten egg whites, mixing lightly. Generously butter baking dish, add ½ the rice mixture, top with 1–1½ lbs. strawberries, blueberries, or raspberries prepared as above. Sprinkle them with ¼ c. powdered sugar and cover with remaining rice mixture. Even out top, cover with aluminum foil and bake in pre-heated 375° oven about 40 min. Serve when done, providing 1-1½ c. sour cream fork-blended into a creamy sauce with ¼ c. powdered sugar.

CHRISTMAS COOKED-WHEAT PUDDING
kutia/kucja

Sort and rinse 1 c. wheat, place in pot, cover with 5–6 c. cold pre-boiled water and let stand overnight. Next day, drain, add fresh water, and cook on low heat 3–4 hrs. or until tender, mixing occasionally. (*Note:* Some cooks drain wheat 2–3 times during cooking, adding fresh boiling water each time, but that isn't really necessary.) Drain the cooked wheat and set aside to cool. Rinse, scald, cook, and grind 1 c. poppyseeds as for noodles & poppyseeds (p. 483). Combine cooled, cooked wheat with poppyseed mixture and add ½ c. powdered sugar, 4 T. honey, ½ t. vanilla extract, the grated rind of 1 scrubbed and scalded lemon, ⅔ c. plumped raisins, and ½ c. coffee cream or half & half. Mix well and chill before serving. *Note*: This somewhat unusual sweet dish is a traditional Christmas Eve favorite in Eastern Poland.

CHRISTMAS COOKED-WHEAT PUDDING WITH WALNUTS
kutia/kucja z orzechami

Prepare wheat and poppyseeds as above. Mix together and add ½ c. honey, ½ c. plumped raisins, ½ c. ground walnut meats, a little vanilla extract, and ½ c. coffee cream or half & half. Mix well, chill, and serve.

CHRISTMAS COOKED-WHEAT PUDDING
WITH SOUTHERN FRUITS & NUTS
kutia/kucja z bakaliami

Prepare wheat and poppyseeds as in 1st recipe. Mix together, add ½ c. powdered sugar, ½ c. honey, 1 c. ground walnut meats, ½ c. coarsely ground blanched almonds, ½ c. plumped raisins, 4–5 chopped figs, and 4–5 chopped pitted dates. (*Note:* Figs and dates should be scalded with boiling water and allowed to soak until soft before draining and chopping.) Add the grated rind of 1 scrubbed and scalded lemon, mix ingredients well, chill, and serve. *Note*: Cooked whole-grain barley may be substituted for wheat in any of the above kucja recipes. Since the Old Polish gentry regarded both these grains as "low-brow", kucja was usually prepared in their manor houses with cooked rice.

SHORTCUT WHEAT PUDDING
kutia najłałwiejsza

If the prospect of finding wheat in your area and cooking it from scratch seems a bit overwhelming, here is a "short-cut" recipe that approximates how this Old Polish pudding is supposed to taste. Simply combine 4–5 c. plain puffed wheat with about 1 c. canned poppyseed filling and flavor to taste with a little honey, several drops vanilla extract, grated rind of ½ lemon, and about ½ c. ground walnuts. Mix in just enough cold half & half to get a thick consistency. Mix well, refrigerate, and serve chilled on Christmas Eve.

POTATOES & POTATO DISHES

When Columbus first discovered the potato on the Island of Hispaniola in the Caribbean, little did he know that this "exotic" plant would revolutionize the world's eating habits and save generations of his fellow Europeans from starvation. It was Poland's King Jan Sobieski who is believed to have brought this New World tuber to his homeland after successfully saving Europe from the Turks at Vienna (1683). At first it was viewed as a botanical curiosity or decorative plant. Some tried to use it for medicinal purposes or to prepare sweet dessert-type dishes. In time, it took the country and the rest of Europe by storm, and the culinary scene hasn't been the same ever since.

Potatoes have had various names over the centuries: *kartofle* in eastern and central Poland, *ziemniaki* in the south, *pyrki* in the western Great Poland region, and *grule*, a dialectic slang equivalent of taters or spuds. Today, Poland is the world's second largest potato producer, surpassed only by Russia. Poland's per capita potato consumption is over 300 pounds, compared with about 230 pounds for Great Britain, 150 pounds for West Germany, and a scant 50 pounds for the U.S.

Potatoes are used to make vodka, starch, and confectioner's syrup, as well as serving as hog feed. Perhaps that's one of the reasons why Polish ham is more juicy, tender, and flavorful than that produced from corn-fed pigs. Potatoes have a wide range of uses in the kitchen, to mention only potato pancakes and a wide variety of dumplings and may even be added to cheesecake. Still, they are served first and foremost as a hot accompaniment to meat and fish entrées or even egg dishes, in some families on nearly a daily basis. They can also be used to make tasty soups and casseroles.

The still widely held notion that potatoes consist of nothing but fattening starch is debatable. A 100-gram (roughly 3½ oz.) serving produces only 80–100 calories, but potatoes provide the body with highly digestible carbohydrates, and contain a fair amount of vitamin C, some vitamin A, B_1, B_2, and trace elements. What little protein they contain is of the highest quality and compares with that of egg whites.

Of course, the nutritional value of potatoes depends on how they are prepared. The worst way is to soak peeled potatoes in cold, salted water an hour or so before cooking—the way many Polish grandmothers still do. Most of their nutrients dissolve in the water and are poured down the drain. The healthiest potatoes are those cooked *w mundurkach*, in jackets, or as the Poles say, in uniforms. This is also the most convenient method, because slipping the skins off the hot cooked potatoes under cold running water takes less time than peeling raw potatoes. If you do peel potatoes, use the parings to make your own potato meal (see end of chapter) instead of throwing them out. This can be added to potato-pancakes batter in place of flour and eggs to make cholesterol-free pancakes with a more "potato-ey" taste to boot.

Speaking of potato pancakes, please look for them in the dumpling & noodle chapter. It was a toss-up whether to list them in this chapter, using their common roots as the criterion, or to include them among dishes of similar structure: noodles, dumplings, pancakes, loaves, etc. We decided on the latter.

* * *

BOILED POTATOES
kartofle z wody

Wash, peel, and cut in half or into quarters (if they are very large) 2 lbs. potatoes. Rinse well, place in pot, add boiling water to cover and 1–2 t. salt and bring to boil. Reduce heat to med. and cook until fork tender. When done, drain, return to heat, and shake pot until all moisture steams away. Serve plain with gravy dishes or herring. A sprinkling of chopped fresh dill and/or parsley will enhance the flavor, look, and nutritional value of your potatoes. *Note*: In the old days, it was common to soak the peeled potatoes in cold, salted water an hr. or so before cooking. This is not recommended, since too many of the nutrients dissolve in the water and are poured away.

HURRY-UP BOILED POTATOES
kartofle gotowane naprędce

When in a hurry, dice the peeled potatoes and they will cook in much less time. Use this method only in emergencies, however, since diced potatoes absorb more water and tend to get mushy. Also, more of the nutrients are lost while draining.

BOILED POTATOES WITH BUTTER OR PORK NUGGETS
kartofle z masłem lub skwarkami

Cook potatoes the regular way or according to the hurry-up method (above). After the cooked potatoes are drained and steamed dry, dot with butter (or butter substitute), or sprinkle with fried salt-pork or bacon bits and as many drippings you like. Chopped dill, parsley, or chives always greatly enhance the flavor of potatoes. Serve with boiled, gravy-less main courses, or as a meal in itself with a bowl of cold sour milk or buttermilk on the side.

POTATOES COOKED IN MILK
kartofle gotowane w mleku

Peel and dice 8 potatoes, place in pot, scald with boiling water to cover, bring to boil, and drain. Drench potatoes with 1 c. boiling milk, add 1–2 t. salt and cook until tender. Transfer to platter with slotted spoon, sprinkle with 2–3 T. melted butter and some finely chopped greens.

BOILED POTATOES WITH SOUR CREAM & ONIONS
kartofle ze śmietaną i cebulą

Slice 2 med. onions wafer thin and add to ¾–1 c. fork-blended sour cream. Season to taste with salt, pepper, and a little sugar. Cover and let stand at room temp. 30 min. Meanwhile, peel and cook about 8 potatoes in boiling salted water, drain, and steam dry. Transfer to serving platter and top with sour cream-onion mixture. This dish is likely to remind you of creamed herring and boiled potatoes.

BOILED POTATOES WITH CHOPPED HARD-BOILED EGGS
kartofle z jajkiem siekanym

Peel and cook 2 lbs. (about 8) potatoes in boiling salted water the normal way, but do not overcook. When done, but still firm, drain and steam dry. Cut into small cubes and toss with 2–3 finely chopped hard-boiled eggs. On serving platter sprinkle with 3 T. melted butter and (optional) 2 T. sweet cream. Garnish with chopped dill and/or parsley. A meal in itself!

POTATOES IN JACKETS
kartofle w mundurkach

Choose 2 lbs. small or med. potatoes of roughly equal size. Scrub well with brush under running water to remove all grit. Transfer to pot, cover with boiling water, and cook on rather high heat until tender. Drain well, steam off moisture and serve immediately with salt and unsalted butter. These are excellent with a bowl of kapuśniak (sauerkraut soup) or herring. More flavorful and nutritious potatoes in jackets are preferred (after peeling) in salads, cutlets, croquettes, casseroles, etc.

MASHED POTATOES
kartofle tłuczone

Wash, peel, and halve or quarter 2 lbs. potatoes. Rinse, place in pot, cover with boiling water, add salt as desired, and cook until tender. Drain, return pot to heat, and shake it until moisture steams away. Mash well and serve with gravy dishes or topped with butter or fried salt-pork or bacon bits. *Note*: For most families in today's Poland, this is the most common way of serving potatoes. Butter and milk are not added, because the gravy or melted topping add sufficient richness. Mashed potatoes with butter and milk added are known in Polish cookery as puréed potatoes (below).

COUNTRY-STYLE POTATOES
kartofle po wiejsku

Peel and cook 2 lbs. potatoes in salted boiling water to cover until tender, then drain and steam dry. Separately, fry up ⅛ lb. diced slab bacon or salt pork until nicely browned and pour over potatoes in pot. Mash well, sprinkle with chopped greens of choice if desired, and serve with a bowl of cold sour milk or buttermilk on the side. May also accompany meat dishes without gravy. *Variation*: Add 1 finely chopped onion to the nearly fried bacon or salt pork and simmer until tender.

MASHED POTATOES À LA MASURIENNE (WITH CARROTS)
kartofle tłuczone po mazursku

In separate pots, cook 5–6 peeled potatoes and 2 peeled, cut-up carrots in boiling salted water until tender. Drain and steam dry. Combine the potatoes and carrots, add several T. golden-brown salt-pork or bacon nuggets and as much of the drippings as you like, plus several pinches pepper. Mash well so the potatoes and carrots blend evenly. Sprinkle with chopped parsley on serving dish. *Variation*: Cooked rutabaga may be used in place of or in addition to the carrots. A change-of-pace way to perk up those same old, bland mashed potatoes!

PURÉED OR WHIPPED POTATOES
kartofle purée

Wash, peel and rinse 2 lbs. potatoes and cook in boiling, salted water as with boiled potatoes. When tender, drain, return to heat, and shake pot until moisture steams away. Add 2–3 T. butter (or butter substitute) and 6–10 T. boiling milk. Mash well. Transfer to serving platter or use ice-cream scoop to make a border of potato balls round the rim of your meat platter. In either case, sprinkle generously with finely chopped chives, dill or parsley, or a combination of any two or all three.

CREAMY PURÉED POTATOES
kartofle purée ze śmietaną

Wash, peel, rinse, cook, drain, and steam dry 2 lbs. potatoes as above. Add 1 heaping T. (more or less) sour cream and mash well. Salt & pepper to taste. *Optional*: 1 t.–2 T. raw grated onions will perk up the flavor of these potatoes. Naturally, this and most other potato dishes may be freely garnished with chopped greens of choice. *Note*: Calorie counters can substitute low-fat yogurt for the sour cream.

MULTI-COLORED PURÉED POTATOES
kartofle purée wielokolorowe

Prepare 3 lbs. puréed or whipped potatoes as above. Divide potatoes into 4 or 5 batches and color as follows: 1. Into 1 batch blend in 2 T. tomato paste; 2. To another add just enough beet juice (from canned beets) to get a nice pinkish hue; 3. Color the 3rd batch with 1–2 raw egg yolks or several pinches saffron; 4. Cook ½ lb. chopped fresh or frozen spinach in small amount of water 10 min. Strain through sieve and use liquid to color 4th batch; 5. Leave 1 batch of potatoes uncolored. Using ice-cream scoop, pile scoops of multi-colored potatoes in a pyramid on serving platter or use them to make a border around your meat platter.

PURÉED POTATOES & POPPYSEEDS
kartofle purée z makiem

Scald 3 T. poppyseeds with boiling water, cover, and let stand until cooled to room temp. Drain well. Crush with spoon or grind in poppyseed grinder if you have one. Cook 10 med. peeled potatoes in boiling, salted water until tender, drain and steam dry. Mash well. Add the ground poppyseeds and 3 T. butter and, stirring constantly, gradually pour in ¾ c. hot boiled milk. When fully absorbed, heat briefly and serve. This dish was once popular among the peasantry of Poland's southeast borderlands annexed by the Soviet Union.

FLUFFY RICED POTATOES
kartofle puchowe

Cook 2 lbs. potatoes (7-8 med.-sized potatoes), drain, and steam dry. Force through ricer directly onto serving platter. Drench with melted butter and sprinkle with chopped parsley, dill, and/or chives. A border of such potatoes may be used to decorate the rim of the meat platter.

BOILED NEW POTATOES
młode kartofelki

These are the season's first tiny potatoes and the best are walnut-sized or smaller. Rather than peeling, use a nylon scrubber to remove their delicate skins under cold running water.

Place 2 lbs. scrub-peeled new potatoes in pot, cover with boiling water, add 1 T. salt, and cook under cover over fairly high heat 20–30 min., checking them for doneness. Drain, steam off moisture, dot with butter, and sprinkle with chopped fresh dill. This Polish summertime favorite is an excellent accompaniment to roast chicken or breaded pork cutlets. In the authors' household, dilled and buttered new potatoes are a hot weather treat, served with bowls of creamy, cold sour milk.

NEW POTATOES WITH SHEEP'S-MILK CHEESE
młode kartofelki z bryndzą

Scrub 2 lbs. walnut-sized new potatoes with nylon scrubber under cold running water to remove skins and cook in salted boiling water to cover until tender. Drain and steam dry. Transfer to platter and top with 4 T. melted butter, ¼ c. grated sheep's-milk cheese (bryndza), feta or farmer's cheese, and chopped dill and/or parsley. *Note*: Cubed mature potatoes can be used in any of the recipes calling for new potatoes and, conversely, new potatoes can be substituted for regular potatoes in all dishes except mashed, pureed, or French-fried potatoes.

STEAMED NEW POTATOES
młode kartofelki gotowane na parze

Scrub 2 lbs. tiny new potatoes with nylon scrubber to remove skins. Place potatoes in top half of steamer pot over boiling water, cover tightly, and cook 30–40 min. or until tender. Transfer to platter, dot with butter, and sprinkle with chopped dill. Another way is to spoon sour cream over the hot potatoes. *Note*: If you don't have a steamer pot (something like a double boiler except the top pot has a perforated bottom to let steam in), simply place potatoes in metal sieve or colander over pot of boiling water and cover tightly. Steamed potatoes are not only tasty but retain more vitamins and minerals than those boiled in water.

BAKED NEW POTATOES
młode kartofelki pieczone

Scrub 2 lbs. tiny new potatoes with nylon scrubber under cold running water to remove skins. Place in baking dish, dot with butter (about 2–3 T.), and sprinkle with about 1 T. chopped dill and 1 T. chopped parsley. Cover baking dish and wrap tightly with aluminum foil to make it airtight. Bake in 375° oven for about 45 min. Potatoes may be salted before or after baking.

MOCK NEW POTATOES
młode kartofelki fałszywe

Even when real walnut-sized new potatoes are out of season or otherwise not available, you can simulate this gourmet delight as follows. Simply scoop out balls from large, mature potatoes and proceed according to the recipes calling for new potatoes. Ideally, use scoops of varying size, since real new potatoes are never all identical.

BOILED POTATO BALLS
kartofle drążone z wody

Peel and wash 2 lbs. large, regularly shaped potatoes. Use melon scoop to make potato balls the size of a cherry. (Freeze up leftover potato scraps for future use in soups, stews, etc.) Place potato balls in pot, cover with salted, boiling water, and cook about 15 min. or until tender. Cook on medium-low heat so potato balls do not fall apart. Drain and steam off moisture. Use potato balls to rim the edge of meat platters or serve them on their own platter. In either case, drench with melted butter and garnish with freshly chopped greens of choice. Buttered bread crumbs (Polonaise topping) are another possibility. This is considered a gourmet side dish that nicely accompanies beef tenderloin.

BUTTER-FRIED POTATO BALLS
kartofle drążone smażone w maśle

Peel and wash 2 lbs. large, regularly shaped potatoes and scoop into cherry-sized balls with melon scoop. Place in pot and scald with boiling water, drain well in colander, and dry on absorbent paper or dish towel. In skillet melt 3–4 T. butter, add potato balls, sprinkle with salt, and simmer on low heat until they are golden on all sides and tender on the inside. Be sure to stir frequently and watch that the butter doesn't burn. Turn out and garnish with chopped dill and/or parsley. *Note*: To prevent butter from burning and to reduce the amount of saturated fat in this recipe, first heat 1 T. olive oil or other high-grade cooking oil in skillet before adding about 2 T. butter.

CREAMED POTATOES
kartofle duszone w śmietanie

Scrub 2 lbs. potatoes of roughly equal size and cook unpeeled (in jackets) until tender. Quickly peel hot potatoes under cold running water. Slice or cut into cubes and place in skillet. Sprinkle with salt, add 1 level T. butter, and stir in 1 heaping T. sour cream. Mix gently and simmer under cover 15 min. *Note:* If dieting, use butter substitute and low-fat yogurt instead.

MASHED-POTATO BALLS & POPPYSEEDS
skubanki kartoflane z makiem

Peel and cut 8 potatoes into cubes. Place in pot, scald with unsalted boiling water to cover, and cook until slightly underdone (hard on the inside). Drain, reserving the water. Mash well, stir in ¾ c. flour and add ½ of the poured-off potato water. Cover and keep on very low heat about 15 min. Pour off any remaining water. Sprinkle with ½ t. salt and mix well. Scoop teaspoonfuls of mixture onto serving platter, sprinkle with 3 T. melted lard, about 1 T. sugar, and 1 T. ground poppyseeds. Although this may sound like an unusual combination, it can be rather tasty.

FRIED POTATOES
kartofle smażone

Peel and rinse well 2 lbs. potatoes and dry on absorbent paper. In large skillet melt 3–4 T. lard or salt-pork or bacon drippings and fry sliced potatoes until golden brown on one side. Turn over and continue frying until the other side becomes a nice golden brown. For best results, fry only a single layer at a time. When done, dry on absorbent paper, sprinkle with salt, and serve immediately.

FRIED POTATOES & PORK CRACKLINGS
kartofle smażone ze skwarkami

Fry up ¼ lb. or less diced salt pork or slab bacon to a nice golden brown. Remove golden-brown nuggets with slotted spoon and set aside. Pour off all but about 4 T. of the drippings. In drippings fry 2 lbs. peeled, washed, dried, and sliced potatoes as above. When done, add the fried nuggets (cracklings) and toss gently. Salt & pepper to taste. A sprinkling of chopped garden greens (dill, parsley and/or chives) is always good. For variety, season with a pinch or 2 ground caraway. *Variation*: Toss the sliced raw potatoes with 1–2 finely chopped onions before frying.

FRIED POTATOES & MUSHROOMS
kartofle smażone z grzybami

In several T. lard, bacon, or salt-pork fat (or oil if you are cutting down on animal fats) fry potatoes as above. Separately, wash well and slice 16 oz. fresh, wild, or cultivated mushrooms and simmer with 1 chopped onion in 2 T. butter about 15 min., stirring frequently, until tender. Combine the fried potatoes and mushrooms, salt & pepper to taste, and garnish with chopped parsley and/or dill. With a crispy salad on the side, this can be a complete meal.

FRIED PRE-COOKED POTATOES
kartofle odsmażane

Melt 3–4 T. bacon or salt-pork drippings in large skillet. Add 1 finely chopped onion and simmer until just transparent. Add about 8 sliced or diced cooked potatoes (either freshly boiled or cold leftovers) and fry on med. heat until a golden crust begins to form. Flip over with spatula and fry the other side until crusty. Salt & pepper to taste and garnish with chopped greens of choice. Personally, we feel the tastiest fried pre-cooked potatoes are prepared from potatoes slightly undercooked in jackets.

FRENCH-FRIED POTATOES/CHIPS
frytki

What Americans call french fries and the British refer to as chips are known in Polish as frytki (from the original French "frites," short for "pommes frites" or fried potatoes). It was a toss-up whether to include them here, but the fact is that they have become naturalized citizens in today's Polish cuisine, much the same way that pizza is now regarded as something very American. Peel and wash 2 lbs. potatoes, slice into sticks, and dry on absorbent paper or dish towel. In deep skillet or pot, heat ½ lb. lard or enough oil so potatoes will be able to float freely. Add potatoes to hot fat in batches and cook, turning gently, until they become golden and begin to brown around the edges. Transfer with slotted spoon to plate lined with several layers of absorbent paper, cover with more absorbent paper, press down gently, and keep in warm oven as you fry the remaining potatoes. When all have been fried, dry them with fresh absorbent paper, sprinkle with salt, and serve immediately.

BAKED POTATOES IN JACKETS
kartofle pieczone w mundurkach

Scrub thoroughly under cold running water 8–12 medium-sized potatoes (do not use new potatoes!) of roughly regular shape. Place on baking sheet in pre-heated 425° oven and bake 40-60 min., testing them for doneness with fork. Sprinkle baking sheet with a little water several times during baking. Serve with fresh, unsalted creamy butter and salt.

BAKED POTATOES
kartofle pieczone

Peel 8–12 medium sized potatoes of roughly uniform shape and rinse well. Dry on absorbent paper or dish towel. Place on greased baking sheet, sprinkle with salt, and bake in 400°–425° oven 40–60 min., or until done.

BAKED POTATOES WITH CARAWAY
kartofle pieczone z kminkiem

Wash, peel, and rinse 2 lbs. small to medium-sized potatoes. Dry with dish towel or absorbent paper. Rub potatoes with cooking oil and place on baking sheet. Sprinkle each with salt and caraway seeds and bake in 400° oven 45–60 min. or until done. Large potatoes can be halved or quartered and baked the same way. The smaller the potato, the less time it needs to cook. *Variation*: Omit the oil and sprinkle the potatoes with salt, caraway seeds, and flour.

POTATOES BAKED WITH CHEESE
kartofle pieczone z serem

Peel, rinse, and dry 8 potatoes. Slice each only ⅔ of the way down so potatoes hold together. Place on baking sheet sliced side up. Sprinkle each potato with salt and brush with melted butter. Bake in 400° oven until they turn golden brown, 25–45 min. depending on their size. Meanwhile, mix 2 T. bread crumbs with 2–3 T. grated sharp yellow cheese (tilsit, brick, etc.). Top each potato with a little of the mixture and bake another 5–10 min. or until topping browns.

FISHERMAN'S POTATO POT
kartofle po rybacku

Peel, rinse, and slice or cut into small cubes 2½–3 lbs. potatoes or as much as needed to fill a medium-sized pot with tightly fitting lid. Dice ¼ lb. or so slab bacon and fry until golden without browning. Add 2–3 chopped onions and simmer briefly, stirring constantly, but do not cook. Mix the bacon, onions, and drippings with the potatoes, place in pot (leaving about 1 inch headspace), salt & pepper, cover pot, and wrap tightly in several layers of preferably heavy-duty aluminum foil. This procedure should be timed for when your wood or charcoal fire has turned to glowing coals and hot ashes. Dig a pit slightly larger and at least 10 inches deeper than your pot. Shovel a thick layer of hot coals and ash into pit and place pot directly on top. Add coals around the sides of pot and a nice layer on top, cover with earth, and stamp down. When you get back several hrs. later and open the pot, it will fill the whole campsite with the most heavenly, mouth-watering aroma. This is a favorite with Polish campers and fishermen which we're sure you'll also enjoy. *Note*: Sliced, skinned, smoked kielbasa or any diced cold cuts you have on hand may freely be added to pot before baking.

CAMPFIRE BAKED POTATOES
kartofle pieczone w ognisku

These are usually baked under rather primitive conditions at the edge of the field after a day of potato digging, so the freshly dug potatoes usually go into the fire just as they are, without washing. But no matter, the skins are not eaten anyway. Place potatoes among the glowing ashes of a dying wood fire, cover with more of the embers and wait: 20, 30, 40 min. It all depends on the size of the potatoes and the temp. of the embers. When cool enough to handle, break open and enjoy. Naturally, a little butter will make them tastier, but usually a sprinkle of salt is the only seasoning available on such occasions. Just as Americans fondly recall the wiener roasts and corn roasts of their childhood, Poles nostalgically remember such outdoor potato bakes, along with the requisite campfire songs and fellowship which took place back when they were boy scouts or farm youths.

BAKED POTATOES FOR THE ROAD
kartofle pieczone na drogę

Scrub 6, 8, 10, or whatever number of potatoes you need and bake in 400° oven 30 min. more or less (depending on size of potatoes) until still underdone. Wrap each potato in several layers of aluminum foil and continue baking until tender. Immediately wrap each potato tightly with several layers of paper towel, then in a cloth napkin or dish towel, and finally in plastic wrap or another sheet of foil. Place potatoes together tightly in plastic bag and roll into a bundle with beach towel or blanket. These will stay hot for hrs. and can be enjoyed while traveling, at picnics, or wherever. Add a piece of ready-to-eat kielbasa or hard-boiled egg and a tomato, and you'll have a balanced meal.

POTATO & HEMPSEED CASSEROLE
kartofle zapiekane z konopiami

Cook 12 well-scrubbed potatoes in jackets in boiling water until slightly underdone. Cool, peel, and slice or cut into small cubes. In 5 T. butter cook 3 coarsely chopped onions until they just begin to brown. Mix potatoes with onions, add ¼ c. ground hempseeds, and salt to taste. Mix lightly and transfer to baking dish. Bake covered in 375° oven 35–45 min. Dishes containing hempseed, although no longer very common, were once typical of Polish peasant cookery.

POTATO & SALT PORK SAUSAGE
kiełbasa kartoflana ze słoniną

Peel and grate 16 potatoes or cut peeled potatoes into cubes and shred in blender. Sprinkle mixture with salt. Separately, dice ¾ lb. salt pork or slab bacon and fry up with 2–3 chopped onions. Mix potato mixture with salt pork and onions and season with a little pepper and (optional) several pinches of marjoram or savory. Fill pork casing with mixture, tie both ends with strong thread, and brown on both sides in remaining pan drippings. Transfer to baking pan and bake in 375° oven about 45 min. Test a piece for doneness. Serve hot with sour cream. This tasty, stick-to-the-ribs dish will appeal to potato-pancake lovers, but is hard to digest and not recommended for those with delicate stomachs.

FRIED POTATO BALLS
kulki kartoflane smażone

Peel, rinse, and cook 7 potatoes in salted boiling water to cover, drain, and steam dry, then mash thoroughly. Separately pour ½ c. cold water into pot, add 3 T. butter and 2 t. salt and bring to boil. Remove from heat and sift in ½ c. flour, stir until smooth, then cook on med. heat 1-2 min., stirring constantly. Set aside to cool. Stirring constantly, add 4 raw eggs one at a time. When fully blended, add the mashed potatoes and mix well to uniform consistency. In skillet, heat 2 c. lard, vegetable shortening or oil. Scoop up bits of dough with teaspoon and fry to a nice golden brown. Dry on absorbent paper. These potato balls may accompany meat or fish dishes, or be a meal in themselves with a little sour cream.

POTATO PUFFS
pączki kartoflane

Dissolve 1 t. dry yeast or ⅓ cake compressed yeast in 2 T. room-temp. sour cream. Cook 8 scrubbed potatoes in jackets, peel under cold running water, force through sieve, or grind and set aside to cool. Combine potatoes, yeast mixture, 2 eggs, about 4 T. flour, 2 t. salt, and several pinches of pepper; mix well until mixture is smooth and fully blended. Heat 2 c. fat or oil of choice in pan or skillet small enough to allow puffs to float freely. Between floured palms roll pieces of dough into balls the size of large cherries and fry in hot fat to a nice golden brown. Remove with slotted spoon and drain on absorbent paper. In better Polish restaurants, these puffs are often served with such gourmet dishes as roast pheasant or fillet steak.

POTATO "ANGEL WINGS"
chrust z kartofli

Cook 6 peeled potatoes in boiling salted water to cover, drain, steam dry, and grind or mash very thoroughly. Mix with 3 c. flour and 1 raw egg yolk, then gently fold in 1 stiffly beaten egg white. On floured board roll out very thin, less than ⅛ inch thick if possible. With pastry cutter or knife, cut dough sheet into 1 inch wide strips, then cut each strip at an angle every 3–4 inches. Make a 1–1½ inch vertical slit in each strip and pull 1 of the ends through the opening as with ordinary faworki (chruściki), sometimes referred to in English as angel-wing pastries. Fry in plenty of hot fat or oil (so they can float freely) to a nice golden color. This should be only a matter of seconds. Turn over and fry a bit longer on the other side. Remove carefully to absorbent paper and sprinkle with a little salt and (optional) ground caraway. They are usually washed down with hot milk, but they also make a nice snack with cold beer. *Variation*: Instead of salt or caraway, they may be dusted with powdered sugar and enjoyed as a dessert pastry.

GRATED RAW POTATOES AS A FOOD-THICKENER
kartofle tarte do zagęszczania potraw

Here is another illustration of the fact that the austere measures of yesteryear can become today's healthful alternative. A cookbook published in Warsaw during World War II, for instance, urged homemakers to replace then hard-to-get eggs in various groundmeat dishes with grated raw potatoes. Simply work 1 raw, peeled, grated potato into about 1 lb. ground meat when preparing meatballs, minced cutlets, meatloaf, and the like, and you can omit the eggs. You not only reduce cholesterol but may even find the finished product tastier than ever. This method can also be used in gołąbki (stuffed cabbage rolls), especially the kind that contain ground meat, rice, or groats. A raw grated potato or two may also be added to a pot of bigos in place of a roux or flour to take up excess moisture.

POTATO-PEEL MEAL
mączka z obierzyn kartoflanych

No matter how thin you manage to peel your potatoes, some of the nutrients will invariably be lost if you throw out the parings. They can be used to prepare an easy homemade potato meal that will make for a tastier and (attention dieters!) 100% cholesterol-free potato pancake. Before peeling, scrub potatoes very well with a brush under cold running water. Place peelings on baking sheet in 350° oven and keep them there an hr. or more, until they are completely brittle and no longer limp. Don't let them burn! Grind the dried peelings or pulverize to a powder in blender, sift and store in sealed jar. You can keep adding meal to jar each time you prepare another batch of potato parings in this way. When preparing potato-pancake batter, add about 1 T. of your potato meal for each grated raw potato instead of flour or eggs. Also use the meal in various potato noodles, dumplings, cutlets, etc.

* * *

Look for more potato recipes in the chapters devoted to appetizers (potato salads), noodles & dumplings, and meat and vegetable dishes, as well as among the soups. You can even find a few among the desserts, cakes, and breads.

NOODLES, DUMPLINGS, PANCAKES & C.

The very length of this chapter attests to the importance that *farinaceous* (or pasta) dishes have traditionally held in Polish cookery. While it might have seemed logical to lump them together in the chapter devoted to groats, as many cookbooks do, we felt that would have made it unwieldy and unmanageable.

In the U.S., undoubtedly the best-known Polish representative of this large food family are *pierogi*, which are increasingly turning up in the frozen-food cases and deli sections of American supermarkets, especially in larger metropolitan areas. They have been variously described as filled dumplings, dough pockets, or even "Polish ravioli", but their Polish name is gaining in popularity. Other Slavic groups prepare similar dishes, to mention only the Ukrainian *perohy* and Russian *pirozhki*.

In the more than 15 years the author has run his Polish Chef column in over a dozen American newspapers, one of the most typical pieces of "fan mail" contained the query: "Could you please print the recipe for *pierogi*?" That seemingly simple question required a bit of research, since there is no "one" recipe for *pierogi*. Not only is there an endless variety of fillings, but even the pasta dough that encases them can be prepared in a number of different ways which influence the finished product's flavor, texture, and manageability. After studying the techniques presented in scores of cookbooks, some going back to the mid-19th century, and conducting numerous culinary experiments, we came up with seven varying dough recipes and nearly 40 different fillings. Also included are a dozen different toppings.

We might add that "pierogi" is probably the only Polish dish that seems to have its own patron saint. "*Święty Jacek z pierogami!*", (St. Hyacinth and his pierogi!) is an old expression of surprise, roughly equivalent to the American "good grief!" or "holy smokes!" Nobody seems to know what the connection between these dumplings and the saintly 13th-century monk was all about.

In addition to *pierogi*, Polish cuisine contains a large variety of other noodles, dumplings, dough balls, and the like, many of which defy easy translation into English. Among them are *leniwe pierogi, kluski, kopytka, knedle, kołduny, pyzy, gałeczki, gałuszki, hałuski, dziatki, łazanki, zacierki, śliziki, prza śniki*, and probably many more.

The translator faces a similar problem in the field of pancakes. It is true that American English uses such terms as pancake, hot cake, wheat cake, griddle cake, and flapjack interchangeably to denote roughly the same type of batter fried in a skillet. By contrast, such Polish terms as *naleśniki, placki, racuchy,* and *bliny* are used to describe quite distinct types of pancakes. Whether or not linguistic problems are your cup of tea, we think you will enjoy these and many of the other dishes presented in this chapter.

* * *

STANDARD PIEROGI DOUGH
ciasto pierogowe zwykłe

Sift about 2½ c. flour onto breadboard. Sprinkle with ½ t. salt. Make a volcano-like crater in the flour mound and deposit 1 egg into it. Work ingredients into a dough, gradually adding about ½ c. cold water in a thin stream. (Some Polish cooks prefer lukewarm or even hot water.) Knead dough on floured board until firm and smooth, roll it into a ball, and let it rest 10 min. or so beneath a warm inverted bowl. Take ⅓ of the dough at a time (leaving the rest beneath the bowl) and roll out thin. With glass or biscuit-cutter cut dough into circles. Place a spoonful of filling on each circle slightly off center, fold in half, and press edges together with fingers, crimping to ensure a tight seal. Drop small batches of pierogi into a fairly large pot of boiling salted water, making sure not to crowd them. When boiling resumes, reduce heat to a slow boil and cook about 10 min. Test one to see how well dough is cooked. Remove to colander with slotted spoon and rinse lightly with cold water. Serve hot with topping of choice (see below) or let them cool and then fry them in butter to a nice golden brown. These dough recipes make 25–30 pierogi or roughly 4 servings.

2-EGG PIEROGI DOUGH
ciasto pierogowe dwujajeczne

Proceed as above, but use 2 eggs in the dough. The amount of water may be reduced to about ⅓ c. This depends however, on many factors like the size of the eggs, the dryness of the flour, and the hardness or softness of the water in your area, so play it by ear. The main thing is that the dough should not be dry and crumbly (meaning that too little liquid was used) nor damp and sticky (too much liquid).

PIEROGI DOUGH WITH OIL
ciasto pierogowe z olejem

Sift 2¼–2½ c. flour onto board, make crater-like indentation in peak and into it pour in a thin stream about ½ c. hot water, heaping the flour from the sides into the moistened center with a knife. When ½ the flour is still dry, add 1 egg yolk, 1 T. cooking oil and ½ t. salt. Quickly work all ingredients into a smooth, elastic dough and leave on floured board beneath a warm inverted bowl 10 min. Then roll out in batches, cut out, fill, and cook as above.

SOUR-CREAM PIEROGI DOUGH
ciasto pierogowe ze śmietaną

Combine 2½ c. flour with ½ t. salt and sift together on board. Deposit 1 egg in "crater" and fold in ½ c. fork-blended sour cream and ¼ c. melted butter. Work into a smooth, elastic dough. Chances are you won't need to add any water, but if the dough feels too hard, a sprinkle wouldn't hurt. *Variation*: For a raised-dough effect, add ½–1 t. baking powder into flour before sifting.

MILK PIEROGI DOUGH
ciasto pierogowe mleczne

Beat 1 egg, ¼ c. milk, ¼ c. water, and ¼ t. salt in bowl. Mix in 2 c. or slightly more sifted flour 1 c. at a time until fully blended. Knead on floured bread board until smooth and leave under inverted bowl 10–15 min. Then proceed as above. *Note*: Pierogi made with this dough should cook several min. longer than those above. As always, check one for doneness.

LUXURY PIEROGI DOUGH
ciasto pierogowe wykwintne

Prepare dough using 2¼–2½ c. flour, 2 egg yolks, 1 T. soft or melted butter, ½ t. salt, and about ½ c. water. For easier sealing, add 1 whole small egg and reduce the amount of water or increase flour slightly to get a nice workable dough.

LEAN PIEROGI DOUGH
ciasto postne na pierogi

Combine 2½ c. flour with ½ t. salt and about 1 c. water. Work into a dough and proceed as above. Adding ½ an egg white to the dough will make the pierogi easier to seal. These pierogi take about 12–15 min. to cook. Try out the above pierogi-dough recipes to see which you like best. They differ in taste, texture, and ease of handling. Here are a few pierogi-dough hints which you may find helpful:
—Adding 1 T. salad oil to standard pierogi dough will make it extra smooth and tender.
—For a very soft dough, add about 1 T. sour cream to standard recipe (i.e. the first pierogi-dough recipe presented above).
—A Polish-American innovation for getting a smooth, pliable dough is to add 1–2 T. room-temp. Philadelphia cream cheese.

—Whichever recipe you choose, remember that the dough should be firm, smooth and elastic. If it is moist and sticky to the touch, sprinkle with and work in a little more flour. If, on the other hand, the dough is dry, floury, and crumbly, moisten with a little water and knead until you get the desired consistency.

—If the dough feels a bit dry when you are sealing your pierogi, moisten your fingers with water when pinching the edges together. It is absolutely essential that no filling protrudes from the seam. If that occurs, the pierogi are likely to fall apart during cooking. Or they may become water-logged and the filling may wash out, leaving only an empty pasta shell.

—Since you cut circles from the sheet of dough, there will obviously be dough left over. You can combine it and roll it out again to make a few more pierogi or roll up the dough sheet tightly, jelly-roll fashion, and slice it thin to make noodles.

—There will be less leftover dough if you cut the dough sheet into 2 inch squares rather than circles. This will produce triangular pierogi.

—Cooked, drained, cooled pierogi freeze up very well in plastic bags. When ready to serve, place frozen pierogi in skillet, add 1 c. boiling water, cover and steam until fully heated through. Or, allow to thaw at room temp. and brown in butter. They can also be reheated in a microwave.

SAVORY CHEESE PIEROGI FILLING
pierogi z serem na słono

Fill dough rounds prepared according to any of the above dough recipes with a mixture made by combining 1 lb. ground farmer cheese (or dry cottage cheese) with 1 whole egg, 1 extra egg yolk, and salt & pepper to taste. 1 t. sugar may be added (optional). If neither farmer cheese nor dry cottage cheese are available, drain and press out all moisture from ordinary creamed cottage cheese, which can be pulverized in a blender or ground. If filling is too wet, stir in some bread crumbs. *Variations*: Add 1–2 T. finely chopped chives to mixture and feel free to vary the taste with different spices like a pinch or two homemade herb pepper, hunter's seasoning, powdered caraway, crushed, dried mint leaves, etc. Remember: The art of improvisation and the personalized touch is what Polish cuisine is all about!

SAVORY CHEESE PIEROGI FILLING ANOTHER WAY
pierogi z serem na słono inaczej

Fork-blend 3 T. sour cream with 1 egg yolk and salt & pepper. Mix with 1 lb. ground farmer cheese (or dry cottage cheese) into a smooth filling. *Variations:* 1 whole egg or 2 egg yolks may also be used and the amount of sour cream may be increased slightly. The main thing is that the filling should not be mushy. If it turns out too moist, firm it up with a sprinkling of flour, potato starch, or sieved bread crumbs. A finely chopped onion browned in butter or some chopped chives may be added.

SWEET CHEESE PIEROGI FILLING
pierogi z serem na słodko

Combine 1 lb. ground farmer cheese (or ground dry cottage cheese) with ¼–⅓ c. sugar, 1 egg, 1 extra yolk, ½ t. vanilla extract and a dash of salt. Fill dough rounds and proceed as above.

SWEET CHEESE PIEROGI FILLING ANOTHER WAY
pierogi z serem na słodko inaczej

Combine 1 lb. ground farmer cheese (or dry cottage cheese) with 1 egg yolk, 1–2 T. melted butter, and several T. sour cream (or enough to get a thick, smooth filling). Add sugar to taste and sprinkle with a little cinnamon.

SWEET CHEESE & RAISIN PIEROGI FILLING
pierogi z serem i rodzynkami

To either of the above two sweet-cheese fillings add ¼–½ c. steamed raisins. To steam raisins, place in bowl, scald with hot water to cover, and let stand 10–15 min. Drain well and add to cheese filling.

LITHUANIAN-STYLE CHEESE PIEROGI FILLING
litewskie pierogi z serem

Combine 1 lb. ground farmer cheese with 2 eggs, 1 T. butter, and 1 t. tarragon. Salt & pepper to taste.

YELLOW CHEESE PIEROGI FILLING
pierogi z żółtym serem

Combine 2 c. grated yellow cheese (tilsit, edam, gouda, munster, brick, or similar) with 2 eggs and several T. bread crumbs, enough to get a moist but firm filling. Salt & pepper to taste. *Variation*: Run ½ lb. yellow cheese and 1–2 c. cold mashed potatoes through meat grinder. To mixture, add 1 finely chopped onion browned in butter, mix well, and salt & pepper to taste.

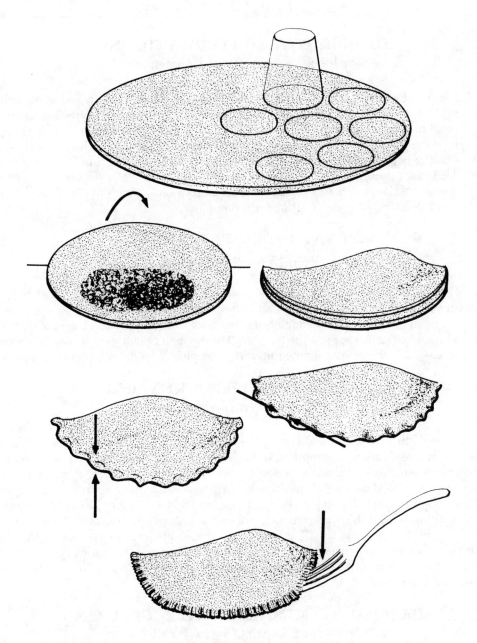

Shown above is the formation of pierogi. Start by cutting circles out of the rolled-out dough sheet. Place filling on each circle and fold in half. Pinch edges together as shown. Then, either crimp seal of hand-held pierogi with fingers or place on firm surface and make pattern along seal with fork.

CHEESE & POTATO PIEROGI FILLING
pierogi z kartoflami i serem

Cook 1 lb. potatoes in skins until tender, peel under cold running water, and mash well or grind together with ¼–½ lb. farmer cheese. (The proportion of potatoes to cheese is a matter of preference and may be varied according to taste.) In 2 T. butter lightly brown 2 finely chopped onions and add to mixture. (For non-fast days, onions may be browned in bacon or salt-pork drippings.) Salt & pepper to taste. A dash or 2 of paprika and/or homemade herb pepper will provide added zest. These are the very favorite pierogi of many Poles on both sides of the Atlantic. They are believed to have originated in the eastern borderlands of Old Poland, hence Poles often call them "ruskie pierogi" (Ruthenian dumplings).

POTATO PIEROGI FILLING
pierogi z kartoflami

Cook 1½ lbs. peeled potatoes or potatoes in jackets (skins), and peel under cold running water. Mash well or put through ricer and set aside to cool. Meanwhile, lightly brown 2 finely chopped onions in 2–3 T. butter. Combine the potatoes with the onions, 1 egg, 2 T. bread crumbs, and (optional) 2 T. chopped chives. *Note:* The egg and bread crumbs may be omitted. For non-fast days, the onions may be fried up with a heaping T. of diced bacon or salt pork.

GRATED POTATO PIEROGI FILLING
pierogi z tartymi kartoflami

Dice fine ⅛–¼ lb. slab bacon and fry in skillet until nuggets are golden brown. Remove nuggets and set aside. In bacon drippings, lightly brown 2 chopped onions. Grate 6 potatoes (like for potato pancakes), let mixture settle, then pour off liquid that appears on top. Transfer to sieve and allow excess moisture to drip away. Combine grated potatoes with onions, pan drippings, and bacon bits, stir in 1 egg, and add 1 or more T. bread crumbs to ensure a firm filling. Combine ingredients well and salt & pepper to taste. These pierogi must cook in gently boiling water 15–20 min. for the raw potatoes to get cooked through, so make sure they are well sealed before placing in boiling water. These pierogi will be enjoyed by hearty eaters (especially potato-pancake lovers), but may be a bit too heavy for those with delicate stomachs.

SAUERKRAUT & MUSHROOM PIEROGI FILLING
pierogi z kapustą i grzybami

Soak 1 oz. dried Polish mushrooms 2–3 hrs. in 1½ c. water, then cook in same water until tender. Chop mushrooms fine, return to water, and cook to reduce liquid. When you have no more than about 2 T. of almost syrupy mushroom liquid left, switch off heat and set aside.

Rinse well in cold water 2 well-packed c. sauerkraut, drain in colander, press out excess moisture, chop fairly fine, place in pot, scald with boiling water to cover, and cook on med. heat 20 min. Meanwhile, simmer 1 finely chopped onion in 2 T. butter until transparent or slightly browned. To sauerkraut add the mushrooms and their liquid, the browned onions, and (optional) ½ t. sugar. Simmer on low heat under cover another 30 min. or until tender, stirring frequently to prevent burning. When tender, uncover and allow moisture to steam away. Salt & pepper to taste then transfer to sieve, pressing out all moisture. If you like the sauerkraut very fine, you may run it through your meat grinder. 1–2 T. bread crumbs may be added to mixture. This is a favorite Wigilia dish! *Note*: For non-fast days, sauerkraut may be cooked in meat stock and onions can be fried up with bacon or salt-pork nuggets. These pierogi are an excellent way to use up left-over stewed sauerkraut or even bigos. Simply heat your sauerkraut dishes, adding about ½ c. boiling water, and steam away most of the liquid. Transfer to sieve and press out all moisture. Chop or grind if sauerkraut strands are on the long side. A T. or so bread crumbs may be added to firm up mixture. Fill pierogi when mixture has cooled.

CABBAGE PIEROGI FILLING
pierogi ze słodką kapustą

Shred 1 lb. (small head) of cabbage, scald with boiling water to cover, bring to boil, and cook 3 min. Drain. Cover with boiling water again and cook on med. heat 20 min. Separately, in skillet simmer 1 chopped onion in 3 T. butter until tender, add cabbage to onions in skillet, stir to mix ingredients, salt & pepper to taste, and simmer under cover until tender. Uncover and simmer a while longer, stirring constantly until moisture evaporates. Transfer to sieve and press out excess moisture. Chop fine or grind. Besides salt & pepper, other seasoning possibilities include about 1 t. or so chopped dill, or ¼ t. crushed caraway seeds.

CABBAGE & MUSHROOM PIEROGI FILLING
pierogi ze słodką kapustą i pieczarkami

Proceed as above but simmer 8 oz. or more washed, chopped fresh mushrooms with the onions in 3 T. butter or bacon drippings until tender before adding to cabbage.

CABBAGE & (DRIED) MUSHROOM PIEROGI FILLING
pierogi ze słodką kapustą i grzybami

Shred fine 1 small head cabbage and cook in boiling salted water until tender. Drain well and chop. Soak 1 oz. dried Polish mushrooms 2–3 hrs. in 1½ c. water, then cook in same water until tender. Chop mushrooms, return to liquid, and simmer uncovered until very little liquid is left. Sauté 1 chopped onion in 2–3 t. butter until tender, then add mushrooms, simmer briefly, and add to cabbage. Mix ingredients and continue simmering until nearly all moisture evaporates. Transfer to sieve and press out remaining moisture. Salt & pepper to taste and firm up filling with 1 T. or so bread crumbs if necessary.

POLISH (DRIED) MUSHROOM PIEROGI FILLING
pierogi z grzybami

Soak 3 oz. or more dried Polish mushrooms in 2 c. water 2–3 hrs. then cook in same water until tender. Chop mushrooms, return to liquid, and simmer to reduce liquid. Sauté 2 finely chopped onions in 3 T. butter until transparent, add the mushrooms and whatever liquid remains, and simmer until nearly all moisture has evaporated. Run the mushrooms and onions through grinder together with 1 stale, un-soaked kaiser roll. Add 1 egg to mixture, season generously with salt & pepper and (optional) 1 T. chopped parsley. Mix ingredients well. Sprinkle in some bread crumbs if mixture appears too mushy. Since imported dried mushrooms are on the pricey side, the recipe below provides a more economical way to enjoy much the same taste.

FRESH MUSHROOM PIEROGI FILLING
pierogi ze świeżymi grzybami

Wash, slice, or chop and simmer 16 oz. fresh, wild, or store-bought mushrooms in 4 T. butter, together with 2 finely chopped onions under cover about 15 min., stirring occasionally. Uncover and continue simmering until moisture evaporates and mushrooms begin to sizzle. Run mushrooms and onions through meat grind together with 1 stale, unsoaked kaiser roll. Add 1 egg to mixture, mix well, salt & pepper, add a little chopped parsley (optional), and firm up with a little bread crumbs if necessary. *Variation*: We feel adding 1 or even ½ oz. dried Polish mushrooms (pre-soaked, cooked, and chopped as usual) greatly improves the flavor of this dish. Another possibility is to use 8 oz. of the white, store-bought mushroom (pieczarki) and 8 oz. oyster mushrooms (boczniaki), available at Oriental markets, specialty food shops, etc.

MEAT PIEROŻKI FILLING
pierożki z mięsem

Grind 1 lb. or so boiled or roast beef or equivalent amount of assorted, cooked leftover meat. Simmer 2 finely chopped onions in 2 T. butter until slightly browned. Soak a stale kaiser roll in ½ c. milk until soggy and grind together with the onions. Combine ingredients well, salt & pepper to taste, and sprinkle with MSG. Other seasoning possibilities include a sprinkle of garlic powder, paprika, and/or marjoram, a dash of beef seasoning or hunter's seasoning. *Note*: Polish dumplings or dough-pockets filled with meat are usually called pierożki (little pierogi) because they are somewhat smaller in size. Use a juice glass or smaller biscuit-cutter to cut out the rounds of dough. The smaller pierogi, whatever their filling, are considered daintier and more elegant.

MEAT & MUSHROOM PIEROŻKI FILLING
pierożki z mięsem i grzybami

Soak 1 oz. dried Polish mushrooms in water 2–3 hrs., cook in same water until tender, chop, return to water, and simmer some more so most liquid steams away. Sauté 2 chopped onions in 3 T. butter until tender, then add mushrooms and cook until moisture evaporates. Grind mushrooms and onions with stale kaiser roll soaked in milk, mix with up to 1 lb. ground cooked meat and proceed as above. *Note*: Fresh chopped mushrooms, anywhere from 12–16 oz., simmered in butter with onions may be used instead of or in addition to the cooked dried mushrooms. In fact, that's a good way to stretch the filling if you don't have much cooked meat for your dumplings.

LITHUANIAN MEAT DUMPLINGS
kołduny litewskie

Grind ⅓ lb. boneless lamb, ⅓ lb. beef tenderloin (or cheaper cut), and ¼ lb. beef suet that has been chilled several hrs. Add 1 raw grated onion, 1–2 buds garlic, minced and mashed with salt, 1 t. or more marjoram, a pinch of sugar and salt & pepper to taste. Work by hand to blend all ingredients, adding 2–3 T. cold meat stock or broth to bind the mixture. Use the standard (1-egg) pierogi dough or the lean (eggless) variety and roll out very thin. Cut dough circles with a wine glass, fill with mixture, seal, and place in boiling salted water. When boiling resumes, cook at a slow boil 5–6 min., testing one for doneness. Remove with slotted spoon to colander. After they have dripped dry, transfer to serving platter and dot with unsalted butter. These bite-sized dumplings are usually eaten with a spoon. Some people prefer them served in a bowl of broth. *Note:* Kołduny is simply the name for pierogi used in the northeastern reaches of Old Poland, once known as the Grand Duchy of Lithuania. *Variation*: If beef suet is not available, beef marrow or salt pork may be used instead.

SIMPLIFIED LITHUANIAN MEAT DUMPLINGS
kołduny litewskie uproszczone

Instead of grinding your own meat, simply combine just under ½ lb. each ground lamb and hamburger from your butcher or supermarket meat counter. Do not use ground round or sirloin because they lack the suet of ordinary low-cost hamburger needed to properly bind the filling. Otherwise proceed as above.

HAM & MUSHROOM DUMPLINGS À LA TYSZKIEWICE
kołduny tyszkiewiczowskie

Soak 3–4 oz. dried Polish mushrooms in 3 c. water 2–3 hrs., then cook in same water until tender. If more than just a little mushroom liquid has remained, reduce it by cooking a bit longer. In skillet, simmer 2 finely chopped onions until tender, then add mushrooms and continue simmering until moisture has evaporated. Grind the mushrooms and onions with ½ lb. fairly fat ham. If ham is on the lean side, grind in a 1 inch square of salt pork. To mixture, add 1 egg and work well to thoroughly blend ingredients. Salt & pepper to taste.

LUNG PIEROZKI FILLING
pierożki z płuckami

Wash 1 lb. pork or veal lungs, trimming away windpipe and any veins or gristle if still attached. Cube lungs, scald with boiling water to cover, and cook 15 min. Drain, add 4 c. cold water, 1 quartered onion, 1 bay leaf, several peppercorns, and 1 T. salt, and cook covered on low heat 1 hr. or until tender. Drain in colander. When dry, grind with 2 chopped onions browned in butter and combine with enough bread crumbs to firm up the mixture. Salt & pepper to taste and add several dashes nutmeg. *Note*: If you make your filling from 1 part boiled beef and 1 part cooked lungs, even squeamish eaters will be convinced they are eating pure beef pierogi!

FISH PIEROGI FILLING
pierożki z rybą

Simmer 2 finely chopped onions in 2–3 T. butter until slightly browned. Run the onions and ¾–1 lb. fried or otherwise cooked fish fillets through grinder. Into mixture work 1 beaten egg and 2 T. or so bread crumbs—enough to get a filling that is not too moist. Sprinkle in 1–2 T. chopped dill and salt & pepper to taste. This is an excellent way to use up that leftover cooked fish and come up with an interesting new dish at the same time! *Variation*: Boneless smoked fish may be used instead.

FISH & MUSHROOM PIEROGI FILLING
pierożki z rybą i pieczarkami

Assuming you have less than the ¾–1 lb. cooked fish called for in the above recipe, you can make up the difference by frying up some fresh sliced mushrooms with the onions and grinding them together with the fish. A hard-boiled egg or two may also be added. If you have no mushrooms on hand, add only 2–3 hard-boiled eggs. A little cooked rice may be used as a filler. This is yet another illustration that Polish cookery means creative improvisation, not the slavish following of recipes!

EGG PIEROGI FILLING
pierogi z jajami

Lightly brown 2 chopped onions in 2–3 T. butter and grind together with 6 or more hard-boiled eggs. To mixture add 2 T. bread crumbs, 1 small raw egg, 1–2 T. chopped dill, and/or parsley and salt & pepper (generously) to taste. A little cooked rice may be used as a stretcher, enabling you to reduce the number of hardboiled eggs to 4 or 5.

BUCKWHEAT-GROAT PIEROGI FILLING
pierogi z kaszą gryczaną/tatarczaną

Combine 2 c. cooked buckwheat groats with 1 c. mashed potatoes and 1 c. crumbled farmer cheese. Lightly brown 1–2 onions in 3 T. butter. Run groats, potatoes, cheese, and onions through grinder. Work in 1 egg, salt & pepper, and sprinkle with ¼ t. dried crushed mint leaves. Blend ingredients into a uniform mixture.

LENTIL PIEROGI FILLING
pierogi z soczewicą

Soak 2 c. lentils in 3 c. water several hrs. or overnight. Add a crumbled bay leaf and cook in same water until lentils are tender but not disintegrated. (Cooking time for lentils varies depending on their type, size, and dryness and may run anywhere from 30–60 min. If they are not very dry, they may not need to be pre-soaked.) Separately, soak ½–1 oz. Polish dried mushrooms 2–3 hrs. and cook in same water until tender. Chop mushrooms very fine, return to their water, and reduce until little liquid remains. Lightly brown 2 finely chopped onions in 2–3 T. butter, add the mushrooms, and simmer until liquid evaporates. Combine lentils and onion-mushroom mixture and salt & pepper to taste. A small egg may be added to better bind the filling. Instead of butter, the onions and mushrooms may be fried up with a little diced bacon. These pierogi are typical of the Podlasie area of northeast Poland.

PEA OR BEAN PIEROGI FILLING
pierogi z grochem lub fasolą

Soak 1 c. navy beans, lima beans, or dried yellow peas in 5 c. water overnight, then cook in same water until tender but not disintegrated. Drain in colander and allow to cool. Brown a heaping T. diced bacon, remove nuggets, and lightly brown 2 chopped onions in drippings.

Grind the beans or peas and combine with browned onions and bacon nuggets. Season with salt, pepper, savory, and/or marjoram. ***Note***: The beans or peas may also be prepared with mushrooms like the lentil filling (above).

BLUEBERRY PIEROGI FILLING
pierogi z jagodami

Wash, drain, and drip dry 1 pt. blueberries. Some cooks sprinkle the blueberries with sugar before filling pierogi, but that makes the filling quite runny. We feel it is better to fill them with just the blueberries and then sprinkle the cooked pierogi with powdered or granulated sugar on serving platter. This is a great summertime favorite, the more so that the small wild blueberries found in Poland's forests are far tastier than the commercially grown variety available in America. ***Note***: Your blueberry pierogi will be less runny if you sprinkle the berries with 1–2 T. flour or potato starch.

CHERRY PIEROGI FILLING
pierogi z wiśniami lub czereśniami

Remove stems, wash and pit 1 lb. or so sweet or sour cherries. Place in colander and gently press out some of the juice, taking care not to damage fruit. Fill pierogi with 3–6 cherries each, depending on the size of your dough rounds. Sprinkling cherries with flour or potato starch will help take up some of the juice and make your pierogi less runny. ***Variation***: If fresh fruit is not available, canned cherry-pie filling or cherry preserves containing whole cherries may be used instead. Place 2 c. pie filling or preserves (or 1 cup of each) in a pot and heat to just below boiling. Drain in sieve, and when dripping stops, use the fruit to fill pierogi. Use the leftover cherry syrup as a topping for ice cream or pudding, add a little to hot tea, or combine with cold club soda for a refreshing cherry drink.

PLUM PIEROGI FILLING
pierogi ze śliwkami

Wash, dry, and remove pits from about 1 lb. ripe, smallish Italian plums (węgierki) and place 1 in each dumpling. A little sugar (about ½ t.) may be added to the cavity from which the pit was removed as well as a pinch of cinnamon if you like.

POLISH PLUM-JAM PIEROGI
pierogi z powidłami

Fill each dumpling with a spoonful of powidła, the thick Polish plum jam you can almost cut with a knife. The thinner American-style plum jam should not be used as is because it will liquify during cooking and ooze onto your plate when you cut into your pierogi. If genuine Polish style powidła is not available, you can make do with store-bought jam, but cook it down to remove excess moisture and thicken. Cool to room temp. Jam is thick enough if a spoonful turned upside down clings to spoon.

PRUNE PIEROGI FILLING
pierogi z suszonymi śliwkami

Soak 2 c. or so prunes overnight in water to cover. Add 1–2 T. sugar and 1 T. lemon juice. Cook on low heat until tender. Remove pits, place prunes in sieve, and press out excess moisture, then fill pierogi.

APPLE PIEROGI FILLING
pierogi z jabłkami

Peel and coarsely grate 5 cooking apples. Sprinkle with a heaping T. powdered sugar and a dash or two of cinnamon.

HONEYED APPLE & RAISIN PIEROGI FILLING
pierogi z jabłkami i rodzynkami w miodzie

Peel, core and coarsely grate 4 cooking apples. Place in pot with ½ c. rinsed, drained raisins, 2–3 ground dried figs, 2½ T. honey and a pinch of cinnamon. Simmer briefly, remove from heat and stir in enough bread crumbs to get a rather firm filling. *Optional*: ½ t. grated orange rind may be added to mixture as it simmers.

DATE PIEROGI FILLING
pierogi z daktylami

Grind 12 oz. pitted dates and 4 oz. blanched almonds. Cream 2½ T. butter with 2 hard-cooked egg yolks (sieved) and 1 raw egg yolk. Combine with date-almond mixture and flavor with 1 T. rum or ½ t. rum extract.

POPPYSEED PIEROGI FILLING
pierogi z makiem

Scald 1 c. poppyseeds with boiling water and cook covered on very low heat until poppyseeds fall apart when rubbed between fingers. Drain well and run through grinder 2–3 times. Mix with

½ c. powdered sugar, ½ c. soaked, drained raisins, ½ c. ground or finely chopped walnuts, 1 beaten egg, and ½ t. grated orange rind. *Note:* Canned poppyseed filling, "doctored" with the above ingredients, may be used when there isn't time to make it from scratch.

PIEROGI TOPPINGS
okrasa do pierogów

—melted butter: Melt 2–5 T. unsalted butter in saucepan but do not brown and pour over any of the savory (non-sweet) or sweet pierogi.

—browned butter: Brown 2–5 T. butter (the salted variety is O.K.) in saucepan; best with savory pierogi.

—browned buttered bread crumbs: To 3–5 T. melted butter in skillet add 2–3 T. bread crumbs and simmer, stirring constantly, until lightly browned; Poland's well-known Polonaise topping is excellent over all savory and sweet pierogi.

—sour-cream: Fork-blend 1 c. or so dairy sour cream into a thick, pourable topping; good over potato-filled and both sweet and savory cheese pierogi.

—sweetened sour cream: Fork-blend 1 c. sour cream with 1–2 heaping T. powdered sugar; the ideal topping for fruit-filled pierogi with sugarless fillings.

—heavy sweet cream: Use about 1 c. just as it comes from your dairy counter over sweet cheese pierogi, any of the fruit pierogi with sweet fillings (prune, jam, apple, date), and the poppyseed pierogi.

—sweetened heavy cream: Fork-blend 1 c. heavy sweet cream with 1 heaping T. or more powdered sugar and pour over unsweetened berry- or cherry-filled pierogi.

—sugar: Granulated or sifted powdered sugar is good sprinkled over berry- or cherry-filled pierogi, especially after they have been drenched with melted butter.

—fruit syrup: Homemade or commercial fruit syrup (berry, cherry) is best over unsweetened berry- or cherry-filled pierogi or any of the gourmet dessert pierogi (last four recipes).

—salt-pork or bacon nuggets: Fry up a heaping T. (about ⅛ lb.) diced salt pork or slab bacon to a nice golden brown and pour the hot cracklings and as much of the drippings as you like over any of the savory pierogi.

—cracklings & onions: Fry up diced salt pork or bacon as above; when golden brown, remove nuggets and lightly brown 1 small, finely chopped onion in drippings; add the nuggets and pour over potato, sauerkraut, or meat pierogi.

—browned onions: Finely chop 1 medium onion and brown in 3–5 T. salt-pork or bacon drippings; best over meat, sauerkraut, groat, lentil, and bean pierogi; on Wigilia (Christmas Eve) and other fast days, brown onions in butter or oil.

* * *

BUCKWHEAT PIEROGI WITH CHEESE FILLING
pierogi gryczane z serem

Mix together 1½ c. ordinary white flour and 1½ c. buckwheat flour and sift onto breadboard. Sprinkle with 1 t. salt, make well (crater) in top of mound, deposit 2 eggs into it, and work into a smooth dough as with ordinary pierogi, adding just enough water to make it smooth and pliable. Roll out, cut into circles, and fill with savory cheese or cheese & potato filling (above), and cook in boiling salted water as with standard pierogi. *Note*: The dough should be rolled out a bit thicker than for the standard-type pierogi. Serve with melted butter and/or sour cream according to preference.

FRIED PIEROGI
pierogi smażone

Spread 2 c. flour along the bottom of a large, dry skillet, sprinkle with 1 t. salt and heat, stirring frequently, until flour is lightly browned. Remove from heat. Slowly stir in just enough boiling water to bind the flour into a dough, return to heat, and mix well until dough comes away from skillet. Set aside to cool. Roll dough by hand on board into a long, narrow, even roll. Slice roll into ½-inch rounds one at a time, flatten between palms into a small pancake, fill with a spoonful of savory cheese filling of choice, fold over, and pinch edges together. Fry in 1 c. hot lard, vegetable shortening, or oil to a nice golden brown on both sides, drain on absorbent paper and serve immediately, topped with liquified sour cream. *Note*: Savory cheese filling is most commonly used in this recipe, but if you like these crispy, fried dumplings, there's no reason why you shouldn't try some of the other fillings listed above.

YEAST-RAISED PIEROGI, OVEN BAKED
pierogi drożdżowe

Scald ½ c. milk, pour into bowl, and cool to lukewarm. Crumble in ½ cake yeast and mash with fork (or use ½ packet dry yeast), add 1 t. sugar, 5 T. flour and mix ingredients. Mixture should have the consistency of thick pancake batter, so stir in a bit more milk if needed. Let stand in warm place to rise. To yeast mixture add 2 lightly beaten eggs, 2½ c. sifted flour, and 1 t. salt; work into a dough. Knead well until air blisters appear, gradually add ½ stick melted butter and continue to knead until it is fully absorbed and dough is smooth and silky. Place dough in bowl, cover with clean dish towel, and let rise in warm place until doubled in bulk (about 1 hr). Roll out dough about ¼ inch thick, cut into circles and fill with mushrooms, savory cheese, sauerkraut, buckwheat-groat, hard-boiled-egg or meat filling of choice, fold in half, and pinch edges together to seal. Place on greased baking sheet and bake in 350° oven about 30 min., or until golden brown.

YEAST-RAISED SOUR-CREAM-DOUGH PIEROGI
pierogi drożdżowe na śmietanie

Dissolve ½ packet dry yeast in ¼ c. hot (105–115°) water. Beat 4 eggs with 1 t. salt and 1 T. melted butter until nice and fluffy. Combine the yeast mixture and egg mixture, beat in 1 c. fork-blended sour cream, and gradually add 3¾–4 c. flour, or enough to get a firm but pliable dough, stirring constantly. Transfer to lightly floured breadboard and knead well until air blisters appear. Place dough in bowl, cover with clean dish towel, and let rise in warm place until doubled. Roll out ¼ inch thick, cut into circles, and proceed as above.

YEAST-RAISED PIEROGI THE EASIEST WAY
pierogi drożdżowe najłatwiejsze

Break open 2 packages of refrigerator crescent-roll dough (from your supermarket). Spread the sheets of dough out on a board and with floured fingers press down to obliterate the manufacturer's perforations showing where to separate the dough for crescent rolls. Cut into circles with glass or biscuit-cutter, then fill, seal, and bake according to manufacturer's directions on package. *Optional*: For a shiny crust, brush the pierogi with beaten egg before baking. Chances are your family won't suspect that you didn't make these tasty baked pierogi from scratch and they will probably ask for seconds!

LAZY (UNFILLED) CHEESE PIEROGI
leniwe pierogi

Grind 1 lb. (or slightly more) farmer cheese. Add 3 lightly beaten raw egg yolks and 2 T. soft butter. (Butter may be omitted if you're cutting down on fat!) Mix ingredients into a uniform mass and fold in 3 stiffly beaten egg whites. Stirring constantly, work in 1 c. flour, add ½–1 t. salt, and mix lightly. Turn dough out onto lightly floured board and roll by hand into a long 1-inch roll. Even up sides and flatten top with a wide-blade knife and cut at an angle into 1–1½ inch pieces. Drop the dumplings in batches into boiling salted water so as not to crowd them in pot. After they float up, cook them at a slow boil about 3 min. Remove with slotted spoon and serve immediately with melted butter or Polonaise topping. Some people also like to sprinkle them with sugar or vanilla sugar, and sweet-pierogi lovers may enjoy adding a pinch of cinnamon. Plain sour cream or sour cream and sugar are also possibilities.

LAZY CHEESE & POTATO PIEROGI
leniwe pierogi z kartoflami

Cook 2–3 potatoes (½–¾ lb.) in jackets in boiling water until fork tender. Peel under cold running water and place in colander to cool. Grind potatoes with 1 lb. (more or less) farmer cheese. Sift 1 c. flour with 2 T. potato flour and mix with the ground cheese & potato mixture, 1–2 eggs and 1 t. salt. When ingredients are fully blended, transfer to floured board, roll by hand into a long roll, even up sides, and flatten top with knife. Cut into dumplings at an angle and cook in boiling salted water as above.

LAZY CHEESE & POTATO PIEROGI ANOTHER WAY
leniwe pierogi z kartoflami inaczej

Cook 2–3 potatoes with skins left on in boiling water until tender. Peel under cold running water and transfer to colander to cool. Grind together with 1 lb. farmer cheese. Separately cream 3 T. soft butter, gradually adding 3 raw egg yolks one at a time while stirring constantly. Add the cheese & potato mixture, and mix until smooth and well blended. Fold in 3 stiffly beaten egg whites, 4 T. potato flour, and 1 t. salt, and mix into a uniform dough. Transfer to floured bread board and proceed as above.

"LAZIEST" CHEESE & POTATO DUMPLINGS
"najleniwsze" pierogi z kartoflami

Leniwe pierogi (lazy pierogi) are so called because they are less time-consuming than the traditional filled variety. But a well-known convenience item and a modern appliance join forces in this recipe to make them even easier. Simply pulverize 1 c. crumbled farmer cheese or low-fat dry cottage cheese (the creamless kind) in blender to a fine powder. Combine 1 c. instant mashed potatoes (straight from the package) with ½ c. lukewarm water, 1 egg, and 7 T. sifted flour plus 1 t. salt. Work into a dough, transfer to floured board, form into a roll, slice, and cook as above.

LAZY CHEESE & BREAD CRUMB PIEROGI
leniwe pierogi z bułką

Grind 1 lb. farmer cheese and combine with 1 c. bread crumbs, 2 T. soft butter, 3–4 eggs, 1 t. sugar, and ½ t. salt. Work into a uniform dough, sprinkle in a little flour if mixture feels mushy. Turn onto floured board and proceed as above. Cook in boiling salted water 5–6 min., testing one for doneness.

BATTER DUMPLINGS
kluski kładzione

Sift 2 c. flour into bowl. Make a crater-like depression in flour and into it deposit 1–2 eggs. Sprinkle with ½ t. salt and work into a thick batter with wooden spoon, gradually adding ½–¾ c. warm water. When batter is smooth, drop spoonfuls into boiling salted water, moistening spoon in boiling water before scooping up the next spoonful of batter. When boiling resumes, reduce heat to a slow boil and cook covered 5–10 min. depending on the size of your dumplings. Transfer to colander and rinse with hot water. Drain. Serve garnished with browned salt-pork nuggets and pan drippings or melted butter. These dumplings can also accompany meat dishes in place of potatoes, rice, or groats. You can also top them with crumbled farmer cheese.

CHEESE-BATTER DUMPLINGS
kluski kładzione z serem

Sift 3 c. flour. Grind ½ lb. farmer cheese, sprinkle with 1 t. salt, mix in 2 eggs, and gradually add the flour. Stirring constantly with spoon, add just a little milk—enough to get a firm but not stiff batter. Cook spoonfuls of batter in boiling salted water as above. Transfer to platter with slotted spoon and serve with melted butter, fried bacon or salt-pork nuggets.

BUCKWHEAT DUMPLINGS SERVED WITH CHEESE
kluski gryczane z serem

Sift 1½ c. buckwheat flour into pot. Scald with boiling water, add ½ t. salt, and, stirring constantly, gradually add ¾ c. ordinary white flour. Use only enough water to get a thick batter similar to the batter dumplings (above). Drop spoonfuls of the batter into boiling salted water, dipping spoon in boiling water between spoonfuls. Cook covered at a slow boil about 5–7 min., testing one to see if cooked. Transfer to colander, rinse with hot water, drain, place on platter, and pour melted butter over dumplings. Top with crumbled farmer cheese. Sour cream can be served separately for those who like it.

RAISED DUMPLINGS
kluski półfrancuskie

Cream 3 T. butter. Stirring constantly, gradually add 3 eggs and ½ t. salt; mix until smooth. Sift 2 c. flour and stir into mixture together with about ½ c. warm milk or water. Stir vigorously with wooden spoon until air blisters appear and then stir in ½ t. baking powder. With a spoon, scoop small, elongated dumplings from batter and drop into boiling salted water, dipping spoon in boiling water between scoops. Cook covered on fairly low heat for about 5 min. Transfer to colander, rinse with hot water, and drain. Serve with browned salt-pork nuggets and crumbled farmer cheese. These dumplings are also excellent drenched with meat-based gravies, or as an accompaniment to meat dishes in place of potatoes.

COOKED POTATO DUMPLINGS
kopytka/kluski kartoflane

Cook about 6 potatoes (1½ lbs.) in jackets and peel under cold running water. Grind or mash thoroughly and transfer to floured breadboard to cool. Add 1½ c. sifted flour, 1–2 eggs and ½–1 t. salt; work into a dough. Between floured palms of hands roll pieces of dough into long rolls about ½ inch thick. Cut at an angle into 1½–2 inch pieces and drop into boiling salted water. When all the dumplings are in pot, bring to boil, reduce heat, and cook 1 min. or so. Remove from heat and drain in colander. Rinse with hot water, drain, and transfer to platter. Top with buttered bread crumbs or browned salt-pork nuggets. These dumplings are also excellent with meat gravy or mushroom sauce of choice. In Silesia they are frequently added to stewed sauerkraut, cabbage, or even bigos. They can also accompany meat dishes in place of potatoes.

COOKED POTATO DUMPLINGS ANOTHER WAY
kluski kartoflane inaczej

Cook about 6 potatoes in jackets, peel, mash well, and transfer to board as above. Sprinkle with ⅓ c. bread crumbs and ½–1 t. salt. Work in 2 raw egg yolks, gradually adding ⅓ c. flour, sifted. When ingredients are well mixed, fold in 2 egg whites beaten to a stiff froth, and mix well. Between floured palms roll into rolls about ½ inch thick, cut into 1½–2 inch pieces, and cook as above. *Optional:* Your dumplings will be even tastier if you lightly brown a chopped onion in about 2 T. butter and add to the dough. Add an extra sprinkle of flour if the addition makes the dough too soft.

GRATED POTATO DUMPLINGS
pyzy/kluski z tartych kartofli

Cook 6 potatoes in jackets, peel under cold running water, and grind or mash very well. While they are still cooking, grate 6 peeled potatoes by hand or in blender. Transfer grated potatoes to fine sieve or cloth bag and allow to drain, gently pressing out moisture. When dripping stops, pour liquid into small bowl and allow it to settle. Carefully pour off clear liquid at top, but retain the sediment and add it to the grated raw potatoes. (The sediment is potato starch which is needed to bind the dumplings.) Combine the cooked potatoes with the raw potato mixture, add 1 egg, 1 t. salt, and work into a dough. Between floured hands roll pieces of dough snowball-fashion into walnut-sized balls. Make an indentation in each with your index finger and cook in boiling salted water 5–8 min. (*Kuchnia Polska*, the standard cookbook in today's Poland, suggests you cook only one to test it before dropping all the dumplings into the pot. If it is too soft or falls apart, work 3–4 T. ordinary flour or 1 T. potato flour into dough.) When they are cooked, remove to colander with slotted spoon, rinse with hot water, and, after they drip dry, place on platter. Serve with browned salt-pork nuggets and onions. Many people make a special trip to Warsaw's open-air market, *Bazar Różyckiego* (Różycki's Bazaar), where women vendors shouting "*Pyzy, gorące pyzy, komu pyzy!*" sell these homemade dumplings in twist-off jars. They are eaten standing up, right from the jar with a plastic fork. A bottle of beer purchased from a nearby vendor helps wash them down.

MEAT-FILLED GRATED POTATO DUMPLINGS
pyzy nadziewane mięsem

Prepare potato dough as in preceding recipe. Between floured palms roll pieces of dough snowball-fashion into golfball-sized balls. Flatten each ball into a patty, place a spoonful of cooked-meat or meat & mushroom filling like that given for pierogi, fold in ½, pinch edges together, and roll into balls. Cook in boiling salted water somewhat longer than the unfilled pyzy above because of their larger size. As always, test one for doneness. Remove with slotted spoon to serving platter, draining off any water that collects on platter. Garnish with fried chopped onions, browned salt-pork nuggets, or a combination of the two. *Variation:* Ground, skinned, ready-to-eat smoked kiełbasa also makes a good filling.

GRATED POTATO DUMPLINGS (WITHOUT COOKED POTATOES)
pyzy (bez gotowanych kartofli)

Grate 2 lbs. peeled potatoes and allow to drip dry in fine sieve or cloth bag; gently press out moisture. Let the leftover liquid settle, pour off the clear liquid at top, and add the sediment (starch) to grated potatoes. Stir in 1 egg and 5 T. flour and work into a moist but firm dough. If it feels too mushy, adding a sprinkle of flour won't hurt. Transfer dough to moist board, form walnut-sized balls between floured hands, and cook in boiling salted water.

MOUNTAINEER POTATO DUMPLINGS WITH HOT MILK
hałuski z mlekiem

Prepare dough exactly as in the above recipe. The difference is that instead of rolling it into balls, use a teaspoon to scoop up small portions of dough or simply pinch pieces of dough with fingers and cook in boiling salted water several min., testing one for doneness. Serve in bowl of hot milk and salt to taste. Dishes such as this were once dietary mainstays in the poor mountain regions of southern Poland.

SIMMERED GRATED POTATO & CHEESE DUMPLINGS
pyzy z serem duszone

Grate 8 (about 2 lbs.) peeled raw potatoes and drain in fine sieve, pressing out excess moisture until dripping stops. After liquid settles, carefully pour off clear liquid at top and add remaining sediment (starch) to grated potatoes. Grind ¼–½ lb. farmer cheese and combine with grated potatoes, adding 1 t. salt. Work ingredients into a uniform dough. (*Optional*: 1 egg and 1 T. potato flour may be added for more body, but this isn't really necessary.) Between floured hands roll pieces of dough into balls the size of a small walnut or small, oblong dumplings. Brown on all sides briefly in hot lard or oil and transfer to Dutch oven or casserole. Add 2 T. butter and 4 T. fork-blended sour cream. Simmer on low heat or bake in pre-heated 325° oven about 30 min.

GRATED POTATO & BARLEY DUMPLINGS
pyzy z kaszą jęczmienną

Soak 1 c. fine (cracked) barley in 1 qt. lukewarm water several hrs. Drain. Grate 12 peeled potatoes (about 1½ lbs.), drain in fine sieve or cloth bag, pour off the clear liquid after it settles, but add the sediment (starch) to grated potatoes. Form a dough from the barley and grated potatoes and add 1 t. salt. Between floured hands roll pieces of dough snowball-fashion into walnut-sized balls and drop into boiling salted water. Cook at a gentle boil about 30 min. Remove with slotted spoon and serve topped with fried bacon bits and onions.

MOUNTAINEER POTATO DUMPLINGS & CHEESE
dziatki (kluski góralskie) z bryndzą

Peel and cut about 2 lbs. potatoes into cubes. Place in pot, cover with boiling water, and cook until tender. Do not drain but mash the potatoes with whatever water is left. Stir in just enough flour to get a workable dough that is neither mushy nor stiff. Roll small pieces into elongated dumplings and cook in boiling salted water several min., testing one for doneness. Transfer to platter after draining well, top with crumbled sheep's milk cheese (bryndza). If you can't get real bryndza, a passable substitute may be found in Greek or Balkan markets, e.g. feta cheese. You can also use that old Polish standby: farmer cheese. In either case, drench the cheese-topped dumplings with browned salt-pork nuggets and drippings.

PLUM-FILLED POTATO DUMPLINGS
knedle ze śliwkami

Cook about 1½ lbs. potatoes in jackets, peel under cold running water, and grind or mash thoroughly. While potatoes are cooking, wash, drain and pit 1 lb. or slightly more fairly ripe Italian plums (węgierki). Into cooled mashed potatoes sift 1½ c. flour, add 1 egg, and ½ t. salt, and quickly work into a uniform dough. Divide dough into 3 parts. Turn each part onto floured board and form by hand into a 1½ inch thick roll, evening off sides and flattening top with knife. Cut into 1½ inch pieces, flatten between palms into a small patty, place a plum on top, fold dough over it, pinch edges together, and roll between hands snowball-fashion into a ball. Drop dumplings into boiling salted water, stir gently, and cover. When boiling resumes, uncover and cook at slow boil about 2–3 min. Test one to see if the plum inside is cooked. Remove to platter with slotted spoon and top with bread crumbs browned in butter. Our family prefers them drenched with 1 c. sour cream fork-blended with a heaping T. or two powdered sugar into a creamy sauce. This is a favorite August dish in the Strybel household, especially when the plum tree in our back garden produces a bumper crop.

POTATO DUMPLINGS WITH OTHER FILLINGS
knedle z różnym nadzieniem

Prepare dough as in preceding recipe but use other sweet or savory ingredients to fill your dumplings. Typical sweet fillings include fresh, pitted cherries, *powidła*, or prunes. Prunes should be soaked several hrs. in water, dried, and pitted before using. The best savory fillings for knedle are cooked ground meat and/or mushrooms (see pierogi fillings). Savory cheese filling is also good.

POTATO DUMPLINGS THE EASY WAY
knedle najłatwiejsze

Combine 2 c. instant mashed potato (crystals, flakes, powder) just as they come from the package with 7 T. sifted flour, 1–2 eggs, 1 t. salt, and 1 c. water. Mix ingredients and work into a uniform dough. Turn onto floured board and roll by hand into a 1½ inch thick roll, flattening top and sides with knife blade. Cut into 1½ inch slices, flatten between hands into a patty, add filling of choice, fold dough over filling, pinch edges together to seal and roll between palms snowball-fashion into a ball. Cook as above.

SILESIAN BREAD DUMPLINGS
knedle bułczane ze Śląska

Slice 1 lb. loaf french bread and leave out overnight to turn stale. Place in bowl. Brown ¼ lb. diced salt pork and set aside. In about 2 T. of the salt-pork drippings simmer 2 finely chopped onions until tender and transparent and add to bread. Add 1 T. finely chopped fresh parsley and a pinch of marjoram. Drench with 1½ c. very warm milk and let stand until all the milk is absorbed. Add 2 eggs, ¾ c. flour, 1 t. salt, and work by hand into a uniform dough. Tear pieces of dough and roll between hands snowball-fashion into balls the size of large plums or small apples. Drop into boiling salted water and cook at a slow boil uncovered about 20 min. Remove with slotted spoon and serve drenched with the salt-pork nuggets and drippings. This is also the classic companion to a favorite Silesian dish: pork & pears. *Note*: If you prefer slightly firmer dumplings, add ½–¾ c. more flour to dough and work it in well.

BOHEMIAN BREAD DUMPLINGS
knedle czeskie

Finely dice ¼ lb. slab bacon and heat in large skillet. When bacon turns golden, add 6 oz. (about 6–8 slices depending on their thickness) french bread, cut into croutons, and simmer until golden brown. Set aside. Crumble 1 cake yeast into ¾ c. lukewarm milk (or use 1 packet dry yeast). Sift in 1½ c. flour, add 2 lightly beaten eggs and 1 t. salt, and mix ingredients well. Add the bacon and croutons, mix with hand into a soft, uniform dough and between moist hands roll snowball-fashion into golfball-sized dumplings. Cook in boiling salted water 10–15 min. Remove with slotted spoon and top with buttered bread crumbs. May be a meal in itself or as accompaniment to roast meat, goulash, stewed sauerkraut, etc. These dumplings are a national specialty in neighboring Czechoslovakia and are best known along Poland's southern border.

SILESIAN POTATO DUMPLINGS
kluski śląskie/gałuszki

Cook about 2 lbs. peeled potatoes in salted water until tender, drain, return pot to heat, and shake it until all moisture steams away. Mash very well, add ½–1 t. salt, and sift in 1½ c. potato flour. Mix thoroughly to blend potatoes and flour into a uniform dough. Tear off pieces and roll between palms into oblong dumplings about 2 inches in length. Drop into boiling salted water and when boiling resumes, cook about 5 min. Remove with slotted spoon. In Silesia these dumplings are the traditional accompaniment to roast goose and are also good with pork dishes. You may be surprised the first time by their somewhat gummy texture, unlike anything found in standard American cookery, but that's how they're supposed to be. *Variation*: 1–2 eggs may be mixed into dough for richer flavor. Besides being a side dish, these dumplings can be a main course when topped with browned salt-pork or bacon bits.

DILLED CREAM OF WHEAT DUMPLINGS
kluski z manny z koperkiem

Mix 1 c. uncooked cream of wheat with ¼ c. lukewarm water, add 2 beaten eggs, ½ t. salt, and mix to blend ingredients. Let stand 15 min. Add 1 T. finely chopped fresh dill and, if you like, mix in an equal amount chopped parsley. Drop spoonfuls of batter into boiling salted water. They will be even tastier if cooked in meat stock or court bouillon. When they float up, cook another min. Remove with slotted spoon. *Variation*: ½–¾ c. ground farmer cheese and a chopped onion simmered in butter may be added to dough.

OAT DUMPLINGS
kluski owsiane

In bowl, cover 1 c. uncooked oatmeal with ½ c. lukewarm water and let stand 15 min. Meanwhile bring ½ c. milk and 1 t. butter to boil. Remove from heat and add the soggy oats, stirring the mixture well. Set aside to cool. Add 1 egg, 2 T. sifted flour, and ½ t. salt; work into a uniform dough. Drop spoonfuls of dough into boiling salted water. When boiling resumes, cook several min. Serve with browned salt-pork or bacon nuggets and top with crumbled farmer cheese or bryndza.

BAKED POTATO & CHEESE DUMPLINGS
kluski kartoflane z serem pieczone

Grate 2 lbs. (about 8) peeled potatoes and drain in fine sieve to drip dry. Add the settled starch from liquid as above and combine grated potatoes with ¾–1 lb. ground farmer cheese. Add 1 egg, 2 T. sweet cream or evaporated milk, and 1 t. salt and work into a uniform dough. Between floured palms roll into golfball-sized balls, place on greased baking sheet, and bake in 375° oven about 30 min. or until nicely browned. Serve hot with melted butter.

BAKED CHEESE DUMPLINGS
kluski serowe pieczone

Mix 1½ c. flour with 1 level T. baking soda and sift into 1 lb. ground farmer cheese. Add 1 egg and ½ t. salt and work into a uniform dough. *Optional*: Flavor with a sprinkle of ground caraway or ground dried mint leaves according to preference and/or several dashes freshly ground pepper. Turn dough onto floured board, form into a 1½ inch thick roll, flattening sides and top with knife, and cut into 2–3 inch dumplings. Place on greased baking sheet and bake in 375° oven about 25–30 min. or until golden brown. Serve hot with melted butter and/or sour cream.

BAKED COOKED POTATO DUMPLINGS
kluchy kartoflane pieczone

Cook 8 potatoes (about 2 lbs.) in jackets, peel under cold running water, and grind or mash thoroughly. Mash ½ cake yeast and dissolve in ¼ c. warm milk (or use ½ packet dry yeast) and add to potatoes. Mix together and set aside in warm place to rise slightly. Sift in ½ c. flour and 1 t. salt, mix ingredients, and allow to rise again. Grease a baking sheet and sprinkle it lightly with flour. Place fairly large spoonfuls of dough on baking sheet and bake in 375° oven 20–25 min. or until nicely golden brown. Serve hot with melted butter, browned bacon bits and drippings or mushroom sauce.

PUFF DUMPLINGS
kluski ptysiowe

Bring 2 c. water and 1 stick (¼ lb.) butter or oleo to boil and remove from heat. Sift in 1½ c. flour, stirring constantly with wooden spoon or with hand-held electric mixer at lowest speed until smooth. Heat briefly on low flame, stirring constantly, until mixture is glossy.

Remove from heat. Beat in 4 eggs, 1 at a time, mixing until the egg is fully blended before adding the next. Set aside for 15 min. Drop spoonfuls of dough into boiling water, dipping spoon in boiling water between spoonfuls. Cover and cook at slow boil 6–8 min. Remove dumplings with slotted spoon to platter and serve with creamed mushrooms or stewed meats. Unlike the peasant dishes above, this is a gourmet dumpling that would not be out of place on the most elegant banquet table!

EGG NOODLES
kluski krajane

Sift 2 slightly heaped c. flour onto breadboard. Make a crater-type indentation in top of flour mound, drop in 2–3 eggs and 1 t. salt, and mix with knife, adding ¼–½ c. lukewarm water. Work by hand until dough is smooth. If you cut the dough in half, you should not see any flecks of unabsorbed flour. Roll dough out thin with rolling pin on lightly floured board and sprinkle with a little flour. Cut the sheet of dough into strips 2 inches wide. Lay the strips one on top of the other and cut, according to preference, "na zapałkę" (the width of a wooden match) or up to ¼ inch in width. Scatter the noodles around the floured board and let stand several min. Cook in boiling salted water. After boiling resumes, cook at a slow boil 5–10 min., depending on thickness. The only sure rule of thumb is to test a few for doneness. Drain in colander and rinse with hot water. Serve as accompaniment with braised meat (in gravy) in place of potatoes or as a meal by itself with mushroom sauce, fried bacon, salt-pork nuggets, or simply melted butter. A few other suggestions follow.

NOODLES & FARMER CHEESE
kluski z serem

In boiling salted water cook homemade or store-bought egg noodles, allowing about 1 c. uncooked noodles per person. Drain, rinse with hot water, drain again, and transfer to serving platter when dripping stops. Pour browned salt-pork or bacon nuggets over the noodles and as much of the drippings as you like and top with crumbled or grated farmer cheese. A nice change of pace from the same old meat and potatoes, this dish is usually served in our home once or twice a month. We think you will also enjoy it. Some people say it tastes a little like cheese-filled pierogi, except that it's a lot easier to prepare. Those who like can add a dollop of sour cream to their portions.

NOODLES & SAUERKRAUT OR CABBAGE
kluski z kapustą

Heat up cooked sauerkraut or cabbage prepared with meat or mushrooms according to any of the recipes in the vegetable chapter and toss with an equal amount of cooked drained egg noodles. Sprinkle with several punches of crushed caraway seeds if your sauerkraut or cabbage does not contain them already or with a T. chopped fresh dill. Allow about 1 c. cooked noodles and 1 c. sauerkraut or cabbage per person, although appetites do vary.

NOODLES & YELLOW CHEESE
kluski z żółtym serem

Transfer 4–5 c. cooked, drained egg noodles to serving platter, dot generously with unsalted butter, and toss with 1–1½ c. grated yellow cheese (tilsit, edam, gouda, munster, even white American cheese if you like bland cheeses). Garnish with 1–2 T. fresh chopped parsley and/or chives. *Variation*: Simmer 1 finely chopped onion in 2 T. butter until tender but not browned and pour over hot noodles before tossing with cheese. Chopped onions fried with bacon or salt-pork nuggets are another possibility.

PLAIN NOODLES & POPPYSEEDS
kluski z makiem zwykłe

Place 1 c. poppyseeds in pot, fill pot with cold water, stir a few times, and let stand briefly, then pour off any impurities that float up. Drain in sieve, rinsing under cold running water and draining again until dripping stops. Return to pot. Scald with boiling water, of which there should be about an inch more than poppyseeds, cover, and let stand 15 min. Place pot on burner and simmer on med.-low heat at a gentle boil about 30 min. Poppyseeds are ready when they disintegrate when rubbed between fingers. Drain and grind once in poppyseed-grinder or 2–3 times in ordinary grinder. Into poppyseed mixture stir about ½ c. powdered sugar. Mix with 5–7 c. cooked, drained egg noodles, homemade or store-bought. This is a traditional Christmas Eve dessert that may be served hot, warm, room temp., or chilled, according to preference. *Optional*: Those who want may pour a little cold coffee cream over their portions.

NOODLES & POPPYSEEDS WITH RAISINS
kluski z makiem wykwintne

Rinse, scald, cook, and grind 1 c. poppyseeds as above. Into poppyseed mixture stir ½ c. honey and ½–¾ c. plumped raisins. A little grated lemon rind may be added if desired. Toss mixture with 4–7 c. cooked drained egg noodles and serve as above. *Optional:* May be topped on serving platter with ground or finely chopped walnuts or blanched almonds.

NOODLES & POPPYSEEDS THE EASY WAY
kluski z makiem najłatwiejsze

Use as much canned poppyseed pastry filling (like Solo brand) as you like to flavor 5–7 c. cooked, drained egg noodles. Use filling as is or "doctor" it up to taste with some honey, raisins, chopped nuts, vanilla, etc.

BAKED DUMPLINGS & POPPYSEEDS
śliziki z makiem

Make a dough by combining 1 c. flour and anywhere from ¼–⅓ c. slightly sweetened, cold, pre-boiled water. Divide dough in 2 and between palms of hands roll each piece into finger-thick roll. Slice into ¼ inch dumplings and bake on floured baking sheet in 350° oven until golden. When baked, transfer dumplings to dish and keep warm. Meanwhile, rinse, scald, cook, and grind 1 c. poppyseeds as in preceding recipes. Place poppyseed mixture in bowl and scald with 3 c. boiling water, mix, sweeten to taste, and set aside in cool place. About 3–4 hrs. before the Wigilia supper is due to begin, add the baked dumplings so they can soak and get soft. Serve in bowls and eat with soup spoon. *Note*: This is a now little-known peasant version of noodles and poppyseeds from the northeastern Wilno region. For softer śliziki, instead of baking, cook like noodles in boiling water, drain, and serve like kluski z makiem.

POPPYSEED DUMPLINGS WITH POPPYSEED MILK
praśniki z mlekiem makowym

Grind 2 c. dry poppyseeds without pre-soaking. Mix in 1 egg and just enough flour to get a workable dough. Roll out ⅛ inch thick and cut into small squares. Cook in boiling, lightly salted water several min., checking to see if cooked. Drain and serve drenched with poppyseed milk (see sweet sauces in dessert chapter.) This is another old Wigilia dish.

NOODLES & STRAWBERRIES
kluski z truskawkami

Place 4–5 c. cooked, drained egg noodles on platter and top with 3 c. or more hulled, washed, drained, and sliced strawberries. Fork-blend 1½ c. sour cream with 2 heaping T. powdered sugar into a thick sauce. Allow each guest to top his portion with as much as he or she likes. *Optional*: 1 t. vanilla extract or 1 t. vanilla sugar may be added to sauce if you like.

APPLE & NOODLE CASSEROLE
kluski zapiekane z jabłkami

Combine 5 c. or so cooked egg noodles, 4 peeled and coarsely grated apples, ½ c. sugar (more or less to taste), and 5 T. butter. Toss ingredients lightly and transfer to buttered casserole sprinkled with bread crumbs. Flavor with several pinches cinnamon or ½ t. vanilla extract, cover, and bake about 30 min. in pre-heated 350° oven or until apples are cooked. Serve hot as is or topped with sweet cream, sour cream fork-blended with powdered sugar, or fruit syrup. A little honey is another possible topping. If you like, you can add several T. honey to mixture before baking.

EGG NOODLES WITH VARIOUS ADDITIONS
kluski z różnymi dodatkami

Cooked egg noodles, whether homemade or store-bought, lend themselves beautifully to a wide variety of dishes, both savory and sweet. The hot noodles can simply be tossed with the desired ingredients before serving, or baked in a casserole. Some examples:
—*Leftover meat*: If you have anywhere from ½–2 c. leftover cooked meat or fowl on hand and the pan drippings in which they were cooked, you can whip up a meal in no time at all. Remove all but about 1 T. congealed fat from refrigerated drippings. Place the gelled drippings in pot and heat to liquify. Strain to remove any whole spices or bits of burned meat. Add enough boiling water to make 2 c., add the meat, diced, and simmer several min. Taste the liquid and adjust to taste with salt, pepper, other spices of choice, Maggi liquid, etc., and thicken with a little flour, stirring so lumps don't form. Simmer another min. or so and pour over hot egg noodles. Add 1 small can drained peas & carrots or leftover cooked vegetables, diced, and you have instant goulash!
—*Mushrooms*: Simmer 8–16 oz. washed, sliced, or diced fresh mushrooms in several T. butter with some chopped onion until fully cooked. Salt & pepper to taste and toss with hot noodles. Garnish with chopped dill and/or parsley.
—*Cherries*: Simply heat a can of cherry-pie filling to boiling and pour over hot buttered noodles. In some families, this is one of the sweet dishes served on Christmas Eve. Naturally, the cherry sauce is made from scratch because canned fruit fillings are not available in Poland. Try the noodles with blueberry or apple-pie filling as well. Top cherries or other fruit with a dollop of sour cream or whipped cream if desired.
—*Dried fruit compote*: If you have some of the traditional dried-fruit compote left over after Christmas, it can be used to make a light meal that will be a change of pace after all that high-powered feasting. Drain compote and add to liquid enough boiling water to make 2 c. If the refrigerated compote has absorbed nearly all the liquid, add 2 c. boiling water to the stewed fruit and bring to boil. Cover and set aside 10 min. Drain again. To room temp.

liquid add several t. potato flour and stir until dissolved. Return to pot and simmer several min. Pour over hot buttered noodles.

* * *

Give vent to your creative fantasy and come up with other noodle combinations of your own. Your imagination is the only limit!

* * *

EGG NOODLE SQUARES
łazanki

Prepare the dough exactly the same way as for egg noodles (p.482). After the sheet of thinly rolled-out dough has dried, cut it into ½, ¾, or 1 inch strips. Place the strips one on top of the other and slice into squares. Scatter the square noodles about the floured board to dry out about 15 min. Cook as you would egg noodles. Use in any of the above egg-noodle recipes. If you have a good eye for language, you may have guessed that the word "łazanki" comes from the Italian "lasagna." Like many foreign imports, these noodles have long since blended into the Polish culinary landscape.

NOODLE SQUARES & CHEESE CASSEROLE
łazanki zapiekane z serem

Butter a casserole and sprinkle with bread crumbs. When cooked and drained noodle squares are cool enough to handle, line the bottom of casserole with a layer so they fit snugly end to end or slightly overlap. Spread with thin layer of sweet or savory cheese filling of choice (see pierogi fillings). Top with another layer of noodle squares, spread with cheese filling, and continue layering ingredients until they are used up. Noodles should form top layer. Dot with butter, sprinkle with bread crumbs, and bake covered at 350° 30–40 min. Serve with sour cream. If using sweet cheese filling, you can dust your casserole with powdered sugar and serve with sour cream or sweet heavy cream. Some people say this dish tastes almost like cheese-filled pierogi.

CRÊPES
naleśniki

Beat 2 eggs, 1 c. milk, and ¼ t. salt with wire whisk or egg-beater until well blended and creamy. Gradually add 1 slightly heaped c. flour, sifted, a little at a time, beating constantly.

Batter is sufficiently beaten when all lumps of flour have disappeared and air bubbles appear on surface. Mix in about 1 c. water. Add only as much water as needed to get a thin batter that easily spreads along the bottom of skillet. A quicker way is to place all ingredients in blender and give them a whirl for 30–40 seconds. *Hint*: Your naleśniki will fry better and be more pliable (easier to fold) if you add 1–2 t. oil to batter. Heat a 7–10 inch skillet until fairly hot and grease it with a cube of salt pork impaled on fork. Pour a little batter into skillet, tilting it so batter covers entire surface. Fry until golden on bottom, then flip over and fry other side to same color. Place an inverted dinner plate on your counter-top and place the fried crêpe on top. Grease skillet with salt pork, fry next naleśnik as above, and continue until all batter is used up. Grease skillet before each addition of fresh batter and stack the finished crêpes one on top of the other on the dinner plate. If you don't plan to use them immediately, keep them stacked on the dinner plate, cover with plastic wrap, and refrigerate. When ready to use, spread with filling of choice, roll up or fold, and brown in butter seam side down. When nicely golden brown on one side, brown on the other. Another way is to place in well-buttered baking dish in layers, drench with melted butter (or dot with cold butter), and bake at 350° about 30 min. Polish cooks roll and fold naleśniki in any of four different ways known as: rulon, rulonik, chusteczka, and koperta.

—*Long roll*: After spreading crêpe with filling of choice, roll up tightly jelly-roll fashion. This produces a nice long naleśnik, but if you're using jam or fruit filling it may run out the ends during frying or baking. With these fillings the next method is recommended.

—*Short roll*: Spread crêpe with filling, keeping it 1 inch from the edge. At 2 opposite sides of the crêpe, fold the 1 inch unspread edge towards the center, then roll up tightly, starting at one of the unfolded ends.

—*Handkerchief fold*: Spread filling over only one half of the naleśnik, keeping it 1 inch from the edge. Fold empty half over filled half, then fold once again, bringing the 2 pointed ends together. This produces an elegant semi-triangular naleśnik similar to the handkerchief gentlemen wear (or used to wear) in their left-hand suit-coat pocket. This fold is good for thicker fillings, not for jams or runny fruit fillings.

—*Envelope fold*: Spread only center of crêpe with filling, leaving a 1 inch border around the edge. Fold one end to cover ⅔ of filling, fold opposite end to overlap first end by about 1 inch. Then fold unfolded ends towards center to form your "envelope." Some Polish cooks refer to this fold as "książeczka" (little book).

CRÊPE FILLINGS
nadzienie do naleśników

Naleśniki are good with most any of the sweet or savory fillings recommended for pierogi. Favorites include fillings made of farmer cheese, sauerkraut, meat, mushrooms, and fruit. Jam, preserves, sliced sugared strawberries, canned fruit-pie filling, applesauce, or your own homemade apple-cake filling (jabłka na szarlotkę) will surely be enjoyed by those who like sweet dishes. Those who prefer savory food might consider fillings made with buckwheat groats, hard-boiled eggs, or spinach purée.

CRÊPES WITH BEATEN EGG WHITES
naleśniki z pianą

Beat by hand until smooth (or whirl in blender) 2 egg yolks, 1 c. milk, 1 c. water, and ½ c. flour, sifted. Beat whites to a froth, fold into batter, mixing lightly, then add ½ c. or trace more flour and ½ t. salt. Mix into a smooth batter and fry as above.

SCALDED CRÊPES
naleśniki parzone

Sift 1 slightly heaped c. flour into bowl. Pour ¼ lb. (1 stick) hot melted butter into flour, stirring to blend ingredients. Gradually pour in 1 c. hot milk, mixing constantly. Add 3 egg yolks one by one, mixing to absorb each yolk before the next one is added. Beat 3 egg whites to a froth and fold in, sprinkle with ½ t. salt, and mix to blend. Fry as above until lightly golden brown on both sides. Spread hot crêpes with jam or preserves of choice, roll up, and serve. Sprinkle with powdered sugar and top with whipped cream.

SPONGE CAKE CRÊPES
naleśniki biszkoptowe

Cream 3 egg yolks with 2½ T. powdered sugar. Stir in 1 c. milk, about ⅔ c. water, and 1 slightly heaped c. flour, sifted, beating well to get a smooth batter. Fold in 3 beaten egg whites, add ½ t. salt, and mix to blend ingredients. Fry as above to a nice golden brown on both sides, spread with jam, preserves, or fruit filling of choice, roll up and dust with powdered vanilla sugar.

LUXURY CRÊPES
naleśniki luksusowe

Cream 4 egg yolks with 2½ T. powdered sugar and beat in 1 c. sour cream. Beating constantly, sift in ¾ c. flour and 2½ T. melted butter and mix into a smooth batter. As usual, grease hot skillet with salt pork, pour in enough batter to cover surface, tilting so it spreads evenly, and fry to a nice golden brown on both sides. Spread with jam, preserves, or fruit filling. Roll up carefully, because this type of naleśnik tears easily, and serve immediately topped with whipped cream. *Note*: Since only yolks are used in this recipe, refrigerate or freeze whites for some other use. These delicious, rich-tasting naleśniki are recommended to those not particularly concerned about calories and cholesterol. Weight-watchers may prefer the leaner milk-free or eggless crêpes below.

LEAN MILK-FREE CRÊPES
naleśniki postne bez mleka

With wire whisk or egg-beater beat 1 c. water, 1 egg, 1 c. sifted flour, 2 T. salad oil, and ½ t. salt (or mix in blender) to get a nice, creamy batter. Fry as above. Spread with filling of choice, roll up or fold, and serve immediately. Naturally you can fry or bake the filled naleśniki as in the first recipe, but if you're dieting it's best to forego the extra fat. The following recipe is for crêpes not containing a single egg. *Note*: These will be even tastier if you use whey in place of some or all of the water.

LEAN EGGLESS CRÊPES
naleśniki postne bez jaj

Make batter by beating 1 c. flour, 1 c. milk, 3 T. salad oil, ½ t. salt and 2 pinches baking powder. Grease hot skillet with salt pork and pour a little more batter into it than for standard naleśniki (first recipe). They must be a shade thicker without the egg for binding, otherwise they may fall apart. Fry on both sides, then fill, roll up, and enjoy. Naturally they won't have the nice golden hue of the other naleśniki presented here, but if you must really avoid eggs, you can still have your crêpes and eat them too!

CRÊPE CAKE
torcik naleśnikowy

Prepare crêpes according to any of the above recipes, but double or triple the recipe. Place the first fried crêpe in a buttered baking pan and spread it with sweet cheese or fruit filling of choice, leaving a 1 inch border around the edge. Cover with the next crêpe, spread with filling, and continue until crêpes are used up. Do not spread the top naleśnik with filling. Dot top with butter and bake in 350° oven 20–30 min. Dust top with powdered sugar and cut into serving-size wedges as you would any round cake. Provide sour cream or whipped cream as a topping if you wish. *Note*: Savory fillings (cheese, meat, mushroom, sauerkraut) may also be used, but prepare naleśniki only according to first recipe or the last two (no-milk and eggless). Do not dust with powdered sugar but provide sour cream. The meat, mushroom, or sauerkraut versions can be drenched with meat gravy or mushroom sauce of choice.

1.

2.

3.

4.

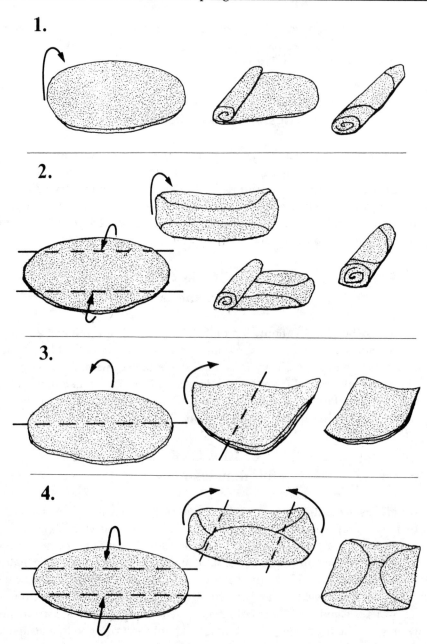

The four most common ways of forming naleśniki (crêpes) are: 1. Long roll; 2. Short roll; 3. Handkerchief fold; and 4. Envelope fold.

CRÊPE CROQUETTES
krokiety naleśnikowe

Prepare naleśniki according to the basic (first) recipe and stack on inverted plate. Spread each with meat, mushroom, or sauerkraut filling of choice (see pierogi), leaving a 1-inch border around the edge. Roll into short rolls, dredge in flour, dip in beaten eggs, and roll in bread crumbs, pressing in breading. Place seam side down in hot fat about ½ inch deep and fry to a nice golden brown on all sides. Drain briefly on absorbent paper and serve hot, with sour cream if desired. These croquettes are also great with a cup of hot clear soup (beet, mushroom, tomato, or bouillon).

CRÊPE NOODLES
kluski naleśnikowe

Tightly roll up 3 stacked crêpes, hot or cold, and cut into noodles of desired width just as in egg noodle recipe. Use as you would ordinary egg noodles in soups or stews, with mushrooms or sauerkraut, or topped with grated farmer cheese. Excellent cold with sliced, sugared strawberries topped with sour cream or whipped cream. To warm up crêpe noodles, simmer in a little butter, steam in covered skillet by adding several T. water or use microwave. This is a good way to use up leftover naleśniki. *Variation*: Cut stacked naleśniki into ½–1 inch wide strips, stack the strips, and cut into ½–1 inch squares and you'll have crêpe noodle squares (łazanki naleśnikowe).

SOUR-MILK PANCAKES
racuchy

Beat 1½ c. sour milk with 2 eggs until creamy, sift in 1 slightly heaped c. flour, add ½ t. salt and 1¼ t. baking powder, and mix into a smooth batter. In skillet heat 4 T. oil or lard and spoon batter into it. Fry to a nice light golden brown on both sides. Dust hot pancakes with powdered sugar on platter or serve with jam or fruit syrup of choice. *Variation*: Add ½–1 t. grated lemon rind to batter.

YEAST-RAISED PANCAKES
racuszki drożdżowe

Crumble ¼ cake yeast into a bowl and mash with 2 T. sugar. Stir in ½ c. lukewarm milk, add 3 T. flour, and set aside to rise. Meanwhile, beat 3 egg whites to a stiff froth, adding 3 T. sugar and 3 egg yolks and mixing the whole time. When yeast mixture rises, add 2⅓ c. flour, 1 T. melted butter and the egg mixture and beat into a smooth batter. Set aside in warm place to rise. In large skillet heat lard or oil which should be about ¼ inch deep. Spoon portions of batter into skillet, smoothing out tops of pancakes with spatula, and fry to a nice golden brown on both sides. Drain on absorbent paper, transfer to serving platter, and dust with powdered vanilla sugar or top with jam or fruit syrup. In some families, these pancakes are among the sweet dishes served on Christmas Eve. Naturally, on that occasion they should be fried in oil.

APPLE PANCAKES
racuszki z jabłkami

To batter for sour milk pancakes (above) add 2 peeled, coarsely grated cooking apples and fry as directed. Serve dusted with powdered sugar. If desired, flavor with pinch of cinnamon.

SOUR-CREAM PANCAKES
racuszki śmietanowe

Beat 1 c. sour cream and 3 egg yolks until smooth. Sift in 1½ c. flour, add ¼ t. salt and mix into a smooth batter. Lastly, fold in 3 beaten egg whites and mix. Fry in hot fat to a nice golden brown on both sides. Drain on absorbent paper and serve immediately dusted with powdered sugar or topped with preserves.

CHEESE PANCAKES
racuszki z serem

Prepare batter as for sour-milk pancakes or sour-cream pancakes. After spooning batter into hot fat in skillet, place a thin slice of farmer cheese on top of each pancake. (The cheese slice should be smaller than the pancake!) Cover cheese with a little more batter. When fried to a nice golden brown on one side, flip over and fry the same way. Drain on absorbent paper and serve dusted with powdered sugar and sour cream. Savory food lovers (i.e. those who aren't particularly fond of sweet dishes) may prefer to salt pancakes to taste and eat with just sour cream, skipping the powdered sugar.

COOKED-BATTER CHEESE PANCAKES
racuszki zaparzane z serem

Bring 1¾ c. milk and 2 T. butter to boil and remove from heat. Sift in ¾ c. flour and stir over low heat until you get a smooth, glossy batter. Remove from heat and continue beating several min. if using electric mixer or up to 10 min. by hand. Add 4 eggs one at a time, beating constantly. Do not add another egg until the previous one has been fully absorbed by batter. Separately, grind ⅓–½ lb. farmer cheese, mix well with ½ c. sweet cream and 2½ T. powdered sugar, then add to batter, mixing to combine ingredients. *(Optional*: Add ½ t. vanilla extract.) Heat 4 T. fat in skillet and spoon batter in to form small round pancakes. Fry on both sides to a nice golden brown. Serve dusted with powdered sugar and a dollop of sour cream.

PRUNE PANCAKES
placuszki z suszonymi śliwkami

Soak 8 oz. prunes in 2 c. lukewarm water several hrs. Drain, remove pits, and dry. (You can use pitted prunes, if you like.) In bowl combine 1 c. flour, 1 egg, 2–3 T. sour cream, ¼ t. salt, and ½–¾ c. water, enough to make a fairly thick batter. Mix well until batter is smooth and lump-free. Add the pre-soaked and dried prunes and mix into batter. Fry in 4–5 T. hot oil to a nice golden brown on both sides. Serve hot, dusted with powdered sugar. *Variation*: If you prefer a fluffier pancake, add 1½ t. baking powder to batter.

STRAWBERRY PANCAKES
placuszki z truskawkami

Beat together 1½ c. sour milk and 2 eggs. Sift in 1 c. flour, add ¼ t. salt, and mix well into a smooth batter. Stir in 1½ t. baking powder and set aside. Prepare 1 c. sliced strawberries. Hull and wash strawberries, drain, and dry with absorbent paper. Quickly slice strawberries and add to batter. Fry in several T. oil to a nice golden brown on both sides. Dust with powdered sugar and serve sour cream on side. Some may prefer these pancakes dusted with powdered sugar and topped with whipped cream. *Note*: Do not use frozen, sliced strawberries or fresh, sugared strawberries, because they contain too much liquid and will dilute your batter. *Variation*: Instead of strawberries, add 1 c. peeled, thinly sliced apples to batter.

YEAST-RAISED BUCKWHEAT PANCAKES
bliny

Mash ¼ cake yeast with fork and mix with ½ c. warm milk, 1 T. flour, and 1 t. sugar. Set aside to rise. Beat 3 eggs with ¼ c. milk, add yeast mixture, sift in 1 c. buckwheat flour, 1 c. ordinary flour, and ½ t. salt; work into a uniform mixture. Finally work in 3 T. melted butter. Fry in small, well-greased skillet (5–6 inches in diameter), pouring in enough batter so it is ¼ inch thick. Fry to a nice golden brown on both sides and serve immediately. These pancakes were created for savory food lovers and are traditionally served with caviar, anchovy butter, melted butter, or sour cream. Another topping is chopped hard-boiled eggs mixed with a little finely chopped onions sautéd in butter. Serve as an elegant hot appetizer at a gourmet dinner or as a supper dish. *Variation*: Your bliny will be fluffier if you let the completed batter rise until doubled before frying. Whether or not you include that step, these pancakes can also be baked in an oven.

BEER & BUCKWHEAT PANCAKES
bliny na piwie

Beat 5 egg yolks until creamy and pale and mix in 12 oz. beer. Mixing constantly, gradually sift in 1 c. ordinary flour and 1 c. buckwheat flour, add ½ t. salt, and at the end fold in 5 egg whites beaten to a froth. Fry in small 5–6 inch skillet as above.

YEAST-RAISED POTATO & BREAD PANCAKES
bliny kartoflane

Grate 6–7 peeled potatoes by hand or in blender. Dice 4 slices fresh french bread and combine with grated potatoes. Mash ½ cake yeast with 1 T. sugar and add to mixture. Mix in 1 c. sour cream, 3 beaten egg yolks, 5 T. flour, and ½ t. salt. When ingredients are blended, fold in 3 stiffly beaten egg whites. Set aside to rise until roughly doubled in bulk. Fry in several T. hot fat until nicely browned on both sides. Use a small 5–6 inch skillet. The difference between bliny and other Polish pancakes is that the former must be perfectly round, hence batter must cover entire surface of skillet wall-to-wall.

POTATO PANCAKES THE TRADITIONAL WAY
placki kartoflane tradycyjne

Grate about 8 peeled potatoes and transfer to sieve to drip dry. When drippings have settled, pour off clear liquid and add remaining sediment (starch) to grated potatoes. To mixture add 2 eggs, 2 heaping T. flour, 1 t.–1 T. grated onion, and ½–1 t. salt. Add a pinch of freshly ground pepper if desired. Mix into a uniform batter and spoon into hot lard or oil in skillet. Flatten each pancake gently with spatula, as they should be on the thin side. Fry to a crisp golden brown on both sides and serve immediately. Poles generally don't drain these on absorbent paper, but feel free to do so if you are dieting. Some like their potato pancakes sprinkled with a little salt and topped with sour cream. Others prefer them sprinkled with just sugar or sugar and sour cream. *Variations*: For a complete meal, serve unsugared pancakes with sauerkraut or red-cabbage salad on the side. They can also be topped with mushroom sauce for a different flavor twist. However you prefer them, if you like potato pancakes, you have plenty of company. In Polish cities and at folk fairs you can often run into stands selling these crispy delights straight from the griddle.

POTATO PANCAKES THE EASY WAY
placki kartoflane łatwiejsze

Peel and dice about 8 potatoes. In blender place 1–2 eggs, 1 quartered onion, ½–1 t. salt, and about 1 c. diced potatoes. Whirl until blended, before adding remaining potatoes 1 c. at a time. Add 1 level T. potato starch and 2 heaping T. flour and blend briefly to get a uniform batter. Fry and serve as above. *Note*: In addition to onion, other flavorings might include 1 bud crushed garlic or about 2 T. chopped parsley, but only for savory pancakes not eaten with sugar. Some say even onion should be added only to pancakes that are not sugared, but we feel that a little onion is not really noticeable even in sweet pancakes and only mellows their flavor.

POTATO PANCAKES WITH BACON
placki kartoflane z boczkiem

Peel and grate (or whirl in blender) 8–10 potatoes. In skillet brown ¼ lb. or less finely diced slab bacon. Drain through metal sieve (a plastic one will melt!) and add browned bacon nuggets to grated-potato mixture. Add 2 raw egg yolks, ¾–1 c. flour, sifted, 1 t. salt, and a pinch or 2 pepper. Mix well to blend ingredients and fry to a nice golden brown on both sides in the remaining bacon drippings. Serve with sour cream, but not sugar. *Variation*: Add ½–¾ c. grated farmer cheese to above batter. Another way is to fry pancakes as above and top with grated farmer cheese on serving platter.

POPPYSEED POTATO PANCAKES
placuszki kartoflane z makiem

Cook about 4 peeled potatoes in boiling salted water to cover. When tender, drain and mash extremely well. While potatoes are still cooking, grate an equal amount peeled raw potatoes. Combine the 2 mixtures, add 1 egg, 1 T. flour, 1 t. salt, and ½–¾ c. washed, drained poppyseeds. Mix ingredients well and fry small pancakes in hot lard or oil to a nice golden brown on both sides. Serve hot with sour cream. They are also a nice accompaniment to a bowl of cold sour milk or buttermilk.

MOUNTAINEER POTATO CAKE
moskol/góralski placek kartoflany

Mix well 2–4 c. cold mashed potatoes, 1½–2 c. flour, 1–2 eggs, 1–2 t. baking powder or soda and 1 t. salt. Flatten by hand into 1 oblong ½ inch thick cake or several smaller ones and bake in 375° oven 45 min. or until nicely browned. Enjoy hot or cold, with or without butter. *Note*: Polish shepherds often take a sackful of these cakes to keep body and soul together as they follow their grazing flocks along the mountain slopes. For more urban eaters, this is a good travel snack.

ZAKOPANE POTATO CAKE
moskol zakopiański

Dissolve 1 packet dry yeast or 1 cake compressed yeast in 2 c. lukewarm milk, add 1 T. sugar and allow to rise. Mix well 4–5 c. mashed potatoes with 6–7 c. flour, add yeast mixture and 2 eggs and work well to blend ingredients. Form 1 large or several smaller cakes 1 inch thick and bake in 375° oven to a nice golden brown, turning frequently.

HOT SAVORY SAUCES, GRAVIES & TOPPINGS

Hot sauces and gravies add flavor, eye-appeal, and nutritional value to foods, and can turn otherwise bland or uninteresting foods into a real treat. Even the freshest poached fish might be pretty boring and unpalatable without a bit of sauce, if only some melted butter and lemon juice. What would mashed potatoes, groats, or noodles be without a nice thick gravy? It is no wonder that the French way back when christened sauces *la poésie de la cuisine* (poetry of the kitchen).

Many Americans seem overwhelmed by the confusing varieties and apparent complexity of sauce-making. They instinctively reach for a canned gravy, condensed soup, or bottle of spaghetti sauce. When they do, they are usually overpaying for a product inferior to that of which can easily be whipped up in no time right at home. Many sauces are really little more than a bit of flour sautéd in butter diluted with some liquid, and flavored according to preference. To illustrate this point, we urge you to master the simple steps required to create the first two sauces presented in this chapter: basic white sauce and hot cream sauce. These two serve as the basis for a limitless variety of genuinely Polish-style *sosy no gorąco*.

The sauces of France—*béchamel, velouté, soubise, lyonnaise, bordelaise, revigote, mornay,* and many more—have influenced the cuisine of Poland and a great many other countries. There they underwent various modifications dictated by local eating habits and available ingredients, often evolving into true native specialties.

Old Polish cookery, for instance, did make use of grape wine for flavoring, but did so more sparingly than the French. It also was more likely to season sauces with beer or *miód pitny* (honey wine). Other popular flavorings included honey, crushed honey-spice cake (*piernik*), and *powidła* (thick plum jam). A typical representative of this family is the subtly tangy and slightly sweet *szary sos* (gray sauce) which additionally contains raisins and almonds and, contrary to its name, is actually brown. Other Polish favorites included cream sauces flavored with horseradish, mustard, pickles, and sorrel.

Two of the best-known Polish creations, which are identified as *à la Polonaise* or simply *Polonaise* (i.e. Polish) on menus across the globe, are not really sauces but toppings. One is toasted, buttered crumbs used to garnish cooked vegetables and other dishes. The other is buttered, dilled, chopped, hard-boiled eggs which usually serve as a topping for poached fish.

We have not forgotten those who love sauces but fear that all that cream, butter, and flour must be fattening. Included in this chapter are ways to replace sour cream with low-fat or non-fat yogurt and prepare sauces without the traditional roux.

* * *

ROUX
zasmażki

This is nothing more than flour cooked with fat to form a paste of various coloration from light to dark brown. Although not a sauce in itself, the zasmazka is used to thicken most savory sauces, gravies, stews, various fricassees, vegetable dishes, etc. Polish cookery distinguishes 4 basic types of roux, depending on whether raw or browned flour is used. Light or white roux is made with unbrowned flour; pale-golden roux uses flour barely browned to a light golden hue; golden roux incorporates flour that has been browned to a nice golden color; and brown roux is made from flour that is med. brown but not burnt. The browned roux have a deeper flavor than that made with unbrowned flour. Although some like the dusky, robust flavor of brown roux, it is rather hard to digest. In general, roux are made with an equal part of fat (butter, margarine, lard, pan drippings) and flour.

WHITE (LIGHT) ROUX
zasmażka biała

Melt but do not brown 2 T. fat in skillet. Add 2 T. flour and simmer on low heat, stirring constantly, several min. Set aside to cool slightly. To make sauce, gradually stir in 1 c. or more cold liquid (usually milk or stock) and simmer on low heat, whisking constantly, until you get a smooth bubbly sauce. Stir in flavoring ingredients, simmer briefly for flavors to blend and season to taste. To thicken soups or fricassees, gradually whisk about 1 c. soup or pan liquid into roux. When fully blended, add to soup pot, Dutch oven, or whatever. Simmer thickened dish at least 1 min. before serving. *Note*: With many roux-thickened soups and sauces, it's a good idea to let them stand covered a few min. after switching off heat before serving for a more mellow and rounded flavor.

PALE GOLDEN ROUX
zasmażka jasnozłota

Brown 2 T. flour on baking sheet in oven or, better yet, in a dry skillet on your stovetop, so you can better regulate the browning. Stir constantly with fork to mix browned and unbrowned flour. Remove from heat the minute the flour begins taking on a pale-golden hue and proceed as above.

GOLDEN ROUX
zasmażka złota

Brown 2 T. flour in dry skillet, stirring constantly until it turns golden, then proceed as with white roux above.

BROWN ROUX
zasmażka rumiana

Brown 2 T. flour a trifle longer than for golden roux until it turns brown (somewhere between tan and med. brown is best). Stir constantly to mix browned and unbrowned flour. Do not overbrown, because your roux will become bitter.

INSTANT FREEZER-STORED ROUX
zasmażka błyskawiczna z zamrażarki

Although roux takes only minutes to prepare, there may be times when it would be good to have some at your fingertips with no additional fuss. Frozen roux is the answer. Prepare any of the above roux as indicated but use ½ c. flour and ½ c. fat. Simmer several min., stirring constantly, but when smooth, stir in ¼–½ c. stock. Simmer and stir several min. until you get a smooth, uniform paste. Set aside to cool to room temp. Spoon heaping T. portions onto baking sheet and place in freezer overnight. Next day transfer frozen roux wafers to plastic bag and store in freezer. If you have more than 1 type of roux (e.g. white, golden, brown), be sure to label it accordingly. A frozen roux wafer or 2 can be dropped into stock, soup, stewed sauerkraut, stews, fricasseed dishes, etc. or can be used to thicken cream sauce, white sauce, or other savory gravies. Since it is already fully cooked, the frozen roux will blend with and thicken your liquid as soon as it melts.

BASIC WHITE SAUCE/BÉCHAMEL SAUCE
beszamel/sos mleczny

Prepare white roux using 2 T. flour and 2 T. butter or margarine as directed above. Stir in 1 c. cold milk or ½ c. half & half and 1 c. stock, simmering over low heat until smooth and bubbly. Season with salt and white pepper to taste. A sprinkle of lemon juice or a pinch of citric-acid crystals will enhance its flavor. Use over cooked vegetables and meat, in casseroles, etc. This is also the basis for many other sauces whose color and flavor depend on what you add to it. *Note*: If sauce is thicker than you want, dilute it with a little milk, stock, or water. *Optional*: For a richer-tasting, golden-tinged sauce, beat 1 raw egg yolk with 1 T. cold milk and stir into cooked sauce. Heat briefly, stirring constantly, but do not boil.

HOT CREAM SAUCE
sos śmietanowy na gorąco

Dilute white or pale-golden roux with ½ c. cold meat or vegetable stock and heat on low flame, stirring constantly until smooth. Salt to taste, add 1 t. or more lemon juice (depending on tartness desired), season with a pinch or 2 white pepper, and stir in ½ c. fork-blended sour cream. Simmer gently several min., stirring constantly. Excellent over boiled meat, cooked vegetables, hot hard-cooked eggs, etc. *Note*: For a change of pace, use it over gołąbki instead of the more conventional tomato sauce. *Optional*: Stir in 1 egg yolk beaten with 1 T. milk.

YOGURT-BASED CREAM SAUCE
sos śmietanowy na jogurcie

Whereas yogurt may be used just as it comes to replace sour cream in cold sauce, its use in hot sauces is trickier, because it has a tendency to curdle when heated. The chances of curdling can be reduced if the whey is drained away and some potato flour or cornstarch is whisked into the yogurt. Yogurt should be added at the very end, simmered very briefly and at lowest possible heat, while whisking the whole time. Over 190° it may separate despite the above precautions. Let ½ c. plain, regular, low-fat, or non-fat yogurt stand at room temp. 1 hr., then pour off whey (liquid) that comes to top. Fork-blend ½ c. strained room temp. meat or vegetable stock with 1 T. flour and simmer about 5 min. Remove from heat and allow to cool slightly. Fork-blend ½ c. yogurt with 1 t. potato starch or cornstarch and stir into stock with whisk. Salt & pepper to taste, add a little lemon juice and a pinch or 2 sugar. Heat very gently, whisking constantly, but do not boil. *Note*: Just between you and us, this sauce is definitely low in calories, but taste-wise is far inferior to the traditional cream sauce, especially when used as is. Its deficiencies can be disguised somewhat with flavorings (horseradish, mustard, tomato paste, garden greens, sorrel, spices, etc.).

HOT HORSERADISH SAUCE
sos chrzanowy na gorąco

To 2 c. white sauce or hot cream sauce (above) add 2–4 T. freshly grated horseradish root or 4–8 t. prepared non-creamed horseradish. The exact amount depends entirely on the potency of your horseradish and how sharp you want the sauce to be. Season to taste with a little sugar and simmer briefly. Cover and let stand about 1 min. before serving for flavors to blend. The perfect sauce for boiled beef, tongue, poached fish, and hot, hard-boiled eggs. *Note*: Feel free to additionally season sauce to taste with salt, white pepper, paprika, lemon juice, or a dash of Maggi seasoning. Best when made with egg-yolk option (above).

HOT MUSTARD SAUCE
sos musztardowy na gorąco

Into 2 c. white sauce or hot cream sauce stir 3–4 t. brown prepared mustard. Add a little sugar to taste and a bit more salt, pepper, and lemon juice if desired. Simmer briefly until smooth and bubbly. Good over boiled beef, tongue, pork hocks, and hot, hard cooked eggs. *Optional*: A T. onion juice (squeezed from grated onion) or horseradish juice (either squeezed from freshly grated horseradish root or the marinade from prepared horseradish) may be added for more zest.

HOT TOMATO SAUCE
sos pomidorowy na gorąco

Wash and dry 3–4 tomatoes, dice, place in pot with ½ c. boiling water and 1 T. grated onion, add a little salt, and simmer on low heat until tomatoes disintegrate. Sieve mixture into 2 C. white sauce or hot cream sauce and simmer briefly. Season to taste with salt, pepper, a pinch of Polish hunter's seasoning, sugar, and lemon juice. Simmer a while longer and let stand covered several min. before serving for flavors to blend. Good with stewed kidneys, meatballs, boiled meat, tongue, and casseroles. *Variation*: An easier way to prepare this sauce is to use 4–8 T. tomato concentrate instead of stewing fresh tomatoes from scratch. *Note*: Polish style tomato sauce is lighter colored and milder than the familiar Italian (Bolognese) variety.

HOT SORREL SAUCE
sos szczawiowy na gorąco

Wash a handful of sorrel leaves well, trim off stems and rinse. Chop fine and place in pot with 1 T. butter. Simmer on low heat, stirring, until tender. Sieve into 2 c. cream sauce and simmer several min. Salt & pepper to taste and (optional) add a pinch tarragon. Serve with boiled beef, hard-boiled eggs, egg cutlets, potato cutlets, etc. *Variation*: Spinach may be used in place of sorrels, but a little lemon juice should be added. You can also use 1 part sorrel and 1 part spinach.

HOT DILL SAUCE
sos koperkowy na gorąco

To standard portion (about 2 c.) basic white sauce or hot cream sauce (preferably with raw egg yolk added), add 2–3 T. chopped fresh dill. Heat briefly and season with a sprinkle lemon juice if desired. After removing from heat, let stand covered a min. or so for flavors to blend. Pour over poached meatballs, boiled chicken, veal, or hot hard-boiled eggs as well as egg cutlets and potato cutlets.

HOT CHIVE SAUCE
sos szczypiorkowy na gorąco

Prepare as above but use 2–3 T. fresh chopped chives instead of dill. *Variation*: A garden green sauce may be prepared identically using 2 t. each chopped dill, chives, and parsley.

HOT GHERKIN SAUCE
sos korniszonowy na gorąco

Grate 4 zesty gherkins and simmer with 1–2 T. meat stock about 10 min. or until tender. Add to 2 c. hot cream sauce, season with a pinch of chopped dill, and (optional) tarragon. A pinch of sugar is also recommended. Mix ingredients, simmer briefly, and let stand covered several min. for flavors to blend. *Optional*: A t. or so gherkin marinade may be added. Serve over boiled beef and tongue.

HOT CARAWAY SAUCE
sos kminkowy na gorąco

Partially crush 1–2 t. caraway in mortar and add to 2 c. white sauce or hot cream sauce (preferably made with egg yolk). Simmer briefly and season to taste with a little lemon juice and sugar. Let stand covered a min. or so for flavors to blend. *Optional*: Stir in a little (¼–½ t.) caramel coloring if desired. Serve with meatballs, pork, and lamb (mutton) dishes. Also good with fresh or smoked, boiled or baked kiełbasa.

HOT MUSHROOM SAUCE
sos grzybowy na gorąco

Soak 1 oz. dried boletes or other mushrooms in 3 c. water several hrs. or overnight and cook in same water until tender. Chop mushrooms fine and set aside. Boil liquid down to 1 c. if necessary and use it to prepare 2 c. cream sauce in place of the stock. Simmer briefly and season with additional salt & pepper if desired. *Note*: Mushrooms may be added to sauce or used in some other dish. This is a meal in itself served over potatoes, groats, noodles, or dumplings. Also good with meatballs, roasts, potato pancakes, or potato cutlets. *Optional*: We feel this sauce will be tastier if you add 1 minced onion sautéed in a little butter.

ECONOMICAL HOT MUSHROOM SAUCE
sos grzybowy oszczędny

Soak 3–4 dried boletes in 2 c. water several hrs., then cook in same water until tender. Chop mushrooms fine, return to liquid, and boil down to 1 c. Meanwhile, sauté 2 med.

chopped onions in 1 T. butter until tender. Use mushroom liquid to prepare 2 c. cream sauce instead of stock. Add sautéed onions and simmer briefly. Salt & pepper to taste and (optional) add 1–2 t. chopped dill. *Note:* This is a milder flavored version of the sauce given above, hence it is best with meat dishes. For blander foods like potatoes, groats, dumplings, etc. it's better to use the sauce made with 1 oz. mushrooms. *Hint:* Dried mushrooms should always be scrubbed well and rinsed in plenty of cold running water before soaking. Even then, some embedded grit may remain in the cracks and crevices. Some cooks strain mushroom liquid through several thicknesses of cheese cloth, linen napkins, or even a coffee filter before adding to sauce.

HOT FRESH MUSHROOM SAUCE
sos pieczarkowy

Wash well and dry 8 oz. fresh mushrooms. Sauté in 1 T. butter and 1–2 chopped onions about 15 min., stirring frequently. Add 2 c. basic white sauce or hot cream sauce (preferably made with egg yolk), stir, salt & pepper to taste, and heat gently a min. or so. Cover and let stand briefly for flavors to blend. *Optional:* 1 T. dry white wine may be added to mushrooms before combining with sauce. Before serving, sprinkle sauce with a little chopped dill and/or parsley. Serve over potatoes, rice, noodles, dumplings, potato cutlets, etc. Great with meatballs and in casseroles.

WHITE ONION SAUCE
sos cebulowy biały

Melt 1 T. butter in skillet, add 2 large or 3 med. onions very finely chopped and mix to coat with butter. Sauté on low until transparent, add 2 T. stock, and simmer covered several min. longer. Add onions straight from skillet or sieved to 2 c. basic white sauce or hot cream sauce. Heat gently, stirring to prevent scorching. Good over potatoes, poached fish, and egg cutlets.

BROWN ONION SAUCE
sos cebulowy rumiany

Sauté 2 large or 3 med. finely chopped onions in 3 T. butter until golden. Add 2 T. flour, browned in dry skillet and simmer on low heat several min., stirring constantly. Let cool slightly, then stir in 1–1½ c. cold meat stock. Heat gently, stirring with whisk until smooth. Season to taste with salt, pepper, a pinch of ground bay leaf, sugar, vinegar, and a little caramel coloring. Bring to boil, reduce heat, and simmer several min. Serve with boiled beef, meatballs, or potato cutlets. *Optional*: Sieve before transferring to gravy boat.

HOT ANCHOVY SAUCE
sos sardelowy na gorąco

To 2 c. basic white sauce or hot cream sauce add 2–3 very finely chopped and mashed canned anchovy fillets. Heat sauce to gentle boil and season with a little lemon juice if desired. Serve with boiled beef, roast veal, or poached fish.

HOT CAPER SAUCE
sos kaparowy na gorąco

Melt 1 T. butter, stir in 1 T. flour, and brown, lightly, stirring constantly with whisk and bringing to boil. Reduce heat and simmer several min. Add 2 T. capers (more or less), bring to boil, remove from heat, and cover. Fork-blend ½ c. sour cream with 1 raw egg yolk and stir into sauce. Heat gently but do not boil. Season with a little salt, sugar, and lemon juice. Serve with vegetarian cutlets, in casseroles, over savory puddings, and hot hard-boiled eggs.

HOT CRAYFISH SAUCE
sos rakowy

Melt 2 T. crayfish butter (see chapter on cold sauces, dressings etc.) in saucepan and stir in 2 T. flour to get a smooth roux. Stir in 1–1¼ c. crayfish, fish, or vegetable stock (court bouillon), heat, whisking until smooth, and simmer 5 min. Add ¼–⅓ c. diced, cooked crayfish meat, season with a little lemon juice and chopped dill. Bring to boil and serve immediately over cooked crayfish meat on a bed of hot rice, poached fish, or hard-boiled eggs.

HOT CAVIAR SAUCE
sos z kawioru

Make a white roux with 1½ T. butter and 2 T. flour, stir in 1 c. beef or fish stock, whisk until smooth, and simmer several min. Add juice of ½ lemon and bring to boil. Stir in ½–1 oz. caviar and serve immediately with boiled beef or poached fish.

HOT HERB SAUCE
sos ziołowy

To 2 c. basic white sauce or hot cream or hot cream sauce, add anywhere from 1–2 t. of any of your homemade Polish meat, fowl, or fish seasonings. Stir into sauce and simmer gently until bubbly. Use beef seasoning if sauce is meant for beef, poultry seasoning for poultry, etc. You may also use 1 part of your specific meat, fowl, or fish seasoning and 1 part mild or sharp Polish herb pepper. Polish hunter's seasoning may be used for any meat, fish or fowl. If sauce is meant for meat or fowl, feel free to add about 1 t. Maggi seasoning. A sprinkling of chopped parsley, dill, or chives will enhance the flavor of any sauce. For a quick mushroom sauce add to hot cream sauce 1 t. or more mushroom powder, liquid mushroom extract, or several homemade frozen mushroom cubes.

HOT VEGETABLE SAUCE
sos jarzynowy

Peel and grate ½ a small celeriac, 1 small parsley root, 1 med. carrot, and 1 onion. Add 1 peeled diced potato. Simmer in 1½ c. meat or fish stock (from poached fish) until tender. Sieve, stir in white or golden roux made from 3 T. butter and 2 T. flour, add juice of ½ lemon and ¼ t. caramel coloring. Bring to boil, add 1 T. chopped dill, and salt & pepper to taste. If too thick, thin with a little stock. Serve with poached fish or fish cutlets.

HOT POTATO SAUCE
sos kartoflany

Peel and dice fine 3 med. potatoes, cover with 1 c. boiling water, and cook until done but not falling apart. Meanwhile, lightly brown 1 chopped onion in 3 T. fat, add 2 T. flour and simmer several min., stirring to form a roux. Dilute with 1½ c. meat stock and simmer 5 min., whisking to get a smooth sauce. Add the drained potatoes and a pinch ground bay leaf, bring to boil, reduce heat, and simmer several min. Season to taste with salt, pepper, lemon juice, and sugar to taste. Add 1 T. chopped parsley just before serving. Serve over boiled beef. *Note*: The number of sauces recommended for boiled beef is a dead giveaway that this dish is a Polish favorite.

BROWN GRAVY FOR MEAT DISHES
sos rumiany do mięs

Heat 3 T. pan drippings from your roast or fried meat and in it lightly brown 1 finely diced onion. Sprinkle in 3 T. flour and simmer on very low heat several min., mixing frequently with whisk. Add 1½–2 c. meat stock and cook on low heat 5 min., whisking until smooth. Add ½ t. caramel coloring or enough to get the color you want. Season to taste with salt, pepper, mushroom powder, Polish hunter's seasoning, and (optional) a pinch or 2 sugar. *Optional*: Remove from heat and stir in 1–2 T. sour cream. Mix well and heat but do not boil. Other possible flavorings include a dash of paprika, Maggi seasoning, or garlic powder. Serve with roast beef, pork, and game.

ROAST-MEAT SAUCE
sos z pieczystego

Whereas the brown gravy above is meant for meat dishes, this one actually contains meat and is served over bland-tasting meatless dishes like dumplings, noodles, and vegetable cutlets. In 4 T. pan drippings (strained to remove spices, bits of burnt meat, etc.) lightly brown 1 finely chopped onion. Add 3 T. flour, simmer, and stir to make a roux. Add 1½–2 c. meat stock and whisk until smooth and lump-free. Simmer several min. and add about 1 c. ground roast meat (pork, beef, veal, poultry etc.). Simmer on lowest possible heat covered 10 min. Season to taste with salt, pepper, ½–1 t. lemon juice, a pinch tarragon and several dashes Polish goulash seasoning or hunter's seasoning and (optional) a little Maggi extract. If sauce is too thick, dilute it with a little more stock to get the consistency you want. Simmer 1 min. or so and let stand covered a brief while for flavors to blend. This is a meal in itself when served over meatless dumplings, potatoes, noodles, groats, bean cutlets, navy beans or potato cutlets. For added flavor, garnish with about 1 T. chopped garden greens of choice.

OLD POLISH (RAISIN & ALMOND) GRAY SAUCE
szary sos staropolski

Lightly brown 1 finely minced onion in 3 T. butter. Add 3 T. flour (browned in dry skillet to a nice golden hue) and simmer on very low heat several min., whisking until roux is smooth. Stir in 2 c. stock, whisking until smooth. (**Note**: Since this sauce is used almost exclusively with boiled beef tongue or poached fish, use the tongue stock or fish-poaching stock as the stock called for above.) Add ¼–⅓ c. ground honey-spice cake (piernik), bring to boil, reduce heat, and simmer until cake crumbs have disintegrated. Add 1 jigger dry red wine, ½–¾ c. raisins, ¼ c. blanched almonds sliced into thin slivers, and a little caramel coloring. Season to taste with salt, pepper, and lemon juice, and sugar to get a sweet, sour, and winey taste with spicy undertones. Simmer covered on very low heat 10 min., then let stand covered several more min. for flavors to blend. *Variation*: A little honey and/or Polish plum jam (powidła) may be used as the sweetener instead of sugar. Serve over boiled, sliced beef tongue or poached fish, especially carp. This interesting sauce was a favorite of the Old Polish nobility centuries ago and continues to have many devotees. *Note*: For a version of the sauce incorporating fresh fish blood, see carp in gray sauce in fish chapter.

OLD POLISH GRAY SAUCE THE EASY WAY
szary sos codzienny

Even when you don't have the time and all the necessary ingredients, you can still enjoy a reasonable facsimile of this classic Polish sauce. Prepare roux with 2 T. butter and 2 T.

flour, simmer and stir until smooth, then stir in 1½–2 c. stock, whisking until smooth. Bring to boil, add ½ c. raisins, ½–1 t. Polish honey-spice cake seasoning, and ½ t. caramel coloring, reduce heat, and simmer covered 10 min. Season to taste with salt, pepper, lemon juice, and sugar, and simmer a bit longer. Serve as above.

HUSSAR SAUCE FOR BEEF
sos husarski do wołowiny

In pot melt 3 T. butter. Add 2 finely chopped onions, 1 coarsely grated med. carrot, 1 coarsely grated small parsley root, 1 t. sugar, a pinch basil, and 1 bay leaf. Stir to coat vegetables evenly and sauté until they are fully cooked and golden. Add 1 T. flour and simmer, stirring constantly to form a roux. Add 1½ c. meat or vegetable stock, mix well until roux is fully blended, cover, and simmer on low heat 20 min. Add juice of ½ lemon, 1 jigger dry red wine and 1 bud crushed garlic. Bring to boil, sieve into another pot, and bring to boil. Purée 1 washed tomato in food processor and force into mixture through sieve fine enough to retain tomato seeds and skins. Place 3 thin slices of boiled ham on top of one another, cut in ½, then slice into thin strips. Add to sauce along with 2 T. freshly grated horseradish. Bring mixture to boil, salt to taste, and serve over boiled beef, beef tongue, or roast beef.

MUSHROOM & CAULIFLOWER SAUCE À LA SOBIESKI
sos à la Sobieski

In 3 T. butter sauté until lightly browned ½–¾ c. washed, drained, diced, fresh cultivated mushrooms. Remove mushrooms and set aside. Into mushroom drippings stir 3 T. flour and mix into a roux without browning. Add 1½ c. meat stock, stir vigorously with whisk until smooth, add mushrooms, and simmer covered 10 min., stirring occasionally. Fork-blend a heaping T. sour cream with ½ c. of the sauce until smooth and add to pot together with ½ c. cooked (fresh or frozen) peas and ¾ c. cooked cauliflower flowerets. Heat briefly and season to taste with salt & pepper, a grating of nutmeg, and a pinch of lovage or its modern counterpart: a dash or Maggi extract. Garnish with chopped dill before serving. *Note*: This sauce was a favorite of Poland's famous 17th-century King Jan Sobieski, who was known as both a valiant military leader as well as a legendary epicurian. Then as now, this sauce is best served with domestic or wild fowl.

ROYAL (MUSHROOM, CRAYFISH & TONGUE) SAUCE
sos królewski

Make a white or pale-golden roux with 3 T. butter and 3 T. flour and stir in 2 finely chopped shallots and 1 t. chopped parsley. Set aside. Cook ½ c. washed, sliced, fresh, cultivated mushrooms in 1½ c. strong meat stock 10 min. Stir stock (minus mushrooms) into roux, heat and whisk until smooth, and simmer covered 10 min., stirring occasionally. Sieve sauce, add ¼ c. Madeira wine, juice of ½ lemon, ½–¾ t. sugar and salt to taste. Slice into thin strips the mushrooms, 1 zesty gherkin, ¼–⅓ c. cooked crayfish meat (or canned crabmeat), and 1–2 thin slices cooked, smoked tongue and add to sauce. Bring to boil and serve over domestic or wild fowl.

PRUNE & ALMOND SAUCE À LA RADZIWIŁŁ
sos à la Radziwiłł

Soak ¾ c. pitted prunes in water to cover 15 min., then cook in same water until they nearly disintegrate. Sieve and set aside. Dice a 3 inch square of slab bacon and sauté in skillet without browning. Add 2 finely chopped onions and simmer until lightly browned. Remove from heat, sprinkle with 3 T. flour, stir into a roux, and simmer until lightly browned. Stir in 1½ c. meat or vegetable stock. Heat and whisk vigorously until smooth. Bring to boil. Reduce heat, cover and simmer 10 min. Add sieved prunes, 1 jigger dry red wine, and ¼–½ c. sliced blanched almonds. Season with salt, pepper, sugar, and lemon juice to taste. Serve with pork, beef, poultry, and game dishes. *Note*: This now exotic-sounding combination of prunes, almonds, bacon, and onions was typical of the foods favored by the Polish nobility of yesteryear. The Radziwiłłs were among Poland's most powerful and illustrious aristocratic families.

ROUXLESS SAUCES FOR DIETERS
sosy bez zasmażki dietetyczne

Most hot Polish sauces and gravies are made with roux which gives them their deep, rich taste. However, it does mean added calories and some people find them a bit hard to digest. If you love sauces, but don't need the extra calories, here is the next best thing. Fork-blend 1 c. strained, room-temp. meat or vegetable stock (with any congealed fat removed) with 4 T. plain or golden-browned flour. When flour has dissolved, transfer mixture to saucepan, heat until bubbly, whisking occasionally, then add another c. stock, bring to boil, reduce heat and simmer covered several min. Add flavoring ingredient (sieved tomatoes or sorrel, onions sautéed until tender in several T. stock, raisins, mushrooms, or whatever) and simmer covered 5 min. Season to taste and stir in 1 heaping T. sour cream. Heat briefly but do not boil. *Note*: If preparing mushroom sauce with dried mushrooms, use 1 c. stock and 1 c. of the liquid in which mushrooms were soaked and cooked. Garden greens (dill, parsley, chives, etc.) should be added towards the end. *Variations*: ½ c. plain, regular, low-fat or non-fat yogurt may be used in place of sour cream, but remember to fork-blend it with 1 t. potato starch or cornstarch before stirring into sauce. Heat on very low flame, whisking constantly, until heated through, but do not boil, or it may separate.

HOT GOOSEBERRY SAUCE
sos agrestowy na gorąco

Wash and remove stems from 1 c. green (underripe) gooseberries. Place in pot. Scald with 1 c. boiling meat stock and cook uncovered until gooseberries fall apart. Sieve mixture into another pot. Fork-blend ½ c. sour cream with 1 raw egg yolk and 2 T. flour until smooth and stir into puréed gooseberries. Salt and sugar to taste and simmer gently several min. Serve with chicken, turkey, or veal.

HOT CURRANT SAUCE
sos porzeczkowy na gorąco

Remove stems and rinse in colander 1 c. red or black currants and puree in blender. Sieve into saucepan. Add 1 c. meat stock, ¼ c. dry red wine, ¼ c. sugar, and a pinch cinnamon. Simmer on low heat 5 min. Dissolve 2 t. potato starch in 3 T. cold water and add to sauce. Simmer several min., stirring frequently. Season with a little salt and let stand a min. or so covered for flavors to blend. Serve with game dishes or roast pork. *Optional*: 1–2 T. pan drippings may be added to and cooked with sauce. *Variation*: Instead of fresh currants, this sauce can be made with ½–¾ c. red or black currant jam or jelly, in which case omit the sugar. You need not blend or sieve jam or jelly but combine directly with stock and wine, then proceed as above.

HOT CHERRY SAUCE
sos wiśniowy na gorąco

In pot combine 1 c. cherry jam (preferably one that isn't excessively sweet), ½ c. meat stock, ¼ c. dry red wine, a pinch ground cloves, and 1–2 T. pan drippings from roast. Mix well, bring to boil, reduce heat, and simmer covered several min. Salt & pepper to taste and add a little lemon juice if you find sauce too sweet. If it is too runny, dissolve 1 t. potato starch in 3 T. cold water, add to sauce, stir well, and simmer several min. Serve with roast boar or pork as well as poultry and boiled beef.

HOT PLUM SAUCE
sos śliwkowy na gorąco

In pot combine 1 c. preferably sugarless Polish jam (powidła), ¼ c. dry red wine, ½ c. meat stock, 1–2 T. pan drippings, and several pinches Polish hunter's seasoning. Heat gently to a boil, reduce heat and simmer covered 5 min. Season to taste with salt, pepper, and lemon juice. If thinner than you want, dissolve 1 t. potato starch in 3 T. cold water, stir into sauce, and simmer several min. Serve with roast pork, beef, game dishes, duck or goose. *Note*: In a pinch, American-style plum jam may also be used.

HOT HAWTHORNBERRY SAUCE
sos głogowy na gorąco

Proceed as for hot plum sauce (above), but use hawthornberry jam. This may be easier to find in European food and specialty shops than in the run-of-the-mill supermarket. *Note*: Hawthorn berries are the reddish berries of the spiny hawthorn shrub found in gardens and parks.

HOT JUNIPER SAUCE FOR GAME DISHES
sos jałowcowy do dziczyzny

Sauté 1 finely minced onion and 1 small grated carrot in 2 T. fat until tender. Sprinkle in 2 T. flour and simmer on low heat, stirring frequently several min. Stir in 1½ c. meat stock, whisk until smooth, add 1 tomato (puréed in blender and sieved) and ½–1 t. ground juniper (pounded in mortar and sieved). Mix well, bring to boil, reduce heat, and simmer covered on low heat 10 min. Add several T. dry red wine, season with salt, pepper, a little sugar, lemon juice, and (optional) 1 bud mashed garlic. Add a little caramel coloring and simmer briefly. After removing from heat, let stand covered a min. or so for flavors to blend. *Optional*: A small piece of grated celeriac may be sautéed at the start with the other vegetables. *Note*: Although, as its name implies, this sauce is meant chiefly for game dishes, it is also good on roast pork, beef, mutton, and poultry. Don't be surprised if one of your guests remarks "this tastes something like gin." The reason is that gin's main flavoring ingredient is juniper.

POLONAISE (BUTTERED BREAD CRUMB) TOPPING
bułka zrumieniona z masłem

We conclude this chapter on sauces with a few typically Polish toppings. Internationally, the best known is this simple but elegant hot garnish which in France, America, and other countries is often referred to as "polonaise" (Polish). In Poland it is so common that it has no name, but is simply described as "bread crumbs browned in butter." Preparing it is the height of simplicity. In saucepan melt about 3 T. butter, add 2–3 T. plain bread crumbs, and simmer briefly, stirring constantly until bread crumbs are a nice golden brown. Immediately spoon topping over cooked cauliflower or other vegetables, boiled potatoes, dumplings, noodles, etc. Gourmet elegance never was this easy!

BUTTER TOPPINGS
masło na okrasę

Purely in terms of taste (health warnings notwithstanding) many Poles feel there is no more noble and flavorful topping than butter. Hot cooked vegetables, dumplings, noodles, potatoes, groats, poached fish, and other dishes may simply be dotted with bits of cold butter which lazily melt in golden trickles. Butter may simply be melted or lightly browned in saucepan before pouring over food. To clarify butter, melt in saucepan and set aside for the milk sediment to settle at bottom. Then spoon clear butter from top over whatever dish you like. This is especially good with poached fish and seafoods. Clarified butter may also be flavored with a little lemon juice or chopped garden greens. It may also be browned in another saucepan for the deeper, more pronounced flavor that many gourmets enjoy. *Note*: There are countless margarines and butter substitutes on the market which some people use in place of real butter. We leave it to you (and your taste buds) to decide whether it's worth it, especially for use as a topping.

POLONAISE EGG TOPPINGS FOR FISH
jajka w maśle do ryby po polsku

In skillet, melt 3–4 T. butter but do not brown. Switch off heat and add 3–4 chopped, hard-boiled eggs. Toss to coat evenly with butter and warm through, but do not cook because egg whites may turn rubbery. Salt & pepper to taste, sprinkle with 2 T. chopped dill (or 1 T. chopped dill and 1 T. chopped parsley), and toss lightly. Use topping to garnish about 4 portions of poached fish, which should first be sprinkled with a bit of lemon juice. *Note*: This is another typical Polish garnish—simple, elegant, and very delicious—that will turn that run-of-the-mill frozen fillet into a gourmet delight. *Variation*: You may sauté a small, finely chopped onion in the butter until tender before adding the eggs.

PORK CRACKLINGS/BROWNED SALT-PORK NUGGETS
skwarki/słonina smażona

In contrast to the above polonaise topping, this is a hearty garnish that is also extremely popular in Poland. If using salted fat back (salt pork), scrape off excess salt from all surfaces before dicing. Dice 3 inch square salt pork and sauté in skillet until nuggets become a nice crunchy golden brown. Spoon nuggets and as much of the drippings as you like over boiled or mashed potatoes, groats, noodles, savory pierogi, and other dumplings as well as cooked vegetables (especially purees). Pork cracklings are sometimes added to meatless soups.

Variation: For a smoky flavor, fry up diced slab bacon and use as above. *Note*: Nowadays, weight-conscious people often use only a little of the drippings as a garnish and reserve the rest for frying, roux, etc. In olden-day Poland, however, every last drop of the drippings was cherished as a rare treat and energy-booster, and often there wasn't enough to go around.

PORK CRACKLINGS & ONIONS
skwarki smażone z cebulką

Sauté diced 3 inch square of salt pork in skillet until it just begins to turn golden. Add 1–2 chopped onions and continue simmering until pork nuggets and onions are lightly browned. Onion-lovers will enjoy this simple topping over potatoes, noodles, dumplings, and groats. Also good over cooked navy beans, bean cutlets, and puréed peas. *Variation*: Onions may also be browned in bacon drippings, lard, meat pan drippings, and oil, although the latter is the least tasty.

HORS D'OEUVRES, appetizers and a wide array of cold starter courses are an important feature of the Polish entertainment scene where pre-dinner drinks are not very popular and most drinking is done while seated at a table during dinner. Shown above is a platter of canapés (open-face sandwiches) featuring eggs, cheese, fish, meat and a variety of colorful embellishments. In the foreground is an apple stuck with skewered hors d'oeuvres, including such contrasting components as green peas and red cranberries.

BIGOS, Poland's fabled hunter's stew, contains a variety of meat, sausage, mushrooms and other ingredients, gently simmered in sauerkraut, to which fresh shredded cabbage is often added. No two families make it exactly the same. Bigos is served as a hot appetizer or main course at casual gatherings or family meals, and even as an early-morning eye-opener just before a party ends.

ZRAZY ZAWIJANE, or steak roll-ups, are an Old Polish dish that continues to have many devotees to this day. The pounded pieces of round steak are spread with any of a variety of fillings (including mushrooms, bacon, bread crumbs, pickles, mustard and others), rolled up, browned, then simmered until tender. Traditional accompaniments are buckwheat groats and braised beets. Here the zrazy are served in a hollowed-out loaf of black bread to keep them hot (the scooped-out bread may be used in the filling).

"Dumplings" describe a variety of filled and unfilled dough balls and potato noodles for which the Polish language has such names as pierogi, pierożki, kluski, kolduny, pyzy, kopytka, knedle, gałuszki and numerous regional variations. Shown above are (left to right) leniwe pierogi (lazy unfilled dumplings), pyzy (raw-potato dumplings) and kopytka ("little hooves"—cooked-potato dumplings).

PIEROGI, translated as "filled dumplings," "dough pockets" or even "Polish ravioli," rank among the most popular dishes in Poland and neighboring Slavic countries. The basic flour-egg-water dough may encase a wide variety of fillings, and they are often fried in butter after draining and cooling.

PĄCZKI AND FAWORKI rank among the best-known Polish pastries and both are associated with Karnawał.Pączki are a kind of doughnut, usually filled with preserves or jam. The faworki (also known as chrust or chruściki) are melt-in-your-mouth sugar-dusted pastries sometimes referred to in America as angel wings, bow-knot pastries, bow ties or crullers

FAVORITE POLISH CAKES include keks (left) and babka. The keks, which might be called a Polish fruit cake, usually contains nuts, dates, raisins, figs, prunes and some candied fruits and rinds for added color, but in general it is more cake and less fruit than the English-style fruit cakes. The term babka (grandmother) may describe a variety of cakes baked in a tall tube-pan, but the best known is the yeast-raised egg cake, often studded with raisins, which many Americans refer to as coffee cake.

IT MAKES NO DIFFERENCE whether you use the traditional hand-cranked coffeemill (left) or a modern electric model. For a truly good cup of coffee, the important thing is to grind the coffee beans just before brewing.

HERBATA OR TEA, Poland's favorite hot beverage, is usually served
with lemon in glasses. The essence method, in which a strong tea
concentrate is steeped in a small teapot above a kettle of boiling water,
is the traditional way of brewing it. That makes it easy to produce the
strength desired by first pouring a little essence into each glass and
topping up with freshly boiled water. The Russian-originated samovar
(seen in background at right) became a standard fixture in Polish
homes in the 19th century, but it is basically an elegant way of storing
boiling water so that escaping steam warms an essence-filled teapot.

POLISH BREAD is usually made of coarser cracked-grain rye and/or wheat flour which means that it contains more fiber, minerals and other natural nutrients than American white bread. The standard Polish bread is a round or oblong loaf that is pale grayish-brown inside and shiny golden-brown on the outside (right rear). Coarsely-textured whole-grain breads in varying shades contrast with kaiser rolls (kajzerki) and croissants (rogale), which are breakfast favorites.

CANNED FRUITS AND VEGETABLES are an excellent way of stocking the Polish pantry with pickles, relishes, jams and other treats that are both tastier and less expensive than those bought in the store. Included are ćwikła, brine-cured dill pickles, pickled pumpkin, marinated mushrooms, horseradish and spiced plums.

SAUSAGES AND OTHER CURED MEATS are widely available commercially, but connoisseurs claim that they are no match for those made from scratch at home. In addition to being more economical, they allow the sausage-maker to create a product that reflects his personal tastes. Hanging in back are (left to right) kabanosy (thin dried sausage), a fatty country-style sausage and a smoked sausage similar to that which passes for "polska kiełbasa" in America. On platter are headcheese, roast bacon, ham, smoked pork loin, baleron (a marbled bladder-encased ham) and krakowska.

WIECZERZA WIGILIJNA or Christmas Eve supper is more than a meal and more than just another family gathering. It is a unique experience full of religious symbolism, a climate of warmth and togetherness and an opportunity to enjoy many culinary delights that are considered too special to serve at any other time. Typical dishes include clear, ruby-red beet soup with tiny ear-shaped, mushroom-filled dumplings (uszka), herring, fried fish, pierogi, poppyseed noodles, dried-fruit compote and traditional holiday cakes.

TYPICAL CHRISTMAS TREATS include makowiec (poppyseed roll) and piernik w czekoladzie (chocolate-covered honey-spice cake). Smaller, often heart-shaped honey-spice cakes are traditionally passed out by Święty Mikołaj (St. Nicholas) when he visits youngsters on his feastday (December 6th). In the foreground the Christ Child overlooks opłatki symbolically placed on a bed of hay and evergreens.

HOME-MADE CORDIALS add a festive touch to any gathering, especially when served from sparkling crystal decanters.

FOOD IN ONE FORM OR ANOTHER has played an important role in Polish tradition. One example is the Dożynki (harvest fest), where grain, vegetables, fruits and herbs are blessed by a priest or bishop.

COOKED VEGETABLES

It would be pretty hard to imagine Polish cuisine without cauliflower Polonaise, lettuce dressed with sour cream, or *gołąbki* (stuffed cabbage rolls) simmered in thick tomato sauce. And yet, these and other vegetables were little known in Poland prior to the reign of its Italian-born Queen Bona Sforza. After marrying King Zygmunt the Old in 1518, she proceeded to import seeds, plants, and master chefs from her native Italy that in time revolutionized Polish eating habits.

Even today, Poles consume less leafy greens than their Italian counterparts due largely to climate, for these are plentiful at reasonable prices only during the summer months. As a result, the bulk of the vegetables eaten in Poland continue to be the old standbys: beets, carrots, cabbage, and legumes (beans, peas, lentils). Polish cooks have therefore developed many interesting ways of preparing these foods, which only recently have been rediscovered in America as important sources of necessary fiber, nutrients and flavor.

Carrots are universally acclaimed as the good eyesight vegetable because of their fantastic vitamin A content, but fewer people realize that the lowly cabbage contains more vitamin C than grapefruit. In addition to supplying calcium and iron, beets are alkaligenous, a fancy word meaning that they neutralize an acid stomach. That is probably why braised beets are a traditional accompaniment to high-acid meats like beef and wild game.

Beans have more vitamin B_1 than any other vegetable and are a true storehouse of all the important minerals: calcium, iron, magnesium, and phosphorous. One of the best ways of preparing wax beans is "Poznań style" (see recipe in this chapter), which retains most of this vegetable's valuable nutrients.

Special mention should be made of sauerkraut, salt-cured, shredded cabbage, whose preparation has remained largely unchanged for over 1,000 years. To this day it is cured in wooden barrels and sold by the kilo (2.2 pounds). Of course the *kapusta kiszona* exported by Poland is packed in glass jars. Besides all the tasty ways it can be prepared (some of which are found in this chapter), in the winter months it is an important source of vitamin C.

Strictly from a flavor standpoint, our family favorites include beets braised with apples, garlicky spinach, floured carrots, sauerkraut and mushrooms, hearty, stick-to-the-ribs pea purée, and nearly all cooked vegetables (cauliflower, string beans, brussels sprouts, etc.) with Polonaise topping.

If you yearn for something new try boiled radishes, stewed cucumbers, or any of the pumpkin recipes. Stewed sorrel and lettuce is another old recipe that may seem unusual by modern standards, and we conclude the chapter with fruits which serve as cooked vegetables: cooked apples and pears.

* * *

COOKED VEGETABLES
warzywa z wody

In general, most vegetables are cooked in similar fashion. After being washed, peeled, hulled, or whatever, they are placed in a pot and scalded with just enough salted, boiling water to cover, then cooked on medium heat until tender. Usually 10–30 min. is enough, and cooking time depends on the type and freshness of the vegetable and whether it is cooked whole or cut up (sliced, diced, cubed). Vegetables of the cabbage (Brussels sprouts, cauliflower) and turnip (kohlrabi, rutabaga) families are best cooked uncovered at least part of the time so their strong odor boils away. Cooking vegetables in broth or bouillon improves their flavor. Adding a little sugar (1–2 t. or so) replaces the natural sweetness that is lost after vegetables are picked. When vegetables are tender, drain well and dot with butter, garnish with butter-browned bread crumbs (Polonaise topping) or sprinkle with finely chopped dill, parsley or a little of both. A little sour cream is often stirred in, and for special occasions the vegetables may be drenched with a gourmet sauce. On less festive occasions a sprinkle of flour or a simple roux (*zasmażka*—a little flour simmered in butter) usually suffices. Many vegetables are delicious topped with *skwarki* (crunchy, golden nuggets of fried salt pork).

CARROTS POLONAISE
marchewka po polsku

Place 1½ lbs. peeled, washed, sliced, or diced carrots in pot, scald with boiling, salted water to cover, add 1–2 t. sugar and 1 T. butter, and cook covered about 10 min. or until tender. Meanwhile, melt 3 T. butter in saucepan, add 2 T. bread crumbs, and brown. Drain carrots and top with breadcrumb mixture.

FLOURED CARROTS
marchewka oprószana

Cook carrots as above, drain briefly to retain some of the moisture and return to pot. Dot generously with butter, toss lightly, sprinkle with flour and toss to coat the carrots. Simmer briefly, stirring constantly. Serve as is or garnished with a little chopped dill and/or parsley.

CREAMED CARROTS
marchewka w śmietanie

To floured carrots (above) stir in 2–3 T. sour cream and simmer until a bubbly sauce begins to form.

BABY CARROTS À LA MASURIENNE
karotka po mazursku

Use nylon scrubber to remove the skin from 1½ lbs. baby carrots (about 2–3 in. long) under running water. Place in pot whole, scald with salted water, add 1–2 t. sugar, and cook covered until tender. Meanwhile, in skillet fry up 1 heaping T. finely diced salt pork until golden brown. Drain carrots, return to pot, and drench with salt-pork nuggets and drippings. Toss. Sprinkle with a little flour and toss to coat evenly. Simmer briefly. Top with finely chopped parsley. *Note*: Mature, sliced carrots may be prepared the same way.

CARROT PURÉE
purée z marchwi

Cook 1½ lbs. diced carrots in boiling, salted water with a little sugar added until tender. Drain and mash well or force through sieve. In saucepan, melt 2–3 T. butter, lard, or bacon (or salt-pork) drippings and simmer 2 T. flour in them, but do not brown. Add to carrots together with 2–3 T. sour cream and briefly simmer, stirring the whole time. Stir in 1 raw egg yolk. Mix well. Use ice-cream scoop to form nice, even balls of your purée and sprinkle with chopped dill and/or parsley on serving platter. Your purée-carrot balls can also form part of an elegant meat platter garnish.

CARROTS AND PEAS
marchew z groszkiem

Peas have long been a favorite companion to carrots in the cuisines of many different countries. Simply cook fresh or frozen peas in a small amount of boiling salted water with a little sugar added (optional) until tender. Drain and add to cooked carrots prepared in any of the ways recommended above (except puréed carrots). To perk up the flavor, stir in ½ t. lemon juice.

CREAMED CARROTS & POTATOES
marchew z kartoflami w śmietanie

Place 1½ c. diced carrots in pot, scald with boiling milk to cover, and cook covered about 10 min. Add 1–1½ c. peeled, diced, raw potatoes, mix with carrots, add enough boiling water to cover mixture (a crushed bouillon cube may also be added), and cook covered another 10–15 min. or until tender. Drain, reserving 2 T. liquid. Toss with 1 T. flour, stir in 2–3 T. sour cream, and simmer briefly until a nice, bubbly sauce forms. Garnish with chopped greens: parsley, dill, and/or chives.

CARROTS & KOHLRABI POLONAISE
marchew z kalarepą

Wash, peel, and dice 1 lb. carrots and 1 lb. young kohlrabi. Instead of dicing, you can cut the vegetables into balls using a small fruit scoop. Scald with boiling salted water to cover, add 1 T. butter, and cook covered about 20 min. or until tender. Drain. Garnish with browned, buttered bread crumbs (Polonaise topping) and sprinkle with garden greens of choice. This dish is also good floured or creamed according to the recipes above.

DILLED PEAS
groszek z koprem

Scald 1½ lbs. fresh or frozen peas with boiling salted water to cover, add 1–2 t. sugar and 1 T. butter and cook covered until nearly tender. Drain, retaining some of the moisture, and return to pot. Dot generously with butter, add 1 T. finely chopped dill, toss gently, and allow to set covered about 5 min. for flavors to blend.

CREAMED PEAS
groszek w śmietanie

Proceed as above, but after draining, sprinkle peas with a little flour and stir in 2–3 T. sour cream. Simmer briefly. *Note:* Cooked peas are also good with browned, buttered bread crumbs.

PEAS & BACON
groszek z boczkiem

Cook peas as above in boiling salted water with a little sugar added until tender. Drain. In skillet, fry up 1–2 heaping T. diced bacon until golden brown. Drench peas with bacon bits and drippings, sprinkle with a little flour, toss gently, simmer briefly, and season with paprika. In a pinch, use canned peas in any of the above recipes.

PEA PURÉE
groch purée

In pot combine 2 c. dried, yellow, split peas, 8 c. water, several peppercorns, and ½ a bay leaf, cook 1½–2 hrs. or until tender. Meanwhile, finely dice ¼ lb. slab bacon and fry up to a nice golden brown. Remove bacon bits and in drippings lightly brown 1–2 minced onions. Drain peas, force through sieve, or put through food mill. Add the bacon bits, onions, and drippings and season with salt, pepper, and marjoram to taste. Mix well. Pea purée is a traditional side dish for boiled pork hocks (golonka).

(FRESH) LIMA BEANS & PORK CRACKLINGS
fasola "Jaś" (świeża) ze skwarkami

Shell and wash 1½ lbs. fresh lima beans and cook covered in a small amount of boiling salted water 20–30 min. or until tender. Dice ¼ lb. or less salt pork or bacon and fry to a nice golden brown. Drain beans and drench with fried cracklings and drippings. Season to taste with salt, pepper, and a pinch or two savory. This vegetable is known in Polish not as Lima beans but "Johnny beans".

(DRIED) LIMA BEANS & PORK RINDS
fasola "Jaś" (sucha) ze skórką wieprzową

Soak 2 c. dried Lima beans in water overnight, then cook in same water 1–1½ hrs. or until tender. Drain. Before you even start cooking the beans, cut up the rind from a 1½ lb. slab of bacon or salt pork into several slices and cook separately in water until tender. This may take several hours. Cut the soft rind into small strips and mix with drained cooked beans. Add ½–1 c. water in which rind was cooked, bring to boil, remove from heat, cover, and allow to set 15–20 min. Mix in a little flour to thicken sauce, season to taste with salt, pepper, and savory, and simmer briefly. The author's maternal grandmother often prepared this hearty dish, which illustrates how Polish cookery found tasty uses for many culinary leftovers. *Optional*: Season with a sprinkling of lemon juice.

NAVY BEANS WITH BACON OR BUTTER
biała fasola z boczkiem lub masłem

Soak 2 c. dried navy beans in 8 c. water overnight. Add 1 T. salt and cook in same water 1½ hrs. or until tender. Drain. Drench with ¼ lb. fried diced bacon and the drippings. A diced onion may also be fried up with the bacon. Season to taste with salt, pepper, and a pinch or 2 marjoram and/or savory. For added tang, sprinkle with a little vinegar. On fast days the beans are drenched with melted butter with or without onions. Some families serve the butter-drenched version on Wigilia.

NAVY BEANS ANOTHER WAY
biała fasola inaczej

Soak and cook navy beans until tender as above and drain. Drench with tomato, mushroom, or gray sauce.

BEANS OLD POLISH STYLE
fasola po staropolsku

Soak 2 c. dried Lima or navy beans overnight and cook as above until tender. While they cook, dice ¼ lb. slab bacon and fry up 2 finely chopped onions. Soak 8–12 prunes in hot water 10 min. Drain bacon and onions, setting them aside. In drippings, lightly brown 2–3 T. flour. If you don't have enough drippings left over, add a little lard or butter. Dilute the roux with enough bean water to form a pourable sauce. To sauce return bacon and onions, add drained and chopped prunes, ¼ c. raisins, 1 T. honey, and 2 t. caramelized sugar (caramelize by browning in dry saucepan and diluting with several T. boiling water). Salt & pepper and season with several pinches marjoram or your homemade hunter's seasoning. Simmer under cover 10 min. and pour over drained beans. A sprinkle of vinegar or lemon juice will give your beans added zest. This and the other dried bean dishes are usually served as a meal in themselves for dinner or supper.

WAX BEANS POLONAISE
fasolka szparagowa z tartą bułką

Wash 1½ lbs. wax beans, cut off ends, and remove strings. Cook in just enough salted boiling water to cover 10–15 min. Fork-test them for doneness. Beans may be cooked whole or—if they are on the long side—cut in half or even three pieces. Drain, remove to platter, and drench with Polonaise topping.

DILLED WAX BEANS
fasolka szparagowa z koperkiem

Cook wax beans as above, drain, and return to pot. Add 1–2 T. chopped dill, 2 T. butter, ¼ c. broth or bouillon and 1 t. sugar. Cover and simmer several min.

WAX BEANS POZNAŃ STYLE
fasolka szparagowa po poznańsku

Wash 1–1½ lbs. wax beans, cut off ends, remove strings, and cut each pod into 2–3 pieces. Place in pot and add just enough water to barely cover beans. Bring to boil and cook on med. heat until tender. Meanwhile, dissolve 1 T. flour in 1/2 c. milk, add to beans, bring to boil, and simmer 1 min. or so. Season to taste with salt, savory and a bit of sugar. Those who like their beans slightly tart may sprinkle with a little lemon juice. Besides being very tasty, this is one of the healthiest ways of preparing wax beans, because the nutrients remain in the dish rather than being poured down the sink.

WAX BEANS STEWED WITH TOMATOES
fasolka szparagowa duszona z pomidorami

Wash, cut off ends, and remove strings from 1½ lbs. wax beans, and cut into 2 or 3 pieces. Slice 2 small onions wafer thin and simmer in 3 T. butter or oil until transparent. In pot, mix beans with onions and drippings, add 2 T. boiling water, sprinkle with pepper, and (optional) a pinch of savory, and simmer covered on low heat about 10 min. Add a little more boiling water if beans begin to sizzle. Scald 3–4 small tomatoes and remove skins, dice, and add to beans together with 2 buds mashed garlic. Toss gently, cover, and continue to simmer until fully cooked. Salt to taste and serve garnished with chopped dill.

CREAMED GREEN BEANS
fasolka zielona ze śmietanką

Wash 1½ lbs. green beans, cut off ends, remove strings, cut into 1 inch pieces, and cook hot broth or bouillon to cover about 10–12 min. or until tender. Drain, reserving stock. Return beans to pot. Lightly brown 1–2 T. flour in a heaping T. butter. Stir in ½ c. sweet cream or ½ c. fork-blended sour cream. Simmer briefly, adding enough of the liquid in which the beans were cooked to form a thick sauce. Season sauce with salt & pepper and 1–2 t. sugar and drench beans. Simmer briefly under cover, then switch off heat and allow to set about 5 min. for flavors to blend. *Note*: Recipes for wax beans and green (string) beans may be used interchangeably.

ASPARAGUS POLONAISE
szparagi z tartą bułką

Gently scrub 2 lbs. asparagus and scrape away skin, starting at the bottom. Cut away tough bottoms if any. (Fresh supermarket asparagus may already be trimmed and ready to cook.) Cover with salted boiling water and cook 10–15 min. or until tender. Another way is to tie the asparagus into bundles with strong white thread, stand upright in pot, and cook in boiling salted water 20 min. or until tender. Either way, a t. or so sugar may be added to boiling water and ½ c. milk may be added to pot. Drain and remove to serving platter. Remove threads if you have used the bundle method. Drench with browned, buttered bread crumbs. A sprinkle of chopped dill may be added.

ASPARAGUS IN BÉCHAMEL SAUCE
szparagi pod beszamelem

Cook as above, drain, transfer to serving platter, and drench with thick, creamy béchamel sauce, a French import that has won many devotees in Poland over the years. An easy way to make it is to melt 3 T. butter in saucepan, stir in 3 T. flour and dilute with ½ c. broth or bouillon. Simmer, stirring constantly, and gradually add 1 c. or more light cream or half & half. Simmer until smooth and lump-free, cover and set aside. Beat 1–2 raw egg yolks, add ½ c. hot sauce 1 t. at a time, beating constantly. Add to sauce, stir well, and heat thoroughly but do not boil. Season with salt, white pepper, and a pinch of mace or nutmeg. *Variation*: Transfer cooked, drained asparagus to baking dish, drench with sauce, top with a little grated cheese, and bake in medium hot oven until cheese melts and sauce begins to bubble and brown.

BROCCOLI
brokuły/kapusta szparagowa

Many Polish cooks like to place their broccoli or cauliflower into a pot of cold water and add 1–2 T. vinegar. In about 15 min. any insects hidden in the various crevices will float out. Drain broccoli, cut stems into 1 inch pieces, and break top up into flowerlets. Place stems in pot, cover with salted boiling water, add 1 t. sugar, and cook about 8 min. Add the flowerlets and cook another 8 min. or until your broccoli is tender. The reason for this is that the stems take longer to cook than the tender flowerlets. Drain and serve topped with bread crumbs browned in butter or béchamel sauce.

CAULIFLOWER POLONAISE
kalafior po polsku

Place whole cauliflower in water-vinegar bath as above if desired. Remove outer leaves and tough stem if still attached. Place in pot and cover with boiling salted water. Add 1–2 t. sugar and cook uncovered 20–30 min. depending on the size of your cauliflower. Drain. Divide into 4 portions and drench each with butter-browned bread crumbs. *Optional:* Garnish with a bit of chopped dill. On hot summer days, when nobody is in the mood for a heavy, meaty dinner, this is often a meal in itself in the Warsaw household of the Strybel family. Usually some sliced tomatoes are served on the side along with a cool fruit compote to wash it all down.

CAULIFLOWER IN BÉCHAMEL SAUCE
kalafior pod beszamelem

Cook cauliflower as above, drain, divide into portions, and drench with béchamel sauce.

BRUSSELS SPROUTS POLONAISE
brukselka/kapusta brukselska po polsku

Remove yellowed, wilted leaves from 2 lbs. Brussels sprouts, wash well, place in pot, cover with salted boiling water with 1 t. sugar added, and cook uncovered 10–15 min. or until tender. Drain. Top with browned, buttered bread crumbs. *Variation*: After draining, sprinkle with a little lemon juice and drench with melted butter. These tasty little cabbages are also good with béchamel sauce.

KALE & BACON
jarmuż z boczkiem

Cut away the tough stems from 2 lbs. of kale. Cook the curly-leaved tops in salted boiling water until tender (10–12 min. should suffice). Drain and serve drenched with browned bacon bits and the drippings. *Variation:* Kale is also good topped with butter-browned bread crumbs or cream sauces like béchamel. It can be cooked together with diced tomatoes or prepared like spinach (see p. 536). Outside of the Poznań region, kale is rarely served as a vegetable and is sometimes used to decorate meat platters.

BRAISED CABBAGE & APPLE
biała kapusta z jabłkami

Discard green outer leaves from a 2 lb. head of cabbage. Shred cabbage, transfer to pot, and scald with boiling water. Cook uncovered 5–10 min. Drain. Fry up 1 heaping T. diced salt pork and add 1 finely chopped onion when salt-pork nuggets just begin turning pale yellow. When nicely browned, add fried salt pork and onions to cabbage together with 2 peeled and diced cooking apples. (1–2 peeled, diced tomatoes may also be added). Salt & pepper, and simmer covered 10–12 min. or until cabbage and apples are tender. Sprinkle with a little flour, stir, and simmer briefly. An excellent companion to hot, fresh, or smoked kiełbasa.

CREAMED CABBAGE
biała kapusta w śmietanie

Shred or chop 1–2 lb. head of cabbage. Place in pot and scald with salted boiling water to cover. Add 1–2 t. sugar and 2 T. fat (bacon or salt-pork drippings, lard or butter), cover, and bring to boil. Uncover, reduce heat, and cook until cabbage is tender. Remove from heat. Fork-blend ¼–½ c. sour cream with 2 T. flour and stir in. Simmer briefly. Season with salt, pepper, and lemon juice to taste. *Optional*: Sprinkle with chopped dill or crushed caraway seeds. A grated cooking apple may also be added at the start of cooking.

LENTEN CABBAGE
biała kapusta postna

Shred a 2 lb. head of cabbage. Scald with boiling salted water to cover and bring to boil. Drain. Add 1 t. sugar, 2 T. cooking oil and (optional) ½ t. caraway seeds; cook on low heat until tender. Adjust to taste with salt, pepper, and lemon juice. Serve with boiled potatoes and/or fish on fast days and with meat at other times. Crinkly Savoy cabbage (kapusta włoska) may be used in any of the cabbage recipes presented here.

CABBAGE & MUSHROOMS IN BEET JUICE
biała kapusta z grzybami na smaku burakowym

Shred 2 lb. head of cabbage and scald with boiling water. In a skillet melt a heaping T. butter, add 1 minced onion, ½–1 c. chopped fresh mushrooms (wild or store-bought), a heaping T. grated celeriac and 1 small grated parsnip. Simmer and stir over low heat until vegetables are tender. Drain cabbage and add the vegetables, 1 c. clear beet soup, or ½ c. juice from canned beets and ½ c. water. Sprinkle with salt and cook covered about 30 min. or until tender. Add 1–2 t. sugar and simmer until dissolved. Stir in heaping T. sour cream, sprinkle with flour, mix well, and simmer briefly.

CABBAGE & ROUX PEASANT STYLE
biała kapusta z zasmażką po chłopsku

Shred 2 lb. head of cabbage, cover with salted boiling water and cook covered 10 min. Uncover and continue cooking until tender (5–10 min.). Meanwhile, in saucepan fry up a heaping T. diced salt pork until golden brown. Remove salt pork and simmer 1 finely chopped onion in drippings until tender. Add salt-pork nuggets and 2 T. flour and simmer until smooth. Dilute with enough cabbage water to get a thick sauce and stir into cabbage. Salt & pepper and sour to taste with a little sauerkraut juice, vinegar, or lemon juice. *Optional*: Sprinkle with a little caraway and/or add 1 bud crushed garlic. Mix well and simmer on very low heat covered another 10–15 min. In poorer families this cabbage served with boiled potatoes is a meal in itself, and you too might find it an interesting change of pace. On fast days butter or oil are used instead of salt pork.

CABBAGE WITH RAISINS À LA UHLAN
biała kapusta po ułańsku

Shred 2 lb. head of cabbage and cover with salted boiling water. Add 1 T. bacon fat and continue cooking 2–3 minutes, add ¼–⅓ c. raisins, cover, and cook until tender. Fry 1 small, finely chopped onion to a nice golden brown in 2 T. drippings, add 2 T. flour, brown slightly, and stir into cabbage. Mix well and simmer briefly. Add a heaping T. sour cream, 1 level T. tomato paste, and 1 T. chopped parsley. Mix well, season with salt, pepper, and a pinch or 2 of paprika and simmer covered on very low heat another 5 min. Let stand covered another 5 min. for flavor to blend. A sprinkle of lemon juice will perk up the flavor.

CABBAGE FRIED IN BATTER OR BREADING
kapusta smażona w cieście lub panierze

Remove core from 2 lb. head of cabbage and discard wilted outer leaves. Cut into quarters, place in pot, cover with salted boiling water, add 1 t. sugar, and cook covered 5 min. Uncover and continue cooking about 10 min. or until tender. Remove with slotted spoon and let drip dry in colander. When dry, sprinkle with pepper, dredge in flour, dip in beaten eggs, and roll in bread crumbs, pressing breading in with hand so it doesn't fall off during frying. Another way is to dip cooked cabbage quarters impaled on fork in rather thick crêpe batter (ciasto naleśnikowe). Fry in about ¼ inch of hot lard or salt-pork drippings until golden on all sides. Then reduce heat and simmer another 5 min. or so. Drain on absorbent paper before serving if you like. All cooked-cabbage dishes are tastier when cooked in meat stock or *kiełbasa* water rather than plain water.

CREAMED CABBAGE & POTATOES
kapusta "parzybroda"

Remove core from 1½ lb. cabbage. Dice cabbage and 1 lb. peeled potatoes. Place in pot, scald with 2 c. boiling water, and cook uncovered until potatoes and cabbage are tender. Meanwhile, fry up 1 heaping T. diced salt pork until golden. Remove from heat, stir in 3 T. flour, mix until smooth and, stirring constantly, add 1 c. whole milk or ½ c. sour cream fork-beaten with ½ c. milk. Add mixture to cabbage, mix well, salt & pepper, and simmer briefly. *Optional*: Season with a pinch or 2 caraway seeds or marjoram and/or garnish with a little chopped dill. A somewhat watered-down version of this dish is served as a soup. Its somewhat humorous name (parzybroda literally means "chin-stinger") suggests that it should be served so hot that anything trickling down will burn your chin!

BRAISED RED CABBAGE
czerwona kapusta zasmażana

Cut up 2 lb. red cabbage, removing core and tough veins, and shred. Place in pot. Scald with 1 c. boiling water, add 1 T. salt-pork or bacon drippings, and simmer on very low heat, stirring from time to time. Meanwhile, fry 1 heaping T. diced salt pork until golden. Remove salt-pork nuggets and simmer 2 finely chopped onions in the drippings until tender. Stir in 2 T. flour and brown slightly. Add to cabbage together with salt-pork nuggets, mix well, season with salt, pepper, and lemon juice and simmer briefly. This and other forms of cooked red cabbage are traditionally served with beef, duck, goose, and wild game.

STEWED RED CABBAGE (SWEET & SOUR)
czerwona kapusta duszona

Remove wilted outer leaves and core from 2 lb. head of red cabbage and shred. Place in pot, sprinkle with 1 T. salt, toss, cover, and let stand 15 min. Meanwhile, melt a heaping T. butter in skillet, add 1 finely chopped onion, a small slice of celeriac grated, and 1 small grated parsnip; simmer until vegetables are tender. Drain cabbage and add the vegetables, 1 c. meat stock or bouillon, and simmer on very low flame until tender (10–15 min.). Add 2 T. vinegar, 2 T. sugar, or a bit more to get the sweet & sour taste you want, 2 pinches ground cloves, a pinch or 2 pepper, and 1 pinch ground allspice. Stir in 1 T. flour, mix well, and simmer under cover about 5 min. Let stand covered another 5 min. for flavors to blend. *Optional*: ¼–½ c. dry red wine may also be added for a gourmet touch.

RED CABBAGE WITH CURRANTS & CRANBERRIES
czerwona kapusta z porzeczkami

Prepare and shred red cabbage as above, place in pot, scald with 1 c. boiling water, add 1 T. fat of choice, and cook on very low heat covered until tender. Melt 2 T. butter or lard in saucepan, add 2 T. flour, and simmer without browning. Add to cabbage together with ¼–½ c. sieved fresh red currants and 1 heaping T. canned, whole-style cranberry sauce. Salt & pepper and adjust to taste with a little sugar and lemon juice. Mix well and simmer covered several min. longer.

RED CABBAGE & RAISINS
czerwona kapusta z rodzynkami

Remove wilted outer leaves and core from 2 lb. head of red cabbage. Shred, place in pot, add ½ c. meat stock, 3 T. dry red wine, and 1 T. fat, and simmer on very low heat under cover until tender, stirring frequently. Melt 2 T. fat in saucepan, stir in 2 T. flour, and simmer briefly without browning. Add to cabbage along with ½–¾ c. soaked, drained raisins and 1 heaping T. cherry jam. Mix well. Season with salt, pepper, a pinch of ground cloves (optional), and a little lemon juice. Simmer covered several min. longer.

STEWED SAUERKRAUT
kapusta kwaszona/kiszona zasmażana

Drain 1 qt. sauerkraut, reserving juice. Rinse in plenty of cold running water, drain in colander, and press out excess moisture. Transfer to pot as is or chop, depending on consistency desired. Cover with boiling water, add 1 T. fat and 1 t. sugar. Cover and bring to boil, reduce heat, and cook 10 min. uncovered, then cover and cook another 30–40 min. The sauerkraut is cooked when it is no longer in the least crunchy. In skillet fry up 1 heaping T. diced salt pork to a nice golden hue. Push fried nuggets off to one side of skillet and simmer 1 small chopped onion in the drippings until golden and tender. In separate dry saucepan lightly brown 3 T. flour, then stir into fried salt pork & onions, mix, and add to sauerkraut. A pinch or 2 of caraway seeds (preferably crushed) may be added. Simmer covered on very low flame about 5 min. For darker color and deeper flavor add 1 t. liquid Maggi seasoning. This kapusta is the perfect accompaniment to pork dishes, including kiełbasa. *Note*: Individual brands of sauerkraut commercially available in America (in cans, jars, plastic bags, and straight from the barrel) differ greatly in acidity. Some can be used just as they are, while others are so sour they must be not only rinsed but also scalded, brought to a boil, and drained. If your finished sauerkraut dish is not as tart as you like, simply sour it to taste with the reserved sauerkraut juice. Store any leftover sauerkraut juice tightly sealed in your fridge and use as a souring agent for salads, soups, sauces, and other savory dishes (but not cakes and desserts!) that call for vinegar, lemon juice, or citric acid crystals. It is certainly healthier than vinegar, which in general should be used sparingly.

SAUERKRAUT & MUSHROOMS
kapusta z grzybami

Soak 1 oz. or more dried Polish mushrooms in 2 c. water several hrs. or overnight. Cook in same water until tender (about 30 min.). Slice into thin strips, return to water in which they cooked, and let stand. Drain, rinse, and press dry 1 qt. sauerkraut as above and transfer to pot whole or chopped. Add mushrooms and the water in which they cooked, cover, bring to boil, cook uncovered 5 min., then cover and continue cooking on medium low heat another 35–45 min. or until sauerkraut is tender. In saucepan melt 2 T. butter (or use 2 T. oil, especially for *Wigilia*), add 1 small, finely chopped onion and simmer until golden and tender. Stir in 2–3 T. flour and brown slightly, then dilute with a little sauerkraut liquid from pot, mix well to blend, and return to pot. Season to taste with a little pepper. *Optional*: If you like your sauerkraut more aromatic, 3–4 peppercorns, 1–2 grains allspice, and ½ a bay leaf may be added at the start of cooking. This is one of the traditional dishes served at Poland's festive Christmas Eve (*Wigilia*) supper. On non-fast days this recipe can be prepared with salt-pork or bacon drippings in place of butter or oil.

SAUERKRAUT & PEAS
kapusta z grochem

Soak 1 c. whole, yellow, dried peas in 5 c. pre-boiled, lukewarm water 24 hrs. Next day add 1 t. salt and cook in same water until tender. (Depending on the size, age, and dryness of the peas this may take anywhere from 2–4 hrs.). A quicker way is to use split yellow peas which usually take 1½–2 hrs. to cook. Soak 3–5 dried Polish mushrooms in 1 c. water overnight and cook in same water until tender. Slice thin or chop and return to mushroom water. Drain, rinse, and press dry 1 qt. sauerkraut and place in pot as is or chopped. Add mushrooms and their liquid, ½–¾ c. meatless court bouillon or water, several peppercorns, ½ a bay leaf, 1 t. sugar, bring to boil under cover, remove cover, and cook 5 min., then replace cover and cook on medium low heat about 30 min. Stir occasionally to prevent burning and add a little liquid if most has evaporated. Simmer 2 T. flour in 2 T. oil or butter to form a roux and add to pot. Mix well and season with a little pepper. Simmer several min. longer covered on very low heat. Like all sauerkraut dishes, sauerkraut & peas is better prepared a day ahead and reheated when ready to serve. This is another traditional Christmas Eve specialty.

SAUERKRAUT OLD POLISH STYLE (WITH PRUNES & MUSHROOMS)
kapusta po staropolsku

Drain, rinse, and press dry 1 qt. sauerkraut as in above recipes. Transfer to pot as is or chopped, add 3–5 pre-soaked, cooked, and chopped dried Polish mushrooms and their water, 1 c. court bouillon, 10 pitted prunes, chopped, and 1 T. salt-pork or bacon drippings. Bring to boil under cover, uncover, and cook 5 min., replace cover, and cook on fairly low heat (about 40 min.) until tender. Fry up a heaping T. diced salt pork or slab bacon until golden, stir in 2 T. flour, and brown slightly then add to sauerkraut. Mix well. Season with a little pepper, 1 t. Maggi, and ½–1 t. sugar and simmer another 5–10 min. A pinch or 2 of marjoram or your homemade hunter's seasoning may be added.

SAUERKRAUT WITH RAISINS & WINE
kapusta z rodzynkami i winem

Drain, rinse, press dry, and chop 1 qt. sauerkraut. Scald with boiling water to cover, add 1 T. fat, cover and bring to boil. Reduce heat and cook uncovered 10 min., allowing strong odor to evaporate. Cover and cook on med.-low heat another 40 min. or until tender. Fry 1 heaping T. diced salt pork or slab bacon until golden and brown 1 T. flour in drippings, then stir into sauerkraut. Add ½ c. raisins and ⅓ c. dry white wine, season to taste with salt, pepper and a little sugar and simmer about 5 min. longer.

SAUERKRAUT & FRESH MUSHROOMS
kapusta z pieczarkami

Drain, rinse, press dry, and chop 1 qt. sauerkraut, scald with boiling water to cover, add 1 T. butter, and bring to boil covered. Cook 5–10 min. uncovered, then cover and cook another 20 min. Meanwhile in 2–3 T. butter simmer 6–8 oz. fresh diced mushrooms, adding 1 finely chopped onion when mushrooms begin to brown. Stir in 2 T. flour, mix well, and dilute with several T. sauerkraut stock, then add to pot. Salt & pepper, add 1 t. sugar, and cook covered on low heat another 10–15 min. or until sauerkraut is tender. *Optional*: Flavor with 1 t. Maggi seasoning and/or mushroom powder.

SAUERKRAUT STEWED WITH MEAT
kapusta duszona w wywarze mięsnym

In pot combine 5 c. water, 1 pig's foot, 1 small pork hock, several pork ribs or some pork neck bones, bring to boil, and simmer 30 min., skimming off scum until it stops forming. Add a small portion of soup greens (carrot, celeriac, parsnip, onion), 3–5 peppercorns, ½–1 bay leaf, and 1 T. salt, and cook covered on low heat until meat is tender. Remove from heat and let stand covered until cooled to room temp. Refrigerate until fat coagulates. Remove and reserve fat. Heat stock and strain. Drain, rinse, press dry, and chop 1–1½ qts. sauerkraut. Scald with boiling stock to cover and cook uncovered 30 min. Remove meat from bone, dice, and add to sauerkraut. (If your sauerkraut is to be a side dish, add only some of the meat and freeze the rest for future use.) Add 1 t. sugar and cook under cover another 30 min. or until sauerkraut is tender. In dry saucepan lightly brown 2–3 T. flour. Separately, lightly brown 1 finely chopped onion in 2 T. reserved meat stock fat and combine with browned flour. Stir in enough sauerkraut stock from pot to get a thick sauce, simmer briefly, stir into sauerkraut and cook another several min. Season with pepper and a little liquid Maggi seasoning. A sprinkle of mushroom powder enhances the taste of every sauerkraut dish.

BRAISED BEETS WITH SALT PORK OR BUTTER
buraczki zasmażane

Scrub 2 lbs. beets well with brush under running water, but do not peel. Cook in water or bake in oven until tender. Peel while hot under cold running water. Grate coarsely and place in pot. Fry up 1 slightly heaping T. finely diced salt pork until golden (or slightly brown 2–3 T. butter) and pour over beets. Fork-blend 2 T. flour with ¼ c. sour cream until smooth and add to beets. Stir to blend ingredients, season to taste with salt, pepper, a little

little sugar, and lemon juice, and simmer covered on very low heat 10–15 min. Let stand another 5 min. before serving.

BRAISED BEETS ANOTHER WAY
buraczki zasmażane inaczej

Scrub, cook , peel, and grate 2 lbs. beets as above. Lightly brown 2 T. flour in the golden salt-pork nuggets or melted butter and pour over beets. Cover and simmer on very low heat 10 min. (*Optional*: Stir in a slightly heaping T. sour cream). Salt & pepper to taste and adjust flavor with souring agent of choice (lemon juice, vinegar, pickle juice, sauerkraut, citric acid crystals) and just enough sugar to get the sweet & sour taste you want. Simmer covered another 5–10 min. This second variant is probably the more widely encountered of the two.

CREAMED BEETS
buraczki ze śmietaną

Scrub, cook, peel, and grate 2 lbs. beets as above. Fork-blend 3 T. flour and ⅓–½ c. sour cream and stir into beets. Add 2–3 T. water and bring to boil. Remove from heat. Season to taste with salt, sugar, and cider vinegar. Simmer covered on low heat another 5–10 min.

BEETS WITH APPLES
buraczki z jabłkami

Prepare cooked, grated beets as above, place in pot, and add 2 peeled, coarsely or finely grated tart cooking apples. Drench with 2 T. flour lightly browned in salt pork or butter (as above). Add 2–3 T. meat stock, milk or water, mix ingredients, cover pot, bring to boil, then reduce heat and cook 10 min. Season to taste with salt and sugar. (If the apples have not made the beets sufficiently tart, add a sprinkle of lemon juice or pinch of citric acid crystals). Simmer covered several min. longer. *Optional*: Stir in a heaping T. sour cream.

BEETS WITH APPLES DIET STYLE
buraczki z jabłkami dietetyczne

Those who love beets and know how healthy they are, but don't need the extra calories or avoid such things as roux and sour cream, should enjoy this recipe. Polish dieticians recommend it to patients who must restrict their diet to foods low in fat and easy to digest.

Scrub 2 lbs. beets and cook in water with skins left or removed. (Beets cooked after peeling have a less earthy taste, are more mild, and possibly a trace more digestible!) Cooking time may be anywhere from 1–1½ hrs. or more, depending on the size and age of beets. Cooking them in a microwave or pressure cooker will cut the time considerably. When beets are cooked, drain, rinse with cold water, drain again, and grate fine. Add 2 finely grated cooking apples, mix well, cover, and bring to boil, then reduce heat and simmer several min. Season to taste with a little salt and sugar. If you prefer a thicker, creamier consistency, but must avoid sour cream, dissolve 1½–2 T. flour in ¼ c. milk, stir into beets, and simmer briefly.

OLD POLISH-STYLE BEETS FOR WILD-GAME DISHES
buraczki po staropolsku do dziczyzny

Following a dish meant for convalescents and delicate eaters, we present a completely different beet recipe, a hearty Old Polish specialty. Scrub, cook in water, or bake in oven 2 lbs. beets. Peel under cold running water, grate coarsely, and place in pot. In saucepan simmer 1 heaping T. diced salt pork until golden and add 1 grated onion, stirring until tender. Stir in 3 T. flour and brown slightly. Stirring constantly, add ½ c. meat stock, bring to boil, and pour over beets. Add 1 bud mashed garlic and simmer covered on low heat 5 min. Salt to taste, add ½–1 t. sugar, and 1–2 T. dry red wine. Cover and cook on very low heat another 10 min. If necessary, sour to taste with a little lemon or pickle juice. *Optional*: For creamier beets, stir in 1 heaping T. sour cream. This and the other beets presented here are traditionally served with beef and wild-game dishes. *Variation*: ¼–½ t. crushed caraway seeds or dill seeds, ¼–½ t. hunter's seasoning or 1 T. fresh chopped dill will add an interesting flavor twist to the above beet recipes.

LENTEN BEETS WITH RAISINS
buraczki postne z rodzynkami

Peel and grate your boiled or baked beets (2 lbs.). Finely chop 1 onion and simmer in 2 T. oil or butter until golden and tender. Soak ½ c. raisins in warm water 10 min. then drain. Add onions and raisins to beets, mix, cover, and simmer on low heat about 15 min., stirring frequently to prevent scorching. For a sweeter taste add 1–2 t. sugar and 1–2 T. court bouillon if mixture appears too thick. Season to taste with salt and a little vinegar. A Polish cookbook published in the late 19th century recommends this dish as the perfect accompaniment for such fast-day dishes as fried fish or fried mushrooms.

QUICK & EASY HURRY-UP BEETS
buraczki naprędce

When you don't have the time to scrub, cook, and peel fresh beets from scratch, use whole canned beets. Simply grate coarsely and proceed according to recipe of choice. Save the canned-beet liquid for soup or sauces.

STEWED KOHLRABI
kalarepa duszona

The tastiest of these are the season's first kohlrabi between the size of a golfball and large plum or nectarine. Wash, peel, and rinse 2 lbs. kohlrabi. Slice, dice, or cut into sticks, scald with boiling meat stock to just barely cover, add 2–3 T. butter, 1 T. sugar, and cook covered 10 min., then uncover and continue cooking another 10 min. or until tender. If necessary, replace evaporated liquid with a little boiling water. If most of the moisture has not been absorbed by the vegetables, drain, sprinkle with flour, stir to coat evenly, and simmer briefly. Salt to taste, add a bit more sugar if needed, and serve garnished with chopped parsley and/or dill. *Variation:* For creamed kohlrabi, instead of sprinkling with flour, fork-blend ½ c. sour cream with 2 T. flour, stir into vegetables, and simmer briefly.

BOILED KOHLRABI WITH TOPPINGS OF CHOICE
kalarepa z wody okraszana

Wash, peel, and rinse 2 lbs. kohlrabi, dice or cut into sticks, cover with salted boiling water, add 1 T. sugar, and cook 20–25 min. or until tender. As with all vegetables of the turnip family, cook part of the time uncovered to release the strong odor. Drain and transfer to serving platter. Drench with either the delicate and elegant Polonaise topping (bread crumbs browned in butter), the heartier country style golden salt-pork nuggets and drippings (*skwarki*) or simply melted butter plus a generous sprinkling of fragrant, freshly chopped dill.

COOKED RADISHES DIFFERENT WAYS
rzodkiewka na różne sposoby

If you think of radishes as only a crispy salad ingredient, you've got another thing coming! They are also excellent as a cooked vegetable worthy of the most elegant banquet table. Remove the stems and tails from 2 lbs. radishes (if still attached) and wash well. Place in pot. Scald with salted boiling water to cover, add 1–2 T. sugar, and cook (preferably uncovered most of the time) about 20 min. or until tender. Replace water of it boils away. Drain and transfer to serving platter.Top with bread crumbs browned in butter or melted butter and chopped dill and/ or parsley. *Variation:* Serve in any of the ways recommended for kohlrabi (above). Cooked radishes are the ideal accompaniment to tenderloin steak (polędwica).

STEWED TURNIPS
rzepa duszona

Wash, peel, and rinse well 2 lbs. young turnips. Dice, place in pot, and cover with salted boiling water and add 1 T. sugar. Cook 20 min. or until tender, at least half of the time uncovered. Drain. In saucepan combine 2 T. melted butter with 1 T. flour, heat and stir, but do not brown. Add several T. milk (enough to get a thick, pourable sauce) and 1 T. sugar and simmer until smooth and bubbly. Season with a little salt if desired (the turnips were cooked in salted water so they may be salty enough), some white pepper and (optional) a pinch of citric-acid crystals, simmer briefly until smooth and bubbly. Pour over cooked, drained turnips, mix, and simmer covered 5–10 min. or so. Good with pork dishes.

RUTABAGA PUREE (WITH POTATOES) MAZURIAN STYLE
brukiew po mazursku

Wash, peel, and cut into cubes 1¼ lbs. rutabaga. Place in pot, scald with 1 c. boiling milk and enough boiling water to cover, add ½ t. salt, 2 t. sugar, and cook about 20–25 min. (some of the time uncovered) until rutabaga is only half done. Add ¾ lb. peeled, cubed potatoes, and continue cooking until both rutabaga and potatoes are done. Cook covered, adding a little more water if most evaporates, but not too much. The vegetables should not "swim" in water but simmer in enough liquid to prevent them from burning. Mash well and drench on serving platter generously with fried bacon bits and their drippings. Garnish with chopped parsley and/or dill.

STEWED RUTABAGA
brukiew duszona

Wash, peel, and cut into cubes 2 lbs. rutabaga. Place in pot and cover with plenty of cold water. Bring to boil and allow to cook 30 sec., then drain. Cover with hot meat stock, add 1 t. salt, 2 t. sugar and cook on low heat 20–40 min. or until tender. Drain. In saucepan combine 2 T. melted butter and 1 T. or so flour, simmer briefly, stirring to get a smooth paste, and add to rutabaga. *Optional*: 1–2 T. meat stock or milk may be added to roux in saucepan and briefly simmered before adding to pot. Simmer rutabagas covered on very low heat several min. *Note*: The previous recipe (rutabaga puree) as well as the other vegetables of the turnip family (turnips, kohlrabi) may also be started by placing the diced or cubed vegetables in a large amount of cold water, bringing to boil, and draining. Then proceed as indicated. This helps diminish the strong, pungent cabbage odor these vegetables sometimes have.

PARSNIPS WITH POLONAISE TOPPING OR ROUX
pasternak z tartą bułką lub zasmażką

Wash 2 lbs. parsnips, peel very thin or scrape, rinse well, and slice like carrots. Place in pot, scald with plenty of boiling water, bring to boil, remove from heat, bring to boil again, and drain. Cover with hot meat stock, add ¼ t. or more salt (depending on how salty the meat stock is) and 2–3 grains allspice. Cook on low heat 15–20 min. or until tender. Drain. Drench with bread crumbs browned in butter. Or, in saucepan combine 1 T. melted butter and 1 T. flour. Add 1–3 T. meat stock and simmer briefly, stirring into a smooth sauce. Salt & pepper to taste and pour over cooked parsnips. Simmer briefly. Either way, this strong-flavored vegetable nicely contrasts with rather bland boiled beef or tongue. In classic Polish cookery, the parsnips are placed on a platter and surrounded with slices of the beef or tongue. Other cooked vegetables are also served this way, especially on formal occasions.

COOKED LEEKS
pory z wody

Cut away the green tops from 2 lbs. leeks and cut off the "whiskers" at the root's base if still attached. (The reason for the "if still attached" remark recurring now and again is that we don't know whether you'll be getting field-fresh leeks at a farmer roadside stand or in a supermarket produce department where many vegetables come already trimmed, cleaned, and packaged.) Place only the white bottoms in pot, covered with salted boiling water, add 1 t. sugar and cook about 20–25 min. or until tender. This depends on the size and freshness of the leeks. Drain, remove to platter, and drench with Polonaise topping or béchamel sauce. *Note*: The green leek tops are too stringy to eat but, used as a soup green, they will give a nice flavor to most any soup, so freeze them for future use.

BATTER-FRIED LEEKS
pory smażone w cieście

Trim and cook 2 lbs. leeks as above, but reduce cooking time to 8–10 min. Meanwhile, in bowl beat 2 eggs, gradually adding ⅔ c. flour and ½ c. sour cream. Add ¼ t. salt and ⅓ t. baking powder and mix into a nice, thick batter. Drain the leeks and dry on absorbent paper. When cool, slice in half lengthwise. Impale each piece on a fork, dip in batter, and fry in fairly hot oil ¼ inch deep in skillet. When nicely golden brown, drain on absorbent paper quickly so they don't get cold, and transfer to platter. Serve with hot tomato or sour-cream sauce on the side.

BREADED FRIED CELERIAC
selery smażone w panierze

Scrub 2 lbs. celeriac roots with brush under running water. Peel off skin, rinse, place in pot, scald with 1 c. hot milk and enough salted boiling water to cover. Cook about 25–30 min. or until almost done. Drain. Slice into rounds ¼ inch thick. Sprinkle with salt & pepper, dredge in flour, dip in beaten eggs, and roll in fine bread crumbs, pressing in breading with hand. Fry in hot oil ¼ inch deep in skillet until golden on both sides, then reduce heat and cook about 5 min. longer. Drain on absorbent paper and serve immediately while still hot.

CREAMED ONIONS
cebula w śmietanie

Peel 2 lbs. onions of roughly equal size. Cut larger onions into quarters, smaller ones in half (very small ones may be left whole). Scald with salted boiling water, add 1 t. sugar, bring to boil uncovered, then cover and cook on low heat 25–35 min. or until tender. Drain. Dot with butter, sprinkle with flour, and toss gently to coat evenly. Stir in a heaping T. sour cream, mix to blend ingredients and simmer covered on low heat another 5 min. Sprinkle with chopped parsley and/or dill.

BATTER-FRIED ONIONS
cebula smażona w cieście

Beat 2 eggs, stirring in ½ c. sour cream, about ⅔ c. flour, ⅛ t. baking powder, ¼ t. salt, and several T. beer. The batter should be smooth and thick—thicker than for crêpes (naleśniki). Peel 1½ lbs. medium onions of equal size and slice about ¼ inch thick. Dip onion slices in batter and fry in about ¼ inch hot oil to a nice golden brown on both sides. Test one to see if the onion is as tender as you want. If not, simmer a bit longer. Drain on absorbent paper and salt & pepper. Serve on the side with meat dishes, as a meal in itself, drenched with tomato sauce, and a fresh salad, or as a tasty snack anytime. Cold beer, sparkling wine, or other fizzy beverages make the perfect accompaniment.

FLOURED PUMPKIN
dynia oprószana

Peel and wash 2 lbs. pumpkin. Cut into small cubes, scald with salted boiling water to barely cover, add 1 T. butter, and cook covered about 10 min. or until tender but still firm.

(Overcooking will make it mushy!) Remove from heat, sprinkle with flour, toss carefully to coat evenly, add 1 t. Maggi seasoning, dot with butter, and simmer briefly. Sprinkle with 1 T. or so chopped parsley. Salt & pepper if desired.

CREAMED PUMPKIN & TOMATOES
dynia z pomidorami w śmietanie

As a cooked vegetable, pumpkin is on the bland side, so it is often combined with zestier ingredients for added tang. Cut several washed tomatoes (about ½ lb.) into cubes or quarters, scald with ½ c. boiling water, add 1 T. butter, and simmer covered 10 min. Then force through sieve. Cook pumpkin as in previous recipe and combine with sieved tomatoes. Salt to taste. Fork-blend ½ c. sour cream and 2 T. flour and add to vegetables. Mix and simmer briefly. Garnish with chopped parsley or dill.

CREAMED PUMPKIN & PEPPERS
dynia z papryką w śmietanie

Thinly slice 1 onion and place in pot. Wash, clean, and cut up 2 green or yellow peppers. Scald with ½ c. boiling salted water, add 1 t. sugar, 1 T. butter, and simmer covered on low heat until nearly done. Add 1½ lbs. diced fresh pumpkin and simmer covered another 8–10 min. or until done. Add a little more boiling water if needed. Fork-blend ½ c. sour cream and 2 T. flour and add to vegetables. Simmer briefly. Salt & pepper and garnish with chopped chives or other greens of choice.

PUMPKIN & APPLES
dynia z jabłkami

Peel and wash 1½ lbs. pumpkin, cut into small cubes, scald with ½ c. water, and cook covered until done but still slightly firm. While it cooks, melt 2 T. butter in skillet, add several (about 1 lb.) peeled, sliced cooking apples, several T. boiling water, and simmer covered until tender. Combine with cooked pumpkin, sprinkle with flour (about 1 T.), dot with butter, and mix gently to coat. Salt & pepper to taste. (*Optional*: Add 1 bud mashed garlic.) Bring to gentle boil and serve sprinkled with chopped dill.

SUMMER SQUASH OR ZUCCHINI DIFFERENT WAYS
kabaczki lub cukinie na różne sposoby

Summer squash and zucchini are also rather bland-tasting vegetables and can be prepared according to any of the recipes given for pumpkin (above).

FRIED ZUCCHINI & ONIONS
cukinie smażone z cebulą

Wash 2 lbs. zucchini and slice ¼ inch thick. (They should not be peeled, as the skin keeps the zucchini from falling apart and is fully edible when cooked.) Sprinkle the rounds with salt & pepper, dredge in flour, shaking off excess and lightly brown on both sides in hot oil, then reduce and cook a bit longer. Transfer to plate lined with absorbent paper, cover with another piece of the paper and keep warm in low oven. In the oil in which the zucchini was cooked, cook 2–3 onions sliced wafer thin until tender and golden. Transfer zucchini to serving platter, interlace with the fried onions, salt & pepper to taste, and garnish with chopped parsley. *Note*: Zucchini made its appearance in Poland around the 1970s and over the next two decades, gradually caught on among many home gardeners, cooks, and home canners. The latter often use it to make marinated pickles and relishes in place of the more traditional cucumbers.

FRIED EGGPLANT
bakłażany smażone

Wash and peel 2 lbs. eggplant and cut into ½ inch slices. Dredge in flour, dip in beaten eggs, and roll in bread crumbs, pressing in breading so it doesn't fall off during frying. Fry in hot oil about ¼ inch deep to a nice golden brown on both sides. Drain in absorbent paper, salt & pepper to taste, and serve immediately. *Optional*: Before breading the eggplant, rub each slice with a little mashed garlic (1–2 buds should suffice for a 2 lb. eggplant). With dilled new potatoes and a crispy salad, this is a tasty summer meal in itself and a great favorite in the Strybel home. We usually sprinkle the eggplant with Parmesan cheese on our dinner plates.

EGGPLANT STEWED WITH TOMATOES
bakłażany duszone z pomidorami

Wash and peel 1½–2 lbs. eggplant, cut into cubes, sprinkle with salt & pepper, and brown on all sides in a little hot oil. Separately scald 3–4 tomatoes with boiling water and peel when they are cool enough handle. Dice or cube the tomatoes and add to eggplant. Remove from heat, add 2 buds garlic mashed with salt, mix lightly, cover and simmer on low heat about 20 min. Sprinkle with a little flour if vegetables are too soupy and simmer briefly. Garnish generously with chopped garden greens of choice before serving.

STEWED CUCUMBERS AS A COOKED VEGETABLE
ogórki duszone na jarzynkę

Although cucumbers are usually eaten raw in salads or cured into pickles, they also make a nice cooked vegetable. One 19th-century recipe for these goes as follows: Wash and peel 2 lbs. cucumbers, slice or dice, sprinkle with 1 T. or slightly more salt and let stand at room temp. 30 min. Drain, pouring away the liquid. In skillet melt 1 T. butter and simmer in it 1 finely chopped onion until golden and tender. Add the cucumbers and simmer until they are tender. (Test a piece to see if it is no longer crunchy.) Sprinkle with a little flour, add ¼ c. meat stock and simmer covered a few min. Garnish with chopped dill. *Variation*: Instead of sprinkling with flour and adding meat stock, fork-blend ½ c. sour cream and 1 T. flour, add to cooked cucumbers, and simmer briefly. Season with a little freshly ground pepper.

STEWED PICKLES
duszone ogórki kiszone

Peel 2 lbs. brine-cured dill pickles and slice, dice, or cube. In 2 T. melted butter simmer 1 finely chopped onion until golden and tender. Add the pickles, mix with onion, and simmer covered several min. longer. Taste your stewed pickles before adding any salt & pepper, because they may already be seasoned enough. This tart and tangy side dish complements rather bland-tasting meats like boiled beef or tongue.

SPINACH POLISH STYLE
szpinak po polsku

If you are using field-fresh spinach purchased at a roadside stand or farmers' market, it must be washed very thoroughly to remove all sand and the stems should be cut off. The packaged spinach sold in supermarket produce departments has been trimmed and washed but still should be rinsed well. Cook 2 lbs. spinach in boiling water to cover 5 min., drain in colander, and press out all moisture. Chop spinach very fine or grind. In pot or skillet melt 2–3 T. butter, stir in 2 T. flour, and simmer without browning. Stir in 1–2 buds crushed garlic, ⅔ c. sour cream, and the spinach. Remove from heat, stir in 1–3 beaten eggs, mix well, and simmer on low heat several min. or until spinach is fully cooked. Do not overcook. Salt & pepper to taste. A sprinkle of lemon juice will provide added zest. Perhaps the reason many Americans don't care for spinach is because it is often simply boiled and served. Doctored up the Polish way, spinach becomes a very tasty and interesting dish, and eggs (in one form or another) are nearly always included.

STEWED (CREAMED) SPINACH
szpinak zasmażany

Bring a large pot of water to boil and add 2 lbs. washed, trimmed spinach. Cook on high uncovered 2–3 min. or until tender. Drain well, pressing out moisture. Combine 4 T. flour with 3 T. melted butter or lard and stir in 1 c. milk (or ½ c. sweet cream) and bring to boil, stirring so no lumps form. Add the drained spinach, 1 t. sugar, 1–2 buds crushed garlic, and salt to taste. Cook several min. This can be a meal in itself. Simply transfer spinach to platter and surround with coddled or fried (sunny-side-up) eggs. Or, garnish with 2–3 chopped, hard-boiled eggs and plenty of chopped dill. *Variation*: A handful of young radish leaves may be cooked together with the spinach, then chopped or ground and stewed as above.

STEWED SORREL & SPINACH
szczaw duszony ze szpinakiem

Although this sour, spinach-like grass is best known in Polish cookery in the form of cream of sorrel soup, served with hard-boiled egg wedges, it also makes a zesty cooked vegetable. Cooked alone, it may be too tart for many, but combining it with some spinach helps to blunt its sour edge. Cook 1 lb. washed and chopped spinach in boiling water about 3 min. Wash 1 lb. sorrel well, chop very fine, and add to 3 T. melted butter in skillet. Toss lightly, simmer on low heat, and stir frequently until tender (about 5–10 min.) Add the cooked, drained spinach, mix well, and remove from heat. Stir in ½ c. sour cream fork-blended with 2 T. flour and season to taste with salt and a little sugar. Simmer briefly. An excellent accompaniment to veal dishes.

STEWED SORREL & LETTUCE
szczaw duszony z sałatą

Wash well and chop fine 1 lb. sorrel and 1 head Boston lettuce. Rinse again in plenty of cold water, drain in colander, and press out moisture. In skillet melt 2 T. butter, add the greens, toss well, cover, and simmer on low heat until tender. Remove from heat. Sprinkle with a little flour, add about 1 T. sugar and 2–3 T. sour cream, mix well, simmer briefly, and salt to taste.

STEWED BABY BEET GREENS
botwina/boćwina duszona

Unless you have your own vegetable garden, you may have trouble finding these greens on the market, except perhaps in certain big-city ethnic food stores. Use only the greens of immature beets, whose roots have not yet developed or are no larger than the size of a very small radish. Wash 2 lbs. baby beet greens very well to remove all sand, cut away the stems, chop fine, place in pot, and scald with salted boiling water or boiling meat stock to cover. Cook uncovered 5 min., then cover and cook several min. longer or until tender. Drain, add to skillet in which 2–3 T. butter have been melted, toss, and simmer a bit longer. Sprinkle with flour and stir in 2–3 T. sour cream. Mix and simmer briefly. Adjust to taste with salt, pepper, sugar, and lemon juice.

MIXED VEGETABLES
mieszanka warzywna

Peel 1 small rutabaga and 2–3 kohlrabi, cut into balls with a small melon scoop, place in pot, add 4 c. cold water, 1 T. salt and 1 T. sugar, bring to boil, and cook uncovered 10 min. Drain. Cut 2–3 peeled potatoes and 1–2 large carrots into balls with melon scoop. Melt 3 T. butter in skillet, add the vegetable balls, and simmer briefly, stirring to coat vegetables. Add 2 c. hot meat stock, 2 t. sugar, salt & pepper, and 2 T. chopped dill, bring to boil, then reduce heat and simmer until vegetables are tender. Sprinkle with flour to thicken sauce and simmer briefly. Feel free to add a small can of peas, drained. Only your imagination and the leftover cooked vegetables you have on hand limit what can be done with this dish. Cooked Brussels sprouts or cooked green or wax beans cut into 1 inch pieces are an excellent addition, as is cauliflower broken up into flowerlets.

APPLES AS A COOKED "VEGETABLE"
jabłka na jarzynkę

Peel, core and cut into halves or quarters 2 lbs. cooking apples. Place in pot, add several T. stock, 1 T. butter, a pinch of sugar and salt and (optional) a sprinkling of marjoram. Cook covered on med. heat until tender (several min.) and serve with pork dishes or fried fish.

PEARS AS A COOKED "VEGETABLE"
gruszki na jarzynkę

Peel 5–8 firm, slightly underripe pears, preferably of a less sweet variety. Cut into quarters, remove the core and seeds, place in pot, scald with boiling water to cover, and cool until tender but not mushy. Drain and drench on serving platter with butter-browned bread crumbs (Polonaise topping). We thus conclude our survey of Polish-style cooked vegetables with a dish that today is somewhat forgotten, but certainly deserves to be revived. Cooked pears are the perfect companion to all pork dishes and are also good with poultry.

FRESH DINNER SALADS

The main reason for this chapter's modest length is that we have included another entitled COLD-APPETIZER & SUPPER SALADS at the start of the book among the cold-appetizer and starter courses. They could, of course, have all been lumped together, but we felt that would have disrupted the chronological order in which courses are ordinarily served: appetizers, soups, main courses and their accompaniments (cooked vegetables and fresh salads), etc.

Modern-day Polish clearly distinguishes between the two. Cold-table salads containing mainly pre-cooked ingredients are called *sałatki* (singular: *sałatka*), whereas those made largely from fresh greens and raw vegetables are referred to as *surówki* (literally: raw stuff). As the two chapter titles indicate, each serves a different purpose, the former being served with cold dishes and the latter to accompany hot dinner courses.

Today the most typical Polish fresh salads would be *mizeria* (sliced cucumber salad), *zielona sałata* (lettuce), alone or with a few other veggies, and *sałatka z pomidorów* (tomato salad) which is really little more than sliced tomatoes garnishes with chopped onions and seasoned with salt, pepper, and lemon juice. For some unknown reason the term *sałatka* has been retained for fresh tomatoes, although it is now mainly reserved for pre-cooked salads as indicated above.

Salads remain a largely seasonal dish, since fresh greens are truly plentiful and moderately priced only between late spring to early autumn. In the colder months the root crops take over, forming the basis for a variety of grated-vegetable salads. Our winter favorites include grated carrots, apples & horseradish, leek salad, any of the various cole slaws, and sauerkraut salad.

Admittedly a diet of nothing but Polish-style one- and two-vegetable salads could be pretty monotonous, but they can provide a convenient alternative when the crisper drawer is nearly bare. Perhaps you will even find some of them to be interesting alternatives to the same old tossed salad with bottled dressing.

We suggest you try the radish salads—one savory, the other slightly sweet—as well as the tangy green-onion salad, the perfect accompaniment to bland-tasting meat and fish. In fact, as you will see, onions, dill pickles, apples, pears, sauerkraut, beets, celeriac, leeks, hard-boiled eggs, and many other ingredients can go to make genuine Polish-style salads that add crunch, zest, and nutrients to any hot meal.

On a final note, dinner salads, as their name implies, are always eaten during, not before or after, the main hot course. When greens and raw vegetables were first introduced by Poland's Italian-born Queen Bona Sforza in the 16th century, most Poles wanted no part of such "rabbit food" at any time of day.

* * *

PLAIN LETTUCE SALAD
zielona sałata

Break off the stem from 1–3 heads Boston lettuce to separate leaves and wash well in cold running water. Drain and place on serving platter. Fork-blend ½–⅔ c. sour cream to liquify and season to taste with a little salt, sugar, and lemon juice or vinegar. Dress lettuce with sauce just before serving. *Note*: This recipe is meant to serve 4–5, so the number of heads depends on their size, which can vary greatly.

LETTUCE & RADISH SALAD
zielona sałata z rzodkiewką

Proceed exactly as above, but intersperse lettuce leaves with thin radish slices in whatever quantity you desire. *Note*: For variety add ½ a peeled, thinly sliced cucumber.

LETTUCE & EGG SALAD
zielona sałata z jajami

Garnish lettuce leaves on platter with hard-boiled egg slices, sprinkling each with a little pepper and/or paprika. *Variation*: Instead of sour cream, an excellent dressing for this salad is made by fork-blending ⅓ c. sour cream with ⅓ c. mayonnaise. Use as is or season to taste with salt, white pepper, lemon juice, or vinegar and (if desired) a sprinkle of sugar. *Note*: This is a classic Polish salad.

LETTUCE & GARDEN GREEN SALAD
zielona sałata z zieleniną

Prepare lettuce as in any of the above recipes but garnish generously with finely chopped green onions, chives, and/or dill. Dress with sour cream or sour cream-mayonnaise sauce.

LETTUCE & TOMATO SALAD
zielona sałata z pomidorami

Place washed lettuce leaves on platter as for plain lettuce salad and top with smallish tomato wedges. If tomatoes are a thick-skinned variety, first plunge into boiling water for a min. or so, then peel under cold running water before cutting into wedges. Dress with sour cream or sour cream-mayonnaise sauce. *Variation*: For added zest, intersperse tomato wedges with wafer-thin onion slices or top with chopped green onions before dressing.

SPRING LETTUCE SALAD
zielona sałata wiosenna

Ideally you should have small heads of young Boston lettuce, allowing 1–2 heads per serving. If only mature lettuce is available, after washing and draining, cut leaves into strips. Top with 1 small peeled cucumber and 1 bunch radishes—both diced—and garnish with 2 chopped hard-boiled eggs. Salt & pepper, drench with ⅔ c. fork-blended sour cream and garnish with fresh chopped dill. *Note*: If you can get baby radishes with their greens left intact, wash greens well, trim away stems, chop fine and add to salad.

LETTUCE WITH VINAIGRETTE (LEMON & OIL)
zielona sałata z winegretem

Instead of a creamy sauce, dress any of the above lettuce salads with a quick & easy vinaigrette whipped up as follows. With fork or wire whisk beat in cup 4–5 T. olive oil (or other oil), 4 T. cold pre-boiled water, juice of ½ lemon, 1 t. sugar, ¼ t. salt, and several pinches pepper. *Variation*: To sauce add 1 bud mashed garlic and/or 1 t. sharp brown mustard. *Note*: For other lettuce dressings, please consult the chapter on sauces and toppings.

LETTUCE WITH YOGURT DRESSING
sałata w jogurcie

Wash and drain lettuce leaves and place on platter. Soak a heaping T. raisins in 1 c. warm water until they plump, then drain well. Coarsely grate 1 peeled apple, chop fine 1 bunch green onions, and combine with 1 c. plain regular or low-fat yogurt. Mix well and season to taste with salt, pepper, and a little lemon juice. Dress lettuce with sauce, sprinkle with raisins, and garnish with chopped parsley.

LETTUCE & BACON POZNAŃ STYLE
sałata z boczkiem po poznańsku

For this salad it is best to use a firmer variety than Boston lettuce, such as that all-American standard: iceberg (head) lettuce. Wash leaves, drain, break up into pieces, and place on platter. Dissolve 1 T. sugar and ½ t. salt in ¼ c. boiling water, add 2–4 T. vinegar and ⅛ t. pepper. *(Optional:* 1–2 pinches marjoram or ground caraway may also be added.) Dice 2–3 inch square of slab bacon and fry up in skillet until nuggets are golden brown, add 1 T. grated onion and vinegar mixture. Be careful you don't get splattered, as the vinegar and hot drippings will churn up a storm! Immediately scald lettuce with boiling mixture. *Note*: This very tasty concoction is something between a fresh salad and a cooked vegetable; with a shirted egg or two and some boiled potatoes it can be a complete meal.

CLASSIC POLISH CUCUMBER SALAD
mizeria klasyczna

Peel and slice thin 2–3 cucumbers and place into serving bowl. Sprinkle with salt & pepper and a little sugar and lemon juice, garnish with chopped dill (optional), toss lightly, and drench with ½–¾ fork-blended sour cream. *Note:* This has long been one of Poland's most popular summer salads, and it's the perfect company to roast stuffed chicken. It should be prepared just prior to serving, as the cucumbers release a lot of liquid if allowed to stand any length of time.

CUCUMBER SALAD ANOTHER WAY
mizeria inaczej

Peel, slice thin, and place in bowl 2–3 cucumbers. Salt generously and toss. Let stand at room temp. at least 30 min. Pour off liquid that has formed, season as above, and dress with sour cream. *Note*: Cucumbers prepared this way are less crunchy and more tender, and some claim they cause less bloating. It is also true that many of their healthful nutrients are lost when the liquid is poured off.

CUCUMBER SALAD WITH VINEGAR
mizeria z octem

Peel and slice thin 2–3 cucumbers. Sprinkle with salt, sugar, and chopped dill, and splash with 1 or more spoonfuls vinegar. The amount of individual flavoring ingredients is strictly a matter of personal preference. *Variation*: Toss 1 small chopped onion or several chopped green onions with cucumbers.

CUCUMBER SALAD RZESZÓW STYLE
mizeria po rzeszowsku

Peel and slice thin 2 cucumbers, add 1 bunch sliced radishes, and 1 bunch chopped green onions. Salt & pepper, add 1–3 c. grated farmer cheese, toss ingredients, and lace with as much sour cream as you like. Rather than just a salad to accompany a main course, this light but nutritious dish can be a spring or summer meal in itself when served with rye bread and unsalted butter for breakfast and dilled, buttered new potatoes for dinner.

TRADITIONAL POLISH TOMATO SALAD
sałatka z pomidorów tradycyjna

Slice about 1 lb. tomatoes and place slices next to one another on serving platter. Sprinkle with salt, pepper, a little lemon juice or vinegar, and top each slice with 1 t. or so finely minced onions, wafer-thin onion slices, or finely chopped chives. Drench tomatoes prepared as above with about ½ c. fork-blended sour cream. If you do, serve immediately so salad does not become soupy.

TOMATO & CUCUMBER SALAD
sałatka z pomidorów i ogórków

Peel and slice 2 cucumbers. Slice tomatoes whose slices are roughly the same size as the cucumbers and slice onions of similar size wafer thin. There should be about as many cucumbers as tomato and onion slices. On serving platter alternate tomato, cucumber, and onion slices in even parallel rows. The number of rows will depend on the width of platter. Sprinkle with salt, pepper, lemon juice (or vinegar), and a little sugar and dress with fork-blended sour cream (about ½–¾ c.). Garnish with chopped dill and/or chives. *Note*: This is one of the author's favorite summer salads. *Variation:* Instead of just sour cream, the sour cream-mayonnaise combination is excellent. Also try it with vinaigrette.

TOMATO & PICKLE SALAD
sałatka z pomidorów i kiszonych ogórków

Slice 4 small tomatoes, 2 brine-cured dill pickles, and 2 onions no larger than the tomatoes. Arrange on platter in rows alternating as follows: tomato, onion, tomato, pickle, tomato, onion, etc. Sprinkle with a little salt and (optional) sugar and drench with about ½ c. fork-blended sour cream, sour cream-mayonnaise combination, or just mayonnaise. Garnish with chopped parsley. This tangy salad is a natural with rather mild-tasting foods like boiled meat or poultry, poached or fried fish.

PICKLE SALAD
sałatka z kiszonych ogórków

This is the kind of salad most people make the first time simply because they have no fresh salad greens on hand, but often it becomes an immediate hit and a regular item on the family menu. Simply slice 4–5 brine-cured dill pickles and 2–3 small onions. Alternate pickle and onion slices in rows on platter and drench with about ½ c. mayonnaise-sour cream sauce. Brine-cured pickles are usually sufficiently salty, so additional salt will probably not be needed. This is a very good accompaniment to boiled beef or tongue. *Note*: Vinegar-cured pickles (like the supermarket variety) may also be used, but the brine-cured ones are better.

RADISH SALAD
surówka z rzodkiewki

Slice thin 2–3 bunches radishes with knife or on slicer blade of hand-held vegetable grater or, if you prefer, grate coarsely. Sprinkle with salt, dress with about ½ c. liquified sour cream, and garnish with 1 T. or so chopped dill.

SWEET RADISH SALAD
surówka z rzodkiewki na słodko

Slice or grate 2–3 bunches radishes as above. Place in serving dish, sprinkle with about 1 t. lemon juice, dust through sieve with 1–2 T. powdered sugar, and drench with ½ c. fork-blended sour cream. *Note*: This salad beautifully complements pork dishes.

LEEK SALAD
surówka z porów

Slice 4–5 leeks (only the white portion) into rounds as thinly as possible. Sprinkle with lemon juice, salt and a little sugar and dress with sour cream-mayonnaise sauce.

LEEK & APPLE SALAD
surówka z porów i jabłek

Thinly slice white portion of 2–3 leeks into rounds. Peel and coarsely grate 2 apples and combine ingredients. Sprinkle with lemon juice, salt (sparingly), and sugar, and dress with ½ c. fork-blended mayonnaise. *Note*: For a gourmet touch, sprinkle salad with several T. chopped walnuts. *Variation:* Use pears instead of apples for an interesting new flavor twist.

CHICORY (BELGIAN ENDIVE) SALAD
surówka z cykorii

Cut 3–4 heads Belgian endive into strips, but be sure to discard the extremely bitter base portion near the stem. Sprinkle with lemon juice, salt and sugar, dress with ½ c. mayonnaise, and garnish with 1 T. chopped parsley. A t. sharp brown mustard may be blended into mayonnaise. *Variation*: 2 peeled, finely chopped apples may be added to salad to mellow the chicory's bitter edge, which not everybody (including our son Leszek) enjoys. In fact, the recipe below was developed by the authoress to disguise the chicory.

MIXED FRUIT & VEGETABLE SALAD
surówka warzywno-owocowa

After washing and trimming vegetables, dice into pieces of roughly equal size. Use 1 head Belgian endive, 1–2 leeks, 2 firm tomatoes (preferably skinned after scalding), 1 peeled cucumber, 1 small pepper (optional), and 2 peeled apples or pears (or 1 apple and 1 pear). Toss ingredients lightly, season with salt, pepper, sugar, and lemon juice and dress with sour cream-mayonnaise sauce.

GREEN-ONION SALAD
surówka z młodej cebulki

Chop fine 2–3 bunches green onions. Season with salt (rather generously) and a little pepper, sprinkle with about 1 T. vinegar, add 2–3 chopped, hard-boiled eggs. Toss to blend ingredients. Season to taste with salt, pepper, sugar, and lemon juice, and dress with mayonnaise, mayonnaise-sour cream combination, or sour cream with 1 t. brown mustard added.

COLE SLAW
surówka z białej kapusty

Discard wilted outer leaves from 1 small head cabbage. Grate cabbage, combine with 2 peeled, finely chopped or coarsely grated apples and 2–3 chopped hard-boiled eggs. Toss ingredients. Season to taste with salt, pepper, sugar and lemon juice and dress with mayonnaise, mayonnaise-sour cream combination or sour cream with 1 t. prepared brown mustard added. *Optional*: Add 1 grated carrot.

COLE SLAW ANOTHER WAY
surówka z białej kapusty inaczej

Shred 1 small or ½ a large cabbage and combine with 2 grated carrots and 1 finely chopped onion. A coarsely grated, peeled apple may be added (optional). In cup fork-blend 4 T. olive oil or other oil, juice of 1 lemon, 1 t. brown mustard, and salt, pepper, and sugar to taste. A bud crushed garlic may be added if desired. Pour sauce over cabbage and let stand at least 30 min. before serving. Garnish with about 1 T. chopped parsley.

RED CABBAGE SALAD
surówka z czerwonej kapusty

Shred 1 small head red cabbage, place in pot, scald with boiling water to cover, and, when boiling resumes, parboil 1–2 min. Drain and sprinkle with lemon juice. Add 1 peeled, coarsely grated apple and 1 small finely chopped onion. Toss ingredients, adjust to taste with salt, pepper, and sugar, and dress with 4 T. olive oil or other salad oil. A typical side dish with pork dishes, goose and duck.

RED CABBAGE & LEEK SALAD
surówka z czerwonej kapusty i porów

Do not shred but grate 1 small head red cabbage and combine with 1 finely chopped leek (white part only). Mix immediately with sauce made by fork-blending ⅔ c. mayonnaise, ⅔ c. sour cream, 1 T. brown mustard, plus lemon juice, salt, and sugar to taste.

SAUERKRAUT SALAD
surówka z kiszonej kapusty

Drain 1 pt. sauerkraut, reserving liquid. Rinse in cold water, drain in colander, pressing out moisture. Chop and sprinkle lightly with sugar. Combine sauerkraut with 1 small minced onion and 3–4 T. oil. Place on serving platter and sprinkle with about 1 T. chopped parsley. Serve with fish or boiled meat.

SAUERKRAUT SALAD ANOTHER WAY
surówka z kiszonej kapusty inaczej

Drain, rinse, and chop 1 pt. sauerkraut as above. Combine with 1 finely grated carrot and 1 peeled, coarsely grated apple. Sprinkle sugar and dress with 3–4 T. oil. *Variation*: Several T. beet liquid (from canned beets) will give your salad a more interesting hue.

SAUERKRAUT SALAD WITH MAYONNAISE
surówka z kiszonej kapusty z majonezem

Drain, rinse, and chop 1 pt. sauerkraut. Season with pepper and sugar and dress with ¼ c. mayonnaise-sour cream combination. Garnish with chopped chives and/or parsley.

CARROT & APPLE SALAD
surówka z marchwi i jabłek

Combine 4 finely grated carrots with 2 peeled, coarsely grated apples. Sprinkle with 1–2 t. sugar and a little lemon juice to taste. Lace with several T. sour cream. *Note*: Grated salads such as this and those that follow are winter-time favorites when fresh greens are less plentiful and overpriced.

CARROT, APPLE & HORSERADISH SALAD
surówka z marchwi i jabłek z chrzanem

Proceed as above but add 1–3 T. prepared horseradish. *Note*: This tangy and refreshing salad is a favorite of the authors, especially with pork dishes.

CELERIAC & PEAR SALAD
surówka z selerów i gruszek

Peel 1 small celeriac (celery root) and grate fine. Sprinkle with lemon juice to prevent discoloration. Peel and coarsely grate 2 firm pears and 1 apple and mix with celeriac. Sprinkle with sugar and a pinch or 2 salt and transfer to serving dish. Drench with about ½ c. mayonnaise or mayonnaise-sour cream combination and garnish with about 1 t. chopped parsley.

BEETROOT SALAD
surówka z buraków

Wash and peel 2 med. size beets. Grate fine and immediately sprinkle with sugar and lemon juice. Peel and coarsely grate 1 apple and 1 brine-cured dill pickle. Finely chop 1 onion and combine all ingredients. Salt & pepper and adjust taste with additional sugar and lemon juice if necessary. Place on serving dish and sprinkle with about 3 T. olive oil or other oil. Garnish generously with chopped parsley (about 3 T.)

MIXED GRATED SALAD
surówka mieszana

Combine about ½ c. each: finely grated carrots, finely grated celeriac, coarsely grated apples and pears. Stir in 1–3 T. prepared horseradish and dress with about ½ c. mayonnaise-sour cream sauce.

GARDEN-CRESS SALAD
surówka z rzeżuchy

Wash well and drain 1 bunch garden cress and chop very fine. You should have about ½–¾ c. when chopped. Finely chop 1 small onion, 1–2 bunches chives, mix with cress and place on serving platter. Coarsely grate 1 peeled apple and mix with ½ c. sour cream. Add 1 bud mashed garlic and season to taste with salt, sugar, and lemon juice. Pour sour-cream mixture over greens on platter. *Note*: Do not confuse the tiny-leaved garden cress with the larger-leaved watercress (rukiew wodna) which is more common in America but in Poland is regarded as an inedible swamp weed.

POLISH SALADS WITH AN AMERICAN ACCENT
polskie surówki z amerykańskim akcentem

For a change of pace, try some of the salads in this chapter with some of the popular American bottled dressings (French, Taystee, Creamy Italian, Thousand Island, etc.). Who knows? You may come up with a hybrid that will really strike your fancy. After all, such cultural cross-fertilization is something very Polish.

EGGS & EGG DISHES

Ever since Homer described the beautiful Helen of Troy as having been hatched, the egg—that singular marvel of nature—has been surrounded by a certain mystique. Old German legend spoke of an *Osterhase*, a magic hare that went around laying eggs, and from this evolved the Easter Bunny tradition. English superstition held that misfortune would befall anyone who dared lend, borrow, give, or receive an egg on Sunday.

In Polish Catholic tradition, the egg has long symbolized Christ's Resurrection and the New Life his followers could expect. To this day on Easter Sunday, Poles across the globe share with their loved ones bits of hard-boiled eggs that have been blessed in church the day before.

Still, for all its mystical and ritual significance, since the earliest times the egg has also been hailed as one of nature's most perfect foods. Eggs are a low-calorie, high-protein food chock full of essential nutrients. Two eggs (about 100 gram or 3½ ounces) supply more protein than a pork cutlet of equal weight, but have only 140–150 calories and less than 12 grams of fat. (The cutlet has 45 grams of fat and 450 calories.) They also supply considerably more phosphorous and iron, twice the vitamin B, and a whopping eight times more calcium. It should also be noted that the protein contained in eggs is of the highest possible quality.

Another important virtue of eggs is the short cooking time they require. What gourmet dish can be whipped up in less time than a classic omelet? Eggs can be boiled, fried, scrambled, poached, and simmered in cream, and used to make puddings, soufflés, cutlets, croquettes, dumplings, cabbage rolls, and a great deal more.

One of the best traditional Polish egg dishes we know are hot eggs stuffed in shells. In fact, we have included one recipe for them in this chapter and another in the hot–appetizer chapter. If you also enjoy them, be sure to try the egg cutlets (this chapter), whenever you don't have time to stuff eggshells. For many different ways of serving hard-cooked eggs, please consult the chapter on cold appetizers.

"What about the great cholesterol scare?" you may ask. Obviously, eating bacon & eggs every day for breakfast, as many Americans once did, is not advisable. Neither is succumbing to fads, phobias, and crazes whipped up by advertisers out to cash in on the general confusion. The average healthy adult should limit himself or herself to no more than about five eggs a week, according to Poland's leading food writer Irena Gumowska, and normal growing children and adolescents can increase their intake to seven. The best advice we can offer on this subject is to consult your physician and follow his or her recommendations.

* * *

An easy old method of checking eggs for freshness is to place them in a large bowl or other receptacle of cold water. A truly fresh egg will lie on its side at the bottom, while a slightly older one will stand up. An egg that is several weeks old will float somewhere below the surface, and a several-month-old egg will come to the top like a fisherman's bobber.

FRIED (SUNNY SIDE UP) EGGS ON BUTTER
jaja sadzone na maśle

In medium-size skillet melt about 1 T. butter but do not brown. Break open 4 eggs one at a time and deposit in teacup to check for freshness. If yolk spills apart, do not use egg for frying. (It may be good in other dishes if it does not give off that tell-tale odor of spoiled eggs.) When the eggs are in 4 separate teacups, gently pour each into skillet from just above its surface. Cook gently until the whites are set but not scorched or dried out on the bottom. Polish cooks do not generally cook the eggs covered, because that produces a pale pinkish film over the yolks which they consider unappetizing. Poles like their yolks a bright orange color. Let each diner salt & pepper their eggs according to preference. *Note*: Besides being a simple breakfast or supper dish eaten with rye bread or rolls, such eggs are often used to garnish breaded veal cutlets, chopped spinach, and other dishes. *Note*: There are special egg-frying pans with depressions for each egg which ensure perfectly round fried eggs with no ragged edges.

FRIED EGGS ON BACON OR SALT PORK
jaja sadzone na boczku lub słoninie

Dice about ⅛ lb. (a roughly 2 inch cube) slab bacon or salt pork and fry in skillet until golden or just lightly browned. Gently slip eggs into skillet as above and cook on low heat until set. *Variation*: Fry the diced bacon or salt pork until crunchy, remove the nuggets with slotted spoon, and fry the eggs in only the fat. Garnish the eggs with fried nuggets just before serving. *Note*: We have deliberately used the term "eggs on bacon" rather than the more customary (in English) "bacon & eggs" to emphasize that the bacon is not something added to the eggs but fried together with them, which gives them a deliciously smoky, porky fragrance. Most Polish cooks would fry the eggs in all the fat rendered from the bacon or salt pork, but you can remove all but about 1 t. of the drippings before frying your eggs. After eggs have just begun to set, you can add 1 T. boiling water. That will prevent them from burning when using very little fat.

FRIED EGGS ON HAM OR SAUSAGE
jaja sadzone na szynce lub kiełbasie

Skin and thinly slice a 3–4 inch piece of smoked kiełbasa or dice an equal amount of ham. If you use fatty kiełbasa or ham (and this is preferable), it will render enough drippings in which to fry your eggs without having to add any additional fat. If kiełbasa or ham are too lean, melt a T. bacon or salt-pork drippings in skillet, brown the sausage or ham in it, add the eggs and fry as above.

FRIED-BAKED EGGS
jaja sadzone zapiekane

Proceed as in any of the above recipes, but when the whites just begin to set, slip skillet into pre-heated 400° oven for several min. or until whites are set. Any of the above may be sprinkled with chopped chives if desired.

FRIED EGGS ON TOMATO SLICES
jaja sadzone na pomidorach

Plunge a fairly large tomato into boiling water. After a min. or so, skin can be easily removed under cold running water. Melt a little butter or other fat in skillet and brown as many thin tomato slices as you have eggs. Turn tomatoes over with spatula and deposit 1 egg on each. The tomato slices should be large enough and the eggs small enough so they don't run over the sides. Cover and cook on low heat until whites are set. You can also cook them uncovered in a 400º oven. Garnish with chopped chives, parsley, or garden cress ("rzeżucha").

"OX-EYE" FRIED EGGS
jaja "wole oczy"

Melt a little fat in hot skillet and add slices of bologna or mortadela with skins left on. Fry over hot enough heat for slices to curl up forming a cup. Deposit 1 egg in each, pop into 400° oven and cook until white is set. This is a complete meal with a fresh salad and some good rye bread.

TANGY FRIED EGGS
jaja sadzone na kwaśno

Melt 1 T. butter in skillet, add 1 T. boiling water, and 1 t. 6% distilled vinegar plus ¼ t. salt. Bring to boil and add 4 eggs. Reduce heat and cook covered or uncovered until whites are set.

EGGS COOKED IN SOUR CREAM
jaja sadzone w śmietanie

Fork-blend ½–¾ c. sour cream with 1–1½ T. flour until smooth and heat in skillet until bubbly. Add 4–6 eggs one by one, reduce heat, and cook until whites are set, spooning the hot cream over eggs every so often. Transfer eggs to platter or individual plates and pour the sauce over them. Sprinkle with a little paprika. *Note*: ¼ t. salt may be added to cream while fork-blending or you can let everyone salt their eggs to taste at table.

EGGS COOKED IN SWEET CREAM
jaja sadzone na śmietance

Proceed as above, but cook eggs in ½–¾ c. sweet cream, fork-blended into a smooth sauce with 1–2 T. flour. Serve these or the eggs in sour cream with rye bread, potatoes, or Kraków groats.

FRIED EGGS WITH CHEESE
jaja sadzone z serem

Melt a little butter or drippings in skillet, add eggs and, when whites are slightly set, sprinkle whites with grated yellow cheese of choice (about ½ c.) For an eye-appealing contrast, sprinkle yolks with chopped chives and cook on low heat until done. May also be cooked in hot oven.

FAT-FREE EGGS "SUNNY SIDE UP"
jaja sadzone bez tłuszczu

In small skillet, heat about ¼ c. milk or water (or a combination of the two in whatever proportion you prefer) to boiling. Add 2 eggs, reduce heat, and cook covered until whites are set.

SCRAMBLED EGGS
jajecznica

Beat 4–6 eggs with fork or whisk, adding about ¼ t. salt. In skillet melt about 1 T. butter or drippings or fry up about ⅛ lb. diced salt pork or slab bacon, leaving as much of the drippings as you like. Pour beaten eggs into skillet and cook on low heat. When bottom is set, flip over with spatula. Sprinkling eggs with about 1 T. cold water will replace the evaporated moisture and prevent eggs from scorching. The scrambled eggs are ready when they are just set but still moist. *Note:* Most Polish travellers complain that the scrambled eggs they were served in both American homes and restaurants were too dried out. This, of course, is a matter of personal preference and habit.

GRANDMOTHER'S SCRAMBLED EGGS
jajecznica babci

Heat butter or drippings in skillet or fry up diced slab bacon or salt pork into crunchy nuggets as above. Add 4–6 unbeaten eggs and cook on low heat until whites are nearly set as for fried eggs "sunny side up", then break up with fork, toss, and cook until still slightly moist. *Note*: Unlike the pre-beaten, scrambled eggs which come out a uniform, pale yellow, these eggs are bright yellow flecked with white. The author named them after his late maternal grandmother who hailed from the Lublin region (eastern Poland) and always prepared scrambled eggs in this way.

SCRAMBLED EGGS PEASANT STYLE
jajecznica po chłopsku

Lightly beat 4–6 eggs. Separately, fork-blend ½ c. milk with 1 T. flour until lump-free and mix well with beaten eggs. In skillet melt 1–2 T. butter or drippings or fry up some bacon or salt-pork nuggets. Pour egg mixture into hot skillet, reduce heat, and cook until they are set the way you like. Sprinkle with chopped garden greens of choice and let everyone salt & pepper their own portion to taste.

SCRAMBLED EGGS & TOMATOES
jajecznica z pomidorami

Plunge 1 larger or 2 smaller tomatoes into boiling water and let stand about 1 min. Peel under cold running water, dry in paper towel, and dice coarsely. Melt a little fat of choice in skillet, add tomatoes, and fry briefly, stirring frequently. Pour in 4–6 beaten eggs (plain or with milk and flour as in peasant style), reduce heat, cook, and scramble until set the way you like. Serve with bread or potatoes.

SCRAMBLED EGGS & MUSHROOMS
jajecznica z grzybami

To 2 T. butter or drippings add about 1 c. washed, dried, and thinly sliced chopped, wild or store-bought fresh mushrooms and 1 small, finely minced onion. Toss to coat ingredients and simmer under cover about 15 min. or fry until golden. Pour in 4–6 beaten eggs (plain or peasant style), mix eggs with mushrooms, and salt and pepper while frying or individually, according to preference. Serve with kaiser rolls or rye bread or on French-bread toast.

SCRAMBLED EGGS & SMOKED FISH
jajecznica z wędzoną rybą

Melt 2 T. butter in skillet. Add ½–1 c. flaked or chopped smoked fish with skin and bones removed. (Smoked carp, white fish, or salmon are best, but trout, halibut, and flounder are also good.) Toss fish to coat with butter and simmer briefly, but do not fry. Add 8–10 beaten eggs (plain or peasant style) and cook on low heat until done. Sprinkle with chopped chives or parsley. Taste the cooked eggs before salting, since smoked fish can be on the salty side.

SCRAMBLED EGGS & HERRING
jajecznica ze śledziem

Soak a medium-sized (about 12 oz.) salt herring in cold water overnight, changing water once. Next day, remove skin and bones and chop herring. Beat 8–10 eggs with ⅓ c. milk, add herring, 1–2 T. chopped chives, and a pinch or 2 pepper and paprika. Melt 2–3 T. butter or drippings in skillet, add egg mixture, and cook until set. Taste cooked eggs before seasoning with salt. This dish hails from the Baltic region or Kashub country.

SCRAMBLED EGGS SHEPHERD STYLE
jajecznica po bacowsku

From the Baltic Coast in the north we move to Poland's southern Tatra Mountains, where this egg dish is a favorite of local shepherds. Dice and fry up into golden nuggets a 2–3 inch cube of salt pork. Add ¾–1 c. cubed black bread and brown slightly in drippings, Beat 8 eggs with 2–3 T. milk and about ½ c. grated oszczypek (smoked sheep's milk cheese). Pour beaten egg mixture into skillet, salt & pepper, and cook on low heat until done, stirring frequently. Garnish with fresh chopped parsley and serve with boiled potatoes or groats of choice.

SCRAMBLED EGGS & MINT LEAVES
jajecznica z miętą

Fry up diced salt pork (a 2 or 3 inch cube) until golden and add 8 unbeaten eggs. Sprinkle with salt and some dried mint leaves and cook on low heat until whites are just barely set. Break eggs up with fork, scramble lightly, and cook until done but still moist and glistening. Serve with black bread. This dish also hails from the Tatra Mountains.

SCRAMBLED EGGS & MATURE OR GREEN ONIONS
jajecznica z cebulką

Melt 2–3 T. butter or bacon or salt-pork drippings in skillet, add 1 finely chopped onion, and simmer until golden or just slightly browned. If using green onions, finely chop the white bottoms and simmer until golden, then add the chopped greens and simmer a while longer. Add 8 beaten eggs (plain or with milk and flour) or 8 unbeaten eggs and cook as above until set. Salt & pepper to taste. For variety, season a pinch or 2 of savory or ground caraway.

FAT-FREE SCRAMBLED EGGS (DIETETIC)
jajecznica bez tłuszczu (dietetyczna)

Heat 3–4 T. milk in top part of double boiler over boiling water. Lightly beat in milk 3–5 eggs with 1 T. water and several pinches salt. (If on a salt-free diet, try adding several pinches of savory /cząber/—a natural salt & pepper substitute.) Pour beaten eggs into hot milk, stir and cook until as firmly or loosely set as you like.

PLAIN OMELET
omlet naturalny

Briefly beat 3–6 very fresh eggs, adding 1 T. cold water for each 3 eggs used plus several pinches salt. In fairly heavy skillet heat 1 T. unsalted butter for each 3 eggs. Heat until butter is quite hot and fragrant but not browned and pour egg mixture into skillet. (Use 7-inch skillet for 3 eggs and proportionately larger one for 4–6 eggs.) Cook omelet on low heat, picking up sides with spatula to let some of the runny egg mixture from the top flow to the bottom. When you have lifted omelet with spatula, slip a pat of butter or 2 underneath.

Omelet is ready when bottom is lightly browned and top is glistening and soft. Fold in half and transfer to warm platter. Serve as is or sprinkled with some chopped chives.

PLAIN OMELET ANOTHER WAY
omlet naturalny inaczej

Briefly beat 3-6 fresh eggs with 1 T. cold water per egg and pinch or 2 of salt & pepper. In heavy skillet, melt 1 t. butter per egg and heat until fragrant but unbrowned and add egg mixture. As omelet cooks on very low heat, swirl egg mixture with fork in circular motion, taking care not to scrape bottom. Cover and continue cooking on very low heat until bottom is firmly set and top is still soft and glistening. Fold in half and serve as above.

FILLED OMELET
omlet nadziewany

Omelets prepared in either of the two ways above may be filled with variety of fillings. When omelet is done, simply spread filling on one half, fold the other half over the filling and serve. Here are some favorites in quantities for 6-egg omelet.

OMELET WITH WILD OR CULTIVATED MUSHROOMS
omlet z grzybami lub pieczarkami

Wash well 8-12 oz. wild or domestic mushrooms, slice thin or dice, and simmer in several T. butter with 1 finely chopped onion under cover about 15 min. Uncover and stir to allow moisture to steam away. When mushrooms begin to sizzle, remove from heat, salt & pepper to taste, and use to fill omelet.

OMELET WITH CREAMED MUSHROOMS
omlet z grzybami w śmietanie

Slice thin or dice 8-12 oz. wild or store-bought fresh mushrooms that have been thoroughly washed to remove all grit. Place in skillet, add 1 finely chopped onion and 3 T. water, bring to boil, then reduce heat to medium, cover, and simmer about 10 min. Fork-blend 2 T. flour with ½ c. sour cream and several T. cold meat stock or court bouillon and add to mushrooms. Add 1 T. chopped dill and/or parsley, salt & pepper to taste, and simmer briefly. Drain, reserving drippings. Use the mushrooms that remain in sieve to fill omelet. Transfer to platter and pour the remaining sauce over it.

OMELET WITH CARROTS
omlet z marchewką

Fill omelet with about 1-1½ c. hot floured carrots (see vegetables), peas & carrots, or peas.

OMELET WITH SPINACH
omlet ze szpinakiem

Cook 1 package chopped frozen spinach according to directions on package, drain, pressing out moisture, run through meatgrinder or whirl in blender. In skillet melt 2 T. butter and make a roux with 2 T. flour. Simmer without browning and gradually stir in about ¼ c. milk. Simmer until bubbly, add spinach, 1 bud mashed garlic, and salt & pepper to taste. If mixture appears too thick, thin with a bit of spinach water left over after draining spinach. *Optional*: Sprinkle with a little lemon juice for added tang. Use mixture to fill omelet.

OMELET WITH HAM
omlet z szynką

In 1–2 T. melted butter simmer ¾-1 c. diced, boiled ham or other smoked meat (skinned kiełbasa, krakowska, frankfurters, bologna, Spam, or any combination thereof) until it begins to brown. Fill omelet with fried ham or other meat. *Optional:* When ham or other meat begins to brown, stir in 3-4 T. sour cream and simmer until bubbly. A sprinkling of chopped chives or parsley is highly recommended.

OMELET WITH BACON
omlet z boczkiem

Dice up ⅛-¼ lb. slab bacon or salt pork (roughly 2 by 4 inch piece) and fry until it turns into crunchy, golden-brown nuggets. Set aside. In separate skillet fry a 6-egg omelet in 2 T. of the bacon or salt pork drippings as above. When done, sprinkle 1 side with the fried nuggets, fold over, and serve. *Optional:* Add 1 chopped onion to the browning nuggets and simmer until golden or slightly browned. A sprinkling of chopped chives or parsley will greatly enhance the flavor.

OMELET WITH CAULIFLOWER & OTHER FILLINGS
omlet z kalafiorem lub innym nadzieniem

Fill cooked omelet with 1-2 c. cooked, diced cauliflower, asparagus, wax or green beans, even Brussels sprouts, for an excellent way of using up yesterday's leftover vegetables. Or, scald and skin a large tomato, dice and simmer in a little butter, then salt & pepper and use to fill omelet, adding some sautéed minced onion if you like. Another possibility is ½–1 c. grated yellow cheese, farmer cheese, bryndza (sheep's milk cheese), oszczypek (smoked sheep's milk cheese), or a similar amount of diced, boneless smoked fish, 1-2 T. finely chopped canned anchovy fillets, or (if you can afford it) several T. caviar. What about yesterday's leftover casserole? Why not? The classic omelet has limitless potential for turning even the most prosaic ingredients into a gourmet dish. Give vent to your creative urge and you may come up with a real winner. *Remember*: A flair for creative improvisation is the essence of Polish cookery!

SPRING (GARDEN-GREEN) OMELET
omlet wiosenny

Lightly beat 4-6 eggs, adding a heaping T. finely chopped garden greens: dill, parsley, chives, and (optional) garden cress. Season with salt as desired and pour mixture into skillet containing 2 T. hot butter. Cook on low heat, carefully lifting sides with knife to let runny egg mixture flow down. Omelet is ready when bottom is golden and top is still moist, soft, and glistening. Fold in half and serve on lettuce-lined platter garnished with radish slices. A wonderful spring treat, especially if using the season's first greens straight from your garden!

SOUR-CREAM OMELET COUNTRY STYLE
omlet po wiejsku

Beat 5 very fresh eggs and 3 extra egg whites well, adding a generous sprinkling of chopped dill and/or parsley and several pinches salt. Heat 2 T. butter in skillet to just below browning point and pour in egg mixture. Cook on low heat briefly (no more than 1 min), then pop skillet into pre-heated 425° oven and bake until it turns slightly golden brown. As it bakes, combine in saucepan 1 c. sour cream, 1 T. melted butter, 3 raw egg yolks, ½ T. flour, 1 T. sugar, and a pinch of cinnamon. Mix well and heat until bubbly, stirring constantly. Fold omelet in half the usual way and transfer to baking dish. Drench with sour-cream sauce and bake in hot oven about 15 min. This rather unusual (parsley & cinnamon?!) baked omelet originated in the northeastern Lithuanian borderlands of the Old Royal Republic.

OLD POLISH BREAD OMELET
staropolski omlet bułczany

Bring 1 qt. milk to boil in heavy-bottom pot (to prevent scorching) and cool to lukewarm. To milk, add 2 c. bread crumbs, 10 beaten egg yolks, ½ t. ground caraway, and ½-1 t. salt. Mix ingredients until well blended. Beat 10 egg whites to a froth, gently fold into milk, yolk, and crumb mixture together with 5 T. sifted flour. In large, heavy skillet or 2 smaller ones brown ¼ lb. diced salt pork. Pour omelet batter into skillet (or skillets), and cook on low heat, occasionally picking up sides to let runny batter flow down. When golden on the bottom and partially set on top, flip over and lightly brown other side. *Note:* This is actually quite an economical dish (milk and bread crumbs are cheaper than eggs!) which can easily serve 12-16 people.

SWEET SPONGE-CAKE OMELET
omlet biszkoptowy na słodko

Separate 6 very fresh eggs and beat the whites into a stiff froth. Add the yolks and 4 T. sifted flour to beaten whites, mix lightly, and season with a pinch or 2 salt. Heat 1½ T. butter in skillet, add egg mixture, and cook on low heat, occasionally picking up sides with spatula so runny egg mixture can flow to bottom of skillet. When omelet is set on bottom but still soft on top, pop it into a hot oven for 5 min. or until it gets lightly browned. Spread one half of omelet with cherry preserves, jam, sugared berries, etc., fold over other half, and serve dusted with powdered sugar. The kids will love this one! *Note:* This omelet can also be filled with savory filling (bacon, mushrooms, spinach, etc.) of choice, in which case do not dust with powdered sugar, but garnish with chopped greens.

APPLE SPONGE-CAKE OMELET
omlet biszkoptowy z jabłkami

Cream 7 raw egg yolks with ½ c. powdered sugar, ½ t. vanilla extract, or 1 t. vanilla sugar and ½ t. grated orange rind. Beat the 7 whites to a froth and gradually fold into yolk mixture, alternating with 5 T. flour. Stir in 3 c. peeled, thinly sliced, cooking apples. Butter 10-12 inch skillet, sprinkle with bread crumbs, pour in egg mixture, and bake in pre-heated 325° oven about 30 min. Dust with powdered sugar and serve. *Variation:* Instead of apples, try this omelet with sliced fresh strawberries or other berries. *Note:* All omelets turn out best if made with room temp. eggs, so take eggs out of fridge at least 2 hrs. before using; other ingredients (milk, butter, etc.) should also be at room temp.

SWEET BATTER OMELET
grzybek słodki

Cream 2 T. soft butter with ½ c. powdered sugar and 8 raw egg yolks. Beat the 8 whites to a froth and gradually fold into yolk mixture, alternating with 3 T. flour. Mix lightly. Heat 1 T. butter in skillet and pour in egg mixture. Cook on low heat until set on bottom, then flip over whole omelet and fry until just lightly browned. Do not fold in half, but top with cherry or other preserves, jam, marmalade, fruit syrup, sugared berries, etc.

BATTER OMELET WITH GARDEN GREENS
grzybek z zieleniną

Beat 8 raw yolks with 2 T. soft butter and add 2 T. chopped chives and dill. Beat the 8 whites to a froth and gradually fold into yolk mixture, alternating with 3 T. flour. Heat 1 T. butter in skillet and pour in egg mixture. Cook on low heat until set and slightly browned on bottom, then flip over and lightly brown other side. Serve topped with creamed peas & carrots, other cooked vegetables, or mushroom sauce.

SOFT-BOILED EGGS
jaja na miękko

Place room temp. eggs in boiling water to cover. When boiling resumes, reduce heat, cover and cook 2-4 min., depending on the size of eggs and firmness desired. Serve in egg-cups and provide salt, pepper, and unsalted butter.

EGGS IN GLASS VIENNESE STYLE
jaja w szklance po wiedeńsku

Cook eggs as above. Place as many juice glasses as needed in pot of boiling water. Tap and peel away top of eggshells and with teaspoon carefully scoop 2 eggs into each glass, taking care not to break yolk. Add 1 t. butter and a pinch of salt to each glass. This is a more convenient way of enjoying soft-boiled eggs than struggling with the eggshell. Personally, we prefer the method below, where the eggs are actually cooked in the glass.

EGGS IN GLASS POLONAISE
jaja w szklance po polsku

Use 1 med.-sized drinking glass per serving. Line inside of pot with several thicknesses of dish towel, fill pot ½ full of water, and switch on heat. Meanwhile, rub inside of each glass, especially bottom ½, with about ½ t. butter, break two very fresh eggs into each and place glasses in hot water in pot. Water should be a bit below the level of the eggs, otherwise glasses may tip during cooking. Cover and cook on med. heat until whites set round walls of glass. With spoon scrape set whites from wall of glasses and stir eggs gently. Continue cooking (very briefly!) until eggs are set the way you like. They should have the consistency of soft-boiled eggs. Serve eggs in the glasses, preferably in small bowls of boiling water to keep them hot. Serve with breakfast rolls or bread. Provide salt & pepper.

SHIRTED (POACHED) EGGS
jaja w koszulkach

In pot combine 4 c. water, 1-2 t. salt, and 1-2 T. distilled vinegar; bring to boil. Use pot in which the water is at least 3 inches deep. Break 4 very fresh eggs into 4 saucers or demitasses and slip eggs into boiling water one by one. Reduce heat, cover, simmer 2-4 min., depending on size of eggs and firmness desired. Carefully remove with slotted spoon and serve immediately. These slightly tart poached eggs are excellent for breakfast with bread or rolls. For supper, they can be served with cooked vegetables or in various sauces (tomato, sour cream, horseradish, mushroom, dill, etc.). *Note:* In Polish these are called shirted eggs because, if properly made, the eggs come out with their yolk entirely enveloped by a white "shirt." These eggs can also serve as additions to clear soups, especially bouillon and clear tomato or beet soup.

BREADED SHIRTED EGGS
jaja w koszulkach panierowane

Cook eggs as above. When done, gently transfer with slotted spoon to colander and allow to drip dry. Salt & pepper. Carefully dredge in flour, dip in beaten raw eggs, and roll in bread crumbs. Fry in med. hot oil about ¼ inch deep in skillet until breading is a nice golden-brown on all sides. Drain on absorbent paper and serve immediately with cooked spinach, braised beets, stewed tomatoes & pumpkin, or a vegetable bouquet.

MEDIUM-BOILED EGGS
jaja na półtwardo/mollet

Place eggs in cold water to cover on med.-high heat and bring to boil. Reduce heat, cover, and cook 4-5 min. Another way is to switch off heat when boiling begins and let stand covered about 6 min. Either way, plunge the medium-cooked eggs into cold water and, when cool enough to handle, carefully remove shell. Serve like shirted eggs or wrap each egg in thin strip of boiled ham or smoked salmon. If properly cooked, the white is fully set and the yolk is a thick semi-liquid. *Note:* They may also be served in egg-cups like soft-boiled eggs.

HARD-BOILED EGGS
jaja na twardo

Place eggs in cold water to cover on med.-high heat and bring to boil. Reduce heat, cover, and cook 6-10 min., then immediately plunge into cold water. When cool, remove shells. *Note:* Do not overcook, or the white may become rubbery and the yolk mealy with a greenish film on the outside. Hard-boiled eggs have endless uses in Polish cookery and lifestyles. They are among the main culinary attractions on the traditional Easter table and have long been a favorite of travelers and outdoorsmen (picnickers, mushroom-hunters, fishermen, etc.). A few ways of serving them are presented below.

HARD-BOILED EGGS IN SAUCE
jaja na twardo w sosie

Shell and cut in half lengthwise 6 cold, hard-boiled eggs and place cut-side-up on lettuce-lined platter. Spoon sauce on eggs and top each with a radish slice or sprinkle with chopped chives, dill, and/or parsley or paprika. You can quickly whip up an easy but very delicious sauce by fork-blending ½ c. mayonnaise (or the sweeter Miracle Whip-type salad dressing) with ½ c. sour cream. Season to taste with salt, white pepper, sugar, and lemon juice. 1 t.-1 T. prepared horseradish or sharp brown mustard will give your sauce added zest. See sections on cold appetizers and cold savory sauces for more such suggestions.

FRIED STUFFED EGGSHELLS
jaja faszerowane

Soak 2 slices stale french bread or kaiser roll in ½ c . cold milk until soggy. Tap 4 cold, hard-boiled eggs (still in their shells) with a heavy, sharp knife lengthwise, place on several thicknesses of dish towel on cutting board and cut egg in half, shell and all. With small spoon gently dislodge the eggs, taking care not to damage the shell. Discard any jagged shell fragments around the rim of shell. Set empty shells aside and remove eggs from remaining ones. (This recipe calls for 4 eggs, but you can always reduce ingredients proportionately for a smaller quantity). Squeeze excess moisture out of soggy bread and run through meat grinder together with whites & yolks. Add 2 T. finely chopped chives and 2 T. finely chopped parsley, 1 raw egg, and salt & pepper to taste. Mix well and use mixture to fill egg-shells. Gently press mixture down into shells with spoon and dip each open side down into bread crumbs, pressing them in with spoon. In hot butter (or olive oil and butter) fry eggs filled side down, reducing heat so they don't burn. Eggs are ready when a golden-brown crust forms on the bottom and shells are hot to the touch, meaning contents have been heated through. Serve as a main course with mashed or pureed potatoes, cooked spinach, and /or a fresh salad. *Note*: Although this recipe may seem a bit involved before you get the hang of it, this is truly one of the tastiest dishes known to Polish cookery. Look for additional recipes in the chapter on hot appetizers.

EGG CUTLETS
kotlety z jaj

Hard-boil but do not overcook 7 eggs and plunge into cold water for several min. when done. Remove shells. Soak 1 stale kaiser roll or 2 slices stale french bread in ½ c. milk until soggy, then run through meat grinder with the eggs. Sauté 1 chopped onion in a little butter until tender and add to egg mixture. Add 3 T. chopped dill and 1 T. chopped chives, 1 raw egg and salt & pepper to taste. Mix well and form into small balls or patties. Roll in bread crumbs and fry to a nice golden brown on all sides in butter (or butter and oil). Serve with potatoes or groats and a fresh salad for a complete meal. The egg cutlets may also be drenched with sour cream, tomato, or mushroom sauce.

DAIRY PRODUCTS,
HOME CHEESE MAKING
& DAIRY DISHES

The earliest Roman and Arab merchants, who traveled to the Baltic Coast in pursuit of amber and left chronicles behind to prove it, described the territory of the ancient pre-Christian Poles as a country of game-filled virgin forests and fish-filled rivers—a land flowing with milk and honey. Despite all the historical vicissitudes experienced by the Polish people since that time, Poland continues to be one of Europe's top milk producers, and dairy products remain crucial to the Polish diet.

Since dairy products are found throughout this book, not excluding the chapter on cordials & liqueurs, we thought it advisable to focus here a bit on the nature and workings of milk and its various derivatives. By the time you get to the actual casseroles, cutlets, soufflés, pancakes, and other true dairy dishes, we think you will have achieved a better understanding of what various milk products are all about and what they can do.

A characteristic feature of Polish cuisine is its extensive use of such fermented milk products as sour cream, sour milk, buttermilk, and also very tasty and nutritious whey. Although even adults should ideally drink two or, at the very least, one glass of milk a day, many people over 30 find that fresh milk upsets their stomach. Strange as it may seem, these same people experience no adverse sensations when they drink the more digestible sour milk instead. Sour milk, which is nothing more than a type of liquid yogurt, also contains more vitamin C than fresh milk and helps counteract harmful bacteria in the intestinal tract.

Sour milk is also the basis of various curd cheeses, and many Polish households continue to make their own to this day. It really isn't all that difficult, and we think you might even find it a rewarding experience. Once you have made your own white cheese, you will find countless recipes on these pages in which to use it. Worth noting is the fact that farmer cheese has considerably less calories and only half the fat of yellow cheese but supplies more vitamins B_1 and B_2. On the other hand, yellow cheese contains more proteins, minerals, and vitamin A than its white unaged counterpart.

Sour cream is another essential component of Polish cookery. It often serves as a cold topping and goes into many salad dressings and sauces. It is used to cream soups, vegetables, gravies, casseroles and fricassees as well as in baking. For the benefit of weight-watchers and cholesterol-counters, we have included a number of ways to enjoy the rich, tangy taste of sour cream without subverting their diet.

* * *

FRESH MILK
mleko słodkie/świeże

From a purely nutritional standpoint, the healthiest milk you can drink comes *prosto od krowy* ("straight from the cow"). Unitiated city-slickers and suburbanites often complain that it's too rich and can even "clean you out!" The bulk of the milk consumed in America these days is processed by commercial creameries and is sold in the dairy case of food shops and supermarkets. Since milk plays such an important role in cooking and human nutrition, it's worth taking a closer look at some of the varieties available.

Whole milk: Whenever milk is referred to in this book, it means (unless otherwise specified) whole milk, which has a butterfat content of 3.5-4%. Whole milk contains all of milk's natural vitamins and minerals, and tastes delicious hot or cold. It makes baked goods light and flavorful, gives a rich taste and appetizing color to hot beverages like cocoa and white coffee, and imparts a glossy sheen to creamed soups and gravies.

Jersey milk: This is the richest milk commercially available. It has a higher butterfat content than regular whole milk and this gives it its pale golden tinge. In these days of obsessive weight-watching and cholesterol scares, Jersey milk has lost its former popularity, but it is recommended for many convalescents who need to build up their strength. No recipes in this book specifically call for Jersey milk, but feel free to use it if cooking for convalescents.

Low-fat milk: Also known as 2% milk, this is milk from which about half the fat of whole milk has been removed. Although obviously watered down, its taste is still acceptable to many. When the fat is removed, most of the fat-soluble natural vitamins A, D, E, and K are also lost, so synthetic ones have to be added at the dairy. If you use 2% milk in baking, it's not a bad idea to add about 1 level t. butter per c. to make up for the removed butterfat.

Skim milk: This is milk with a butterfat content of 1% or less. It is about as tasty as chalk water and imparts an unappetizing, grayish color to soups, gravies, and hot beverages. This watery and nutritionally worthless swill has to be artificially enriched with vitamins and minerals in the form of chemical additives. Do not use this milk in any of our recipes. The only recommendation we have concerning skim milk is to forget it.

Homogenized milk: All milk, regardless of butterfat content, can be homogenized. All this means is that the fat is broken down into such small particles that there is no cream separation. It is, of course, pasteurized to destroy harmful microorganisms.

Pasteurized milk: Although homogenized milk constitutes the bulk of the milk sold today, some dairies still produce milk that is only pasteurized. That means the raw milk is heated to well below the boiling point (140°-160°), kept at that temp. for a set period of time, and then quickly cooled. When allowed to stand, this milk produces a cream line round the neck of the bottle and should be shaken before using to evenly distribute the cream.

Evaporated milk: This is canned milk from which half the moisture has been removed. To reconstitute, simply combine 1 part of evaporated milk with 1 part of water, and use in all recipes as you would fresh whole milk.

Powdered milk: Available in both whole and skim-milk versions, these are dry milk solids sold in the form of a powder or crystals. To reconstitute, combine powder or crystals with the amount of water specified on the package and use like ordinary fresh milk. Nearly everyone can distinguish its characteristically dry-milk taste when consumed as is, but in cooking or baking the difference is harder to detect.

BUTTERMILK
maślanka

Natural buttermilk is the liquid left over from butter-churning, hence it is plentiful in rural Poland, where butter is churned by hand to this day. Unless you have your own cow, however, chances are you will get cultured buttermilk in the dairy case of your favorite supermarket. Chilled buttermilk is a refreshing and nutritious beverage as is. Poles enjoy it in the hot summer months served in soup bowl with dilled, buttered new potatoes, or buckwheat groats garnished with pork cracklings on the side. It can be used in place of sour milk in various soups, hot and cold, as well as in pancakes and baking.

HOMEMADE BUTTERMILK
maślanka domowym sposobem

In crockery bowl, combine 1 qt. 2% low-fat milk (or 1 qt. milk made from low-fat powdered milk) with 1 c. store-bought buttermilk. Leave out at room temp. overnight or until fully clabbered. Stir until smooth and refrigerate until ready to use. If you want to have a steady supply of buttermilk on hand, reserve 1 c. of your homemade buttermilk, add to 1 qt. fresh low-fat milk and keep at room temp. until clabbered.

BUTTER
masło

The authoress grew up in a small Polish town where butter-making was a normal household routine. Although raised in Detroit, the author also recalls back in the 1940's and '50s how his paternal grandfather would occasionally furiously shake fresh cream straight from the farm in a large glass jar for what seemed like an awfully long time. Eventually a yellowish mass would emerge and become the tastiest butter imaginable. The leftover liquid was delicious natural buttermilk. If you have access to farm-fresh cream, you can try your hand at making your own butter, using the above-mentioned jar-shaking method or in a manual or electric butter-churn. We strongly suspect, however, that most readers of this book will get their butter from the nearby food store. **Remember**: Use only sweet, unsalted butter in the recipes in this book that call for butter. If you have ever wondered why unsalted butter is more expensive than the salted variety, the answer is simple. Salt is used as a preservative to prevent old and inferior butter from going rancid. But the best answer of all is a simple taste test: unsalted butter has a pale-yellow color and a light, fresh, delicious taste; by contrast, salted butter is darker yellow in color and has a heavy, oily taste.

MARGARINE, BUTTER SUBSTITUTES
margaryna, namiastki masła

Like butter, regular margarine has a fat content of about 80%. It can therefore be used in most recipes that call for butter as a less expensive substitute. Although hard to detect when used in baking, margarine (often referred to as oleo by the older generation) lacks the fresh creamery tasty of butter in many dishes, from pan-fried mushrooms to scrambled eggs. In the 1980's and '90s, the U.S. market became flooded with a variety of butter substitutes. The sales pitch capitalized on current fat and cholesterol scares, and promised a more natural, buttery taste than conventional margarines. If you find the taste acceptable, feel free to use these products as a spread on bread or a melted topping over various foods, but they should not be used in baking. The same holds true for the various low-fat, low-calorie, and light margarines. Like the butter substitutes, they contain plenty of water and lack the fat content of butter and regular margarine necessary to achieve light and flavorful baked goods.

COFFEE CREAM
śmietanka

This sweet cream with a butterfat content of about 20% is commonly known in the U.S. as coffee cream. That term is not used in Poland, since most Poles take their coffee black. It can be used to cream soups and gravies as well as in baking and sweet dessert sauces. It is good as is over fresh, sugared fruit.

HALF & HALF
śmietanka chuda

Although the common American name suggests that this product is half milk and half cream, this is nothing more than a low-fat cream with a butterfat content of about 12%. It can be used in place of coffee cream over fruit, pudding, etc. To cream soups and gravies in place of sour cream use a trifle more flour than called for in the recipe. If used to replace coffee cream in baking, add about 1 level T. butter to make up for the missing butterfat.

SOUR CREAM
śmietana

Sour cream is a basic staple regularly found in the refrigerator of nearly every Polish family. If you have leafed through this book, you know that its uses are limitless. It is the main ingredient or the base of salad dressings and sauces, hot and cold. Sour cream is used more widely in Polish cuisine to cream soups and gravies than milk or sweet cream. It is used in stews, casseroles and creamed dishes, in cold-buffet salads and canapé spreads, as a topping for various dumplings, noodles, crêpes, pancakes, fresh fruit, and dessert dishes. It can be added to scrambled eggs and omelets and is used to poach eggs. It also widely used in baking. *Note:* If you read the label, you will know that American dairy sour cream is artificially thickened with gelatin, tapioca flour, and soybean additives. In most recipes, therefore, it has to be liquified by fork-blending. Simply place dairy sour cream in cup and stir vigorously with fork until you get a thick, pourable liquid. If all the artificial thickeners turn you off, you can make your own sour cream, which will be more natural and less adulterated than the store-bought variety (see below).

HOMEMADE SOUR CREAM
śmietana domowym sposobem

Pour 2 c. coffee cream (18-20% butterfat) into crockery bowl and stir in 2-3 T. dairy sour cream or cultured buttermilk. To prevent dust from getting in, cover with clean dish towel and let stand in warm room (75-80°) 24 hrs. or until fully clabbered. Refrigerate 24 hrs. before using. *Variation:* For a reduced-fat sour cream, use half & half instead of coffee cream. *Note:* Either way, you get a purer, more natural sour cream than what is commercially available. Commercial coffee cream may contain a spoilage retardant, but it is free of gelatin, tapioca flour, soybean additives, and other artificial thickeners found in American store-bought sour cream.

LOW-FAT HOMEMADE SOUR CREAM
chuda śmietana domowa

If you use the half & half variation in the above recipe, you will get a fairly lean sour cream with a butterfat content of about 12% . You can get an even leaner sour cream with a butterfat content of 8% if you stir ½ c. liquified dairy sour cream into 1 ½ c. whole milk and let it stand overnight at room temp. or until fully clabbered. Anything lower than 8% would no longer qualify as sour cream and would be more like a rich sour milk. *Note:* Due to its low butterfat content, this low-fat sour cream is best when used as a cold topping or a cold salad-dressing ingredient. In hot dishes it may curdle. It blends beautifully with an equal part of mayonnaise into a creamy sauce.

LOW-FAT HOMEMADE SOUR CREAM ANOTHER WAY
chuda śmietana domowa inaczej

In blender, combine 1 c. grated farmer cheese, dry cottage cheese, or small-curd creamed cottage cheese, about ⅓ c. buttermilk and 1 T. freshly squeezed lemon juice. Whirl several seconds until smooth and creamy. *Note:* Use only as a cold topping or cold salad-dressing ingredient, not to cream hot soups or gravies.

EMERGENCY SOUR CREAM
śmietana awaryjna

Into glass or crockery bowl pour 1 c. room-temp. canned, evaporated milk. Stir in 1 T. 6% distilled vinegar and let stand uncovered at room temp. or slightly warmer until fully clabbered. *Note:* Use only in cold salad dressings containing mayonnaise or other ingredients to disguise its flavor which is less reminiscent of real sour cream than the above 2 recipes.

EASY HOMEMADE YOGURT
jogurt domowy łatwy

Dissolve 3 heaped T. dried milk powder in 1 c. fresh milk, stirring until smooth and completely dissolved. Combine mixture with 1 c. fresh milk in pot and heat very gently to 180°. Then allow to cool to 110°. Stir in no more than 1 level t. plain, natural (not low-cal!) store-bought yogurt. Keep mixture at that temperature at least 4 hrs. or until thick and custardy. This can be best accomplished with an electric yogurt-maker. If you don't own one, the mixture can be kept warm in warm oven or in a thermos-type container or in the pot in which it was heated, wrapped in quite a few thicknesses of blanket and smothered with pillows. Care should be taken to jostle the yogurt as little as possible. *Note:* The secret of yogurtmaking is the temperature. If it is too high or too low, it will not succeed. When yogurt is thick, stir a bit, then refrigerate overnight before using. If you plan to make yogurt frequently, reserve a little as the starter for your next batch.

YOGURT AS A SOUR CREAM SUBSTITUTE
jogurt zamiast śmietany

Plain yogurt, either regular or low-fat, may be used in place of sour cream as a cold topping or in cold salad dressings. *Note:* It requires special handling when used to cream hot soups or gravies (see chapter on hot savory sauces).

YOGURT CHEESE
serek z jogurtu

As this book was being written, a product known as yogurt cheese made its appearance on the American market. Essentially, this is little more than yogurt from which the whey has been removed. You can therefore quite easily make a reasonable facsimile of it right in your kitchen by placing plain yogurt in a cloth-lined sieve and letting it drip dry. Yogurt cheese is used by some as a low-fat sour-cream substitute. One example is the *Fromage Blanc* (French for white cheese), produced by a creamery in Vermont.

SOUR MILK
zsiadłe mleko

When Polish soldiers were stationed in Britain during World War II, their British and Scottish counterparts looked with revulsion on Polish servicemen who actually drank "spoiled" milk. They were even more perplexed when they saw the Poles putting perfectly good fresh milk out to sour. Since then, Britons, Americans, and other people of the English-speaking world have wised up to the distinctive taste and health benefits of fermented dairy products such as sour cream, yogurt, and buttermilk—something Poles and other Slavs have known right along. Cold, creamy sour milk is a refreshing and healthy drink just as it is or can be a meal in itself when served in a bowl along with boiled potatoes, buttered and dilled or topped with crunchy pork cracklings, or with buckwheat groats. Whirled in a blender with sliced, sugared strawberries or other berries (1 part berries to 3-4 parts cold sour milk), it makes a delicious milk shake. It can be used in all recipes that call for buttermilk. Making it at home is extremely simple. Simply pour 1 qt. whole or 2% milk into a crockery bowl, let stand until warmed to room temp. and add a heaping T. dairy sour cream. Let it stand overnight or until fully clabbered, then refrigerate. A steady diet of sour milk (1-2 c. a day) is said to retard aging, improve one's complexion, promote digestion and prevent irregularity, because its beneficial lactic enzymes help to restore the body's proper chemical balance. *Note:* In Poland, a glass of cold sour milk is a popular eye-opener the morning after an overabundance of partying. It is also the basis for homemade farmer cheese (see below).

SOUR MILK MADE FROM DRY MILK
zsiadłe mleko z proszku

Prepare 1 qt. milk using dry milk crystals or powder according to package directions. (If the tap water in your area is heavily chlorinated, boil it first and cool to room temp. before adding dry-milk crystals.) Place milk in crockery bowl, add a heaping T. sour cream, and let stand at room temp. overnight or until fully clabbered. *Note:* When souring milk according to any method, best results are achieved in warmer than room temp. surroundings of 75-80°. It takes longer to sour and is less tasty if set out at below 70°. That is probably the reason sour milk is mainly associated with the hot summer months, when rapid fermentation is possible.

HURRY-UP SOUR MILK
zsiadłe mleko naprędce

If you occasionally need a c. of sour milk for racuszki (pancakes), chlodnik (cold creamed soup), or whatever purpose, but haven't the time to wait for it to sour naturally overnight, try this method. To 1 c. room temp. milk (whole or 2%) add 1 T. or slightly less lemon juice or 6% vinegar. Let stand in warm place 2-4 hrs. or until nicely clabbered.

HOMEMADE FRESH CURD CHEESE
świeży twarożek domowy

This cheese is best made in summer in a fairly hot room of around 80°. Pour 2 qts. whole milk into crockery bowl and let stand until warmed to room temp. Mix to liquify 1 c. sour cream, which should also be at room temp., and add to milk. Let stand 24 hrs., or until curds float up and separate from whey. Gently pour mixture into sieve lined with linen napkin. The sieve should be place over a pot to collect the drippings (whey). When drippings stops, cheese is ready. Serve sweet or savory. Typical savory seasonings include salt, pepper, paprika, caraway, chopped chives, etc. Those with a sweet tooth may prefer this creamy cheese with sugar, vanilla sugar, raisins, or sliced, sugared strawberries. For a richer taste, stir in a heaping T. sour cream. *Note:* Do not discard the whey, which has numerous uses (see below).

HOMEMADE CURD CHEESE
twarożek domowy

When the term "handle gently" is used in reference to cheese-making, it is not just a figure of speech. Excessive jostling of the curds will reduce the amount of cheese produced, since a larger percentage of the curds will get dissolved in and drain away with the whey. If properly made, you can count on about ¾ lb. cheese from 2 qts. milk. It is therefore best to sour the milk in the same unchipped enameled metal pot or heat-proof glass bowl or pot in which it will eventually be heated. If possible, place the container of milk to be soured on the switched-off burner of your range, on which it will be cooked. To 2 qts. milk add 1-3 heaping T. fork-blended sour cream and leave out overnight or until fully clabbered. Both milk and sour cream should be at room temp. Next day, very gently heat the sour milk on lowest possible heat to around 100° and keep it at that temp. about 1 hr. or until curds separate from whey and float to the top. Switch off heat and allow to stand several hrs. until pot has cooled to room temp. and is no longer warm to the touch. Place a fine-mesh sieve large enough to contain the cheese over another pot and pour the curds and whey into it. When dripping stops, let stand another 15 mins., then serve immediately or refrigerate. Mixed with a little sour cream, salted and peppered and garnished with some chopped chives, green onions, radishes, etc., this makes a tasty breakfast cheese spread. *Note:* This cheese is too soft and moist for use in pierogi, naleśniki, cheese cake, etc., for which farmer cheese should be used. Also, pour the whey into a clean jar, seal, and refrigerate for future use!

HOMEMADE CURD CHEESE (HOT-WATER METHOD)
twarożek domowy parzony

This method takes a little less time than that presented above, but the results are similar. Sour 2 qts. milk as above. When fully clabbered, add to sour milk 2-3 c. boiled water that has been cooled to about 150°. Switch on the lowest possible heat and keep mixture at about 100° for 1 hr., or until curds float up and separate from whey. Too high a temp. will cause the cheese to become rubbery. Drain through fine sieve and, when dripping stops, serve as above. If you line the sieve with a linen napkin, it will take longer to drain, but you will get a moister cheese. Season as above.

FRESH-MILK CURD CHEESE
twarożek ze słodkiego mleka

When you can't wait for milk to curdle overnight, try this quicker method. Heat 2 qts. milk to about 100°, stir in 5-6 T. freshly-squeezed lemon juice, cover with dish towel, and keep in warm (75-80°) place about 3 hrs. or until it thickens. Place pot of clabbered milk into a larger pot of boiling water and heat until curds separate from whey and float up. Place curd pot into larger pot of cold water and allow to cool 15-20 min. Carefully pour mixture into fine sieve positioned over an empty bowl. Ready to use when dripping stops.

QUICKEST CURD CHEESE
twarożek błyskawiczny

This method is quickest only if you have 1 qt. sour milk on hand. Bring 1 qt. fresh milk to boil, taking care that it doesn't scorch. Add 1 qt. sour milk and mix well with wire whisk. Reduce heat, count to 100, and switch off heat. Let stand about 30 min. or until curds separate from whey. Pour into sieve lined with linen napkin to drain. Your cheese is ready when dripping stops.

HOMEMADE BUTTER CHEESE
twarożek maślany

Combine 1 part homemade curd cheese (prepared according to any of the above methods) with ½-1 part unsalted room temp. butter. Mix well until you get a smooth creamy texture, and salt to taste. Use as a spread on bread or rolls. If you like, you can add more zest to this mild flavored cheese with such seasonings as pepper (white & black), paprika, ground caraway, chopped dill, a little grated onion, or mashed garlic. Chances are your whole gang will really go for this one! *Note:* Margarine or butter substitutes may be used in place of butter, but some of the flavor will be sacrificed.

HOMEMADE FARMER CHEESE
twaróg domowy

The only difference between twarożek (curd cheese) and twaróg (farmer cheese) is the amount of moisture they contain. The former is moist and soft, while the latter is firm and dry and can be sliced with a knife. Proceed exactly as with twarożek, but instead of draining the hot curds and whey through a sieve, pour them into a linen sack and allow to drip dry. Simply suspend sack and let it drip into a pot. Be sure to reserve the whey! When dripping stops, squeeze sack gently to extract additional moisture. Then place sack between two boards and weight down with something heavy to remove additional whey, positioning boards at an angle so the drippings end up in the pot. If you plan to make your own farmer cheese on a regular basis, it would be a good idea to hinge 2 med. wooden cutting boards together at one end and possibly attach a wing-nut tightener at the other. A cheese press of this type will enable you to keep tightening the boards when dripping stops to extract more moisture and ensure a nice dry cheese. Refrigerate cheese overnight, preferably between boards. This is undoubtedly Poland's favorite cheese. It is as likely to turn up on the breakfast table as it is in supper dishes. It is used in various dumplings, crêpes, casseroles, salads, cakes, and even in some soups. *Note:* Even if you don't make your own, you can enjoy all the recipes in this book that call for farmer cheese by buying it at your food store. It also goes by such names as pot cheese, curd cheese, Dutch cheese, pressed cottage cheese, and baker's cheese. You can use dry cottage cheese, but for most Polish uses, it must be ground or blended to get rid of those little globs. Italian ricotta is another substitute for farmer cheese. Incidentally, some Poles refer to twaróg as biały ser (white cheese).

CARAWAY CHEESE
twaróg kminkowy

Proceed as with homemade curd cheese (p. 573). When curds in sieve stop dripping, mix in ½-¾ t. salt and ½ t. caraway seeds, whole or partially crushed in mortar. For a soft caraway cheese, serve as is or with a little sour cream mixed in for added creaminess. For a firm caraway cheese, transfer mixture to linen sack and squeeze out additional moisture between 2 cutting boards or in cheese press as with farmer cheese (above).

RICH CREAM CHEESE
tłusty serek śmietankowy

In crockery bowl combine 1½ qts. whole milk, 1 c. whipping cream (unwhipped), and 1 c. liquified sour cream—all at room temp. Leave out at room temp. overnight. Next day, place bowl on rack in pan of boiling water and keep curds at temp. of 85° until they float up and come away from sides of bowl. Switch off heat and let stand until cooled to room temp., then pour through sieve. When dripping stops, cover cheese and chill the whey. When whey is thoroughly chilled, scoop up the buttery substance on the surface and work it back into the cheese until mixture is smooth. Serve this cheese with any of the sweet or savory flavorings listed above, or use it in any of your recipes calling for Philadelphia brand cream cheese. *Note:* For a firmer cheese, transfer mixture to sack and extract additional moisture in cheese press.

WHEY
serwatka

The above recipes have urged you to reserve the whey, so it's about time to define this cheese byproduct. Many Americans not connected with the dairy industry invariably associate this term with the nursery rhyme about Little Miss Muffet. Whey is a treasure chest of valuable vitamin and mineral nutrients which should definitely not go down the drain of your kitchen sink. It is a healthful and refreshing drink when chilled, and some Poles use it to cure a hangover. (This is no old wives' tale! The whey simply replaces some of the B vitamins that alcoholic beverages destroy!) To the uninitiated, a little sugar and a few raisins will help enhance the tangy, winey flavor of serwatka. It can be used in various soups (see soup section) and makes an excellent marinade for meat. Whey tenderizes meat, enhances its taste, and neutralizes any off-flavors that may occur. It is used in bread-baking and serves as a substitute for wine in most any recipe. Add several T. to most any gravy or soup, sprinkle a little over roast meat or fowl, fish, or green salads. It can be added to creamy sauces and, chances are, you'll be able to come up with a few uses of your own. So, whenever you make cheese, pour whey into a clean jar, seal, and refrigerate until ready to use. The górale (mountaineers) of southern Poland, who are known for their cheese-making, frequently stew pork ribs, goose meat, or kielbasa in whey which gives their dishes a delightfully different flavor. Why not try it some time?

RENNET
podpuszczka

Rennet is the inner lining of the fourth stomach of suckling calves. An extract thereof is widely used in commercial cheese-making. Its purpose is to cause the rapid and thorough curdling of milk, which is subsequently heated to separate the curds from the whey. In the above recipes, we have called for sour cream as a curdling agent, but rennet may also be used in home cheese-making. It ensures swifter curdling and greater productivity, i.e. less of the curds are lost with the whey. This substance, usually in the form of household rennet tablets, is available at cheesemaking supply houses, food specialty shops, and larger drug stores. You may use it in any of the above recipes according to package directions. If the instructions specify, for example, ½ a rennet tablet per gallon of milk, then use ¼ of a tablet in the above recipes calling for 2 qts. of milk. Simply dissolve the rennet in ¼ c. cold, pre-boiled water and add to fresh room temp. milk. Do not omit the sour cream, but the amount you use may be cut in half. Instead of the sour cream, you can use ¼ c. cultured buttermilk.

POLISH (COOKED-MILK) CHEESE
ser polski (z gotowanego mleka)

Without scorching, bring 2 qts. milk to a boil, remove from heat, pour into unchipped, enameled pot or flame-proof bowl and let cool to room temp. Add 1 c. liquified room-temp. sour cream and let stand 24 hrs. Gently heat to 100° and keep at that temp. until curds float up. Switch off the heat and let stand until cooled to room temp. Pour into linen sack. When dripping stops, place in cheese press or between 2 boards weighed down with a brick or other heavy object for about 12 hrs. Remove from sack, sprinkle with salt on all sides, and dry in sunlight in a well-ventilated place. This may be done outdoors, but the cheese must be brought inside at night to protect it against rain, dew, and insects. The drying takes 3-4 days and cheese should be sprinkled with fresh salt at the start of each day. If sunlight is too intense, cracks may appear in the cheese, so it's best to keep it in the shade during the hottest hrs. of the afternoon. During drying, turn cheese over every few hrs. *Note:* When fully dried, this cheese will keep a good long time. Simply wrap in parchment paper or foil and refrigerate or store in cool, dry cellar. Thinly sliced, it is excellent with bread and butter and, when grated, may be used in recipes calling for grated cheese. The outside skin is rather tough and should be removed before serving. *Variation:* ¼ t. freshly ground pepper or ½ t. crushed caraway seeds, dill seeds, or dried mint leaves may be mixed with curds before transferring to linen sack. If you choose this option, first pour curds into sieve, stir in flavoring, then transfer to sack.

DRIED ROUND CHEESE
gomółka

To 4 qts. room-temp. milk in enameled pot or flame-proof bowl add 2 c. liquified room-temp. sour cream and leave out overnight. Next day, heat gently to 100° and keep mixture at that temp. until curds float up. Switch off heat and let stand until pot in which curds were heated is no longer warm to the touch. Pour mixture into fine sieve over a pot to collect the whey. When dripping stops, sprinkle cheese with 1 t. salt and 1 t. whole or crushed caraway seeds. (If freshly crushed in mortar, the seeds release much more flavor.) Stir in 1 T. sour cream and mix to distribute ingredients. Divide cheese into 3 parts. Place each part on a piece of clean cheesecloth and roll into a ball, twisting it to extract moisture. When no more can be extracted, place cheese balls in their cheesecloth between 2 boards and weight down with something heavy overnight. Next day, remove cheesecloth and dry the 3 cheeses outdoors in direct but not too intense sunlight. (The best place is a screened sun porch or breezeway.) After two days, sprinkle cheeses with fresh salt every 2 days. After a week of drying, place the 3 cheeses in a clean crockery bowl, surrounded with beer-soaked cheesecloth. Cheeses are ready to eat within a week. They may be stored in beer-soaked cheesecloth in covered container for months in refrigerator or cool cellar. The longer they're aged, the sharper they get!

DRIED WHITE & YELLOW ROUND CHEESE
gomółka z twarogu i żółtego sera

Grind in meat grinder or pulverize to a fine powder in food processor 1 lb. homemade or store-bought farmer cheese. Add ½ lb. grated ementhaler or other natural, unprocessed yellow cheese (like edam or gruyère), ¼ lb. (1 stick) unsalted room-temp. butter, ½ t. salt and ¾-1 t. caraway seeds. Mix well by hand with wooden spoon or electric mixer on low speed to achieve a smooth and uniform consistency. Dip hands in cold water and form cheese snowball-fashion into 3 balls. Flatten them slightly to get an oval shape and dry outdoors or on well-ventilated sun porch 3-4 days, turning frequently to ensure even drying. Store in covered container in refrigerator until ready to use.

BEER CHEESES
kwargle

Combine 2½ qts. milk and 1 c. liquified sour cream and leave out at room temp. until clabbered. Heat to 100° until curds float up and pour into sieve. When dripping stops, sprinkle with salt and caraway seeds, mix well, transfer cheese to cheesecloth, and roll up tightly, jelly-roll fashion. Place between 2 boards, adding thin slats on the sides so cheese does not become flattened. Next day, roll cheese in cheesecloth on counter top to get a long, cylindrical roll about 2 inches in diameter. Carefully remove cheesecloth, slice into rounds about ½ inch thick, and place on rack outdoors or on sun porch to dry. After several hrs. brush with beer on both sides and continue drying. Dry about 2 days, brushing with beer occasionally. Store cheeses in layers in covered crockery bowl in fridge.

LITTLE CHEESES FROM LWÓW
serki lwowskie

Grind or pulverize in blender 1 lb. farmer cheese and place in pot. Heat over low flame, stirring constantly, until a little whey appears, then transfer to sieve and with saucer press out as much moisture as possible. (*Important*: The cheese must not be allowed to melt and become gooey—something that may occur if too high heat is used!) Into cheese stir ½-1 t. caraway seeds, and 5 lightly beaten raw egg yolks. Mix ingredients well to blend with wooden spoon or hand-held electric mixer on low speed. Place on low heat and gently bring to boil, stirring constantly with wooden spoon. The min. mixture boils, remove from heat and pour into tiny tart pans or demitasses to create variously shaped little cheeses. Ready to use as soon as it cools to room temp. Wrap unused cheeses in plastic wrap and store in refrigerator.

ZESTY FRIED CHEESE
pikantny ser smażony

Grind, pulverize in blender, or mash well with fork 1 lb. homemade farmer cheese. Spread evenly across surface of dinner plate, salt lightly, and cover with pot lid. (*Note*: We have found that plastic wrap also works well, but leave a tiny opening or two so the seal is not completely air tight.) Keep in warm place, 75°-85°, out of direct sunlight 2-3 days, stirring cheese each day. Cheese is ready to fry when it is sticky and gooey. Don't think it has spoiled if it gives off a pungent, yeasty aroma reminiscent of stale beer, because that's exactly how it's supposed to smell before frying. In heavy skillet melt 5 T. butter, add the cheese, and fry on very low heat, stirring constantly. Stir with fork, mashing any curds as finely as possible until they are blended into a smooth, somewhat gummy mass. Season with a little salt and caraway seeds, stirring constantly. Remove from heat. Gradually mix in 2 slightly beaten room-temp. egg yolks, stirring until they're completely absorbed. Return to heat and cook 30 seconds longer, stirring constantly. Pour mixture into tiny tart pans or demitasses. Serve hot on bread or toast or let it cool, slice thin, and use on canapés. *Variation*: Other flavor possibilities include paprika (about ½ t.) and/or 1 bud mashed garlic. *Note*: This strong-flavored cheese will definitely go over better with connoisseurs, adventurous eaters, and he-man types.

MOUNTAINEER'S SHEEPMILK CHEESE
bryndza

Into unchipped, enameled pot or flame-proof bowl pour 4 qts. fresh sheepmilk or 3 qts. sheepmilk and 1 qt. regular whole cowmilk. Dissolve in ¼ c. cold, pre-boiled water as much rennet as indicated on package to curdle 1 gallon milk. Add to milk and let stand in warm place (75°-80°) 24 hrs. Transfer curds that have separated from whey to linen sacks to drip dry. When dripping stops, squeeze out additional moisture between hands or boards. Remove cheese from sacks, place in large pan, crumble with fork (mountaineer cheesemakers crumble it with their hands!) and dry in the sun. As with the other cheeses that require sun-drying, a breezy sun porch is the best place for such an operation. Let dry about 3 days, frequently mashing any lumps that form. At this stage the cheese should have taken on a yellow hue. Transfer to mixing bowl, sprinkle with 1 T. salt or more and 2-3 t. caraway seeds, and mix with wooden spoon quite a while until mixture achieves a smooth and uniform consistency. Transfer mixture to small earthenware crock (the kind some fancy Wisconsin cheeses come in are great for this purpose!), cover with saucer that snugly fits in the crock, press cheese mixture down slightly, and store in cool, dry cellar no warmer than 50° 4-6 weeks. If you lack such a cellar, store in warmest part of your fridge. After that time, remove cheese from crock and place in mixing bowl. Stirring constantly with wooden spoon (this mixture is probably too thick for your electric mixer to handle!), gradually add about 2 jiggers medium-dry sherry ½ a t. at a time. When mixture is smooth, cover bowl with dish towel and let stand at room temp. about 6 hrs. for flavors to blend. Transfer mixture back to crock, cover with saucer and store in cool, dry cellar another 4 weeks or longer. This smooth but slightly grainy cheese with a pungent flavor is likely to appeal to those with a more sophisticated palate and yen for the exotic. Bryndza is a great appetite-stimulant on canapés and is also used in many simple and hearty peasant dishes from the mountainous regions of southern Poland. Mead or *miód pitny* (Polish honey wine) may be used in place of sherry in its preparation.

MOUNTAINEER'S SHEEPMILK CHEESE AN EASIER WAY
bryndza łatwiejsza

This is a simpler way of making bryndza, more typical of humble peasant cookery than gourmet cuisine. Pour 4 qts. fresh sheepmilk or 3 qts. sheepmilk and 1 qt. regular whole cowmilk into crockery bowl. Add rennet dissolved in ¼ c. cold pre-boiled water and let stand until mixture clabbers. Transfer curds to linen sacks and allow to drip dry. When dripping stops, place between 2 boards and weight down or use cheese press to extract moisture. After 2 hrs. remove cheese from sacks and run through meat grinder. *Important*: The meat grinder (as well as other cheesemaking utensils) should be absolutely spotless and scalded several times with boiling water before using; the least impurity may harm the flavor of your bryndza and significantly reduce its shelf life. Sprinkle ground cheese with salt rather generously, mix well, and pack into small earthenware crocks. Store as above. Ready to use in 4-6 weeks. For longer storage cover with melted paraffin the way you would homemade jelly. Polish górale use melted beef suet for this purpose. *Note*: Bryndza, which is of Romanian origin, may be found in Balkan food markets in larger U.S. cities. In Romanian, it is spelled *brindsa*.

MOUNTAINEER'S SMOKED SHEEPMILK CHEESE
oszczypek

If you want to try your hand at Polish style cheesemaking, don't start with this recipe, which is rather involved. Until you get the hang of it, it would be better to first tackle the simpler curd cheeses, farmer cheese or bryndza, especially the fairly easy recipe above. Oszczypek (which the górale themselves pronounce *oscypek* because their dialect lacks the "sz" and "cz" sounds) is a small, tapered, cylindrical cheese with a ruddy-brown skin on the outside (from smoking) that is traditionally decorated with geometric motifs. These are imprinted by the special wooden cheese molds used in their preparation. The inside is white to pale yellow with a somewhat rubbery texture that actually produces a faint squeak when the cheese is chewed. Dissolve in ¼ c. cold, pre-boiled water as much rennet (probably only a fraction of a tablet) as indicated on package for curdling 1 gallon milk. Add to 4 qts. preferably freshly milked sheepmilk and let stand 1 hr. Add 3-4 c. boiling water, stir gently, and let stand until pot is no longer warm to the touch. Transfer curds to linen sacks, drip dry, then extract additional moisture between 2 boards or in cheese press as above. Place cheese in wooden oszczypek molds, pressing down so mixture fills all the decorative crevices. *(Note*: Finding such molds in the U.S. may be next to impossible, but if you know someone in Poland, perhaps you could ask them to send you some formy do oszczypków, also known as łupki; if not, maybe you can find a reasonable substitute at a cheesemaking supply store or specialty shop.) When cheese is set, remove from molds, place on slotted spoon, and dip into boiling water for a few seconds several times. When cheeses have cooled to room temp., transfer them to a pot of cold brine. Dissolve 1½ c. salt in 4 c. boiling water, then add to 3 qts. cold, pre-boiled water and chill. Keep cheese in cold brine 24 hrs. Remove from brine and dry on rack. Place on rack or truss with twine and hang up in smoker. Smoke in cold smoke until skin turns a nice ruddy brown. Oszczypki prepared properly can be stored indefinitely in a cool, dry cellar.

YELLOW CHEESES
sery żółte

Unlike the soft curd cheeses, farmer cheese and sheepmilk cheese presented above, yellow or hard cheeses for all intents and purposes cannot be readily prepared in the home. Their preparation requires expensive equipment, elaborate techniques, and controlled-temperature aging, hence you will have to depend on those supplied by your supermarket, delicatessen, or cheese shop. The most typical Polish yellow cheese available in America is *tylżycki* (tilsit or tilsiter), a medium-sharp cheese dotted with tiny pockmarks rather than the large holes found in Swiss cheese. Besides tilsit, in any of the recipes calling for yellow cheese, also feel free to use gouda, edam, emmenthaler, gruyère, or brick. Munster is also usually acceptable, although being on the soft side, it tends to melt too quickly. Processed "cheese foods," American cheese, and cheddar are not recommended for use in Polish recipes.

FARMER CHEESE & GARDEN GREENS
biały ser z zieleniną

Fresh garden greens add color, zest, and vitamin nutrients to mild-tasting farmer cheese, and leave plenty of room for creative invention. Fork-mash, grind, or pulverize to a powder in blender about ¾ lb. farmer cheese. Add anywhere from ½-1 c. of any or all of the following greens: finely chopped chives or green onions, thinly sliced radishes (and a sprinkling of finely chopped unwilted greens from baby radishes), and peeled, diced cucumbers. Stir in ½-¾ c. fork-blended sour cream and salt & pepper to taste. *Variation*: Add 1-2 chopped or fork-mashed, hard-boiled eggs and this becomes a complete meal. This is one of our family's favorite spring and summer breakfasts. We usually enjoy it with bakery rogale (Polish crescents) and in the U.S. with hot crescent rolls, made from refrigerator crescent-roll dough, and unsalted butter. Biała kawa (white coffee or café au lait) is the perfect companion.

FARMER CHEESE WITH EGGS & GREEN ONIONS
biały ser z jajkiem i cebulką

Combine ¾ lb. ground farmer cheese with 1 bunch finely chopped green onions. Add 1 or more ground or mashed hard-boiled eggs, and 1-3 t. chopped fresh dill. Cream with enough sour cream to get the consistency you want and salt & pepper to taste. *Variation:* A little whole or ground caraway will add character to the above cheese salads, and a pinch or 2 dried mint leaves will give them a refreshing twist. A crushed bud of garlic is another flavor option.

FARMER CHEESE & RAISINS
biały ser z rodzynkami

Scatter ½ c. or more rinsed, dried raisins over ¾ lb. ground farmer cheese. Drench with ¾ c. of fork-blended sour cream and sprinkle with sieved powdered sugar or granulated sugar to taste. A t. or so vanilla sugar may be added. *Note*: Polish mothers often prepare this simple, dessert-like dish for youngsters, who might otherwise not want to eat their cheese, an important source of calcium and other nutrients.

FARMER CHEESE & PEARS
biały ser z gruszkami

Combine ¾ lb. ground farmer cheese with 4 peeled, cored, diced juicy pears and stir in ½-¾ c. fork-blended sour cream. Add just a sprinkle of salt. A little sugar may be added, but this isn't necessary, as this dish should have just the hint of sweetness provided by the pears. *Variation*: 8 drained canned pear halves may be used if fresh fruit is not available.

FARMER CHEESE & BAKED APPLES
twaróg z pieczonymi jabłkami

Bake 4 whole, unpeeled apples in 375° oven 45-60 min., or until tender, then force through sieve and allow to cool. Combine with ¾ lb. ground farmer cheese and sugar lightly to taste. Flavor with a pinch of cinnamon, if desired. Serve as is or with a little sweet cream or fork-blended sour cream poured over. *Variation*: When there's no time to bake apples, use applesauce instead. *Note*: The above sweet cheeses may be served for breakfast, as an after-dinner dessert, or light supper.

MIXED CHEESE SALAD
sałatka z twarogu i żółtego sera

Combine 1-1½ c. diced farmer cheese and an equal amount of diced yellow cheese of choice with a bunch of finely chopped green onions. Salt & pepper lightly and drench with sauce made by fork-blending ½ c. sour cream and ½ c. mayonnaise. Garnish with small tomato wedges on serving platter. If desired, sprinkle with a little chopped dill.

CHEESE & LEEK SALAD
sałatka z żółtego sera z porami

Wash and trim 2-3 leeks and cut the white root portion in half lengthwise. (Freeze the leek greens for use in stock-making.) Slice the white portions wafer thin and combine with

1 peeled, cored, diced apple (or 2 apples if small) and 2 c. diced yellow cheese of choice. Salt & pepper and drench with mayonnaise or 50-50 combination of mayonnaise and sour cream. A t. brown mustard and a sprinkle of sugar and/or lemon juice will provide added zest. This is one of our favorites!

CHEESE & GREEN PEPPER SALAD
sałatka z żółtego sera z papryką

Combine 2 c. diced yellow cheese, 1 diced green pepper, 1 finely chopped onion, 2-3 skinned diced tomatoes (scald to remove skins) and 3 T. chopped fresh parsley. Fork-blend ⅓ c. mayonnaise and ⅓ c. sour cream with 1 t. brown mustard, salt & pepper to taste, sweeten slightly with a bit of sugar (optional), and pour over salad.

CHEESE & HAM SALAD
sałatka z żółtego sera z szynką

Combine 2 c. diced yellow cheese (or slice cheese into match-sticks), 1 c. diced boiled ham, and 1 bunch thinly sliced or coarsely grated radishes. Dress with ¾ c. mayonnaise and serve on leaves of Boston lettuce or tomato slices.

CHEESE & FRANKFURTER SALAD
sałatka z żółtego sera z parówkami

Combine 1½ c. diced yellow cheese (a mild variety is best in this recipe), 1½ c. diced skinless frankfurters, and 2 diced dill pickles. Fork-blend 3 T. olive oil, juice of ½ lemon, and 1 t. brown mustard. Add a little sugar, if desired. Sprinkle salad with sauce and decorate with tomato wedges.

CHEESE & PEA SALAD
sałatka z żółtego sera z groszkiem

Combine ¼ lb. diced or coarsely grated yellow cheese, 2 diced dill pickles, 1 leek cut in ½ lengthwise and sliced wafer thin, 1-2 chopped, hard-boiled eggs, and 1-2 c. drained canned peas. Toss gently so as not to damage the peas and dress with mayonnaise. Season to taste with a little salt and sugar and garnish with chopped fresh parsley.

BRYNDZA & CUCUMBER SALAD
sałatka z bryndzy z ogórkiem

Mix about ¼ lb. bryndza (mountaineer's sheepmilk cheese) with 2-3 T. sour cream to get a smooth consistency. Combine with 1 med. peeled, diced cucumber and garnish with chopped fresh dill.

BRYNDZA-MAYONNAISE SPREAD
pasta majonezowa z bryndzy

Mix ¼ lb. bryndza with a heaping T. mayonnaise (homemade or store-bought) until smooth. Add 1 chopped hard-boiled egg and 3 T. chopped chives. Use as spread on rye or black bread (preferably small canapé-size rounds, squares, or triangles) and serve with chilled vodka.

"DAREDEVIL'S" BRYNDZA SPREAD
pasta z bryndzy "awanturka"

In mixing bowl mash ½ lb. bryndza with ½ can smoked Baltic sprats (or sardines), including ½ the oil. When smooth, add 1 finely diced dill pickle, 1 small finely chopped onion, and generously season with paprika. Use as a canapé spread. *Note:* This potent and piquant concoction is a drinking man's treat if there ever was one; in fact, we have never run across a teetotaler who liked it. Serve on canapés, topped with dill-pickle slices, as a bite-down for well-chilled Wódka Wyborowa. *Variation:* Use capers instead of or in addition to dill pickles in this spread.

* * *

Although the cheese salads and spreads could have been included in the appetizer section. We listed some of them here so they wouldn't get lost among the various canapés, spreads, starter courses, and cold-buffet salads which are so much a part of Polish lifestyles. We suggest you treat them as orientational guidelines rather than hard-and-fast recipes; feel free to alter the proportions and doctor them up according to preference. Since cheese blends so nicely with various ingredients, you will probably be able to come up with improvisations of your own. Creative improvisation, after all, is what Polish cookery is all about!

* * *

POTATOES, NOODLES, OR GROATS & CHEESE
kluski, kartofle lub kasza z serem

This is not so much a recipe as an illustration of the way old peasant cookery made use of cheese to add flavor and nutrition to these common staples. These simple dishes, however, can provide a refreshing change of pace from the super-processed high-tech foods which are the steady diet of far too many Americans. Simply drizzle a plate of steaming hot noodles or any of the unfilled dumplings, boiled potatoes, or cooked buckwheat groats with crunchy, golden fried salt-pork nuggets and as much of the drippings as you like. Top with crumbled or grated farmer cheese or bryndza in whatever quantity you like, salt & pepper to taste, and enjoy. A glass or bowl of cold sour milk or buttermilk on the side will turn this into a complete meal. *Optional*: Garnish noodles with a little chopped dill, potatoes with chopped dill or crushed caraway seeds, and groats with a pinch of dried mint leaves.

POTATO & FARMER CHEESE CASSEROLE
kartofle zapiekane z twarogiem

Cook 7-8 med. potatoes in jackets. When done, peel under cold running water and set aside. Mix 1 lb. ground farmer cheese with 1 c. milk. In several T. bacon or salt-pork drippings simmer 1 large chopped onion until tender and slightly browned and stir into milk & cheese mixture. Butter a casserole and sprinkle with bread crumbs. Slice potatoes and place a layer along bottom of casserole. Salt & pepper. Top with a layer of cheese mixture, then another layer of potatoes, etc. until ingredients are used up. Top layer should be potatoes. Brush top layer generously with soft butter, sprinkle with bread crumbs. Bake in pre-heated 350° oven about 30 min. Sprinkle with chopped dill and/or parsley and serve with sour cream and fresh salad for a complete meal.

CHEESE, BEAN & MUSHROOM CASSEROLE
zapiekanka z sera, fasoli i pieczarek

In 3 T. salt-pork or bacon drippings, simmer 1 onion sliced wafer thin until just golden, add 8 oz. washed, drained, diced fresh mushrooms, toss with onions, and simmer covered about 5 min. Sprinkle with 1 T. flour, stirring so it is absorbed by pan drippings. Add 1 c. milk and bring to boil. Beat 1 c. cold milk with 1 egg, add ¾ c. grated yellow cheese of choice, and 6-8 T. mixed chopped greens (parsley, chives, garden cress, celery tops). To mushroom mixture add ½ c. cooked or canned, drained navy beans or pea beans, and 1½ c. more grated cheese. Gently toss ingredients to mix and season to taste with salt, pepper, and savory. Butter baking dish and sprinkle with bread crumbs, transfer mixture to dish, and drench with milk & egg mixture. Sprinkle with bread crumbs and bake in 350° oven 35-45 min. Serve as is with a green salad or with sour cream or tomato sauce.

CHEESE PUDDING WITH FRUIT SYRUP
budyń z twarożku z sokiem

Grind or sieve ¾ lb. soft curd cheese. Mix 2 T. soft butter until creamy, adding a little of the cheese at a time until fully blended. Salt mixture lightly. Fold in 3 stiffly beaten egg whites and stir in 4-5 T. uncooked cream of wheat. Mix lightly. Butter a pudding mold and sprinkle with bread crumbs. Transfer mixture to mold, which should be no more than ¾ full. Seal lid, place in large pot of boiling water, which should reach ¾ of the way up the side of mold. When boiling resumes, cover pot and cook 40-45 min. Remove mold from water and set aside to cool slightly, then remove lid and slip pudding onto serving dish. This tall tapered pudding, drenched with red cherry or raspberry syrup trickling down the sides, is a sight to behold. It is an easily digestible dish ideal for small children and convalescents. *Note*: If you do not own a classic pudding mold with snap-on lid, you can place mixture in an ordinary pot with tight-fitting lid so that it fills the pot no more than ¾ full. Then place it in pot of boiling water and proceed as above. This pudding can also be baked in pre-heated 325° oven about 45 min.

SWEET FARMER-CHEESE PUDDING
budyń z twarogu na słodko

Grind or sieve 2 cooked potatoes together with ¾ lb. farmer cheese. Cream 4 T. butter with ½ c. sugar, gradually adding 4 egg yolks until fully blended. Combine cheese & potato mixture with butter, sugar and yolk mixture, add ¼ c. rinsed, drained raisins, and 1 t. finely chopped candied orange rind. Mix ingredients well. Fold in 4 beaten egg whites and mix lightly. Butter pudding mold, sprinkle with bread crumbs, and add mixture which should reach ¾ of the way up. Seal mold and cook in covered pot of boiling water 45 min. from the time boiling resumes. Remove pudding to warm serving platter. Serve dusted with powdered sugar or drenched with sweet cream.

SAVORY FARMER-CHEESE PUDDING
budyń z twarogu na ostro

Grind or sieve 2 cooked potatoes together with just under 1 lb. farmer cheese. Cream 2 T. butter, gradually adding 4 egg yolks one by one. Mixing constantly, pour in 1 c. milk, add cheese & potato mixture, ¾ c. flour, several T. chopped parsley, and salt & pepper to taste. Mix well to blend ingredients. Fold in 4 stiffly beaten egg whites. Butter pudding mold, sprinkle with bread crumbs, and fill ¾ with mixture. (Choose pudding mold or pot the right size so that mixture reaches only ¾ of the way up!) Cook in covered pot of boiling water 45 min. After removing to warm plate, garnish with a little more chopped parsley. Serve drenched with sour-cream sauce or tomato sauce. With a seasonal salad on the side, this is a complete meal.

CHEESE, RICE & MUSHROOM PUDDING
budyń z sera, ryżu i grzybów

Wash, drain, and chop 8–12 oz. fresh mushrooms and simmer in 3 T. olive oil with 2 finely chopped onions until tender. Combine mushrooms with 2–2½ c. cooked rice, ½ lb. ground or sieved farmer cheese, or ¼ lb. grated yellow cheese, 5 beaten egg yolks, and several T. chopped parsley. Mix well. Beat 5 egg whites to a stiff froth with 1-2 t. sugar and fold into mixture. Salt & pepper to taste and mix lightly. Cook in buttered pudding mold sprinkled with bread crumbs as above 50-60 min. *Note*: Instead of water-bath cooking, pudding can be baked in 325° oven about 50 min. Serve with sour-cream sauce or mushroom sauce with a salad on the side.

FARMER CHEESE SOUFFLÉ
suflet z twarogu

Grind slightly more than 1 lb. farmer cheese twice or force through sieve. Add 2 T. butter, 4 egg yolks, and ½ c. sugar, and mix vigorously until smooth and fully blended. Add 4 T. potato starch, ½ c. fork-blended sour cream, and 4 egg whites beaten to fairly stiff froth. Mix lightly. Transfer to buttered baking dish and bake in pre-heated 350° oven about 30 min., or until nicely set. Serve immediately.

YELLOW-CHEESE SOUFFLÉ
suflet z żółtego sera

Cream 1 stick (¼ lb.) butter, adding 3 egg yolks, one at a time. Add 1 scant c. grated yellow cheese of choice, 1 t. sugar, and salt & pepper to taste. Fold in 3 stiffly beaten egg whites and mix lightly. Transfer mixture to buttered baking dish and bake in pre-heated 350° oven about 25 min., or until set. As with all soufflés, serve immediately. For added zest, season with garden greens, pepper, paprika, etc.

FRIED CHEESE & RICE CAKES
serniki ryżowe

Combine ¾ lb. ground farmer cheese with 3 egg yolks creamed with ½ c. sugar. Add ½ t. vanilla extract (optional). Mix with 1 c. preferably milk-cooked rice (see chapter on groats & grains). Beat 3 egg whites until stiff, adding 4 T. flour, fold into mixture and mix lightly. Between palms of hands form mixture into ½ inch thick oval patties and fry in 4 T. butter (or oil-butter combination) until nicely golden on both sides. Serve hot, drenched with fruit syrup of choice.

SAVORY BAKED CHEESE PANCAKES
placuszki z żółtego sera

In pot combine 2 c. milk and 6 T. butter. Bring to boil, stirring to prevent scorching. Reduce heat and through sieve sift in ¾ c. flour, stirring to prevent lumping until mixture begins coming away from sides of pot. Switch off heat and continue stirring until cooled somewhat. Stir in 3-4 whole eggs and 1¾ c. or slightly more grated yellow cheese and continue mixing until ingredients are well blended. Refrigerate 30 min. Place spoonfuls of mixture on greased baking sheet and bake in 375° oven about 30 min., or until cakes are a nice golden brown. Serve hot, sprinkled with a little more grated cheese.

BREADED CHEESE CUTLETS
kotlety z żółtego sera

Dredge 8 ½-inch-thick slices yellow cheese of choice in flour, dip in beaten egg, and roll in bread crumbs. *Optional*: Cheese slices may be seasoned with pepper, paprika, and/or ground caraway before breading. Fry in 4 t. hot oil to a nice golden brown on both sides, drain on absorbant paper if desired, and serve immediately with potatoes or rice and salad as a main course. Do not overfry, as cheese should be only partially melted. *Note*: This change-of-pace dish packs protein and energy and, in addition, is rich in one important nutrient that meat lacks: bone-building calcium. It is also less expensive than meat!

HONEY-SIMMERED CHEESE
żółty ser duszony w miodzie

Bring 2 t.–1 T. honey to boil in skillet and switch off heat. Place 8 ½-inch-thick slices yellow cheese in skillet, turning over to coat with honey on both sides. Keep cheese in skillet only long enough for it to soften and not melt completely. Serve immediately. This unusual snack makes a nice breakfast or light supper when served with rolls or french bread.

BUTTER-SIMMERED FARMER CHEESE
twaróg duszony w maśle

Melt 3 T. butter in skillet. Add 8 ½-inch-thick slices farmer cheese and heat briefly until cheese is softened and warmed through but still unmelted. Serve with bread or rolls. *Note:* If desired, cheese may be seasoned with salt, pepper, paprika, or ground caraway before or after simmering, or garnished with chopped chives just before serving.

BUCKWHEAT & BRYNDZA CASSEROLE
kasza gryczana zapiekana z bryndzą

Wash and trim 2 leeks, reserving greens for soup. Cut whole bottom sections in half lengthwise and slice wafer thin. Simmer in several T. fat until tender. Mix leeks with 3 c. cooked buckwheat groats, 1½-2 c. bryndza, 2 beaten eggs, 3 T. sour cream, 2 T. bread crumbs, and season to taste with salt, pepper, and marjoram. Grease baking dish and sprinkle with bread crumbs, add mixture to dish, and bake in 350° oven 30-40 min. Transfer to serving platter and drizzle with fried golden salt-pork nuggets and as much of the drippings as you like. Serve with a fresh salad for a complete meal.

FRIED FARMER CHEESE PATTIES
kotleciki z twarogu

Combine 2 egg yolks with 1 lb. ground or sieved farmer cheese and mix until well blended. In sieve combine ¾ c. flour and 2 T. potato starch and sift into cheese mixture, stirring constantly until completely absorbed. Fold in 3 stiffly beaten egg whites, mix lightly, and form into small, round or oval patties. Fry in butter or oil (or a combination of the two) on med. heat until lightly browned. Savory-food lovers (like the author) prefer these seasoned with a little salt and topped with a dollop of sour cream. Youngsters may prefer them dusted with powdered sugar or drenched with fruit syrup.

BREADED CHEESE & POTATO PATTIES
kotleciki z sera i kartofli

Peel and cook in boiling salted water 3 med. potatoes. Drain and cool. Grind potatoes together with 1 lb. farmer cheese. In 2 T. fat simmer 1 finely chopped onion until tender and add to cheese-potato mixture. Add 2 eggs and ⅓ c. bread crumbs and mix well to blend ingredients. Salt & pepper to taste. *Optional*: Other flavorings could include a sprinkling of crushed caraway seeds, several dashes paprika, or 2-3 T. chopped parsley. Form into small oval patties about ⅓ inch thick and roll in bread crumbs. Fry to a nice golden brown on both sides in several T. lard or oil. Serve with hot sour-cream sauce or cold sour cream with a tomato, green-onion or leek salad on the side.

CRUNCHY CHEESE OMELET
chrupiący omlet z serem

Melt 4 T. butter in skillet and add 4 slices french bread cut into croutons. Fry croutons on med. heat until nicely browned on all sides. Beat 7-8 eggs with 3 T. coffee cream, add 1-2 c. grated yellow cheese, and salt & pepper to taste. Pour egg mixture into skillet and fry on low heat. Pick up sides with spatula while tilting skillet slightly and let runny omelet batter flow to bottom. Omelet is done when bottom is nicely browned and top is set but still glistening and moist. Sprinkle with chopped chives, fold omelet in half, and slip onto serving platter. *Note*: After bottom of omelet is lightly browned you can slip skillet into 375° oven for about 10 min. or until top is set. For other omelet recipes, see chapter on egg dishes.

PUDDINGS, KISIELS, JELLIES & OTHER DESSERTS

Poles have always been fond of sweet dishes, and over the centuries have eagerly enhanced their own native repertoire with successive waves of foreign novelties. Even the hard-drinking he-man types, whose palate runs to sausage, dill pickles, and herring—traditional Polish bite-downs—have been known to develop the occasional sweet tooth.

Our chapter opens with the simplest dessert of all: compote. This is nothing more than fruit cooked in water and sugar to produce what Americans commonly refer to as canned fruit. Of course, there are also the thinner compotes meant for drinking, and these are included in the beverages chapter.

Other even simpler but still highly delightful desserts are fresh sugared fruits, usually topped with a dollop of sour cream or whipped cream. (But, please, do not spoil your dish of fresh berries with an artificial topping!)

Among the entries are jellies (gelatin desserts), mousses, crèmes, soufflés, and a variety of classic steamed and baked puddings. There is also the indigenously Polish kisiel, or jelly-pudding, which is something like a jelly although it has a taste and texture all its own.

For those who enjoy preparing their own ice cream from scratch, we have collected a number of interesting recipes, ranging from the rich classic versions to the leaner varieties, dieters may prefer. To round things off, there is a good selection of sweet sauces and toppings which will highlight the flavor of any pudding, kisiel, or ice.

This chapter would have been considerably longer, if we had included various sweet dishes. Although these double as desserts and light supper courses, we have decided to list them in chapters devoted to their principal ingredients.

For example, let's consider that old Polish favorite, rice baked with apples. To the authoress and many other Poles, it is a hot supper dish, whereas the author, who is not especially partial to sweet foods as the main course, prefers to enjoy it for dessert. Ultimately, you will have to look for it among the grain dishes. One could argue that it should be listed among the fruits, which only goes to show the major dilemma facing any cookbook author: where to list what in the many borderline cases the writer invariably encounters.

As a result, that classic Christmas Eve dish *kluski z makiem* is found in the pasta section, but another Wigilia favorite, *kutia*, is listed in the chapter devoted to grain dishes. When in doubt, simply consult the index at the back of the book.

* * *

COMPOTES
kompoty

Compotes, a favorite light and refreshing dessert after a heavy meal, are little more than fruit cooked in water with a little sugar. What Americans refer to as canned peaches the Pole would call "kompot z brzoskwiń" (peach compote). To stick with the canned fruit just a bit, you know they come in light, medium, or heavy syrup, which simply refers to the amount of water and sugar in which the fruit was cooked. The compotes in this chapter are served as desserts in dessert bowls or dishes. The thinner drinking compotes so popular in today's Poland are listed in the beverage chapter, but any of the following can also be drunk if diluted with pre-boiled water. According to preference, compotes may be lightly flavored with vanilla, cinnamon, cloves, or nutmeg. If they come out too sweet, a pinch of citric-acid crystals will give them added tang. Compotes may be served hot, warm, at room temp., or chilled.

APPLE OR PEAR COMPOTE
kompot z jabłek lub gruszek

Wash, peel, and quarter 1 lb. apples or pears, remove cores, and slice fruit. In pot bring to boil 2 c. water and 3–4 T. sugar. Add the fruit and 1–3 cloves if desired. If using apples, you may add a pinch of cinnamon instead. Cook covered on low heat until fruit is tender. This should be only a matter of min. If preparing pear compote, a pinch citric-acid crystals or 1 T. lemon juice may be added. Let stand covered until cooled to room temp. Transfer to compote serving dish and chill before serving. *Optional*: Cook with 1 inch piece of vanilla pod if desired.

BERRY COMPOTE
kompot z owoców jagodowych

Wash, hull, and rinse 1 lb. berries (strawberries, raspberries, gooseberries, or currants). Bring 2 c. water and 4–5 T. sugar to boil, add drained fruit, reduce heat, and cook about 2 min. Cool covered to room temp. and serve as above. *Note*: The actual amount of sugar should be adjusted to the tartness of the fruit and the taste you desire. Reduce the amount of water if a heavier syrup is preferred.

CHERRY COMPOTE
kompot z wiśni

Stem and wash 1 lb. sour or sweet cherries. Remove pits if desired. Bring 2 c. water and 4 T. sugar (for sweet cherries) or 7–8 T. sugar (for sour cherries) to boil. Add fruit, reduce heat, and cook covered 3–4 min. Cool to room temp. under cover, transfer to compote serving dish, chill, and serve. *Optional*: 1 clove or a dash of cinnamon may be added during cooking.

PLUM, PEACH OR APRICOT COMPOTE
kompot ze śliwek, brzoskwiń lub moreli

Wash 1 lb. plums, peaches, or apricots. If using peaches, peel them. Halve plums and discard pits. Halve peeled peaches and peeled or unpeeled apricots, discard pits, and slice. Bring 2 c. water and 4–6 T. sugar to boil, add fruit, and cook until tender. Cool covered to room temp., transfer to compote serving dish, chill, and serve. *Note*: A tart compote made with tiny, yellow wild plums (mirabelki) is good to quench that morning-after thirst!

MIXED COMPOTE/"POLISH FRUIT COCKTAIL"
kompot mieszany

Use 1 lb. of mixed fruit. Wash, hull, and rinse berries or currants. Remove stems and (optional) pits from cherries. Halve and pit plums. Peel, core, and slice apples or pears. Peel, pit, and slice peaches. Pit and slice peeled or unpeeled apricots. Bring 2 c. water to boil with 3–4 T. sugar. Add larger fruit, bring to boil, then add smaller fruit (berries, cherries, currants) and cook under cover about 2 min. Cool covered to room temp., transfer to compote serving dish, and chill before serving. *Optional*: Flavor lightly with any of the above spices if desired.

FRESH STRAWBERRY COMPOTE
kompot surówkowy z truskawek lub poziomek

Wash, hull, rinse, and drain 1 lb. cultivated or wild strawberries. Place whole wild strawberries or sliced domestic strawberries in compote serving dish, sprinkle with 2 T. powdered sugar, cover, and refrigerate 2-3 hrs. Bring 2 c. water and 2 T. sugar to boil and set aside to cool. Pour over fruit, mix lightly so as not to damage fruit, and chill another hr. before serving. *Note*: None of the vitamins are lost during cooking which is saying quite a lot, considering that strawberries have more vitamin C than citrus fruit!

FRESH BRANDIED RASPBERRY COMPOTE
kompot surówkowy z malin z koniakiem

Carefully clean, wash, and drain 1 lb. raspberries—handle them gently because they're quite fragile!—place in compote serving dish, sprinkle with 1 jigger cognac (brandy) or rum, cover, and refrigerate 1 hr. Bring 1–1½ c. water to boil with 3–4 T. sugar, cool only slightly, and pour over raspberries while still rather hot. Mix gently, cover, and chill thoroughly before serving.

FRESH APRICOT OR PEACH COMPOTE
kompot surówkowy z moreli lub brzoskwiń

Scald 1 lb. apricots or peaches with boiling water, drain, rinse with cold water, and peel. Cut in ½, discard pits, and slice. Place in compote serving dish. Bring 2 c. water to boil with 3–4 T. sugar, cool only slightly, and pour while still quite hot over fruit. Cool to room temp. covered. Sprinkle with 1 T. lemon juice, mix gently, and chill at least 2 hrs. before serving.

FRESH ORANGE COMPOTE WITH WINE
kompot surówkowy z pomarańcz z winem

Peel 4 oranges, slice, and cut each slice into 4 pieces, discarding seeds. Place in compote serving dish. Dust with 4 T. powdered sugar, cover, and refrigerate 1 hr. Mix ½ c. cold, pre-boiled water with ¼–½ c. dry red wine and pour over oranges. Mix gently and chill at least 2 hrs. before serving.

PRUNE COMPOTE/STEWED PRUNES
kompot z suszonych śliwek

Drench 1 lb. prunes with cold, pre-boiled water to cover and soak at room temp. covered overnight. Add a little water if all has been absorbed by prunes. Next day add 1 heaping T. sugar, a small piece cinnamon bark, and a piece of lemon rind; cook about 15 min. Cool to room temp. and chill before serving. Compote made of prunes and other dried fruit are typical desserts of Christmas Eve.

CHRISTMAS DRIED-FRUIT COMPOTE
wigilijny kompot z suszu

In pot combine 1 c. mixed dried fruit, 1 c. prunes, and (optional) ½–1 c. raisins. Cover with lukewarm, pre-boiled water and soak covered overnight at room temp. Add a heaping T. sugar and a piece of lemon rind and cook 10 min. Cool and serve as above. *Note*: Another way is to drain the fruits after they have soaked overnight, reserving liquid. Add 1 heaping T. sugar and a piece of lemon rind, bring to boil, reduce heat, and simmer 10 min. Place fruit in compote serving dish and pour the liquid over it. Cool to room temp., then chill before serving.

CHRISTMAS PRUNE & FIG COMPOTE
wigilijny kompot ze śliwek suszonych i fig

In 2 separate containers soak 8 oz. prunes and 8 oz. dried figs overnight in pre-boiled lukewarm water to cover. Next day, combine the 2 mixtures, add 2–3 heaping T. sugar, 2 t. lemon juice, and a small piece of cinnamon bark; simmer about 10 min. Cool to room temp. and chill before serving.

12-FRUIT CHRISTMAS COMPOTE
kompot wigilijny z dwunastu owoców

Soak 1 lb. dried fruit in pre-boiled, lukewarm water to cover overnight. Use prunes, apricots, pears, apples, peaches, cherries, raisins, currants, figs, and dates, as far as the dried fruit are concerned, plus a whole small lemon and whole small orange, sliced rind and all. (*Note*: When using citrus fruit with rinds, first scrub well with stiff brush in plenty of hot soapy water, rinse, scald with boiling water, and dry.) Next day add 1–2 heaping T. sugar, a small piece of cinnamon bark, and cook 10 min. Cool to room temp. and chill before serving. *Note*: If you don't have 10 different dried fruits but want to uphold tradition, fresh fruit (apples, pears, etc.) may be used but should be added after compote has cooked and cooled to room temp. Some say this dish originated in memory of the 12 Apostles.

FRUIT & CREAM
owoce ze śmietanką

Wash 1 lb. fruit (apricots, peaches, raspberries, blueberries). Peaches or apricots should then be scalded with boiling water, peeled, pitted, and sliced. With berries, simply drain in colander until dry. Place fruit in dessert dishes, parfait glasses, etc. and chill. Mix 1 c. cold coffee cream or half & half with 1–2 level or slightly heaped T. powdered sugar (depending on tartness of fruit and sweetness desired), pour over chilled fruit, and serve immediately.

BERRIES WITH SOUR CREAM
owoce jagodowe ze śmietaną

Tart and tangy sour cream seems to be ideally suited to berries. Wash 1 lb. strawberries (cultivated or wild) or blackberries, hull, rinse, and drain. Place in dessert dishes of choice.

Fork-blend 1 c. cold sour cream with 2–3 T. powdered sugar and pour over fruit. *Note*: Crème fraîche, a slightly tart cream, is also excellent over berries, but use a little less sugar.

BERRIES WITH WHIPPED CREAM
owoce jagodowe z bitą śmietaną

Wash, hull, rinse, and drain 1 lb. strawberries, raspberries, blueberries, or blackberries. Place in dessert cups or bowl and chill 30 min. Beat ½ c. cold whipping cream with 2 T. powdered sugar and place a dollop on each serving.

APRICOTS & WALNUTS
morele z orzechami

Wash, scald, and rinse with cold water 1 lb. ripe apricots. Peel, halve, and pit. Set aside the ripest apricot and slice the rest. Place sliced apricots in dessert cups. In blender, whirl the reserved apricot with ¾ c. coffee cream and about 3 T. powdered sugar until creamy. Pour over sliced apricots and chill. Top each portion with ground walnuts, of which you will need about ½ c.

PEACHES IN WINE
brzoskwinie w winie

Scald 4 large ripe peaches with boiling water, rinse with cold water immediately, then peel, halve, and pit. Slice thin, then cut each slice in ½. Arrange in compote serving dish, dust with 4 T. powdered sugar through sieve, and sprinkle with ¼–½ c. dry or semi-dry white wine. Cover and refrigerate 2 hrs. before serving. Top each portion with a dollop of whipped cream if desired.

SUGARED STRAWBERRIES
truskawki cukrzone

Wash, hull, rinse, and drain well 1 qt. strawberries. Slice into bowl and sprinkle with 2–4 T. granulated or powdered sugar. (Personally, we prefer sifting powdered sugar over berries since it dissolves more completely.) Cover and let stand at room temp. 30-60 min. Serve with a dollop of sour cream, crème fraîche, or whipped cream. Chill in fridge before serving if desired. *Note*: If more liquid has formed than desired, pour some off and use it as a topping for ice cream, pudding, etc.

STRAWBERRIES IN VANILLA SAUCE
truskawki w sosie waniliowym

Wash and hull, rinse, and drain well 1 qt. preferably small strawberries. Arrange in compote serving dish and drench with vanilla sauce (see sweet sauces at end of chapter). Serve immediately with plain wafers or tea cakes of choice.

APPLES OR PEARS IN VANILLA SAUCE
jabłka lub gruszki w sosie waniliowym

Drain well 20 cooked apple quarters or 10 pear halves from compote (or use canned pears), arrange on compote serving dish and drench with vanilla sauce. Chill at least 1 hr. before serving.

PEARS IN CHOCOLATE
gruszki w czekoladzie

Drain well 10 cooked or canned pear halves, arrange on serving dish, and drench with chocolate sauce. Chill 1 hr. before serving. Top each portion with a dollop of whipped cream if desired.

COMPOTE (CANNED) FRUIT IN VARIOUS WAYS
owoce kompotowe na różne sposoby

Drained fruit from homemade compote or store-bought canned fruit affords various opportunities to prepare quick, easy, and tasty desserts. Whenever our apple tree has a bumper crop, we frequently have compote. Since we prefer the thin, drinking variety, there are always plenty of cooked apples left over. For a quick dessert, these need only be drained, dusted with powdered sugar, and topped with a dollop of sour cream or whipped cream. If compote was made without cinnamon, a pinch will perk up the flavor. Drained canned pear halves may be filled with a spoonful of preserves for an instant dessert. Peach and apricot halves are also good. Use your imagination and you'll surely come up with your own new ways to serve them. (*Note*: The leftover syrup makes a nice gelatin dessert.) Several more examples follow.

PEACHES IN ALMOND SAUCE
brzoskwinie w sosie migdałowym

Drain well 10 canned peach halves, arrange on serving dish, and drench with almond sauce (see cold sauces at end of chapter).

FRUIT IN CREAMY WHITE-WINE SAUCE
owoce w sosie szodonowym

Arrange 4 c. drained fruit from mixed compote (or store-bought, large-chunk fruit cocktail) in serving dish, drench with hot, creamy white-wine sauce (see end of chapter) and serve at once.

CHOCOLATE-GLAZED PEARS
gruszki w polewie czekoladowej

Peel 8 pears, leaving stems intact. Place upright in pot, and scald with boiling water which should reach ½ way up. Cover, bring to gentle boil, and simmer several min. Remove and drain pears, then chill 1 hr. in fridge. In double boiler, melt 2–3 squares (oz.) sweetened chocolate, stirring constantly, and set aside to cool slightly. Arrange pears in serving dish and pour warm melted chocolate over them, letting it trickle down the sides. Chill at least 30 min. Before serving, sprinkle with 2–3 T. rum.

BAKED APPLES
jabłka pieczone

Wash well and drain 4 apples. Stand stem side down and scoop out core, leaving a thin wall at stem end. Fill openings with sugar mixed with a pinch of cinnamon; honey; cherry preserves; or black-currant jam. Place apples in baking dish, sprinkle with several T. boiling water, and bake in pre-heated 375° oven 20–30 min. or until apples are tender but still intact. Serve hot dusted with powdered sugar, topped with a little honey or fruit syrup. *Note*: Fill openings with drained preserves before baking and spoon the leftover syrup over hot baked apples.

WINE-BAKED APPLES
jabłka pieczone w winie

Wash, peel, halve, and core 4 tart cooking apples. Remove a thin slice from bottom so they do not wobble and place cored side up in baking dish. Scald and drain 3 T. raisins, mix with 3 T. chopped walnuts, and fill apple cavities with mixture. Dissolve 4 T. powdered sugar in ¾ c. red wine (dry or sweet) and pour over apples. Bake in pre-heated 375° oven 15–20 min. When cooled to room temp., chill in fridge and serve in dish in which they were baked.

EASY HOMEMADE DESSERT JELLY/GELATIN DESSERT/"JELLO"
galaretka owocowa szybka

Homemade flavored gelatins are more natural than the artificially colored and flavored store-bought "jello"-type mixes. They are also far more economical (enabling you to use up leftover canned-fruit liquid, the syrup from drained preserves etc.) and surprisingly easy to prepare. Simply soak 1 T. plain gelatin in ½ c. cold water 10–15 min. In pot, combine 1½ c. bottled fruit syrup (cherry, raspberry, strawberry) and 1 c. water, heat until quite hot, add gelatin mixture, bring to boil, stirring to dissolve gelatin. Pour into individual dessert dishes, fruit cups, etc. When cooled to room temp. chill 2-3 hrs. or until firmly set before serving. Serve as is or topped with fruit syrup, vanilla sauce, or whipped cream. *Variation*: Bottled or canned fruit juice or fruit drink (cherry, strawberry, cranberry, cranberry-apple, apple, grape) also make a tasty gelatin dessert. Remember, 1 packet unflavored gelatin gels 2 c. liquid. Make sure to count the water in which the gelatin was soaked before being added to hot liquid.

JELLIED COMPOTE
kompot w galarecie

Drain well 1 qt. compote or canned fruit. Arrange fruit in compote serving dish or gelatin mold. Soak 1 packet gelatin in ½ c. cold water 10–15 min. Heat compote or canned fruit liquid of which there should be 1½ c., adding water if necessary to obtain that quantity. Add gelatin mixture and bring to boil, stirring occasionally. Allow gelatin mixture to cool to lukewarm, then pour over fruit. When cooled to room temp. refrigerate 2–3 hrs. or until nicely set. If using gelatin mold, dip it briefly in boiling water to loosen gelatin dessert and turn out onto serving dish. Top with whipped cream if desired. *Note*: To give a blush of color to pear or peach gelatins, which are a bit grayish on their own, add 1–2 t. cherry syrup to hot liquid before adding gelatin. For a bit more tang, add 1 t. or so lemon juice to hot liquid. *Variation*: Just the liquid from canned fruit can be used to make a jellied dessert, when fruit is needed for other purposes.

JELLIED FRUIT
galaretka z owoców

Soak 3 t. gelatin in ½ c. cold water 10-15 min. Place 2 c. washed, trimmed, and (where applicable) peeled fruit in pot. These may be strawberries, raspberries, apples, apricots, or peaches. (*Note*: The 2 c. refers of course to diced apples, apricots, or peaches.) Add 1½ c. water and 4–5 T. sugar and cook until tender (5–10 min.). Drain, reserving liquid, and place fruit in dessert dishes. Add gelatin mixture to hot liquid and bring to boil, stirring occasionally. Pour gelatin liquid after it has cooled somewhat over fruit, cool to room temp., and chill 2-3 hrs. Serve with whipped cream or sweet sauce of choice.

JELLIED FRUIT HEALTH DESSERT
galaretka z owoców witaminowa

Soak 3 t. gelatin in ½ c. cold water 10–15 min. Wash and hull 2 c. strawberries or raspberries (or 1 c. of each), purée in blender and sieve. Pour 1 c. water over pulp left in sieve into another pot, mixing pulp vigorously with wooden spoon to force through as many fruit particles as possible and scraping into pot sieved mixture that clings to bottom of sieve. To sieved mixture add gelatin and 4–5 T. sugar and bring to boil. Place pot into a larger pot of cold water to cool quickly. When cooled to lukewarm, add the pureed berries and mix in well. Pour into serving dish or individual dessert bowls and chill 2–3 hrs. before serving. Serve with whipped cream or sweet sauce of choice.

LEMON GELATIN
galaretka cytrynowa

This is a nice, light, and refreshing dessert to crown a heavy meal! Soak 3 t. gelatin in ½ c. cold water 10-15 min. Scrub 2 lemons with brush in hot soapy water. Rinse and dry. Grate rind of 1 lemon, place in pot, add 1½ c. water, 5–6 T. sugar and gelatin mixture, and bring to boil, stirring occasionally. Set aside to cool somewhat. Stir in juice of 2 lemons and (optional) 2–3 T. dry white wine, mix very well, and pour into serving bowl or individual dessert dishes. Chill 2–3 hrs. before serving. Decorate tops of servings with thin lemon wedges. *Note*: Adding 1 t. cherry syrup together with lemon juice will improve the color of your dessert.

ORANGE GELATIN
galaretka pomarańczowa

Proceed as with lemon gelatin, but use grated rind and juice of 1 orange and juice of ½ lemon and reduce sugar to 3–4 T.

TEA & RUM JELLY
galaretka ponczowa

Soak 3 t. gelatin in ½ c. cold water 10–15 min. Sweeten 1½ c. hot fairly strong tea (made with 2 level t. loose tea or 1 teabag) to taste with sugar, add gelatin mixture and bring to boil. Cool slightly, add 2–3 T. rum and 1 T. lemon juice and mix well. Pour into dessert cups and chill 2-3 hrs. Decorate tops with thin lemon slices or top with vanilla or creamy white-wine sauce.

CREAMY COFFEE GELATIN
galaretka kawowa

Soak 3 t. gelatin in ½ c. cold water 10–15 min. Place 2 heaping t. powder-fine ground coffee in pot, scald with ½ c. boiling water, bring to boil, remove from heat, strain through fine sieve, and set aside. In pot combine 1¼ c. milk, the brewed coffee, and 2-4 T. sugar. Heat, add gelatin mixture, and bring to boil, stirring. Cool somewhat and pour into individual dessert cups. Chill 2–3 hrs. or until set. Serve with chocolate or rum sauce.

CREAMY VANILLA GELATIN
galaretka mleczna waniliowa

Soak 3 t. gelatin in ½ c. cold water 10–15 min. Bring 1 c. milk and ½ a cut-up vanilla pod to boil, stirring frequently so as not to scorch milk. Strain. Add ½ c. coffee cream or half & half, 2–3 t. sugar and gelatin mixture and bring to boil while stirring. Cool somewhat and pour into dessert cups. When cooled to room temp. chill 2-3 hrs. Serve with chocolate sauce or other sweet sauce of choice.

TANGY CREAMY GELATIN
galaretka z zsiadłego mleka

Soak 3 t. gelatin in ½ c. cold water 10–15 min. With wire whisk beat 1½ c. sour milk with ½ c. powdered sugar, ½ c. sour cream, and ½–1 t. vanilla extract. (**Variation**: For creamy lemon gelatin, substitute 2 T. lemon juice for vanilla.) Transfer gelatin mixture to sauce pan and heat on low flame until completely dissolved. Remove from flame, cool somewhat, and slowly add to milk mixture, whisking or beating with egg-beater. Pour into dessert cups and chill 2-3 hrs. Serve with fruit syrup of choice.

CREAMY STRAWBERRY DESSERT
galaretka mleczno-truskawkowa

Soak 3 t. gelatin in ½ c. cold water 10–15 min. Wash, hull, rinse, and drain ½–¾ c. fresh strawberries. Heat gelatin mixture over low flame, stirring constantly, until completely dissolved and set aside to cool. Whirl in blender strawberries, 2 c. sour milk, 4–5 T. powdered sugar, and gelatin mixture until creamy. Pour into dessert cups and chill 2–3 hrs. Decorate each portion with small, washed and hulled strawberries. *Note:* This dessert may also be made with thawed frozen strawberries, strawberry preserves, or jam, but omit or reduce sugar if using preserves or jam.

KISIEL/JELLY-PUDDING
kisiel

This very old dessert, which predates the widespread use of gelatin in the kitchen, was originally thickened with oat starch or millet starch. Nowadays, potato starch is the customary thickener. Kisiel is cloudier than gelatin desserts and its texture could be described as slightly "gooey" and grainy. Translating it into English also poses a problem. Since it seems like a cross between gelatin desserts and American pudding mixes that come in a box, we considered "jelly-pudding" but find that a bit clumsy. "Fruit gel" was another possibility, but not every kisiel is made from fruit. We finally decided to simply stick to the original, the way we have with pierogi and a number of other dishes. Besides, it should be rather easy for every English speaker to say KEY-shell. *Note:* Cornstarch may be used in place of potato starch in any of the following kisiel recipes.

EASY FRUIT KISIEL
kisiel owocowy łatwy

In pot combine 1½ c. fruit syrup (cherry, strawberry or raspberry are best) with 1 c. water and bring to boil. Dissolve ¼ c. potato starch in ½ c. cold water, stir into hot fruit-syrup mixture and bring to boil, mixing constantly. Pour kisiel into dessert dishes rinsed with cold water, cool to room temp. and chill. Serve with cold coffee cream. *Note:* To prevent a skin from forming, sprinkle tops with cold water and keep covered as it cools.

FRUIT KISIEL
kisiel owocowy

Wash well and drain 2 c. fruit (strawberries, raspberries, blackberries, cherries, from which pits should be removed), cut in half, place in pot, add 2 c. water and 4–5 T. sugar, and cook about 5 min. Sieve mixture, forcing through with wooden spoon and scraping sieve bottom until no more liquid matter appears. Dissolve ¼ c. potato starch in ½ c. cold water and slowly pour into cooking sieved fruit, stirring constantly and bringing to boil. Pour mixture into dessert bowls rinsed with cold water. Decorate tops with several whole cherries or berries from which kisiel was made. Cool to room temp., chill until set, and serve with cold sweet sauce of choice or coffee cream.

VITAMIN-RICH FRUIT KISIEL
kisiel witaminowy

This kisiel retains much of the fruit's vitamins because it is not really cooked. Wash, hull, rinse, drain, and (in the case of cherries) pit 2 c. fruit. Puree in blender and sieve, forcing puree through with wooden spoon until bottom of sieve is scraped clean and all dripping stops. Transfer pulp leftover in sieve to pot, add 1½ c. water and 4–5 T. sugar, bring to boil, and sieve again. Add ¼ c. potato starch dissolved in ½ c. water and bring to boil, stirring constantly. Remove from heat, add juice (i.e. liquid obtained from sieving blender-puréed fruit), and mix well with whisk or egg-beater. Transfer to dessert dishes rinsed with cold water, cool, chill, and serve as above.

CHRISTMAS CRANBERRY KISIEL
kisiel żurawinowy wigilijny

This is one of the desserts traditionally served in many Polish families on that most festive of occasions, Christmas Eve. Wash and drain 2 c. fresh cranberries, place in pot, add 2 c. water, bring to boil, and cook about 5 min. or until cranberries burst. Sieve mixture, mashing with wooden spoon and scraping sieve bottom into pot. Sweeten to taste, stir in ¼ c. potato starch dissolved in ½ c. water, and bring to boil, stirring frequently. As with all kisiels, for a smoother texture, beat vigorously with whisk or egg-beater. Pour mixture into dessert dishes rinsed with cold water, cool, and chill before serving. Serve with poppyseed sauce (see end of chapter). *Variation:* Puree raw cranberries in blender before cooking and they'll be easier to sieve.

CHRISTMAS OAT KISIEL
kisiel owsiany wigilijny

This is another traditional Christmas Eve dessert. In pot combine 1 c. rolled oats and 5 c. water, bring to boil, reduce heat and simmer uncovered on low flame about 45 min., stirring occasionally. Strain into another pot, stirring oat mixture to extract all liquid and scraping sieve bottom into pot. To sieved mixture add 4–5 T. sugar, ½–1 t. vanilla extract. Heat, adding 1–2 T. potato starch dissolved in ¼ c. water and bring to boil. Beat briefly with egg-beater or whisk and transfer to dessert dishes pre-rinsed in cold water. Cool to room temp. and chill. Serve with poppyseed milk (see end of chapter). *Note*: Feel free to slightly increase or reduce amount of potato starch in all kisiel recipes, depending on texture desired. In this recipe, using 1 T. will produce the "gooier" consistency many Poles prefer. Two T. will give it a firmness comparable to American "out-of-the-box" pudding.

VANILLA KISIEL
kisiel waniliowy

In pot combine 2½ c. milk and ½ chopped-up vanilla pod (or 1 t. vanilla extract). Bring to boil, stirring constantly to prevent scorching. Strain (if using vanilla pod), and dissolve 3–4 T. sugar in hot milk. Dissolve ¼ c. potato starch in ½ c. cold milk and add in thin stream to hot milk, stirring constantly. Bring mixture to boil, remove from heat, add 1 T. butter or margarine, and beat briefly with whisk or egg-beater. Pour into damp, pre-rinsed dessert cups, cool to room temp., and chill. Serve topped with preserves, fruit syrup, or chocolate sauce. *Note*: This kisiel is quite similar in taste and texture to "out-of-the-box" vanilla pudding. *Hint*: When kisiel has cooled to lukewarm, cover top with thin layer of fruit syrup which will prevent a skin from forming.

CARAMEL KISIEL
kisiel karmelowy

Caramelize 3 T. sugar in dry saucepan to a nice golden color, remove from heat. Carefully stir in 3 T. hot water, simmer while stirring until caramelized sugar fully dissolves, and bring to boil. Heat 2½ c. milk and 2–3 T. sugar until sugar dissolves. Stir in ¼ c. potato starch, add caramel liquid, and bring to boil. Beat briefly with whisk or egg-beater and pour into dessert dishes pre-rinsed with cold water. Cool, chill, and serve with cold sauce of choice.

CHOCOLATE KISIEL
kisiel kakaowy

Fork-blend 2–3 T. cocoa with about ⅓ c. sugar and ½ c. cold milk into smooth paste. Combine in pot with 2 c. milk and bring to boil, stirring constantly to prevent scorching. Dissolve ¼ c. potato starch in ½ c. cold milk and stir into hot mixture. Add 1 T. butter and ½ t. vanilla extract and simmer briefly. Beat with whisk or egg-beater and pour into damp dessert cups. When cooled to room temp., chill 2 hrs. or so. Serve with cherry preserves, cherry syrup or vanilla sauce.

COFFEE KISIEL
kisiel kawowy

In small pot combine 1 heaping t. coffee, ground flour fine, and ⅓ c. water, bring to boil, remove from heat, and let stand covered until cooled slightly. Strain through fine sieve and discard grounds. Bring 2½ c. milk and 4 T. sugar to boil and add coffee. Dissolve ¼ c. potato starch in ½ c. cold milk and add in thin stream to hot mixture, stirring constantly. Bring to boil. Remove from heat, add 1 T. butter, and beat briefly with whisk or egg-beater. Pour into pre-rinsed dessert cups, cool, and chill as above. Serve with cold coffee cream or chocolate sauce.

ALMOND KISIEL
kisiel migdałowy

In pot combine 2½ c. milk and 3–4 T. sugar, and 1 c. ground blanched almonds. (*Note*: For better flavor, replace 1 t. ground almonds with equal amount ground bitter almonds.) Bring to boil, stirring to prevent scorching. Dissolve ¼ c. potato starch in ½ c. cold milk and stir into hot mixture. Bring to boil and simmer briefly. Add 1 T. butter and ¼ t. vanilla extract and beat briefly with whisk or egg-beater. Pour into damp, pre-rinsed dessert cups, cool, chill, and serve with preserves or fruit syrup. *Note:* An almond-flavored kisiel may be prepared by using several drops almond oil or ½ t. or more almond extract instead of ground almonds.

SOUTHERN-FRUIT KISIEL
kisiel bakaliowy

Soak in water to cover 3 T. raisins, 2 dried figs, and 2 dried apricots several min. Drain well and chop figs and apricots fine. In pot combine 2½ c. milk, dried fruit, 2 T. ground almonds, and 3–4 T. sugar and bring to boil. In thin stream, add ¼ c. potato starch dissolved in ¼ c. cold milk and bring to boil, stirring frequently. Add 1 T. butter and ¼ t. vanilla or rum extract and beat briefly with whisk or egg-beater. After cooling to room temp. and chilling, top individual portions with chopped almonds or walnuts or grated chocolate.

MOUSSE
mus

Long a naturalized citizen on the Polish culinary scene, this French import is a light dessert usually made with pureed fruit, beaten egg whites, and flavorings and stiffened with gelatin. There are also varieties that do without egg whites or gelatin. A small sampling from the extensive mousse family follows.

COOKED-FRUIT MOUSSE
mus z owoców gotowanych

Soak 2 t. gelatin in 2 T. cold water 10–15 min. Wash and pit (where applicable) 1 lb. fresh fruit: apples, plums, peaches, apricots, cherries, gooseberries, etc. Discard seed portions from apples but do not peel. Dice fruit, place in pot, add 2 T. water and cook on low heat, stirring constantly, until fruit disintegrates. Sieve mixture to extract all flavor, making sure to scrape sieve bottom clean. To mixture add ⅓ c. powdered sugar and mix well. Place soaked gelatin on low flame (a metal cup is ideal for this purpose) and heat, stirring constantly until gelatin completely dissolves. Set aside to cool. Beat 3 egg whites to stiff froth, then gradually add ⅓ c. powdered sugar, gelatin mixture, and sieved fruit. Beat until mixture is smooth and fluffy. Transfer mixture to dessert serving dish and chill in fridge 1 hr. Serve immediately, garnished with drained fruit from preserves or drenched with coffee cream. Plain wafers are a nice accompaniment.

FRESH-FRUIT MOUSSE
mus z owoców surowych

Soak 2 t. gelatin in 2 T. cold water 10–15 min., preferably in metal or heat-proof glass cup. Wash, hull, drain, and sieve 1 lb. fresh strawberries or raspberries. (**Note**: Fruit may be pureed in blender before sieving.) Heat gelatin mixture over low flame, stirring, until dissolved and set aside to cool. Beat 3 egg whites to stiff froth. Beat into froth gradually ½–⅔ c. powdered sugar, gelatin mixture, and sieved fruit. Beat until ingredients blend and mixture becomes smooth and fluffy. Transfer to dessert serving dish and chill 1 hr. Serve immediately as is or decorated with whole fresh berries or berries from drained preserves.

SOUR-CREAM MOUSSE
mus z kwaśnej śmietany

Soak 3 t. gelatin in 3 T. water 10–15 min., heat to dissolve, and set aside to cool. Beat 2 c. sour cream until creamy, adding ⅔ c. powdered sugar and ½–1 t. vanilla extract. Beat in 2 t. finely chopped, candied orange rind and cool gelatin mixture. Transfer to damp, pre-rinsed parfait or champagne glasses and chill 1 hr. before serving. Decorate with preserves of choice.

CREAM OF WHEAT MOUSSE
mus z kaszy manny

Mix 1 c. water with ½ c. uncooked cream of wheat. In pot combine 2 c. water and ½ c. sugar and heat to boiling. Add cream of wheat mixture to boiling syrup, reduce heat, and cook about 15 min., stirring frequently. Remove from heat and beat until fluffy. Add 2 t. lemon juice and mix in well. Transfer to damp, pre-rinsed serving dish. When cooled to room temp., chill at least 1 hr. before serving. Serve topped with fruit syrup. *Variation*: Replace 2–3 T. sugar with equal amount of honey or fruit syrup when preparing sugar syrup. Instead of 2 t. lemon juice, flavor with 1 t. vanilla extract, and 1 t. lemon juice.

CREAM OF WHEAT MOUSSE ANOTHER WAY
mus z kaszy manny inaczej

Mix ½ c. uncooked cream of wheat with 1 c. cold milk. Bring another c. milk to boil, add cream of wheat mixture, stir, and simmer on low heat about 15 min., stirring. Dissolve 4–5 T. sugar in mixture, add ½–1 t. vanilla extract and remove from heat. Beat until fluffy. Fold in 3 beaten egg whites, mix well, and transfer to serving dish or individual dessert dishes pre-rinsed with cold water. When cooled to room temp., chill about 1 hr. Serve with vanilla or chocolate sauce or fruit syrup. *Variation*: For chocolate mousse, dissolve 2-3 T. cocoa in 1 c. milk before bringing to boil and adding cream of wheat mixture.

LEMON CRÈME
krem cytrynowy

The crème is a light and fluffy dessert richer than mousse because it also contains egg yolks. The following lemony dessert is sure to be a winner. Start by soaking 2½ t. gelatin in 3 T. cold water 10–15 min. Add 2 T. boiling milk and stir until gelatin dissolves. Beat 3 egg yolks with ½ c. sugar until white, gradually adding juice of 1 large lemon as well as gelatin mixture. Beat 3 egg whites to stiff froth, add the yolk mixture, and mix lightly. Transfer to sundae or parfait cups or champagne glasses dusted with powdered sugar and chill at least 1 hr. Decorate tops with whipped cream and thin lemon wedges. Plain wafers are often served on the side.

STRAWBERRY CRÈME
krem truskawkowy

Soak 2½ t. gelatin in 3 T. cold water 10–15 min. Place container containing gelatin mixture in pot of hot water and stir until gelatin completely dissolves. Wash, hull, drain, and sieve ½ lb. strawberries. Beat 3 egg yolks with ½ c. powdered sugar until white, gradually adding sieved strawberries and gelatin mixture. Fold in 3 beaten egg whites and 1 T. powdered sugar and mix well. Transfer to powder-sugar-dusted parfait glasses, etc., and chill 1 hr. before serving. Top each serving with a dollop of whipped cream and crown with one whole strawberry.

VANILLA CRÈME
krem waniliowy

Soak 2½ t. gelatin in 3 T. cold water 10–15 min., then place bowl or cup containing gelatin into pan of hot water and stir gelatin until it dissolves. Beat 3 egg yolks and ¼ c. powdered sugar until white, adding 2 T. homemade vanilla sugar (or 1 t. vanilla extract) and gelatin mixture. Whip ½ c. ice-cold whipping cream and stir into yolk mixture. Beat 3 egg whites until stiff, adding 2 T. powdered sugar towards end, add to yolk mixture, and mix ingredients well. Transfer to powder-sugar-dusted dessert cups and chill well. Before serving, garnish with grated chocolate.

CHOCOLATE CRÈME
krem czekoladowy

Prepare as above, but melt 2 squares semi-sweet chocolate with 1 T. milk in double-boiler and add to whipped cream before folding it into yolk mixture.

COFFEE-FLAVORED CRÈME
krem kawowy

In pot, combine 2 heaping T. finely ground coffee and ½ c. water, bring to boil. Remove from heat, cover, and allow to cool. Strain through fine sieve and add to whipped cream before folding it into yolk mixture. Otherwise proceed as in vanilla crème (above).

VANILLA CUSTARD
mleczko waniliowe

Custard, which is known in Polish as mleczko (little milk), has long been a favorite dessert of many and is surprisingly easy to prepare. Combine 2 c. milk and ½ cut-up vanilla pod in pot and bring to boil. Strain and set aside to cool slightly. Beat 3 eggs into bowl, add 4 T. sugar, and beat well with whisk. Gradually add warm milk to beaten eggs., whisking until fully blended. Pour mixture into dessert cups or coffee cups ¾ full and cover each with a piece of aluminum foil, making sure you have a tight seal. Place in pan of boiling water reaching half way up the cups, cover pan, and cook on low heat 30-40 min. Check for doneness with wooden pick. Allow to cool in cups, then chill. Turn out upside down onto serving platter or individual dessert dishes. Top with preserves or sweet sauce of choice.

CHOCOLATE CUSTARD
mleczko czekoladowe

In pot, combine 1½ squares semi-sweet chocolate and 1¾ c. milk, heat to melt chocolate, stirring constantly, and bring to boil. Set aside to cool somewhat. Beat 3 eggs with 2–3 T. sugar, add to warm chocolate mixture, and beat well to blend. Then proceed as above.

WALNUT OR ALMOND CUSTARD
mleczko orzechowe lub migdałowe

Proceed as with vanilla custard (above), but instead of vanilla pod bring 2 c. milk to boil with ½ c. ground walnuts or almonds.

APPLE SOUFFLÉ
suflet z jabłek

Grease an oven-proof baking dish with butter and sprinkle with bread crumbs. Pre-heat oven to 350°. Peel, core, and quarter 1 lb. tart cooking apples, place in pot, add 2 T. water, and cook until they disintegrate. Sieve, add 1 c. powdered sugar to sieved mixture and cook on low heat until it thickens. Beat 6 egg whites to stiff froth and fold into warm apple mixture; mix lightly. Transfer to baking dish, which should be placed in pan of hot water, and bake about 25 min. Serve immediately in baking dish in which soufflé was baked. *Note*: Although this may seem pretty straightforward, soufflés can be tricky and have a tendency to collapse before they get to the table. Only practice can ensure a fair degree of more or less regular success.

LEMON SOUFFLÉ
suflet cytrynowy

Butter heat-proof baking dish, sprinkle with bread crumbs, and pre-heat oven to 375°. Beat 4 egg yolks and ½ c. powdered sugar until white, then mix in juice of 1 lemon, 2 T. finely chopped walnuts, and 2 T. flour. Beat 4 egg whites to stiff froth, add ½ c. powdered sugar towards end, and continue beating another 1–2 min. Fold beaten whites into yolk mixture and mix thoroughly but delicately, for all soufflés must be handled with care.

Transfer mixture to baking dish, which should be placed in pan of hot water, and bake about 25 min. Serve immediately because it tends to collapse.

PEACH OR APRICOT SOUFFLÉ
suflet brzoskwiniowy lub morelowy

Butter oven-proof baking dish, sprinkle with bread crumbs, and set oven at 350°. Wash, cut into eights, 1 lb. ripe peaches or apricots. Combine in pot with 2–3 T. water, cook until fruit disintegrates, and sieve. To sieved fruit add ¾ c. sugar and simmer on low heat, stirring, until mixture thickens. Set aside to cool. Stiffly beat 4 egg whites, adding 4 T. powdered sugar, and beating another 2 min. Fold into warm fruit mixture and mix thoroughly but delicately. Transfer to baking dish set in pan of hot water and bake about 30 min. Serve immediately with coffee cream.

CHOCOLATE SOUFFLÉ
suflet czekoladowy

Cream 3 T. room-temp. butter with 4 T. powdered sugar, adding 4 egg yolks one by one and beating constantly. Add ½ t. vanilla extract and beat to blend in. In double-boiler, melt 3 squares (oz.) semi-sweet chocolate in 2 T. milk, add to yolk mixture and beat well. Beat 4 egg whites until stiff, adding 4 T. powdered sugar. Sprinkle yolk mixture with 4 T. bread crumbs, fold in beaten whites, and mix thoroughly but delicately. Transfer to baking dish set in pan of hot water and bake about 30 min.

WALNUT PUDDING
budyń orzechowy

In Polish, the term "budyń" (pudding) is usually reserved for desserts cooked in classic, tapered pudding molds with tight-fitting snap-on lids. If you don't own one, a tall tapered gelatin mold or even a coffee can may be used, its top tightly sealed with heavy-duty aluminum foil. You will also need a large pot with tight-fitting lid that, when covered, accommodates the entire mold. Butter mold and sprinkle with bread crumbs. Beat 4 egg yolks and ⅔ c. powdered sugar until white, gradually adding 1 c. ground walnuts and beating constantly. Add ½ c. sifted bread crumbs and fold in 4 stiffly beaten egg whites, mixing ingredients thoroughly but delicately. Transfer to pudding mold, which should be no more than ¾ full, snap on lid (or seal top with foil), and place in large pot of boiling water reaching half way up side of mold. Cover pot and cook on low heat about 60 min. Check for doneness with pick. Allow to cool in form 10–15 min., then turn out onto serving dish.

Pudding may be served warm, room temp., or chilled according to preference. Serve with sweet-cream sauce.

RUM PUDDING
budyń ponczowy

Butter pudding mold and sprinkle with bread crumbs. Beat 4 egg yolks, gradually adding 1¼ c. powdered sugar, 2 T. lemon juice, and 2 T. rum. Sprinkle mixture with 8 T. bread crumbs and ⅓ c. ground, blanched almonds. Beat 4 egg whites until stiff, fold into mixture, and mix gently but thoroughly. Transfer to mold, snap on lid, place in pot of boiling water, cover, and cook as above about 1 hr. When slightly cooled, remove from mold and serve with wine sauce or rum sauce (see end of chapter).

SPONGE-CAKE PUDDING
budyń biszkoptowy

Butter pudding mold and sprinkle with bread crumbs. Beat 4 egg yolks with ⅔ c. powdered sugar until white, adding 1 t. lemon juice towards end. Beat 4 egg whites to stiff froth. Fold beaten whites little by little into yolk mixture, alternating with ⅔ c. sifted flour. Mix to blend ingredients, transfer to mold, seal, and cook in hot-water bath as above about 60 min. Remove from mold when slightly cooled and serve with red-wine sauce or other sweet sauce of choice.

CHOCOLATE PUDDING
budyń czekoladowy

In double-boiler combine 3 oz. broken-up, unsweetened or semi-sweet chocolate and ½ c. coffee cream, stirring over boiling water until chocolate melts. Set aside to cool. Meanwhile, beat 4 egg yolks with ⅔ c. powdered sugar and 3 T. soft butter until smooth and creamy. Add lukewarm chocolate mixture and beat a while longer. Add ½ c. ground blanched almonds or walnuts, ⅔ c. bread crumbs, and 4 stiffly beaten egg whites. Mix gently but thoroughly. Transfer to pudding mold and cook in hot-water bath about 60 min. Serve with vanilla sauce or fruit syrup.

CHEESE PUDDING
budyń z sera

Cream ½ stick soft butter with 1 c. powdered sugar and 4 egg yolks until fluffy. Add 1 lb. ground farmer cheese a little at a time, beating continuously. Stir in 2 T. finely chopped blanched almonds and 1 T. finely chopped candied orange rind, fold in 4 stiffly beaten egg whites and mix lightly. Transfer to mold and cook in hot-water bath about 60 min. Serve with chocolate sauce or raspberry sauce.

POPPYSEED PUDDING
budyń z maku

Rinse and drain 1 c. poppyseeds. Place in pot, scald with 2 c. boiling water, and cook at gentle boil about 30 min. or until poppyseeds can be crushed between fingers. Drain well and grind in poppyseed grinder once or in ordinary meat grinder (with finest strainer attached) 3 times. Grind ½ c. blanched almonds and mix into poppyseeds. Separately, beat 3 T. room-temp. butter with ⅔ c. powdered sugar, 2 T. vanilla sugar (or ½ t. vanilla extract), and 3 egg yolks until fluffy. Add ground poppyseeds and almonds and mix in well. Fold in 3 stiffly beaten egg whites and mix lightly. Transfer to mold and cook in hot-water bath about 60 min. Serve with vanilla, almond, or chocolate sauce.

BAKED VANILLA PUDDING
legumina waniliowa

The term "legumina" in Polish designates a kind of pudding usually thickened with flour and baked rather than cooked in a hot-water bath. In English we might refer to these as dessert casseroles. Countless varieties have been developed over the years, of which we can list only a handful. To prepare baked vanilla pudding, start by splitting a small vanilla pod lengthwise and cooking it several min. in 1 c. coffee cream. Set aside to cool. Beat 5 egg yolks with ½ c. sugar until fluffy. Add 2 t. of the vanilla-flavored coffee cream and gradually stir in ⅔ c. flour, sifted, beating until fully blended. Place in pot, add strained coffee cream and heat, stirring until mixture thickens. Remove from heat to cool. When lukewarm, fold in 5 stiffly beaten egg whites and mix gently. Transfer to buttered baking dish, smooth top, and bake in pre-heated 375° oven 30–40 min. Check for doneness with pick. Serve topped with preserves or sweet-cream sauce.

BAKED ALMOND PUDDING
legumina migdałowa

Bring to boil ¼ c. water and 4½ T. sugar, add ½ c. ground, unblanched almonds (i.e. with skins left on), mix, and set aside to cool slightly. Add 4 egg yolks and beat until smooth and fluffy, add ¼ c. sifted bread crumbs, fold in 4 stiffly beaten egg whites, and mix lightly. Transfer to buttered baking dish and bake in pre-heated 375° oven 30–40 min. Serve hot or cold with raspberry sauce or red-wine sauce.

BAKED PLUM-JAM PUDDING
legumina z powideł

Place 1 c. bread crumbs in bowl, pour ¼ c. melted butter over them, add ½ c. sour cream, mix, and set aside. Beat 6 egg yolks with ½ c. sugar until white, add ⅓ c. Polish plum jam (powidła), and 1 t. grated orange rind, combine with bread-crumb mixture and mix well. Fold in 6 stiffly beaten egg whites, mix lightly, and transfer to buttered baking dish. Bake in pre-heated 350° oven about 1 hr. Serve with sour cream or whipped cream.

BAKED RUM PUDDING FLAMBÉ
płonąca legumina rumowa

Cream ⅓ c. butter or margarine with ¾ c. sugar, adding ½ t. grated lemon rind and 8 egg yolks one at a time. After adding each yolk, beat until fully absorbed before adding the next. When mixture is smooth and creamy, add ¼ c. rum, fold in 8 stiffly beaten egg whites, sift in 1½ c. flour, and mix gently to blend ingredients. Transfer to buttered tube pan and bake in pre-heated 350° oven about 1 hr. Check for doneness with pick. To serve, turn out onto serving dish, sprinkle top and sides of "crater" with 1 T. grain alcohol, light, and bring flaming into darkened room. A true conversation piece that also tastes good!

BAKED CHERRY PUDDING
legumina wiśniowa

Cream ⅓ c. room-temp. butter. When fluffy, add ½ c. sugar, beating continuously, then 2 eggs, one at a time, and 4 egg yolks. Add ½ t. grated lemon rind and mix in 1 c. flour, sifted. Add 1 lb. washed, drained, canned, pitted, sour cherries (or equal amount of cherries from well drained, canned cherry-pie filling). Mix ingredients lightly, transfer to buttered baking dish and bake in pre-heated 350° oven about 1 hr. Serve with cold sour cream on the side. *Note:* If you have used the canned pie-filling option, the leftover liquid will make a nice pudding topping.

OTHER PUDDINGS, SWEET DISHES, AND DESSERT CASSEROLES
inne leguminy, słodkie potrawy i zapiekanki deserowe

Many other dishes qualifying as "leguminy" are found in the grain and noodle chapters. Among them are such typical Christmas Eve desserts as noodles & poppyseeds and cooked-wheat pudding. These could easily have been included in this chapter, except that many of them, including rice & apple casserole, are frequently served as a light supper meal in themselves. The same holds true for many of the crêpes (naleśniki) and other pancakes which double as desserts and main courses.

HOMEMADE ICE CREAM
lody domowe

Despite the wide availability of ice creams on the market of every color, flavor, and description, there will always be those who prefer making their own, at least some of the time. Usually it is made in a hand-cranked or electric ice cream freezer. If you own one, you know all about packing the freezer with ice and rock salt and how to operate it. We won't go into the details here, limiting ourselves to providing several typical Polish ice cream mixtures. If you don't own such a device but plan to get one, simply follow the manufacturer's instructions. Even if you have no immediate plans to invest in an ice cream freezer, you can still produce homemade ice cream that requires no churn-freezing. In fact, we begin our presentation with non-churned ice cream proposed by the Grande Dame of Polish Cuisine, Madame Lucyna Ćwierczakiewiczowa.

ĆWIERCZAKIEWICZOWA'S VANILLA ICE CREAM
lody waniliowe Ćwierczakiewiczowej

Beat 3 egg yolks and ⅓ c. sugar until white. In saucepan combine ½ vanilla pod, split lengthwise and chopped, with ½ c. milk. Bring to boil and strain. Pour hot milk into yolk mixture in thin stream, beating continuously and heating on low flame until mixture thickens. Do not boil! Remove from heat and place in pan of cold water to cool quickly. When cooled to room temp., place in freezer for 1 hr. Beat 1 c. ice cold whipping cream and ⅓ c. powdered sugar until fluffy. Combine the whipped cream and frozen mixture, mix well, and return to freezer for several hrs. Mix well 2 times during freezing to beat air into mixture, ensuring its light texture. *Optional*: Vary the flavor of your ice cream by adding ½ c. of any of the following: ground walnuts, hazelnuts, or almonds; raisins; grated unsweetened chocolate or sieved fresh fruit, especially berries, black cherries, or peaches.

LOWER-CALORIE VANILLA ICE CREAM
lody waniliowe chudsze

Beat 2 egg yolks with 5 T. sugar and 2 T. homemade vanilla sugar until white. Bring 2 c. milk to boil and, after it has cooled a bit, pour in thin stream into yolk mixture, mixing continuously. Place mixture in pot and heat, stirring constantly, until mixture thickens, but do not boil. Remove from flame and cool quickly in pan of cool water. When cooled to room temp., transfer to freezer for 1 hr. Beat 2 egg whites to stiff froth, adding 1 T. vanilla sugar. Fold froth into frozen mixture and mix gently. Place in freezer for 1 hr., remove, and mix well. Return to freezer for another 2 hrs. before serving. *Variation*: Add any of the flavorings indicated in preceding recipe if desired; instead of vanilla sugar, flavor with 3 T. rum.

TRADITIONAL VANILLA ICE CREAM (CHURN-FROZEN)
lody waniliowe tradycyjne (kręcone)

Beat 2 eggs and 2 yolks with ¾ c. sugar over boiling water in double-boiler until fluffy. Bring 2 c. milk to boil with ½ cut-up vanilla pod. Strain. Pour hot milk in thin stream into egg mixture, beating constantly until mixture thickens. Remove top part of double-boiler and plunge into pot of cold water. When cooled to room temp., chill in fridge. (*Note*: Refrigerate overnight for best results.) Transfer to ice cream freezer (machine) and churn-freeze according to manufacturer's directions. Remember to fill the machine's container only ¾ full with mixture as it expands during churning.

PLAIN WHITE ICE CREAM
lody śmietankowe

Proceed as above, but omit vanilla pod or flavor milk with only about ¼ t. vanilla extract. The latter would be close to what most Americans refer to as "vanilla ice cream". Traditional Polish "lody waniliowe" are more like "French vanilla".

CHOCOLATE OR COCOA ICE CREAM
lody czekoladowe lub kakaowe

Proceed as in traditional vanilla ice cream (above), but melt 1½ squares broken-up, unsweetened chocolate in 2 c. hot milk. Or dissolve 2 T. cocoa in ¼ c. cold milk before adding to rest of milk in pot. Several drops rum or almond extract may be added for flavoring. Cool mixture to room temp. in cold water as above, chill, and churn-freeze. *Optional*: Add about ½ c. coarsely ground walnuts or blanched almonds after 1st 5 min. of churning.

STRAWBERRY ICE CREAM
lody truskawkowe

Wash, hull, rinse, and drain well 1 qt. fresh strawberries (cultivated or wild.) Sieve or puree in blender before sieving. Mix ¾–1 c. sugar with sieved mixture, cover, and chill in coldest part of fridge 2 hrs. Combine with 2 c. coffee cream and 2 c. unwhipped whipping cream, both of which should be very cold. Transfer to ice cream freezer and churn-freeze as directed. *Note:* For raspberry ice cream, use fresh raspberries in place of strawberries.

EASY, ECONOMICAL, LOW-FAT ICE CREAM
lody łatwe, oszczędne i chude

The advent of the blender has made it possible to create homemade ice cream that is fairly simple, economical, lower in calories than the traditional kind, and more than acceptable in flavor. Beat 2 eggs with scant ⅓ c. sugar and ½ t. vanilla extract until creamy. Heat 1½ c. milk. In ½ c. cold milk dissolve 3–4 T. powdered-milk crystals and 2 T. instant vanilla pudding powder. Add to hot milk and bring to boil, stirring constantly. In thin stream add thickened milk mixture to egg mixture, beating constantly. Transfer to blender and whirl briefly. Transfer to metal tin, cool to room temp., chill, and place in freezer. After 1–2 hrs., when mixture begins to freeze around edges, place in blender and whirl a few seconds, then return to tin, freeze, and when mixture freezes around edges, blend again. Repeat process 1 more time. After final blending, return mixture to container, seal with aluminum foil, and keep in freezer 3–4 hrs. before serving. *Variations*: Different flavors can be achieved by adding 2–3 T. cocoa or 1 heaping t. instant coffee to milk. For fruit-flavored ice cream, add ½ c. sieved fresh fruit, sugared to taste with powdered sugar, after initial blending of partially frozen mixture. Other possibilities include ground nuts, grated chocolate, chopped raisins, or other southern fruits. Several t. finely diced, candied orange rind and several drops orange extract will produce an orange-flavored ice cream.

FRUIT ICE
lody owocowe

The Polish term "lody" encompasses both traditional ice cream as well as fruit ices made without milk, cream, or eggs. Wash, hull, rinse, and drain well 1 lb. fresh strawberries or raspberries or wash, dry, peel, pit and dice 1 lb. ripe peaches. It is best to use only 1 type of fruit. Puree fruit in blender but do not overblend. Bring 1 c. water and 1-2 c. sugar to boil, stirring to dissolve sugar, and set aside to cool. Lightly beat 2 egg whites. To pureed fruit in blender add syrup and egg whites and whirl briefly to blend. Chill mixture thoroughly, transfer to ice-cream freezer, filling its container only half full with mixture, and churn-freeze. This ice can also be prepared without an ice-cream freezer. Transfer mixture to metal bowl and place in freezer for 1 hr. or until mixture begins to freeze around edges. Whirl in blender several seconds, return to bowl, and place in freezer for another hr. Blend again, then keep covered in freezer several hrs. until fully set.

ICE CUPS
puchary lodowe

The European ice cup is essentially the same as the American sundae, i.e. ice cream served with various toppings. Serving your ice cream, whether homemade or store-bought, in glass or crystal ice cups or parfait glasses (saucer-type champagne glasses may be used in a pinch!) will give your frozen dessert a touch of elegance. In season, fresh berries beautifully complement plain white or vanilla ice cream. Ice cream of most any flavor responds nicely to cherries, strawberries, or raspberries from drained preserves. You can simply top your ice cream with a generous dollop of whipped cream. The sweet sauces that follow shortly are also worth considering. The top dollop of whipped cream can be sprinkled with chopped nuts or grated chocolate. A t. rum, cognac, wiśniówka (cherry cordial), or other liqueur may be poured over ice cream before crowning dollop of whipped cream is added. 1 T. very strong coffee or 1–2 t. strong sweetened tea & rum can also lend zest and variety to ice cream. If fresh or preserved fruit is used in the ice cup, it is customary to crown it with a single whole berry or cherry. A nice continental touch is provided by plain wafers stuck into the ice cream. These are baked in simple rounds or fingers as well as figure 8's and various whimsical swirls. We conclude our encounter with Polish ice cream by presenting what, at the time of this writing, is Warsaw's most popular ice cup. Named after ambrosia, the "food of the gods" in Greek mythology, it is the specialty of the Hortex frozen-food firm which operates a number of ice cream parlors and an umbrella-shaded outdoor café in Warsaw's quaint Old Town Square.

AMBROSIA ICE CUP
puchar "ambrozja"

For each serving use 1 scoop each vanilla, chocolate, and fruit-flavored ice cream, and intersperse scoops with about ½ c. mixed fruit. These vary according to season, but in summer they typically include fresh strawberries, blueberries, seedless grapes, diced, drained canned pineapples and peaches, as well as chopped raisins. Drench with 1–2 t. fruit syrup and (optional) 1 t. rum or cognac. Top with ½ c. whipped cream and garnish with 1 T. chopped walnuts and 1 T. grated chocolate. Insert a fancy swirled wafer into whipped cream and enjoy!

RASPBERRY SAUCE
sos malinowy

Wash, drain, and sieve 1½ c. fresh or thawed frozen (unsugared) raspberries. Combine in saucepan with 3 T. sugar and bring to boil, stirring. Dissolve 1 T. potato starch in 4 T. cold water and add to simmering fruit mixture gradually, stirring continuously and bringing to boil. Remove from heat and continue stirring to cool somewhat. Stir in ⅓ c. sweet red wine and serve hot or cold over ice cream, puddings, etc.

STRAWBERRY SAUCE
sos truskawkowy

Proceed as in raspberry sauce but use fresh or thawed frozen strawberries. *Note*: In both cases, wine may be omitted.

CHERRY SAUCE
sos wiśniowy

Wash, pit, and crush ½ lb. sour cherries and place in saucepan with a tiny piece of cinnamon bark and 1 c. water. Cook until tender. Force through sieve, return to pot, add 5–6 T. sugar, ½ c. sweet or dry red wine, and simmer briefly. Dissolve 2 T. potato starch in 3 T. cold water, add to mixture, stirring and simmering a bit longer. Serve hot or cold over puddings and other desserts of choice. *Variation*: Sieve canned cherry-pie filling, season with a pinch cinnamon and a little wine if desired, and you have "instant cherry sauce!"

APRICOT SAUCE
sos morelowy

Wash, pit, and slice ¾ lb. ripe apricots, place in pot, add ½ c. water, and cook on low heat covered until fruit is tender. Sieve. Beat 2 egg yolks with 4 T. powdered sugar until fluffy, gradually adding sieved apricots. Beat ½ c. very cold whipping cream until peaks form and stir into apricot mixture. Serve cold over fruit, puddings, vanilla ice cream, etc.

EASY FRUIT SAUCE
łatwy sos owocowy

Along the lines of the easy cherry sauce (above), a quick fruit sauce can be whipped up in no time at all by sieving cherry or berry preserves. If necessary, dilute with just enough cold, pre-boiled water to get the pourable consistency you want. If desired, season with a pinch of cinnamon or cloves or 1–2 t. wine. Sieved apricot preserves are very good flavored with 1 t.–1 T. cognac or brandy per cup. Powidła (Polish plum jam) needs nothing more than a little water and perhaps a pinch ground cloves to produce a nice sauce. In most cases, however, preserves are better than jams for this purpose because the latter are less fruity.

CREAMY DESSERT SAUCE
słodki sos śmietankowy

Bring 1 c. coffee cream and ½ t. vanilla extract to boil, remove from heat and set aside to cool. Beat 2 egg yolks and 2 T. powdered sugar until fluffy, combine with cream and heat on low flame, stirring constantly until mixture thickens. Place pot in pan of cold water and continue stirring until cool. Serve cold over dark-colored puddings, kisiels, gelatins and chocolate ice cream.

VANILLA SAUCE
sos waniliowy

Combine ½ c. coffee cream or milk and ½ cut-up vanilla pod in saucepan and bring to boil. Strain. Dissolve 2 t. potato starch in ½ c. cold coffee cream or milk, stir into hot cream (or milk) and bring to boil, stirring constantly. Beat 2 egg yolks and 2–3 T. powdered sugar until fluffy, gradually adding hot milk, stirring constantly. Place saucepan in pan of cold water and stir until cooled. Serve cold over dark-colored puddings and kisiels and fresh fruit.

RUM SAUCE
sos rumowy

Proceed as with vanilla sauce (above), but omit vanilla pod and flavor hot sauce with 2 T. rum or several drops rum extract. Serve as above.

ALMOND SAUCE
sos migdałowy

In saucepan, combine ½ c. ground blanched almonds and ½ c. milk, heat until very hot but do not boil. Dissolve 2 t. potato starch in ½ c. cold milk and add to hot milk & almond mixture, stirring constantly, and bringing to boil. Beat 2 egg yolks and 3 T. powdered sugar until fluffy, gradually adding hot mixture and beating continuously. Place saucepan in pan of cold water and cool, stirring frequently. Serve cold over puddings and other desserts.

CHOCOLATE SAUCE
sos czekoladowy

Combine 2 squares (oz.) broken up chocolate with 1 c. milk in saucepan and bring to boil. Dissolve ½ T. potato starch in ½ c. cold milk and stir into chocolate-flavored milk. Bring to boil, stirring frequently. Beat 2 egg yolks with 4 T. powdered sugar until fluffy, gradually adding hot sauce in thin stream and beating constantly. Place in pan of cold water and continue stirring until cooled. Serve cold over light-colored puddings, kisiels, ice cream, etc.

EASY, YOLKLESS DESSERT SAUCES
łatwe sosy deserowe bez żółtek

Pour 1 c. cold milk into small bowl, add 1 t. vanilla instant-pudding powder and beat with egg-beater, whisk, or hand-held electric mixer. Continue adding pudding powder 1 t. at a time until you get a sauce of pourable consistency. That's all there is to it. It'll do when there isn't time to prepare a cooked sauce from scratch and may be a boon to those who wish to avoid egg yolks, but still it's nowhere near as good as the real thing. You can't have everything! *Note*: Easy chocolate sauce is prepared the same way using chocolate instant-pudding powder.

WHITE-WINE SAUCE
sos szodonowy

In saucepan, beat 3 egg yolks and ½ c. powdered sugar until fluffy. Separately heat 1 c. dry white wine and pour it in thin stream into yolk mixture, beating continuously. Heat, stirring, in double-boiler until sauce thickens. Serve hot over puddings. *Note*: If you prefer a sauce with less "kick", use ½ c. wine and ½ c. water.

RED-WINE SAUCE
sos z czerwonego wina

In saucepan, combine 1 c. dry red wine, 3 T. sugar, ¼ t. cinnamon, and 3–4 cloves. Bring to boil and strain. Dissolve ½ T. potato starch in 2 T. water and stir into hot wine. Bring to boil, stirring. Add ½ c. rinsed, drained raisins and serve hot or cold over puddings and rice-based dessert casseroles. *Note*: Replace part of the wine with water for a less potent sauce.

POPPYSEED SAUCE
sos makowy

This sauce, which is served almost exclusively over cranberry kisiel and oat kisiel on Christmas Eve, is usually made with a little of the pre-soaked or cooked, ground poppyseeds meant for other Wigilia dishes like noodles & poppyseed rolls. It simply wouldn't make sense to drag out and mess up your grinder for this small amount. In saucepan combine ½ c. milk, 1 T. sugar, and 1 T. vanilla sugar or ¼ t. vanilla extract. Bring to boil. Add 2–3 T. poppyseeds ground once in poppyseed grinder or 3 times in ordinary grinder, mix, and set aside to cool. Use as topping for kisiel.

POPPYSEED MILK
mleczko makowe

Place 1 c. ground poppyseeds in bowl, add 1 c. boiling water or milk, mix, cover, and let stand until cooled to room temp. Drain, reserving liquid and force out all moisture. Sweeten poppyseed milk with powdered sugar to taste and add ¼ t. vanilla extract if desired. Chill. Spoon over oat kisiel or cranberry kisiel.

BABKAS, MAZURKAS, TORTES
& OTHER CAKES

In Poland, culinary nostalgia largely revolves around the mouth-watering fragrance of cake-baking time. The unmistakable aroma of yeast-raised egg dough baking in the oven invariably evokes visions of majestically tall, delicately tapered, frosted *babkas* towering over the *święcone* (blessed Easter Food) on crystal pedestals. On the other hand, the pleasing pungency of honey-spice cakes, mingling with the scent of the Christmas tree, is a dead giveway that the festive *Wigilia* supper cannot be far away.

Nothing turns a house into the kind of home everyone enjoys coming back to like cake-baking. In fact, Poland's leading food and nutrition writer, Irena Gumovska, once half-jokingly suggested that so many marriages nowadays might not be on the rocks if that tantalizing, heart-warming fragrance wafted in from the kitchen a little more frequently.

Since time immemorial, the *babka* and other yeast-raised delights like the *strucla*, *placek* and *kołacz* have been Polish classics—the crowning culinary touch of Christmas, Easter, weddings, and other festive occasions. But the term *babka* in Polish also refers to other cakes that do not necessary incorporate yeast. In fact, the only requirement for a cake to be called a babka is that it must be taller than it is wide and narrower at the top than at the bottom. To produce one, you will therefore need a classic *babka* pan, although Bundt and *brioche* pans are sometimes also used for this purpose.

Another classic Polish cake is the *mazurek*, a flat square or rectangular cake, usually associated with Easter. Beginners will be happy to note that the flaky-dough *mazurka* is nearly fool-proof. At any rate, it is far easier to produce than any of the yeast-raised cakes which require a certain cooking knack. An even simpler mazurka is that made with store-bought wafer sheets.

There is also *szarlotka*, an apple-cake, which in Poland enjoys a popularity similar to that of America's apple pie. Others are just crazy about cheesecake, for which a number of different recipes have been provided. We strongly urge you to try *poemat*, a cross between an unbaked cheesecake and a pudding, which many feel is the world's tastiest dessert.

Also included are fruitcakes (*keksy*) and honey-spice cakes (*pierniki*), usually associated with Christmas, and a good selection of luscious tortes of both the baked and unbaked variety.

Adventurous cake hobbyists may enjoy tackling the traditional *sękacz* (log cake), which is baked on a spit in front of a roaring fire, although simpler versions are also included. The *strudel*, which also requires a certain degree of know-how, is similarly presented in both classic and streamlined versions. Throughout this chapter you will find plenty of traditional, rich cakes full of eggs, cream, and butter, but wherever possible, we have sought to supplement them with leaner alternatives with weight- and cholesterol-watchers in mind.

Many of the cakes in this chapter are quite involved. Even those cooks who feel up to trying their hand at them will probably do so only on special occasions. Thus, we have also included a number of simpler everyday cakes like easy lemon cake, "5-of-everything" apple sponge cake, and some of the unbaked tortes. Of course, even these will probably require a bit more effort than the store-bought cake mixes. The major advantage here is the absence of that monotonous cake-mix taste!

BRIDE'S-VEIL BABKA
babka tiulowa

Beat 7 egg yolks with 1½ c. powdered (confectioner's) sugar until white. Dissolve 2 cakes yeast in 1 c. lukewarm milk and stir into yolk mixture. Into separate bowl sift 3½ c. flour, add the yolk & yeast mixture, mix well, cover, and let stand in warm place until doubled. Work in 1½ sticks melted butter and knead about 30 min. Generously butter babka pans (see note below) and fill them ⅓ full with dough. Allow to rise in warm place until dough nearly comes up to rim of pan, then bake in pre-heated 350° oven about 50 min. As always, less baking time is needed if dough has been placed in 2 smaller pans than in 1 larger one. Test to see if cooked with wooden toothpick. Allow babkas to cool slightly in their pans, then remove them very carefully and glaze as desired (see glazes at end of chapter). Let stand until fully cooled before slicing. As their name suggests, these babkas have a delicate, porous texture and easily collapse if roughly handled. *Note*: A genuine babka pan produces a cake that is taller than it is wide and tapers at the top. These seem difficult to come by in America, hence we have seen people using Bundt pans, brioche pans, angel-food pans, and others for this purpose. Perhaps one of those fancy metal molds for molded gelatin salads might also do the trick, but some type of tube would probably have to be improvised to ensure even baking.

SCALDED BABKA
babka parzona

Sift 1 c. flour into bowl and scald with 1½ c. boiling milk. Mix well until smooth and lump-free. When slightly cooled, add 2 cakes yeast mixed with 1 T. sugar and let rise in warm place, covered with dish towel. Meanwhile cream 7 egg yolks with 1½ c. powdered sugar until fluffy, add to sponge (yeast mixture), sift in 3 c. flour, work well by hand into a uniform dough, and knead until air blisters appear. Gradually work in 1½ sticks warm melted butter or margarine and continue kneading until dough no longer sticks to hands and sides of bowl. Add ¾ c. washed, dried raisins and ½–1 t. vanilla extract. Mix well to evenly distribute raisins. Transfer dough to babka pan or pans, which should be no more than ⅓ full, cover with cloth, and let rise in warm, draftless place. When dough has risen nearly to top of pan, bake in pre-heated 350° oven about 50 min. Remove from pans when cooled and glaze or simply dust with powdered sugar. *Note*: Scalded-dough cakes, if properly made, have a nice, light texture and stay fresh for a long time.

HOLIDAY BABKA
babka świąteczna

Mash 1 cake yeast with 1 T. sugar and combine with 1 c. lukewarm milk and 1 c. flour. Mix well, cover with cloth, and leave in warm (80°) place for sponge to rise (10–15 min.). Separately cream 5 egg yolks with ¼ t. salt using low speed of electric mixer. Add ¾ c. powdered sugar and 2 T. vanilla sugar and mix at high speed until mixture becomes thick and fluffy. Into bowl sift 3 c. flour, add the sponge and egg mixture and work well by hand until smooth and glossy. Add 1 stick (½ c.) warm melted butter and continue kneading until air blisters appear and dough easily comes away from hands and sides of bowl. Add 1½ c. washed, dried raisins and knead a bit longer to evenly distribute them. Cover with cloth and leave in warm place until double in bulk (about 1 hr.). Fill generously buttered and flour-dusted babka pans ½ full with dough, cover with cloth, and let rise in warm place again. When doubled, bake in 375° oven about 45 min. When cooled, remove from pans and cover top and sides with almond glaze. *Optional*: Chopped almonds may be sprinkled over babkas before glaze sets. This is a traditional Easter cake.

LEMON BABKA
babka cytrynowa

Prepare as above, but add 1 T. grated lemon rind to dough. Decorate the baked babka with lemon glaze.

RUM BABKA
babka ponczowa z rumem

Mash 1 cake yeast with 1 T. sugar, mix with 1 c. warm milk and 1 c. flour, and set aside to rise in warm place 10–15 min. Beat 5 egg yolks with ½ t. salt at low speed with electric mixer, add ½ c. powdered sugar, and beat at high speed until fluffy. Separately cream 1 stick room-temp. butter, gradually increasing speed and adding yolk mixture a little at a time plus 1 t. vanilla extract. Add sponge, 2½ c. sifted flour, and 5 stiffly beaten egg whites. Work ingredients into a smooth dough. It should be glossy, smooth, and full of air blisters. Fill greased babka pans with dough ½ full, cover with cloth, and allow to double in warm place. Bake in pre-heated 375° oven to a nice golden color (about 50 min.). Remove babkas from pans after they have cooled. Cover with plastic wrap and store at room temp. overnight. Drive wooden skewer deep into babka in quite a few places and pour rum syrup over cake slowly until it is absorbed. It is prepared as follows. In pot combine 1⅓ c. water and ¾ c. sugar. Heat and stir until sugar dissolves and simmer on low heat several min. When cooled to lukewarm, stir in 1 t. lemon juice and 4–5 T. rum. *Variation*: For a more pronounced rum flavor, bring ½ c. sugar and ¼ c. water to boil. When cooled to lukewarm, stir in ½ c. rum. *Note:* This cake was a favorite of Poland's 18th-century King Stanisław Leszczyński who introduced it in France where it became an immediate hit. It is best known worldwide by its French name: *baba au rhum.*

PODOLIAN (PLUM) BABKA
babka podolska

Mash 1 cake yeast with 1 T. sugar. Stir in 1 c. warm milk and 1 c. flour, mix well, cover with cloth, and leave in warm place to rise. Beat 2 egg yolks and 1 whole egg with 1 c. powdered sugar and 2 T. vanilla sugar until nice and fluffy. Into separate bowl sift 3 c. flour, add sponge, egg mixture, and ½ t. salt. Work well by hand until dough is smooth and glossy. Add ¾ stick melted butter and continue kneading until dough no longer sticks to hands and sides of bowl. Cover with cloth and leave in warm 80° place to rise. Meanwhile, wash, halve, and pit about 1 lb. Italian plums (węgierki). Place in colander to drain. Transfer risen dough to floured board, divide in ½ , and with floured hands flatten each piece into a rectangle. Spread plums over dough up to 2 inches from edges, bring long side of rectangle up and roll dough up jelly-roll fashion. Seal ends by pinching them together and transfer each roll to buttered babka or bundt pan, joining ends together. Choose the size pan in which dough fills it only half full. Cover with cloth and allow to rise in warm place. Bake in 375° oven about 1 hr. Cool in pan, remove, and dust with powdered sugar.

SPONGE BABKA
babka biszkoptowa

Beat 4 egg yolks and 4 T. sugar until fluffy. Continue beating while adding 4 heaping T. potato starch (also known as potato flour), 4 heaping T. ordinary flour, 2 T. melted butter,

1 t. vanilla extract, and 1 T. baking powder. Beat 4 egg whites to a stiff froth and gently mix into dough. Grease babka pans and place dough into them so they are no more than ⅔ full. Bake in pre-heated 350° oven 30-40 min. Remove from pan when cooled and dust with powdered sugar or cover with plain or flavored glaze of choice.

BUTTER BABKA
babka maślana

Place 5 eggs and 1 c. sugar in top part of double-boiler immersed in boiling water and beat at high speed with hand-held electric mixer until thick and fluffy. (This may take 10–15 min.). Remove from heat and continue beating until mixture cools. In separate bowl, cream 2½ sticks (¾ lbs.) room-temp. butter, increasing speed as mixture grows fluffy and adding 2 T. vanilla sugar and the egg mixture. Gently stir in 1 c. sifted flour, mixing until blended. Butter babka pans and sprinkle with bread crumbs. Fill pans ⅔ full with dough and bake in pre-heated 350° oven about 40–50 min. Remove babkas from pans when cooled and dust with powdered sugar.

RAISIN BABKA
babka z rodzynkami

Cream 1½ sticks room-temp. butter and 1 c powdered sugar on high speed until fluffy. Continue beating and add 2 egg yolks, 2 T. baking powder, 1 t. lemon extract, 2 c. flour, and ½ c. sour cream. Beat 2 egg whites to a froth and fold into batter. Wash, drain, and dredge in flour 1½ c. raisins and mix into batter to evenly distribute. Transfer batter to greased babka pans, which should be no more than ⅔ full, even off tops and bake in pre-heated 350° oven 40–45 min. Remove cakes from pans when cool and dust with powdered sugar or glaze. If you like a "raisiny" babka, sprinkle glaze with additional raisins before it sets. Some chopped nuts (walnuts, hazelnuts, almonds) may also be sprinkled over the freshly glazed babkas.

SAND BABKA
babka piaskowa

Grease babka pans and line bottom with greased parchment paper. Cream 1½ sticks room-temp. butter or margarine with electric mixer, gradually increasing speed as it becomes increasingly fluffy. Continue beating, gradually adding 5 eggs one by one, 1 c. powdered sugar, ½ c. coffee cream, and finally 1⅓ c. flour and 1⅓ c. potato starch, mixed together and sifted, plus 2 T. baking powder and 1 t. vanilla extract or 2 T. vanilla sugar. Fill pans with mixture ⅔ full and bake in pre-heated 350° oven about 45–50 min. Check for doneness with wooden pick. Allow to cool in pans, remove, and cover with chocolate glaze and (optional) chopped nuts of choice.

CHOCOLATE SAND BABKA
babka piaskowa kakaowa

Proceed exactly as with sand babka (above), but add 1–2 heaping T. cocoa and ½ t. rum extract to beaten mixture.

SOUTHERN FRUIT BABKA
babka bakaliowa

Prepare dough as for sand babka but, before placing it in baking pans, stir in about 1½ c. mixed southern fruit dredged in flour. This may include any combination of the following: raisins (whole), chopped nuts of choice, chopped pitted prunes, finely diced candied orange rind, chopped figs, chopped pitted dates, dried currants (whole), and the like.

MARBLE BABKA
babka marmurkowa

Prepare dough as for sand babka but beat into ⅓ of it 2–3 T. cocoa until color is uniform throughout. Place light-colored dough in pan, and top with ring of cocoa-flavored dough, which should trickle into light-colored dough during baking to create a marble effect. Bake as above. Dust baked, cooled babkas with powdered sugar.

CHOCOLATE BABKA
babka czekoladowa

In pot, combine 2½ sticks butter or margarine, 3 heaping T. cocoa, 4 T. pre-boiled water and 1½ c. sugar. Place on very low heat, stirring until ingredients blend. When mixture is smooth, remove from heat and set aside to cool. Separately, sift 2 c. flour and 2 T. baking powder into a bowl, gradually adding chocolate mixture and stirring constantly. Add 4 yolks and work well until fluffy. Add 1 t. vanilla extract, fold in 4 beaten egg whites, and mix gently. Grease babka pans and sprinkle with bread crumbs. Fill pans ⅔ full and bake in pre-heated 350° oven 40–45 min. Remove from pans when cool and cover with chocolate glaze.

BLACK-BREAD BABKA
babka chlebowa

Grind through fine strainer of grinder about 2 slices dry black bread or enough to get ½ c. bread crumbs. Butter babka pan and line bottom and sides with greased parchment paper. Beat at high speed 4 eggs, 5 T. powdered sugar and 2 T. vanilla sugar until mixture is thick and fluffy. Add 2 heaping T. cocoa and beat briefly until fully blended. Add ½ c. sifted black bread crumbs and 2 T. potato starch, mixing lightly. Transfer dough to pan, in which it reaches only ⅔ of the way up, and bake in pre-heated 350° oven 35–40 min. Check for doneness with wooden pick or skewer. Allow to cool in pan. Remove from pan, peel off parchment paper, and slowly pour ½ c. rum or orange liqueur over it until absorbed. Sprinkle top with chopped nuts.

YEAST-RAISED CRUMB CAKE/PLAIN COFFEE CAKE
placek drożdżowy z kruszonką/posypką

Mash 1 cake yeast with 1 T. sugar, add 1 c. lukewarm milk and 1 c. flour and mix well. Cover with dish towel and set aside to rise in warm place about 10–15 min. Beat 4 egg yolks with ½ t. salt, add 8 T. powdered sugar, and beat at high speed until fluffy. Separately, sift 2½ c. flour into bowl, add sponge, ½ t. vanilla extract, and yolk mixture, work into a uniform dough and knead until smooth and glossy. Add 1½ sticks melted butter and continue kneading until dough no longer stick to hands and bowl. Cover with cloth and let rise in warm (80°) place until doubled. Transfer dough to greased loaf pans so they are ⅓ full, smooth tops, sprinkle with crumb topping (see p. 668), cover with cloth, and allow to rise again. For crumb topping, dice ½ stick cold butter with 3 T. sugar, 1 T. vanilla sugar and ½ c. flour until mixture resembles coarse groats. Chill 30 min. in fridge, then sprinkle over cake. When cake has risen and filled pan, bake in 375° oven about 50 min.

YEAST-RAISED PLUM CAKE
placek drożdżowy ze śliwkami

Prepare dough as in preceding recipe. When it has doubled in bulk, roll it out ½ inch thick into the shape of your square or rectangular baking pan. Grease pan and transfer dough to it on rolling-pin. Wash about 2 lbs. Italian plums, cut in half, and remove pits.

Drain well. Place plum halves cut side down on top of dough, cover with cloth, and let rise in warm place until doubled. Bake in 375° oven about 50 min. Dust generously with powdered sugar when cake is still hot. *Variation*: May also be made with apricots or peaches, but it won't be as good.

YEAST-RAISED BLUEBERRY CAKE
placek drożdżowy z jagodami

Sift 3 c. flour into bowl. Add ¾ c. warm milk mixed with 1 crushed cake yeast, ¾ c. powdered sugar, 2 T. vanilla sugar, and 3 egg yolks. Work ingredients into a smooth dough. Add 1 stick melted butter or margarine (slightly cooled) and knead dough until it easily comes away from hands and bowl. Cover with cloth and let stand in warm place until doubled. Transfer risen dough to floured bread board. Roll ⅔ of dough out ½ inch thick in the shape of your pan. Transfer on rolling-pin to greased pan. Take pieces of remaining dough and roll between floured palms into finger-thick (¼–½-inch) rolls, using them to form a latticework on top of cake. Wash and drain very well 1 lb. blueberries. Mix them with 1 T. bread crumbs and fill the squares of your latticework with them. (*Optional*: Before adding berries, the dough may be brushed with lightly beaten egg whites.) Cover with cloth and allow to rise in warm place. Bake in 375° oven about 50 min. After baking, dust generously with powdered sugar. *Note*: This cake is best the day it is baked.

YEAST-RAISED SOUTHERN-FRUIT CAKE
placek drożdżowy z bakaliami

In pot combine 1 c. milk and 1 stick margarine, heating gently until margarine melts. Remove from heat and cool to lukewarm. Add 1 cake crushed yeast and 1 T. sugar and mix well. Separately, beat 2 eggs with 1 c. powdered sugar until fluffy. Add yeast mixture and 1 t. ginger and sift in 4 c. flour. Work well by hand to combine ingredients and knead until smooth and glossy. Add 1 c. scalded and completely drained raisins and finely diced figs and knead a while longer. Cover with cloth and set aside in warm place to double. Transfer risen dough to floured board and divide dough into 4 equal parts with floured hands. Between palms roll each piece into a 1-inch diameter roll. Place 2 of the rolls side by side and twist together. Repeat with remaining 2 rolls. Arrange dough roll in the form of a snail-like spiral, starting at center of greased round cake pan. Add the remaining roll spiral fashion until entire pan bottom is covered. Choose a size pan in which dough rolls cover its entire surface. Brush dough with beaten egg, and sprinkle with ½ c. chopped walnuts, ½ c. chopped, blanched almonds, and 2–3 T. finely chopped orange rind. Lightly press down chopped nuts and rind so they are embedded in dough. Cover with cloth and set aside to rise. Bake in 375° oven about 35 min. Remove from oven, sprinkle with ½ c. granulated sugar, and return to oven for another 10–15 min. Serve as soon as cake has cooled to room temp.

OLD-POLISH (YEAST-RAISED) WHEEL CAKE
kołacz weselny

In Old Poland this cake was associated with weddings, holidays, and other festive occasions but today has all but been forgotten. It is made with the same type of dough used in yeast-raised babkas and coffee cakes and gets its name from the Polish word "koło" (wheel). Mash 1½ cakes yeast with 1 T. sugar, mix in 1¾ c. warm milk and 1 c. flour, and set aside to rise in warm place 10–15 min. Beat 4 eggs and 1 c. powdered sugar until fluffy. Into egg mixture sift 4 c. flour, add the sponge, and work well by hand until dough is smooth and glossy. Gradually add 2 sticks of melted lukewarm butter, and continue kneading until air blisters appear. Cover dough and let stand in warm place until doubled. Grease a fairly large, round, tall-sided cake pan (the spring-form type is excellent!), roll dough out into a 1-inch-thick round and place in pan. (*Note*: Choose a pan of the right size to accommodate the dough round.) Cover and leave in warm place to rise. Make indentation in dough with dinner plate and fill with cheese or other filling. Smooth top, brush with beaten egg, and bake in pre-heated 375° oven about 50 min. *Optional*: Sprinkle cake with crumb topping (see yeast-raised crumb cake p. 627) before baking.

Cheese filling: Grind 1½ lb. farmer cheese. Separately, beat 4 egg yolks with 1 c. powdered sugar and 1 t. vanilla extract (or 2 T. vanilla sugar) until smooth. Gradually add ground cheese, mixing well and adding 3 T. potato starch, 4 T. melted butter, and ½–1 c. washed, drained raisins. Fold in 4 egg whites beaten to a froth and mix lightly.

Poppyseed filling: See poppyseed roll (p. 630). After cake is baked, dust with powdered sugar. Allow to cool to room temp. before slicing, as goes for all yeast-raised cakes.

LITTLE-WHEEL CAKES WITH CHEESE FILLING
kołaczyki/kołaczki z serem

This miniaturized version of the above is made as follows. Dissolve 1 cake mashed yeast in ½ c. warm milk, add 1 T. sugar, stir in ½ c. flour, cover, and leave in warm place to rise (10–15 min.). Beat 4 egg yolks with ½ c. powdered sugar and 2 T. vanilla sugar. Separately, sift 3 c. flour into bowl, add sponge and yolk mixture, work well to blend ingredients, and knead until dough is smooth and glossy. Add ½ stick melted lukewarm butter or oleo, kneading constantly until air blisters appear and dough no longer sticks to hands. Cover with cloth and let rise in warm place until doubled. Transfer risen dough to floured board and roll out 1 inch thick, sprinkling top with a little flour. With glass or biscuit-cutter cut dough into rounds and place them on greased baking sheet 1 inch apart. Cover with dish towel and let stand in warm place until double. While it rises, prepare filling. Cream ½ stick room-temp. butter with ½ c. powdered sugar and 1 egg yolk, then add 1 T. vanilla sugar and ¾ lb. ground farmer cheese. Mix well into a smooth filling. When cakes have risen, make an indentation in each with bottom of juice glass and fill with cheese mixture. Smooth tops, brush with beaten egg, and bake in 350° oven about 30 min.

FRUIT-FILLED LITTLE-WHEEL CAKES
kołaczyki/kołaczki z nadzieniem owocowym

Proceed as in preceding recipe, but fill indentations with powidła (thick plum jam), raspberry, apricot, or other jam of choice. Top each with grated-dough topping made as follows. Mix 1 c. flour with ½ c. granulated sugar, add ¼ t. vanilla or rum extract, and cut in 1 stick room-temp. butter. Quickly work ingredients into a stiff dough, cover with plastic wrap, and chill in fridge 30 min. Grate on coarse side of hand-held grater and sprinkle gratings over fruit filling, pressing in lightly. Bake in pre-heated 350° oven about 30 min.

POPPYSEED ROLL
strucla z makiem/makowiec/, makownik

Place 2 c. cleaned poppyseeds in pot, scald with boiling water which should cover poppyseeds by 2 inches and heat on very low flame, preferably on insulated pad. (*Note*: Asbestos pads were formerly used until they were found to be cancer-causing!) Simmer very gently 30 min., drain, and grind 3 times through fine strainer. (*Note*: If you use poppyseeds often, it might be a good idea to get a special poppyseed grinder available in import and specialty shops.) In clean pot, combine 3 T. butter, the ground poppyseeds, ¾ c. powdered sugar, 4 T. honey, ½ –1 c. soaked and drained raisins, ½ c. ground walnuts, and (optional) 1 T. finely diced candied orange rind. Heat mixture on low flame about 10 min., stirring constantly. Remove from heat and cool. Add 3–4 drops almond oil, 2 eggs, and mix ingredients well. For the dough, mash 1 cake yeast with 1 T. sugar and dissolve in ½ c. lukewarm milk. Add 1 c. flour and 1 T. sugar, mix well, cover with cloth and leave in warm place to rise. Meanwhile, beat 5 egg yolks with ½ t. salt until smooth and lemony. Continue beating while adding ¾ c. powdered sugar and beat until fluffy. Separately, sift into bowl 4 c. flour, add sponge and yolk mixture and work well until smooth and glossy. Gradually work in 1 stick melted butter and 1 t. vanilla extract and knead until dough easily comes away from hands and bowl. Cover with dish towel and let rise in warm place until doubled in bulk. Then transfer to floured board, divide in 2, and roll into ¼-inch-thick rectangles, sprinkling tops with a little flour. Spread ½ the poppyseed mixture on each rectangle, leaving a 1-inch space round the edges. Roll each up tightly, jelly-roll fashion, pinch ends shut and fold them under. Place cakes on sheets of greased parchment paper and roll up loosely leaving ends open. Place cakes side by side in baking pan and let rise until doubled. The rolled-parchment method causes the dough to expand out the open sides, forming long, elegant poppyseed rolls. Bake in parchment in pre-heated 350° oven about 45 min. When fully cooled, glaze and sprinkle with ground walnuts, sliced almonds, finely diced candied orange rind, or raisins. The freshly glazed cakes may also be sprinkled with whole poppyseeds. *Note*: This cake is traditionally served on Christmas Eve, Poland's most festive family occasion of the year.

WALNUT ROLL
strucla z orzechami

Prepare dough as above. Spread dough rectangles with the following filling. With wooden spoon mix well 3 c. ground walnut meats, 1 c. powdered sugar, and 2 unbeaten egg whites (or ½ c. sour cream). When mixture is nice and smooth, add about 1 c. soaked and drained raisins and (optional) 1 T. finely chopped candied orange rind. Mix to evenly distribute ingredients and proceed as with poppyseed filling. *Variation*: Ground blanched almonds may be used in place of walnuts. When cakes have baked and cooled, sprinkle fresh glaze with chopped walnuts, if cake contains walnut filling, or slivered almonds if filled with almond mixture.

FRUIT ROLL
strucla owocowa

Use the same dough indicated for poppyseed roll, but spread the rectangles with about 3 c. fairly thick fruit filling. This could include homemade apple-cake filling (jabłka na szarlotkę), powidła (thick Polish-style plum jam) or other thick jams. Preserves, especially cherry or strawberry are good but should be heated, drained, and cooled before spreading on dough. Canned pie fillings (apple, cherry, blueberry, peach) are another possibility, but they too should first be heated and drained to reduce excessive liquid. Cool before spreading on dough rectangles. Several T. bread crumbs or ground nuts may be added to fillings, and some raisins are a nice addition to apple filling. Fruit fillings may be flavored with a pinch or 2 cinnamon or cloves. After filling, roll up, let rise, bake, cool, and glaze as above.

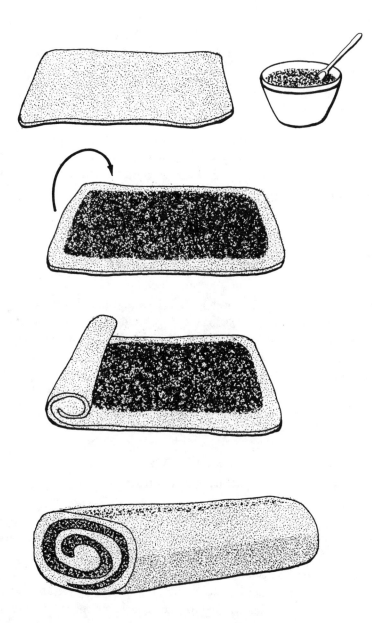

The above illustration shows how to apply filling and roll up a sheet of rolled-out dough when preparing poppyseed roll (strucla z makiem, makowiec) and other roll-type cakes.

FLAKY-DOUGH PLUM CAKE
kruchy placek ze śliwkami

Sift 2½ c. flour onto board, cut into it 2 sticks cold butter and dice to combine ingredients. Sprinkle with 1 t. baking powder, add 2 T. vanilla sugar and 2 egg yolks and quickly work into a dough. Wrap in aluminum foil and chill in fridge 1 hr. Roll out into a ¼ -inch-thick square or rectangle the size of your pan and transfer on rolling pin to pan. Form a small rim with the dough on all 4 sides. Wash and drain well about 1 lb. Italian plums (węgierki). Cut plums in half and discard pits. Brush top of cake with egg white which will prevent plum juice from soaking dough during baking. Arrange plum halves cut side up on dough side by side. Bake in pre-heated 400° oven 25–30 min. After baking, dust rather generously with powdered sugar. When cool, cut into squares. Just the thing for an occasional podwieczorek (afternoon tea).

FRUIT-FILLED PASTRY SQUARES/"POLISH FRUIT PIE"
kruchy placek z owocami

This is probably the closest thing to American-style fruit pie found in Polish pastry cookery. The main difference is that the crust is tastier and is served cut into squares. Sift 2 c. flour onto board, cut in 1 stick butter or margarine, add 2 egg yolks and 1 t. grated lemon rind (zest). Combine ingredients with knife or pastry blender and then work by hand very quickly into a dough. Roll into ball, wrap in dish towel or foil, and chill in fridge 10–15 min. Roll out ⅔ of dough (returning rest to fridge) into ¼-inch-thick square or rectangle to fit pan. Press dough into pan, stretching to form ½-inch rim round the sides of pan. Pop into pre-heated 375°– 400° oven for only as long as needed for dough to take on a faintly golden hue. Cool. Spread with thick fruit filling of choice: drained preserves, thick jam like powidła, drained canned fruit-pie filling, etc. Coarsely grate remaining dough onto fruit filling, distributing it evenly across surface. Bake 20–25 min. at 400°. When cool, cut into squares and spread with lemon or vanilla glaze.

FLAKY-DOUGH POPPYSEED SQUARES
kruchy placek z makiem

Prepare dough exactly as above. After chilling, set ⅓ of it aside. After baking pastry bottom as above, cool and spread crust with several T. thick jam. Cover with ¼–½-inch thick layer of poppyseed filling (see poppyseed roll) and smooth top. Roll the remaining dough out thin, cut into strips, and use it to arrange a latticework on top of cake, sealing edges. Brush latticework with beaten egg. Bake in pre-heated 375° oven about 20 min. to a light golden brown. When cake has cooled, spread with almond icing.

CHOCOLATE-COVERED PASTRY SQUARES
kruchy placek z polewą czekoladową

Prepare dough and bake as indicated for flaky-dough plum cake but omit plums. When pastry has cooled, spread with chocolate icing. Cut into serving-size squares and enjoy!

"RAGGED" FLAKY-DOUGH CAKE
kruchy placek "strzępiasty"/"pleśniak"

Grated pastry dough gives this cake its unusual name and texture, but it's really very good and is a specialty of the author's aunt from Biłgoraj. Simply sift 4 c. flour onto board, sprinkle with 2 t. baking powder, and cut in 2½ sticks cold butter. Add 5 egg yolks and briefly work ingredients together with knife or pastry cutter. Sift in ½ c. powdered sugar and quickly work by hand into a dough. Mix 1 heaping T. cocoa with 1 level T. sour cream, beat until smooth and blend into ⅓ of dough. Wrap 2 dough balls in separate dish towels or sheets of aluminum foil and chill in fridge 1 hr. Roll half the light-colored (cocoa free) dough out thin to fit baking pan and line its bottom with dough sheet. (*Note*: It's usually best to transfer dough from board to pan on rolling-pin.) Spread dough with thin layer of thick tart jam of choice. Grate cocoa-flavored dough on coarse side of grater onto jam and smooth it by hand. Beat 5 egg whites and 1 c. powdered sugar to a stiff froth and spread over dough evenly. Cover with the remaining dough which should also be coarsely grated. Bake in pre-heated 375° oven 45–50 min.

NAPOLEON PASTRIES
kruche napoleonki

Into bowl sift 1 c. flour and cut in 1 stick cold butter, blending until you get a texture like that of fine groats. Set aside. Separately sift 1 c. flour onto board, mix in 1 egg yolk and 4 T. sour cream, and quickly work into a dough. Cut in ½ and roll 1 part out very thin into rectangle. Sprinkle dough sheet with ½ the grainy flour-butter mixture, roll up jelly-roll fashion, then curve roll into snail-like spiral. Flatten dough with hand, sprinkle board and dough with a little flour and roll out thin to fit round baking pan. Transfer to pan on rolling-pin. Proceed identically with remaining dough, placing it in another pan. Bake both pans in pre-heated 375° oven about 20–25 min. or until golden. While they bake, prepare filling. Beat 2 eggs with 5 T. sugar until white. Continue beating, gradually adding 6 heaping

t. flour. Bring 2 c. milk and ¼–½ t. vanilla extract to boil carefully without scorching. In thin stream slowly pour hot milk into egg mixture, stirring briskly. Place mixture in pot and gently simmer on low heat, stirring until thick and bubbly. Stir in 1 T. butter and mix to blend. Set aside to cool slightly. Pour the warm filling over one of the baked crusts left in its pan and smooth top of filling. Carefully remove remaining crust, which is very fragile. The best way is to place a folded-up dish towel over it, hold down with hand, and gently invert pan. Cover filling with remaining crust. Dust with powdered sugar and cut into wedges when thoroughly cooled. Delicious, but very crumbly! *Note*: This is one of several cakes named after the French emperor who many Poles had hoped would help free their country from the German, Russian, and Austrian occupation forces. Unlike the short-lived Duchy of Warsaw (1807-1812), which Napoleon did indeed set up on a portion of Poland's pre-partition territory, his name has lived on much longer in the pastry field. The above recipe has been adapted from the 19th-century Grand Dame of Polish cuisine, Lucyna Ćwierczakiewiczowa.

POLISH APPLE CAKE
szarlotka

In terms of popularity, the szarlotka is to Poles what apple pie is to Americans. There are a great many ways of preparing it, of which we have chosen three. Begin by peeling 2½ lbs. preferably tart cooking apples. Grate on coarse side of grater. Place in pot with about ½ c. sugar and simmer on low heat, stirring often, until you get a nice thick filling. You may add a bit more sugar, but the mixture need not be too sweet, because the sweet pastry crust will offset the tartness of the filling. Flavor with a pinch or 2 cinnamon if desired and set aside to cool. Meanwhile, mix 4 c. flour with 1 T. baking powder and sift onto board. With knife or pastry blender cut in 2½ sticks cold butter and quickly combine ingredients. Sprinkle with 1 c. powdered sugar and 2 T. vanilla sugar and blend in. Fork-blend 2 egg yolks and 1 whole egg with ½ c. sour cream, pour over dough and quickly combine, rolling into ball. Cut off and set aside ⅓ of the dough. Lightly sprinkle remaining dough with flour and roll out on floured board into ¼-inch-thick rectangle or square just a shade larger than your pan. Line greased baking pan with dough, bringing it up to form a roughly ½ -inch wall along sides of pan. Top with apple filling, roll out remaining dough, and place on top of apple mixture, sealing edges with floured fingers. Sprinkle top with ½ c. preferably large-crystal granulated sugar and bake in pre-heated 375° oven about 45 min. Cut into squares when cool.

POLISH APPLE CAKE ANOTHER WAY
szarlotka inaczej

Prepare apples as above. For the crust, beat 1 c. room-temp. butter and ½ c. powdered sugar until fluffy and velvety, gradually adding 1 c. sour cream and 1 c. flour. When nice and smooth, sift in another c. flour and work by hand into a dough. Cover and refrigerate 2 hrs.

Turn dough out onto generously floured board, cut in ½ , sprinkle 1 portion with flour, and roll out ¼-inch thick to fit your baking pan. Transfer dough sheet to buttered baking pan, lining its bottom and about 1½ inch of its sides. Bake in pre-heated 375° oven 20–30 min. Meanwhile, keep remaining dough in fridge. When bottom is baked, remove from oven, cover with apple filling and set aside. Roll out and bake remaining dough the same way. Cover apples with 2nd baked crust and dust with powdered sugar. To serve, cut into squares.

EASIEST (DOUGHLESS) APPLE CAKE
szarlotka najłatwiejsza (bez ciasta)

Peel, core, and quarter 2½ lbs. tart cooking apples. Spread baking pan with butter and add the apples. In bowl, combine ½ c. flour, ½ c. sugar, ½ c. bread crumbs, and ½ t. baking powder. Sprinkle mixture over apples and dot with ¾ stick cold butter, diced. Bake in pre-heated 375° oven 45–50 min. Serve warm or cold with a dollop of whipped cream (optional). *Note*: We have found that this cake tastes best when chilled overnight and served the next day, allowing flavors to blend. *Optional*: Apples may be flavored with a pinch or 2 cinnamon, ground cloves, and /or grated nutmeg before covering with dry mixture and baking. After baking, cake may be dusted with powdered and vanilla sugar if too tart.

MAZURKA/FLAT EASTER CAKE
mazurek

The mazurka undoubtedly ranks among the best-known typically Polish cakes. It has been baked for centuries, hence a seemingly endless variety has developed over the years. No matter how they are made and decorated, mazurkas have one thing in common: they rarely exceed a height of 1 inch. What's more, they are invariably associated with Easter. One of the most common types is based on a flaky-dough crust prepared as follows. Sift 2 c. flour onto board and cut in 1½ sticks cold butter, adding ½ c. powdered sugar and 1 T. vanilla sugar. When mixture has been diced with knife, 2 knives, or pastry-blender into groat-like consistency, add 2 raw egg yolks, and quickly combine ingredients into a dough. Roll into ball and chill in fridge 30 min. Turn out onto lightly floured board, cut off and set aside ⅓ of the dough and roll the larger portion out ¼-inch-thick into a rectangle the size of your pan. (*Optional*: Since smaller mazurkas are more attractive, roll dough into 2 smaller rectangles.) Transfer on rolling-pin to pan or pans. Roll remaining dough between palms into finger-thick roll and use it to form a rim round the edge of dough sheet in pan, pressing down lightly so it adheres. Use fork to apply decorative pattern to dough rim or pinch with fingers at equal intervals for interesting effect. For glazed effect, brush rim with beaten egg or yolk. Bake in pre-heated 375° oven about 20 min. or until nicely golden. When cool, remove from pan and fill and decorate as below. To serve, cut into squares.

ICED RASPBERRY MAZURKA
mazurek malinowy lukrowany

Spread the cooled mazurka, baked as above, with raspberry jam. With wooden spoon hand-blend 1 c. powdered sugar with 2 T. lemon juice into a smooth icing. Spread over the jam. Decorate top with strips of candied orange rind and cherries from drained preserves. For Easter, mazurkas are often decorated with holiday motifs: the inscriptions "Wesołego Alleluja" or simply "Alleluja"; an Easter Lamb with the cross-emblazoned banner of Resurrection; or pussy willows. Use a decorator tube to apply the desired design. An easy icing for writing inscriptions on the white iced surface is made by mixing 4 T. butter with 2 T. powdered sugar and 1 t. vanilla sugar until smooth. Add 2 t. cocoa and continue mixing until fully blended. To draw a white, fleecy lamb, omit cocoa and apply lamb to darker frosted surface.

WALNUT MAZURKA
mazurek orzechowy

Prepare mazurka as in first recipe and bake in 375° oven 10 min. While it bakes, mix well 2 c. ground walnuts with ½ c. powdered sugar and 6 T. coffee cream. Spread top of partially baked mazurka with mixture and bake another 10–15 min. Decorate top with walnut-meat halves.

APRICOT-WALNUT MAZURKA
mazurek morelowo-orzechowy

Prepare basic mazurka as in first recipe and bake in 375° oven 10 min. Meanwhile mix 1 c. thick apricot jam with 1 c. ground walnuts. Spread mixture over partially baked mazurka and pop into oven for another 10–15 min.

ORANGE-WALNUT MAZURKA
mazurek pomarańczowo-orzechowy

Prepare and bake mazurka as in first recipe. While it bakes, scrub 3 oranges and 1 lemon with brush in hot soapy water. Rinse well and scald with boiling water. Dry. Cut into quarters and remove all pits. Grind, hand-grate or pulverize in food-processor rinds and all. To mixture add 2 c. granulated sugar and cook on low heat until transparent. It is ready when a drop of cooled mixture dropped on plate stays put rather than turning into a little puddle.

Top baked mazurka with hot mixture and sprinkle top with 1 c. coarsely ground walnuts. *Note*: Although this mazurka is quite easy to prepare, it is really one of the best!

GELLED ORANGE MAZURKA
mazurek pomarańczowy z galaretką

Bake basic mazurka as in first recipe and top with orange-lemon mixture as in preceding recipe. Decorate with fresh, peeled orange segments. (*Suggestion*: Make an orange-segment flower at center and arrange 3 orange segments flaring in out of each corner.) Fill spaces between orange segments with rinsed, dried raisins and cover with partially set fruit gelatin made with 1½ c. strained liquid from canned peaches or pineapples and 1 envelope gelatin soaked in ⅓ c. water. Keep in cool place until firmly set but not fridge as refrigeration turns dough hard. *Variation*: Instead of fresh orange segments, top may be decorated with drained, sliced, canned peaches or pineapple pieces before covering with gel: peach-flavored if using sliced peaches and pineapple-flavored if using pineapple. *Note*: To accommodate cooked orange filling, fruit decoration, and gel, you may need a slightly higher rim of dough round the mazurka pastry shell.

APPLE MAZURKA
mazurek jabłkowy

In pot, combine 2 c. applesauce, 2 T. finely chopped, candied orange rind, ½ c. raisins, ½ c. sugar, and a pinch cinnamon. Simmer on low heat, stirring frequently, until mixture begins to gel. Spread over baked mazurka pastry shell, decorate with white icing, and chopped, candied orange rind.

TURKISH-FUDGE MAZURKA
mazurek kaimakowy

Spread baked mazurka with thin layer of tart jam and top with Turkish fudge (kaimak), prepared in any of the following ways:
Traditional Turkish fudge: In pot combine 2 c. milk and 2 c. sugar and cook on low heat, stirring frequently with wooden spoon, until mixture is reduced by half. It is ready when a drop transferred to plate congeals and is no longer sticky to the touch. Remove from heat and stir until somewhat cooled, then add a half stick butter and mix until blended. Fill mazurka shell with mixture, smoothing top with knife and decorating with raisins, almonds, and (if desired) candied orange rind. *Note*: Halved or slivered blanched almonds are excellent for creating flowers or other designs on darker backgrounds.

Quick Turkish fudge: Melt 2½ sticks margarine on low heat, add 1 c. powdered milk and 1 c. sugar and simmer, stirring frequently until ingredients fully dissolve. Remove from heat, cool slightly, then mix in 2 egg yolks, stirring until completely blended. Immediately fill mazurka shell with mixture, smooth top, and decorate as desired.

Quick low-fat Turkish fudge: Mix 1 c. powdered milk with 1 t. cocoa until free of lumps and set aside. Place ¾ c. sugar in pot, add ½ c. milk and cook on low heat, stirring frequently, until sugar dissolves and you get a thick syrup. Add 3 T. cooking oil and the powdered milk mixture and simmer on very low heat, stirring constantly, until mixture is nice and smooth. Immediately fill mazurka shell with mixture, smooth top, and decorate as above.

CHOCOLATE-WALNUT MAZURKA (WAFER TYPE)
mazurek czekoladowy z orzechami (na waflu)

Beat 3 egg whites to stiff froth, gradually adding 1 c. powdered sugar 1 spoon at a time. Mix in 3 squares (3 oz.) grated semi-sweet chocolate, 1 c. finely chopped or coarsely ground walnuts and 1 t. cherry syrup. Spread mixture about ½ inch thick over plain wafer (see note below), smooth top, and dry in 250° oven 25–30 min. Cut into serving-size squares when cool. *Note*: Plain wafer squares or rectangles, made from ice cream cone-type dough, are available at gourmet shops, confectioner's-supply stores and some pastry shops. Or, try your hand at baking your own (next recipe).

HOMEMADE MAZURKA WAFERS
wafle domowe do mazurków

Cream 6 egg yolks with 1 c. powdered sugar until white, stir in 1 stick clarified butter and ½ t. vanilla extract or ¼ t. grated lemon rind, add 1¼ c. sifted flour and beat vigorously until fluffy. Batter should be pourable to cover surface of wafer iron. If too thick, dilute with a little coffee cream. Place wafer iron over gas or electric burner on med. heat, brush with butter. Just before baking, fold in 6 beaten egg whites. Spoon just enough batter into iron to cover surface, close top, and bake about 1½ min., then turn iron over and bake another 1½ min. When cool, top with filling and bake in slow oven as above. *Note*: Roughly 4 by 6 inch rectangular wafers are ideal for mazurkas. If you cannot get one, you can use a round krumkake or gaufrette iron available at gourmet-supply and European import shops. We don't see why you can't use your old American-style electric waffle iron, although the wafer will come out thicker than what is normally used for mazurkas.

WHITE-WAFER MAZURKAS
mazurki na opłatku

In addition to golden store-bought, or homemade wafers, opłatek, the plain white wafer traditionally broken and shared on Christmas Eve, can also be used as a mazurka base. It can be used interchangeably with the golden wafer in any mazurka of this type.

WALNUT MAZURKA
mazurek orzechowy

Grind 2 c. walnut meats. Cream 1 stick butter or oleo, while adding a little at a time, 3 egg yolks, 1¾ c. powdered sugar, the ground walnuts, and ⅔ c. flour. Finally, beat in ½ t. vanilla extract and 1 T. lemon juice. Spread mixture over wafers, smoothing top and evening out sides. Beat 2 egg whites to froth, gradually beating in 1 c. powdered sugar. Spread beaten whites over nut topping and bake in 350° oven about 30 min. Cut into servings when cool.

GYPSY (FRUIT & NUT) MAZURKA
mazurek cygański

Rinse and drain ⅔ c. raisins and equal amount dried figs. Slice figs, ½ c. pitted dates, ¼ c. candied orange rind, and ⅔ c. walnut meats into thin strips and mix with raisins. Cream 5 egg yolks and 1½ c. powdered sugar until fluffy, fold in 5 beaten egg whites, add the fruits and nuts, sift in ⅔ c. flour, and mix to blend ingredients. Spread mixture over wafers, smooth top and even out sides, and bake in pre-heated 350° oven 30 min. Cut into servings when cool.

CHOCOLATE-ALMOND MAZURKA
mazurek migdałowy z czekoladą

Cream 1 stick butter or oleo, adding 1 c. powdered sugar a little at a time. Add 1 c. ground, blanched almonds, ⅔ c. sifted flour, and 3 egg whites beaten to a stiff froth. Mix all ingredients and transfer mixture to greased baking pan in which its height does not exceed ½ inch. Bake in pre-heated 325° oven 30 min. While it bakes, combine in saucepan 3 squares semi-sweet chocolate, 2 T. butter, and 4 T. milk. Heat and stir until ingredients melt and blend. Top the baked, slightly cooled mazurek with chocolate mixture, smooth top, even out sides, and allow to cool. *Note:* The chocolate background is perfect for inscribing "Alleluja!" with white icing or using it to draw an Easter Lamb and/or pussywillows.

ROYAL (COOKED-YOLK) MAZURKA
mazurek królewski

Cream 3½ sticks butter or margarine and ⅔ c. powdered sugar until fluffy, sifting in 2⅓ c. flour, 1 c. finely chopped, blanched almonds, 4 cold, cooked egg yolks, sieved, 1 raw egg, and 1 pinch salt. Work ingredients into a dough and chill in fridge 30 min. Roll out into ¾ -inch-tall rectangle, transfer to lightly greased baking sheet, even out sides with flat of knife. Brush top and sides of mazurka with beaten egg and bake in pre-heated 375° oven 40–45 min. or until beautifully golden. Make latticework on top of cooled mazurka with white icing and, when it sets, place a cherry (from drained preserves) in each square.

POPPYSEED MAZURKA
mazurek makowy

Rinse in plenty of water 1 c. poppyseeds, stirring with hand and pouring off any hulls or other impurities until no more float up. Drain. Place in pot, scald with boiling water which should cover poppyseeds by 1 inch, and let soak overnight. Next day, drain well and grind in poppyseed grinder once or in ordinary meat grinder 3 times. Beat 1 c. powdered sugar with 3 egg yolks, add the ground poppyseeds, and beat a while longer. Add 2 T. bread crumbs and several drops almond oil and fold in 3 stiffly beaten egg whites. Mix ingredients lightly. Line 2 small rectangular baking pans with greased parchment paper, pour in batter to a height of ¾ inch, and bake in 350° oven about 25 min. Top with vanilla or lemon icing and sprinkle with chopped almonds or walnuts.

CHEESECAKE ON FLAKY CRUST
sernik na kruchym spodzie

Onto bread board sift 1½ c. flour and cut in 1 stick cold butter or margarine. Mix 2 eggs with 4 T. powdered sugar and add to flour mixture. Sprinkle with 2 t. baking powder and 2 T. milk. Quickly work ingredients into a dough and chill in fridge 30 min. Meanwhile, cook 2 med. peeled potatoes in lightly salted water, drain, mash, and set aside to cool. Grind or pulverize in blender 1½ lbs. farmer cheese, dry cottage cheese or ricotta together with the cold potatoes. Cream 1½ sticks butter or margarine with 1 c. powdered sugar and ½ t. vanilla extract. Continue mixing, gradually adding 5 egg yolks and cheese mixture. When nicely blended, add 1½ c. rinsed, drained raisins, 2 T. finely chopped, candied orange rind, and 3 T. potato starch. Fold in 3 stiffly beaten egg whites and lightly mix ingredients. Transfer dough to board, cutting off and setting aside ⅓. Roll out ¼-inch thick into rectangle the size of your pan and transfer to lightly greased pan. Top with cheese filling and smooth top. Use the remaining ⅓ dough to roll pencil-thin rolls between palms and arrange in latticework on top of cheese. Brush top with beaten egg and bake in pre-heated 350° oven about 50 min.

VIENNESE CHEESECAKE
sernik wiedeński

Prepare dough as above and roll all of it out (after chilling) into ¼-inch-thick rectangle to fit your pan. Transfer to lightly greased pan. For the filling, grind 2 lbs. farmer cheese (or dry cottage cheese or ricotta) twice. Cream 2 sticks butter with 1 c. powdered sugar until fluffy, then gradually mix in half the cheese a little at a time. Separately, beat 8 egg yolks and 1 c. powdered sugar, gradually stirring in the remaining cheese and mixing until smooth. Combine cheese & butter and cheese & yolk mixtures, mix well, sprinkle in 2 heaping T. flour, 2 heaping T. potato starch, 1 T. baking powder, and 1 t. vanilla extract. Mix to blend ingredients well. Fold in 8 beaten egg whites, and mix lightly. Place mixture on pastry shell, smooth top, and bake in pre-heated 350° oven 50–60 min. When it has cooled, spread top with thin layer of jam of choice. In saucepan bring to boil 1 T. water, ½ stick butter and 1 heaping T. cocoa. Spread cheesecake with cocoa topping and sprinkle generously with rinsed, dried raisins. In many families this is an Easter favorite.

CHOCOLATE CHEESECAKE
sernik kakaowy

Place 1 c. sugar in bowl, add 2½ sticks melted margarine and mix. Sift in 3 c. flour, add 3 egg yolks, 1½ T. baking powder, 2 T. cocoa, and several drops rum or almond extract. Work ingredients into a dough, divide in half, wrap each piece in foil or plastic wrap and place in freezer for the time it takes to prepare cheese filling. Grind 3 lbs. farmer cheese, dry cottage cheese, or ricotta. Cream 1½ sticks butter or oleo with 1 c. powdered sugar, adding 4 egg yolks one at a time. Combine mixture with ground cheese, add a little vanilla extract for flavoring, and mix ingredients well. Stiffly beat 7 egg whites, adding 2 T. powdered sugar towards end. Fold into cheese mixture and mix lightly. Remove 1 piece of dough from freezer and grate it over greased baking pan to cover entire surface. Distribute evenly and press down with hand. Top grated dough with cheese mixture and smooth top. Grate the remaining piece of frozen dough over entire surface of cheese mixture. Bake in pre-heated 325° oven about 50 min.

ECONOMICAL CHEESECAKE
sernik oszczędny

Sift ¾ c. flour into bowl, cut in 1 stick cold oleo, add 1 egg and 4 T. powdered sugar, blend with knife, then quickly work into a dough by hand. Chill in fridge 30 min. Meanwhile, grind 1½ lbs. farmer cheese and gradually mix in 2 eggs and 2 T. milk. Add ¾ c. sugar, ⅓ c. flour, sifted, and several drops lemon extract. Mix until smooth and set aside. From dough cut off and set aside about ⅓. Roll out larger piece ⅛-inch thick into rectangle to fit your pan. Carefully transfer to pan on rolling-pin, pressing down with fingers so it fills the corners and comes an inch up the sides. Bake in 350° oven 20 min. or until golden. Fill with cheese mixture, smoothing top. Roll out remaining dough and cut into ¼-inch strips, arranging diagonal latticework on top of cheese. Brush top with beaten egg and bake in 375° oven 50–60 min.

CRUSTLESS CHEESECAKE
sernik bez spodu

Rinse and drain 2 c. raisins. Cream 2½ sticks butter or margarine with 1 c. powdered sugar. Separately beat 8 egg yolks with ½ c. powdered sugar. Combine the 2 mixtures, adding 2 lbs. ground farmer cheese, 5 T. potato starch, ½–1 t. vanilla extract, and mix well. Add raisins. Beat 8 egg whites to a stiff froth, beating in 1 T. powdered sugar towards end. Fold into cheese mixture and mix lightly. Place mixture in 2 narrow, well-buttered loafpans and smooth tops. Bake in pre-heated 350° oven 45–50 min.

UNBAKED FRUIT-GEL CHEESECAKE
sernik bez pieczenia z owocami

Cream ½ stick butter with ½ c. powdered sugar. Separately beat 3 egg yolks with 1 c. powdered sugar until fluffy. Combine the 2 mixtures and continue beating, adding 1 lb. ground farmer cheese a little at a time. Soften 1 T. gelatin in 4 T. milk, then heat until gelatin completely dissolves. Stir into cheese mixture and mix well to distribute evenly. Stiffly beat 3 egg whites and fold into mixture, mixing gently. Cover bottom of round cakepan (the spring-form type is good) with a thin layer of plain crushed teacakes like vanilla wafers or Lorna Doone's. Add cheese mixture and smooth top. Decorate top with fresh, hulled, washed and drained small strawberries or well-drained, canned, sliced peaches. Prepare strawberry or orange gelatin dessert (jello) according to package direction, but use ¼ c. less water than called for, and chill. When it has gelled somewhat, pour it over fruit. Refrigerate until set. *Note*: Use strawberry gelatin for strawberries and orange gelatin for peaches.

PASCHAL CHEESECAKE
pascha

This crustless cheesecake, which is more a gelled cheese dessert than a cake, is widely served at Easter in Eastern Poland and adjoining parts of Ukraine. As its name indicates (Pascha is Polish for Passover), it was originated by Jews of the Slavic world. To prepare it, start by grinding 1 lb. farmer cheese (or dry cottage cheese or ricotta) twice. Beat 4 egg yolks with 1 c. sugar into a fluffy cream. Transfer mixture to pot, gradually add ½ c. coffee cream, stirring constantly and heating on low flame to just below boiling point. *Important*: Do not boil because too high heat may curdle yolks. Remove from heat and continue mixing until slightly cooled. Add butter mixture and cheese, stirring well until mixture is smooth. Wash, drain, scald with boiling water, and drain again anywhere from 2–3 c. southern fruits: raisins, walnuts, almonds, dates, figs, candied orange rind. Dice fine and add to cheese mixture together with a little flavoring of choice, e.g. vanilla, rum, almond, orange or lemon extract. Mix well. Line colander with 2 thicknesses cheesecloth, place mixture thereon, and twist into a tight ball. Cover with plate and weight down with something heavy. Place over pot or bowl and refrigerate overnight. Next day, when ready to serve, turn out onto round serving dish. Decorate pascha with cherries (from drained preserves), walnut meats, slivered almonds, or grated chocolate. Cut into wedges and enjoy!

"PURE POETRY" CHEESECAKE
"poemat"

Like pascha (above), this is also closer to a dessert than a cake. It differs from the former in that you make your own cheese during its preparation. Although all this may sound a bit involved, we think it is well worth the effort. In fact, many people say this is the best dessert they ever ate, and those remarks come even from those who don't care much for cheesecake of any kind. Break 6 eggs into a 3 qt. pot and mix lightly with whisk but do not beat. Add 2 c. sour cream and 1 t. vanilla extract, whisking to blend ingredients. Stir in 2 quarts warm whole milk, place on lowest possible flame, and heat, stirring occasionally with wooden spoon. Mixture should not boil! When curds separate from whey and float up, pour mixture into colander lined with 2 thicknesses cheesecloth and place over bowl. When dripping stops and mixture cools to room temp., refrigerate 15 min. Meanwhile, cream 3 sticks room-temp. butter and 2 c. powdered sugar until fluffy. Gradually add homemade cheese mixture 1–2 T. at a time, beating continuously until fully blended and creamy. Transfer ⅓ of mixture to separate bowl, add 3 T. cocoa, and beat until smooth. To unflavored ⅔ of mixture add 1 c. ground walnuts and 1 c. washed, drained raisins. Mix lightly. Line 2 narrow loafpans with damp cheesecloth large enough so its ends extend over sides. Into each pan place a layer of nut & raisin mixture, a layer of cocoa-flavored mixture, and a final top layer of nut & raisin mixture. Smooth tops, cover with ends of cheesecloth, and refrigerate overnight. When ready to serve, remove cake by cheesecloth ends gently, unwrap it, slice, and arrange shingle-fashion on serving dish. *Note*: Suspecting that American dairy products might behave differently than their Polish counterparts, we had this dessert specially kitchen-tested in the U.S. Our test cook reported that the American homogenized milk took nearly 2 hrs. to produce curds, but the finished product was nonetheless "pure poetry."

CLASSIC APPLE STRUDEL
strudel z jabłkami tradycyjny

This classic central European specialty now has devotees the world over. Although its preparation requires considerable skill, we nevertheless present the traditional version for purists and food hobbyists, followed by simplified method. Sift 3 c. flour onto board, add 1 egg, ½ t. salt, and work into a dough, adding in thin stream about 1 c. warm, pre-boiled water. Use only as much water as needed to get a nice workable dough. The exact amount will depend on the type and dryness of your flour. Knead until it no longer sticks to fingers. Old Polish cookbooks suggested that you beat the dough against board until air bubbles form. Place dough beneath warm inverted bowl and let stand 2–3 hrs. in warm place. Place inverted dinner plate at center of table, cover with table cloth or sheet and dust with flour. Roll dough ball out slightly, place on plate and gently pull dough away from center. Stretch dough out as thinly as possible in all directions, meaning that you'll have to work your way around the table. Take care not to cause too many tears in dough sheet. If you stretch dough properly it may well cover your entire table top. Leave dough sheet to rest on table 15 min. Trim off ragged edges and use trimmings to patch any tears. Peel, core, and thinly slice 7 large apples. Melt 10 T. butter and sprinkle dough sheet with 5 T., reserving the rest. Place apples on dough sheet. Mix 1 c. powdered sugar with 2 t. grated lemon and/or orange rind and 2 t. cinnamon, and sprinkle over apples more or less evenly. Sprinkle entire surface with about 5 T. bread crumbs browned in dry skillet. (**Optional**: Some ground walnuts and/or almonds as well as rinsed, drained, dried raisins ½–¾ c. of each—may be added.) Pick up 1 side of dough through table cloth and roll up not too tightly without touching dough with hands. In large bread ovens the whole strudel used to be baked in one stretch, but normally it is placed in a greased pan sprinkled with bread crumbs after being rolled into a snail-like coil or shaped into a horseshoe. Brush strudel with remaining melted butter and bake in pre-heated 375° oven about 50 min. If it browns too quickly, brush with some more butter and reduce heat to 350°. After baking, dust with powdered sugar. *Note*: Strudel may be filled with poppyseed, nut, and other cake fillings found in this book. There is even a savory strudel filled with sauerkraut and mushrooms and served as a soup accompaniment.

EASIER APPLE STRUDEL
strudel z jabłkami łatwiejszy

Sift 2 c. flour onto board, add 4½ T. cooking oil, 1½ T. sugar, ¼ t. salt, and about ¾ c. lukewarm water. Combine ingredients into a dough and work well by hand. Roll into ball, sprinkle with flour and cover with warmed bowl. Keep in warm place about 2 hrs. Peel, core, and coarsely grate 4 large apples, mix with 2 T. powdered sugar and ½ t. cinnamon (more or less to taste). Roll dough out as thin as possible, sprinkling with flour, and transfer on rolling-pin to lightly floured tablecloth. Stretch it out additionally by hand, taking care not to tear it. Cover dough sheet with apple mixture and roll up through tablecloth. Bake as in preceding recipe. *Note*: If even this simpler recipe is too involved, you may want to get ready-to-use strudel dough. Some cooks make strudel using store-bought phyllo dough (available at Greek foodmarkets).

FRUIT-TOP CAKE
placek ucierany z owocami

Clean (hull, pit, etc.) 1½ lbs. fruit (cherries, strawberries, raspberries, blueberries), wash, and drain. If apples are used, peel and slice thin. Butter a long narrow loafpan and sprinkle with bread crumbs. Cream 1½ sticks butter or margarine with 1½ c. powdered sugar until fluffy. Add 3 eggs one at a time, mixing continuously, 2 c. sifted flour a little at a time, 1 T. baking powder, ½ c. sour milk, or plain yogurt and several drops lemon extract. Beat until mixture is glossy. Transfer mixture to loafpan, arrange fruit on top, and bake in pre-heated 375° oven 40-45 min. until cake begins to brown. When cool, dust with powdered sugar.

ORANGE CAKE
ciasto pomarańczowe

Cream 2 sticks room-temp. butter or oleo with 1½ c. powdered sugar until fluffy. Continue beating while adding 4 eggs, one at a time. Sift in 3½ c. flour mixed with 3 T. baking powder. Add grated rind (zest) and juice of 1 orange, 1 t. orange extract, and 1 c. sour cream and mix until nice and smooth. Stir in 1 c. ground walnuts and 1 c. scalded, drained, and dried raisins. Mix well. Grease 2 narrow loafpans and sprinkle with bread crumbs. Fill pans with mixture no more than ¾ full and bake in pre-heated 375° oven about 40-45 min. Test for doneness with wooden pick. Cool cakes in pans about 10 min., then gently transfer to sheets of aluminum foil and let stand until completely cooled. Meanwhile, prepare glaze by fork-blending 1½ c. powdered sugar, ¼ t. orange extract, 1 T. lemon juice, and 2 T. orange juice until nice and smooth. Glaze top and sides of cakes. When glaze sets, wrap cakes in foil and refrigerate for 7–14 days. This delicious moist cake improves in flavor the longer it stands.

HOLIDAY FRUITCAKE
keks świąteczny

Prepare 1 lb. southern fruits: wash and drain raisins, prunes, dried apricots, figs, and dates, then dice (all except raisins); add broken-up walnut meats, whole shelled hazelnuts, and chopped, candied orange rind. Place nuts & fruits in plastic bag, add 1 c. flour, and shake to thoroughly coat. Transfer to colander and shake gently to remove excess flour. Line 2 narrow loafpans with aluminum foil so it protrudes beyond rim 2 inches. Generously butter foil inside pans. In large bowl cream 2 sticks room-temp. butter with 1½ c. powdered sugar, gradually increasing mixer speed. Mixing constantly, gradually add 5 egg yolks, 1 T. baking powder, ½ lb. flour, sifted (about 2 c.), and vanilla extract. Beat 5 egg whites to stiff froth and fold into batter. Add nuts & fruits and mix lightly. Transfer batter to pans and bake in pre-heated 350° oven 15–20 min. until cakes begin turning golden. Reduce heat to 300°–325° and bake another 30–40 min. If they brown too quickly, cover with protruding foil flaps. Check for doneness with wooden pick. When cool, wrap in foil, place in plastic bags, and chill in fridge overnight before serving. They will stay fresh refrigerated for a week. To serve, cut into thin slices with serrated knife. This is an annual Christmas favorite in our household and many Polish homes as well.

EVERYDAY FRUITCAKE
keks popularny

Prepare 1 lb. fruits & nuts as above. In bowl lightly beat 5 eggs, removing 1 T. mixture for brushing cake. Transfer eggs to double boiler and beat over boiling water with 1 c. powdered sugar until mixture is thick and fluffy. (*Note*: A hand-held electric mixer at high speed is good for this purpose!) Remove from heat and continue beating until mixture cools. Separately cream 1½ sticks room-temp. margarine, gradually adding egg mixture and 2 c. sifted flour. When fully blended, add flour-coated fruit & nuts and mix lightly. Transfer to buttered, foil-lined narrow loafpans as above and smooth tops. Brush tops with reserved beaten egg. Bake in pre-heated 350° oven 15–20 min. Then reduce heat to 300°–325° and bake another 30–40 min.

SPONGE FRUITCAKE
keks biszkoptowy

Prepare ½ lb. fruits & nuts as above. Beat 5 egg yolks and 1 c. powdered sugar until fluffy, adding 1 T. white 6% vinegar towards end. Beat 5 egg whites to a froth. Fold beaten whites into yolk mixture, sifting in 1¼ c. flour and adding floured fruits & nuts. Mix gently. Place mixture in buttered, foil-lined narrow loafpans and bake in pre-heated 300° oven 15 min. Increase heat to 350° and bake another 15–20 min. Check for doneness with pick. *Note*: In every Polish keks the proportion of nuts & fruits is variable. Depending on what you prefer or have on hand, feel free to use just prunes and raisins, add almonds or pecans, include mixed, dried fruits, or a little finely chopped, mixed, candied fruits & rinds.

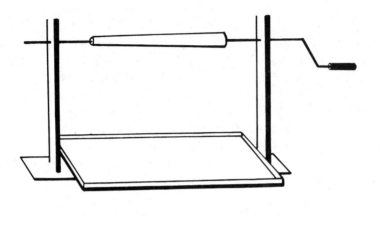

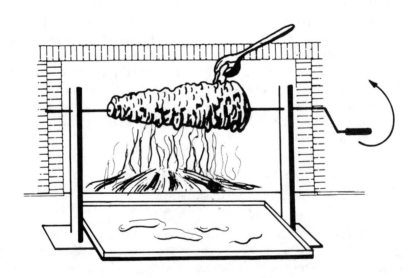

The traditional "sękacz" or log cake is made on a hand-cranked spit fitted with a tapered wooden spindle, a device most any handy man can put together at home. Batter is gradually applied to the hot surface and the spindle is slowly rotated and cranked back and forth until it gets flame-baked in front of a hot fireplace or other such heat source. Only then is more batter spooned on.

SPIKED HOLIDAY LOG CAKE (BAUMKUCHEN)/PYRAMID CAKE
sękacz świąteczny z kolcami/dziad

This old-style cake, baked on a spit for both Christmas and Easter (as well as weddings and other festive occasions), takes a little doing, but one taste will convince you that it's really worth the effort. You will need a hand-cranked spit fitted with a smooth wooden spindle tapering at one end (see illustration) and a roaring fireplace to set it next to. A drip pan should be positioned below spit to collect any batter that drips during baking. Run clean white cord from narrow to wide end of spit. One person should hold cord against narrow end, while another wraps cord tightly in 1 layer round spit from wide to narrow end of spit. (*Note*: The cord will enable you to easily remove cake from spit after baking.) Wrap cord-covered spit tightly with parchment paper and tie with string at both ends and center. Grease parchment with butter. To prepare batter, cream 1 lb. (4 sticks) room-temp. butter and 2 c. powdered sugar until fluffy. Continue beating and add a total of 30 egg yolks, 2–3 at a time. Towards end add 1–2 t. vanilla extract and ½–1 t. grated nutmeg. Sift in 3 c. flour and ⅔ c. potato starch, gradually adding 1 c. heavy cream. Separately beat 30 egg whites to froth and gently mix into yolk batter. Place spit near flame and when it is hot, ladle some batter the full length of top. Turn spit slowly toward flame, cover bare top with batter, turn toward flame, and continue procedure until surface is covered by baked batter. Ladle some more batter onto spit, turning it this way and that for "spikes" to form. Icicle-type drips of batter will set in heat, forming increasingly larger "spikes" with each successive ladling of batter. Turn spit slowly so entire surface gets evenly baked. As the log cake gets thicker, it should be turned ever more slowly. It is ready when surface is a nice golden brown. Move spit and rack away from flame and let cake cool to room temp. Remove spit with baked cake encasing it and stand on table narrow side up. Have someone gently tug protruding cord at top and unravel string. This loosens cake which can be lifted up, leaving spit behind. This 15–18-inch-tall cake makes a spectacular centerpiece on any festive holiday table. To serve, cut into 3–4-inch-tall rounds, starting at top, then cut rounds into fairly thin slices. If you can't use it all up at once, cut remainder into rounds, wrap in foil, and refrigerate up to 1 week. It also freezes up well and keeps indefinitely in freezer.

GLAZED LOG CAKE
sękacz glazurowany

Proceed as above, but reduce the number of eggs in batter to 20. Heat buttered, parchment-covered spit and apply three 1½ –2 inch vertical bands of batter round the spit at equal intervals. Bake near flame, cranking slowly until batter sets and begins to brown. Then ladle some batter the full length of spit and allow it to bake. Continue ladling and baking batter until all is used up. When last layer is lightly browned, move rack away from heat and allow to cool. After removing spit from cake (as above), brush cake with the following glaze. In saucepan combine ½ c. water and 1 T. white vinegar. Add 2 c. granulated sugar, heat to dissolve sugar, and bring to gentle boil. Simmer about 3 min. Brush cake with hot glaze 2–3 times until all is used up. *Note*: Proper preparation of the traditional sękacz requires feel and flair, and is definitely not recommended for anyone who has never done much baking. In fact, in today's Poland, few people take the time and trouble to bake them from scratch and usually rely on those offered by professional cake shops. Some, however, have obtained satisfactory results from the simplified versions below.

EASY (BROILED) LOG CAKE
sękacz ułatwiony (z prodiża)

Cream 4 sticks room-temp. butter or margarine until fluffy. Continue beating and gradually add a total of 8 eggs, 3 c. flour, and 2½ c. powdered sugar. Add eggs one at a time and flour and sugar 1 T. at a time beating until fully absorbed before each new addition. Towards the end sprinkle in 1 T. baking powder and 2 t. vanilla extract. Butter bottom of tube pan, sprinkle with bread crumbs. Pour in 5 T. batter and place pan under pre-heated electric broiler or broiling segment of oven. Top of pan should be about 5 inches from flame. Broil until batter turns light golden brown, remove from heat, add 5 more T. batter, broil until light golden brown, and keep repeating until all is used up. *Note*: Depending on the heat, you may need 1–2 min. to bake each layer. After baking about 3 layers, test for doneness with wooden pick. As cake gets taller and comes closer to flame, you may want to use the next lowest oven-rack level. Allow to cool somewhat in pan, then remove and let cool completely. Serve cake just as is, glaze as in preceding recipe, or dust with powdered sugar.

SOUR CREAM LOG CAKE
sękacz łatwy na śmietanie

Proceed as above but prepare batter with 4 sticks butter, 1 c. powdered sugar, 4 c. flour, 6 eggs, 1 c. sour cream, 2 t. vanilla extract, and 2 t. baking powder.

LOW-FAT LOG CAKE
sękacz łatwy chudszy

Cream only 2 sticks room-temp. butter or oleo until smooth and fluffy, gradually add one by one, 7 egg yolks, alternating with 1¼ c. flour, 1¼ c. powdered sugar, and ¾ c. potato starch, which should be added 1 T. at a time. Towards end, add 2½ t. baking powder, 2 t. vanilla extract, and 2 T. vodka, cognac, or light rum. Add ingredients 1 T. at a time and do not add the next until batter has absorbed previous addition. Pre-heat broiler, butter tube-pan bottom, and sprinkle with bread crumbs. Divide batter in 2, beat to a moist froth

3½ egg whites and fold into one portion of batter, mixing lightly. Pour 5 heaping T. batter into pan and bake in broiler as in easy (broiled) log cake (above). While last layer bakes, beat another 3½ egg whites to a froth and fold into remaining batter. Bake in layers until all is used up. When cool, serve plain, glaze, or dust with powdered sugar. *Note*: One of the advantages of pan-baked log cakes is that you can correct inadequate doneness by finishing cake up in oven. Baking layers of batter under broiler is tricky, because sometimes surface browns too quickly while inside is not fully baked. When you have completed broil-baking your cake, test it for doneness with wooden pick. If not fully baked, pop into 375° oven for 15–30 min. or however long is necessary for wooden pick to come out clean.

CARPATHIAN (PUFF-PASTRY) MOUNTAIN CAKE
karpatka

This popular Polish cake gets its name from the rugged Carpathian Mountains, because after it is dusted with powdered sugar, its top resembles irregular, snow-covered peaks and crags. In pot combine 1 c. water and 1¼ sticks butter or margarine and bring to boil. Remove from heat, sift in 1 c. flour, and mix with wooden spoon until smooth and free of lumps. Return to heat and simmer, stirring constantly until mixture loses its raw-flour taste and becomes glossy (about 2 min.). Remove from heat and cool to lukewarm. To lukewarm mixture add 5 large or 6 small eggs one at a time, mixing with hand-held electric mixer at low speed until each egg is fully absorbed before adding the next. At the end, add 1 t. baking powder and mix briefly. Line bottom of 2 square or rectangular baking pans with parchment paper and grease with butter. Pour ½ the batter into each in fairly thin layer and do not smooth tops. They are supposed to be craggy and mountainous! Pop into pre-heated 500° oven and bake 25–30 min. Do not open oven during first 15 min. Reduce heat slightly if tops brown too quickly. While they bake, prepare filling. Bring 1 c. milk to boil and dissolve ½ c. potato starch in 1 c. cold milk. In thin stream add cold milk and starch mixture to hot milk, stirring constantly and simmering on low heat several min. until a glossy, pudding-like mixture is obtained. Set aside to cool. Cream 1¼ sticks butter and 1¾ c. powdered sugar. Mixing constantly, gradually add 2 egg yolks and the cold pudding-like mixture, 1 t. vanilla, and 1 T. lemon juice. Spread mixture over surface of one of the cakes, cover with the other cake "mountain-side-up", and allow to cool. Dust with powdered sugar and cut into squares to serve.

HONEY-SPICE CAKE
piernik/miodownik

Like Nuremberg, Germany, the Polish city of Toruń has been known since the Middle Ages for its legendary honey-spice cakes. To this day Toruń bakers turn out these cakes in the shape of decorative hearts and intricate figures of saints, knights, and maidens which look almost too nice to eat and are actually suitable for framing. We, however, will stick to those that you can bake and consume. Some examples follow.

TORUŃ HONEY-SPICE CAKE OLD POLISH STYLE
staropolski piernik toruński

This cake is meant to be prepared 3 weeks before Christmas or whatever other festive occasion you're planning. In saucepan combine 1⅓ c. honey and 1–2 T. honey-spice-cake seasoning, bring to boil, and set aside to cool somewhat. Sift 2 c. flour (preferably a slightly coarser, milled variety than the standard all-purpose type) onto board, making well at center of mound. Pour in warm honey and cut flour into it with knife until blended. Cut in ½ stick butter until blended and let stand 15 min. Sprinkle dough with 1 t. potassium carbonate (a baking powder used solely for pierniks) and 4 t. baking soda. Add 1 jigger rum and 3 eggs beaten with 2 c. powdered sugar and grated rind of ½ lemon. Work ingredients by hand for a full hr. Transfer dough, which by now should be very elastic, to narrow loafpans, filling them only half full. Cover dough in each pan with several thicknesses of dish towel and keep in cool place (cellar or fridge) 1 week. Remove towels, decorate tops with blanched almond halves, and bake in pre-heated 425° oven 1 hr. or longer, checking for doneness with wooden pick. If tops brown too quickly, cover with greased parchment paper or aluminum foil and reduce heat slightly. After baking, remove from pans and let cool on board. Wrap in dish towels and refrigerate 2 weeks before serving. Just before serving, glaze or dust with powdered sugar. *Note*: The piernik is just about the healthiest cake you can eat. It is low in fat and cholesterol, and the combination of honey and spices stimulates digestion. That is probably why it fits so nicely into Christmas, a time when overindulging in rich foods is the order of the day.

LAYERED TORUŃ HONEY-SPICE CAKE
piernik toruński przekładany

Into bowl sift 1½ c. rye flour and 2 c. all-purpose (wheat) flour. Bring 1 c. honey to boil in saucepan, pour over flour, and mix well with wooden spoon. Beat 4 egg yolks and 1 c. powdered sugar until fluffy and add to flour-honey mixture together with 1 t. cinnamon and 1 t. ground cloves. Mix all ingredients well. When mixture cools to room temp., dissolve ½ T. baking soda in 2 T. cold water and mix into dough. Line narrow loafpan with aluminum foil, grease it, and sprinkle with bread crumbs. Fill ½ full with dough. Use more than 1 pan if needed. Brush top of dough with water, decorate with about ¼ c. blanched almonds (whole or halved) and bake in pre-heated 325° oven about 1 hr. When cake has cooled, cut into 3 horizontal layers. Spread bottom layer with powidła or Polish-style marmalade (see

Home-canning, Pickling, and Preserving chapter), top with middle layer, spread with some more jam or marmalade, and cover with almond-studded top. Press down gently to stick layers together. *Variation*: Instead of jam, spread layers with nut filling. In dry skillet lightly toast 1 c. walnut meats or shelled hazelnuts or some of both, then grind. Beat 1 egg yolk and 3 T. powdered sugar until fluffy, adding ¼ c. honey, 1 T. lemon juice, 1 T. rum, 2 T. finely grated chocolate, and the ground nuts. Mix until uniform and spread layers of piernik with mixture. *Optional*: Cover all over with chocolate glaze.

SOUTHERN FRUIT HONEY-SPICE CAKE
piernik bakaliowy

Chop ¼ lb. walnut meats and ¼ lb. blanched almonds. Wash, drain, and dry ¾ c. raisins. Wash, drain, dry, and dice ¼ lb. pitted prunes. (*Optional*: Some chopped dates and/or figs may be used in place of some of the raisins and prunes.) Mix nuts & fruits with about 1 c. flour and set aside. Sift 2½ c. ordinary or rye flour into bowl. Bring ¾ c. honey to boil and pour it over flour, mixing with wooden spoon until smooth. Melt 1 stick butter and add to mixture together with 1 T. honey-spice-cake seasoning. Mix well with wooden spoon to obliterate all lumps and let cool. Beat 6 egg yolks with 1 c. sugar until white. To dough add nuts & fruits and all the flour with which they were mixed, the yolk mixture, and 4 T. sour cream and work well. When a thick, uniform dough is obtained, add 1 t. ammonium carbonate (a kind of baking powder) dissolved in 2 T. water and 6 egg whites beaten to a stiff froth with 2 T. powdered sugar added towards end of beating. Mix ingredients lightly. Line narrow loafpans with aluminum foil, grease, and fill half full with dough. Bake in pre-heated 325° oven about 1 hr.

ALMOND (MARZIPAN) HONEY-SPICE CAKE
piernik z marcepanem

Mix well 1 c. honey, 1 stick room-temp. butter, and ¾ c. powdered sugar until smooth. Beating constantly, add 2 eggs one at a time, 2 T. ground walnuts, 2 T. ground hazelnuts, ¼ t. cinnamon, ¼ t. ginger, ¼ t. ground cloves, 2 T. cocoa, and 1 T. strong coffee extract (1 level t. instant coffee dissolved in 1 T. water). Mix ingredients well, adding 2 T. baking powder. Continue mixing, sifting in gradually 4¼ c. flour. Mix until dough is uniform. Place in bowl, cover with several thicknesses of dish towel, and refrigerate 2–7 days—the longer the better. Divide dough into 3 parts and roll out each ¼–½-inch thick to fit 3 separate pans. Place each in greased pan and bake in pre-heated 325° oven about 25 min. (*Note*: Bake one at a time if your oven cannot accommodate all three at once.) When cool, spread 1 layer with powidła or thick Polish marmalade, cover with next layer, and spread it thinly with the same jam, and top with layer of almond filling (marzipan–see below). Cover with top layer and spread it thinly with jam and then almond filling. Cover with waxed paper and weighted-down board. Leave at room temp. overnight and serve the following day. To prepare almond filling, grind ½ lb. blanched almonds twice. In saucepan combine almonds, 2 c. powdered sugar, 1 T. cognac or vodka and 2 T. lemon juice. Beat until smooth mixture is obtained. Heat gently without boiling until mixture easily comes away from bottom of pot. Remove from heat, cool somewhat, and spread cake, including sides, with warm mixture.

WALNUT HONEY-SPICE SPONGE CAKE
piernik biszkoptowy z orzechami

Cream 1½ sticks room-temp. butter and 1½ c. powdered sugar, gradually adding 5 egg yolks and 1 c. honey and mixing until fully absorbed. Coarsely chop 8 oz. walnut meats, mix with 1½ c. flour, and add to above mixture. Stir in 1 T. honey-spice cake seasoning, ⅔ c. sour cream, and 1 T. baking soda; mix well. Fill 2 narrow greased and floured loafpans with mixture no more than ⅔ full. Bake in pre-heated 325° oven 30 min. without opening oven door. Increase heat to 350° and bake another 20 min. without opening oven door, checking for doneness with wooden pick. Remove from pans when cool and spread with white, chocolate, or rum-flavored glaze.

2-WEEK HONEY-SPICE CAKE
piernik dojrzewający 2 tygodnie

In dry saucepan melt and brown (caramelize) 4 T. sugar, add 4 T. hot water and stir until dissolved. Add 1 c. honey, 1½ sticks margarine, and 1 c. sugar. Simmer on low heat, stirring constantly until ingredients dissolve and blend. Set aside to cool. Transfer to bowl and gradually sift in 3½ c. flour, add 2 eggs, 1 T. honey-spice cake seasoning and ½ c. milk in which 1 t. baking soda has been dissolved. Mix well and place dough in crockery bowl or enameled pot. Cover top with parchment paper and secure with large rubber band. Refrigerate 2 weeks. Line narrow loafpans with aluminum foil, butter, and sprinkle insides with bread crumbs. Fill pans half full with dough and bake in pre-heated 325° oven about 50 min.

FAT-FREE HONEY-SPICE CAKE
piernik bez tłuszczu

This cake is recommended for those on fat-restricted diets. It contains no fat whatsoever, except for the small amount of butter used to grease pans to prevent sticking. Even this can be eliminated if you use a non-stick baking spray. Combine ½ c. raisins and diced prunes with ½ c. chopped walnuts and 4 T. flour. In saucepan combine 1 c. crystalized honey and

1 c. milk, heating and stirring until blended, then set aside to cool. In mixture dissolve 1 t. baking soda and 1 t. ammonium carbonate. Sift 3 c. flour into bowl. Separately beat 4 eggs with 1 c. powdered sugar and add to flour together with honey & milk mixture and 1 T. honey-spice cake seasoning. Mix ingredients well until blended, add floured fruits & nuts, and mix to distribute evenly. Line 2 narrow loafpans with aluminum foil, grease with a little butter, sprinkle with bread crumbs, and fill with dough which should reach no more than ½ way to top. Bake in preheated 350° oven about 1 hr. Check for doneness with pick. *Note*: For more zing, add ¼–½ t. freshly ground pepper to this or any of the other honey-spice cakes in addition to the other spices.

CARROT SPICE CAKE
piernik "marchwianka"

Brown 4 T. sugar in dry skillet, carefully add ¼ c. boiling water so it doesn't splatter, stir to dissolve caramel, bring to boil, and set aside to cool. Peel and finely grate 1¼ lbs. carrots. Cream 1 stick room-temp. margarine, gradually adding 4 egg yolks, 1 c. sugar, and 1½ c. flour mixed with 2 t. baking powder and sifted, caramel, grated carrots, 1 t. vanilla extract, and ⅓ t. each: cinnamon, ground cloves, and ground coriander (or 1 t. honey-spice cake seasoning). Mix well until smooth, fold in 4 beaten egg whites, sifting in another 1½ c. flour and mixing lightly. Grease and sprinkle with bread crumbs 2 narrow loafpans, transfer dough to pans, and bake in 450° oven about 1 hr. Cover with foil and reduce heat if tops brown too quickly. Test for doneness with pick.

EASY LEMON CAKE
łatwy placek cytrynowy

Break 5 eggs into bowl and beat lightly with fork or whisk. Add 1 c. powdered sugar and 1 stick cooled, melted butter. Mix 1½ c. flour with 2 t. baking powder and sift into above mixture, adding 1 t. grated lemon rind and several drops lemon extract. Mix ingredients and pour into generously buttered tube pan sprinkled with bread crumbs which should be no more than half full. Bake in pre-heated 350° oven about 40 min. Test for doneness with pick. When cool, spread with lemon icing. This is a very simple cake at which even youngsters can try their hand.

FRUIT SPONGE CAKE
placek biszkoptowy z owocami

This cake can be made with cherries, strawberries, plums, or apricots. Wash and drain fruit (hull strawberries, pit cherries, pit and halve plums, or pit and slice apricots). Grease square or rectangular pan and sprinkle with bread crumbs. Beat 4 egg whites to a stiff froth.

Add 3 heaping T. powdered sugar and 4 egg yolks one by one, and beat until fluffy. Mix 1 T. baking powder with 4 slightly heaped T. flour and 2 T. potato starch, sift into egg mixture, and mix lightly. Transfer to baking pan in layer not exceeding 1 inch and arrange fruit on top. Bake in pre-heated 375° oven 30–40 min.

"5-OF-EVERYTHING" APPLE SPONGE CAKE
placek biszkoptowy z jabłkami "wszystkiego po 5"

This is another easy cake which frequently turns up on the dinner table whenever the apple tree in our back garden produces a bumper crop. Peel, core, and thinly slice 5 large tart apples. Beat 5 egg yolks at high speed until fluffy, adding 5 T. powdered sugar and 5 T. sifted flour. Top mixture with 5 stiffly beaten egg whites and lightly mix together. Pour ½ the batter into greased tube pan, top with apples, cover with remaining batter, and bake in pre-heated 375° oven 30–40 min. (*Note*: Batter should fill only half the pan before baking.) Remove from pan when partially cooled, dust with powdered sugar, and serve warm or after it has cooled completely. *Note*: Depending on the quantity you need you can make this cake with 4, 6, 7, etc. of everything.

FILLED SPONGE-CAKE ROLL
rolada biszkoptowa

Grease rectangular pan (a jelly-roll pan if you have one), cover bottom with parchment paper or aluminum foil and grease. Beat 4 egg yolks and 4 T. sugar until fluffy, sift in 4 T. flour, fold in 4 stiffly beaten egg whites and lightly mix ingredients. Pour batter in ⅓ -inch layer into pan, pop immediately into pre-heated 350° oven and bake about 15 min. or until it becomes lightly golden. Remove from oven, sprinkle lightly with powdered sugar, invert pan and turn out onto clean dish cloth lightly dusted with powdered sugar. Roll up jelly-roll-fashion together with cloth and let stand until cooled nearly to room temp. Unroll cake, spread with jam, Polish marmalade or cake filling of choice (see cake fillings towards end of chapter), roll up again, and keep in fridge until thoroughly chilled. Dust with powdered sugar just before serving.

SPONGE-CAKE ROLL ANOTHER WAY
rolada biszkoptowa inaczej

Beat 4 eggs and 4 T. sugar in double boiler over boiling water until mixture thickens. Remove from heat and continue beating until mixture cools. Sift in 4 T. flour and mix lightly. Transfer to greased baking pan lined with parchment or aluminum foil and proceed as above.

Sponge cake is sliced into layers which are spread with fillings and reassembled to create a torte.

ECONOMY CAKE ROLL
rolada oszczędna

Beat 2 egg yolks, adding 2 T. boiling water and mixing until mixture becomes fluffy. Gradually add ½ c. powdered sugar and beat until fluffy. Beat 2 egg whites to a stiff froth, add 1 T. powdered sugar, and beat a bit longer. Into yolk mixture sift ¼ c. flour, 3 T. potato starch, and 1 t. baking powder, top with beaten whites and lightly mix ingredients. Transfer to pan lined with greased parchment paper or aluminum foil. Batter should be only about ¼ inch high in pan because it rises. Bake in pre-heated 350° oven about 15 min. or until light golden. Proceed as in first sponge cake roll recipe.

TORTES
torty

These light, moist, delicious, and often elegantly decorated cakes have been long a Central European specialty, and nearly all Polish homemakers have one or more torte recipes in their repertoire. If you have never prepared them, we strongly urge you to read through the following pointers before trying the actual recipes for sponge-cake tortes.

—It is best to bake cake a day ahead. The next day, when ready to fill, cut it horizontally with a long, sharp knife into 3 layers of equal size. Set layers aside separately.

—Line the edge of serving platter on which torte is to be placed with roughly 2-inch-wide strips of parchment paper or foil so as not to spatter platter while decorating torte. After it is decorated, the paper is discarded.

—The middle layer of cake is placed on serving platter first. It is usually sprinkled with flavored torte liquor (poncz) (see p. 663), spread with a thin layer of tart jelly (red-currant, raspberry, cherry, etc.) and then topped with thin layer of cake filling (also known as pastry creme).

—The top layer of sponge cake goes on top. It too is sprinkled with flavored torte liquor and spread with filling.

—Filling should be at room temp. when spreading over layers and entire outside surface of torte. The remainder should be placed in pastry tube and chilled. Use chilled filling in decorator tube to decorate torte with flowers, swirls, and other embellishments (see torte decorations).

—Usually a single filling is used for inside and outside of torte. However, a fancier effect can be achieved by using contrasting fillings. For instance a torte filled and frosted with chocolate filling may be decorated with a white filling and vice-versa.

—The final decorative touches can be added using candied fruit, well-drained fruit from preserves, fresh berries, almonds, or other nuts.

—The completed torte should be chilled in fridge before serving.

—Before serving, cut into serving-size wedges in kitchen but bring torte to table intact and it will draw oohs and ahs from your guests. Portion it out at table after your guests have feasted their eyes upon your masterpiece.

—When there is a decorative centerpiece on top of torte, it is common to cut a (1½ –2-inch circle) around it with a small glass, and slice portions from outside of circle. That way the decoration remains intact.

BASIC SPONGE CAKE TORTE
tort biszkoptowy podstawowy

By starting with a basic yellow sponge cake, cut into 3 layers, you can produce many different tortes by simply varying the torte liquors, filling, and decorations. Start by greasing a springform pan. Cut a circle of parchment paper to fit pan bottom and make a parchment-paper wall extending 1 inch above pan rim round the sides. Parchment will adhere to greased sides. Grease parchment (bottom and sides) with butter. Over boiling water in double boiler beat 7 eggs and 1 c. powdered sugar with whisk or hand-held electric mixer until mixture thickens, whitens, and achieves a temp. of 100°–110°. Remove from heat and continue beating until cool. Sift in 1 c. + 2 T. flour, mix gently, and pour into pan. It should fill only ½ the pan, not counting parchment collar. Place in pre-heated 325° oven and bake 15 min. Increase temp. to 400° and bake another 20–25 min. A properly baked cake will come away from sides and a wooden pick inserted in center will come out clean. Tread lightly, i.e. do not open oven, jostle cake, or bang things during baking because cake may collapse. Allow cake to cool in pan. When cool, remove from pan and preferably let stand covered with foil overnight. Then cut into 3 layers, fill, and decorate as indicated in torte-baking pointers (preceding entry).

CHOCOLATE TORTE
tort czekoladowy

You can prepare a chocolate torte by filling and frosting the basic yellow sponge cake with chocolate filling or you can choose this double-chocolate torte in which both cake and filling are chocolatey. Beat 7 eggs over boiling water in double boiler with 1 c. sugar and ¼ c. hot water until smooth and fluffy. Remove from heat and continue beating until mixture cools. Towards end beat in 4 T. cocoa. Sift in 1 c. flour and mix lightly. Otherwise, proceed as with basic sponge cake torte (above). When assembling, sprinkle with cocoa- or rum-flavored torte liquor (see p. 663) and fill and frost top and sides with chocolate, rum, walnut or southern-fruit filling (see pp. 664-666).

NUT TORTE
tort orzechowy

Butter springform pan, line with parchment and butter again as in basic sponge-cake torte recipe (above). In nut-grinder grind 2 c. walnut meats and/or hazelnuts. Over boiling water in double-boiler beat 7 eggs with 1¼ c. powdered sugar until mixture thickens and whitens, then remove from heat and continue beating until cooled. Add ground nuts and 8 T. bread crumbs and mix lightly. Transfer to pan, filling it ¾ full and bake in pre-heated 375° oven about 35 min. Leave in pan to cool, remove from pan, discard parchment. Next day, cut it into 3 layers. Sprinkle with rum or arrack-flavored torte liquor (see p. 663) and spread layers. Frost entire torte with walnut, chocolate, cocoa, rum, or coffee-flavored filling (see pgs. 664-665). Decorate with walnut meats. *Variation:* Sprinkle top and sides with ground nuts or nuts ground with equal amount of stale white bread.

BREAD TORTE
tort chlebowy

Prepare springform pan as above. Grind several slices stale black bread—enough to get 1 c. crumbs. Over boiling water in double-boiler beat 8 eggs with 1 c. sugar until mixture thickens and whitens. Remove from heat and continue beating until cool. Add almond extract (several drops–¼ t. depending on intensity desired) and sifted black-bread crumbs and mix lightly. (*Variation*: Torte will be lighter if only yolks are beaten with sugar and the beaten whites are folded into room-temp. yolk mixture.) Transfer batter to pan, filling it ¾ full, and bake in pre-heated 350° about 40 min., checking for doneness with wooden pick. Next day, cut into 3 layers, sprinkle with rum-flavored torte liquor (see p. 663) and fill and frost with chocolate or cocoa filling (see p. 665). Decorate top with halved blanched almonds.

POPPYSEED TORTE
tort makowy

Prepare springform pan as usual. Rinse and drain 2 c. poppyseeds, place in pot, scald with boiling water to cover by 1 inch and simmer on low heat 10–15., switch off heat, cover, and let stand 1 hr. Drain and run through poppyseed grinder once or through ordinary meat grinder twice. Beat 8 egg yolks and 2 c. powdered sugar until light and fluffy. Continue beating and add gradually ground poppyseeds, 1 T. honey, ½ c. bread crumbs, 2 t. baking powder, and ¼–½ t. vanilla extract. Towards end, fold in 8 stiffly beaten egg whites and mix lightly. Fill pan ½ full with mixture and bake in pre-heated 350° oven about 40 min. Cool in pan, remove when cool, discard parchment, and let stand overnight. Next day, cut into 3 layers. Sprinkle with tea-flavored torte liquor (see p. 663) and fill and frost with cognac, nut, or coffee-flavored filling (see p. 665). *Note*: Tart jelly may be applied to bottom and middle layers of this and other tortes after sprinkling with liquor but before applying filling.

SAND TORTE
tort piaskowy

Prepare springform pan as usual. Cream 2 sticks room-temp. butter with 1⅓ c. powdered sugar, gradually adding 6 egg yolks one at a time, 2 T. vanilla sugar, 1 t. baking powder, ⅔ c. flour, ⅔ c. potato starch—both sifted. Fold in 6 stiffly beaten egg whites and mix delicately. Fill pan with batter ⅔ full and bake in pre-heated 325° oven 15 min. Increase heat to 375° and bake another 25–30 min. Proceed as with other tortes. Next day, cut into layers and fill and frost with vanilla torte filling (see p. 664). *Variation*: Filling may be divided in half with 2 T. cocoa or 2 T. instant coffee added to 1 portion. Fill torte with lighter filling and frost outside with cocoa– or coffee-flavored filling. Torte liquor is not used in this recipe. *Note*: In Polish cake-baking, the term "sand" is used to describe babkas, tortes, and other cakes made with potato starch which gives them their delightfully grainy texture.

LEMON SAND TORTE
tort piaskowy cytrynowy

As always, when planning to grate citrus-fruit rind, scrub 1 lemon with stiff brush in hot soapy water, rinse, scald with boiling water, and dry. Prepare batter as for sand torte (above), but towards the end add grated lemon rind and juice of 1 lemon. Bake as above and fill and frost torte with lemon filling (see p. 664). Do not sprinkle with torte liquor.

EASY UNBAKED TORTES
łatwe torty bez pieczenia

You can easily prepare any of the tortes calling for yellow sponge cake by cutting plain, store-bought sponge cake into rounds rather than baking it from scratch. Store-bought teacakes (cookies) and wafers can also be used for this purpose. Some examples follow.

VANILLA-WAFER TORTE
tort z biszkopcików

Line bottom and sides of springform pan of whatever size you like with store-bought or homemade vanilla wafers. Sprinkle with a little torte liquor of choice (see following pages) and cover with a layer of torte filling of choice. Top with another layer of vanilla wafers, sprinkle with torte liquor, spread with another layer of filling, and continue until you reach top of pan. Top layer should be wafers. Cover with board, baking sheet, or other flat surface, weight down and refrigerate 2–3 hrs. until firmly set. Remove sides of pan and frost top and sides with some more filling. Decorate with nuts, fruits, etc. as desired and chill another hr. before serving. *Note*: This torte may be prepared with other plain teacakes like Lorna Doones. Feel free to call your creation "chocolate torte", "almond torte", "lemon torte", or whatever, depending on the filling you use. Only the most perceptive guests will suspect you didn't bake it from scratch!

CREAMY PEACH TORTE (VANILLA-WAFER TYPE)
torcik brzoskwiniowy (z biszkopcików)

Prepare 1 package peach gelatin dessert (jello) but use the juice of drained canned peaches in place of water. Set aside to cool to room temp. Prepare 1 package vanilla pudding according to directions. This can be instant or the cooked type, but in the latter case set aside to cool. Cream 2 sticks room-temp. butter or margarine with ¼ c. powdered sugar until fluffy. Add juice of 1 small lemon and continue beating, adding pudding a T. at a time until completely absorbed. Mix 1 T. rum with ¾ c. water, dip vanilla wafers in solution and use them to line bottom and sides of springform pan. Cover with layer of filling and continue layering wafers (dipped in rum solution) and filling until filling has been nearly used up. (Reserve enough to frost sides of cake later.). Smooth filling on top with knife dipped in warm water and top with well-drained, sliced, canned peaches. Cover with room-temp. peach gelatin and chill in fridge 2–3 hrs. (*Important*: Layer wafers and filling, leaving space near top of pan for peaches and gelatin.) When set, remove sides of pan, frost sides of torte with remaining filling, and chill at least 1 hr. before serving.

STEPHANIE'S (UNBAKED) CHOCOLATE TORTE
torcik "Stefanka" bez pieczenia

Line bottom and sides of springform pan with vanilla wafers, Lorna Doone-type biscuits, or other plain teacakes. Cover with layer of chocolate or cocoa torte filling (see torte fillings) and continue layering until you reach top of pan. Top layer should be wafers or teacakes. Cover top with flat surface, weight down and refrigerate at least 2 hrs. Remove sides of pan and frost top and sides of torte with filling. Decorate top with halved or whole blanched almonds. Chill another hr. before serving.

EASY WAFER TORTES
łatwe torciki waflowe

Besides plain teacakes, tortes that require no baking can be made with gaufrette or krumkake-type wafer rounds available at gourmet and food-specialty shops. Or, you can bake your own at home (see homemade mazurka wafers). Spread wafer with torte filling of choice,

choice, cover with another wafer, and continue layering until torte reaches the height you want. Top layer should be wafer round. Cover with board or other flat surface and weigh down. Chill at least 2 hrs. Frost top and sides with additional torte filling or spread with icing if you prefer. *Note:* Especially popular in Poland is the "torcik wedlowski", a chocolate wafer torte produced by the E. Wedel Chocolate Co. of Warsaw.

TORTE LIQUORS
poncze do nasączania tortów

To flavor the average torte you will need just over 1 c. torte liquor, a liquid flavored with spirits, and other ingredients which accounts for the delicate moistness of your finished product. Here are a few examples:

TEA-FLAVORED TORTE LIQUOR
poncz herbaciany

Sweeten 1 c. hot weak tea with 6 T. sugar and allow to cool. Stir in 1 T. lemon juice and 1 T. 190-proof grain alcohol (spirit) or 2 T. cognac or less expensive French brandy.

RUM-FLAVORED TORTE LIQUOR
poncz rumowy

Bring 1 c. water to boil with 4 T. sugar and allow to cool. Add 2–3 T. rum. *Variation:* Instead of rum, use 2–3 T. arrack (arak), a Middle Eastern brandy.

COGNAC-FLAVORED TORTE LIQUOR
poncz koniakowy

Bring 1 c. water and 4 T. sugar to boil and set aside to cool. Add 2–3 T. cognac or less expensive French brandy.

COCOA-FLAVORED TORTE LIQUOR
poncz kakaowy

Mix 6 T. sugar and with 2 T. cocoa, gradually adding 1 c. hot water and a pinch citric-acid crystals. When cool, add 2 T. rum.

BASIC TORTE FILLING & FROSTING
masa tortowa podstawowa

Over boiling water in double-boiler beat 4 eggs and 1½ c. powdered sugar until mixture is fluffy, whitens, and achieves a temp. of 100°. Remove from heat and continue beating until cooled to room temp. Cream 4 sticks room-temp. butter (or 2 sticks butter and 2 sticks margarine) until fluffy, gradually adding egg mixture and beating until mixture is light and fluffy. To this basic filling various spirits and flavorings are added to obtain any of the below.

COGNAC FILLING
masa koniakowa

Towards end of beating to basic torte filling (above) add 1 t. lemon juice and 4 T. cognac or less expensive French brandy.

RUM FILLING
masa rumowa

Towards end of beating to basic torte filling add 4 T. rum and (if a more intense flavor is desired) several drops rum extract.

ARRACK FILLING
masa arakowa

Proceed exactly as with rum filling, but use 4 T. arrack (Middle Eastern brandy) and (if desired and available) several drops arrack extract.

VANILLA FILLING
masa waniliowa

Towards end of beating to basic torte filling add 1 t. or more vanilla extract and 2 T. 190-proof grain alcohol or 3–4 T. 100-proof vodka.

LEMON FILLING
masa cytrynowa

Beat into basic filling grated rind and juice of 1 lemon and 2 T. 190-proof grain alcohol.

ORANGE FILLING
masa pomarańczowa

To basic filling add 1 T. lemon juice, 4 T. orange juice, ½ t. grated orange rind, and 2 T. rum. *Note*: Add several drops orange extract for more intense flavor.

COCOA FILLING
masa kakaowa

Dissolve 3 T. cocoa in 2 T. hot milk. When cool, add 2 T. cognac or less expensive French brandy and beat into basic filling.

CHOCOLATE FILLING
masa czekoladowa

Over boiling water in double boiler melt 3–4 oz.(squares) unsweetened or semi-sweet, broken-up chocolate in ⅓ c. milk and 2 T. rum or cognac. When cool, add to basic filling.

COFFEE FILLING
masa kawowa

In ¼ c. strong coffee dissolve 1 t. instant coffee powder or crystals. When cool, add 1 T. 190-proof grain alcohol and beat into basic filling.

ALMOND FILLING
masa migdałowa

Mix ½ c. ground blanched almonds with several drops almond extract and 1 T. 190-proof grain alcohol or 2 T. rum. Add to basic filling.

NUT FILLING
masa orzechowa

Mix 1 c. ground nuts (walnuts, hazelnuts, and/or pecans) with 3 T. rum and beat into basic filling.

SOUTHERN-FRUIT FILLING
masa bakaliowa

Finely dice 1 c. of southern fruits (raisins, prunes, dates, figs, candied orange rind), mix with 2 T. 190-proof grain alcohol and add to basic filling towards end.

FRESH-FRUIT FILLING
masa owocowa

Wash, dry, hull, or pit enough fruit to get 1 c. puree. These can be strawberries, raspberries, peaches, or apricots. Puree in blender and mix into basic torte filling. *Note*: No matter how you slice it (no pun intended!), a torte with any of the above fillings is rich and fattening. If you love tortes from time to time but don't need the extra calories, cut the filling recipes in half and fill and frost torte less generously. Or, try the filling below which calls for 1½ sticks butter instead of 4.

TURKISH-FUDGE FILLING
masa kaimakowa

Cook 3 c. milk and 3 c. sugar on low heat, stirring constantly so mixture doesn't scorch, until it is reduced by half. It is ready when a drop of mixture dropped on plate sets immediately and is not sticky to the touch. Cool mixture. Cream 1½ sticks butter until fluffy, gradually adding fudge and ½–1 t. vanilla extract.

SIMPLEST CAKE ICING
lukier do ciast najłatwiejszy

Sift 1 c. powdered sugar, add about 2 T. liquid, mix until smooth and spread over cake. Use: hot water or milk; very strong hot coffee (1 t. instant coffee dissolved in 2 T. brewed coffee); 2 T. lemon juice plus grated rind of ½ lemon; 1 T. hot water mixed with 1 T. rum, cognac or arrack and a few drops of corresponding extract; 2 t. vanilla extract mixed with 4 t. hot water or milk produces a nice vanilla-flavored glaze; for a chocolate-flavored glaze, dissolve 1–2 T. cocoa in 2 T. hot water before blending with powdered sugar. *Note*: For finest texture use 10X confectioner's sugar. Spread icing over cake with knife dipped in hot water.

BASIC COOKED ICING
lukier gotowany podstawowy

Place 1½ c. granulated sugar in pot, add ½ c. water and ½ t. 6% distilled (white) vinegar and simmer on low heat (about 30 min.) until a drop of syrup leaves a trail of wispy threads when dropped from a height. Sprinkle syrup with a little cold water, place pot into bowl of cold water. When syrup cools to 140°, mix it with wooden spoon until smooth. If too thick, add a few drops of hot water. Flavor if desired with vanilla, rum, lemon juice, cognac, extracts, etc. Heat in double-boiler over boiling water and apply warm to cake.

EGG-WHITE ICING
lukier na białkach

Mix 1 egg white and ⅔ c. powdered sugar, sifted, until mixture is thick and fluffy (about 3–4 min. with electric mixer). The iced cakes should be placed in a warm (150°–200°) oven until icing dries, but it should not brown. This icing is good over babkas, mazurkas, and small honey-spice cakes. Flavoring of choice may be added.

CHOCOLATE ICING
polewa czekoladowa

Cream 2 sticks room-temp. butter with 1½ c. powdered sugar until fluffy, adding 3 egg yolks one at a time. Dissolve 4 T. cocoa in 3 T. milk and bring to boil. When cool, add to butter mixture together with 1 jigger cognac or brandy and 1 T. finely chopped walnuts. Mix well. Spread over cake with wide-blade knife dipped in hot water.

CHOCOLATE GLAZE
glazura czekoladowa

In saucepan combine 3–4 oz. (squares) semi-sweet chocolate and ½ –1 stick butter. Sprinkle with a little water and heat, stirring constantly, until smooth and glossy. Spread cake with hot glaze immediately.

CAKE GARNISHES
posypki do ciast

Before icing or glaze have set, you may sprinkle surface with a variety of different garnishes. Among the most common are ground nuts (walnuts, hazelnuts, almonds, pecans) which you can apply by cranking your nut grinder directly over cake. To "stretch" nuts, add cubes of stale white bread to grinder. Poppyseeds sprinkled over unset white icing provide an interesting color contrast. The same holds true for grated chocolate. Finely diced southern fruits (candied orange rinds, raisins, dates, figs, etc.) are another possibility

SUGAR-DUSTING CAKES
posypywanie ciast cukrem-pudrem

The simplest of all cake decoration is a dusting of powdered sugar which is recommended for plain, unfrosted cakes. Simply place powdered sugar in sifter and apply as generously or skimpily as you like. An ordinary sieve filled with powdered sugar and shaken over cake will do just as well. Dust a cool cake with powdered sugar and it will resemble freshly fallen snow. If you dust a hot cake straight from the oven, the powdered sugar will melt somewhat and provide an interesting glazed effect.

BUTTER-CRUMB TOPPING/STREUSEL
kruszonka

Sift ½ c. flour onto board and cut in ½ stick cold butter, dicing to blend. Add 4 T. powdered sugar and 1 T. vanilla sugar, mixing to combine ingredients and roll into ball. Grate over cake before baking. This topping is often used on plain, yeast-raised cakes and can also replace the top crust of fruit-filled cakes such as szarlotka.

BUTTER-CRUMB NUT TOPPING/STREUSEL ANOTHER WAY
kruszonka z orzechami

Mix ½ c. flour and ⅔ c. powdered sugar and sift together into bowl. Stir in several T. ground nuts of choice, ½ t. vanilla extract, and 1 t. lemon juice. Drench mixture with 1 stick hot melted butter and mix well. Chill at least 1 hr. On board break up by hand into little lumps and sprinkle over cake before baking. *Optional:* Several T. bread crumbs or cake crumbs may be added to mixture and a pinch or 2 cinnamon may be included.

PASTRIES, DOUGHNUTS & TEACAKES

A great many small Polish cakes and pastries are highly seasonal delights and many have an almost ritual significance. That certainly is true of *pączki* (Polish doughnuts) and *faworki* (angel-wing pastries) which highlight the final festivities of *zapusty* or *karnawał (Mardi Gras)* before the onset of Lent.

Needless to say, quite a few entries in this chapter are connected with Christmas, which in many countries is the traditional time for cookie baking. For your Yuletide enjoyment, you will find the traditional honey-spice cakes, including one you can hang on your Christmas tree, as well as one of our family's holiday favorites, cheese-dough apple cakes. Among the oldest Christmas treats are *makagigi* (poppyseed or nut crunch) and *tłuczeńce* (honey-rye wafers), while honeyed Christmas wafers are undoubtedly the easiest.

Blueberry rolls and strawberry tarts by contrast would normally be baked in summer, when fresh berries are in season, although they can be prepared at other times of year using jam or fruit filling.

Many other cakes could be encountered all year round, especially in the tradition-minded families that still observe the quaint, old *podwieczorek* (afternoon tea). *Bezy* (meringues) are usually baked when there are egg whites left over from other cakes or dishes.

This chapter includes Polish adaptations of pastries with which you are probably familiar, such as cream puffs, chocolate eclairs, tarts, and napoleons. There is even something we have called "Polish brownies", although they are probably a bit different than what you're used to. On the other hand, unless you were raised in a traditional Polish family, such entries as poppyseed squares, Carpathian Mountain cake, carnival rosettes, and the poppyseed "hedgehog" are likely to be something new.

If you're a cookie-lover, we strongly urge you to try the Polish jelly cookies whose secret ingredient, sieved, hard-boiled egg yolks, gives them a taste and texture all their own.

With the exception of the yeast-raised cakes, which can always be a bit tricky, many of the entries in this chapter take only minutes to prepare and a few more minutes to bake. They are ideal for beginners, and even the kids may enjoy giving them a try. In addition to natural ingredients and superior flavor, both the simple and more involved recipes have one main advantage over store-bought cakes: the satisfaction you'll get from knowing that you baked them yourself.

* * *

POLISH-STYLE DOUGHNUTS
pączki

Although these luscious doughnuts are available year-round at Polish pastry shops, they reign supreme on Tłusty Czwartek (Fat Thursday), which begins the final fling of the pre-Lenten karnawał of zapusty (Mardi Gras season). More pączki are sold on that one day than at any other time of the year. You can try your hand at making your own by proceeding according to this and the following recipes. Dissolve 2 cakes crushed yeast in 1 c. lukewarm milk, sift in 1 c. flour, add 1 T. sugar, mix, cover, and let stand in warm place to rise. Beat 8 egg yolks with ⅔ c. powdered sugar and 2 T. vanilla sugar until fluffy. Sift 2½ c. flour into bowl, add sponge, egg mixture, and 2 T. grain alcohol (spirit) or 3 T. rum, and knead well until dough is smooth and glossy. Gradually add 1 stick melted lukewarm butter and continue kneading until dough no longer clings to hands and bowl and air blisters appear. Cover with cloth and let rise in warm place until doubled. Punch dough down and let it rise again. Transfer dough to floured board, sprinkle top with flour, and roll out about ½ inch thick. With glass or biscuit-cutter cut into rounds. Arrange on floured board and proceed in either of the following ways:

Small pączki: Place a spoonful of fruit filling (rose-hip preserves, cherry preserves, powidła, or other thick jam) off center on each round. Raise edges of dough and pinch together over filling, then roll between palms snowball fashion to form balls. Let rise in warm place until doubled.

Large pączki: Place a spoonful of fruit filling as above on only ½ the dough rounds, cover each with another round, pinch edges together to seal, and roll between palms to form a ball. Let rise until doubled in warm, draftless place. Heat 1½–2 lbs. lard in deep pan so pączki can float freely during frying. It is hot enough when a small piece of dough dropped into hot fat immediately floats up. Fry pączki under cover without crowding several min. until nicely browned on bottom, then turn over and fry uncovered on the other side another 3 min. or so. *Note*: If using electric fryer, set temp. at 360°–375°. If frying in stove top pan and fat begins to burn, add several slices of peeled raw potato which will both lower the temp. and absorb any burnt flavor. Transfer fried pączki to absorbent paper and set aside to cool. When cool, dust generously with powdered sugar, glaze, or icing. *Variation*: Pączki may also be fried in oil, but lard produces the tastiest results. If you are cutting down on animal fats, you can compromise by using a lard & oil combination.

EXQUISITE OLD WARSAW PĄCZKI
wyborne pączki warszawskie

This is an old recipe specially modified for those who prefer using granulated, active dry yeast to the more traditional compressed fresh yeast called for in most of our recipes. Beat 12 egg yolks with 1 t. salt at high speed until thick and lemony. Dissolve 2 packets dry yeast in ¼ c. 110° water. Separately, cream ⅓ c. room-temp. butter with ½ c. granulated sugar until fluffy and beat into yeast mixture. Scald 1 c. whipping cream and cool to lukewarm. Gradually add 2 c. flour and the cream plus 3 T. French brandy, beating constantly. Then add 2 more c. flour and finally the yolk mixture. Knead well until air blisters appear. Cover with cloth and let stand in warm place until doubled. Punch down, and let rise again. Roll out on floured board, sprinkling top of dough with a little flour, about ¾ inch thick. Cut into 2 inch rounds and top half of them with spoonful of fruit filling (see preceding recipe). Cover with remaining rounds, pinch edges together to seal. (*Note*: If dough is dry, moisten edges with water before pinching together.) Place pączki on floured board, cover with cloth, and let rise until doubled. Fry as above, drain on absorbent paper and, when cool, dust with vanilla sugar or cover with glaze, preferably containing some grated orange rind.

OLD POLISH (UNFILLED) PĄCZKI
pączki staropolskie

Add a pinch saffron to 2 T. 190-proof grain alcohol and let stand several hrs. In bowl, sift 1 c. flour and scald it with 1 c. boiling milk, mixing with wooden spoon until smooth and lump-free. Set aside to cool. Meanwhile, mix 1 stick room-temp. butter, ⅓ c. honey, and 1 cake yeast. Stir in 2½ c. flour, add 1 pinch salt, knead until smooth, cover with cloth, and allow to rise in warm place. When it has doubled, work in 1 T. rum, the strained, saffron-flavored alcohol, and 1 T. finely chopped, candied orange rind. Knead again briefly and set aside to rise once more. Tear off walnut-sized pieces of dough and roll between floured palms into balls. Arrange on floured board, cover with cloth, and allow to rise until doubled. Fry in hot fat, drain on absorbent paper and, when cool, dust with powdered sugar or glaze as above.

FRUIT-FILLED BUNS
buchty

Dissolve 1 cake yeast in 1 c. lukewarm milk, add 1 T. sugar and 1 c. flour, mix well, cover, and let rise in warm place (10–15 min.). Beat 1 egg, 3 yolks, and 2 T. vanilla sugar into fluffy cream. Into bowl sift 2½ c. flour, add sponge, 1 stick melted butter, and egg mixture, kneading well until air blisters appear. Cover with cloth and let rise until doubled in warm place. Dip hands in a little melted butter and form apricot-sized round buns. Fill with drained cherry preserves, soaked, drained, chopped, pitted prunes, powidła or other thick jam. Seal and re-form into round bun. Place buns in greased baking pan that will accommodate them snugly side by side. Cover with dish towel and let rise in warm place until doubled. Bake in pre-heated 375° about 40 min. Serve warm, dusted with powdered sugar, or as a kind of dessert drenched with hot chocolate or vanilla sauce (see sweet sauces in dessert chapter). *Note*: These buns can also be made without the fruit filling.

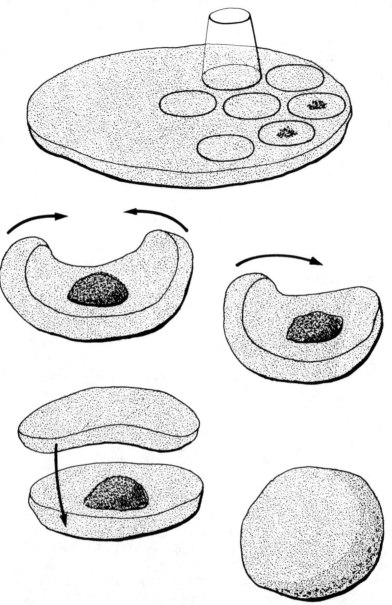

Top illustration shows rolled-out *pączki* dough being cut into circles with glass or biscuit-cutter. Small doughnuts are formed by either placing a spoonful of filling at center and pinching ends together over it (left) or placing filling towards one side, folding the other side over it and pinching shut (right). Larger *pączki* are formed by sandwiching filling between two dough rounds and pinching them together (bottom illustration).

SWEET RAISED ROLLS
słodkie bułeczki drożdżowe

Prepare dough exactly as for fruit-filled buns (above). After it has doubled in bulk, transfer to floured board and roll into a 1½ -inch diameter roll. Cut into 1–1½ -inch rounds and form into round cakes in floured hands. Unlike the buchty, arrange them in greased baking pan about 1–1½ inches apart. Cover with cloth and allow to double in bulk in warm place. Then, brush with beaten egg and sprinkle with poppyseeds or crumb topping. Bake in pre-heated 375° oven to a nice golden color, about 20–25 min.

BLUEBERRY ROLLS
jagodzianki

Prepare dough as for buchty (fruit-filled buns). After it has risen, transfer to floured board and roll into a 2-inch roll. Slice into oval cakes, making an indentation at center. Separately, wash and drain 1 lb. blueberries, sprinkle with 5 (level or heaping) T. sugar, depending on sweetness desired, and toss lightly. Fill indentations with blueberries. With floured hands bring up sides of dough over berries, pinch together to seal, and shape into slightly flattened oval rolls. Place in greased baking pan seam-side-down, leaving a 1-inch space between them. Cover with cloth and let rise until doubled in warm place. When they have risen, brush with beaten egg and bake in 375° oven about 25–30 min. These rolls have long been a favorite of Polish school children. *Variation*: Other thick fruit fillings like drained preserves, powidła, etc. may also be used.

RAISED CRESCENT ROLLS
rogaliki drożdżowe

Dissolve 1 cake yeast in 1 c. lukewarm milk, add 1 T. sugar and 1 c. flour, mix, and allow to rise covered in warm place (10–15 min.). Beat 3 egg yolks with 1 c. powdered sugar until light and fluffy. Sift 3 c. flour into bowl, add sponge and yolk mixture, and knead thoroughly until nice and smooth. Add 1 stick melted lukewarm butter, kneading constantly until air blisters appear. Cover with cloth and let rise until doubled in warm place. Turn out onto floured board and roll into a ¼-inch-thick circle. Starting at center, cut into triangles the way you would slice a pie. Place a spoonful of thick jam or other fruit filling of choice at base of each triangle and roll up towards peak. Arrange on greased baking sheet, bending ends of dough towards each other to form crescents. Cover with cloth and allow to rise in warm place until doubled. After they rise, brush with beaten egg or an egg white mixed with 1 t. milk. Bake in pre-heated 375° oven about 20 min. Good anytime with tea, coffee, or cocoa.

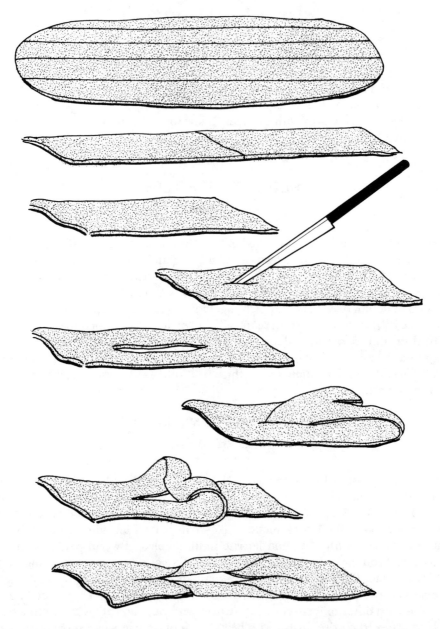

To form angel-wing pastries a thinly rolled-out dough sheet is first cut into strips which are cut at an angle into individual pastries. A slit is made in each piece and one end is pulled through it to create a bow.

ST. MARTIN'S WHITE-POPPYSEED CRESCENTS
marcinki

In the western region of Poznań (also known as Wielkopolska or Great Poland), these tasty crescents are traditionally baked and consumed in large quantities on St. Martin's Day (Nov.11), much the way pączki are enjoyed in abundance on Fat Thursday. The reason is also similar. Just as Tłusty Czwartek marks the final fling of self-indulgence before the penitential days of Lent, so too St. Martin's Day once ushered in Advent, which centuries ago used to last 6 weeks. Advent has long since been shortened to 4 weeks, but the crescent-baking tradition has remained. Prepare the dough exactly as for raised crescent rolls (above), but instead of fruit filling use poppyseed filling (see poppyseed roll), preferably made with white poppyseeds. If unavailable, use ordinary poppyseeds. After baking, apply plain, white glaze.

ANGEL WINGS/BOW-KNOT PASTRIES/CRISPS/POLISH CRULLERS/FAVORS
faworki/chrust/chruściki

Like pączki (Polish doughnuts), these flaky, sugar-dusted pastries are invariably associated in Poland with the pre-Lenten carnival, but among Polish Americans they are also served at weddings and other festive occasions. Sift 2 c. flour onto board, making a well at center of mound. In it place 5 egg yolks, a pinch salt, 1 T. butter, 2 T. sour cream, and 1 T. 190-proof grain alcohol or 6% distilled vinegar. Work ingredients into a dough and work thoroughly by hand until it is uniform, glossy, and full of small holes when cut in half. It should be kneaded about 15 min. to force as much air into dough as possible. Occasionally beat dough vigorously with rolling-pin on both sides and knead some more. Roll out as thin as possible on floured board, sprinkling top lightly with flour. Cut dough sheet into 1-inch strips, then cut strips at an angle into 5-inch-long pieces. Cut a 1½-inch vertical slit down center of each piece and carefully pull 1 end of dough through slit to form a bow. Set completed faworki on floured corder of board. Heat 1½ lbs. lard in electric or stove-top skillet or pan long enough to set on 2 burners. It is hot enough when a small piece of dough floats up immediately. Fry the pastries in the fat in small batches so they can float freely without touching. When bottoms turn golden, turn pastries over with long fork and fry the other side. Each angel wing takes about 1 min. (more or less) to fry. Remove with fork to absorbent paper and fry next batch. When cool, dust with powdered sugar to which some vanilla sugar may be added. *Note:* Faworki may be fried in vegetable shortening or oil instead of lard, but they won't be as tasty. The choice is yours.

ANGEL WINGS ANOTHER WAY
faworki inaczej

Beat 5 egg yolks and 2 T. powdered sugar until white. Continue beating while gradually adding 6 T. sour cream, 2 T. melted room-temp. butter, and 2 T. 190-proof grain alcohol or 6% distilled vinegar, Sift 3 c. flour onto board, add yolk mixture, and work ingredients into dough. Knead vigorously 5-7 min., then beat with rolling-pin about 10 min, until texture is silky. Roll out as thin as possible and proceed as above.

ANGEL WINGS ECONOMY TYPE
faworki oszczędne

Sift 1½ c. flour onto board. Cut in 3½ T. cold soft-type margarine (the kind that comes in plastic tubes rather than sticks) and dice to a fine, groatlike consistency. Add 2 egg yolks and a scant ½ c. sour cream, and mix to blend ingredients. Sprinkle with ¼ t. salt and 1 t. vinegar, kneading until smooth and uniform. Roll out very thin and proceed as in preceding recipes. *Note:* Alcohol or vinegar is used in all faworki recipes to prevent dough from absorbing hot fat during frying.

CARNIVAL ROSETTES
róże karnawałowe

These fancy, fried pastries are on the order of angel wings but differ in shape and, like the roses after which they are named, burst into bloom as they fry. Like faworki, they are a traditional Mardi Gras treat. Start by sifting 3½ c. flour onto board. Make a volcano-like crater at center and in it deposit 6 egg yolks, 1 whole egg, ½ t. salt, 1 T. powdered sugar, and 2 T. 190-proof grain alcohol (spirytus) or 6% white vinegar. Combine ingredients into a dough and knead well 5–7 min. Then beat with rolling-pin about 10 min. to obtain a silky texture. Roll out as thin as possible on floured board, sprinkling top slightly with flour. Cut into equal number of rounds in 3 different sizes, using shot glass, wine glass, and water glass or pastry-cutters with a diameter of 1½, 2, and 2½ inches. Score large and med. circles in 6 places (see illustration) and small circles in 4 places. With finger dab a little egg white at center of large circles, cover with med. circles, press down to join, dab with some more egg white and top with small circles, pressing down at center so they stick together. Fry in hot fat small circle down until golden (a min. or less). Fat is hot enough when a small piece of dough dropped into it floats up at once. With long fork carefully turn over rosettes to fry tops. *Note:*Fry in batches so they float freely without touching. Remove with slotted spoon to absorbent paper. When cool, dust with powdered sugar and place a cherry from well-drained preserves at center of each.

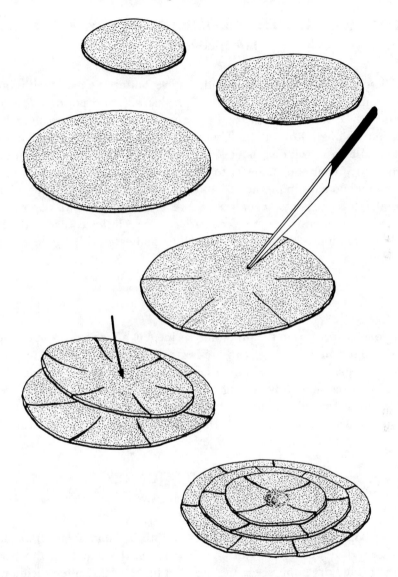

Carnival rosettes are made with a dough identical or similar to that used for faworki. However, instead of being cut into strips, the dough sheet is cut into rounds of three different sizes. The circles are scored at intervals as shown above and three circles of different size are placed on top of each other (with the largest at bottom) to form a rosette. A dab of egg white is applied to center of bottom two circles and an indentation is made with thumb at center of top circle which is pressed down to seal all three together.

BUTTER CAKES TO ACCOMPANY POPPYSEED FILLING
łamańce z makiem

Sift 3 c. flour onto bread-board, top with 2 sticks butter and cut in with knife of pastry-blender until mixture resembles fine groats. Sprinkle with ¾ c. powdered sugar and 1–2 T. vanilla sugar (or ½ t. vanilla extract), add 1 egg yolk and 1 T. sour cream and quickly work ingredients into a dough. Roll into boll, wrap in aluminum foil and refrigerate 1 hr. Turn out onto floured board. Roll out about ¼ inch thin with floured rolling pin into square or rectangle the size of your pan. Transfer to pin on rolling-pin. In pan cut into 1-inch squares with pastry cutter and bake in pre-heated 400° oven about 15 min. When cool, remove from pan and break into squares along cut lines. Serve as go-together with poppyseed filling (see poppyseed roll or noodles & poppyseeds). *Note:* These little teacakes, usually served on Christmas Eve, are dipped in the poppyseed filling and eaten chip-dip fashion.

POPPYSEED "HEDGEHOG"
"jeżyk" makowy

Prepare dough exactly as in the preceding recipe, but after rolling out cut into ¼ inch by 2 inch fingers. Bake on baking sheet in pre-heated 400° oven about 15 min. or less if they begin to brown. Mound poppyseed filling (as for poppyseed roll or noodles & poppyseeds) on serving dish to resemble a hedgehog, shaping one end into a little snout with a cherry (from drained preserves) for the nose. Stud the mound with the baked fingers at the angle sloping away from the head. Although this novelty dessert tastes no different than the preceding recipe, your kids are sure to enjoy it!

POPPYSEED SQUARES
łamańce makowe

Drench 1 c. poppyseeds with 4 c. cold water and stir by hand. Pour off any hulls or other impurities that float up, pour off water and rinse again. Drain and dry thoroughly. Sift 3 c. flour onto board, add dry poppyseeds and mix. Cut in 2½ sticks butter, dicing until blended. Add 1 egg, ½ c. sour cream and 2 c. powdered sugar, work ingredients into a dough and roll thin on lightly floured board. On rolling-pin transfer dough sheet to greased baking sheet and cut into 1-inch squares. Pierce each square 2–3 times with fork and bake in 400° oven about 15 min. When they cool slightly, break into squares along cut lines. *Note*: These differ from the butter-cake squares in that the dough already contains poppyseeds, hence they would not normally be served with poppyseed fillings like the plain version.

POPPYSEED SQUARES ANOTHER WAY
łamańce makowe inaczej

Sift 2 c. flour onto board and mix with 1½ c. dry poppyseeds. Cut in 1 stick butter or oleo and blend to a fine, groat-like consistency. Add ½ c. powdered sugar and ⅔ c. sour cream mixed with 2 t. baking powder and a pinch salt. Work ingredients into a dough and roll out thin. Transfer dough sheet on rolling-pin to greased baking pan and cut into 1-inch squares. Brush with lightly beaten egg white, pierce each square in several places with fork, and bake in pre-heated 400° oven about 15 min.

AMMONIA CAKES
amoniaczki

Admittedly, the English translation for these tasty cookies may not sound too appetizing, but the name simply refers to the type of baking powder (ammonium carbonate) used in their preparation. Sift 2 c. flour onto board in a ring. In center, place 1 stick soft butter or margarine, 2 eggs, 1 t. ammonium carbonate dissolved in 2 T. water, 2 T. vanilla sugar, 2 T. sour cream, and ½ c. powdered sugar. Work ingredients into uniform dough, wrap in aluminum foil, and refrigerate overnight. Next day, roll out one-fifth inch thick on floured board, sprinkling top of dough with a little flour. Cut into rounds with biscuit-cutter or glass, pierce each in several places with fork, and place on lightly greased and floured baking sheet. Bake in pre-heated 350° oven about 15 min. or until they just begin to brown. Store in tightly sealed glass jar or tin.

GINGER CAKES
imbirki

Sift ¾ c. flour into bowl. Cut in 1 stick plus 2 T. butter, add 1 c. sugar, ½ t. grated lemon rind and ½–1 t. ginger. Mix ingredients to get uniform dough, roll out thin on floured board, cut into rounds or other shapes and place on baking sheet. Let stand 3 hrs. Bake in pre-heated 375° oven 10–12 min.

CINNAMON CRESCENTS
cynamonki

Sift 2 c. flour onto board and sprinkle with about 1 t. cinnamon. Cut in 1 stick butter or oleo, add ⅔ c. powdered sugar, 1 egg, and 1 t. baking powder. Work ingredients by hand into a uniform dough and roll out thin on floured board. Cut into 3 inch strips and arrange on baking sheet, bending each to form a horseshoe. Bake in pre-heated 375° oven about 10 min.

CRISPY TEACAKES
kruche ciasteczka

Sift 3½ c. flour onto broad and cut in 2½ sticks butter or oleo until mixture achieves a groatlike consistency. Sprinkle with 1 c. powdered sugar and 1–2 T. vanilla sugar and dice a bit longer. Add 2 egg yolks and quickly combine ingredients into a dough that can easily be rolled into a ball. Wrap in aluminum foil and chill in fridge 1 hr. Turn out onto floured board and roll out with floured rolling-pin ¼ inch thin. With cutter of choice cut into stars, crescents, circles, triangles, etc. Lightly beat 2 egg whites and brush tops of cakes. Sprinkle with large-crystal sugar, ground walnuts, ground almonds, poppyseeds, etc. (*Note*: Sprinkling a single shape with one of these toppings will create the illusion of a large variety of different cakes.) Place on ungreased baking sheet and bake in pre-heated 400° oven 15–20 min.

POLISH JELLY COOKIES
ciasteczka polskie z galaretką

The term "Polish crumbly dough" ("kruche ciasto polskie") is used to describe pastry dough made with sieved hard-boiled eggs which frequently form the basis for mazurkas. It also makes tasty cookies, of which these are an example. Sift 3 c. flour onto board, cut in 2 sticks butter or margarine, and dice with knife until groat-like. Add 3 cooked, sieved egg yolks and sift in ¾ c. powdered sugar, quickly working ingredients into a dough. Place in bowl, cover, and chill 10 min. in fridge. Roll out ¼ inch thick, cut into 2-inch rounds or stars, place on baking sheet, and make a depression at center of each with finger. Bake in 350° oven for 12–15 min. or until golden. While they bake, heat ½–¾ c. red-currant jelly, cooking it down slightly. Place a dab of warm jelly in depressions of baked cookies and allow to cool. *Variation*: Proceed as above but omit the depression. When cookies are baked, thinly spread bottom of ½ of them with warm jelly, covering with bottom side of remaining ones to form little sandwiches.

CRISPY CHOCOLATE TEACAKES
kruche ciasteczka czekoladowe

Prepare as above but add 2 T. cocoa to the powdered sugar before sprinkling over flour-butter mixture. *Note:* Both these and the preceding teacakes will keep well in an airtight tin at room temp., but should not be refrigerated because they harden. The unbaked dough, however, wrapped in foil, may be refrigerated up to 1 week. *Variation*: The same dough may be used to bake a tasty plum or cherry cake. Place rolled-out dough in baking pan, brush with lightly beaten egg white, and top with about 1 lb. halved, pitted plums or whole, pitted cherries. Bake 25–30 min. When cool, dust with powdered sugar, cut into squares and serve.

CRISPY VANILLA WAFERS
kruche ciasteczka waniliowe

Sift 1⅓ c. flour onto board and cut in 1½ sticks butter or margarine until mixture resembles fine groats. Add 1 egg yolk, 1 T. sour cream, and ½ t. vanilla extract. Combine ingredients just enough so they roll into a ball. Wrap in aluminum foil and refrigerate 1 hr. Roll out wafer thin and cut into small rounds and place on baking sheet. Beat 2 egg whites, gradually adding 1 c. powdered sugar and ½ t. vanilla extract, until you get a thick mixture. Spread tops of wafers with mixture and bake in pre-heated 425° oven about 10 min. After wafers are baked, spread tops with thin layer of tart jam (gooseberry, black currant, rose-hip) and stick jam-covered surfaces together to form little sandwiches. Dust with home-made vanilla sugar. We consider these among the tastiest teacakes found in this book.

"CAT"S-EYE" SANDWICH COOKIES
"kocie oczka"

Sift 3 c. flour onto board and cut in 2 sticks butter or margarine until mixture resembles fine groats. Add 2 T. vanilla sugar and 1 c. sour cream and quickly work into a dough. Roll out thin on floured board and cut into circles with biscuit-cutter or water glass. At center of half the rounds, cut out smaller circles with shot glass. Place cookies on lightly floured baking sheet and puncture each in several places with fork. Bake in pre-heated 425° oven 10–15 min. When they have cooled, spread the whole cookies thinly with jam of choice, cover each with a round that has an opening at center, press down gently, and dust with powdered sugar.

FLAKY APPLE CAKES
jabłka w kruchym cieście

Sift 2 c. flour onto board and cut in 1½ sticks butter until mixture resembles fine groats. Sprinkle with ½ c. powdered sugar and 1 T. vanilla sugar and dice together. Add 1 egg yolk and 1 T. sour cream and quickly work into a ball. Wrap in aluminum foil and chill in fridge 1 hr. Roll dough out ¼ inch thick on floured board and cut into 4–5 inch squares. Peel 4–5 tart apples, cut in ½ horizontally, and scoop out core and seeds with small spoon. Place an apple half cut side down at center of each dough square, bring 2 opposite ends of square together over apple, and stick together, then do same with remaining 2 ends. With spatula transfer cakes to baking sheet and bake 25 min. in pre-heated 425° oven. Remove carefully and dust with powdered sugar and (optional) a pinch cinnamon. These taste best on the day they were baked!

CHEESE-DOUGH APPLE CAKES
ciasteczka serowe z jabłkami

Sift 1⅔ c. flour onto board and mix with ½ lb. ground farmer cheese. Cut in 2½ sticks butter, mix in 5 T. sour cream, and quickly combine ingredients into a dough. Roll out thin and cut out circles with juice glass. Peel 4 tart apples, cut in quarters, scoop out core portions, and cut each quarter in two or, if using larger apples, into 3 slices. Place apple slices on half of each dough circle with narrower end at center (see illustration) and fold the other dough flap over it to form semi-circles. Arrange on ungreased baking sheet half inch apart and bake in pre-heated 400° oven until golden (about 15 min.). After baking, dust with powdered sugar. They are best the next day, but they keep nicely at room temp. covered with foil 3–4 days. They should not be refrigerated! These tasty little teacakes are a Christmas time favorite in the Strybel household.

CHEESE-DOUGH APPLE TURNOVERS
rożki serowe z jabłkami

Prepare dough as above but, after rolling out, cut into 2-inch squares. Place apple slices (prepared as above) on squares diagonally, bring 2 opposite ends of dough over apple and pinch together along seam to seal. Place on ungreased baking sheet and bake in pre-heated 400° oven to a nice golden color (about 15 min.). After baking, dust with powdered sugar.

CHEESE-DOUGH PLUM-JAM CAKES
ciasteczka serowe z powidłami

Prepare dough as for cheese-dough apple cakes, roll out thin, and cut into 2-inch squares. Place a spoonful of thick plum jam (powidła) at center of each, bring 2 opposite points of dough over jam, and pinch together, then bring together and seal in similar fashion remaining 2 points. Place on baking sheet and bake in pre-heated 400° oven about 15 min. or until nicely golden. Dust with powdered sugar. *Variation*: Instead of plain powidła, combine jam with an equal amount of ground walnuts and flavor with a pinch cinnamon if desired. *Note*: These cakes may also be filled with many other fillings, including drained preserves, poppyseed filling, nut filling, almond paste, chopped dates mixed with a little honey... Let your imagination be your guide!

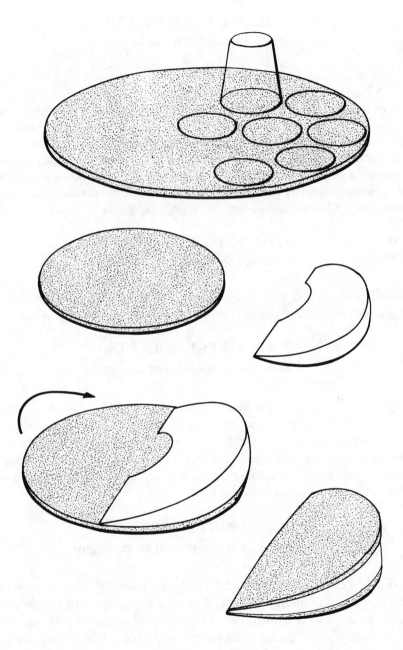

The rolled-out dough for cheese-dough apple cakes is cut into circles. An apple slice is placed on one half of each circle and the other half is folded over it as shown above.

FLAKY TART SHELLS
kruche babeczki

Sift 1⅓ c. flour onto board, cut in 1 stick butter or oleo, and blend to groat-like consistency. Sprinkle with 1 T. powdered sugar and 1 T. lemon juice or 190 proof grain alcohol. Work in 1 egg yolk. Quickly combine ingredients into a dough and roll into a ball. Wrap with foil and refrigerate 1 hr. Brush tart pans with melted butter (about 1 T. all told). Roll dough out thin, cut into circles, and press dough circles into tart pans, trimming with knife any dough protruding beyond rims. Combining dough trimmings, roll out and cut into additional circle or circles. Place tart pans on baking sheet and bake in pre-heated 400° oven until nicely golden. After they have cooled somewhat, carefully remove from pans and allow to cool completely. Fill with any of the cold fillings below.

WHIPPED-CREAM TARTS
babeczki z bitą śmietaną

Fill baked tart shells with cold, plain, or sweetened whipped cream (about 2 c. all told). Sprinkle each with about ½ t. grated chocolate, ground walnuts, or almonds. Serve at once.

FRESH-FRUIT TARTS
babeczki ze świeżymi owocami

Wash about 1½ c. fresh strawberries or raspberries, drain, chop, and fill tart shells. Dust generously with powdered sugar and top with a dollop of cold whipped cream. Place a whole small berry on top of the cream. *Note*: Peeled, chopped ripe peaches or apricots may also be used. *Variation*: Instead of powdered sugar, tarts may be topped with just enough homemade or store-bought fruit gel (gelatin dessert, jello) to cover fruit. Chill tarts until fully gelled, top with whipped cream, and serve immediately.

FRUIT TARTS
babeczki z nadzieniem owocowym

When you don't have fresh fruit, fill tarts with partially drained preserves, partially drained, canned fruit-pie filling, or drained canned fruit (especially peaches or pineapple), topped with a little partially chilled fruit gel. Poppyseed filling topped with whipped cream is another possibility. If you glance through this chapter, chances are you will run into other possible fillings that will make very nice tarts.

CREAM TARTS
babeczki śmietankowe

Beat 3 egg yolks with 2 T. granulated sugar, 1 T. flour, and ¼ t. vanilla extract. Stir in 1 c. coffee cream or half and half and heat over low flame, stirring constantly, until mixture comes to boil. Set aside to cool. For the crust, cream 2 sticks room-temp. butter or margarine with ⅔ c. powdered sugar, adding 2 eggs one at a time and mixing until smooth. Stir in 2 c. flour and work into a dough by hand. Brush tart pans lightly with melted butter. Tear off pieces of dough, flatten in palm into patties, and press into tart pans. Fill with cream filling, cover with another hand-flattened round of dough, pinching ends together to seal. Place filled tarts on baking sheet and bake in pre-heated 350°–375° oven about 25 min. When somewhat cooled, carefully remove from pans. Arrange on serving dish upside down.

CREAM PUFFS
kremówki/ptysie

Bring to boil ⅔ c. water, 1 stick butter, and 1 pinch salt. Remove from heat, sift in 1 c. flour, beating vigorously with wooden spoon to obliterate any lumps. Place on low heat and simmer 2–3 min., stirring constantly, until mixture resembles smooth, glossy, whipped potatoes. Remove from heat, mix to cool, and add 6 eggs one at a time, stirring until one is fully absorbed before adding the next. Towards the end, stir in 1 level t. baking powder and beat until batter doubles in bulk. Set aside for 10–15 min. Heat oven to 500° and grease baking pan. With spoon or pastry tube, place golf-ball-sized mounds of batter in pan at least 1 inch apart. Pop pan into oven and bake 10 min. without opening oven door. Reduce heat to 400° and bake another 10–15 min. or until pale golden. Properly baked puffs are hard to the touch and hollow on the inside. When they have cooled, cut off top ⅓, fill with cold whipped cream, replace tops, dust with powdered sugar, and serve immediately.

CHOCOLATE ECLAIRS
eklery

Prepare dough as for cream puffs (above), but use pastry bag to place 1-inch by 3-inch bars of batter in greased pan at least 1 inch apart. Bake as above. Cut the cooled puff fingers in half lengthwise, fill bottoms with cold whipped cream, replace top, and cover with chocolate glaze. In double boiler melt 3½ oz. broken-up sweet chocolate with ½ stick butter or margarine, mixing until smooth. Remove from heat and cool slightly, then pour warm glaze over eclairs. Chill in fridge until glaze is set and serve immediately. *Variation:* Instead of whipped cream, eclairs may be filled with pudding-like filling used in Carpathian cake (see cake chapter).

NUT CRESCENTS
rożki orzechowe

Cream 2 sticks room-temp. butter with ⅔ c. powdered sugar. Add ⅔ c. ground walnuts or hazelnuts, sift in 2 c. flour, and mix well to blend ingredients. Transfer to lightly floured board, knead briefly, and roll into ball. With floured rolling-pin roll out into ¼-inch-thin rectangle. Trim with knife so sides are perfectly straight. With water glass cut out crescents along edges of dough. Crescents should be ¾ inch wide at widest point. Place on greased baking sheet and bake in pre-heated 375° oven for about 20 min. Transfer to plate and allow to cool. Meanwhile, in saucepan melt 3 oz. (squares) bitter or semi-sweet chocolate, add 2 t. butter, 2 t. powdered sugar, and 2 T. coffee cream. Heat gently until ingredients are blended, stirring frequently. Dip ends of crescents in chocolate glaze and set aside to cool.

POLISH "BROWNIES"
krajanka czekoladowa

Cream ¼ c. room-temp. butter. Add 1 c. sugar, 3 eggs, and 4 oz. finely grated semi-sweet chocolate. Sift in 1 c. flour, add 1⅓ c. chopped, unblanched almonds (i.e. with skins left on), and mix to blend ingredients with wooden spoon or spatula. Transfer mixture to greased narrow loafpan and bake in pre-heated 350° oven 25–30 min. Remove from pan when still somewhat warm and slice. Arrange slices on ungreased baking sheet and dry on both sides in 250° oven 15–20 min.

CHOCOLATE HEARTS
serduszka czekoladowe

Beat 1 egg white with ¾ c. sugar, mixing in 1 c. ground unblanched almonds, 3 squares (oz.) grated unsweetened chocolate and the juice and grated ring of ½ a lemon. On sugar-sprinkled board roll into finger-thick rolls and form into hearts or pretzels. Bake on baking sheet in 325° oven 15-20 min. Spread with white or chocolate glaze and (optional) sprinkle with poppyseeds before glaze sets.

SPONGE FINGERS/LADYFINGERS
biszkopty

Beat 5 egg yolks with 1 c. powdered sugar and 2 T. homemade vanilla sugar into a thick cream. Mix 1 t. baking powder with 2 c. flour and sift into bowl. Beat 5 egg whites until stiff, adding 2–3 T. powdered sugar towards end. Stir yolk mixture into flour, fold in beaten whites, and mix gently. Line baking sheet with wax paper and dust with powdered sugar.

Place dough in pastry bag and pipe 3–4-inch fingers onto baking sheet so they don't touch. Bake in 325°–350° oven, pre-heated of course, 10–15 min. or until nicely pale golden. Serve with ice cream, crèmes, and other such desserts.

SPONGE SANDWICH COOKIES
biszkopty przekładane

Prepare dough as above. Pipe 1–1½-inch rounds onto wax-paper-covered baking sheet dusted with powdered sugar and bake as above. When cool, spread ½ the bottoms with thick jam or marmalade and press bottoms of remaining cookies onto it to form sandwiches. *Optional:* Dust with powdered sugar or glaze with melted chocolate mixture as in nut crescents.

LESS SWEET SPONGE FINGERS
biszkopty mniej słodkie

Beat 7 egg yolks with ½ c. granulated sugar until thick and whitish. Combine ⅔ c. flour and ⅔ c. potato starch and sift into yolk mixture. Beat stiffly 7 egg whites, fold half of them into batter and mix well. Fold remaining beaten whites into batter and mix lightly. Onto baking sheet lined with wax paper (parchment paper may also be used), dusted with powdered sugar, pipe 3–4-inch fingers. Bake in pre-heated 325°–350° oven about 10–15 min.

MERINGUES
bezy

Beat 5 egg whites to stiff froth, gradually adding 2 c. powdered sugar and ¼ t. vanilla extract. When froth is stiff enough to tear, beat in 1 T. lemon juice, and beat a bit longer. Pre-heat oven to 220°–250°. Line baking sheet with parchment paper and sprinkle with powdered sugar. With pastry tube squeeze small rounds of froth onto parchment or simply spoon mixture thereon. Pop into oven for 30–40 min. At that low temp. the meringues actually dry rather than bake. Ready when dry and brittle. *Note*: These simple meringues are certainly not the world's most outstanding pastry, but they keep indefinitely and many youngsters enjoy them. Usually they are made when egg whites are left over from babkas and other cakes. Crumbled up, they make an interesting topping over fresh or drained canned fruit in place of sugar. Top your meringue-fruit cup with a dollop of whipped cream.

WALNUT OR ALMOND MACAROONS
makaroniki orzechowe lub migdałowe

Beat 3 egg whites over boiling water in double-boiler with 1¼ c. powdered sugar, sifted. Stir in ½ c. ground walnuts or almonds, mix lightly, and spoon mixture onto parchment-lined baking sheet. Dry in 250° oven about 1 hr.

POPPYSEED MACAROONS
makaroniki makowe

Scald ¾ c. poppyseeds with boiling water, cover, and let stand 10 min. Drain well, mix with 1 c. granulated sugar, and grind mixture twice. Place in double-boiler over boiling water, add 4 unbeaten egg whites, and mix ingredients well. Mix in 1 T. sifted flour, mix well, and spoon portions of mixture onto greased, flour-sprinkled baking sheet and bake in 400° oven about 15 min.

OAT MACAROONS
makaroniki owsiane

Scatter 1¼ c. rolled oats over baking sheet and place in 375° oven until they begin to brown. Crush with rolling-pin. Place in double-boiler, add 4–5 egg whites, 2 c. powdered sugar, 1 T. lemon juice, and ½ t. vanilla extract. Mix well. Sift in 3 T. flour and mix. With pastry bag or simply a sheet of parchment rolled into a cone, place small rounds or bars of mixture on lightly greased baking sheet. Bake in 400° oven 10–15 min. or until they are lightly golden.

POPPYSEED CRUNCH, SNAPS OR BRITTLE
makagigi

In pot combine 1 c. honey and ½ c. sugar. Heat, stirring to dissolve sugar and simmer until slightly browned. Add 1 c. dry poppyseeds and simmer briefly, stirring constantly. Transfer mixture to damp board or, better yet, marble slab (if you've got one). Roll out thin with damp rolling pin. (*Note*: This can be done through wax paper.) When cool, cut into small rectangles or irregular pieces and spread out on wax paper to dry thoroughly. *Note*: For chewier and less brittle makagigi, slightly decrease amount of sugar. This traditional Wigilia confection has long been a favorite with Polish youngsters. *Variation*: Proceed as above, but to browned honey mixture add ¾ c. poppyseeds and ½ c. coarsely ground walnuts.

WALNUT OR ALMOND CRUNCH, SNAPS OR BRITTLE
makagigi orzechowe lub migdałowe

Prepare as above, but instead of poppyseeds add 1½ c. coarsely ground or finely chopped walnuts or blanched almonds to browned honey mixture.

HONEY-RYE WAFERS
tłuczeńce

This is another old Christmas treat which tastes a little like honey-spice cake (piernik). Sift 1 c. rye flour onto board and add in stream just enough water to get a soft dough, working ingredients together well by hand. Place in baking pan and bake in pre-heated 375°–400° oven 30–35 min. or until fully baked. When cool, break up into pieces and either dry until brittle in 200° oven with door left ajar or leave out overnight until it is stale. Grind and sift. In pot combine 2 c. honey, 4 oz. chopped, blanched almonds, and about 2–3 T. very finely diced candied orange rind, raisins, dates and figs. Heat mixture, add ½ c. sifted rye crumbs, season to taste with a little cinnamon, ground cloves, and ginger and simmer until mixture browns slightly, stirring constantly. When partially cooled, spread sheets of opłatek, pressing down carefully so it doesn't crack. Leave out overnight. Next day cut into squares and enjoy.

HONEYED CHRISTMAS WAFERS
opłatki z miodem

This is definitely the easiest Christmas "cake" anyone can prepare. Simply spread sheets of opłatek to form a sandwich wafer. *Note:* The old Polish nobility of yesterday often shared pieces of honeyed opłatek on Christmas Eve.

HONEY-SPICE CAKES/COOKIES
pierniczki

In pot combine 1 stick margarine, 1 c. honey, and spices: ½ t. cinnamon, ½ t. ground cloves, and 1 t. ginger. Heat, stir, bring to boil, and set aside to cool. Beat 2 egg yolks with ½ c. sugar. Caramelize 4 T. sugar with 1 T. water. To yolk mixture gradually add honey mixture, caramel, 3 c. flour (sifted), and 2 t. baking powder, mixing well to blend ingredients. Fold in 2 stiffly beaten egg whites, mix well, sprinkle with a little flour, cover with bowl, and let stand overnight. Next day roll out ¼-inch-thick on floured board with floured rolling-pin.

Rolled-out honey-spice-cake dough can be cut into various shapes with special cutters or free-hand.

Cut into rounds or other shapes of choice and arrange on greased baking sheet. Bake about 10 min. in pre-heated 400° oven. After they cool, store in airtight tin or jar. They become tender as they age. Before serving, decorate with chocolate glaze.

HONEY-SPICE CAKES ANOTHER WAY
pierniczki inaczej

Cream 2 eggs and 1 c. sugar until white. Add 1 T. honey-spice cake seasoning, 1 t. baking soda dissolved in 3 T. water, 1 c. honey, and 3 c. flour sifted. Work ingredients well into a dough, then knead awhile on floured board. Sprinkle with flour and roll out ¼-inch-thick. Cut into rounds or whatever other shapes you like. Place on greased baking sheet and bake in 400° oven about 10 min. Store in airtight tin or jar and glaze before serving. *Note*: Chocolate-covered honey-spice hearts are traditionally passed out to youngsters by Święty Mikołaj (St. Nicholas).

CHRISTMAS-TREE HONEY-SPICE CAKES

Prepare honey-spice cakes according to either of the above recipes. After they have become tender in airtight tin or jar, cover with chocolate glaze. When it sets you can additionally decorate them with white icing in decorator tube. Decorations can include floral designs, straight or squiggly lines, geometric patterns, funny faces, or such inscriptions as "Wesołych Świąt" (Merry Christmas) if you can fit all that writing on a single cookie. Besides cakes, cut with cutters into rounds, hearts, crescents, etc., you can try cutting the unbaked dough sheet free-hand with a knife in the shape of an angel, St. Nicholas, or a large heart. To hang cakes on tree, run a large needle and strong thread through cake near top. Tie thread into loop for hanging. *Note*: In simpler days, Polish Christmas trees, as well as the podłaźniczka (evergreen top suspended upside down from rafter), were highly edible affairs. Their main decorations comprised honey-spice cakes, apples, candies wrapped in colorful paper, walnuts wrapped in shimmering foil and tied with bows, as well as almond-paste (marzipan) confections in various shapes.

* * *

BEVERAGES HOT & COLD

Tea, usually served in glasses with lemon slices and sugar, is undoubtedly Poland's most popular hot beverage, although *herbata* did not really establish itself until the 19th century. Coffee arrived on the scene a century earlier and with considerable fanfare. It was in the early 1700's that the great Johann Sebastian Bach, court composer to Poland's King August III, wrote his Coffee Cantata in praise of the new beverage. To this day, *kawa* has retained its "something special" status as a treat to be sipped and savored. It is never just a "warmer-upper" or something to wash down food with. But, whether or not historical sidelights are your cup of tea (no pun intended!), we have collected in this chapter a number of ways of brewing what we consider superior-tasting tea and coffee for less than you may now be paying.

Long before anyone had heard of tea or coffee, the people of Old Poland would quench their thirst with a variety of "teas" or infusions made by boiling dried fruit and/or herbs in water. Many of them have medicinal properties, although it should be stressed that their health-inducing qualities are very gentle acting. If you like their taste, you can simply enjoy tisanes made from chamomile, linden, or dried raspberries as a thirst-quencher. Then there are the refreshing compotes, good hot or cold. Nothing could be easier to prepare, because a compote is simply a little fruit cooked in water a few minutes and sweetened to taste.

Also included in this chapter are some beverages which by Anglo-Saxon standards may seem unusual or exotic. Among them are recipes calling for dill-pickle brine, beet sour, whey, and sour milk. They not only have a delicious zing all their own, but are also healthy and refreshing. Some have long been used as 'morning-after' cures, because they counteract the dehydration caused by overindulgence and replace the vitamins destroyed by alcohol.

On a cold winter's night, nothing casts a more heartwarming glow over any gathering than a serving of hot wine or beer. For the adventurous, we have even included a few recipes for homemade beer, although you shouldn't expect that fizzy, golden lager that most people associate with the drink these days. Actually, the Polish word *piwo* (beer) once simply meant beverage, and encompassed a broad array of liquids made from different grains and flavored with a variety of honeys, fruits, and spices. According to legend, it was with one such beverage that Poland's King Mieszko toasted the German Emperor Otto at Gniezno in the year 1000. The point of the legend was to show that Poles had mastered the art of beer-brewing way back when, and did not need the Germans to show them how it was done. In reality, the ancient Egyptians already produced a fermented-grain beverage that would also qualify as *piwo*.

There are many more beverages in this chapter. Some are the height of simplicity to concoct, while others require more involved preparation. However, they all have one thing in common. They represent by and large a traditional, natural, more healthful alternative to the chemical-laced, imitation-flavored and artificially-colored diet sodas and drink mixes so prevalent on today's supermarket's shelves.

* * *

TEA
herbata

Both in Poland and America black tea is by far the most popular. This is the standard tea you find in your grocery or supermarket that often has the term "Orange Pekoe" on the label. (That term has nothing to do with oranges or orange flavor, but is simply a trade name used in the tea-growing business to designate the larger leaves that go to make fully fermented black tea.) To brew Polish-style tea, start with a package of loose black tea of whatever brand. You may find that some of the lesser-known brands are more than acceptable, and that can mean a considerable savings compared to the price of the widely advertised name brands. By all means, feel free to mix various brands and come up with the blend that suits you best. For exquisite flavor, mix your supermarket tea with Darjeeling or Oolong. You may want to add a little green tea (not to be confused with mint tea!) for a different flavor twist or a pinch or two Jasmine tea for an aromatic touch. We enjoy adding just a little Earl Grey to our black tea, but no more than 1 t. of the former to 2 T. of the latter. We suggest you stay away from the artificially aromatized teas which are now so plentiful on the market. Flavored and scented teas are so much better when prepared at home from natural ingredients, and nothing could be easier, as the recipes below will show.

TEA BREWED THE POLISH WAY
herbata parzona po polsku

Although Poles normally brew tea in a ceramic teapot, it is quite unlike the well-known British way, in which ready-to-drink tea is poured from the teapot into teacups. Instead, they prepare "esencja" (a strong tea essence or infusion), pour a little into tea cups, and fill them with boiling water. To do this, you will need a small, roughly 2 c. capacity ceramic teapot. Scald it with boiling water and pour it out, add 2–3 T. loose tea, and scald with about ½ c. boiling water. It is best to set covered teapot into the opening of a hot-water kettle, whose boiling water will warm the bottom of the teapot to promote steeping. (The teapot should fit snugly into kettle opening, so you may have to shop around to find ones that match.) After 5 min., fill teapot with boiling water and steep over boiling kettle another 5 min. Pour anywhere from ½–2 jiggers tea essence into cups and fill with boiling water. *Note*: The Polish method of tea brewing is definitely superior to the British way, because it allows everyone to get a cup of tea whose strength is custom-tailored to his or her taste. Some people barely wet the bottom of the cup with essence for a thin, straw-colored brew, while others pour in ¼ c. of essence for a tea of palate-numbing potency. Provide lemon slices and sugar on the side and enjoy! Many Polish families brew a pot of essence for breakfast and leave it on the counter top all day, or until all its flavor has been extracted. Enjoying a cup of hot tea is as easy as boiling some water, without drippy teabags or artificial-tasting instants.

SAMOVAR TEA
herbata parzona w samowarze

The samovar is a fancy, polished metal urn, fitted with a spigot, from which boiling water is drawn for tea. Although invented in Russia, the samovar quickly caught on in Poland, where it became the standard tea-brewing method throughout the 19th century. Essentially, it is no different than the method described above. A small, tea-essence pot is set at the top above the boiling water which promotes steeping. Essence is poured into cups and topped off with boiling water held in the urn. Originally, the water was boiled by a charcoal burner at the base of the samovar, but nowadays, electric models are more common. The main advantage of a samovar (which means "self-boiler" in Russian) is that it enables you to brew tea at or near the dinner table in high style.

TEA WITH FRUIT SYRUP
herbata z sokiem

For a special treat, sweeten your tea (brewed as above) with a natural fruit syrup instead of sugar. Especially good are cherry, raspberry, blackberry, blueberry, and black-currant syrups. If you have no homemade syrups on hand (see pickling & canning chapter), be sure to get a pure and natural syrup imported from Poland, Germany, etc or a quality domestic brand. U.S. supermarket brands of fruit syrups, meant mainly for pancakes and waffles, are often full of artificial flavoring, coloring, thickeners, and other additives. Fruit-flavored tea may be served with or without lemon, according to preference.

TEA WITH PRESERVES
herbata z konfiturami

Besides fruit syrups, tea may also be sweetened with preserves. We feel homemade cherry preserves (konfitury z wiśni) are best, but you may enjoy others as well. If using store-bought preserves, choose the more fruity, top-of-the-line or gourmet brands, rather than the runny or artificially thickened budget varieties. *Note*: Some people prefer to eat their preserves with a spoon from a little dish and wash it down with unsweetened tea with lemon.

TEA WITH HONEY
herbata z miodem

Sweeten hot tea and lemon with honey. This is a real warmer-upper that is sometimes served as a cold, flu, or sore-throat remedy. *Note*: Adding a jigger or so vodka, brandy, rum, or cordial (not to mention 190 proof grain alcohol or "spirytus") is said to greatly boost the curative properties of honeyed tea. Whether or not this is true, it certainly packs a punch!

HONEY & PEPPER TEA
herbata z miodem i pieprzem

Prepare tea with honey with or without alcohol as above but add about 4 ground peppercorns per cup. This is another old cold remedy.

TEA WITH RUM
herbata z rumem

Adding anywhere from 1 t.–1 jigger of good rum produces a cup of hot tea that imparts a festive glow to any occasion. It may be added to plain or lemon-flavored tea, sweetened with sugar, fruit syrup, or honey. An excellent way to dispel those cold-weather blues! *Note*: In a pinch, you can use vodka and a few drops of rum extract, but it won't be as good as genuine rum.

TEA WITH WINE
herbata z winem

Sweeten tea and lemon with honey to taste and add 1–2 jiggers dry red wine to each cup. *Variation*: Omit the honey and add 2 jiggers of Polish honey wine (mead or miód pitny) to each cup of hot tea. Sweeten additionally with honey or sugar as needed.

ORANGE-FLAVORED TEA
herbata pomarańczowa

To tea leaves in essence pot add ½–1 t. orange zest (grated orange rind), then drench with boiling water and allow to steep as usual. You may also use 1 part orange zest and 1 part lemon zest. In any case, be sure to scrub oranges or lemons with soap and hot water, then rinse, scald with boiling water, and dry before grating their rinds. *Note*: This tea may also be flavored with rum or spices according to preference.

SPICED TEA
herbata korzenna

In small pot combine 6–8 cloves, a small piece of cinnamon bark, and a slice of ginger root with ½ c. water. Bring to boil, reduce heat, and simmer covered 5 min. Switch off heat and allow mixture to steep until cooled to room temp. *Note*: May be used in plain tea or flavored with fruit syrup, honey, rum, wine, etc.

TEA WITH MILK
herbata mleczna/"bawarka"

Despite what British and many American tea-fanciers may say, tea with milk has very few devotees in Poland, where it is known as "bawarka," suggesting its Bavarian origins. However, Polish folk medicine extols its alleged restorative properties and recommends it for nursing mothers and convalescents who need to build up their strength. To prepare this concoction, simply flavor a cup of hot milk with enough tea essence to get the strength you want. Sweeten to taste with sugar or honey.

COFFEE
kawa

Rather than consuming large quantities of that flavorless, brownish swill that still passes for coffee in much of mainstream America, we propose a Polish alternative. Regard coffee as something to savor in small amounts for its deep, rich, flavor and aroma, something that uplifts body and spirit and adds a festive touch to solitary interludes and social gatherings alike. This can be summed up in the following "Ten Commandments of Coffee Enjoyment":

1. The darker, French-roasted blends, which come closest to Polish-style coffee in flavor, are the best all-around beans to start with. But, as with tea, do not settle for a single brand. The bulk-food stores usually offer a good selection of blends, so you can combine, let's say, a lb. of French roast with ½ lb. of mild but aromatic mocha and perhaps include a ¼ lb. or so very dark-roasted Italian espresso beans for added zing. With a good collection of beans to choose from, you can come up with your own distinctive blend, but avoid beans artificially impregnated with imitation chocolate, almond, cinnamon, citrus flavoring, or the like. You can easily flavor coffee with natural ingredients when you brew it at home.

2. For peak flavor and aroma, only as many coffee beans as needed should be ground just before brewing, because ground coffee loses much of its bouquet when stored. If you are a true coffee-lover, your best bet is to invest a few dollars in a small, electric coffee-mill rather than using the coffee grinders found in supermarkets. In general, a fine grind not only produces more flavorful coffee but is actually more economical, because you use less. American commercial grinds labeled "all purpose", "automatic drip", or even "fine" contain many gritty particles whose full flavor is not released by the boiling water. The ideal grind for the brewing methods described below is somewhere between "espresso" and "Turkish". When rubbed between fingers, it should feel like coarse flour. If you have your own electric coffee mill, there's no problem grinding the beans as fine as you want. Set supermarket grinders at finest setting and grind twice. If you must store ground coffee, keep it refrigerated in an air-tight container.

3. Start with fresh cold water when brewing coffee. However, if the tap water in your area is heavily chlorinated, it may be better to let it boil a while, then cool it to room temp. before using. Bottled spring water makes an exceptionally good cup of coffee, so it's good to have on hand if only for that purpose. The same, of course, applies to tea.

4. The best coffee is brewed when extremely hot water (at or above the boiling point) is forced through finely-ground, dark-roasted beans a single time, and only espresso-type coffee fits that description. Other methods like boiling, steeping, or drip-brewing produce fair to good coffee. The major flaws of today's highly popular automatic drip coffee-makers are too coarse a grind, insufficiently hot water (below the boiling point) and the paper filter itself which holds back some of the flavor. The worst thing that could be done to coffee is to percolate it, meaning that the coffee is boiled, circulated, re-boiled, re-circulated, etc., until you have a beautifully coffee-scented kitchen but little aroma left in the cup.

5. Coffee should be served as soon as it is brewed, so brew only as many cups as you need. For refills, brew another batch. Coffee loses much of its aroma when kept hot after brewing as in the automatic-drip coffee makers at home, or in restaurant and institutional coffee urns.

6. We recommend smaller portions of full-flavored coffee than larger ones of watered-down swill, hence what could be called the Polish café cup is very good. It contains a roughly 4 oz. serving—midway between the 2 oz. demitasse and the standard American 6 oz. cup—and is often just the amount you need. That way, coffee is rarely left behind in cups. Beautiful, often hand-painted Polish china coffee services provide the proper setting for true coffee enjoyment. Serving this epicurean delight in plastic mugs or paper cups is almost as sacrilegious as drinking cognac from a jelly jar through a plastic straw or spreading caviar on a hamburger bun!

7. Always serve coffee after dinner or as a separate treat with cakes and sweets, never before or during a meal. Gourmets and gastronomes the world over find it abominable the way many American restaurants force coffee on patrons before they have even ordered their meal. Both coffee and iced tap water have palate-numbing properties which dull the taste buds and make the food you eat less flavorful. Before a meal it is best to stimulate, not anesthetize, your taste buds with an aperitif or a glass of appetite-stimulating sparkling mineral water. Also, do not downgrade coffee to the level of something hot with which to wash down a sandwich. Use such utility beverages as tea, beer, compote, juice, or soft drink for that purpose.

8. If you must eliminate caffeine on a doctor's advice, be sure to add some decaffeinated dark Italian-roast coffee to your blend. Darker roasts more effectively disguise the flavor loss that occurs when coffee is chemically treated to remove caffeine. If you are ordered only to cut back on caffeine, then mix normal beans with decaffeinated ones when creating a blend to suit you.

9. Use instant coffee only if you enjoy overpaying for an inferior product. All the high-pressure salesmanship notwithstanding, instant coffee cannot match freshly-brewed coffee for flavor, aroma, and economy. What's more, preparing it is no quicker than brewing coffee from scratch using the single-boil method described below.

10. Some of the above hints may run counter to conventional American coffee wisdom, but it should be remembered that such common notions are molded by the coffee industry whose main purpose is to make money. Coffee producers want you to use as much of their product as possible and are not about to divulge that you can use less coffee if you grind it more finely and employ a different brewing method. The manufacturers of automatic-drip coffee makers have no reason to admit that their product is wasteful (requiring more coffee than needed in other methods) nor that you can get a more flavorful brew by dispensing with paper filters entirely. Try the methods below and see if you don't agree.

ESPRESSO-TYPE COFFEE
kawa z ekspresu

This method is internationally hailed as the very best, because it is the only one in which pressurized boiling water and steam are forced through the coffee a single time, extracting all its flavor. The classic stove-top espresso pot (available in various sizes) is favored by most, but electric models (miniature versions of professional café equipment) may eventually surpass them in popularity. If you get one, follow manufacturer's instructions. To brew coffee in the stove-top pot, pour as much cold water as needed into bottom half of pot. Insert metal filter basket, and 1 heaping t. finely ground French-roasted coffee per ½ c. water, screw on top portion of pot tightly, and place over med. heat. When gurgling stops, the brewed coffee is in the top half of pot ready to enjoy. After pouring coffee, shake or swing pot to force up the last few drops. Serve immediately, preferably in scalded or oven-heated china cups. ***Note***: We have purposely used the term "espresso-type coffee" to indicate using an espresso pot to brew the blend of ground coffee described in "the first commandment" (above). Most Poles and Americans as well find the black-roasted Italian espresso coffee too burnt and bitter to their taste when used alone.

DRIP-POT COFFEE
kawa zaparzona w maszynce

This method is the exact opposite of the espresso pot, in which pressurized boiling water is forced up through the ground coffee and the brew ends up in the top half of the pot. With the drip pot, boiling water poured into the top trickles down over the ground coffee and ends up in the bottom portion. The lack of pressure means that slightly less flavor is extracted from the coffee and you may have to use a bit more to get a brew similar in strength. It is best to place the pot in a pan full of boiling water (but not over direct heat!) or pop it into a 150° oven until dripping stops to prevent brewed coffee from cooling. Reheating ruins the flavor of coffee. *Note*: The best utensil for this method is the Neapolitan drip pot, available in European-import and gourmet-supply shops. Pour brewed coffee into hot, pre-scalded cups and enjoy.

AUTOMATIC-DRIP COFFEE
kawa z zaparzacza (z papierowym filtrem)

Despite the drawbacks of this well-known contraption, you can brew a fairly acceptable cup of coffee by this method if you disregard the manufacturer's instructions and do the following. Use a grind finer than recommended, which should not feel gritty when rubbed between fingers. Instead of a paper filter, use a reusable plastic filter or even a fine sieve that comfortably fits your coffee maker and fill it with ground coffee. This may not be possible in all types of coffee makers, but just using a finer grind is already an improvement. Serve coffee as soon as dripping stops. Storing it on the heating plate for more than several min. spoils its flavor. *Note*: You don't need an expensive appliance to brew coffee in this way. Simply place a sieve filled with ground coffee over a china coffee pot and gradually pour water over it. Return kettle to flame between drenchings to keep the water violently boiling. This actually is preferable to the automatic-drip method, because the water is at higher temp. and ensures more efficient extraction. Sieve-brewed coffee may have a little sediment at bottom, but—especially if taken with sugar—it is so rich in flavor it may actually taste chocolatey.

THERMAL CARAFE COFFEE
kawa parzona w termosie

The thermal carafe, an insulated pot patterned after the familiar thermos bottle, is an easy way to produce fairly good coffee with a minimum of fuss. Measure the contents of your carafe. Fill it with boiling water, seal, and let stand several min. Pour out water, add 1 heaping t. finely ground French-roast coffee per 4–5 oz. c. and fill carafe with rapidly boiling water, leaving at least 1 inch head space. Seal immediately and let stand 10 min. Pour into hot cups and enjoy. If your carafe is an eye-appealing decorator type, use it as is. For added elegance, pour coffee into pre-scalded china coffee pot before bringing to table. *Note*: If you haven't got a thermal carafe, an ordinary thermos bottle will work just as well.

POT-BREWED (ONCE BOILED) COFFEE
kawa zaparzana w rondelku

This is a take-off on the Turkish method that uses a special, small, lidless pot attached to a long handle. Use any cooking pot with handle for this purpose and proceed in 1 of 2 ways. Place finely ground coffee in pot (allowing 1 heaping t. per 4–5 oz. c.), drench with proper amount of boiling water, and heat until boiling resumes. Cover, switch off heat, and let stand 1 min. or more to settle. To prevent cooling, covered pot may be placed in 150° oven. Strain into pre-scalded cups through fine sieve. Another way is to combine coffee with cold water in pot, bring to boil, and proceed as above. Coffee may be brewed with sugar.

CHINA-POT (STEEPED) COFFEE
kawa parzona w dzbanku

Fill your favorite hand-decorated china coffee pot with boiling water and let stand covered 1 min. Pour out water, add coffee (allowing 1 heaping t. per 4–5 oz. c.), cover with rapidly boiling water, replace lid, and let stand in 150° oven 5 min. Give coffee a stir and return to oven for several min. longer for coffee to settle. Pour into pre-scalded cups. *Note*: If the grind is fine enough, sediment will settle to bottom without the need of straining. If you have a tea cozy (an insulated cloth teapot covering meant to retain heat), you can place it over your coffee pot instead of keeping it in oven.

CUP- OR GLASS-BREWED COFFEE
kawa parzona w filiżance lub szklance

This is similar to the preceding method, except that each cup is individually brewed. Simply scald cup or glass with boiling water, pour out, add 1 heaping t. finely ground (preferably very fine Turkish grind) coffee in cup, and cover with boiling water. Cover cup or glass with saucer. Coffee is ready when grounds settle to bottom. *Note*: Although this is by far the most widely used method in today's Poland for brewing a single portion of coffee, we feel that most of the above are preferable. By the time grounds settle, the coffee is no longer extremely hot. Most Americans we have encountered also didn't like the idea of finding a layer of muddy coffee grounds at the bottom of their cup or glass. Poles take this for granted, and some even add sugar to the grounds and eat them with a spoon.

FLAVORED COFFEE
kawa z dodatkami

Full-flavored after-dinner coffee, sweetened to taste with sugar if desired, is a sufficiently delightful treat just as it is, as long as it is freshly brewed and served in hot pre-scalded cups. For variety, however, various flavoring ingredients may be added. These include spices (cinnamon, nutmeg, or vanilla), chocolate (½ t. grated chocolate may be added to each cup), and spirits (brandy, rum, cordials). Hot black coffee served with a dollop of whipped cream is known as "kawa po wiedeńsku" or Viennese-style coffee. If you lighten your coffee with milk, half & half, or cream, be sure they are hot or at least luke-warm so they don't cool the coffee.

ROYAL COFFEE
kawa po królewsku

Sweeten 5 c. hot brewed coffee in china coffeepot with powdered sugar to taste. Add 3 jiggers coffee liqueur and 1 jigger cognac and pour immediately into pre-scalded cups. Top each with a dollop of whipped cream.

SPICED COFFEE
kawa korzenna

Combine a pinch of nutmeg, cinnamon, and ground cardamon each with 3 heaping t. finely ground coffee and brew in any of the above ways. Serve hot, allowing guests to sugar their portions to taste. *Optional*: Add a dollop of whipped cream to each cup.

CHOCOLATE & CHERRY-BRANDY COFFEE
kawa z czekoladą i wiśniówką

To each portion of hot brewed coffee (in 4–5 oz. cups) add ¼ t. powdered chocolate and ½ jigger wiśniówka (cherry brandy or cordial).

COFFEE WITH CHICORY
kawa z cykorią

Following the above gourmet novelties, a more prosaic type of coffee is flavored (some would say adulterated) with chicory, the best known coffee-stretcher. While purists may wince, the addition of a little chicory not only lowers the cost and caffeine content of coffee, but some even claim it mellows the taste. Simply add 2–3 oz. roasted chicory to 1 lb. coffee beans when you grind them. Brew coffee in any of the ways presented above, except espresso pot, which may get clogged up and overheat when anything other than pure coffee is used. *Note*: Coffee with chicory is very good for use in preparing white coffee (see below).

WHITE COFFEE/CAFÉ AU LAIT
biała kawa/kawa mleczna

This hot breakfast drink is prepared in one of two ways. The traditional French method is to have strong brewed black coffee in one pot and hot milk in another and to simultaneously fill cups with an equal amount of both, with guests sugaring their own portions to taste. A popular, more down-home way goes as follows. In cooking pot, combine 2 measuring c. cold water, 1–2 heaping T. ground coffee, and 2–3 heaping T. sugar. Bring to boil, remove from heat, cover, and let stand 1 min. or so. Strain through fine sieve into serving pot containing 2–3 c. hot milk. Add a bit more sugar if desired. Coffee with chicory (above) is very good in this recipe. *Note*: Unlike black after-dinner coffee, white coffee is a hearty and nutritious beverage usually served in larger 6 oz. cups or even 8 oz. mugs.

COFFEE SUBSTITUTE/ERSATZ COFFEE
kawa zbożowa

Known in Polish as grain coffee, this cereal beverage is made from such ingredients as roasted barley, sugar beets, and chicory, and is served as a hearty warmer-upper for breakfast. The best-known American beverage of this type is Postum, although Polish-made Inka (instant grain coffee) has also made an appearance in the U.S. and other countries. As grain coffees go (because in taste and aroma none can compare with real coffee), it ranks quite high. To make 1 qt. add 2–4 heaping t. to 2 c. boiling water, sweeten with 2–3 heaping T. sugar, and combine with 2 c. boiling milk. *Note*: Real instant coffee can be used the same way, alone or mixed with an equal part of instant coffee substitute (Inka, Postum, or whatever). Serve hot in larger cups or mugs.

FROSTED COFFEE
kawa mrożona

Sweeten 3 measuring c. hot brewed coffee with sugar to taste, cover, and let stand until cooled to room temp. Refrigerate until chilled. Combine in blender (or milk shake mixer) with 3 or so scoops French vanilla ice cream and whirl until creamy. Pour into glasses, top with a dollop of whipped cream and garnish with grated chocolate. Serve with straws on hot summer afternoons.

COLD EGG-CREAM COFFEE
zimna kawa z koglem-moglem

Beat 3 raw egg yolks with 4 level T. sugar until creamy and fluffy. Gradually add to 3 measuring c. hot brewed coffee, whisking vigorously to blend. Towards end add 2 jiggers rum, whisk a bit longer, and serve in cups over ice cubes.

MAZAGRAN/COLD COFFEE & COGNAC
mazagran

Sweeten 3 measuring c. hot brewed coffee to taste with sugar. Cover and chill. Add 1–3 jiggers cognac (or more affordable brandy) and serve in glasses over ice. Provide drinking straws.

COCOA
kakao

Long a favorite of children, hot cocoa is a great cold weather warmer-upper for people of all ages and a good way for those who don't like the taste of plain milk to get their Vitamin D. (Cocoa itself is one of the major sources of magnesium, although too much may cause constipation.) For each c. mix 1 heaping t. cocoa with 2 heaping t. sugar, stir in about 2 t. cold milk or water, and mix into a smooth paste. Stir into boiling milk and simmer on lowest possible heat about 5 min. Serve as is or topped with a dollop of egg whites beaten to a stiff froth with sugar (2½ T. sugar per white) or whipped cream. *Variation*: For leaner cocoa use 1 part boiling milk and 1 part boiling water. For richer cocoa, after removing from heat, beat in 1 raw egg yolk for every 1–2 c. hot cocoa just before serving with no additional heating.

COCOA HEALTH DRINK
kakaowy napój zdrowia

Yeast, a treasure-trove of B vitamins (not to mention phosphorous and other minerals), is often prescribed for patients suffering from neuritis, sciatica, and other ailments. The problem is that fresh yeast tastes simply awful, despite attempts to disguise it in hot milk with honey or mock calves brains. We have found that 1 T. fresh yeast can be dissolved in a cup of hot cocoa, which will completely disguise its unpleasant taste and odor and take on a mellow, rounded taste. Something this healthy and nutritious never tasted so good!

HOT CHOCOLATE
czekolada

Although there is no shortage of hot chocolate mixes on the market, we recommend trying the real thing. In pot combine 2 1-oz. squares unsweetened chocolate, ¼ c. sugar, and 1 c. water. Simmer on low heat, stirring until chocolate is melted. Gradually stir in 4 c. milk and heat gently to boil, whisking occasionally. May be served as is or, like cocoa, with a dollop of whipped cream or stiffly beaten egg whites.

HERB AND FRUIT TEAS
napary ziołowe i owocowe

Long before tea, coffee, or cocoa made their appearance, the Polish people quenched their thirst, washed down food, fended off the cold, and helped cure a variety of ailments with various hot beverages flavored with herbs, berries, and other plants. Although a huge repertoire of such drinks has accumulated over the centuries, we have space to list only a few of the more common ones which are still encountered today. Look for them in special herb shops, health-food stores, and old-style pharmacies in ethnic neighborhoods. Herb and fruit teas may be sweetened with sugar or honey to make them more palatable, especially to children, but milk or cream are never added. Herbal teas are sometimes known in English as tisanes (pronounced the French way: tee-ZAHN.)

MINT TEA
napar miętowy

Scald 2 T. mint leaves with 2 c. boiling water. Cover and allow to steep 10 min. Strain and serve as a refreshing after-dinner drink that acts as a mild relaxant and aids digestion, especially after consuming rich greasy foods. For indigestion, drink ½ c, 2–3 times a day.

Drink hot or at room temp., but do not reheat after it has cooled. *Note*: All steeped herbal teas may be made in vacuum flask (thermos bottle.)

ST. JOHN'S WORT TEA
napar z dziurawca

Scald 2 T. St. John's wort (Hypericum perforatum) with 2 c. boiling water. Cover and let steep 20 min. Strain and drink ½ c. 2–3 times a day before meals. It is recommended for gastric ailments, gently dilates blood vessels, relaxes the nerves, and serves as a disinfectant. Applied externally it promotes the healing of cuts. This is one of the oldest still-used herbal remedies and was known to the Ancient Greeks. It gets its English name from the fact that its yellow blossoms bloom around St. John's Day, June 24.

CHAMOMILE TEA
napar rumiankowy

Scald 1 T. chamomile blossoms with 1 c. boiling water, cover, and let steep 15–20 min. Strain and drink ¼ c. 3 times a day. Chamomile counteracts inflammation and fever and is frequently used to soothe gastric distress, including nervous stomach. Its disinfectant properties make it good for gargling against mouth infections and for bathing skin infections.

SAGE TEA
napar z szałwii

Drench 1 T. sage with 1 c. boiling water, cover, and allow to steep 15–20 min. This tisane is used primarily for gargling for a sore throat, or mouth, or gum infections. As a good disinfectant, it is often applied externally on sores, skin infections, cuts, and burns. *Note*: Although Polish cooks of the older generations used a little sage in pork, mutton, and fish dishes, nowadays most Poles associate its smell with something purely medicinal. By contrast, Anglo-American cookery makes wide use of this herb as a seasoning.

LINDEN TEA
napar lipowy

Scald 2 T. linden blossoms with 2 c. water, cover, and steep 15 min. Strain and drink 1 c. 2–3 times a day, one of them just before retiring. Linden tea is chiefly used against colds, flu, and their accompanying congestion of the upper respiratory tract, because it counteracts fever and induces perspiration. It is also good for nervousness and insomnia. Add a double portion (4 T. linden blossoms steeped in 4 c. boiling water and strained) to a hot bath just before going to bed. Many say they sleep like a baby afterwards!

FENNEL TEA
napar z kopru włoskiego

Scald 1 t. crushed fennel seeds with 1 c. boiling water. Cover and steep 10–15 min. Drink about ⅓ c. after meals to promote digestion and counteract flatulence (gas). Nursing mothers who drink fennel tea can help prevent gas pains in their infants. A milder version of this tea (1 T. steeped strained tisane per ½ c. pre-boiled water) is given to infants for the same purpose.

WORMWOOD TEA
napar piołunowy

Although the English name may sound none too appetizing, wormwood (Artemisia absinthium) is the herb from which Absinthe, France's world-famous bitter-liquorice-flavored liqueur is made. Scald a scant t. wormwood leaves with 1 c. boiling water and steep covered about 20 min. Strain. To stimulate the appetite and promote digestion, take 1 T. of this tisane before meals. For indigestion, drink ¼ c. before meals three times a day. A t. honey per c. will help mellow the taste of this horribly bitter but effective tisane. This potent remedy is not meant for children, and adults should not use it uninterrupted for more than three weeks.

RASPBERRY TEA
herbatka malinowa

A delightful hot tea, especially good on cold winter nights, can be prepared as follows. Into china or glass coffee pot or thermal carafe place 3 T. dried raspberries and 4 T. dried raspberry leaves. Drench with 5 c. boiling water, cover, and steep 10 min. Strain and serve. Allow guests to sweeten their tea with sugar, pure raspberry juice, or honey. Add ½ jigger vodka per cup if desired. *Variation*: For medicinal purposes, let stand 20 min. Strain and drink just before retiring for colds. A jigger rum or vodka may be added. This tisane induces sweating, so patient should remain warmly covered all night.

ROSE-HIP TEA
herbatka z dzikiej róży

Place 2 T. dried chopped rose hips, 1 T. dried rose petals, and 1 T. dried rose leaves in pot or thermal carafe, scald with 4–5 c. boiling water, and steep 15 min. Strain and serve sweetened with honey to taste if desired. *Note*: Rose hips are extremely high in vitamin C, hence they are recommended to prevent or relieve colds.

MIXED FRUIT TEA
herbatka owocowa mieszana

Prepare your own fruit-tea blend by combining 3 T. dried chopped rose hips, 2 T. dried hawthorn berries, 2 T. dried elderberries, 2 T. dried raspberries, 2 T. dried raspberry leaves, and 1 T. dried mountain-ash berries. Store in dry place in air tight container. To brew tea, use the essence-pot method or in thermos scald tea with boiling water (1 c. water per t. tea), cover, and steep 10 min. Strain and sugar to taste.

APPLE TEA
herbatka jabłeczna

This pleasing hot drink was enjoyed in Poland ages before real tea appeared and seems to provide yet another illustration of the theme that in Polish cookery nothing ever went to waste. This tea will cost you absolutely nothing, because it is made from apple peelings that you normally discard. Make sure to scrub the apples well to remove any traces or pesticides or other protective chemicals. Dry the peels in a warm 150° oven on parchment paper with oven door left ajar. They are ready when they become brittle and lightly browned. Crumble dried peelings and store in dry place in air tight container. Use as you would ordinary loose tea. Sweeten glasses of hot apple tea with sugar or honey to taste. Flavor with a pinch of cinnamon if desired. Excellent for children, the elderly, and others who do not care for the stimulation of real tea.

COMPOTES
kompoty

A compote is nothing more than fruit cooked in sugared water. What Americans call "canned peaches", "canned pears", etc., Poles would therefore refer to as *kompot z brzoskwiń* (peach compote) and *kompot z gruszek* (pear compote). In Poland, compotes have long been favored as a refreshing drink or stewed-fruit dessert after a heavy meal when a rich pastry or pudding would be just too much. To prepare compote, combine 5–6 c. water with roughly ½ c. sugar, bring to boil, and add about 2 c. fresh, cleaned fruit. Cook covered on med. low heat 5–15 min., depending on type of fruit used. It should be fully cooked but still firm, not falling apart. Use less water for a dessert-type compote and more for a fruit-drink compote served in glasses. The amount of sugar also depends on the type (i.e. tartness) of the fruit you use. Compotes may be flavored with a little vanilla extract (or cooked with a small piece of vanilla pod), cinnamon, or cloves. They may be served hot, warm, room temp., or chilled. *Optional*: A jigger wine may be added before portioning it out. *Note*: A few specific recipes follow, but in general use your imagination and whatever fruit you happen to have on hand. Compotes may be made from one or more varieties of fruit. If you ever have any liquid left over from canned fruit, do not discard it. Mix it with as much cold, pre-boiled water (or sparkling water) as needed to cut its sweetness and enjoy it as a refreshing fruit drink.

APPLE OR PEAR COMPOTE
kompot z jabłek lub gruszek

Combine 7–8 c. water with 4 heaping T. sugar and a small piece of vanilla pod and bring to boil. Add 4 or so peeled, sliced apples or pears. Reduce heat and cook covered about 4 min. Serve as above. *Variation*: Omit vanilla and season cooked compote with a pinch of cinnamon or nutmeg. A piece of orange or lemon rind may be added at start of cooking.

SOUR-CHERRY COMPOTE
kompot z wiśni

Bring 6 c. water and ¾ c. sugar to boil, add 2 c. washed, stemmed, whole sour red cherries (the kind used for American cherry pie!), reduce heat, and cook 2–3 min. Cool and serve at room temp. or chilled, allowing several cherries per serving of liquid compote. *Note*: If using sweet cherries, decrease sugar to about ½ c. *Variation*: Proceed the same way for berry compotes. Strawberries, raspberries, blueberries, blackberries, currants, or any combination thereof are especially good. Gooseberries may take a bit longer to cook.

QUICK COMPOTE
kompot na poczekaniu

When in a hurry, you can prepare this very tasty fruit drink in no time at all. In pitcher combine 1 large can sliced pears and 1 small can sweet black cherries, including their liquids. Add an equal part of cold, pre-boiled water, or as much needed to get a refreshing, not-too sweet compote. Season with pinch of cinnamon or ground cloves or a few drops of vanilla extract if desired. Chill before serving.

STRAWBERRY DRINK
napój z truskawek

Bring 3 c. water and ⅓–½ c. sugar to boil and set aside to cool. Hull, wash and drain 1 pt. strawberries and puree in blender. Add puree to cool syrup, stir and strain into serving pitcher. Chill well before serving or serve over ice. *Note*: An electric juicer may be used to extract juice from strawberries which is mixed with syrup without additional straining.

BLUEBERRY DRINK
napój z czarnych jagód/czernic

Bring 2½ c. water, ¼ vanilla pod, and ½ c. sugar to boil, cover, and set aside to cool. In blender puree 1 pt. washed, drained blueberries, add to cool sugar solution, stir, and strain into serving pitcher. Chill well before serving or pour into glasses containing 2–3 ice cubes. *Variation*: Bring only 2 c. water to boil with sugar and vanilla. When combining sieved, blended fruit with liquid, add ½ c. dry red wine.

CRANBERRY OR CURRANT DRINK
napój z żurawin lub porzeczek

Bring 4 c. water to boil. In 1 c. dissolve ½–¾ c. sugar. Heat if necessary to dissolve sugar, then set aside. In blender crush ½ lb. washed, drained cranberries or red or black currants. Transfer to bowl and add 3 c. cold, pre-boiled water. Cover and refrigerate 1 hr. Strain into syrup, mix, and pour into ice-filled glasses. *Note*: If you're economy minded and don't mind a cloudier drink, bring the remaining pulp (left in sieve) to boil with 1 c. water and strain again into beverage. Mix and serve with ice.

RHUBARB & HONEY DRINK
napój z rabarbaru/rzewienia z miodem

Bring 4 c. water to boil set aside to cool, and stir in ½ c. honey. Wash, dry, and cut into cubes 1 lb. young rhubarb and crush in blender. Place in bowl, cover with 3 c. lukewarm water, cover, and refrigerate 2 hrs. Strain through sieve into water-honey mixture, stir, and chill, or pour as is into glasses containing ice cubes. *Variation*: For rhubarb compote proceed as with apple or pear compote, but omit spices and increase sugar to taste.

LEMONADE
lemoniada

In pot combine 2 c. water, 3–5 T. sugar, and ½ t. grated lemon rind (zest). Bring to boil, remove from heat, and let stand covered until cooled to room temp. Add juice of 2 lemons and 2 c. cold pre-boiled water or (for sparkling lemonade) 2 c. cold club soda, and serve immediately over ice cubes. Add 1 lemon slice and a drinking straw to each glass.

QUICK LEMONADE
lemoniada naprędce

For each serving, combine juice of ½ lemon with 1 c. club soda or other sparkling water, sweeten to taste with powdered sugar, and serve with ice cubes and straw. *Note*: Lemonade prepared in either of the two above ways may be flavored with a little pure raspberry or red-currant syrup to taste.

ORANGEADE
oranżada

Dissolve ½–¾ c. sugar in 4 c. boiling water. Add grated rind of 1 orange, juice of 2 oranges and 1 lemon, cover, and chill. Serve cold with or without ice cubes, adding an orange slice to each glass.

OLD POLISH LEMON & HONEY DRINK
napój staropolski (cytrynowo-miodowy)

Dissolve ½ c. or more honey in 3 c. lukewarm pre-boiled water. Cover and set aside to cool. Add juice of 2 lemons, stir and serve. *Note*: In Old Poland this healthful and refreshing drink was usually served at room temp. or only slightly cooled.

TANGY STRAWBERRY MILK SHAKE
cocktail mleczno-truskawkowy

Hull, wash, and slice about 1 lb. strawberries and mix with about ¾ c. powdered sugar. Let stand 30 min. or until juice forms, then chill in fridge. Combine strawberries and their liquid with 1 qt. cold sour milk in blender and whirl until creamy. Serve immediately. *Optional*: Several drops vanilla extract may be added before blending. For a richer shake, add 1 heaping T. sour cream before blending. *Note*: This shake may be made with other berries of a single type or mixed varieties. When fresh or frozen berries are not available, you can replace them with preserves or jam, using 1 heaping T. (more or less) per c. cold sour milk and omitting sugar.

STRAWBERRY-WINE COOLER
cocktail winno-truskawkowy

Slice ¾ lb. strawberries, raspberries, or 1 part each, sprinkle with 3 heaping T. powdered sugar. Place in blender with 1 c. cold coffee cream or half & half, 1 c. semi-dry red wine, and 2 c. cold club soda. Whirl until creamy and serve immediately with or without ice.

ALMOND MILK
orszada

Crush ½ lb. blanched almonds and 3 bitter almonds in mortar with a few t. water. Or use your blender, also add several t. cold water and switch it on in brief spurts, rather than pulverizing them to a paste. Place crushed almonds in bowl, add 2 c. cold pre-boiled water, let stand several min., and drain into serving pitcher through napkin-lined sieve. Return almonds to bowl, add another 2 c. water, stir, and strain into pitcher. Sweeten to taste with powdered sugar and chill well before serving as is or over ice cubes.

SWEET WHEY COOLER
napój z serwatki na słodko

Flavor fresh, ice-cold whey to taste with pure cherry or raspberry syrup for an interesting thirst-quencher with a subtly winey tang.

TART WHEY COOLER
napój z serwatki na kwaśno

Combine 2–3 c. fresh ice-cold whey with about 1 c. beet sour or dill pickle juice (from brine-cured dill pickles) or ½ c. sauerkraut juice. Add a sprinkling of chopped dill or chives and a pinch of salt and drink immediately. *Note*: This and similar tart & tangy beverages are not likely to appeal to youngsters brought up on soft drinks and chocolate milk, but the morning-after crowd may find them to be a satisfying thirst-quencher.

TOMATO-SAUERKRAUT DRINK
napój pomidorowy z kwaśnicą

Mix 3 c. cold tomato juice with 1 c. cold sauerkraut juice. Add 1 T. chopped dill and a pinch of sugar to taste. Serve ice cold, especially the morning after. *Variation*: Combine 2 c. cold tomato juice with 2 c. dill-pickle juice (brine-cured type) or with 1 c. dill-pickle juice and 1 c. sauerkraut juice.

CUCUMBER DRINK
napój ze świeżych ogórków

Peel, cube, and place in juicer 3 lbs. cucumbers. Drink the extracted juice flavored with pinch of salt and sugar.

BEET SOUR DRINK
napój z kiszonych buraków

If you don't have any beet sour (called for in the tart whey cooler recipe above), here's an easy way to make some. Wash, dry, and peel 2 lbs. beets. Slice thin and place in 1½ qt. jar. Add 1 sliced bud garlic and a slice stale black bread, crumbled up. Bring 4 c. water to boil, cool to luke warm and pour over beets. Cover mouth of jar with cheesecloth, fasten with rubber band, and let stand in room-temp. place or warmer (preferably at 75°–80°) about 3 days. Strain beet sour into serving pitcher, season with a little salt, sugar, and chopped dill, chill and serve. May be strained into bottle without seasoning, sealed and refrigerated. *Note*: This is the same kind of beet sour used to make barszcz (beet soup).

CREAMY SOUR-MILK DRINK
roztrzepaniec

Vigorously mix 1 qt. ice-cold sour milk with 1–2 T. sour cream until creamy. Stir in a little finely chopped dill and/or chives. Serve immediately as a refreshing hot-weather drink. This can be a meal in itself with a plate of boiled potatoes, garnished with fried salt-pork nuggets on the side. *Variation*: For added zing, mix in about 1 c. beet sour or dill-pickle brine. Buttermilk may be used in place of sour milk.

TANGY BREAD DRINK
kwas chlebowy

Cut ¼ lb. black bread into cubes and dry in warm oven until hard. Transfer bread cubes to large jar and drench with 8 c. boiling water. When liquid cools to lukewarm, dissolve 1 T. sugar in ½ c. lukewarm water, add ⅛ cake crumbled yeast, mix well and add to jar. Also add ⅓ c. sugar, cover with cloth napkin or dish towel and let stand in warm place 24 hrs. Strain into bottles with twist-off caps, add ¼ c. raisins, seal, and store in cool place 3 days before serving.

HOT SUGARED BEER
piwo grzane z cukrem

Combine 3 c. beer and ¼–⅓ c. sugar in pot and heat to just below boiling, stirring to dissolve sugar. Add 1 c. room-temp. beer and serve immediately. *Note*: This and other hot beer drinks are not only great cold-weather warmer-uppers, but they give you a nicer glow than a similar amount of cold beer. *Variation:* Sweeten hot beer to taste with pure cherry or raspberry syrup. Since this version is a good sweat inducer, folk-medicine advocates recommend drinking a glass or two and sweating it out under a featherbed overnight. If you don't feel better the next day, repeat procedure until cold goes away!

HOT SPICED BEER
piwo grzane z korzeniami

In pot combine 3 c. beer, 5–7 partially crushed cloves, a piece of cinnamon bark, and a slice of ginger root. Cover and simmer on low heat about 2 min. Sweeten to taste with sugar, fruit syrup, or honey and heat a bit longer. Mix in 1 c. room temp. beer, strain, and serve at once. *Note*: A thermos of this sweet & spicy brew is a great pick-me-up for those engaged in outdoor winter activities.

HOT EGG-CREAM BEER
grzane piwo korzenne z żółtkami

Bring 2 c. beer to boil with 2–3 partially crushed cloves and a small piece of cinnamon bark. Remove from heat and set aside covered. In top part of double boiler over boiling water beat 2 egg yolks with ¼ c. sugar until fluffy. Add a little strained hot beer at a time and continue beating until mixture begins to thicken. Gradually stir in remaining beer and serve immediately. *Note*: You don't have to be a beer-lover to enjoy this delightfully creamy and spicy hot drink.

HOMEMADE BEER
piwo domowe

Without special equipment, beer is not the easiest beverage to prepare at home from scratch. For those interested in giving it a try anyway, we have selected the simplest recipes we could find. One was presented by the Grande Dame of Polish cuisine, Lucyna Ćwierczakiewiczowa, in the 1885 edition of her famous "*Jedyne praktyczne przepisy*" where she wrote that this "superb, easy-to-prepare home made beer is light, refreshing, tasty and sparkles like champagne." The following is a modernized version of this recipe.

In large, dry skillet brown 1–1¼ lbs. whole-grain barley until coffee colored. Add to pot containing 16½ qts. water. Sew ⅔ oz. hops into small linen bag, add to pot, and gently cook mixture 2 hrs. Add 1–1½ c. sugar and cook another 30 min. When liquid cools to lukewarm, add ½ cake mashed yeast, stir gently, and let stand at room temp. 24 hrs. Skim off any foam from top of liquid. Strain through cheesecloth-lined sieve into another container and ladle through funnel into bottles leaving an inch or more head space. Seal tightly and store in cool place 3 weeks before serving. *Note*: Due to the pressure that builds up inside, it is best to use champagne bottles or other thick-walled bottles with twist-off caps or stoppers that can be wired in place. Incidentally, this will not be the clear, golden, store-bought lager you are used to. Instead, it may turn out a bit cloudy and show traces of yeast sediment at bottom, but that's how it's supposed to be. Today's pale, fizzy lagers did not gain prominence until the 1900's, whereas beer-like beverages go back thousands of years.

HOMEMADE DARK BEER
ciemne piwo domowe

Brown in dry skillet or roast in oven in pan 2.2 lbs. (1 kilogram) whole-grain barley until light brown and grind in coffee grinder or processor. Place barley in pot containing 6½ qts. water and cook 3 hrs. In separate pot combine ⅔ oz. hops in 2 qts. water same length of time and in third pot simmer 1¼ c. sugar in 3 qts. water about 30 min. Combine all 3 liquids and let stand until cooled to room temp. Strain through cheesecloth into another vessel. Crumble ¼ cake yeast into 1 c. liquid. When it starts bubbling, add to remaining liquid in pot. Let stand 24 hrs. at room temp. Ladle into thick-walled bottles, seal tightly, and store in cold cellar or warmest part of fridge one week before drinking. *Note*: This may not be a Guinness Stout, but you'll probably feel a sense of satisfaction after your first crack at home brewing anyway!

HOMEMADE HONEY BEER
piwo domowe na miodzie

In large dry skillet brown ½ lb. whole-grain barley, stirring until it is coffee colored. Grind coarsely in coffee grinder. Place barley, 1 c. honey, and ⅔ oz. hops in large pot. (*Note*: It is best to add hops in a linen bag, as this makes for a clearer brew that does not require filtration.) Add 6½ qts. water and simmer until about 1 qt. of liquid evaporates. Pour off 1 c. of mixture, and when cooled to lukewarm, stir in ½ cake yeast. When yeast mixture starts bubbling vigorously, add it to pot with remaining ingredients. Let stand at room temp. 12 hrs. Strain through cheesecloth-lined sieve into another pot, then ladle through funnel into bottles, leaving about 10% head space in each. Seal and refrigerate 5–6 days before drinking. *Note*: Small champagne bottles or other thick-walled bottles with twist-off caps are recommended for this and all other homemade beers.

VARIOUS HOMEMADE FLAVORED BEERS
różne domowe piwa smakowe

In the olden days, there was an infinite variety of beers flavored with a great many different herbs, berries, and other ingredients. You can duplicate the flavor of some of them as follows. Prepare beer as in above recipe (honey beer), but to pot add 1 t. partially crushed juniper berries, mint leaves, or melissa (also known in English as lemon balm.) Cook together with roasted barley, hops, honey, and water.

NEAR-MEAD/HONEY WINE
niby-miód

In pot, combine ½ c. honey and ½ c. cold pre-boiled water. Simmer gently 20 min., stirring occasionally. Remove from heat, cover, and let stand until cooled to room temp. Mix in 1 qt. dry white wine, pour into clean bottle, seal, and let stand at room temp. overnight. Next day strain through cotton-filled funnel into serving decanter and serve at room temp. This is not a real Polish miód pitny (mead), but it may be the next best thing. *Note*: We considered including recipes for genuine mead and other homemade wines, but decided against it. This requires a good theoretical background, expensive equipment, and hard-to-find supplies and would necessitate a long and involved list of do's and don'ts, and mustn'ts. If you would like to try your hand at home wine-making anyway, we suggest consulting a specialized manual like *The Art of Wine Making* by Stanley Anderson and Raymond Hall, Hawthorn-Dutton (publishers), New York, 1970. It contains recipes for mead, elderberry wine, currant wine, gooseberry wine, and others produced by home wine-makers in Poland. An easier way is to pick up genuine imported Polish mead and fruit wines at stores in may Polish neighborhoods.

OLD POLISH HOT HONEY-SPICE CORDIAL
krupnik staropolski

In pot combine 3–4 cloves, a small piece cinnamon bark, a sliver of nutmeg, 2 grains allspice, 1 inch piece vanilla pod, and 1 c. honey. Simmer until honey just begins to brown. Stir in 1 c. hot water, bring to boil, remove from heat, and let stand covered several min. Stir in 2 c. 190 proof grain alcohol. *Warning*: Be sure there is no open flame anywhere nearby, because alcohol vapors could ignite! Add 1 small piece of orange rind (with bitter white inner skin removed). Pour mixture including spices, into bottle, seal, and let stand at room temp. 24 hrs. Filter into serving decanter through cotton-filled funnel and serve hot or cold. *Note*: We have included krupnik in the beverage chapter because it is meant for quick consumption. Long-life cordials and brandies are presented in the following chapter.

HOT SPICED WINE
wino grzane z korzeniami

In pot combine 1 qt. dry red wine, ½ c. sugar, 5 partially crushed cloves, a piece of cinnamon bark, and ½ a bay leaf. Heat, stirring to dissolve sugar, bring to boil, strain, and serve. Guaranteed to give a mellow glow to any winter gathering!

OLD POLISH HOT SPICED WINE
wino grzane po staropolsku

Heat but do not boil 4 c. dry red wine with 5–6 partially crushed cloves and 4 T. honey. Beat 4 egg yolks with 2 T. sugar until fluffy. Continue beating, while adding hot strained wine gradually in thin stream. Adding it too quickly may cause yolks to curdle. Serve immediately.

WINE PUNCH
kruszon

In crystal pitcher or punch bowl combine 1 qt. ice-cold, dry white wine, 1 c. freshly squeezed orange juice, juice of 1 lemon, and ¾ c. powdered sugar. Stir to dissolve sugar and add 1 qt. iced-cold club soda. Add lemon and orange slices and some ice cubes (or serve over ice block in punch bowl.)

CHAMPAGNE PUNCH
kruszon szampański

In punch bowl or pitcher combine 1 bottle cold dry or semi-dry champagne or sparkling wine with 1 c. strained pineapple liquid (from canned pineapple slices) and ½ c. freshly squeezed orange juice. Stir in 1 qt. ice-cold club soda or other sparkling water. Decorate with several pineapple slices and a few spiced cherries and serve at once so fizz is not lost. This is a light, refreshing drink, perfect for a garden or patio party on a hot summer day, when thirst-quenching takes precedence over any serious drinking.

FIERY WINE & RUM PUNCH
poncz ognisty

Unlike the preceding 2 drinks, the following would be preferable on a cold winter's night to add a warm glow to your gathering. Heat 1 qt. dry red wine with 1⅓ c. sugar but do not boil. Stir in 1 c. freshly squeezed orange juice and 1 c. rum. Heat briefly. Slice 1 well-scrubbed orange with rind and place in punch bowl. Drench with hot punch and serve immediately.

CORDIALS, BRANDIES & LIQUEURS

It was in 16th-century Poland, not Russia, that the world's first *wódka* (literally: "little water") was distilled, giving rise to the *nalewka* (homemade cordial) tradition that is still much in evidence today. Originally these alcohol-based extracts were used largely for medicinal purposes, and the manor houses of yesteryear would employ a special keeper to guard over them. It was he or she that held the keys to the cupboard where the various herbal cordials, tinctures, and elixirs for what ailed one were kept.

Very early on, many of these medicinal potions also doubled as popular tipples to mark special occasions. Except that these occasions were somehow never in short supply. Besides annual holidays, weddings, christenings, and funerals, there always seemed to be reasons to celebrate. Old Polish hospitality meant that both the arrival of a visitor as well as his departure had to be marked with a liquor-laced feast. If things turned out badly, one could always drown one's sorrows.

To this day, many men of the house pride themselves in this or that *nalewka* which adds a warm, hospitable touch to any gathering. This is a tradition which we feel may well catch on among many do-it-yourself enthusiasts in America. Anyone can go down to the liquor store and pick up a bottle of scotch, brandy, gin, fruit cordial, or what have you, but a homemade cordial or liquor is an entirely different ballgame.

It is a custom-made product bearing your own personalized stamp and it evokes a certain sense of bonhomie that store-bought liquor cannot match. When poured from a sparkling crystal carafe into matching cordial glasses, it also adds its own touch of elegance to the simplest meal or get-together.

Like many areas of Polish cuisine, the blending of homemade cordials enables you to give reign to your imagination, experiment, and play around with ingredients until you achieve precisely the color, flavor, aroma, and potency you desire. Unlike other culinary fields, there is nothing to burn, oversalt, or otherwise spoil. You may prefer one recipe to another, but a cordial or liquor will never go bad because the alcohol acts as a fool-proof preservative.

So go ahead and give it a try. Start with some of the simpler recipes before tackling those that are more involved. As always, feel free to improve on any of the spirits listed on the following pages and come up with original recipes all your own. Although there are nearly 50 cordials, flavored vodkas, brandies, and liquors in this chapter, they by no means exhaust the variety of home-blended spirits the Poles have long enjoyed.

* * *

CHERRY CORDIAL THE EASY WAY
wiśniówka łatwa

In bottle or jar combine anywhere from ¼–1 c. homemade or imported (preferably Polish or German) cherry syrup and 1 qt. 100-proof (or stronger) vodka. Shake well, seal, and store 2–3 months. Shake bottle every few days. Strain through cotton-filled funnel into serving decanter. *Note*: Additional flavoring may include a small piece of lemon rind (minus white inner skin) or 1 clove both of which are added when syrup and vodka are first mixed.

CHERRY-HONEY CORDIAL
wiśniówka na miodzie

Combine 1 qt. 100-proof vodka with ½ c. cherry syrup, ½ c. honey, and 1–2 cloves. Seal and store at room temp. 2–3 months, shaking occasionally. Carefully strain through cotton-filled funnel into another bottle, taking care to leave sediment behind and let stand several days. Strain again into serving decanter.

CHERRY-RUM OR CHERRY-BRANDY CORDIAL
nalewka wiśniowa na rumie lub koniaku

Combine 2 c. 100-proof vodka, 1 c. light rum, or 1 c. French brandy (cognac if you can afford it!) and 1 c. cherry syrup. Seal bottle or jar, shake and store 2–3 months, shaking occasionally. Strain through cotton-filled funnel into carafe. *Note*: This and other cordials may be stored in cool, dry place almost indefinitely, as they improve in flavor with age.

VARIOUS EASY FRUIT CORDIALS
łatwe nalewki owocowe różne

Easy cordials can be prepared according to the above recipes with other fruit syrups such as blackberry, blueberry, raspberry, red & black-currant, etc. If you have not prepared your own homemade syrup, get commercially available syrups imported from Poland or other European countries. Do not use the supermarket brands of fruit syrup meant for pancakes—they may contain corn syrup, artificial coloring, and other additives.

CHERRY CORDIAL THE TRADITIONAL WAY
wiśniówka tradycyjna

Pit, wash, and drain just over 2 lbs. dark sour cherries, leaving 5–6 cherries with pits intact. Place in jar. Add 1 heaping c. sugar and 2 c. spirits* or 1 qt. 100-proof vodka. Seal, shake, and to mix ingredients and let stand at room temp. 3–4 months or even up to 6 months. Strain through cotton-filled funnel into decanter. For greater clarity, strain into another bottle, let stand 1 day, then strain again into decanter. *Optional*: At start of process, mixture may be flavored with 4 cloves, 1 pinch cinnamon, or ¼–½ t. vanilla extract.

---

* Spirits (in Polish "spirytus") in this chapter means roughly 190 proof grain alcohol.

DRY CHERRY CORDIAL
nalewka wiśniowa wytrawna

Wash, discard stems, and drain 2¼ lbs. dark sour cherries. Remove pits from all but about 15–20 of the cherries. Place in large glass jar. Mix 3 c. spirits and 2 c. cold, pre-boiled water and pour over cherries. Seal and store in room-temp. or slightly warmer place 2–3 months, shaking jar occasionally. Strain through cotton-filled funnel. Separately, dissolve ½ c. sugar in 1 c. boiling water. When cool, combine with 1 c. spirits and add to cordial. Seal and store another 4–6 weeks before serving. *Note*: The leftover cherries may be covered with 100-proof vodka, sealed, and allowed to stand several weeks to get a dry cherry vodka. After straining into bottle, sweeten to taste with a little sugar syrup.

CHERRY BRANDY
wiśniak

Wash and drain 2 lbs. dark sour cherries, leaving pits intact. Remove pits from 3–4 cherries and crush pits in mortar. Place cherries and crushed pits in jar, cover with 2 c. sugar, shaking so it gets evenly distributed. Seal and let stand at room temp. 3–4 weeks, shaking occasionally. Pour syrup that forms into bottle, seal, and set aside. Fill jar containing cherries with 100-proof vodka or 3 parts spirits to 2 parts cold pre-boiled water. Next day, combine vodka mixture with cherry syrup, seal, and let stand several days. Strain through cotton-filled funnel into another bottle or bottles, taking care to leave sediment at bottom of first bottle. Store in cool, dark cellar several months before serving.

RASPBERRY CORDIAL
malinówka

Fill large jar ½ full with hulled, washed, drained raspberries. Fill jar nearly to top with spirits, seal, let stand at room temp. 4–6 weeks. Strain liquid through cotton-filled funnel into bottles, seal, and set aside. Cover leftover fruit in jar with sugar, using 1 part sugar to 2 parts fruit by weight. (Fruit should be weighed at beginning before being drenched with spirits.) Seal and let stand another 4–6 weeks, shaking occasionally. Strain into bottles through cotton-filled funnel, seal, and let stand several days. Combine with first mixture and strain again into bottles, seal, and allow to age several weeks or months. *Note*: Instead of raspberries, you may use blueberries, blackberries, lingonberries, wild strawberries, and other berries.

OLD POLISH PLUM CORDIAL
śliwowica staropolska

Fill jar with ripe, washed, drained, unpitted Italian plums (węgierki) and cover with spirits. Seal and let stand 4–6 weeks at room temp. Pour off liquid, straining through cotton-filled funnel into bottles. Seal and set aside. To plums add sugar to cover, seal, and let stand about 2 weeks or until sugar completely dissolves. Pour off syrup and combine with spirit mixture. Strain through cotton-filled funnel into bottles, seal and store in cool, dark cellar from several months to half a year—the longer the better.

PRUNE CORDIAL
śliwowica na suszonych śliwkach

Place 8 oz. pitted prunes in jar and cover with 5 c. 100-proof vodka and 1 c. spirits. For best results, dice the prunes first. Seal and let stand at room temp. 4–6 weeks, shaking occasionally. Pour liquid off through cotton-filled funnel into bottles, seal and set aside. To prunes in jar, add 1 c. cold, pre-boiled water, seal, and let stand overnight. Next day filter through cotton-filled funnel into first mixture, seal, and age in cool, dark place several months.

SOUTHERN-FRUIT CORDIAL
nalewka bakaliowa

In qt. jar place 1–2 c. mixed southern fruits (raisins, chopped prunes, dates, and figs) in whatever proportion you like, and add a piece of orange and lemon rind with white inner skin removed. Drench with 1 c. spirits and fill jar nearly to top with 100-proof vodka. Seal and store at room temp. 3–4 weeks, shaking occasionally. Strain through cotton into bottles, seal, and set aside. Add 1 c. cool, pre-boiled water to fruits, seal, and let stand several days longer. Strain through cotton-filled funnel and combine with fruit-flavored vodka. Seal and let stand another day. Strain again through cotton into bottle or decanter.

DRIED-FRUIT CORDIAL
nalewka z suszu

Prepare like southern-fruit cordial (above) but use 1–2 c. raisins, prunes, dried apricots, pears, apples, etc. Packaged mixed dried fruits are good in this recipe, as are other fruits not found in such mixtures, such as dried Zante currants, dried cherries, etc.

CRANBERRY CORDIAL
żurawinka

Wash, hull, and drain 1 c. strawberries and 1 c. raspberries. Slice, place in bowl, sprinkle with 1 c. sugar, cover, and let stand at room temp. 24 hrs. Drain berries, reserving syrup. Mix syrup with 1 c. commercial cranberry juice and pour into bottle containing 1 c. spirits and 100-proof vodka. Seal, shake well, and let stand 24 hrs. Strain through cotton-filled funnel into decanter. Requires no aging and may be served at once.

SLOEBERRY CORDIAL
tarniówka/tarkówka

Fill qt. jar or larger slightly more than half full with washed, drained sloeberries. These are best after the first frost, but you can achieve the same effect by keeping them in the freezer overnight. Fill jar with 100-proof vodka and ½ c. spirits, seal, and let stand at room temp. 4–6 weeks, shaking occasionally. Filter through cotton into bottle, seal, and store—the longer the better. *Variation*: For a sweeter cordial, add 1 part sugar to 4 parts of sloeberries left in jar, seal and let stand 6 weeks. Strain syrup into first mixture, seal, shake, and let stand overnight. Carefully strain through cotton into another bottle and leave in cool, dark place to age several months. *Note*: Sloeberries (tarnina) are what the English use to make their sloe gin.

MOUNTAIN-ASH CORDIAL
jarzębiak

Wash, trim off stems, and drain about 1 c. mountain-ash berries. These are the bright, orange-red berries that grow in clusters on the mountain-ash trees which many people have in their gardens. (*Important*: Do not use berries growing along heavily-traveled roads since they may be contaminated with car-exhaust fumes.) Use berries picked after the first frost or place them in freezer overnight. Place in pot, scald with boiling water (to remove excess bitterness), drain, and place in jar. Cover with 2 c. spirits, seal, and let stand at room temp. 4–6 weeks, shaking occasionally. Strain through cotton into bottle, seal, and set aside. Dissolve ⅔ c. sugar in 2 c. hot water and pour over berries left in jar. Seal and let stand 2 weeks. Strain through cotton into first mixture. Seal and keep in cool, dark place several weeks. For greater clarity, filter through cotton into decanter when ready to serve. *Optional*: Several prunes and several T. raisins may be added to sloeberries before drenching them with alcohol.

STRONG JUNIPER VODKA/"POLISH GIN"
jałowcówka mocna

In mortar partially crush 2 slightly heaped T. dried juniper berries and add to bottle containing 4 c. spirits and 1 c. cold pre-boiled water. Seal and let stand 7–8 days, shaking occasionally. After that time, dissolve ¾ c. sugar in 2 c. boiling water. When cool, add spirit mixture filtered through cotton-filled funnel, mix, and pour into bottles. Seal and age 5–6 months. This potent spirit, made with the same juniper berries used to flavor English gin, will help digest those hearty game dishes. *Note*: If this 116-proof vodka is too strong for your taste, simply use an additional 1–1½ c. water when dissolving sugar.

DRY CARAWAY VODKA
kminkówka wytrawna

Dissolve ¼ c. sugar in 2 c. boiling water and set aside to cool. Mix syrup with 2 c. spirits. Place 1–2 t. caraway seeds in bottle and drench them with syrup-spirit mixture. Seal and let stand 5 days. Filter through cotton into bottle. Ready to serve immediately. A nice accompaniment to those heavy sauerkraut and pork dishes, since it stimulates digestion. *Note*: For a less dry vodka, up to 1 c. sugar may be used when preparing the syrup.

PEPPER VODKA
pieprzówka

Place 25 peppercorns in bottle and drench with 2 c. spirits. Seal and let stand 12 days, shaking occasionally. Dissolve ¼–½ c. sugar in 2 c. boiling water. When syrup cools in room temp., pour it into bottle. Through cotton-filled funnel add spirits, seal, shake, and let stand 3–4 days. *Note*: In Polish folk medicine, this was a traditional remedy for stomachaches, and many Polish immigrants to the U.S. took a few bottles along to fend off seasickness during the trans-Atlantic crossing. *Optional:* Several drops caramel may be added to improve color.

BISON-GRASS VODKA
żubrówka

Place 5–6 strands of Polish bison grass (trawa żubrowa—available at herb shops in Polish ethnic neighborhoods) into 1 qt. 100-proof vodka, seal, and let stand 15–20 days. Transfer through cotton-filled funnel to another bottle, add 1 t.–1 T. simple syrup and several drops caramel, seal, shake, and let stand two days. A strand of bison grass may be added to bottle to identify your spirit as żubrówka. This is another favorite drink that traditionally accompanies bigos and game dishes.

WALNUT CORDIAL
orzechówka

Take 3–4 unripe green walnuts and cut each into 4 parts. (*Note*: In temperate climates similar to Poland's unripe walnuts are just right in August; for this cordial both the green outer skin and the immature nut inside are used and both are soft enough to be cut with an ordinary knife.) Place in jar and cover with 4 c. spirits and 1 c. cold, pre-boiled water. Seal and keep in warm place about a week. Dissolve ½–1 c. sugar in 2–3 c. boiling water and, when cool, combine with filtered alcohol mixture. Pour into bottles and age 10–12 months. This is another traditional digestive stimulant. *Optional*: 2–4 cloves may be added to nuts before drenching with alcohol.

HONEY CORDIAL
miodówka

In pot combine 1 c. honey, 1 c. water, and small piece of lemon rind (minus white inner skin) and bring to boil. Reduce heat, simmer several min., and set aside to cool. Combine with 2 c. spirits or 1 qt. 100-proof vodka and pour into bottle, remembering to add lemon rind. Seal and let stand 1 week. Pour into another bottle through cotton-filled funnel, seal, and let stand another week. Filter once again carefully to leave sediment that forms at bottom behind. Ready to use at once, but it improves with aging.

HONEY-RUM CORDIAL
miodówka na rumie

In pot lightly brown 1⅓ c. honey. Add 1¼ c. water and bring to boil. Remove from heat. Add 1 c. rum (light or dark) and ½ c. strong coffee. Mix in 4 c. vodka and pour into bottles. Seal and let stand 5–6 weeks. Filter through cotton into bottles or decanter.

POLISH HONEY-SPICE CORDIAL
krupnik polski

In small pot combine 1 c. water, ½ vanilla pod, ½ stick cinnamon, ¼ t. freshly grated nutmeg, 10–12 cloves, a pinch or 2 mace, and bring to boil. When mixture is just about to boil, add 1 t. grated orange rind. Cover and set aside. Separately, bring to boil 2 c. honey and 1 c. water, skimming off scum until no more forms. Remove from heat and switch off all heat sources. (*Warning*: There should be no open flames around whenever pouring 190-proof grain alcohol (spirits), because even its fumes can ignite!) Into hot honey mixture stir 4 c. spirits and spice mixture including spices. Pour into clean jar, seal, and let stand overnight. Next day pour through cotton-filled funnel into bottle or serving carafe. This mellow and spicy cordial is often served hot on Christmas Eve and is guaranteed to cast a nice, warm glow over any gathering. It is also good at room temp. To serve hot, pour in pot and heat but do not boil. *Optional*: When heating krupnik, you may add 2–3 T. butter, allowing it to melt. Some regard the buttery version of krupnik as a good cold remedy. *Variation*: A weaker krupnik can be made using 1 qt. 100-proof vodka instead of spirits.

LITHUANIAN HONEY-SPICE CORDIAL
krupnik litewski

This version of krupnik hails from the northeastern borderlands of Old Royal Poland but is quite similar to the preceding recipe. In pot combine 1⅓ c. honey, ½ vanilla pod, 5 cloves, a piece of cinnamon bark, 5 grains allspice, and ¼ t. freshly grated nutmeg. Simmer mixture until honey begins to brown, add 2 c. water, and bring to boil. Switch off flame, remove from heat, and stir in 4 c. spirits, add a piece of finely diced orange rind (minus white inner skin), and—if desired—a piece of diced lemon rind. Pour mixture into jar, seal, and let stand at room temp. 24 hrs. Filter through cotton-filled funnel into bottle or decanter. Serve hot or room temp. as above. *Optional*: For added zing, several peppercorns may be included with the other spices in both krupnik recipes.

OTHER HONEY-BASED CORDIALS
inne nalewki na miodzie

Honey may be used in place of sugar in almost any of the preceding or following cordials, and many feel it gives the finished product a more mellow, rounded, and subtly aromatic flavor. *Remember*: Honey has almost twice the sweetening power of sugar, so be sure to use less. If a recipe calls for 1 c. sugar, you will achieve roughly the same sweetening by using just over ½ c. honey.

CARAMEL CORDIAL
karmelówka/przypalanka

Into bottle or jar place 1 chopped green walnut, 1 t. raisins, 3–4 chopped pitted prunes, 4–5 chopped blanched almonds, and ¼–½ vanilla pod. Add 4 c. spirits, seal, and let stand 2–4 weeks, shaking occasionally. After that time, in dry saucepan caramelize 1½ T. sugar. Remove from heat and carefully stir in several T. boiling water, stirring until caramel is dissolved. Add 2 c. cold, pre-boiled water. Combine with spirit mixture and pour into bottles through cotton-filled funnel. Seal and let stand at least 5 days before serving. ***Note***: The caramelized sugar dissolved in 2 T. boiling water can be used to flavor plain vodka minus the other ingredients. During the American Prohibition, Polish immigrants sometimes added caramel to moonshine, which softened its harsh flavor and gave it a nice, amber color similar to that of whisky.

LEMON CORDIAL
cytrynówka

Scrub 2 lemons with brush in plenty of hot, soapy water, rinse well, and scald with boiling water. When dry, carefully peel just the outer yellow skin, leaving the bitter white inner skin behind. Dissolve 1¼ c. sugar in 2 c. boiling water, bring to boil, and pour over chopped lemon rinds. Cover and let stand at room temp. 24 hrs. Combine with 2 c. spirits and strain through cotton into bottles. Ready to use in several days.

ORANGE CORDIAL
pomarańczówka

Proceed as for lemon cordial (above) but use rinds of 2 oranges and ½ lemon.

DRY LEMON OR ORANGE CORDIAL
cytrynówka lub pomarańczówka wytrawna

Proceed as for lemon or orange cordial (above), but reduce amount of sugar to ¼ c.

LEMON OR ORANGE CORDIAL THE EASY WAY
cytrynówka lub pomarańczówka najłatwiejsza

As always, when using the rinds of fresh citrus fruits, scrub well and scald to remove chemical preservatives. To 1 qt. 100-proof vodka add colored outer rind (minus white inner rind) of ½ orange or lemon or a combination of both. Add 2–3 t. sugar, seal, and shake vigorously to dissolve sugar. Set aside for 4 days, shaking occasionally. Pour into another bottle through cotton-filled funnel.

DARK BEER CORDIAL
porterówka

To do justice to this delightful old cordial, a true, heavy, dark porter like Guinness Stout should be used, but thinner dark beers like Bock are also acceptable. In pot combine 3 c.

dark beer and anywhere from 2 t.–2 T. sugar, depending on sweetness or dryness desired. Heat to just below boiling point, stirring to dissolve sugar, remove from heat, and switch off flame. Pour in 3 c. spirits in thin stream, stirring as you pour. Transfer mixture to bottles, seal, and let stand about 4 days. Filter through cotton into bottles, seal, and age several months before serving.

HOMEMADE BRANDY
"koniak" domowy

In jar combine ½ c. raisins, 2–3 prunes, ¼-inch piece vanilla pod, 1-inch piece orange rind (minus white inner skin), and 1–2 green oak leaves or several oak-wood shavings. Drench with 1 c. spirits and 3 c. 100-proof vodka, seal, and keep at room temp. about 30 days, shaking every few days. Strain mixture, add 1 c. inexpensive French brandy, and 1 c. cold, pre-boiled water, filter through cotton into bottles, seal, and store in cool, dark place. It improves with age and is best after a year or more, but it can also be served after 3–4 months.

OLD POLISH BRANDY
starka

In dry skillet brown 2 slices rye bread cut into cubes. Place browned bread into jar and cover with 4 c. spirits. Seal and let stand 30 days. Strain through cotton-filled funnel into another jar containing several oak-wood shavings, seal, and store several months or up to a year. Combine with equal amount cold pre-boiled water. Strain through cotton into bottles, seal, and store several months or more, as it improves with age. *Note*: Adding 1–2 t. simple syrup will mellow the flavor.

BLACK-BREAD CORDIAL
chlebówka

Cut ½ lb. black bread (razowiec) into cubes and dry on baking sheet in warm oven until brittle. Place in jar, add 1 c. spirits, and 3 c. 100-proof vodka (or simply 4 c. vodka and no spirits), seal, and keep in warm (75°–80°) place 3–4 days. Pour through cotton-filled funnel into bottles and seal. Ready to serve immediately, although like most cordials, its flavor will mellow after several days or—better yet—weeks.

LIQUEURS
likiery

Cordials and flavored vodkas differ from liqueurs mainly in sugar content. As a result, the drier cordials are often served during meals, whereas liqueurs usually accompany the coffee and dessert. They are also a nice treat when someone drops in for coffee. Most of the cordials have a liqueur counterpart, so we will mainly present those that are unique.

COFFEE LIQUEUR
likier kawowy

Grind ½ c. dark-roasted coffee beans powder fine, place in jar, and cover with 2 c. spirits. Seal and let stand 1 week. Dissolve 3½ c. sugar in 3–4 c. boiling water and bring to boil. Switch off heat and pour coffee-spirit mixture into hot syrup in thin stream, mixing all the while. Filter mixture through cotton into bottles. Your coffee liqueur is ready to enjoy when it cools to room temp.

RATAFIA/MULTI-FRUIT LIQUEUR
ratafia/likier wieloowocowy

This is usually prepared over the summer months and even on into autumn as various fruits come into season. All fruits should be trimmed of leaves, stems, etc., washed and drained before using. When strawberries become abundant (around June in temperate climates), place 1 c. in large jar, cover with 1½ c. sugar, seal, and keep at room temp. Add 1 c. raspberries when they come into season plus 1½ c. sugar. Proceed the same way, adding cherries, currants etc. as they become cheap and plentiful. In August, you can add Hungarian plums. If you want to add mountain ash berries around October, use only ½ c., place overnight in freezer, then scald with boiling water and drain well before adding. Also top them with 1½ c. sugar. Shake jar occasionally. Sugar dissolves best when jar is kept on window ledge in direct sunlight, but this destroys Vitamin C. When sugar has dissolved, pour syrup into bottles, seal, and keep in cool, dark place or refrigerate. Cover fruit left in jar with spirits, seal, and let stand 1 week. Pour liquid off through cotton. Place leftover fruit in large sieve lined with several thicknesses of cheesecloth and squeeze out as much liquid as possible. Combine spirit mixture with equal amount of fruit syrup and pour into bottles through funnel. Seal and store in dark, cool cellar about 4 months. *Note*: Since you may end up with more syrup than spirit mixture, use the former to flavor vodka.

PEAR LIQUEUR
likier gruszkowy

Wash 2 lbs. pears, drain, dice, and mash—skin, core, and all—and place in jar. Cover with 4 c. spirits, seal, and keep at room temp. 6–8 weeks, shaking occasionally. Pour off spirit extract into bottles, seal, and set aside. Add 2 c. boiling water to pears left in jar, stir, and strain into pot through cheesecloth-lined sieve, pressing down to extract as much moisture as possible. Discard leftover pears. To pear liquid in pot add 4 c. sugar and ½ vanilla pod and simmer, stirring, until sugar dissolves. Remove from heat, switch off stove, and into mixture pour the spirit extract. Mix well and pour into bottles through cotton-filled funnel. Seal and set aside. When sediment settles to bottom and liqueur is completely clear, filter once again through cotton into another bottle.

APPLE LIQUEUR
likier jabłkowy

Proceed as above, but use apples instead of pears.

RASPBERRY LIQUEUR
likier malinowy

Fill qt. jar ¾ full with washed, trimmed, drained raspberries. Add spirits to cover them by ½ inch, seal, and set aside for 24 hrs. Pour off spirits. Fill another clean jar ¾ full with more fresh raspberries and drench with raspberry-flavored spirits, i.e. those poured off from the first batch. Seal and let stand at room temp. 24 hrs. Pour raspberry extract into bottle, seal, and set aside. Dissolve 2 c. sugar in 1½ c. boiling water. Remove from heat, switch off flame, and mix spirit extract with hot syrup. Filter through cotton into bottle, seal, and store 3 months before serving.

PEACH OR APRICOT LIQUEUR
likier brzoskwiniowy lub morelowy

Wash, dry, dice, and mash 4 lbs. peaches or apricots and place in large jar. Add 2–4 crushed pits, cover with 1 qt. spirits, seal, and let stand at room temp. 10 days. Pour spirits off through cotton-filled funnel into bottle, seal, and set aside. To fruit add a piece of cinnamon bark and 2 c. boiling water, seal, and let stand 4 days. Strain mixture through cheesecloth-lined sieve into pot, pressing down to extract all moisture. Discard fruit. To pot add 3–4 c. sugar and heat until it dissolves. Bring to boil, remove from heat, and switch off stove. Add spirit-fruit extract to hot syrup, stir well, and pour into bottles through cotton-filled funnel. Seal and let stand until sediment settles to bottom and liqueur becomes clear. Filter through cotton once again into another bottle, seal, and store several months before serving.

EGG LIQUEUR/EGG BRANDY
jajokoniak/ajerkoniak/likier jajeczny/likier żółtkowy

In heavy pot bring 1½ c. milk to boil, stirring frequently with wooden spoon so it doesn't scorch. Set aside to cool to room temp. Beat 5 egg yolks and 1 c. powdered sugar until fluffy and stir into cooled milk with whisk until mixture is smooth. Stir in ½–1 t. vanilla extract and pour mixture into bottle large enough to accommodate 2 more c. liquid. Add 1 c. French brandy and 1 c. spirits, seal, and shake vigorously to blend ingredients. Refrigerate 4 days. Serve ice-cold and shake vigorously before pouring into liqueur glasses, because ingredients have a tendency to separate. A nice accompaniment to black coffee.

CHOCOLATE-EGG LIQUEUR
likier jajeczno-kakaowy

Prepare as in preceding recipe but add 3 T. cocoa to powdered sugar when beating with egg yolks. *Note*: Even the cholesterol-wary need not worry about either of the above liqueurs, because each 1-oz. serving contains only about ⅛ of a yolk.

VODKA-BASED CORDIALS & LIQUEURS
nalewki i likiery na wódce

In many parts of the U.S., legally obtaining 190-proof grain neutral spirits or grain alcohol, which we have referred to only as spirits, is a problem. Vodka, which is nothing more than grain alcohol diluted with an equal part of water, may be used instead, but the quantity should be doubled. Use 100-proof vodka or stronger if available. (We have seen 102- and 104-proof vodka on sale in some areas.) The results will not always be as good, but they should be acceptable. Even strong vodkas are not potent enough to release all the flavor of various ingredients, including citrus-fruit rinds, unripe walnuts, and certain herbs. Since you have to use twice as much vodka as spirits, the flavoring ingredients will be less pronounced. If you use the same amount of vodka as spirits, then your finished product will be very weak.

Still, as the Poles say, *"Na bezrybiu i rak ryba!"* (In a fishless place, even a crayfish passes for a fish.) If you have no access to spirits, then vodka will have to do. Incidentally, a few of the recipes above expressly stipulate vodka rather than grain alcohol, so that's a good place to start.

VARIOUS QUICK & EASY LIQUEURS
różne łatwe likiery

We began this chapter with a few easy cordials, so we will end it with a few tips on preparing short-cut liqueurs. The simplest way is to combine 2 c. fruit syrup of choice with 3 c. 100-proof vodka this will produce a 60-proof liqueur. You will get a weaker 57-proof liqueur by combining 3 c. syrup with 4 c. vodka. These can then be flavored with several drops of any extracts or aromatic oils you like such as vanilla, almond, rum, lemon, orange, etc., enabling you to come up with an endless variety of liqueurs. In fact, if you prepare a cordial or liqueur the traditional way but happen to lack one of the ingredients, you can replace the almonds, lemon rind, or whatever with the appropriate extract.

HOME-CANNING, PICKLING, & PRESERVING

Since time immemorial people have preserved food in one way or another. At first it was a question of sheer survival, especially in northern climates, where plant life and many game species went into deep hibernation during the long, winter months. Only those who had planned ahead and stockpiled dried meat and berries had any chance of making it.

Later on, economics entered the picture. Various foods were sold at medieval market stalls and by roving peddlers, but not everyone could afford them. The less affluent lived largely off the land on wild berries, mushrooms, fish, and game and preserved what they couldn't use—mainly by drying and salting—for the lean period ahead.

Today food preservation at home is a question of both economics and culture. Most produce is quite inexpensive when in season, but prices begin to climb at times of the year when it has to be trucked a great distance or raised in hothouses. In addition to providing your family with a variety of fruits, vegetables, and mushrooms, home-canning also can mean having on hand products that are not readily available at any price. And then, there is always the added sense of satisfaction of treating family and friends to jams, pickles, and relishes that you made yourself.

Home-canning remains a popular pastime in Poland, and even big-city families frequently put up some jars of brine-cured dill pickles, spiced plums, or marinated mushrooms. Naturally, more produce is home-processed in small towns and rural areas where many people have large vegetable patches as well as numerous berry bushes and fruit trees.

In many parts of the U.S. and Canada, fresh dill is hard to come by even in summer. You can enjoy the bright flavor accent of Poland's most popular herb by freezing or salting it. Also, genuine Polish dill pickles, naturally brine-cured without a drop of vinegar, are surprisingly easy to prepare in a large jar on a kitchen counter. There is little more to do than drench cucumbers with brine. The cucumbers do the rest on their own.

If your backyard plum tree produces a bumper crop some year, that may be the time to put up some jars of *powidła*, that thick, dark, almost paste-like jam that is so widely used in Polish cookery. Easy to make, it requires no water-bath processing (pasteurization); neither do other brine-cured, sour-cured, or salted goods as well as products preserved by sugar or strong marinades. Sugar-steeped fruit syrups are a good example. Simply combine cherries or berries with sugar in a jar and let them stand in a kitchen corner until you get a pure, vitamin-rich syrup. It can be used as a dessert topping and to flavor tea, vodka, or soda water. It's also good over pancakes, whether they be American-style flapjacks or Polish *racuszki* (sour-milk pancakes).

Many other products do require pasteurization to prevent spoilage, but that may not be as complicated as it sounds. If you already own fancy pressure-canning equipment and a wide array of special canning jars, by all means use them. If you don't, no problem. In recent years Polish homemakers have found that ordinary twist-off jars—the kind that you get store-bought pickles, relishes, and jams in—work just as well. Any large kettle can be used for pasteurization following a few pointers.

The bottom of the kettle should be lined with several thicknesses of dish towel (in the olden days Polish cooks used straw for this purpose), to insulate the jars against the direct heat. Jars should be placed in water of the same temperature. Cold jars should be placed in cold water and warmer ones in water of higher temperature, so they don't crack. During processing, jars should not touch each other nor the sides of the kettle, and another dish towel can be used to separate them. In many cases, lids are only lightly screwed on during water-bath processing and tightened after jars are removed from kettle.

It is very important that jars be air tight, since it is air-borne bacteria that cause products to go bad. An easy way to check is to stand jars, after removing from water-bath, on their lids to check for leaks. Any leaking lid must be replaced with a new one that has been scalded and dried. Even jars that don't leak should be additionally tightened before storing. Home-canned goods store best in cool cellar or other cool, dark, dry place, and 40°–45° is the ideal storing temperature. It should not exceed 50° nor fall below 35° for any length of time.

One parting thought: ideal cleanliness must be maintained during all stages of food-processing. Spoons, pans, and other utensils, as well as jars and lids, should be sterilized by scalding with boiling water. They can also be sterilized in a hot oven. The home-canner's hands should be frequently scrubbed in hot, soapy water.

The whole thing may sound rather complicated to the novice, but with a little practice it'll soon become second nature. We're sure that you will find in this chapter recipes that suit your taste and dietary requirements to a tee, whether your preferences run to the sweet or savory, the tart or tangy.

* * *

THICK, COOKED-DOWN, LOW-SUGAR JAMS/"POWIDŁA"
powidła

Powidła is a thick fruit spread or filling which requires very little or no sugar and is obtained by gently cooking down fruit into a smooth uniform paste without straining. Plum powidła is the classic representative of this group, although cherries can also be used. Plum powidła is widely used in Polish cuisine and not only for spreading on bread. It is used to flavor bigos and various sauces, as a glaze for pork and water fowl, and in pastries and desserts. By spooning some over hot rice or noodles you will have a quick light meal or hot dessert. There is even a soup, powidlanka, make from thick plum jam. If you ever have access to ripe plums, we strongly urge you to try making powidła. It is one thing no Polish cook should ever be without, and the homemade variety is much better that what comes from a store. *Note*: Powidła is not a true jam because it is cooked down to a state in which no particles of fruit remain visible; neither is it the typical English fruit butter which is usually strained; this accounts for the rather unwieldy English translation in the above heading.

THICK PLUM JAM/POLISH PLUM BUTTER (IN INSTALLMENTS)
powidła śliwkowe (na raty)

Wash, drain, pit, and halve 4 lbs. ripe Italian (węgierki) or damson plums. Place in wide stainless-steel or enameled pan and simmer on low heat. As mixture thickens, stir ever more frequently with wooden spoon. When quite a bit of the moisture has evaporated but mixture is still runny, switch off heat and let stand uncovered until cooled to room temp. or overnight. Continue simmering on low heat, stirring occasionally, until mixture cooks down to just over half of the original bulk. Add 1–2 c. sugar, stir well, and let stand until cooled to room temp. First add 1 c. sugar and when it dissolves, taste mixture to see if more sugar is needed. This will depend entirely on the sweetness of your plums. Before cooking mixture again, wash, and rinse jars, and place upside down on dish towel to dry. Simmer the powidła until they get thick, stirring frequently. It is thick enough when bubbles begin erupting at surface and a spoonful of jam drops back into pot in a single blob. Another rule of thumb for sufficient thickness is when the spoon leaves a trace on the surface. Pack hot mixture into jars and seal. When cooled to room temp., store in cool pantry. *Note*: Although good powidła takes many hrs. to cook, this is done in installments which can be adjusted to your schedule; you can start it in the evening, leave it out overnight, then simmer it in the morning while preparing to go to work, leave it out to cool and finish it up when you get back; it can also be simmered only once a day for 3 or more days in a row.

THICK PLUM JAM ANOTHER WAY
powidła śliwkowe inaczej

Although the traditional method (above) gives the best results, powidła can also be made in a single uninterrupted process. Wash, drain, pit, and halve 4 lbs. ripe Italian or damson plums, place in wide pot, and simmer on low heat. As mixture thickens, stir with wooden spoon with increasing frequency so it does not burn. As it simmers, you can attend to other kitchen chores. When mixture cooks down to just over half of its original level, add 1–2 c.

sugar. Taste powidła after adding 1st c. sugar, and add the rest only if you don't find it sweet enough. After sugar is added, mixture temporarily becomes thinner. Continue simmering until mixture is as thick as or thicker than it was before sugar was added. Use the methods in first recipe to test for proper thickness. Pack into washed, scalded, dry jars, seal, cool to room temp., and store in cool pantry or cellar. *Note*: Although this method is accomplished in a single day, it requires more actual cooking time than the first one in which some evaporation occurs during cooling periods.

SUGARLESS THICK PLUM JAM
powidła śliwkowe bez cukru

For this recipe, you will need very ripe Italian plums (4 lbs.) which already show signs of wrinkling around the stem. Wash, drain, pit, and halve and simmer as above—either in installments or uninterrupted—until nice and thick. Pack into jars, seal, cool to room temp., and store in cool, dark place. *Note*: By sugarless we mean that no ordinary sugar (sucrose) is added; in reality this jam contains plenty of natural fruit sugars, fructose and glucose, which are far healthier than cane or beet sugar.

SELF-MAKING POWIDŁA (OVEN METHOD)
powidła samosmażące się (w piekarniku)

Wash and drain well 5 lbs. very ripe Italian plums. When dry, halve and discard pits. Place in low, wide pan, pressing plums down to extract some of their juice. Place uncovered in pre-heated 250° oven and let them simmer several hrs. When plums get soft, stir, reduce temp. slightly, and let them gently simmer 12 hrs. or longer. Stir every so often. (*Note*: It's best to start in the morning; at night, after switching off heat, leave mixture in oven overnight with oven door ajar.) Next day, simmer on stove top until cooked down to ⅓ of original bulk. Add 1½ c. sugar (optional) and continue heating and stirring until mixture thickens to pre-sugar consistency (3–4 min.). Pack into dry, sterilized jars as above. *Note*: This nearly fool-proof method is great for beginners because it does not require constant stirring and attendance; many experienced Polish cooks also like it because it allows them to perform other chores and, above all, produces an excellent powidła.

THICK CHERRY JAM/POLISH CHERRY BUTTER
powidła wiśniowe

Wash, drain, and pit 4 lbs. sour cherries. Place in wide pot and simmer on low heat, stirring as they begin to thicken. Add about 2 c. sugar and continue simmering and stirring until nice and thick, using the rule of thumb provided in 1st thick plum jam recipe. Pack into ½-pt. or smaller jars, seal, cool to room temp., and store in cool cellar.

POLISH MARMALADES/FRUIT BUTTERS
marmolady

Rather than the diced citrus rinds in a jelly-like suspension that English-speakers think of when "marmalade" is mentioned, Polish "marmolada" is a kind of fruit butter or strained jam that usually, but not always, contains apples. This is a good way to use up windfalls, from which bruised or wormy portions should be trimmed. The fruit is cooked using very little water until it disintegrates, then it is sieved and cooked with sugar until it thickens. Frequent stirring is necessary to prevent scorching. After sugar is added usually only 15 min. of cooking is needed, and the entire process takes only about 1 hr. There are 2 basic types of marmolada: soft, which spreads easily, and hard, which can be sliced with a knife and is often used in pastries. The latter requires longer simmering. To test for doneness, place a drop of hot marmalade on a dry dish. Soft marmalade is thick enough when it stays put and is soft and sticky to the touch. A drop of hard marmalade can be removed from dish with knife and should feel springy between fingers. Also, the mark made by a spoon in pot of hot hard marmalade remains visible for a while. High-pectin fruits such as apples, gooseberries, black currants and quinces make the best Polish marmalades. It can be made from almost any fruit, but apples or other high-pectin fruits should account for at least ⅓ thereof. Soft marmalades are packed into jars when hot and sealed immediately. When cool, store in cold cellar or fridge. Hot hard marmalade should be packed into square or rectangular glass containers with lids (the kind leftovers are often refrigerated in). When it cools, store in fridge. Since hard marmalade is meant to be sliced, it would be difficult to remove from an ordinary jar.

APPLE MARMALADE
marmolada z jabłek

Wash 4 lbs. apples and drain. If using windfalls, trim away bruised or wormy portions. Cut apples into quarters, skin, core, and all. Place in pot, add 1½–2 c. water and cook covered about 20 min. or until they disintegrate, stirring occasionally. Strain through sieve. Cook strained mixture over very low heat, preferably over insulating pad, and heat to boil, stirring frequently. Add 2½ lbs. sugar about 10 min. after mixture boils and continue simmering and stirring until proper thickness is achieved (see above entry).

PEAR MARMALADE
marmolada z gruszek

Wash and drain 4 lbs. pears, trimming off any damaged portions. Cut pears into quarters, skin, core, and all, place in pot, add 1–2 c. water, and cook under cover until they fall apart (20–30 min.), stirring occasionally. Sieve into wide pot and heat over very low flame on insulated pad, stirring frequently, until pureé cooks down to half of its original bulk. Add 1½–2 lbs. sugar and continue simmering until proper thickness is obtained.

BLACK-CURRANT MARMALADE
marmolada z czarnych porzeczek

Wash and drain 4 lbs. black currants (trimmed of stems), puree in blender, and sieve. Transfer mixture to wide pot and heat on low through pad until it starts to boil. Simmer 10 min. longer, stirring frequently. Add 2 lbs. sugar and continue simmering and stirring until the right consistency is achieved.

MIXED FRUIT MARMALADE
marmolada z owoców mieszanych

Marmalades can be prepared from two or more different fruits, but high-pectin apples should constitute one of them. Individual fruits should be cooked separately with only a little water until they disintegrate and then they are sieved. Then the sieved mixtures are combined in a single pot. Simmer on low heat about 20 min., add sugar, and continue simmering until proper consistency is achieved. The following chart shows the recommended proportion of apple puree to those made with other fruits. This is where a kitchen scale will come in handy.

apple puree 1 lb.	plum puree 2 lbs.	sugar 2 lbs.
apple puree 1–½ lbs.	strawberry puree 2 lbs.	sugar 2 lbs.
apple puree 2 lbs.	peach puree 2 lbs.	sugar 2 lbs.
apple puree 1 lb.	cherry puree 2 lbs.	sugar 1½ lbs.
apple puree 1 lb.	apricot puree 2 lbs.	sugar 1½ lbs.
apple puree 2 lbs.	raspberry puree 2 lbs.	sugar 1½ lbs.

A 3-fruit marmalade can be made using 2 lbs. apple puree, 3 lbs. currant puree, 1 lb. cherry puree and 3–4 lbs. sugar.

JAMS
dżemy

Jams are of Anglo-Saxon origin, as indicated by the Polish term for this product: "dżem". Being rather easy to prepare, they have become naturalized citizens in the Polish pantry alongside the more traditional powidła, marmolady, and konfitury (preserves). Jams are cooked in wide, preferably enameled pots, and high-pectin fruits are best. Fruits that contain little natural pectine (strawberries, raspberries) should be combined with high-pectin ones like apples, currants, mountain-ash berries, or quinces. The washed, drained, and pitted (in case of fruits containing pits) fruit should be placed in pot and covered with sugar. Ordinarily, the sugar accounts for 60%–70% of the fruit's weight. It is best to prepare jam in batches not exceeding 5 lbs. of fruit, in which case about 3 lbs. of sugar is needed. Larger quantities require longer cooking time, during which more vitamins are destroyed and the flavor and aroma are impaired. The sugared fruit can be cooked uninterrupted for about 30 min., or in 3 installments of 10 min. each. After each installment, they are allowed to cool to room temp. During cooking foam should be skimmed from top of mixture. Jam is ready when the particles of fruit are glossy and the syrup has the right consistency. A drop of syrup should stay put when dropped on a dinner plate and not spill into a little puddle. The jam's temp. should be 223°–225°. The hot jam should be transferred to pre-scalded, dry jars and sealed with pre-scalded dry lids. Store in cool, dark place.

GOOSEBERRY-RASPBERRY JAM
dżem agrestowo-malinowy

Wash and drain well 1 lb. gooseberries and ½ lb. raspberries. Place in pot, cover with 1 lb. sugar and let stand 1 hr. Cook gently about 30 min., in single stretch or in 3 10-min. installments, stirring frequently and skimming off any foam that forms on top. Pack into pre-scalded dry jars and seal immediately.

CHERRY JAM
dżem czereśniowy

Wash, drain, and pit 2 lbs. sweet black cherries, place in pot, add 2 lbs. sugar, and cook about 20 min. or until cherries become glossy. Meanwhile, in another pot place 1½ lbs. washed, drained white or red currants and cook about 10 min. Sieve currants into cherries, bring mixture to boil, and simmer gently another 10 min., stirring frequently and skimming off foam. Pack into jars and seal immediately.

GRAPE-APPLE JAM
dżem winogronowo-jabłkowy

Separate 2 lbs. red or purple grapes from cluster, wash, drain, and place in pot. Crush slightly and bring to boil. Add ¼ t. citric acid so grapes don't lose their nice color. Sieve grapes into another pot and heat until reduced by ¼. Add 1½ lbs. sugar, bring to boil, and skim off foam. Peel and coarsely grate 1½ lbs. tart cooking apples, add to grapes, and cook until jam thickens and apple particles become glossy and transparent. Pack hot jam into dry, pre-scalded jars and seal at once.

CRANBERRY-PUMPKIN JAM
dżem żurawinowo-dyniowy

Wash and drain 1½ lbs. cranberries, place in pot, add 1½ lbs. sugar and heat gently to a boil. Add 1½ lbs. coarsely grated pumpkin rind (with skin and pulpy portions removed). Cook until jam thickens and pumpkin particles become nice and glossy. Stir frequently and remove foam from top the whole time. Pack into jars and seal as always.

ROSE-HIP JAM
dżem z dzikiej róży

Wash and drain 2 lbs. rose hips. (*Note*: These are best after the season's first good frost!) Place in pot with about 2 c. water, bring to gentle boil, and simmer until tender. Sieve into another pot. Add 2 lbs. sugar and simmer until nice and thick, stirring frequently and skimming off any foam from top. Pack into jars and seal. *Note*: Rose-hip jam is often used to fill pączki (doughnuts).

LOW-SUGAR JAMS
dżemy niskocukrowe

Use one fifth as much sugar as fruit by weight, i.e. for 5 lbs. fruit use 1 lb. sugar. These jams do not contain enough sugar to act as a natural preservative, hence they must be pasteurized to prevent spoilage.

LOW-SUGAR BLACK-CURRANT JAM
dżem z czarnej porzeczki niskocukrowy

Wash and drain 2½ lbs. black currants and place in pot. Add ½ lb. sugar, bring to gentle boil, and simmer about 20 min. Pack into sterilized, dry jars, cover with lids but do not tighten them. Pasteurized 15 min. at 195°. (*Note:* Water into which jars are placed should be fairly hot, otherwise jars may crack.) After pasteurizing, tighten lids. Leave jars in water bath until water cools to room temp., then remove, dry jars, and store.

LOW-SUGAR GOOSEBERRY JAM
dżem agrestowy niskocukrowy

Prepare like black-currant jam above, but use 2½ lbs. ripe gooseberries.

LOW-SUGAR STRAWBERRY-CURRANT JAM
dżem truskawkowo-porzeczkowy niskocukrowy

Wash, hull, and drain 2½ lbs. strawberries. Place in pot together with 1½ c. red-currant juice (obtained by cooking and sieving red currants with several T. water) and ½ lb. sugar. Cook gently to boiling point, stirring and skimming as always, then simmer another 20 min. Pack into jars, cover with lids, and pasteurize 20 min. at 200°.

LINGONBERRY JAM/SAUCE (RELISH FOR MEAT)
borówki (do mięsa)

Clean, wash, and drain 6 lbs. lingonberries (mountain cranberries), scald with boiling water, and drain again. Place in large, wide pot, add 4 lbs. sugar, and cook on high flame about 20 min. Add 2 lbs. peeled, diced pears, mix well and simmer another 20 min. until mixture boils. Stir and skim the whole time. Pack into pre-scalded dry jars and seal. *Note*: This is a traditional Polish relish served with meat and fowl. *Variation*: 2 lbs. apples or 1 lb. apples and 1 lb. pears may be used instead of 2 lbs. pears.

CRANBERRY JAM/SAUCE (RELISH FOR MEAT)
żurawiny (do mięsa)

Wash and drain 6 lbs. cranberries. In blender purée ⅓ of the berries and sieve into pot. Add 3–4 lbs. sugar and bring mixture to boil. Add remaining cranberries and simmer on low heat about 10 min. Add 2 lbs. peeled, cored, and diced firm pears and simmer, stirring and skimming, until fruit becomes glossy and falls to bottom of pot and syrup is nice and thick. Pack hot mixture into jars and seal immediately. *Note*: Pears may be omitted, but the dish won't be as good because they give the sauce a nice aroma and mellow flavor.

APPLE-CAKE FILLING
jabłka na szarlotkę

You can conveniently whip up szarlotka and other cakes requiring apple filling if you put up some jars of these stewed apples in the autumn when apples are plentiful and inexpensive. Wash, peel, and core 5 lbs. tart cooking apples and dice. In large, wide pot pour 1 c. water, add the apples and cook, stirring frequently, about 10 min. Add about 2 lbs. sugar and continue simmering, stirring, and skimming, 10–15 min. Transfer to dry, sterilized jars and seal immediately.

PRESERVES
konfitury

The best Polish preserves contain whole, glossy cherries or berries in a fairly thick syrup. We like cherry preserves the best, but other varieties are also very good if properly made. They have a wide range of uses in Polish cuisine. Some eat them from a little dish like a dessert, washing it down with hot tea; others prefer to add it to their tea instead of sugar. They make a nice topping for ice cream, kisiel, and pudding. The well-drained fruit are often used to decorate cakes and desserts. Preserves rank among the "nobility" of fruit products and require fruit of the highest quality that is very fresh, unbruised, ripe but not overripe. While they cook, preserves should not be stirred, because care must be taken to leave fruit intact. Instead, the pot should be shaken in a circular motion from time to time to ensure that the fruit floating up to top is constantly immersed in syrup. Foam should be skimmed off as it forms. Preserves are ready when fruit is glossy and evenly distributed throughout syrup. The boiling point of completed preserves is 223°.

CHERRY PRESERVES
konfitury z wiśni

Wash, drain, and pit 4½ lbs. large, dark, sour cherries which should weigh in at about 4 lbs. after pitting. Place in wide pot and add 4 lbs. sugar, cover, and let stand overnight at room temp. Next day, heat gently to boil, removing pot from heat and shaking it in circular motion 2–3 times before boiling point is achieved. Remove boiling preserves from heat and set aside to cool to room temp. To cold mixture add 1½ lbs. more sugar, place on low heat, gently bring to boil and simmer several min. Cooking is completed when foam comes together at center of pot, rather than forming round its sides; also when a spoonful of syrup falls back into pot in a thick stream and a drop of syrup dropped on plate sets rather than spill. Remove scum and let preserves cool uncovered to 90°. Transfer to jars, seal, and store in cool, dark cellar.

The step-by-step preparation of gooseberry preserves is shown in the following series of illustrations: A) Stems and blossom ends are removed; B) Trimmed gooseberries are placed in acidulated cold water, so they don't discolor while the remainder are being hulled; then they are drained; C) Berries are punctured all over with sharp toothpick or pin; a cork imbedded with needles makes the job quicker; D) A large pot of water is brought to boil and sugar is added to make a syrup;

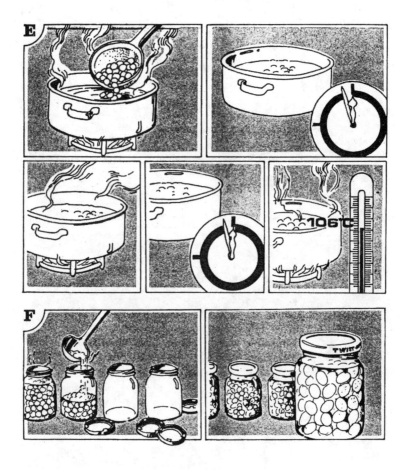

E) Gooseberries are added to syrup which is brought to boil, heat is switched off, and mixture is allowed to stand overnight; next day the process is repeated and cooking ends when mixture reaches a temperature of 222° (106° C); F) Hot preserves are packed into hot, sterilized jars and sealed immediately; they are transferred to cool, dark cellar when they cool to room temperature. *Note:* As indicated in recipe, gooseberries may be seeded or halved according to preference.

CHERRY PRESERVES (SYRUP METHOD) THE TRADITIONAL WAY
konfitury z wiśni (na syropie) tradycyjne

This is the traditional way of preparing preserves. Its main advantage is that the cherries remain almost perfectly round, whereas in the above method they tend to lose their shape. The disadvantage is that it produces what we consider too much syrup. However, those who use preserves frequently as a dessert topping may not consider this a drawback. Wash, drain, and pit 4½ lbs. dark sour cherries. Dissolve just under 4½ lbs., sugar in 2 c. hot water and bring to boil while stirring. Add cherries to boiling syrup, bring to boil, reduce heat, and simmer on low about 30 min. Do not stir while they simmer, but shake pot in circular motion several times and remove scum with slotted spoon. Let mixture stand uncovered in cool place overnight. Next day, cook on low heat, shaking pot occasionally and skimming off any scum. It is cooked when cherries are glossy and transluscent. Pour into jars, seal tightly, and store in cool, dark place.

CHERRY PRESERVES (INSTALLMENT METHOD)
konfitury z wiśni (na raty)

Wash and drain 4½ lbs. cherries as above, place in pot, and let stand 1 hr. Pour off juice that forms. You should get about 2 c. If less is obtained, add enough water to get 2 c. liquid. Pour juice into wide pot, heat, and gradually add 4 lbs. sugar, stirring until dissolved, bring to boil, remove scum, and set aside to cool. To room-temp. syrup add cherries and bring gently to boil, shaking pot 2–3 times in the meantime. Set aside to cool once again, then bring to boil, simmer 3–4 min. and cool. Add 1–1½ lbs. sugar and again gradually bring to boil. Simmer several min. until cherries become glossy and syrup thickens. Skim off foam, cool to 90°, and transfer to jars. Seal immediately. *Note*: Compared with the traditional sugar-syrup method (preceding recipe), this method produces a fruitier syrup and requires less cooking time.

CHERRY SYRUP BY-PRODUCT
sok wiśniowy jako produkt uboczny

This dual-purpose method produces fruitier preserves plus a bonus of high-quality cherry syrup thrown into the bargain. Prepare preserves as in preceding recipe, but after second simmering pour off about ½ the syrup into small, dry, sterilized bottles with twist-off caps. Seal and store. After mixture left in pot cools to room temp., add 1 lb. sugar and continue simmering as above until proper consistency is achieved. Pack, seal, and store as above.

GOOSEBERRY PRESERVES
konfitury z agrestu

Remove stems from 4 lbs. large, green, slightly underripe gooseberries wash and drain well. Gooseberries may be used seeded or with seeds left in. To seed, make slit down side and remove seeds. The berries may also be halved and seeded. If using whole gooseberries, prick each in several places with sharp toothpick to prevent bursting. Place gooseberries in bowl. Dissolve 3 T. citric acid crystals in 1 c. warm water, combine with 7 c. cold water, and pour liquid over gooseberries. (This will prevent them from discoloring). Place in fridge for 3 hrs. In wide pot prepare syrup from 2 c. water and 3 lbs. sugar, bring to boil, remove foam, and set aside to cool slightly. Add gooseberries and let stand until pot cools to room temp., shaking it several times. Strain, add ½ lb. sugar to cool syrup, bring to boil, and pour over berries. Allow to cool slightly, then place pot containing gooseberries and syrup on burner and bring to boil. Simmer on low heat several min., then set aside to cool. Simmer one last time several min. until gooseberries appear translucent and are suspended in syrup. Pour into dry, pre-scalded jars and seal immediately. It may seem like quite a lot of fuss and bother, but we think it's worth it.

RASPBERRY PRESERVES
konfitury z malin

The word "carefully" appears a number of times in this recipe, because raspberries are the most fragile berries of all and care must be taken not to crush them. Carefully rinse 4 lbs. large, undamaged raspberries. The best way is to line sieve with single layer of berries at a time, dip into water, and drain well. When berries have drained, transfer to wide pan so they aren't layered too high. Separately cook 2 c. water and 4 lbs. sugar into syrup and skim off foam. Carefully pour hot syrup over berries and let cool to room temp. Carefully pour off syrup into pot, add 1 lb. sugar, bring to boil, and pour over raspberries. Let cool to room temp. Repeat this process as many times as needed until berries are suspended in clear syrup. Transfer hot mixture to dry, sterilized jars and seal at once. *Note*: Although this method is a bit involved and time-consuming, its advantage is that the fruit retains the flavor and most of the vitamins of fresh raspberries. The method below is simpler, but involves some loss of quality.

RASPBERRY PRESERVES ANOTHER WAY
konfitury z malin inaczej

Crush and strain through cheesecloth-lined sieve enough washed, drained raspberries to get 2 c. syrup. In pot combine syrup and 2½ lbs. sugar, bring to boil, and remove foam. You should use a very wide pan for this purpose so the raspberries can float in a single layer. To boiling syrup add 2 lbs. raspberries, a little at a time. When all are submerged, set aside to cool to room temp. Bring to boil and let cool again. Repeat 3–4 times, skimming off foam as they cool and shaking pan in circular motion. Transfer hot preserves to dry, sterilized jars and seal at once.

STRAWBERRY PRESERVES
konfitury z truskawek

These can be prepared according to either of the ways given for raspberry preserves (above). Since strawberries are not as fragile as raspberries, you may double the quantity of all the ingredients.

GREEN-WALNUT PRESERVES
konfitury z orzechów włoskich

These rather exotic-sounding preserves are an Old Polish delicacy worth recalling. To prepare it you will need immature, green walnuts, which in a Polish-like climate are ready in July. The walnuts are right if you can easily run a toothpick through the green outer skin and the unformed nut at center. Take 4 lbs. green walnuts and pierce each several times with fork. Place in container and cover with cold water. Let stand 36 hrs. changing water several times. Drain, place in pot, cover with fresh cold water, and cook until tender. Drain. In pot combine 4½ c. water, 5 lbs. sugar, 1 t. cinnamon, and 10 cloves. Bring to boil and skim off foam. Add the walnuts, remove from heat, and let stand 24 hrs. After that time, heat mixture to just below boiling and set aside until cooled to room temp. Repeat this process several times. Preserves are ready when soft, brown walnuts are suspended in thick syrup. Pour while hot into dry, sterilized jars and seal immediately.

CURRANT-RASPBERRY JELLY
galaretka z porzeczek i malin

Jellies are far less popular in Poland than in America and, rather than being used as a spread for bread, they are often eaten as a dessert. We present only two recipes for jelly, but others can be prepared similarly using at least one high-pectin fruit. Rinse and drain 2¼ lbs. red or white currants and 1¼ lbs. raspberries. Place in pot and crush with potato-masher. Add 2 c. water and cook about 5 min. Strain through cheesecloth-lined sieve. If you allow it to strain until dripping stops, you will get a clearer jelly. You will get more juice if you press down on fruit in strainer, but jelly may turn out a bit cloudy, although it will be more fruity in taste. Cook 4 c. syrup about 15–20 min. alone, then add 4 c. sugar and continue simmering, stirring occasionally with wooden spoon and skimming off foam as it forms. Jelly is ready when a drop placed on room-temp. saucer sets at once. Pour hot jelly into small dry, sterilized jars and let stand uncovered until cool. Cut a piece of parchment paper into a circle to fit the jar, moisten it with grain alcohol, place on top of jelly, seal lid, and refrigerate. *Note*: You can use melted paraffin to cover the jelly before sealing instead of alcohol-soaked parchment.

GOOSEBERRY-STRAWBERRY JELLY
galaretka z agrestu i truskawek

Wash, drain, and hull 2¼ lbs. underripe gooseberries and 1¼ lbs. strawberries. Run gooseberries through grinder or pureé in blender. Crush strawberries with potato-masher. Combine pulp in pot, add 3 c. water, and cook about 10 min. Strain through cheesecloth-lined sieve. To 4 c. juice add 3½ c. sugar and cook gently, stirring, skimming until proper consistency is obtained. Test for doneness as above.

FRUIT SYRUPS
soki owocowe

Fruit syrups have many uses in Polish cuisine. Besides being the obvious topping for ice cream, desserts, and pancakes, they are used to sweeten tea, flavor vodka, and make a nice drink when combined with soda water or plain, pre-boiled water. The most popular is the sugar-steeping method, widely encountered both in Poland as well as in Polish neighborhoods in America. Its advantages include its simplicity as well as the delicious finished product which retains nearly all the flavor and nutrients of fresh fruit. Syrups prepared in this way may be stored up to a year in a cool, dark place, and we have syrups on hand that are still delicious after several years. Pasteurization lengthens the shelf life of a syrup but also destroys some of its vitamins. The cooked-syrup method is nutritionally the least advisable, but we have included it just for the record.

FRUIT SYRUPS (SUGAR-STEEPED)
soki owocowe (zasypywane cukrem)

Scrub a gallon-sized glass jar with hot, soapy water, rinse well, scald with boiling water, and turn upside down to dry on dish towel. Syrup can be made with a single or more than one variety of fruit. All fruit should be washed and drained and any stems or leaves should be discarded. Weigh fresh fruit and allow 1 lb. sugar per lb. fruit. Place a 2–3 inch layer of fruit at bottom of jar, press down lightly, and cover with layer of sugar. Add more fruit, press down, cover with sugar, and continue layering until ingredients are used up. Top layer should be sugar. Cover mouth of jar with triple layer of cheesecloth or gauze and fasten it in place with rubber band. Leave in warm place but out of direct sunlight 3–4 months. After that time pour syrup off through funnel into dry, sterilized pt. or qt. bottles, seal, and store in cool, dark cellar. *Note*: Although various fruits may be used, the best syrups are made from sour cherries and berries. The old-timers still place these fruit out to sugar-steep on sun-drenched window ledges, but direct sunlight destroys the syrup's vitamin C and is thus not advisable.

PASTEURIZED FRUIT SYRUPS
soki owocowe pasteryzowane

Prepare as above. When sugar dissolves, pour off syrup through funnel into dry, sterilized bottles, and cover with caps without tightening. Place in pot of cold water on several thicknesses of dish towel and use another towel to keep bottles from touching each other and sides of pot. Water should reach just below level of juice inside bottles. Heat to 185° and keep at that temp. 20 min. for pt. bottles and 30 min. for qt. bottles. Remove bottles from hot-water bath, tighten caps, and stand on dish towel until cooled to room temp. Store in cool, dark place.

COOKED FRUIT SYRUPS
soki owocowe gotowane

Wash, drain, and trim fruit as above, removing pits where applicable. Extract juice from fruit in juicer. Weigh the juice and allow 1 lb. sugar for each lb. juice. Combine juice and sugar in pot and bring to boil, stirring occasionally. Pour hot syrup into dry, sterilized bottles and seal immediately. *Note*: In all syrup recipes twist-off caps must also be pre-scalded to sterilize and dried.

COMPOTES/CANNED FRUIT
kompoty

What the American calls "canned peaches" the Pole refers to as "kompot brzoskwiniowy." Regardless of what it's called, a compote is nothing more than pasteurized fruit in sugar syrup. It can be served as a dessert or, after draining, used in various desserts, or as decoration on cold-meat platters. Poles often turned home-canned fruit into a refreshing after-dinner beverage by combining them with an equal part or more cold, pre-boiled water. All compotes are made roughly the same, and only the proportions of water and sugar vary depending on the moisture content and acidity of different fruits. Fruit meant for compote should be ripe, but not overripe, firm, uncracked, and unblemished. All fruit should be washed and drained and any stems or leaves should be discarded. Certain fruits require special handling:

—apples & pears: peel, halve, scoop out core portion, and blanche, i.e., parboil in 4 c. boiling water containing 1 t. citric acid crystals from 1–3 min., depending on firmness of fruit; apples usually require less blanching and pears slightly more.

—cherries and plums may be used whole with pits left in or halved and pitted.

—peaches and apricots should be halved and pitted.

For each 2 lbs. of fruit, prepare a syrup using the proportions indicated in the chart below, skimming off all foam that forms at top. Place fruit in dry, sterilized pt. jars, leaving 2 inches head space. Add hot syrup which should cover fruit by ½ inch. Cover with lids but do not tighten. Pasteurize as above, taking care to place very warm jars into water baths of similar temp. Gradually heat to 185° and maintain that temp. 20 min. After pasteurizing, remove jars immediately, tighten caps, wipe jars dry, and stand upside down. That prevents fruit from floating up and shows if any jar has a damaged lid causing it to leak. When jars are cool, store right side up in cool, dark place.

Amount of water and sugar per 2 lbs. fruit:

FRUIT	WATER	SUGAR
apples	2⅓ c.	2 c.
apricots	2 c.	2–2½ c.
blueberries	2½ c.	1½–2 c.
cherries, sour, sweet	2 c. 2½ c.	2–2½ c. 1 c.
gooseberries	2½ c.	1½–2 c.
peaches	2 c.	1½–2 c.
pears	3 c.	1–1¼ c.
plums, Italian greengage yellow wild (mirabelki)	2½ c. 3 c. 2½ c.	2–2½ c. 1½–2 c. 2–2½ c.
raspberries	2 c.	1½–2 c.
strawberries	2½ c.	2–2½

PICKLED FRUITS, VEGETABLES & MUSHROOMS
marynaty

A characteristic of Polish-style home entertaining is the abundance of cold roast and smoked meats, pâtés, aspic dishes, etc. which pair up so nicely with various tangy marinated vegetables, spiced fruits, pickled mushrooms, and relishes. As a result, the average home-canner in Poland will nearly always have on hand spiced plums, ćwikła, pickled cucumbers of various types, marinated salads, pickled pumpkin, as well as a few house specialties of his own. Most are preserved in a vinegar-based marinade and require no pasteurization. Since vinegar is not very stomach-friendly, the nutrition-conscious prefer lighter vinegar marinades or those made with citric-acid crystals, but these require pasteurization to prevent spoilage. Below, we present some of both.

SPICED PLUMS
śliwki w occie

Wash and drain 2 lbs. ripe but still firm Italian plums. Leave pits in or remove them by making a slit along the side and easing them out, as you prefer. Puncture each plum in several places with toothpick and place in dry, sterilized pt. jars, leaving 1½ inch head space. In pot combine ½ c. water, 2 c. 6 % distilled (white) vinegar*, 3 c. sugar and a doz. cloves. (Other spices according to preference may include a broken-up piece of cinnamon stick and several grains allspice.) Cover pot, bring to boil and simmer 2–3 min. Pour hot marinade over plums in jars, leaving 1 inch head space, and evenly distribute spices. Seal immediately. When cooled to room temp. store in cool, dark cellar.

LIGHT SPICED PLUMS
śliwki w zalewie niskooctowej

Prepare 2 lbs. plums as above and place in pt. jars. In pot combine 1 c. water, spices as above and 2½ c. sugar and bring to boil under cover. Add ½–⅔ c. vinegar and bring to boil again. Pour hot marinade over plums, evenly distribute spices, and cover with lids without tightening. Pasteurize in hot-water bath 20 min. at 195°.

----

* Unless otherwise indicated, the term "vinegar" in this chapter means 6% distilled (white) vinegar.

SPICED CHERRIES
czereśnie w occie

Wash and drain 2 lbs. sweet black cherries. Stems may be removed or left on. Leaving them on makes for an interesting relish easy to pick up by guests. Place in jars, leaving 1½ inch head space. In pot combine 2 c. vinegar, 3 c. sugar, and several cloves; bring to boil. Pour marinade over cherries, evenly distribute spices, and seal at once. Leave about 1 inch head space.

SPICED CHERRIES WITHOUT VINEGAR
czereśnie marynowane bez octu

Prepare 2 lbs. cherries and place in jars as above. In pot combine 2 c. water, 2½ c. sugar, 2 t. citric-acid crystals, and several cloves. Bring to boil and pour hot marinade over cherries. Cover with lids without tightening and pasteurize in hot-water batch 20 min. at 185°. Tighten lids and, when cool, store in cool, dark place.

SPICED HONEYED APRICOTS
morele marynowane z miodem

Wash, drain, halve, and pit 3 lbs. just barely ripe but still rather firm apricots and place in pt. jars, leaving 1½ inch head space. In pot combine 2 c. water, 2 c. sugar, ½ c. honey, ¾ c. vinegar, several cloves, 2 grains allspice, and a pinch cinnamon. Bring to boil, simmer briefly, and pour hot marinade over apricots, evenly distributing spices. Cover with lids but do not tighten. Pasteurize at 195° 20 min. Tighten lids, allow to cool, then store in cool cellar.

SPICED PEARS
gruszki w occie

Wash, drain, and peel 4 lbs. firm pears, cut in half and scoop out core portions. Dissolve 1 T. citric-acid crystals in 1 c. warm water, combine with 7 c. cold water, and place pear halves in solution to prevent their discoloration as you peel and trim the rest. In pot combine 2 c. water, 3 c. vinegar, 5 c. sugar, and 1 t. cloves. Bring to boil and simmer covered briefly. Drain pears and transfer to marinade. Simmer in marinade 30–40 min. or until pears become translucent. Place pears in pt. jars and cover with hot marinade, leaving one inch head space. Seal at once, allow to cool, then transfer to cool, dark place.

PREPARED HORSERADISH
chrzan tarty

Scrub a roughly 1-lb. horseradish root with brush under cold running water. The best roots are those freshly dug up. If the root seems somewhat dry, soak it in cold water several hrs. Peel the root and grate fine. (*Note*: This task is generally performed near an open window or even outdoors because the fumes can be overpowering.) Another way of preparing horseradish is to cut root into cubes and run through meat grinder directly into a plastic bag fastened to the grinder's opening with a rubber band. In pot combine ¾ c. water, ¾ c. vinegar (or 1 T. citric-acid crystals), 1 T. salt, and 2–4 T. sugar. Bring to boil. Transfer grated horseradish to bowl, pour hot marinade over it, and mix well. Pack into ½ pt. or smaller jars, seal, and store in fridge. *Note*: Traditional horseradish made with vinegar is good 3–4 months, whereas the kind with citric acid should be used up within 2–3 weeks.

BEET & HORSERADISH RELISH
ćwikła z chrzanem

This is undoubtedly the most typically Polish relish which adds zest to ham, sausage, and other cold meats. It is also served as a kind of salad with hot kiełbasa, boiled beef, pork hocks, roast pork, and other hot meats. Scrub and rinse 2 lbs. beets under cold running water, but do not peel. Place in pot, cover with boiling water, bring to boil, and cook on med. heat 45 min. or until fork-tender. Drain and plunge into cold water to cool. Peel and grate coarsely. Toss grated beets with anywhere from several T. to 1 c. homemade prepared horseradish. The exact amount depends entirely on the potency of your horseradish and how sharp you want your ćwikła to be. Pack mixture into ½ pt. jars, leaving 1 inch head space. In pot combine 1 c. water, 1¼ c. vinegar, 1 T. salt, and 1–4 T. sugar. Bring to boil and pour hot marinade over mixture. Tap jars against solid surface lightly so marinade flows to bottom and add more if needed to cover ćwikła. Seal, cool to room temp., and store in fridge.

OLD POLISH BEET & HORSERADISH RELISH
ćwikła staropolska

Cook and peel 2 lbs. beets as above, but slice on slicer blade of hand-held grater. Place beets at bottom of jars and sprinkle with freshly grated horseradish root (about ¼ lb. all told). Continue layering beets and horseradish until used up, leaving 2 inch head space. Bring to boil 1 c. water, 1½ c. vinegar, 3–4 peppercorns, a piece of bay leaf, ¼ t. caraway or dill seeds (partially crushed in mortar) and anywhere from 2 T.–¼ c. sugar. Simmer briefly and pour over mixture in jars, evenly distributing spices. Marinade should cover ćwikła by at least ½ inch. Seal, cool, and store in fridge.

PASTEURIZED "ĆWIKŁA"
ćwikła pasteryzowana

For a less vinegary ćwikła with an extended shelf life, proceed as in either of the above two recipes but prepare a weaker marinade. Use 1¾ c. water and ¾ c. vinegar plus the same seasonings as desired. After drenching ćwikła with hot marinade, cover with lids loosely and pasteurize 15 min. at 195°. Seal, cool, and store in cellar.

PICKLED BEETS
buraczki marynowane

Wash 2 lbs. small, golfball-sized beets, place in boiling water with skins left on, and cook until fork tender. Cool in cold water and peel. Place cooked beets in pt. jars. In pot combine 2 c. water, ¾ c. vinegar, 1 T. salt, and 2 T. sugar. Bring to boil and drench beets with marinade. Cover with lids without tightening and pasteurize in hot-water bath at 195° 15 min. Tighten lids, cool, and store in cellar. *Optional*: For zestier beets, 1–2 buds garlic and a sliver of horseradish root may be added to each jar before drenching with marinade.

PICKLED ONIONS
cebulka marynowana

Peel and wash 2 lbs. small onions of uniform size, place in pot of boiling water, and parboil 2 min. Drain, rinse with cold water, drain, and place in dry, sterilized ½ pt. jars. In pot combine 2½ c. water, ½ c. vinegar, ½ t. salt, 2 peppercorns, 2 grains allspice, ½ bay leaf, and 1 clove. Bring to boil, simmer briefly, and pour over onions, evenly distributing spices. Cover with lids and pasteurize 20 min. at 195°. Tighten lids, cool, and store in cool, dark place.

PICKLED PUMPKIN
dynia w occie

Peel 2 lbs. pumpkin and scrape away traces of the mushy inner pulp. Cut into ¾-inch cubes or cut into balls with melon scoop. In pot combine 3½ c. water, 1½ c. vinegar, 1½ c. sugar, and 1 t. cloves. Bring to boil. Place pumpkin in marinade, bring to boil, reduce heat, and simmer on low heat about 30 min. or until pumpkin becomes glossy. Pour mixture into pt. jars, seal, cool, and store in cellar.

PASTEURIZED PICKLED PUMPKIN
dynia w occie pasteryzowana

Prepare pumpkin as above. Place in colander and immerse in pot of boiling water for 2–3 min. Drain and transfer to jars. Separately bring to boil 4 c. water, 1 c. sugar, 1 t. citric-acid crystals, ½ t. salt, 5–6 cloves, and pinch cinnamon. Pour over pumpkin, cover with lids, and pasteurize 20 min. at 195°.

MARINATED MUSHROOMS
grzyby marynowane

Both store-bought white mushrooms as well as wild mushrooms (especially King Boletes, honey mushrooms, and butterballs) can be marinated. Wash 2 lbs. mushrooms well, taking care to remove embedded grit. Just the caps of large mushrooms are usually marinated with the stems used for other purposes. Small mushrooms may be marinated whole, but hardened base of stem should be trimmed off. If using butterballs (maślaki), be sure to peel the caps before proceeding. Prepare marinade by bringing to boil 1½ c. vinegar, 2 c. water, 1 T. sugar, 1 crumbled bay leaf, and several peppercorns and grains allspice. Simmer briefly and set aside covered. Place mushrooms in another pot, drench with plenty of boiling water, add 1 quartered onion, and 1 T. salt and simmer 30 min. Transfer mushrooms with slotted spoon to marinade, bring to boil, and simmer several min. Place mushrooms in ½ pt. jars, cover with marinade, seal, cool, and store in cool cellar or fridge. *Optional:* Several cloves and/or pieces of chopped cayenne pepper may also be cooked in marinade as desired.

MARINATED MUSHROOMS, PASTEURIZED
grzyby marynowane pasteryzowane

Wash and trim 2 lbs. fresh mushrooms as above, place in pot, drench with boiling water, add 1 t. salt, and cook 10–12 min. Drain in colander, rinse with cold water, and place in ½ pt. jars. Separately, combine 2 c. water, ¼ c. vinegar, 1 T. salt, 1 bay leaf, and several peppercorns and allspice grains. (*Optional*: 1–2 T. sugar may be added if desired.) Bring to boil and pour over mushrooms, leaving 1 inch head space. Evenly distribute spices. Cover loosely with lids and pasteurize 30 min. at 190°. Tighten lids, cool, and store in cool cellar. *Note*: Marinated mushrooms are among the most common Polish relishes. Besides being served in relish trays and used to decorate cold-meat platters, they are often chopped and added to various cooked-vegetable type salads.

GREEN TOMATO RELISH
sałatka z zielonych pomidorów

This relish or pickled salad apparently originated when people were stuck with an abundance of unripe tomatoes in years of early autumn frosts. Now some people like it so much that they go out of their way to pick green tomatoes before they can ripen. The best thing about this recipe is that it's quite easy to prepare. Wash 2 lbs. green tomatoes and slice. Peel and slice thin 1 lb. onions. Combine with tomatoes in bowl, sprinkle with 1½ T. salt, cover, and let stand at room temp. overnight. Next day, drain and pack into small jars. In pot combine 1¼ c. water, ¼ c. sugar, ½ c. vinegar, several peppercorns, several grains allspice, and 1 bay leaf. (*Optional*: Several cloves and a few grains mustard seed may also be added.) Bring to boil and pour hot marinade over tomatoes. Loosely cover with lids and pasteurize 20–25 min. at 195°. Seal tightly, cool, and store in cool place.

MARINATED CUCUMBER SALAD
mizeria marynowana

Wash and peel 2 lbs. young cucumbers. The season's first mature cucumbers with underdeveloped seed portions are best. Slice into thin rounds, place in bowl, sprinkle with 1½ T. salt, ¼ c. vinegar, and ¼ t. pepper. Toss and let stand at room temp. 1 hr. Pack into ½ pt. dry, sterilized jars, pressing down, and cover with liquid that formed while standing. Cover loosely with lids and pasteurize 20 min. at 195°. Tighten lids, allow to cool, and store in cool cellar or fridge. Good straight from the jar as a zesty relish. To use as a salad, drain, rinse in colander under cold running water, drain well, and lace with sour cream to taste.

PICKLED CUCUMBERS
pikle z ogórków

Wash and peel 2 lbs. large, yellowed, late-season cucumbers. Cut in half, scoop out seed portions and adjoining jelly-like substance. Slice cucumbers into ½-inch pieces and place in bowl. Sprinkle with 3 T. salt, cover and refrigerate overnight. Next day drain, transfer cucumbers to ½-pt. jars, add a small sliver of horseradish or two and 1 bud sliced garlic to each jar. In pot combine 1 c. water, ⅔ c. vinegar, ½ c. sugar, ½ a bay leaf, several peppercorns, and ¼ t. mustard seed. Bring to boil and pour over cucumbers. Pasteurize 15 min. at 195°. Tighten lids, cool, and store in cool pantry or cellar.

ZESTY GHERKINS
korniszony

Wash 2 lbs. tiny cucumbers 1½–2 inches in length and soak in cold water 1 hr. Drain well. Place in bowl and cover with ¾ c. salt, cover with inverted plate that fits over cucumbers, weight down with something heavy (like a qt. jar filled with water), and refrigerate overnight. Next day, rinse and drain, place in ½-pt. jars and add several slices slightly undercooked carrot to each. Bring to boil 1½ c. water, 1½ c. vinegar, 4–5 T. sugar, 10 partially crushed peppercorns, 8 grains allspice and 4–5 crumbled bay leaves. Pour hot marinade over pickles, cover loosely with lids, and pasteurize 15 min. at 185°. Tighten lids and store.

MUSTARD PICKLES
ogórki z gorczycą

Wash, peel, and cut in half lengthwise 2 lbs. large, yellow cucumbers. Scoop out and discard seed portion. Cut in ½ crosswise and slice each piece into several spears. Place in bowl, cover with 1 c. salt, cover, and refrigerate overnight. Next day, rinse away salt under cold running water in colander and let cucumbers drip-dry. Place in ½-pt. jars and add ¼ t. mustard seed and several slivers of horseradish root to each. In pot bring to boil 1½ c. vinegar, ½ c. water, 5 T. sugar, 1 bay leaf, and 6–8 peppercorns. Pour hot marinade over pickles to cover. Add 1 T. olive oil to each jar and seal at once. When cool, store in cool cellar.

DILL PICKLES (VINEGAR TYPE)
ogórki konserwowe

Wash and drain 2 lbs. pickling cucumbers about 3 inches long. Stand cucumbers upright in pt. jars. To each add 1 head of dill, 2–3 peppercorns, 1 grain allspice, a pinch of mustard seeds, a sliver of horseradish root, and 1 bud garlic, sliced. In pot, combine 2½ c. water, ½–⅔ c. vinegar, 1 T. salt, and 1–3 T. sugar. Bring to boil and pour over cucumbers, leaving 1 inch head space. Cover loosely with lids and pasteurize in hot-water bath 20 min. at 195°. Tighten lids, allow to cool, and store in cool place. *Note*: Dill pickles made along these lines are often labeled "polski wyrób" in American supermarkets and are also prepared by many Polish-American home-canners. The real Polish dill pickles are the brine-cured variety that don't contain a drop of vinegar. Some recipes for these follow.

POLISH BRINE-CURED DILL PICKLES
ogórki kiszone/kwaszone

The classic Polish dill pickle, whose preparation goes back well over 1,000 years, is naturally cured, hence it is a far healthier alternative than any of the pickles pickled with vinegar. It is extremely versatile, since it produces several products in a single container: the crunchy, several-day undercured pickles some people like, tart and tangy fully-cured pickles, and very tart and soft overcured pickles, which are good for eating and a required ingredient in dill-pickle soup. The leftover dill-pickle juice is a vitamin and mineral-rich beverage as is, or in combination with other ingredients (see dill-pickle brine below) and can be used to give a delightful tang to soups, sauces, and meat dishes. Above all, ogórki kiszone are so delicious that they will quickly disappear from your counter-top crock. They are also easy to prepare. Wash and drain 4 lbs. roughly 4-inch, green pickling cucumbers. Any larger than 6 inches are not used. If you have cucumbers of varying size, put the large ones at bottom of jar, since they take longer to cure. The best cucumbers to brine-cure are those picked the same day. If yours are not, soak them in cold water 2–3 hrs. Wash, dry, scald with boiling water, and dry again large glass jar or crock big enough to accommodate the pickles. At bottom of container, place 3 stalks mature pickling dill (heads or seed clusters as well as stems). Stand cucumbers in container upright. Add 3–5 buds garlic, several small pieces of horseradish root, and several fruit leaves (cherry, black-currant or grape are best!). Bring to boil 6 c. water and 3 T. pickling salt. When cooled slightly, pour warm solution over cucumbers. Cover with inverted plate and weight down so cucumbers are submerged. Cover with cheesecloth and that's all there is to it. They should be fully cured in 7–10 days. You may leave them on counter until all are used up (and remove them with tongs, never with fingers!), or transfer to fridge. *Optional*: Other flavorings may include: 1 horseradish leaf, 1–2 green oak leaves (this gives pickles a barrel-like taste), 1 bay leaf, a pinch of mustard seeds or unground coriander, a small piece of chili pepper, a slice of celeriac or parsley root. Do not use all these flavorings in a single batch of pickles, but experiment on successive batches to see which combination suits you best. Personally, we feel the basic recipe is good just as it is.

DILL-PICKLE BRINE
sok ogórkowy/solanka ogórkowa

When the above pickles are used up, skim off any whitish foam from surface and strain leftover brine through cheesecloth into jar or bottle. Seal and refrigerate until ready to use. Its uses have been described above, but we might add that this makes the ideal thirst-quenching and regenerative "morning-after" drink. Fill glass ½ full with ice-cold pickle brine and top it off with ice-cold club soda. Drink in a single gulp if possible. It has long been known that any liquid helps offset the dehydration that results from drinking alcoholic beverages, but the latest findings show that salt helps speed up the cure.

Illustrations show preparation of traditional Polish-style pickles packed in jars:
A) Pickling cucumbers are scrubbed and set aside to drain: if they have not been picked the same day, it is best to first soak them in cold water several hours; B) Cucumbers are placed upright in jars and interspersed with dill, garlic, slices of horseradish root, and other flavoring according to preference; C) The right proportion of pickling salt (2–2½ T. per qt water) is added to boiling water and brine is allowed to cool;

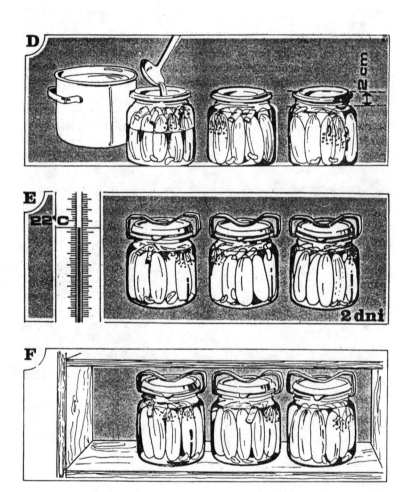

D) Brine is poured over cucumbers, leaving about ¾ inch head space. E) Jars are sealed and kept at room temperature anywhere from two to four days; F) Pickles are removed to cool, dark cellar for storage.

CRUNCHY UNDERCURED (LOW SALT) DILL PICKLES
ogórki małosolne

This is not a recipe, but a way of using the traditional brine-cured dill pickles described above. Some people, including the author's mother, like crunchy, under-cured pickles, which are low in salt and have a pleasantly bitter after-taste. You can have these by simply eating the above after 3–5 days, or transfer to another jar, cover with strained brine, seal, and refrigerate.

HURRY-UP BRINE-CURED DILL PICKLES
ogórki kiszone błyskawiczne

If you need fully-cured dill pickles in a hurry, do the following. Wash, drain, and soak pickling cucumbers as in the first recipe (Polish brine-cured dill pickles), but cut off ends of cucumbers and puncture each all over with toothpick. Place in jar with dill, garlic, horseradish, etc. as indicated. Bring 4 c. water and 3 T. salt to boil, add 2 c. rye-sour (żur-see chapter on spices & other ingredients), and pour hot liquid over cucumbers. Keep in very warm (75°–80°) place 24 hrs. and enjoy. They will also be good, although more tart, after 36 or 48 hrs. *Variation*: If you haven't any żur (rye-sour), make brine with 6 c. water and 3 T. salt, add several skins from black bread (razowiec), and scald with brine; this method may take longer, however.

QUICK BRINE-CURED DILL PICKLES
ogórki kiszone naprędce jeszcze inaczej

Wash, soak, etc. dill pickles as in first recipe, cut off ends, puncture all over with toothpick, and cut cucumbers in half crosswise or lengthwise into halves or quarters (spears). Place in jar with flavoring ingredients. Bring to boil 4 c. water and 2 T. salt, add 2 c. dill-pickle brine from previous batch of pickles, and pour hot liquid over cucumbers. *Note*: Although quick, the disadvantage of this method is that the pickles lose much of their mineral nutrients in the brine.

CANNED BRINE-CURED DILL PICKLES
ogórki kiszone w słoikach

Whereas the above counter-top pickles are meant for current consumption, you can also put up dill pickles for the long winter and spring months ahead. Wash and soak 5–6 hrs. in cold water 10 lbs. 3–5 inch green, firm, pickling cucumbers. Drain. Into each dry, sterilized qt. jar place 1–2 heads (seed clusters) mature pickling dill, a small slice of horseradish root, a small piece of horseradish leaf and 1–4 buds garlic. (***Optional***: This is the basic recipe, but feel free to add to each jar a small quantity of any of the additional flavorings suggested for Polish brine-cured dill pickles.) Stand cucumbers in jar upright. Bring to boil 12 c. water, ½ c. pickling salt, and 2 T. sugar; set aside until cooled to room temp. Pour brine over pickles to cover, leaving ¾-inch head space. Cover with lids and screw on lightly, but do not tighten. Place jars in pan (to collect drippings that may spill over during early vigorous curing period) and let stand at room temp. (or slightly warmer: 75°–80°) 3–4 days, by which time bubbling should cease. Add extra brine to any jar in which cucumbers are not submerged. Wipe jar and lids with clean cloth and seal tightly. Store in cold cellar or fridge. ***Note***: 35° is the ideal temp. for storing these pickles, but up to 40° is also O.K.

DILL PICKLES FOR SOUP
ogórki kiszone na zupę

Brine-cured dill pickles prepared in any of the above ways may be used for soup when they become very well cured and soft. If you like zupa ogórkowa (dill-pickle soup) as much as we do, you may want to put up pickles especially for this purpose and have them on hand all year. Wash and peel 4 lbs. pickling cucumbers, cut into cubes and place in dry, sterilized ½-pt. jars. (This size jar will make about 4–5 servings of soup.) To each jar add 1–2 buds garlic and ½ a head mature dill, preferably pre-scalded and drained. Bring to boil 3½ c. water and 2 T. salt. When cool, pour over cucumbers and seal jars tightly. Keep at room temp. 2 days and then transfer to cellar and store. Another way is to keep at room temp. 6–7 days, loosen lids, pasteurize 20 min. at 185°–195°, and store in cool place after they have cooled to room temp.

SAUERKRAUT (BASIC RECIPE)
kapusta kiszona/kwaszona (przepis podstawowy)

Let us start by saying that making sauerkraut at home is far more tricky than preparing any of the above brine-cured pickles, which rarely turn out bad. Absolute cleanliness, including frequent scrubbing of hands with hot, soapy water and the scalding of utensils, is very important. Don't try this recipe until you feel quite comfortable and familiar with the preparation of brine-cured pickles. Start with 10 lbs. white cabbage, taking care to select firmly packed heads. Discard wilted outer leaves. Wash, drain, and shred heads, using pre-scalded manual shredder or whatever electric appliance you have that will do the job. Finely grate the cores. Transfer to large sterilized bowl or pan, sprinkle with 5 T. pickling salt, and mix well by hand. Transfer to large gallon jars or crock (in which sauerkraut is to be cured) a little at a time. Start with a 2-inch layer of shredded cabbage at bottom of curing container and pack it down tightly with scalded wooden spoon or bottom of similarly sterilized bottle.

Add another 2-inch layer of cabbage, pack down, and continue layering and packing tightly until all is used up. If cabbage is near top of container, place it in a pan to collect drippings that may spill over during first stage of curing. If crock is less than ¾ full, this shouldn't be necessary. Cover cabbage with dry, sterilized, inverted dinner plate, press down, cover crock with clean dish towel, and let stand at room temp. or slightly warmer 8–12 days, or until vigorous bubbling ceases. Every 2 days run a clean, scalded stick down to bottom of crocks in several places to allow gases to escape. With sterilized wooden spoon, skim off any foam that forms on surface of liquid. When active curing ceases (after 8–12 days), weight plate down with water-filled jar. *Remember:* The jar must also be scrubbed, rinsed, dried, scalded with boiling water, and dried again before coming into contact with sauerkraut juice. Remove to cool cellar (40°-50° is best for storing sauerkraut), cover crock with piece of plastic (polyethylene), and fasten it with large rubber band. When removing some sauerkraut from crock, it's a good idea to re-scald and dry plate and water-filled jar. The inside of crock between juice level and top rim should be wiped with clean cloth moistened in strong fresh brine (3 T. salt dissolved in ¾ c. boiling water) to prevent mold from forming. Be sure you do this with freshly scrubbed hands. Sauerkraut is very suspectable to bacteria, so these precautions are not exaggerated!

SAUERKRAUT WITH APPLES & CARROTS
kapusta kiszona z marchwią i jabłkami

Mix 10 lbs. shredded cabbage with 5 T. salt, ¼ lb. peeled, coarsely grated apples and ¼ lb. peeled, finely grated carrots. *Optional*: Scald ¼–1 t. caraway seeds in sieve and, when dry, add to mixture. Otherwise, proceed as in basic recipe (above).

SAUERKRAUT WITH LINGONBERRIES (MOUNTAIN CRANBERRIES)
kapusta kiszona z borówkami

Mix with shredded, salted cabbage (prepared as above) ¼ lb. washed drained lingonberries, ¼ lb. peeled, coarsely grated apples, ¼ lb. peeled, finely grated carrots and ½ t. caraway seeds. Proceed as in basic recipe.

SAUERKRAUT WITH CRANBERRIES
kapusta kiszona z żurawiną

With 10 lbs. shredded salt cabbage (prepared as in basic sauerkraut recipe) mix 1 lb. washed, drained cranberries, several partially crushed grains allspice, ½ t. partially crushed peppercorns, and 2 broken-up bay leaves. Otherwise proceed as in basic recipe (above).

JAR-CURED SAUERKRAUT
kapusta kiszona w słoikach

Any of the above can be cured in qt. jars. Prepare as indicated above, but pack shredded, salted cabbage (with whatever other ingredients you like) into dry, sterilized jars. Place in pan (to catch drippings), cover with lids, and screw on loosely. Let stand at room temp. 4–7 days or until active curing (bubbling and overflowing) stops. Usually gas escapes on its own from qt. jars, but to make sure, you can run a clean, sterilized stick down to bottom of jars every 2 days. Also skim away any foam that forms at top of liquid. After active curing period, cabbage should be covered with liquid. If it isn't, fill jars with enough brine (1 t. salt dissolved in 1 c. boiling water) to allow ½-inch head space. Wipe sides and tops of jars with clean cloth and seal tightly. Store in cold cellar or fridge.

PASTEURIZED SAUERKRAUT
kapusta kiszona pasteryzowana

After sauerkraut cured in crock achieves the proper taste (this may be several weeks after it was moved to cellar), it can be canned in jars and pasteurized, making it more convenient to use. Taste the sauerkraut, because pasteurization will fix it at exactly that stage of curing. If left in crock, it will slowly continue to become more tart. Pack cured sauerkraut into dry, sterilized qt. jars, making sure there is at least ½ inch of liquid above the tightly packed sauerkraut and another ½ inch head space. Seal tightly, place in pot of cold water, gradually bring temp. up to 185°, and pasteurize 15–20 min. Unpasteurized sauerkraut, if properly handled, is good for 3–4 months, but the pasteurized kind can stand a year or more in cool, dark place.

QUICK-USE SAUERKRAUT
kapusta kiszona do szybkiego użytku

If you are expecting guests next week, this is a short-cut method that reduces curing period from several weeks to several days. Shred 5 lbs. cabbage as indicated in first recipe and mix by hand in pan with 2½ T. pickling salt and (optional) ¼ t. caraway seeds. Pack into crock or gallon jar, pressing down with scalded wooden spoon, potato-masher, or bottle every several-inch layer. When all cabbage has been used up, scald with 5–6 c. boiling water in which potatoes were cooked. There should be 1 inch of this liquid above the packed-down sauerkraut. Cover crock with dish towel and let stand in very warm place (78°–80° is best). It should be ready to cook in 4–6 days. *Note*: Although quicker than conventional sauerkraut, it doesn't keep well, so prepare only as much as you need for 1 or 2 days.

SALAD SAUERKRAUT
kapusta kiszona sałatkowa

Although prepared the same way as basic crock-cured sauerkraut, this version contains a combination of flavoring ingredients that makes it ideal for salads. Shred 10 lbs. cabbage as above and mix with 5 T. salt, ½ lb. peeled, coarsely grated apples, ½ lb. peeled, finely grated carrots, ½ lb. washed, drained, whole fresh cranberries, 1 t. caraway seeds, 1 t. dill seeds, and the following spices crushed in mortar and sieved: several peppercorns and grains allspice, 2 bay leaves, and 1 t. juniper berries. Otherwise proceed as in basic sauerkraut recipe. When fully cured, sprinkle with some chopped onions, sweeten to taste with a little sugar, and dress with salad oil.

SOUR-CURED BEETS
buraki kiszone

Wash, dry, and peel 4 lbs. beets which should be the size of plums or golfballs. Small beets can be used whole, larger ones should be quartered, sliced, or cubed. Place in large jar which should be no more than ¾ full. Bring 8 c. water and 7–8 T. pickling salt to boil. Remove from heat and stir in ¾ t. citric-acid crystals. Pour over beets. Cover with dry, sterilized plate or saucer and weight down so beets are submerged. Keep at room temp. or slightly warmer until active fermentation (vigorous bubbling) ceases, then transfer to cool cellar. Cover with dish towel. Skim off any white foam that forms on surface of liquid. *Note:* These can be used in soups, as cooked vegetables, and in salads.

SOUR-CURED APPLES
jabłka kwaszone

For this recipe, choose small, firm, tart, unbruised, and unblemished apples. Wash and drain enough apples to fill a crock or large glass jar ¾ full. For 5 lbs. apples bring to boil 6 c. water, 1½ T. pickling salt, and 3 T. sugar. When cooled to lukewarm, stir in 3 T. rye flour and let stand in warm place overnight. Line bottom of crock or jar with washed, drained black-currant leaves, add the apples, cover with more black-currant leaves, and drench with souring liquid. Cover with dry, sterilized, inverted plate and weight down with sterilized, water-filled jar to keep apples fully immersed. Keep at room temp. during active fermentation (3–5 days). When vigorous bubbling stops, store in cool cellar. As apples are used, wipe inside of container with clean cloth moistened with strong brine (1 T. salt dissolved in ½ c. boiling water) to prevent mold from forming. Cover with dish towel during storage. *Note*: Diced sour-cured apples can be used in all cooked-vegetable salads that call for fresh diced apples. They are good as a relish and can be cooked with pork roasts and pork stews (slice and add during last 5 min. of cooking).

SOUR-CURED MUSHROOMS
grzyby kwaszone

Any fresh domestic or wild mushrooms (King Bolete, honey mushrooms, chanterelles, etc.) can be used for sour-curing, but only one variety should be included in a single crock. Wash well, trim away any hardened stem bottoms and wormy portions, and drain 4 lbs. mushrooms. Par-boil in large pot of lightly salted water 3–5 min., drain in colander, and allow to dry and cool. (*Note*: Just the caps may be sour-cured with stems reserved for some other purpose.) Place dry mushrooms in crock or jar large enough to accommodate them. Sprinkle each layer of mushrooms with a little pickling salt and sugar. (For 4 lbs. mushrooms you will need 2 T. salt and 1 t. sugar. If desired, 2 bay leaves and several peppercorns and grains allspice may be added.) Cover mushrooms with dry, sterilized, inverted plate and weight down with sterilized, water-filled jar. Cover jar with clean dish towel and let stand at room temp. 3–4 days or until active fermentation ends. Mushrooms should be always submerged in liquid that forms. If there is not enough (this might occur if you happen to get fresh mushrooms that have dried out), add a little cold brine (1 t. pickling salt dissolved in 1 c. boiling water). Store in cool cellar. *Note*: When they are cured, mushrooms may be transferred to small ¼-pt. jars and pasteurized about 15 min. Sour-cured mushrooms serve as a relish and may be diced and added to cooked-vegetable salads much the same way as marinated mushrooms are. These are healthier because they contain no vinegar!

SALTED MUSHROOMS
grzyby solone

King Boletes, lactarius (milky caps or rydze), honey mushrooms (opieńki) or chanterelles (kurki) are best for salting. Wash, trim, rinse, and drain mushrooms. Cook in large pot of boiling salted water about 5 min., drain, and allow to dry and cool. Line bottom of dry, sterilized crock or large glass jar with layer of pickling salt. Add a layer of mushrooms, sprinkle with salt, and continue layering so that top layer is salt. *Note*: Use 5 T. pickling salt per lb. fresh mushrooms. Press down with dry, sterilized, inverted plate and weight down with water-filled jar. Leave at room temp. until mushrooms are covered with their natural brine (about 12 hrs.). If this does not occur, add some cold brine (1 t. salt dissolved in 1 c. boiling water), because mushrooms will spoil if they are not submerged. *Note*: Some cooks add a 1 inch-layer of salad oil to insulate mushrooms against air-borne bacteria. Store in cool, dark cellar. To use, remove as much as you need with dry, sterilized, slotted spoon and soak mushrooms in cold water 30 min. Then drain and use as you would fresh mushrooms.

CANNED MUSHROOMS
grzyby pasteryzowane

Both domestic white mushrooms and their wild counterpart, meadow mushrooms, as well as other wild species (King Bolete, lactarius, chanterelles, etc.) may be used for canning, but use only 1 variety per batch. Wash well, drain, trim, and rinse 4 lbs. fresh mushrooms (or use only the caps and reserve stems for other purposes). Slice mushrooms, place in wide, shallow pot, cover with 2 c. boiling water, add 1 T. salt, 2–3 grains allspice, and simmer 15–20 min. Towards the end add 1 T. sugar, ¼ t. ground pepper, and ½ t. citric-acid crystals. Transfer mixture to ½-pt. dry, sterilized jars, leaving about ¾ inch head space, seal tightly, and pasteurize in hot-water bath at 195° about 1 hr. from the time boiling begins. Remove from bath and allow to cool at room temp. Jars may be placed upside down to check if all are well sealed. Pasteurize again about 30 min. When cooled to room temp., store in cool, dark cellar. *Note*: Cook the canned mushrooms in their liquid about 15 min. before adding to soups, sauces, stews, etc.

CANNED BUTTER-STEWED MUSHROOMS
grzyby duszone w maśle pasteryzowane

Use domestic or wild mushrooms in this recipe. Oyster mushrooms are also good prepared this way. Wash, trim, rinse, and dry 4 lbs. fresh mushrooms. (Or use just the caps and reserve stems for other purposes; be sure to weigh caps if using them alone and adjust recipe accordingly). Slice mushrooms, place in pot containing 2 sticks (½ lb.) melted, unsalted butter, add ½ lb. diced onions, salt lightly, and simmer on low 10–12 min. or until most of the liquid evaporates. Dissolve 1 t. citric-acid crystals in ¼ c. boiling water and add to pot. Season with several pinches ground pepper. Transfer to ½-pt. jars, packing mixture tightly so there are no empty spaces between sliced mushrooms. Leave ½ inch head space. Seal and pasteurize at 195° 1 hr. Allow to cool in water bath to room temp. Remove and wipe jars and place upside down to check for leaks. Tighten lids as necessary and store in cool, dark place.

DRYING MUSHROOMS
suszenie grzybów

Almost any type of mushroom can be dried—a process that both preserves them and intensifies their flavor. It is best to dry caps and stems separately, because they require a different amount of time to dry. Mushrooms for drying should be very fresh, not withered or tough, and free of visible insect bites. They should not be washed, because then they take longer to dry and tend to become very brown. Instead, wipe them thoroughly with damp cloth to remove all grit, grass, and other such impurities. There are several ways to dry mushrooms:

—*Sun & air drying*: On hot, dry, sunny days place mushrooms on clean paper in direct sunlight. Turn them over every so often to ensure even drying. If you start in the morning on a hot day, they may be fully dried by sundown. They are fully dried when brittle. If they are not dry enough, bring them indoors overnight so they don't absorb moisture from the dew, and repeat next day or even a third day if necessary. *Hint*: Instead of drying them on paper on a solid surface, a window screen will ensure better air circulation and quicker drying.

—*Sun & air drying on string*: Run large needle threaded with strong string with a wooden stick tied to its end through center of mushroom cap and pull until mushroom rests against knotted stick. Tie a knot on opposite side of mushroom and run needle and string through next cap, tie another knot and continue threading until you get a 2 or 3-ft. string. The knots separating mushrooms enable air to freely circulate and evenly dry mushrooms. Hang up on hot, sunny day in direct sunlight. Take indoors overnight and repeat another day or more until fully dried. *Note*: Strings of mushroom caps look beautiful hanging in loops at markets, but will lose some of their aroma if permanently stored this way. See following entry on storing dried mushrooms.

—*Indoor air drying*: If weather is rainy, or cloudy, place mushrooms on window screen over radiator, next to hot-air register, furnace, or hot kitchen stove. Dry mushrooms, turning them over occasionally, until brittle. *Note*: If you started drying them outdoors and the weather worsened, you can finish the job indoors as indicated above.

—*Oven drying*: Mushrooms can be dried on small window screen or tray in 120°–150° oven with door left ajar to allow moisture to escape. You can direct a small electric fan at oven-door opening from a distance of several ft. away to ensure air circulation.

—*Air & oven drying*: Polish homemakers often place mushrooms out in the sun to wilt and partially dry, then finish the job up in a warm oven. Vincent Maretka, a leading Polish-American mushroom authority, suggests pre-heating oven to 350°, switching it off and placing mushrooms on tray inside until oven cools to room temp. This reportedly kills any insect eggs or larvae hidden inside. They are then kept in the hot sun until fully dried. *Note*: Although normally wild mushrooms are dried, some Polish Americans also dry fresh, store-bought mushrooms for use in their Christmas Eve soups and sauerkraut dishes. Although nowhere as good as borowiki (King Boletes), they have a more intense aroma than fresh mushrooms.

STORING DRIED MUSHROOMS
przechowywanie grzybów suszonych

When mushrooms are fully dried, i.e. when they become brittle and can be cracked, they can be stored in tightly sealed dark-glass jar or tin and kept in cupboard until ready to use. The jar or tin may also be refrigerated. We feel the best way to store dried mushrooms is in the freezer. Simply place 1–2 oz., the quantity you will need for most recipes, in small jars or plastic containers, seal and store them in freezer until needed. *Note*: Ways of using dried mushrooms are presented in the mushroom chapter as well as sections devoted to soups, meat dishes, sauces, and vegetable dishes.

FREEZING FRESH MUSHROOMS
mrożenie świeżych grzybów

If you're a mushroom-picker who struck the jackpot but haven't the time to preserve them in any of the ways given above, the alternative is to freeze them. Wash, trim, and rinse mushrooms as usual, place in colander, and dip into pot of boiling water for about 20 seconds. Drain until mushrooms are completely cool and dry. Place on baking sheet with enough distance between them so they don't touch and pop into freezer overnight. Next day, transfer to plastic freezer bags, allowing the amount in each bag that you are likely to use a single time: roughly ½ lb. if mushrooms are to be used in a soup, gravy or meat dish, and 1 lb. if they are to be a meal in themselves. Seal bags, label, indicating type of mushroom and date of freezing, and keep in freezer. They will retain natural flavor, texture, and aroma up to 6 months.

PRUNES
śliwki suszone

The best prunes are made from Italian plums which in Polish happen to be known as Hungarian plums (węgierki). Plums should be ripe but not overripe. They are just right when they fall after you gently shake the branch. Any plums that burst or crack on impact should be used for other purposes. Place plums in colander and dip into pot of boiling water for 15–30 seconds, then plunge them immediately into another pot of cold water. This will remove their natural waxy coating which impedes proper drying. (*Note*: Some older cooks add 1 t. baking soda per qt. to the boiling water, which more effectively removes the coating; unfortunately it also destroys some of the B vitamins of which prunes are an important source, so we don't recommend it.) Drain plums until completely dry. On a very hot, dry, sunny day, they may be dried outdoors. After first day, if they are not fully dried, they should be brought indoors overnight and taken out into the sun the next day. A good way is to sun dry them until they wrinkle and then finish the job in a warm oven. They may also be dried entirely in the oven. Place plums on metal tray and pop into 100° oven, keeping them at that temp. until their skins wrinkle. Remove from oven. When cooled to room temp. ease out their pits. (*Note*: Plums may be dried with pits left in, but drying takes longer and plums are less convenient to use.) Increase oven temp. to 120° and keep plums inside with oven door ajar several more hrs. Then increase temp. to 160° until fully dried. Your plums have turned into prunes when they become elastic but dry enough so that not a single drop of juice can be squeezed from them. When in doubt, it's better to overdry than to underdry them, as underdried prunes can turn moldy. *Hint:* The best oven-dried prunes are obtained by interrupting the process at intervals, i.e. removing them from oven and letting them cool to room temp., then returning them to oven. Store in sealed glass jars in cupboard or fridge.

DRIED APPLES
jabłka suszone

Although not as popular in America as prunes, dried apples are very common in Poland where they are used to make compote. For this purpose, the best are firm, tart, unbruised apples. Wash, dry, and peel. (*Note*: Use the peels to make apple tea or homemade vinegar.) Remove cores. There are various apple-coring devices on the market, but a simple one is a 5-inch piece of metal tubing whose diameter encompasses the core. Simply stand apple upright, place tubing at center over core, and press down to surface. The core trapped in the tubing can be forced out with a stick. Slice apples into ⅛-inch rings. To prevent apple rings from discoloring while you core and slice the rest, place the finished rings in a cold, mild brine (¾ t. salt dissolved in 1 qt. boiled water and cooled). Drain apple rings. When completely dry, place on tray or window screen in hot sunlight, turning them over occasionally. They are ready when they become elastic but secrete no more juice. If one day of sun-drying is insufficient to achieve that stage, finish the job in a 190° oven with door left ajar. The entire drying can be done in an oven, but it should be repeatedly interrupted, with apple rings removed to cool off. Additional slow evaporation takes place during the cooling-off period, and that makes for nice dried apples. Store in dark airtight jar or tin in cupboard or fridge.

DRIED PEARS
gruszki suszone

Besides prunes and dried apples, dried pears are among the standard ingredients of the traditional Christmas Eve compote. Pears are easier to dry than apples, because after peeling they are cut into halves or quarters. The pear's core is edible and needs not be removed. Slow drying at about 120° gives the best results in an oven, whose door should be left ajar. They may also be partially air-dried in the hot sun on trays or screens and finished up in oven. *Note*: When pears are partially dried, flatten them with cutting-board or other flat surface to speed up the process. They are ready when they become elastic and completely juiceless.

DRIED CHERRIES & OTHER FRUIT
wiśnie suszone i inny susz owocowy

Use unblemished and unbroken sour cherries. Wash, drain until dry, and discard stems. Place on tray or screen so they don't touch and dry in oven with door ajar at 120° until they wrinkle. Remove from oven to cool, then continue drying at 150°–160°, preferably with interruptions as above. Best results are achieved by a combination of sun and oven drying. Fully dried cherries are elastic but juiceless. *Note*: They will dry more quickly if pits are eased out after cherries partially dry and wrinkled. Flatten pitless cherries between fingers and continue drying until fully dried. Raspberries, blueberries, blackberries, black currants, etc., are dried in much the same way. They are properly dried when elastic, but—like raisins—no juice can be squeezed out of them.

DRIED DILL
koperek suszony

There are three basic ways of preserving dill, undoubtedly the most popular herb used by Polish cooks: drying, salting and freezing. If you're familiar with the dry "dill weed" found in the spice section of supermarkets, you know that it bears little resemblance to fresh dill. Its main advantage is convenience. It can easily be sprinkled over various foods and can be combined with dried herbs to create various seasonings like Polish poultry seasoning (see herb & spice chapter). Wash several bunches fresh young dill (the green, feathery kind, not the mature stalks), shake off moisture, spread loosely on rack to drain. When they are completely free of detectable moisture, chop the feathery leaves very fine, spread them out on tray and keep at room temp. or warmer in well-ventilated place (not in direct sunlight!) until they are brittle and crumbly. Sieve dry dill and store in small sealed spice bottles. *Variation*: An easier way is to dry the entire leaves without chopping them first. When crumbly dry, break them up by hand, sieve, and store.

SALTED DILL
koperek solony

Wash, shake off moisture, and drain completely several bunches dill. Chop leaves very fine. Line bottom of small jar with thin layer of pickling salt, add layer of chopped dill, pack it down, add another layer of salt, then dill, and continue layering and packing down until no more will fit. Top layer should be salt. Seal tightly and refrigerate. This will enable you to enjoy dill that is nearly like the garden-fresh variety all year round. Since it does lose some of its aroma (but far less than dried dill), you will have to use twice the amount to achieve a similar intensity. To use, place a spoonful of salted dill in sieve (re-seal and return the rest to fridge), rinse out salt under cold running water, and add dill to soup, sauce, meat dish, etc.

FROZEN DILL
koperek mrożony

According to some, freezing is the best way to preserve dill, although it loses some of its aroma just as salted dill does. Rinse, shake off water, and spread fresh dill leaves out to drain completely. When free of all detectable moisture, chop leaves very fine. Pack into small jars and freeze. Use a spoonful or two whenever you want the flavor of dill in some dish you're preparing.

PRESERVING PARSLEY & CELERY LEAVES
utrwalanie naci pietruszki i selera

Besides dill, two other flavoring ingredients worth having on hand all year round are parsley and celery leaves (the tops of celery stalks that are often discarded). These may be dried, salted, or frozen the same way as dill. Sprinkle into soups, sauces, meat dishes, etc. *Note*: A very nice, versatile seasoning for poultry, soups, sauces, etc. can be prepared by combining one part each dried and sieved dill, parsley, and celery leaves and storing in tightly sealed spice bottle.

SALTED SORREL
szczaw solony

Trim away and discard stems of fresh sorrel leaves. Wash the leaves well and drain on rack. When completely free of moisture, chop very fine and pack into small jars with pickling salt, layering the way given for salted dill (above). To use, place a spoonful in sieve and rinse out salt under cold running water. Add to soups, sauces, meat dishes, etc. whenever a trace of tartness is desired. An excellent addition to beef broth. *Note*: To prepare sorrel soup, see following recipe.

BOTTLED SORREL
szczaw pasteryzowany

If you love Poland's famous sorrel soup (zupa szczawiowa) the way many people do, you need not limit your enjoyment to summer when fresh sorrel is available. Wash well 2–3 lbs. fresh sorrel, trimming off and discarding stems. Run moist leaves through meat grinder (these could probably be puréed in blender, although we have not tried it). Place ground sorrel in pot, add 1–1½ T. salt and heat gently to just below boiling point. Transfer mixture to small ¼-pt. jars or bottles and pasteurize at 185° 15–20 min. Tighten lids if necessary after sorrel cools to room temp. and store in cool, dark cellar or fridge. Use the entire jar for a pot of soup, because it does not keep well once it is opened.

TOMATO PUREE
przecier pomidorowy

Wash well, discarding stems, 5 lbs. ripe, unblemished tomatoes. Cut in quarters or cubes, place in large, wide pan, crush somewhat with potato masher, and heat gently until they disintegrate. Sieve mixture, adding ½–1 t. salt per qt. puree. Transfer to ½ or ¼-pt. jars (the size you are likely to use for a single dish). Screw lids on jars without tightening and pasteurize at 195° 15–20 min. Remove from water bath, seal tightly and, when cooled to room temp., store in cool, dark cellar. (*Hint*: One way to ensure against spoilage is to add 1 t. cooking oil to each jar after pasteurization.) Use this puree in tomato soup and gołąbki as well as your favorite Italian, Spanish, or other dishes that call for pureed tomatoes or tomato sauce.

CANNED WHOLE TOMATOES
pomidory całe pasteryzowane

Wash, stem, and dry 5 lbs. small (roughly 2 inches in diameter), ripe but firm, uncracked and unblemished tomatoes. Place in colander in batches, immerse in boiling water for several seconds, then plunge immediately into cold water. This will make skins easy to remove. Place into ½–1-pt. jars, leaving two inches head space. To each qt. water add ⅓ t. salt, ¾ t. sugar, and ½ t. citric-acid crystals. Bring to boil and pour hot liquid over tomatoes in jars, leaving ¾ inch head space. Seal lids tightly and pasteurize in hot-water bath at 190° 20 min. for ½-pt. jars and 30 min. for pt. jars. When cool, store in cool, dark cellar.

CANNED TOMATOES IN PUREE
pomidory w przecierze pasteryzowane

Prepare tomatoes as above or cut in half and fill jars, leaving two inches head space. Cover them with hot tomato puree (prepared as above without pasteurizing in water bath). Leave ¾ inch head space. Seal jars tightly and pasteurize at 195° 30 min. Then cool and store as above. *Note:* If using halved tomatoes, do not pack them too tightly, so puree can easily penetrate. These are very good for gołąbki. *Variation:* If you haven't time to prepare puree, whole or halved tomatoes may be covered with canned tomato juice and pasteurized as above.

SAUSAGE-MAKING, MEAT-CURING & SMOKING

To many Americans, the word "Polish" immediately evokes the term "sausage" in much the same way as "Danish" seems to go with pastries and "French" with onion soup. Indeed, Poles have long been known for the preparation of a wide variety of tasty, moderately spiced, and pleasantly garlicky *kiełbasa*. Many of them are available at ethnic meat markets and sausage stores in such heavily Polish-populated North American cities as Chicago, New York, Detroit, and Toronto. On the other hand, what most of the large name-brand meat producers refer to as "Polish sausage" or "*polska kiełbasa*" is usually only vaguely reminiscent of the real thing.

Whether or not you have easy access to genuine Polish sausage, a major advantage of making your own is economy. Home sausage-making is still a widespread practice in rural and small-town Poland, where even people whose livelihood is not hog-raising often keep a pig or two. These are butchered for Christmas, Easter, and weddings, and turned into an assortment of sausages and cold cuts, not to mention roasts, bacon, variety-meat dishes, and other treats.

Of course, it would not be too economical to turn meat purchased at your local supermarket into *kiełbasa*, unless you prepare only a small quantity on rare occasions as a kind of cultural novelty. If, however, you raise your own pigs, know someone who does, or at least have access to cut-rate meat from a wholesale butcher, then sausage-making is both economical and enables you to enjoy a variety of quality meat products not commercially available.

Before trying your hand at making your own *kiełbasa, kiszka, salceson*, or whatever, it is advisable to familiarize yourself with the basics. This includes the necessary equipment and utensils as well as the ingredients and their proper handling, especially at the initial preparation stage, where you are dealing with raw, uncured meat. Absolute cleanliness is essential here. All the utensils, cutting boards, pans, etc., that touch the meat should be sterilized by scalding with boiling water and then re-sterilized in a hot oven. Hands must also be frequently scrubbed in plenty of hot, soapy water. Since meat is highly susceptible to air-borne bacteria, anything but the most sanitary possible conditions can adversely affect the quality and life of your finished product.

As with most everything else, there is a knack to sausage-making and meat curing. If you are a novice to this field, it would not be wise to plunge into an involved recipe that entails numerous ingredients and weeks of careful curing, followed by air-drying and perhaps several more weeks of patient cold-smoking. Above all, do not choose a recipe that calls for a huge amount of meat until you feel up to doing it justice.

Instead, we suggest you start with a simple, unsmoked sausage calling for only 4 lbs. of meat, like the quick fresh *kiełbasa* at the beginning of the chapter, or the easy buckwheat & liver sausage found further on. If you find that home meat processing is your cup of tea, in time you can graduate to the more complex varieties of *kiełbasa* like the various smoked & dried sausages or head cheese and eventually even cure your own ham, pork loin, ribs, beef tongue, goose breast, and fish.

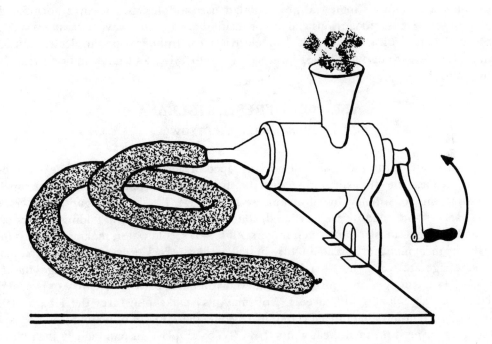

Meat for sausage is cut into cubes, seasoned, and allowed to stand in shallow pan overnight. Then it is stuffed into casing through a special sausage funnel attached to manual or electric meatgrinder.

SAUSAGE CASING
kiełbaśnice/jelita

Sausage casing (salted intestines) are available at your butcher's. Before using they should be rinsed of the salt in cold water. It isn't a bad idea to attach one end of casing to your kitchen tap and run cold water through it to check for holes. Wherever a hole is found, cut the intestine and use for making a shorter piece of sausage. Unless otherwise specified (e.g. sheep casing, large beef intestine, pork stomach etc.), ordinary pork intestines are called for whenever the term "casing" with no added qualifiers is referred to in this chapter.

STUFFING CASINGS
napełnianie kiełbaśnic

Sausage is made by stuffing casings with any variety of fillings. This can be done by hand by attaching one end of casing to narrow end of sausage funnel and forcing filling into it with thumb. The author's maternal grandmother used a hollowed-cut cow's horn for this purpose, but this is rather laborious and time-consuming. A quicker way is to attach a sausage funnel to the front of a hand-cranked or electric meat grinder. Special electric sausage-making machines are also available. Twist sausage into 1½–2 foot links and tie twists with strong white thread.

ALL-PORK FRESH KIEŁBASA
kiełbasa biała wieprzowa

Dice 5 lbs. pork butts and ½ lb. salt pork (scraped of salt) or unsalted fat back. The best way is to cut meat into thin slices, then dice the slices. If you have a food-processor capable of achieving this consistency, by all means use it. Add 2–3 T. salt, 1 t. sugar, and 2–5 buds minced garlic. Work mixture well by hand, clutching meat with palm, folding fingers over meat, and letting it squish out between fingers. Add ½–¾ c. cold water, making sure it is fully absorbed by meat mixture. Spread mixture in shallow glass, crockery, or unchipped enameled pan and refrigerate overnight. Next day stuff casings with mixture, twisting sausages into 1–2 foot links. Hang sausages up to air-dry in cool, well-ventilated place several hrs. or overnight. Puncture any air bubbles with needle. You may also make punctures the length of the kiełbasa to prevent bursting during cooking. To cook, place in pot of boiling water to cover and simmer covered on med. heat about 1 hr. To bake, place in pan, add ½ inch boiling water and bake in 375° oven about 1 hr., or until nicely browned. Turn sausage over midway through baking.

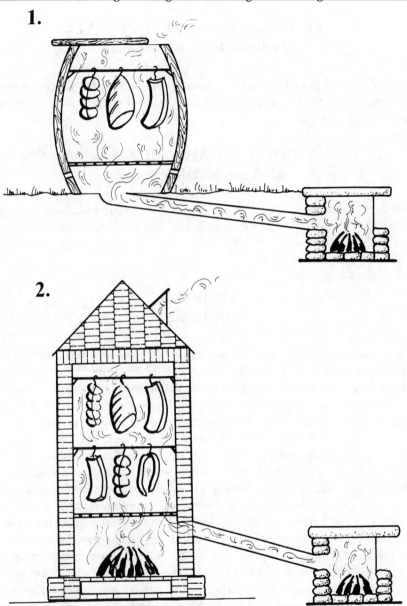

Meats and other products may be smoked in a simple barrel-smoker (1.), which can be easily disassembled, or in a more or less permanent smokehouse (2.).

FRESH KIEŁBASA POZNAŃ STYLE
kiełbasa biała poznańska

Combine 4 lbs. diced pork butts and ½ lb. diced fat back with 1 lb. coarsely ground beef round steak. Add 3 T. salt, ½ t. pepper, 3–4 buds minced garlic, and 1 T. marjoram, then proceed as above.

QUICK FRESH KIEŁBASA
kiełbasa biała naprędce

Combine 3 lbs. store-bought ground pork with 1 lb. ground beef (or ½ lb. ground beef and ½ lb. ground veal). Add 2–3 buds minced garlic, ½ t. pepper, 2 T. salt, and (optional) 1–2 t. marjoram. Mix well by hand, working in ½ c. cold water. Refrigerate at least 1 hr. for flavors to blend, then proceed as above.

SMOKING
wędzenie

Only hardwoods should be used for smoking. The best are oak, beech, alder, maple, linden, pear, apple, cherry, or plum. Birch may also be used but it must first be stripped of its bark which may give the meat a bitter taste. Coniferous wood (pine, spruce, fir) should never be used because they give the meat a bitter, turpentine-like taste and a sticky residue. The only exception is juniper, whose branches, needles, and berries may be added to any smokehouse fire for an exquisite aroma. When smoking, logs, branches, chips, and sawdust may be used. After you have built a good hot fire, it should be smothered with damp wood, which produces plenty of smoke. (*Note*: Packaged smoking chips are available at smoking-supply and many hardware stores.) There are basically three types of smoking which will be repeatedly referred to in this chapter, so they're worth becoming acquainted with:
—*Hot smoking*: This is the quickest smoking method and partially cooks the sausage or other product. This does not preserve the meat but only gives it a nice ruddy color and smoky flavor. For the 1st 30 min. a temp. of 105°–120° is used, then it is decreased slightly to 85°–105° for 30–90 min., and finally heat is increased to 140°–190° for last 10–20 min. After this, sausage is simmered in hot 170° water for 30 min. or so. This is the method preferred by commercial sausage-makers, because the kiełbasa not only does not lose weight but takes it on during hot-water bath. This sausage is ready to eat but cannot be stored for any length of time. Commercial varieties are therefore treated with chemical preservatives.
—*Warm smoking*: This entails smoking kiełbasa from 4–48 hrs. in smoke with a temp. of 80°–115°. The sausage has a longer shelf life than the hot-smoked variety and may be eaten

in some cases without additional cooking. This method is frequently used for cured cuts of pork and other meats.

—*Cold smoking*: This method produces sausage and other smoked meats that can last indefinitely without refrigeration. The products are gently smoked in room-temp. (70°) moist smoke anywhere from 1–2 weeks. To achieve billows of thick, moist smoke, damp sawdust is added to fire and allowed to smoulder. Hams loins, and bacon are usually smoked in this way, as are dry sausages.

SMOKERS
wędzarnie

There are many different types of smokers, but we will focus on only the most common varieties:

—***Barrel smoker***: A simple, inexpensive, and very effective smoker can be made from a wooden barrel or crate, oil drum, or similar such receptacle. It must have a removable lid and the bottom must be removed entirely. This is how to go about it

—Dig 2 small pits anywhere from 3–7 feet apart. The shallower one, about 8 inches deep, is for the barrel to be set over. The other one, 1½–2 feet deep, is for your smoking fire. You may want to have more than one smoking pit, depending on whether you use hot, warm, or cold smoke. The greater the distance between smoking pit and barrel, the cooler the smoke.

—Connect the barrel pit to smoking pit with a small canal (ditch), which should be dug at an angle from the higher barrel pit to smoking pit (see illustration). If you have a small incline anywhere on your property, that is a good place to position a barrel smoker.

—Place a stove pipe or rain pipe of proper length to carry the smoke from smoking pit to bottom of barrel. *Note*: If you have dug more than one smoking pit at various distances from the barrel, you will need several lengths of piping of the proper size.

—Use bricks to build a kind of oven in smoking pit with an iron grate for the fire and a space beneath it to allow for ventilation. An iron or other flame-proof plate should be used to cover top and exposed side of oven so that smoke is forced into pipe and doesn't escape out the sides. *Note*: You may but need not build a permanent oven by sticking bricks together with mortar; bricks may simply be placed on top of each other for quick disassembly.

—Provide flanges near top of barrel on which one or more rods may be positioned; sausage and other items to be smoked are suspended from these rods by S-hooks.

—If you ever plan to smoke items that won't be suspended (meat slices, fish fillets, etc.), you should also fit sides of barrel with flanges about ⅓ of the way up, on which a rack may be placed.

—It is also a good idea to provide flanges towards bottom of barrel for a "catch rack"; that way, if the string on which sausage or other item is suspended happens to break, your meat won't fall into the dirt.

—There should be fresh-air openings at bottom of barrel to promote free circulation of smoke inside. These may be holes drilled in sides of barrel near bottom. An even easier way is to simply position barrel over pit in such a way as to leave a small air crack on one or more sides.

—During smoking, the lid is loosely placed on top of barrel, leaving a crack for smoke to escape. When smoking stops, seal barrel with lid to protect against rain, rodents, or insects. Using a metal screen as your "catch rack" is a good way to prevent uninvited scavengers from entering through ventilation openings at bottom.

—*Smokehouse*: If you have a fair-sized parcel of land and plan to smoke on a more or less regular basis, a smokehouse may be a better solution. For normal, non-commercial smoking all you will need is a structure 7–8 feet tall with sides 3–4 feet long—roughly the size of a telephone booth. It may be square or rectangular. Here are a few pointers:

—The smokehouse may be built of bricks, cement, cinder blocks or even wood. If built of wood, it should have a brick or cement foundation for the fire.

—The roof should have a hinged plate or flap which can be opened to let smoke escape during smoking and closed to keep out rain and pests when smoking has stopped.

—A door on one side of smokehouse will provide easy access to smoked items, but it should be tightly fitted to prevent smoke from escaping out the cracks.

—The inside walls of smokehouse should be fitted with flanges at various heights on which to place rods and racks.

—A perforated metal plate or metal screen should be fitted near bottom to separate smoke pit from smoking area and to act as a "catch rack" in case something falls off its hook. This will also prevent scavengers from getting in through the bottom.

—A grate should be provided on which to build the fire, with a space beneath it for ventilation. Fresh-air holes are needed to ensure free circulation of smoke.

—Build a hardwood or charcoal fire with door open. When it is good and hot, smother it with damp wood, chips, twigs, shavings, sawdust, etc., to create smoke. Do not add sausage or other items to be smoked until interior temp. is right for cold, warm, or hot smoking. You will need a good thermometer to ensure the temp. desired.

—If you plan to do a lot of cold smoking, you can also build an auxiliary smoke pit some distance away from smokehouse and pipe smoke into bottom (as with barrel smoker). *Note*: Whatever kind of smoker you decide on, the items being smoked should hang freely and not touch each other or the walls.

ALL-PORK SMOKE-SIMMERED KIEŁBASA
kiełbasa wieprzowa podwędzana parzona

Dice fine 2¼ lbs. lean pork and ¾ lb. fatty pork, discarding any veins, membranes, or gristle. In saucepan heat 4–5 t. salt until it just begins to turn golden and add to meat. Add

¼ t. saltpeter, ½–1 t. freshly ground pepper, 1 t. marjoram, and 1 bud mashed garlic. Work mixture well by hand until well blended and sticky. Stuff casings with mixture, twisting into links at 12–15 inch intervals. Use sterilized pin or needle to puncture sausage at intervals so trapped air can escape. Hang sausage up in cool (50°–55°), well-ventilated place to air-dry for 2–3 days. Smoke in hot smoke about 90 min., i.e. until sausage takes on a nice ruddy-brown color. Immediately plunge sausage into kettle of hot water and simmer at 170° 30 min. Transfer sausage to pot of cold water for 10 min. Hang sausage up until fully cooled to room temp., then refrigerate. This sausage is perfect for boiling and baking, for smoked-stock soups (żur, kapuśniak, grochówka etc.), and for adding to such dishes as bigos. *Variation*: After hot-smoking, simmering, and cooling, this kiełbasa may be cold-smoked for 7 days to make it keep longer. *Note*: Most of what passes for "polska kiełbasa" in America is prepared roughly along these lines (without the additional cold-smoking). The brief hot-smoking gives the sausage its nice color and smoky flavor without causing much shrinkage and the hot-water bath actually adds weight. You can see, therefore, why this par-smoking & simmering method is preferred by commercial butchers who sell their product by the pound.

ALL-PORK FRYING SAUSAGE
kiełbasa wieprzowa do smażenia

Dice fine 2¼ lbs. lean pork and 2¼ lbs. fatty pork, discarding any veins or the like. Parch 6–7 t. salt in saucepan as above and add to meat together with ½ t. saltpeter, 1½–2 t. freshly ground pepper, 1½–2 t. marjoram, and 2 buds mashed garlic. (*Note*: The amount of pepper and garlic may be adjusted to personal preference, and the marjoram may be eliminated entirely.) Mix meat, stuff casings, air-dry, smoke, simmer, and cool as above. Juicier than the above recipe for lean kiełbasa, this sausage is perfect for frying. Simply slice into rounds and fry in ungreased skillet to a nice golden brown. Fried or scrambled eggs are excellent when cooked with fried sliced sausage and its drippings.

PORK & BEEF SMOKED-SIMMERED KIEŁBASA
kiełbasa wieprzowo-wołowa podwędzana parzona

Dice fine 4½ lbs. lean, fat pork and combine with 2¼ lbs. coarsely ground beef (with some suet included). Sprinkle with 3 T. skillet-parched salt, ½ t. saltpeter, about 2 t. freshly ground pepper, 2 t. or so marjoram, and 2–3 buds mashed garlic. Work meat by hand until sticky, fill casing, air-dry, smoke, simmer, and cool as above.

MARKETDAY (ECONOMY) SAUSAGE
kiełbasa "jarmarczna" (oszczędna)

Sausage-makers have long prepared all-meat kiełbasa "dla siebie" (for themselves and their families) and varieties containing less expensive fillers "na handel" (for sale). It was sold by vendors on marketday, at fairs, and in city streets. It might be just the thing for food concessions or fund-raisers. Combine 4 lbs. ground pork with 2 lbs. ground beef (hamburger is good for this purpose). Add 2½ T. salt, ½ t. saltpeter, 2 t. freshly ground pepper, 1 t. marjoram (optional), and 2 buds mashed garlic. Work well by hand until sticky, spread mixture along bottom of shallow pan, and refrigerate 1–2 hrs. Add 1–2 c. filler (bread crumbs, uncooked instant cream of wheat, or uncooked quick-cooking oatmeal whirled to a powder in a processor). Work in well, adding 1–2 c. water—but only as much as the meat can absorb—and work until fully blended. Fill casings a little more loosely than usual, as filler expands during simmering and may cause sausage to burst. Puncture with pin at intervals and gently roll sausage on board, pressing down lightly, to remove trapped air. Hang up to air dry several hrs. Smoke in hot smoke about 90 min., or until sausage takes on a nice ruddy-brown color. Simmer in hot 170° water about 40 min., plunge into cold water for 10 min., then hang up until completely cooled. *Note*: Although traditional Polish cookery views sausage containing starchy additives as a budget alternative, if properly made it can be very tasty, as the filler absorbs the meat's flavorful juice which would otherwise be partially lost. Also in today's diet-conscious times, any cereal "stretcher" you add means much less red meat and cholesterol. This sausage is served hot with horseradish or mustard. In food-concession conditions, it can be kept hot in steamer or pot of hot water. It is best to prepare this kiełbasa one day and serve it the next, as it is rather perishable.

ECONOMY SAUSAGE ANOTHER WAY
kiełbasa oszczędna inaczej

Another way to prepare a fairly tasty kiełbasa at a reasonable price is to substitute pork head (jowls, rind, ears, snout) for about half of the fresh ground or diced fresh meat in any of the above recipes. The split head (with eyes and gristle discarded and tongue and brains reserved for other use) should be washed well and any bristle should be singed over a flame. Place the split head in pot, add a bay leaf, several peppercorns, 1–2 grains allspice, and 2 t. salt, scald with boiling water to cover, and cook on med. heat 1½–2 hrs. or until tender. During cooking replace water that evaporates so meat is always covered. Drain and cool to room temp., then dice fine or grind coarsely, discarding bones. To prepare kiełbasa, combine one part diced or ground cooked pork head with one part fresh diced or ground pork (with some fresh beef or veal added if desired) season and proceed as with fresh or smoke-simmered kiełbasa (above). *Note*: The leftover stock makes an excellent base for kapuśniak, żur, barszcz, pea, and other meat-based soups. Simply chill, discard congealed fat, and use as you would the ordinary meat-bone stock.

REGULAR SMOKED KIEŁBASA
kiełbasa zwyczajna wędzona

Dice or grind coarsely 15 lbs. pork, including butts as well as some pieces from fresh bacon and ham portions, and 4 lbs. lean beef. Sprinkle meat with ⅔ c. (preferably skillet-parched Kosher) salt, 2½ t. saltpeter, 2–3 T. freshly ground pepper, 1 t. ground allspice, and 6 buds mashed garlic. Mix and work well by hand until mixture is fully blended and somewhat sticky. Fill casings with mixture, twisting to form links every 12 inches or so. Remove any air bubbles by piercing with pin or needle dipped in grain alcohol. Hang up in cool (40°–45°) cellar overnight, then air-dry 6 hrs. Cold-smoke 2–3 hrs. a day for 1 week. This sausage will keep 6–8 months, possibly up to 1 year, if stored in a cool, dry, slightly ventilated place. It is primarily meant to be eaten cold as a lunch meat with rye bread, horseradish, ćwikła, or mustard. *Note*: This recipe is in larger quantity for the benefit of those who feel it isn't worth all the fuss and bother to make just a few lbs. of sausage at a time. Another such recipe slightly down-scaled follows.

REGULAR ALL-PORK SMOKED KIEŁBASA
kiełbasa wieprzowa zwyczajna wędzona

Combine 2 lbs. ground pork butts, 4 lbs. finely diced pork butts and 2 lbs. finely diced pork fat back. Sprinkle with ½ c. salt, 2 t. saltpeter, 1–2 T. freshly ground pepper, 1 t. ground allspice, and 1 t. sugar. Mix well and place in large shallow glass, crockery, or unchipped enameled pans in which meat mixture reaches a height of no more that 2 inches. Cover lightly with dish towel and keep in cool place or on lowest shelf of fridge overnight. Next day, mash 3–4 buds minced garlic with 1 t. salt into a paste, add to meat mixture, and work well by hand until fully blended and sticky. Fill casings with mixture, twisting into links every 12–15 inches. Tie ends with strong cotton thread and cut sausage into 2-link loops. Eliminate any air bubbles by piercing with sterilized pin or needle. Hang up in open non-smoking smokehouse overnight to dry. Next day, cold-smoke 2–3 times a day for 1 week.

SUPERB COUNTRY SAUSAGE
kiełbasa wiejska wyborowa

Finely dice 2 lbs. lean pork (butts with an addition of loin and ham portion trimmings are good), ½ lb. tender beef and ½ lb. pork fat back. As always, discard any bone chips, sinews, etc. Sprinkle meat with 4 t. salt, ¼ t. saltpeter, ¼–½ t. freshly ground pepper, ¼ t. marjoram, 1 pinch ground allspice, and 1 pinch grated nutmeg. Work well by hand until uniform and place mixture in thin, packed-down layer in shallow pan. Keep in coolish (55°–60°) place 24 hrs. Mash 1 bud garlic, add to mixture and work well by hand until it gets sticky. Fill casings with mixture rather tightly, twisting into links every 25 inches or so. Tie each twist with strong cotton thread and cut into individual links. Bring tied ends of each link together to form a loop and tie. Eliminate any air bubbles by piercing as above. Hang sausage up to air-dry several hrs. in cool, breezy place. Then smoke in thin cold smoke 3–5 hrs., in warm thick smoke 90 min. and finally in hot (185°) smoke 45–60 min. Hang up to cool in cool, well-ventilated place. This delicious sausage is ready to eat cold or re-heated.

KRAKÓW SAUSAGE
kiełbasa krakowska

Cut 4½ lbs. pork shoulder butts or pork neck into roughly ¾ inch cubes, trimming away sinews, veins, bone chips, etc. Combine with 1½ lbs. coarsely ground beef rump. Sprinkle with 2¾ T. salt, ½ t. saltpeter, 1 t. freshly ground pepper, 8 grains allspice mortar-pounded and sieved, ½ t. coriander, 1 pinch marjoram, and 1 bud mashed garlic. Work well by hand until well blended, pack mixture down in thin layer in shallow pan, cover with dish towel, and keep in cool place 24 hrs. Fill casings (middle beef intestines are best) with mixture rather tightly. Twist into roughly 20-inch links and secure twists with strong cotton thread. Cut into 2-link pieces, pierce any air bubbles with sterilized pin, and roll lightly with hands on board to remove all air. Hang sausage up in cool place to dry about 1 hr. Smoke in hot smoke about 2 hrs. them immediately plunge into kettle of hot 170° water and keep it at that temp. 1 hr. Transfer sausage to pot of cold water and let it stand 10 min. Hang sausage up in cool breezy place until completely cooled.

DRY KRAKÓW SAUSAGE
kiełbasa krakowska sucha

Proceed as with ordinary Kraków sausage (above), but after keeping sausage in 170° hot-water bath 1 hr., hang up to cool and dry. Then cold-smoke 6–12 days, 2–3 times a day. You can easily test whether it has been smoked enough, because the final weight should not exceed 60% of the fresh sausage you started with before the first hot-smoking. If it exceeds that weight, hang it up in a cool, airy place until it has dried sufficiently. *Note*: If properly made, this tasty sausage is nice and hard and should be sliced very thin. It will last many months if stored in hanging position in cool, slightly ventilated cellar. *Important*: If a thin layer of mold begins to form on the casing of this or any other smoked sausage, wipe it off with a damp cloth, cold-smoke another day or two, and air-dry one day before returning to storage.

HAM SAUSAGE
kiełbasa szynkowa

Finely dice 2 lbs. lean pork from ham portion, ½ lb. fatty pork shoulder butts, and 1 lb. baby beef rump. Sprinkle with 1½ T. salt, ½ t. saltpeter, ¼ t. freshly ground pepper, ⅛ t. coriander, and a pinch or 2 grated nutmeg. Work well by hand until blended and pack mixture in thin layer into shallow pan. Cover and keep in cool place 24 hrs. Work mixture by hand again until it becomes sticky. If very thick, work in 1–2 T. dry red wine. Tightly fill middle beef intestine with mixture, tie both ends with strong thread or string, pierce with sterilized needle, and roll gently on board to remove air. Hang up in cool place for 2 hrs., then hot-smoke about 2 hrs. The sausage should turn a nice light brown with shades of pink. Plunge into cold water for 10 min. then hang up to dry. Refrigerate and serve as a luncheon meat. *Variation*: For longer life, after drying, cold-smoke for several days. *Optional*: Sausage mixture may be additionally seasoned with a pinch of ground bay leaf and/or ground cloves.

JUNIPER/HUNTER'S SAUSAGE
kiełbasa jałowcowa/myśliwska

Dice, discarding sinews, bone chips, etc., 2 lbs. lean pork (butt or ham portion), 2 lbs. fatty pork butts, 2 lbs. baby beef and ½ lb. pork fat back. Sprinkle with 2¾ T. salt, 1 scant t. saltpeter, and 1 t. freshly ground pepper. Work well by hand and pack into shallow pan in thin layer. Cover with dish towel and keep in cool place 24 hrs. Meanwhile, place 1 T. juniper berries in small bowl and cover with 10 T. lukewarm water. Let stand 24 hrs. Next day, drain berries if they have not absorbed all the water, pound to a pulp in mortar, combine with any leftover water, stir in 1½ t. sugar, mix well, and add to meat mixture. Work very well by hand until mixture·becomes sticky. Fill casings with mixture tightly, twisting into 20-inch links, tying ends, and forming links into loops. Remove air by piercing with pin. Hang up in 60° place for 3 hrs. Hot-smoke at about 110° 90 min., then increase heat to 185° for 30 min. Sausage should have taken on a nice brown color by then. Cool in well-ventilated place. Cold-smoke in juniper smoke 2–3 days. Sausage should not exceed 75%

of its original weight. Dry in cool, well-ventilated place a day or so, then store in cool, slightly ventilated cellar. Hunter's sausage is always eaten cold and was apparently so named because it is the ideal addition to a hunter's rucksack.

CARAWAY SAUSAGE
kiełbasa kminkowa

Prepare like Kraków sausage (above), but omit allspice, coriander, marjoram, and garlic. After meat has "aged" in a pan in cool place for 24 hrs., add 2–3 t. whole or partially crushed caraway seeds and 1 small grated onion, then work well by hand until sticky, filling casings and proceed as indicated. *Note*: Sausage containing onion or other vegetable additives other than garlic does not keep well even when refrigerated and should be eaten within several days.

EASTERN-BORDERLANDS (VODKA) SAUSAGE
kiełbasa kresowa

Coarsely grind 10 lbs. lean pork and 4 lbs. tender beef. Sprinkle with 2–3 T. freshly ground pepper, 2 T. marjoram, 1 t. ground allspice, and 1 t. ground cloves. Scorch ¾ c. Kosher salt in dry skillet as indicated previously, mix with 2 t. saltpeter, and sprinkle over meat. Work well by hand, gradually adding about 1 c. vodka or light rum. Continue working rather vigorously until mixture is smooth and uniform. Add 3 lbs. diced fat back, preferably the harder variety from neck area, and mix until evenly distributed. Fill casings tightly with mixture, rolling sausage lightly with rolling-pin to eliminate empty spaces. Tie ends of casing with strong thread, place sausage on board, cover with another board, and weight down with several bricks or other heavy objects. Let stand at room temp. 2 days, then transfer to cool, dry, ventilated cellar and keep it there 2 weeks. Hang sausage up to air-dry in cool breezy place, then cold-smoke for 7 days. Store by hanging in cool cellar. This long-life sausage is eaten cold like a lunch meat. To serve, slice very thin and enjoy with rye bread and hot lemon tea or "coś mocniejszego" (something stronger)!

DRY SAUSAGE
kiełbasa sucha

Dice 2½ lbs. pork butts, ¾ lb. tender beef and ¾ lb. pork fat back. Sprinkle with 1 T. salt, ¼ t. saltpeter, ¼–½ t. freshly ground pepper and a pinch or two nutmeg. (*Optional*: A pinch of marjoram or ground allspice may also be added). Work well by hand until mixture becomes sticky and fill casings very tightly. Twist into links every 12–15 inches, tie every second link, and cut into 2-link loops. Hang up to air-dry several days in cool breezy place, then cold-smoke 6–10 days, as always for 2-hr. periods 2–3 times a day. Air-dry some more until sausage weighs only 55%–60% of what it did before smoking. In this case, if you started with 4 lbs. of fresh sausage, you should have no more than 2¼–2½ lbs. after it has been sufficiently cold-smoked and air-dried. It will keep a good long time in hanging position in cool ventilated cellar or pantry. Slice very thin and serve cold.

THIN DRY SAUSAGE
kabanosy

Dice 2½ lbs. lean pork (preferably ham portion) and 1¼ lbs. fatty pork butts. Sprinkle with 1 T. salt and ¼ t. saltpeter and work by hand briefly to blend. Line mixture along bottom of shallow pan and keep 24 hrs. in cool, well-ventilated place. Season with ½–1 t. freshly ground pepper, ¼ t. partially crushed caraway seeds, a pinch of ground allspice, and ½ bud mashed garlic. Work mixture well by hand until sticky. Fill thin sheep's casings with mixture tightly, as always eliminating any air pockets with sterilized needle. Hang up to air-dry several hrs. Hot-smoke at about 110° about 60 min., then increase heat in smokehouse to 185° for 20 min. Hang up to dry in cool breezy place for several days. They are ready when they weigh only 55% of what they did when fresh. *Note*: These finger-thick sausages are very delicious and can be enjoyed as a cold snack any time. They are best when sufficiently dried and brittle so they crack when bent. Like other dry sausages, they require no refrigeration and are best stored by hanging in cool cellar. In the fridge, they take on moisture and become limp.

POLISH SALAMI
salami polskie

Cut into small cubes 3 lbs. lean pork from ham and loin portions, 1¼ lbs. lean beef and 1¼ lbs. fat back. Air-dry in breezy place several hrs. so it loses some of its moistness. Grind fine, sprinkle with 1 T. salt, ½ t. saltpeter, 1 t. freshly ground pepper, and ½ t. paprika. Work ingredients by hand very well into smooth uniform mixture, gradually adding ¼ c. grain alcohol or vodka. Pack mixture tightly into pan in thin layer and let stand 24 hrs. in cool, airy, place. Tightly fill beef casings with mixture, twisting and tying every 20 inches. Cut salami into sticks, place on table, cover with weighed-down board, and let stand overnight in cool place. Hang up to air-dry in cool, breezy place about 4 days, then cold-smoke 6–12 days. Dry them by hanging in cool breezy place another several days. These will keep almost indefinitely if stored in hanging position in cool place. *Note*: Feel free to vary the flavor of your salami with such seasonings as a pinch of ground bay leaf, nutmeg, or cloves and 1–2 buds crushed garlic. *Variation*: Some purists insist that the meat for salami should be scraped rather then ground, but this is a rather tedious process. The choice is yours!

GOOSE SAUSAGE
kiełbasa z gęsiny

Finely dice 1½ lbs. uncooked skinned goose meat from drumsticks, 3½ lbs. pork butts and 1½ lbs. lean beef. Grind ½ lb. uncooked goose fat and add to meat. Sprinkle with 4 T. salt, ½ t. saltpeter, 1 t. freshly ground pepper, and a pinch or 2 ground allspice, marjoram, and coriander or cloves. Work ingredients into uniform mixture, place in glass or crockery bowl, cover snugly with inverted dinner plate, weight it down with something heavy and keep in cool place 3 days. Fill casings with mixture very tightly, piercing to remove air bubbles, twist, and tie into 20-inch links and air-dry in cool, breezy place 3 days. Cold-smoke 8–9 days. This sausage should keep up to 2 months if properly prepared. *Note*: Polish Jews used to make a similar sausage without the pork.

DUCK OR TURKEY SAUSAGE
kiełbasa z kaczki lub indyka

Since duck drumsticks are not very meaty, use breast and thigh portions, but otherwise proceed as with goose sausage (above). For turkey sausage, substitute uncooked, skinned, dark turkey meat for goose and use ½ lb. finely diced pork fat back in place of goose fat. Otherwise, mix, season, stuff casings, air-dry, and cold-smoke as indicated for goose sausage.

RABBIT SAUSAGE
kiełbasa z królika

Finely dice 4½ lbs. rabbit meat, discarding veins and membranes. Cut 1¼ lbs. pork fat back into slightly larger cubes and combine with diced (or coarsely ground) rabbit. Mix ¼ t. saltpeter with ¼ c. salt and sprinkle over meat mixture. Add ¼ t. freshly ground pepper and ⅛ t. sugar. (*Optional*: ¼ t. ground allspice may also be added.) Work mixture well by hand, adding only as much cold pre-boiled water as the meat will absorb. Fill casings with mixture, twisting into links every 12–15 inches. Hot-smoke about 1 hr., then plunge into hot 170° water and keep it at that temp. for 30–40 min. Hang up to cool and dry in airy place. *Note*: Rabbit sausage, while quite tasty, is on the perishable side and should be stored in fridge no more than 3–4 days. Naturally, like all sausage, it can be stored indefinitely in freezer.

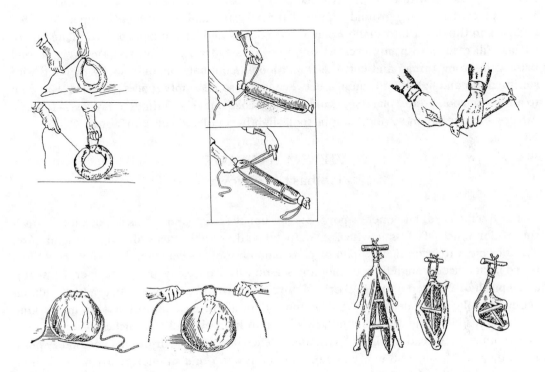

Illustrations show top row left to right: fitting a ring of kiełbasa serdelowa (Vienna sausage) with a loop of string by which it will be suspended during smoking and drying; trussing a thicker-casing lunch-meat-type sausage with string; and fastened ends of sausage with skewers. Bottom row shows sewing and tightening of bladder filled with head-cheese mixture and the proper way to prepare fowl for smoking, using sticks to expose inner surfaces to smoke penetration.

WILD-BOAR SAUSAGE
kiełbasa z dzika

Cut 4 lbs. fresh wild boar meat into cubes, trimming away veins, gristle, etc., then grind coarsely. Combine with 2 lbs. finely diced pork fat back, sprinkle with ¼ c. salt mixed with 1 t. saltpeter, 1 t. freshly ground pepper, 1 t. marjoram, and ½ t. ground juniper. Mix well and pack in thin layer into shallow pan. Cover loosely and let stand in cool, ventilated place 24 hrs. Fill casings with mixture, twisting into links every 12–15 inches. Tie every second twist with strong thread and cut into 2-link loops. Eliminate air bubbles by piercing with sterilized pin and lightly roll sausage between hands so all empty spaces get filled. Hang up to air-dry in cool, breezy place several days, then cold-smoke 2–3 times a day for 7–10 days. Air-dry another day or so and hang in cool, slightly ventilated cellar to store.

VIENNA SAUSAGE
kiełbasa serdelowa

Cut 6½ lbs. med. fat boneless pork, 3⅓ lbs. boneless veal and 1 lb. salt pork into ¾-inch cubes. Combine 5–6 T. salt with 2 t. saltpeter and sprinkle meat all over with mixture. Transfer meat to large shallow pan or pans, smooth top, and let stand in cool place 24 hrs. Grind meat twice through fine strainer and season with 1 t. freshly ground pepper, 1 t. sugar, and a pinch or 2 grated nutmeg. Work mixture well by hand until uniform, gradually adding about 2 c. cold, pre-boiled water, but no more than mixture can absorb. Continue working until sticky. Fill casings with mixture, twisting into links every 30–35 inches. Tie both ends of each link with thread, cut links apart, and tie each into a loop. Air-dry in cool, breezy place 1 hr., then warm-smoke 3 hrs. Plunge into boiling water and simmer gently below boiling point 45 min. Hang up until dry and cooled to room temp. Refrigerate and use within several days or freeze. To serve, cook in gently boiling water 15–20 min. and enjoy with mustard or horseradish. In Poland, this is a favorite breakfast or supper dish.

KNACKWURST
serdelki

This is essentially a smaller-link version of kiełbasa serdelowa (above), and we present it in more modest quantity for those who don't feel up to preparing nearly 11 lbs. of sausage. Cut 2½ lbs. lean pork, ½ lb. pork fat back and 1¼ lbs. veal (or lean beef) into small cubes and mix with 2¾ T. salt and ¾ t. saltpeter. Let stand in cool place 24 hrs. Next day grind through med. strainer and a second time through fine strainer. Sprinkle with ½ t. sugar, ½

t. freshly ground pepper, and a pinch grated nutmeg. Add about 1 c. water (or as much as meat will absorb) and work vigorously by hand until mixture is smooth and sticky. Fill casings with mixture, twisting into links every 4 inches. Hang chains of serdelki out to air-dry an hr. or so. Then, either hot-smoke 40 min., cool in breezy place, and refrigerate, or warm-smoke 40 min. and transfer to kettle of hot water below boiling point for 10 min. Hang up to cool and dry, then refrigerate. To serve, cook in gently boiling water 15–20 min.

FRANKFURTERS
parówki

Cut 5½ lbs. veal, 2½ lbs. fatty pork butts and 1 lb. pork fat back into cubes, sprinkle with ⅓ c. salt and 2 t. saltpeter, mix and let stand in cool place 12 hrs. or overnight. Grind mixture 3 times, first through coarse, then med., and finally fine strainer. Work mixture well, adding only as much cold, pre-boiled water as it can absorb. Add 2 t. (more or less) freshly ground pepper, several pinches ground allspice, and grated nutmeg. Work well by hand until smooth and glossy. Fill thin sheep's casing with mixture, twisting into links every 4–5 inches. Hot-smoke 30–35 min., then plunge into hot 190° water and keep them at that temp. about 8–10 min. Hang up in airy place to cool and dry, then refrigerate. To serve, cook in boiling water as you would store-bought franks. *Note*: These can be stored refrigerated only for several days but they freeze very well. *Variation*: For more "porky" frankfurters, feel free to reverse the proportions of pork and veal.

BUCKWHEAT SAUSAGE/BLOOD SAUSAGE/BLACK PUDDING/"KISZKA"
kiszka kaszana/kaszanka

Place in pot 1 lb. salt-pork rinds, 1 pork lung, ½ lb. pork jowls and ¾ lb. lean and fatty pork trimmings. Cover with water, add 1 t. salt and cook on med. heat until tender, replacing water that evaporated so meat is covered the whole time. Drain, reserving stock. When meat is cool enough to handle, trim away any bones, veins, and gristle and grind coarsely. Strain stock, add enough water to make 10 c., add 1 t. salt, bring to boil, and gradually add 6 c. buckwheat groats. Cook on med. heat until water is absorbed, cover, and bake in 375° oven 30 min. To hot groats add ground meat, 2 c. sieved pork blood, 1 t. freshly ground pepper, and 1 t. or more marjoram. Add a little more salt if desired. Mix ingredients well and stuff into large hog intestine, sewing ends shut or fastening them with wooden skewers. Place kiszka into kettle of warm water, gently bring to boil, then reduce heat and simmer 40 min. Hang up in cool, airy place to dry and cool. May be eaten hot or cold. To serve hot, slice and fry in a little fat or in vegetable oil spray if dieting.

BAKED COUNTRY-STYLE BUCKWHEAT SAUSAGE
kaszanka wiejska pieczona

In 8 c. hot water cook pork lungs, heart, and spleen (totaling about 2¼ lbs.) until tender. While they cook, in skillet fry up ½ lb. diced salt pork (or unsalted fat back) into crunchy, golden-brown nuggets, drain, and set aside. (Reserve drippings for other purposes). Drain tender variety meats, reserving stock. Cut up lungs, heart, and spleen, trimming away and discarding veins and gristle. Coarsely grind meat and pork nuggets. In 6 c. boiling stock cook 4 c. buckwheat groats until liquid is absorbed, cover, and simmer on very low heat about 20 min. or bake in oven. Combine groats and meat, add 1 c. sieved pork blood, 1½–2 T. salt, 2 t. marjoram, 1 t. pepper and ¼ t. ground allspice. Mix well and fill large hot intestine with mixture and sew ends shut or fasten with wooden skewers. Place in greased shallow baking pan and bake in 350°–375° oven about 90 min. May be served hot straight from the oven. Or, cool to room temp., refrigerate, and reheat before serving. It can also be sliced and served cold as a lunch meat.

LUXURY BUCKWHEAT SAUSAGE
kiszka kaszana wyborowa

Cook 2¼ lbs. pork jowls and 2¼ lbs. pork head (snout, lips, ears) in gently boiling water 1 hr. Add 2¼ lbs. pork or veal lights and continue cooking until tender. Drain, reserving stock. Cut up meat, discarding veins and gristle. Grind meat together with 1 raw quartered onion. Cook 4 c. buckwheat groats in 6 c. stock until fluffy. Soak 1 c. bread crumbs in a little of the stock and combine with groats and ground mixture. Add 1 trimmed pork liver, ground twice through fine strainer, and 3 c. sieved pork blood. Sprinkle with 4–5 T. salt, 1 T. freshly ground pepper, 1–2 T. marjoram, and 1 T. ground allspice. (*Optional*: A little MSG will enhance the flavor of this and other buckwheat sausages; in this recipe use ½–1 t. if you like). Mix all ingredients until fully blended and fill 15-inch lengths of large hog intestines with mixture. Sew ends shut or fasten with wooden skewer. Gently simmer kiszka in kettle of hot water for 10 min., then set on rack in cool place to cool and dry. Refrigerate until ready to use. *Note*: May also be baked in oven as above instead of being cooked in hot water.

BLOOD SAUSAGE/BLACK PUDDING
kiszka krwista/czarna

Bring 1 qt. milk to boil, switch off heat, and add 1¼ lbs. broken-up stale french bread, mixing until milk is absorbed. Add 1⅓ qts. fresh pork blood, mix well, and run mixture through meat grinder. Add 1¼ lbs. finely diced fat back, 2 med. onions finely diced and sautéed in 2 T. lard, 2 t. salt, 2 t. marjoram. 1 t. MSG, and from 1 pinch–¼ t. ground allspice. Mix ingredients well, transfer to heavy pot, and heat to gentle boil, stirring constantly so mixture doesn't burn. Set aside to cool and use it to fill large hog intestines only half full. Mixture will expand during cooking! As usual, sew up ends or fasten with skewers, plunge into a kettle of hot water, and simmer below boiling point about 30 min. Remove and cool on rack, then refrigerate until ready to use. Good hot or cold. *Variation*: Instead of poaching in water, these sausages may be fried on all sides in salt-pork drippings about 20 min.

PORK-JOWL SAUSAGE
kiszka podgardlana

Cover 2¼ lbs. pork jowls with boiling water and cook 1 hr. Add 1 lb. pork or veal lungs and continue cooking until meat is tender. Towards the end add ½ lb. pork liver and cook about 5 min. longer. Drain, reserving stock. In 2 c. stock, soak 2–3 stale kaiser rolls or other white bread. When meat is cool enough to handle, cut up into chunks, discarding any veins or gristle. Run meat through grinder together with the soggy rolls. Replace coarse or med. strainer with fine strainer on grinder and grind ½ lb. raw pork liver twice. Mix all ingredients, adding ¼ lb. diced lard. Sprinkle with 2 T. salt, ½–1 t. pepper, 1–2 t. marjoram, and ¼ t. ground allspice. Mix well and fill large hog intestines of whatever length you prefer. (*Hint*: 10–12-inch stretches of intestines make just the right-sized sausage for 3–4 people at a single meal). Sew ends shut or fasten with skewers and cook in water below boiling point 30–40 min. The shorter the sausages, the shorter the cooking time. Plunge into cold water for 10 min. Transfer to scalded (sterilized) board, cover with another board, weight down and keep in cool, well-ventilated place overnight. Refrigerate until ready to use. *Variation*: For a different flavor twist and longer life, this sausage may be warm-smoked for a couple hrs. or cold-smoked 1–2 days.

EASY BUCKWHEAT & LIVER SAUSAGE
łatwa kaszanka wątrobiana

If you have never made buckwheat sausage before or if you don't happen to have on hand all the ingredients required in the other recipes, this is the version you should definitely try. Place 2–3 lbs. (or whatever amount you want) sliced liver of choice in pot or bowl and scald with boiling water to cover. Let stand 1 min. and drain. Grind liver and mix with equal amount cooked buckwheat groats or barley, preferably cooked in meat stock. Add 1 level T.

lard, salt-pork drippings, or bacon drippings per qt. of mixture, season with salt, pepper, marjoram, ground allspice (optional), and MSG to taste. Mix ingredients well and loosely stuff 12-inch lengths of large hog intestines, sewing or skewering ends as always. Plunge into hot water and simmer gently 30–40 min. Hang up in cool place to dry and cool. *Variation*: Most any ground, cooked leftover meat may be added to mixture before filling casings. *Note*: Cooked barley may be used in any of the sausages calling for buckwheat groats, but they won't be as good.

SILESIAN BUCKWHEAT SAUSAGE
krupnioki śląskie

Place 2 lbs. pork hocks in pot, cover with water, bring to boil, and simmer 2 hrs. Add ½ lb. pork jowls and 1½ lbs. pork lights, add enough hot water so meat is covered, add 2 t. salt and several grains allspice, and cook until meat is very tender. Strain, reserving stock. Bring 6 c. stock to boil, adding enough water to make 6 c. if you have less. Add 4 c. buckwheat groats and simmer until water is absorbed. Cover, and simmer on very low heat another 20 min. Cut up the cooked, cooled meat, discarding any bones or gristle, and grind it together with ½ lb. raw pork or other liver, drained golden salt-pork nuggets obtained by frying up ½ lb. diced salt pork, and 1 quartered onion. Mix with groats, add 2 lbs. sieved pork blood, mix well and season to taste with salt, pepper, and about 1–2 t. marjoram. Stuff mixture loosely into ordinary pork casing (the kind used for kiełbasa), twisting every 8 inches so each link makes 1 average serving. Simmer in hot water 45–50 min. Serve hot straight from the pot or dry and cool on rack and refrigerate until ready to use. Reheat by frying in a little fat or grilling. In Poland, these sausages are sold at sidewalk stands with mustard or horseradish and rye bread. In keeping with Silesian tradition, a stein of beer would be the perfect companion. *Variation*: Instead of cooking in water, krupnioki may be baked in oven. Prick each sausage in several places with pin, place in pan, add 1½ c. water, and bake at 375° 1 hr., turning them over after first 30 min. For a soft skin, cover pan with foil during baking.

LIVER SAUSAGE
kiszka lub kiełbasa pasztetowa/pasztetówka

Cut 1 lb. pork jowls into small cubes, discarding gristle, place in pot, add 1 quartered onion, cover with water, simmer until meat is tender. At end of cooking, add 1¼ lbs. sliced pork, baby beef, or calf's liver, and keep it in pot only long enough for it to lose its redness. It should not cook! Drain and set aside to cool. In leftover stock soak 2 broken-up kaiser rolls until soggy and grind through fine strainer with jowls and liver twice. Add 1 whole egg and 1 T. bread crumbs, season to taste with salt, pepper, and a little grated nutmeg and work well by hand until smooth. Fill stretches of large hog intestine with mixture, sewing or skewering ends shut. Simmer in hot water about 40 min., then cool on rack and refrigerate. *Note*: For a smoky flavor and longer life, air-dry in cool, breezy place 3 hrs., then cold-smoke 10–12 hrs.

LIVER SAUSAGE ANOTHER WAY
kiszka wątrobiana/wątrobianka/pasztetówka

For this recipe, you will need a whole pork liver, which should be washed, cut up into chunks, and trimmed of any veins, membranes, etc. You will also need half that amount by weight of pork-belly fat (sadło), which should likewise be trimmed of veins and membranes and cut up. Grind the liver and pork-belly fat twice. Soak 1 lb. stale, broken-up rolls (or about 3½ c. bread crumbs) in 2 c. coffee cream or half & half. When soggy, grind and add to meat mixture together with any cream not absorbed by the rolls. Mix well and run entire mixture through fine strainer of grinder. Sprinkle with 1–2 t. salt, 1 t. freshly ground pepper, ½ t. ground allspice, 1–2 t. marjoram, and ¼ t. grated nutmeg. Add ½ lb. fat back cut into thin strips and mix well. Fill 15-inch stretches of large hog intestines with mixture ¾ full, sewing up or skewering ends. Place in kettle of hot water and simmer at gentle boil about 45 min. from the time simmering begins. Remove, rinse with cold water, and place on board. Cover with another lightly weighted-down board and keep in cool place overnight. Ready to use as is or it may be cold-smoked 12 hrs.

POMERANIAN PORK SAUSAGE
kiełbasa pomorska/metka

Grind 5 lbs. pork and 1 lb. pork fat back twice, using the fine strainer the second time. Season to taste with salt, freshly ground pepper, and paprika, work well by hand until smooth, and fill casing with mixture, twisting into links of desired length. Air-dry about 4 hrs., preferably in cool, brisk wind, then cold-smoke 3–4 hrs. Air-dry briefly again and refrigerate. This sausage is meant to be eaten cold.

WHITE HEAD CHEESE
salceson biały

In large pot, place 1 cleaned, split pig's head (with eyes discarded and brains reserved for other uses), 1 lb. fat back, the fat-back rind (skin), pork heart, and tongue. Add 2 t.–1 T. salt, 10–15 peppercorns, 1 bay leaf, and 4–6 grains allspice. Cover with hot water and cook at gentle boil, skimming scum from top. After 30 min. remove fat back (leaving its rind in pot) and set aside. Continue cooking remaining ingredients 1½–2 hrs. or until soft but not falling apart. Drain, reserving stock. Cut tongue and reserved par-boiled fat back into ½-inch or so cubes, the remaining meat into thin strips and rind into "matchsticks." Discard any membranes, veins, gristle, bones, etc. when slicing cooked meat. Mix cooked meat with the strained stock and season to taste with a little marjoram, several gratings nutmeg, 1 bud crushed garlic, and additional salt & pepper if desired. Transfer mixture to cleaned pork stomach. (**Note**: All openings other than the one through which mixture is placed in stomach should be tightly sewn up.) Sew up last opening with string, pull together, and tie (see illustration). Depending on the size of stomach, there may be too much or too little mixture. Stomach is properly filled if it gives when pressed with finger. If it doesn't, stomach is packed too tightly and may burst while cooking. Place in hot but not boiling water and cook 1 hr. at gentle boil from the time boiling begins. Remove from pot, rinse in cold water, place on board, cover with another weighted-down board, and keep in cool, dry, ventilated place overnight. Refrigerate. To serve, slice and use as a lunch meat. *Note:* Head cheese should be consumed within a week as it does not keep well. *Variations:* Head cheese may also be stuffed into cleaned bladders or large pork or beef intestines. For leaner head cheese, replace fat back with 1 lb. various pork, veal, or beef trimmings and de-grease stock before mixing with cut-up meat prior to stuffing.

HEAD-CHEESE LOAF
salceson z formy

Not having access to a pork stomach, bladder, or intestines need not prevent you from making homemade head cheese. Loafpans can also do the job. In pot, place 1 pork tongue, 1 pork heart, 1 pork ear, and a piece of pork jowl totaling 2½ lbs. Add ½ lb. rindless fat back, 1 onion, 2 carrots, 1 parsley root, a slice of celeriac, and 1 kohlrabi (optional), 2 T. salt, 15 peppercorns, 2 bay leaves, and 4 qts water. Bring to boil, reduce heat, and cook about 40 min. Remove fat back and set aside. Continue simmering remaining ingredients 2½ hrs. or until meat begins to fall apart. Drain, reserving stock, and place meat in pan to cool. Discard spices and use vegetables in other dishes. Strain stock of which there should be no more than 6 c. Let stand and skim off grease from top. Mash 2–3 buds garlic and add to stock. Cut tongue, heart, and fat back into small cubes and remaining meat into thin strips. Mix with stock and season to taste with a few pinches pepper and marjoram as needed, and a ½ t. MSG also won't hurt. Pour mixture into loaf pans and, when cooled to room temp., refrigerate. Scrape off and discard any congealed fat that collects at top when head cheese is set. Slice thin and serve. Horseradish or sprinkle of lemon juice or vinegar are common accompaniments. *Optional*: For a slightly tart head cheese, add 2 pinches citric-acid crystals to mixture before stuffing.

BLACK HEAD CHEESE
salceson czarny

Prepare as indicated for white head cheese (first head-cheese recipe), but add 2 c. fresh pork blood to cut-up meat and stock mixture. Mix well and stuff pork stomach, bladder, or intestines, and sew up tightly. Cook 1 hr. in gently boiling water. To check doneness, pierce with long needle reaching center of head cheese. If juice that runs out is still red or pink, cook a while longer. Otherwise, proceed as with white head cheese.

RICE (PORK & RAISIN) SAUSAGE
kiszka ryżowa

Cook 2 lbs. pork jowls in water until tender, trim away gristle, and grind. In 4 c. of the stock cook 2 c. rice the usual way. Combine rice and ground mixture, add ½ c. melted lard, and 1 c. washed, drained raisins. Season to taste with salt, ground allspice, and a pinch cinnamon, add 1 bud crushed garlic, and mix well. Fill large hog intestines with mixture loosely, sewing up or skewering ends. Simmer in hot water 30–40 min. Cool on rack and refrigerate. To serve, slice and fry in a little butter or vegetable-oil spray until heated through.

HAM & OTHER SMOKED MEATS
szynka i inne wędzonki

Juicy, tender, pink ham, seasoned and smoked to perfection, has been a Polish favorite for centuries. However, if you have never cured your own, don't think you will achieve such results by picking any old fresh ham from the nearest supermarket. The best hams come from hogs specially bred, fed, and handled for this purpose, so rely on a reputable butcher or meat wholesaler to supply the proper raw materials. Best effects are achieved by using meat from a freshly slaughtered hog that is still warm. As with all home cured meats, absolute cleanliness is essential in their preparation, as we stressed in this chapter's introduction. Each stage of the operation—from trimming and/or deboning to the curing, air-drying and smoking process—contributes to the quality of your final product. This, of course, also applies to other smoked meats such as bacon, pork hocks, beef tongue, and rolled goose breast, to mention but a few of the entries found in this chapter.

COUNTRY-STYLE HAM
szynka wiejska

Mix 13 T. salt (preferably scorched in dry skillet until it crackles) with 4½ t. saltpeter, 1 t. freshly ground pepper, 1 t. ground allspice, 1 t. sugar, 4–5 ground cloves, and 4–5 crumbled bay leaves. Rub half the curing mixture (i.e. salt, saltpeter, and spices) into a fresh, 11 lb. bone-in ham. Continue rubbing all over until surface of meat becomes quite moist. Place ham to fit snugly in a sterilized, earthenware crock or large crockery or glass bowl. Cover ham with sterilized, inverted dinner plate that snugly fits container, place a bowl on top, and weight it down with something heavy like a 2-qt. jar filled with water. Leave at room temp. 2 days. Remove ham and rub with remaining curing mixture and ½–1 bud crushed garlic. Cover with re-sterilized weighted-down plate and transfer to cool (40° or cooler) place. After 2 days check to see whether ham is covered with its own liquid. If not, dissolve ⅔ c. salt and ½ t. saltpeter in 1 qt. pre-boiled water and pour it over ham so it is just covered. (**Note**: Longest-lasting are hams that produce enough of their own juice; adding salt & saltpeter solution is necessary for those that don't, but they are more perishable). Keep ham in curing solution 14–15 days, turning it over every 3 days. Rinse ham in cold water and air-dry in cool, breezy place 2 days. Cold-smoke 8–14 days. The longer it is smoked, the longer its life. May be sliced and served cold as is or cooked in plenty of boiling water about 5½ hrs. Remove ham from water only when pot has cooled to room temp.

UNSMOKED BOILED HAM
szynka gotowana nie wędzona

Cure 11-lb ham as in preceding recipe, then air-dry in cool, breezy place 3 days. Place ham in large pot of boiling water and simmer about 5 hrs. Ham cooks best when suspended from stick placed across top of pot (see illustration) so that it does not rest against bottom. Leave ham in pot until water cools to room temp. Refrigerate and use as you would store-bought boiled ham.

BEER-CURED SMOKED HAM
szynka wędzona piwna

Pour 1 c. salt into measuring cup. Scorch 5 T. thereof in dry skillet and mix with 5 t. saltpeter and 1 T. sugar. Rub fresh 11-lb. bone-in ham all over with mixture, place snugly into sterilized crock or crockery or glass bowl, cover with weighted-down plate, and let stand at room temp. 12 hrs. In separate pot combine 4¼ c. beer (a full-bodied brew like Poland's Żywiec or Okocim or a dark beer like Guinness stout is best !), the remaining salt, 4 T. sugar, 1 T. freshly ground pepper, and 5–6 ground cloves. Bring to boil and set aside to cool somewhat. Pour lukewarm spiced beer over ham until fully submerged. Cover with plate and keep in cool place 2 weeks. Remove ham from beer marinade, air-dry in cool wind 4–5 hrs. and cold-smoke 14 days.

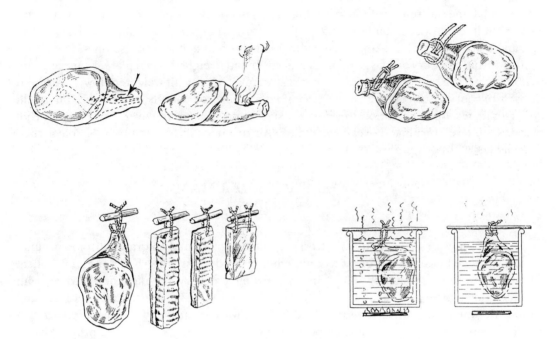

The incision made in cured ham meant for smoking should be filled with pickling mixture (salt, saltpeter, and spices) to ensure against spoilage which usually starts near the bone. Hams are then fitted with loops for hanging in smokehouse. Bottom left illustration shows ham, bacon, and salt pork properly suspended without touching each other in smokehouse. Illustration at bottom right presents the best way of cooking ham, suspended from a stick placed across top of pot to ensure that boiling water can freely circulate. After cooking, ham is left in water to cool.

BONELESS TRUSSED SMOKED HAM
szynka bez kości sznurowana wędzona

Remove bone from 11-lb. fresh ham (or have it removed). Rub meat all over with half the curing mixture called for in country-style smoked ham (see above), most generously in area from which bone was removed, since it is the most susceptible to spoilage. You can leave ham as is or cut it lengthwise in half to get 2 smaller hams. Roll up ham or hams tightly, skin side out, and truss with cord, making 6–10 widthwise loops and 2–4 lengthwise ones. Place ham in snug-fitting crockery or glass container and cover with weighed-down plate. Leave at room temp. 2 days. Rub ham with remaining curing mixture, cover with weighted-down plate, and transfer to cool 40° place for 2 days. Check if ham is covered with its own liquid. If not, add enough salt & saltpeter solution (see country-style smoked ham) to cover. Cure ham in cool place 14–15 days, turning it over ever 3 days. Air-dry in cool, breezy place 2–3 days, then cold smoke 10–14 days.

SMOKED SHOULDER HAM
baleron wędzony

Mix 4 T. salt with 1 t. saltpeter, 1 t. freshly ground pepper, and 15 grains allspice, ground. Trim any ragged bits of meat or fat from 2¼ lbs. fresh boneless pork shoulder and rub meat all over with curing mixture. Place in snug-fitting crockery or glass bowl, cover with weighted-down plate and keep in cool 40°–45° place 15 days. Turn meat over each day and baste with liquid that forms. Remove meat, rinse in warm water, and air-dry in breeze 3–4 hrs. Place meat on a piece of cleaned pork-belly-fat membrane (skin) of the proper size to accommodate it and roll up tightly. Truss with cord and warm-smoke 4 hrs. Slice thin and serve as a cold cut.

BOILED SHOULDER HAM
baleron gotowany

Rub 2¼ lb. fresh, boneless pork shoulder all over with mixture of 5 T. salt, 1 t. saltpeter, and 1 t. freshly ground pepper. Place in glass or crockery container, cover with weighted-down plate, and keep in 45°–50° place. After 24 hrs., dissolve 7 T. salt, 1 t. saltpeter and ½ t. sugar in 4 c. pre-boiled water and pour over meat to cover. Cover with weighted-down plate and cure 6–10 days at 45°–50°, turning meat over every 2 days. Remove meat from curing solution, soak in cold water 2 hrs., then air-dry 2–3 hrs. Roll up tightly in pork-belly-fat membrane and truss with cord. Hot-smoke 3–4 hrs., then cook in boiling water 2½ hrs.

Allow to cool to room temp. in pot, hang up to dry out 1–2 hrs., then refrigerate. Serve as a cold cut.

VEAL HAM
szynka cielęca

Prepare curing mixture by combining 2 T. salt and ½ t. saltpeter per 1 kilogram (2.2 lbs) of meat. Rub fresh veal ham all over with mixture, place in sterilized crockery or glass container, and let stand at room temp. 24 hrs. Separately combine 6–7 c. water, 2 T. salt, 10 peppercorns, 10 grains allspice, 4 cloves, and 2 bay leaves. Bring to boil, cool to lukewarm, and pour over meat to cover. Cover snugly with weighted-down plate and keep in cool 40° or cooler place 2–4 weeks, turning meat every 3 days. Remove meat from curing solution and air-dry in cool breeze 4–5 hrs. Your veal ham may then be cold-smoked 6 hrs. or hot-smoked 1 hr. Instead of smoking, it may be boiled in water or baked in oven. *Note*: Veal ham is very delicious but is less durable than pork ham.

SMOKED PORK LOIN
polędwica wieprzowa wędzona

Mix 3 T. salt, 1½ t. saltpeter, 1 t. freshly ground pepper, and 25 grains allspice, ground. Cut 6½–7 lb. fresh, boneless, pork loin into 10-inch lengths and rub all over with curing mixture. Snugly place meat in glass or crockery container and cover with weighted-down plate. Cure in cool place 8–10 days, turning meat over daily and basting with liquid that forms. Remove meat, rinse with warm water, and air-dry 3–4 hrs. Roll each length of loin in a piece of pork-belly-fat membrane tightly and truss with cord. Warm-smoke 3–4 days.

SMOKED PORK LOIN ANOTHER WAY
polędwica wieprzowa wędzona inaczej

Cut 6½–7 lb. fresh, boneless pork loin into 10-inch lengths, place in glass or crockery container, and drench with fresh pork blood to cover. Keep in cool place 2 days. Remove meat, discard blood, and wipe loin dry with clean cloth. Rub meat all over with curing mixture as in preceding recipe, adding 1 t. marjoram if desired. Reserve a little of the mixture to sprinkle over top of meat after placing snugly in glass or crockery bowl. Cover with weighted-down plate and keep at room temp. 2 days. Turn meat over and transfer to cold place for 10 days, turning meat every two days. Remove from curing container, wipe dry with clean cloth, and slide snugly into lengths of beef intestine large enough to accommodate meat. Air-dry 6 hrs. then cold-smoke 14 days. After 2 weeks of cold-smoking twice a day you will have a long-life pork loin that can be stored by hanging in a cool, well-ventilated place.

SMOKED BACON
boczek wędzony

Cut 11 lbs. fresh boneless slab bacon into 6 by 4 inch rectangles. Combine 15 T. salt with 1 t. saltpeter, ½ t. sugar, and ½ t. ground pepper, and rub bacon well on all sides with mixture. Place bacon in glass or crockery container. Bottom layer should be skin side down, next layer should be skin up, then skin side down, etc. Sprinkle each layer with salt (a total of 5 T.). Cover and keep in cool place 6 days. Re-arrange bacon, bringing bottom layer to top and vice-versa, but making sure that adjoining layers touch meat to meat and skin to skin. Cure another 6 days, re-arrange bacon again, and leave in cool place 4 more days. Total curing time is 16 days. With knife, scrape off excess salt and soak bacon in cold running water up to 4 hrs. Wash in warm water, then place on rack to dry 2–3 hrs. Run a loop of cord through one end of each piece and air-dry in lightly ventilated dark place 1–2 days. Cold-smoke 7–10 days. This bacon has a long life but may be on the salty side. It is good for frying, baking, and boiling.

SMOKED PORK RIBS
żeberka wieprzowe wędzone

Cut 4½ lbs. fresh pork ribs into 3–6-rib pieces, trimming away any ragged bits of meat or fat. Place in glass or crockery container. Bring 3¼ qts. water to boil with 10 grains allspice, 2 crumbled bay leaves, and 1 T. marjoram. Remove from heat and dissolve 21 T. salt and 3 t. saltpeter in solution. When cooled to lukewarm, pour curing solution over ribs to completely cover, cover with weighted-down plate, and transfer to cool place for 3–5 days. Remove ribs from solution and soak in cold running water 1 hr. Run loop through one end of ribs and hang up to air-dry 2–3 hrs. If ribs are to be used within several days, warm-smoke 3–4 hrs. For longer life, cold-smoke 4–5 days. These are excellent when cooked with sauerkraut.

SMOKED PORK HOCKS
golonka wędzona

Trim 11 lbs. fresh pork hocks of any ragged bits of meat or fat. Arrange snugly in glass or crockery container. Bring 3¼ qts. water to boil with 25 grains allspice, 1 crumbled bay leaf, and 2 t. marjoram. When cooled slightly, dissolve 26 T. salt and 3 t. saltpeter in solution. When cooled to lukewarm, pour over hocks to cover. Cover with weighted-down plate and keep in cool place 6–10 days. Larger hocks require more time to cure than smaller ones. After removing from brine, scrape with knife to remove any bristle, and trim away any dangling bits of meat or fat. If you plan to use them within several days, air-dry 2 hrs. and warm-smoke 3–4 hrs. For longer life, air-dry 3–4 hrs. and cold smoke 4–5 days. Like smoked ribs, smoked pork hocks are delicious with sauerkraut. Simply cook hocks in plenty of water until tender, discard water, and simmer several min. with cooked sauerkraut.

SMOKED BEEF TONGUE
ozór wołowy wędzony

Wash 1–2 beef tongues in warm water to remove any traces of blood and other impurities. Lard with thin sticks of frozen salt pork, cutting off any protrusions so lardoons do not stick out. Combine 1 t. each ground pepper, marjoram, basil, and rosemary with 1 pinch saltpeter. Sprinkle tongue all over with mixture, place in crockery or glass bowl, and let stand at coolish room temp. (65°) about 6 hrs. Vigorously rub spices into tongue. Bring 2 qts. water to boil and dissolve in it 16 T. salt and 2 t. saltpeter. When cooled to lukewarm, pour over tongue which should be completely submerged. Cover with weighted-down plate and keep in cool (40°) place 14–21 days. Drain on rack until completely dry. Run loop about ¾ inch from tip of tongue and cold-smoke 2–3 days. The addition of juniper wood to smoking fire will enhance the flavor. To prepare, cook in gently boiling water until tender the same as with fresh beef tongues. Good hot or cold.

SMOKED GOOSE BREASTS
półgęski wędzone

Remove breasts from 3–4 meaty, well-fattened geese, taking care not to damage skin. Combine 5 T. salt, 1 t. saltpeter, 1 t. ground coriander, ½ t. ground pepper, ½ t. ground allspice, ¼ t. ground cloves, and several pinches ground bay leaf. Rub goose breasts well all over with mixture and place in crockery or glass container snugly. Cover with weighted-down plate and leave at room temp. 36 hrs. Transfer to cool cellar (40°) for 2 weeks, turning meat over every 2 days. Remove from curing containers, wipe dry with clean cloth, and hang up to air-dry in breezy place 6–12 hrs. Cold-smoke 7–8 days. This is a real Old Polish specialty that is sliced thin and served cold as a true gourmet treat. When in Warsaw, try it at the Forum Hotel. *Note*: If properly cured and smoked, these can be stored suspended for months in a cool cellar without refrigeration.

SMOKED DUCK
kaczki wędzone

Trim off necks and wings from 2 large, meaty, dressed ducks and reserve them for other uses. With poultry shears, split ducks along spine and spread them breast side down on board. With sharp, narrow knife, carefully remove all bones, taking care not to puncture skin or damage breasts. Combine 6 t. salt, ½ t. saltpeter, ½ c. ground pepper, 1 t. marjoram, ¼ t. ground allspice, 2–3 buds crushed garlic, and 2 pinches ground cloves. Rub deboned ducks with mixture all over. Place 1 duck, skin side down, in crockery container, top with the other duck, skin side up, so meaty portions of ducks face each other. Cover with weighted-down plate and keep in cool place 5 days, turning meat over daily. Wipe ducks dry with clean cloth. Roll up each duck tightly, skin side out, taking care to have meatiest portion at center. Truss with cord and hang up to air-dry in cool, breezy place 6–8 hrs. Cold-smoke 7 days. Slice thin and serve as a gourmet cold meat.

SMOKED FISH
ryby wędzone

Scale and gut 5–6 lbs. very fresh (preferably freshly caught) fish. Slime can be removed from surface by rubbing lightly with clean sand. Rather than rinsing, wipe inside and out with clean cloth. (**Important**: Whenever cleaning any fish, be careful not to damage gall bladder; if the bile spills, it will give the fish an unpleasantly bitter taste!). Scorch 1 c. salt in dry skillet, then add 1 t. ground pepper, ¼ t. ground bay leaf, and 1 t. marjoram or sage. Rub fish all over with mixture, reserving about ¼ c. Sprinkle half the reserved salt & spice mixture on bottom of crockery or glass bowl, add the fish, and sprinkle with remaining mixture. Cover snugly with weighted-down plate and keep in cool 35°–40° place (including warmest part of fridge) 3 days. Turn fish over daily to ensure even curing. Wipe off excess salt with clean cloth and hang fish up to air-dry about 12 hrs. in cool breezy place. Use small, clean sticks to keep cavity open so air and smoke can penetrate better. Wrap fish in parchment paper and fasten with string, leaving an opening at top and bottom for smoke to circulate freely. Cold-smoke 8–10 days. *Note*: Whole large fish will require longer smoking than smaller ones or fillets. Besides fillets (with skin left on), fish steaks (i.e. roughly 2-inch crosswise slices) of larger fish may be smoked on a rack and require less smoking time. Fish is fully smoked when it takes on a nice golden-brown or ruddy color. Fatter species like carp, whitefish, and salmon are better for smoking than leaner fish such as a pike and walleye, since the latter tend to dry out too much.

SMOKED EEL
węgorz wędzony

Gut 5–6 lbs. freshly caught eel. Rub off slime from skin with clean sand, then wipe inside out with clean cloth. Combine 1 c. salt (preferably pre-scorched) with 1 t. pepper, ½ t. savory, and ¼ t. ground bay leaf; rub eels well inside and out with mixture. If head is left on, be sure to rub mixture into gills, mouth, and base of neck, since spoilage begins with the head. Place in crockery or glass bowl, cover with weighted-down plate and keep in cool place 3 days, turning fish daily. Wipe off excess salt, position several small clean sticks (wooden matches with heads broken off or toothpicks with sharp points broken off may be used) in cavity of each eel to give it added exposure to air and smoke. Hang up and air-dry several hrs., wrap in parchment, and tie it with string in several places, leaving top and bottom open. Cold-smoke about 4 days or until eel take on a nice orange hue. Smoked eel is a true delicacy that feels right at home next to the caviar and smoked salmon of the most elegant gourmet banquets!

SMOKED HERRING
śledzie wędzone

Soak 4–5 lbs. large, meaty salt herring in plenty of cold water 24 hrs., changing water 3 times. Wipe dry with clean cloth. Wrap each in parchment, tie in place with string, and hang up by tails to smoke in cold smoke 3–4 days, or until they take on a nice golden hue.

BREAD & ROLLS

Bread, unlike any other food, has since time immemorial been the staff of life, the symbol of human sustenance. *"Chleba naszego powszedniego"* ("Our daily bread") is the daily plea of millions in every imaginable language. Breaking bread is the ultimate token of friendship and hospitality. In Polish tradition, it was customary to trace a cross on a loaf of bread with a knife before slicing it. Letting a piece fall to the ground was nearly a sacrilege, and the bread would be tenderly picked up and kissed, whenever that occurred. To this day, Polish newlyweds as well as honored visitors are traditionally welcomed with bread and salt. Furthermore, the high point of the solemn Christmas Eve gathering is the breaking and sharing of the *opłatek*, a plain wafer of unleavened bread, a sign of love and reconciliation.

Linguistics also enter the picture. In Polish tradition, only loaves containing at least some rye flour are referred to as *chleb* (bread). The English language is far more capacious in this regard and uses the term "bread" to describe baked goods (e.g. date bread, nut bread, raisin bread, etc.) which by Polish standards are viewed as cakes. In fact, such things as french bread are referred to in Polish as *bułka paryska* (Parisian loaf) and various other white breads are usually termed *bułki pszenne* (wheat loaves) or *białe bułki* (white loaves).

Over the ages, health and culture were on opposite sides of the social barricade. Dark, heavy, coarsely milled, whole-grain breads were traditionally regarded as something fit only for peasants, whereas lighter and whiter loaves made of highly refined flour were associated with the more well-to-do. The term "pumpernickel" was said to have been originated by Napoléon during his march through Poland. *"Pain pour Nickel"* he was said to have sneered upon being served a dense, heavy, black bread during an overnight stop in one Polish village. Nickel was the name of his steed, and the French emperor felt that such bread was fit for only a horse. Nowadays, however, most everyone knows that the super-refined white breads are mostly pure starch, a steady diet of which can clog the intestines and lead to serious health problems. It is the once frowned upon darker breads that are high in fiber and full of natural nutrients. They also have more flavor, body, and character.

Historical anecdotes and health considerations aside, home bread-baking ranks among the most difficult of culinary tasks, especially where the traditional Polish-style sourdough rye bread is concerned. This is because so many unpredictable variables are involved, including the age, quality, grind, dryness and gluten content of a given type of flour, not to mention the other ingredients. The human factor is also extremely important. An experienced baker takes a handful of flour, examines it, smells it, rubs it between his fingers, and immediately has a pretty good idea how much liquid, leavening agent, and baking time will be needed to produce a decent bread. The way the dough behaves during the kneading will tell him the rest of the story.

Another factor is the bread oven itself, which it quite unlike what is found in the typical gas or electric range. It not only has the proper heat, but also just the right degree of humidity and ventilation needed to siphon off the gases given off by bread during baking. As a result, it may take quite some doing to produce a Polish-style rye bread as good as what you find in your local Polish, Jewish, or Russian bakery.

An American husband and wife team, Vrest and Ellen Orton, prefaced the bread chapter of their interesting book, *"Cooking with Wholegrains"*, with the following statement: "The best recipes in the world will not make a good bread-baker. There is a knack in making good bread which, like many other good things in life, comes to one by doing after no little trial and error." We endorse that statement 100% and can only add that home bread baking is not for those who become easily discouraged.

"After you have followed a recipe for bread religiously," to quote the Ortons again, "and it doesn't come out right, don't despair or suspect that the recipes are wrong. Try again. And then, some bright Tuesday morning, you will enter the kitchen, put some things together and bake a bread that is so wonderful you wonder how it ever happened. Once you do this, you will have the knack. Like learning to ride a bicycle, you can keep it with you as long as you like."

If that has not scared you off, you are ready to enter the world of Polish home style bread-baking. Before plunging headlong into the rather complicated sourdough ryes, which have to be gently nursed along for two to three days, we suggest you start with the easier white loaves that begin the chapter. When you achieve success, you can gradually ease yourself into the more exacting yeast-raised rye, rye & wheat, and whole-rye breads. Only then will you be ready to graduate to the temperamental and demanding sourdoughs.

In fact, to make this easier, we have arranged the recipes in this chapter according to their degree of difficulty. With the exception of the last two novelty recipes for bagels and unleavened Old Slavic bread, the first entries are the easiest to bake and are followed by progressively more difficult breads.

"Życzymy powodzenia!" (We wish you luck!)

*　*　*

HOLIDAY POPPYSEED CRESCENT
rogal świąteczny z makiem

This is a nice, light bread, ideal for serving with butter, honey, or jam at that festive Sunday or holiday breakfast. Prepare sponge by mashing 1 cake yeast with 1 T. sugar. Add 1 c. warm milk and ½ c. flour, mix well, cover with cloth, and let stand in warm place to rise about 15–20 min. Beat 3 egg yolks with 3 heaping T. sugar until fluffy. Sift 4 c. all-purpose flour into bowl, add sponge and yolk mixture, and work well by hand until dough becomes smooth and elastic. Add 1 stick melted butter and continue working until dough comes away from hands and sides of bowl. Cover with cloth and let rise until doubled in bulk (60–90 min.). Turn dough out onto floured board and roll into ½-inch-thick square. Cut square diagonally into 2 triangles and roll up each, starting with base of triangle. Curve each into a crescent and place in greased baking pan, preferably each crescent in a separate pan. Cover with cloth and let rise until doubled (about 1 hr.). Brush surface with beaten egg and sprinkle with poppyseeds. (*Variation*: For sweeter crescents, instead of poppyseeds, sprinkle with large crystal sugar or crumb topping.) Bake in pre-heated 375° oven to a nice golden brown (about 30 min.). Check for doneness with wooden skewer.

HOLIDAY POPPYSEED WREATH
wieniec świąteczny z makiem

Prepare dough exactly as above. After it has doubled in bulk, roll out on floured board into rectangle. Roll up long side of rectangle jelly-roll fashion, bring ends together to form a circle, and place in greased round pan. Cover with cloth and let rise in warm place. Brush with beaten egg, sprinkle with poppyseeds, (or large-crystal sugar or crumb topping) and bake as above.

HOLIDAY POPPYSEED LOAF
bułka świąteczna z makiem

As you can see, considerable mileage can be obtained from a single dough recipe by simply altering the shape. For 2 long loaves, prepare dough as in first recipe. After it has risen, divide in half and roll each piece out on floured board in ½-inch thick rectangles. Roll long side of each up jelly-roll fashion to form loaves. Place in greased pan or on baking sheet, cover with cloth, and let rise until doubled. Brush with beaten egg, sprinkle with poppyseeds, and bake in pre-heated 375° oven about 30 min.

SMALL POPPYSEED CRESCENTS
rogaliki z makiem

Prepare dough as in first recipe. After it has risen, transfer to floured board and divide in half. Roll out each half into a ½-inch thick circle. Cut each circle into 8 wedges and roll each up towards point of wedge. Curve into crescents, place on greased baking sheet, cover with cloth, and let rise until doubled (about 1 hr.). Brush with beaten egg, sprinkle with poppyseeds, crumb topping, or large crystal sugar, and bake in pre-heated 375° oven 20-25 min. or until nicely golden brown.

BRAIDED EGG BREAD
chałka

This delicious, faintly sweet egg bread was originated by Poland's once 3.5-million-strong Jewish community, for whom it had a ritual significance. It has long been a standard fixture on the Polish culinary scene, and we're sure you too will enjoy it. To make the sponge, sift 2½ c. all-purpose flour and heat 2 c. milk to lukewarm. In large 5–6 qt. bowl mash 1 cake yeast with 1 T. sugar, add the milk and flour, and mix well. Cover with cloth and let rise in warm place 15–20 min. Meanwhile, combine in blender 4 eggs, ½ t. salt, and 1 c. powdered sugar and whirl 2–3 min. When sponge doubles in size, add egg mixture, sift in 6 c. all-purpose flour, and work well by hand about 30 min. Add 1 stick melted butter or margarine and continue working until butter is fully absorbed and the silky dough no longer sticks to hand and comes away from sides of bowl. Cover with cloth and let stand in warm place until doubled (1½–2 hrs.). Transfer dough to floured board and divide in half. (Each ½ is meant for 1 chałka). From each ½, roll between palms of hands 4, 20-inch strands and 4, 18-inch strands of dough, which should be slightly thicker at center and taper of towards ends. Braid 4 longer strands, pinching ends and tucking them under. Place in greased pan sprinkled with flour. Braid the four shorter strands the same way and place it on top off the braided longer strands in pan. Repeat process for second chałka. Cover both pans with cloth and let rise in warm place 30–40 min. When nearly doubled in bulk, brush with beaten egg and sprinkle with poppyseeds, large crystal sugar, or crumb topping. You may just brush with egg and leave it plain without additional topping. Bake in pre-heated 375° oven about 45 min. to a nice golden brown. Test with wooden skewer. If it comes out clean, your chałkas are baked. *Note*: This recipe produces two large egg breads, but you can divide the dough to make 3 or even 4 smaller chałkas, in which case baking time should be reduced to 25–35 min.

DIET (YOLKLESS) EGG BREAD
chałka dietetyczna na białkach

For the benefit of the diet-conscious, we have developed this less sweet, butter-free, and yolkless chalka, which is also very good. Mash ½ cake yeast with 1 T. sugar, add 1 c. lukewarm milk and 1 c. sifted flour, mix well, cover with cloth, and set aside to rise in warm place 15–20 min. Sift 3 c. flour into bowl, add sponge, 2 beaten egg whites, and 1 t. salt. Work well by hand until dough is smooth and elastic and no longer sticks to hands. If too thick to handle, work in about ¼ c. lukewarm milk. Cover with cloth and let rise in warm place about 1 hr. When doubled, turn out onto floured board and kneed briefly. Divide dough into two unequal parts. Between palms of hands roll larger part into three strands, thicker near center and tapering off towards ends. Braid, pinching and tucking ends under. Similarly roll smaller part into 3 strands, braid, tuck ends under, and place on top of previously braided dough. Place in greased pan, cover with cloth, and let rinse until just about doubled (app. 1 hr.). Brush with beaten egg and sprinkle with poppyseeds, large crystal sugar, or crumb topping. Bake 40–45 min. in pre-heated 400° oven.

BRAIDED WREATH ROLLS
obwarzanki plecione

The above dough can also be used to make small, braided, circular rolls. Prepare dough as indicated above. After it has risen the first time, turn out onto floured board. Between palms of hands roll small pieces of dough into 10-inch pencil-thin strands. When all is used up, place two strands together and twist into a braid, then form into a circle and pinch ends together. Brush dough circles with beaten egg. For breakfast rolls, sprinkle with poppyseeds, large crystal sugar, or crumb topping. For a beer snack, sprinkle with coarse kosher salt, caraway seeds, or salt and poppyseeds. Place in greased baking pan, cover with cloth, and let rise in warm place about 1 hr. Bake in pre-heated 400° oven 20–25 min. or until golden brown. *Note*: Instead of circular wreaths, dough strands may be formed into a figure "8" or pretzel as desired.

WHITE WHEAT LOAF WITH POPPYSEEDS
bułka pszenna z makiem

This is a nice, all-purpose, white wheat loaf similar to Vienna bread. Mash 1 cake yeast with 1 t. sugar, add 2 c. lukewarm water, and mix well. Add 1 c. sifted, all-purpose flour, mix again, cover with cloth, and let rise in warm place 15–20 min. Into bowl sift 5½ c. all-purpose flour. In blender mix 2 eggs with 2 t. salt. To flour add sponge and egg mixture and work well by hand about 30 min. until dough is smooth and elastic. Add 3 T. cooking oil and work another 3–4 min. Cover with cloth and let stand in warm place until doubled (60–90 min.). Turn out onto floured board and knead several min. Divide into two equal parts and roll out each into a ½-inch-thick rectangle. Roll each of the longer sides up to form two loaves. Grease a large baking sheet and place the loaves thereon, leaving a large space in between so they don't touch. Cover with cloth and let rise in warm place 60–90 min. Brush with beaten egg and sprinkle with poppyseeds. Place pan containing 1 inch boiling water at bottom of pre-heated 400° oven. Place loaves in oven and bake about 30 min.

BREAKFAST CRESCENT ROLLS
rogale, rogaliki śniadaniowe

Prepare dough as for white wheat loaf (above). After it has risen the first time, turn out onto floured breadboard, divide in two and roll out each piece into a ½-inch-thick circle. Cut each circle into 4 equal parts for large crescents or 8 wedges for 8 smaller ones. Arrange on greased baking sheet so they don't touch, cover with cloth, and let rise in warm place until doubled. Brush with beaten egg, sprinkle with poppyseeds if desired (optional), and bake in pre-heated 400° oven 25–35 min. to a light golden brown. Test for doneness with pick.

KAISER ROLLS
kajzerki

The same white-wheat-loaf dough is also used in this recipe. After it has doubled in bulk, tear off pieces the size of apricots and roll into balls between hands snowball fashion. Place on greased baking sheet, cover with cloth, and let rise in warm place until doubled. With knife cut a ½-inch-deep cross on top of each roll, brush with beaten egg, sprinkle with poppyseeds, and bake in pre-heated 400° oven 25–30 min.

ROLLS FOR CRUMBS & STUFFING
bułka tarta i do farszu

Many recipes in this book call for stale kaiser rolls, which are soaked until soggy in milk, water, or stock, ground, and added to stuffing, meatballs (and other ground meat dishes), desserts, etc. You can use both your own homemade kajzerki or the store-bought type for this purpose. Naturally, the white wheat loaf and breakfast crescent rolls (made from the same dough) are just as good, because it's the dough, not the shape, that counts. Stale rolls also make excellent bread crumbs. Of course, commercial french bread, Vienna bread, white bread, hamburger buns, hot dog rolls etc, can also be used for both crumbs and stuffing.

ONION ROLLS
cebulaki

Before World War II, these zesty rolls were a specialty of Polish Jewish bakeries, but they continue to have many devotees to this day. In small bowl, mash ½ cake yeast with 1 t. sugar, add ¾ c. lukewarm milk, and ½ c. all-purpose flour, sifted. Mix well, cover with cloth, and let stand in warm place to rise about 10–15 min. Sift 2 c. all-purpose flour into a larger bowl, add yeast mixture, 3 T. cooking oil, 1 beaten egg, and ½–1 t. salt. Work by hand into a smooth, glossy dough. Cover with cloth and let rise in warm place until doubled (30–45 min.). Transfer to floured board, sprinkle with a little flour, and divide into 8 equal parts. Between floured hands, roll each piece into ball, flatten with palm, and roll each into ¼-inch-thick circle. Place on greased baking sheet, leaving 1½-inch space between rolls. Cover with cloth and let rise in warm place about 60 min. Meanwhile, peel and thinly slice 4 onions and sauté in 2 T. fat (oil, butter, oleo, lard) to a pale golden hue. Add 1 T. water, cover, and simmer 1–2 min. or until liquid evaporates. Salt & pepper to taste and set aside to cool. When rolls have doubled, use floured bottom of drinking glass to make a depression at center of each and fill depression with fried onions. Brush parts of rolls extending beyond onion filling with beaten egg and sprinkle with poppyseeds. Bake in pre-heated 350° oven about 20–30 min. or until golden. These are good hot or cold.

EASIEST ONION ROLLS
cebulaki najłatwiejsze

For the benefit of onion roll lovers, who get the urge but haven't the time to do things up from scratch, we have struck upon something that may well be the next best thing. Proceed as above using store-bought plain pizza dough. Cut into circles, let rise, fill depressions with fried onions, brush with egg, sprinkle with poppyseeds, and bake according to package directions. *Note*: Since rolls are smaller than a whole pizza, they should take less time to bake, so be sure to watch over them so they don't burn.

EASY RYE BREAD (WITH BRAN)
łatwy chlebek żytnio-pszenny (z otrębami)

If you have never baked rye bread before, this is a comparatively simple recipe which produces results similar to the whole-grain peasant breads of yesteryear. By being high in fiber, it can also be considered a kind of health bread. In bowl crush 1 cake yeast with 1 t. sugar. Heat ¾ c. milk and ¾ c. water together until lukewarm. Add to yeast mixture, and mix well. Add ⅔ c. all-purpose flour, mix again, cover with cloth, and let stand in warm place 15–20 min. Into clean bowl sift 1 c. all-purpose flour and 2 c. rye flour. Add 2 c. wheat bran, 1½–2 t. salt, 2 T. oil, and the sponge and work mixture well by hand about 10–15 min. Cover with cloth and set aside in warm place to rise 60–90 min. Transfer dough to narrow, greased, bran-sprinkled loaf pans, in which dough fills ⅓–½ of the pan. Cover with cloth and let rise in warm place until nearly doubled (about 2 hrs.). Brush with lightly beaten egg white and bake in pre-heated 375° oven about 40 min. Check for doneness with wooden skewer.

WHOLE-WHEAT BREAD
chleb pszenno-razowy

This is similar to but a bit lighter than Graham bread (next recipe) with a faintly sweet taste. Mash 2 cakes yeast with 1 T. sugar, add ½ c. warm water, mix well, and let rise covered with cloth in warm place about 15 min. Into bowl sift 2½ c. whole wheat flour and 3½ c. all-purpose flour and mix well. In pot heat to lukewarm 1 c. milk, ¼ c. water, 2 T. honey, 2 T. butter, 2 t. salt, and 2 t. sugar. When all ingredients have dissolved, add to flour and work by hand into a smooth dough (15–20 min.). Grease narrow loafpans and fill ½ full with dough. Cover with cloth and let rise in warm place until dough reaches top of pans. Brush tops with beaten egg and bake in pre-heated 375° oven about 50 min. *Note*: Many recipes call for bread to be brushed with sugared water before and after baking, but this creates a sticky top that we are not fond of. We prefer the shiny crust that beaten egg ensures.

GRAHAM BREAD
chleb Grahama

Graham, a 19th-century American miller, after whom this bread was named, is scarcely remembered in his native land except for the familiar graham crackers. In Poland, by contrast, his name lives on both in this whole-wheat loaf and popular whole-wheat rolls (grahamki). Incidentally, in Polish his name is pronounced GRA-hamm, not GREY-um. Mash 1 cake yeast with 1 T. sugar, add 1–2 T. honey, 1 c. water or whey, and 1 c. whole-wheat flour and mix well. Cover with cloth and let rise in warm place about 15 min. Into bowl sift 6 c. whole-wheat (Graham) flour, add 2 c. water, the sponge, and 1½–2 t. salt. Work well by hand until smooth and elastic (15–20 min.). Cover with cloth and allow to rise in warm place about 1 hr. Transfer to board sprinkled with all-purpose flour, knead briefly, sprinkling dough with a little all-purpose flour while kneeding. Divide into two parts and transfer to narrow loafpans which should be greased and sprinkled with all-purpose flour. The dough should fill the pans only halfway. With moistened hand smooth tops of dough, cover with cloth, and let rise in warm place until doubled (about 1 hr.). Brush tops with water. Bake in pre-heated 375° oven about 50 min., testing for doneness with wooden pick. Allow to cool somewhat before removing from pans. *Note*: A pan of boiling water may be placed at bottom of oven during baking, but this isn't absolutely necessary with this type of bread.

WHOLE-WHEAT ROLLS
grahamki

Prepare dough as above. After it has risen, knead briefly on floured board, roll between palms into small balls, which should fill compartments of greased muffin tin no more than halfway. With moistened hand smooth tops of rolls. Cover and let rise in warm place about 30–40 min. Brush tops with sugared water or beaten egg and bake in pre-heated 375° oven 15–25 min. depending on their size. Check with wooden pick to see if they are fully baked. After a few min., remove from tin and allow to cool thoroughly on rack or tray.

WHOLE-RYE BREAD/BLACK BREAD
razowiec/chleb razowy

This is a delicious, dark bread with just the faintest trace of sweetness and is comparatively easy to bake. Mash 1 cake yeast with 1 T. sugar, add 1 c. lukewarm milk and ½ c. whole-rye flour, sifted. Mix well, cover with cloth, and let stand in warm place about 15 min. Into bowl sift 6 c. whole-rye flour and 1 c. all-purpose flour. Add 1 T. salt, 2 T. honey, and the sponge. Work well about 15 min., gradually adding 1¾–2 c. lukewarm milk a little at a time, mixing until fully absorbed before each new addition. Transfer dough to greased loafpans which should be filled only halfway. Cover with cloth and let rise in warm place about 1 hr. Brush tops with beaten egg and bake in pre-heated 375° oven about 75 min. When fully baked, wooden skewer should come out clean and loaf should come away from sides of pan. *Note*: A pan of boiling water may be kept at bottom of oven during baking.

WHOLE-RYE HONEY BREAD
razowiec na miodzie

This bread came out very dense, heavy, and moist to the point of being gummy inside, and we debated whether to include it. Although we found the preceding recipe far superior, personal tastes do differ. It appears that it is the addition of 1 c. all-purpose flour (in the preceding recipe) that makes the difference, because all whole-rye breads such as this one do not rise very well. If you want to try it anyway, here goes. Mash 1 cake yeast with 1 T. sugar, add 1 c. lukewarm water, and ½ c. whole-rye flour. Mix well, cover with cloth, and set aside in warm place for about 15 min. Into bowl sift 6 c. whole-rye flour, add 2 T. salt, 6 T. honey, and the sponge. Work well by hand, adding 1½–1¾ c. lukewarm water a little at a time. Work dough until uniform and fairly smooth. Grease narrow loafpans and sprinkle with all-purpose flour. Transfer dough to pans which should be only half-full. *(Note: This dough is not very eye-appealing and sticks to hands, so dip in water before smoothing tops.)* Cover with cloth and let rise about 1 hr. in warm place. Bake in pre-heated 375° oven about 70–75 min. Allow to cool slightly before removing from pans.

MIXED WHOLE-GRAIN BREAD (SOURDOUGH TYPE)
razowiec mieszany (na zakwasie)

Prepare sourdough starter by pouring ⅔ c. pre-boiled water, cooled to 85°, into qt. bowl or jar. Sift in ⅔ c. whole-rye flour, add a small piece (½-inch square) of onion, mix well, cover with cloth, and set aside in warm place for 24 hrs. When it gives off a faintly sour aroma, it's ready to use. Into a large bowl sift 1½ c. whole-rye flour, add sourdough starter (discarding onion), pour in 1 c. warm water, mix well, and let stand overnight (or 12 hrs.) in warm place to rise. Punch it down, add 2 T. honey, 2 t. salt, 1 c. all-purpose flour, 1 c. whole-rye flour, 3½ c. whole-wheat flour (all flours should be sifted of course!), 1 t. sugar, and 2 c. warm whey or buttermilk . Combine ingredients by hand and work well about 15–20 min. until dough is smooth. Transfer to greased loafpans, which should be only half full, and smooth tops with moistened hand. Cover with cloth and let rise in warm place 4–5 hrs. By that time dough should fill pans. Brush tops with water and bake in pre-heated 350° oven with pan of hot water at bottom about 50 min. Brush tops with beaten egg and bake another 20–25 min. Check for doneness with wooden skewer.

WHEAT & RYE BREAD (YEAST TYPE)
chleb pszenno-żytni (na drożdżach)

Mix 1 c. lukewarm water, 2 T. melted butter, and 2 t. honey. Into bowl sift 4 c. all-purpose flour and 1 c. rye flour. Add 1½ t. salt and ¾ cake crumbled yeast and mix well. Add honey mixture and 1 beaten egg and work well by hand, gradually adding about ½ c. water. When dough is smooth and elastic, cover with cloth and let stand in warm place until doubled in bulk (about 1 hr). Punch down dough and transfer to floured board. Sprinkle with flour and knead briefly, divide in two, then knead each half a bit and form into oval loaf. Place on greased baking sheet, cover with cloth, and let rise until doubled (about 1 hr). Brush with beaten egg or just egg white and bake in pre-heated 375° oven about 45 min. *Variation*: Bake in loafpans if you prefer. *Note*: As it contains only 20% rye flour, this bread can easily be mistaken for an all-wheat loaf. We now move to more typical Polish breads, which may contain up to 100% rye flour.

BUTTERMILK OR SOUR-MILK RYE BREAD
chleb żytni na maślance lub zsiadłym mleku

This is another very flavorful Old World rye bread from the Polish countryside. Heat to lukewarm 2 c. buttermilk or sour milk. Add 1½ cakes crumbled yeast, 1 c. rye flour, sifted, and 1 t. sugar. Mix well, cover with cloth, and set aside in warm place about 15 min. Into bowl sift 6 c. rye flour and warm slightly in warm oven. Add sponge, 2 t. salt, ¼ t. citric-acid crystals, and work well about 15 min. or until smooth and silky. Cover bowl with cloth and let stand in warm place to rise 60–90 min. When it doubles in bulk, punch down and turn out onto floured board, knead briefly, sprinkling with rye flour, and form into two round or oval loaves. Place on greased baking sheet, cover with cloth, and let rise in warm place about 30 min. Brush with hot water, sprinkle with caraway or poppyseeds, and bake about 1 hr. in pre-heated 390° oven with pan of boiling water at bottom.

COUNTRY-STYLE ALL-RYE BREAD (YEAST & WHEY TYPE)
chleb wiejski żytni (na drożdżach i serwatce)

Dissolve 1 cake crumbled yeast in 1 c. lukewarm whey (see dairy chapter on how to obtain whey). Into bowl sift 4 c. rye flour, add whey & yeast mixture, mix well, cover with cloth, and let stand in warm place about 1 hr. When sponge doubles in bulk, beat it down and mix with wooden spoon. (*Note*: At this point you can take and reserve ⅓ c. of sponge which can serve as a sourdough starter for your next batch of bread.) To beaten-down sponge add 4 more c. rye flour, sifted, ¼ t. citric-acid crystals, 1 T. salt, and ¾ c. warm whey. Work ingredients by hand into fairly stiff dough and continue working 30–40 min. Smooth top with moistened hand, sprinkle with rye flour, cover with cloth, and let stand in warm place to rise 60–90 min. Punch down, turn out onto bread board sprinkled with rye flour, and knead until smooth and elastic. Divide in three and form into 3 round or oval loaves as tall as possible. Smooth loaves with moistened hand and place on greased baking sheet. Squeeze sides of loaves gently with both hands to get them as tall as possible. Cover with cloth and allow to rise about 30 min. In that time it should rise about 50%. Brush with lightly beaten egg white and sprinkle with poppy or caraway seeds. Bake in pre-heated 375° oven with pan of boiling water at bottom about 50 min. About 5 min. before end of baking, brush again with egg white and bake 5 min. longer. *Note*: While this is not yet a true sourdough bread, the addition of whey and citric-acid crystals makes it taste like one.

RYE ROLLS (FOR SAUSAGE)
paluszki żytnie (na kiełbaski)

Rolls such as these are very popular at various Polish-American festivals for serving portions of hot kiełbasa in hot dog style. Prepare dough as above. Rather than dividing it into 3 loaves, divide into 24 small pieces. Roll each first into a ball and then into a 5-inch long roll about 1 inch in diameter. Place on greased baking sheet, brush with water, cover with lightly beaten egg white, sprinkle with poppy or caraway seeds if desired, and bake in pre-heated 375° oven for 25–30 min. Don't forget the pan of boiling water!

REGULAR POLISH (RYE & WHEAT) BREAD, SCALDED TYPE
chleb zwykły (żytnio-pszenny) parzony

This bread comes close to today's standard Polish bread and to what Americans expect when they think of "Polish bakery rye." Sift 3½ c. rye flour into large bowl, scald with 4 c. boiling water. Mix well with wooden spoon until free of lumps, cover with cloth, and let stand at room temp. or slightly warmer overnight (10–12 hrs.). Next day crumble ¾ cake yeast into small bowl, add ½ c. lukewarm water, and ½ c. all-purpose flour. Mix well, cover with cloth, and let stand in warm place 10–15 min. Combine flour & water mixture (that stood out overnight) with sponge (yeast mixture), add 5 c. all-purpose flour, sifted, 1–1½ T. salt, and ¼–½ t. citric-acid crystals. Combine ingredients by hand and work dough until elastic. The dough should be fairly stiff, so you can add ½–1 c. all-purpose flour if necessary. Cover with cloth and let stand until doubled (60–90 min.). When doubled in bulk, turn out onto floured bread-board and knead 1–2 min., sprinkling dough with flour. Divide into 3 or 4 parts, knead each briefly, and form into tall oval loaf. Place on greased baking sheet sprinkled with flour or wheat bran, cover with cloth, and let rise in warm place 60–90 min. Place pan of boiling water at bottom of oven and pre-heat to 375°. Brush loaves with lightly beaten egg white and bake 60–75 min. *Note*: If this or other rye bread expands sideways rather than rising before being placed in oven, return to board, knead briefly and place in greased loafpan. Let it rise again in warm place and bake as directed. It may not have the nice shape of typically Polish round or oval loaves, but the taste will be the same.

POLISH (RYE & WHEAT) BREAD, SOURDOUGH TYPE
chleb zwykły (żytnio-pszenny) na zakwasie

For this recipe, you will need ⅓ c. sourdough starter. You can use the ⅓ c. of the sponge from country-style, all-rye bread (p. 814) or get some from your local European-style bakery. Sift 6 c. rye flour and 2½ c. all-purpose flour into large bowl and mix well. In small bowl, mix well ⅓ c. sourdough starter with 2½ c. lukewarm, pre-boiled water. Add ¼ cake crumbled yeast, and 3 c. of the flour (above). Mix well, cover with cloth, and leave in warm place to ferment 4–8 hrs. The longer it ferments, the more tart the bread will taste. To fermented sourdough add remaining flour and 2 t. salt and work by hand 40–50 min. until dough comes away from hand. Smooth top with moistened hand, cover with cloth, and leave in warm place until doubled (2–3 hrs.). Punch down risen dough, turn out onto floured board, knead briefly, divide into 3 parts, knead each briefly, and form into round or oval loaf. Transfer to greased baking sheet, which may be sprinkled with wheat bran if desired. Brush loaves with lightly beaten egg white, boiling water, or 1 T. rye flour mixed with 1 c. room-temp. water. (*Note*: The egg white produces the shiniest crust!). Sprinkle with poppyseeds, caraway seeds, or black cumin (czarnuszka) if desired, and bake in pre-heated 400° oven about 1 hr. *Remember*: All rye and rye & wheat breads bake best in oven containing pan of boiling water at bottom.

ALL-RYE SOURDOUGH BREAD
chleb żytni na zakwasie

If you cannot get sourdough starter from a bakery and have not previously baked a rye bread whose dough serves the same purpose, you can make a sourdough starter from scratch as follows. Bring 2 c. water to boil, pour into 2–qt. bowl, and cool to 85°. Add 2 c. rye flour, sifted, and ¼ bud garlic, 1 thin ring of onion slice or 5–10 caraway seeds. Mix well, cover with cloth, and keep in warm place about 24 hrs. Mixture should rise and fall during this time. When mixture gives off a faintly sour odor, it is ready for use in your bread dough. Into large, 15–qt. container (an earthenware bowl is best) sift 10 c. rye flour. Scald with 6 c. boiling water, mixing constantly with wooden spoon. When water is absorbed by flour, cover bowl with thick towel or blanket, and let stand in warm place 3 hrs. To fermented sourdough starter (first mixture) add 2 c. warm water, remove and discard garlic or onion, and mix well. Add this mixture to flour & water mixture (that has been kept in warm place 3 hrs.) and work well, obliterating any lumps, until dough is smooth. Smooth top of dough, sprinkle with rye flour, and cover with several thick towels or blankets. Let stand in warm place 20 hrs. After the time, when the dough has risen, punch down at. (*Note*: At this point, you can take some of dough as a sourdough starter for your next batch of bread.) Gradually add 16 c. warmed and sifted rye flour and 2–3 T. salt. Work dough well after each addition of flour and do not add more until previous addition is fully absorbed. When dough is smooth and elastic, cover with cloth and leave in warm place 3 hrs. Punch down and turn out onto board sprinkled with rye flour. Knead dough until springy. Divide into 8 parts. Briefly knead each portion and shape into tall, round, or oval loaf. Place on greased baking sheets which may be sprinkled with wheat bran, cover with cloth, and let rise in warm place about 1 hr. Brush with lightly beaten egg white and bake in pre-heated 375° oven with pan of boiling water at bottom about 75 min. *Optional*: Sprinkle with poppyseeds, caraway seeds, dill seeds, or black cumin before baking. *Note*: If properly baked, this bread is very delicious, but it requires considerable skill. If dough is too soft, it will expand sideways during rising period. If too hard, it will crack. A certain feel is required to achieve just the right consistency, and that only comes with practice. A safer way for the novice baker is to bake bread in loafpans. This recipe can be followed according to the quantities specified only if you have more than one oven. Those who have a working range in their basements can bake 4 loaves upstairs and the other 4 downstairs. If you have only one oven, then cut recipe in half.

CARAWAY RYE BREAD
chleb kminkowy

Caraway seeds, along with poppyseeds and black cumin, are frequently sprinkled over rye and rye & wheat breads before baking. Caraway seeds may also be added to the dough. If you like their taste, feel free to add 1–2 t. caraway seeds to any of the above doughs before you begin to work them by hand. To the preceding recipe, which is for 8 loaves, add 1–2 T. caraway seeds. Dill seed, whose flavor is similar to that of caraway, may be used instead. Poppyseeds and black cumin are almost never added to the dough and are reserved for sprinkling over the tops of loaves just before baking.

RING BISCUITS/BAGELS
obwarzanki

In Kraków, Warsaw, and other Polish cities, street vendors sell strings of these chewy, ring-shaped biscuits which people like to munch on as they sight-see or window-shop. You can enjoy them at home by following this fairly simple recipe. Onto board sift 2 c. all-purpose flour, sprinkle with ¼ c. sugar, and make a crater at center. Into it deposit 3 eggs and work ingredients by hand until fully blended. Knead well about 5–7 min. or until dough is smooth and springy, sprinkling it and the board with a little more flour if necessary. Take bits of dough and between palms roll them into pencil-thin strands 3–4 inches long. Join ends to form circles and pinch together. Place a few at a time into a large pot of boiling salted water. When they float up, remove with slotted spoon, cool under cold running water, and place on ungreased baking sheet. When all are arranged on baking sheets without touching, place in pre-heated 400° oven and bake 10 min. on 1 side. Turn over and bake another 5–7 min. on remaining side. They are done when pale golden in color.

OLD SLAVIC UNLEAVENED BREAD
podpłomyczki

We conclude this chapter as well as this book with a primitive bread that was known to the ancient Slavic forerunners of today's Poles. It hearkens back to a time when yeast breads were unknown and, as the Polish name implies ("płomyczek" means flame), was once baked on stones heated by a campfire. If it reminds you of Middle Eastern pita bread, that only goes to show that the breads of ancient tribes were often quite similar. This is a slightly modernized (oven-baked) version of this ancient recipe. Sift 2 c. all-purpose flour onto board. Make crater at center, deposit 2 eggs therein and sprinkle with ½ t. salt. Work ingredients into a dough, gradually adding about ½ c. milk. Knead well until dough is smooth and elastic, sprinkling board and dough with a little flour as you go. Divide into 6 parts and roll out each into a ¼-inch-thick-circle. Place on ungreased baking sheet and bake in pre-heated 400° oven about 10 min. Flip over and bake another 5–10 min. on other side. Podpłomyczki are best served hot straight from the oven with a little butter. You can also split them and slip a slice of ham, cheese, or something else, inside for an interesting hot sandwich.

THE END

CONVERTING COOKING WEIGHTS, MEASURES & TEMPERATURES

Many Americans, who think they know the language of their immigrant ancestors, are often in for a surprise the first time they open a cookbook printed in the Old Country. "What in the world is a 'dag.'?" is a query I have repeatedly received from readers over the years. How much is "250 ml. milk" or "3 gr. saltpeter"? Or what if a recipe calls for something to be cut into "1 cm. strips" or baked at "200° C."? The problem arises, because most of the world is now on the metric system and Celsius (formerly Centigrade) temperatures. But, as of this writing, the United States still follows the British-derived system known as "Standard U.S. Weights and Measures" as well as the Fahrenheit scale. Further complications may arise if you ever try to use a cookbook from Britain. The American and English weights given in ounces and pounds are identical but the British liquid measures (cups, pints, quarts etc.)* are larger by one-fifth (20%) than their U.S. counterparts. Hopefully the following information will help clear up some of the confusion.

* * *

WEIGHTS

1 gram (1/1000 kilogram)	.035 oz.
1 decagram (10 grams or 1/100 kilogram)	.35 oz.
5 decagrams or 50 grams or 1/50 kilogram)	1.8 oz.
10 decagrams (100 grams or 1/10 kilogram)	3.5 oz.
25 decagrams (250 grams or ¼ kilogram)	8.8 oz.
50 decagrams (500 grams or ½ kilogram)	17.6 oz.
75 decagrams (750 grams or ¾ kilogram)	26.3 oz.
100 decagrams (1,000 grams or 1 kilogram)	35.3 oz.
1 ounce (1/16 lb.)	28 grams
4 ounces (¼ lb.)	113 grams
8 ounces (½ lb.)	226 grams
12 ounces (¾ lb.)	340 grams
16 ounces (1 lb.)	450 grams

* A British teaspoon is equivalent to about 1¼ U.S. teaspoons and the British tablespoon = 1¼ American tablespoons. The British measuring cup is 10 fluid oz., but since a British fluid oz. is .96 of a U.S. fluid oz., it contains 9.6 U.S. fl. oz. Similarly an Imperial pint = 19.2 U.S. fl. oz. (20 British fl. oz.) and an Imperial gallon = 153.7 U.S. fl. oz. (160 British fl. oz.). In other words, the Imperial units are 20% larger than their American counterparts. A British Imperial quart = 1.2 U.S. quarts. Despite the inroads made by the metric system, the Imperial measures are still in use in the British Isles and countries with historic links to the British Commonwealth.

CAPACITY

1 milliliter (1/1000 liter)	.034 fluid oz.
5 milliliters (1/200 liter or 1 teaspoon)	.169 fluid oz.
15 milliliters (1/66 liter or 1 tablespoon)	.507 fluid oz.
25 milliliters (1/40 liter, app. 1 jigger)	.845 fluid oz.
100 milliliters (1/10 liter, small wine glass)	3.4 fluid oz.
250 milliliters (1/4 liter, measuring cup)	8.4 fluid oz.
500 milliliters (1/2 liter)	16.9 fluid. oz
1,000 milliliters (1 liter)	33.8 fluid oz.

1 fluid ounce (1/8 cup or 1/32 quart)	=	29 milliliters
4 fluid ounces (1/2 cup or 1/8 quart)	=	118 milliliters
8 fluid ounces (1 cup, 1/2 pint or 1/4 quart)	=	236 milliliters
16 fluid ounces (2 cups, 1 pint or 1/2 quart)	=	473 milliliters
32 fluid ounces (4 cup, 2 pints or 1 quart)	=	946 milliliters (app. .95 liter)
128 fluid ounces (4 quarts or 1 gallon)	=	3,785 milliliters (app. 3.8 liters)

* * *

VOLUME AND WEIGHT OF COMMON FOODS

Product	1 metric cup** (250 ml.)	
	app. weight in decagrams	app. weight in ounces
Barley, uncooked	20	7
Beans, dry white	23	8
Bread crumbs	15	5.3
Buckwheat groats, uncooked	19	6.6
Butter	24	8.4
Cooking oil	23	8

Cream of wheat, uncooked	19	6.6
Eggs, whole (4–6)	25	8.8
Egg whites (8–11)	25	8.8
Egg yolks (12–14)	25	8.8
Flour	17	5.9
Honey	30	10.5
Lard	23	8
Margarine	24	8.4
Nuts, chopped	13	4.5
Peas, dry split	22	7.7
Peas, dry whole	20	7
Poppyseeds	16	5.6
Potato starch/flour	18	6.3
Raisins	15	5.3
Rice uncooked	23	8
Rolled oats	9	3.1
Salt	30	10.5
Sour cream	25	8.8
Sugar, granulated	22	7.7
Sugar, powdered	15	5.3

** The "szklanka" (Polish for drinking glass) is the customary measure of capacity in Polish cooking and is the equivalent of the metric cup (250 ml. or 8.2 U.S. fl. oz). It contains roughly 17 tablespoons or about 1 T. more than the standard 8-ounce U.S. measuring cup (236 ml.). ***Note***: All the recipes in this book are given in standard American weights and measures. The above chart is meant for those who wish to quickly convert metric weights found in foreign cookbooks into volume.

LENGTHS

1 millimeter (1/10 centimeter or 1/1000 meter) = 0.39 inch
1 centimeter (10 millimeters or 1/100 meter) = .39 inch
10 centimeters (100 millimeters) or 1/10 meter) = 3.94 inches
50 centimeters (500 millimeters or 1/2 meter) = 19.68 inches
100 centimeters (1,000 millimeters or 1 meter) = 39.37 inches (3.28 feet)

1 inch (1/12 foot or 1/36 yard) = 2.5 centimeters
6 inches (1/2 foot or 1/6 yard) = 15.2 centimeters
12 inches (1 foot or 1/3 yard) = 30.5 centimeters
36 inches (1 yard) = 91.4 centimeters (.914 meter)

Note: Centimeter, inches and fractions thereof are often used in recipes to designate the lengths and width into which certain foods are to be cut or the thickness into which dough should be rolled out. Feet are occasionally used to indicate such things as sausage links, but rarely are length in excess of one yard or meter encountered, hence miles and kilometers are not found in our conversion tables.

TEMPERATURES

	Celsius (formerly Centigrade)	Fahrenheit
Boiling point of water	100°	212°
Freezing point of water	0°	32°
Ideal storage temperature for most foods in cold cellar or pantry	1.7°–10°	35°–50°
Room temperature	20°–22°	68°–72°
"Warm place"***	24°–30°	75°–85°
Drying temperature	35°–65°	95°–150°
Very slow oven	120°–135°	248°–275°
Slow oven	150°–165°	302°–329° ****
Moderate oven	180°–190°	356°–374°

Hot oven	200°–220°	392°–428°
Very hot oven	230°–250°	446°–482°
Broiling temperature	260°–275°	500°–527°

Note: For temperatures not listed in the above chart, simply do the following:
To get Fahrenheit, multiply Celsius temperature by 1.8 and add 32.
To get Celsius, subtract 32 from Fahrenheit temperature and multiply the result by 5/9.

COMMON METRIC ABBREVIATIONS

milligram	— mg
gram	— gr.
decagram	— dag. (in some Polish cookbooks also "dkg")
kilogram	— (in colloquial speech often called "kilo")
milliliter	— ml.
liter	— l.
millimeter	— mm.
centimeter	— cm.
meter	— m.

*** Such "higher than room temperature" surroundings are ideal for yeast doughs to rise in as well as for various types of fermentation such as souring milk, brine-curing pickles and preparing rye or beet sour.
**** When following a foreign cookbook that gives Celsius temperatures, simply use the closest setting marked on your American oven. If, for instance, 150° C (exact conversion 302° F.) or 190° C (374° F.) are called for, set your oven at 300° F and 375° F respectively.

BOOKS OF CULINARY INTEREST

This is not a bibliography in the conventional sense but simply a list of works that were consulted in one way or another as this book was being prepared. We have therefore forgone the practice of starting the entries with authors' names, which would mean little to the average reader of Polish Heritage Cookery. Instead, we have compiled the titles in alphabetical order and provided translations of the Polish ones to give at least a rough idea of what the books are about. The non-Polish cookbooks listed below were consulted mainly for English weights, measures, and temperatures, comparable terminology, and signs of cultural cross-fertilization.

Apteczka Ziołowa (Herb Cupboard), Leszek Marek Krześniak, Wydawnictwo "Sport i Turystyka," Warszawa 1968.

American Family Cookbook, Lily Wallace Books, New York 1954.

(The) Art of Polish Cooking, Alina Żerańska, Doubleday & Co., Garden City, NY, 1968.

As the World Cooks, International Institute of Lowell, Lowell, MA, 1938.

(The) Best of Polish Cooking, Karen West, Hippocrene Books, New York 1983.

Betty Crocker's Cookbook, Collective work, Bantam Books, New York 1974.

Białko nie tylko w mięsie (Protein Not Only in Meat), Zofia Zawistowska, Wydawnictwo Watra, Warszawa 1972.

Ciasta słodkie i wytrawne (Cakes Sweet and Savory), Helena Lipińska & Andrzej Woźniakowski, Wydawnictwo Spółdzielcze, Warszawa 1990.

Co dzisiaj jeść i jak gotować (What to Eat Today and How to Cook), M. Halska, Gebethner & Wolff, Warszawa 1942.

Cooking the Polish-Jewish Way, Eugeniusz Wirkowski, Interpress Publishers, Warsaw 1988.

Cooking the Polish Way, Danuta Zamojska-Hutchins, Lerner Publications, Minneapolis 1984.

Cooking with Wholegrains, Ellen & Vrest Orton, Farrar, Straus & Young Publishers, New York 1951.

(La) Cuisine, Encyclopédie Populaire Illustrée (Cuisine: a Popular Illustrated Encyclopedia), Société Française d'Éditions d'Art, Paris 1899.

Cymes czyli kuchnia żydowska (Tzimes or Jewish Cookery), Katarzyna Pospieszyńska, Warszawskie Wydawnictwo Prasowe, Warszawa----.

Czy wiesz, co jesz? (Do You Know What You're Eating?), Irena Gumowska, Wydawnictwa "Alfa," Warszawa 1989.

Dania rybne (Fish Dishes), Mieczysław Łazarek, Wydawnictwo Watra, Warszawa 1982.

Desery zimne (Cold Desserts), Małgorzata Borczak, Agencja Presspol, Warszawa 1988.

Dieta łatwo strawna (An Easy-to-Digest Diet), Roman Połeć & Zofia Zawistowska, Państwowy Zakład Wydawnictw Lekarskich, Warszawa 1989.

Dietetyczna książka kucharska (Diet Cookbook), Zofia Wieczorek-Chełmińska, Państwowy Zakład Wydawnictw Leczniczych, Warszawa 1987.

Dobra kuchnia (Good Cookery), Collective work, Wydawnictwo Watra, Warszawa 1987.

Dom, kuchnia i ja (The Home, Kitchen, and I), Magda Szarecka, Instytut Prasy i Wydawnictw "Novum," Warszawa 1988.

Domowe ciasta i ciasteczka (Homemade Cakes and Cookies), Ilona Dąbrowska & Kinga Ośmycka, Wydawnictwa Naukowo-Techniczne, Warszawa 1988.

Domowe przetwory z mięsa (Home-Processed Meats), Władysław Poszepczyński, Wydawnictwa Naukowo-Techniczne, Warszawa 1989.

Domowe przetwory z owoców i warzyw (Home-Processed Fruits and Vegetables), Andrzej Mering, Wydawnictwo Watra, Warszawa 1975.

Domowe wina, nalewki, likiery i owoce w alkoholu (Homemade Wines, Cordials, Liqueurs, and Brandied Fruits), Biruta Markuza-Bienicka, Warszawskie Wydawnictwo Prasowe, Warszawa, 1989.

Domowe wyroby mięsne (Home-Style Meat Products), Tadeusz Kłossowski, Wydawnictwo Watra 1975.

(The) Eight-week Cholesterol Cure, Robert E. Kowalski, Harper & Row Publishers, New York 1987

Feasting with Tradition, Holy Family Polish National Catholic Church, McKeesport, PA, 1977.

(The) Food & Cooking of Russia, Lesley Chamberlain, Penguin Books, Hammondsworth, Middlesex (England) 1982.

Food Smoking the Easy Way, Bob Musselman, Kalamazoo, MI, 1986.

Gawędy o jedzeniu (Chats About Food), Maria Iwaszkiewicz, Wydawnictwo Watra, Warszawa 1972.

(The) Gold Cookbook, Louis P. De Gouy, Greenburg Publishers, New York 1947.

Gospodarstwo domowe (Home-Making) Kamilla Chłoniewska, Wydawnictwo M. Arcta, Warszawa 1929.

Grzyby (Mushrooms), Jaroslav Klán & Bohumil Vančura, Państwowe Wydawnictwo Rolnicze i Leśne, Warszawa 1988.

How to Eat Better for Less Money, James Beard, Simon & Schuster Publishers, New York 1954.

Jak gotować (How to Cook), Maria Disslowa, Instytut Wydawniczy Związków Zawodowych, Warszawa 1988.

Jedyne praktyczne przepisy (The only Practical Recipes), Lucyna Ćwierczakiewiczowa, Gebethner & Wolff, Warszawa 1885.

Joy of Cooking, Irma S. Rombauer & Marion Rombauer-Becker, Plume Books, New York, 1973.

Kalendarz polski (Polish Calendar), Józef Szczypka, Instytut Wydawniczy PAX, Warszawa, 1984.

Koktajle, nalewki, wina, miody i piwa (Cocktails, Cordials, Wines, Meads, and Beers), Alojzy Cerski, Wielkopolskie Wydawnictwo Prasowe, Poznań (year of publication not listed)

Kompoty, marynaty, dżemy, (Compotes, Pickles, Jams), Zdzisława Skrodzka, Wydawnictwo Watra, Warszawa 1981

Krupnioki i moczka (Silesian Specialties), Wera Sztabowa, Wydawnictwo "Śląsk," Katowice 1990.

Książka kucharska (Cookery Book), Zofia Zawistowska, Wydawnictwo Watra, Warszawa 1981.

Kucharka litewska (The Lithuanian Cook), Wincenta Zawadzka, Wydawnictwo Pojezierze, Olsztyn 1985

Kucharz polski (The Polish Cook), Maria Śleżańska, Księgarnia J. Leitgebera i S-ki, Poznań 1932

Kuchenka mickrofalowa (The Microwave Oven), Jerzy & Marek Zubrzycki, Wydawnictwo Prywatne "Żubr", Warszawa 1991

Kuchnia białoruska (Byelorussian Cookery), Collective work, Państwowe Wydawnictwo Rolnicze i Leśne, Warszawa 1986

Kuchnia dla wszystkich (Everyone's Cookery), Jadwiga Kłossowska, Wydawnictwo Watra, Warszawa 1980

Kuchnia domowa (Home Cooking), Zofia Zawistowska, Instytut Wydawniczy Związków Zawodowych, Warszawa 1986

Kuchnia i zdrowie (Cookery and Health), Anna Szczepańska, Anna Ners & Zofia Zawistowska, Państwowy Zakład Wydawnictw Lekarskich, Warszawa 1988

Kuchnia litewska (Lithuanian Cookery), Nicole i Maciej Druto, Krajowa Agencja Wydawnicza, Warszawa 1987

Kuchnia myśliwska (Hunter's Cookery), Collective work, Wydawnictwo Polonia, Warszawa 1971

Kuchnia Neli (Nela's Cuisine), Nela Rubinstein, Wydawnictwo Polonia, Warszawa, 1990

Kuchnia oszczędnej gospodyni (A Thrifty Homemaker's Cookery) Barbara Bytnerowiczowa, Wydawnictwo Watra, Warszawa 1989

Kuchnia pod chmurką (Outdoor Cookery), Irena Gumowska, Wydawnictwo PTTK "Kraj," Warszawa 1986

Kuchnia polska (Polish Cuisine), Maria Librowska et al., Państwowe Wydawnictwo Ekonomiczne, Warszawa 1980

Kuchnia to moje hobby (Cooking is My Hobby), Renata Pacer, Wydawnictwo Watra, Warszawa 1989

Leksykon sztuki kulinarnej (Lexicon of the Culinary Arts), Maciej E. Halbański, Wydawnictwo Watra, Warszawa 1987

Miód w kuchni (Cooking with Honey), Leszek Rum, Państwowe Wydawnictwo Rolnicze i Leśne, Poznań 1990

Moučniky a sladkosti (Cakes and Sweets), Maria Teplá, Nakladelství Hynka Buchbauma, Mor. Ostrava (Czechoslovakia) 1934.

Mushrooms: Wild and Edible, Vincent Maretka, W. W. Norton & Co., New York, 1980.

Najnowsza kuchnia (The Latest Cuisine), Marta Nortowska, Gebethner & Wolff, Warszawa 1904.

Nasze ryby (Our Fish), Jósef Mihálik & František Reisner, Wydawnictwo Rolnicze i Leśne, Warszawa 1990

Nie tylko dla jaroszów (Not Only for Vegetarians), Zofia Zawistowska, Instytut Wydawniczy Związków Zawodowych, Warszawa 1987

Obiady na cztery pory roku (Dinners for All Four Seasons), Barbara Szczepańska & Krystyna Tarnowska, Państwowe Wydawnictwo Rolnicze i Leśne, 1989.

Obiady u Kowalskich (Dinners at the Kowalskis), Jadwiga Kłossowska, Wydawnictwo Watra, Warszawa 1987

Od ananasa do ziemniaka (From Pineapples to Potatoes), Irena Gumowska, Instytut Wydawniczy CRZZ, Warszawa 1976

Old Warsaw Cookbook, Rysia, Roy Publishers, New York, 1958, Hippocrene 1991

Owoce na każdą okazję (Fruits for Every Occasion), Alicja i Paulina Fedak, Wydawnictwo Watra, Warszawa, 1972

Pieczenie ciast i ciasteczek (Baking Cakes and Pastries), Irena Głowacka, Wydawnictwo Watra, Warszawa 1972

Piekę ciasta i ciasteczka (I Bake Cakes and Pastries), Wanda Piotrowiakowa, Państwowe Wydawnictwo Ekonomiczne, Warszawa 1987

500 potraw z ziemniaków (500 Potato Dishes), W. A. Bołotnikowa & L. M. Wapielnik, Państwowe Wydawnictwo Rolnicze i Leśne, Warszawa 1985

Polish Cookbook, Arts Institute, Consolidated Book Publishers, Chicago 1978

Polish Cookbook, Children of the Piekło Family (in memory of their immigrant mother, Anna Dziengiel-Piekło), Creative Composition, (place of publication not listed) 1977

Polish Cookbook, Zofia Czerny, Państwowe Wydawnictwo Ekonomiczne, Warszawa, 1975

Polish Cooking, Marianne Olszewska-Heberle, HPBooks, Los Angeles 1985

Polska Wigilia (Polish Christmas Eve), Hanna Szymanderska, Wydawnictwo Watra, Warszawa 1989.

Potrawy jarskie (Vegetarian Dishes), Wanda Piotrowiakowa, Państwowe Wydawnictwo Ekonomiczne, Warszawa, 1988

Potrawy mało znane (Little Known Dishes), Anna Czerny, Wydawnictwo Watra, Warszawa, 1987

Potrawy mięsne na polskim stole (Meat Dishes on the Polish Table), Danuta i Henryk Dębscy, Instytut Wydawniczy Związków Zawodowych, Warszawa 1988

Potrawy niskokaloryczne (Low-Calorie Dishes), Zofia Zawistowska, Wydawnictwo Watra, Warszawa 1990.

Potrawy staropolskie i regionalne (Old-Polish and Regional Dishes), Barbara Snaglewska & Irmina Zahorska, Wydawnictwo Watra, Warszawa, 1989

Potrawy z drobiu i dzikiego ptactwa (Poultry and Wildfowl Dishes), Irena Krawczyk & Anna Rościszewska-Stoyanow, Wydawnictwo Watra, Warszawa 1973

Potrawy z jaj (Egg Dishes), Joanna Mosingiewicz, Wydawnictwo Watra, Warszawa 1974

Potrawy z królików (Rabbit Dishes), Wojciech Tatarczych, Wydawnictwo Watra, Warszawa 1987

Potrawy z sera (Cheese Dishes), Joanna Słowikowska, Wydawnictwo Watra, Warszawa 1972

Praktyczny kucharz warszawski (The Practical Warsaw Cook), Collective work, Ferdynand & Hoesick, Warszawa 1906

Produkcja wyrobów garmażeryjnych (The Production of Delicatessen Food), Kazimierz Krata, Wydawnictwo Watra, Warszawa 1969

Przekąski zimne i gorące (Hors D'Oeuvres Hot and Cold), Barbara Bytnerowiczowa, Wydawnictwo Watra, Warszawa 1987

Przepisy kulinarne dla oszczędnej gospodyni (Recipes for the Thrifty Homemaker), Jadwiga Łukasik, Wydawnictwo Spółdzielcze, Warszawa 1990.

Przewory domowe dawne i nowe (Home-Processed Foods Old and New), Zofia Zawistowska, Instytut Wydawniczy Związków Zawodowych, Warszawa, 1990.

Przetwory w gospodarstwie domowym (Home-Processed Foods in the Household), Kazimiera Pyszkowska, Państwowe Wydawnictwo Rolnicze i Leśne, Warszawa 1988.

Rośliny źródłem przypraw (Plants as a Source of Seasonings), Anton Šedo & Jindřich Krejča, Państwowe Wydawnictwo Rolnicze i Leśne, Warszawa

Ryby w codziennym żywieniu (Fish in Daily Nutrition), Leonard Duklewski, Wydawnictwo Watra, Warszawa 1971.

Słodkie dania obiadowe i desery (Sweet Dinner Courses and Desserts), Henryk Dębski, Wydawnictwo Watra, Warszawa 1979.

Smacznie i zdrowo od rana do wieczora (Tasty and Healthy from Morning to Night), Jadwiga Kłossowska, Wydawnictwo Spółdzielcze, Warszawa 1989.

Spiżarnia i zapasy domowe (The Pantry and Winter Supplies), Marta Nortowska, Gebethner & Wolff, Warszawa 1902.

600 potraw z jaj (600 Egg Dishes), Henryk Dębski, Wydawnictwo Watra, Warszawa 1983.

Śląska kucharka doskonała (The Perfect Silesian Cook), Elżbieta Łabońska, Fundacja dla Śląskiego Instytutu Naukowego, Katowice 1989.

Treasured Polish Recipes fo: Americans, Polanie Club, Polanie Publishing House Co., Minneapolis 1961.

Treasured Polish Christmas Customs and Traditions, Polanie Publishing House Co., Minneapolis 1974.

365 obiadów (365 Dinners), Lucyna Ćwierczakiewiczowa, Nakład Jana Fiszera, Warszawa 1911.

Vegetable Cookery, Myra Waldo, Bantam Books, New York 1962.

Wenus i atleta (Venus and the Athlete), Irena Gumowska, Wydawnictwa "Alfa," Warszawa 1990.

Więcej warzyw w ogródku, spiżarni i na talerzu (More Vegetables in the Garden, Pantry, and on the Dinner Plate), Maria Dudzik, Jadwiga Kowalska, Kazimiera Pyszkowska & Helena Spalona, Wydawnictwo Watra, Warszawa 1973.

Wina domowe, nalewki i likiery (Homemade Wines, Cordials, and Liqueurs), Bronisław Adacz, Wydawnictwo Watra, Warszawa 1987.

Współczesna kuchnia domowa (Contemporary Home Cooking), Alina Gniewkowska, Stowarzyszenie Pracowników Księgarskich, Warszawa 1927.

Współczesna kuchnia polska (Contemporary Polish Cooking), Henryk Dębski, Wydawnictwo Interpress, Warszawa 1979.

W staropolskiej kuchni (In the Old Polish Kitchen), Maria Lemnis & Henryk Vitry, Wydawnictwo Interpress, Warszawa 1979.

Wypieki domowe (Homemade Baked Goods), Komitet Gospodarstwa Domowego Ligi Kobiet Polskich, Warszawa 1990.

Yummy Tummy Tempters, School of Christian Living & PTA, Blessed Virgin Mary Polish National Catholic Church (Fall River, MA), Walter's Cookbooks, Weseca, MN, 1988.

Zapasy na zimę (Stocking the Pantry for Winter), Maria Monatowa, Krajowa Agencja Wydawnicza, Poznań 1988.

Zioła w domu (Herbs in the Home), Danuta Tyszyńska Lownacka, Wydawnictwo Współczesne, Warszawa.

Ziołowe przyprawy kuchenne (Herb Seasonings), Zenon Węglarz & Krystyna Suchorska, Wydawnictwa, "Alfa", Warszawa 1988.

Ziółka i my (Herbs and Us), Irena Gumowska, Wydawnictwo PTTK "Kraj," Warszawa 1983.

RECIPE INDEX

RECIPE INDEX IN POLISH

From Spanish salsas to Russian pirogi, from Israeli delicacies to Hungarian pastries, **HIPPOCRENE INTERNATIONAL COOKBOOK CLASSICS** provide an array of tantalizing recipes from across the globe.

ALL ALONG THE DANUBE
by Marina Polvay
0491 ISBN 0-7818-0098-6 $11.95pb

THE ART OF BRAZILIAN COOKERY
by Dolores Botafogo
0250 ISBN 0-7818-0130-3 $12.95pb

THE JOY OF CHINESE COOKING
by Doreen Yen Hung Feng
0288 ISBN 0-7818-0097-8 $8.95pb

THE BEST OF FINNISH COOKING
by Taimi Previdi
0354 ISBN 0-7818-0284-9 $19.95hc

THE HONEY COOKBOOK
by Maria Lo Pinto
0283 ISBN 0-7818-0149-4 $8.95pb

THE ART OF HUNGARIAN COOKING
by Paula Pogany Bennett & Velma R. Clark
0165 ISBN 0-7818-0202-4 $8.95pb

THE ART OF ISRAELI COOKING
by Chef Aldo Nahoum
0252 ISBN 0-7818-0096-X $9.95pb

THE ART OF PERSIAN COOKING
by Forough Hekmat
0125 ISBN 0-7818-0241-5 $9.95pb

THE BEST OF POLISH COOKING
Revised Edition
by Karen West
1391 ISBN 0-7818-0123-3 $8.95pb

OLD WARSAW COOKBOOK
by Rysia
0536 SBN 0-87052-932-3 $12.95

THE BEST OF RUSSIAN COOKING
by Alexandra Kropotkin
0251 ISBN 0-7818-0131-1 $9.95pb

THE BEST OF SMORGASBORD COOKING
by Gerda Simonson
0207 ISBN 0-7818-0407-8 $14.95pb

A SPANISH FAMILY COOKBOOK
Revised Edition
by Juan and Susan Serrano
0642 ISBN 0-7818-0546-5 $11.95pb

THE ART OF TURKISH COOKING
by Neset Eren
0162 ISBN 0-7818-0201-6 $9.95pb

THE BEST OF UKRAINIAN CUISINE
by Bohdan Zahny
0124 ISBN 0-7818-0240-7 $19.95pb

(Prices subject to change.)
TO PURCHASE HIPPOCRENE BOOKS contact your local bookstore, or write to: HIPPOCRENE BOOKS, 171 Madison Avenue, New York, NY 10016. Please enclose a check or money order, adding $5.00 shipping (UPS) for first book and .50 for each additional book.

THE BEST OF
POLISH COOKING
Revised
by Karen West

This delightful compilation of traditional Polish fare is arranged in an easy-to-use menu format. The author has placed complementary and harmonious foods together and arranged them to follow the seasonal cycle.

• Spring offers delectable recipes for the beautiful foods which abound: Braised Spring Lamb with Cabbage, Baby Carrots Polonaise, Almond Babka, Wild Strawberries with Whipped Sour Cream.

• Summer's menus are cool and light, using fresh fruits and vegetables: Frosty Artichoke Salad, Individual Oyster Souffles, Fresh Peas with Dill Butter, Chilled Blueberry Soup.

• Autumn's recipes bring warmth and harvest's bounty to your kitchen and table: Polish Sausage Simmered in Wine, Apple Raisin Cake, Hunter's Stew, Rye Bread with Sweet Butter.

• Winter is full of hearty fare brimming with holiday flavor: Christmas Almond Soup, Smoked Salmon Omelets, Christmas Eve Bread.

Sprinkled throughout these seasonal delights are plenty of recipes for barshch, mazureks, sausages, babkas, potato pancakes—all the foods for which the Polish are justly famous, including a traditional Easter menu.

Twenty-nine menus are included, complete with *all* required recipes. Most can be prepared in advance—perfect for entertainment enjoyment. So, whether you're Polish or simply adventuresome, invite your guests, choose your menu, steep your vodka and enjoy! *Smacznego!*

"A charming offering of Polish cuisine with lovely woodcuts throughout."
    —*Publishers Weekly*

"Ethnic cuisine at its best."   —*The Midwest Book Review*

$8.95 • 219 pages • 0-7818-0123-3

All prices subject to change.

TO PURCHASE HIPPOCRENE BOOKS contact your local bookstore, or write to: HIPPOCRENE BOOKS, 171 Madison Avenue, New York, NY 10016. Please enclose check or money order, adding $5.00 shipping (UPS) for the first book and $.50 for each additional book.

Also available from Hippocrene . . .

POLISH HERBS, FLOWERS & FOLK MEDICINE
Sophie Hodorowicz Knab

Besides taking the reader on a guided tour through monastery, castle and cottage gardens, this book provides details on over one hundred herbs and flowers and how they were used in folk medicine as well as in everyday life, traditions, and customs.

207 pages   illustrations, woodcuts, bibliography, glossary, index
0-7818-0319-5 $19.95 hardcover (573)

POLISH WEDDINGS: CUSTOMS & TRADITIONS
Sophie Hodorowicz Knab

A unique planning guide for Americans who want to organize and celebrate a Polish-style wedding. Sections entitled Engagement, Bridal Flowers, Wedding Clothes, Ceremony, Reception, and even Baby Names, will assist the bride- and groom-to-be through every step of the wedding process. Special tips on "How to Draw from the Past" at the end of each chapter provide helpful suggestions on how to incorporate Polish tradition into the modern wedding, to make it a truly distinctive and unforgettable event.

250 pages
0-7818-0530-9 $19.95 hardcover (641)

POLISH CUSTOMS, TRADITIONS, AND FOLKLORE, Revised Edition

Sophie Hodorowicz Knab

with an Introduction by Rev. Czesław Krysa

Now in its fourth printing!

Best selling author Sophie Hodorowicz Knab has updated her first book to include a new chapter on "Customs for Kids"!

This unique reference book is arranged by month, covering the various occasions, feasts and holidays. Beginning with December, it includes Advent, St. Nicholas Day, the *Wigilia* (Christmas Eve), nativity plays, caroling as well as the New Year celebrations, and those of the shrovetide period to Ash Wednesday, Lent, the celebrations of spring, Holy Week customs, superstitions, beliefs and rituals associated with farming, Pentecost, Corpus Christi, midsummer celebrations, birth and death.

Delicate line drawings complete this rich and varied treasury of folklore.

PRAISE FOR *POLISH CUSTOMS, TRADITIONS, AND FOLKLORE:*

"There is nothing on the subject that even approaches this book in its breadth and authority. A prodigious amount of research has gone into the work, as well as sheer education and enthusiasm that keeps an author going, and searching and reading."—*Zgoda*

"This collection is a tremendous asset to understanding the ethnic behavior of a people. Highly recommended."—Florence Waszkelewicz-Clowes, *Polish American Journal*

"Eagerly awaited...comprehensive and definitive....Most [readers] will be delighted to discover the many regional variations which enrich this informative guide."—*Polish Heritage*

$19.95 • 340 pages • 12 b/w illustrations • ISBN 0-7818-0515-5

POLISH DICTIONARIES AND LANGUAGE BOOKS
Modern • Up-to-Date • Easy-to-Use • Practical

POLISH-ENGLISH/ENGLISH-POLISH PRACTICAL DICTIONARY (Completely Revised) *by Iwo Cyprian Pogonowski*. Contains over 31,000 entries for students and travelers. Includes a phonetic guide to pronunciation in both languages, a handy glossary of the country's menu terms, a bilingual instruction on how-to-use the dictionary, and a bilingual list of abbreviations.
0450   ISBN 0-7818-0085-4 $11.95 pb

POLISH-ENGLISH/ENGLISH-POLISH CONCISE DICTIONARY (Completely Revised) *by Iwo Cyprian Pogonowski*. Contains over 91,000 completely modern, up-to-date entries in a clear, concise format.
0268   ISBN 0-7818-0133-8 $9.95 pb

POLISH-ENGLISH/ENGLISH-POLISH STANDARD DICTIONARY
0298   ISBN 0-7818-0282-2 $19.95 pb

POLISH PHRASEBOOK AND DICTIONARY (New Edition) *by Iwo Cyprian Pogonowski*, 252 pages. Revised and re-typeset, this handy guide for the English speaking traveler in Poland is now more useful than ever.
0192   ISBN 0-7818-0134-0 $9.95 pb

ENGLISH CONVERSATIONS FOR POLES (New Edition) *by Iwo Cyprian Pogonowski*, 250 pages. This handbook of our bestselling dictionary author includes 3,300 practical, up-to-date entries, indexed by main entry, with useful expressions for every need. It also features a phonetic guide to pronunciation and a dictionary with over 6,500 entries.
0225   ISBN 0-87052-873-4 $9.95 pb

AMERICAN ENGLISH FOR POLES: In Four Parts, *Institute of Applied Linguistics in Warsaw and the Center for Applied Linguistics in Virginia*, 828 pages in set. The set includes a Teacher's Guide, Exercises, Dictionary, Student's Textbook: 20 integrated units with 3,500 word vocabulary.
0441   ISBN 83-214-0152-X $24.95 for the set

ENGLISH FOR POLES SELF-TAUGHT *by Irena Dobrzycka*, 496 pages. Contains 455 lessons with dictionary of over 3,600 entries.
0317   ISBN 0-7818-0273-3 $19.95 pb

MASTERING POLISH (New) *by Albert Juszczak*, 288 pages. A teach-yourself set perfect for the serious traveler, student or business executive. Imaginative, practical exercises in grammar are accompanied by cassette tapes for conversation practice. Juszczak teaches Polish at the New York University.
0381   ISBN 0-7818-0015-3 $14.95 (paperback book)
0389   ISBN 0-7818-0016-1 $12.95 (2 cassettes)
0414   ISBN 0-7818-0017-X $24.90 (paperback and cassettes)

AMERICAN PHRASEBOOK FOR POLES/ROZMOWKI AMERYKANSKIE DLA POLAKOW, Revised Edition *by Jacek Galazka*, 154 pages. "The book meets in an extraordinary way the needs of today's world. And it is so practical; ...it anticipates the situations likely to confront the arriving Pole...."—*Nowy Dziennik* (Polish Daily) New York
644   ISBN 0-7818-0554-6 $8.95 pb